PRETRIAL
LITIGATION
LAW, POLICY AND PRACTICE
Fifth Edition

■ ■ ■

By
R. Lawrence Dessem
Dean and Professor of Law
University of Missouri

AMERICAN CASEBOOK SERIES®

WEST®
A Thomson Reuters business

Mat #40918597

American Casebook Series is a trademark registered in the U.S. Patent and Trademark Office.

COPYRIGHT © 1991, 1996 WEST PUBLISHING CO.
© West, a Thomson business, 2001, 2007
© 2011 Thomson Reuters

    610 Opperman Drive
    St. Paul, MN 55123
    1–800–313–9378

Printed in the United States of America

ISBN: 978–0–314–23791–0

The first edition was dedicated
To Beth

The book's second edition was dedicated
To My Parents

The book's third edition was dedicated
To Judge William K. Thomas

The book's fourth edition was dedicated
To My Children: Matthew, Lindsay and Emily

This fifth edition is dedicated
**To the lawyers and judges who work to make
Equal Justice Under Law a reality for us all.**

PREFACE

Despite popular misconceptions perpetuated by television and the movies, practicing attorneys spend very little of their time in the courtroom. Nevertheless, to the extent that law schools have attempted to teach lawyering skills, they traditionally have focused on courtroom skills involved in trial and appellate advocacy. Because most legal textbooks contain reported judicial opinions, law students have further reason to believe, incorrectly, that most cases end in trial.

One of my reasons for writing this book originally was to correct such misperceptions. In the twenty years since the publication of the book's first edition, great attention has been paid to the civil pretrial process. Congress, the judiciary, the bar, and legal scholars have focused on the pretrial process and offered various suggestions for reforming that process. These developments, especially the 1993 and 2000 amendments to the Federal Rules of Civil Procedure, were incorporated in the second and third editions of the book, while the book's fourth edition considered the 2006 amendments to the Federal Rules concerning electronic discovery. This fifth edition incorporates the many significant developments over the last four years, including the further evolution of electronic discovery law and practice, the refashioning of pleading pursuant to the Supreme Court's decisions in *Bell Atlantic Corp. v. Twombly* and *Iqbal v. Ashcroft*, and the 2010 Rules amendments concerning expert witnesses and summary judgment.

Rather than focus on the trial of civil actions, this text systematically considers the civil pretrial process. The text explores pretrial activities such as interviewing clients and witnesses, drafting pleadings, drafting and responding to discovery requests, preparing and responding to motions, and negotiating settlements. Of necessity, the text considers both the formal and informal lawyering that occurs prior to trial. So that students can better understand the pretrial process and the interrelationships among the various aspects of that process, the book includes many exercises that place students in simulated settings similar to those that they will encounter as practicing lawyers.

A course in pretrial litigation provides excellent opportunities for employing teaching techniques other than the Socratic and lecture formats traditionally used in American legal education. This text can be used in small classes, either with or without the writing and simulation exercises contained in each chapter. However, because of its mix of cases, textual material, forms, and problems, the book effectively can be used in a larger class by a professor utilizing more traditional teaching methods. The first four editions of the book were used successfully in upper-level pretrial litigation courses, in more comprehensive civil procedure offerings, and in legal writing courses.

Multiple exercises have been included to give the professor maximum flexibility in using the book. In most chapters, one or more exercises can be discussed in class while another exercise can be assigned for independent student work. Included are exercises that students can perform with one another outside of class or that students, professors, or attorneys can perform during classroom sessions.

Many of the exercises in this book are based upon a single, complex civil case. The major advantages of drawing exercises from a single case are that (1) students can concentrate on the procedural aspects of the pretrial process, rather than upon the differing fact patterns and governing law that inevitably will be raised by different cases, and (2) if the class is taught in a problem or workshop fashion, students can better see how decisions made early in the pretrial process can affect, and limit, later choices in that same case.

The civil action chosen as the basis for many of this text's problems, *Prince v. The Pittston Company*, Civil Action 3052 (S.D.W.V. filed Sept. 3, 1972), was brought by and on behalf of several hundred individuals injured or killed by the 1972 collapse of a mining dam in Logan County, West Virginia. This litigation was chronicled by plaintiffs' attorney Gerald Stern in *The Buffalo Creek Disaster*, and it has been written about by others as well. The use of supplemental materials, particularly Stern's book, should enhance students' understanding of many of the factual exercises contained in the text. However, the text is self-contained and does not presuppose the reading of any outside materials.

Much of a lawyer's work in the pretrial process occurs outside the presence of the court and, sometimes, outside the presence of other lawyers. It therefore is particularly important that students receive a strong foundation in the ethics of pretrial litigation. Accordingly, each chapter of this text explicitly raises ethical concerns that arise during the pretrial process.

The procedural law underlying this text is that which is set forth in the Federal Rules of Civil Procedure. Local rules of court are cited throughout the text to illustrate some of the practice alternatives that can be decreed by courts or adopted by counsel. In citing to these local rules, I have not specifically designated them as the civil (as opposed to criminal or general) local rules of the federal district court in question. No text in pretrial litigation could do justice to its subject without a consideration of how law is practiced, as opposed to how the drafters of the Federal Rules envisioned that it would be practiced. For this reason, I also have integrated into the text illustrative pleadings, motions, and practice forms.

Much can be learned about pretrial litigation, and about legal practice generally, by examining case studies of lawyers and judges at work. This book includes excerpts from other books describing how law is actually practiced. These excerpts include nonfiction accounts of alleged document destruction in the *Berkey v. Kodak* litigation, Judge Jack Weinstein's efforts to settle the *Agent Orange* class actions, the pretrial investigation by a court-appointed lawyer that led to freedom for Clarence Earl Gideon, and an excerpt from

Anatomy of a Murder that raises important issues concerning the ethics of interviewing.

There are increasing numbers of quality CDs, videotapes and other supplemental aids that can enhance a course in pretrial litigation and give students a sense of what a deposition or a motion hearing actually looks like in practice. These supplemental materials easily can be integrated into a pretrial litigation course taught from this text. Supplemental materials that I have used in my own course, as well as other teaching suggestions, are contained in the Teacher's Manual written in connection with this book.

Because so many cases are resolved by the parties short of trial, a text in pretrial litigation is a natural place in which to discuss alternative dispute resolution. The text contains a final chapter devoted to this subject, and throughout the book students are asked to consider whether formal adjudicatory resolution of various disputes is in the best interests of the persons involved.

Case and statute citations, as well as footnotes, have been omitted from documents reprinted in the text without so indicating. The footnotes in the motion for a protective order reprinted in Chapter 10 have been designated by asterisks rather than by the numerals that were used in the original motion. While I have not added the first names of the authors of the many law review articles that I have cited, I have identified the authors of student work where possible.

A truly scientific method was used to determine the gender of the attorneys, clients and judges referred to in this book. I flipped a coin. As a result of that coin flip, the text generally refers to attorneys as females and judges and clients as males.

As I tell the students in my own classes, I welcome any thoughts, criticism, or suggestions concerning this text. I hope that it is as useful a teaching device for others as it has been for me.

R. LAWRENCE DESSEM

Columbia, Missouri
March 1, 2011

ACKNOWLEDGEMENTS

Writing a book makes you realize the debt that you owe to other people. Any author should thank the parents, friends, teachers and others who have nurtured and taught him over the years, and I do so now. I also must thank those who taught me about the practice of law: Judge William K. Thomas, my friends in the General Counsel's Office of the National Education Association, and, especially, my former colleagues and continuing friends in the Federal Programs Branch of the Civil Division of the United States Department of Justice.

I owe a special debt to my former colleagues at the University of Tennessee College of Law for all that they taught me about law teaching, legal education, and life. Dean Richard Wirtz was especially supportive of the first two editions of this book, as were Deans John Sebert and Marilyn Yarbrough in connection with the book's first edition. I also thank Professor Lawrence Grosberg, who has graciously shared with me and others Buffalo Creek litigation documents and his experiences using the Buffalo Creek factual scenario in classroom exercises.

My family is worthy of special mention. I could not have written any of the editions of this book without the help of my wife Beth, who is a gifted teacher, inspirational leader, and valued friend. She read the first edition of this book in draft untold times and always offered valuable commentary (including pithy comments such as "This is why some people hate lawyers!"). My three children have been very supportive, and I thank Matthew ("the advocate"), Lindsay ("the investigator"), and Emily ("the settlement judge"). They continue to teach me about the many things in life that are more important than pretrial litigation.

I have been blessed with outstanding research assistance in connection with all five editions of this book. Daniel Graves, Josh Scott, and Allyson Walker made invaluable contributions to this fifth edition, just as Jessica Gunder, Whitney Pile, Kathy Birkhofer, Cullen Sheppard, Rhonda Wilcox, Ann–Riley Caldwell and Patricia Nicely did a superb job on the book's first four editions. Their many hours of hard work on this project have improved both the style and substance of this text.

Among those who have been of special assistance in the preparation of the book's fifth edition are Judy Tayloe and Robin Nichols in my own office and Randy Diamond, Cindy Bassett, John Dethman, Needra Jackson, Steve Lambson, Cindy Shearrer and their colleagues within the Law Library of the University of Missouri School of Law. John Dethman was particularly resourceful in tracking down material for this edition on very short order. Debbie Manly, Patsy Tye, and the librarians and staff of the Mercer University School of Law and Patricia Hurd, LaVaun Browder, Jacqueline Bonvin, and the librarians and staff of the University of Tennessee College of Law provided invaluable help with the earlier editions of the text. Both the students in my own pretrial litigation classes and those who have taught pretrial litigation at the University of Tennessee have been quite helpful with their suggestions, especially Judges Robert Murrian and Thomas Phillips.

Finally, I thank those who have permitted me to reprint excerpts from the following articles and books:

American Bar Association, " ' . . . *In the Spirit of Public Service:' A Blueprint for the Rekindling of Lawyer Professionalism,*" 112 F.R.D. 243 (2006), Copyright 2006 © by the American Bar Association. Reprinted with permission. This information or any portion thereof may not be copied or disseminated in any form or by any means or stored in an electronic database or retrieval system without the express written consent of the American Bar Association.

American Bar Association, *Model Rules of Professional Conduct*, 2010 Edition. Copyright © 2010 by the American Bar Association. Reprinted with permission. Copies of the ABA *Model Rules of Professional Conduct* are available from Service Center, American Bar Association, 321 North Clark Street, Chicago, IL 60654, 1–800–285–2221. This information or any portion thereof may not be copied or disseminated in any form or by any means or stored in an electronic database or retrieval system without the express written consent of the American Bar Association.

American Bar Association, *Formal Ethics Opinions 94–389 and 93–379.* Copyright © 1994 and 1993 by the American Bar Association. Reprinted with permission. Copies of the ABA Formal Ethics Opinions are available from the Service Center, American Bar Association, 321 North Clark Street, Chicago, IL 60654, 1–800–285–2221.

American Bar Association, *Civil Discovery Standards* (2004). Copyright 2004 © by the American Bar Association. Reprinted with permission. This information or any portion thereof may not be copied or disseminated in any form or by any means or stored in an electronic database or retrieval system without the express written consent of the American Bar Association.

American Bar Association, *Principles for Juries and Jury Trials*, Principle 13(H) (2005). Copyright 2005 © by the American Bar Association. Reprinted with permission. This information or any portion thereof may not be copied or disseminated in any form or by any means or stored in an electronic database or retrieval system without the express written consent of the American Bar Association.

American Law Institute, *Proceedings* (1984). Copyright © 1985 by The American Law Institute. Reprinted with the permission of The American Law Institute.

Association of the Bar of the City of New York, *Lectures on Legal Topics* (1926). Copyright © 1926 by the Association of the Bar of the City of New York.

Barber, "California Taxes Punitive Damage Awards," *Litigation News*, September 2005, at 5. © 2005 by the American Bar Association. Reprinted with permission. All rights reserved. This information or any portion thereof may not be copied or disseminated in any form or by any means stored in an electronic database or retrieval system without the express written consent of the American Bar Association.

Beckerman, "Confronting Civil Discovery's Fatal Flaws," 84 *Minn. L. Rev.* 505 (2000).

Bell et al., "Automatic Disclosure in Discovery—The Rush to Reform," originally published at 27 *Ga. L. Rev.*1 (1992) and reprinted with permission.

Belli, "Pre–Trial: Aid to the New Advocacy," 43 *Cornell L. Q.* 34 (1957). Copyright © 1957 by Cornell University and Fred B. Rothman & Co. All rights reserved.

Bender's Forms of Discovery (2009). Reprinted from *Benders Forms of Discovery*, "Animals," No. 4, with permission. Copyright 2009 Matthew Bender & Co., Inc., a member of the LexisNexis Group. All rights reserved.

Bench–Bar Proposal to Revise Civil Procedure Rule 11, 137 F.R.D. 159 (1991). Reprinted with permission of West Group.

Bernstein, "Understanding the Limits of Court–Connected ADR: A Critique of Federal Court-Annexed Arbitration Programs," 141 *U. Pa. L. Rev.* 2169 (1993). Copyright © 1993 by the University of Pennsylvania Law Review.

D. Binder & S. Price, *Legal Interviewing and Counseling: A Client–Centered Approach* (1977). Reprinted with permission of West Group.

Brazil, "Civil Discovery: How Bad Are the Problems?," *A.B.A.J.*, April 1981, at 450. Reprinted by permission of the *ABA Journal*.

Brazil, "Civil Discovery: Lawyers' Views of Its Effectiveness, Its Principal Problems and Abuses," 1980 *Am. B. Found. Res. J.* 787. Copyright © 1980 by the American Bar Foundation.

Brazil, "The Adversary Character of Civil Discovery: A Critique and Proposals for Change," 31 *Vand. L. Rev.* 1295 (1978). Copyright © 1978 by the Vanderbilt Law Review.

Brazil, "Views from the Front Lines: Observations by Chicago Lawyers About the System of Civil Discovery," 1980 *Am. B. Found. Res. J.* 217. Copyright © 1980 by the American Bar Foundation.

W. Brazil, *Settling Civil Suits* (1985). Copyright © 1985 by the American Bar Association. Reprinted by permission of the American Bar Association.

Bronsteen, "Against Summary Judgment," 75 *Geo. Wash. L. Rev.* 522, 551 (2007).

Buchmeyer, "Discovery Abuse and the Time Out Rule," *Tex. B. J.* Feb. 1983. Copyright © 1983 by Jerry Buchmeyer and the Texas Bar Journal.

Buchmeyer, "How to Use a Deposition at Trial," *Tex. B. J.* April 1995. Copyright © 1995 by Jerry Buchmeyer and the Texas Bar Journal.

Burbank, "Vanishing Trials and Summary Judgment in Federal Civil Cases: Drifting Toward Bethlehem or Gomorrah?," *J. Emp. Legal Studies* 591, 620 (2004).

Burger, "Agenda for 2000 A.D.—A Need for Systematic Anticipation," 70 F.R.D. 83 (1976). Copyright © 1976 by West Group.

Chayes, "The Role of the Judge in Public Law Litigation," 89 *Harv. L. Rev.* 1281 (1976).

Childress, "A New Era for Summary Judgments: Recent Shifts at the Supreme Court," 116 F.R.D. 183 (1987). Copyright © 1987 by Steven Alan Childress and West Group.

Clark, "To an Understanding Use of Pretrial," 29 F.R.D. 454 (1961). Copyright © 1961 by West Group.

R. Cochran & T. Collet, *Cases and Materials on the Legal Profession* 173 (2d ed 2003).

Coleman, "The *Celotex* Initial Burden Standard and Opportunity to 'Revivify' Rule 56," 32 *S. Ill. U.L.J.* 295, 320–321 (2008).

Commercial and Federal Litigation Section, New York State Bar Association, *Report on Discovery Under Rule 26(b)(1),* 127 F.R.D. 625 (1990). Reprinted with permission from 127 F.R.D. 625, copyright © 1989, 1990 by the Commercial and Federal Litigation Section, New York State Bar Association and West Group.

Committee to the Judicial Conference for the District of Columbia, "Pretrial Procedure," 1 F.R.D. 759 (1941). Copyright © 1941 by West Group.

Cooper, "Simplified Rules of Civil Procedure?," 100 *Mich. L. Rev.* 1794 (2002).

Crist, "The E–Brief: Legal Writing for an Online World," 33 *N.M. L. Rev.* 49 (2003).

Davis, "The Argument of an Appeal," *A.B.A.J.,* Dec. 1940, at 895. Reprinted by permission of the *ABA Journal.*

Dayton, "Case Management in the Eastern District of Virginia," 26 *U.S.F. L. Rev.* 445 (1992). Reprinted with permission of the University of San Francisco Law Review.

Dayton, "The Myth of Alternative Dispute Resolution in the Federal Courts," 76 *Iowa L. Rev.* 889 (1991), reprinted with permission.

Dixon & Gill, *Changes in the Standards for Admitting Expert Evidence in Federal Civil Cases Since the Daubert Decision* xiii (RAND Institute for Civil Justice 2001). Copyright 2001 by the RAND Corporation.

Drummond, "The Electronic Courthouse," *Litigation News,* Volume 23, 1998. © 1998 by the American Bar Association. Reprinted with permission. All rights reserved. This information or any portion thereof may not be copied or disseminated in any form or by any means stored in an electronic database or retrieval system without the express written consent of the American Bar Association.

Drummond, "Michigan Legislation Creates First Virtual Courtroom," *Litigation News*, Volume 27, No. 3, March 2002. © 2002 by the American Bar Association. Reprinted with permission. All rights reserved. This information or any portion thereof may not be copied or disseminated in any form or by any means stored in an electronic database or retrieval system without the express written consent of the American Bar Association.

Ehrenbard, "Cutting Discovery Costs Through Interrogatories and Document Requests," *Litigation*, Volume 1, No. 2, Spring 1975. © 1975 by the American Bar Association. Reprinted with permission. All rights reserved. This information or any portion thereof may not be copied or disseminated in any form or by any means stored in an electronic database or retrieval system without the express written consent of the American Bar Association.

Elliott, "Managerial Judging and the Evolution of Procedure," 53 *U. Chi. L. Rev.* 306 (1986). Copyright © 1986 by the University of Chicago Law Review.

Fairman, "The Myth of Notice Pleading," 45 *Ariz. L. Rev.* 987 (2003). Copyright 2003 by Arizona Board of Regents and Christopher Fairman. Reprinted with permission of the author and publisher.

Fiss, "Against Settlement," 93 *Yale L. J.* 1073 (1984). Reprinted by permission of The Yale Law Journal Company and Fred B. Rothman & Company from The Yale Law Journal, Vol. 93, pp. 1073–1090.

J. Flanagan, *Pleadings, Motions and Papers from the Buffalo Creek Case* (1986). Copyright © 1986 by James F. Flanagan.

Flynn & Finkelstein, "A Primer on 'E-vide-n.c.e.,'" *Litigation*, Volume 28, No. 2, Winter 2002. © 2002 by the American Bar Association. Reprinted with permission. All rights reserved. This information or any portion thereof may not be copied or disseminated in any form or by any means stored in an electronic database or retrieval system without the express written consent of the American Bar Association.

J. Foonberg, *How to Start and Build a Law Practice* (4th ed. 1999). Copyright © 1999 by Jay G. Foonberg.

J. Frank, *Courts on Trial: Myth and Reality in American Justice* (1949). Copyright © 1949 by Jerome Frank; copyright © renewed 1976 by Princeton University Press.

Frankel, "The Adversary Judge," 64 *Tex. L. Rev.* 465 (1976). Published originally in 64 *Tex. L. Rev.* 465–87 (1976). Copyright © 1976 by the Texas Law Review Association. Reprinted by permission.

Friedman, Note, "An Analysis of Settlement," 22 *Stan. L. Rev.* 67 (1969). Copyright © 1969 by the Board of Trustees of the Leland Stanford Junior University and Fred B. Rothman & Co.

Galanter, "Reading the Landscape of Disputes: What We Know and Don't Know (and Think We Know) About Our Allegedly Contentious and Litigious Society," 31 *UCLA L. Rev.* 4 (1983). Originally published in 31

UCLA L. Rev. 4, copyright © 1983, The Regents of the University of California. All rights reserved.

Goldberg, "Playing Hardball," *A.B.A.J.*, July 1, 1987, at 48. Reprinted by permission, © 1987. The *ABA Journal* is published by the American Bar Association.

J. Goulden, *The Superlawyers* (1971). Copyright © 1971, 1999 by Joseph C. Goulden. Reprinted by permission of Brandt & Hochman Literary Agents, Inc.

Grady, "Trial Lawyers, Litigators and Clients' Costs," *Litigation*, Volume 4, No. 3, Spring 1978. © 1978 by the American Bar Association. Reprinted with permission. All rights reserved. This information or any portion thereof may not be copied or disseminated in any form or by any means stored in an electronic database or retrieval system without the express written consent of the American Bar Association.

Hazard, "From Whom No Secrets Are Hid," 76 *Texas L. Rev.* 1665 (1998).

G. Hazard & W. Hodes, *The Law of Lawyering* (2d ed. 1990). Reprinted by permission of Panel Publishers, a division of Aspen Publishers, Inc., 36 W. 44th Street, Suite 1316, New York, New York 10036. Copyright 1990 by Panel Publishers.

K. Hegland, *Introduction to the Study and Practice of Law in a Nutshell* (4th ed. 2003). Copyright © 2003 by West Group.

Helland & Tabarrok, "Contingency Fees, Settlement Delay, and Low–Quality Litigation: Empirical Evidence from Two Datasets," 19 *J. L. Econ. & Org.* 517, 517 (2003).

Honeyman & Schneider, "Catching up with the Major–General: The Need for a 'Canon in Negotiation,' " 87 *Marq. L. Rev.* 637 (2004).

Jackson, "Tribute to Country Lawyers: A Review," *A.B.A.J.*, March 1944, at 136. Reprinted by permission, © 1944. The *ABA Journal* is published by the American Bar Association.

F. James et al., *Civil Procedure* (5th ed. 2001).

Joseph, "Rule Traps," *Litigation*, Volume 30, No. 1, Fall 2003. © 2003 by the American Bar Association. Reprinted with permission. All rights reserved. This information or any portion thereof may not be copied or disseminated in any form or by any means stored in an electronic database or retrieval system without the express written consent of the American Bar Association.

Kakalik et al., "Discovery Management: Further Analysis of the Civil Justice Reform Act Evaluation Data," 39 *B.C. L. Rev.* 613 (1998). Copyright © 1998 by the *Boston College Law Review*.

J. Kakalik et al., *Just, Speedy and Inexpensive? An Evaluation of Judicial Case Management Under the Civil Justice Reform Act* (Rand Institute for Civil Justice 1996). Copyright © 1996 by the RAND Corporation.

Shapiro, "Some Problems of Discovery in an Adversary System," 63 *Minn. L. Rev.* 1055 (1979). Copyright © 1979 by David L. Shapiro and the University of Minnesota Law Review.

Shepherd, "An Empirical Study of the Economics of Pretrial Discovery," 19 *Int'l Rev. L. & Econ.*, 245 (1999). Copyright © 1999, reprinted with permission from Elsevier Science.

Sofaer, "Sanctioning Attorneys for Discovery Abuse Under the New Federal Rules: On the Limited Utility of Punishment," 57 *St. John's L. Rev.* 680 (1983). Copyright © 1983 by Abraham D. Sofaer and the St. John's Law Review.

Special Project, "The Work Product Doctrine," 68 *Cornell L. Rev.* 760 (1983). Copyright © 1983 by the Cornell Law Review.

Stein, "Believe Me It Happened. I Was There," *Litigation*, Volume 15, No. 2, Winter 1989. © 1989 by the American Bar Association. Reprinted with permission. All rights reserved. This information or any portion thereof may not be copied or disseminated in any form or by any means stored in an electronic database or retrieval system without the express written consent of the American Bar Association.

Steinman, "The Pleading Problem," 62 *Stan. L. Rev.* 1293, 1299 (2010).

Sternlight, "Separate and Not Equal: Integrating Civil Procedure and ADR in Legal Academia," 80 *Notre Dame L. Rev.* 681 (2005). Reprinted by permission. Copyright © by the *Notre Dame Law Review*, University of Notre Dame, which bears no responsibility for any errors in reprinting or editing of the reprinted portion of this article.

J. Stewart, *The Partners* (1983). Reprinted by permission of International Creative Management, Inc., Copyright © 1983 by James Stewart.

L. Stryker, *The Art of Advocacy* (1954). Copyright © 1954 by Simon & Schuster, Inc.

Sunderland, "The New Federal Rules," 45 *W.Va. L. Q.* 5 (1938). Copyright © 1938 by the West Virginia Law Review.

Sunderland, "The Theory and Practice of Pre–Trial Procedure," 36 *Mich. L. Rev.* 215 (1937). Copyright © 1937 by the Michigan Law Review.

D. Suplee & D. Donaldson, *The Deposition Handbook* (4th ed. 2002). Copyright © 2002 by Dennis R. Suplee, Diana S. Donaldson, and Aspen Law Publishers, Inc. Reprinted with permission.

"The Line of Gratitude," 7 *Law Office Economics & Management* (1966). Copyright © 1966 by Law Office Economics and Management (Callaghan Publishing Co.).

Thomas, "The Story of Pre-trial in the Common Pleas Court of Cuyahoga County," 7 *W. Res. L. Rev.* 368 (1956). Copyright © 1956 by the Case Western Reserve Law Review.

Thornberg, "Sanctifying Secrecy: The Mythology of the Corporate Attorney–Client Privilege," 69 *Notre Dame L. Rev.* 157 (1993). Reprinted with permission by the *Notre Dame Law Review*, University of Notre Dame, which bears no responsibility for any errors in reprinting or editing of the reprinted portion of this article.

Tobias, "Local Federal Civil Procedure for the Twenty–First Century," 77 *Notre Dame L. Rev.* 533 (2002). Reprinted with permission © by the *Notre Dame Law Review*, University of Notre Dame, which bears no responsibility for any errors in reprinting or editing of the reprinted portion of this article.

R. Traver, *Anatomy of a Murder* (1958). Copyright © 1958, 1983 by the author and reprinted by permission of St. Martin's Press, LLC.

Trubek et al., "The Costs of Ordinary Litigation," 31 *UCLA L. Rev.* 72 (1983). Originally published in 31 *UCLA L. Rev.* 72. Copyright © 1983, The Regents of the University of California. All rights reserved.

Wald, "Summary Judgment at Sixty," 76 *Tex. L. Rev.* 1897 (1998). Copyright © 1998 by the University of Texas Law Review.

Webber, Comment, "Mandatory Summary Jury Trial: Playing by the Rules?," 56 *U. Chi. L. Rev.* 1495 (1989).

Weissbrod, Comment, "Sanctions Under Amended Rule 26–Scalpel or Meat-ax? The 1983 Amendments to the Federal Rules of Civil Procedure," 46 *Ohio St. L. J.* 183 (1985). Copyright © 1985 by The Ohio State University.

Will et al., "The Role of the Judge in the Settlement Process," 75 F.R.D. 203 (1976). Copyright © 1976 by West Group.

C. Wright et al., *Federal Practice and Procedure*. Copyright © 1990, 1994, 1998 & 2004 by West Group.

Wright, "The Pretrial Conference," 28 F.R.D. 141 (1960). Copyright 1960 by West Group.

Summary of Contents

TABLE OF CONTENTS

TABLE OF CASES

The principal cases are in bold type. Cases cited or discussed in the text are in roman type. References are to pages. Cases cited in principal cases and within other quoted materials are not included.

TABLE OF MODEL RULES OF PROFESSIONAL CONDUCT

PRETRIAL LITIGATION
LAW, POLICY AND PRACTICE
Fifth Edition

CHAPTER 1

AN OVERVIEW OF THE PRETRIAL PROCESS: "AND YOU CALL YOURSELF A *TRIAL* LAWYER?"

■ ■ ■

In the beginning * * *.

Genesis 1:1.

These [Federal Rules of Civil Procedure] * * * should be construed and administered to secure the just, speedy, and inexpensive determination of every action and proceeding.

Rule 1 of the Federal Rules of Civil Procedure.

Analysis

I. INTRODUCTION

There are many skills that attorneys must possess, and many roles that attorneys must play, to be successful in the pretrial litigation process. Attorneys must know how to draft pleadings, conduct both oral and written discovery, prepare and argue motions, and negotiate on behalf of their clients. These skills are the subject of the following chapters of this book. Before plunging into a discussion of the many separate tasks that attorneys perform in the pretrial process, this chapter looks briefly at the system as a whole.

The first major section of the chapter briefly examines the civil pretrial process. Contrary to popular belief, it is within the pretrial

1

process, rather than in the more formal courtroom setting, that most "trial lawyers" spend most of their time. More than ninety percent of the civil lawsuits filed each year are settled or otherwise resolved short of trial.[1]

The chapter also considers the various tasks that attorneys perform within the pretrial process. This section of the chapter sketches the relationships among the different parts of the pretrial process and the various pretrial skills and tasks. By remaining aware of these relationships, a more integrated, and thus more successful, pretrial advocacy should be achieved.

Finally, this chapter introduces the Buffalo Creek disaster litigation that forms the basis for many of the exercises and problems contained in this book. By drawing upon this single factual scenario for exercises and problems, a more concrete appreciation of pretrial tasks and skills, as well as the relationships among those tasks and skills, should be gained.

II. AN OVERVIEW OF THE PRETRIAL PROCESS

Civil lawsuits often involve a great deal of pretrial activity. In too many lawsuits, this activity is unrelated to other pretrial activity or to trial. When handled properly, however, pretrial proceedings should be coordinated with other pretrial and trial activity in the case. Pretrial litigation also must be understood against the backdrop of the system of civil litigation of which it is one part. In order to fully understand the pretrial process, one must understand the system by which civil disputes are adjudicated in this country.

Of some help in appreciating civil litigation is an understanding of a "typical" civil dispute. Such a dispute has been described as follows in one comprehensive study of federal and state cases:

> [F]irst, the very fact that a dispute has reached the court and not been settled without litigation makes it unusual. Viewed against the baseline of potential lawsuits, litigation is not frequent, since for every dispute in the court records there are nine others that never

---

1. For the 12 month period that ended March 31, 2010, only 1.2% of the civil actions, other than land condemnation cases, that were terminated in the federal courts reached trial. Admin. Office of the U.S. Courts, *Federal Judicial Caseload Statistics: March 31, 2010* (2010) (Table C4). In a major study of trial trends in 22 state courts, civil jury trials as a percentage of total civil dispositions decreased from about 1.8% in 1976 to 0.6% in 2002, while bench trials decreased from 34% to 15%. Considering just torts, contract, and real property rights cases, the percentage of jury trials per total dispositions was 1.3% in 2002, while the percentage of bench trials was 4.3%. Ostrom et al., "Examining Trial Trends in State Courts: 1976–2002," 1 *J. Emp. Legal Studies* 755, 768–771 (2004). *See also* Eisenberg et al., "Litigation Outcomes in State and Federal Courts: A Statistical Portrait," 19 *Seattle U. Law Rev.* 433, 444 (1996); Grossman et al., "Measuring the Pace of Civil Litigation in Federal and State Trial Courts," 65 *Judicature* 86, 106 (Table 6) (1981). So few cases are now resolved by trial that the American Bar Association and others have expressed concern about the "Vanishing Trial" phenomenon. *See generally* Galanter, "A World Without Trials?," 2006 *J. Disp. Resol.* 7; Symposium, "The Vanishing Trial," 1 *J. Emp. Legal Studies* 459 (2004).

even reach the filing stage. Second, the cases in courts of general jurisdiction are modest. The parties are usually fighting over money, and the amounts at stake are $10,000 or less. Third, the typical case is procedurally simple and will be settled voluntarily without a verdict or judgment on the merits. This case will involve some pretrial activity, but no trial. Each side's lawyer spends about thirty hours on the case, mostly gathering facts and negotiating a settlement. Judicial involvement, either ruling on motions or rendering judgment, will be rare.[2]

The mere fact that a dispute is in the courts makes that dispute a statistical rarity. Moreover, even if a person invokes formal adjudicatory mechanisms by the filing of a civil complaint, it is likely that the lawsuit will be resolved by the same informal settlement techniques as are disputes that never result in formal lawsuits.[3]

Although there is no single route by which all civil lawsuits proceed to trial, there are some generalities that can be made about the steps in the civil pretrial process. For instance, the complaint almost always is filed before discovery is undertaken and after the client has been interviewed and at least some informal investigation undertaken.[4] As illustrated in Figure 1–1, the chapters of this book are organized to reflect the typical pretrial stages in a civil case. This pretrial case progression should be kept in mind as individual chapters of the book are studied.

Although much, if not most, civil litigation proceeds in roughly the order set forth in Figure 1–1, there are numerous exceptions to this sequence. Because this book focuses on pretrial litigation under the Federal Rules of Civil Procedure and state counterparts to those Rules, procedures in a state which has not adopted a variant of the Federal Rules may differ somewhat from those set forth in Figure 1–1. Even in jurisdic-

---

2. Trubek et al., "The Costs of Ordinary Litigation," 31 *UCLA L. Rev.* 72, 83–84 (1983). *See also* Galanter, "Reading the Landscape of Disputes: What We Know and Don't Know (And Think We Know) About Our Allegedly Contentious and Litigious Society," 31 *UCLA L. Rev.* 4 (1983).

Although judicial involvement in most civil cases is rare, the aggregate governmental cost of the judicial processing of civil cases was approximately $1.9 billion for state cases in fiscal year 1980 and $287 million for federal cases in fiscal year 1981. J. Kakalik & R. Ross, *Costs of the Civil Justice System* xix–xx (1983). In addition to these governmental costs are the much greater costs borne by the private litigants in the civil justice system.

3. Of the 285,126 non-land condemnation cases terminated in the federal courts during the twelve month period that ended March 31, 2010, 55,286 cases were terminated with no court action. Admin. Office of the U.S. Courts, *Statistical Tables for the Federal Judiciary: March 31, 2010* (2010) (Table C4). In addition, Professor Marc Galanter has noted that "[o]ver 30% of cases in American courts of general jurisdiction are not formally contested." Galanter, *supra* note 2, at 26.

The informal settlement of lawsuits within the formal judicial process has been referred to as "bargaining in the shadow of the law." Mnookin & Kornhauser, "Bargaining in the Shadow of the Law: The Case of Divorce," 88 *Yale L. J.* 950 (1979). *See also* H. Ross, *Settled Out of Court: The Social Process of Insurance Claims Adjustment* (2d ed. 1980).

4. This sequence need not always be followed, however. Federal Rule of Civil Procedure 27(a) permits depositions to be undertaken before the filing of an action in certain circumstances, while the statute of limitations or the physical or mental condition of one's client may limit the extent of the client interview or other investigation that can be undertaken prior to the filing of a civil complaint.

tions that have adopted the basic provisions of the Federal Rules of Civil Procedure, there may be good reasons to vary the pretrial litigation stages to best suit the needs of individual cases.

FIGURE 1-1

TYPICAL PRETRIAL STAGES IN A CIVIL CASE

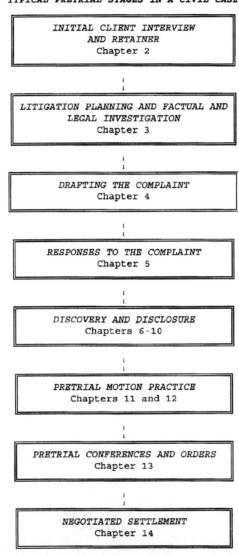

Not reflected in Figure 1–1 is the fact that different pretrial proceedings may be conducted simultaneously. For example, discovery on one issue may proceed simultaneously with the briefing of motions to dismiss or for summary judgment on other issues. Moreover, many pretrial activities may be undertaken at several points prior to trial. There often will be several client interviews, and factual investigation and legal research generally will be conducted throughout the entire pretrial period.

In addition to the pretrial activities set forth in Figure 1–1, Chapter 15 of this book considers possible alternatives to the formal adjudication of civil claims. Not only can these alternative dispute resolution mechanisms be invoked prior to resort to the courts, but they can be employed at various stages of the pretrial process. Indeed, you may want to read Chapter 15 before starting through the chapters concerning specific aspects of the pretrial process. Counsel always should be alert to opportunities to resolve a dispute, whether prior to the filing of a lawsuit or at any stage of a lawsuit that actually is filed.

III. THE LAWYER'S ROLE IN THE PRETRIAL PROCESS

The fact that most cases are resolved prior to trial has important ramifications for the tasks to which civil litigators devote their time. In one study of civil litigation,[5] the following breakdown of attorney time was found:

AVERAGE PERCENTAGE OF LAWYER TIME DEVOTED TO ACTIVITIES

Activity	% of Time Spent
Conferring with Client	16.0
Discovery	16.7
Factual Investigation	12.8
Settlement Discussions	15.1
Pleadings	14.3
Legal Research	10.1
Trials and Hearings	8.6
Appeals and Enforcement	.9
Other	5.5
	100.0

This data supports the assertion that with the "burgeoning of pretrial and post-trial activities like motions, discovery, hearings, conferences, post-conviction proceedings, hearings about lawyer's fees, etc., the trial is no longer the center of gravity of common law litigation."[6] Thus while

---

5. Trubek, et al., *supra* note 2, at 91 (Table 3). A study of federal civil cases in the 1990s found that lawyers spent their time on: trials (11%); alternative dispute resolution after filing (3%); discovery after filing (36%); motion practice (16%); other pretrial conferences or talks with judicial officer (3%); other time worked after case filing (24%); and time worked before filing case (7%). Kakalik et al., "Discovery Management: Further Analysis of the Civil Justice Reform Act Evaluation Data," 39 *B.C.L. Rev.* 613, 637 (1998). A Federal Judicial Center study of civil cases terminated in 2008 found that attorneys representing primarily plaintiffs spent, on average, 42.7% of their time in discovery-related activities, while attorneys representing primarily defendants spent, on average, 47.7% on such activities. E. Lee & T. Willging, *Federal Judicial Center National, Case–Based Civil Rules Survey: Preliminary Report to the Judicial Conference Advisory Committee on Civil Rules* 11 (2009).

6. Galanter, *supra* note 2, at 45. Statistics cited by Professor Galanter show a decline in the percentage of civil cases terminated during or after trial in United States district courts from

earlier generations of lawyers prided themselves on being "trial lawyers," many of today's law firms boast of their extensive "litigation departments."

This is not to suggest that modern litigators can be ignorant of trial and appellate practice. The Federal Rules of Civil Procedure and Federal Rules of Evidence, which govern the trial and pretrial stages of civil lawsuits, are premised upon the assumption that civil litigation culminates in formal adjudication by a judge or jury.

In addition, as Professor Marc Galanter has noted, "Litigation * * * profoundly affects what happens at earlier [prelitigation] stages by providing cues, symbols, and bargaining counters which the actors use in constructing (and dismantling) disputes."[7] Or, as was more pragmatically put by attorney Melvin Belli, "I have to maintain my advocacy in court on trial in order to keep up my settlement value."[8] Although the great majority of lawsuits are resolved short of trial, it is the possibility of trial that leads to many of these pretrial case resolutions.

The relationship of pretrial to trial proceedings should be kept in mind as pretrial skills and proceedings are considered in the subsequent chapters of this book. Although there are quite distinct pretrial activities and proceedings, they should not be considered in isolation. Just as there are relationships among the various pretrial proceedings themselves, pretrial proceedings are part of a much more comprehensive process for the eventual resolution of civil claims at trial.

IV. THE BUFFALO CREEK DISASTER LITIGATION

At approximately 8:00 a.m. on February 26, 1972, a coal refuse retaining dam on the Middle Fork in Logan County, West Virginia failed. As a result of this dam failure, over 130 million gallons of water were released into the narrow Buffalo Creek Valley. The resulting flood killed

---

15.2% in 1940 to 6.5% in 1980. *Id.* at 44 (Table 2). For the 12 month period that ended on March 31, 2010, only 1.2% of the civil actions, other than land condemnation cases, that were terminated in the federal courts reached trial. Admin. Office of the U.S. Courts, *Statistical Tables for the Federal Judiciary: March 31, 2010* (2010) (Table C4).

However, as Professor Galanter notes, "[F]or the minority of matters that run the full course, adjudication is more protracted, more elaborate, more exhaustive, and more expensive." Galanter, *supra* note 2, at 44. *See also* Galanter, "The Vanishing Trial: An Examination of Trials and Related Matters in Federal and State Courts," 1 *J. Emp. Legal Studies* 459, 477–78 (2004) (civil trials lasting at least four days constituted 15% of federal civil trials in 1965, but 29% of federal civil trials in 2002); R. Posner, *The Federal Courts: Crisis and Reform* 66–68 (1985) (percentage of federal civil cases reaching trial declined from 11.4% in 1962 to 5.4% in 1983, but average length of federal civil trials rose from 2.2 days in 1960 to 3.1 days in 1983). *But see* Clark, "Adjudication to Administration: A Statistical Analysis of Federal District Courts in the Twentieth Century," 55 *S. Cal. L. Rev.* 65, 80–81 (1981) (average length of time from civil case filing to final termination in the federal courts dropped from approximately 3.5 to 1.16 years from 1900 to 1980).

7. Galanter, *supra* note 2, at 12.

8. Belli, "Pre-trial: Aid to the New Advocacy," 43 *Cornell L. Q.* 34, 44 (1957).

125 men, women, and children, destroyed over 500 homes, and left approximately 4000 people homeless.[9]

The devastation was described by an investigator for the United States Senate some ten days after the flood:

> It is virtually impossible to describe what one sees in something like this, and even the photographs cannot convey the impression one gets from being at the scene and personally viewing the damage. The damage varies from houses being loosened from their foundations (at the lower end of the hollow) to complete obliteration of whole settlements. Everywhere one looks, and in all directions, there are wrecked houses, tons of debris, black mud, and hundreds of mutilated automobiles.[10]

Senate investigators received the following account of the flood from one of its victims:

> At approximately 8:00 a.m., Miss Gibson heard the sound of rushing water coming from the direction of the slate pile. She went out the back door with two babies under her arms and started running up the mountain. Looking back, Miss Gibson saw an ocean of water hit the burning slate and a loud explosion sounded. She said that a pile of slate and water bigger than two trailers flew in the air together with smoke and gas. * * * She said the water and slate crashed over the church at the right of the dam. Miss Gibson estimated that the water was at least 20 feet high at this point. After the church was crushed, the water moved onto a course following the road down the hollow.[11]

The experiences of other residents of the Buffalo Creek Valley were similar:

> The morning was clear and light. Bennie Wilson went to the bathroom in [Tom] Sparks' house and Harold Sloane watched the water coming over the dam. As Mr. Wilson left the bathroom, he heard the water rushing over the dam and when he went outside he saw the water hit a hot slag dump piled on the outside of the dam approximately 100 yards from Sparks house across the road at the right of the dam. Mr. Wilson said the slag dump exploded, carrying water and slag 100 feet in the air. * * * Mr. Wilson yelled to Tom Sparks who was in the hog house and all three men ran across the highway, across the railroad tracks and up the mountain directly opposite Sparks house. * * *

---

9. Task Force to Study Coal Waste Hazards, U.S. Dept. of the Interior, *Preliminary Analysis of the Coal Refuse Dam Failure at Saunders, West Virginia, February 26, 1972* 1 (March 12, 1972), *reprinted in Buffalo Creek (W.Va.) Disaster, 1972: Hearings before the Subcomm. on Labor of the Senate Comm. on Labor and Public Welfare*, 92d Cong., 2d Sess. 867, 870 (1972); T. Nugent, *Death at Buffalo Creek* 146 (1973). *See also* Governor's Ad Hoc Commission of Inquiry, State of West Virginia, *The Buffalo Creek Flood and Disaster* (1972).

10. *Buffalo Creek (W.Va.) Disaster, 1972: Hearings before the Subcomm. on Labor of the Senate Comm. on Labor and Public Welfare*, 92d Cong., 2d Sess. 867, 870 (1972) (Memorandum to Files (Roy Wade)) [hereinafter *Senate Hearings*].

11. *Senate Hearings*, *supra* note 10, at 1249 (Memorandum of Interview (Sherry Elaine Gibson)).

From a perch approximately 30 feet up the mountain, they watched the water * * * take out the church near the right side of the dam. The water then moved to the left, sweeping away Harold Sloane's house, Tom Sparks house, his pig house, pigs and truck. Mr. Wilson said the water, which was about 30 feet high at this point, moved down the hollow wiping out everything in its path. * * *

* * * Mr. Wilson and Mr. Sparks [eventually] went to the road across from Bennie Wilson's house[,] * * * [which] was filled with unclothed bodies, mangled cars and an assortment of rubbish.[12]

As a result of this disaster several lawsuits were filed. One of these lawsuits, *Prince v. The Pittston Company*,[13] was brought on behalf of approximately 600 plaintiffs by attorney Gerald Stern and is described in his 1976 book *The Buffalo Creek Disaster*. In this suit the plaintiffs sought injunctive relief, punitive damages, and compensatory damages under traditional tort theories for loss of property, personal injuries, and wrongful death. Attorney Gerald Stern also retained expert witnesses to testify concerning the "survivors' syndrome" and loss of community from which those plaintiffs who had survived the flood were suffering.[14] Because the lawsuit ultimately was settled for $13,500,000, there was no trial of this action.

The Buffalo Creek flood and the litigation that it spawned provide the basis for many of the pretrial litigation exercises and problems throughout this book.

V. CONCLUSION

This chapter has introduced, albeit quite briefly, the system of civil adjudication of which modern pretrial litigation is one part. Attorneys involved in pretrial litigation, as well as students attempting to master the various pretrial litigation skills, need to be aware of the relationships among different aspects of the pretrial process and the lawsuit of which individual pretrial processes are one part. To paraphrase John Donne, no element of the pretrial process is "entire of itself;" instead, each element is "a part of the main," *i.e.,* of a comprehensive procedural system for the resolution of civil actions. Understanding not only the individual aspects of the pretrial process, but also their interrelationships and their place within a system of civil adjudication, is the challenge posed to the civil litigator.

---

12. *Senate Hearings, supra* note 10, at 1325–26 (Memorandum of Interview (Bennie Wilson)).

13. Civil Action 3052 (S.D.W.Va. 1972).

14. One of these experts, sociologist Kai Erickson, has described the plaintiffs' psychological injuries in his book *Everything In Its Path: Destruction of Community in the Buffalo Creek Flood* (1976). *See also* G. Gleser et al., *Prolonged Psychological Effects of Disaster: A Study of Buffalo Creek* (1981); "Special Section: Disaster at Buffalo Creek," *Am. J. Psychiatry,* March 1976, at 295; Lifton & Olson, "The Human Meaning of Total Disaster," *Psychiatry,* Feb. 1976, at 1.

A more general description of the Buffalo Creek flood is provided in Nugent, *supra* note 9.

VI. CHAPTER BIBLIOGRAPHY

D. Baum, *Art of Advocacy: Preparation of the Case* (1981).

M. Berger et al., *Pretrial Advocacy: Planning, Analysis, and Strategy* (3d ed. 2010).

Committee on Continuing Professional Education, American Law Institute–American Bar Association, *ALI–ABA's Practice Checklist Manual on Trial Preparation* (1996).

Committee on Continuing Professional Education, American Law Institute–American Bar Association, *ALI–ABA's Practice Checklist Manual on Trial Preparation II* (1999).

Committee on Continuing Professional Education, American Law Institute–American Bar Association, *The Practical Lawyer's Manual on Pretrial Preparation* (1985).

Committee on Continuing Professional Education, American Law Institute–American Bar Association, *The Practical Lawyer's Manual on Pretrial Preparation No. 2* (1986).

R. L. Dessem, *Pretrial Litigation in a Nutshell* (4th ed. 2008).

S. Gold, *Fundamentals of Federal Court Pre–Trial Techniques* (1982).

J. Hartje & M. Wilson, *Lawyer's Work: Counseling, Problem Solving, Advocacy and Conduct of Litigation* (1984).

R. Haydock et al., *Fundamentals of Pretrial Litigation* (8th ed. 2011).

D. Karlen, *Procedure Before Trial in a Nutshell* (1972).

The Litigation Manual: Pretrial (J. Koelt & J. Kiernan eds. 3d ed. 1999).

T. Mauet, *Pretrial* (7th ed. 2008).

National Institute for Trial Advocacy, *Training the Advocate: The Pretrial Stage* (1985) (videotapes).

C. Rose & J. Underwood, *Fundamental Pretrial Advocacy* (2008).

R. Simon, *A Complete Course in Pretrial Litigation* (1987).

J. Tanford, *The Pretrial Process* (2003).

CHAPTER 2

INTERVIEWING AND THE ESTABLISHMENT OF THE ATTORNEY-CLIENT RELATIONSHIP: "HOW DO YOU DO?"

■ ■ ■

Let us allow plenty of time and a place of interview free from interruption to those who shall have occasion to consult us, and let us earnestly exhort them to state every particular off hand, however verbosely or however far he may wish to go back; for it is a less inconvenience to listen to what is superfluous than to be left ignorant of what is essential.

Roman Rhetorician Quintilian, *quoted in* L. Stryker, *The Art of Advocacy* 7–8 (1954).

Yes, * * * we can doubtless gain your case for you; we can set a whole neighborhood at loggerheads; we can distress a widowed mother and her six fatherless children and thereby get you six hundred dollars to which you seem to have a legal claim, but which rightfully belongs, it appears to me, as much to the woman and her children as it does to you. You must remember that some things legally right are not morally right. We shall not take your case, but will give you a little advice for which we will charge you nothing. You seem to be a sprightly, energetic man; we would advise you to try your hand at making six hundred dollars in some other way.

Abraham Lincoln, *quoted in* 2 W. Herndon & J. Weik, *Herndon's Lincoln* 345–46 n* (1889).

Analysis

Sec.

I. INTRODUCTION

Much of modern American legal education involves a consideration of the decisions of appellate courts, from which decisions students are expected to extract governing principles of law. Because of this focus on appellate decisions, students sometimes forget that there were real people involved in the cases now digested in their casebooks and that those people initially came to attorneys seeking help with their real world problems. Harry Tompkins consulted an attorney to obtain money from the Erie Railroad to compensate him for the loss of his arm, rather than because of any great interest in the relationship between the federal and state judicial systems.[1] Carl Hansberry pursued his litigation to the United States Supreme Court to secure the right to live in Chicago's South Park neighborhood, rather than to establish a major Supreme Court precedent concerning the application of constitutional due process to class actions.[2]

In contrast to the top-down view of litigation sometimes fostered by traditional law school casebooks, the focus of this chapter of the present text is on clients. Initially considered is an attorney's first meeting with her client and how to interview the client so that the best legal representation can be provided. The chapter then examines the ethical ground rules governing client interviews. Finally, the chapter considers the client's retainer of the attorney and the agreements and understandings commonly existing between attorney and client.

As noted in the prior chapter, the attorneys surveyed in one study spent sixteen percent of their time conferring with their clients.[3] That figure is even more significant when the time devoted to other attorney litigation tasks is considered. The attorneys surveyed devoted more time to only one other task (discovery, which occupied 16.7 percent of attorney case time), while the time spent with clients was almost twice as much as the 8.6 percent of attorney time spent in trials and hearings.[4] Attorneys who slight interviewing may be disadvantaged in those cases that do reach trial, as well as in cases that are resolved prior to trial, if their clients have not shared all relevant facts with them.

Client interviewing thus is not only an important pretrial litigation task, but one to which attorneys devote significant amounts of their time. Accordingly, the skills and ethics of client interviewing are worthy of close attention by attorneys and law students alike.

---

1. *Erie R.R. v. Tompkins,* 304 U.S. 64 (1938). For a discussion of the background of this case see Younger, "Observation: What Happened in *Erie*," 56 *Tex. L. Rev.* 1011 (1978).

2. *Hansberry v. Lee,* 311 U.S. 32 (1940). For a discussion of the background of this case see Kamp, "The History Behind *Hansberry v. Lee*," 20 *U.C. Davis L. Rev.* 481 (1987).

3. Trubek et al., "The Costs of Ordinary Litigation," 31 *UCLA L. Rev.* 72, 91 (Table 3) (1983).

4. *Id.*

II. THE INITIAL CLIENT INTERVIEW

Client interviews are important for many reasons. Among the purposes of the client interview are: (1) obtaining information from the client; (2) testing the client's version of the facts; (3) explaining the legal process to the client; (4) explaining the likely course and consequences of the present lawsuit or of any lawsuit that the client may file; (5) exploring non-adjudicative dispute resolution alternatives; (6) evaluating the client as both a client and as a witness at deposition and at trial; (7) conveying the attorney's professionalism and competence to the client; (8) working to obtain the active participation of the client in the matter; and (9) generally developing attorney-client rapport.

In order to conduct effective client interviews and achieve these multiple goals, attorneys must pay attention to the structure of the interviews and their own questioning and listening techniques. Both interview structure and technique now will be considered.

A. THE STRUCTURE OF THE INITIAL CLIENT INTERVIEW

Different attorneys conduct initial client interviews in different ways. Interview structures that work well for one attorney may not be as successful for other attorneys. Because of the importance of client interviews, however, attorneys should be aware of the interview structure, explicit or implicit, that they use.

The present section of this chapter suggests one possible manner in which initial client interviews can be structured. The suggested structure includes (1) introductions and introductory remarks; (2) the client's problem definition; (3) the client narrative; (4) a description of the relief sought by the client; (5) follow-up questioning by the attorney; and (6) concluding remarks.[5]

1. Introductions and Introductory Remarks: "Glad to Meet You"

As is the case with most activities, it is best to begin client interviews at the beginning. This can mean different things for different attorneys in different types of practices.

---

5. For other suggested interview structures *see* D. Binder & S. Price, *Legal Interviewing and Counseling: A Client–Centered Approach* 53–103 (1977); R. Cochran et al., *The Counselor-at-Law: A Collaborative Approach to Client Interviewing and Counseling* 58–59 (2d ed. 2006); J. Tanford, *The Trial Process: Law, Tactics & Ethics* 51–52 (3d ed. 2002). *See also* D. Binder et al., *Lawyers as Counselors: A Client–Centered Approach* 80–207; 234–246 (2d ed. 2004).

There also are legal settings (such as legal aid and public defender offices) in which attorneys are required to use an interview check list. While these forms give a structure to legal interviews, they can inhibit attorney-client communication. This may occur if the client believes that the attorney is more interested in the interview form than in him, the client does not understand why the form seeks certain information, or the attorney misses important non-verbal cues from the client due to a preoccupation with the form. Thus, while interview forms and check lists can be quite helpful, they should be used with care.

At the time that he arranged his appointment with counsel, the client may have provided limited background information, including a preliminary definition of his legal problem, to a secretary or paralegal. The office's conflicts index may have been checked to ensure that no conflict of interest stemming from the office's other representations prevents acceptance of this case. In a legal aid office, the client may have been required to provide income and other information to determine his eligibility for the legal assistance being sought. In other situations, the client may have been informed about the charge for the initial attorney consultation.

Presuming such preliminary matters have been completed, the attorney and client will now meet (in most cases for the first time). Because many clients are not familiar with the legal system, the attorney should attempt to put the client at ease as soon as possible. Most of us learn such techniques well before coming to law school: a friendly smile, a warm handshake, the offer of a comfortable chair and, perhaps, a cup of coffee.

Physical surroundings can either ease or create discomfort for the client. It's not a terrific idea to sit clients in straight back chairs with bright lights shining in their eyes as in the old detective thrillers shown on the late show. Clients also may feel more comfortable relating their problems to attorneys who are not barricaded behind their desks, but who instead sit opposite them around a conference table or in a corner of the office. The attorney, too, must be comfortable with the physical surroundings, while striving to maintain an office that does not heighten the anxieties that most people feel when initially dealing with an attorney.

In a further effort to put her client at ease, the attorney should consider explaining to the client exactly what will happen during the interview. An attorney might tell her client something like this:

> Mr. Jones, what I'd like to do during this interview is to learn about your problem. After you've told me all about the problem, I'll have some questions for you. Then we'll talk some about your situation and about your legal options. I've had my secretary hold my calls, so that we should have the next hour to talk. You also should know that everything you tell me is privileged, which means that, generally, the court can't require either one of us to reveal our conversation.

> Before we begin, do you have any questions about the interview?

Once the client is aware of the anticipated structure of the interview, the attorney and client should get to the matter at hand, *i.e.,* determine what the problem is that has caused the client to seek legal help.

2.   The Client's Problem Definition: "What's the Matter?"

To give at least some focus to the interview, the attorney should ask the client at the outset of the interview to describe his problem in a sentence or two. Such a summarization of the client's problem should not only help the client in relating his later, detailed narrative, but also should help the attorney in following such a narrative. The initial problem definition from a client may be no more than a statement that "I just was fired from my job because of my age."

Attorneys should not accept at face value the problem definition that the client gives. For example, although a client may believe that he was fired from his job due to his age, the employer's action may have been taken because of the client's religion, gender, or incompetence. The client's actual problem may be non-legal in nature or may be a problem for which there is no available legal remedy. As more facts are uncovered during the pretrial process, the original problem definition may change.

Nevertheless, it is helpful to have the client initially give his perception of the existing problem. It is the client who has consulted the attorney, and the attorney can provide the best representation if the client, himself, initially defines the problem that has caused him to seek legal assistance.

3.   The Client's Narrative: "Tell Me About It"

Once the preliminaries have been taken care of and the client has summarized his legal problem, it is time for the client to tell his story. As Quintilian stresses in the quotation that begins this chapter, clients should be encouraged to "state every particular off hand, * * * for it is a less inconvenience to listen to what is superfluous than to be left ignorant of what is essential." The client thus should be asked to tell his story. The attorney must know the specific reasons why the client has come to her for help.

The narrative should be more than the mere summarization of the problem that the client already has given. Instead, the client should be asked to elaborate on his problem: "Can you tell me a little more about what happened?" If the client is not encouraged to further describe his problem, the attorney may never obtain information that could help her best represent her client. Both attorney and client need to be aware that it is the lawyer, with her knowledge of the governing law, who ultimately must determine what facts are legally relevant and what facts are not. This only can be done if all the facts are shared with the attorney.

During the initial client narrative, it is best to avoid distractions that may cause the client to limit the information provided to counsel. The client may perceive fidgeting by the lawyer or telephone interruptions as indications that the lawyer is not interested in his problem. Not only may such a perception preclude the attorney from obtaining valuable information from her client, but such a belief may undermine effective attorney-client relations more generally.

Although some lawyers will not permit their clients to say anything that is not immediately written down on a legal pad, note-taking can be distracting, especially to a client who is unfamiliar with the legal system. For this reason, some lawyers do not take notes during the initial client narrative, but ask their clients to tell their stories twice and only take notes as the client's story is told a second time. The attorney's attention to, and eye contact with, the client should encourage him to more fully recount his problem. In addition, the attorney may pick up significant "body language" from the client that would be lost if she had her head in her notes. By watching a client tell his story, the attorney also can make mental notes concerning how the client will appear to opposing counsel at a deposition or to a judge or jury at trial.

Counsel must be alert to any hesitancy on the client's part and consider gently prodding the client to tell his story fully. This is not to say that an attorney should push a client to reveal information of a personal or sensitive nature at the very outset of an interview. However, the attorney must be aware that there is information that the client is not sharing with her, and she must seek that information once the client is more comfortable with her as an attorney. At the end of the client's narrative, the attorney may want to more generally prod her client by asking, "Is there anything else that I should know?"

4. A Description of the Relief Sought by the Client: "What Do You Want Me to Do for You?"

Once the basic facts have been set forth by the client, he will, quite appropriately, expect the attorney to address the possible legal avenues open to him. However, not only should the client initially define his own problem, but he alone can decide the relief that he would like to obtain from the legal system. Presuming the client's objectives are legal, counsel are to "abide by a client's decisions concerning the objectives of representation."[6]

Some clients will not be aware of the legal redress potentially available to them. Other clients may be less than realistic concerning the relief to which they are entitled ("I want to sue that guy for a million dollars!"). One of the important services that lawyers provide is to counsel clients concerning the options available to them. During such counseling, attorneys should not presume that a client desires any particular legal resolution of his problem. Rather than immediately telling a client that "We can sue Acme for $10,000," it is best to ask the client to state precisely what it is that he wants.

Once the client has stated what it is that he seeks, the attorney can discuss the possibility of obtaining such an outcome. In addition, counsel should suggest alternative courses that might be pursued (based upon the limited information available at the time of the initial client interview). In particular, counsel should inform the client about alternative dispute resolution possibilities for resolving the matter (about which many clients will be unaware).[7] However, before she does so, the attorney undoubtedly will have to question the client concerning the specifics of his narrative.

---

6. Model Rules of Prof'l Conduct Rule 1.2(a).

7. In some states, lawyers are required to advise their clients about alternative forms of dispute resolution in matters likely to involve litigation. *E.g.*, Colorado Rules of Prof'l Conduct Rule 2.1. *See also* Comment 5 to Rule 2.1 of the Model Rules of Prof'l Conduct: "[W]hen a matter is likely to involve litigation, it may be necessary under Rule 1.4 to inform the client of forms of

5. Attorney Follow–Up Questioning: "Let Me Ask You a Few Questions"

Once the client has finished his narrative and told the attorney what relief he desires, it's time for the attorney to ask some questions. Follow-up questioning can be thought of as a loop, in which additional information from the client generates additional questions from the attorney (which, in turn, generate additional information from the client).

Follow-up questions should be targeted at particular aspects of the client's narrative, but, at least initially, they should remain as open-ended as possible. Rather than try to pin the client down to specific facts, he first might be asked to "Tell me more about [a particular matter mentioned in his narrative]." In his narrative the client presumably has set forth the basic structure of his problem, and it is now the attorney's job to flesh out important aspects of that structure through follow-up questioning. Attorneys also can use follow-up questions to learn the specific facts supporting the more general conclusions that the client may have offered in his initial narrative.

Follow-up questions can be used to test aspects of the client's narrative, as well as to gain additional information. Not only does Rule 11(b) of the Federal Rules of Civil Procedure require counsel to conduct "an inquiry reasonable under the circumstances," but it is best to find out both the good and bad facts early in the legal representation. The attorney should stress to the client that she needs to know *everything* about his problem—not just the facts that he believes are favorable or relevant.

The client's narrative usually can, and should, be tested in as non-accusatorial a fashion as possible. The initial client interview is not a good time to practice cross-examination technique. The attorney might merely ask for clarification or further explanation concerning aspects of the client narrative that don't ring true: "I'm sorry, but I'm not sure why you believe you were fired on the basis of your age. Are there some facts that you haven't told me that lead you to believe that this is the reason you were fired?"

Follow-up questions should be used to learn more than "the facts, and just the facts." In addition to the facts, the client's explanations and theories about particular facts can be sought, as well as the reactions of individuals to the facts described in the client narrative. While client speculation on such matters may not be admissible at trial, it may be very helpful in guiding further factual investigation and in developing a theory of the case.

Although specific follow-up questions should be based upon the client's narrative and desired relief, there are certain matters that should be probed in any legal representation. If the filing of a legal action on

---

dispute resolution that might constitute reasonable alternatives to litigation." *See also* Breger, "Should an Attorney be Required to Advise a Client of ADR Options?," 13 *Geo. J. Legal Ethics* 427 (2000); Cochran, "ADR, the ABA, and Client Control: A Proposal that the Model Rules Require Lawyers to Present ADR Options to Clients," 41 *S. Tex. L. Rev.* 183 (1999).

behalf of the client is a possible option, the dates of significant occurrences must be nailed down so that any potential statute of limitations problems can be ascertained. Names and addresses of potential witnesses also should be acquired so that the attorney can conduct further factual investigation.

The client must understand that interviewing is a process that is ongoing throughout the legal representation. In most cases the attorney will continue to question her client concerning certain matters throughout the case, and the client's responses often will spark still further questions. Even with the adroit use of follow-up questions, a truly complete client narrative usually is not obtained at the initial client interview. Clients therefore should be advised to keep track of additional information that comes to mind after the initial interview, perhaps by keeping a note pad at their bedside to record information that comes to them in the evening hours.

The attorney's major interview goal should be to obtain as complete a factual statement from her client as possible. To achieve this goal, not only must she facilitate a complete client narrative in the initial interview, but she must ask appropriate follow-up questions and encourage her client to supplement his narrative as the legal relationship progresses.

6.   Concluding Remarks: "Let Me Hear How You Want Me to Proceed on This"

By the conclusion of the initial client interview, it is important that the client's immediate concerns have been addressed and that he knows what to expect from his attorney and the legal system in the future. The concluding portion of the interview therefore should be used to summarize any decisions made during the interview, as well as the possible client options as they then appear.

Probably of greatest importance to the client is the likelihood that the lawyer can help him obtain the relief that he seeks. The attorney thus should summarize the available options, as they appear based upon what the client has told her. In presenting possibilities to the client, the attorney should help to guide him among the alternatives rather than dictate the relief that she believes is most appropriate for the client. The attorney should stress that any legal strategy recommended and adopted at the initial client interview may well change based upon additional factual and legal investigation. In discussing possible strategies with the client (as well as in all other aspects of attorney-client relations), counsel should speak in plain English and avoid the use of legal jargon.

Clients always should be informed about the likely course of any contemplated litigation, particularly about the lengthy delays inherent in civil litigation. The client should be told about the extent to which he will be required to participate in the litigation through, for example, the completion of discovery responses or the giving of deposition testimony. Legal fees also should be addressed, although the client should be informed that in many situations no accurate estimation of total legal fees can be given with any assurance. Some attorneys provide a booklet containing an explanation of the legal process for clients to read at their leisure.[8]

Certain requests should be made of the client. For instance, the client should be asked to provide the attorney with relevant documents and to sign releases authorizing counsel to obtain records from third-parties. If the client is a business, its representative should be asked to suspend company policies that might result in automatic destruction of relevant documents. The client also should be warned about the potential dangers from talking about his legal problem (and potential litigation) with others.

The client should clearly understand when he will hear back from the attorney. If the client has decided to retain this particular attorney, a future appointment can be set. If the client wants to think about whether to retain this attorney, a specific time should be set by which he should contact the attorney if he desires her services. The initial client interview should conclude with both attorney and client understanding exactly what they are to do and by when.

To avoid later misunderstandings, some attorneys send clients a letter after an initial interview summarizing any advice given, decisions made, and the terms of the contemplated representation.[9] Especially if the interview was lengthy, the attorney also may want to dictate a summary of the interview in a memorandum to the file.

B. ATTORNEY QUESTIONING AND LISTENING TECHNIQUES

Regardless of the structure employed for client interviews, it is important that attorneys consciously consider and adopt the particular questioning and listening techniques that will ensure the most effective client interview. While lawyers may differ as to what the "most effective client interview" means in different settings, at a minimum such an interview is one in which the attorney has been able to garner all the facts necessary for her to competently and professionally represent her client.

Client interviews, though, should be considered more than opportunities to gather objective facts. The time spent interviewing clients should be seen as an opportunity in which to establish rapport with clients. Such rapport can be important for several reasons. Most clients are unfamiliar with the legal system, and many persons (including some lawyers!) are intimidated by the prospect of litigation. This anxiety may be heightened due to the age, gender, race, and ethnicity of the client. To the extent that

---

8. *E.g.,* "You and Your Lawyer," *The Compleat Lawyer*, Spring 1994; "You're Going to Trial," *The Compleat Lawyer*, Winter 1993. *See also* L. Fox & S. Martyn, *Your Lawyer: A User's Guide* (2006).

9. A sample representation letter is set forth in Section IV(A), *infra* p. 41. If a potential case is turned down, a letter may be used to confirm that the attorney is not representing the individual in question.

a client trusts and believes in his attorney, the client's anxieties about the legal process may be lessened.

The establishment of attorney-client rapport may have benefits that go beyond making the litigation experience more agreeable for the client. There is empirical evidence that clients who actively participate in the handling of their personal injury claims ultimately receive better results than clients who passively delegate decision-making responsibilities to their attorneys.[10]

Attorneys also should benefit from effective working relationships with their clients. The significant decisions in a lawsuit are the client's,[11] and the establishment of a good attorney-client relationship may result in a client who is both more willing and better able to make these important decisions. Even if the attorney views the client interview as merely a means to obtain factual information, it seems likely that clients will be forthcoming with more relevant facts if they are comfortable with their attorney.

Nor should attorneys ever forget that in contested cases the courts ultimately rule against fifty percent of all litigants. A litigant may be better able to accept an unsuccessful case outcome, and the attorney's role in that outcome, if a strong attorney-client rapport previously had been established.

The client interview is both an opportunity for the attorney to question her client and for the client to tell his story. While attorneys must ask questions and impart information during client interviews, the bulk of attorney time in most successful interviews involves listening rather than speaking. The following selection is from the classic text *Legal Interviewing and Counseling: A Client–Centered Approach* by Professors David Binder and Susan Price. Carefully consider these authors' suggestion that "active listening" can be used by attorneys to ensure full client participation in the attorney-client relationship and, thus, more effective legal representation and advocacy. Also consider the possible uses of active listening in other settings, such as a civil discovery deposition.

D. BINDER & S. PRICE, LEGAL INTERVIEWING AND COUNSELING: A CLIENT–CENTERED APPROACH

20–32; 36–37 (1977).[12]

It may seem that to listen is a very simple and easily accomplished task. Most people, when told to listen, believe that all one needs to do is to sit back and hear what is said. From the viewpoint of effective interviewing and counseling, this belief is incorrect. First, listening involves much

---

10. D. Rosenthal, *Lawyer and Client: Who's in Charge?* (1977).

11. Model Rules of Prof'l Conduct Rule 1.2.

12. Reprinted from D. Binder & S. Price, *Legal Interviewing and Counseling: A Client–Centered Approach* (1977) with permission of the West Group. *See also* D. Binder et al., *Lawyers as Counselors: A Client–Centered Approach* (2d ed. 2004).

more than sitting back and hearing. Second, listening is not a task easily performed. Rather, it is one which requires enormous concentration and affirmative action.

* * *

[P]roviding a client with the feeling that he/she has been heard, understood, and yet not judged, often has an enormously facilitating effect. What we wish to stress here is that listening, when properly carried out, is the technique through which empathetic understanding is most readily communicated to the client. Thus, listening is important not simply to insure that the lawyer hears and understands what has occurred, but also to provide the client with the motivation for full and complete communication.

* * *

When an individual views or participates in an event, the individual typically observes the various details which make up the incident and often simultaneously experiences various feelings about the occurrence. In recalling the event, the individual will, therefore, often describe both the content of what occurred and the feelings associated with the event. Moreover, recalling the event during an interview may trigger still further emotional reactions. "I didn't think about it much then, but now every time I think about it, I get mad." Accordingly, in an interview a lawyer can listen for both *content* and current and past *feelings*.

* * *

Identifying Content and Feelings

* * *

Although from a legal point of view the lawyer may be primarily interested in the content of a client's report (time, place, transactions), the lawyer can usually provide full empathetic understanding only if he/she also identifies and responds to the client's feelings. The following example[ ] can be used for practice in identifying both content and feelings.

Client * * *:

> "My husband and I sat down years ago and wrote a will together, but I guess I never really thought we'd use it. Then they called to say my husband had had a heart attack at work. He died two days later. When he died, I felt overwhelmed. Lately, I've been worrying about our finances. It's hard to think of money at a time like this, but I feel like I should. I don't sleep at night and I just sit around depressed all day. Other times, when I think about him, I start crying and it seems like it will never stop. On top of all this, the children are saying they are going to contest the will. They've already hired a lawyer. I'm really surprised, I never expected this."

What is the content of the client's situation?

What are the client's past and current feelings?

* * *

Here is how you might have conceptualized [this] * * * case[ ]:

* * *

Content:	Husband died unexpectedly and wife must assume responsibility for family finances. Children plan to contest the will and have already hired a lawyer.
Feelings:	Sad, overwhelmed, depressed, worried, surprised.

* * *

Having discussed why listening is important and what should be listened for, let us now turn to matters of technique. How does one listen effectively? As a technique, listening can be broken down into two types—passive and active. Though our discussion will involve both types, we will stress "active listening." We do so for two reasons. First, active listening is probably more effective in providing empathetic understanding. Second, the technique, unlike those involved in passive listening, is generally not one used in normal social conversation. As a consequence, it is a technique that will require substantial effort to master.

Passive Listening

Silence

Silence is defined here as a brief but definite pause in the conversation. The client makes a statement and then there is a pause, typically two to five seconds, before the client continues speaking. Many lawyers feel uncomfortable allowing a period of silence. They seem to feel that a good interview must have a constant flow of words, and silence is thus a sign of their incompetence in not knowing the right thing to say. To cope with their discomfort, lawyers often ask a series of rapid questions just to keep the client talking. This failure to allow silence can interrupt a client's stream of association and make the client feel cut off or hurried. Effective lawyers will often wait out the pause and allow the client time to reflect before continuing with the story. Effective lawyers seem to use silence to communicate the message, "I'm listening, go ahead at your own speed."

Non–Committal Acknowledgements

Silence sometimes can have an inhibiting effect on a client. The client may feel anxious, on the spot, and pressured to keep talking if there is no reassurance the client is being heard. To let clients know that the lawyer is listening and taking in what is being said, the lawyer can respond with brief expressions which tend to communicate acknowledgement of the client's content or feelings. These include such brief comments as:

"Oh"

"I see"

"Mm-hmm"

"Interesting"

"Really"

"No fooling"

"You did, eh"

These are considered non-committal responses because they acknowledge that the lawyer is listening without giving any indication about how the lawyer might be evaluating the client's messages.

Open–Ended Questions

Sometimes a long pause can indicate the client has finished with a particular topic. To get the ball rolling again, the lawyer may ask a brief open-ended question—a question which permits the client to continue to respond in a narrative manner. Open-ended questions * * * include such things as:

"What else happened?"

"What other reasons are there?"

"Can you tell me some more about that?"

These techniques—silence, non-committal acknowledgements, and open-ended questions—are basically *passive* listening techniques. They function primarily to give the client space in the interview to freely communicate his or her thoughts and feelings. However, they do *not* tend to communicate that the lawyer truly understands or accepts the client's messages.

Active Listening

Active listening is the process of picking up the client's message and sending it back in a *reflective statement which mirrors what the lawyer has heard.*

> Client: "When I asked him for the money, he had the nerve to tell me not to be uptight."
>
> Lawyer: "Rather than telling you about the money, he suggested you were somehow wrong for asking. I imagine that made you angry."

Note the lawyer does not simply repeat or "parrot" what was said. Rather, the lawyer's response is an affirmative effort to convey back the essence of what was heard. It is a response which, by mirroring what was said, affirmatively demonstrates understanding. Further, since the statement only mirrors, it does not in any way "judge" what has been said. In short, it is a completely empathetic response.

The active listening response differs from the passive response in important particulars. By reflecting back what has been heard, the active response explicitly communicates that what the client said was actually heard and understood. Passive responses, such as "Mm-hmm" or "Tell me some more about that," can only imply the lawyer has heard and understood. In contrast, a reflective statement—one which mirrors back the essence of what has been said—constitutes an explicit form of expression, demonstrating lawyer comprehension.

Moreover, insofar as the empathetic ideal of "non-judgmental acceptance" is concerned, active responses are probably more effective than passive ones. Affirmatively demonstrating understanding through the reflective statement probably carries with it a greater implication of non-judgmental acceptance than do passive remarks such as, "Oh, I see," "Tell me more," or "Mm-hmm."

The active listening response can be used to mirror both content and feelings.

Let us turn now to two common problems lawyers can expect to encounter in endeavoring to reflect feelings: (1) Many people do not actually express their feelings. They leave them completely unstated ("How long will the appeal take?") or reveal them only in the form of non-verbal cues—tears, smiles, etc. (2) Often, to the extent feelings are expressed, they are not clearly articulated. Rather, the feelings are stated in very vague terms, "I felt weird." "I felt uptight."

Vaguely Expressed Feelings

When a client expresses feelings in a vague or obscure manner, the lawyer can be most empathetic by reflecting the feelings in a precise way. Specific labeling of the feelings helps the client better understand his/her own emotional reactions. Here are some examples of client statements which are vague, abstract, or general, and responses by a lawyer which attempt to identify and label the specific feelings:

> Client: "I felt *bummed out* when I found out she was having an affair with him. I thought our marriage meant something. *I guess I was wrong.*"
>
> Lawyer: "You felt *hurt* and *disappointed* when she told you about the affair."
>
> Client: *"I've felt out of it* ever since I moved to Los Angeles. *I don't have friends* here or even neighbors to talk to."
>
> Lawyer: *"You've felt lonely* and *isolated* since you came to Los Angeles."

* * *

Note how, in each case, the lawyer listens to what the client has to say and then attempts to restate in more specific terms what the client is feeling. * * *

* * *

Unstated Feelings

No lawyer's task is more difficult to learn than that of recognizing and reflecting unstated feelings. This is not so because the technique is difficult, but because the lawyer is often not aware that feelings are present or being expressed. Frequently, clients will discuss situations, which, for most people, would be emotionally charged, without ever expressing any emotions. Consider this example. A woman charged with child abuse is recounting to her lawyer her version of how the child came to the attention of the authorities. She has previously explained that the child was injured in a fall.

> Client: I decided to take her (the child) to the County hospital. I had no car, but finally I got in touch with my aunt. She came over about an hour later. The baby kept crying. It took about an hour to get to the hospital.
> Lawyer: Then what happened?
> Client: I told them what happened. They said we would have to wait. It took almost two hours for me to see a doctor. I kept saying my baby was hurt bad, but the people at the desk kept saying it wasn't an emergency. Finally, a nurse came and took the baby. She told me I would have to wait. I couldn't go with the baby.

Without verbalizing any emotional reaction, the client has just described a situation which, for most people, would be extremely stressful. At this juncture, the lawyer has a choice. The lawyer can proceed directly to gather more data. Or, the lawyer may attempt to gather data indirectly by increasing rapport—i.e., providing an empathetic response before asking for more content. If the lawyer chooses the former, the next lawyer response will either be a question—e.g., "What happened next?"—or a reflection of content—e.g., "So they took the baby and left you waiting." If the lawyer chooses the latter, the next lawyer response will be an attempt to identify and reflect feelings—e.g., "I imagine you were very angry and quite worried about your baby."

* * *

Non–Verbal Expressions of Feelings

There is a second way in which a lawyer may be able to identify a client's unstated feelings. Frequently, the lawyer can gain an impression of a client's feelings by carefully listening to and observing the client's non-verbal cues. These cues are generally of two types—auditory and visual. Auditory cues include such things as intonation, pitch, rate of speech, and pauses in the conversation. Visual cues include posture, gestures, facial expressions, and body movements such as fidgeting fingers and constantly shifting positions. Some nonverbal cues are quite easily identified: tears typically indicate sadness; wringing hands usually indicate worry; a smile usually indicates pleasure. However, at times nonverbal cues can be quite difficult to detect. The client may be trying very hard to "maintain composure" and therefore inhibit non-verbal expressions. However, the observant lawyer may nonetheless be able to detect some of the client's feelings since the client usually cannot repress all non-verbal expression. Thus, a client may be able to avoid any facial expression but nonetheless be unable to hide body movements, such as drumming fingers or rapid changes in position which belie feelings of anxiety. Additionally, the lawyer may be able to detect inconsistencies between what the client says he/she feels and what the client's body movements suggest the client is feeling. For example, a client may state, "No, it doesn't make me mad" while tightly clenching his/her fists. Or the client may state, "It's perfectly all right with me," in a disgusted tone of voice.

* * *

Once the lawyer has a fairly good idea of what emotion the client is expressing by the client's non-verbal behavior, the lawyer can then provide a reflective response. As with any reflective response to unstated feelings the lawyer's statement, even if inaccurate, may still serve to facilitate and clarify communication.

* * *

Non–Empathetic Responses

Often, when a lawyer identifies a client's feelings, the lawyer fails to reflect the understanding non-judgmentally. Consider the following client statement and lawyer responses.

> Client: When I came home, I discovered she had moved out. She took everything. All the furniture was gone; the house was empty. I was pissed.
>
> Lawyer:
> No. 1:   I don't blame you.
> No. 2:   But I guess after a while you calmed down.
> No. 3:   I guess you felt you deserved better.

Lawyer No. 1 has judged the appropriateness of the reaction. Lawyer No. 2 has treated the feeling as irrelevant and shifted the discussion to another time frame. Lawyer No. 3 has played amateur psychologist. He has attempted to analyze the reason for the reaction. None has simply mirrored back what was said—"You were really furious." Consider this further example.

> Witness: Every time I think about that woman rushing over to her child, my eyes get misty.
>
> Lawyer:
> No. 4:   I'm sure the feeling will pass with time. Most people who see an accident like this feel that way at first.
>
> No. 5:   That's probably because you think it could have been you and your daughter.
>
> No. 6:   You certainly have a right to feel that way; it was a shocking thing.

Again, the lawyers do not merely reflect back the essence of what was said—"It makes you sad to think about it." Rather, there was advice (Lawyer No. 4), analysis (Lawyer No. 5), and judgment (Lawyer No. 6).

To reflect feelings in a non-judgmental manner requires practice accompanied by constructive feedback. All we can do here is to point up the fact that lawyers often substitute their own advice, analysis, or judgment in place of a simple reflective statement. * * *

* * *

How Much Active Listening?

The purpose of the active listening response is to provide non-judgmental understanding and thereby stimulate full client participation. The technique is to be used to help the client feel free to discuss and reflect upon his/her problem in a comfortable and open manner. In short, the technique is to be used to develop rapport.

A client's feelings will typically emerge throughout the interview. When the client is reporting the past transaction from which the problem emanates and when the client is identifying and discussing the potential consequences of proposed solutions, the client's emotional reactions will be continually in evidence. Given this kind of continual emotional presence, how often should the lawyer reflect feelings? Should feelings be reflected every time they seem to emerge? There is no single, right, or easy answer to these questions.

The amount of non-judgmental understanding that will be helpful in developing rapport will vary from client to client and case to case. A client who feels comfortable talking openly about one case may feel much more inhibited in talking about another. * * * Furthermore, while some aspects of a case can be confronted quite readily, other aspects of the case may pose a much greater problem. * * *

To use active listening effectively, the lawyer must employ his/her judgment in gauging the amount of client rapport that needs to be developed. Is the client talking fully, freely, and openly? Are there some matters which obviously bear discussion and yet are being omitted from the dialogue? Is an incident which certainly must have stirred some feelings being reported without any obvious emotional reaction? Even those people who perceive themselves as totally rational and objective experience feelings. They experience feelings even though they may not often discuss them or show them. On occasion, even these "totally rational" people welcome the opportunity to share their feelings with someone who can respond with non-judgmental understanding.

Good judgment must ultimately be relied upon in deciding how frequently it will be helpful to reflect a client's feelings. Hopefully, constructive feedback about performance as an interviewer and counselor, both in simulated classroom exercises and in actual interactions with clients, will prove to be an aid in developing judgment about when and how often to reflect a client's stated and unstated feelings.

NOTES AND QUESTIONS CONCERNING ACTIVE LISTENING

1. What do Binder and Price see as the advantages of active listening? Do you agree with their assessment? Are there any disadvantages to active listening? Are there situations in which active listening would be inappropriate?

2. Is active listening for everyone? Why don't all attorneys make use of active listening techniques? Why might some attorneys feel uncomfortable using such techniques? Should professionals such as attorneys be concerned with clients' feelings as well as with litigation-related facts?

3. Are there clients who may be uncomfortable with active listening? What impact should the reactions of a client have upon attorney interviewing techniques?

4. How can attorneys attempt to avoid being judgmental in their client interviews? While Binder and Price criticize attorneys for being judgmental, aren't clients in fact seeking judgment from the attorneys with whom they consult?

5. Can an attorney not be judgmental enough in her client interviews? While client autonomy should be preserved during the interviewing process, some attorneys are so deferential to client desires that they become mere "hired guns" who exercise no independent professional judgment on behalf of their clients. *See generally* J. Heinz & E. Laumann, *Chicago Lawyers: The Social Structure of the Bar* 151–166 (rev. ed. 1994); Heinz, "The Power of Lawyers," 17 *Ga. L. Rev.* 891 (1983). *See also* "Ethics Symposium: What Do Clients Want?," 52 *Emory L. J.* 1053 (2003).

6. In addition to the "client centered" approach to legal representation advocated by Binder and Price, others have argued that attorneys should be more directive with respect to moral issues arising during the representation or that they should adopt a collaborative approach to client representation under which moral issues are resolved through moral discourse between attorney and client. "Symposium: Client Counseling and Moral Responsibility," 30 *Pepp. L. Rev.* 591 (2003). Is one of these three models of lawyering appropriate in all situations? With which type of legal representation are you most comfortable?

7. Empirical studies in the social sciences highlight both problems and opportunities concerning client interviewing and the attorney-client relationship. *E.g.,* Relis, " 'It's Not About the Money!': A Theory on Misconceptions of Plaintiffs' Litigation Aims," 68 *U. Pitt. L. Rev.* 341 (2006) (finding attorney misperceptions of clients' litigation aims); Sternlight & Robbennolt, "Good Lawyers Should be Good Psychologists: Insights for Interviewing and Counseling Clients," 23 *Ohio St. J. On Disp. Resol.* 437 (2008) (applying psychological findings to client interviewing and counseling).

Exercise Concerning the Critique of a Client Interview[13]

Presume that the following interview took place in Charleston, West Virginia in April 1972, the Buffalo Creek disaster having occurred on February 26, 1972. Read the interview transcript with a critical eye, considering both the good and the bad aspects of the attorney's interviewing performance.

Secretary: "Mr. Attorney, this is Mrs. Jones, the ten o'clock appointment."

Attorney: "Sorry to have kept you waiting. I'll be with you in a minute. I've just got to finish this document so that I can get it filed this afternoon." [pause]

Attorney: "Now then, I understand that you're one of the survivors of the flood down in Logan County. That was a terrible tragedy. How are you doing?"

Client: "Oh, we're doing O.K. We're living with friends, and my husband is back at work."

Attorney: "Good. So, what can I do for you?"

Client: "Well, our house was pretty much destroyed by the flood, and we thought we ought to see a lawyer about trying to get some money to rebuild."

Attorney: "Have you talked to any lawyers in Logan County?"

Client: "Not really."

Attorney: "Well, there'll be quite a few lawsuits filed as a result of that flood. In fact, some cases have been filed already. Did you lose anything other than your house? Anybody hurt in the flood?"

Client: "Well, my husband's little cousin was staying with us, and he was hurt pretty badly."

Attorney: "I'm sorry to hear that. Nobody in your immediate family was hurt, though?"

Client: "No."

Attorney: "That's too bad. I mean, for your lawsuit, that's too bad. For you that's very good. Anybody in your family see a doctor?"

Client: "No."

Attorney: "Hold on just a minute. I have to take this call."

Attorney: [talking on telephone] "Hey Dan, how're you doing? Listen, I've got somebody with me in my office now, but I wanted you to know that the company rejected our last offer. Those jerks don't know a good deal when they see one. So it looks like we better get ready for trial. I'll transfer you to my secretary, so that she can set a time for you to come in next week to talk about where we go from here. Take care. See you next week."

Attorney: "I'm sorry, but that guy wanted to know whether he's going to have to go to trial, which he is. Now, you were

---

13. This is a hypothetical interview transcript. Although the interview and other simulation exercises in this book are based on the facts surrounding the February 26, 1972, Buffalo Creek disaster, unless specifically noted to the contrary the individuals portrayed in the exercises are fictitious and are not meant to represent any actual persons either living or dead.

	telling me you want to bring a suit for the damage to your house. Is it totally destroyed?"
Client:	"Yes sir."
Attorney:	"What do you think it was worth?"
Client:	"We paid $10,000 for it back in 1963. It was worth a whole lot more than that before the flood."
Attorney:	"Well, what I want you to do is to bring me all of the documents that you have relating to the value of the house. Things like tax records or appraisals. If you want me to take the case, I'll poke around and find out what other cases have been filed. I can't predict how any lawsuit will come out, but I'd say that we ought to be able to get Pittston to build you a new house. Do you want me to try?"
Client:	"I guess so."
Attorney:	"Well, you think about it. I'm sorry that I'm so busy today. What we can do is set up an appointment sometime next week and talk more about this. You've got a lot of time before any lawsuit needs to be filed. Maybe you can bring your husband back with you next week, too."
Client:	"Sure."
Attorney:	"This is the kind of case that we take on what's known as a contingency basis. You only pay us if we get a recovery for you. If there is a recovery, our attorney fees are one-third of the amount we recover. I'll ask my secretary to give you a copy of our fee agreement so you can talk it over with your husband. I think you'll find it's pretty standard. Now, are there any other questions you've got for me?"
Client:	"When do you think you could get us any money?"
Attorney:	"That's a tough one. Usually in these types of cases the defendant won't really offer much in settlement until right before trial. But we could try to get you a settlement right away if you really needed it."
Client:	"Well, that's why I came today, to see how quickly we could get money to rebuild our house. Maybe we can talk about that next week."
Attorney:	"Yes, let's do that. The other thing you've got to do, whether you employ me or another lawyer, is not talk to anybody; especially anybody from Pittston."
Client:	"My husband talked with people from Pittston right after the flood."
Attorney:	"Did he sign anything?"
Client:	"I think he did."
Attorney:	"That probably wasn't too smart. Why don't you bring along a copy of what he signed to your next appointment. And don't you or he sign anything else that anybody from Pittston asks you to sign."
Client:	"O.K."
Attorney:	"Listen, I really want to help you out on this. If you need money quickly, I'll do what I can for you. Why don't you set up an appointment with my secretary for next week, and then if you think about it and want to go with

another attorney, just call in and cancel the appointment. Does that make sense to you?"

Client: "Yes, that makes sense."

Attorney: "I hope I'll see you next week. Anything else I can tell you now?"

Client: "No, I guess not."

Attorney: "O.K., then, you take care of yourself. So long."

Client: "Thank you very much."

Your critique of the above interview should consider both its positive and negative aspects, including such matters as interviewing technique, substance, and ethics. Consider, also, the needs and feelings of the client and how they were or were not addressed by the attorney. Finally, consider the apparent goals of the attorney conducting the interview and the extent to which they either were or were not achieved.

III. THE ETHICS OF INTERVIEWING

If the attorney does not permit her client to tell his own story, vital facts may never become known to that attorney. Attorneys who do not engage in active listening techniques or otherwise facilitate full client communication risk embarking upon litigation without all the relevant facts. The attorney's ignorance concerning the real facts can have disastrous consequences, particularly if those facts are revealed for the first time by the opposing party at or near the time of trial.

While some attorneys may not learn all the facts from their clients due to poor interviewing techniques, other attorneys actually may not want to know all of the true facts. In certain situations attorneys may be tempted to mold the factual narrative they receive from their clients. At some point an attorney's efforts to structure a client's version of the facts crosses the line from poor interviewing technique to a violation of generally acceptable ethical norms.

Perhaps the best example of an attorney's attempt to help his client structure facts in a particular manner is contained in the novel *Anatomy of a Murder*. Although this book concerns a criminal defense attorney, the situation portrayed occurs in both civil and criminal litigation. Robert Traver, the listed author of the novel, was the pen name of John D. Voelker, who was an associate justice on the Michigan Supreme Court at the time the novel was written.

R. TRAVER, ANATOMY OF A MURDER
32; 35–39; 40; 42–43; 44–47 (1958).

I paused and lit a cigar. I took my time. I had reached a point where a few wrong answers to a few right questions would leave me with a client—if I took his case—whose cause was legally defenseless. Either I stopped now and begged off and let some other lawyer worry over it or I asked him the few fatal questions and let him hang himself. Or else, like any smart lawyer, I went into the Lecture. I studied my man, * * * delicately fingering his Ming holder, daintily sipping his dark mustache. He apparently did not realize how close I had him to admitting that he was guilty of first degree murder, that is, that he "feloniously, wilfully and of his malice aforethought did kill and murder one Barney Quill." The man was a sitting duck.

* * *

"Sit down," I repeated, "and listen carefully. Better break out your Ming holder. This is it."

"Yes, sir," said Lieutenant Manion, obediently sitting down and producing the Ming holder. His lawyer was making ready to deliver the Lecture.

And what is the Lecture?

The Lecture is an ancient device that lawyers use to coach their clients so that the client won't quite know he has been coached and his lawyer can still preserve the face-saving illusion that he hasn't done any coaching. For coaching clients, like robbing them, is not only frowned upon, it is downright unethical and bad, very bad. Hence the Lecture, an artful device as old as the law itself, and one used constantly by some of the nicest and most ethical lawyers in the land. "Who, me? I didn't tell him what to say," the lawyer can later comfort himself. "I merely explained the law, see." It is a good practice to scowl and shrug here and add virtuously: "That's my duty, isn't it?"

* * *

"As I told you," I began, "I've been thinking about your case during the noon hour."

"Yes," he replied. "You mentioned that."

"So I did, so I did," I said. "Now I realize there are many questions still to be asked, facts to be discussed," I went on. "And I am not prejudging your case." I paused to discharge the opening salvo of the Lecture. "But as things presently stand I must advise you that in my opinion you have not yet disclosed to me a *legal* defense to this charge of murder."

I again paused to let this sink in. It is a necessary condition to the successful lecture. My man blinked a little and touched both sides of his mustache lightly with the tip of his tongue. "Could it be you are advising me to plead guilty?" he said, smiling ever so slightly.

"I may eventually," I said, "but I didn't quite say that. I merely want at this time for you to have the trained reaction of a man who—" I paused "—who is not without experience in cases of this kind." I was getting a

little overwhelmed by the sheer beauty of my own modesty and I fought
the impulse to flutter my eyelashes.

* * *

* * * "But unwritten law or no, doesn't a man have a legal right to
kill a man who has raped his wife? Isn't that the *written* law, then?"

"No, only to prevent it, or if he has caught him at it, or, finally, to
prevent his escape." We were treading dangerous ground again and I
spoke rapidly to prevent any interruption. "In fact, Lieutenant, for all the
elaborate hemorrhage of words in the law books about the legal defenses
to murder there are only about three basic defenses: one, that it didn't
happen but was instead a suicide or accident or what not; two, that
whether it happened or not you didn't do it, such as alibi, mistaken
identity and so forth; and three, that even if it happened and you did it,
your action was legally justified or excusable." I paused to see how my
student was doing.

The Lieutenant grew thoughtful. "Where do I fit in that rosy picture?" he responded nicely.

"I can tell you better where you don't fit," I went on. "Since a whole
barroom full of people saw you shoot down Barney Quill in apparent cold
blood, you scarcely fit in the first two classes of defenses. I'm afraid we
needn't waste time on those." I paused. "If you fit anywhere it's got to be
in the third. So we'd better bear down on that."

"You mean," Lieutenant Manion said, "that my only possible defense
in this case is to find some justification or excuse?"

My lecture was proceeding nicely according to schedule. "You're
learning rapidly," I said, nodding approvingly. "Merely add *legal* justification or excuse and I'll mark you an A."

"And you say that a man is not justified in killing a man who has just
raped and beat up his wife?"

"Morally, perhaps, but not legally. Not after it's all over, as it was
here." I paused, wondering why I didn't go to Detroit and lecture in night
school. That way, too, I would be close enough to go see all my old school's
home football games. "Hail to the victors valiant...." "You see, Lieutenant," I went on, "it's not the *act* of killing a man that makes it murder; it
is the circumstances, the time, and the state of mind or purpose which
induced the act." I paused, and could almost hear my old Crimes professor, J. B. "Jabby" White, droning this out in law school nearly twenty
years before. It was amazing how the old stuff stuck.

The Lieutenant's eyes narrowed and flickered ever so little. "Maybe,"
he began, and cleared his throat. "On second thought, maybe I *did* catch
Quill in the act. I've never precisely told the police one way or the other."
His eyes regarded me quietly, steadily. This man, I saw, was not only an
apt student of the Lecture; like most people (including lawyers) he
indubitably possessed a heart full of larceny. He was also, perhaps

instinctively, trying to turn the Lecture on his lawyer. "I've never really told them," he concluded.

A lawyer in the midst of his Lecture is apt to cling to the slenderest reed to bolster his wavering virtue. "But you've told *me*," I said, pausing complacently, swollen with rectitude, grateful for the swift surge of virtue he'd afforded me. "And anyway," I went on, "you would have had to dispatch him then, not, as you've already admitted, an hour or so later. The catching and killing must combine. And that's true even if you'd actually caught him at it—which you didn't. I've just now told you that *time* is one of the factors in determining whether a homicide is a murder or not. Here it's a big one. Don't you see?—in your case *time* is the rub; it's the elapsed *time* between the rape and the killing that permits the People to bear down and argue that your shooting of Barney Quill was a deliberate, malicious and premeditated act. And that, my friend, is no more than they've charged you with."

Stoically: "Are you telling me to plead guilty?"

"Look, we've been over that. When I'm ready to advise you to cop out you'll know it. Right now I want you to realize what you're up against, man."

The Lieutenant blinked his eyes thoughtfully. "I'm busy realizing," he said.

"Try to look at it this way, Lieutenant," I went on, warmed to my lecture. "Just as murder itself is one of the most elemental and primitive of crimes, so also the law of murder is, for all the torrent of words written about it, still pretty elemental and primitive in its basic concepts. The human tribe learned early that indiscriminate killing was not only poor for tribal decorum and well-being but threatened its very survival and was therefore bad in itself. So murder became taboo. Are you still with me?"

"Go on."

"At the same time it was seen that there were occasions when a killing might nevertheless still be justified. Stated most baldly it all pretty much boiled down to this: Thou shalt not kill—except to save yourself, your property, or your loved ones. That simple statement still embraces by far most of the modern defenses to murder. If a man tries to take my life or my wife or my cow I may kill him to prevent it. But if I chase him off or, more like your situation, if he should steal my wife or my cow while I am away fishing (or sleeping in my trailer) I must pursue other tribal remedies when I discover it. I must do so because I did not catch him at it, the damage is done, the danger is past, the culprit may be dealt with later and at leisure.["]

　　* * *

Quietly: "You don't want to take my case, then?"

"Not quite so fast, I'm not ready to make that decision. Look, in a murder case the jury has only a few narrow choices. Among them, it *might* let you go. It *might* also up and convict you. A judge trying you without a jury would surely have to, as I have said. Now do you want to go into court with the dice loaded? With all the law and instructions stacked against you?" I paused to deliver my clincher. "Well, whether you're willing to do so, I'm not. I will either find a sound and plausible legal defense in your case or else advise you to cop out." I paused thoughtfully. "Then there's one other possible 'or else.'"

"Or else what?"

A chastening hint, a light play on the client's fear that the lawyer of his choice might walk out on him is also sound strategy during the Lecture. It tends to keep the subject both alert and appropriately humble. "Or else, Lieutenant, you can find yourself another lawyer," I said, waiting for him to squirm.

* * *

Lieutenant Manion produced the Ming holder and studied it carefully, as though for the first time. "What do you recommend then?" he said.

It was a good question. "I don't know yet. So far I've been trying to impress you with the importance, the naked necessity, of our finding a valid legal defense, if one exists, in addition to the 'unwritten law' you so dearly want to cling to. Put it this way: what Barney Quill might have done to your wife before you killed him may present a favorable condition, an equitable climate, to a possible jury acquittal. But alone it simply isn't enough." I paused. "Not enough for Paul Biegler, anyway."

"You mean you want to find a way to give the jurors some decently plausible legal peg to hang their verdict on so that they might let me go— and still save face?"

My man was responding beautifully to the lecture. "Precisely," I said, adding hastily: "Whether you have such a defense of course remains to be seen. But I hope, Lieutenant, I have shown you how vital it is to find one if it exists."

"I think you have, Counselor," he said slowly. "I rather think now you really have." He paused. "Tell me, tell me more about this justification or excuse business. Excuse me," he added, smiling faintly, "I mean *legal* justification or excuse."

* * *

I looked hopefully at the man. Was it barely possible that he possessed a rudimentary sense of humor? "Well, take self-defense," I began. "That's the classic example of justifiable homicide. On the basis of what I've so far heard and read about your case I do not think we need pause too long over that. Do you?"

"Perhaps not," Lieutenant Manion conceded. "We'll pass it for now."

"Let's," I said dryly. "Then there's the defense of habitation, defense of property, and the defense of relatives or friends. Now there are more ramifications to these defenses than a dog has fleas, but we won't explore them now. I've already told you at length why I don't think you can invoke the possible defense of your wife. When you shot Quill her need for defense had passed. It's as simple as that.''

"Go on," Lieutenant Manion said, frowning.

"Then there's the defense of a homicide committed to prevent a felony—say you're being robbed—; to prevent the escape of the felon— suppose he's getting away with your wallet—; or to arrest a felon—you've caught up with him and he's either trying to get away or has actually escaped.''

At this point I paused and blinked thoughtfully. An idea no bigger than a pea rattled faintly at the back door of my mind. Let's see. . . . Wouldn't it be true that if Barney Quill actually raped Laura Manion *he* would be a felon at large at the time he was shot? The pea kept faintly rattling. But so what, so what? "Hm. . . ." I said. It would bear pondering.

The Lieutenant's eyes gleamed and bored into mine. "Who—what do you see?" he said. It was becoming increasingly clear that this soldier was no dummy.

"Nothing," I lied glibly. "Not a thing." The student was getting ahead of the lecturer and that would never do. And wherever my idea might drop into the ultimate defense picture, I sensed that now was not the time to try to fit it. "I was just thinking," I concluded.

"Yes," Lieutenant Manion said. "You were just thinking." He smiled faintly. "Go on, then; what are some of the other legal justifications or excuses?''

"Then there's the tricky and dubious defense of intoxication. Personally I've never seen it succeed. But since you were not drunk when you shot Quill we shall mercifully not dwell on that. Or were you?''

"I was cold sober. Please go on."

"Then finally there's the defense of insanity." I paused and spoke abruptly, airily: "Well, that just about winds it up." I arose as though making ready to leave.

"Tell me more."

"There is no more." I slowly paced up and down the room.

"I mean about this insanity."

"Oh, insanity," I said, elaborately surprised. It was like luring a trained seal with a herring. "Well, insanity, where proven, is a complete defense to murder. It does not legally justify the killing, like self-defense, say, but rather excuses it." The lecturer was hitting his stride. He was also on the home stretch. "Our law requires that a punishable killing—in fact, any crime—must be committed by a sapient human being, one capable, as the law insists, of distinguishing between right and wrong. If a man is insane, legally insane, the act of homicide may still be murder but the law excuses the perpetrator."

Lieutenant Manion was sitting erect now, very still and erect. "I see—and this—this perpetrator, what happens to him if he should—should be excused?"

"Under Michigan law—like that of many other states—if he is acquitted of murder on the grounds of insanity it is provided that he must be sent to a hospital for the criminally insane until he is pronounced sane." I drummed my fingers on the Sheriff's desk and glanced at my watch, the picture of a man eager to be gone.

My man was baying along the scent now. "How long does it take to get him out of there?"

"Out of where?" I asked innocently.

"Out of this insane hospital!"

"Oh, you mean where a man claims he was insane at the time of the offense but is sane at the time of the trial and his possible acquittal?"

"Exactly."

"I don't know," I said, stroking my chin. "Months, maybe a year. It really takes a bit of doing. Being D.A. so long I've never really had to study that phase of it. I got them in there; it was somebody else's problem to spring them. And I didn't dream this defense might come up in your case."

My naβvete was somewhat excessive; it had been obvious to me from merely reading the newspaper the night before that insanity was the best, if not the only, legal defense the man had. And here I'd just slammed shut every other escape hatch and told him this was the last. Only a cretin could have missed it, and I was rapidly learning that Lieutenant Manion was no cretin.

"Tell me more," Lieutenant Manion said quietly.

"I may add that the law that requires persons acquitted on the grounds of insanity to be sent away is designed to discourage phony pleas of insanity in criminal cases."

"Yes?"

"So the man who successfully invokes the defense of insanity is taking a calculated risk, like the time you took the chance that the old German lieutenant was alone behind his ruined chimney."

I paused and knocked out my pipe. The Lecture was about over. The rest was up to the student. The Lieutenant looked out the window. He studied his Ming holder. I sat very still. Then he looked at me. "Maybe," he said, "maybe I was insane."

Very casually: "Maybe you were insane when?" I said. "When you shot the German lieutenant?"

"You know what I mean. When I shot Barney Quill."

Thoughtfully: "Hm.... Why do you say that?"

"Well, I can't really say," he went on slowly. "I—I guess I blacked out. I can't remember a thing after I saw him standing behind the bar that night until I got back to my trailer."

"You mean—you mean you don't remember shooting him?" I shook my head in wonderment.

"Yes, that's what I mean."

"You don't even remember driving home?"

"No."

"You don't even remember threatening Barney's bartender when he followed you outside after the shooting—as the newspaper says you did?" I paused and held my breath. "You don't remember telling him, 'Do you want some, too, Buster?'?"

The smoldering dark eyes flickered ever so little. "No, not a thing."

"My, my," I said, blinking my eyes, contemplating the wonder of it all. "Maybe you've got something there."

The Lecture was over; I had told my man the law; and now he had told me things that might possibly invoke the defense of insanity. It had all been done with mirrors. Or rather with padded hammers.

NOTES AND QUESTIONS CONCERNING THE ETHICS OF INTERVIEWING

1. Why may it be considered unethical for an attorney to inform a client about the governing law before establishing the relevant facts? Won't legally sophisticated clients have a general sense of the governing law even before the attorney says anything? Why penalize less sophisticated clients by refusing to give them the same general legal background that other clients bring to the initial interview?

2. Even if a client tells his story before the attorney provides legal advice, isn't it reasonable to assume that at least some clients will tailor their stories based upon what they *presume* to be the governing law? For example, most persons are aware that theft is illegal, and at least some civil and criminal defendants may slant their factual narratives to take account of this knowledge. In light of this potential problem, how can the attorney ensure that she is receiving the "real" facts from her client?

3. Don't most attorneys give at least subtle indications as to the answers that they hope their clients will give to important interview questions? What message is sent to a client if his attorney frowns upon receipt of a particular answer or asks the client if he is certain about his answer? Should attorneys attempt to guard against such verbal and non-verbal cues? Is this really possible?

4. What if a client's interview questions are not about past conduct, but about contemplated future actions? Presume, for instance, that a client is balking at responding to discovery requests. The court has granted a final extension of time for the responses to be filed, and the client asks his attorney

quite detailed questions about what is likely to happen if he doesn't comply with the court's order. How should the attorney respond to these questions?

5.   Although this topic will be discussed more fully in Chapter 4 in the context of pleading, attorneys should be aware that Rule 11 of the Federal Rules of Civil Procedure may be implicated by their initial client interviews. Rule 11(b) provides that, by signing any pleading, motion, or other litigation paper, an attorney certifies that "to the best of the person's knowledge, information, and belief, formed after an inquiry reasonable under the circumstances[,] * * * the factual contentions have evidentiary support * * *."

This suggests that attorneys should not simply "take their client's word for it" before filing litigation papers. Most people prefer to appear in a good light and avoid admitting personal failings and embarrassing incidents. For this reason, attorneys may need to question and confirm facts related by a client. While the attorney should not cross-examine her new client in an offensive manner, a healthy skepticism expressed at the outset may save both attorney and client later embarrassment and needless expense. Rule 11's "reasonable inquiry" requirement also may require the attorney to attempt to verify a client's story by checking with third-parties or examining documents or other physical evidence. In *Belleville Catering Co. v. Champaign Market Place, L.L.C.*, 350 F.3d 691 (7th Cir. 2003), counsel improperly relied upon a lease referring to the citizenship of the corporate plaintiff rather than independently confirming such citizenship. In vacating a judgment of $220,000 and remanding for a dismissal of the case for lack of subject-matter jurisdiction, the court of appeals directed that no clients should be charged for "any further services that are necessary to bring this suit to a conclusion in state court, or via settlement." 350 F.3d at 694.

6.   Regardless of the quality of client interviewing, it is the lawyer who ultimately will craft the legal positions taken on behalf of the client. For a discussion of the manner in which lawyers transform the "lay stories" of their clients into "law stories," see Menkel–Meadow, "The Transformation of Disputes by Lawyers: What the Dispute Paradigm Does and Does Not Tell Us," 1985 *J. Disp. Resol.* 25, and the articles discussed therein.

7.   In England, witnesses are interviewed by solicitors, who prepare extensive witness statements that are exchanged with other parties prior to trial. Since 1995, these witness statements are typically offered in lieu of direct examination at trial, with the witness then being subject to cross examination. Trial evidence is presented by barristers, who rarely have direct contact with witnesses (other than their lay clients and experts) before trial, in order to preserve the distinction between solicitors and barristers, avoid suspicions of witness coaching, and preclude possible contamination of the witness's testimony. Wydick, "The Ethics of Witness Coaching," 17 *Cardozo L. Rev.* 1, 5–8 (1995). Does this bifurcated system solve the possible problems of witness coaching?

Exercises Concerning Client Interviewing

1.   Mr. Thomas Eakins has contacted your small law firm in Nashville, Tennessee concerning possible claims that he may have as a result of

the collapse of the dam in the Buffalo Creek Valley approximately one year ago on February 26, 1972. Your secretary has set up an appointment for you with Mr. Eakins on January 30, 1973. In setting this interview, your secretary learned that Eakins is an unemployed coal miner who has lived for the last nine months in Nashville, but was visiting his sister and brother-in-law in Logan County, West Virginia when the dam burst. Although the house in which he was staying was destroyed in the flood, Eakins, himself, was not physically injured. Assume that you are familiar, generally, with the Buffalo Creek disaster, as well as with the fact that a lawsuit has been filed against the Pittston Company in the United States District Court for the Southern District of West Virginia.

Prepare to conduct the initial client interview of Mr. Eakins and actually conduct that interview in class.

2.   You are an associate in a fifty person law firm in Richmond, Virginia. Your firm has been contacted by Ms. Mary Cassatt, the owner of a construction firm that does work in Virginia and West Virginia. Ms. Cassatt has come to your firm because of concern that her company, Heavy Equipment, Inc., might be named as a defendant in the litigation that is just beginning to be filed as a result of the Buffalo Creek disaster. Although this fact is not generally known, Heavy Equipment, Inc. supplied some of the earth moving equipment and heavy equipment operators that were used in the initial work in building the dam that collapsed in Logan County, West Virginia. While Ms. Cassatt and Heavy Equipment, Inc. in the past have used another Richmond law firm for their legal work, Cassatt has come to your firm because of dissatisfaction with that other firm and because of your firm's expertise in construction litigation.

Prepare to conduct the initial client interview of Ms. Cassatt and actually conduct that interview in class.

3.   At a party you are introduced to someone who, upon learning that you are an attorney, begins to question you about a dispute that he is having with the construction company that is building his new house.

   a.   How should you respond to this person at the party?

   b.   Prepare to conduct the interview of this person in your office the next day and actually conduct that interview.

4.   As you are about to leave your law office at the end of a long day, the telephone rings. Before you can tell the caller that your office is closed, he begins to tell you about an automobile accident in which his son recently was involved. What should you tell this distressed father over the telephone?

5.   You are in the process of establishing your own office for the private practice of law. Write a memorandum to your new secretary explaining the manner in which calls from prospective clients should be handled. In your memorandum specify the information that your secretary should obtain from, and give to, callers when scheduling them for initial client interviews. Be sure to consider the implications of your instructions

for the interviews that you ultimately will have with these potential clients.

IV. THE CLIENT'S RETAINER OF THE ATTORNEY

Not only is the initial client interview important for obtaining facts concerning the client's problem and for establishing client rapport, but this should be the time when the formal terms of the attorney-client relationship are established or at least discussed. In particular, agreement should be reached at the outset of the attorney-client relationship concerning the terms of the client's retainer of the attorney.

A. THE REPRESENTATION AGREEMENT

The attorney representation agreement is a contract between attorney and client. This agreement should specify what the attorney agrees to do for the client. Indeed, it is a good idea to set forth explicitly what is *not* covered within the scope of the attorney's engagement (for instance, that the attorney only contracts to perform work in the trial court and not to handle any resulting appeals).

In addition to describing what the attorney will do for the client, the representation agreement should describe all responsibilities of the client. The most significant client agreement (at least for most attorneys!) is the promise to pay the attorney and reimburse the costs of suit pursuant to the terms set forth in the agreement. The representation agreement also may include an explicit client promise to cooperate in the prosecution or defense of the contemplated litigation.

The representation agreement may contain various other terms. Such terms may govern the termination of the agreement, require the submission of attorney-client disputes to arbitration by bar counsel or others, establish billing and payment schedules, specify who within a law firm will do the work on a case, specify whether client files will be maintained in paper or electronic format, and state how an attorney will dispose of client files and provide client access to them.[14]

Although there are many variants on these themes, the three basic types of attorney compensation arrangements provide for (1) the payment of a flat fee for certain specified work (such as the handling of an uncontested divorce), (2) compensation of the attorney on an hourly basis for the time spent on a matter, and (3) a contingent fee arrangement, under which the attorney will receive a fixed percentage of any recovery obtained in the lawsuit.[15] The decision as to which of these attorney

---

14. On these latter points, see Thompson, "You Have to Share," *A.B.A.J.*, Sept. 2008, at 30.

15. Attorneys also may agree to accept retainers under which they will provide legal services for a particular period of time for a set fee. Moreover, certain clients may be eligible for the services of legal aid attorneys, who generally receive a salary or other payment from a private or

compensation provisions will be utilized in any particular case depends upon the preferences of the attorney and client, the client's ability to pay, the type of case involved, and local custom and practice.

Because they are legal contracts, and because of their possible complexity, attorney representation agreements are best put into writing.[16] Putting the terms of the representation into a written contract should help to ensure that both attorney and client appreciate what it is to which they are agreeing. Written specificity at the outset of the attorney-client relationship may help to avoid later possible misunderstandings.

Although the representation agreement is a legal contract, many such contracts take the form of letter agreements. Letter agreements are favored by some attorneys because of their less formal nature, while other attorneys perceive this as a disadvantage in certain cases. Another reason that letter agreements often are used is because they provide a convenient way to summarize the attorney's initial client interview. Such a memorialization can be helpful both at the outset of the attorney-client relationship and if later disputes or questions arise between attorney and client.

The following annotated representation letter contains illustrative terms that may be included in a letter representation agreement.[17] Note that the letter contemplates a combination of both a fixed attorney fee for certain specified work and hourly fees for work beyond that specified in the letter.

J. FOONBERG, HOW TO START AND BUILD A LAW PRACTICE

219–224 (4th ed. 1999).

John Client
123 Main Street
Anytown, U.S.A.

(1)   RE: Jones vs. Smith; breach of contract

Dear Mr. Jones:
This letter will confirm our office discussion

---

governmental organization. Finally, all attorneys are to render public interest legal service and may represent certain clients for no fee or for a reduced fee. *See* Model Rules of Prof'l Conduct Rule 6.1.

16. Model Rule of Prof'l Conduct 1.5(b) provides: "When the lawyer has not regularly represented the client, the basis or rate of the fee shall be communicated to the client, preferably in writing, before or within a reasonable time after commencing the representation."

Some states have gone beyond the precatory language of Model Rule 1.5(b) to require that most legal representations be memorialized by written engagement letters or retainer agreements. *E. g.* N.Y. Comp. Codes R. & Regs. tit. 22 § 1215 (2006).

Model Rule of Prof'l Conduct 1.5(c) requires that contingent fee agreements be put into writing.

17. For other illustrative terms and discussions of representation letters see Becker, "The Client Retention Agreement—The Engagement Letter," 23 *Akron L. Rev.* 323 (1990); Corp. Counsel Section of the New York State Bar Ass'n, "Report on Engagement Letters for Legal Services and a Model Letter," 34 *Law Office Econ. & Mgt.* 284 (1993). Form engagement letters are sometimes provided on bar association websites. *E.g,*, Alternative Billing Comm'n, North Carolina Bar Ass'n, http://www.ncbar.org/about/commissions—task-forces/alternate-billing-forms.aspx.

(2)   of Thursday, January 4th.

It was a pleasure meeting with you in our office.

As I explained to you, it is my opinion that you defin-

(3)   itely need the assistance of a lawyer, whether it be our

(4)   firm or another lawyer. In my opinion, the matter is too complex for you to represent yourself.

(5)   As I explained to you, if you wish us to repre-

(6)(7) sent you, our fee will be $1,500 to prepare the complaint, do written interrogatories, take the deposition of Mr. Smith if necessary, and appear for the first day

(8)   in court. If any additional work is required for such things as motions, additional depositions or additional

(9)   days in court, you will be charged at our hourly rate of $115 per hour. If the case is settled short of trial,

(10)   the fee will still be a minimum of $1,500.

(11)   The above does not include any out-of-pocket costs which may be incurred, such as court filing fees, sheriff's fees, deposition costs, photocopying, etc. We estimate, but cannot guarantee, that these costs will

(12)   run between $250 and $350, and, as explained, these costs are in addition to our fee and are *not* included in the $1,500 fee.

(13)   We shall have the right to engage other attorneys to assist us at our sole expense and at no additional cost to you.

(14)   You indicated that you wished to pay in installments of $350 fees and $100 costs to begin work, and $150 fees and $50 costs the first of each month until you are current, and then, additional fees and costs will be paid monthly, as billed.

This schedule is acceptable to us, so long as you understand that if you terminate payments, we may

(15)   terminate our services and withdraw from the case.

(16)   You are also agreeing to cooperate and participate in the conduct of your case and to truthfully and immediately notify us as to anything that may occur that could affect the case. You understand we are relying on the facts as given to us by you.

(17)   As I indicated to you, based on the facts as you related them to me in the office, you should win, and you should be awarded a judgment of between $9,500 and $15,000, unless the case is settled at a different sum. Obviously, depending upon the facts as they are developed, our opinion could change and you could be awarded more or less, or even lose. You

(18)   also understand that getting a judgment is not the same as getting cash and that you may have to expend additional costs and fees to collect the judgment.

(19)   You asked me if spending money on legal fees in this case is throwing good money after bad, and I told

you that at this point, I couldn't give you an answer, and that you should understand that there are no guarantees of winning or collecting.

(20) It is my opinion, however, that whether you use our firm or other lawyers, you should proceed with your case. Please do not delay. If you delay the commencement of your suit, you may at some point be barred from bringing it.

(21) If the above properly sets forth our agreement, please sign and return the enclosed copy of this letter, along with a check in the amount of $450, payable to my trust account. I will draw $350 toward my fees, and leave $100 toward costs as

(22) outlined above. Trust account funds are deposited to our Trust Account in accordance with the rules governing lawyers in our state including IOLTA (Interest On Lawyer Trust Accounts) rules as well as our fiduciary duty to you as a client. If funds are sufficient enough to earn net interest for the period of time held, we will consult with you for instructions. A self-addressed, postage-paid envelope is enclosed for your convenience.

(23) If we do not receive the signed copy of this letter, and your check, within 30 days, I shall assume that you have obtained other counsel, and shall mark my

(24) file "closed" and do nothing further.

(25) If any of the above is not clear, or if you have any question, please do not hesitate to call.
Very truly yours,

_____

To be typed on the copy of the letter:
The above is understood and agreed to, and my check in the amount of $450, payable to Jane Attorney Trust Account is enclosed.

(26) Dated: _____

_____
John Client

Essential Points to the Fee and Representation Letter

Obviously, the fee-representation letter must be tailor-made to the particular facts of the matter and the fee. Whatever form you decide to use, your letter should include the following:

(1) *The Matter Involved.* Perhaps your client has several legal matters, and has not told you about any of them except the Smith matter. This should prevent a later claim that you were responsible for *more* than this matter.

(2) *Your Interview Date.* This establishes when you had an interview to get the facts. This is for your protection in the event you are sued by your client or another party.

(3) *Whether or Not a Lawyer Is Required.* This avoids the interviewee claiming that you said no lawyer was necessary and that he or she should "forget about it."

(4) *Suggesting Other Lawyers.* Suggest the client may wish to see another lawyer. This relates to not representing the client until the agreement is returned. (See point 21 * * *.)

(5) *If You Wish Us to Represent You.* This reinforces that you are not yet the lawyer, and don't yet have responsibility.

(6) *The Amount of the Fee.* This establishes what I call the "Basic Fee."

(7) *Describing the Work the Fee Covers.* This discusses what you will do for the Basic Fee.

(8) *What the Basic Fee Does NOT Cover.* This describes what is not included in the Basic Fee.

(9) *Additional Work Fee Arrangement.* How you will charge for the work that is *not* included in this Basic Fee.

(10) *Minimum Fee.* What the minimum fee will be.

(11) *Out–of–Pocket Costs.* The client will not understand the difference between costs and fees, unless you explain it. This reinforces your explanation.

(12) *Addition to Fees.* Reinforce that out-of-pocket costs are in addition to fees.

(13) *Engaging Other Attorneys to Assist.* This allows you to get help at your expense if you are in over your head and need help.

(14) *Payment Schedule.* Set forth the cash flow that you have agreed upon, to avoid later misunderstandings.

(15) *Right to Terminate Services.* It is important that the client understands your right to terminate services for nonpayment. In some jurisdictions there may be ethical considerations in domestic relations and criminal matters. This portion should satisfy the requirements of DR 2–110(C)(1)([f]) so that you can withdraw when the client stops paying.

(16) *Agreeing to Cooperate and Be Truthful.* This may be the basis of your motion to be relieved as counsel at a later time.

(17) *Your Opinion of the Merits of the Case.* Repeat in a letter what you told the client in the office, and that what you said was based upon the facts that were given you. (Obviously, you may use this part of your letter to state that you are not yet in a position to express an opinion as to the outcome, or that you won't be able to express an opinion until research is done or until discovery is underway or completed.) In some types of work, you can quote dollar amounts. In some types, such as personal injury, you should not. Always repeat in writing what you did or did not say in the office to prevent later problems when the client claims you quoted a large recovery.

(18) *Explain Judgments.* Be sure the client is aware that winning a case and getting a judgment for fees and costs is not the same as getting cash, and that many judgments are uncollectible.

(19) *No Guarantees.* The client should understand that you have not guaranteed the outcome, and that it is possible that the funds expended on legal fees won't guarantee results.

(20) *Tell Client Not to Delay.* Warn the prospective client in lay language not to delay. Warn the prospective client that laches or a Statute of Limitations can prejudice the case if there are delays. Do not express an opinion on the statute date, unless you are engaged to do so. If you gave the client the wrong date, you could have malpractice liability.

(21) *Signing and Returning Copy of Letter.* Obviously, the signed copy in effect becomes a fee contract when returned to you.

(22) *Trust Account Rules—Explain IOLTA.* IOLTA rules may vary from state to state. You have to comply with your IOLTA rules and also comply with your fiduciary duties to your client. In some states IOLTA is mandatory. In some states it is optional or "opt-out." Be careful when the amount of net interest that could be earned on your client's funds might exceed bank charges. Refer to your local IOLTA rules and *The ABA Guide to Lawyer Trust Accounts* * * * .

(23) *Repeat* that both letter and check should be returned.

(24) *Set Date for Return of Engagement Letter.* Clearly indicate that you will assume the "client" has obtained other help to prevent the "client" coming in two years later claiming you undertook the case even though you never heard from the client again. Let there be no misunderstanding that you are doing nothing further until you receive the signed fee agreement and the check.

(25) *Clarify Any Loose Ends.* Give the client an opportunity to ask if anything is not clear.

(26) *Have the Client Sign the Fee Agreement, and Get Your Retainer for Fees and Costs.* Upon execution and return of the fee agreement, you have a client, and the client has a lawyer.

While every attorney will use his or her own form of representation agreement, the preceding agreement gives a good indication of what such agreements may look like. However, two comments concerning this agreement should be made.

Although the author of the agreement suggests that clients not be told when the statute of limitations will run on their claims, there may be situations in which the mere admonition "Please do not delay" may not sufficiently protect a potential client's claim. If the attorney reasonably believes that the statute of limitations may run in the very near future, the client should be told specifically of the earliest possible date by which suit may have to be filed.

Many lawyers also are more explicit than is the preceding agreement in stressing that, although in their professional opinion there is merit to the potential client's claim, they do not, and cannot, guarantee the results of any litigation. Attorneys should be careful about making statements such as the one set forth at note 17 that "you should win." Some representation agreements contain clauses (sometimes in boldface type) in which the potential client acknowledges that the attorney has made no assurances as to the eventual outcome of any litigation.

The preceding representation letter contains provisions for payment of counsel at both a flat rate (for the specified initial work on the case) and an hourly rate (for work beyond the specified initial work). The following paragraph is from a contingent fee contract that was cited in *Zauderer v. Office of Disciplinary Counsel*.[18]

IV. ATTORNEY FEES

"I hereby agree to pay P. Q. Z. & A as attorney fees for such representation, which fees are deemed by me to be reasonable:

"*Thirty–Three and One–Third Per Cent* of the gross amount recovered by way of settlement or compromise prior to trial;

"*Forty Per Cent* of the gross amount recovered by way of settlement or compromise or judgment if a trial or any part thereof commences, and an appeal is not necessary;

"*Forty–Five Per Cent* of the gross amount recovered by way of settlement or compromise or judgment if a trial or any part thereof commences, and an appeal is necessary.

"The term 'gross amount' shall mean the total amount of money recovered, prior to any deduction for expenses, and shall include any interest awarded or recovered.

"IT IS AGREED AND UNDERSTOOD THAT THIS EMPLOYMENT IS UPON A CONTINGENT FEE BASIS, AND IF NO RECOVERY IS MADE, I WILL NOT BE INDEBTED TO P. Q. Z. & A FOR ANY SUM WHATSOEVER AS ATTORNEY FEES (EXCEPT AS PROVIDED IN SECTION VIII HEREOF.)["]

In this agreement the "gross amount" of any recovery which is the basis for calculating the attorney's contingent fee is specified quite precisely. In addition to such a provision concerning attorneys' fees, contingent fee representation agreements may contain explicit provisions that the client is responsible for the payment of any non-fee costs or expenses resulting from the contemplated litigation. In some jurisdictions it is considered unethical for attorneys to agree to advance legal costs (as

---

18.   471 U.S. 626, 662 n. 6 (1985) (Brennan, J., concurring, in part, and dissenting, in part).

opposed to attorneys' fees) for which the client is not ultimately responsible.[19]

Whatever the specific terms of an attorney representation agreement, they should be clearly set forth in a written agreement at the outset of the attorney-client relationship. Over time, attorneys develop representation forms that best protect both themselves and their clients and that can be tailored to the needs of particular cases.

B. SETTING LEGAL FEES

ABA Model Rule of Professional Conduct 1.5(a) provides:

A lawyer's fee shall be reasonable. The factors to be considered in determining the reasonableness of a fee include the following:

(1) the time and labor required, the novelty and difficulty of the questions involved, and the skill requisite to perform the legal service properly;

(2) the likelihood, if apparent to the client, that the acceptance of the particular employment will preclude other employment by the lawyer;

(3) the fee customarily charged in the locality for similar legal services;

(4) the amount involved and the results obtained;

(5) the time limitations imposed by the client or by the circumstances;

(6) the nature and length of the professional relationship with the client;

(7) the experience, reputation, and ability of the lawyer or lawyers performing the services; and

(8) whether the fee is fixed or contingent.

Can Model Rule 1.5(a) be used to define precisely a "reasonable" fee for any particular case? Is such a definition really possible? Or must the test for unreasonable attorneys' fees be similar to Justice Stewart's test for pornography: "I know it when I see it."[20] As difficult as it may be to precisely determine a reasonable attorneys' fee, the task has become increasingly important both for attorneys in initially setting fees and for

---

19. *E.g.*, Mich. Rule of Prof'l Conduct 1.8(e)(1). However, Model Rule 1.8(e)(1) provides that "a lawyer may advance court costs and expenses of litigation, the repayment of which may be contingent on the outcome of the matter." Even if the representation contract provides that the client is ultimately responsible for all litigation costs, attorneys generally do not proceed against their clients to recover litigation costs if the client does not prevail in the lawsuit.

Another way in which costs and expenses may be covered in a contingent case is through "nonrecourse" lending, pursuant to which a company loans funds to cover costs and expenses but the client is not required to repay this loan if the lawsuit is unsuccessful. *See* Libby, "Whose Lawsuit Is It?," *A.B.A.J.*, May 2003, at 36. Such loans may create ethical issues for attorneys involving client confidentiality and the attorney's independence of professional judgment. *Id.*

20. *Jacobellis v. Ohio*, 378 U.S. 184, 197 (1964) (Stewart, J., concurring).

courts asked to approve attorneys' fee requests under federal and state fee-shifting statutes.

NOTES AND QUESTIONS CONCERNING THE SETTING OF ATTORNEYS' FEES

1. Consider the reasonableness of the attorneys' fees in the following story about Washington, D. C. lawyer Clark Clifford:

> There is a story, perhaps apocryphal, of the corporation general counsel in the Midwest who asked Clifford what his company should do concerning certain tax legislation. After several weeks Clifford responded, "Nothing," and enclosed a bill for $20,000. Unaccustomed to the Clifford style, the general counsel testily wrote that for $20,000 he certainly was entitled to a more complete explanation of the recommendation. He got it. "Because I said so," Clifford said in letter two, and billed the corporation for another $5,000.

J. Goulden, *The Superlawyers* 71 (1972).

2. Does the type of fee arrangement make a difference in the manner in which an attorney handles a case? It has been suggested that attorneys who are employed on an hourly basis may expend more hours on a case than attorneys who are employed on a contingent fee basis. Johnson, "Lawyers' Choice: A Theoretical Appraisal of Litigation Investment Decisions," 15 *Law & Soc'y Rev.* 567 (1980–81). However, an empirical study has found this to be true only for cases with less than $10,000 at stake; in cases with greater stakes, contingent fee attorneys actually appeared to devote more hours to a case than did attorneys paid on an hourly basis. Kritzer et al., "The Impact of Fee Arrangement on Lawyer Effort," 19 *Law & Soc'y Rev.* 251 (1985). *See also* Helland & Tabarrok, "Contingency Fees, Settlement Delay, and Low–Quality Litigation: Empirical Evidence from Two Datasets," 19 *J. L. Econ. & Org.* 517, 517 (2003) ("contingency fees increase legal quality and decrease the time to settlement").

Are there factors other than economic self-interest that influence how much time attorneys devote to their cases? Should there be?

3. What is the rationale for permitting attorneys to represent clients on a contingent fee basis? Consider the story told by attorney Melvin Belli about the attorney informing his client that "I'm not going to charge you one single cent as a fee for representing you—as a matter of fact, to prove to you how generous we lawyers really are, I'm going to give you half of everything we collect from your lawsuit!" Belli, "Pre–Trial: Aid to the New Advocacy," 43 *Cornell L. Q.* 34, 36 (1957).

4. If attorneys may be seen as investing in the outcome of a lawsuit by agreeing to a contingent fee, are different issues presented when litigation funding is provided by outside investors who, in effect, purchase shares in an individual's legal claim? *See* Gillers, "Waiting for Good Dough: Litigation Funding Comes to Law," 43 *Akron L. Rev.* 677 (2010); Steinitz, "Whose Claim Is This Anyway? Third Party Litigation Funding," 95 *Minn. L. Rev.* 101 (2011); Appelbaum, "Taking Sides in a Divorce, Chasing Profit," *N. Y. Times,*

Dec. 5, 2010, § 1, at 1 (firm providing litigation funding for individuals in domestic relations suits in return for a share of the lawsuit proceeds).

5. In *Haines v. Liggett Group, Inc.*, 814 F.Supp. 414 (D.N.J. 1993), counsel sought to withdraw from representing a plaintiff in litigation against several tobacco companies because of the millions of dollars of fees and expenses that already had been expended on the case and that still would be necessary to bring the case to its final resolution. In denying the motion to withdraw the court stated: "If lawyers—after assessing the likelihood of recovery, negotiating a contingency fee and raising the expectations of their client—are permitted to withdraw when contingency fee representation becomes unprofitable or even costly, the purpose of contingency fee litigation will be defeated." 814 F.Supp. at 427–28.

6. Are there situations in which a contingent fee is generally not appropriate? See Rule 1.5(d) of the Model Rules of Professional Conduct (proscribing contingent fees in criminal and certain domestic relations cases). Are there other situations in which contingent fee arrangements might be inappropriate? Will it sometimes be to a client's advantage to compensate an attorney on a non-contingent fee basis? What if the client has a very strong claim (for example, is a victim of an airplane crash) and is financially able to pay an attorney on an hourly basis? What if the client nevertheless prefers for the case to be handled on a contingent fee basis? *See generally* Brickman, "Contingent Fees Without Contingencies: *Hamlet* Without the Prince of Denmark?," 37 *UCLA L. Rev.* 29 (1989). Such situations were considered in ABA Formal Ethics Opinion 94–389, which concluded: "It is not necessarily unethical to charge a contingent fee when liability is clear and some recovery is anticipated" so long as "the fee is appropriate and reasonable and * * * the client has been fully informed of all appropriate alternative billing arrangements and their implications."

7. Plaintiffs are not the only litigants to whom contingent fee arrangements may be attractive. Under "reverse contingent fee" agreements, attorneys receive in compensation the difference between the amount that is being demanded from their client and the amount that the client ultimately pays in settlement or judgment. As with plaintiff contingent fee agreements, reverse contingent fee agreements can be abused to the disadvantage of the client. However, these agreements can be appropriate "where the contingency rests on the amount of money, if any, saved the client, provided the amount saved is reasonably determinable, the fee is reasonable in amount under the circumstances, and the client's agreement to the fee arrangement is fully informed." ABA Formal Ethics Opinion 93–373 (Apr. 16, 1993).

8. Aren't there also problems with billing clients on an hourly basis? Should clients be expected to compensate attorneys on the basis of attorney efforts rather than results? Judge John Grady of the Northern District of Illinois has asserted that "[m]uch pretrial work is done primarily for the purpose of generating fees. Most pretrial work is billed on a time basis. In some law offices, hourly fees tend to generate hours of work." Grady, "Trial Lawyers, Litigators and Clients' Costs," *Litigation,* Spring 1978, at 5, 58.

9. Consider ABA Formal Ethics Opinion 93–379, interpreting Model Rule 1.5:

[A] lawyer may not bill more time than she actually spends on a matter, except to the extent that she rounds up to minimum time periods (such as one-quarter or one-tenth of an hour) * * * .

A lawyer who spends four hours of time on behalf of three clients has not earned twelve billable hours. A lawyer who flies for six hours for one client, while working for five hours on behalf of another, has not earned eleven billable hours * * * .

It goes without saying that a lawyer who has undertaken to bill on an hourly basis is never justified in charging a client for hours not actually expended.

If it "goes without saying that a lawyer who has undertaken to bill on an hourly basis is never justified in charging a client for hours not actually expended," why did the ABA Committee on Ethics and Professional Responsibility believe that it was necessary to say this? Forty percent of the lawyers surveyed in one study admitted that they had performed legal tasks in order to bill for such tasks. W. Ross, *The Honest Hour: The Ethics of Time–Based Billing by Attorneys* 29 (1996).

10. Reginald Heber Smith, working with the Harvard Business School, developed the hourly billing system, and attorney time sheets, during his leadership of the Boston Legal Aid Society and, subsequently, at the law firm of Hale and Dorr. McCollam, "The Future of Time," *The American Lawyer*, Nov. 2005 (Litigation Supplement), at 64, 66–68. In the almost 100 years since this development, hourly fees have been criticized by both attorneys and clients. In response to the "corrosive impact of [the] emphasis on billable hours," American Bar Association President Robert Hirshon appointed an ABA Commission on Billable Hours. Commission on Billable Hours, American Bar Association, *ABA Commission on Billable Hours Report* 5 (2002) (available at http://www.abanet.org/careercounsel/billable/toolkit/bhcomplete.pdf). The report considered such alternatives to hourly billing as fixed or flat fees, blended hourly rates, fee discounts for volume legal work, retainers, task-specific fees, and contingent fees. *See also Winning Alternatives to the Billable Hour: Strategies That Work* (M. Robertson & J. Calloway 3d ed. 2008); *Beyond the Billable Hour: An Anthology of Alternative Billing Methods* (R. Reed ed. 1989).

11. In response to the recession that began in December 2007, some large corporations reduced their legal bills by insisting that increasing amounts of legal work be billed on a flat fee basis or under other alternatives to hourly billing. Glater, "Billable Hours Giving Ground at Law Firms," *N. Y. Times*, Jan. 30, 2009, at A1; Koppel & Jones, " 'Billable Hour' Under Attack," *Wall St. J.*, Aug. 24, 2009, at A1. Even before the recession, some attorneys had moved away from hourly billing to "value billing," under which clients are billed for the "value" of legal services provided rather than for attorney hours expended. *See* Reed, "Value Billing," *Legal Econ.*, Sept. 1988, at 20. However, not all clients are enthusiastic about value billing. One corporate vice president, who was presented with a legal bill for $1,000,000 without any documentation of the work done, considers value billing to be the "greatest threat to controlling outside legal costs in recent years." Terence Gallagher, Vice President of Legal Administration for Pfizer Co., *quoted in* Marcotte,

"Corporations Cut Legal Costs," *A.B.A.J.*, Feb. 1989, at 22, 22. Other clients, however, have welcomed law firm offers to handle blocks of matters (such as all of a client's discovery responses or all litigation within a certain geographic region) for a flat rate. Klein, "Got Case? They'll Travel," *National Law Journal*, Aug. 25, 1997, at A1, A21.

12.   Under what circumstances is an attorney obligated to accept as a client someone who does not have the money to pay the attorney's customary fees? Are there ways other than representing individual clients by which attorneys can help to ensure that those who cannot afford legal counsel are able to obtain it? *See* Model Rules of Prof'l Conduct Rule 6.1. Should attorneys be able to decline to represent indigent persons because of their monetary contributions to such representations? Because of other public interest activities?

13.   Can (and should) the courts compel attorneys to accept appointments to represent indigent persons? See the majority and dissenting opinions in *Mallard v. United States District Court*, 490 U.S. 296 (1989), in which the Supreme Court held that one federal statute, 28 U.S.C. § 1915, does not give federal district courts the power to compel attorneys to represent *in forma pauperis* claimants.

14.   Are there circumstances under which an attorney should refuse to undertake legal representation? Can an attorney refuse to represent a potential client with an apparently meritorious claim? Are there situations in which a client's best interests might be served by not filing even a meritorious claim? Is it the attorney's job to do more than determine the potential legal merit of a claim?

In this regard, consider the quotation from Abraham Lincoln at the beginning of this chapter. What impact upon the adversary system would Lincoln's views have if they were shared by all attorneys? *See* Model Rules of Prof'l Conduct Rule 1.16(b)(3) (permitting attorneys to withdraw from representation if "a client insists upon pursuing an objective that the lawyer considers repugnant or imprudent"); Simon, "Ethical Discretion in Lawyering," 101 *Harv. L. Rev.* 1083 (1988) (advocating that attorneys should have ethical discretion to refuse to assist clients in the pursuit of legally permissible courses of action if such assistance would not further justice).

C. CLIENT BILLING

Presuming that agreement is reached on the terms of the representation and legal services are performed on the client's behalf, there comes a time for billing the client. It's a good idea to bill clients on a regular basis. These bills should specifically describe the work done by the attorney. For example, a bill might state that it is for "legal research concerning defendant's motion to dismiss (June 2–3; 3 hours); drafting opposition to motion to dismiss (June 3–4; 4 hours); court hearing concerning motion to dismiss (June 12; 1 hour)," rather than merely demanding: "For professional services rendered: $1200.00."

Specific descriptions of legal activity require that counsel keep detailed and contemporaneous time records. These records are not only useful for client billings, but may be essential in obtaining court-awarded attorneys' fees under the numerous federal and state statutes that provide for the shifting of legal fees to unsuccessful litigants.

Clients will be much happier (?) with their bills if they have been kept informed of the work that is being done on their behalf as the case progresses. If the client was provided with a copy of a document at the time that it was filed, he should not be surprised to later receive a bill for that work. Even more importantly, if clients are to meaningfully participate in their cases, they must be kept informed of significant case developments as they occur.

Figure 2–1 graphically illustrates the precise moment when a client should be billed for legal services.[21] This table should be taken in the light-hearted manner in which it is offered. Under no circumstances should it be left out where clients can see it.

---

21. 7 *Law Office Econ. & Mgt.* 62 (1966).

In some situations a billing schedule may be included in the retainer agreement or created by client expectations. Some corporations require law firms to bill them electronically, which not only expedites attorney payment but also permits the corporation to electronically scrutinize firm billings and billing patterns. Carter, "Do it the DuPont Way," *A.B.A.J.*, April 2004, at 27.

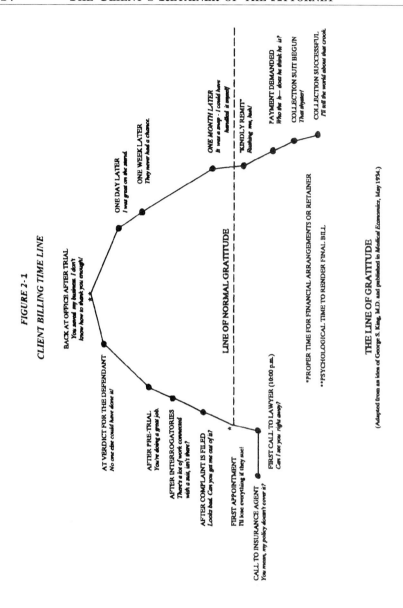

FIGURE 2-1
CLIENT BILLING TIME LINE

Exercise Concerning the Attorney–Client Relationship

You graduated from law school one year ago and are attempting to establish a solo private practice in Logan County, West Virginia. With the exception of a basic course in constitutional law, you have had no training or experience in the area of civil rights. Instead, your current legal "specialty" is criminal law. The only cases that you have handled in federal court have been court appointments under the Criminal Justice Act (which provides for the payment of counsel fees to attorneys handling cases for indigent federal criminal defendants). In both of these federal cases your client pled guilty prior to trial. In fact, the only trial that you have handled was a small land condemnation case referred to you by the Logan County Prosecuting Attorney's Office.

You have just had an initial interview with James Jones, a prospective client who was referred to your office by a federal district judge. Although the federal district court has no formal plan for the assignment of counsel to represent indigent persons in civil cases, the judge sent you a letter in which he requested that you "See what you can do for Mr. Jones."

In your interview with Mr. Jones, you learn that he has filed a *pro se* civil rights action against Logan County, West Virginia and several of its office holders. In this action Jones has alleged that he was dismissed from his position in the county maintenance department because of a letter that he wrote to the local newspaper criticizing the county for its clean-up efforts after the Buffalo Creek flood. During your interview with Jones, he can point to no specific facts that support his claim other than his discharge several months after the publication of his letter to the editor. Jones, however, does tell you that two of the other employees at the maintenance department also recently were discharged, and one of these men was highly critical of the county's flood clean-up efforts.

Not only are you somewhat skeptical of the allegations made by Mr. Jones, but you find him to be a generally obnoxious person (at least in part because of his comment during the interview that "I might be better off handling my case myself, rather than trusting it to a greenhorn like you."). In addition, you have concerns that handling this case might disrupt your practice, which finally is beginning to grow.

What should you do with respect to the case? Draft a letter to Mr. Jones explaining your proposed course of action. If there are any other documents that you would prepare, draft them as well.

V. CONCLUSION

Regardless of the type of litigation practice that a lawyer chooses, she will spend great amounts of time interviewing clients. In many practice settings, the attorney will regularly enter into representation agreements and set legal fees. While effective client interviews cannot guarantee successful litigation outcomes, ineffective client interviews will make unsuccessful litigation outcomes more likely. Lack of attention to representation agreements also can lead to less than satisfactory client relations and case outcomes. By becoming conscious of interviewing techniques and client relations, the chances for both a successful and satisfying litigation practice should be enhanced.

VI. CHAPTER BIBLIOGRAPHY

R. Aronson, *Attorney–Client Fee Arrangements: Regulation and Review* (1980).

R. Bastress & J. Harbaugh, *Interviewing, Counseling, and Negotiating* (1990).

A. Benjamin, *The Helping Interview* (3d ed. 1980).

D. Binder & S. Price, *Legal Interviewing and Counseling: A Client–Centered Approach* (1977).

D. Binder et al., *Lawyers as Counselors: A Client–Centered Approach* (2d ed. 2004).

R. Cochran et al., *The Counselor-at-Law: A Collaborative Approach to Client Interviewing and Counseling* (2d ed. 2006).

"Client Counseling and Legal Interviewing: Special Issue," 18 *Creighton L. Rev.* 1329 (1985).

Commission on Billable Hours, American Bar Association, *ABA Commission on Billable Hours Report* (2002).

Committee on Continuing Professional Education, American Law Institute–American Bar Association, *The Practical Lawyer's Manual on Lawyer–Client Relations* (1983).

Earl, "Conducting the Initial Interview," *Trial*, April 1993, at 58.

Fey & Goldberg, "Legal Interviewing from a Psychological Perspective: An Attorney's Handbook," 14 *Willamette L. J.* 217 (1978).

H. Freeman & H. Weihofen, *Clinical Law Training: Interviewing and Counseling* (1972).

R. Gorden, *Interviewing: Strategy, Techniques, and Tactics* (4th ed. 1987).

Haig & Caley, "What's a Fair Fee for a Litigator?," *Litigation*, Fall 1993, at 37.

G. Herman & J. Cary, *A Practical Approach to Client Interviewing, Counseling, and Decision–Making: For Clinical Programs and Practical Skills Courses* (2009).

Howarth & Hetrick, "How to Interview the Client," *Litigation*, Summer 1983, at 25.

F. Jandt, *Effective Interviewing* (1990).

S. Krieger & R. Neumann, Jr., *Essential Lawyering Skills: Interviewing, Counseling, Negotiation, and Persuasive Fact Analysis* (3d ed. 2007).

J. McRae, *Legal Fees and Representation Agreements* (1983).

M. Nelken et al., *Problems and Cases in Interviewing, Counseling and Negotiation* (3d ed. 1986).

P. Pedersen & A. Ivey, *Culture–Centered Counseling and Interviewing Skills: A Practical Guide* (1993).

Rebuen, "Getting the Truth from the Client," *Litigation,* Fall 1987, at 11.

R. Redmount & T. Shaffer, *Legal Interviewing and Counseling* (1980).

D. Rosenthal, *Lawyer and Client: Who's in Charge?* (1977).

M. Schoenfield & B. Schoenfield, *Interviewing and Counseling* (1981).

T. Shaffer & J. Elkins, *Legal Interviewing and Counseling in a Nutshell* (4th ed. 2005).

Smith & Nester, "Lawyers, Clients, and Communication Skill," 1977 *BYU L. Rev.* 275.

Sobelson, "Interviewing Clients Ethically," *Prac. Law.*, Jan. 1991, at 13.

Sternlight & Robbennolt, "Good Lawyers Should be Good Psychologists: Insights for Interviewing and Counseling Clients," 23 *Ohio St. J. On Disp. Resol.* 437 (2008).

"Symposium: Client Counseling and Moral Responsibility," 30 *Pepp. L. Rev.* 591 (2003).

A. Watson, *The Lawyer in the Interviewing and Counseling Process* (1976).

Wernz, "Getting Paid," *Litigation*, Summer 1996, at 27.

Winning Alternatives to the Billable Hour: Strategies That Work (M. Robertson & J. Calloway 3d ed. 2008).

CHAPTER 3

PRETRIAL PLANNING AND INVESTIGATION: "LET'S START AT THE BEGINNING."

■ ■ ■

Mr. Smith, do you not think by introducing a little order into your narrative you might possibly render yourself a trifle more intelligible? * * * I should like to stipulate for some sort of order. There are plenty of them. There is the chronological, the botanical, the metaphysical, the geographical, why even the alphabetical order would be better than no order at all.

Great Britain's Mr. Justice Maule, *quoted in* Stein, "Believe Me It Happened. I Was There," *Litigation,* Winter 1989, at 42, 59.

The really difficult problem in the preparation of the case is to learn what the facts are * * * . The law seldom decides the issue, the facts do; and as contrasted with the ascertainment of the facts, the law is relatively easy to discover.

L. Stryker, *The Art of Advocacy* 11 (1954).

Analysis

I. INTRODUCTION

Even after a client has been interviewed and the attorney decides to take a case, a great amount of work must be done before a lawsuit or a responsive pleading or motion actually is filed. This chapter deals with these pretrial tasks of litigation planning, factual and legal investigation and research, and the development of a case theory and theme.

An attorney's immediate concern after the initial client interview should be to determine whether there are factual and legal predicates to support a claim or defense on behalf of her new client. Prior to jumping into extensive factual investigation or legal research, however, the attorney should develop an initial litigation plan to focus her pretrial activity. Only after completion of a litigation plan should more extensive factual investigation and legal research be undertaken. Finally, in addition to conducting this investigation and research, the attorney must choose a persuasive case theory and theme.

At these preliminary stages of litigation, there generally are no definitive rules, such as the Federal Rules of Civil Procedure, governing attorney behavior. Instead, the attorney has wide latitude in planning, investigating, and researching the lawsuit. Attorney diligence and creativity concerning these tasks can pay handsome dividends later in the case. Similarly, lack of attention to, or interest in, the pretrial tasks discussed in this chapter can result in decisions that both attorney and client later will regret.

II. LITIGATION PLANNING

While serendipity may bring pleasant surprises to even lawyers from time to time, it is not a wise litigation strategy to assume that "Things will come out O.K. in the end." Instead of making it up as you go along, it's best to devise a litigation plan at the very outset of each case. These plans may be encompassed in a memorandum setting forth the governing law and facts, the potential witnesses and exhibits, the factual and legal matters that must be investigated and researched, and the pleadings, motions, and other pretrial and trial activity anticipated in the case. Important parts of most litigation plans are a timetable for the execution of the pretrial and trial tasks included in the plan and an estimate of the expenses that the plan will entail.

A. WHY PLAN LITIGATION?

One of the reasons why lawyering can be such a creative activity is because of the enumerable choices available to attorneys in shaping litigation. However, decisions made very early in a lawsuit often will greatly restrict later options. The witness not interviewed, the discovery not undertaken, or the motion not made may have a significant impact upon the final shape, and thus the final outcome, of the lawsuit.

The prerequisites for many pretrial activities make litigation planning a must. For instance, a court order or the consent of counsel is required to obtain the physical or mental examination of a party pursuant to Rule 35 of the Federal Rules of Civil Procedure. Attorneys therefore must plan for the eventuality that opposing counsel will insist upon an order before producing her client for examination. Not only will the requisite motion have to be prepared, but other pretrial activities must be scheduled to allow sufficient time for the court to rule upon the Rule 35 motion.

In addition, all pretrial actions have the potential for stimulating numerous reactions from other counsel or the court. If the physical or mental examination of a party is taken pursuant to Rule 35(a), the examined party is entitled under Rule 35(b)(1) to a copy of the examining physician's report. The consequence of requesting a copy of the report, though, is that the examined party then must make available any other reports concerning the same condition pursuant to Rule 35(b)(3). In order to enhance chances of litigation success, pretrial decisions thus should be based upon a consistent, overall plan, rather than made on an ad hoc basis.

Not only should litigation planning enable counsel to achieve better litigation outcomes, it can be an effective means of litigation cost control. For this reason, many corporations require their attorneys to prepare litigation plans and budgets that project not only anticipated attorneys' fees but litigation costs such as the expense of deposition transcripts, travel, copying, and expert witnesses.[1] These plans can provide an informed basis for settlement decisions and help businesses anticipate and prepare for the disruptions often caused by litigation events. Attorneys can use litigation plans and budgets to help focus clients on the non-monetary costs of litigation, such as the client's time and peace of mind that will be consumed by the pretrial and trial stages of a civil action.

Presenting a litigation plan to a client in a complex case may head off possible billing controversies that might result if the client were merely billed for a course of action after the fact. In addition, litigation plans may get clients more involved in the significant decision-making in a case. A corporate client might decide that it is not cost effective for counsel to attend all depositions involving co-defendants in a complex case. Discussion of litigation plans with a client also can lead to the identification of systemic problems with the client's operations that, if not changed, may lead to continuing litigation in the future. For example, a manager's habit of making promises that his corporate employer cannot keep may lead to future, as well as existing, lawsuits.

Litigation plans should be updated periodically as the litigation progresses. Reports to a client can show the litigation activity and costs that were planned for a particular period, the litigation activity and costs that actually occurred during that period, and the litigation activity and costs predicted for the next reporting period.

---

1. *See, e.g.,* Subcomm. on Budgeting for Litigation, Comm. on Corporate Counsel, American Bar Association Section of Litigation, *Case Histories on Budgeting for Litigation* (1988). Proposed litigation budgets have become increasingly important in choice of counsel decisions by corporate clients. *See* L. Smith, *Inside/Outside: How Businesses Buy Legal Services* 151–69 (2002); Decker, "Economics and Litigation: View from the Inside Looking Out," *Litigation*, Summer 1998, at 36. In developing such budgets, counsel should be certain to consider the increasing cost of electronic discovery and the possibility of the shifting of the cost of such discovery pursuant to Federal Rule of Civil Procedure 26(b)(2)(B). *See* Svetz, "Electronic Discovery: Cost Shifting Calls for Earlier Discovery Planning," *Construction Lawyer*, Summer 2003, at 9.

Litigation planning makes sense for several reasons and should be undertaken at the very outset of civil litigation.

B.   GENERAL PLANNING CONSIDERATIONS

Before turning to the specifics of the litigation plan, certain general planning considerations should be addressed. Perhaps most importantly, the pretrial process should not be considered a discrete end in itself, but as one aspect of the total litigation process. The strategies employed at the pretrial stage should be consistent with those that will be employed at trial. Attorneys should not expect a judge to reopen discovery on the eve of trial to permit the pursuit of a new case theory that was not previously developed.

Pretrial litigation always must be considered in the context of the particular court and judge before whom it is conducted. Not only should the attorney familiarize herself with the local rules of court, but she should attempt to learn the idiosyncrasies of the judge who will hear the case. Before settling on a motion for summary judgment as the centerpiece of her pretrial strategy, counsel should consider the summary judgment requirements imposed by local rules of court and the proclivities of the judge to grant summary judgments.

Attorneys quickly learn that the most frequent pretrial decisions concern which courses of action *not* to pursue. While law schools train students about the many possible motions they *can* make, practicing attorneys must determine which motions they actually *should* make. Judges and other counsel are not impressed by attorneys who file every conceivable motion or seek every conceivable bit of discovery. Nor are clients impressed by the charges for such litigation overkill.

Attorneys soon realize that the time and money spent in the early stages of a case on planning may save even greater amounts of time and money in the later stages of the case. While it might take some time, and cost some money, to determine whether certain discovery should be pursued, this preliminary investigation may result in a decision that the discovery should not be undertaken at all.

The long run benefits from planning must not be overlooked, because in a litigation practice there always are other tasks that have to be done immediately. There exists the very real possibility that the urgent (the tasks with immediate deadlines) may displace the truly important (longer run litigation planning). While some attorneys contend that they do not have the necessary time to devote to litigation planning, a fairer assessment may be that busy attorneys do not have the time *not* to plan.

Attorneys must be careful to organize their cases so that their litigation plans can be effectuated. The development of a chronology of important events underlying a case can be helpful in organizing information and in highlighting the information that isn't yet known. Most attorneys keep separate files for different aspects of a case. In major cases, an attorney may have a pleadings file, a file containing court orders, a discovery file, indexed files to documents requested and produced, files for legal research and investigation, and files for each witness. While different attorneys have different filing systems, the aim of any system should be to permit an attorney to quickly assess the status of a case and locate particular documents and information when needed.

Attorneys need to develop a "tickler system" so that their calendars will indicate upcoming litigation deadlines. Not knowing that a brief or motion must be filed until the day that it is due is usually not sufficient. The attorney's calendar should be arranged to set aside time in advance so that the brief can be completed by the date that it must be filed with the court.

Pretrial planning makes sense for both attorneys and their clients. Consideration of the above suggestions in the development of pretrial litigation plans should result in plans that are even more effective in ensuring litigation success and containing litigation costs.

C. THE SPECIFIC LITIGATION PLAN

To be most successful, a litigation plan must be developed as early in the case as possible. Plaintiff's counsel should develop a litigation plan before filing any lawsuit. One of plaintiff's major litigation advantages is being able to take control of a case at the outset. This advantage should not be squandered by having to plan and attend to other preliminary matters after suit has been filed. Many attorneys open their case files with a memorandum setting forth the governing law, the facts then known, potential witnesses, documentary and other physical sources of proof, and the various factual and legal matters that still must be investigated and researched.

The objectives of one's client must be the starting point for any litigation plan. By the conclusion of the initial client interview, the attorney should know what relief her client desires, as well as whether the client wishes to pursue a strategy more oriented to settlement or to trial. Counsel then must conduct preliminary legal research to determine the availability of the desired relief. Counsel must consider the potential defendants, the possible jurisdictions in which an action could be filed, and the various pretrial motions available to all potential parties.

In the course of this research, counsel should determine the elements of the possible claims that may afford the desired relief. Plaintiff's counsel then must decide exactly how each element will be established. Not only must plaintiff's counsel know, specifically, what plaintiff must prove to prevail, but defense counsel, too, must know each and every element of plaintiff's case. Once defense counsel has this information, she can determine which of these elements plaintiff will have the greatest difficulty proving (and, therefore, the elements upon which the defense should focus). Both plaintiff's and defendant's counsel should consider potential affirmative defenses and counterclaims and determine the legal elements of such defenses and counterclaims.

After conducting preliminary legal research to determine the elements of plaintiff's claims and all potential defenses, an element check list should be developed. One helpful starting place in developing such a check list are pattern jury instructions, the sample instructions in which list the elements for most major causes of action.[2] For instance, in a simple negligence action, the legal elements would be defendant's negligence, proximate or legal causation of injury, and proof of resulting damages.[3]

Once an element check list has been developed, it is often helpful to diagram the elements of a case by creating a litigation grid. Such a grid should list the elements that must be proven and the witnesses and other sources of proof that will be used to establish each of these elements. A preliminary litigation grid in the Buffalo Creek disaster litigation might look something like Figure 3–1.

Several things should be noted about the litigation grid set forth in Figure 3–1. First of all, it portrays a very preliminary litigation plan. The grid is based only upon the initial client interview and the most preliminary legal research. Therefore the grid is a plan for further pretrial investigation, rather than a complete listing of trial witnesses and exhibits.

This litigation grid could be expanded to include other boxes. For example, rather than a single box concerning defendant's negligence, the grid might be further divided to organize the proof of negligence in terms of defendant's duty to plaintiffs and defendant's breach of that duty. Boxes could be added to the grid to show the estimated cost of establishing the elements of plaintiffs' case, the time for completion of the research, investigation, and discovery contemplated by the proof shown on the grid, and sources of proof other than witnesses or documents (such as party stipulations or judicial notice).

Not just plaintiffs' witnesses and documents have been included in the preliminary litigation plan illustrated in Figure 3–1. This plan presumes that certain elements of plaintiffs' case will be established through the testimony of defense officials (called as adverse witnesses) and through defense documents (obtained through discovery). Some of the exhibits (such as the charts, models and reports of the experts) do not now exist but must be created specifically for this litigation. The litigation plan also presumes that some witnesses (such as the plaintiffs and their experts) will testify concerning more than one element of plaintiffs' case.

---

2. *See, e.g.,* 3–3C K. O'Malley et al., *Federal Jury Practice and Instructions (Civil)* (5th ed. 2000–2001); Comm. on Pattern Jury Instructions, District Judges Ass'n, United States Court of Appeals for the Fifth Circuit, *Pattern Jury Instructions: Civil Cases* (2006); Comm. on Pattern Jury Instructions of the Seventh Circuit, United States Court of Appeals for the Seventh Circuit, *Federal Civil Jury Instructions of the Seventh Circuit* (2009). Federal pattern jury instructions also are collected on the Federal Evidence Review website at http://federalevidence.com/evidence-resources/federal-jury-instructions.

3. 3 O'Malley et al., *supra* note 2, at § 120.

FIGURE 3–1

PLAINTIFFS' PROOF IN BUFFALO CREEK LITIGATION

Element of Plaintiffs' Case	Possible Witnesses to Testify Concerning Element	Possible Exhibits to Offer Concerning Element

Defendant's Negligence	Pittston Employees Who Constructed Dam
	
	Pittston Officials (adverse witnesses)
	
	Plaintiffs' Expert Witnesses:
	    Engineers
	    Hydrologists
		Pittston Records:
		    Other Dam Breaks
		    Engineering Data
		    Absence of Records
		
		Government Safety Standards
		
		Charts and Models Prepared by Experts

Proximate or Legal Causation	Plaintiffs
	
	Eyewitnesses
	
	Plaintiffs' Expert Witnesses:
	    Engineers
	    Hydrologists
		Photographs of Flood
		
		Before and After Photographs
		
		Charts and Models Prepared by Experts

Resulting Damages	Plaintiffs Plaintiffs' Doctors Appraisers Psychologists Community Members	Doctors' Bills Drug Prescriptions Reports of Doctors and Psychologists Photographs

Once a preliminary determination is made as to the possible witnesses, documents, and physical items that can be used to establish the elements of a claim or defense, counsel must decide how to obtain each piece of evidence. If reliance is to be made upon documents or statements of opposing parties, Rule 34 document production requests or Rule 30 depositions may have to be planned. Information from third-parties, though, may be obtained by informal discovery. Thus the first part of the litigation grid shown in Figure 3–1 might be refined in the manner shown in Figure 3–2.

FIGURE 3–2

PLAINTIFFS' PROOF IN BUFFALO CREEK LITIGATION (DEFENDANT'S NEGLIGENCE)

Element of Plaintiffs' Case	Possible Witnesses to Testify Concerning Element	Possible Exhibits to Offer Concerning Element
Defendant's Negligence	Pittston Employees Who Constructed Dam [**interviews**]	Pittston Records: Other Dam Breaks Engineering Data Absence of Records [**Rule 34 requests**]
	Pittston Officials (adverse witnesses) [**depositions**]	Government Safety Standards [**library research**]
	Plaintiffs' Expert Witnesses: Engineers Hydrologists [**interviews/ reports**]	Charts and Models Prepared by Experts [**experts**]

A litigation time table must be established as one part of any litigation plan. This can be done by adding a series of boxes to the litigation grid or by creating a separate chart or list of the pretrial litigation tasks included on that grid. The litigation time table should represent counsel's best estimate of the time necessary to complete informal and formal discovery, file pretrial motions, and join additional parties or amend the pleadings. In determining the time that will be necessary for these tasks, the attorney must consider both the initiatives that she plans to undertake and the likely responses from opposing counsel and the court. For instance, counsel should consider both (1) when her own motion for summary judgment can and should be filed and (2) when a probable cross-motion for summary judgment might be filed by opposing counsel.

The Federal Rules of Civil Procedure can be a major help in litigation scheduling. In many cases, the parties will be required to prepare a joint discovery plan pursuant to Rule 26(f). In addition, Rule 16(b) requires district courts to enter scheduling orders in most cases establishing time limitations for joining parties, amending the pleadings, filing motions, and completing discovery and other pretrial tasks. Attorneys therefore often can seek acceptance of their proposed pretrial litigation schedules by other parties pursuant to Rule 26(f) and ask the judge to enter those schedules as Rule 16 court orders.

Before seeking the agreement of other parties or the court to proposed pretrial deadlines, counsel should be sure that they will be able to adhere to those deadlines. However, litigation schedules, as well as the more general litigation plans of which they are one part, often must be modified as a case develops. The completion dates for various pretrial tasks usually are tied to one another. If discovery is not completed by the scheduled deadline, it may be necessary to seek an extension of the deadlines for the filing of dispositive motions and final amendment of the pleadings.

Attorneys should not be inflexibly tied to a litigation plan, but should continuously update the plan to reflect ongoing factual investigation, legal research, and pretrial proceedings. Just as the trial attorney must be able to adapt her cross-examination to the answers she receives from the witness, effective litigation planning requires sufficient flexibility to adjust to ongoing case developments.

Litigation plans and schedules are essential to maintain any chance of control over developing litigation. While time and effort are required to develop litigation plans, the alternatives to not planning usually are not welcome. Generally the choice is not between following a litigation plan or not following a litigation plan. Instead, the choice may be to develop and attempt to follow your own litigation plan or be required to adhere to a plan developed by the court or opposing counsel.

Exercises Concerning Litigation Planning

1.   You are a civil practitioner in a small law firm in Nashville, Tennessee. Thomas Eakins (whom you interviewed in exercise 1 of the Exercises Concerning Client Interviewing in Chapter 2, *supra* p. 38 has consulted you about possible claims stemming from the collapse of the dam in the Buffalo Creek Valley approximately one year ago on February 26, 1972. The failure of this dam is described in the first chapter of this book.

Eakins, an unemployed coal miner, has lived for the last nine months in Nashville, but was visiting his sister and brother-in-law in Logan County, West Virginia when the dam burst. Eakins's car, a 1965 Oldsmobile, was washed away in the flood, but Eakins was himself uninjured. He saw several people drown in the flood waters, and, from high ground, watched the house where he had been staying collapse in the flood.

Eakins informed you during your initial interview with him that his sister and brother-in-law are being represented in the major action that has been filed on behalf of several hundred flood victims in the United States District Court for the Southern District of West Virginia. You have called counsel in that case, and he has talked with you briefly about that litigation.

Your assignment is to write a memorandum to your partner proposing the litigation plan that you would employ on Thomas Eakins's behalf. Because you have only limited information concerning Mr. Eakins's situation and you have not had time to do extensive legal research, your memorandum may raise issues that it does not definitively resolve. Your litigation strategy should be premised upon what you believe the applicable facts and governing law will be and upon your general familiarity with such subjects as torts, civil procedure, and evidence.

In your litigation memorandum, you should outline the factual investigation, both formal and informal, that should be undertaken and the legal research that should be done on Eakins's behalf. In addition, consider where and against whom a possible suit might be brought (including the advantages and disadvantages of suing various defendants in particular jurisdictions), the relief that should be sought, any pretrial motions that might be filed by the parties, and the general course of action that you would recommend to Eakins. Be sure to include in your litigation plan a tentative pretrial scheduling proposal.

2. You recently interviewed Mason Charles, who has just been sued by his former employer, Allied Industries, Inc. Mr. Charles worked for Allied for thirty-five years, most recently as a district sales manager. Six months ago Charles was asked to take a newly-created position with Allied. Although he was told that this new position was a promotion, it involved longer hours, less responsibility, and only slightly higher pay than his position as district sales manager. Rather than accept this new position, Charles resigned from Allied three years before he would have been entitled to retirement with full pay. The position of district sales manager was filled by Sally Samuels, the thirty-two year old daughter-in-law of Allied's president.

After his resignation from Allied, Charles accepted a sales position with Consolidated Corporations, Inc., one of Allied's major competitors. While this is a supervisory position that does not involve Charles in direct sales activity, he has dealt with some of his former Allied customers from time to time in this new position.

Charles has asked you to represent him in the suit that Allied has brought against him alleging (1) violation of a term of his former Allied contract in which he agreed not to compete with Allied for a period of five years after he left that company and (2) common law tort and contract violations premised upon his alleged use of information gained in his prior position to the disadvantage of Allied. Allied has filed this suit in state court and seeks both a permanent injunction and legal damages.

You have agreed to write a letter to Mason Charles setting forth the manner in which you believe his lawsuit should be defended. Write this letter, describing the pretrial investigation and research, pleadings, motions, and discovery that you will pursue on his behalf. Be sure to give Charles an estimate of the cost of this defense and an approximate time schedule for the pretrial course of action that you recommend.

3. You have been engaged to represent several plaintiffs who were seriously injured or killed in automobile accidents that apparently were caused by a defect in the tires on these late-model cars. The theory of your case is that these tires are unsafe when underinflated and the cars are driven at high speeds in hot weather. Both the defendant automobile manufactures and the manufacturer of the tires deny liability, and no serious settlement offers have been forthcoming. Despite your efforts to

expedite pretrial proceedings, it appears that it will be at least two years until these actions will be tried.

As plaintiffs' counsel, should you report these alleged defects to the National Highway Traffic Safety Administration (NHTSA), which is the federal agency charged with investigating such safety defects? Should your decision be influenced by the fact that NHTSA recently closed several tire investigations without finding any defect? By the fact that NHTSA might be unlikely to order a recall involving such a huge number of tires? Is this a question on which your clients should be consulted?

III. FACTUAL INVESTIGATION

As *Dragnet*'s Sergeant Joe Friday was fond of saying, "Just the facts, Ma'am; Just the facts." Most attorneys' jobs would be significantly easier if they, too, could uncover "just the facts" in all of their cases. However, in real life "the facts" are not provided to the lawyer as they are on a law school examination. Nor are most attorneys as adept and lucky at factual investigation as Joe Friday, Perry Mason, and other fictional attorneys and sleuths.

To be successful in modern civil litigation, counsel must have at her disposal as many of the potentially relevant facts as possible. In order to obtain these facts, the attorney either must be a good investigator herself or have access to a good investigator. Professor James McElhaney suggests that good investigators possess three basic personal characteristics: curiosity, suspicion, and understanding.[4]

This section of the chapter addresses factual investigation. After an initial consideration of how to structure and implement a good factual investigation, one particular investigative technique, the witness interview, is analyzed in more depth. Finally, the actual handling of an historic case is examined in order to show the significance of a thorough factual investigation.

A. THE STRUCTURE AND IMPLEMENTATION OF THE FACTUAL INVESTIGATION

As with other litigation tasks, it is best to approach factual investigation with a plan rather than to hope to stumble upon important facts by chance. While a successful investigation is not guaranteed by a well structured and implemented investigative plan, such a plan should make successful pretrial investigations much more likely. In turn, successful factual investigations should lead to greater chances of success at trial or in dispositions short of trial. Not only do thorough factual investigations constitute good legal practice, but Rule 11 of the Federal Rules of Civil Procedure requires that an "inquiry reasonable under the circumstances" be conducted to ensure that case pleadings, motions, and other litigation documents have "evidentiary support."

---

4. McElhaney, "Informal Investigation," *Litigation,* Spring 1982, at 51.

The investigative structure suggested in this chapter requires the attorney to consider the what, who, where, how, and when of any factual investigation. The attorney must determine (1) the factual information that should be sought; (2) the source from which to seek the information; (3) the person to whom the request for information should be directed; (4) how to seek the information; and (5) when the information should be sought. Why a particular investigation is being pursued (*e.g.,* to establish an essential case element or merely to uncover corroborative evidence) will influence the answer to each of the other five questions.

1. What Factual Information Should Be Sought?

Before jumping into any factual investigation, it is best to determine exactly what facts are needed. As easy as this sounds, many attorneys undertake investigations without explicitly determining just what facts they are after. While investigative plans must be altered and refined to accommodate new facts and law as the investigation develops, an initial decision must be made as to the facts that the attorney would like to elicit during pretrial factual investigation.

In deciding what facts to seek, there are two extremes to be avoided. The first mistake that some attorneys make is to be too restrictive in the information that is sought. For instance, attorneys may decide that it is not worth the time or effort to explore certain factual possibilities. While other factual possibilities may be explored, they may not be pursued to the fullest extent possible. The attorney may be satisfied with her client's answer to a particular question rather than take the time to contact others with direct knowledge about an event.

A second mistake that attorneys increasingly make is to be too expansive in the facts that they seek. One of the reasons that Edward Bennett Williams became a trial legend was because of his belief that "There is no substitute for knowing everything."[5] However, factual investigation can become very expensive, very rapidly. There is always one more witness who can be interviewed or one more deposition that can be taken. The skillful investigator will not only seek to uncover existing facts but will consider any helpful facts that can be created at the pretrial stage. By inspecting a site soon after an accident or conducting computer analyses of a corporation's employment patterns, the attorney can preserve or create litigation facts that otherwise would not be available at trial.

In order to avoid either a too narrow or too sweeping factual investigation, attorneys should determine at the outset of a case (1) what information they *must* have to be successful in the case and (2) what information they would *like* to have because it would increase their chances of litigation success. The client then should be consulted and informed about the estimated cost to do a minimally sufficient factual investigation (items in category 1) as well as the estimated costs to obtain

---

5. McElhaney, "Fault Lines," *A.B.A.J.*, Oct. 2001, at 64, 65.

additional, helpful information (items in category 2). Applying such a cost/benefit analysis to the universe of factual possibilities, attorney and client can agree on the scope of a factual investigation that maximizes the chances for litigation success while minimizing client costs.

Third-parties can be helpful in suggesting some of the information that should be sought in the factual investigation. An expert can be particularly useful in formulating both formal and informal discovery requests. The expert may need specific information upon which to base an opinion, and this information should be sought during pretrial investigation. Sympathetic non-managerial employees of a corporation or other organization may be helpful in suggesting relevant records that might be requested from the institution. A focus group of "typical jurors" might be constituted to talk with counsel about facts that would make her client's case most sympathetic; such facts then can be sought in formal or informal pretrial discovery.[6]

Third-parties can help conserve valuable attorney time during the investigation. A secretary, law clerk, or paralegal may be able to search records as efficiently as an attorney, but at significantly less cost. For more difficult situations, an investigator may prove useful. These third-persons later can testify at trial, while trial counsel usually cannot.[7]

No matter how carefully an attorney has determined what facts she will seek in her pretrial investigation, she must be prepared to adjust her plan as the investigation develops. Adjustments may be necessary if information that originally was desired no longer appears to be relevant or if information that the attorney did not at first seek later seems worth obtaining.

2. From What Source Should the Information Be Sought?

Once the attorney determines that certain factual material should be obtained, she must decide the source from which that information should be sought. This decision is necessary because many times the same information can be obtained from more than one source.

In a personal injury action, plaintiff's counsel presumably will need to obtain information concerning the physical condition of the plaintiff. The possible sources of this information might include (1) the plaintiff himself; (2) doctors who treated the plaintiff after his injury; (3) doctors who now may be employed to examine the plaintiff and reach a conclusion concerning his physical condition; and (4) other persons, such as a spouse, coworker, or friend, with direct knowledge of plaintiff's condition. Because of the many possible individuals with relevant information, a decision must be made as to which possible sources of information should be pursued.

---

6. McElhaney, "Don't Be a Discovery Walrus," *A.B.A.J.*, Dec. 1999, at 70, 71.

7. Model Rules of Prof'l Conduct Rule 3.7(a). *See generally* Milford, "From Streets to Suites: Private Investigators in Civil Cases," *Litigation*, Spring 2004, at 18.

The plaintiff in a personal injury action should be questioned about his physical condition during the initial client interview. Because this condition will be at issue in the lawsuit, a plaintiff's description of his injuries will be one of the major factual bases underlying the suit. An attorney may not have complied with the "reasonable inquiry" requirement of Rule 11 of the Federal Rules of Civil Procedure if she has not thoroughly interviewed her client concerning his physical injuries.

In addition to interviewing one's own client, efforts should be made to verify his statements by talking to others who may have seen the plaintiff's injuries or been told of them by plaintiff. Such additional sources either may corroborate plaintiff ("The cuts and bruises looked awful.") or contradict him ("He was back at work the next day and said that he'd never felt better.").

There may be individuals, such as doctors, who can provide facts about which even the plaintiff is unaware. For instance, while the plaintiff may be able to testify that he had a severe pain in his chest, a doctor who has taken x-rays may be able to testify that plaintiff had seven broken ribs and describe the medical implications of his condition.

Once the possible sources of particular information have been identified, the attorney must choose among those sources. In so doing, she should consider: (1) whether more than one source of information should be consulted; (2) the relative costs of obtaining information from the various sources; and (3) whether there is a tactical advantage or disadvantage in obtaining information from a particular source.

In a personal injury case it might be helpful to consult several witnesses to establish with some certainty the extent of plaintiff's injuries. However, there will be additional costs of obtaining information from some sources (*e.g.,* doctors' bills). Perhaps even more importantly, the more wide-ranging a factual investigation is, the more likely it is that opposing counsel will learn of the investigation (possibly by interviewing the same third-party witnesses). After considering the above factors, the attorney might decide to initially gather information concerning plaintiff's injuries from the plaintiff himself, a few of the many lay witnesses who can confirm the injuries, and the treating physician. A similar analysis must be undertaken, and decision reached, with respect to significant information in other cases as well.

3. To Which Person Should the Request for Information Be Directed?

Once a decision is made to request certain information from a particular source, the method and timing of the request can be addressed. In some situations there may be several persons within an entity from whom the desired information can be requested.

Corporations, governmental bodies, and private associations typically are made up of many people, creating multiple possibilities for obtaining information from those entities. The possibilities with respect to a corporation may include a letter to the corporation itself, formal contacts with individual corporate officers, an email to the corporation's website, and informal contacts with lower-level corporate employees. Indeed, it often will be the lower-level employees who have the direct knowledge that is most needed. When litigating against a corporation, it typically is only senior corporate officials who are covered by the prohibition against communicating with another party without consent of counsel.[8]

Different subdivisions or offices of a corporate or governmental entity also may vary in their sympathy toward certain parties or lawsuits. Those individuals charged with civil rights enforcement within a governmental body may be more ready to release statistics showing enforcement deficiencies than would officials in a central office who will be criticized once such statistics are made public. All organizations are made up of people. When requesting information from organizational entities, always consider which persons within the organization will be most sympathetic to your cause and thus most likely to release the information that you seek.

4. How Should the Information Be Sought?

Once it is determined what information should be sought and from whom it should be requested, there still remains the question as to how the information should be sought. There frequently is more than one manner in which a given set of facts can be obtained.

Informal discovery always should be considered by the party seeking information. Informal discovery usually is much less expensive than formal discovery. It costs much less to interview a witness informally than to take that person's deposition. In addition, informal discovery can be undertaken prior to the filing of a lawsuit, and, although an opposing party may learn of such discovery, there is no requirement that the opposing party be formally notified of the investigative efforts.

Informal discovery can take many forms. One of the most common means of informal investigation is the witness interview, which is discussed in the next subsection of this chapter. Helpful information also can be obtained by reviewing public records and other documents.[9] Records in a state secretary of state's office should disclose the internal structure of companies incorporated or doing business within the state and list corporate officers and directors. Other important information can be obtained from title and land records, court dockets, and police and accident reports. It's also a good practice to check the local media for any mention of the events underlying the dispute in question.

In determining what documents to seek, counsel should visualize the possible conduct of the party in question and think of records that may have been created in the course of that conduct. If an individual made a telephone call, a record of that call may exist. If a person met with

---

8. Model Rules of Prof'l Conduct Rule 4.2 comment.

9. *See generally The Sourcebook to Public Record Information* (P. Weber & M. Sankey eds. 10th ed. 2009).

someone, there may be a notation in an appointment book recording that meeting. Many people do believe everything they read, which makes contemporaneous records very powerful evidentiary and cross-examination tools at trial. In examining and obtaining documents, however, the attorney must consider the possible need for the authentication of the documents at trial by a live witness. A document that is self-authenticating or that can be authenticated by a friendly witness may be more useful than other documents that cannot be so easily authenticated.

There often are relevant records that are not publicly available, but to which an attorney may have access through her client. A client's medical, employment, or police records may be very useful, but can only be obtained with a written release from the client. For this reason, clients should be asked to sign releases at the initial client interview or soon thereafter.

The attorney is not limited to speaking with witnesses and reviewing documents. It's often the case that "a picture is worth a thousand words." There may be no substitute for an attorney actually viewing the scene of a particular occurrence or transaction. This is typically done in cases in which some physical mishap, such as an accident, took place. However, by visiting a business office valuable information may be gained about the people who work there. Not only can a site visit help the attorney's initial understanding of a case, but the knowledge gained from the visit may help the attorney to appreciate the significance of facts that only become known in the later stages of a lawsuit.

If a scene is worth visiting, it may make sense to preserve what was observed by taking photographs. If there is a possibility that photographs may be useful to preserve a scene, someone should accompany the attorney to take the photographs. If this practice is followed, this individual later can authenticate the photographs. If the attorney is the only person who can authenticate the photographs, her testimony might require that she withdraw as counsel.[10] Digital cameras have made photographic preservation of evidence much easier, but the photographic images should be carefully preserved to prevent any later charges that the photographs were electronically altered.

Despite the advantages of informal factual investigations, there may be times when a more formal record of the discovery undertaken is desired. In such cases, formal discovery is preferred. Before undertaking formal discovery, however, the attorney should attempt to determine whether the discovery sought will be favorable to her client. It usually makes sense to interview third-party witnesses before they are deposed. Favorable information should be preserved for trial, while there generally is no reason to similarly create a record concerning information that is unfavorable to your client and unknown to opposing counsel.

In addition to informal and formal case discovery, useful information may be available pursuant to a state or federal freedom of information act.

---

10. Model Rules of Prof'l Conduct Rule 3.7.

The federal Freedom of Information Act[11] provides, with certain exceptions, a right of access to federal agency records. Counterpart acts in many states provide a means of obtaining information from governmental bodies outside the confines of a civil action.[12] However, it may take some time to receive a governmental response pursuant to these statutes, so that information requested may not be received as quickly as it is needed. A tremendous amount of information is now available on the Internet, however, and the ability to access such information instantaneously (and, often, anonymously) makes the Internet a fertile tool in any legal investigation.[13]

There are often several ways to obtain the same basic information. Available alternatives should be considered to ensure that the information sought is obtained in the most efficient, least costly, and most useful manner.

5. When Should the Information Be Sought?

Once it is decided that particular information will be sought from a particular person in a particular manner, the attorney still must decide when to seek the information. Both strategic and practical considerations govern exactly when pretrial factual investigation should be undertaken.

As a general rule, the earlier an attorney learns of relevant information the better. This is the case with respect to both favorable and unfavorable information. If an attorney is not aware of favorable information, she may not litigate the claim as aggressively as is warranted or may accept a lesser settlement than she otherwise might obtain. It also is best to learn of unfavorable information in the early stages of a case, because this will give the attorney the most time to either meet the information or attempt to negotiate a favorable settlement.

Over time memories fade, documents become lost, and physical settings change. It may be important to view the scene of an accident before the snow melts, skid marks or oil stains disappear, a new handrail is constructed, or the lighting is improved.

If counsel can be the first to talk to third-party witnesses, she may gain their support before they are interviewed by opposing counsel. Witnesses may be more ready to talk about a matter before it has led to

---

11. 5 U.S.C. § 552 (2006). *See* General Services Administration, *Your Rights to Federal Records* (2004), http://www.pueblo.gsa.gov/cic—text/fed—prog/foia/foia.pdf.

12. *Access to Government in the Computer Age: An Examination of State Public Records Laws* (M. Chumbler ed. 2007).

13. *See* C. Levitt & M. Rosch, *The Lawyer's Guide to Fact Finding on the Internet* (3d ed. 2006). Government agencies are putting increasing amounts of information on the Internet, thus expediting the time and effort otherwise required to obtain these public documents. *See generally United States Government Internet Manual 2008* (P. Garvin ed. 2008); P. Hernon et al., *U.S. Government on the Web: Getting the Information You Need* (3d ed. 2003). Pursuant to the electronic public access service PACER (http://pacer.gov), individuals can register to obtain electronic access to documents in federal appellate, district and bankruptcy court cases rather than having to review such records at the federal courthouses where these documents have been filed.

the filing of litigation. It therefore is generally best to begin a factual investigation as soon as possible.

Certain evidence, such as public records or physical evidence controlled by a client, can be examined without alerting the opposing party to the possibility of legal action. Other information, however, cannot be obtained without running the risk that opposing counsel will learn that the information is being sought. If a third-party is interviewed prior to filing an action, the potential defendant may be alerted that a lawsuit is in the works. If a party prefers that the opposing party not learn of such plans, this type of investigation should be deferred as long as possible.

There often is a logical sequence to investigations. It usually makes more sense to talk to one's client about a matter before interviewing third-parties. Attorneys also should be sensitive to sources of information to which they will have access only one time. If an attorney knows that a witness is likely to speak to her only once, it may make sense to pursue other related investigation first so that the witness interview will be as thorough as possible.

Finally, there may be quite practical reasons that dictate the timing of certain investigative work. It may be cheaper and more efficient to interview out-of-town witnesses who are in a particular city on the same trip. However, there also may be witnesses who can see an attorney only at certain times, and whose schedules will have to be accommodated in the attorney's investigative plans.

The timing of pretrial investigation should not be taken for granted. An investigative plan should be developed in which the attorney has considered investigative timing, as well as the information that will be sought, the sources of that information, and the manner of obtaining the information.

Exercises Concerning the Structure and Implementation of Factual Investigations

1. It is February 28, 1972, you are an attorney employed by the Pittston Company, and the dam on the Middle Fork in the Buffalo Creek Valley has just collapsed. You have been assigned the task of investigating exactly what happened and the results of the dam failure. Presume for the purposes of your investigation that lawsuits will be filed on behalf of those individuals who died and were injured in the flood.

Your assignment is to write a memorandum to Pittston's general counsel concerning the investigation that you plan to pursue. Your memorandum should address the structure of the investigation you have planned, the specific information you will seek, the sources from which the information will be sought, the investigative methods you will employ, what Pittston employees or other individuals you will use in the investigation, when certain information will be sought, and in what sequence you will seek different types of information.

2.   You have been contacted by the mother of a twenty-one year old man who was recently arrested for driving under the influence of alcohol, reckless driving, and assaulting an officer. The man was arrested late at night and was found dead in his jail cell the next morning, hanging from the ceiling of the cell. Write a memorandum to the file setting forth the factual investigation that you would pursue in this case. The memorandum should list the specific information that you will seek, the sources of this information, the investigative methods you will employ, when the information will be sought, and the sequence in which the information will be obtained.

B.   WITNESS INTERVIEWS

Perhaps the most frequently used means of obtaining information prior to the filing of a suit is interviewing third-parties who have relevant information. Third-party witness interviews are not only frequently used, but they are very important in pretrial case investigation. Both the ways in which third-party witness interviews differ from client interviews and the means by which such interviews should be recorded are discussed in this section.

1.   Differences Between Client and Witness Interviews

The prior chapter of this book is largely devoted to client interviewing. While the client interview may be the most important interview that an attorney conducts, in most cases many more third-party than client interviews will be conducted. Many of the techniques and skills necessary for a successful client interview apply to witness interviews. However, witness and client interviews differ in several important respects.

First of all, because a witness is not the attorney's client, he probably will have less incentive to speak with the attorney than does her client. Motivating a witness to talk therefore often will be necessary in order to obtain information from non-client witnesses. This can be as difficult as prying information out of a school child at the end of the day, when the child's consistent answer to the question "What did you do in school today?" is "Nuthin."

There are several techniques that can be used to attempt to motivate third-party witnesses to cooperate. If properly approached by an attorney, many individuals will be more than happy to contribute information that is relevant to a legal dispute. Indeed, witnesses who are not antagonistic to a client may be motivated by being told that only they can help the client by providing the unique information that they possess. Efforts to personalize the client may make a witness more likely to cooperate: "Mr. Smith, my name is Perry Mason and I'm a lawyer representing Jimmy White. Jimmy is the little boy who was struck by a delivery truck last week outside your house. He's in the hospital and needs your help. I wonder if you'd be willing to take a few minutes to talk to me about what you saw last week?"

Even when dealing with friendly third-party witnesses, it is best to approach them at a time and place when they will feel free to talk. It's usually best to call friendly witnesses to schedule an appointment at their convenience, rather than merely showing up unexpectedly at the witness's work place ("Mr. Jones, there's an attorney here to see you … "). Unsympathetic witnesses, though, may be most effectively approached without advance notice of the attorney's arrival.

While an interview appointment may be made over the telephone, witnesses often will provide more information if interviewed in person. By meeting personally with the witness, the attorney has the option of asking him to sign a witness statement right on the spot. Personal interviews also permit the attorney to evaluate how the witness will present himself at a deposition or at trial.

The setting of the interview always should be considered. Witnesses may be more relaxed if interviewed at home and thus may provide more helpful information than if questioned elsewhere. On the other hand, the attorney may pick up valuable information by seeing the witness in his or her work setting. Whether the interview is conducted at the witness's home or workplace, efforts should be made to ensure that the attorney can speak with the witness without interruption and without the presence of others.

Not all witnesses will be sympathetic to your client, and appeals to help your client may be unavailing with unsympathetic witnesses.[14] However, an appeal to civic duty and the need for all persons to present all relevant information may motivate some unsympathetic third-persons to cooperate. Other witnesses may be motivated by asking them to put themselves in the shoes of your client and provide the same cooperation that they would expect others to give in that situation.

Those witnesses who are not so high-minded may need to be subtly informed that there are ways by which you can compel their testimony. These witnesses can be told that everyone's time will be saved if they speak with you voluntarily:

> Mrs. Jones, I represent Jim Smith in connection with the accident that he had at work last month. Because I haven't heard back from you in response to my phone calls, I thought that I'd stop by to see you. I only need to talk with you for about half an hour. I thought that this would be simpler than having the court issue a subpoena requiring you to come downtown and give formal deposition testimony. If you'll talk with me now, you may not need to be involved any further in this dispute.

If the witness still refuses to cooperate, the attorney might inform her that all she's after is the truth. Later trial cross-examination then can

---

14. Attorneys should be wary of witnesses who are so sympathetic to their client that they bend the facts in that client's favor. These witnesses should be informed that you need "the truth, the whole truth, and nothing but the truth" and that anything less may harm your client.

stress that the witness refused to be interviewed despite the assurance that the attorney merely wanted to learn the truth.

A witness may be more inclined to talk if other persons have talked with the attorney about that witness's participation in the dispute in question. This is the approach sometimes used by newspaper reporters: "Mrs. Jones, I've met with Fred Hawkins about what happened back on December 7th, and he talked with me about what you did on that day. The reason I'd like to talk with you now is to give you a chance to give your own statement about what happened."

This suggests that it may be important to question witnesses in a certain order, speaking first with the witness whom you believe is most likely to provide you with useful information. While the information obtained from the initial witnesses can be used in an attempt to obtain information from later witnesses, counsel may not want to reveal to some witnesses that they have talked to others. The attorney-client privilege doesn't protect conversations between an attorney and third-party witnesses, and the attorney should presume that anything she says to these witnesses might be passed on to opposing counsel.[15]

Not only may third-party witnesses have less incentive to talk with an attorney than do that attorney's clients, but there may be only one chance to speak with third-parties. Thus decisions whether to ask witnesses to sign statements often must be made on the spot and without the opportunity to reflect on the precise language in the witness statement.

Counsel also may not have the full amount of time for a single interview that she had expected; as the attorney sits in the reception room waiting to see the witness, she may realize that her hour interview now will be no more than fifteen minutes. This makes it extremely important to plan witness interviews carefully. The attorney should know exactly what information she needs from a witness and not approach him until other preliminary factual investigation has been completed.[16]

Finally, client and third-party witness interviews differ because the attorney-client privilege extends only to an attorney's clients. Any conversations between an attorney and a non-client witness are fair game for discovery by opposing counsel. In fact, valuable information sometimes can be obtained about opposing counsel's strategy by questioning witnesses who are not represented by an attorney about their conversations with opposing counsel. Third-party witnesses also may give to counsel copies of their witness statements or other documents originally given to, or obtained from, opposing counsel. Witnesses should be asked for such

---

15. However, there may be situations in which the attorney will want opposing counsel to be aware of the scope of her investigation. In a case that is likely to settle, settlement leverage may be increased if opposing counsel knows that an attorney has conducted a thorough investigation and has located favorable third-party witnesses.

16. This is not to say that the attorney should not attempt to contact third-party witnesses as the case progresses. One of the first things that should be done in any case is to create a list of witness addresses and contact information so that the attorney can locate witnesses. Witnesses should be asked where and when they can be contacted and if there is someone else (perhaps a relative) who will know their location if the attorney cannot reach them.

documents, as well as any other documents that corroborate or otherwise relate to their statements.

Despite the differences between client and witness interviews, these types of interviews are more alike than they are different. Active listening techniques, open-ended questions, and catch-all phrases ("Is there anything else you can remember?") can be effective in any interview. Well-planned interviews conducted in a professional manner should yield valuable information from clients and third-parties alike.

Exercise Concerning the Critique of a Witness Interview

After reviewing the material in the previous chapter concerning interviewing techniques, consider the following interview conducted by investigators for the Subcommittee on Labor of the Committee on Labor and Public Welfare of the United States Senate. This interview is one of many conducted with Buffalo Creek residents in connection with the hearings concerning the Buffalo Creek disaster before the Senate Subcommittee on Labor on May 30 and 31, 1972.[17]

MEMORANDUM TO FILES

BUFFALO MINE DISASTER

DATE: MARCH 28, 1972

My name is MICHAEL PAUL GRIMMETT, I live at Kistler. I was in the Logan County jail when the flood was going on, and we got several reports there, about the dam and everything. We got reports that it was breaking, we got a report that there was someone there with a bulldozer trying to cut an edge in the dam to let some of the water to drain off. I guess after that we didn't hear too much except that it had broke. There was a lot of confusion down there, I guess there was everywhere.

ROY WADE: NOW LETS GO BACK TO THE BEGINNING: ABOUT WHAT TIME DID YOU GET TO THE SHERIFF'S OFFICE THAT MORNING?

MICHAEL GRIMMETT: About 1:00 a.m. We got the report and . . . .

WADE: AS I UNDERSTAND IT, YOUR CAR WAS STRANDED THERE AT THE GAS STATION.

GRIMMETT: Yes.

WADE: WHERE?

GRIMMETT: Black Bottom.

WADE: THEN YOU WENT TO THE SHERIFF'S OFFICE TO GET HELP TO GET IT OUT, IS THAT CORRECT. THAT WAS AT 1:00 a.m. IN THE MORNING?

---

17. *Buffalo Creek (W.Va.) Disaster, 1972: Hearings before the Subcomm. on Labor of the Senate Comm. on Labor and Public Welfare*, 92d Cong., 2d Sess. 1251–54 (1972) (Appendix A) (interview with Michael Paul Grimmett).

GRIMMETT: Yes.

WADE: THEN DID YOU GO BACK TO THE CAR?

GRIMMETT: No, the water had already gotten it.

WADE: SO YOU STAYED UP AT THE SHERIFFS OFFICE FROM 1:00 a.m. ON, ALL THE WAY THROUGH, YOU WERE THERE. NOW, WHAT WAS LARRY SPRIGGS DOING ALL THIS TIME?

GRIMMETT: Well, he was busy answering phones, taking complaints, this and that. We got one report that someone [was] floating down Mud Fork on the top of a truck. The National Guard was there. He was busy all the time.

WADE: [WERE] YOU THERE WHEN MR. SPRIGGS CALLED YOUR FATHER TO GET PERMISSION TO CALL UP THE NATIONAL GUARD?

GRIMMETT: Yes.

WADE: YOU WERE ALSO THERE WHEN SOMEONE CALLED ON THE PHONE AND TOLD HIM THE DAM WAS BREAKING, AND HE HAD YOUR FATHER CALL HIM BACK? DO YOU KNOW WHO THAT WAS?

GRIMMETT: To the best of my knowledge, I think it was Jack Kent from Lorado.

WADE: NO, I MEAN, THE FIRST CALL, WHEN SOMEONE CALLED HIM AND SAID THAT THE DAM WAS GOING TO BREAK WHICH MADE THEM WARN THE PEOPLE.

GRIMMETT: We started getting the deputies out there about, I think, 5:00 a.m.

WADE: NOW, YOU MENTIONED JACK KENT'S NAME, NOW JUST WHAT HAPPENED THERE—DID YOU TAKE THE PHONE CALL FROM HIM?

GRIMMETT: No, I didn't.

WADE: YOU DIDN'T, WHO TOOK THE PHONE CALL?

GRIMMETT: Larry Spriggs.

WADE: LARRY TOOK THE PHONE CALL HIMSELF? WHAT WAS YOUR INTERPRETATION OF WHAT HE WAS SUPPOSED TO HAVE SAID?

GRIMMETT: Well, that the dam, they had been working on the dam, and it had broke, and then just then he took for granted what was happening.

WADE: YOU MEAN, THAT WAS AFTER THE DAM HAD BROKE?

GRIMMETT: Well now, he had called once before, I think, and warned us, but ... then someone called back, I believe it was him again, that it had broke.

WADE: WHEN THEY WARNED YOU, YOU SAY THEY HAD CALLED BEFORE AND WARNED YOU? DO YOU RECALL WHAT THEY HAD SAID?

GRIMMETT: Well, they said that, from my interpretation, that the dam was full, and it was in bad shape, so to watch, be careful and try to get everything ready for it if it does break.

WADE: DO YOU RECALL ANYTHING THAT HAD BEEN SAID ABOUT WHAT TYPE OF WORK THEY WERE DOING OR WERE GOING TO DO?

GRIMMETT: Well, about all I know they took a bulldozer down there, now I'm not for sure of what I'm saying, but they took a bulldozer down there, and tried to let some of the water drain off, cut it, and we looked at each other and we figured if they do that, it's out for sure and then the next thing we knew, I guess, it had broke.

WADE: IN OTHER WORDS, WHAT YOU ARE SAYING—IN THE PHONE CALL, DID THEY SAY THEY WERE DOING THIS OR THEY WERE GOING TO DO IT. THAT'S WHAT I WAS TRYING TO GET DOWN TOO, OR DO YOU REALLY REMEMBER?

GRIMMETT: Well, the best I think, is they had the bulldozer on the way down there to it.

WADE: DO YOU KNOW WHAT TIME THAT WAS?

GRIMMETT: I would say about 6:30 a.m. or something like that.

WADE: YOU DIDN'T ACTUALLY TAKE THE PHONE CALL YOURSELF?

GRIMMETT: No.

WADE: I UNDERSTAND THAT YOU WERE PRETTY BUSY DOWN THERE THAT MORNING? ANYWAY, PEOPLE SAID YOU DID A REAL GOOD JOB DOWN THERE? VERY COMPLEMENTARY.

GRIMMETT: A lot of phones calls there.

WADE: HOW ABOUT THE CB RADIOS?

GRIMMETT: We run those too.

WADE: WAS THERE ANYONE SET UP TO HANDLE A CENTRAL CONTROL POINT FOR THE CB NETWORK OR WAS EVERYBODY CALLING IN WHO HAD ONE?

GRIMMETT: Everybody called in.

WADE: BUT THERE WAS NO ORGANIZATION SET UP RIGHT THERE, EMERGENCY RADIO OR SOMETHING LIKE THAT?

GRIMMETT: No real big thing or nothing like that.

WADE: WHO WAS IN CHARGE OF THAT?

GRIMMETT: Dennie Napier, Accoville.

WADE: DOES HE STILL LIVE THERE OR DID HE GET WASHED OUT?

GRIMMETT: No, he still lives there.

WADE: OK, [DO] YOU HAVE ANYTHING ELSE THAT YOU WOULD LIKE TO SAY FOR US?

GRIMMETT: Well, no.

WADE: ANYTHING THAT YOU THINK THE SENATORS OUGHT TO KNOW ABOUT THIS?

GRIMMETT: Well, I guess the most important thing was this bulldozer.

MCDONNELL: LIKE WHICH PHONE CALL OR WHO WAS THE PHONE CALL FROM THAT MENTIONED ANYTHING ABOUT A BULLDOZER?

GRIMMETT: They called us there, and it was somebody who had something to do with the Coal Company. I think it was Jack Kent, I'm not positive.

WADE: NOW WHEN YOU SAY YOU THINK IT WAS JACK KENT, WHAT MAKES YOU THINK SO?

GRIMMETT: Oh, it was a series of calls and all the information, we were pretty well kept up on it. It had to be somebody from up there and he was calling.

WADE: HE WAS CALLING? HE CALLED EARLIER BEFORE AND YOU REMEMBER THAT THERE WERE CALLS FROM JACK KENT. PUTTING TWO AND TWO TOGETHER YOU ARE ASSUMING IT WAS HIM.

ROY M. WADE
DONALD MACDONNELL

———

Write a short critique of this witness interview. In your critique address not only the interview technique generally, but also the following specific questions.

1. Based upon the types of questions asked by the Senate investigators, do you think that they had talked with Mr. Grimmett before this interview was transcribed? Why or why not?

2. Presuming that the investigators had never spoken with Mr. Grimmett before, are there any problems with the substance of the questions asked by the investigators? Are there problems with the form of the questions?

3. Does it appear that these investigators were obtaining the maximum information from Mr. Grimmett? In this respect, consider the length of many of Mr. Grimmett's responses. What could the investigators have

done differently to encourage Mr. Grimmett to provide them with more information?

4.   In the event that this had been one of the first interviews conducted by the investigators, was there additional information that should have been elicited from Mr. Grimmett?

5.   Of what apparent significance is the information actually obtained from Mr. Grimmett?

2.   Recording the Witness Interview

One of the important questions that must be answered in connection with any witness interview is in what, if any, manner the interview should be recorded. There are several possible choices, none of which will be appropriate for all interview situations.

There may be situations in which it is not immediately apparent that a witness interview needs to be recorded at all. If the witness has nothing to contribute concerning a case, there may be little reason to memorialize this fact. However, the very fact that the witness has no relevant information may be significant in and of itself, especially if the witness later appears at trial with a greatly improved memory. In effect, the witness's lack of knowledge concerning the case may be a fact that is favorable to your client.[18]

There may be other situations in which the witness has information, but it is unfavorable to your client. In these situations, it may make little sense to preserve the unfavorable witness testimony, particularly if there is some question as to whether opposing counsel is aware of the information. Only once you know what a witness will say can you definitely determine whether to preserve that witness's testimony.

Figure 3–3 illustrates one way in which attorneys can determine whether, and in what manner, witness testimony should be preserved or presented to the court. Note that the attorney does not proceed to the next higher level of investigative formality unless there is good reason to believe that the facts in question will be favorable to her client. Thus if the witness provides only unfavorable information in the initial witness interview, there may be no reason to take a witness statement. Similarly, there may be no reason to depose a witness whom the other side is unlikely to call at trial if that witness has provided only unfavorable testimony in his witness statement. The same general principle applies to expert witnesses, who may be asked to consult orally with counsel before creating written documents that are unfavorable to the client on whose behalf they have been retained.

---

18.   Consider the words of one of the premier investigators of all times, Sherlock Holmes:

"Is there any other point to which you [Holmes] would wish to draw my attention?"

"To the curious incident of the dog in the night-time."

"The dog did nothing in the night-time."

"That was the curious incident," remarked Sherlock Holmes.

A. Doyle, "The Adventure of Silver Blaze" (1892).

FIGURE 3-3
FORMALIZATION OF FAVORABLE FACTS

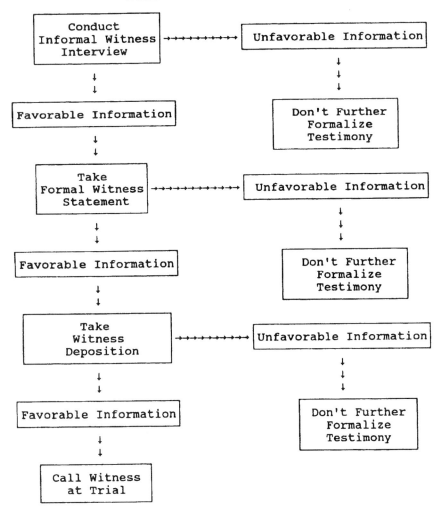

Figure 3–3 presumes that there is some question as to whether opposing counsel is aware of the witness from whom information is sought. If an attorney is certain that her opposing counsel knows about an important witness, it usually will be wise to formalize even the unfavorable testimony of that witness. To take an extreme example, defense counsel must presume that the plaintiff and his trial witnesses will offer evidence that is, on balance, unfavorable to the defendant. Nevertheless, defense counsel should seriously consider deposing these individuals to nail them down to specific stories and to preserve facts suggesting possible bias or error in their testimony.

Most witness interviews should be memorialized in some fashion. It is a good practice to at least summarize all witness interviews in the attorney's own file. Even witnesses with unfavorable information usually should be pinned down to a specific statement if it is likely that their testimony will be offered by opposing counsel.

There should be someone, such as a law clerk, paralegal, or secretary, present other than the attorney when witnesses are interviewed. By bringing another person to witness interviews, the possibility of future attorney testimony can be avoided.[19] By having the attorney directly involved in the interview, however, the attorney work-product protection should be assured and the attorney herself can follow-up on witness testimony and evaluate individuals as potential trial witnesses.

Even before memorializing her own witness interview, the attorney should ask the witness if he has given a statement to any other person. It usually is helpful to review any prior statements before a new witness statement is drafted. The present statement then can be used to address or clarify aspects of the prior statement.

While the attorney's own memorandum may be useful for some purposes, it cannot effectively be used to impeach a witness unless it is somehow adopted by the witness. Therefore, it usually makes sense to obtain a witness statement in a form that the witness cannot later disown. The major alternatives are statements prepared or signed by the witness or recorded or videotaped witness statements.

A recording (either audio or video) of the witness can be very effective in later settlement negotiations or at trial. However, these recordings may not be ideal for later impeachment. Not only may portions of a recording be unintelligible, but it often is awkward to find and use a specific portion of a recording. Additionally, witnesses may be hesitant to permit themselves to be recorded. If this hesitancy on the part of a witness can be overcome, however, a recording may provide a basis for a written witness statement that the witness can sign or otherwise adopt.

The written witness statement is the second major alternative for preserving the witness's testimony in a fashion that he cannot credibly disavow. Written witness statements can be prepared in several different ways.

The witness can be asked to write his own narrative of the events in question. While such a statement in the witness's own hand should have the greatest impact on the trier of fact, there are potential problems with these statements. Most significantly, because the witness writes the statement himself, the attorney has no control over what is written. The statement may not be written in as persuasive and effective a manner as if the attorney had drafted it in the first instance. Furthermore, the witness may not clearly understand what facts are relevant to a case, and the witness's own narrative may include extraneous matter (as well as omit other, relevant material).

It therefore is usually preferable for the attorney to interview the witness and then draft a statement summarizing the relevant facts. This

---

19. *See* Model Rules of Prof'l Conduct Rule 3.7.

statement can be typed or written out on the spot, or, if the attorney is confident that the witness will sign the statement, returned to the witness for signature at a later time. Some attorneys send a letter to witnesses after they have been interviewed, asking them to sign a copy of the letter if it accurately reflects the facts at issue. However, because witnesses sometimes change their minds about signing statements (especially if they have been in contact with opposing counsel), the safest course is to have the statement signed at the same time that the initial witness interview is conducted.

The witness statement, at a minimum, should include (1) the identity of the witness, (2) the witness's narrative set forth in a clear fashion, and (3) some indication that the witness understands what he or she is signing. To the extent possible, the narrative should include facts, as opposed to conclusions or opinions. Rather than have the witness state that a person "was driving recklessly," the statement should be that the person "was weaving from one side of the road to the other and struck Mr. Brown's mailbox." The witness also can be asked to draw a map or diagram and attach it to his statement.

Asking a witness for specifics about an event is one way of testing the witness's narrative. If the witness states that he sees someone "all the time," ask him when the last time was that he saw that person. It usually is a bad idea to include specific details on minor points in the written narrative, however. If the witness is incorrect on these minor details, the credibility of the entire statement may be undermined.

To increase the authority of the witness statement, it can be notarized or signed under the penalty of perjury pursuant to 28 U.S.C. § 1746. The pages of the statement should be consecutively numbered, and some attorneys ask witnesses to initial each page so there can be no later contention that intermediate pages were switched after the statement had been signed. Another technique to accomplish the same purpose is to be sure that sentences don't end on the bottom of any page, but instead run over onto the next page.

A final sentence should be included in the witness statement indicating that the witness has read and understands his statement. Such a statement might provide: "I have carefully read this statement of five pages, I understand it, and I have had a chance to make any necessary corrections. The statement is true and accurate as signed by me."

Some attorneys deliberately make minor errors in witness statements, such as misspelling the witness's name or incorrectly listing his street address. In reading such a statement, these errors are caught by the witness, corrected, and initialed. The fact that the witness corrected these errors can be used later by the attorney to establish that the statement was read, carefully, by the witness before signing.

Once the statement has been signed, the attorney should give a copy of it to the witness. The witness has a right to a copy of his statement pursuant to Rule 26(b)(3)(C) of the Federal Rules of Civil Procedure.

Providing the witness with a copy of the statement also may increase his confidence in the attorney. Were the attorney to refuse to provide the witness with a copy of the statement that he has just signed, serious questions might be raised in the witness's mind as to the integrity of the attorney.

Finally, it's generally a good practice to leave your card, or at least your telephone number or other contact information, with the witnesses whom you interview. Witnesses then can be asked to contact you if they remember anything else or if they are contacted by other counsel. Efforts should be made to maintain contact with witnesses during the pretrial period, so that they continue to identify with you and your client.

Exercises Concerning Witness Interviews

1.   You are an associate in a medium-sized law firm in New York City that represents the Pittston Company's insurance carrier. You have been asked to investigate the circumstances surrounding the dam collapse on the Middle Fork of the Buffalo Creek. In the course of your investigation, you have learned that the former Buffalo Mining employee who supervised the initial construction of the dam is now living in Harrisburg, Pennsylvania. You believe that other counsel have not yet talked with this individual, Charles Keller, who is retired and draws a small pension from the Buffalo Mining Company.

Plan the manner in which you will attempt to interview Mr. Keller. Also consider the following questions concerning the ethical limitations on witness interviews.

a.   What will you tell Mr. Keller as to why you are interested in talking with him? What will you tell him as to whom you represent?

b.   Is it appropriate to affirmatively misrepresent who you are or why you want Keller's testimony? What if you say nothing as to who you are, but dress in a United Mine Workers' jacket? Can you hire a miner or an old friend of Mr. Keller's to obtain a statement from him? Can you secretly record your conversation with Mr. Keller?

c.   Is there an affirmative duty to tell Keller that you are an attorney and that you are interested in information concerning the collapse of the dam?

d.   Can you tell Mr. Keller that you do not represent the Pittston Company or the Buffalo Mining Company? Can you tell him only this? Can you tell him that you represent the insurance company that is trying to get money to those injured in the flood?

e.   Is it significant for the purposes of your interview that a legal action has not yet been filed? Is it significant that your client, the insurance carrier, may not be named as a party in any potential litigation?

f. Can you suggest to Mr. Keller that he should not talk to other attorneys about the dam? Can you inform him that he is under no legal obligation to do so? Can you tell him that you'd like to be present if he does decide to talk to counsel for those injured in the flood?

g. Can you inform Mr. Keller of the many practical burdens (such as travel to West Virginia and the need to give deposition and trial testimony) that might be placed upon him if he becomes involved in the Buffalo Creek litigation? Can you offer to hire him as an expert consultant concerning dam construction and safety?

h. What if Mr. Keller has a son who was injured in the flood? What if Keller, himself, has a potential claim against Pittston for damage to property in Logan County, West Virginia? What if Keller has retained an attorney to pursue a claim against Pittston and the Buffalo Mining Company concerning a dispute about his pension? What are your duties if Keller tells you that he has an appointment next week to talk to an attorney about a possible claim against Pittston stemming from the dam collapse?

i. If Mr. Keller has a Facebook account, can you or a third party working on your behalf "friend" Mr. Keller in order to obtain information on his site?

j. If the above investigation tactics are ethically permissible, are there other reasons why an attorney might decide not to employ them?

k. What if you represent the plaintiffs, rather than Pittston's insurance carrier, in the Buffalo Creek disaster litigation? Are you free to interview Mr. Keller?

2. You represent a thirteen-year-old boy who was struck by a hit-and-run driver. Conduct a telephone interview with the following witnesses to the accident, each of whom you believe can give testimony favorable to your client.

a. Sarah Garrety is twenty years old and is about to return to college in a distant state. While she is sympathetic to your client, she does not want to have to return home to provide testimony in any legal action.

b. Michael Johnson is a busy business executive who is sure that you can find better witnesses than him to testify in the case.

c. Charles Clark is a thirty-two year old delivery man who had a good view of the accident. However, he is reluctant to provide testimony because he witnessed the accident while outside of his delivery zone, on an extended lunch hour, with an unauthorized rider in the truck.

3. You represent an automobile manufacturer that has been sued as the result of a car accident. Your preliminary investigation suggests that

the car's brakes may have failed because of some work that was done on them at a small, independent service station. Plan and conduct the interview that you have decided to hold with the mechanic who worked on the car's brakes shortly before the accident.

C. THE SIGNIFICANCE OF A THOROUGH FACTUAL INVESTIGATION

In *Gideon v. Wainwright*[20] the United States Supreme Court held that indigent criminal defendants are entitled to appointed counsel in state felony prosecutions. Although the Supreme Court overturned Clarence Earl Gideon's criminal conviction because he had not been appointed counsel, Florida was permitted to retry Gideon after the appointment of counsel. The following selection is the Epilogue to *Gideon's Trumpet,* in which Anthony Lewis describes the retrial of Mr. Gideon in Panama City, Florida.

In reading this selection consider (1) the factual investigation conducted by Gideon's appointed lawyer; (2) the way in which Gideon's lawyer built upon that pretrial investigation at trial; and (3) whether the appointment of counsel made any difference in the outcome of the second trial.

A. LEWIS, GIDEON'S TRUMPET
223–238 (1964).

Resolution of the great constitutional question in *Gideon v. Wainwright* did not decide the fate of Clarence Earl Gideon. He was now entitled to a new trial, with a lawyer. Was he guilty of breaking into the Bay Harbor Poolroom? The verdict would not set any legal precedents, but there is significance in the human beings who make constitutional-law cases as well as in the law. And in this case there was the interesting question whether the legal assistance for which Gideon had fought so hard would make any difference to him.

Soon after the decision Abe Fortas wrote Gideon suggesting that in the future a local Florida lawyer should represent him. Fortas said he had written to a Florida Civil Liberties Union attorney about the case. This lawyer was Tobias Simon of Miami, who had signed the *amicus* brief presented to the Supreme Court by the American Civil Liberties Union. Gideon, who before the decision had expressed the hope that the A.C.L.U. would give him a lawyer, wrote Simon on April 9, 1963.

"I humbly am asking you for any help that you can give me in the present situation," Gideon said. "Because no one knows any better than me of what I am up against. I have no reason to believe now that I would receive a fair trial in the same court than I did before even with a court

---

20. 372 U.S. 335 (1963).

appointed attorney. I have my plea already to make but it probably will be denied me."

Simon replied on April 15th that someone from the Civil Liberties Union would represent him at his new trial. Gideon acknowledged that letter with thanks on April 29th, adding that he wondered how long the Supreme Court of Florida could take to act on his case now "without becoming contemptible of the United States Supreme Court."

A few days later Simon went to Raiford and interviewed Gideon for an hour and a half. He found Gideon to be "an irascible but spunky white male." Gideon spoke even more forcefully than in his letters. He was under the illusion that a new trial would constitute double jeopardy and that the Florida Supreme Court should already have released him outright. (A new trial won by a prisoner as a result of his own appeal is not double jeopardy under American law.) He said he could never get a fair trial in Panama City, and when Simon tried to reassure him Gideon "became exceedingly bitter and refused to discuss his case any further." But he "did agree that we would be able to represent him in the forthcoming new trial," Simon reported to the A.C.L.U.

The Florida Supreme Court had received the official notice of the United States Supreme Court decision—the mandate—in April; and on May 15th it issued an order entitling Gideon to a new trial. The circuit court of Bay County set July 5th as the trial date.

On July 4th Simon went to Panama City with Irwin J. Block, an experienced criminal lawyer, until recently the chief assistant prosecutor in Miami, who had agreed to help him. They interviewed some witnesses and former neighbors of Gideon who seemed to have "admiration for a man who fought so hard against odds so great." Then they went to see Gideon, who had been brought from Raiford to the local jail. Mr. Simon described the meeting.

"Gideon refused to be represented by either of us; he refused to be tried; he stated that the court had no power to try him, and that his trial in Panama City would only mean his return to the penitentiary. All efforts to calm him and to have him place some trust in us failed."

The next morning, the time set for trial, Simon and Block met with the prosecutors in the chambers of Robert L. McCrary, Jr., the judge who had presided over Gideon's first trial and was to handle the second. Gideon was also present. Judge McCrary began by noting that Simon had signed some papers and was appearing as defense counsel.

"I didn't authorize Mr. Simon to sign anything for me," Gideon said. "I'll do my own signing. I do not want him to represent me."

Judge McCrary asked warily, "Do you want another lawyer to represent you?"

"No," said Gideon. After a pause he added: "And I'm not ready for trial."

There must have been a touch of bewilderment in the judge's next question. "What do you want, then?"

"I want to file for an order to move my case from this court," Gideon replied. "I can't get a fair trial in this court; it's the same court, the same judge, everything, and everybody connected with the court is the same as it was before and I can't get a fair trial here. . . . You're not even going to let me plead my case."

At this point Simon explained his position in the case, reading to the judge, among other documents, Gideon's letter "humbly asking" for help. But Simon said that of course he and Block did not want to represent Gideon if he did not want them.

Gideon repeated his wish: "I want to plead my own case. I want to make my own plea. I do not want them to make any plea for me."

"You don't want Mr. Simon and Mr. Block to represent you?" Judge McCrary asked, making absolutely certain that all this was really happening.

"No," said Gideon, "I don't want them to represent me. I DO NOT WANT THEM." (The court reporter used capitals.)

The judge excused Simon and Block, but he also made clear that under no circumstances did he want Gideon to try his own case again. After ascertaining that Gideon had no money to hire a lawyer of his own choice, Judge McCrary asked whether there was a local lawyer whom Gideon would like to represent him. There was: W. Fred Turner.

"For the record," Judge McCrary said quickly, "I am going to appoint Mr. Fred Turner to represent this defendant, Clarence Earl Gideon."

A member of the prosecuting staff suggested that the public defender just appointed for that judicial circuit under the new Florida public-defender law assist Fred Turner.

"I don't want him in it," Gideon said, evidently preferring a private attorney with no touch of welfare.

The judge said, "We will just let Mr. Turner handle this case." Then he advised Gideon to get in touch with his new lawyer to file any motions he desired.

"I want to file my own motions," Gideon said. "If this is to be a matter of just sending me back to the penitentiary I want to do it my own way. It has been more than two years now since this crime is alleged to have been committed, and if I'm going back to the penitentiary for the same crime I want to do it my way. I want to file my own motions."

He pulled from his hip pocket two crumpled pages, typewritten single-spaced, that were the motions he had prepared. Judge McCrary asked Gideon to read them to the court reporter. The motions were full of legalistic language, and Gideon seemed to have some trouble reading them; finally the judge called a short recess to let Gideon look them over before reading them to the stenographer. These long documents made two main points: That a new trial was barred by the rule against double jeopardy and by Florida's two-year statute of limitations on his alleged crime. (The statute of limitations does not, in fact, apply when an appeal results in a new trial.)

Judge McCrary listened attentively during the reading of the motions and said he would rule on them later. Then he set a new trial date, August 5th, exactly one month later. The judge offered to free the prisoner on $1,000 bail, but Gideon could not raise it and was returned to the penitentiary.

Simon later wrote a report on the episode for the Florida Civil Liberties Union, which he subtitled, "How the Florida Civil Liberties Union Wasted $300, and How Two Attorneys Each Traveled over 1200 Miles and Killed an Otherwise Perfectly Enjoyable July Fourth Weekend." But by the end of the report his anger seems to have softened. He wrote:

"It has become almost axiomatic that the great rights which are secured for all of us by the Bill of Rights are constantly tested and retested in the courts by the people who live in the bottom of society's barrel. Thus, many of our freedom-of-religion cases developed out of efforts by members of small sects to force religious tracts upon people who did not want them; our freedom-of-speech cases have developed from the efforts of the police to jail persons who ranted and raved against others, including Catholics, Jews and Negroes. . . .

"In the future the name 'Gideon' will stand for the great principle that the poor are entitled to the same type of justice as are those who are able to afford counsel. It is probably a good thing that it is immaterial and unimportant that Gideon is something of a 'nut,' that his maniacal distrust and suspicion lead him to the very borders of insanity. Upon the shoulders of such persons are our great rights carried."

Gideon's new lawyer, Fred Turner, wrote to Judge McCrary on July 12th asking that the trial be postponed three weeks. He said there were "many, many legal problems" in this case—a case once considered so simple that the defendant could be required to try it himself on a few minutes' notice. Judge McCrary refused the postponement.

On August 1st the judge denied a series of motions including Gideon's own, presented by Turner, to dismiss the charges. Courtroom observers thought Gideon looked pleased at the denial and was looking forward to the new trial. Judge McCrary warned him not to interfere with Turner or try to take over his own defense.

The courthouse in Panama City is a large brick building, painted yellow, with peeling white columns. It stands on a rather seedy square set with palms. The courtroom is a simple, good-looking room with pale green walls and seats for about one hundred and fifty. It is air conditioned, a necessity in Panama City in August.

The trial began promptly at nine A.M. on August 5th. After the sheriff's traditional opening (". . . God save the United States of America, the State of Florida and this honorable court"), Judge McCrary read a prayer ending "and help us to do impartial justice, for Christ's sake. Amen." Forty-eight years old, with black hair, informal and gracious in his dealings with the lawyers but decisive when necessary, McCrary was not an awesome figure in his robes. To his left and below him was the court reporter, Mrs. Nelle P. Heath, a motherly figure with firmly upswept hair and pearl earrings. ("I reported this case originally, and I thought it was just another run-of-the-mill case. I never thought that Gideon was different from anyone else—that he would just keep on goin' and goin' and goin'.") The prosecution table was just in front of the bench. The original prosecutor, Assistant State Attorney William E. Harris, a tanned, bulky man, again sat there. But this time, indicating the importance the case had acquired, his boss was there, too—the state attorney for the circuit, J. Frank Adams, a foxy-looking figure in a bow tie—and also another assistant, J. Paul Griffith. The prosecutors seemed confident. Adams said, "If he'd had a lawyer in the first place, he'd have been advised to plead guilty."

Judge McCrary announced "the case of State of Florida versus Clarence Earl Gideon. Is the state ready for trial?" Harris said it was. Turner, who was sitting with Gideon at a table back near the rail that separated the spectators from the trial area, got up without waiting to be asked. "We're ready, your Honor," he said, enthusiastically rolling a pencil between his two flattened hands. Turner was thin and dapper, reminiscent of Fred Astaire, "forty-one summers" old, he said when asked.

Ordinarily a jury of six is used in Florida. There was a panel of twenty-eight white men in the courtroom. (Why no Negroes? "They just don't call any," a local newspaper man explained.) The first six men were called forward and questioned first by Harris for possible prejudice. Harris was satisfied with all of them. Then Turner questioned the same six; they said they had no prejudices in the case, and they agreed that they would give the defendant the benefit of any reasonable doubt. Without explanation, Turner excused two of the six. Later he said, privately, that he had gone over the whole jury list in advance—"you've got to know who they are, what they think"—and dropped the two men because he knew that one didn't like alcohol and that the other was "a convicter."

The jury was sworn just before ten A.M. Harris made a two-minute opening statement to the effect that the state expected to prove Gideon had broken in the Bay Harbor Poolroom through a rear window; a witness had seen him inside and in an alley after leaving. Turner waived his right to make an opening statement.

Henry Cook, the eyewitness, was the first to take the stand. He turned out to be a sallow-faced youth of twenty-two, with greasy black hair cut in a pompadour and long sideburns. Under Harris's questioning he told the same story he had at the first trial. He had come back to Bay Harbor from a dance in Apalachicola, sixty miles away, at five-thirty that morning and had spotted Gideon inside the poolroom; he had followed

Gideon down the alley to a telephone booth, then back to the poolroom; Gideon's pockets bulged.

Turner began his cross-examination by asking who had driven Cook back from Apalachicola that night. When Cook had trouble remembering, Turner suggested some names. (Turner had driven to Apalachicola a few days earlier to try, without success, to find the other young men who had been in the car.) Cook said the car was "an old model Chevrolet."

"Why did they put you off two blocks from your home when they'd driven you sixty miles?" Turner asked.

Cook mumbled inaudibly, then said, "I was going to hang around there till the poolroom opened up—seven o'clock."

Turner began addressing the witness with irritating familiarity, "Well now, Henry ... ," and took him back over the events of that night. Cook said he had had a beer or two, but then the stores had closed in Apalachicola at midnight. This brought Turner back to the question of why Cook and his friends had stopped outside the Bay Harbor Poolroom. Turner had a suggestion—an accusation.

"Mr. Cook," he said, "did you go into the Bay Harbor Poolroom?"

"No, sir."

"Did you all get a six-pack of beer out of there?"

"No, sir."

Turner led Cook over a detailed discussion of the geography of Bay Harbor and the poolroom, indicating an intimate acquaintance with it himself. (He had spent a day nosing around Bay Harbor and talking with people, to prepare for the trial.) Weren't there some advertising boards in the front window? How could Cook have seen past them and spotted Gideon, as he claimed? Weren't the windows on the alley too high to see through?

"You did not call the police then or later," Turner asked. It was as much a comment as a question.

"That's right."

After more questions, Turner asked, "Ever been convicted of a felony?"

"No, sir, not convicted. I stole a car and was put on probation."

That answer set off a long wrangle between the lawyers. At the first trial, when Gideon asked whether he had ever been convicted of a felony, Cook had answered: "No, sir, never have." Turner said that was a false answer that reflected on Cook's character and credibility as a witness. State Attorney Adams popped up and said it was not necessarily false because Cook had evidently pleaded guilty; that was not the same as being "convicted." Turner said it was the same. There was a suggestion that the plea might have been in a juvenile court, where there are no formal convictions. Finally the judge allowed this exchange, which closed the cross-examination:

Turner: "Have you ever denied being convicted of a felony?"

Cook: "Yes, sir."

Turner: "When and where did you deny your criminal record?"

Cook: "Right here—at his last trial."

On redirect examination Harris got Cook to say he had not understood the question about a felony at the first trial. Turner moved to strike this testimony, saying "I don't think this should go to the jury with any excuses or any embellishments. . . . I don't care if he's ignorant of the law or I am, that still doesn't change the spots on the leopard. He's a convicted felon." Judge McCrary let Cook's explanation stand, but Turner had made the score he wanted—impressing the jury with Cook's record.

The prosecution's second witness was the man who had operated the Bay Harbor Poolroom, Ira Strickland, Jr., twenty-nine years old, growing bald. He was no longer in the poolroom business; now he was a stock clerk. Questioning him, State Attorney Adams went into much greater detail about the poolroom and Gideon's relationship to it than at the first trial. Had Gideon worked for Strickland? "Never on the payroll," but he had helped out sometimes.

"Was he authorized to be in the poolroom on the morning of the third day of June, 1961?"

"No."

On cross-examination Turner asked whether others had not operated the poolroom for Strickland.

"Occasionally."

"Even this defendant, Gideon, operated it sometimes, didn't he?"

"Well, occasionally." There was no further explanation.

Turner pressed Strickland to say exactly what he missed from the poolroom when he arrived that morning, but Strickland said he could not be precise.

"Are you sure there was money in that cigarette machine [the night before]?"

"Yes."

"How can you be sure?"

"I bought a pack myself."

Shortly before noon Judge McCrary recessed the trial for lunch. Afterward the state called the detective who had arrested Gideon in 1961. Duell Pitts was a square-faced, handsome man, thirty-seven years old, wearing a sports jacket and salmon-colored tie. Like the other prosecution witnesses, he seemed to have no animus toward Gideon; indeed he spoke rather gently of him. On direct examination he testified that he had been called by the policeman who discovered the break-in, was given Gideon's name at the scene by Cook, and arrested Gideon in a downtown Panama City bar the same morning.

Under cross-examination Pitts produced his notes of what Strickland had told him was missing from the poolroom that morning: four fifths of wine, twelve bottles of Coca Cola, twelve cans of beer, about five dollars from the cigarette machine and sixty dollars from the juke box. Then Turner asked a question that boomeranged: "When you arrested Clarence Earl Gideon that morning, how much money did he have on him?"

Pitts answered, "Twenty-five dollars and twenty-eight cents in quarters, nickels, dimes and a few pennies."

On redirect, that damning point was re-emphasized: "This twenty-five dollars and twenty-eight cents—he had no bills?"

"Not that I remember."

Preston Bray, the cab driver who was called by Gideon the morning of the crime and drove him downtown, testified that Gideon had paid him six quarters. He said that Gideon had told him: "If anyone asks you where you left me off, you don't know; you haven't seen me." But on cross-examination he said Gideon had told him the same thing on other occasions.

"Do you know why?"

"I understand it was his wife—he had trouble with his wife." There were these further exchanges between Turner and Bray:

Q: "What was his condition as to sobriety?"

A: "What's that?"

Q: "Was he drunk or sober?"

A: "He was sober."

Q: "Did he have any wine on him?"

A: "No, sir."

Q: "Any beer?"

A: "No, sir."

Q: "Any Coca Cola?"

A: "No, sir."

Q: "Did his pockets bulge?"

A: "No, sir."

That was the prosecution's case. The jury was sent out; and then Turner moved for a directed verdict of acquittal, arguing that the evidence went only to show Gideon in the poolroom, not breaking into it. Judge McCrary listened politely and then said without hesitation: "The motion will be denied. Call the jury back."

Turner produced a surprise defense witness who had never appeared in the case before. He was J.D. Henderson, owner of the grocery in Bay Harbor. Between eight and nine on the morning of June 3, 1961, Henderson said, Henry Cook had come into his store and told the grocer that "the law had picked him up for questioning" about the break-in.

"Picked who up?" Turner asked with an air of mock disbelief.

"Henry Cook."

Henderson said Cook had told him about seeing someone in the poolroom but was "not sure who it was. He said, 'It looked like Mr. Gideon.'" If such a statement had been made by Cook, it was much less positive than his subsequent testimony.

On cross-examination Harris asked whether Henderson had ever had "any trouble with Henry Cook."

"No."

"Does he owe you any money?"

"He owes a grocery bill, forty-one dollars, for almost a year."

The second and last witness for the defense was Clarence Earl Gideon.

Q: "On the morning of June 3, 1961, did you break and enter the Bay Harbor Poolroom?"

A: "No, sir."

Q: "What was the purpose of your going into town?"

A: "To get me another drink."

Q: "Where'd you get the money?"

A: "I gambled."

Q: "What kind of games?"

A: "Mostly rummy."

Q: "Did you ever gamble with Henry Cook?"

A: "Sure, I gambled with all those boys."

Q: "Did you have any wine with you?"

A: "I don't drink wine."

Q: "Any beer? Any Coke?"

A: "No."

Q: "What did you purchase in town?"

A: "I didn't purchase nothin' except somethin' to drink."

Q: "That's what I mean. What did you purchase to drink?"

A: "Four or five beers, and I bought a half-pint of vodka."

Q: "What do you say to this charge that you broke and entered the pool hall?"

A: "I'm not guilty of it—I know nothing about it."

On cross-examination, Harris asked where Gideon was employed at the time. "I wasn't employed. I was gambling." There was a long exploration of when Gideon had last held a regular job. He had painted some rooms at the Bay Harbor Hotel and was given free rent (a $6–a–week room) in exchange. He had run poker games for Strickland in the poolroom. There followed some questions about gambling that Gideon answered with a puzzled air, as if bewildered at Harris's failure to understand.

Q: "Why did you have all that money in coins?"

A: "I've had as much as one hundred dollars in my pockets in coins."

Q: "Why?"

A: "Have you ever run a poker game?"

Q: "You would carry one hundred dollars in coins around for a couple of days at a time?"

A: "Yes sir, I sure wouldn't leave it in a room in the Bay Harbor Hotel."

Q: "Did you play rummy that night?"

A: "No—I was too busy drinking."

Q: "Have you ever been convicted or pled guilty to a felony?"

A: "Yes, five times, including this one."

At two-forty P.M. the testimony was all in. Judge McCrary recessed the trial and called the lawyers and Gideon into his chambers to discuss how he should charge the jury. The lawyers wrangled for half an hour, ending with a squabble over how much time they would have for closing arguments. Judge McCrary settled this by allowing each side forty-five minutes; as it turned out, neither used that much.

In his address to the jury Turner was the model of the practiced criminal lawyer—dramatic but not too dramatic. His whole argument focused on Henry Cook.

"This probationer," he said scornfully, "has been out at a dance drinking beer.... He does a peculiar thing [when he supposedly sees Gideon inside the poolroom]. He doesn't call the police, he doesn't notify the owner, he just walks to the corner and walks back [as Cook had testified].... What happened to the beer and the wine and the Cokes? I'll tell you—it left there in that old model Chevrolet. The beer ran out at midnight in Apalachicola.... Why was Cook walking back and forth? I'll give you the explanation: He was the lookout."

Having accused Cook and his friends of actually committing the crime, Turner turned to the defendant.

"Gideon's a gambler," he said, "and he'd been drinking whiskey. I submit to you that he did just what he said that morning—he walked out of his hotel and went to that telephone booth [to call the cab]. . . . Cook saw him, and here was a perfect answer for Cook. He names Gideon."

For the state, Assistant Prosecutor Griffith had made a straightforward closing argument, summarizing the testimony without dramatics. Now, in rebuttal to Turner, Harris got a little more folksy.

"Twenty-five dollars' worth of change," he said, "that's a lot to carry in your pocket. But Mr. Gideon carried one hundred dollars' worth of change in his pocket." He paused and raised his eyebrows. "Do you believe that? . . . There's been no evidence here of any animosity by Cook toward Gideon. There's no evidence here that Cook and his friends took this beer and wine."

The jury went out at four-twenty P.M., after a colorless charge by the judge including the instruction—requested by Turner—that the jury must believe Gideon guilty "beyond a reasonable doubt" in order to convict him. When a half-hour had passed with no verdict, the prosecutors were less confident. At five twenty-five there was a knock on the door between the courtroom and the jury room. The jurors filed in, and the court clerk read their verdict, written on a form. It was *Not Guilty*.

"So say you all?" asked Judge McCrary, without a flicker of emotion. The jurors nodded.

Judge McCrary had written of Gideon's first trial: "In my opinion he did as well as most lawyers could have done in handling his case." But Gideon had not done as well as Fred Turner. He had none of Fred Turner's training, or his talent, or his knowledge of the community. Nor could he prepare the case as Turner had, because he had been in prison before his trial.

Turner had spent three full days before trial interviewing witnesses and exploring the case. He went out in the backyard and picked pears with Cook's mother to see what he could find out about the prosecution's star witness. Actually, Turner already knew a good deal about Cook because he had twice been Cook's lawyer—a coincidence that was not a great surprise in a small town like Panama City, where part of a lawyer's job is to know everyone. He had represented Cook in a divorce action and defended him successfully against a charge of leading a drunk out of the Bay Harbor Poolroom, beating him up and robbing him of $1.98. Gideon's insistence on having a local lawyer—Fred Turner—may well have won the case for him. It is doubtful that the Civil Liberties Union lawyers from Miami could have been so effective with a Panama City jury.

After nearly two years in the state penitentiary Gideon was a free man. There were tears in his eyes, and he trembled even more than usual as he stood in a circle of well-wishers and discussed his plans. His half-brother, the Air Force sergeant, was coming home from Japan and would adopt Gideon's children. Gideon would see the children the next day, then go off to stay with a friend in Tallahassee. That night he would pay a last, triumphant visit to the Bay Harbor Poolroom. Could someone let him have a few dollars? Someone did.

"Do you feel like you accomplished something?" a newspaper reporter asked.

"Well I did."

NOTES AND QUESTIONS CONCERNING *GIDEON'S TRUMPET*

1. How is it that Clarence Earl Gideon was represented by Abe Fortas in the United States Supreme Court? *See* Model Rules of Prof'l Conduct Rule 6.1. Did Fortas have a responsibility to represent Gideon after the Supreme Court's decision? *See* Model Rules of Prof'l Conduct Rule 1.1. Were there any other barriers to Fortas's representation of Gideon in the Florida courts?

2. In his Supreme Court argument, Fortas argued eloquently that basic fairness required the appointment of counsel in state felony prosecutions because the adversary system "means that counsel for the State will do his best * * * to present the case for the State, and counsel for the defense will do his best, similarly, to present the best case possible for the defendant, and from that clash there will emerge the truth." Transcript of Oral Argument at 4, *Gideon v. Cochran* (Jan. 15, 1963). Are indigents therefore entitled to the appointment of counsel in civil actions? *See Lassiter v. Department of Social Services,* 452 U.S. 18, 26–27 (1981) ("[A]n indigent litigant has a right to appointed counsel only when, if he loses, he may be deprived of his physical liberty.").

3. Did the appointment of counsel for Clarence Earl Gideon make a difference in his second trial? In what way? What advantages did attorney Fred Turner have in conducting the pretrial investigation that Gideon did not? Critique the investigation conducted by Gideon's counsel.

4. Are there any ethical issues raised by the manner in which Fred Turner gained information concerning Henry Cook? *See* Model Rules of Prof'l Conduct Rules 1.6(a), 1.8(b), 1.9(c).

5. Did Gideon have a right *not* to be represented by counsel? Why did the Florida judge want to ensure that Gideon was represented by counsel for his retrial? Was Gideon right to insist upon counsel other than the Florida Civil Liberties Union attorneys who originally volunteered to represent him? Does *Gideon* "guarantee[ ] no more than that 'a person who happens to be a lawyer is present at trial alongside the accused?' " *Mitchell v. Kemp,* 483 U.S. 1026, 1026 (1987) (Marshall, J., dissenting), *quoting Strickland v. Washington,* 466 U.S. 668, 685 (1984). Has the promise of *Gideon* been fulfilled? *See Gideon's Broken Promise: America's Continuing Quest for Equal Justice* (2004) (A.B.A. Standing Comm. on Legal Aid and Indigent Defendants); A. Butcher & M. Moore, *Muting Gideon's Trumpet: The Crisis in Indigent Criminal Defense in Texas* (2000) (Comm. on Legal Services to the Poor in Crim. Matters, State Bar of Texas); S. Bright, *Promises to Keep: Achieving Fairness and Equal Justice for the Poor in Criminal Cases* (2000) (Southern Center for Human Rights).

6. What if disagreements had arisen between Gideon and his counsel concerning pretrial or trial strategy? Is it an attorney's duty to shield a client from making a "bad" litigation decision? *See* Model Rules of Prof'l Conduct Rule 1.2(a). Consider also the state attorney's comment: "If [Gideon had] had a lawyer in the first place, he'd have been advised to plead guilty."

IV. LEGAL RESEARCH

By now in your law school career, you have had instruction in legal research. Indeed, entire courses and books are devoted to this subject.[21] This book's discussion of legal research is therefore restricted to a consideration of the manner in which such research is conducted by practicing attorneys within the pretrial process.

Perhaps the major difference between legal research as taught in law school and legal research as conducted in practice is that in practice legal research is an ongoing activity. The facts in any lawsuit are not set, and, as the facts change, so, too, should the corresponding legal research. Legal research is a fluid activity that cannot be restricted to a one-time analysis based upon a static set of facts.

In practice there is a symbiosis between legal research and factual investigation. Not only does the initial factual investigation in a case suggest avenues for legal research, but a general understanding of the governing law in an area also should suggest possibilities for factual investigation. There is a continuous loop (or, depending upon your perspective, a vicious cycle), in which additional factual investigation suggests possibilities for additional legal research, which in turn suggests possibilities for additional factual research.

The subjects researched in practice may be somewhat different from those that typically are the basis of law school legal writing exercises. While practicing attorneys must research and be concerned about the substantive law governing a claim or defense, they also may need to research applicable procedural rules.

For example, a plaintiff's attorney cannot merely focus on whether plaintiff has a good cause of action under the common law of tort, but must consider the procedural rules under which the claim can be asserted. Indeed, the choice of law rule, or statute of limitations, or available remedies may be more significant than the substantive law in many cases. All of this law must be carefully researched, so that not only the substantive, but also the procedural, law that is most favorable to a client can be invoked. Before legal research is complete, the attorney must check local

---

21. Among the many recent treatments of legal research are J. Armstrong & C. Knott, *Where the Law Is: An Introduction to Advanced Legal Research* (3d ed. 2008); S. Barkan et al., *Fundamentals of Legal Research* (9th ed. 2009); R. Berring & E. Edinger, *Finding the Law* (12th ed. 2005); D Bouchoux, *Legal Research Explained* (2008); M. Cohen & K. Olson, *Legal Research in a Nutshell* (10th ed. 2010); C. Kunz et al., *The Process of Legal Research* (7th ed. 2008); M. Murray & C. DeSanctis, *Legal Research and Writing* (2005).

rules of court, standing orders issued by individual judges, and any particular requirements of the local clerk's office.

Nor should legal research only be conducted in response to actions taken by opposing counsel. At the very outset of the lawsuit (before its filing, for plaintiff's counsel) the possible future course of the action should be predicted and corresponding legal research conducted. If it is important that a case be heard in a particular state forum, the possibility of the defendant removing the action to federal court should be investigated and researched before the action is filed.

Legal research may be a much less formal affair in practice than the research projects assigned in the law school classroom. Rather than working for extended periods on lengthy legal memoranda, attorneys often perform much more cursory legal research. This research may be only to confirm counsel's initial belief as to the governing law or to find a particular case or statute that establishes the legal point in question.

If there is governing law on a subject, the attorney generally will not continue in law review fashion to explore the historic development of the law or what the law might be in other jurisdictions. If the judge to whom your case is assigned has spoken on a subject, all the learning of the other members of the bench may be quite beside the point. Computer data bases can be very helpful in quickly narrowing one's research to relevant opinions from a particular jurisdiction or judge. Computer searches also may reveal positions taken by opposing counsel in prior cases; very effective arguments sometimes can be based upon the statements of opposing counsel in other cases.

The Internet provides many opportunities for creative attorneys in connection with both factual and legal research.[22] As with other research, however, electronic research should be conducted in a planned and systematic fashion.

Despite the cursory nature of certain legal research, a record of all research should be made. If this is not done, the attorney may come back to an area previously researched but be unable to determine exactly what research was done. In this event, there may be no alternative but to start the research again from scratch. Time usually will be saved in the long run if short notations are made concerning the scope of research undertaken and the results of that research, even if the research does not appear to have any immediate relevance. Legal research done in one case may be of use in other cases and should be preserved for this reason as well.

What if existing law is not favorable to your client's position? In this situation, an attorney may decide to do further research to determine what state of facts *would* support a good claim or defense under existing

---

22. *See, e.g.,* K. Biehl & T. Calishain, *The Lawyer's Guide to the Internet* (2000); C. Levitt & M. Rosch, *The Lawyer's Guide to Fact Finding on the Internet* (3d ed. 2006); K. Kozlowski, *The Internet Guide for the Legal Researcher* (3d ed. 2001); H. Ramy & S. Moppett, *Navigating the Internet: Legal Research on the World Wide Web* (2000).

law. Once this is determined, the attorney can conduct further factual investigation searching for these facts. As the old saying goes, "If the facts are not in your favor, pound on the law; If the law is not in your favor, pound on the facts; and if neither the law nor the facts are in your favor, pound on the table."

There is another route open to the attorney whose legal research indicates no colorable claim or defense under existing law; she can argue that existing law should be changed. How far can counsel go in this regard? Rule 11(b)(2) of the Federal Rules of Civil Procedure provides that an attorney's signature on a court paper constitutes a certification that "the claims, defenses, and other legal contentions are warranted by existing law or by a nonfrivolous argument for extending, modifying, or reversing existing law or for establishing new law." Rule 3.1 of the Model Rules of Professional Conduct permits attorneys to advance claims that are supported by a "good faith argument for an extension, modification, or reversal of existing law."

The practical meaning of these provisions is explored in the following exercise.

Exercise Concerning Legal Research

In the lawsuit brought on behalf of those injured and killed in the Buffalo Creek disaster, plaintiffs' attorney Gerald Stern asserted claims on behalf of at least some individuals who neither were themselves physically injured nor witnessed others sustaining injury in the flood. *See* G. Stern, *The Buffalo Creek Disaster* 244–51 (1976). These claims were asserted despite the fact that the West Virginia Supreme Court, in an opinion overturning a jury verdict predicated on mental suffering unaccompanied by physical injury, had stated: "In 1 *Am. & Eng. Enc. Law,* 862, we find the rule of law stated thus: ' * * * [M]ental suffering alone * * * cannot sustain an action for damages, or be considered as an element of damages. Anxiety of mind and mental torture are too refined and too vague in their nature to be the subject of pecuniary compensation in damages, except where, as in case of personal injury, they are so inseparably connected with the physical pain that they cannot be distinguished from it, and are therefore considered a part of it.' " *Davis v. Western Union Tel. Co.,* 46 W.Va. 48, 53, 32 S.E. 1026, 1028 (1899).

In 1945 the West Virginia Supreme Court relied upon *Davis* in overturning a jury verdict based upon mental and emotional injury, without physical injury, due to the defendant's simple negligence. *Monteleone v. Co–Operative Transit Co.,* 128 W.Va. 340, 36 S.E.2d 475 (1945). More recently, in a 1967 opinion, Judge Christie of the United States District Court for the Southern District of West Virginia relied upon *Davis* and *Monteleone* for the proposition that "under West Virginia law, one may not have a recovery for mental suffering alone, and unaccompanied by any physical injury." *Bishop v. Byrne,* 265 F.Supp. 460, 465 (S.D.W.Va. 1967).

Although Gerald Stern's action was filed prior to the 1983 and 1993 amendments to Rule 11 of the Federal Rules of Civil Procedure, would the assertion of claims on behalf of "absent plaintiffs" be proper under the current version of Rule 11? Even if the assertion of such claims can be defended under Rule 11, does that Rule nevertheless create potential problems for plaintiffs' counsel? What efforts would you make, as plaintiffs' counsel, to ensure that Rule 11 sanctions are not later levied? Must you cite the older West Virginia precedents? In what manner would you do so? Presuming that the above cases are the West Virginia precedents most directly on point, what other legal research would you conduct?

After considering the above questions, plan what you would tell your clients about the assertion of claims on behalf of individuals who did not witness the Buffalo Creek dam failure. Then draft a letter to your clients explaining the course of action that you would pursue.

V. DEVELOPING A CASE THEORY AND THEME

As discussed earlier in this chapter, litigation planning is essential so that the attorney will know exactly what facts must be proven (or not proven) in order for her client to prevail. As factual investigation and legal research progress, however, the attorney must move beyond a simple check list of necessary legal and factual elements. Counsel also must develop a case theory, or explanation, of (1) exactly what, factually, happened and (2) why, legally, defendant either is or is not liable for plaintiff's alleged injuries. In addition, counsel will want to refine that case theory to a much simpler case theme, or persuasive case summary, in order to most effectively present her case to the judge or jury.

Case theories and themes typically have been recommended as the most effective way in which to present a case at trial.[23] However, case theories, in particular, should be developed early in the pretrial process.

There are several reasons why this is so. If a case theory or explanation is not adopted early in a case, sufficient evidence may not be developed during pretrial to permit the theory to be presented at trial. For example, there are many types of both formal and informal discovery that could be undertaken to support the theory that the defendant in an automobile accident case was intoxicated at the time of the accident. However, if plaintiff does not come up with a case theory until the eve of trial, he may be effectively foreclosed from even advancing the theory at trial.

Case theories can be of benefit within the pretrial process itself. The great majority of cases are resolved short of trial. Development of effective

---

23. Imwinkelried, "The Development of Professional Judgment in Law School Litigation Courses: The Concepts of Trial Theory and Theme," 39 *Vand. L. Rev.* 59 (1986); McElhaney, "The Theory of the Case," *Litigation,* Fall 1979, at 51. *See generally,* E. Oliver, *Facts Can't Speak for Themselves: Reveal the Stories that Give Facts their Meaning* (2006).

case theories during pretrial may increase a case's settlement value or make the court less likely to grant an opponent's dispositive motion.

There are a myriad of factual and legal issues that can be investigated in connection with any case. Case theories help focus pretrial investigation and research on those selected issues that are most likely to bear fruit at trial or during the pretrial process. Because Rule 26(b)(1) generally limits the scope of permissible discovery to matters "relevant to any party's claim or defense," the theories advanced in the pleadings serve to focus, and limit, formal discovery as well.

The development of case theories or explanations begins with the initial client interview. As the client gives his narrative, the attorney often subconsciously will consider both (1) the credibility of the factual narrative being offered and (2) the legal ramifications of those facts. For example, initial attorney questioning of a survivor of the Buffalo Creek disaster probably would focus on possible tort claims, rather than pursue facts relevant to a contract cause of action. Additionally, attorney questioning should test any elements of the client's factual narrative that do not ring true.

Although even inconsistent pleading is permitted by Rule 8(d)(3) of the Federal Rules of Civil Procedure, effective trial advocacy usually requires the choice of either a single case theory or of at least closely related and consistent theories. While legally permissible, it may not be wise to argue to a jury that the defendant never ran over the plaintiff, but, even if he did, the plaintiff darted in front of defendant's car.

Nor does it normally make sense to advance too many theories at trial, even if they are consistent. Your trial advocacy will be weakened if you attempt to assert a "top ten list" of reasons why your client should prevail in the litigation. A lawsuit is not like a law school examination, on which points may be awarded for every conceivable issue that is spotted.

This certainly does not mean that multiple or inconsistent case theories should not be pursued during the pretrial period. In fact, one of the purposes of pretrial is to permit the parties to explore various explanations of the facts underlying the suit. Promising initial theories may have to be discarded after factual investigation. For this reason it usually makes sense to initially explore multiple case theories. However, as the pretrial period progresses, counsel should focus on fewer numbers of possible theories. It is from these theories that remain at the end of the pretrial period that the actual trial theory or theories should be chosen.

How should an attorney choose among possible case theories? The case theories or explanations that are most effective are those that are most credible or believable. Consider, for instance, the various explanations as to why dinosaurs became extinct. Is it more credible that dinosaurs died out due to a change in the earth's climate, a meteor striking the earth, or, as cartoonist Gary Larson has suggested, because they smoked cigarettes? While at least two of these three theories may be worthy of extended investigation, as the facts develop over time one theory should appear more credible than the others.

Case theories sometimes become less credible due to developments during the pretrial process. While such developments usually are not good news, it's better to obtain bad news sooner rather than later. When a document that totally contradicts one's case theory first appears on the eve of trial, it may be too late to develop a new case theory. Instead, it's probably time to settle the lawsuit. For this reason, early, ongoing investigations usually are best.

In choosing case theories, attorneys must be conscious of what they actually can prove at trial. In the dinosaur hypothetical, it may be very difficult to definitively prove any single theory. In other cases, however, certain theories may be more easily established than others. Other things being equal, these are the theories that should be developed during the pretrial process.

In determining which theories can be proven at trial and which theories are the most credible, a good deal of common sense is quite helpful. At the simplest level, this means that there is no reason to pursue theories that do not pass the proverbial "laugh test." Until we discover fossilized cigarette butts, there probably is little need to investigate possible links between dinosaurs and smoking. At a more sophisticated level, common sense must be applied to determine which case theories make the most logical and intuitive sense.

Case theories are explanations of how something occurred and the legal consequences of that occurrence, but counsel also need to think ahead to a case theme by which a case can most persuasively be packaged and presented to the trier of fact. While the case theory should encompass every fact that must be proven (or not proven) to justify a particular legal outcome, the case theme is a much more general summarization of the party's strongest point or points.[24] Although the case theory in the antitrust action brought by the United States to break up American Telephone and Telegraph undoubtedly was rather complicated, the case theme was simple and to the point. Government counsel asserted in opening statement that whenever A. T. & T. had the chance it "reached out, reached out, and crushed someone." To be effective, case themes must be simple (but not simplistic). One helpful way to develop case themes is to consider how you would describe your case to a friend or acquaintance in a sentence or two. Think back to those fill-in-the blank questions from grammar school: "This is a case about * * * ."

The quality and persuasiveness of both your case theories and themes will be directly related to the thoroughness of your factual investigation and the creativity of your legal research. Pretrial litigation is an area in

---

24. *See* Imwinkelried, *supra* note 23, at 60–65; McElhaney, "The Big Idea," *A.B.A.J.*, Aug. 2006, at 24; McElhaney, "Hit Themes," *A.B.A.J.*, Aug. 1998, at 88; Baum, "Creating a Theme," *Trial*, Mar. 1994, at 66.

which hard work is not only its own reward, but pays significant dividends to the diligent attorney.

Exercises Concerning Case Theory and Theme

1. Based upon the facts contained in exercise 1 of the Exercises Concerning Litigation Planning, *supra* p. 65, develop several possible case theories that counsel for Thomas Eakins could use to structure an action on Eakins's behalf. Then determine which of these theories should be the most effective and why. Finally, decide upon a case theme by which Eakins's claim(s) could most understandably and persuasively be presented to the trier of fact.

Set forth your conclusions in a memorandum to the file.

2. Based upon the facts contained in exercise 1 of the Exercises Concerning Litigation Planning, *supra* p. 65, develop several possible case theories that counsel for the potential defendant the Pittston Company could use to structure its defense against a claim by Thomas Eakins. Then determine which of these theories should be the most effective and why. Finally, decide upon a case theme by which Pittston's defense(s) could most understandably and persuasively be presented to the trier of fact.

Set forth your conclusions in a memorandum to the file.

3. You have preliminarily investigated the facts underlying the dispute described in exercise 2 of the Exercises Concerning Litigation Planning, *supra* p. 66. Your preliminary investigation suggests several contradictory case theories: (1) Mason Charles did not compete with his former employer; (2) While Mason Charles may have attracted customers from his former employer, he did not intend to do so; and (3) Mason Charles intended to take business from his former employer because he believed that company had wronged him. Write a memorandum discussing whether all three of these theories should be developed during the pretrial process or whether a single theory should be chosen at some point, and, if so, when.

VI.   CONCLUSION

While the popular media celebrates the attorney who displays flashes of courtroom brilliance, lawsuits are not necessarily won by the quickest wit or the flashiest cross-examiner. Instead, modern civil litigation often turns on an attorney's attention to the pretrial tasks discussed in this chapter: litigation planning, factual investigation, legal research, and the development of case theories and themes.

Thomas Edison reputedly attributed his success to "one percent inspiration and ninety-nine percent perspiration." So it is with pretrial litigation.

VII. CHAPTER BIBLIOGRAPHY

R. Akin, *The Private Investigator's Basic Manual* (1976).

Allen & Hazelwood, "Preserving the Confidentiality of Internal Corporate Investigations," 31 *Corp. Prac. Com.* 76 (1989).

J. Armstrong & C. Knott, *Where the Law Is: An Introduction to Advanced Legal Research* (2d ed. 2006).

S. Barkan et al, *Fundamentals of Legal Research* (9th ed. 2009).

Baum, "Creating a Theme," *Trial*, Mar. 1994, at 66.

R. Berring & R. Edinger, *Finding the Law* (12th ed. 2005).

K. Biehl & T. Calishain, *The Lawyer's Guide to the Internet* (2000).

D. Binder & P. Bergman, *Fact Investigation: From Hypothesis to Proof* (1984).

M. Cohen & K. Olson, *Legal Research in a Nutshell* (10th ed. 2010).

Decker, "Economics and Litigation: View from the Inside Looking Out," *Litigation*, Summer 1998, at 36.

Giller, "Choosing and Using an Investigator," *Litigation,* Summer 1989, at 35.

Gladstone & Bernardo, "How to Prepare a Pretrial Litigation Budget," *Prac. Law.,* April 1990, at 83.

A. Golec, *Techniques of Legal Investigation* (1976).

Goodwin, "Informal Witness Investigation," *Litigation,* Summer 1987, at 8.

S. Gottlieb, *Systematic Litigation Planning* (1978).

Grant et al., "Dive Early, Dive Deep: The Importance of Pre-suit Investigation," *Litigation* (2009).

Imwinkelried, "The Development of Professional Judgment in Law School Litigation Courses: The Concepts of Trial Theory and Theme," 39 *Vand. L. Rev.* 59 (1986).

R. Haydock & P. Knapp, *Lawyering: Practice and Planning* (3d ed. 2011).

C. Kunz et al., *The Process of Legal Research* (6th ed. 2004).

Kuppens, "The Game is Afoot: Tips on Non–Discovery Investigation," *For the Defense*, Jan. 1995, at 14.

Lay, "A Trial Lawyer Speaks to the Investigator," *Prac. Law.,* Jan. 1974, at 59.

C. Levitt & M. Rosch, *The Lawyer's Guide to Fact Finding on the Internet* (3d ed. 2006).

McElhaney, "Hit Themes," *A.B.A.J.*, Aug. 1998, at 88.

McElhaney, "Informal Investigation," *Litigation*, Spring 1982, at 51.

McElhaney, "The Theory of the Case," *Litigation,* Fall 1979, at 51.

Milford, "From Streets to Suites: Private Investigators in Civil Cases," *Litigation*, Spring 2004, at 18.

E. Oliver, *Facts Can't Speak for Themselves: Reveal the Stories that Give Facts their Meaning* (2006).

Office of Information and Privacy, United States Department of Justice, *Freedom of Information Act Guide and Privacy Act Overview* (2004).

Practicing Law Institute, *Conducting Complex Fact Investigations: Techniques and Issues for Lawyers* (1987).

R. Scheff, "Getting Witnesses to Talk," *Litigation*, Summer 2001, at 38.

The Sourcebook to Public Record Information (P. Weber & M. Sankey eds. 10th ed. 2009).

Tillers & Schuman, "A Theory of Preliminary Fact Investigation," 24 *U.C. Davis L. Rev.* 931 (1991).

P. Zwier & A. Bocchino, *Fact Investigation: A Practical Guide to Interviewing, Counseling, and Case Theory Development* (2000).

CHAPTER 4

DRAFTING THE COMPLAINT: "LET'S MAKE A FEDERAL CASE OUT OF THIS!"

■ ■ ■

Pre-trial civil procedure under the English common-law system consisted only of pleading. Whatever the rules of pleading could accomplish in the way of defining and restricting issues contributed to the efficiency of the trial. What could not be done by the rules of pleading could not be done at all.

Sunderland, "The Theory and Practice of Pre–Trial Procedure," 36 *Mich. L. Rev.* 215, 216 (1937).

Just as patience is requisite in the temperament of the individual judge, so it must be an attribute of the judicial system as a whole. Our annoyance at spurious and frivolous claims, and our real concern with burdened dockets, must not drive us to adopt interpretations of the rules that make honest claimants fear to petition the courts.

Business Guides, Inc. v. Chromatic Communications Enterprises, Inc., 498 U.S. 533, 570 (1991) (Kennedy, J., dissenting).

Analysis

I. INTRODUCTION

You have diligently investigated the facts of your client's claim and carefully researched the governing law. A litigation plan has been prepared, and you have selected the most promising case theories for pretrial development. Only one thing remains to move your case from the prefiling to the pretrial litigation stage. You still need to draft a complaint. It is with this subject that this chapter deals.

Before actually drafting a complaint, counsel must determine whether the prerequisites for a civil lawsuit exist and the substance of the claims that should be asserted and the relief that should be sought in the complaint. The first major section of this chapter therefore deals with the basic prerequisites for a civil suit: subject matter jurisdiction, personal jurisdiction, venue, and filing and service of process. Even if the basic suit prerequisites are met, important decisions still must be made concerning which claims to assert in the action and the specific relief to request. These topics are discussed next.

Once this basic groundwork has been laid, the chapter considers the modern pleading regime established by the Federal Rules of Civil Procedure. Because attorneys also must be concerned with the particular pleading requirements imposed by Rule 11 of the Federal Rules of Civil Procedure, Rule 11 and the ethics of pleading are considered in the final major section of the chapter.

Contrary to the traditional English common law system described in the quotation opening this chapter, pretrial procedure no longer consists only of pleading. Nevertheless, pleading remains a very important aspect of modern civil procedure. Through pleading, the attorney translates the fruits of her factual investigation and legal research into a civil action seeking judicial redress for her client. Pleading is therefore a subject that bears close attention by all attorneys.

II. SUIT PREREQUISITES

Whether an action is filed in state or federal court, there are certain suit prerequisites that must be satisfied. While other specific requirements may apply depending upon the type of case and the court in question, before any court can entertain a civil action there must be (1) subject matter jurisdiction, (2) personal jurisdiction, (3) venue, and (4) filing and service of process. These prerequisites to suit now will be considered.

A. SUBJECT MATTER JURISDICTION

The first requirement for a civil action is that the court have power to hear the particular type of claim at issue. The court's power over a claim is called its subject matter jurisdiction. In a state court of general jurisdiction, subject matter jurisdiction normally does not present a problem; all the attorney need do is check the relevant jurisdictional statutes to ensure that the claim has not been excluded from the court's general jurisdiction. For example, state courts of general jurisdiction may not have the power to entertain claims for less than a certain monetary amount.

Some state courts and the federal district courts are courts of limited jurisdiction; that is, they only possess the subject matter jurisdiction that specifically has been conferred upon them. If such a court has not been given subject matter jurisdiction over a particular claim, it cannot entertain that claim. The attorney must check the statute conferring subject matter jurisdiction to ensure that there is a specific jurisdictional provision that extends to the claim in question.

The two major categories of federal subject matter jurisdiction are federal question jurisdiction and diversity of citizenship jurisdiction. In determining whether a federal district court can exercise federal question or diversity jurisdiction, the jurisdictional statutes must be checked. Section 1331 of Title 28 of the United States Code provides that the district courts have the power to entertain "all civil actions arising under the Constitution, laws, or treaties of the United States," while 28 U.S.C. § 1332(a) provides, *inter alia,* that the federal courts can entertain civil actions between citizens of different states "where the matter in controversy exceeds the sum or value of $75,000, exclusive of interest and costs."

A recent example of a much more targeted jurisdictional statute is the Multiparty, Multiforum Trial Jurisdiction Act of 2002,[1] which grants jurisdiction based upon minimal diversity in certain actions arising from a single accident in which "at least 75 natural persons have died in [an] accident at a discrete location."[2] However, even if the statute's jurisdictional requirements are met, district courts are to abstain from hearing such cases if "the substantial majority of all plaintiffs are citizens of a single State of which the primary defendants are also citizens" and "the claims asserted will be governed primarily by the laws of that State."[3]

The attorney's first job in drafting a civil complaint is to check the relevant jurisdictional statutes and ensure that there is a basis for subject matter jurisdiction.

B. PERSONAL JURISDICTION

In addition to jurisdiction over the type of case, a court cannot entertain a civil action unless it also has personal or territorial jurisdiction over the parties to the suit. Generally, there is no question concerning the court's power over the plaintiff, who is considered to have submitted to the court's personal jurisdiction by the filing of suit.[4] Nor are there

---

1. Pub.L. No. 107–273, § 11020(b)(1), 116 Stat. 1826 (codified as amended at 28 U.S.C. §§ 1369, 1697). Venue in such cases has been expanded to include "any district * * * in which a substantial part of the accident giving rise to the accident took place." 28 U.S.C. § 1391(g).

2. 28 U.S.C. § 1369(a).

3. 28 U.S.C. § 1369(b).

4. *See Keeton v. Hustler Magazine, Inc.,* 465 U.S. 770, 779–81 (1984).

usually any serious issues concerning personal jurisdiction over defendants who are physically present within the forum state.[5] Questions may arise, though, concerning the court's power to bind defendants who are not physically present within the forum state.

A court's power to bind absent parties breaks down into two separate questions: (1) Is there a statute or rule that establishes the court's personal jurisdiction over the parties? and, if so, (2) Is the exercise of personal jurisdiction pursuant to the statute or rule constitutional?

The first of these requirements usually is not difficult to satisfy. Most states have adopted long-arm statutes providing their courts with the authority to exercise personal jurisdiction over out-of-state defendants who have some ties or contacts with the forum state. In fact, some state statutes have gone as far as to provide: "A court of this state may exercise jurisdiction on any basis not inconsistent with the Constitution of this state or of the United States."[6] Rule 4(k)(1) of the Federal Rules of Civil Procedure provides that federal district courts can exercise personal jurisdiction over out-of-state parties pursuant to both federal statutes and long-arm statutes or rules of the state in which the federal court sits. With respect to federal question claims, Rule 4(k)(2) permits federal courts to exercise personal jurisdiction over a defendant who is not subject to the personal jurisdiction of any state but whose aggregate contacts with the United States are sufficient to subject that defendant to the constitutional exercise of the federal judicial power.[7]

Once a basis for asserting personal jurisdiction over the defendant has been located, it still must be determined whether the exercise of personal jurisdiction is constitutional. The modern constitutional due process test was formulated in *International Shoe Co. v. Washington*,[8] under which personal jurisdiction constitutionally can be asserted if the defendant has "minimum contacts" with the forum state, the claim sought to be asserted arises from those contacts, and the maintenance of suit does not offend "traditional notions of fair play and substantial justice."[9] While the Supreme Court has refined this constitutional due process test in recent years, if personal jurisdiction is sought to be asserted over an absent

---

5. *Burnham v. Superior Court,* 495 U.S. 604 (1990); *Pennoyer v. Neff,* 95 U.S. 714 (1877).

6. Cal. Code Civ. Proc. § 410.10 (West 2004). The long-arm statutes or rules in many other states have been interpreted to extend to the constitutional limits. McFarland, "Dictum Run Wild: How Long–Arm Statutes Extended to the Limits of Due Process," 84 *B.U. L. Rev.* 491 (2004).

7. *E.g., Graduate Management Admission Council v. Raju,* 241 F.Supp.2d 589 (E.D.Va. 2003) (although defendant's contacts with any individual state were insufficient to establish personal jurisdiction with any state, defendant's website was directed to the United States, generally, and provided a basis for Virginia federal district court to exercise personal jurisdiction over plaintiff's federal question claims).

8. 326 U.S. 310 (1945).

9. 326 U.S. at 316, *quoting Milliken v. Meyer,* 311 U.S. 457, 463 (1940). Subsequent to *International Shoe* the Supreme Court has upheld the exercise of general jurisdiction, involving the assertion of personal jurisdiction over claims which do not arise from the defendant's forum contacts. *Perkins v. Benguet Consol. Mining Co.,* 342 U.S. 437 (1952). *See also Helicopteros Nacionales de Colombia, S.A. v. Hall,* 466 U.S. 408, 414 (1984); *LSI Industries Inc. v. Hubbell Lighting, Inc.,* 232 F.3d 1369 (Fed. Cir. 2000).

defendant some contacts between the defendant and the forum are necessary.[10]

Therefore, in determining whether personal jurisdiction can be asserted over absent defendants, an attorney must identify the appropriate jurisdictional (long-arm) statute or rule as well as judicial decisions delimiting the constitutional reach of the jurisdictional provision.

C. VENUE

Once it is determined that a court system has the constitutional and statutory authority to entertain a case, the particular courts within that court system that can entertain the case must be identified. State and federal venue requirements allocate cases to the individual courts within a court system.

Many federal statutes contain specific venue provisions establishing the courts that can hear particular federal statutory causes of action.[11] In addition, 28 U.S.C. § 1391 is the general federal venue statute establishing venue for those claims that are not covered by a special venue statute.

Under Section 1391 there are somewhat different venue choices depending upon the basis of the subject matter jurisdiction of the underlying cause of action. If subject matter jurisdiction is founded only on diversity of citizenship, 28 U.S.C. § 1391(a) provides that venue is proper in

> (1) a judicial district where any defendant resides, if all defendants reside in the same State, (2) a judicial district in which a substantial part of the events or omissions giving rise to the claim occurred, or a substantial part of property that is the subject of the action is situated, or (3) a judicial district in which any defendant is subject to personal jurisdiction at the time the action is commenced, if there is no district in which the action may otherwise be brought.

If the jurisdictional basis of the civil action is not solely diversity of citizenship, venue choices (1) (based on defendants' residence) and (2) (based on where the claim arose or property is situated) still exist pursuant to 28 U.S.C. § 1391(b). However, the third possible venue for a non-diversity claim is not premised directly upon personal jurisdiction, but is available in "a judicial district in which any defendant may be found, if there is no district in which the action may otherwise be brought." While this final venue choice for cases not solely based on diversity of citizenship is somewhat different from the final venue choice for diversity cases, both 1391(a)(3) and 1391(b)(3) are "fall-back" provisions that only come into

---

10. In addition, constitutional due process requires that the defendant receive notice and an opportunity to be heard. *Phillips Petroleum Co. v. Shutts,* 472 U.S. 797, 811–12 (1985); *Mullane v. Central Hanover Bank & Trust Co.,* 339 U.S. 306 (1950). This constitutional requirement is generally satisfied by compliance with state and federal service of process requirements.

11. *E.g.,* 15 U.S.C. § 78aa (federal securities claims); 42 U.S.C. § 2000e–5(f)(3) (federal discrimination claims); 29 U.S.C. § 160(e) (federal unfair labor practice claims).

play "if there is no district in which the action may otherwise be brought" under 1391(a)(1) and (2) or 1391(b)(1) and (2).

In some cases there will be no real options as to venue. Even if a particular venue choice is presented under 28 U.S.C. § 1391, suit cannot be brought in a district in which personal jurisdiction doesn't also exist. Moreover, the apparent options under Section 1391 may not really exist in practice if, for instance, the events or omissions giving rise to the claim occurred in the same district in which the defendant resides. Nevertheless, alternative venue possibilities do exist in many cases. In such cases, the strategic advantages and disadvantages of each possible venue should be carefully considered. Among the considerations relevant to venue selection are client, witness, and counsel convenience; the judges who may be assigned a case; the type of jurors that may hear a case; the substantive, procedural, and evidentiary rules that will be applied; and possible delay in reaching a case on the trial docket.[12]

Counsel should research the possibility that opposing counsel will be able to transfer an action from the court in which it originally is filed to another district. Section 1404(a) of Title 28 of the United States Code provides that for "the convenience of parties and witnesses, in the interest of justice, a district court may transfer any civil action to any other district or division where it might have been brought." While a Montana plaintiff may feel some momentary satisfaction from filing his action in Montana, if the defendant and all of the witnesses and physical proof are in Maine he should not be surprised when the defendant moves for a change of venue under 28 U.S.C. § 1404.

Counsel should be aware of any rules for allocating cases within a given venue. There may be a local rule concerning the specific city within a federal judicial district where particular actions should be filed.[13] Local rules of court are especially significant in determining whether a particular judge within a district is assigned a given case. Many courts have related case rules, under which a new case will be assigned to the judge handling any pending related case (rather than being randomly assigned by the clerk's office).[14] If counsel can craft a suit so that it is related to a pending action, she may ensure the assignment of that case to a particular judge.

Counsel should be generally aware of the manner in which cases are assigned to specific judges. In some courts, cases are not randomly

---

12. *See* Rothschild, "Forum Shopping," *Litigation*, Spring 1998, at 40. *See generally* R. Casad, *Jurisdiction and Forum Selection* (2d ed. 2005).

One study found that plaintiffs' ultimate success rate dropped significantly in federal cases in which defendants had been successful in obtaining a change of venue. Clermont & Eisenberg, "Exorcizing the Evil of Forum–Shopping," 80 *Cornell L. Rev.* 1507 (1995). *But see* Steinberg, "Simplifying the Choice of Forum: A Response to Professor Clermont and Professor Eisenberg," 75 *Wash. U. L. Q.* 1479 (1997); Clermont & Eisenberg, "Simplifying the Choice of Forum: A Reply," 75 *Wash. U. L. Q.* 1551 (1997).

13. *E.g.*, Rule 3.8(b) of the United States District Court for the Northern District of Ohio (allocating actions to cities within the district based upon the residence of defendants).

14. *E.g.*, Rule 40.5 of the United States District Court for the District of Columbia.

assigned. Instead, every third case might be assigned to a particular judge. In these jurisdictions, another attorney's offer to permit you to step in front of her in the clerk's office filing line may not be motivated by humanitarian concerns. Instead, the seemingly courteous attorney may be waiting to file her action until she is sure that it will be assigned to a particular judge.[15]

As previously discussed, suit only can be brought in a court that has subject matter jurisdiction, personal jurisdiction, and venue. Venue and other case allocation rules may provide attorneys with options as to where suit can be filed and, possibly, which judge will hear the case. Those options should be thoroughly investigated in order to obtain the maximum strategic advantage for one's client.

D. FILING AND SERVICE OF PROCESS

Once the complaint has been drafted, it still must be filed and served.[16] Before this is done, however, other prefiling actions may be taken by plaintiff's counsel.

First of all, counsel may make a final attempt to settle plaintiff's claim by sending a demand letter to opposing counsel.[17] This demand letter might summarize the causes of action relied upon by plaintiff or actually include a draft of the civil complaint that will be filed if a settlement is not reached. Regardless of the form of the demand letter, the letter should make it clear that if a settlement is not reached by a date certain plaintiff's civil action will be filed. The letter and any accompanying complaint must be carefully drafted so that plaintiff's demand is taken seriously by the defendant and defense counsel. A demand letter should not contain idle threats. On the other hand, counsel should not squander any opportunities to seriously explore the possibility of settlement or other non-judicial dispute resolution.

Secondly, a prerequisite to the filing of some claims is the exhaustion of administrative remedies, often by the filing of an administrative com-

---

15. Sometimes it will seem more important to avoid a particular judge than to insure that a specific judge hears the case. In *In Re BellSouth Corp.*, 334 F.3d 941 (11th Cir. 2003), the Eleventh Circuit Court of Appeals refused to issue a writ of mandamus to overturn a district court order disqualifying an attorney and his law firm from representing the defendant BellSouth. The trial court had concluded that the attorney, a nephew of the judge to whom the case had been assigned, had been retained in order to require the recusal of that judge.

16. Fed. R. Civ. P. 3, 4, 5.

17. See generally Rappaport, "A Shot Across the Bow: How to Write an Effective Demand Letter," 5 *J. ALWD* 32 (2008).

In an opinion explicitly restricted to the facts of the case before it, the Eleventh Circuit Court of Appeals affirmed a district court's denial of attorneys' fees to a prevailing plaintiff because there had been no pre-suit demand or other notice to the defendant law firm. *Sahyers v. Prugh, Holliday & Karatinos P.L.*, 560 F.3d 1241 (11th Cir. 2009). The Court of Appeals noted, "As the district court saw it, this conscious disregard for lawyer-to-lawyer collegiality and civility caused (among other things) the judiciary to waste significant time and resources on unnecessary litigation and stood in stark contrast to the behavior expected of an officer of the court." 560 F.3d at 1245.

plaint. For example, plaintiffs cannot file employment discrimination claims under the Civil Rights Act of 1964 unless they first have filed an administrative complaint with the Equal Employment Opportunity Commission or a comparable state agency.[18]

Once any such prefiling requirements have been satisfied, it's time to actually file the complaint. This is easily accomplished, although there usually is a fee required for the filing of any civil action.[19] In addition to filing the complaint with the clerk's office, a civil cover sheet such as the one used in the federal district courts and shown in Figure 4–1 often must be completed. Cover sheets generally can be obtained in advance from the clerk's office and should be completed and brought to the clerk's office along with the complaint.

---

18. 42 U.S.C. § 2000e–5. *See also* 28 U.S.C. § 2675 (Federal Tort Claims Act); 42 U.S.C. § 6972(b) (citizen suits under Resource Conservation and Recovery Act of 1976).

19. Pursuant to 28 U.S.C. § 1915, a federal court can authorize the filing of suits without the prepayment of fees by those persons whom the court determines to be unable to pay these fees.

FIGURE 4–1

⬟JS 44   (Rev. 12/07)   **CIVIL COVER SHEET**

The JS 44 civil cover sheet and the information contained herein neither replace nor supplement the filing and service of pleadings or other papers as required by law, except as provided by local rules of court. This form, approved by the Judicial Conference of the United States in September 1974, is required for the use of the Clerk of Court for the purpose of initiating the civil docket sheet.   (SEE INSTRUCTIONS ON THE REVERSE OF THE FORM.)

I. (a) PLAINTIFFS	DEFENDANTS
(b) County of Residence of First Listed Plaintiff _____ (EXCEPT IN U.S. PLAINTIFF CASES)	County of Residence of First Listed Defendant _____ (IN U.S. PLAINTIFF CASES ONLY) NOTE: IN LAND CONDEMNATION CASES, USE THE LOCATION OF THE LAND INVOLVED.
(c) Attorney's (Firm Name, Address, and Telephone Number)	Attorneys (If Known)

II. BASIS OF JURISDICTION   (Place an "X" in One Box Only)

☐ 1 U.S. Government Plaintiff	☐ 3 Federal Question (U.S. Government Not a Party)
☐ 2 U.S. Government Defendant	☐ 4 Diversity (Indicate Citizenship of Parties in Item III)

III. CITIZENSHIP OF PRINCIPAL PARTIES(Place an "X" in One Box for Plaintiff
(For Diversity Cases Only)   and One Box for Defendant)

	PTF	DEF		PTF	DEF
Citizen of This State	☐ 1	☐ 1	Incorporated or Principal Place of Business In This State	☐ 4	☐ 4
Citizen of Another State	☐ 2	☐ 2	Incorporated and Principal Place of Business In Another State	☐ 5	☐ 5
Citizen or Subject of a Foreign Country	☐ 3	☐ 3	Foreign Nation	☐ 6	☐ 6

IV. NATURE OF SUIT   (Place an "X" in One Box Only)

CONTRACT	TORTS		FORFEITURE/PENALTY	BANKRUPTCY	OTHER STATUTES
☐ 110 Insurance ☐ 120 Marine ☐ 130 Miller Act ☐ 140 Negotiable Instrument ☐ 150 Recovery of Overpayment & Enforcement of Judgment ☐ 151 Medicare Act ☐ 152 Recovery of Defaulted Student Loans (Excl. Veterans) ☐ 153 Recovery of Overpayment of Veteran's Benefits ☐ 160 Stockholders' Suits ☐ 190 Other Contract ☐ 195 Contract Product Liability ☐ 196 Franchise	**PERSONAL INJURY** ☐ 310 Airplane ☐ 315 Airplane Product Liability ☐ 320 Assault, Libel & Slander ☐ 330 Federal Employers' Liability ☐ 340 Marine ☐ 345 Marine Product Liability ☐ 350 Motor Vehicle ☐ 355 Motor Vehicle Product Liability ☐ 360 Other Personal Injury	**PERSONAL INJURY** ☐ 362 Personal Injury - Med. Malpractice ☐ 365 Personal Injury - Product Liability ☐ 368 Asbestos Personal Injury Product Liability **PERSONAL PROPERTY** ☐ 370 Other Fraud ☐ 371 Truth in Lending ☐ 380 Other Personal Property Damage ☐ 385 Property Damage Product Liability	☐ 610 Agriculture ☐ 620 Other Food & Drug ☐ 625 Drug Related Seizure of Property 21 USC 881 ☐ 630 Liquor Laws ☐ 640 R.R. & Truck ☐ 650 Airline Regs. ☐ 660 Occupational Safety/Health ☐ 690 Other	☐ 422 Appeal 28 USC 158 ☐ 423 Withdrawal 28 USC 157 **PROPERTY RIGHTS** ☐ 820 Copyrights ☐ 830 Patent ☐ 840 Trademark	☐ 400 State Reapportionment ☐ 410 Antitrust ☐ 430 Banks and Banking ☐ 450 Commerce ☐ 460 Deportation ☐ 470 Racketeer Influenced and Corrupt Organizations ☐ 480 Consumer Credit ☐ 490 Cable/Sat TV ☐ 810 Selective Service ☐ 850 Securities/Commodities/ Exchange
REAL PROPERTY ☐ 210 Land Condemnation ☐ 220 Foreclosure ☐ 230 Rent Lease & Ejectment ☐ 240 Torts to Land ☐ 245 Tort Product Liability ☐ 290 All Other Real Property	**CIVIL RIGHTS** ☐ 441 Voting ☐ 442 Employment ☐ 443 Housing/ Accommodations ☐ 444 Welfare ☐ 445 Amer. w/Disabilities - Employment ☐ 446 Amer. w/Disabilities - Other ☐ 440 Other Civil Rights	**PRISONER PETITIONS** ☐ 510 Motions to Vacate Sentence **Habeas Corpus:** ☐ 530 General ☐ 535 Death Penalty ☐ 540 Mandamus & Other ☐ 550 Civil Rights ☐ 555 Prison Condition	**LABOR** ☐ 710 Fair Labor Standards Act ☐ 720 Labor/Mgmt. Relations ☐ 730 Labor/Mgmt. Reporting & Disclosure Act ☐ 740 Railway Labor Act ☐ 790 Other Labor Litigation ☐ 791 Empl. Ret. Inc. Security Act **IMMIGRATION** ☐ 462 Naturalization Application ☐ 463 Habeas Corpus - Alien Detainee ☐ 465 Other Immigration Actions	**SOCIAL SECURITY** ☐ 861 HIA (1395ff) ☐ 862 Black Lung (923) ☐ 863 DIWC/DIWW (405(g)) ☐ 864 SSID Title XVI ☐ 865 RSI (405(g)) **FEDERAL TAX SUITS** ☐ 870 Taxes (U.S. Plaintiff or Defendant) ☐ 871 IRS—Third Party 26 USC 7609	☐ 875 Customer Challenge 12 USC 3410 ☐ 890 Other Statutory Actions ☐ 891 Agricultural Acts ☐ 892 Economic Stabilization Act ☐ 893 Environmental Matters ☐ 894 Energy Allocation Act ☐ 895 Freedom of Information Act ☐ 900 Appeal of Fee Determination Under Equal Access to Justice ☐ 950 Constitutionality of State Statutes

V. ORIGIN   (Place an "X" in One Box Only)

☐ 1   Original Proceeding   ☐ 2   Removed from State Court   ☐ 3   Remanded from Appellate Court   ☐ 4   Reinstated or Reopened   ☐ 5   Transferred from another district (specify)   ☐ 6   Multidistrict Litigation   ☐ 7   Appeal to District Judge from Magistrate Judgment

VI. CAUSE OF ACTION
Cite the U.S. Civil Statute under which you are filing (Do not cite jurisdictional statutes unless diversity):
Brief description of cause:

VII. REQUESTED IN COMPLAINT:	☐ CHECK IF THIS IS A CLASS ACTION UNDER F.R.C.P. 23	DEMAND $	CHECK YES only if demanded in complaint: JURY DEMAND: ☐ Yes ☐ No

VIII. RELATED CASE(S) IF ANY   (See instructions):   JUDGE _____   DOCKET NUMBER _____

DATE _____   SIGNATURE OF ATTORNEY OF RECORD _____

FOR OFFICE USE ONLY

RECEIPT # _____   AMOUNT _____   APPLYING IFP _____   JUDGE _____   MAG. JUDGE _____

Traditionally, the complaint had to be formally served upon the defendant, typically by an official such as a sheriff or federal marshal. More recently, many jurisdictions have permitted service by mail in order to avoid the expense of personal service. In 1993, Rule 4 of the Federal Rules of Civil Procedure was amended to provide for waiver of formal service of process.[20]

Under Rule 4(d)(1), a plaintiff can request that competent adults, corporations, and associations waive formal service of process. Pursuant to

---

20. For a discussion of the extensive 1993 amendments to Rule 4 and the resulting changes in service of process see Sinclair, "Service of Process: Amended Rule 4 and the Presumption of Jurisdiction," 14 *Rev. Litig.* 159 (1994); Siegel, "The New (Dec. 1, 1993) Rule 4 of the Federal Rules of Civil Procedure: Changes in Summons Service and Personal Jurisdiction," 151 F.R.D. 441 (Part I); 152 F.R.D. 249 (Part II) (1994).

Rule 4(d)(1), the plaintiff can send to these defendants by first-class mail a copy of the complaint and a written request that they waive formal service of process.[21] Rule 4(d)(1)(F) gives most defendants 30 days in which to return the waiver form, although defendants addressed outside a federal judicial district are given 60 days from the date on which the request is sent. If a defendant does not return the waiver form within 30 or 60 days, the plaintiff must formally serve the defendant pursuant to the provisions of Rule 4(e)–(j).

Why would a defendant make it easier for the plaintiff by waiving formal service of process? First of all, such a Rule 4(d) waiver does not waive any jurisdictional or venue defenses the defendant may have, but only constitutes a waiver of the Rule 12(b)(4) and (5) defenses of insufficiency of process and insufficiency of service of process.[22] Rule 4(d) also includes both a carrot and a stick encouraging waiver of formal service. Rule 4(d)(2) provides that if a domestic defendant fails, without good cause, to comply with the waiver request of a domestic plaintiff, "the court must impose on the defendant: (A) the expenses later incurred in making service; and (B) the reasonable expenses, including attorney's fees, of any motion required to collect those service expenses." Rule 4(d)(3) further provides that defendants who do timely return requested waivers are not required to answer the complaint until 60 (90, in the case of a foreign defendant) days after the request for waiver of service was sent. Otherwise, Rule 12(a)(1)(A)(i) gives defendants who decline to waive service of process only 21 days after service to respond to the complaint.

The waiver of service provision of Rule 4(d) can save all parties the expense of formal service, and with a foreign defendant, in particular, this can be a significant savings. However, waiver cannot be requested from infants and incompetents; the United States and its agencies, corporations and officers; and foreign, state, or local governments.[23] Even with respect to defendants subject to Rule 4(d), a plaintiff may choose not to exercise its right to seek a waiver of service. The plaintiff may decide to formally serve a particular defendant based on a belief that the defendant will not waive service or because of plaintiff's desire to expedite the lawsuit and not afford the defendant the automatic extension of time provided by Rule 4(d)(3). The plaintiff also should be careful not to seek a waiver if there is a need to effect service of process on the defendant to satisfy either an impending statute of limitations or Rule 4(m)'s 120 day time limit for service of process.[24]

---

21. The complaint and waiver request also can be sent by "reliable means" other than first-class mail. Fed. R. Civ. P. 4(d)(1)(G). These can include private messenger services and electronic facsimile transmission, which may be particularly efficient and cost-effective when seeking a waiver of service from a foreign defendant. Advisory Committee Note to 1993 Amendment to Rule 4, 146 F.R.D. 401, 563–64 (1993).

22. Fed. R. Civ. P. 4(d)(5); Advisory Committee Note to 1993 Amendment to Rule 4, 146 F.R.D. 401, 563 (1993).

23. Fed. R. Civ. P. 4(d)(1), (g), (i), (j).

24. *See* Advisory Committee Note to 1993 Amendment to Rule 4, 146 F.R.D. 401, 564–65 (1993). Rule 4(d)(4) provides that the summons and complaint are to be considered as having

If waiver of service is not requested or is declined, plaintiff's counsel must prepare a summons for each defendant. Rather than drafting your own summons, it's much easier to obtain from the clerk's office blank summons forms. The summons must be signed by the clerk or a deputy clerk and list the plaintiff, the name and address of the defendant who is being summoned, and the name and address of plaintiff's counsel. If a federal summons and complaint are not served upon a defendant within 120 days after the filing of the complaint, Rule 4(m) provides that the court must, absent good cause, dismiss the action as to that defendant or, if good cause is shown, direct that service be effected within a specified time. Defendants should be served as soon as possible, because under Rule 12(a)(1)(A)(i) a defendant's time for responding to the complaint does not start to run until he has been served with the summons and complaint. If the defendant has waived formal service, Rule 12(a)(1)(A)(ii) provides that defendant's 60 or 90 day response time begins when the request for waiver was sent.

While the requirements for service of process vary from jurisdiction to jurisdiction, they generally are not difficult to master. The local clerk's office may have a handout or page on its website listing service and other filing requirements, or a friendly clerk's office employee may help smooth your initial case filings and service of process. The trickiest aspect of service of process may be learning where the defendant can be served.[25]

E.   SUIT PREREQUISITES CHECK LIST

Until such analysis becomes second nature, it may help to develop a chart or check list setting forth the prerequisites for any civil action. One way in which to organize this material is illustrated in Figure 4–2. In addition to the general suit prerequisites shown in Figure 4–2, counsel should consider more particularized prerequisites for the filing of specific claims. Counsel should determine, for example, whether there is a requirement that notice be given or an administrative claim be filed prior to suit. Most significantly, the statute of limitations for the claim in question must be determined as soon as possible. By using a chart such as Figure 4–2, attorneys can test their complaints before filing and can anticipate possible defense responses to those complaints.

---

been served at the time the completed waiver is filed with the court, not at the time that the request for waiver is served or the defendant receives the request.

25. *See United States ex rel. Mayo v. Satan and His Staff,* 54 F.R.D. 282 (W.D.Pa. 1971) (complaint dismissed because plaintiff did not include with it directions for serving defendant Satan). *See generally* Yablon, "Suing the Devil: A Guide for Practitioners," 86 *Va. L. Rev.* 103 (2000).

In a lawsuit stemming from the September 11, 2001, attack on the World Trade Center, a federal district judge authorized service upon Osama Bin Laden and Al Qaeda by publication in several Afghani and Pakistani newspapers and on broadcast networks in the Middle East and around the world. *Smith v. Islamic Emirate of Afghanistan,* 2001 WL 1658211 (S.D.N.Y. 2001).

FIGURE 4–2
PREREQUISITES FOR A FEDERAL CIVIL ACTION *

SUIT PREREQUISITE	Subject Matter Jurisdiction Rule 12(b)(1)	Personal Jurisdiction Rule 12(b)(2)	Venue Rule 12(b)(3)	Process Rule 12(b)(4)	Service of Process Rule 12(b)(5)
TEST(S)	1) Fed. Question: action "arise[s] under the Constitution, laws or treaties of the United States," 28 U.S.C. § 1331; or 2) Diversity of Citizenship: complete diversity of citizenship and more than $75,000 in controversy, 28 U.S.C. § 1332.	Minimum contacts test of International Shoe Co. v. Washington, 326 U.S. 310 (1945): 1) Minimum contacts with forum state; 2) Suit arises from contacts (unless general jurisdiction exists); and 3) Suit does not offend "traditional notions of fair play and substantial justice."	1) Specified in substantive statute; or 2) 28 U.S.C. § 1391: a) where any defendant resides (if all in same state); b) where a substantial part of events/omissions giving rise to claim occurred or subject property is situated; or, if no other venue, (c) where any defendant is subject to personal jurisdiction (diversity) or where any defendant may be found (non–diversity).	Federal Rule of Civil Procedure 4(a) and (b) and Form 3.	Federal Rule of Civil Procedure 4(c)–(n) and Forms 5 and 6.

* In addition to the prerequisites shown, the complaint must state a claim upon which relief can be granted (Rule 12(b)(6)) and any Rule 19 indispensable parties must be joined (Rule 12(b)(7)). There also are special federal statutes governing subject matter jurisdiction and venue that have not been shown.

F. CIVIL ACTIONS IN CYBERSPACE

The prerequisites for a civil action have changed over the years, although the changes have been evolutionary rather than revolutionary in nature.

1. How does the Internet change a plaintiff's ability to obtain personal jurisdiction over a defendant? *Compare Mink v. AAAA Development LLC*, 190 F.3d 333 (5th Cir. 1999) (website containing information about defendant's products and services but through which orders cannot be placed does not constitute sufficient presence in Texas to subject defendant to personal jurisdiction) *with Zippo Manufacturing Co. v. Zippo Dot Com*, 952 F.Supp. 1119 (W.D.Pa. 1997) (use of defendant's website to transact business with Pennsylvania subscribers to its Internet news service subjects defendant to personal jurisdiction in Pennsylvania). Applying traditional personal jurisdiction principles, courts have concluded that the mere creation of a site on the World Wide Web is not sufficient to subject one to personal jurisdiction wherever that site can be viewed.

Cybersell Inc. v. Cybersell Inc., 130 F.3d 414 (9th Cir. 1997). *See also Griffis v. Luban*, 646 N.W.2d 527, 536 (Minn. 2002) ("The mere fact that messages posted to the newsgroup *could* have been read in Alabama, just as they *could* have been read anywhere in the world, cannot suffice to establish Alabama as the focal point of the defendant's conduct."). *See generally* J. Zittrain, *Jurisdiction (Internet Law Series)* (2005); Symposium, "Personal Jurisdiction in the Internet Age," 98 *Nw. U. L. Rev.* 409 (2004); "Developments in the Law—The Law of Cyberspace," 112 *Harv. L. Rev.* 1574 (1999); "Internet Law Symposium," 19 *Pace L. Rev.* 1 (1998).

2. While at least one court has suggested that "attempting to apply established trademark law in the fast-developing world of the internet is somewhat like trying to board a moving bus," *Bensusan Restaurant Corp. v. King*, 126 F.3d 25, 27 (2d Cir. 1997), others have suggested that, while the technology has changed, the governing legal principles remain the same. Redish, "Of New Wine and Old Bottles: Personal Jurisdiction, the Internet, and the Nature of Constitutional Evolution," 38 *Jurimetrics J.* 575 (1998); Stein, "The Unexceptional Problem of Jurisdiction in Cyberspace," 32 *Int'l Lawyer* 1167 (1998).

3. Rule 5(d)(3) of the Federal Rules of Civil Procedure authorizes district courts to adopt local rules permitting or requiring papers to be "filed, signed, or verified by electronic means." Acting pursuant to Rule 5, electronic filing has been authorized in virtually all federal district courts. *E.g.*, Rule 5.1 of the United States District Court for the Northern District of Ohio; *In re Electronic Filing Procedures*, Administrative Order 97–12 (E.D.N.Y. Oct. 22, 1997). Through companies such as E-filing.com, complaints and other legal documents can be filed in many state courts as well. Judge Marvin Aspen has predicted that soon "all filing will be electronic, and status and motion calls will be by telephone or videoconferencing." Drummond, "The Electronic Courthouse," *Litigation News*, March 2000, at 4. The 2006 amendments to Rule 5 authorized federal courts to require (rather than just permit) electronic filing; Rule 5(d)(3) now provides: "A local rule may require electronic filing only if reasonable exceptions are allowed." This provision was added to the 2006 amendments to Rule 5(e) because "[s]everal major bar associations, including the American Bar Association, expressed concern during the public comment period that mandatory electronic case filing would pose hardships for litigants who do not have access to a personal computer and suggested that the national rules require that any local rule include appropriate exceptions." Report of the Judicial Conference Committee on Rules of Practice and Procedure, 234 F.R.D. 219, 270 (2006). *See, e.g.*, Rule CV–5 of the United States District Court for the Eastern District of Texas (requiring electronic filing of all documents in civil actions, except for, *inter alia*, proof of service of the initial papers in a civil action and filings from pro se litigants).

4. Rule 5(b)(2)(E) permits electronic service of papers and pleadings other than the complaint upon parties who have consented to such service in writing. This written consent can be provided electronically, but con-

sent cannot be implied from the mere listing of an email address on a law firm letterhead. Advisory Committee Note to the 2001 Amendment to Rule 5, 200 F.R.D. 52, 76 (2001). Rule 5(b)(2)(E) also provides that electronic service is complete on transmission, "but is not effective if the serving party learns that it did not reach the person to be served." By consenting to electronic service pursuant to Rule 5(b)(2)(E), a party also consents to electronic service of orders and judgments from the court pursuant to Federal Rule of Civil Procedure 77(d).

5.   Rule 5(b)(3) authorizes local rules pursuant to which parties can use the court's own transmission facilities to effect service upon other parties. Under such a rule, a party can electronically file one document with the court, and that document then is electronically served upon other parties by and through the court's own transmission facilities.

Electronic service pursuant to Rule 5(b)(2)(E) requires written consent by the party to be served. As an incentive to such consent, Rule 6(d) gives a party who is served electronically three additional days in which to respond to the served document. The Advisory Committee Note to the 2001 Amendment to Rule 5, 200 F.R.D. 52, 73 (2001), suggests, "A district court may establish a registry or other facility that allows advance consent to service by specified means for future actions."

6.   Court papers other than the complaint thus can be served electronically, so long as the person served has consented in writing to such service. However, Rule 4 of the Federal Rules of Civil Procedure, rather than Rule 5, governs service of the summons and complaint. Is there a way in which to achieve electronic service pursuant to Rule 4(d)?

What if the defendant refuses to consent to electronic service of process (due to lack of access to electronic communications or for other reasons)? Several United States courts have upheld electronic service of process upon defendants outside the United States pursuant to Federal Rule of Civil Procedure 4(f)(3), "by other means not prohibited by international agreement, as the court orders." *E.g.*, *Rio Properties, Inc. v. Rio Int'l Interlink*, 284 F.3d 1007, 1014–1019 (9th Cir. 2002); *Williams v. Advertising Sex LLC*, 231 F.R.D. 483 (N.D.W.Va. 2005); *Ryan v. Brunswick Corp.*, 2002 WL 1628933 (W.D.N.Y. 2002); *Broadfoot v. Diaz (In re Int'l Telemedia Associates, Inc.)*, 245 B.R. 713, 717–22 (Bankr. N.D.Ga. 2000).

Outside the United States, a British judge has authorized email service of an injunction upon an unknown individual who had sent harassing emails to a British rock star from somewhere in Europe. Staib, "British Court Authorizes E-mail Service of Process," *Litigation News*, Nov. 1996, at 3. *See generally* Stewart & Conley, "E–Mail Service on Foreign Defendants: Time for an International Approach?," 38 *Geo. J. Int'l L.* 755 (2007); Colby, "You've Got Mail: The Modern Trend Towards Universal Electronic Service of Process," 51 *Buff. L. Rev.* 337 (2003); Tamayo, "Catch Me If You Can: Serving United States Process on an Elusive Defendant Abroad," 17 *Harv. J. L & Tech.* 211 (2003); Tamayo,

"Are You Being Served?: E–Mail and (Due) Service of Process," 51 *S.C. L. Rev.* 227 (2000). More recently, service via Facebook has been authorized by judges in Australia and New Zealand. Keall, "Could you get served via Twitter?," *Nat'l Bus. Rev.*, Mar. 17, 2009, http://www.nbr.co.nz/article/could-you-get-served-twitter–83171.

7. Before serving complaints, briefs, or other papers electronically, counsel should be aware of just what information they may be sharing with others. Modern software makes it possible to uncover changes to, and earlier drafts of, many word-processed documents. Opposing counsel therefore may be able to determine claims or arguments that were discarded in composing a document, as well as notes that may have been made regarding that document during its preparation. To reduce such risks, counsel can convert documents to rich text format (RTF) or portable document format (PDF) before they are sent to others. Beckman, "Word Processing Documents Reveal Drafters' Secrets," *Litigation News* (Nov. 2003), at 1. Indeed, an attorney's duty to exercise reasonable care not to reveal client confidences or secrets may in some circumstances require the attorney to remove metadata from documents before they are exchanged with opposing counsel. N.Y. State Bar Ass'n Comm. on Prof'l Ethics, Op. 782 (2004).

8. Not only can electronic filing and service save parties time and money, but court websites can be quite useful in searching dockets, obtaining copies of orders and opinions, obtaining local rules, standing orders, and forms, checking the court's calendar, and learning about the judges. *See, e.g.*, Website of the United States District Court for the Northern District of Georgia, http://www.gand.uscourts.gov. Through the Federal Judiciary Homepage (http://www.uscourts.gov), the homepages of individual federal courts of appeal and district courts easily can be located.

9. The United States District Court for the Northern District of California requires that designated documents in class actions governed by the Private Securities Litigation Reform Act of 1995, Pub. L. No. 104–67, 109 Stat. 737 (1995), must be posted on a designated Internet site. Rule 23–2(a) of the United States District Court for the Northern District of California. One such site, the Stanford Law School Securities Class Action Clearinghouse (http://securities.stanford.edu), contains copies of complaints filed in securities fraud actions, as well as other litigation documents, docket sheets, settlement agreements, articles, statistics, and other information concerning securities fraud actions.

III. THE CLAIMS ASSERTED

Even after determining that the prerequisites for a civil action can be satisfied, counsel still must determine what the scope of plaintiff's action should be and what specific claims should be asserted. As with other aspects of pretrial litigation, both legal and strategic considerations should guide counsel in making these determinations.

Proof check lists were discussed in Chapter 3.[26] These check lists should help counsel organize both prefiling legal research and factual investigation. Commercial form books may be useful in suggesting potential claims. Based upon preliminary research and investigation, counsel should be aware of the possible claims that plaintiff can assert. In drafting the complaint, counsel must choose those claims that actually *should* be asserted by plaintiff.

Initially, counsel should consider whether the prerequisites to suit discussed in the previous section of this chapter have been met for each potential claim. Even if the suit prerequisites can be satisfied for each claim individually, there may be no single forum in which all of the possible claims can be heard. Plaintiff may have claims against several defendants, but there may be no forum in which all defendants are subject to personal jurisdiction. In such a situation, counsel must determine whether to file separate lawsuits or proceed with as many of the claims as possible in the most advantageous forum.

It's also possible that the assertion of a particular type of claim may permit the court to entertain additional claims that it otherwise could not consider. A party may be able to use interpleader to bring several property claimants into a single forum despite difficulties with subject matter jurisdiction, personal jurisdiction, venue, or service of process that otherwise would preclude party joinder.[27] Under 28 U.S.C. § 1367, a federal court with original subject matter jurisdiction may be able to exercise supplemental jurisdiction over additional, constitutionally-related claims that it otherwise could not entertain.[28]

Counsel must be sure to determine the statutes of limitations applicable to all potential claims. Instead of a single statute of limitations governing all claims, there may be separate statutes of limitations governing, for instance, tort and contract claims.[29]

Rule 8(d) of the Federal Rules of Civil Procedure may have a bearing upon the claims that can be asserted in the complaint. Rule 8(d)(2) provides that a party "may set out two or more statements of a claim or defense alternately or hypothetically," while Rule 8(d)(3) allows a party to

---

26. *See* Figures 3–1 and 3–2, *supra* pp. 63; 64.

27. 28 U.S.C. §§ 1335, 1397, 2361; Fed. R. Civ. P. 22.

28. Section 1367 represented an attempt by Congress to codify the doctrines of pendent and ancillary jurisdiction recognized in *United Mine Workers v. Gibbs,* 383 U.S. 715, 725 (1966) (pendent jurisdiction) and *Moore v. New York Cotton Exchange,* 270 U.S. 593 (1926) (ancillary jurisdiction). However, important questions concerning the interpretation of that statute, and the scope of supplemental jurisdiction, remain. *See* Oakley, "Joinder and Jurisdiction in the Federal District Courts: The State of the Union of Rules and Statutes," 69 *Tenn. L. Rev.* 35 (2001); Pfander, "Supplemental Jurisdiction and Section 1367: The Case for a Sympathetic Textualism," 148 *U. Pa. L. Rev.* 109 (1999); Symposium: "A Reappraisal of the Supplemental–Jurisdiction Statute: Title 28 U.S.C. § 1367," 74 *Ind. L. J.* 1 (1998).

29. Some state statutes of limitations draw even finer lines than this. In *Owens v. Okure,* 488 U.S. 235 (1989), the Supreme Court had to determine whether the appropriate New York statute of limitations that a federal court should borrow in an action brought under 42 U.S.C. § 1983 was the statute of limitations governing intentional torts or the residual statute of limitations for personal injury claims not covered by other, specific statutes of limitations.

"state as many separate claims or defenses as it has, regardless of consistency." Although there is no requirement that the complaint contain only consistent claims, it is important to have a relatively simple and consistent theory of the case by the time the action is presented at trial. There may not be enough information available at the time that the complaint is drafted, though, to permit counsel to confidently reject all inconsistent claims. In that case, Rule 8(d)(3) allows counsel to plead inconsistent claims until discovery permits an intelligent choice to be made among the possibilities.

Counsel must consider the defendant's likely response to any of the claims that plaintiff might assert. If plaintiff decides to file claims in state court, can the defendant remove them to federal court? Will the filing of a particular claim permit the defendant to obtain information in discovery that plaintiff would rather protect from disclosure? Will the defendant respond to the action by seeking a stay or by attempting to bring third-parties into the suit?

The assertion of a particular claim by the plaintiff may permit or encourage the defendant to assert certain claims that he otherwise would not. Federal Rule of Civil Procedure 13(b) permits a defendant to assert permissive counterclaims against the plaintiff, while Rule 13(a)(1)(A) requires the defendant to assert most claims that "arise[ ] out of the transaction or occurrence that is the subject matter of the [complaint]." Rule 13(c) provides that counterclaims can request more and different relief than that sought in plaintiff's complaint. In addition, the defendant's assertion of a counterclaim can limit the plaintiff's ability to voluntarily dismiss his action.[30]

Always of great significance is the choice of defendants who will be sued. To the extent that there are indispensable parties or others can successfully intervene in an action, the plaintiff may not be able to control the parties to the suit. Where these problems don't exist, it is in plaintiff's interest to consider carefully who will be named as a defendant.

The same basic relief often can be sought from several potential defendants. Monetary damages may be available both from a governmental unit and from individual government officials. In such a case, naming the officials as defendants in their individual capacities actually may weaken the plaintiff's case at trial; the individual defendants not only may possess qualified immunities but a jury may be concerned that they will be financially ruined by a sizeable plaintiff's verdict. Similar concerns are rarely felt for governmental institutions.

Some of the benefits of naming a person as a party may be obtainable in other ways. One of the advantages of naming a person as a defendant is that the individual is then subject to all of the discovery devices recognized under the Federal Rules of Civil Procedure. However, it may be possible to reach an agreement under which a person will provide discovery voluntarily if he is not named as a defendant in the lawsuit.

---

30.   See Fed. R. Civ. P. 41(a)(2).

There are, though, litigation benefits that only can be obtained by naming individuals as plaintiffs or defendants. Federal diversity jurisdiction can be created or destroyed depending upon the parties to the suit. Even if there is diversity among the parties, removal from state court can be prevented pursuant to 28 U.S.C. § 1441(b) by naming as a defendant a citizen of the state in which suit is brought. However, the naming of parties must be done in good faith. Not only must counsel satisfy the requirements of Rule 11, but a federal statute specifically precludes collusive party joinder to invoke the jurisdiction of the federal courts.[31]

A possible judicial venue may be defeated if all defendants do not reside in the same state.[32] The venue in which a claim is heard can be quite significant. The sympathies of judges and juries, as well as the time it may take to get a case to trial, vary from jurisdiction to jurisdiction, and the "home court advantage" is important in any lawsuit. In addition, the choice of law rule (and, thus, the governing substantive law) may vary depending upon the venue of the suit.

Plaintiff's counsel should both consider the jurisdictional implications of naming certain defendants and assess the manner in which an action will be defended by each potential defendant. While a large corporation may present a classic "deep pocket" into which a plaintiff would like to dip, the ferocity of the defense that such a corporation will raise may give plaintiff's counsel second thoughts about naming the corporation if other, fiscally sound, defendants exist.

Plaintiff's counsel also should consider the probable interaction among various potential defendants. Pitting defendants against one another generally will work to plaintiff's advantage, as will the naming of a defendant who is likely to settle quickly and offer the plaintiff help in his claims against the remaining defendants.

The relief, including attorneys' fees, that can be awarded under any particular claim is of major significance in claim selection, and it is specifically considered in the next section of this chapter. Counsel also should be alert to any possible procedural hurdles that may be created by the manner in which the lawsuit is crafted. A fraud claim must be pled with greater specificity than other claims,[33] while there are several procedural prerequisites for the bringing of a shareholder derivative action.[34]

Counsel's aim should be to ultimately take plaintiff's strongest claims before the trier of fact. Which claims are the "strongest" will depend upon factors such as the possible relief that can be obtained in connection with each claim, the ease or difficulty of proving individual claims, the appeal to the judge or jury of each claim, and the extent to which the pleading of

---

31.   28 U.S.C. § 1359. *See also* Federal Rule of Civil Procedure 23.1(b)(2), which provides that, in a shareholder derivative action, a verified complaint must allege "that the action is not a collusive one to confer jurisdiction that the court would otherwise lack."

32.   *See* 28 U.S.C. § 1391(a)(1), (b)(1).

33.   Fed. R. Civ. P. 9(b).

34.   Fed. R. Civ. P. 23.1.

one claim will make it more or less difficult to plead other claims. In selecting among the possibilities, it's better to go with fewer, stronger claims than to clutter the complaint with every colorable claim that a creative attorney can devise.

NOTES AND QUESTIONS CONCERNING THE CLAIMS ASSERTED

1. An example of selecting particular defendants to ensure a specific forum occurred in *World–Wide Volkswagen Corp. v. Woodson,* 444 U.S. 286 (1980), in which Justice Blackmun "confess[ed] that [he was] somewhat puzzled why the plaintiffs in this litigation are so insistent that the regional distributor and the retail dealer * * * be named defendants." 444 U.S. at 317. Plaintiffs' counsel later explained that his interest had not been in obtaining any additional damages from these defendants, but in destroying diversity of citizenship that otherwise would have permitted defendants to remove the action to federal court from an extremely favorable plaintiff's forum in state court. Weintraub, "Due Process Limitations on the Personal Jurisdiction of State Courts: Time for Change," 63 *Or. L. Rev.* 485, 500 n.98 (1984).

2. Another, unsuccessful, example of this same tactic involved Pete Rose's attempt to enjoin the Commissioner of Baseball from disciplining him. Rose's state court action named not only Commissioner Giamatti but the Cincinnati Reds and Major League Baseball as defendants. Although complete diversity of citizenship did not exist upon the face of the complaint, a federal district judge held that the Cincinnati Reds and Major League Baseball were nominal parties whose citizenship should be ignored in determining diversity jurisdiction. The case therefore was held to have been properly removed to federal court, and Rose's claims were decided in that court rather than before a very sympathetic elected state court judge. *Rose v. Giamatti,* 721 F.Supp. 906 (S.D.Ohio 1989). *See generally* Rosenthal, "Improper Joinder: Confronting Plaintiffs' Attempts to Destroy Federal Subject Matter Jurisdiction," 59 *Am. U. L. Rev.* 49 (2009).

3. There were approximately 600 plaintiffs in the major Buffalo Creek lawsuit filed in the United States District Court for the Southern District of West Virginia. Why wasn't this action filed as a class action?

4. How much input should plaintiffs have in the selection of the particular claims that will be asserted in the complaint? Are attorneys required to consult with, or advise, clients concerning the selection of claims?

IV. THE RELIEF REQUESTED

Remedies is a subject worthy of separate, and extended, study by all litigation attorneys. This section merely touches on some of the major points that should be considered by counsel in selecting among the possible remedies available in a civil action.

Attorneys should never forget that, while they may be very proud of creatively pled complaints, the bottom line for most clients is the relief that they ultimately do or do not recover. Attorneys must be diligent to ensure that the relief sought is what their clients really desire. There often are strategic advantages in prosecuting a case as a class action. However, because of the potential costs and delays that class action treatment usually entails, many plaintiffs may not be well served by class certification. A client's desire for a specific type of relief, as well as the immediacy with which relief is needed, should guide the attorney's pleading and prosecution of all cases.

A. THE POSSIBLE RELIEF

The relief available in a civil action may be legal, equitable, or declaratory in nature. In addition, a prevailing plaintiff may be entitled to the recovery of attorneys' fees and costs. One of counsel's major jobs is to determine which types of relief may be available in a given action and then to consult with the client so that the most appropriate relief can be requested and ultimately obtained.

The most common form of legal relief is monetary damages. Within the category of damages, however, there are several different subcategories. The most common damages are compensatory damages, which are to compensate an individual for a loss that he or she has suffered. A major difficulty with compensatory damages is attempting to determine what amount of monetary relief will compensate an individual for certain injuries. Not only can it be difficult to place a monetary value on some losses, but implicit in the very concept of compensatory damages is the assumption that a fair market value can be placed upon anything. Contrary to this assumption, a person may not be willing to part with a photograph or family heirloom for an objectively determined fair market value, even if such an objective value could be established.

Compensatory damages can be further subdivided into general and special damages. Both general and special damages result from the defendant's actions, but special damages are to compensate plaintiff for injuries that are not the necessary consequence of those actions. While pain and suffering is considered an element of general damages in a personal injury suit, medical bills and harm to earning capacity usually are classified as special damages.[35] The major significance of the not-too-neat categorization of compensatory damages as general or special is that Federal Rule of Civil Procedure 9(g) requires that special damages be specifically pled. What this means will vary from case to case, but the specificity requirement of Rule 9(g) usually will be considered satisfied if the opposing party has been provided with sufficient information to prepare his responsive pleading and defense.[36]

In certain cases the plaintiff may be entitled to punitive, as well as compensatory, damages. Punitive damages are not to compensate the

---

35. *Restatement (Second) of Torts* § 904 (1979). *See also* 5A C. Wright & A. Miller, *Federal Practice and Procedure* § 1310 (3d ed. 2004).

36. 5A C. Wright & A. Miller, *Federal Practice and Procedure* § 1311 (3d ed. 2004).

injured plaintiff, but instead are to punish the defendant and deter conduct such as defendant's in the future. Punitive damages may be particularly attractive to plaintiffs who are entitled to relatively little compensatory relief. However, the plaintiff must establish that the defendant's conduct was willful or reckless to obtain an award of punitive damages.[37]

Monetary damages also may be limited, or liquidated, either by private party agreement or by statute. The parties' contract may have provided for specific liquidated damages upon breach of the contract. For that matter, plaintiff may be barred from bringing a civil action because of an agreement to submit his claim to arbitration rather than to the courts.[38]

The damages recoverable for certain statutory violations also may be statutorily fixed. The federal Truth in Lending Act sets the recoveries for certain lending violations as "twice the amount of any finance charge in connection with the transaction, or * * * 25 per centum of the total amount of monthly payments under the lease, except that the liability under this subparagraph shall not be less than $100 nor greater than $1000."[39] The provision for the award of costs and attorneys' fees in successful enforcement actions[40] is to encourage private parties to initiate lawsuits to enforce the act.

In certain cases a party may be able to recover nominal damages. Nominal damages may be awarded to a plaintiff when his monetary loss is difficult to measure or prove.[41] While the actual nominal damages recovered may be only $1.00, the significance of such a recovery may be that, under certain fee-shifting statutes, the prevailing party thereby becomes entitled to an award of attorneys' fees.[42]

If legal relief would be an inadequate remedy, the plaintiff may be entitled to equitable relief. As its name indicates, equitable relief was developed in the English courts of equity, which were able to tailor relief more precisely than could the English law courts. Rather than ordering the defendant to pay money to the plaintiff, equitable decrees generally require the defendant to take some other, specific act. The equitable relief most often of interest to modern attorneys is the injunction.[43]

---

37. *Browning–Ferris Industries v. Kelco Disposal, Inc.*, 492 U.S. 257, 279 n. 24 (1989). *See generally* J. Kircher & C. Wiseman, *Punitive Damages, Law and Practice* (2d ed. 2000).

38. *E.g., Rodriguez de Quijas v. Shearson/American Express, Inc.*, 490 U.S. 477 (1989); *Shearson/American Express, Inc. v. McMahon*, 482 U.S. 220 (1987).

39. 15 U.S.C. § 1640(a)(2)(A)(ii).

40. 15 U.S.C. § 1640(a)(3).

41. *E.g., Carey v. Piphus*, 435 U.S. 247 (1978).

42. *Nephew v. City of Aurora*, 830 F.2d 1547 (10th Cir.1987) (*en banc*), *cert. denied*, 485 U.S. 976 (1988); *Milwe v. Cavuoto*, 653 F.2d 80 (2d Cir.1981). *But see Farrar v. Hobby*, 506 U.S. 103 (1992) (while plaintiff who sought compensatory damages of $17,000,000 but received only $1.00 in nominal damages is "prevailing party" under 42 U.S.C. § 1988, he should receive no fee award under that statute).

43. Concerning injunctions generally see O. Fiss, *The Civil Rights Injunction* (1978); Denlow, "The Motion for a Preliminary Injunction: Time for a Uniform Federal Standard," 22 *Rev. Litig.*

Under Federal Rule of Civil Procedure 65, federal district courts have the authority to issue permanent injunctions, preliminary injunctions, and temporary restraining orders. While the violation of any injunction may be punished as contempt, the major distinguishing features of the different types of injunctions are their duration and the procedural requirements established by Rule 65 for their issuance.

Permanent injunctive relief issues after full adjudicatory proceedings and usually takes the form of a permanent order to a party to take or refrain from taking certain action. A preliminary injunction, on the other hand, is a court order of limited duration that often issues after a truncated judicial hearing. Preliminary injunctions usually are issued merely to preserve the status quo until the court can hear the merits of a case.

Different types of injunctions can be sought and granted in the same case. In the *Pentagon Papers* litigation, the United States sought not only (1) permanent injunctions prohibiting the defendant newspapers from publishing information concerning the conduct of the Vietnam War but also (2) preliminary injunctions enjoining publication until its requests for permanent injunctions could be decided and (3) temporary restraining orders enjoining publication until preliminary injunction hearings could be held.[44]

Rule 65(b) of the Federal Rules of Civil Procedure recognizes and establishes certain requirements for temporary restraining orders. Temporary restraining orders typically are sought when there is not enough time for the court to hear a motion for a preliminary injunction and the moving party will suffer irreparable injury if the restraining order does not issue. A temporary restraining order might be sought by a person who is about to be evicted from an apartment building or deported from the country for allegedly illegal reasons. The temporary restraining orders sought in these cases would be to prevent the landlord from evicting the plaintiff or the government from deporting the plaintiff until the court can hold a hearing on a preliminary or permanent injunction.

While even preliminary injunctions cannot issue in the federal courts without notice to the opposing party,[45] temporary restraining orders can in certain circumstances.[46] However, Rule 65(b) contains numerous procedural requirements for the issuance of temporary restraining orders and provides that these orders only can last for 14 days (unless extended during the initial 14 day period for an additional 14 days).

---

495 (2003); Leubsdorf, "The Standard for Preliminary Injunctions," 91 *Harv. L. Rev.* 525 (1978); "Developments in the Law—Injunctions," 78 *Harv. L. Rev.* 994 (1965).

In appropriate cases, attorneys should consider other equitable remedies such as specific performance, rescission, restitution, and reformation.

44. *See New York Times Co. v. United States,* 403 U.S. 713 (1971) (per curiam).

45. Fed. R. Civ. P. 65(a)(1).

46. *See* Fed. R. Civ. P. 65(b)(1).

The final major type of relief on the merits is a declaratory judgment. Such a judicial declaration of the rights and obligations of the parties has the same force as any other final judgment.[47] In the federal courts, declaratory relief is addressed in 28 U.S.C. §§ 2201 and 2202 and Federal Rule of Civil Procedure 57. In contrast to equitable relief, a declaratory judgment can be awarded despite the adequacy of other relief.[48] A declaratory judgment may be of great importance to a person who is about to embark on a course of conduct but would first like a judicial declaration of the legal consequences of the conduct.[49] Declaratory judgment claims also sometimes are filed as an offshoot of other litigation to determine the extent of the litigants' insurance coverage.

If a plaintiff prevails on the merits of his claims, he may be entitled to an award of attorneys' fees and costs. Rule 54(d)(1) of the Federal Rules of Civil Procedure provides that, generally, "costs—other than attorney's fees—should be allowed to the prevailing party." However, 28 U.S.C. § 1920 defines recoverable "costs" quite narrowly, limiting costs to such items as fees of the clerk and marshal, docket fees, and fees for transcripts and copies of papers "necessarily obtained for use in the case."

The most significant legal cost, the cost of counsel, may not be recoverable by the prevailing party. At common law the American Rule traditionally precluded the prevailing party from the recovery of attorneys' fees, but in recent years the Congress and state legislatures have enacted laws specifically providing for the recovery of attorneys' fees by prevailing parties.[50] In addition, some of the Federal Rules of Civil Procedure may operate to shift fees and costs in specific situations.[51]

The preceding discussion is merely a summary of the various types of relief that may be available in certain civil actions. Attorneys must carefully consider the types of relief available in each particular case and choose the relief best suited to the needs of their individual clients.

B. PRACTICAL CONSIDERATIONS CONCERNING THE RELIEF REQUESTED

Before requesting relief, the attorney should be sure that all of the prerequisites for the award of that relief have been met. A temporary restraining order hearing may be counsel's first appearance before the judge, who may not be happy about the manner in which the hearing

---

47. 28 U.S.C. § 2201(a).

48. Fed. R. Civ. P. 57.

49. In order for a declaratory judgment to issue, though, there must be an actual "case or controversy" between the parties. In *Int'l Longshoremen's & Warehousemen's Union v. Boyd,* 347 U.S. 222 (1954), the Supreme Court held that a district court could not issue a declaratory judgment concerning the proper interpretation of an immigration statute until the plaintiff aliens had left the mainland United States and sought readmission under that statute.

50. *See Alyeska Pipeline Service Co. v. Wilderness Society,* 421 U.S. 240, 260 n. 33 (1975) (listing more than 30 federal statutory exceptions to American Rule).

51. *See* Fed. R. Civ. P. 11, 16(f), 26(g), 37, 41(d), 68.

intrudes upon pending trials or other proceedings. Counsel therefore should not seek relief such as a temporary restraining order unless she is fairly certain that her client is entitled to that relief.

Plaintiff's counsel also should be realistic concerning the relief that is demanded. Counsel should restrain themselves in drafting the prayer for relief and be reasonable in the amount of damages requested.[52] Indeed, there often is an inverse relation between the damages sought and the seriousness of the action. In deciding upon the relief to be requested, consider whether opposing counsel could ridicule your entire case by reading plaintiff's prayer to the jury. Not only has a federal court of appeals upheld the imposition of Rule 11 sanctions due to an inflated prayer for relief,[53] but Rule 54(c) provides that, except for default judgments, every final judgment "should grant the relief to which each party is entitled, even if the party has not demanded that relief in its pleadings."

In drafting a demand for damages, counsel should consider requesting damages in a very precise amount. The prayer for relief might request $997,956.43 rather than $1,000,000. While the first figure presumably has been quite precisely calculated, the request for the round amount of one million dollars may strike the judge or jury as inflated and less principled. By providing listings of damage awards for specific types of cases in a given jurisdiction, jury verdict reporting services can help counsel determine a reasonable prayer for relief.

Counsel should consider the possible effect that a request for relief may have upon discovery. A request for punitive damages may entitle plaintiff to discovery concerning defendant's financial resources, while a preliminary injunction request may provide a basis for obtaining discovery sooner than otherwise would be possible under the Federal Rules of Civil Procedure.

In addition to carefully considering the specific relief requested, counsel should consider the procedures that will be employed to resolve plaintiff's claims. For example, attorneys should be aware of the provisions for prosecuting an action *in forma pauperis* in the federal courts. Under 28 U.S.C. § 1915, a civil action may be prosecuted without the normal prepayment of court fees and the indigent party may be provided with a record of the trial court proceedings for the purposes of appeal.

A major decision in any case is whether to request a jury trial. This decision will depend upon such factors as the judge who otherwise will decide the case, the "jury appeal" of plaintiff's case, the potential delay if a jury is utilized, and any differences in the evidence that will or will not be admitted if a jury, rather than a judge, hears the case. Here, too, jury

---

52. In some courts plaintiffs are prohibited from including in the complaint a demand for a specific unliquidated damages award. *E.g.,* Rule 8.1 of the United States District Court for the District of New Jersey; Michigan Court Rule 2.111(B)(2).

53. *Hudson v. Moore Business Forms, Inc.,* 836 F.2d 1156 (9th Cir. 1987).

verdict reporting services, as well as judicial directories, can assist counsel in deciding whether to request a jury.

Counsel should be aware that under Rule 39(c)(2) of the Federal Rules of Civil Procedure in most cases the court, with the consent of the parties, may order a trial by jury even in actions in which the parties are not entitled to a jury as a matter of right. The parties also may consent to the trial of federal civil actions by a United States magistrate judge, rather than by a federal district judge.[54] Whether to consent to trial before a magistrate judge generally will depend on quite practical considerations. Among the relevant considerations are the relative abilities and dispositions of the magistrate and district judge who might hear the case, the possible delay if a federal district judge is demanded, and the relative advantages and disadvantages of an earlier (or, in a few districts, later) trial before a magistrate judge.

Unfortunately, some of the choices counsel must make concerning the relief requested and other pretrial matters may have to be based on guesswork concerning future events. The successful attorney, however, will attempt to make only educated guesses.

NOTES AND QUESTIONS CONCERNING THE RELIEF REQUESTED

1. How should compensatory damages be determined in the absence of a functioning market? Are there some things in life that money just can't buy? What about the value of life itself? Should a plaintiff be able to recover damages for loss of enjoyment of life, or "hedonic damages," in addition to damages for loss of earnings and pain and suffering? *Compare Boan v. Blackwell*, 343 S.C. 498, 541 S.E.2d 242 (2001), and *Sherrod v. Berry*, 629 F.Supp. 159 (N.D.Ill. 1985), *rev'd on other grounds,* 856 F.2d 802 (7th Cir. 1988) (en banc) (yes) *with McDougald v. Garber*, 73 N.Y.2d 246, 538 N.Y.S.2d 937, 536 N.E.2d 372 (1989) (no). *See also Gregory v. Carey*, 246 Kan. 504, 511–514, 791 P.2d 1329, 1334–36 (1990) (loss of enjoyment of life compensable as an element of disability, pain, and suffering). Even if such damages are available, are there problems in proving hedonic damages? *See* Kuiper, Note, "The Courts, *Daubert*, and Willingness-to-Pay: The Doubtful Future of Hedonic Damages Testimony under the Federal Rules of Evidence," 1996 *U. Ill. L. Rev.* 1197. *See also* Posner et al., "Measuring Damages for Lost Enjoyment of Life: The View from the Bench and the Jury Box," 27 *Law & Hum. Behav.* 53 (2003).

2. Is there any limitation upon the amount of punitive damages that can be assessed against a defendant? What about a case in which a jury awards compensatory damages of $51,146 and punitive damages of $6 million? *See Browning–Ferris Industries v. Kelco Disposal, Inc.,* 492 U.S. 257 (1989). What procedural protections are necessary before punitive damages constitutionally can be imposed? *See Honda Motor Co. v. Oberg,* 512 U.S. 415 (1994); *TXO Production Corp. v. Alliance Resources,* 509 U.S. 443 (1993); *Pacific Mut. Life*

---

54. 28 U.S.C. § 636(c).

Ins. Co. v. Haslip, 499 U.S. 1 (1991). *See also Cooper Industries, Inc. v. Leatherman Tool Group, Inc.*, 532 U.S. 424 (2001).

In *B.M.W. v. Gore*, 517 U.S. 559 (1996), the Supreme Court concluded that a state court could not impose punitive damages based upon a defendant's conduct that was lawful in other states (although unlawful in the forum state) and had no impact upon residents of the forum state; the Court evaluated the punitive damages award based upon the reprehensibility of the defendant's conduct, the disparity between the harm suffered by the plaintiff and the amount of punitive damages, and the difference between the punitive damages and civil or criminal penalties authorized in comparable cases. While refusing to adopt a mathematical ratio limiting the amount by which punitive damages can constitutionally exceed compensatory damages, the Supreme Court subsequently noted "that, in practice, few awards exceeding a single-digit ratio between punitive and compensatory damages, to a significant degree, will satisfy due process." *State Farm Mutual Automobile Ins. Co. v. Campbell*, 538 U.S. 408, 425 (2003).

In *Philip Morris USA v. Williams*, 549 U.S. 346 (2007), the Supreme Court concluded that "the Constitution's Due Process Clause forbids a State to use a punitive damages award to punish a defendant for injury that it inflicts upon nonparties or those whom they directly represent, *i.e.*, injury that it inflicts upon those who are, essentially, strangers to the litigation." 549 U.S. at 353. The Court concluded that, while a jury may not "use a punitive damages verdict to punish a defendant directly on account of harms it is alleged to have visited on nonparties," a plaintiff could, though, "show harm to others in order to demonstrate reprehensibility." 549 U.S. at 355. Are juries capable of making such a distinction? *See generally* Colby, "Clearing the Smoke from *Philip Morris v. Williams*: The Past, Present, and Future of Punitive Damages," 118 *Yale L. J.* 392 (2008); Symposium, "Punitive Damages, Due Process, and Deterrence: The Debate After *Philip Morris v. Williams*," 2 *Chas. L. Rev.* 287 (2008).

3. Punitive damages have been widely criticized in recent years, with political and business leaders and others calling for punitive damages reform. Symposium: "Reforming Punitive Damages," 38 *Harv. J. Legis.* 469 (2001); 39 *Harv. J. Legis.* 121 (2002); "Developments in the Law, The Paths of Civil Litigation: Problems and Proposals in Punitive Damages Reform," 113 *Harv. L. Rev.* 1752, 1783 (2000). Unfortunately, these calls for reform, and the reforms actually enacted, typically have not been informed by empirical data or studies of punitive damages decision-making. Robbennolt, "Determining Punitive Damages: Empirical Insights and Implications for Reform," 50 *Buff. L. Rev.* 103 (2002). For a collection of empirical studies concerning jury decision-making with respect to punitive damages see C. Sunstein et al., *Punitive Damages: How Juries Decide* (2002). Despite the intensity of the political debate concerning punitive damages in recent years, such damages are awarded in only two to four percent of civil cases in which plaintiffs prevail. Luban, "A Flawed Case Against Punitive Damages," 87 *Geo. L. J.* 359, 360 (1998); Galanter, "Shadow Play: The Fabled Menace of Punitive Damages," 1998 *Wis. L. Rev.* 1, 2.

4. Does the assessment of multiple punitive damage awards against a defendant for a single course of conduct violate that defendant's constitutional right to due process? *Compare Juzwin v. Amtorg Trading Corp.,* 705 F.Supp. 1053, 1060–65 (D.N.J.), *vac'd on other grounds,* 718 F.Supp. 1233 (D.N.J. 1989) (yes) *with Leonen v. Johns–Manville Corp.,* 717 F.Supp. 272, 281–86 (D.N.J. 1989) (no). If so, what remedy will best protect a defendant's right to due process? *See Juzwin v. Amtorg Trading Corp.,* 718 F.Supp. 1233 (D.N.J. 1989); Denmark, "Seeking Greater Fairness When Awarding Multiple Plaintiffs Punitive Damages for a Single Act by a Defendant," 63 *Ohio St. L. J.* 931 (2002) (suggesting that defendants should be able to claim a dollar-for-dollar setoff for punitive damage awards already paid for a single act or course of conduct); Gash, "Solving the Multiple Punishments Problem: A Call for a National Punitive Damages Registry," 99 *Nw. U. L. Rev.* 1613 (2005). Are there litigation strategies that defendants can pursue to prevent multiple punitive damage awards? *See generally* Phillips, "Multiple Punitive Damage Awards," 39 *Vill. L. Rev.* 433 (1994).

5. Realizing that "there are some things in life that money can't buy," some plaintiffs have not wanted to receive punitive damage awards that juries otherwise might award them. Can a jury be told that, if that jury awards punitive damages, the plaintiff will provide those damages to a foundation that will use the funds to remedy the problem that led to the injury in question (such as, for instance, an unsafe railroad crossing)? *See* McDonough, "Handing Down Help: In Ohio, 'Curative Damages' Are Embraced by Tort Plaintiffs and the Supreme Court," *A.B.A.J.,* Oct. 2005, at 24. Some states have enacted "split recovery" laws, under which a percentage (typically 50 to 75%) of punitive damages awards goes to the state, rather than to the plaintiff. Barber, "California Taxes Punitive Damages Awards," *Litigation News,* Sept. 2005, at 5. "Because the law applies only to damages awarded on a final judgment, plaintiffs have reason to settle rather [than] take a punitive damages claim to trial." *Id.*

6. A California jury returns a verdict of $107 million in compensatory damages and $4.9 billion in punitive damages against the manufacturer of a car that exploded in flames when rear-ended by a drunk driver. Plaintiffs, who were horribly burned in the crash, would like to "trade" the bulk of the punitive damages award for an agreement that the cars in question be recalled because of the fuel tank design problems that allegedly caused plaintiffs' injuries. What is your response to the plaintiffs as their counsel? What is your response as counsel for the automobile manufacturer? *See* Van Voris, "Tort Lawyers Give up Punies," *Nat'l L. J.,* Sept. 20, 1999, at A1.

7. Unfortunately, the relief awarded by a court may not be immediately paid to the plaintiff. If a defendant does not satisfy a money judgment entered against him, plaintiff may have to execute on the judgment. Under Rule 69(a)(1) of the Federal Rules of Civil Procedure, "The procedure on execution—and in proceedings supplementary to and in aid of judgment or execution—must accord with the procedure of the state where the court is located, but a federal statute governs to the extent it applies." While execution procedures vary from state to state, typically a writ of execution will issue from the clerk of court and a local law enforcement official acting pursuant to this writ will enforce it by seizing property or income of the judgment debtor.

E.g., Conn. Gen. Stat. § 51–52(a)(7) (2005); Neb. Rev. Stat. § 25–1501 (1995 Reissue).

Exercise Concerning the Relief Requested[55]

For the purposes of this assignment, presume that you represent the Pittston Company in the major civil action brought against it by the victims of the Buffalo Creek disaster in the United States District Court for the Southern District of West Virginia.

After carefully reading Rule 65 of the Federal Rules of Civil Procedure, develop the responses, written and otherwise, that you would make to the following motion.

IN THE UNITED STATES DISTRICT COURT FOR THE SOUTHERN DISTRICT OF WEST VIRGINIA At Huntington

DENNIS PRINCE, individually and as Administrator of the estate of Margie Prince, et al., Plaintiffs)))))) v.)) THE PITTSTON COMPANY, a Delaware) and Virginia Corporation,) Defendant)	CA No. 3052

PLAINTIFFS' MOTION FOR A TEMPORARY RESTRAINING ORDER

Pursuant to Rule 65 of the Federal Rules of Civil Procedure, plaintiffs Dennis Prince, et al., hereby request the court to temporarily restrain the defendant Pittston Company from further construction of a dam on the Upper Fork of the Buffalo Creek. A hearing on this motion has been set for February 12, 1973, at 10:00 a.m. in Courtroom 300 in the United States Courthouse in Charleston, West Virginia. In support of this motion, plaintiffs submit the attached Memorandum of Points and Authorities, the Affidavits of Michael L. Rivers and C. Darrow, and a proposed order.

Respectfully submitted,

s/ _____
C. Darrow
525 Main Street
Charleston, West Virginia
(304) 974–6793
Counsel for Plaintiffs

---

55. This exercise is based upon a negotiation exercise developed by Professor Lawrence Grosberg of New York Law School and presented at the Association of American Law Schools Civil Procedure Conference in June 1988. In contrast to the other court papers included in this book, the following papers, and the facts set forth in them, are purely fictitious except insofar as they refer to the Buffalo Creek dam failure on February 26, 1972.

IN THE UNITED STATES DISTRICT COURT
FOR THE SOUTHERN DISTRICT OF
WEST VIRGINIA At Huntington

DENNIS PRINCE, individually and as   )
    Administrator of the estate of   )
    Margie Prince, et al.,   )
              Plaintiffs   )
)   CA No. 3052
            v.   )
)
THE PITTSTON COMPANY, a Delaware)
    and Virginia Corporation,   )
              Defendant)

ORDER

This matter came on to be heard on Plaintiffs' Motion for a Temporary Restraining Order at a hearing on February 12, 1973. Having heard the argument of counsel at that time, and having considered the written submissions of counsel at that hearing, the court finds (1) that there is a strong likelihood that plaintiffs ultimately will prevail on the merits of their claims; (2) that plaintiffs will suffer irreparable injury unless a temporary restraining order issues; (3) that no harm will occur to the defendant by the issuance of immediate injunctive relief; and (4) that the injunctive relief sought by plaintiffs would be in the public interest.

The Court therefore hereby Orders, at ___ ___.m. on February 12, 1973, that:

Plaintiffs' motion for a temporary restraining order is granted and the defendant, the Pittston Company, is hereby enjoined from engaging in any further construction of its waste dam on the Upper Fork of the Buffalo Creek in Logan County, West Virginia or from dumping any mining waste into the Buffalo Creek.

Pursuant to Rule 65(c) plaintiffs will post a cash or surety bond in the amount of $100.00 with the clerk of court.

This order shall expire on ___, 1973, at ___ ___.m.

_____

United States District Judge

_____

IN THE UNITED STATES DISTRICT COURT
FOR THE SOUTHERN DISTRICT OF
WEST VIRGINIA At Huntington

DENNIS PRINCE, individually and as   )
    Administrator of the estate of   )
    Margie Prince, et al.,   )
                Plaintiffs   )
)   CA No. 3052
         v.   )
)
THE PITTSTON COMPANY, a Delaware   )
    and Virginia Corporation,   )
                Defendant   )

MEMORANDUM OF POINTS AND AUTHORITIES IN
SUPPORT OF PLAINTIFFS' MOTION FOR A
TEMPORARY RESTRAINING ORDER

I. INTRODUCTION

By their motion for a temporary restraining order, plaintiffs request that this court restrain the defendant Pittston Company from further construction and expansion of a dam on the Upper Fork tributary of the Buffalo Creek. This dam is frighteningly similar to Dam 3 on the Middle Fork tributary of the Buffalo Creek, which collapsed on February 26, 1972, killing over one hundred men, women, and children. Not only is Pittston's expanding dam on the Upper Fork a public nuisance, but continued construction of the dam is in violation of safety regulations issued by the Bureau of Mines pursuant to the Federal Coal Mine Health and Safety Act of 1969. Plaintiffs ask this court to enjoin further construction of this dam until a preliminary injunction hearing concerning this matter can be held.

II. STATEMENT OF THE CASE

As the February 5, 1973, Affidavit of Michael L. Rivers ("Rivers Affidavit") indicates, the Pittston Company is constructing and expanding a dam on the Upper Fork tributary of the Buffalo Creek. This earthen dam is adjacent to Pittston's "Upper Fork Mine" and is being constructed from the solid and semi-solid wastes from the coal washing operations at that mine. Rivers Affidavit ¶ 5.

While this dam on the Upper Fork has existed for some time, Pittston had stopped dumping its wastes behind the dam after the collapse of Dam 3 on the Middle Fork tributary of the Buffalo Creek on February 26, 1972. Instead, these wastes were dumped into a small quarry. However, on approximately December 20, 1972, this quarry became full and Pittston once again began dumping mining wastes into the Upper Fork and thereby expanding the size of the dam. Rivers Affidavit ¶ 5.

This expanding dam is approximately 20 feet high and stretches approximately 200 feet across the Upper Fork and the surrounding banks and land area. It is approximately 100 feet wide from the front to the back of the dam. Rivers Affidavit ¶ 5. Although a spillway has been constructed for this dam, apparently no engineers have been consulted concerning either the dam or the spillway. Rivers Affidavit ¶ 6.

By their Motion for a Temporary Restraining Order, plaintiffs ask this court to restrain Pittston from continuing to expand this dam on the Upper Fork tributary of the Buffalo Creek.

III. ARGUMENT

This Court Should Restrain Construction of the Dam on Buffalo Creek's Upper Fork in order to Prevent another Disastrous Dam Collapse.

The test for temporary injunctive relief in this circuit was set forth in *Airport Commission v. Civil Aeronautics Board*, 296 F.2d 95 (4th Cir. 1961). In deciding whether to issue injunctive relief, a court must address four questions:

> (1) Has the petitioner made a strong showing that it is likely to prevail on the merits . . .?

> (2) Has the petitioner shown that without such relief it will be irreparably injured?

> (3) Would the issuance of a stay substantially harm other parties interested in the proceeding?

> (4) Where lies the public interest?

296 F.2d at 96. *Accord First–Citizens Bank & Trust Co. v. Camp*, 432 F.2d 481, 483 (4th Cir. 1970). *See also Virginia Petroleum Jobbers Ass'n v. Federal Power Commission*, 259 F.2d 921 (D.C.Cir. 1958).

The answers to the above questions mandate the issuance of a temporary restraining order in this case.

> A. *The plaintiffs have a substantial likelihood of success on the merits of their claims.*

There is a strong likelihood that plaintiffs will succeed upon the merits of their claims that the Upper Fork dam construction is both a public nuisance and in violation of regulations issued under the Federal Coal Mine Health and Safety Act of 1969. Regulations promulgated by the United States Bureau of Mines pursuant to the Federal Coal Mine Health and Safety Act of 1969 provide:

> Refuse piles shall not be constructed so as to impede drainage or impound water.

> If failure of a water or silt retaining dam will create a hazard, it shall be of substantial construction and shall be inspected at least once each week.

30 C.F.R. §§ 77.215(e) and 77.216(a) (1972).

Pittston presumably will argue that these regulations are not applicable because it, Pittston, does not consider the obstruction of the Upper Fork to be a "dam" and because it has a separate "refuse pile" at the side of that creek rather than directly in it. However, the purpose of the Federal Coal Mine Health and Safety Act would be thwarted by such a cramped construction of these regulations. Only if these regulations are interpreted to apply to the obstruction Pittston has thrown across the Upper Fork of the Buffalo Creek can the public and private safety that Congress intended to protect be assured. In addition, Pittston's new dam creates a public nuisance which this court has the power to enjoin.

Because of the likelihood that plaintiffs will prevail on the merits of their claims, the court should issue the requested temporary restraining order to preserve the status quo until it can hear plaintiffs' requests for preliminary, and ultimately permanent, injunctive relief.

B.   Plaintiffs will be irreparably injured if a temporary restraining order does not issue.

If this court does not issue the temporary restraining order they seek, plaintiffs will be irreparably injured in at least two separate ways. First of all, there is a very real chance that the dam on the Upper Fork of the Buffalo Creek may collapse as did the dam on Buffalo Creek's Middle Fork. Plaintiffs' trial evidence will show that Pittston did not take the necessary precautions to prevent the dam collapse of February 26, 1972. This court has it within its power to prevent a similar tragedy in connection with the dam on the Upper Fork. While that dam may not fail today, or tomorrow, it will be months, if not years, until the merits of this case are heard. Emergency injunctive relief is needed at this time to preserve the status quo now existing in the Buffalo Creek Valley.

Even if the dam on the Upper Fork does not fail, plaintiffs are nevertheless subjected to irreparable injury due to the continued construction of that dam. The plaintiffs who survived the flood of February 26, 1972, are now attempting to resume somewhat normal lives. Although they have been permanently scarred by the disaster they survived, they are attempting to put the disaster of one year ago behind them. To permit Pittston to build another dam on the Buffalo Creek will reopen the wounds that only now have begun to heal. In the words of plaintiff Michael Rivers, "I am in great fear that the dam on the Upper Fork of the Buffalo Creek will collapse in the same manner, and with the same tragic results, as did Dam 3 on the Middle Fork of Buffalo Creek." Rivers Affidavit, ¶ 7.

Plaintiffs will suffer irreparable harm if a temporary restraining order does not issue.

C.   The harm to defendant will be minimal if a temporary restraining order is granted.

In contrast to the irreparable injury plaintiffs will suffer if a temporary restraining order does not issue, the harm to Pittston from such an order would be minimal. Indeed, the only possible harm to Pittston would be the temporary dislocation caused by the potential suspension of its mining operations at the Upper Fork Mine.

Such possible economic harm to Pittston provides no basis for denying the order sought. Plaintiffs will demonstrate at the trial of this action that the tragedy of February 26, 1972, was caused, at least in part, by Pittston's preoccupation with profits over human lives. Even if Pittston has to shut down its Upper Fork Mine for the short time that a temporary restraining order can run, that is a minor price to pay to prevent further death and suffering in the Buffalo Creek Valley.

The minimal potential harm to Pittston, especially when balanced against the threat to human life posed by its continuing dam construction, is no basis upon which to deny the restraining order sought by plaintiffs.

D. Issuance of a temporary restraining order would serve the public interest.

It is difficult to envision a temporary restraining order that would be more in the public interest than the order sought in this case. No one, plaintiffs or defendant Pittston, wants a repeat of the disaster of February 26, 1972. This court has it within its power to prevent a similar disaster due to a collapse of the dam on the Upper Fork of the Buffalo Creek.

In order to protect the public, as well as the plaintiffs in this action, the court should enjoin Pittston from further expansion of its dam.

IV.   CONCLUSION

For the above reasons, plaintiffs request that the temporary restraining order sought be granted and that a preliminary injunction hearing be scheduled by the court at its earliest convenience.

Respectfully submitted,

s/ ———
C. Darrow
525 Main Street
Charleston, West Virginia
(304) 974–6793
Counsel for Plaintiffs

V.   MODERN PLEADING AND PRACTICE

At common law in medieval England, pleadings initially were oral and relatively straightforward. Common law pleading eventually became so complex, though, that parties hired "special pleaders" to plead their causes. The proper common law procedural writ depended upon the substance of the claim asserted, and many claims were dismissed not upon their merits but due to procedural technicalities. Pleadings were very inflexible; pleading in the alternative was not permitted, there were severe restrictions upon joinder of claims and parties, and proof had to conform quite precisely to the pleadings.[56]

Because of the difficulties with common law pleading, code pleading developed during the mid-nineteenth century. Under the resulting codes, such as the Field Code, the forms of action were abolished and common law issue pleading was replaced with fact pleading. However, eventually code pleading developed its own technicalities, and it became very important that pleadings be neither too general ("conclusory") nor too specific ("evidentiary").[57] In reaction to these problems with code pleading, the Rules Enabling Act[58] was enacted in 1934 and provided the basis for the Federal Rules of Civil Procedure.

A. PLEADING REQUIREMENTS UNDER THE FEDERAL RULES

Pleading under the Federal Rules of Civil Procedure is quite different than under common law or code pleading systems. The basic requirements for claims for relief are set forth in Rule 8(a) of the Federal Rules of Civil Procedure. The three requirements of Rule 8(a) are:

(1) a short and plain statement of the grounds for the court's jurisdiction, unless the court already has jurisdiction and the claim needs no new jurisdictional support;

(2) a short and plain statement of the claim showing that the pleader is entitled to relief; and

(3) a demand for the relief sought, which may include relief in the alternative or different types of relief.

The simplicity with which these requirements can be met is illustrated by the Appendix of Forms to the Federal Rules of Civil Procedure. Rule 84 of the Federal Rules of Civil Procedure provides: "The forms in the Appendix suffice under these rules and illustrate the simplicity and brevity that these rules contemplate." So who needs those expensive form books?[59]

Form 7 in the Appendix of Forms sets forth sample allegations sufficient to satisfy Rule 8(a)(1)'s initial requirement of "a short and plain

---

56. *See, generally,* F. James et al., *Civil Procedure* § 3.2 (5th ed. 2001); R. Field et al., *Civil Procedure* 1069–76 (10th ed. 2010).

57. James et al., *supra* note 56, at § 3.5, 3.7–3.9; Field et al., *supra* note 56, at 1117–23.

58. 28 U.S.C. § 2072.

59. The California Judicial Council has gone beyond the Federal Rules of Civil Procedure by adopting form complaints that merely require attorneys or parties to check the relevant boxes and fill in occasional blanks. California Judicial Council, *California Judicial Council Forms* http://www.courtinfo.ca.gov/cgi-bin/forms.cgi.

For both state and federal practice, the best form books are the ones that attorneys themselves develop. Newly admitted attorneys often can obtain good samples of complaints from colleagues or from opposing counsel (in actions filed against their clients). Over time, counsel can supplement their stock of forms with complaints that they, themselves, have filed. Commercial form books also can be useful, although any form must be tailored to the specific case at hand.

statement of the grounds for the court's jurisdiction." Form 7, for instance, contains the following sample jurisdictional allegation for a diversity of citizenship case:

> The plaintiff is [a citizen of *Michigan*] [a corporation incorporated under the laws of *Michigan* with its principal place of business in *Michigan*]. The defendant is [a citizen of *New York*] [a corporation incorporated under the laws of *New York* with its principal place of business in *New York*]. The amount in controversy, without interest and costs, exceeds the sum or value specified by 28 U.S.C. § 1332.[60]

Form 11 in the Appendix of Forms illustrates the simplicity with which the requirements of Federal Rule of Civil Procedure 8(a) can be satisfied:

COMPLAINT FOR NEGLIGENCE

(Caption–See Form 1.)

1. (Statement of Jurisdiction–See Form 7).

2. On *date*, at *place*, the defendant negligently drove a motor vehicle against the plaintiff.

3. As a result, the plaintiff was physically injured, lost wages or income, suffered physical and mental pain, and incurred medical expenses of $____.

Therefore, the plaintiff demands judgment against the defendant for $_____, plus costs.

(Date and sign—See Form 2.)

In addition to the general requirements of Rule 8, Rule 10 governs the form of federal pleadings.[61] Rule 10(a) provides that all pleadings are to contain a caption setting forth the name of the court, the title of the action, the file number, and a designation of the pleading. Rule 10(b) requires that averments of claims and defenses be made in numbered paragraphs "each limited as far as practicable to a single set of circumstances" and that each claim and defense generally should be set forth in a separate count or defense.

Finally, Rule 10(c) permits the adoption by reference in one part of a pleading of a statement made elsewhere in the pleading; Rule 10(c) also provides that copies of written documents (such as an administrative complaint or a contract that is at issue in the suit) can be attached to the pleading and will be considered a part of the pleading for all purposes. In addition to the requirements of Rule 10, counsel should consult the local

---

60. In state courts of general jurisdiction, the pleading of jurisdictional allegations may not be necessary. *E.g.*, Rule 8(A) of the Indiana Rules of Trial Procedure; Rule 8.01 of the Tennessee Rules of Civil Procedure.

61. Federal Rule of Civil Procedure 7(a) defines pleadings to include "(1) a complaint; (2) an answer to a complaint; (3) an answer to a counterclaim designated as a counterclaim; (4) an answer to a crossclaim; (5) a third-party complaint; (6) an answer to a third-party complaint; and (7) if the court orders one, a reply to an answer."

rules of their jurisdiction for any supplemental requirements concerning form.[62]

Are there circumstances in which counsel are required to plead their complaint with greater specificity than that generally required by Rule 8(a)? Yes, there are. The Federal Rules of Civil Procedure, judicial decisions, and federal statutes require additional specificity in the pleading of certain claims.[63]

Rule 8's general requirements are modified by the additional requirements of Rule 9 of the Federal Rules of Civil Procedure. In particular, Rule 9(b) requires that the circumstances constituting fraud or mistake must be stated "with particularity," while Rule 9(g) similarly requires that items of special damages such as medical expenses be "specifically stated." These specificity requirements usually are not too difficult to satisfy.[64]

In addition to cases falling within the specific requirements of Rule 9, during the 1980s increasing numbers of federal courts began to require that certain other claims be pled with greater specificity than that required by Rule 8.[65] Most prominent in this latter category of claims were civil rights actions.[66] However, in 1993 the Supreme Court rejected such a heightened pleading standard as applied to a civil rights claim asserting municipal liability under 42 U.S.C. § 1983.[67] The *Leatherman* Court concluded: "We think that it is impossible to square the 'heightened pleading standard' applied * * * in this case with the liberal system of 'notice pleading' set up by the Federal Rules.[68]

---

62. *See, e.g.,* Rule 3–4(c) of the United States District Court for the Northern District of California (governing the size of paper to be used for all court filings and the spacing of text and footnotes); Rule 8.1 of the United States District Court for the Middle District of Pennsylvania (if unliquidated damages are sought, complaint's demand for judgment shall not claim any specific sum).

63. In light of the many specific pleading requirements for certain types of federal claims, one commentator has asserted: "Notwithstanding its foundation in the Federal Rules and repeated Supreme Court imprimatur, notice pleading is a myth." Fairman, "The Myth of Notice Pleading," 45 *Ariz. L. Rev.* 987, 988 (2003).

64. *See* Form 21 of the Appendix of Forms to the Federal Rules of Civil Procedure (complaint on a claim for a debt and to set aside a fraudulent conveyance).

65. *See* Marcus, "The Revival of Fact Pleading Under the Federal Rules of Civil Procedure," 86 *Colum. L. Rev.* 433 (1986).

66. *See generally* Blaze, "Presumed Frivolous: Application of Stringent Pleading Requirements in Civil Rights Litigation," 31 *Wm. & Mary L. Rev.* 935 (1990).

67. *Leatherman v. Tarrant County Narcotics Intelligence and Coordination Unit,* 507 U.S. 163 (1993). *See also Swierkiewicz v. Sorema N.A.,* 534 U.S. 506 (2002) (no heightened pleading standard for employment discrimination suits).

68. 507 U.S. at 168. Even after *Leatherman,* lower federal courts continued to impose a heightened pleading standard in damage actions brought against individual government officers entitled to a qualified immunity defense. *See* Blum, "Heightened Pleading: Is There Life After *Leatherman*?," 44 *Cath. U. L. Rev.* 59 (1995). Courts also required greater specificity by ordering plaintiffs to file a Rule 7(a) reply or by granting a Rule 12(e) motion for a more definite statement. *Crawford–El v. Britton,* 523 U.S. 574, 598 (1998). *See generally* Fairman, "Heightened Pleading," 81 *Tex. L. Rev.* 551 (2002).

In addition to these judicial decisions, Congress has demanded greater specificity in certain federal securities fraud actions, requiring that complaints "shall, with respect to each act or omission alleged to violate [these federal provisions], state with particularity facts giving rise to a

Despite the Supreme Court's praise for "notice pleading" in *Leatherman*, more recently the Court "retired" the long-standing language in *Conley v. Gibson* that "a complaint should not be dismissed for failure to state a claim unless it appears beyond doubt that the plaintiff can prove no set of facts in support of his claim which would entitle him to relief."[69] In *Bell Atlantic Corp. v. Twombly* the Court noted: "[T]his famous observation [from *Conley*] has earned its retirement. The phrase is best forgotten as an incomplete, negative gloss on an accepted pleading standard: once a claim has been stated adequately, it may be supported by showing any set of facts consistent with the allegations in the complaint. * * * *Conley*, then, described the breadth of opportunity to prove what an adequate complaint claims, not the minimum standard of adequate pleading to govern a complaint's survival."[70]

Subsequently, in *Iqbal v. Ashcroft*, the Supreme Court stated: "To survive a motion to dismiss, a complaint must contain sufficient factual matter, accepted as true, to 'state a claim to relief that is plausible on its face.' * * * A claim has facial plausibility when the plaintiff pleads factual content that allows the court to draw the reasonable inference that the defendant is liable for the misconduct alleged."[71] The Court further explained:

> Two working principles underlie our decision in *Twombly*. First, the tenet that a court must accept as true all of the allegations contained in a complaint is inapplicable to legal conclusions. Threadbare recitals of the elements of a cause of action, supported by mere conclusory statements, do not suffice. * * * Second, only a complaint that states a plausible claim for relief survives a motion to dismiss. * * * Determining whether a complaint states a plausible claim for relief will, as the Court of Appeals observed, be a context-specific task that requires the reviewing court to draw on its judicial experience and common sense."[72]

The Court also concluded: "Our decision in *Twombly* expounded the pleading standard for 'all civil actions,' and it applies to antitrust and discrimination suits alike."[73]

---

strong inference that the defendant acted with the required state of mind." 15 U.S.C. § 78u–4(b)(2). *See Tellabs, Inc. v. Makor Issues & Rights, Ltd.*, 551 U.S. 308, 314 (2007) ("To qualify as 'strong' within the intendment of § 21(D)(b)(2), we hold, an inference of scienter must be more than merely plausible or reasonable—it must be cogent and at least as compelling as any opposing inference of nonfraudulent intent."). *See generally* Symposium, "The Implications of the Private Securities Litigation Reform Act," 76 *Wash. U. L. Q.* 447 (1998). *See also* Parness et al., "The Substantive Elements in the New Special Pleading Laws," 78 *Neb. L. Rev.* 412 (1999); Marcus, "The Puzzling Persistence of Pleading Practice," 76 *Tex. L. Rev.* 1749 (1998).

69.   355 U.S. 41, 45–46 (1957).

70.   550 U.S. 544, 563 (2007).

71.   556 U.S. ___, ___ (2009), quoting *Bell Atlantic Corp. v. Twombly*, 550 U.S. 544, 556 (2007).

72.   *Id.* at ___.

73.   *Id.* at ___, quoting Rule 1 of the Federal Rules of Civil Procedure.

Within fifteen months after its decision by the Supreme Court, *Iqbal* had been cited nearly 11,000 times by the federal courts,[74] while Judge Richard Posner quipped that the Court's decision in *Twombly* was "fast becoming the citation du jour in Rule 12(b)(6) cases."[75] A great deal of commentary also followed these two decisions.[76]

Among the critiques following these decisions was concern that the pleading standard they enunciated would make it particularly difficult for plaintiffs to survive motions to dismiss in civil rights and employment discrimination actions and in other cases in which it may be difficult for plaintiffs to make detailed factual pleadings without the opportunity for some initial discovery.[77] Proposed legislation also was introduced in Congress to overturn the heightened pleading standard announced in these cases.[78] As Charles Clark, reporter for the original advisory committee for the Federal Rules of Civil Procedure, noted back in the 1950s, "[E]very little while there seems a recurring hope or belief that we can somehow tie the parties up and avoid trial by requiring detailed pleading."[79] Although the Supreme Court's recent pleadings decisions ultimately may be limited or modified by future action of the Supreme Court, amendment of the Federal Rules, or congressional enactment, the federal courts, and federal pleading, are now in a period such as noted by Judge Clark.

Whatever the pleading standard, both governing substantive law and practical considerations may influence whether a party is required to plead a specific matter as an element of his cause of action. In *Gomez v. Toledo*[80] the Supreme Court held that the plaintiff in an action brought

---

74. Kuperman, *Review of Caselaw Applying Bell Atlantic Corp. v. Twombly and Ashcroft v. Iqbal* 1, n.2 (July 26, 2010).

75. *Smith v. Duffey*, 576 F.3d 336, 339–40 (7th Cir. 2009).

76. *E.g.*, Miller, "From *Conley* to *Twombly* to *Iqbal*: A Double Play on the Federal Rules of Civil Procedure," 60 *Duke L. J.* 1 (2010); Bone, "Plausibility Pleading Revisited and Revised: A Comment on *Ashcroft v. Iqbal*," 85 *Notre Dame L. Rev.* 849 (2010); Clermont & Yeazell, "Inventing Tests, Destabilizing Systems," 95 *Iowa L. Rev.* 821 (2010); Hartnett, "Taming *Twombly*, Even After *Iqbal*, 158 *U. Pa. L. Rev.* 473 (2010); Symposium, "Pondering *Iqbal*," 14 *Lewis & Clark L. Rev.* 1 (2010); Symposium, "Reflections on *Iqbal*: Discerning Its Rule, Grappling with Its Implications," 114 *Penn. St. L. Rev.* 1257 (2010).

77. *E.g.*, Schneider, "The Changing Shape of Federal Civil Pretrial Practice: The Disparate Impact on Civil Rights and Employment Discrimination Cases," 158 *U. P. L. Rev.* 517, 527–36 (2010); Seiner, "The Trouble with *Twombly*: A Proposed Pleading Standard for Employment Discrimination Cases," 2009 *U. Il. L. Rev.* 1011 (2009). *But see* Steinman, "The Pleading Problem," 62 *Stan. L. Rev.* 1293, 1299 (2010) ("[P]roperly understood, the post-*Iqbal* pleading framework is not fundamentally in conflict with notice pleading, because the most significant pre-*Twombly* authorities on federal pleading remain good law and because the troublesome plausibility standard is rendered irrelevant when a plaintiff provides nonconclusory allegations for each element of a claim.").

78. Senator Arlen Specter introduced the Notice Pleading Restoration Act of 2009, S 1504, 111th Cong., 1st Sess. (2009), which provided:

Except as otherwise expressly provided by an Act of Congress or by an amendment to the Federal Rules of Civil Procedure which takes effect after the date of enactment of this Act, a Federal court shall not dismiss a complaint under rule 12(b)(6) or (e) of the Federal Rules of Civil Procedure, except under the standards set forth by the Supreme Court of the United States in Conley v. Gibson, 355 U.S. 41 (1957).

See also Open Access to Courts Act, H.R. 4115, 111th Cong., 1st Sess. (2009).

79. Clark, "Pleading Under the Federal Rules," 12 *Wyo. L. J.* 177, 181 (1957).

80. 446 U.S. 635 (1980).

under 42 U.S.C. § 1983 need not allege that the defendant had acted in bad faith in taking certain action against him. The Court reached this conclusion due to, *inter alia,* the liberal construction to be afforded Section 1983 and the fact that a public official's state of mind is a fact peculiarly within the control of the official.[81]

While the pleading requirements of the Federal Rules of Civil Procedure have tightened in recent years, the Federal Rules provide for the liberal amendment of pleadings. Under Rule 15(a)(1), a complaint can be amended once as a matter of right within 21 days after service of a responsive pleading (*i.e.,* an answer) or of a Rule 12(b), (e), or (f) motion (whichever is earlier). Otherwise, the complaint only can be amended with the written consent of the adverse party or leave of court. However, in considering motions to amend, Rule 15(a)(2) provides "The court should freely give leave when justice so requires." In *Foman v. Davis,* the Supreme Court stressed that "this mandate [of Rule 15(a)] is to be heeded. * * * If the underlying facts or circumstances relied upon by a plaintiff may be a proper subject of relief, he ought to be afforded an opportunity to test his claim on the merits."[82]

Attorneys should not be lulled into a false sense of security due to the liberality of Rule 15. Courts can, and do, deny leave to amend pleadings, particularly when leave is not sought in a timely fashion and the opposing party will be prejudiced by the amendment.[83] Moreover, even if amendment is permitted, there still may be a question concerning whether the amended pleading relates back in time to the filing of the original pleading.[84] It's therefore always best to plead properly and completely in the first instance.

B. PRACTICAL PLEADING CONSIDERATIONS

Not only does the filing of the complaint initiate the civil action, but the complaint may serve other strategic purposes as well. The complaint sets the outer bounds on permissible discovery, it can be used to obtain admissions from the defendant, and it can play an important role in the resolution of an action short of trial. Attorneys should think of the complaint not merely as a legal necessity, but as an advocacy document.

Rule 26(b)(1) of the Federal Rules of Civil Procedure provides that parties "may obtain discovery regarding any nonprivileged matter that is

---

81. *Id.* at 638–41. *See generally* Cleary, "Presuming and Pleading: An Essay on Juristic Immaturity," 12 *Stan. L. Rev.* 5 (1959).

82. 371 U.S. 178, 182 (1962).

83. *E.g., Zenith Radio Corp. v. Hazeltine Research, Inc.,* 401 U.S. 321, 325–33 (1971); *Earlie v. Jacobs,* 745 F.2d 342, 345 (5th Cir. 1984). In addition, once a pretrial order is entered, a party may have to show good cause under Rule 16 to amend that order as well as satisfy the requirements of Rule 15(a) for amending the pleadings. *Southwestern Bell Tel. Co. v. City of El Paso,* 346 F.3d 541, 546–47 (5th Cir. 2003); *Sexton v. Gulf Oil Corp.,* 809 F.2d 167, 170 (1st Cir. 1987); *Forstmann v. Culp,* 114 F.R.D. 83, 85–86 (M.D.N.C. 1987). *But cf. Alvin v. Suzuki,* 227 F.3d 107 (3d Cir. 2000) ("case management concerns" and failure to follow prior court order not sufficient basis to deny motion to amend complaint).

84. *See* Fed. R. Civ. P. 15(c).

relevant to any party's claim or defense * * * ." Thus the scope of permissible discovery ultimately depends upon the claim or claims asserted in the complaint. Nor is the plaintiff the only party whose right to discovery is dependent upon the claims asserted. The defendant, too, will be entitled to expanded discovery as plaintiff's claims are broadened; Rule 26(b)(1) also provides, "For good cause, the court may order discovery of any matter relevant to the subject matter involved in the action." In addition, pursuant to Rule 26(a)(1)(A) parties also must disclose the names of individuals likely to have discoverable information, as well as documents, data compilations, and tangible things that support their claims or defenses. Plaintiff's counsel therefore should not make allegations in a complaint unless she is prepared to permit other parties to obtain discovery and disclosure concerning those allegations.

The prayer for relief also may entitle the parties to specific discovery. Although a defendant's financial condition normally is not a proper subject for discovery, if punitive damages are sought then discovery concerning defendant's finances is permissible.[85] Because many of the discovery devices only can be used against other parties,[86] counsel's decision as to the defendants to name may be guided, at least in part, by discovery considerations.

The complaint can even serve as a discovery tool itself. Rule 8(b) requires a defendant to specifically address the averments of the complaint in his or her answer. Accordingly, pleading specific factual matters in a complaint may result in early defense admissions that will narrow the scope of disputed issues and perhaps prove significant in ultimately resolving the action.

If counsel hopes to obtain admissions, however, the complaint must be drafted with sufficient specificity so that defense counsel cannot legitimately deny allegations or claim lack of knowledge or information to either admit or deny the allegations. Separate sentences should be used to set forth separate matters, so that the defendant will be forced to admit as many individual facts as possible. One way to test whether the complaint is as tight as it might be is to actually answer the complaint yourself before it is filed; if you can find holes and ambiguities in your complaint, so can defense counsel.

A detailed and specific complaint may have a major impact upon opposing counsel and the court. A professionally drafted complaint evidences the importance of a case to plaintiff's counsel, as well as the depth of the legal research and factual investigation that she has undertaken. As

---

85. *Charles O. Bradley Trust v. Zenith Capital LLC*, 2005 WL 1030218, 1–4 (N.D.Cal. 2005); *Krenning v. Hunter Health Clinic, Inc.*, 166 F.R.D. 33, 34 (D.Kan. 1996); *Miller v. Doctor's General Hosp.*, 76 F.R.D. 136, 140 (W.D.Okla. 1977); *Vollert v. Summa Corp.*, 389 F.Supp. 1348 (D.Haw. 1975). *See also City of Newport v. Fact Concerts, Inc.*, 453 U.S. 247, 270 (1981) ("[E]vidence of a tortfeasor's wealth is traditionally admissible as a measure of the amount of punitive damages that should be awarded * * * .").

86. Fed. R. Civ. P. 33 (interrogatories); 34 (production requests and entry upon land); 36 (admission requests).

a result, opposing counsel may be more inclined to settle an action than they otherwise would have been.

The judge, too, may have occasion to read the complaint in connection with a pretrial motion to dismiss or for summary judgment. An important judgment as to the seriousness of the action, and as to the professionalism of plaintiff's counsel, may be made based upon the judge's assessment of the complaint. First impressions can be important, and the complaint may be the basis for both opposing counsel's and the judge's first impression of you and your client's lawsuit.

Counsel should remember that the complaint is a public document that will be filed with the court. While the complaint should not be written or treated as a press release, counsel should be aware that the contents of a complaint may be reported in the trade or general media and thereby shape public opinion concerning your client. In addition to satisfying applicable pleading requirements, the complaint should tell the story of your case.[87]

If there are compelling facts supporting plaintiff's cause of action, it may make sense to get these facts before the judge at the earliest stages of a case. Counsel should be careful, however, to avoid characterizations, as opposed to objective facts, in the complaint. Avoid allegations such as this: "In perhaps the greatest outrage of all, defendant, in a frenzy of rage, sadistically beat the plaintiff." Defense counsel presumably will not admit that there was any "outrage" committed or that his client acted "in a frenzy of rage" or "sadistically."

Instead of using the above characterizations, consider merely alleging: "Defendant then hit Steven Smith at least seven times in the face with the butt of his revolver." Defense counsel should have a difficult time denying such objective facts (presuming that they are, in fact, true). Note, too, that by referring to the plaintiff by name this sentence personalizes the victim of the assault perpetrated by the nameless and impersonal defendant.

The most effective advocacy usually is somewhat understated and deals in facts rather than characterizations. Instead of telling the judge that defendant's conduct was an outrage, counsel should attempt to structure the facts so that the judge will himself exclaim "That's an outrage!" while reading the complaint.

There are reasons, however, why a complaint should not contain too many specific facts. Most plaintiffs are interested in a speedy adjudication on the merits, and extensive factual allegations in the complaint may delay such a determination by creating a basis for unnecessary discovery and pretrial motions. In addition, although they may not be required to do so as a matter of law, there is an assumption that plaintiffs will be able to prove all that they have alleged in their complaints. Counsel should think twice before alleging matters that they may not be able to prove.

---

87. *See* Armon, "A Method for Writing Factual Complaints," 1998 *Det. C. L. Mich. St. U. L. Rev.* 109.

The complaint also can serve as an excellent source of discovery for other parties. If counsel presumes that a case will settle, she may decide to be quite detailed in the complaint and attempt to use the complaint for settlement leverage. However, if settlement is unlikely, plaintiff's counsel may not want to lay all her cards on the table at the very outset of the case. Judicial complaints are public records that can be examined by the general public and may be of interest to competitors, the media, or the parties in other actions involving the plaintiff.

The allegations of the complaint should be sufficient to withstand a Rule 12 motion to dismiss, and they may go beyond the minimal requirements of the Federal Rules of Civil Procedure in appropriate cases. However, the complaint should not be verbose, and there should be a reason for every allegation.

The complaint should have a logical organization and be easily understood. Complaints often are organized chronologically, but need not be. Well drafted complaints can be organized by the elements of the case; in a torts case the major substantive sections of the complaint might concern duty, breach, and injuries.

Some attorneys begin their complaints with a short paragraph describing the action in a sentence or two. This can be particularly useful to a judge or judicial law clerk in working with complaints in complex actions. A possible introductory paragraph in a complaint brought as a result of the Buffalo Creek disaster might be:

Introduction

1. This action is brought as a result of the failure of a mining dam on the Middle Fork of the Buffalo Creek in Logan County, West Virginia on February 26, 1972. Plaintiffs are among the 125 men, women, and children who were killed and the more than 4000 people who were left homeless due to the resulting flood. The defendant Pittston Company ("Pittston") was responsible for the failed dam through its wholly-owned subsidiary, the Buffalo Mining Company.

After such an introductory paragraph, either a description of the parties or the jurisdictional basis of the suit may be set forth. Rule 8(a)(1) requires the complaint to state "the grounds for the court's jurisdiction," and it often makes sense to describe the parties in connection with the jurisdictional allegations.[88] Even in federal question cases in which the court's jurisdiction is not dependent upon the parties' citizenship, the complaint may be more understandable if the parties are described at the very outset.

These initial paragraphs should be followed by paragraphs containing the separate causes of action or counts of the complaint and the prayer for relief. Different theories of recovery typically are pled in separate counts of the complaint. A consumer dispute may result in a complaint with

---

88. *See* Form 7 of the Appendix of Forms to the Federal Rules of Civil Procedure, *supra* p. 143.

separate counts alleging breach of contract, quasi contract, violation of a consumer protection statute, and common law fraud. Separate counts usually are numbered with Roman numerals and often are labeled with a descriptive heading. A typical heading might be:

Count I

Breach of Contract

If different types of relief are sought in connection with the separate counts of the complaint, individual demands for relief can follow each count. For example, a contract count might be followed by a request for monetary damages and a count alleging a statutory violation might be followed by a request for injunctive or declaratory relief. Otherwise, a single demand for relief can be used after all of the claims have been alleged. This demand may specify that certain relief is being sought in connection with particular counts of the complaint:

> The plaintiff demands judgment in his favor and asks the court to award him:
>
> (1) a permanent injunction requiring defendant to abate its public nuisance pursuant to Count I of the complaint;
>
> (2) monetary damages in the amount of $175,550 pursuant to Count II of the complaint;
>
> (3) reasonable and necessary costs, including attorneys' fees; and
>
> (4) further relief as is appropriate.

The attorneys' signature lines required by Rule 11 should conclude the complaint. If trial by jury is desired, a jury demand also should be included at either the beginning or the end of the complaint.[89]

Because Rule 10(c) permits adoption by reference, the broadest cause of action often is set forth first in the complaint. The facts underlying all counts of the complaint can be set forth in the initial count and then relied upon and adopted by reference in the succeeding counts. It often makes sense to define certain events, parties, or other terms only once in the complaint; latter references to these matters then can be by a shortened form. In the Buffalo Creek disaster litigation, plaintiffs' counsel might define terms such as "Dam 3," "The Buffalo Creek Disaster," and "Pittston" to make the complaint more readable.

In order to be easily understood, plain language is a must. While it sometimes may be necessary to use specific statutory language (for example, to paraphrase the governing substantive law), the plainer the complaint's language the better. The sentences and paragraphs of the complaint should be no longer than necessary. Headings can be used for each of the separate sections of the complaint (*e.g., Jurisdiction, Prayer for Relief*). Headings also can be used to summarize particular subsections of

---

89. *See* Fed. R. Civ. P. 38(b). Local custom or rules of court may provide guidance as to where on the complaint the jury demand should be endorsed.

a lengthy complaint; such a subheading in a torts case might be *Defendant's Failure to Exercise Due Care.* The complaint should be self-contained and not refer to documents that are not attached to it.

One way to test whether the complaint is understandable is to have another attorney read it for you. While no one will ever win the Nobel Prize in Literature for drafting a complaint, there's no reason why complaints can't be written in simple, effective English.

C. THE BUFFALO CREEK COMPLAINT

Below is a portion of the federal complaint filed on behalf of many of the victims of the Buffalo Creek disaster by attorney Gerald Stern. The reproduced portion of the complaint includes the introductory paragraphs, the first and second counts or causes of action, the allegations of plaintiffs' injuries, and the prayer for relief. Because there were several hundred plaintiffs, they were listed in an appendix to the complaint rather than in the case caption. While the caption contains the civil action number for the case (3052), this number was assigned to the case at the time of its filing rather than placed on the complaint by counsel.

As you read the complaint consider (1) its compliance with the pleading requirements of the Federal Rules of Civil Procedure; (2) the factual investigation and legal research that presumably was done before the filing of the complaint; (3) the strategic decisions that led to the drafting of the complaint in the manner that it was drafted; (4) any pleading techniques that were used in the complaint because of the size and scope of the Buffalo Creek disaster litigation; and (5) why the complaint is so different from the barebones complaint shown in Form 11 of the Appendix of Forms to the Federal Rules of Civil Procedure.

**IN THE UNITED STATES DISTRICT COURT
FOR THE SOUTHERN DISTRICT OF
WEST VIRGINIA At Huntington**

DENNIS PRINCE, individually and as)
  Administrator of the estate of)
  Margie Prince;)
ROLAND STATEN, individually and as)
  Administrator of the estates of)
  Gladys Staten, Kevin Staten and)
  the unborn child of Gladys Staten;)
BOGLE TRENT, individually and as)
  Administrator of the estates of)
  Henry Trent, John Trent, Gene)
  Trent and Dellie Trent; and)
)
ADDITIONAL PLAINTIFFS LISTED IN)
  APPENDIX A,)
                   Plaintiffs)
) Civil Action

                                    v.   )
) No. 3052
THE PITTSTON COMPANY, a Delaware)
    and Virginia Corporation,   )
250 Park Avenue   )
New York, New York 10017,   )
                                    Defendant)

COMPLAINT

Plaintiffs for their complaint bring this civil action by their attorneys and complain and allege as follows:

1. The jurisdiction of this Court arises under 28 U.S.C., Section 1332.

2. The matter in controversy exceeds, for each of the individually named plaintiffs, the sum or value of $10,000, exclusive of interest and costs.

I. LIABILITY

FIRST CAUSE OF ACTION

Parties

3. All plaintiffs are citizens of the State of West Virginia or of a state other than the states in which the defendant, The Pittston Company, is incorporated or has its principal place of business.

4. The defendant, The Pittston Company, is a corporation incorporated under the laws of the states of Delaware and Virginia, and has its principal place of business in a state other than the State of West Virginia. Pittston's principal executive offices are at 250 Park Avenue, New York, New York 10017, and Pittston's principal operating offices are in Dante, Virginia. Pittston is licensed to do business in the State of West Virginia and is doing business in the Southern District of West Virginia.

5. All plaintiffs are persons who suffered grievous injury as a direct and proximate result of the defendant's actions and failures to act, as more particularly alleged hereafter.

6. Defendant, The Pittston Company ("Pittston") has been in the coal mining business for many years and is one of the largest coal companies in the United States. On or about June 1, 1970, Pittston acquired the Buffalo Mining Company, which also has been in the coal mining business for many years.

7. Pittston is liable to the plaintiffs for Pittston's own acts and failures to act, as a joint tortfeasor with Pittston's wholly-owned subsidiary, the Buffalo Mining Company.

8. Pittston also is liable to the plaintiffs for Pittston's own acts and failures to act, and for the acts and failures to act of Pittston's wholly-owned subsidiary, the Buffalo Mining Company, which is the alter ego and

business conduit of Pittston, dominated, directed, and controlled by Pittston and maintained by Pittston in corporate form and name only.

9.   Pittston also is liable to the plaintiffs for Pittston's own acts and failures to act of Pittston's wholly-owned subsidiary, the Buffalo Mining Company, on the basis of *respondeat superior*.

The Buffalo Creek Disaster

10.   Prior to and on February 26, 1972, the defendant conducted a coal mining operation in Logan County, West Virginia, in the immediate vicinity of the town of Saunders, West Virginia, and of two watercourses— Middle Fork and Buffalo Creek. This coal mining operation will be referred to hereafter as the "Buffalo Creek Coal Mining Operation."

11.   Prior to and on February 26, 1972, the defendant's Buffalo Creek Coal mining operation included a number of coal mines (underground, strip and auger coal mines), an enormous burning coal refuse pile (hereafter referred to as the "Burning Refuse Pile") approximately 200 feet high and over 1,000 feet long, located near the mouth of the Middle Fork of Buffalo Creek, Logan County, West Virginia, plus three refuse piles used as dams along the Middle Fork above this Burning Refuse Pile. The first refuse pile dam ("Dam 1"), constructed from coal mine refuse, was approximately twenty feet high. The second refuse pile dam ("Dam 2"), also constructed from coal mine refuse, was approximately twenty feet high. The third refuse pile dam ("Dam 3"), also constructed from coal mine refuse, was approximately forty-five to sixty feet high and was still being enlarged by the dumping of coal mine refuse immediately prior to its failure on February 26, 1972.

12.   Except for the Burning Refuse Pile and Dams 1, 2 and 3, Middle Fork would be a natural drain or watercourse, approximately six feet wide and six inches deep. As Dams 1, 2 and 3 were constructed and enlarged, the water that ran unobstructed down Middle Fork to Buffalo Creek was impounded.

13.   By February 26, 1972, the base of Dam 3 stretched 378 feet across Middle Fork Valley and was about 327 to 498 feet thick from front to back. The bank of Dam 3 was about 43 feet high on the right (northeast) abutment, and rose gradually to the southwest where it was sixty feet high.

14.   The refuse pile herein referred to as Dam 3 impeded drainage and impounded water, and as more and more coal mine refuse was dumped on top of and behind Dam 3, drainage through Dam 3 became more and more impeded and obstructed and water began to be impounded behind Dam 3 to a greater and greater extent. By February 26, 1972, approximately 21 million (21,000,000) cubic feet, or approximately 130 million (130,000,000) gallons, of water and 200,000 cubic yards of sludge and silt were impounded behind the refuse pile herein referred to as Dam 3.

15. For some time prior to February 26, 1972, up until approximately 8:00 a.m. on February 26, 1972, the defendant negligently and willfully did:

(a) use coal mine refuse to obstruct a natural watercourse and negligently permit a fire to burn in coal mine refuse in front of large bodies of water;

(b) design, construct, operate, maintain, use and/or enlarge the burning refuse pile, Dams 1, 2 and 3, the impoundment of water behind Dam 3, and the pools of water behind Dams 1 and 2;

(c) fail to inspect the burning refuse pile, Dams 1, 2 and 3, the impoundment of water behind Dam 3, and the pools of water behind Dams 1 and 2;

(d) fail to reinforce Dam 3 and to construct an emergency spillway around Dam 3;

(e) fail to warn the residents of Buffalo Creek Valley of the impending danger that Dam 3 would fail or of the failure of Dam 3; and

(f) interfere with, obstruct and deter others from warning the residents of Buffalo Creek Valley of the impending danger that Dam 3 would fail.

16. Paragraphs 17 through 30 contain some of the facts demonstrating the above-alleged negligent and willful acts and failure to act of the defendant.

17. Defendant knew or should have known, for many years, not to use coal mine refuse to obstruct a watercourse and not to permit a fire to burn in coal mine refuse in front of a large body of water.

18. Defendant knew or should have known that on October 21, 1966, in Aberfan, South Wales, United Kingdom, a massive coal mine refuse pile shifted and slid down upon the community of Aberfan, destroying a school, eighteen houses and other property and killing 144 men, women and children, of whom 116 were children.

19. Defendant knew or should have known that, as a result of the Aberfan disaster, the U.S. Geological Survey and the U.S. Bureau of Mines conducted an investigation of coal mine refuse piles in the United States to see if the Aberfan disaster could repeat itself in the United States; and that on December 9, 1966, the U.S. Geological Survey and the U.S. Bureau of Mines inspected the coal mine refuse pile (Dam 1) at Middle Fork, the only dam then in existence on Middle Fork, and found that the impoundment of 5 million cubic feet of water behind Dam 1, for settling of material and wash water, lacked an adequate spillway and could overtop Dam 1. Defendant knew, or should have known, of the report of this 1966 inspection.

20. Subsequent to and despite the 1966 report of the U.S. Geological Survey and the U.S. Bureau of Mines, Dam 1 was substantially increased in elevation, and Dams 2 and 3 were constructed.

21. On at least one occasion, one of the dams cracked and/or was overtopped causing some damage in the town of Saunders, West Virginia, immediately below the dams and the burning gob pile.

22. In 1971 a small failure occurred on the downstream side of Dam 3 toward the right abutment side, causing the coal mine refuse from Dam 3 to slide into Pool 2 from Dam 3; the defendant simply replaced this lost material by dumping more coal mine refuse on Dam 3.

23. The defendant improperly designed, constructed, operated, maintained, used and enlarged Dam 3.

24. Dam 3 was unstable under the conditions imposed upon it by defendant.

25. For approximately a year or more prior to February 26, 1972, "boils" of black water of about the color of the pool upstream of Dam 3 emerged into the relatively clear water of Pool 2 between Dam 3 and Dam 2. These boils indicated that excessive seepage had eroded a small flow path, or "pipe" in the foundation of Dam 3. Such piping is a well known danger signal. Nevertheless, defendant made no effort to inspect Dam 3 or the pool of water in front of Dam 3 to check for evidence of "piping" in the foundation of Dam 3.

26. The defendant did not provide an adequate program of technical inspections of Dams 1, 2 and 3, and the burning refuse pile, and did not continuously monitor Dams 1, 2 and 3 during periods of high precipitation.

27. The defendant constructed no emergency spillway or other adequate water-level controls for Dam 3 to permit the runoff of any of the 21 million cubic feet or 130 million gallons of water not needed by it, and took no measures to allow normal drainage to occur past Dam 3.

28. The defendant did not formulate any emergency plan for negating the hazard of rising water behind Dam 3 and warning persons downstream of possible flooding from Dam 3, although defendant knew or should have known, *inter alia,* that Dams 3 and 2 had failed on prior occasions, that Dam 3 was a hazard, that there were apparently impending dangers with respect to Dam 3, that residents of Buffalo Creek Valley had been concerned as to the stability of Dam 3, that a coal refuse pile was the cause of the 1966 Aberfan disaster, that in 1966 a United States Government report on Dam 1 had indicated that Dam 1 lacked an adequate spillway, and that the State of West Virginia officials thought Dam 3 needed reinforcement and an emergency spillway.

29. The defendant did not alert or warn, in any way, the residents of the Buffalo Creek Valley, the plaintiffs, the deceased persons represented by the plaintiffs, local public officials, local radio stations or TV stations, state public officials, or federal public officials, including the National Guard and the Bureau of Mines, (a) of the apparent impending dangers and Pittston's concern and alarm, on February 24, 25 and the morning of

February 26 prior to the dam's failure, for the stability of Dam 3, and (b) of the failure of Dam 3.

30. The defendant interfered with, obstructed and deterred efforts by concerned persons to learn of the impending dangers and concern and alarm for Dam 3's stability and to alert and warn other persons of the impending dangers and concern and alarm for Dam 3's stability.

31. The defendant's acts and failures to act, as alleged above in paragraphs 6 through 30, were negligent, grossly negligent and in wanton, willful, reckless and intentional disregard of the lives and property of plaintiffs and plaintiffs' decedents.

32. On February 26, 1972, as a direct and proximate result of the defendant's negligence, gross negligence, and wanton, willful, reckless and intentional disregard of the lives and property of the plaintiffs and plaintiffs' decedents, as alleged above in paragraphs 6 through 31, Dam 3 failed, Dams 1 and 2 failed, the burning refuse pile exploded, and an estimated 130 million (130,000,000) gallons of water and about one million (1,000,000) tons of refuse material descended upon the persons and property downstream of Dam 3—killing at least 118 men, women and children, some of whom are still missing; seriously, and in many cases, permanently, injuring thousands of persons in body and mind, totally destroying over five hundred homes and over forty mobile homes; damaging over 250 additional homes; destroying approximately 1,000 automobiles and trucks; leaving approximately 4,000 persons homeless, without water, electricity, telephone, or transportation; destroying community and family life nurtured over many generations; forcing numerous coal miners out of work; and directly and proximately causing the damages suffered and continuing to be suffered by plaintiffs and plaintiffs' decedents, as more particularly set forth in Section II and Appendix B attached hereto.

SECOND CAUSE OF ACTION

33. Plaintiffs repeat and re-allege paragraphs 3 through 32 hereof.

34. The defendant designed, constructed, used, and was in complete control of, an ultra-hazardous activity, i.e., the dumping of coal mine refuse, the maintenance of a burning refuse pile, the impoundment of massive amounts of water, and the obstruction of a natural watercourse, as more particularly alleged above. Therefore, defendant is absolutely liable, as a matter of law, for the damages suffered by plaintiffs and plaintiffs' decedents, as the direct and proximate result of defendant's ultra-hazardous activity.

35. Defendant's ultra-hazardous activity was and is the direct and proximate cause of the damages suffered and continuing to be suffered by plaintiffs and plaintiffs' decedents, as more particularly set forth in Section II and Appendix B attached hereto.

[The third through fifth causes of action then were alleged.]

II. COMPENSATORY DAMAGES

51. As a direct and proximate result of the defendant's negligent acts and failures to act, and as a direct and proximate result of the defendant's ultra-hazardous activity, * * * as more particularly alleged in Section I above:

A. The deceased persons whom plaintiffs represent suffered intense physical pain and mental anguish and lost their lives by drowning and/or in other ways, and lost all of their personal and/or real property; and

B. Plaintiffs suffered intense physical pain and mental anguish, and/or the loss of immediate members of their family and/or close personal friends; and/or lost all, or a large part, of their personal and/or real property; and/or lost their previous community and family life; and/or lost their physical and/or mental health; and/or received injuries to their bodies (all or a portion of said injuries being permanent in nature); and/or suffered and continue to suffer extensive medical expenses; and/or lost wages from employment; and/or suffered in their ability to make a living; and/or incurred and continue to incur great expense in attempting to support and maintain the remaining members of their families; and/or have been forced to live in undesirable and severely depressing circumstances at great expense of time, money and effort; and/or lost the companionship, services, society and/or consortium of immediate members of their family and/or close personal friends of themselves or their children; and/or suffered humiliation, insult and aggravation; and/or suffered in their efforts to educate themselves and/or other members of their family.

52. More particularly, plaintiffs have suffered damages in the amounts set forth in Appendix B attached hereto.

III. EXEMPLARY DAMAGES

53. Pittston's actions and failures to act in connection with Dam 3, Dams 1 and 2, the burning refuse pile, the massive impoundment of water behind Dam 3, and the pools of water behind Dams 1 and 2, as more particularly alleged in Sections I and II above, and as further alleged in this Section III, were done wantonly, willfully, intentionally, recklessly, maliciously, consciously, and in complete disregard of the consequences to the lives and property of plaintiffs and plaintiffs' decedents; and Pittston's gross negligence and wanton, willful, intentional, reckless, conscious and malicious conduct in complete disregard of the consequences to plaintiffs and plaintiffs' decedents was the direct and proximate cause of the damages suffered by plaintiffs and of the deaths of plaintiffs' decedents. Accordingly, in addition to compensatory damages due them, plaintiffs are entitled to damages of an exemplary and punitive nature.

54. In order to punish Pittston for its wanton and reckless disregard of human life and property and to deter Pittston from continuing such wanton and reckless disregard of human life and property, exemplary damages must be calculated in such a way and in such an amount,

together with compensatory damages, so as to provide an effective punishment and deterrence of Pittston.

[Exemplary damages of "at least $21 million" then were requested in paragraphs 55 through 58.]

IV. INJUNCTIVE RELIEF

59. Plaintiffs repeat and re-allege paragraphs 1 through 50 hereof.

[In paragraphs 60 and 61 the plaintiffs alleged that the Pittston Company was continuing the practices that led to the dam failure and that there was no adequate remedy at law "to compensate plaintiffs for these continuing hazards and perils."]

PRAYERS FOR RELIEF

WHEREFORE, plaintiffs pray:

1. Judgment against Pittston for compensatory damages in the approximate amount of $31 million as set forth in Appendix B attached hereto and made a part hereof;

2. Judgment against Pittston for exemplary damages of $21 million to be apportioned among plaintiffs in proportion to their compensatory damages;

3. To the extent that monetary damages do not provide complete relief, a permanent injunction requiring Pittston to provide plaintiffs with the same or equal housing and community facilities they enjoyed prior to February 26, 1972;

4. A permanent injunction enjoining and restraining Pittston from constructing refuse piles in the vicinity of its Buffalo Creek mines so as to impede drainage or impound water; from constructing water or silt retaining dams out of coal refuse; from failing to construct water or silt retaining dams of substantial construction; from failing to inspect at least once each week all of its water or silt retaining dams; * * * from maintaining and continuing to use the burning refuse piles in the vicinity of the Buffalo Creek mines; from failing to extinguish forever any and all fires burning in any of its burning refuse piles in the vicinity of its Buffalo Creek mines; from damming or obstructing or continuing to dam or obstruct any natural watercourse in the vicinity of its Buffalo Creek mines without obtaining design or construction approval from the Public Service Commission of the State of West Virginia; and from failing to establish and to maintain an emergency warning system to provide accurate and sufficient warning to all residents in the vicinity of its Buffalo Creek mines of the imminence of any hazard or danger arising out of the operations of its Buffalo Creek mines; from failing to drain all of its water impoundments, wherever they may be, constructed of coal mine refuse; and from failing to extinguish forever all fires in all of its coal mine refuse piles, wherever they may be.

5. Such other, further and additional relief as to the Court may seem just and proper, together with the interest, costs and disbursements of this action, including just and reasonable attorneys' fees and expenses.

s/ _____
Gerald M. Stern

s/ _____
Harry Huge
Arnold & Porter
1229 Nineteenth Street, N.W.
Washington, D.C. 20036
Tel: 202/223–3200

s/ _____
Willis O. Shay
Steptoe & Johnson
10th Floor
Union Bank Building
Clarksburg, West Virginia 26301
Tel: 624–5601

Of Counsel:

Arnold & Porter
1229 Nineteenth Street, N.W.
Washington, D.C. 20036

Steptoe & Johnson
10th Floor
Union Bank Building
Clarksburg, West Virginia
26301

PLAINTIFFS DEMAND A JURY TRIAL AS TO SECTIONS I, II AND III AND PARAGRAPHS 1 AND 2 OF THE PRAYERS FOR RELIEF

Exercises Concerning Complaint Drafting

1. You are an associate in a small law firm in Nashville, Tennessee. Your assignment is set forth in the following memorandum.

MEMORANDUM

TO: LITIGATION ASSOCIATE
FROM: LITIGATION PARTNER
DATE: JANUARY 30, 1973
RE: THOMAS EAKINS LAWSUIT

This memorandum will confirm our conversation concerning the drafting of a civil complaint on behalf of Thomas Eakins. As you will remember, Mr. Eakins is an unemployed coal miner who was visiting his sister in Logan County, West Virginia at the time of the Buffalo Creek disaster on February 26, 1972. On the morning of the flood Eakins had been left in charge of his young nephew, and, although Eakins, himself, survived the flood, his nephew drowned. Eakins also lost his 1965 Oldsmobile and various items of personal property in the flood, saw several people die, and watched his sister's house collapse from the flood waters.

As you suggested, I have obtained and attached a copy of the complaint filed by Gerald Stern in the United States District Court for the Southern District of West Virginia. I'd like you to improve on this complaint if you can and see if there aren't additional claims that we can assert on Eakins's behalf. Remember that we have decided to file Eakins's action against the Pittston Company in the United States District Court for the Middle District of Tennessee.

In addition to drafting the complaint you should (1) prepare the necessary civil summons; (2) complete a civil cover sheet; and (3) prepare a short memorandum explaining the differences between your complaint and the one drafted by Gerald Stern and the reasons for such differences. While I don't expect extensive legal research, please use your memorandum to explain the reasons for suing the defendants and adopting the legal theories that you have. Your memorandum also should flag any additional factual investigation that should be done before filing the complaint.

———

2. Your neighbor, Rita Wagner, bought a new and quite expensive sports car nine months ago. Unfortunately, she has had a series of major problems with the car and would like to be rid of it. The car dealer from whom she bought the car will not take it back, and efforts to resolve her dispute with the dealer have proven unsuccessful. Making reasonable assumptions as to any necessary additional facts, draft a short complaint on behalf of Rita Wagner.

3. Find a newspaper article describing an accident or other event that has the potential to lead to civil litigation. Draft a complaint on behalf of one of the parties to this incident. Along with your complaint, hand in a short memorandum describing the investigation that you would conduct before filing suit and any factual assumptions that you have made in drafting the complaint. Attach to your memorandum a copy of the newspaper article on which the complaint is based. While suitable articles can be found in any newspaper, the exercise will be more fun if the article is chosen from one of those papers sold in the grocery store check-out line.

VI.   RULE 11 AND THE ETHICS OF PLEADING

The Preamble to the ABA Model Rules of Professional Conduct recognizes "the lawyer's obligation zealously to protect and pursue a client's legitimate interests, within the bounds of the law, while maintaining a professional, courteous and civil attitude toward all persons involved in the legal system." When does an attorney's devotion to a client run afoul of duties to other parties, other counsel, the courts, and our system of civil justice? Although sometimes the answers to these questions are not easy, the bench and bar have attempted in at least two separate ways to delineate the boundaries within which modern civil adjudication is to be conducted.

In addition to the pleading requirements of Rules 8, 9, and 10, Rule 11 of the Federal Rules of Civil Procedure requires attorneys to perform factual investigation and legal research before filing court documents and forbids the filing of documents for improper purposes. To give teeth to these requirements, Rule 11(c)(1) provides that district courts may impose sanctions upon "any attorney, law firm, or party that violated [Rule 11] or is responsible for the violation."

In contrast to the sanctions approach taken by Rule 11, bar associations, other professional groups, and courts have adopted codes of litigation conduct and creeds of professionalism. These codes often concern not only attorneys' dealings with clients and the courts, but their duties to fellow counsel. In this section, both Rule 11 and the efforts to police and improve attorney conduct through codes of conduct and professionalism are considered.

A. RULE 11 OF THE FEDERAL RULES OF CIVIL PROCEDURE

Rule 11 of the Federal Rules of Civil Procedure has been extremely controversial in recent years.[90] While largely ignored for the first 45 years of its existence, after its amendment in 1983 Rule 11 became a major concern both among lawyers and judges. As amended in 1983, Rule 11 for the first time established an objective, rather than a subjective, standard for attorney conduct. Perhaps even more significantly, the 1983 version of the Rule provided that, if this objective standard of reasonableness was violated, sanctions had to be imposed by the courts.

As a result of the 1983 amendments to Rule 11, there was a tremendous increase in litigation under that Rule.[91] There also was criticism that

---

90. However, the notion behind Rule 11 is not new. "The genesis of the rationale supporting the rule is generally attributed to Justice Joseph Story, who believed that counsel's signature served to guarantee that 'there is good ground for suit in the manner in which it is framed.' J. Story, *Equity Pleadings* § 47 (1838)." *Golyar v. McCausland*, 738 F.Supp. 1090, 1097 n. 11 (W.D.Mich. 1990).

91. From the adoption of the Federal Rules in 1938 until the amendment of Rule 11 in 1983, there were approximately two dozen reported decisions involving that Rule. Stempel, "Sanctions, Symmetry, and Safe Harbors: Limiting Misapplication of Rule 11 by Harmonizing it with Pre–Verdict Dismissal Devices," 60 *Fordham L. Rev.* 257, 257 (1991). As of 1988, only five years after the amended Rule 11 took effect, there were over 100 federal appellate decisions and over 1000 reported decisions in all federal courts dealing with Rule 11. Section of Litigation, American Bar Association, *Sanctions: Rule 11 and Other Powers* (2d ed. 1988); Committee on Trial Practice, Section of Litigation, American Bar Association, "Standards and Guidelines for Practice Under Rule 11 of the Federal Rules of Civil Procedure," 121 F.R.D. 101, 104 (1988).

Rule 11 was having a differential impact upon civil rights plaintiffs and had become a deterrent to the filing of legitimate civil rights actions.[92] Both opponents and proponents of the 1983 version of the Rule argued that the Rule deterred certain litigation conduct and required attorneys to "stop and think" before filing a paper, advocating a position, or taking a case.[93] Critics differed, though, as to whether this deterrence was a good or a bad development.[94] There also was a concern that "the financial cost of satellite litigation resulting from imposing sanctions perhaps exceeded the benefits resulting from any increased tendency of lawyers to 'stop and think.' "[95]

Due to the wide-spread criticism of the 1983 amendments to Rule 11, the Advisory Committee on Civil Rules initiated a study of the Rule in 1990, which included a solicitation of written comments and a 1991 public hearing.[96] In response to this study and debate, the Advisory Committee recommended amendments to Rule 11, and those recommended amendments became effective in 1993. The current version of Rule 11 differs from the 1983 version of the Rule both in terms of what conduct constitutes a violation of Rule 11 and in regard to what, if any, sanction should be imposed by the court when a Rule 11 violation occurs.[97]

The growth in Rule 11 decisions and sanctions led to the founding of newsletters and treatises devoted to that rule and other sanction developments. *See Attorney Sanctions Newsletter* (Shepard's/McGraw–Hill, Inc.); G. Joseph, *Sanctions: The Federal Law of Litigation Abuse* (4th ed. 2008); G. Vairo, *Rule 11 Sanctions: Case Law, Perspectives and Preventive Measures* (3d ed. 2004).

The expansion of Rule 11 litigation and sanctions in recent years has impacted popular culture as well. *E.g., Christian v. Mattel, Inc.*, 286 F.3d 1118, 1121 (9th Cir. 2002) ("In her wildest dreams, Barbie could not have imagined herself in the middle of Rule 11 proceedings.").

92. *See* Committee on Rules of Practice and Procedure, Judicial Conference of the United States, *Call for Written Comments on Rule 11 of the Federal Rules of Civil Procedure and Related Rules*, 131 F.R.D. 335, 347 (1990) [hereinafter *Call for Written Comments on Rule 11*] ("Particular concern has been expressed about the effect [of Rule 11] on civil rights plaintiffs.").

93. Arthur R. Miller, *The August 1983 Amendments to the Federal Rules of Civil Procedure: Promoting Effective Case Management and Lawyer Responsibility* 15 (1984).

94. Just as there are both "good" and "bad" types of cholesterol, there are "good" and "bad" types of deterrence. While Rule 11 should operate to deter frivolous and harassing litigation, that Rule should not have the effect of deterring legitimate legal theories and factual contentions.

95. *Call for Written Comments on Rule 11, supra* note 92, 131 F.R.D. at 346.

96. *Call for Written Comments on Rule 11, supra* note 92, 131 F.R.D. at 344–45. *See also* Federal Judicial Center, *Rule 11: Final Report to the Advisory Committee on Civil Rules of the Judicial Conference of the United States* (1991); Marshall et al., "The Use and Impact of Rule 11," 86 *Nw. U. L. Rev.* 943 (1992); Task Force on Federal Rule of Civil Procedure 11, United States Court of Appeals for the Third Circuit, *Rule 11 in Transition: The Report of the Third Circuit Task Force on Federal Rule of Civil Procedure 11* (1989).

97. In recent years Members of Congress have attempted to overturn the 1993 "kinder and gentler" version of Rule 11. *E.g.*, Job Creation Act of 2010, H.R. 4513, 111th Cong., 2nd Sess. (2010); Lawsuit Abuse Reduction Act of 2005, H.R. 420, 109th Cong., 1st Sess. (2005). Such proposed legislation would, *inter alia*, return Rule 11 to its 1983 form, under which judges were required to impose sanctions on attorneys who violated that Rule and there was no 21–day "safe harbor" period during which attorneys can withdraw objectionable pleadings to avoid sanctions. Such efforts have been opposed by the ABA's Section of Litigation and an overwhelming majority of federal judges who participated in a Federal Judicial Center survey. Stevenson, "Federal Judges Favor Rule 11 As Is," *Litigation News*, Sept. 30, 2005, at 1.

In addition to these efforts to legislatively amend Rule 11, in the Private Securities Litigation Reform Act of 1995, Pub. L. No. 104–67, 109 Stat. 737 (1995), Congress provided that federal

1. What Conduct Violates Rule 11?

Rule 11(a) of the Federal Rules of Civil Procedure requires that every "pleading, written motion, and other paper" must be signed by at least one attorney of record or, if a party is not represented by counsel, by the party. By "presenting" such a paper to the court (which may occur by signing, filing, submitting, or later advocating the paper), an attorney or unrepresented party certifies to the court that, "to the best of the person's knowledge, information, and belief, formed after an inquiry reasonable under the circumstances:"

(1) [the document] is not being presented for any improper purpose, such as to harass, cause unnecessary delay, or needlessly increase the cost of litigation;

(2) the claims, defenses, and other legal contentions are warranted by existing law or by a nonfrivolous argument for extending, modifying, or reversing existing law or for establishing new law;

(3) the factual contentions have evidentiary support or, if specifically so identified, will likely have evidentiary support after a reasonable opportunity for further investigation or discovery; and

(4) the denials of factual contentions are warranted on the evidence or, if specifically so identified, are reasonably based on belief or a lack of information.[98]

As was the case prior to 1993, Rule 11 certifications fall into three basic categories. By presenting a court paper, the presenter certifies certain things concerning both the legal and factual bases underlying that paper, as well as certifying that the paper is not being presented for an improper purpose.

Rule 11 applies an objective standard to attorney and party conduct. It is no defense to an alleged violation of Rule 11 that the presenter of the offending paper believed that the paper complied with the Rule. Lawyers cannot invoke a subjective "empty-head pure-heart" defense to alleged violations of Rule 11.[99] Rule 11(b) requires that attorneys and parties conduct an "inquiry reasonable under the circumstances" before presenting a paper to the court. There thus is an affirmative duty upon a lawyer to conduct factual investigation and legal research before filing lawsuits and taking positions in court documents.

Prior to 1993, courts differed as to whether Rule 11 imposed a "continuing duty" upon counsel and, therefore, whether that Rule could be violated even though a document complied with Rule 11 at the time that it had been filed with the court.[100] Under the current version of the

---

district courts "shall impose" sanctions for non-compliance with Rule 11(b) in connection with certain litigation pursuant to the federal securities acts. 15 U.S.C. §§ 77z–1(c)(2) and 78u–4(c)(2).

98. Fed. R. Civ. P. 11(b).

99. Advisory Committee Note to 1993 Amendment to Rule 11, 146 F.R.D. 401, 586–87 (1993).

100. *Compare Herron v. Jupiter Transp. Co.*, 858 F.2d 332, 335–36 (6th Cir. 1988) (continuing duty) *with Corporation of the Presiding Bishop v. Associated Contractors*, 877 F.2d 938, 942–43

Rule, there is no question that a continuing duty exists. The Rule now is triggered by "presenting" a paper to the court, and "presenting" is defined by Rule 11(b) to include "signing, filing, submitting, or later advocating" a particular court paper. The Advisory Committee explained in its note to the 1993 amendment to Rule 11 that "a litigant's obligations with respect to the contents of [court] papers are not measured solely as of the time they are filed with or submitted to the court, but include reaffirming to the court and advocating positions contained in those pleadings and motions after learning that they cease to have merit."[101] However, while later conduct may trigger an attorney's duty concerning a previously-filed paper, Rule 11 does not apply to situations in which no paper ever has been filed with or submitted to the court.[102]

Rule 11 recognizes that counsel may be uncertain concerning particular facts at the very outset of an action when the complaint and answer are filed. Rule 11(b)(3) provides that if a party or counsel is not, at the time a paper is filed or submitted, yet certain about the evidentiary basis underlying an allegation or factual contention, the matter nevertheless can be pled if it is "specifically so identified" and "will likely have evidentiary support after a reasonable opportunity for further investigation or discovery." Rule 11(b)(4) is a counterpart provision for those opposing a claim, providing that denials can be asserted even if they are not then known to be warranted on the evidence so long as they are "specifically so identified" and are "reasonably based on belief or a lack of information."

However, the Rule 11 duty remains:

> Tolerance of factual contentions in initial pleadings by plaintiffs or defendants when specifically identified as made on information and belief does not relieve litigants from the obligation to conduct an appropriate investigation into the facts that is reasonable under the circumstances * * * . Moreover, if evidentiary support is not obtained after a reasonable opportunity for further investigation or discovery, the party has a duty under the rule not to persist with the contention.[103]

Although the offending document need not be amended or withdrawn, it is a violation of Rule 11 to premise advocacy upon a court document that, despite a reasonable opportunity for investigation or discovery, is without evidentiary support.

While improper discovery conduct may be considered pursuant to Rules 26 through 37, Rule 11(d) explicitly provides that Rule 11 does not apply to disclosures and discovery requests, responses, objections, and

---

(11th Cir. 1989) (no continuing duty). Even absent the recognition of a continuing duty under the pre–1993 version of Rule 11, "Rare is the case that goes from complaint and answer to trial without an intervening filing. Updating occurs in the course of these filings." *Pantry Queen Foods v. Lifschultz Fast Freight*, 809 F.2d 451, 454 (7th Cir. 1987).

101. Advisory Committee Note to 1993 Amendment to Rule 11, 146 F.R.D. 401, 585 (1993).

102. *Id.*

103. *Id.* at 585–86.

motions. However, Rule 11 otherwise is very broad, applying not only to written pleadings and motions but extending to any "other paper" presented to the court.[104]

NOTES AND QUESTIONS CONCERNING RULE 11 VIOLATIONS

1. May attorneys be sanctioned under Rule 11 for failure to cite adverse authority? *Compare Golden Eagle Distrib. Corp. v. Burroughs Corp.*, 801 F.2d 1531, 1541–42 (9th Cir. 1986) (no) *with Jorgenson v. County of Volusia*, 846 F.2d 1350 (11th Cir. 1988) (per curiam) (yes). *See also* Model Rules of Prof'l Conduct Rule 3.3(a)(3). The following test has been suggested to provide guidance as to whether an adverse precedent must be disclosed: "[T]he more unhappy a lawyer is that he found an adverse precedent, the clearer it is that he must reveal it." 2 G. Hazard et al., *The Law of Lawyering* § 29.11, at 29–18 (3d ed. 2011). *See also* Howard, Comment, "The Duty to Cite Adverse Authority," 16 *J. Legal Prof.* 295 (1991).

2. In connection with the duty to cite adverse authority, consider the following argument made by an attorney to the Illinois Supreme Court:

> This is the first case that I have ever had in this court, and I have therefore examined it with great care. As the Court will perceive by looking at the abstract of the record, the only question in this case is one of authority. I have not been able to find any authority to sustain my side of the case, but I have found several cases directly on point on the other side. I will now give these authorities to the court, and then submit the case.

W. Herndon & J. Weik, *Herndon's Lincoln* 323 (1889). Was the attorney, Abraham Lincoln, required to make such a presentation to the court? Why was this position apparently taken for the first time on appeal?

3. Prior to its 1993 amendment, the portion of Rule 11 concerning the legal sufficiency of court papers tracked the language of Disciplinary Rule 7–102(A)(2) of the Model Code of Professional Responsibility. The 1983 version of Rule 11 thus provided that attorneys should not take positions unwarranted by existing law unless they were supported by a "good faith argument for the extension, modification, or reversal of existing law." As amended in 1993 and 2007, Rule 11(b)(2) now requires that contentions be "warranted by exiting law or by a nonfrivolous argument for extending, modifying, or reversing existing law or for establishing new law." *Cf.* Model Rules of Prof'l Conduct Rule 3.1 ("A lawyer shall not bring or defend a proceeding, or assert or controvert an issue therein, unless there is a basis for doing so that is not frivolous, which includes a good faith argument for an extension, modification or reversal of existing law."). *See generally* Johnson, "Integrating Legal Ethics & Professional Responsibility with Federal Rule of Civil Procedure 11," 37 *Loy. L.A. L. Rev.* 819 (2004).

4. Can counsel assert a legal position that she knows the trial court must reject because of binding precedent to the contrary in that jurisdiction? *See Hunter v. Earthgrains Co. Bakery*, 281 F.3d 144 (4th Cir. 2002) (Rule 11

---

104. Fed. R. Civ. P. 11(b).

sanction overturned because, despite binding appellate decision to the contrary, majority of other courts of appeals (and, ultimately, the Supreme Court) had resolved this legal question to the contrary).

5. Must attorneys in their court papers explicitly differentiate an argument "warranted by existing law" from a "nonfrivolous argument for extending, modifying, or reversing existing law or for establishing new law?" *Compare Golden Eagle Distrib. Corp. v. Burroughs Corp.*, 801 F.2d 1531, 1539–41 (9th Cir. 1986), and *Mary Ann Pensiero, Inc. v. Lingle*, 847 F.2d 90, 96 (3d Cir. 1988) (no) *with DeSisto College, Inc. v. Line*, 888 F.2d 755, 766 (11th Cir. 1989), *cert. denied*, 495 U.S. 952 (1990) (yes).

6. One consequence of recent Rule 11 activity has been a federalization of certain aspects of legal ethics, which historically have been primarily matters of state concern. *See* McMorrow, "Rule 11 and Federalizing Lawyer Ethics," 1991 *B.Y.U. L. Rev.* 959. *See also* Kramer, "Viewing Rule 11 as a Tool to Improve Professional Responsibility," 75 *Minn. L. Rev.* 793, 798 (1991) (arguing that "Rule 11 thus offers the federal courts an opportunity to enforce professional responsibility rules that state disciplinary bodies have been unable or unwilling to enforce."). Is this a good trend?

7. Does knowledge that other attorneys have withdrawn from a case create a duty for prospective counsel to inquire as to the reasons for change of counsel? *See Brown v. Federation of State Medical Boards*, 830 F.2d 1429, 1436 (7th Cir. 1987) (yes). *See also Bakker v. Grutman*, 942 F.2d 236 (4th Cir. 1991) (lawyer did not violate Rule 11 by entering frivolous lawsuit as replacement counsel and signing motions for extensions of time).

8. Do some court papers only become a violation of Rule 11 based upon the response of the opposing party? Can a plaintiff assert time-barred claims in her complaint or must she withhold such claims and presume that the defendant will raise the affirmative defense of the statute of limitations? *See Brubaker v. City of Richmond*, 943 F.2d 1363, 1383–85 (4th Cir. 1991) (plaintiff's lawyer cannot engage in "cat and mouse" game with defendant by filing time-barred claims and only withdrawing them once statute of limitations defense is asserted). *See generally* Taylor, "Filing with Your Fingers Crossed: Should a Party be Sanctioned for Filing a Claim to Which There is a Dispositive, Yet Waivable, Affirmative Defense?," 47 *Syracuse L. Rev.* 1037 (1997).

9. How do clients and potential clients feel about the fact that attorneys have been sanctioned for Rule 11 violations? *Compare* Burton, "Rule 11 Sanctions and Lawyer Advertising: A Modest Proposal," 45 *Ark. L. Rev.* 309 (1992) (suggesting as a potential sanction a requirement that attorneys must disclose Rule 11 sanctions in any advertising) *with* United States Court of Appeals for the Second Circuit, *Annual Judicial Conference*, 136 F.R.D. 233, 257 (1990) (relating anecdote concerning client who retained attorney who had been sanctioned four times in the past).

10. During the Rules revision process, it was suggested that Rule 11 should be amended so that violations would be determined based upon "the paper taken as a whole." *Bench–Bar Proposal to Revise Civil Procedure Rule 11*, 137 F.R.D. 159, 165 (1991). Under such an amendment, "If the paper as a whole reflects reasonable inquiry and reasonable presentation of law or a non-

frivolous proposal for change of law, it will meet the requirement; litigation which takes the form of parsing of fragments of the composition is intended to be eliminated." *Id.* at 169. This proposed amendment was not adopted. Should it have been?

11.   Since 1983, bad faith has not been a prerequisite to the imposition of sanctions, and attorneys can not invoke a subjective "empty-head pure-heart" defense. Are there problems with administering an objective standard under Rule 11? With sanctioning attorneys and clients for non-wilful violations of Rule 11? Is wilfulness significant for any purposes under Rule 11? *See also In re Pennie & Edmonds LLP*, 323 F.3d 86, 91 (2d Cir. 2003) (subjective bad faith standard applies to court-initiated Rule 11 sanctions, at least when sanction "was initiated long after [sanctioned law firm] had an opportunity to correct or withdraw the challenged submission").

12.   Rule 11(b)(1)–(4) provides that a court paper can violate Rule 11 in several ways. Prior to the 1993 amendment to Rule 11, at least one court of appeals had held that a motion filed to harass, even though not objectively unreasonable, could violate the "improper purpose" clause of Rule 11. *Aetna Life Ins. Co. v. Alla Medical Services, Inc.*, 855 F.2d 1470 (9th Cir. 1988). Previously this same court of appeals had concluded that an objectively reasonable complaint, even if filed for an improper purpose, could not violate Rule 11. *Zaldivar v. City of Los Angeles*, 780 F.2d 823 (9th Cir. 1986). Is there a basis for differentiating between an objectively reasonable complaint that is filed for an improper purpose and another pleading or paper that is objectively reasonable but filed for an improper purpose? *See also Whitehead v. Food Max of Mississippi, Inc.*, 332 F.3d 796 (5th Cir. 2003) (en banc) (although writ of execution was "well grounded in fact and law," lawyer's improper purpose in obtaining writ (to embarrass defendant and advance his own reputation) provided basis for Rule 11 sanction); *Sussman v. Bank of Israel*, 56 F.3d 450 (2d Cir.), *cert. denied*, 516 U.S. 916 (1995) (so long as complaint is not frivolous, sanctions should not be imposed for allegedly improper motives in its filing).

13.   Is the court's grant of leave to file an amended complaint always a good thing for the plaintiff and his attorney? In *Sprewell v. Golden State Warriors*, 231 F.3d 520 (9th Cir. 2000), the district court dismissed Latrell Sprewell's complaint without prejudice to the filing of an amended complaint but then sanctioned his attorneys for filing "the same baseless claims previously dismissed by the court." 231 F.3d at 525. However, in *Anderson v. Smithfield Foods, Inc.*, 353 F.3d 912 (11th Cir. 2003), sanctions of $128,563 were overturned because, *inter alia*, "[w]hile the district court's first dismissal does state that RICO is not the proper remedy for Plaintiffs to pursue, the order also points out the pleading defects in the Plaintiffs' RICO claims and gives the Plaintiffs leave to file a Second Amended Complaint." 353 F.3d at 916.

The repleading dilemma faced by plaintiff's counsel has been described, and resolved, by one court as follows:

> [A] dismissal with leave to replead is not a final order that is immediately appealable. [citations omitted] In order to appeal, the plaintiff would have to forego the leave to replead granted him, either by allowing the deadline

for repleading to pass or by having the court revoke that leave and enter a final judgment. We disagree with the suggestion that a plaintiff should be penalized for taking the option given him by the court to attempt to replead in a way designed to cure flaws found in his complaint by the court.

Stern v. Leucadia Nat'l Corp., 844 F.2d 997, 1004–1005 (2d Cir. 1988). *See* Joseph, "Sanctions 2002," *Nat'l L.J.*, Feb. 4, 2002, at B11.

2. What Sanctions Should Be Imposed?

Of even greater significance than the 1993 amendments that define Rule 11 violations are amendments from that same year governing Rule 11 sanctions. Those amendments worked great changes not only in the sanctions that can be imposed but in the manner in which sanctions are to be imposed under amended Rule 11.

Rule 11(c)(1) now explicitly provides that sanctions only are to be imposed "after notice and a reasonable opportunity to respond." In addition, a "safe harbor" provision now applies to situations in which sanctions are sought by a party. A party seeking Rule 11 sanctions must request sanctions in a motion, "made separately from any other motion," that describes the specific conduct that allegedly violates Rule 11.[105] However, this motion is not in the first instance to be filed with the court. Instead, Rule 11(c)(2) provides that, while such a motion should be served upon the party against whom sanctions are sought, it "must not be filed or be presented to the court if the challenged paper, claim, defense, contention, or denial is withdrawn or appropriately corrected within 21 days after service or within another time the court sets." Therefore, if the alleged Rule 11 violation is corrected within 21 days after a Rule 11 motion has been served, no sanctions can be awarded. Thus there is an incentive to withdraw papers that may violate Rule 11, and counsel need not fear that the withdrawal of a court paper will be seen as an admission of a Rule 11 violation.

The persons against whom sanctions can be imposed also changed as a result of the 1993 amendments. Rule 11(c)(1) provides that sanctions may be imposed "on any attorney, law firm, or party that violated [Rule 11] or is responsible for the violation." Prior to 1993, only those persons who signed an offending court paper could be sanctioned for the Rule 11 violation.[106] Thus, under the 1983 version of Rule 11, a court could sanction a client who signed a court document violative of Rule 11 but not the law firm's senior partner who ordered the document to be filed but did not sign that document. Rule 11(c)(1) now extends to those "responsible for" any violation of that Rule, specifically providing: "Absent exceptional circumstances, a law firm must be held jointly responsible for a violation committed by its partner, associate, or employee."[107]

---

105. Fed. R. Civ. P. 11(c)(2).

106. *Pavelic & LeFlore v. Marvel Entertainment Group*, 493 U.S. 120 (1989).

107. Apart from possible Rule 11 sanctions, an attorney may be sanctioned for violations of the Rules of Professional Conduct due to the conduct of an associate in his law firm whom the partner was to be supervising. *In re Cohen*, 847 A.2d 1162 (D.C. 2004).

While defendants and defense counsel could be sanctioned under the prior version of Rule 11, there were few instances in which defendants or their counsel actually were sanctioned due to an answer.[108] Because of this unequal application of Rule 11, the most recent version of the Rule explicitly extends to "defenses" as well as "claims" and to "denials" as well as "contentions."[109]

Perhaps most significantly, under the current version of Rule 11 judicial sanctions are no longer mandatory; Rule 11(c)(1) now provides that courts "may" impose sanctions for a violation of the Rule. In addition, Rule 11(c)(4) specifically provides that any sanction "must be limited to what suffices to deter repetition of [the offending] conduct or comparable conduct by others similarly situated."

District courts retain a great amount of discretion concerning the appropriate sanction to be imposed for a violation of Rule 11. As one federal court of appeals noted concerning the 1983 version of Rule 11, sanctions under Rule 11 can include "a warm friendly discussion on the record, a hard-nosed reprimand in open court, compulsory legal education, monetary sanctions, or other measures appropriate to the circumstances."[110] For violating Rule 11, attorneys have been required to send a written apology to the injured party, attend continuing legal education sessions, and, in at least one instance, undertake a "penmanship exercise" requiring the offending attorney to copy Rule 11 100 times.[111]

The Advisory Committee Note to the 1993 amendment to Rule 11 lists numerous factors that might be considered in determining whether to impose a sanction and, if so, what sanction to impose:

> Whether the improper conduct was willful, or negligent; whether it was part of a pattern of activity, or an isolated event; whether it infected the entire pleading, or only one particular count or defense; whether the person has engaged in similar conduct in other litigation; whether it was intended to injure; what effect it had on the litigation process in time or expense; whether the responsible person is trained in the law; what amount, given the financial resources of the responsible person, is needed to deter that person from repetition in the

---

108. For a rare example of such a sanction, in this case due to a grossly inflated prayer for relief in a counterclaim, see *Hudson v. Moore Business Forms, Inc.*, 836 F.2d 1156 (9th Cir. 1987). *See also Bodenhamer Building Corp. v. Architectural Research Corp.*, 989 F.2d 213, 217 (6th Cir. 1993) ("[W]e reject defendants' contention that an answer is not a pleading capable of being sanctioned.").

109. Fed. R. Civ. P. 11(b)(2), (3), (4).

110. *Thomas v. Capital Security Services, Inc.*, 836 F.2d 866, 878 (5th Cir.1988) (en banc).

111. *Rule 11: Final Report to the Advisory Committee on Civil Rules of the Judicial Conference of the United States* § 2C, at 16, 17 (1991). Then there was the lawyer who was ordered to take courses in reading comprehension and legal ethics by a federal judge due to his failure to have a party representative with unlimited settlement authority present at a settlement conference. Harlan, "Remedial Writing May Have Been a Better Choice for This Profession," *Wall St. J.*, May 27, 1992, at B1. *See also Moser v. Bret Harte Union High School Dist.*, 366 F.Supp.2d 944 (E.D.Cal. 2005) (Rule 11 sanction required attorney to obtain 20 hours of continuing legal education credit in ethics and her law firm to provide a minimum of six hours of such training for all attorneys in the firm).

same case; what amount is needed to deter similar activity by other litigants: all of these may in a particular case be proper considerations.[112]

Under the pre–1993 version of Rule 11, quite substantial monetary sanctions had been awarded by the courts.[113] While monetary sanctions still can be imposed under Rule 11, fee shifting under that Rule (as opposed to the payment of a monetary penalty into court) is only authorized by Rule 11(c)(4) "if imposed on motion and warranted for effective deterrence."[114] In addition, monetary sanctions cannot be awarded against a represented party due to lack of legal support for that party's claims, defenses, or contentions.[115] If a party is represented by counsel, any monetary sanction for such a Rule 11 violation must fall upon that party's counsel.

Although the courts retain a great amount of discretion as to appropriate sanctions under Rule 11, amended Rule 11 prescribes specific procedures that must be followed before a court imposes any sanction. While Rule 11 preserves the ability of the court to impose Rule 11 sanctions on its own initiative, this power is carefully circumscribed. There is no "safe harbor" provision as there is when a party seeks Rule 11 sanctions, but Rule 11(c)(3) only permits a court to award sanctions on its own initiative if it first orders "an attorney, law firm, or party to show cause why conduct specifically described in the order has not violated Rule 11(b)." In addition to this requirement that show cause orders be used in connection with court-initiated sanctions, Rule 11 now precludes a court from awarding monetary sanctions on its own initiative unless its show cause order issues before a voluntary dismissal or settlement.[116] When imposing any sanctions, Rule 11(c)(6) requires a court to describe the conduct constituting a Rule 11 violation and explain the basis of the sanction imposed.

---

112. Advisory Committee Note to 1993 Amendment to Rule 11, 146 F.R.D. 401, 587 (1993).

113. *E.g. Avirgan v. Hull*, 932 F.2d 1572 (11th Cir. 1991), *cert. denied,* 502 U.S. 1048 (1992) (sanction "in excess of one million dollars"); *Kunstler v. Britt*, 914 F.2d 505 (4th Cir. 1990), *cert. denied*, 499 U.S. 969 (1991) ($122,834.28 sanction); *Unioil, Inc. v. E. F. Hutton & Co.*, 809 F.2d 548 (9th Cir. 1986), *cert. denied*, 484 U.S. 823 (1987) ($294,141.10 sanction). However, such large monetary sanctions were not typical of the sanctions imposed under Rule 11. Federal Judicial Center, *Rule 11: Final Report to the Advisory Committee on Civil Rules of the Judicial Conference of the United States* § 1B, at 8 (1991) (in 5 districts studied, median Rule 11 monetary sanctions ranged from $1000 to $3776); Marshal et al., "The Use and Impact of Rule 11," 86 *Nw. U. L. Rev.* 943, 957 (1992) (44.6% of monetary sanctions considered in study involved $1500 or less, while 91.3% of sanctions involved $25,000 or less).

114. Thus courts cannot, on their own initiative, award attorneys' fees due to a Rule 11 violation. *Nuwesra v. Merrill Lynch, Fenner & Smith Inc.*, 174 F.3d 87, 95 (2d Cir. 1999) (per curiam); *Johnson v. Waddell & Reed, Inc.*, 74 F.3d 147, 151 (7th Cir. 1996).

115. Fed. R. Civ. P. 11(c)(5)(A).

116. Fed. R. Civ. P. 11(c)(5)(B). This is to prevent situations in which parties settle their case only to have the judge on his own initiative subsequently assess sanctions (which the parties believed they had resolved by their settlement). Advisory Committee Note to 1993 Amendment to Rule 11, 146 F.R.D. 401, 592 (1993). In *Cooter & Gell v. Hartmarx Corp.*, 496 U.S. 384 (1990), the Supreme Court held that district courts had jurisdiction to impose a Rule 11 sanction even after an action had been voluntarily dismissed. *See also Willy v. Coastal Corp.*, 503 U.S. 131 (1992) (although court of appeals later determined that case was not within district court's removal jurisdiction, court nevertheless had power to impose Rule 11 sanctions).

Rule 11 serves as a reminder to attorneys concerning their duties to the court. One federal district judge has remarked concerning Rule 11 that "the idea that the trial judge is responsible to exact from the bar the bar's best, honest effort is and must be stated."[117] Another judge, responding to the same survey, stated that "the existence of Rule 11, not its use, has helped."[118]

NOTES AND QUESTIONS CONCERNING RULE 11 SANCTIONS

1. When should a motion for Rule 11 sanctions be filed with the Court? In *Cooter & Gell v. Hartmarx Corp.*, the Court recognized the power of district courts to adopt local rules governing the time by which Rule 11 motions must be filed. 496 U.S. 384, 398 (1990). *See* Rule 11.3 of the United States District Court for the District of New Jersey (applications for Rule 11 sanctions shall be filed prior to entry of final judgment). Under the 1983 version of Rule 11, some courts had refused to impose Rule 11 sanctions because of delay between the offending conduct and a party's presentation of a Rule 11 motion to the court. *Mary Ann Pensiero, Inc. v. Lingle*, 847 F.2d 90, 100 (3d Cir. 1988); *Stevens v. Lawyers Mut. Liability Ins. Co.*, 789 F.2d 1056, 1061 (4th Cir. 1986). *See also Thomas v. Capital Security Services, Inc.*, 836 F.2d 866, 879 (5th Cir. 1988) (en banc) ("[A]n attorney may not remain idle after a 'motion, pleading, or other paper' filed in violation of Rule 11 by his opponent has come to his attention."); Advisory Committee Note to 1983 Amendment to Rule 11, 97 F.R.D. 165, 200 (1983). This general approach is endorsed in the Advisory Committee Note to the 1993 amendment to Rule 11: "Ordinarily the motion should be served promptly after the inappropriate paper is filed, and, if delayed too long, may be viewed as untimely." Advisory Committee Note to 1993 Amendment to Rule 11, 146 F.R.D. 401, 590 (1993).

2. Can a court impose Rule 11 sanctions based upon factual allegations that have been held sufficient to create a genuine issue for trial and thus defeat entry of summary judgment? *See* Advisory Committee Note to 1993 Amendment to Rule 11, 146 F.R.D. 401, 586 (1993) ("[I]f a party has evidence with respect to a contention that would suffice to defeat a motion for summary judgment based thereon, it would have sufficient 'evidentiary support' for purposes of Rule 11.").

3. It had been argued that under the pre–1993 version of Rule 11 defense lawyers had more of an incentive to threaten Rule 11 sanction motions in response to non-frivolous, rather than frivolous, claims and actions. Stein, "Rule 11 in the Real World: How the Dynamics of Litigation Defeat the Purpose of Imposing Attorney Fee Sanctions for the Assertion of Frivolous Legal Arguments," 132 F.R.D. 309, 312–14 (1991). Have the incentives changed under Rule 11 as amended in 1993? *See also* Armour, "Rethinking Judicial Discretion: Sanctions and the Conundrum of the Close Case," 50 *SMU L. Rev.* 493 (1997).

---

117. Federal Judicial Center, *Rule 11: Final Report to the Advisory Committee on Civil Rules of the Judicial Conference of the United States* § 2C, at 50 (1991).

118. *Id.* at § 1C, at 20.

4. Under the 1983 version of Rule 11, there was a duty on the party seeking sanctions to mitigate its damages. *Dubisky v. Owens*, 849 F.2d 1034, 1037–39 (7th Cir. 1988); *INVST Financial Group, Inc. v. Chem–Nuclear Systems, Inc.*, 815 F.2d 391, 404–405 (6th Cir.), *cert. denied*, 484 U.S. 927 (1987). Under the current version of Rule 11(c)(4), sanctions "must be limited to what suffices to deter repetition of the conduct or comparable conduct by others similarly situated" and orders to pay attorneys' fees and other expenses to the moving party must be "imposed on motion and warranted for effective deterrence."

5. Does a court have authority to impose a Rule 11 monetary sanction against an attorney and forbid reimbursement of that attorney by her client? *Compare Derechin v. State University of New York*, 963 F.2d 513, 519–20 (2d Cir. 1992) (district court did not abuse its discretion in imposing Rule 11 sanctions on state attorney and prohibiting reimbursement under state indemnification statute) *with Blue v. United States Dept. of the Army*, 914 F.2d 525, 549 (4th Cir. 1990), *cert. denied*, 499 U.S. 959 (1991) (district court was without authority to forbid NAACP Legal Defense Fund from reimbursing Rule 11 sanctions imposed on private counsel). Whether legal malpractice insurance extends to Rule 11 monetary sanctions may depend upon the specific contractual language in question. *E.g.*, *Wellcome v. Home Ins. Co.*, 257 Mont. 354, 849 P.2d 190 (1993) (no coverage of judicial sanctions because policy excluded payment for "fines or statutory penalties whether imposed by law or otherwise").

6. In *Cooter & Gell v. Hartmarx Corp.*, 496 U.S. 384, 399–405 (1990), the Supreme Court held that appellate courts are to apply a unitary abuse of discretion standard to all Rule 11 determinations (concerning legal issues, factual issues, and the sanction imposed). Of what significance is the appellate standard of review in Rule 11 cases? What sort of a record must be made in the district court to permit meaningful appellate review?

7. What impact does Rule 11 have upon attorney-client relations? Should attorneys attempt to protect themselves against sanctions by cross-examining their clients concerning their factual allegations? By confirming the facts their clients have told them in detailed retention letters? What happens to the attorney-client relationship when a Rule 11 motion is filed and sanctions are sought against both party and attorney? *See* Beck, Note, "Rule 11 and Its Effect on Attorney/Client Relations," 65 *S. Cal. L. Rev.* 875 (1992).

8. Despite the focus on non-monetary sanctions under amended Rule 11, will there still be a great amount of litigation once sanctions are imposed under that Rule? Is it the amount or type of a sanction or the simple fact that a sanction has been imposed that causes attorneys to litigate Rule 11 issues? *See Golden Eagle Distrib. Corp. v. Burroughs Corp.*, 801 F.2d 1531 (9th Cir. 1986) (major law firm retained lawyer from another major law firm to appeal sanction of $3155.50); *Aetna Life Ins. Co. v. Alla Medical Services, Inc.*, 855 F.2d 1470 (9th Cir. 1988) (appeal to challenge $750 sanction).

9. What happens to the relationship between opposing counsel once a Rule 11 motion is served? Are Rule 11 motions more likely to be filed in cases in which opposing counsel do not have an ongoing relationship? If an apparent violation of Rule 11 has occurred, is counsel obligated to serve a

Rule 11 motion upon the offending party? If a Rule 11 motion is filed, is counsel required to seek monetary sanctions to compensate her client for any expenses incurred as a result of the challenged conduct?

10. In addition to increased activity under Rule 11 since its 1983 amendment, some federal courts have rediscovered 28 U.S.C. § 1927, which permits the imposition of sanctions against any attorney who "multiplies the proceedings * * * unreasonably and vexatiously." *E.g., In re TCI Ltd.,* 769 F.2d 441 (7th Cir. 1985); *McCandless v. Great Atlantic & Pacific Tea Co.,* 697 F.2d 198 (7th Cir. 1983). *See* Josselyn, Note, "The Song of the Sirens—Sanctioning Lawyers under 28 U.S.C. § 1927," 31 *B.C. L. Rev.* 477 (1990). *See also* Hart, "And the Chill Goes On–Federal Civil Rights Plaintiffs Beware: Rule 11 vis-a-vis 28 U.S.C. § 1927 and the Court's Inherent Power," 37 *Loy. L.A. L. Rev.* 645 (2004) (suggesting that, after Rule 11 was amended in 1993, the number of Rule 11 cases in certain federal districts declined while the number of cases involving 28 U.S.C. § 1927 and the court's inherent power to sanction increased, perhaps due to parties "sidestepping" the new procedural requirements of Rule 11).

11. Section 1927 of Title 28 illustrates the fact that attempts to control litigation delay and expense are not a new phenomenon. The original version of Section 1927 was enacted in 1813, apparently at least in part to curb litigious United States Attorneys who were then paid on a piece-work basis. *See Roadway Express, Inc. v. Piper,* 447 U.S. 752, 759 (1980).

3. Preventive Lawyering Under Rule 11

By its terms, Rule 11 merely requires good lawyering and reminds attorneys of their duties to the court. Attorneys should not file court papers without investigating both the factual and legal basis for those papers. In addition, attorneys should take precautions to minimize the amount of Rule 11 litigation in which they otherwise might become enmeshed.

Rule 11 should encourage attorneys not only to conduct reasonable prefiling inquiries but to memorialize those inquiries in anticipation of a possible later Rule 11 motion. Such record-keeping makes sense totally apart from Rule 11, because it will facilitate both the litigation of an action and client billing. Attorneys themselves should examine relevant documentary evidence and talk to potential witnesses, rather than merely rely upon their clients concerning important matters.

If an attorney has questions about the propriety of an action, it may be wise for her to compose, in her own mind, the Rule 11 affidavit that she would file with the court if the conduct were later challenged. An inability to explain your conduct in this fashion may be an indicator that the contemplated action is questionable under Rule 11.

Not only should individual attorneys read every paper they sign, but law firms should consider adopting internal review procedures to ensure that firm members are not filing documents that may expose the firm to liability. Clients should be counseled concerning Rule 11, so that they understand the duties placed upon their attorneys and themselves (including the potential for Rule 11 sanctions).

If it is another party who apparently has violated Rule 11, a measured approach should be undertaken in attempting to obtain correction of the apparent violation. While Rule 11(c)(2) requires that parties file a written motion to seek Rule 11 sanctions, in most cases "counsel should * * * give informal notice to the other party, whether in person or by a telephone call or letter, of a potential violation before proceeding to prepare and serve a Rule 11 motion."[119] The aim should be to correct the allegedly offending conduct, not to show up the other party, shift fees, or gain a tactical advantage for a client. Not only will the courts not permit counsel to play such games, but in most instances your client will be saved fees, and probably time, by contacting opposing counsel informally before drafting a Rule 11 motion.

Rule 11(c)(2) in part provides: "If warranted, the court may award to the prevailing party the reasonable expenses, including attorney's fees, incurred for the motion." Before filing a Rule 11 motion, counsel therefore should consider not only the possibility that the motion may be denied but the likelihood that such a denial may result in the award of sanctions to the other party.

Finally, whether asserting or defending against a Rule 11 claim, counsel should be aware of and be certain to comply with any local rules governing Rule 11 motions.[120]

Exercises Concerning Rule 11

1. On February 25, 1973, Homer Hanson limps into the office of Dean James, a sole practitioner in Logan County, West Virginia. Hanson tells James that he was injured on February 26, 1972, in the Buffalo Creek disaster. Because Mr. Hanson had not called to schedule an appointment, James does not have time to conduct a full interview. However, in the fifteen minutes that James spends with him, Hanson states that he lost his car and personal items valued at about $500.00 in the flood. He also tells James that he saw a doctor, whose name he cannot now remember, soon after the flood for injuries to his left leg. The doctor was in Roanoke, Virginia, where Hanson has lived for the past year.

Believing that West Virginia's statute of limitations for intentional torts is only one year, James files a lawsuit later that same day in West Virginia state court. Presume that, unbeknownst to James, the applicable West Virginia statute of limitations recently had been amended to read as

---

119. Advisory Committee Note to 1993 Amendment to Rule 11, 146 F.R.D. 401, 591 (1993).

120. *E.g.*, Rule 11.1 of the United States District Court for the District of Kansas (governing judicial imposition of sanctions generally); Rule 105(8)(b) of the United States District Court for the District of Maryland ("Unless otherwise ordered by the Court, a party need not respond to any motion filed under Fed.R.Civ.P. 11 or 28 U.S.C. 1927. The Court shall not grant any motion without requesting a response.").

follows: "Effective January 1, 1973, the statute of limitations for claims of intentional tort shall be two years."

Upon receipt of Hanson's complaint, Sally Samuels, counsel for Pittston, serves James with a Rule 11 motion for sanctions. In the letter accompanying this motion, Samuels invites James to call her to discuss the motion before it is filed. In the motion Pittston asserts that Hanson is a former mental patient and a former employee of the Buffalo Mining Company who has unsuccessfully sued Buffalo Mining on employment-related claims four times over the last ten years. When James calls Hanson to question him about these allegations, he learns that Hanson's telephone has been disconnected.

> a. Presume that you are an attorney in a Charleston, West Virginia law firm and have had no connection with the Buffalo Creek disaster litigation. Dean James telephones you for advice about the above situation. Write a letter to James giving that advice. In this letter you also may seek clarification from James concerning any relevant facts.

> b. What if it is not James, but Samuels, who calls you in Charleston? Presume that she tells you that, after mailing the Rule 11 motion to James, she learned that Hanson actually was injured in the dam collapse? What if she also tells you that it is unlikely that James will be able to verify this fact? Write an advice letter to Samuels.

2. You are house counsel to Acme Corporation and are sent the draft of a complaint and a demand letter from an attorney representing Achilles, Inc., one of Acme's competitors. The draft complaint contains several factual allegations that you know are not true. The accompanying demand letter says that if the attorney for Achilles does not hear from you in three weeks, the draft complaint will be filed against Acme.

Write a memorandum to Acme's general counsel recommending the response that Acme should make to the demand letter.

3. You have been asked to file a personal injury action on behalf of Pamela Rogers, who was injured several years ago in a car accident and recently has begun to experience neck pains that she believes were caused by the accident. You have spoken with Ms. Rogers's personal physician who says that it is "quite possible" that her injuries were caused by the accident. Your legal research convinces you that the potential defendant has a very strong statute of limitations defense.

Write a letter to Pamela Rogers explaining why you will, or will not, take her case.

B. CODES OF LITIGATION CONDUCT AND CREEDS OF PROFESSIONALISM

Judicial imposition of Rule 11 sanctions has not been the only response to perceived problems with abusive litigation conduct. Former

Chief Justice Warren Burger and other judges and attorneys have led a movement that has established several hundred American Inns of Court, in which judges, attorneys and law students discuss and debate issues of professionalism and legal ethics.[121] The Standing Committee on Ethics and Professional Responsibility of the American Bar Association Center for Professional Responsibility addresses professionalism through its newsletter, *The Professional Lawyer*, and its other activities.[122] Newly admitted lawyers in Virginia and several other states are required to attend a course on professionalism,[123] while more than 40 states require training in legal ethics or professionalism as a component of mandatory continuing legal education.[124]

Various bar associations and attorney organizations have adopted codes of litigation conduct and creeds of professionalism. In 1998 the American Bar Association adopted its *Guidelines for Litigation Conduct*, which are "purely aspirational and are not to be used as a basis for litigation, liability, discipline, sanctions, or penalties of any type."[125]

In addition to the many bar associations that have promulgated codes of professionalism, the United States District Court for the Northern District of Texas has adopted the following standards of practice for attorneys appearing in that court:

> (A) In fulfilling his or her primary duty to the client, a lawyer must be ever conscious of the broader duty to the judicial system that serves both attorney and client.

> (B) A lawyer owes, to the judiciary, candor, diligence and utmost respect.

> (C) A lawyer owes, to opposing counsel, a duty of courtesy and cooperation, the observance of which is necessary for the efficient administration of our system of justice and the respect of the public it serves.

> (D) A lawyer unquestionably owes, to the administration of justice, the fundamental duties of personal dignity and professional integrity.

> (E) Lawyers should treat each other, the opposing party, the court, and members of the court staff with courtesy and civility and conduct themselves in a professional manner at all times.

---

121. *See* Jenkins, "The American Inns of Court: Preparing Our Students for Ethical Practice," 27 *Akron L. Rev.* 175 (1993).

122. These include the ABA Ethics Research Service, ETHICSearch, which will research ethical questions, often for free, for lawyers and other legal professionals such as law students and law clerks. http://www.abanet.org/cpr/ethicsearch/.

123. "Virginia Requires Professionalism Course for New Lawyers," *The Professional Lawyer*, Spring 1989, at 6; 17A Ariz. Rev. Stat., Sup. Ct. Rule 34(f).

124. Center for Continuing Legal Education, American Bar Association, "Summary of State MCLE Requirements," http://www.abanet.org/cle/mcleview.html.

125. "Guidelines for Litigation Conduct," *Litigation News*, Aug. 1998, at 5. In 1999 the ABA House of Delegates adopted separate and more specific guidelines governing civil discovery practice. American Bar Association, *Civil Discovery Standards* (1999) (revised 2004).

(F) A client has no right to demand that counsel abuse the opposite party or indulge in offensive conduct. A lawyer shall always treat adverse witnesses and suitors with fairness and due consideration.

(G) In adversary proceedings, clients are litigants and though ill feeling may exist between clients, such ill feeling should not influence a lawyer's conduct, attitude, or demeanor towards opposing lawyers.

(H) A lawyer should not use any form of discovery, or the scheduling of discovery, as a means of harassing opposing counsel or counsel's client.

(I) Lawyers will be punctual in communications with others and in honoring scheduled appearances, and will recognize that neglect and tardiness are demeaning to the lawyer and to the judicial system.

(J) If a fellow member of the Bar makes a just request for cooperation, or seeks scheduling accommodation, a lawyer will not arbitrarily or unreasonably withhold consent.

(K) Effective advocacy does not require antagonistic or obnoxious behavior and members of the Bar will adhere to the higher standard of conduct which judges, lawyers, clients, and the public may rightfully expect.[126]

The judges in the Northern District of Texas adopted the above litigation standards out of concern that "valuable judicial and attorney time is consumed in resolving unnecessary contention and sharp practices between lawyers. Judges and magistrates of this court are required to devote substantial attention to refereeing abusive litigation tactics that range from benign incivility to outright obstruction."[127] As a result, the court advised counsel that violations of the above standards would result in such sanctions as "a warm friendly discussion on the record, a hard-nosed reprimand in open court, compulsory legal education, monetary sanctions, or other measures appropriate to the circumstances."[128]

While not enforceable by judicial sanctions, the United States Court of Appeals for the Seventh Circuit has adopted standards for professional conduct that are to be received by every lawyer admitted to practice in any federal court in the Seventh Circuit.[129] These standards, which were the model for the ABA *Guidelines for Litigation Conduct*,[130] concern not only

---

126. *Dondi Properties Corp. v. Commerce Savings & Loan Ass'n,* 121 F.R.D. 284, 287–88 (N.D.Tex. 1988) (per curiam) (en banc). *See also* the *Texas Lawyer's Creed* adopted by the Texas Supreme Court and Court of Criminal Appeals (which is an appendix to Reavley, "Rambo Litigators: Pitting Aggressive Tactics Against Legal Ethics," 17 Pepp. L. Rev. 637, 656 (1990)).

127. 121 F.R.D. at 286.

128. 121 F.R.D. at 288, *quoting Thomas v. Capital Security Services, Inc.,* 836 F.2d 866, 878 (5th Cir.1988) (en banc). *See also* Rule 83.12.1 of the United States District Court for the District of Wyoming (containing standards of litigation conduct which are enforceable by judicial sanctions).

129. Committee on Civility, United States Court of Appeals for the Seventh Circuit, *Final Report*, 143 F.R.D. 441, 448 (1992) (Appendix A).

130. "Guidelines for Litigation Conduct," *supra* n. 125, at 5.

lawyers' duties to other lawyers and to the court, but courts' duties to lawyers and judges' duties to each other.[131] The standards were prompted by a survey in which more than 41% of responding Seventh Circuit judges and lawyers agreed that lack of civility was a problem in the federal courts in that judicial circuit.[132]

Codes and creeds such as those adopted by the Northern District of Texas and the Seventh Circuit have been prompted by sentiments such as those expressed by Illinois Judge Richard Curry: "Zealous advocacy is the buzz word which is squeezing decency and civility out of the law profession."[133] On the other hand, Professor Monroe Freedman has asserted that "I don't think there has been a lessening in civility. * * * Civility in that context is simply a euphemism for the old boy network * * * ."[134] Attorney Gerry Spence also has been characterized as having "no patience with lawyers who do a workmanlike job but don't pull out all the stops in presenting their cases. 'They don't love their clients. They won't take any risks. They only want to do a job that someone can't criticize.' "[135]

Not only will the debate concerning professionalism continue within the legal profession for the foreseeable future, but individual litigators will continue to be required to deal with the tension between "professionalism" and "zealous advocacy" in their own practices.

NOTES AND QUESTIONS CONCERNING CREEDS OF PROFESSIONALISM

1. What has caused the perceived breakdown in attorney civility and professionalism that has spurred the adoption of litigation codes and creeds of professionalism? The judges in *Dondi Properties* noted: "Whether the increased size of the bar has decreased collegiality, or the legal profession has become only a business, or experienced lawyers have ceased to teach new lawyers the standards to be observed, or because of other factors not readily categorized, we observe patterns of behavior that forebode ill for our system of justice." 121 F.R.D. at 286. Are there other explanations for the perceived problems?

2. Are there any problems with the judicial adoption of a creed of professionalism in *Dondi Properties?* Is it clear that the adoption of such a creed will reduce the amount of judicial time needed to referee attorney disputes concerning litigation tactics? Are these the sort of standards that should be adopted by judges in individual judicial districts?

3. Do creeds such as the one adopted in *Dondi Properties* add anything to the more general requirements of the Model Rules of Professional Conduct? Do these creeds attempt to delineate even more fundamental standards of

---

131. *Id.* at 448–52.

132. Committee on Civility, United States Court of Appeals for the Seventh Circuit, *Interim Report*, 143 F.R.D. 371, 378 (1991).

133. Sayler, "Rambo Litigation: Why Hardball Tactics Don't Work," *A.B.A.J.,* March 1, 1988, at 79, 81.

134. Goldberg, "Playing Hardball," *A.B.A.J.,* July 1, 1987, at 48, 51.

135. *Id.*

decency and civility than those explicitly spelled out in state disciplinary rules? In how much detail should codes of professionalism or disciplinary rules attempt to regulate attorney behavior?

4. Is it likely that creeds of professionalism will temper zealous client advocacy? If so, is this a point in favor of, or against, adoption of these creeds?

5. Attorneys and judges are not the only persons concerned about the possible abuse of "hardball" litigation tactics. Only six percent of the corporate executives questioned in one survey considered "all or most" attorneys worthy of the title "professionals." Commission on Professionalism, American Bar Association, " '... In the Spirit of Public Service:' A Blueprint for the Rekindling of Lawyer Professionalism," 112 F.R.D. 243, 254 (1986). Fifty-five percent of the state and federal judges questioned in this same survey said that attorney professionalism was declining. *Id.*

6. In a memorandum to all lawyers representing Xerox Corporation, President David T. Kearns stated, "We will insist that when you appear on our behalf that you have as one of your primary objectives the support and maintenance of an efficient court system as required by the letter and spirit of the recently amended Federal Rules." Commission on Professionalism, American Bar Association, " '... In the Spirit of Public Service:' A Blueprint for the Rekindling of Lawyer Professionalism," 112 F.R.D. 243, 310 (1986). Attached to that memorandum was another memorandum from Xerox's general counsel reminding attorneys that "Xerox attorneys cannot justify extreme advocacy positions on the ground that the client expects it of us," as well as specific guidelines for Xerox attorneys to follow in handling that corporation's litigation. *Id.* at 312.

7. In addition to creeds of professionalism governing attorney conduct, some individual law firms have adopted creeds setting forth the aspirations and goals of the professionals within the firm. Gering, "Law Firms Adopt Credos," *A.B.A.J.,* Jan. 1989, at 56.

8. Whether or not the courts have adopted a formal creed of professionalism, lawyers quickly develop a reputation within the jurisdictions in which they practice. Consider the following story from an Oklahoma court, in which an attorney repudiated his verbal agreement to a change in the parties' discovery schedule so that he could take advantage of a local rule requiring that all such changes be made in writing.

> The judge felt compelled to order compliance with the original schedule in light of the court rule. However, after rendering his ruling on the schedule, he ordered both attorneys to turn and face the courtroom. * * * When all eyes were focused on the bench the judge introduced the two lawyers, and announced "I just want everyone to know how Mr. X practices law. He orally agreed to postpone certain discovery matters, but now is before this court arguing that his word is not enforceable because the agreement wasn't in writing as required by the local court rules. Take a good look at him now so you will know who you are dealing with in the future."

R. Cochran & T. Collet, *Cases and Materials on the Legal Profession* 173 (2d ed. 2003). *See also* Wendell, "Regulation of Lawyers Without the Code, the

Rules, or the Restatement: Or, What Do Honor and Shame Have to Do with Civil Discovery Practice?," 71 *Fordham L. Rev.* 1567 (2003).

Exercises Concerning Attorney Professionalism

1. You have been asked to draft a code of professionalism for the West Virginia State Bar Association. Prepare a memorandum including:

(a) A draft of the code that you propose, focusing, in particular, upon problems of professionalism that might occur in the pleadings stage of a case;

(b) A proposal for obtaining comments upon your draft, discussing, for instance, the groups that should be invited to comment on the proposals and the groups that might oppose these standards;

(c) A discussion of whether the standards should apply uniformly to all attorneys in all situations; and

(d) Your recommendation as to whether the standards should be enforced by judicial or other sanctions.

In drafting your proposed code, you may wish to consider the several codes and creeds set forth in the appendix to the *Dondi Properties* decision, 121 F.R.D. at 292, as well as the ABA's *Guidelines for Litigation Conduct*.

2. You are a young associate in a large New York City law firm. Recently you and other associates have become concerned about two senior partners who have asked associates to engage in "hardball" litigation tactics that the associates believe is ethically improper. Some of the associates believe that the firm should adopt a code of professionalism addressed to these incidents. You have been asked to draft such a code, as well as a short memorandum discussing both how to present the code to the firm and other approaches that might be adopted to deal with the recent problems.

VII. CONSIDER THE ALTERNATIVES

You've now determined the claims to assert, the relief to request, and the forum in which to assert those claims and request that relief. However, before actually filing a lawsuit, consider the alternatives. Some lawsuits are filed to "gain leverage" with respect to a negotiated settlement that plaintiff's counsel presumes eventually will be reached. However, it may be just as easy to reach that settlement now, rather than after the parties have invested lots of time and money in a lawsuit. Moreover, in many cases it won't be "just as easy" to settle later as now. Lawsuits can take on a life of their own, and the formal involvement of the court in a dispute reduces the amount of control the parties have over the dispute resolution process. The confrontational nature of civil litigation typically causes parties to think less well of opposing parties and lawyers, which may create a barrier to settlement. In addition, parties may believe that they must see a lawsuit through to its formal conclusion once they have invested significant amounts of money, time, and energy in that litigation.

Chapter 15 examines alternative dispute resolution. That chapter could just as well have been the book's first chapter, and it might profitably be read at this point in the text. Lawyers always should be on the alert for alternatives to formal adjudication by which disputes can be resolved more quickly, more cheaply, and with greater client satisfaction than may be possible through formal adjudication. "Windows of opportunity" especially conducive to settlement exist in most lawsuits, typically right before or right after a complaint has been filed. In order to serve their clients most effectively, counsel should not miss these opportunities.

VIII. CONCLUSION

Although legal research and factual investigation have preceded its drafting, the civil complaint is the first paper that formally sets forth plaintiff's claims. The complaint is similar to the blueprint for a house, laying the ground work for all that will follow. Just as a good blueprint doesn't guarantee that the finished house will be perfect, a good complaint does not guarantee later success in the litigation of a civil action. However, just as a poorly prepared blueprint may lead to later construction difficulties, a poorly drafted complaint may cause the plaintiff difficulties in the prosecution of his lawsuit. The time spent in carefully planning a civil action and in drafting the complaint exemplifying that planning will be repaid many times over as the case progresses toward final resolution.

IX. CHAPTER BIBLIOGRAPHY

I. Alterman, *Plain and Accurate Style in Court Papers* (1987).

Armon, "A Method for Writing Factual Complaints," 1998 *Det. C. L. Mich. St. U. L. Rev.* 109.

Bone, "Mapping the Boundaries of a Dispute: Conceptions of Ideal Lawsuit Structure from the Field Code to the Federal Rules," 89 *Colum. L. Rev.* 1 (1989).

Burbank, "The Transformation of American Civil Procedure: The Example of Rule 11," 137 *U. Pa. L. Rev.* 1925 (1989).

B. Child, *Drafting Legal Documents: Materials and Problems* (1988).

Clermont & Yeazell, "Inventing Tests, Destabilizing Systems," 95 *Iowa L. Rev.* 821 (2010).

Commission on Professionalism, American Bar Association, " '. . . In the Spirit of Public Service:' A Blueprint for the Rekindling of Lawyer Professionalism," 112 F.R.D. 243 (1986).

Committee on Civility, United States Court of Appeals for the Seventh Circuit, *Interim Report*, 143 F.R.D. 371 (1991); *Final Report*, 143 F.R.D. 441 (1992).

Committee on Trial Practice, Section of Litigation, American Bar Association, "Standards and Guidelines for Practice Under Rule 11 of the Federal Rules of Civil Procedure," 121 F.R.D. 101 (1988).

A. Conte, *Attorney Fee Awards* (3d ed. 2004).

Cutler, Comment, "A Practitioner's Guide to the 1993 Amendment to Federal Rule of Civil Procedure 11," 67 *Temple L. Rev.* 265 (1994).

"Developments in the Law—Injunctions," 78 *Harv. L. Rev.* 994 (1965).

R. Dickerson, *The Fundamentals of Legal Drafting* (2d ed. 1986).

D. Dobbs, *Law of Remedies* (2d ed. 1993).

Donnici, "The Amendment of Pleadings—A Study of the Operation of Judicial Discretion in the Federal Courts," 37 *S. Cal. L. Rev.* 529 (1964).

Fairman, "Heightened Pleading," 81 *Tex. L. Rev.* 551 (2002).

Federal Judicial Center, *Rule 11: Final Report to the Advisory Committee on Civil Rules of the Judicial Conference of the United States* (1991).

O. Fiss, *The Civil Rights Injunction* (1978).

W. Fortune et al., *Modern Litigation and Professional Responsibility Handbook: The Limits of Zealous Advocacy* (1996).

H. Friendly, *Federal Jurisdiction: A General View* (1973).

Gohn & Oliver, "In Pursuit of the Elusive TRO," *Litigation*, Summer 1993, at 25.

G. Joseph, *Sanctions: The Federal Law of Litigation Abuse* (4th ed. 2008).

Hirt, "A Second Look at Amended Rule 11," 48 *Am. U. L. Rev.* 1007 (1999).

S. Kassin, *An Empirical Study of Rule 11 Sanctions* (1985).

J. Kircher & C. Wiseman, *Punitive Damages, Law and Practice* (2d ed. 2000).

J. Kole, *Pleading Your Case: Complaints and Responses* (2011).

Leubsdorf, "The Standard for Preliminary Injunctions," 91 *Harv. L. Rev.* 525 (1978).

Levin & Sobel, "Achieving Balance in the Developing Law of Sanctions," 36 *Cath. L. Rev.* 587 (1987).

"Litigation Ethics and Professionalism Symposium," 28 *Stetson L. Rev.* 247 (1998).

Marcus, "The Puzzling Persistence of Pleading Practice," 76 *Tex. L. Rev.* 1749 (1998).

Marshall et al., "The Use and Impact of Rule 11," 86 *Nw. U. L. Rev.* 943 (1992).

Napolitano, "Injunctions in the Nineties," *Litigation*, Spring 1991, at 23.

Nelken, "Sanctions Under Amended Federal Rule 11—Some 'Chilling' Problems in the Struggle Between Compensation and Punishment," 74 *Geo. L. J.* 1313 (1986).

Neubauer, "Check–the–Box Pleadings," *Litigation*, Winter 1985, at 28.

Parness, "Fines Under New Federal Civil Rule 11: The New Monetary Sanctions for the 'Stop–and–Think–Again' Rule," 1993 *B.Y.U. L. Rev.* 879.

Parness, "More Stringent Sanctions under Federal Civil Rule 11: A Reply to Professor Nelken," 75 *Geo. L. J.* 1937 (1987).

"Professionalism in the Practice of Law: A Symposium on Civility and Judicial Ethics in the 1990s," 28 *Val. U. L. Rev.* 513 (1994).

Reavley, "Rambo Litigators: Pitting Aggressive Tactics Against Legal Ethics," 17 *Pepp. L. Rev.* 637 (1990).

R. Rossi, *Attorneys' Fees* (3d ed. 2001).

Rothschild, "Forum Shopping," *Litigation*, Spring 1998, at 40.

Schwarzer, "Rule 11: Entering a New Era," 28 *Loy. L.A. L. Rev.* 7 (1994).

Shepard's Causes of Action (2d ed. 1993).

Siegel, "The New (Dec. 1, 1993) Rule 4 of thc Federal Rules of Civil Procedure: Changes in Summons Service and Personal Jurisdiction," 151 F.R.D. 441 (Part I); 152 F.R.D. 249 (Part II) (1994).

Simon, "Ethical Discretion in Lawyering," 101 *Harv. L. Rev.* 1083 (1988).

Sinclair, "Service of Process: Amended Rule 4 and the Presumption of Jurisdiction," 14 *Rev. Litig.* 159 (1994).

J. Solovy, *The Federal Law of Sanctions* (1991).

"Special Issue: The Future of Punitive Damages," 1998 *Wis. L. Rev.* 1.

Stein, "Rule 11 in the Real World: How the Dynamics of Litigation Defeat the Purpose of Imposing Attorney Fee Sanctions for the Assertion of Frivolous Legal Arguments," 132 F.R.D. 309 (1990).

Symposium, "Happy (?) Birthday Rule 11," 37 *Loy. L.A. L. Rev.* 515 (2004).

Symposium, "Pondering *Iqbal*," 14 *Lewis & Clark L. Rev.* 1 (2010).

Symposium, "Reflections on *Iqbal*: Discerning Its Rule, Grappling with Its Implications," 114 *Penn. St. L. Rev.* 1257 (2010).

Symposium, "Who Feels Their Pain? The Challenge of Noneconomic Damages in Civil Litigation," 55 *DePaul L. Rev.* 249 (2006).

Task Force on Federal Rule of Civil Procedure 11, United States Court of Appeals for the Third Circuit, *Rule 11 in Transition: The Report of the Third Circuit Task Force on Federal Rule of Civil Procedure 11* (1989).

Tobias, "The 1993 Revision of Federal Rule 11," 70 *Ind. L. J.* 171 (1994).

Vairo, "The New Rule 11: Past as Prologue?," 28 *Loy. L.A. L. Rev.* 39 (1994).

Vairo, "Rule 11 and the Profession," 67 *Fordham L. Rev.* 589 (1998).

G. Vairo, *Rule 11 Sanctions: Case Law, Perspectives and Preventive Measures* (3d ed. 2004).

T. Willging, *The Rule 11 Sanctioning Process* (1988).

C. Wolfram, *Modern Legal Ethics* (1986).

Zielinski, "How to Draft Effective Complaints," *Prac. Litigator,* March 1990, at 13.

CHAPTER 5

RESPONSES TO THE COMPLAINT: "DAISY, DAISY, GIVE ME YOUR ANSWER DO."

■ ■ ■

[A motion to dismiss] is a wonderful tool on paper, but have you ever looked at the batting average of rule 12(b)(6) motions? I think it was last effectively used during the McKinley administration.

A. Miller, *The August 1983 Amendments to the Federal Rules of Civil Procedure: Promoting Effective Case Management and Lawyer Responsibility* 8 (1984).

Under [the Federal Rules of Civil Procedure] it may happen that no issue will be reached on the pleadings. One might wonder about the utility of starting for a destination if it is a matter of no consequence whether or not it is ever reached. * * * As a matter of fact most issues are reached on the complaint and answer, and the termination of the pleadings before issue can hardly cause serious trouble if there is a means for obtaining a discovery before trial.

Sunderland, "The New Federal Rules," 45 *W. Va. L. Q.* 5, 10–11 (1938).

Analysis

I. INTRODUCTION

Until now this book has considered pretrial litigation primarily from the perspective of plaintiff's counsel. The present chapter deals with the unique skills and judgments required of defense counsel. In particular, this chapter considers the possible responses to the complaint available to the defendant and his counsel.

Initially, the chapter considers the defenses that may be asserted in response to the complaint. Not only should defense counsel investigate the legal and factual merits of plaintiff's substantive allegations, but the possibility of threshold defenses to the action also should be considered. From among the various possible defenses, counsel must choose those defenses that appear most promising.

Once the appropriate defenses have been identified, counsel must decide in what manner they should be asserted. The two major possibilities are by the filing of a preanswer motion or by raising the defenses in the answer. Section III of this chapter considers Rule 12 preanswer motions, while Section IV analyzes the pleading that is the counterpart to the civil complaint: the answer. The final major section of the chapter then considers possible claims that the defendant himself may assert: counterclaims against the plaintiff, crossclaims against co-parties, and third-party claims against persons who are not parties to the suit but who may be liable to the defendant for any part of the plaintiff's claim.

The plaintiff has a distinct advantage in being able to initiate suit and shape the original contours of the civil action. Defendant's responses to the complaint, however, can be equally important in fashioning the lawsuit for ultimate disposition. Defendant's initial responses to the complaint should be carefully planned to be consistent with, and advance, the defendant's overall litigation plan.

II. THE POSSIBLE DEFENSES

Upon receipt of the complaint, defense counsel must begin the same sort of factual investigation and legal research that plaintiff's counsel undertook before filing the complaint. While the major time constraint upon plaintiff's counsel usually is the statute of limitations, defense counsel must respond to the complaint within the time permitted by Rule 12(a). Rule 12(a)(1)(A)(i) gives the defendant just 21 days after being served with the summons and complaint to respond. However, if the defendant has agreed to waive formal service of process pursuant to Rule 4(d), its response time is extended to 60 days from the date the request was sent, while if the request was sent to the defendant outside the United States he has 90 days.[1]

Much work must be done in the time permitted by Rule 12(a). Defense counsel must simultaneously investigate the facts and research

---

1. Fed. R. Civ. P. 12(a)(1)(A)(ii). Rule 12(a)(2) gives the United States and its agencies, officers, and employees 60 days in which to answer complaints.

In appropriate cases, defense counsel may seek an extension of time to respond to a complaint. However, there should be less need for extensions of time after the 1993 amendment to Rule 12 that gave defendants 60 or 90 days to respond to complaints if formal service has been waived pursuant to Rule 4(d). Fed. R. Civ. P. 12(a)(1)(A)(ii).

the law. Based upon this investigation and research, a litigation plan should be developed for the defendant.[2] In developing the defendant's litigation plan, counsel should consider four separate types of defenses.

First, defense counsel should consider whether plaintiff has satisfied all of the normal prerequisites for maintaining a civil action. In the federal courts, Rule 12(b) of the Federal Rules of Civil Procedure provides a quick check list of suit prerequisites. Very early in her investigation of possible defenses, counsel should consider whether there is subject matter jurisdiction (Rule 12(b)(1)), personal jurisdiction (Rule 12(b)(2)), venue (Rule 12(b)(3)), sufficient process and service of process (Rule 12(b)(4) and (5)), and whether the plaintiff has failed to join an indispensable party under Rule 19 (Rule 12(b)(7)).

Second, defense counsel should consider the legal sufficiency of plaintiff's claim. A challenge to the legal sufficiency of the complaint is recognized in Rule 12(b)(6). In ruling upon a motion to dismiss the complaint under Rule 12(b)(6), the facts alleged in the complaint are presumed to be true and must be construed favorably to the pleader.[3] Because plaintiff's allegations are presumed to be true for the purposes of a Rule 12(b)(6) motion, legal research, rather than factual investigation, will be necessary to determine whether this defense can be asserted. The Rule 12(b)(6) defense can be considered a "So what?" defense, because of its implicit assertion to the plaintiff: "So what if everything that you allege in your complaint is true, you are still not entitled to any relief."

Affirmative defenses are the third major category of defenses. They might be characterized as "Yes, but" defenses. Rather than directly controverting plaintiff's allegations, affirmative defenses interject new facts into the case which, the defendant argues, establish affirmative reasons why the plaintiff should not recover. The most common affirmative defenses are listed in Rule 8(c) of the Federal Rules of Civil Procedure and include contributory negligence, laches, release, res judicata, statute of frauds, and the statute of limitations. In fact, the listing of affirmative defenses in Rule 8(c) provides a very convenient check list which counsel can use to ensure that no common affirmative defense has been overlooked.

Fourth, and finally, defense counsel must determine the truth or falsity of the substantive allegations of plaintiff's complaint. Did the defendant actually strike the plaintiff, or fire the plaintiff, or pollute the environment as alleged in the complaint? If some of plaintiff's allegations are not true, defendant should deny those allegations in the answer and thereby assert that there is a factual dispute that must be resolved by the judge or jury.

---

2. *See* Section II of Chapter 3, *supra* p. 58.

3. *Scheuer v. Rhodes,* 416 U.S. 232, 236 (1974). *But see Ashcroft v. Iqbal,* 556 U.S. ___, ___ (2009) (In considering a motion to dismiss, "Threadbare recitals of the elements of a cause of action, supported by mere conclusory statements, do not suffice. . . . [and] only a complaint that states a plausible claim for relief survives a motion to dismiss."); *Bell Atlantic Corp. v. Twombly,* 550 U.S. 544 (2007). *See also* Chapter 4, Section V(A), *supra* pp. 142–147.

Once defense counsel determines which of these defenses are available in a particular case, she still must decide how they should be asserted. The two basic choices are to assert defenses (1) in a preanswer motion or (2) in the answer.

Exercise Concerning the Analysis of Possible Defenses

Your law firm represents the defendant Pittston Company in connection with the litigation that has been brought against it due to the collapse of the Buffalo Mining Company dam in Logan County, West Virginia on February 26, 1972. Your assignment is to write a memorandum to your senior partner outlining the possible defenses that Pittston might raise in this action.

In your memorandum be sure to consider possible Rule 12(b) defenses, affirmative defenses, and defenses on the merits to the complaint set forth in Chapter 4, *supra* p. 152. Your memorandum should consider not only the various possible defenses that could be raised, but should evaluate the relative strengths of those defenses (based on the facts as you now know them) and make a recommendation as to the defenses that actually should be raised with the court.

III.   PREANSWER MOTIONS

The most common manner in which to assert the defenses specified in Rule 12(b) and affirmative defenses such as those listed in Rule 8(c) is by way of a preanswer motion. While these defenses also can be raised in the answer, the answer usually does not trigger any immediate action by the court. If the defenses are raised in a preanswer motion, however, the court will consider them and, if they are found to be valid, will dismiss the complaint. The filing of a preanswer motion may put opposing counsel on the defensive from the very outset of the case, thereby helping defense counsel gain a measure of control in the pretrial proceedings. Preanswer motions going to a threshold defense also may provide a basis for obtaining a stay of discovery concerning plaintiff's allegations on the merits. For these reasons, preanswer motions can be extremely useful to defense counsel in shaping and disposing of lawsuits.

A.   THE MOTION TO DISMISS

Rule 12(b) of the Federal Rules of Civil Procedure provides: "Every defense to a claim for relief in any pleading must be asserted in the responsive pleading if one is required." However, Rule 12(b) also states that a party may assert certain specified defenses by motion. These include "(1) lack of subject-matter jurisdiction; (2) lack of personal jurisdiction; (3) improper venue; (4) insufficient process; (5) insufficient service of process; (6) failure to state a claim upon which relief can be granted; and (7) failure to join a party under Rule 19."

These seven defenses typically are raised by a Rule 12(b) motion to dismiss, the modern equivalent of the common law demurrer. Defense counsel must be familiar with the law and strategy governing motions to dismiss, as well as with the actual drafting of these motions.

1. Governing Law and Strategy

Future defense counsel by now must be licking their chops. A successful motion may result in the dismissal of an action on any of the seven grounds set forth in Rule 12(b). Even an unsuccessful motion may buy some time for the defendant (which usually is to the defendant's advantage). Why not file a motion to dismiss in all cases?

Must comply w/ Rule 11

The requirements of Rule 11 apply to every paper filed in a civil action, and defense counsel have been sanctioned for filing motions to dismiss that do not comply with Rule 11's requirements.[4] In addition, Rule 8(e) of the Federal Rules of Civil Procedure provides: "Pleadings must be construed so as to do justice."

Plaintiff may amend complaint

Even if the complaint is legally deficient, the judge may not dismiss the civil action. As amended in 2009, Rule 15(a)(1)(B) permits the plaintiff to amend the complaint "21 days after service of a responsive pleading or 21 days after service of a motion under Rule 12(b), (e), or (f), whichever is earlier." As explained in the Advisory Committee note to this amendment to Rule 15(a):

> This provision will force the pleader to consider carefully and promptly the wisdom of amending to meet the arguments in the motion. A responsive amendment may avoid the need to decide the motion or reduce the number of issues to be decided, and will expedite determination of issues that otherwise might be raised seriatim. It also should address other pretrial proceedings.[5]

A motion to dismiss therefore may result in a more focused complaint, rather than the end to the lawsuit in the trial court. As Professor Arthur Miller facetiously points out in the quote beginning this chapter, many courts are not predisposed to grant motions to dismiss.[6] A preanswer motion may trigger the judge's first contact with a case. Because first impressions are often lasting, it's usually not a good idea to file motions that are not likely to be granted.

File motions likely to be granted

Having said all this, the motion to dismiss is nevertheless a powerful defense motion. Nor is the likelihood of success with motions to dismiss quite as bleak as suggested by Professor Miller. A study by the Federal Judicial Center found that, in a sample of cases terminated in 1975 in six federal judicial districts, Rule 12(b)(6) motions led to a final disposition of

---

4. *Treadwell v. Kennedy*, 656 F.Supp. 442 (C.D.Ill. 1987); *National Survival Game, Inc. v. Skirmish, U.S.A., Inc.*, 603 F.Supp. 339, 341–42 (S.D.N.Y. 1985); *Booker v. City of Atlanta*, 586 F.Supp. 340 (N.D.Ga. 1984), *aff'd mem.*, 827 F.2d 775 (11th Cir. 1987).

5. Advisory Committee Note to 2009 Amendment to Rule 15, 260 F.R.D. 436, 544–45 (2009).

6. *See also* C. Wright, *The Law of Federal Courts* § 66, at 465 (6th ed. 2002) (citing data from a 1962 survey finding that motions to dismiss were filed in only 5% of cases and that such motions led to a final termination of less than 2% of all cases).

approximately thirty-two percent of cases in which they were filed and that approximately thirty-one percent of all Rule 12 motions to dismiss led to final case dispositions.[7]

This same study suggests that there may be certain types of cases that are particularly suited, or particularly unsuited, to disposition by pretrial motion (including Rule 12 motions to dismiss). While 88.5 percent of the prisoner cases, 59.3 percent of the administrative appeals, and 43.8 percent of the civil rights/constitutional law cases were disposed of by motion, only 7.5 percent of the intellectual property cases, 11.5 percent of the securities cases, and 13.1 percent of the tort cases were similarly disposed of by motion.[8]

In what circumstances does the filing of a motion to dismiss make good strategic sense? If the facts truly are not in dispute, a motion to dismiss can serve the useful purpose of testing the legal sufficiency of the complaint. While the law and facts often are intertwined, in some cases the court's determination of the governing law will decide the case. These are the cases in which Rule 12(b)(6) should be used.

Another type of case in which the defendant may be entitled to judgment at the pretrial stage is an action in which a dispositive affirmative defense exists. If, for instance, it is clear from the complaint that the action has not been filed within the statute of limitations period, this defense generally should be asserted in a motion to dismiss.[9] An affirmative defense such as contributory negligence, however, usually involves issues of fact for the judge or jury and thus is not well suited to resolution by preanswer motion.

With defenses that are not as clear-cut as the statute of limitations or statute of frauds, a balancing of the risks and benefits of a preanswer motion must be undertaken. On the down side, judges may not be as ready to dismiss an action at the very outset of a case as they may be once the plaintiff has had an opportunity for discovery. The motion to dismiss also may educate opposing counsel about the details of defendant's case. On the other hand, it may be beneficial to educate the judge on defendant's theory of the case from the outset.

---

7. P. Connolly & P. Lombard, *Judicial Controls and the Civil Litigative Process: Motions* 71, 74 (Tables 20 and 23) (1980). A later study of cases terminated in 1988 in two federal district courts found that, while Rule 12(b)(6) motions were filed in only 13% of the cases sampled, 52% of those motions were granted. T. Willging, *Use of Rule 12(b)(6) in Two Federal District Courts* 8, 9 n.21, 19 (1989).

8. Connolly & Lombard, *supra* note 7, at 76 (Table 25). Section 1915 of Title 28 provides for the filing of civil actions *in forma pauperis* by those who are unable to pay the fees normally assessed in federal civil actions. However, in such actions "the court shall dismiss the case at any time if the court determines that—(A) the allegation of poverty is untrue; or (B) the action or appeal—(i) is frivolous or malicious; (ii) fails to state a claim on which relief may be granted; or (iii) seeks monetary relief against a defendant who is immune from such relief." 28 U.S.C. § 1915(e)(2).

9. *See* 5 C. Wright & A. Miller, *Federal Practice and Procedure* § 1277, at 634 n.12, 640–43 (3d ed. 2004). *But see Harris v. Secretary, U.S. Dep't of Veterans Affairs*, 126 F.3d 339, 341 (D.C.Cir. 1997) ("Rule 8(c) means what it says: a party must first raise its affirmative defenses in a responsive pleading before it can raise them in a dispositive motion.").

Judicial decision-making is an art rather than a science, and judges sometimes grant motions that counsel did not believe they would. Nevertheless, attorneys should be selective in determining the defenses to raise by a preanswer motion and should carefully choose among the possible defenses. A judge faced with a lengthy motion that raises many defenses, both sound and questionable, may decline to grant the motion merely because counsel has not directed him to the best grounds for dismissal.

Motions should be targeted like a rifle rather than a shotgun. Motion practice, and individual motions, should fit within, and advance, the specific litigation plan adopted by defense counsel.

2. Drafting the Motion to Dismiss

The motion to dismiss generally consists of several separate documents.[10] The motion itself usually is no more than one page long. Form 40 of the Appendix of Forms to the Federal Rules of Civil Procedure illustrates the brevity of such motions:[11]

MOTION TO DISMISS UNDER RULE 12(b) FOR LACK OF JURISDICTION, IMPROPER VENUE, INSUFFICIENT SERVICE OF PROCESS, OR FAILURE TO STATE A CLAIM

(Caption–See Form 1.)

The defendant moves to dismiss the action because:

1. the amount in controversy is less than the sum or value specified by 28 U.S.C. § 1332;

2. the defendant is not subject to the personal jurisdiction of this court;

3. venue is improper (this defendant does not reside in this district and no part of the events or omissions giving rise to the claim occurred in the district);

4. the defendant has not been properly served, as shown by the attached affidavits of _____; or

5. the complaint fails to state a claim upon which relief can be granted.

---

10. Rule 7(b)(1)(A) of the Federal Rules of Civil Procedure recognizes the possibility of oral motions if made "during a hearing or trial." *See Int'l Business Machines Corp. v. Edelstein,* 526 F.2d 37, 46–47 (2d Cir.1975) (interpreting trial judge's order as not precluding oral motions "of necessity made during a trial").

If a complaint is clearly subject to a Rule 12(b) defense, a judge might even dismiss the action at a pretrial conference. *See* Fed. R. Civ. P. 16(c)(2)(A). *But see Fidelity & Deposit Co. v. Southern Utilities, Inc.,* 726 F.2d 692, 693–94 (11th Cir. 1984). Counsel should ensure that a record is made of any oral motions and the court's rulings on those motions.

11. Form 40 does not contain an attorney signature line or the printed name, address, email address, and telephone number of the attorney. Those items are represented in Form 2 of the Appendix of Forms to the Federal Rules of Civil Procedure. For illustrative purposes, Forms 2 and 40 have been combined in this text.

Date: _____   _____
                              (Signature of the attorney or unrepresented party)

                              _____
                              (Printed name)
                              (Address)
                              (E-mail address)
                              (Telephone number)

_____

In addition to the motion, a notice of motion may be required by local rules of court. Prior to the amendment of the Appendix of Forms to the Federal Rules of Civil Procedure in 2007, Form 19 included the following example of a notice of motion:

NOTICE OF MOTION

To: _____
Attorney for Plaintiff.

_____

Please take notice, that the undersigned will bring the above motion on for hearing before this Court at Room ___, United States Court House, Foley Square, City of New York, on the ___ day of ___, 20__, at 10 o'clock in the forenoon of that day or as soon thereafter as counsel can be heard.

Signed: _____
Attorney for Defendant.

Address: _____

_____

Whether a notice of motion is required depends upon the motion practice of individual courts.[12] The local rules in some jurisdictions also require that a form order, granting the relief sought, must be submitted with any motion.[13]

In addition to the motion to dismiss and the notice of motion, counsel generally will be expected to submit a brief or memorandum in support of the motion to dismiss. This document may take some time to prepare, for in it counsel marshals the legal authorities entitling her client to a dismissal of the action. The drafting of briefs and memoranda is discussed in Chapter 11.

Submit a brief memo

---

12. *Compare* Rule 7.1(b) & (f)(1) of the United States District Court for the Southern District of California (requiring written notice of motion setting a motion hearing for the day assigned by clerk assigned to the judge) *with* Rule 7.1(b) of the United States District Court for the Southern District of Florida ("No hearing will be held on motions unless set by the Court.").

13. *E.g.,* Rule 7.1(C) of the United States District Court for the Southern District of Texas; Rule 7(c) of the United States District Court for the District of Columbia.

In certain situations it may be necessary, or may make good strategic sense, to provide the court with some factual material in addition to the motion to dismiss. For example, the fourth defense in the motion to dismiss contained in Form 40 of the Appendix of Forms to the Federal Rules of Civil Procedure challenges the service of process upon the defendant. Because the sufficiency of the service of process cannot be determined on the face of the complaint, defense counsel has supported the motion to dismiss by filing affidavits setting forth the facts concerning service.

In the event that such evidentiary materials are contested, the court can hold a hearing on the motion to dismiss pursuant to Rule 12(i) of the Federal Rules of Civil Procedure. Rule 12(i) also permits a district court to defer the adjudication of any Rule 12(b) defense until trial. A court may be particularly likely to defer resolution of a Rule 12(b) defense if the facts relevant to that defense are intertwined with the merits of the action.[14]

Rule 12(d) provides that, if evidentiary material is considered by the court in connection with a Rule 12(b)(6) motion to dismiss for failure to state a claim upon which relief can be granted, "the motion must be treated as one for summary judgment under Rule 56. All parties shall be given reasonable opportunity to present all the material that is pertinent to the motion." Thus the court is permitted to go beyond the four corners of the complaint in considering a Rule 12(b)(6) motion to dismiss, but if it does so the motion is in effect converted into a motion for summary judgment.[15]

Rule 12(b) creates the possibility of combining a Rule 12(b)(6) motion to dismiss and a Rule 56 motion for summary judgment into a motion to dismiss or, in the alternative, for summary judgment. Such a motion permits counsel to get before the court evidentiary material that otherwise would not be considered in connection with a motion to dismiss. By combining a motion to dismiss and a motion for summary judgment, counsel can argue, implicitly, as follows: "Your honor, there is no legal basis to support this action. In addition, there's no substance to the allegations made on the merits." The judge then can grant the motion to dismiss, having been reassured as to the lack of substance of plaintiff's claims by the summary judgment evidentiary material (or explicitly rely upon the evidentiary material to grant the motion for summary judgment).

---

14. *Eaton v. Dorchester Dev., Inc.*, 692 F.2d 727, 731–34 (11th Cir. 1982). *See also Safe Air for Everyone v. Meyer*, 373 F.3d 1035, 1038–40 (9th Cir. 2004); *Data Disc, Inc. v. Systems Technology Associates, Inc.*, 557 F.2d 1280, 1285 n. 2 (9th Cir. 1977).

15. In certain cases, the court may be able to consider documents supporting the motion to dismiss without converting the motion to a motion for summary judgment. "Documents that a defendant attaches to a motion to dismiss are considered part of the pleadings if they are referred to in the plaintiff's complaint and are central to her claim." *Venture Assocs. Corp. v. Zenith Data Systems Corp.*, 987 F.2d 429, 431 (7th Cir. 1993). *See also Collins v. Morgan Stanley Dean Witter*, 224 F.3d 496, 498–99 (5th Cir. 2000); Fed. R. Civ. P. 10(c) ("A copy of a written instrument that is an exhibit to a pleading is a part of the pleading for all purposes.").

A certificate of service should be appended to every filing after the complaint. This is the certification by the attorney (or a secretary or other employee in the attorney's office) that the document in question has been mailed or otherwise served upon opposing counsel. A typical certificate of service might provide as follows:

CERTIFICATE OF SERVICE

I, [insert name of person who served the document], hereby certify that on this ___ day of _____, 20__, I served the foregoing [insert titles of the documents served] upon [insert name of opposing counsel] by [usually by (1) first class mail, postage prepaid, (2) hand, or (3) electronic means, if the person consented to receipt of electronic service in writing as required by Federal Rule of Civil Procedure 5(b)(2)(E)].

———

[signature of person who served papers]

———

As by now should be clear, a "motion to dismiss" involves quite a bit more than the mere preparation of the motion, itself.

NOTES AND QUESTIONS CONCERNING MOTIONS TO DISMISS

1. What accounts for the differing success rates of motions to dismiss in different types of cases (for instance, in prisoner as opposed to tort cases)? Are these differences due to differences in the types of claims asserted or something else?

2. Motions to dismiss are not just of use for defense counsel. Rule 12(b) provides that the defenses enumerated therein may be asserted in response to "a claim for relief in any pleading," and they thus can be asserted in response to a claim, counterclaim, crossclaim, or third-party claim.

3. Motions to dismiss can be directed to selected claims within a complaint, counterclaim, crossclaim, or third-party claim. A favorable time to discuss settlement may be after the dismissal of a major portion of an opposing party's claim. A quite unfavorable time to attempt to settle a case may be right after the court has denied your motion to dismiss.

4. Not only may the court consider evidentiary material in connection with a motion to dismiss, but the parties may be entitled to discovery concerning the issues raised by such a motion. *Eaton v. Dorchester Dev., Inc.,* 692 F.2d 727 (11th Cir. 1982). *See also Oppenheimer Fund, Inc. v. Sanders,* 437 U.S. 340, 351 n. 13 (1978). In *Ignatiev v. United States,* 238 F.3d 464 (D.C. Cir. 2001), the court of appeals held that, before the district court ruled on the United States' motion to dismiss for lack of subject matter jurisdiction, the plaintiffs were entitled to discovery concerning any internal guidelines relevant to the Secret Service's duty to protect diplomatic missions; the Rule 12(b)(1) motion to dismiss had been premised on the theory that sovereign

immunity had not been waived in this case because any duty to protect the mission was discretionary in nature.

5.　On the other hand, a court may stay discovery on the merits pending the resolution of a motion to dismiss based on threshold defenses. *See* Fed. R. Civ. P. 26(c). *See also Wyatt v. Kaplan*, 686 F.2d 276, 283–85 (5th Cir. 1982). The rationale for such stays is that parties should not be put to the time and expense of responding to discovery if the basic suit prerequisites are not met and the court will not need to consider the merits of the case.

B.　OTHER RULE 12 PREANSWER MOTIONS

In addition to Rule 12(b) motions to dismiss, there are two other preanswer motions of which defense counsel should be aware: the motion for a more definite statement provided by Rule 12(e) and the Rule 12(f) motion to strike. In addition, motions to transfer, notices of removal of a case from state to federal court, and motions for an enlargement of time sometimes are filed prior to the answer. Chapter 11, which deals with the presentation and argument of pretrial motions, discusses these litigation control devices.[16]

Rule 12(e) provides: "A party may move for a more definite statement of a pleading to which a responsive pleading is allowed but which is so vague or ambiguous that the party cannot reasonably prepare a response." Rule 12(e) motions for a more definite statement are generally disfavored by the courts.[17] Under the notice pleading contemplated by the Federal Rules of Civil Procedure, it's the rare pleading that is "so vague or ambiguous that the party cannot reasonably prepare a response."

Rule 12(e) has been strictly interpreted because of the availability of liberal discovery under the Federal Rules of Civil Procedure. For example, Rule II(B)(5) of the standing orders of Senior District Judge Jerry Buchmeyer of the United States District Court for the Northern District of Texas provided: "Except for motions filed under Rule 9(b), Fed. R. Civ. P—i.e., motions complaining of failure to plead fraud or mistake with particularity—a motion for more definite statement may only be filed where the information sought cannot be obtained by discovery." As a matter of pretrial strategy, if a complaint is so ambiguous that a motion for a more definite statement might be seriously considered by the court, the complaint may be subject to a successful motion to dismiss. If that is the case, the wiser course simply is to move to dismiss the complaint, rather than file a Rule 12(e) motion and give the plaintiff a chance to restate its claims.

Rule 12(f) of the Federal Rules of Civil Procedure provides for preanswer motions to strike "from a pleading an insufficient defense or any redundant, immaterial, impertinent, or scandalous matter." As with

---

16.　Chapter 11, Section II(B)(2) and (4), *infra* pp. 480, 484.

17.　*Comm. for Immigrant Rights v. County of Sonoma*, 644 F.Supp.2d 1177, 1190–91 (N.D.Cal. 2009); *Sagan v. Apple Computer, Inc.*, 874 F.Supp. 1072, 1077 (C.D.Cal. 1994); *Faulk v. Home Oil Co.*, 173 F.R.D. 311, 313 (M.D.Ala. 1997).

motions for a more definite statement, motions to strike are generally disfavored.[18] To enhance the chances of its success, the motion to strike should be targeted at specific allegations within a complaint, rather than being used as a substitute for a motion to dismiss. If a complaint is so poorly drafted that it might be subject to a motion to strike, counsel should consider filing a dispositive motion to dismiss.[19]

The motion to strike also can be used to seek the dismissal of a particular demand for relief to which the plaintiff is not entitled (such as damages that exceed a court's jurisdictional maximum). Otherwise, the motion may be best reserved for challenges to the ramblings of a *pro se* plaintiff whose entire complaint is not subject to a motion to dismiss. Nor should defense counsel overlook the possibility that the inclusion of "redundant, immaterial, impertinent, or scandalous matter" within a complaint may work to the defendant's advantage. Such material may suggest that the plaintiff, plaintiff's counsel, or both are pursuing unmeritorious claims in an unprofessional manner.

Rule 12(e) and 12(f) motions do not lead to the final disposition of many major lawsuits. They are, however, motions about which litigators should be aware and should be prepared to use in appropriate situations.

C. THE MOTION FOR JUDGMENT ON THE PLEADINGS

Although not a preanswer motion, the motion for judgment on the pleadings merits a short discussion. This motion logically falls within a discussion of preanswer motions because the defenses asserted in the motion are the same defenses that could have been raised in a motion to dismiss. The discussion is short for this same reason. Instead of filing a motion for judgment on the pleadings, most attorneys usually file a motion to dismiss or a motion for summary judgment.[20]

The motion for judgment on the pleadings is recognized in Rule 12(c) of the Federal Rules of Civil Procedure. Rule 12(c) provides: "After the pleadings are closed—but early enough not to delay trial—a party may move for judgment on the pleadings." In contrast to a motion to dismiss, a motion for judgment on the pleadings can be brought by either the

---

18. *Rosales v. Citibank*, 133 F.Supp.2d 1177, 1180 (N.D.Cal. 2001); *Johnson v. Chrysler Corp.*, 187 F.R.D. 440, 441 (D.Me. 1999); *Oliner v. McBride's Indus., Inc.*, 106 F.R.D. 14, 17 (S.D.N.Y. 1985).

19. While Rule 12(b) of the Federal Rules of Civil Procedure does not provide for motions challenging defenses, Rule 12(f) contemplates motions to strike "from a pleading an insufficient defense or any redundant, immaterial, impertinent, or scandalous matter." Rule 12(f) therefore may be of greater utility for plaintiff's, rather than defendant's, counsel. *See generally* Vitaris, Note, "The Motion to Strike an Insufficient Defense—Rule 12(f) of the Federal Rules of Civil Procedure," 11 *Rut. Cam L. J.* 441 (1980). *See also* Loomis, "Motion to Strike Affirmative Defenses—The Equivalent of Partial Summary Judgment," 13 *Am. J. Trial Advoc.* 645 (1989).

20. Professors Wright and Miller have called the motion for judgment on the pleadings "little more than a relic of the common law and code eras." 5A C. Wright & A. Miller, *Federal Practice and Procedure* § 1369, at 265 (3d ed. 2004).

plaintiff or the defendant.[21] In ruling upon such a motion, a court is to consider as true the well-pled allegations in the pleading of the party opposing judgment.[22] Thus the motion for judgment on the pleadings is for the resolution of legal, rather than factual, issues.

Why file a motion for judgment on the pleadings when the same defenses can be raised by a motion to dismiss? A common reason for not raising the Rule 12(b) defenses in a motion to dismiss is that, for whatever reason, the motion to dismiss could not be prepared within the Rule 12(a) response period. Although an extension of time for responding to the complaint sometimes may be obtained, such an extension may not provide adequate time for the preparation of a polished motion to dismiss in some cases.

If a timely filing of a motion to dismiss is not possible, Rule 12(b) defenses should be preserved by their inclusion in the answer and counsel should continue work on a motion for judgment on the pleadings. Rule 12(c) provides that, so long as trial is not delayed by the motion, a motion for judgment on the pleadings can be filed at any time after the filing of the answer and any reply. Tactical considerations (such as the desire to resolve a case as soon as possible) argue for the speedy filing of a motion for judgment on the pleadings, and case scheduling orders may require that such motions be filed by a date certain. However, there is no hard and fast rule generally limiting the time by which such motions must be filed.

There is another, albeit usually minor, advantage that can be gained from raising Rule 12(b) defenses in a motion for judgment on the pleadings rather than in a motion to dismiss. Under Rule 41(a)(1)(A)(i) of the Federal Rules of Civil Procedure, a plaintiff may, as a matter of right, dismiss an action "before the opposing party serves either an answer or of a motion for summary judgment." Accordingly, by filing an answer, the defendant precludes a plaintiff from voluntarily dismissing its action without leave of court once he sees the strong arguments mustered in a motion to dismiss.[23]

If defense counsel believes that the plaintiff might seek a voluntary dismissal, it may make sense to file an answer and a motion for judgment on the pleadings rather than a motion to dismiss. In order to expedite the disposition of the motion for judgment on the pleadings, it can be filed immediately after, or simultaneously with, the answer.

While the court normally is not to go beyond the face of the pleadings in ruling upon a motion for judgment on the pleadings,[24] Rule 12(d)

---

21. *E.g., National Metropolitan Bank v. United States,* 323 U.S. 454 (1945).

22. *Id.* at 456–57; *Beal v. Missouri Pacific R.R. Corp.,* 312 U.S. 45, 50–51 (1941).

23. Those who believe that there is little practical advantage to "locking in" a plaintiff to a lawsuit by the filing of an answer should read the description of the Pennzoil Company's use of a Rule 41(a) voluntary dismissal in its litigation with Texaco Incorporated. *See* Note 5 of Chapter 11's Notes and Questions Concerning Pretrial Motion Strategy, *infra* p. 487.

24. *United States v. Wood,* 925 F.2d 1580, 1581–82 (7th Cir. 1991) (per curiam); *PVM Redwood Co. v. United States,* 686 F.2d 1327, 1329 (9th Cir. 1982), *cert. denied,* 459 U.S. 1106 (1983); *Barr v. WUI/TAS, Inc.,* 66 F.R.D. 109, 113 (S.D.N.Y. 1975).

provides that if, on a motion for judgment on the pleadings, "matters outside the pleadings are presented to and not excluded by the court, the motion must be treated as one for summary judgment under Rule 56." Thus, as with a motion to dismiss, defense counsel can include evidentiary material along with a motion for judgment on the pleadings. Counsel also might consider a motion for judgment on the pleadings or, in the alternative, for summary judgment. Such a combined motion may make sense if counsel believes that she is entitled to judgment on the pleadings but there is very favorable evidentiary material that she would like to get before the judge.

Because motions for judgment on the pleadings can be filed by plaintiffs as well as defendants, all counsel should consider attempting to resolve litigation short of trial by the use of these motions.

D. CONSOLIDATION OF DEFENSES

Rule 12(b) provides that no defense or objection is waived "by joining it with one or more other defenses or objections in a responsive pleading or in a motion." Rule 12(g)(1) states: "A motion under this rule may be joined with any other motion allowed by this rule." A motion to dismiss therefore could be based upon an alleged lack of (1) subject matter jurisdiction, (2) personal jurisdiction, and (3) failure to state a claim upon which relief can be granted. Similarly, Rule 12(b) permits any combination of defenses to be set forth in an answer.

Rule 12 does not merely permit the consolidation of defenses. In certain circumstances it requires that defenses be consolidated. Rule 12(h)(1) states:

A party waives any defense listed in Rule 12(b)(2)–(5) by:

(A) omitting it from a motion in the circumstances described in Rule 12(g)(2); or

(B) failing to either:

(i) make it by motion under this rule; or

(ii) include it in a responsive pleading or in an amendment allowed by Rule 15(a)(1) as a matter of course.

Accordingly, the defenses of lack of jurisdiction over the person (Rule 12(b)(2)), improper venue (Rule 12(b)(3)), insufficiency of process (Rule 12(b)(4)), and insufficiency of service of process (Rule 12(b)(5)), as well as possible motions for a more definite statement and to strike, are waived if the defendant files a preanswer motion that does not raise these defenses. While there is no requirement that a preanswer motion be filed, if such a motion is filed, all of the above defenses must be consolidated in the motion.

Indeed, Rule 12(h)(1) provides that the four defenses recognized under Rules 12(b)(2) through (5) can be waived in either of two ways: "(A) [by] omitting it from a motion [that raises other Rule 12 defenses]; or (B) failing to either: (i) make it by motion under [Rule 12]; or (ii) include it in a responsive pleading or in an amendment allowed by Rule 15(a)(1) as a matter of course." These four Rule 12(b) defenses are considered personal to the defendant, and if the defendant does not raise the defenses, they are waived.

A second group of Rule 12(b) defenses is specifically protected from the waiver provisions of Rule 12(g) by Rule 12(h)(2). Rule 12(h)(2) provides that the defenses of failure to state a claim upon which relief can be granted (Rule 12(b)(6)) and failure to join an indispensable party (Rule 12(b)(7)), as well as an objection of failure to state a legal defense to a claim, "may be raised: (A) in any pleading allowed or ordered under Rule 7(a); (B) by a motion under Rule 12(c) [for judgment on the pleadings]; or (C) at trial." Accordingly, the Rule 12(b)(6) and (7) defenses, which bear directly on the merits of the underlying claims, are preserved until the time of trial.[25] While defense counsel generally will want to raise these defenses at the earliest possible time, the defenses are not waived (as are the Rule 12(b)(2) through (5) defenses) if not asserted in the answer or a preanswer motion.

The final Rule 12(b) defense, the Rule 12(b)(1) defense of lack of subject matter jurisdiction, cannot be waived. Rule 12(h)(3) provides: "If the court determines at any time that it lacks subject-matter jurisdiction, the court must dismiss the action." Even though not argued by the parties, a federal trial or appellate court can raise lack of subject matter jurisdiction and dismiss the case on those grounds at any time.[26]

Figure 5–1 summarizes the Rule 12(b) defenses and the circumstances under which these defenses are waived. In order to prevent waiver, defense counsel should thoroughly investigate the possible existence of each of the Rule 12(b) defenses at the very outset of the case. If counsel determines that there is a good faith basis for the assertion of any of these defenses, the viable defenses (1) should be consolidated in a preanswer motion if such a motion is filed or (2) should be raised in the answer. Rule 12 merely requires that counsel follow what would be good defensive pleading practice absent the waiver provisions of that Rule.

---

25. However, counsel should be aware of Federal Rule of Civil Procedure 16(d), which provides that a pretrial order "controls the course of the action unless the court modifies it," and Rule 16(e), providing that a court may modify a final pretrial order "only to prevent manifest injustice." Any Rule 12(b)(6) or (7) defenses therefore should be raised in the final pretrial order.

26. *Arbaugh v. Y & H Corp.*, 546 U.S. 500, 514 (2006); *Buethe v. Britt Airlines, Inc.*, 749 F.2d 1235, 1238 n. 3 (7th Cir. 1984); *Paul Marsh, Inc. v. Edward A. Goodman Co.*, 612 F.Supp. 635 (S.D.N.Y. 1985). *See also Giles v. NYLCare Health Plans, Inc.*, 172 F.3d 332, 336 (5th Cir. 1999).

FIGURE 5–1
*RULE 12(b) DEFENSES**

DEFENSE	Lack of Subject Matter Jurisdiction	Lack of Personal Jurisdiction	Improper Venue	Insufficiency of Process or Service of Process	Failure to State a Claim	Failure to Join an Indispens-able Party
Rule 12 Provision	12(b)(1)	12(b)(2)	12(b)(3)	12(b)(4) & (5)	12(b)(6)	12(b)(7)
Rule 12(h)(1): Defense is waived if omitted from a Rule 12 motion that actually is made or from answer.		X	X	X		
Rule 12(h)(2): Defense can be asserted in any pleading permitted or ordered under Rule 7(a), by motion for judgment on pleadings, or at trial.					X	X
Rule 12(h)(3): Defense is never waived.	X					

* In addition to the possible waiver of Rule 12(b) defenses, motions for a more definite statement and to strike cannot be raised after the filing of an answer or a preanswer motion. Federal Rules of Civil Procedure 12(e), 12(f), and 12(g)(2).

Exercises Concerning Preanswer Motions

1. In the litigation filed by attorney Gerald Stern on behalf of several hundred survivors of the Buffalo Creek disaster, defendant Pittston filed a motion for a more definite statement "(i) as to the nature and amount of damages allegedly sustained by [plaintiffs] and (ii) as to the citizenship of each plaintiff, on the ground that the present allegations are so vague and ambiguous that defendant cannot reasonably be required to frame a responsive pleading." Motion of Defendant (A) for Judgment on the Ground that Defendant is Not a Proper Party to this Action, (B) for a More Definite Statement as to Certain Allegations Contained in the Complaint, and (C) to Strike Certain Allegations Contained in the Complaint, at 2, *Prince v. The Pittston Company,* Civil Action No. 3052 (S.D.W.Va. 1972).

As counsel for plaintiffs, write a memorandum about Pittston's apparent purpose in filing this motion for a more definite statement, the wisdom of filing the motion, and how plaintiffs should respond to the motion.

2. Your law firm represents the defendant Pittston Company in connection with the litigation stemming from the collapse of the Buffalo Mining Company dam in Logan County, West Virginia. Working from the memorandum prepared in response to the Exercise Concerning the Analysis of Possible Defenses set forth earlier in this chapter, *supra* p. 189, write a memorandum recommending the manner in which Pittston's various possible defenses should be raised (in a preanswer motion or

otherwise). In your memorandum be sure to address what should be done to ensure that none of Pittston's defenses are waived.

3. You represent Financial Planners, Inc. (FPI), a group of financial planners who have been sued by Harry Simpson in the United States District Court for the District of New Mexico. Mr. Simpson, a retired letter carrier, alleges that FPI pressured him to invest his life savings in speculative stocks and that his investment of $95,000 is now worth only $6500. Mr. Simpson's investment contract with FPI provides that "any dispute concerning the business dealings of customer (Mr. Harry Simpson) and FPI shall be submitted to arbitration. Customer (Mr. Harry Simpson) hereby waives his right to initiate a court action except to enforce or challenge an arbitration award." All of Simpson's dealings with FPI were through the mail, and FPI does not have an office in New Mexico, where Simpson lives. In the Simpson–FPI investment contract, the parties stipulated that a two year New Hampshire statute of limitations would apply to any actions brought concerning that contract. Mr. Simpson's suit was not brought until twenty-six months after his stock reached its lowest value of $3700.

Should a motion to dismiss be filed on behalf of FPI? Presuming that such a motion should be filed, draft the motion and any supporting papers.

4. A federal diversity action has been filed against your client, Industrial Wastes, Inc. This action has been filed by We the People, a coalition of citizen activists. Your research indicates that (1) there is no diversity of citizenship between the parties and (2) the statute of limitations for the public nuisance claim asserted will run in 45 days from the date upon which your client was formally served with the summons and complaint. Your senior partner has suggested that you request a 30 day extension of time from plaintiff's counsel to file a motion to dismiss. Write a memorandum to your senior partner responding to this suggestion.

IV. THE ANSWER

The basic pleadings in any civil action are the complaint and the defendant's answer to the complaint.[27] The defendant's responses in the answer to the allegations of the complaint should delineate the disputed issues in the case. This early definition of the disputed issues establishes the permissible scope for pretrial discovery, as well as the issues to be resolved either before or at trial.

A. THE GOVERNING LAW

Rule 12(a) of the Federal Rules of Civil Procedure prescribes the time by which the defendant must answer the complaint. Rule 12(a)(1)(A)(i) requires a defendant to serve its answer within 21 days after being served with the summons and complaint. Rule 12(a)(1)(A)(ii) governs situations

---

27. Fed. R. Civ. P. 7(a).

in which the defendant has agreed to waive formal service pursuant to Rule 4(d). Rule 12(a)(1)(A)(ii) provides that in such cases the defendant need not serve an answer until 60 days after the request for waiver was sent or, if the request was addressed to the defendant outside the United States, not until 90 days after the request was sent.[28] However, unless the court sets a different time, the filing of a Rule 12 preanswer motion delays the time for the filing of an answer until 14 days after the court denies or defers ruling on the motion or until 14 days after the service of a more definite statement if one is ordered by the court.[29]

Extension of answer after courts ruling on preanswer motion

Three basic types of responses to the complaint may be contained in the answer. First of all, the defendant is required to directly address the individual allegations of the complaint and to admit or deny those allegations (or state that he cannot do so). Secondly, the defendant may assert other, affirmative, defenses that are not directly responsive to the complaint. Finally, the defendant can assert claims of its own, either against the plaintiff (in a counterclaim), against a co-party (in a crossclaim), or against a person not yet a party to the action who may be liable to the defendant for at least a part of plaintiff's claim against the defendant (in a third-party claim). While counterclaims, crossclaims, and third-party claims are discussed in the next section of this chapter, denials and affirmative defenses now will be considered.

3 Responses

Rule 8 of the Federal Rules of Civil Procedure establishes the basic ground rules for admissions and denials in the defendant's answer. A thorough understanding of Rule 8(b), in particular, is important so that all defenses are preserved. Rule 8(b)(1)(A) provides that all defenses must be set forth in the answer "in short and plain terms" while Rule 8(b)(1)(B) more specifically requires the defendant to "admit or deny the allegations asserted against it by an opposing party." Rule 8(b)(2) requires that each denial "fairly respond to the substance of the allegation" in question. Rule 8(b)(4) further requires that when a pleader "intends in good faith to deny only part of an allegation" that party must "admit the part that is true and deny the rest."

---

28. While Rule 4(d) does not permit requests that federal defendants waive formal service, Rule 12(a)(2) gives federal defendants 60 days to serve their answers. Under Rule 5(b)(2)(C), service by mail is complete upon mailing.

29. Fed. R. Civ. P. 12(a)(4). What if the defendant moves to dismiss some, but not all, of the counts of the complaint? Moberly & Lisenbee, "To Plead of Not to Plead?: Assessing the Effect of a Partial Motion to Dismiss on the Duty to Answer," 13 *J. Trial & App. Advoc.* 45 (2008). While the great weight of authority is that an answer need not be filed until after the court's ruling on the motion, defense counsel can protect against entry of a default on any portion of the complaint by combining with the partial motion to dismiss a request for extension of time for filing the answer until 14 days after notice of the court's ruling on the partial motion to dismiss. *Id.* at 80–90.

Nor does Rule 12 specify when an answer must be filed if the court grants a motion to strike a portion of a pleading. However, it would make little sense to require the filing of an answer during the time that a motion to strike is pending. The most reasonable interpretation of Rule 12 is that the defendant has until 14 days after the court grants a motion striking a portion of the complaint to file an answer to the remainder of the complaint. 5B C. Wright & A. Miller, *Federal Practice and Procedure* § 1346, at 46–47 (3d ed. 2004).

The defendant must respond point by point to all of the allegations of the complaint. There is a significant penalty placed upon defendants who do not specifically respond to all of the complaint's allegations. Rule 8(b)(6) provides: "An allegation—other than one relating to the amount of damages—is admitted if a responsive pleading is required and the allegation is not denied."

Nor are general denials of all of the allegations of a complaint permissible unless the defendant "intends in good faith to deny all the allegations of [the complaint]."[30] It is difficult to conceive of an answer which properly could contain a single, general denial; virtually all complaints contain some allegations (such as, perhaps, a description of the parties) that the defendant must in good faith admit.[31]

What if the defendant doesn't know whether certain allegations of the complaint are true or not? Rule 11's requirement that counsel conduct an "inquiry reasonable under the circumstances" to ensure that court papers have both legal and evidentiary support applies not only to complaints, but to every "pleading, written motion, or other paper" filed in connection with a civil action. Rule 11(b)(4) specifically provides that by presenting a paper to the court the attorney is certifying that "the denials of factual contentions are warranted on the evidence, or, if specifically so identified, are reasonably based on belief or a lack of information."

In fact, in one case a defendant and its counsel were sanctioned for *not* raising the defense of federal subject matter jurisdiction. In *Itel Containers Int'l Corp. v. Puerto Rico Marine Management Inc.*,[32] defense counsel knew that diversity of citizenship did not exist. Nevertheless, so that the statute of limitations would run on some of plaintiff's claims, counsel evasively answered the complaint and plaintiff's interrogatories, filed a counterclaim, and defended the action for almost two years before finally raising lack of subject matter jurisdiction. The court dismissed the action due to lack of subject matter jurisdiction, but required the defendant and its counsel to pay more than $40,000 to the plaintiff and $5000 to the United States due to the imposition on the federal judicial system.[33]

In the more typical case, defense counsel's concern will be not that she knows too much, but that she may not know enough. Whether an inquiry sufficient to satisfy the requirements of Rule 11 has been conducted depends upon the specific facts of each individual case. If defense counsel can ascertain the truth of an allegation of the complaint by

---

30. Fed. R. Civ. P. 8(b)(3).

31. Defense counsel can adopt one of two possible styles in setting forth denials and admissions in the answer. Rule 8(b)(3) provides: "A party that does not intend to deny all the allegations must either specifically deny designated allegations or generally deny all except those specifically admitted."

32. 108 F.R.D. 96 (D.N.J. 1985).

33. *Id.* at 105–107. This case does not illustrate a new defense tactic. *See* Wigmore, "Civil Procedure and Football—Defeating a Valid Claim by Pleading and then Demurring, While the Statute of Limitations Runs," 4 *Ill. L. Rev.* 344 (1909).

interviewing individuals or reviewing documents within the defendant's control, such an inquiry should be conducted.

Sometimes defense counsel will not be able to confirm or deny the truth of an allegation quite so easily. What if, for instance, the allegation concerns information to which only plaintiff is privy? Anticipating such situations, Rule 8(b)(5) provides: "A party that lacks knowledge or information sufficient to form a belief about the truth of an allegation must so state, and the statement has the effect of a denial."

Rule 8(c) of the Federal Rules of Civil Procedure is specifically addressed to affirmative defenses. Among the common affirmative defenses listed in Rule 8(c) are contributory negligence, the statute of frauds, and the statute of limitations. These defenses are the modern equivalent of the common law plea of confession and avoidance. However, under the Federal Rules of Civil Procedure, a responding party need not confess (or admit) an opposing party's allegations in order to avoid them by the filing of an affirmative defense. Indeed, Rule 8(d)(2) permits the pleading of defenses alternatively or hypothetically, while Rule 8(d)(3) allows the assertion of inconsistent claims or defenses. Counsel, though, must remember that all allegations of the answer must comply with the obligations of Rule 11.

Rule 8(c)(1) requires that affirmative defenses be set forth affirmatively, and if an affirmative defense is not alleged in the answer it usually will be considered waived.[34] However, the liberal notice pleading standards of the Federal Rules of Civil Procedure apply to the pleading of affirmative defenses,[35] and a Rule 15 amendment of the answer may provide a way to assert an overlooked affirmative defense in certain cases.[36]

What does an answer actually look like? Form 30 from the Appendix of Forms to the Federal Rules of Civil Procedure is a sample answer presenting various Rule 12(b) defenses:

ANSWER PRESENTING DEFENSES UNDER RULE 12(b)

(Caption—See Form 1.)

Responding to Allegations in the Complaint

1. Defendant admits the allegations in paragraphs _____.

2. Defendant lacks knowledge or information sufficient to form a belief about the truth of the allegations in paragraphs _____.

---

34. *Haskell v. Washington Township*, 864 F.2d 1266, 1273 (6th Cir. 1988); *Depositors Trust Co. v. Slobusky*, 692 F.2d 205, 208–209 (1st Cir. 1982). *But see Lafreniere Park Foundation v. Broussard*, 221 F.3d 804, 808 (5th Cir. 2000); *Brinkley v. Harbour Recreation Club*, 180 F.3d 598, 611–13 (4th Cir. 1999) (absent unfair surprise or prejudice to the plaintiff, affirmative defense is not waived because it is first raised in dispositive pretrial motion).

35. *Marine Overseas Services, Inc. v. Crossocean Shipping Co.*, 791 F.2d 1227, 1233 (5th Cir. 1986).

36. *Harris v. Secretary, U.S. Dept. of Veterans Affairs*, 126 F.3d 339, 343–44 (D.C.Cir. 1997); *Gallegos v. Stokes*, 593 F.2d 372, 374–75 (10th Cir. 1979); *Groninger v. Davison*, 364 F.2d 638, 640 (8th Cir. 1966).

3. Defendant admits *identify part of the allegation* in paragraph _____ and denies or lacks knowledge or information sufficient to form a belief about the truth of the rest of the paragraph.

Failure to State a Claim

4. The complaint fails to state a claim upon which relief can be granted.

Failure to Join a Required Party

5. If there is a debt, it is owed jointly by the defendant and *name* who is a citizen of _____. This person can be made a party without depriving this court of jurisdiction over the existing parties.

Affirmative Defense–Statute of Limitations

6. The plaintiff's claim is barred by the statute of limitations because it arose more than _____ years before this action was commenced.

Counterclaim

7. (*Set forth any counterclaim in the same way a claim is pleaded in a complaint. Include a further statement of jurisdiction if needed.*)

Crossclaim

8. (*Set forth a crossclaim against a coparty in the same way a claim is pleaded in a complaint. Include a further statement of jurisdiction if needed.*)

(Date and sign—See Form 2.)

———

Although not required by either the Federal Rules of Civil Procedure or the forms appended to those rules, defense counsel often conclude the answer with a final sentence demanding dismissal of the complaint and requesting the costs of suit and defendant's attorneys' fees. Illustrative of such a demand is the final sentence in the answer filed in the Buffalo Creek disaster litigation: "WHEREFORE, defendant demands judgment of dismissal, and for its costs."[37]

Counsel should not forget that defendants, as well as plaintiffs, have a constitutional right to jury trial on certain claims in federal court. So that it is not overlooked later, defense counsel can include at the end of the answer a Rule 38(b) demand for jury trial. A jury demand should specify the particular issue or issues upon which a jury is sought. For example, defense counsel may desire that a jury determine defendant's counterclaim, but want a judge to hear plaintiff's original claim.

---

37. Answer of Defendant to Plaintiffs' Complaint as Amended, at 13, *Prince v. The Pittston Company*, Civil No. 3052 (S.D.W.Va. 1973).

Rule 11 requires that all papers, including answers, be signed by counsel, while a certificate of service should be appended to the answer to evidence the service required by Rule 5. While answers should be carefully drafted in the first instance, Federal Rule of Civil Procedure 15 creates at least the possibility of later amendment.

In the initial portion of the answer shown in Form 30, all of the denials and admissions are grouped together.[38] Particularly in responding to longer complaints, a more common, and more easily understood, manner of setting forth admissions and denials is to follow the same paragraph numbering system in the answer that was used in the complaint. Illustrative of this system is the first portion of the Pittston Company's Second Defense to the allegations contained in the Buffalo Creek disaster complaint set forth in Chapter 4:[39]

SECOND DEFENSE

For specific answer to the allegations contained and set forth in the Complaint, as amended, by paragraphs numerically designated to correspond to the numerical designations assigned the several paragraphs thereof, defendant:

1. Admits that plaintiffs seek to invoke the Court's jurisdiction under Title 28, United States Code, Section 1332, but save as to that admission, denies Paragraph 1.

2. Is without knowledge or information sufficient to form a belief as to the truth of Paragraph 2.

3. Is without knowledge or information sufficient to form a belief as to the truth of Paragraph 3.

4. Denies that defendant has a single principal operating office and, except as so denied, admits Paragraph 4.

5. Denies Paragraph 5.

6. Denies the characterization of defendant as one of the largest coal companies in the United States, but admits that defendant has been in the coal mining business for many years, that on or about June 1, 1970, defendant became the owner of all the outstanding stock of Buffalo Mining Company ("Buffalo"), and that Buffalo has engaged in the coal mining business for a number of years; affirmatively alleges that Buffalo began its coal mining operations following its incorporation under the laws of the State of West Virginia on the date of June 12, 1964; and except as so admitted and alleged denies Paragraph 6.

7. Denies Paragraph 7.

8. Denies Paragraph 8.

---

38. *Supra* p. 205.

39. Answer of Defendant to Plaintiffs' Complaint as Amended, at 1–2, *Prince v. The Pittston Company,* Civil No. 3052 (S.D.W.Va. 1973). The paragraphs of plaintiffs' amended complaint to which this answer responds are the same as the paragraphs in the original complaint set forth in Chapter 4, *supra* p. 152.

9. Denies Paragraph 9.

———

By tracking the individual paragraphs of the complaint in the above manner, it should be relatively easy for the court and counsel to determine precisely which of the complaint's paragraphs, and portions of paragraphs, are disputed by the defendant. Some attorneys are even more brief in their answers and, instead of paragraphs 7, 8, and 9 above, would merely state:

7. Deny.

8. Deny.

9. Deny.

The same general rules of form and organization that apply to complaints also apply to answers. The Rule 10 requirements of captions and paragraphing must be followed in the answer, although Rule 10(a) provides that in the answer and other papers filed after the complaint only the first party on each side of the case need be listed in the case caption. Rule 10(c) permits defense counsel to adopt by reference statements made in different parts of the answer, just as may plaintiff's counsel in the complaint. Finally, as Form 30 and the excerpt from the Buffalo Creek answer illustrate, headings for separate defenses should be used to make those defenses and the answer easier to understand.

B. PRACTICAL CONSIDERATIONS

As the preceding examples illustrate, the answer is generally a relatively short document. One of the advantages of filing an answer, as opposed to a preanswer motion, is that the answer usually can be drafted rather quickly. Despite the speed with which an answer can be prepared, however, a great amount of time and effort must be devoted to the necessary work preparatory to the drafting of the answer. In particular, both thorough factual investigation and careful legal research are necessary in order to determine what defenses and claims should be asserted in the answer.

Thorough factual investigation and legal research not only are required by Rule 11 but also are necessary because the defendant's initial response to the complaint will frame the issues for later discovery and final adjudication. Defense counsel should avoid asserting defenses for which there is no colorable legal or factual support, while not omitting defenses from the answer that may result in the waiver of those defenses. Rules 8(c) and 12(b) of the Federal Rules of Civil Procedure provide good check lists for possible challenges to the complaint.

Thus the careful preparation of an answer can require a significant amount of factual investigation and legal research. Many cases therefore are settled before the answer is filed. If it is likely that a case will settle, a logical time to discuss settlement is before defense counsel invests the time to prepare an answer or preanswer motion and before both parties are required to invest time and effort in further pretrial proceedings.

If settlement is not reached, defense counsel must decide whether to file an answer or a preanswer motion. Usually it will be to defendant's advantage to raise Rule 12(b) defenses in a preanswer motion and thereby attempt to obtain an early dismissal of the action. In certain circumstances, however, it may be to defendant's advantage not to file an immediate motion to dismiss. Even if the defendant has a reasonably good Rule 12(b)(6) defense, such a defense may become even stronger if buttressed by the factual record that could be developed through discovery. While counsel should not engage in needless discovery, some judges may be less willing to grant a motion for summary judgment if they previously have denied a motion to dismiss based upon the same legal defense. In such circumstances, it may make more sense to file an answer, conduct limited discovery, and then move for summary judgment rather than to file a motion to dismiss.

Sometimes want to get to discovery

There also may be situations in which defense counsel may not wish to expedite the court's resolution of certain defenses and therefore will prefer to file an answer rather than a preanswer motion. The passage of time may work to defendant's advantage if, for example, another court is expected to issue a favorable ruling in a related case or popular sentiment in the local community currently is strongly against the defendant.[40]

If an answer is to be filed, the defendant should be involved in its preparation. In fact, the starting point for drafting the answer should be the defendant's own answers to the allegations of the complaint. Counsel should recognize, however, that her client will not be able to answer all of plaintiff's allegations (such as the complaint's jurisdictional allegations).

Nor should counsel take the defendant's initial answers at face value. Instead, she should discuss those answers with her client to ensure that (1) allegations are not admitted that in good faith can be denied and (2) allegations are not denied that the defendant either knows are true or can confirm are true by conducting, in the words of Rule 11, "an inquiry reasonable under the circumstances." A possible side benefit of admitting facts in the answer is that, once a fact is admitted, the defendant should be able to prevent plaintiff from obtaining discovery concerning that matter.

Defense counsel must be careful in responding to paragraphs of the complaint that should be admitted in part and denied in part. Rule 8(b)(6) provides: "An allegation—other than one relating to the amount of

---

40. This is not to say that a court cannot consider defenses that are set forth in the answer rather than asserted in a preanswer motion. Rule 12(i) of the Federal Rules of Civil Procedure gives the district courts the power to determine the sufficiency of any defense set forth in the answer. However, that same rule permits the court to defer the hearing and resolution of such a defense until trial. While the judge must decide whether to hear Rule 12(b) defenses prior to trial, defense counsel should remember that Rule 12(i) provides that any party can request a pretrial resolution of these defenses by the court.

damages—is admitted if a responsive pleading is required and the allegation is not denied." The answer must be carefully drafted so that there are no inadvertent admissions through the operation of Rule 8(b)(6). For this reason, many lawyers phrase partial admissions in the following terms:

> 1. Deny, except to admit that defendant and plaintiff had a telephone conversation on June 1, 2010.

By starting the response with a general denial, the defendant has admitted nothing other than what he, himself, has specified in the answer. Whatever drafting techniques are used by defense counsel, great care should be taken with both the substance and the style of the answer.

Exercises Concerning Answers

1. You are one of the counsel for the Pittston Company in connection with a lawsuit filed by Thomas Eakins seeking damages as a result of the Buffalo Creek disaster. Eakins's complaint contains the following paragraph:

> Plaintiff Thomas Eakins was surrounded by, and submerged in, the flood waters caused by the collapse of the Middle Fork dam. Eakins struggled in the flood waters in an effort to save his nephew, Matthew Smith. Despite Eakins's efforts, Matthew Smith was torn from plaintiff's arms and drowned.

Draft the answer that you would make to this paragraph under each of the following circumstances:

> (a) Neither you nor Pittston officials have any specific knowledge concerning the matters alleged in this paragraph.

> (b) Other flood survivors have told Pittston investigators that they have heard that Eakins unsuccessfully attempted to save his nephew from the flood waters.

> (c) Other flood survivors have told Pittston investigators that they saw Eakins unsuccessfully attempt to save his nephew from the flood waters.

> (d) A picture in the local paper several days after the flood was captioned: "Mr. Thomas Eakins grieves at the loss of his young nephew, who was torn from Eakins's arms by the flood waters."

> (e) A Pittston official believes that he remembers seeing a short segment on television showing Eakins's nephew being pulled from Eakins's arms by the flood.

> (f) Several days after the flood Eakins made a statement to a Pittston claims representative that he had unsuccessfully tried to save his nephew from the flood.

2. You are representing the Pittston Company in lawsuits brought against it in connection with the Buffalo Creek disaster. In the complaint filed in one of these lawsuits, the plaintiffs allege that Charles Cartwright,

a Pittston engineer, made a statement several weeks before the dam failure to Claude Humphreys, a retired miner, that the dam was "an accident waiting to happen." Both Cartwright and Humphreys died soon after the flood.

Based upon your pretrial investigation, you believe that Humphreys told no one about Cartwright's statement other than the attorney who drafted plaintiffs' complaint. You have been told that plaintiffs' counsel has nothing in writing memorializing Humphreys's statement about the Cartwright conversation. However, in a conversation with you immediately after the flood, Cartwright told you that he had made the statement about the dam to Humphreys but he would "never tell anyone else what [he had] said."

Based upon the above facts, how should Pittston respond to the allegation in plaintiffs' complaint that Cartwright stated that the dam was "an accident waiting to happen?"

3. Write a critique of the portion of the Buffalo Creek answer set forth in Section IV(A) of this chapter, *supra* p. 207.

4. Draft a memorandum describing the steps that you would take as defense counsel in answering the Buffalo Creek complaint set forth in Section V of Chapter 4, *supra* p. 152.

5. Draft the answer to the Buffalo Creek complaint set forth in Chapter 4, *supra* p. 152. Be sure to consider defenses other than denials of the allegations of the complaint.

V. COUNTERCLAIMS, CROSSCLAIMS, AND THIRD–PARTY CLAIMS

The defendant need not merely respond defensively to the complaint, but can adopt the theory that "the best defense is a good offense" and file claims of its own. The three claims available to the defendant are counterclaims (generally filed against the plaintiff), crossclaims (filed against a coparty), and third-party claims (filed against a person not named as a party by plaintiff but who may be liable for at least a part of plaintiff's claim against defendant). These possible claims are illustrated in Figure 5–2 and will be considered in turn.

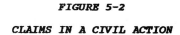

FIGURE 5-2

CLAIMS IN A CIVIL ACTION

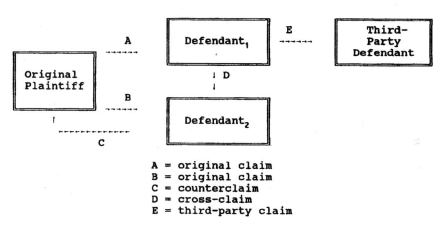

A = original claim
B = original claim
C = counterclaim
D = cross-claim
E = third-party claim

A. COUNTERCLAIMS

Rule 13(b) of the Federal Rules of Civil Procedure provides: "A pleading [in the case of the defendant, the answer] may state as a counterclaim against an opposing party any claim that is not compulsory." If the plaintiff sues a defendant for injuries sustained in an automobile accident, the defendant can assert a counterclaim against that plaintiff based upon a totally unrelated contract breach. Claim C in Figure 5–2 illustrates a counterclaim filed by a defendant against the plaintiff.

Does Rule 13(b) mean that all counterclaims are permissive? Hardly. In fact, Rule 13(a)(1) generally provides that claims that arise from the same transaction or occurrence as the complaint, and that do not require adding another party to the action over which the court cannot acquire jurisdiction, *must* be asserted as *compulsory* counterclaims. While there is no immediate penalty if a compulsory counterclaim is not asserted, the defendant's failure to assert the claim will bar its assertion in any later action.[41] Rule 13(a) compulsory counterclaims are an exception to the general rule that parties are able to choose the forum in which to assert their claims.

The distinction between compulsory and permissive counterclaims also is of significance for jurisdictional purposes. While there must be an independent basis of federal subject matter jurisdiction for a federal court to entertain a permissive counterclaim, compulsory counterclaims generally can be heard pursuant to the district court's supplemental jurisdic-

---

41.   *Crutcher v. Aetna Life Ins. Co.,* 746 F.2d 1076, 1080 (5th Cir. 1984). *See also Baker v. Gold Seal Liquors, Inc.,* 417 U.S. 467, 469 n. 1 (1974).

tion.[42] In the event that the counterclaim is permissive, it must set forth the independent jurisdictional basis upon which it rests.[43]

The counterclaim, either permissive or compulsory, is to be included in the answer.[44] Counsel should be sure to caption the counterclaim so that it is not confused with an affirmative defense (upon which defendant cannot recover affirmative relief). Moreover, Rule 7(a) of the Federal Rules of Civil Procedure only requires that an answer be filed to "a counterclaim denominated as a counterclaim." If the counterclaim is labeled or denominated as such, plaintiff will be required to file an answer setting forth its responses to the counterclaim's allegations.

Rules 13(a) and (b) of the Federal Rules of Civil Procedure require defense counsel to ask two questions when examining any complaint: (1) Are there claims that my client must assert as a compulsory counterclaim under Rule 13(a)? (2) Are there claims that my client may assert as a permissive counterclaim under Rule 13(b)? If a counterclaim is compulsory, it almost always will be asserted. However, whether to file a permissive counterclaim will depend upon a variety of factors.

Among the factors to be considered in deciding whether to file a permissive counterclaim are (1) the favorability of the current forum to defendant, (2) the additional time that might be required to dispose of plaintiff's claims if defendant's counterclaim is also before the court, (3) the additional discovery to which plaintiff might be entitled if defendant asserts its counterclaim, (4) whether the assertion of the counterclaim would make defendant's defense against plaintiff's pending claims more difficult, (5) whether there would be any savings from resolving the counterclaim in the same proceeding with plaintiff's pending claims, (6) the ability of the defendant to wait until its counterclaim can be asserted and resolved in another forum, and (7) practical problems that might occur if the defendant must satisfy a judgment in the present action before its counterclaim can be adjudicated in another forum.

In contemplating the scope of a potential counterclaim, defense counsel should remember that (1) Rule 13(c) permits a counterclaim to seek more or different relief than that sought in the complaint, (2) Rule 13(h) provides that persons other than the parties to the original action can be made parties to the counterclaim pursuant to Rules 19 and 20, and (3) the plaintiff may be able to assert a counterclaim or third-party claim in response to any counterclaim filed by the defendant.[45]

---

42. 28 U.S.C. § 1367. Prior to the enactment of Section 1367, federal courts exercised their ancillary jurisdiction over compulsory counterclaims. *Great Lakes Rubber Corp. v. Herbert Cooper Co.*, 286 F.2d 631 (3d Cir. 1961). *See also Baker v. Gold Seal Liquors, Inc.*, 417 U.S. 467, 469 n. 1 (1974).

In *Jones v. Ford Motor Credit Co.*, 358 F.3d 205, 210–214 (2d Cir. 2004), the Second Circuit Court of Appeals held that 28 U.S.C. § 1367 permits federal district courts to exercise jurisdiction over both compulsory and permissive counterclaims. However, even in the event that a court is considered to have the power to exercise jurisdiction over a permissive counterclaim, the court may still decline to exercise jurisdiction for one or more of the reasons set forth in 28 U.S.C. § 1367(c). 358 F.3d at 214–216. *See also Channell v. Citicorp Nat'l Services, Inc.*, 89 F.3d 379 (7th Cir. 1996); *Mostin v. GL Recovery, LLC*, 2010 WL 668808 (C.D.Cal. 2010).

43. Fed. R. Civ. P 8(a)(1); Fed. R. Civ. P. Form 30, ¶ 7.

44. Fed. R. Civ. P. 13(a)–(b).

45. Fed. R. Civ. P. 13(a)–(b), 14(b).

There are strong reasons for defendants to file counterclaims and thereby resolve several outstanding claims in the same action. However, before filing a counterclaim, counsel should consider carefully any factors arguing against the assertion of that counterclaim in a particular action.

B. CROSSCLAIMS

Rule 13(g) of the Federal Rules of Civil Procedure provides: "A pleading may state as a crossclaim any claim by one party against a coparty if the claim arises out of the transaction or occurrence that is the subject matter of the original action or of a counterclaim, or if the claim relates to any property that is the subject matter of the original action." In addition, Rule 13(h) provides that additional parties may be named in a crossclaim so long as the requirements of Rule 19 or Rule 20 are satisfied. Claim D in Figure 5–2 is a crossclaim brought by one defendant against a codefendant.

In contrast to compulsory counterclaims, all crossclaims are permissive. No independent jurisdictional basis is required for crossclaims, but the federal district courts can exercise supplemental jurisdiction over these claims.[46]

Although there is no requirement that crossclaims be filed within any civil action, it often will conserve both legal and judicial resources if these claims are adjudicated along with plaintiff's original claims. In addition, there is at least the possibility that a determination in the pending action could be used to collaterally estop the defendant in a separate and independent action if it does not file a crossclaim in the initial action. On the other hand, practical considerations such as the unfavorability of the forum to defendant may argue for bringing a potential crossclaim as a separate action in another forum.

The dynamics of a lawsuit and of the defense of a lawsuit can change dramatically upon the filing of a crossclaim. The adjudication of such a claim can divert both legal and judicial resources from the resolution of plaintiff's initial claims and any defense counterclaims. The co-party will have a right to discovery concerning the new claim, and the claim may induce the coparty to file additional claims or motions of its own.

Plaintiffs generally will have an easier time if they can pit defendants against one another. It therefore may be in the defendants' best interests to stand united in the defense of the existing action and, if time and practical considerations permit, resolve any differences among themselves either through negotiation or in a separate, and later, lawsuit.

The same general strategies apply to the filing of crossclaims that apply to any other action taken by counsel during the pretrial process. Before filing any crossclaim counsel should carefully calculate both the

---

46. 28 U.S.C. § 1367. Prior to the enactment of Section 1367, federal courts exercised their ancillary jurisdiction to entertain crossclaims. *United States v. Zima,* 766 F.2d 1153 (7th Cir. 1985). *See also Owen Equip. & Erection Co. v. Kroger,* 437 U.S. 365, 375 n. 18 (1978).

advantages and disadvantages of such a claim, as well as the likely responses to the claim by the other parties to the action.

C. THIRD–PARTY CLAIMS

Rule 14(a)(1) of the Federal Rules of Civil Procedure provides: "A defending party may, as third-party plaintiff, serve a summons and complaint on a nonparty who is or may be liable to it for all or part of the claim against it." Third-party practice, or impleader, is employed in indemnity situations in which, for example, an insurance company, a corporation, or an employer is allegedly liable for at least part of any award that plaintiff may recover. Claim E in Figure 5–2 is a third-party claim.

As with crossclaims, third-party claims are not compulsory but may be filed by a party if the requirements of Rule 14 are satisfied. Also as with crossclaims, third-party claims can be entertained within the court's supplemental jurisdiction.[47] In contrast to crossclaims, however, third-party claims are not set forth in the answer. Because a new person is being brought into the lawsuit by the third-party claim, it must be asserted in a separate third-party complaint and be separately served along with a summons upon the third-party defendant.[48]

A defendant can file a third-party claim without leave of court within 14 days after service of its original answer. If this 14–day period has passed, Rule 14(a)(1) requires that "the third-party plaintiff must, by motion, obtain the court's leave." While Rule 14 does not set a time limit for the filing of third-party claims, local rules of court may do so.[49] Even if the third-party claim is filed within 14 days after service of the answer, the court can decide not to entertain the claim, can sever the claim pursuant to Rule 21 of the Federal Rules of Civil Procedure, or can order a separate trial of the claim pursuant to Rule 42(b) of the Federal Rules of Civil Procedure.[50]

In attempting to convince a court to entertain a third-party claim, counsel should consider whether the adjudication of such a claim in the present action will conserve legal or judicial resources. Judicial efficiency is the rationale for permitting the assertion of third-party claims and

---

47. 28 U.S.C. § 1367. Prior to the enactment of Section 1367, federal courts entertained third-party claims pursuant to their ancillary jurisdiction. *Rogers v. Aetna Casualty & Surety Co.,* 601 F.2d 840, 843 (5th Cir. 1979). *See also Owen Equip. & Erection Co. v. Kroger,* 437 U.S. 365, 375 n. 18 (1978).

48. Fed. R. Civ. P. 14(a)(1). *See also* Fed. R. Civ. P. Form 16.

49. *E.g.,* Rule 14.1(a) of the United States District Court for the Eastern District of Pennsylvania (third-party claims generally must be filed within 90 days after service of claimant's answer); Rule 4.03(a) of the United States District Court for the Middle District of Florida (third-party claims generally must be filed by defendants within 6 months after service of answer or at least 60 days prior to trial date, whichever first occurs).

50. Rule 14(a)(4) of the Federal Rules of Civil Procedure provides: "Any party may move to strike the third-party claim, to sever it, or to try it separately." *See also* Advisory Committee's Note to 1963 Amendment to Rule 14, 31 F.R.D. 621, 636 (1962).

thereby collapsing two separate lawsuits into a single judicial action.[51] There often will be factual support for such an argument, because the alternative to a third-party claim usually is an entirely separate action.

A defendant seeking to assert a third-party claim may be able to show possible prejudice if the third-party claim is not entertained. The defendant might argue that if plaintiff's original claim and defendant's indemnity claim are separately litigated, the actions could result in inconsistent judgments; the defendant might lose the initial lawsuit to plaintiff, only to then lose the second action to the third-party due to an inconsistent factual finding. Possible prejudice to the defendant also could result if the defendant were found liable to plaintiff in the first suit but was without funds to satisfy the judgment in that action because a separate action against the third-party had not yet been resolved.

As with crossclaims and counterclaims, there are both advantages and disadvantages to third-party claims. Any time another party is brought into a lawsuit, pretrial proceedings become more complicated. The new party has the right to participate in discovery and to file claims of its own (including possible third-party claims against persons not yet named as parties to the suit). The new party presumably will be represented by counsel, which may make pretrial proceedings more complicated for scheduling and other purposes.

The decision to file a third-party claim only should be made after careful consideration of the potential risks and benefits of such a claim.

Exercises Concerning Counterclaims, Crossclaims and Third–Party Claims

1. You are the general counsel of the Pittston Company, which has been served with the complaint set forth in Chapter 4, *supra* p. 152. You have just begun your factual and legal research in an effort to develop Pittston's possible defenses to this action. The president of Pittston has asked you to consider the possibility of bringing a third-party claim against the State of West Virginia.

The president's interest in such a claim stems from the fact that the dam that failed had been built to satisfy West Virginia environmental regulations. As with other, similar dams in West Virginia, this dam was meant to act as a giant filter and prevent coal-wash waste water from polluting the Buffalo Creek. Prior to the adoption of West Virginia environmental regulations, Buffalo Mining and other coal companies merely dumped their coal-wash waste water directly into local creeks, rivers, and streams.

Your assignment is to write a memorandum to the president of Pittston concerning a possible third-party claim against the State of West Virginia. In your memorandum consider both the feasibility and the

---

51. *See United States v. Yellow Cab Co.,* 340 U.S. 543, 556 (1951).

wisdom of asserting such a claim. Also consider whether there are alternative ways in which Pittston can raise such a claim and the advantages and disadvantages of asserting the claim. Finally, consider whether there are any other claims that Pittston should consider asserting in the pending action.

2. Several years ago, Charlie Contractor entered into a contract to build a new factory for Atlas, Inc. Charlie entered into contracts with several subcontractors, including Plumwood Plumbers. Charlie was required to post a surety bond, which was underwritten by the American Insurance Company (before January 1, 2006) and the Insurance Company of America (from January 1, 2006, to July 1, 2006). During the construction, Charlie went bankrupt. Plumwood Plumbers then sued the American Insurance Company and the Insurance Company of America for $200,000 to compensate it for work done in 2005 and 2006 but for which it was not paid.

Although the American Insurance Company already has paid $100,000 to Plumwood Plumbers, it now appears that Plumwood did only $50,000 of the work for which it claims compensation before January 1, 2006. American Insurance also has paid $30,000 on a performance bond, unrelated to the bonds at issue in this suit, to the Green Meadow School District due to Plumwood's failure to adequately complete a plumbing job for the school district.

You represent the American Insurance Company in the action filed by Plumwood against American and the Insurance Company of America. Draft any offensive claims that you recommend should be filed on behalf of American.

VI. CONCLUSION

Under our system of civil procedure, the plaintiff has the chance both to initiate and initially structure the civil action. It is therefore especially important that the defendant's response to the complaint, whether by preanswer motion, answer, or the filing of other claims, be well-conceived and executed. In many cases, a preanswer motion may achieve the defendant's ultimate goal: a speedy end to the litigation that has been brought against it. In other cases, the initial defense pleadings and motions should lay the foundation for a successful defense during the later pretrial or trial stages of the case. In all cases, defense counsel must attempt to ensure that defendant's litigation plan is effectively and efficiently executed from the very outset of the case.

VII. CHAPTER BIBLIOGRAPHY

I. Alterman, *Plain and Accurate Style in Court Papers* (1987).

B. Child, *Drafting Legal Documents: Materials and Problems* (1988).

Conway, Comment, "Narrowing the Scope of Rule 13(a)," 60 *U. Chi. L. Rev.* 141 (1993).

"Developments in the Law—Multiparty Litigation in the Federal Courts," 71 *Harv. L. Rev.* 874 (1958).

Feirich, "Third–Party Practice," 1967 *U. Ill. L. F.* 236.

Greenbaum, "Jacks or Better to Open: Procedural Limitations on Co-Party and Third–Party Claims," 74 *Minn. L. Rev.* 507 (1990).

Guy, "Plan Trial Strategy Before You File Your Answer," *For the Defense,* Jan. 1981, at 24.

Hamabe, "Functions of Rule 12(b)(6) in the Federal Rules of Civil Procedure: A Categorization Approach," 15 *Campbell L. Rev.* 119 (1993).

Holtzoff, "Entry of Additional Parties in a Civil Action: Intervention and Third–Party Practice," 31 *F.R.D.* 101 (1962).

Hurd, Note, "The Propriety of Permitting Affirmative Defenses to be Raised by Motions to Dismiss," 20 *Mem. St. U. L. Rev.* 411 (1990).

Kennedy, "Counterclaims under Federal Rule 13," 11 *Hous. L. Rev.* 255 (1974).

J. Kole, *Pleading Your Case: Complaints and Responses* (2011).

McFarland, "In Search of the Transaction or Occurrence: Counterclaims," 40 *Creighton L. Rev.* 699 (2007).

McInerney, "Counterclaims as Self–inflicted Wounds," *Litigation,* Spring 1992, at 17.

Millar, "Counterclaim Against Counterclaim," 48 *Nw. U. L. Rev.* 671 (1954).

"Symposium—Third–Party Practice," 14 *Loy. U. Chi. L. J.* 415 (1983).

Tucker, Comment, "Federal Civil Procedure—Federal Rule 12(e): Motion for More Definite Statement—History, Operation and Efficacy," 61 *Mich. L. Rev.* 1126 (1963).

Vitaris, Note, "The Motion to Strike an Insufficient Defense—Rule 12(f) of the Federal Rules of Civil Procedure," 11 *Rutgers–Cam. L. J.* 441 (1980).

Wright, "Estoppel by Rule: The Compulsory Counterclaim Under Modern Pleading," 38 *Minn. L. Rev.* 423 (1954).

Wright, "Joinder of Claims and Parties under Modern Pleading Rules," 36 *Minn. L. Rev.* 580 (1952).

CHAPTER 6

THE SCOPE OF CIVIL DISCOVERY: "CAN THERE BE TOO MUCH OF A GOOD THING?"

■ ■ ■

If you are a conscientious lawyer, you want to turn over every rock or every bit of evidence. If you get paid by the pebble as you turn over these rocks, it makes it even more congenial to do the turning.

Professor Maurice Rosenberg at the June 1988 Association of American Law Schools Civil Procedure Conference.

Too much of a good thing can be wonderful!

Mae West.

Analysis

I. INTRODUCTION

The next five chapters of this text explore one of the most significant aspects of the entire civil pretrial process: discovery. In this chapter, the general scope of discovery is examined. In the next three chapters, the specific devices by which discovery is obtained from opposing parties and third-persons are considered. Chapter 10 then discusses the court's intervention in the discovery process pursuant to a party's request for a protective order, for an order compelling discovery, or for discovery sanctions.

The broad discovery contemplated by the Federal Rules of Civil Procedure was one of the major innovations of those rules. Liberal discovery was expected to result in better prepared and streamlined trials and eliminate "trial by ambush." It also was expected to lead to settlements, on the assumption that, in most situations, there is little reason to try a case if all parties know the evidence that all other parties possess. These expectations should be kept in mind as the scope of discovery is discussed in this chapter.

II. DISCOVERY AND DISCLOSURE IN THE FEDERAL DISTRICT COURTS

Rules 26 through 37 of the Federal Rules of Civil Procedure govern discovery in the federal district courts. In 1993 and again in 2000 these Rules were amended in major respects. The amendments to Rule 26, in particular, were among the most significant amendments to the Federal Rules of Civil Procedure since the adoption of the Rules. Pursuant to the 1993 amendments to Rule 26(a), individual district courts were given the power to "opt out" of major aspects of the amended Rules, but then, only seven years later, these opt-out possibilities were abolished in favor of national discovery uniformity. In 2006 the Rules were again amended—this time to specifically address the disclosure and discovery of electronically stored information. Most recently, in 2010, Rule 26 was amended to address aspects of expert discovery.

This section will discuss the general discovery framework provided by the Federal Rules of Civil Procedure. Because local rules of court still can significantly impact discovery practice in individual districts, they also will be discussed. In addition, counsel must be aware that they have the power to modify, by party stipulation, many of the discovery provisions of the Federal Rules of Civil Procedure. These subjects all are considered in this section.

A. DISCLOSURE UNDER RULE 26(a)

In order to fully understand the disclosure requirements of Rule 26(a), it's helpful to know something about not only the specific provisions of that Rule but also the Rule's history and background.

1. Mandatory Disclosure in the Federal Courts

While the 1993 amendments to the Federal Rules of Civil Procedure brought major changes in many aspects of the Federal Rules, in no area were there greater changes than in the Rules governing discovery. One member of the United States Supreme Court referred to these changes as "potentially disastrous and certainly premature."[1] A former Attorney

---

1. 113 S.Ct. 194, 197 (1993) (Scalia, J., dissenting from the transmittal of amendments to Congress).

General argued that "the actions of the Advisory Committee and the Judicial Conference are precipitous and unwise and, despite the best intentions of the Committee, will further mire the civil litigation system in costly and inefficient exercises of gamesmanship."[2] On the other hand, a federal district judge who had experimented with the automatic disclosure rules before their adoption as Federal Rules of Civil Procedure did not encounter the attorney opposition or other problems that he had anticipated.[3] The state courts in Arizona, which adopted a mandatory disclosure requirement and discovery limitations in July 1992, also had success with such new discovery rules prior to the 1993 amendment of the Federal Rules themselves.[4]

The 1993 amendments to Rule 26(a) did not address the scope of discoverable matter under the Federal Rules, but instead altered discovery procedures and their availability. In particular, Rule 26(a) was amended to impose upon parties a duty to voluntarily disclose certain relevant, non-privileged material without awaiting a formal discovery request from another party. Parties were required to identify individuals "likely to have discoverable information relevant to disputed facts alleged with particularity in the pleadings" and "documents, data compilations, and tangible things in the possession, custody, or control of the party that are relevant to disputed facts alleged with particularity in the pleadings."[5] Even before these amendments to Rule 26(a) became effective, they were vigorously attacked, particularly because of the requirement to voluntarily identify and produce damaging information to opposing parties and the absence of any required uniformity in the new pretrial disclosure regime.[6]

As a result of these concerns, the Federal Judicial Center conducted a 1997 survey of disclosure and discovery practices,[7] and this survey was relied upon in connection with the 2000 amendments to Rule 26(a). Because of the "widespread support for national uniformity" found in the Federal Judicial Center survey, the ability of individual district courts or judges to "opt out" of disclosure by local rules or standing orders was

---

2. Bell et al., "Automatic Disclosure in Discovery—The Rush to Reform," 27 *Ga. L. Rev.* 1, 58 (1992) (reprinted with permission).

3. Bertelsman, "Federal Judge's Experiment with Proposed Disclosure Provisions Proves Successful," *State–Federal Judicial Observer*, No. 2, at 1, 4 (April 1993) ("The lawyers seemed to know instinctively what they were supposed to disclose and disclosed it without a lot of fuss.").

4. Apple, "Mandatory Disclosure, Arbitration Rules Dramatically Affect Arizona Litigation," *State–Federal Judicial Observer*, No. 2, at 1 (April 1993) (citing decreases in civil caseloads, more frequent settlements, shorter disposition times, and a reduction in discovery motions).

5. Fed. R. Civ. P. 26(a)(1)(A), (B), 146 F.R.D. 401, 431 (1993).

6. *E.g.*, Bell et al., *supra* note 2, at 28–32, 39–48; 113 S.Ct. 194, 198 (1993) (Scalia, J., dissenting) ("By placing upon lawyers the obligation to disclose information damaging to their clients—on their own initiative, and in a context where the lines between what must be disclosed and what need not be disclosed are not clear but require the exercise of considerable judgment—the new Rule would place intolerable strain upon lawyers' ethical duty to represent their clients and not to assist the opposing side.").

7. T. Willging et al., *Discovery and Disclosure Practice, Problems and Proposals for Change* (1997).

eliminated.[8] Rule 26(a)(1) also was amended to require that parties only identify certain individuals, documents, data compilations, and tangible things that the disclosing party may use to support its claims or defenses.

The Federal Rules of Civil Procedure rarely have drawn the attention or sparked the controversy that surrounded the creation, study, and modification of the current required disclosure provisions of Rule 26(a). However, this history and background are quite helpful to a full understanding of the controversial nature of required disclosures in the United States District Courts.

NOTES AND QUESTIONS CONCERNING THE RULES AMENDMENT PROCESS

1. The process by which the Federal Rules of Civil Procedure may be amended is quite lengthy. The following table (from H.R. Rep. No. 103–319, 103d Cong., 1st Sess. 3 (1993)) shows the amendment process.

Action	Date
1. Suggestion for a change in the rules. (Submitted in writing to the Secretary of the Judicial Conference).	At any time.
2. Referred by the Secretary to the appropriate Advisory Committee	Promptly after receipt.
3. Considered by the Advisory Committee and its reporter	Normally at next Advisory Committee meeting.
4. If approved, the Advisory Committee seeks authority from the Standing Committee to circulate to bench and bar for comment.	At the same or subsequent meeting.
5. Public comment period	6 months.
6. Public hearings	During the comment period.
7. Advisory committee considers the amendment afresh in light of public comments and testimony at hearings.	Usually about one month after the close of the comment period.
8. Advisory Committee approves amendment in final form and submits it to the Standing Committee.	Normally at same meeting.
9. Standing Committee approves amendment, with or without revisions, and recommends approval by the Judicial Conference.	Normally at June meeting.

---

8. Advisory Committee Note to 2000 Amendment to Rule 26, 192 F.R.D. 340, 385 (2000). Instead, eight categories of proceedings that are exempt from mandatory disclosure under Rule 26(a) were specifically identified in that Rule. Fed. R. Civ. P. 26(a)(1)(B).

Prior to the 2000 amendment to Rule 26(a)(1) abolishing the ability of individual courts to opt out of the initial disclosure requirements, there was a wide split between the courts that required mandatory initial disclosures and those that opted out of this Rule 26(a)(1) requirement. D. Stienstra, *Implementation of Disclosure in United States District Courts, With Specific Attention to Courts' Responses to Selected Amendments to Federal Rule of Civil Procedure 26*, 182 F.R.D. 304, 310 (1998) (As of March 30, 1998, Rule 26(a)(1) was in effect in 49 district courts (including 7 that had significantly varied the Rule 26(a)(1) requirements) and not in effect in 45 district courts (including 18 districts that provided that judges may order disclosures in specific cases)).

Action	Date
10. Judicial Conference approves amendment, with or without revisions, and submits it to the Supreme Court.	Normally at June meeting.
11. The Supreme Court prescribes and transmits amendment to Congress	By May 1.
12. Congress has a statutory time period in which to enact legislation to reject, modify, or defer the amendment.	By December 1.
13. The amendment to the rules become law	December 1.

2.   There was a difference of opinion among the justices of the Supreme Court concerning both the 1993 discovery amendments and the Court's proper role in the Rules amendment process. In his letter transmitting the amendments to Congress, Chief Justice Rehnquist stated: "While the Court is satisfied that the required procedures have been observed, this transmittal does not necessarily indicate that the Court itself would have proposed these amendments in the form submitted." H.R. Doc. No. 103–74, 103d Cong., 1st Sess. I. (1993) (April 22, 1993, letter from Chief Justice William H. Rehnquist to Thomas S. Foley, Speaker of the House of Representatives).

3.   In a separate statement issued at the time of the transmittal of the proposed amendments to Congress, Justice White stated that the Supreme Court's role is to "transmit the Judicial Conference's recommendations without change and without careful study as long as there is no suggestion that the committee system has not operated with integrity." 113 S.Ct. 188, 192 (1993) (White, J.). Justice White's position was that "the trial practice is a dynamic profession, and the longer one is away from it the less likely it is that he or she should presume to second-guess the careful work of the active professionals manning the rulemaking committees, work that the Judicial Conference has approved." *Id.* at 191.

4.   Justices Scalia, Thomas, and Souter dissented from the Supreme Court order transmitting the 1993 discovery amendments to Congress. These justices were concerned that rather than replacing "the current, much-criticized discovery process * * * it *adds a further layer of discovery*" and that the new rules were likely to increase the burdens on federal district judges. 113 S.Ct. 194, 197 (1993) (Scalia, J., dissenting).

5.   During their tenures on the Court, Justices Black and Douglas suggested that the Rules Enabling Act be amended to shift the Supreme Court's current responsibility to the Judicial Conference of the United States, both because of the resources that the Judicial Conference has to evaluate proposed Rules and to relieve the Court "of the embarrassment of having to sit in judgment on the constitutionality of rules which we have approved and which as applied in given situations might have to be declared invalid." 374 U.S. 865, 870 (1963) (statement of Black & Douglas, JJ.).

6.   Do the Justices have sufficient expertise to second-guess proposed rules that have survived the amendment process? Consider the statement of Justice Douglas in dissenting from an order transmitting proposed amendments to the bankruptcy rules to Congress:

Forty years ago I had perhaps some expertise in the field; and I know enough about history, our Constitution, and our decisions to oppose the adoption of Rule 920. But for most of these Rules I do not have sufficient insight and experience to know whether they are desirable or undesirable. I must, therefore, disassociate myself from them.

411 U.S. 992, 994 (1973) (Douglas, J., dissenting). Responding to this position in his dissent from the transmittal of the 1993 discovery amendments to Congress, Justice Scalia asserted: "It takes no expert to know * * * that a breathtakingly novel revision of discovery practice should not be adopted nationwide without a trial run." 113 S.Ct. 194, 200 (1993) (Scalia, J., dissenting).

7. A bill to delete the mandatory disclosure requirement from the 1993 amendments to the Federal Rules was passed by the House of Representatives but was not considered by the Senate prior to December 1, 1993. H.R. 2814, 103d Cong., 1st Sess. (1993). Therefore Rule 26(a)(1), and the other 1993 amendments to the Federal Rules of Civil Procedure, became effective on December 1, 1993. *See* Hughes, "Congressional Reaction to the 1993 Amendments to the Federal Rules of Civil Procedure," 18 *Seton Hall Legis. J.* 1 (1993).

8. What should be the role of the Supreme Court in the Rules amendment process? Of the Advisory Committee? Of Congress?

2. The Required Disclosures

Required disclosures under Rule 26(a) are of three distinct types: (1) Rule 26(a)(1) initial disclosures; (2) Rule 26(a)(2) expert disclosures; and (3) Rule 26(a)(3) pretrial disclosures.

Initial Disclosures. Rule 26(a)(1) contains a requirement that certain basic information be voluntarily disclosed at the very outset of most cases.[9] The four categories of information falling within the initial disclosure requirement of Rule 26(a)(1)(A) are:

(i) the name and, if known, the address and telephone number of each individual likely to have discoverable information—along with the subjects of that information—that the disclosing party may use to support its claims or defenses, unless the use would be solely for impeachment;

(ii) a copy—or a description by category and location—of all documents, electronically stored information, and tangible things that the disclosing party has in its possession, custody, or control and may use to support its claims or defenses, unless solely for impeachment;

---

9. The 1993 amendments to Rule 26(a)(1) authorized courts to promulgate local rules to exclude categories of cases from initial disclosure. As a result of the 2000 amendments to Rule 26(a)(1), such local rules are no longer authorized. Instead, Rule 26(a)(1)(B) itself exempts from initial disclosure eight specific categories of proceedings, including petitions for habeas corpus, subpoena enforcement actions, student loan collection actions, and actions to enforce arbitration awards. In addition, Rule 26(a)(1)(A) provides that the parties may stipulate or the court may order that the initial disclosures not be required in a particular case.

(iii) a computation of each category of damages claimed by the disclosing party—who must also make available for inspection and copying as under Rule 34 the documents or other evidentiary material, unless privileged or protected from disclosure, on which each computation is based, including materials bearing on the nature and extent of injuries suffered; and

(iv) for inspection and copying as under Rule 34, any insurance agreement under which an insurance business may be liable to satisfy all or part of a possible judgment which may be entered in the action or to indemnify or reimburse for payments made to satisfy the judgment.

Material falling within the Rule 26(a)(1) initial disclosure requirement is rather basic information that typically was requested by means of a formal discovery request before the advent of disclosure in 1993. As a result of the 2000 amendments to Rule 26(a)(1), parties are no longer required to disclose information "relevant to disputed facts alleged with particularity in the pleadings," but only to identify individuals, documents, electronically stored information, and tangible things that the disclosing party may use to support its claims or defenses. As with all Rule 26(a) disclosures, Rule 26(a)(4) provides that initial disclosures are to be "in writing, signed, and served" unless the court orders otherwise.

Rule 26(a)(1)(C) provides that initial disclosures must be made "at or within 14 days after the parties' Rule 26(f) conference unless a different time is set by stipulation or court order, or unless a party objects during the conference that initial disclosures are not appropriate in this action and states the objection in the proposed discovery plan." Rule 26(f)(1) requires that, except "in a proceeding exempted from initial disclosure under Rule 26(a)(1)(B) or when the court orders otherwise," the parties must confer about their case. Rule 26(f)(2) requires the parties to consider the action, the possibility of settlement, and a proposed discovery plan, as well as to make or arrange for the Rule 26(a)(1) initial disclosures. Rule 26(f)(2) further provides that, within 14 days after their conference, the parties are to submit to the court a written report outlining the discovery plan upon which they have agreed.

So when is the Rule 26(f) conference to be held? Rule 26(f)(1) provides that this meeting is to be held "as soon as practicable—and in any event at least 21 days before a scheduling conference is to be held or a scheduling order is due under Rule 16(b)." Next question: When does the court issue its Rule 16(b) scheduling order? Rule 16(b)(2) provides that these orders are to issue "as soon as practicable, but in any event within the earlier of 120 days after any defendant has been served with the complaint or 90 days after any defendant has appeared." Pursuant to Rule 4(m) of the Federal Rules of Civil Procedure, a defendant must be served with the summons and complaint within 120 days after the filing of the complaint. What results is a "House–That–Jack–Built" time sequence for initial discovery disclosures, represented in Figure 6–1. Lawyers are fortunate, though, that the specific times for Rule 26(a) disclosures, Rule 26(f) conferences, Rule 16(b) conferences or for the issuance of Rule 16(b) scheduling orders often are set by party stipulation, court order, or local rules of court.[10]

FIGURE 6–1 *PRETRIAL DEADLINES*		
PRETRIAL ACTION	**TIME LIMIT**	**GOVERNING RULE**
Filing Complaint	varies	Statutes of Limitations
Serving Defendant	within 120 days after filing complaint	Rule 4(m)
Scheduling Order	within earlier of 120 days after any defendant has been served or 90 days after any defendant has appeared	Rule 16(b)(2)
Party Discovery Conference	at least 21 days before scheduling conference or order	Rule 26(f)(1)
Initial Disclosures	at or within 14 days after Rule 26(f) conference	Rule 26(a)(1)(C)
Submission of Written Discovery Plan to Court	within 14 days after Rule 26(f) conference	Rule 26(f)(2)

What if a party does not have all the responsive information at the time by which Rule 26(a)(1) initial disclosures are to be made? Rule 26(a)(1)(E) provides: "A party must make its initial disclosures based on the information then reasonably available to it. A party is not excused from making its disclosures because it has not fully investigated the case or because it challenges the sufficiency of another party's disclosures or because another party has not made its disclosures." Rule 26(e)(1) further provides that when additional information becomes known, the party is under a duty to supplement its earlier, incomplete, disclosures.

Expert Disclosures. In addition to Rule 26(a)(1) initial disclosures, Rule 26(a)(2) requires the disclosure of certain information concerning expert witnesses. Rule 26(a)(2)(A) requires the disclosure of the identity of

---

10. *E.g.* Rule 26.1(d)(2) of the United States District Court for the District of Wyoming (initial disclosures to be exchanged within 30 days after last pleading or dispositive motion is filed); Rule 16.01(d)(1)(a)(1)(a) of the United States District Court for the Middle District of Tennessee (at the time complaint is filed, clerk is to give filing party notice of initial case management conference).

any person who may testify as an expert witness. In addition to this requirement, which applies in all cases, Rule 26(a)(2)(B) provides that, unless the parties stipulate or the court directs to the contrary, the identification of each expert must be "accompanied by a written report— prepared and signed by the witness—if the witness is one retained or specially employed to provide expert testimony in the case or one whose duties as the party's employee regularly involve giving expert testimony." Rule 26(a)(2)(B) further provides that this report is to contain a complete statement of all opinions to be expressed by the expert, including the basis and reasons for those opinions, the facts or data considered by the expert in forming those opinions, any exhibits that will be used by the expert, and the qualifications, compensation, and past testimony of the expert. Even if the expert is not required to provide a written report under Rule 26(a)(2)(B), the party planning to call the expert is required by Rule 26(a)(2)(C) to disclose the subject matter of the expected expert testimony and a summary of the facts and opinions to which the expert is expected to testify.

Whereas the Rule 26(a)(1) initial disclosures are to be made at the outset of the case, Rule 26(a)(2) expert disclosures typically will be made much closer to the time of trial. Rule 26(a)(2)(D) provides that expert disclosures are to be made "at the times and in the sequence that the court orders." In the event that the court does not set or the parties agree to another time, expert disclosures are to be made "at least 90 days before the date set for trial or for the case to be ready for trial" or, "if the evidence is intended solely to contradict or rebut evidence on the same subject matter identified by another party under Rule 26(a)(2)(B) or (C), within 30 days after the other party's disclosure."[11] Rule 26(e)(1) and (2) require supplementation of both expert disclosures and expert reports.

Pretrial Disclosures. Rule 26(a)(3) pretrial disclosures are the third category of disclosures provided by Rule 26(a). Rule 26(a)(3)(A) provides that, in addition to initial disclosures under Rule 26(a)(1) and expert disclosures under Rule 26(a)(2), parties are to disclose the following evidence (unless the evidence is solely for impeachment):

> (i) the name and, if not previously provided, the address and telephone number of each witness—separately identifying those the party expects to present and those it may call if the need arises;

> (ii) the designation of those witnesses whose testimony the party expects to present by deposition and, if not taken stenographically, a transcript of the pertinent parts of the deposition; and

> (iii) an identification of each document or other exhibit, including summaries of other evidence—separately identifying those items the party expects to offer and those it may offer if the need arises.

These Rule 26(a)(3) pretrial disclosures concern information that actually will be offered at trial, rather than information more generally

---

11.   Fed. R. Civ. P. 26(a)(2)(D).

relevant to the parties' claims and defenses. Because trial witnesses and exhibits often are not known until close to the time of trial, Rule 26(a)(3)(B) provides that, unless otherwise directed by the court, pretrial disclosures must be made at least 30 days before trial.

How are the Rule 26(a) disclosure provisions enforced? First, Rule 26(g)(1) requires counsel to sign each Rule 26(a)(1) and (a)(3) disclosure and treats that signature as a certification as to the completeness and correctness of the disclosure. Similarly to the treatment of other court documents under Rule 11, Rule 26(g)(3) provides for the imposition of appropriate sanctions upon attorneys who violate Rule 26(g)(1)'s disclosure certification requirement. In addition, sanctions can be imposed upon a party or counsel pursuant to Rule 37(a) for a failure to comply with Rule 26(a) disclosure requirements. These sanctions can include a court order prohibiting a party from using at a trial, at a hearing, or on a motion any witnesses or evidence falling within Rule 26(a) that was not disclosed.[12] Finally, Rule 26(d)(1) provides that parties generally are not entitled to seek discovery from any source before they have conferred about initial disclosures and the other matters covered by Rule 26(f).

There are thus three types of disclosures that parties are required to make to other parties under Rule 26(a): (1) Rule 26(a)(1) initial disclosures at the very outset of the case; (2) Rule 26(a)(2) expert disclosures that typically are to be made at least 90 days before trial; and (3) Rule 26(a)(3) pretrial disclosures concerning evidence to be offered at trial and that generally are to be made at least 30 days before trial. The Rule 26(a) disclosures are summarized in Figure 6–2.

FIGURE 6–2 RULE 26(a) DISCLOSURES				
Rule 26(a) Provision	Material to be Disclosed	Can Stipulation Supersede Rule?	Can Court Supersede Rule?	When Disclosure is Required
Rule 26(a)(1)(A)(i) Initial Disclosures	Names, Addresses, and Phone Numbers of Persons with Supportive Discoverable Information	Yes	Yes	Unless Otherwise Stipulatedor Ordered or Party Objects, Within 14 Days After Rule 26(f) Conference
Rule 26(a)(1)(A)(ii) Initial Disclosures	Copies or a Description of Relevant Supportive Documents	Yes	Yes	
Rule 26(a)(1)(A)(iii) Initial Disclosures	Computation of Damages by Disclosing Party	Yes	Yes	
Rule 26(a)(1)(A)(iv) Initial Disclosures	Insurance Agreements	Yes	Yes	

---

12. Fed. R. Civ. P. 37(c)(1).

Rule 26(a) Provision	Material to be Disclosed	Can Stipulation Supersede Rule?	Can Court Supersede Rule?	When Disclosure is Required
Rule 26(a)(2)(A) Expert Disclosures	Identities of Experts	No	No	Unless Otherwise Stipulated or Directed by the Court, at Least 90 Days Before Trial
Rule 26(a)(2)(B) Expert Disclosures	Expert Reports	Yes	Yes	
Rule 26(a)(3)(A)(i) Pretrial Disclosures	Identification of Trial Witnesses	No	No	Unless Otherwise Directed by the Court, at Least 30 Days Before Trial
Rule 26(a)(3)(A)(ii) Pretrial Disclosures	Designation of Depositions for Trial	No	No	
Rule 26(a)(3)(A)(iii) Pretrial Disclosures	Identification of Trial Exhibits	No	No	

NOTES AND QUESTIONS CONCERNING REQUIRED DISCLOSURES IN THE FEDERAL COURTS

1. Prior to its amendment in 2000, Rule 26(a)(1) permitted local rules requiring parties to provide initial disclosures beyond those required by the 1993 version of that Rule. *E.g.* Rule 200–5(a)(1)(i) and (ii) of the United States District Court for the District of Montana (1995) (requiring disclosure of "the factual basis of every claim or defense advanced by the disclosing party" and "the legal theory upon which each claim or defense is based"); Rule 35.1(a) of the United States District Court for the District of Massachusetts (1998) (requiring automatic disclosure of medical information by personal injury claimants). As amended in 2000, Rule 26(a)(1) preempts not only local rules by which individual district courts opted out of disclosure, but also local rules such as these that either limited or expanded the disclosure required under Rule 26(a)(1). Advisory Committee Note to 2000 Amendment to Rule 26(a)(1), 192 F.R.D. 340, 385 (2000).

2. In his influential 1978 article, relied upon by the Advisory Committee that recommended the 1993 amendments to Rule 26 that added federal disclosure requirements, Magistrate Judge Wayne Brazil asserted:

> The adversary structure of the discovery machinery creates significant functional difficulties for, and imposes costly economic burdens on, our system of dispute resolution. Because these difficulties and burdens are an inevitable consequence of adversary relationships and competitive economic pressures, they cannot be removed by the kind of limited, nonstructural discovery reforms that have been made in the past and are once again under consideration. To come to terms with these problems will require an assault on their sources; effective reform consequently must include institutional changes that will curtail substantially the impact of adversary forces in the pretrial stage of litigation.

Brazil, "The Adversary Character of Civil Discovery: A Critique and Proposals for Change," 31 *Vand. L. Rev.* 1295, 1296–97 (1978). Should we be confident that Rule 26(a)(1) will "curtail substantially the impact of adversary forces in the pretrial stage of litigation?" What is more important in determining attorney behavior: the Federal Rules of Civil Procedure or the legal culture in which attorneys practice? Can cooperative attorney behavior be mandated by court rules?

3.   Are attorneys likely to be more forthcoming in their Rule 26(a)(1) initial disclosures than in responding to the initial interrogatories that the disclosure requirements replaced? Under the 1993 amendment to Rule 26(a)(1), parties were to disclose information "relevant to disputed facts alleged with particularity in the pleadings," while parties now are to disclose information that they may use to support their claims or defenses. Are attorneys likely to more fully comply with the current version of Rule 26(a)(1) than its 1993 predecessor? What incentives are there for them to do so?

4.   Is it possible that there will be problems with overinclusive discovery disclosures under Rule 26(a)(1), either due to attorneys improperly seeking to inundate opposing counsel with irrelevant material or because these disclosures must be made at the very outset of the case? Consider, too, that at least one study by the Federal Judicial Center concluded that "discovery abuse, to the extent it exists, does not permeate the vast majority of federal filings. In half the filings, there is no discovery—abusive or otherwise." P. Connolly et al., *Judicial Controls and the Civil Litigative Process: Discovery* 35 (1978). *See also* Trubek et al., "The Costs of Ordinary Litigation," 31 *UCLA L. Rev.* 72, 89–90 (1983) (finding no evidence of discovery in over one-half of 1600 federal and state cases studied); Brazil, "Civil Discovery: How Bad Are the Problems?," 67 *A.B.A.J.* 450, 454 (1981) (concluding that "discovery in smaller cases * * * is a very different animal from that in larger cases and that in the smaller matters it is afflicted by substantially less debilitating abuses and problems"). However, in a Federal Judicial Center study of civil cases that terminated in the last quarter of 2008, 86.3% of the respondent attorneys reported at least one type of discovery in their closed cases. E. Lee & T. Willging, *Federal Judicial Center National, Case–Based Civil Rules Survey: Preliminary Report to the Judicial Conference Advisory Committee on Civil Rules* 8 (2009).

5.   Rule 26(a)(1)(A)(i) and (ii) material need not be disclosed if it is "solely for impeachment." Can counsel be confident at the time that initial disclosures must be made that particular individuals or documents will only be needed for impeachment? Why would attorneys not want to disclose potentially impeaching individuals or documents at the very outset of the case? What if counsel withholds material believing that it only will be needed for impeachment and it later is determined to be supportive of her client's claims or defenses?

6.   Are there ways in which counsel can avoid the potential problems of over- or under-inclusive Rule 26(a)(1) initial disclosures?

Exercise Concerning Disclosure Under Rule 26(a)

You represent a young school teacher seriously injured in an automobile accident that resulted from another driver crashing through a red light and striking your client's car. Your senior partner, who is not familiar with the provisions of Rule 26(a), has asked you to write a memorandum concerning the following matters.

(a) You have the option of filing this action in state court or invoking federal diversity jurisdiction and filing the case in federal court pursuant to 28 U.S.C. § 1332. The state court does not require disclosures as are mandated under Federal Rule of Civil Procedure 26(a). Other things being equal, should the action be filed in federal court in order to take advantage of the federal disclosure rules?

(b) Presume that this case actually was filed in federal court and that it is quite likely that opposing counsel has some documents that could be very harmful to your client if offered at trial. These documents, however, were not provided by the defendant in his initial Rule 26(a)(1) disclosures. Should plaintiff's counsel request copies of these documents or say nothing and plan to rely upon Rule 37(c)(1) if defendant later offers the documents at trial?

3. Disclosure of Insurance Agreements

While the other initial required disclosures of Rule 26(a)(1) were first added to Rule 26 in 1993, prior to 1993 Rule 26 explicitly provided that insurance agreements were discoverable. The pre–1993 version of Rule 26(b)(2) did not require the automatic disclosure of insurance agreements, but insurance information was routinely sought by, and provided in response to, discovery requests promulgated pursuant to that Rule. The current version of Rule 26(a)(1)(A)(iv) now includes insurance agreements within that Rule's required initial disclosures. Except to the extent otherwise stipulated or directed by the court, Rule 26(a)(1)(A)(iv) requires that parties automatically provide to other parties "for inspection and copying as under Rule 34, any insurance agreement under which an insurance business may be liable to satisfy all or part of a possible judgment in the action or to indemnify or reimburse for payments made to satisfy the judgment."

As under the pre–1993 Rules, the disclosure of insurance agreements in the pretrial process does not render such evidence admissible at trial.[13] In fact, Federal Rule of Evidence 411 specifically provides: "Evidence that a person was or was not insured against liability is not admissible upon the issue whether the person acted negligently or otherwise wrongfully."

NOTES AND QUESTIONS CONCERNING THE DISCLOSURE
OF INSURANCE AGREEMENTS

1. What kind of a system is it in which a party is entitled to disclosure of insurance agreements, but is not permitted to present the information disclosed at trial? Are there reasons, not related to the presentation of a case at trial, for requiring disclosure of insurance agreements?

2. The 1970 Advisory Committee Note to Rule 26(b)(2) differentiated discovery of insurance coverage from other information concerning a party's financial status:

---

13. Advisory Committee Note to 1993 Amendment to Rule 26(a)(1)(D), 146 F.R.D. 401, 632 (1993).

The amendment is limited to insurance coverage, which should be distinguished from any other facts concerning defendant's financial status (1) because insurance is an asset created specifically to satisfy the claim; (2) because the insurance company ordinarily controls the litigation; (3) because information about coverage is available only from defendant or his insurer; and (4) because disclosure does not involve a significant invasion of privacy.

48 F.R.D. 487, 499 (1970). Are these distinctions convincing?

3.   As the Advisory Committee noted, financial information concerning a party is not automatically subject to discovery under Rule 26. However, "[w]here punitive damages are claimed, it has been generally held that the Defendant's financial condition is relevant to the subject matter of the action and is thus a proper subject of pretrial discovery." *Miller v. Doctor's General Hosp.,* 76 F.R.D. 136, 140 (W.D.Okla. 1977). *See also Rupe v. Fourman,* 532 F.Supp. 344, 350–51 (S.D.Ohio 1981); *Vollert v. Summa Corp.,* 389 F.Supp. 1348, 1351–51 (D.Hawai'i 1975); *Holliman v. Redman Dev. Corp.,* 61 F.R.D. 488 (D.S.C. 1973).

4.   One obvious way to attempt to ascertain the financial status of an adversary is to examine that party's income tax returns. Consider the policy reasons why tax returns have not been held to be generally subject to discovery under Rule 26:

> While tax returns do not enjoy an absolute privilege from discovery, a "public policy against unnecessary public disclosure arises from the need, if the tax laws are to function properly, to encourage taxpayers to file complete and accurate returns." Unless "clearly required in the interests of justice, litigants ought not to be required to submit such returns as the price for bringing or defending a lawsuit."

Tele–Radio Systems Ltd. v. De Forest Electronics, Inc., 92 F.R.D. 371, 375 (D.N.J. 1981), *quoting Premium Serv. Corp. v. Sperry & Hutchinson Co.,* 511 F.2d 225, 229 (9th Cir. 1975), *and Wiesenberger v. W. E. Hutton & Co.,* 35 F.R.D. 556, 557 (S.D.N.Y. 1964).

5.   Why are insurance applications not considered to be part of insurance agreements that must be disclosed pursuant to Rule 26(a)(1)(A)(iv)? *See* Advisory Committee Note to 1993 Amendment to Rule 26(a)(1)(D), 146 F.R.D. 401, 632 (1993); Advisory Committee Note to 1970 Amendment to Rule 26(b)(2), 48 F.R.D. 487, 499 (1970).

Exercise Concerning the Discovery of Insurance Agreements

In the Buffalo Creek disaster litigation, the plaintiffs served the following deposition notice:

In the United States District Court for the Southern
District of West Virginia at Charleston

DENNIS PRINCE, et al.,   )
              Plaintiffs,   )
             v.   )   CIVIL ACTION No. 3052–HN
)
THE PITTSTON COMPANY,   )
             Defendant.)

NOTICE OF TAKING DEPOSITIONS

TO: THE PITTSTON COMPANY, the Defendant in the above-
styled action, and Zane Grey Staker, Esquire, Box 388, Kermit,
West Virginia, 25674; William T. O'Farrell, Esquire, Jackson,
Kelly, Holt & O'Farrell, 1601 Kanawha Valley Building,
Charleston, West Virginia, 25322; and Daniel R. Murdock,
Esquire, Donovan Leisure Newton & Irvine, 30 Rockefeller
Plaza, New York, New York, 10020, Attorneys for Defendant:

Notice is hereby given that plaintiffs will take the testimony, upon
oral examination, before an officer authorized by law to administer oaths,
at the office of Weil, Gotshal & Manges, 767 Fifth Avenue, New York, New
York, 10022, commencing at 10:30 a.m. on February 25, 1974 of (1) Mr. A.
P. Bedell and of (2) one or more officers, directors or managing agents of
Johnson & Higgins, to be designated by Johnson & Higgins.

Pursuant to Rule 30(b)(6), Johnson & Higgins will be asked to
designate one or more officers, directors or managing agents to testify
with respect to:

I. The Pittston Company Umbrella Liability Quotation, expiration:
January 1, 1971 (see the attached November 5, 1970 letter from
Johnson & Higgins to Willis, Faber & Dumas, Ltd.), including
  A. The limitation proposed in the quotation on damage caused by
dams,
  B. The circumstances surrounding the proposed limitation and the
lifting of the limitation, and
  C. Correspondence and communications between Johnson & Higgins and The Pittston Company and between Johnson & Higgins and Willis, Faber and Dumas, Ltd. and/or the leader on the
first million layer with respect to the proposed limitation and its
lifting.

II. The exclusion, under the Pittston Company Umbrella Liability Contract beginning on January 1, 1971, concerning a $500,000 proper-
ty damage limit for dams (See the attached July 30, 1971 letter
from Johnson & Higgins to Willis, Faber & Dumas, Ltd.), including
  A. The circumstances surrounding the $500,000 property damage
limit for dams, and the attempt to delete this exclusion, and
  B. Correspondence and communications between Johnson & Higgins and The Pittston Company and between Johnson & Higgins and Willis, Faber & Dumas, Ltd. and/or the excess underwriters relating to the $500,000 property damage limit for dams
and the attempt to delete this exclusion.

Subpoenas *duces tecum* will be served upon Mr. Bedell and upon Johnson & Higgins. Each subpoena *duces tecum* will require the production of the following materials at the depositions for copying:

Designation of the Materials to Be Produced for Copying

[Documents relating to the matters set forth in sections I and II of the deposition notice then were designated.]

Dated this 6th day of February, 1974.

s/ ———
GERALD M. STERN
Arnold & Porter
1229 19th Street, N.W.
Washington, D.C. 20036

s/ ———
WILLIS O. SHAY
Steptoe and Johnson
Tenth Floor, Union Bank
Building
Clarksburg, West Virginia
26301
Attorneys for Plaintiffs

———

You are an associate in the law firm that represents the insurance brokerage of Johnson & Higgins and its employee A. P. Bedell. Putting to one side any questions about the use of depositions to obtain the information sought, write a short memorandum addressing whether the plaintiffs are entitled to the substance of the discovery sought by the deposition notice.

B. THE RELATIONSHIP OF RULE 26 TO THE OTHER DISCOVERY RULES

Mandatory disclosure under Rule 26(a) is only one way in which information can be obtained under the Federal Rules of Civil Procedure. In addition to Rule 26(a) mandatory disclosures, discovery can be specifically requested by invoking the various discovery devices set forth in Rules 27 through 36. However, unless the parties agree or the court orders to the contrary, in most situations these additional discovery devices cannot be used until a Rule 26(f) discovery conference has been held.[14]

Rule 26 contains the general provisions that govern all discovery in the federal district courts. In particular, Rule 26(b) sets forth the scope and limits of federal discovery that may be sought pursuant to the discovery devices recognized in Rules 27 through 36. In the event that discovery disputes arise between the parties concerning the discoverability of certain information sought pursuant to a Rule 27 through 36 discovery

---

14. Fed. R. Civ. P. 26(d)(1).

device, the district court can resolve these disputes pursuant to a Rule 26(c) protective order, a Rule 37 order compelling discovery or imposing sanctions, or by a Rule 16 pretrial order. Figure 6–3 illustrates the relationship of the discovery rules within the Federal Rules of Civil Procedure.

FIGURE 6-3

DISCOVERY SCOPE AND METHODS

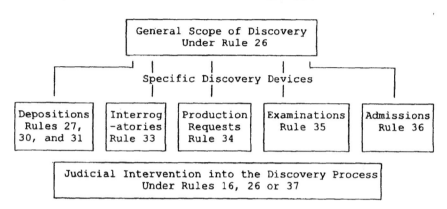

Other provisions of the Federal Rules of Civil Procedure also govern the discovery process. Rule 45 subpoenas can be used to obtain books, documents, electronically stored information, things or deposition testimony from non-parties. The district courts can use their powers under Rule 16 to govern the discovery process, and the major purpose of Rule 26(f) conferences is for the parties to discuss and plan discovery. However, once a case moves beyond the stage of initial disclosures and discovery planning, the Rules shown in Figure 6–3 generally govern discovery.

C. THE EFFECT OF LOCAL RULES OF COURT

Now that you have a general idea concerning discovery under the Federal Rules of Civil Procedure, here's some bad news. Those discovery rules are not applied in the same fashion in each federal district court. All ninety-four United States district courts have the authority under Rule 83 of the Federal Rules of Civil Procedure to promulgate local rules of court. As compiled by one legal publisher, these local rules fill six looseleaf binders and the rules of some individual districts are fifty pages in length.[15]

Local rules serve very important functions in permitting courts to tailor legal practice to local norms and customs and in providing attorneys

---

15. *Federal Local Court Rules* (West 3d ed. 2010); Rules of the United States District Courts for the Southern and Eastern Districts of New York; Rules of the United States District Court for the Eastern District of California. The local rules of individual district courts also are available on the federal judiciary's website, http://www.uscourts.gov/rulesandpolicies/FederalRulemaking/Local CourtRules.aspx.

with detailed information concerning procedures for discovery, motion practice, and other aspects of the pretrial process. However, local rules may undercut the nationwide procedural uniformity within the federal system that the Federal Rules of Civil Procedure were intended to achieve. Such rules also can impede the efforts of states to standardize state and federal practice by the adoption of the Federal Rules of Civil Procedure.[16] Professor Maurice Rosenberg testified before Congress over four decades ago that "[t]he Federal courts of this country are becoming a kind of procedural Tower of Babel because of the differences in local rules."[17]

In the 1990s both Congress and the Judicial Conference opted for more local rules, which resulted in less national uniformity in federal practice. Under the 1990 Civil Justice Reform Act, Congress required that each of the 94 federal district courts adopt a civil justice expense and delay reduction plan.[18] The original version of the bill that resulted in the Civil Justice Reform Act would have mandated that all federal district courts include certain specified, identical provisions in their plans.[19] In response to criticism that there was no "one size fits all" plan that would be appropriate in every federal district court, the requirement for identical cost and delay reduction provisions in each federal district was not adopted. Instead, the version of the Civil Justice Reform Act that ultimately was enacted merely required each district to consider certain "principles and guidelines of litigation management and cost and delay reduction" and "litigation management and cost and delay reduction techniques" and to adopt those principles, guidelines and techniques appropriate for that particular district.[20] Because of the option given individual districts to tailor their expense and delay reduction plans to local needs, 94 separate plans were developed to govern practice in the 94 federal district courts.[21]

In addition to the balkanization of procedure resulting from Civil Justice Reform Act expense and delay reduction plans, individual district courts were given the power to determine whether particular provisions of the 1993 amendments to the Federal Rules of Civil Procedure would apply in particular districts. District courts were given the power to adopt local

---

16. *See generally* Keeton, "The Function of Local Rules and the Tension with Uniformity," 50 *U. Pitt. L. Rev.* 853 (1989); Roberts, "The Myth of Uniformity in Federal Civil Procedure: Federal Civil Rule 83 and District Court Local Rulemaking Powers," 8 *U. Puget Sound L. Rev.* 537 (1985); Flanders, "Local Rules in Federal District Court: Usurpation, Legislation, or Information?," 14 *Loy. L.A. L. Rev.* 213 (1981).

17. *Hearings on S. 915 and H.R. 6111 before the Senate Subcomm. on Improvements in Judicial Machinery*, 90th Cong., 1st Sess. 282 (1967) (testimony of Maurice Rosenberg). *See also* Note, "Rule 83 and the Local Federal Rules," 67 *Colum. L. Rev.* 1251 (1967); Comment, "The Local Rules of Civil Procedure in the Federal District Courts—A Survey," 1966 *Duke L. J.* 1011.

18. 28 U.S.C. § 471 (expired Dec. 1, 1997).

19. S. 2027, 101st Cong., 2d Sess. § 3 (1990) (proposed 28 U.S.C. § 471).

20. 28 U.S.C. § 473 (expired Dec. 1, 1997).

21. Most provisions of the Civil Justice Reform Act expired on December 1, 1997. Judicial Improvements Act of 1990, Pub. L. No. 101–650, § 103(a), 104 Stat. 5089, 5096 (1990). However, in some districts portions of the expense and delay reduction plans were adopted as local rules pursuant to Federal Rule of Civil Procedure 83.

rules opting out of the initial disclosure requirements of Rule 26(a)(1),[22] the discovery meeting requirement of Rule 26(f),[23] and the presumptive limitations on the number of depositions and interrogatories contained in the 1993 amendments to the Rules.[24] In addition to these opportunities for local rules inconsistent with the Federal Rules, the 1993 amendments contained many provisions permitting the parties to modify by stipulation, or individual judges to order changes in, provisions of otherwise applicable Rules in specific cases.[25]

The great concern with this balkanization of federal discovery procedure led to the abolishment of many of the "local options" created for individual district courts by the 1993 amendments to the Federal Rules. In recommending national uniformity in discovery procedure in the 2000 amendments to the Federal Rules, the Advisory Committee on Civil Rules described the difficulties with the lack of national uniformity in discovery practice as follows:

> Many lawyers have experienced difficulty in coping with divergent disclosure and other practices as they move from one district to another. Lawyers surveyed by the Federal Judicial Center ranked adoption of a uniform national disclosure rule second among proposed rule changes (behind increased availability of judges to resolve discovery disputes) as a means to reduce litigation expenses without interfering with fair outcomes.[26]

The recommended amendments were adopted in 2000. While discovery procedures may be tailored to fit the needs of individual cases by court order or party stipulation, district courts no longer have the authority to adopt local rules to opt out of initial disclosures, alter the form of disclosures or the limitations on the numbers or length of depositions or the numbers of interrogatories, or change the timing and sequence of discovery or the Rule 26(f) discovery conference as established by the Federal Rules.

While much greater uniformity thus has been brought to discovery practice, "[a]ttorneys who practice before a district court without familiarizing themselves with the court's local rules do so at their peril."[27] The United States Court of Appeals for the Ninth Circuit has affirmed a district court's assessment of a monetary sanction against an attorney who failed to comply with a local rule requiring the exchange of exhibits and filing of trial briefs at least seven days in advance of trial.[28]

---

22.   Fed. R. Civ. P. 26(a)(1), 146 F.R.D. 401, 431 (1993).

23.   Fed. R. Civ. P. 26(f), 146 F.R.D. 401, 443–44 (1993).

24.   Fed. R. Civ. P. 26(b)(2), 146 F.R.D. 401, 437–38 (1993).

25.   *E.g.*, Fed. R. Civ. P. 26(a)(1) (initial disclosures); 26(a)(2)(A) (disclosure of reports of expert witnesses); 26(a)(3) (timing of pretrial disclosures); 26(f) (party discovery conference). 146 F.R.D. 401, 431, 433, 434, 443 (1993).

26.   Advisory Committee Note to 2000 Amendment to Rule 26, 192 F.R.D. 340, 385 (2000).

27.   *Loman Development Co. v. Daytona Hotel & Motel Suppliers, Inc.*, 817 F.2d 1533, 1537 n. 6 (11th Cir. 1987).

28.   *Toombs v. Leone*, 777 F.2d 465, 470–72 (9th Cir. 1985). *See also Weinberg v. Lear Fan Corp.*, 102 F.R.D. 269, 272 (S.D.N.Y. 1984) ($500 sanction assessed against plaintiffs' counsel for

As amended in 1985 and 1995, Rule 83(a)(1) requires "public notice and an opportunity for comment" before the adoption or amendment of local rules and explicitly provides that local rules must be consistent with federal statutes and rules. As amended in 1995, Rule 83(a)(2) also provides: "A local rule imposing a requirement of form must not be enforced in a way that causes a party to lose any right because of a nonwillful failure to comply." Regardless of the consequences to one's client from ignorance of local rules, it's imperative that counsel check and understand the local rules that apply in any court in which they practice.[29]

In addition to local rules of court, Rule 83(b) of the Federal Rules of Civil Procedure permits individual district judges and magistrate judges to adopt standing orders to "regulate practice in any manner consistent with federal law, [the Federal Rules of Civil Procedure, Evidence, and Bankruptcy Procedure], and the district's local rules." While authorizing the promulgation of such standing orders, Rule 83(b) further provides: "No sanction or other disadvantage may be imposed for noncompliance with any requirement not in federal law, federal rules, or the local rules unless the alleged violator has been furnished in the particular case with actual notice of the requirement."[30]

A creative use of Rule 83 in the discovery context is exemplified by a discovery memorandum and order promulgated by Judge Robert Keeton of the United States District Court for the District of Massachusetts. Judge Keeton's order in part provides:

> The court will not serve, or acquiesce in a magistrate's serving, as a mediator for settlement of disputes over discovery in which each party takes unreasonable positions with the purpose of conceding what is plainly due under the rules only when before the court or magistrate. If counsel make excessive demands or insufficient responses after this cautionary order by the court, an order may be

---

failure to file class action certification motion within 60 days as required by local rules); *Greene v. Union Mut. Life Ins. Co.*, 102 F.R.D. 598 (D.Me. 1984), *vac'd and remanded on other grounds*, 764 F.2d 19 (1st Cir. 1985) (clerk properly granted defendant's motion to dismiss due to failure of plaintiff's counsel to file written objection to defendant's motion within 10 days as required by local rule).

29. Despite the 1985 and 1995 amendments to Rule 83 that required greater national uniformity in local rules and practice, Professor Carl Tobias has concluded that the proliferation of local rules, orders, and practices in recent decades has resulted in a "federal practice [that] is more fractured than at any time since the Supreme Court prescribed the original federal rules during 1938." Tobias, "Local Federal Civil Procedure for the Twenty–First Century," 77 *Notre Dame L. Rev.* 533, 533 (2002). However, procedural variants introduced through local rules have sometimes provided the basis for later amendments to the Federal Rules of Civil Procedure. Marcus, "Discovery Containment Redux," 39 *B.C. L. Rev.* 747, 771 (1998) (noting that "local deviation has de facto become the Advisory Committee's experimental laboratory").

30. A major help in locating the standing orders of federal judges is the *Directory of Federal Court Guidelines* (2010). This directory is regularly supplemented and includes the standing orders, policies and practices of individual district judges, as well as biographical information concerning the judges. This information also is available electronically. See, for instance, the website for the United States District Court for the Northern District of Ohio, http://www.ohnd. uscourts.gov, which includes the civil and criminal practices and procedures and standing orders for individual federal district judges in that district.

entered providing for more stringent controls over discovery, including the following:

(1) Having determined that both sides have been unreasonable, the court may impose an appropriate sanction, pursuant to Fed. R. Civ. P. 26(g) and 37. An appropriate sanction in this case may include an order in which the court declines to undertake the burdensome task of working out some compromise position that is a reasonable accommodation within the range counsel should have agreed upon; the court may instead determine only which side has been more unreasonable and, as a sanction for misconduct, enter an order that discovery proceed in accordance with the other side's position.

(2) The court may award attorney fees against a party, or against counsel.

(3) The court may order that no client be charged for any of the time of counsel on either side spent on the discovery dispute in which counsel on both sides were taking unreasonable positions.[31]

Regardless of the district in which they practice, attorneys must adhere to governing constitutional and statutory provisions, the Federal Rules of Civil Procedure, relevant local rules, any standing orders of the district judge or magistrate judge to whom the case is assigned, and specific orders issued in their particular cases.

D. VARIATION OF DISCOVERY PROCEDURES BY PARTY STIPULATION

A discovery rule with which all civil practitioners should be familiar is Rule 29 of the Federal Rules of Civil Procedure. Rule 29 provides:

Unless the court orders otherwise, the parties may stipulate that:

(a) a deposition may be taken before any person, at any time or place, on any notice, and in the manner specified—in which event it may be used in the same way as any other deposition; and

(b) other procedures governing or limiting discovery be modified-but a stipulation extending the time for any form of discovery must have court approval if it would interfere with the time set for completing discovery, for hearing a motion, or for trial.

The 1970 amendment to Rule 29 provided for the first time that parties could stipulate to discovery modifications other than those concerning depositions. In its note to the 1970 amendment to Rule 29, the Advisory Committee stated: "It is common practice for parties to agree on such variations, and the amendment recognizes such agreements and provides a formal mechanism in the rules for giving them effect."[32]

---

31. For the complete text of Judge Keeton's memorandum and order see Keeton, "The Function of Local Rules and the Tension with Uniformity," 50 *U. Pitt. L. Rev.* 853, 900–902 (1989).

32. 48 F.R.D. 487, 508 (1970).

Under the 1993 amendments to the Federal Rules of Civil Procedure, parties are given additional, explicit authority to stipulate to procedures other than those set forth in the Federal Rules. For instance, parties can agree that formal discovery may commence before a Rule 26(f) discovery conference has been held[33] or that Rule 26(a)(1) initial disclosures not be provided.[34] In addition, parties can use their Rule 26(f) discovery plan to suggest to the court disclosure and discovery rules tailored to their particular case.

As amended in 1993, Rule 29 permits party stipulations concerning even discovery deadlines so long as the extension of a discovery deadline will not "interfere with any time set for completing discovery, for hearing a motion, or for trial." By this 1993 amendment, parties are "encouraged to agree on less expensive and time-consuming methods to obtain information, as through voluntary exchange of documents [and] use of interviews in lieu of depositions."[35] However, Rule 29 provides that the parties' ability to modify discovery procedures can be restricted by court order to the contrary.

What options are available to the parties? Consider the following use of a discovery stipulation:

> This dispute arose during the deposition of Dr. Winton H. Manning, a Vice President of ETS * * * . The plaintiffs deposed Dr. Manning for several days resulting in nearly 2000 pages of transcript. ETS [a non-party] being concerned with plaintiffs' inability to conclude the deposition of this senior officer offered to answer written questions in lieu of continuing the deposition by oral questioning. Plaintiffs agreed and submitted 188 written questions on cross-examination. ETS answered these questions promptly. Thereafter, Dr. Manning submitted to another day of oral cross-examination. Defendants then submitted 174 written questions in lieu of redirect examination by oral questions. Plaintiffs then submitted 54 written questions in lieu of oral re-cross examination which ETS answered.

> Plaintiffs objected to the admission into evidence of the answers to the questions on redirect examination. * * * We hold that the agreement of the parties did not give plaintiffs the exclusive right to use written questions in this regard, and such agreed to procedure is not inconsistent with the Federal Rules, and did not adversely affect the plaintiffs.[36]

Thus, while Rule 29 permits the parties to stipulate to variations in discovery practice, counsel must be careful that any stipulations reached accurately reflect the parties' agreement. One way to be sure of this is to offer to draft the discovery stipulation yourself.

---

33. Fed. R. Civ. P. 26(d)(1).

34. Fed. R. Civ. P. 26(a)(1)(A).

35. Advisory Committee Note to 1993 Amendment to Rule 29, 146 F.R.D. 401, 648 (1993).

36. *United States v. South Carolina*, 445 F.Supp. 1094, 1099 (D.S.C. 1977) (three judge court), *aff'd mem.*, 434 U.S. 1026 (1978).

The "discovery survey" pioneered by Professor Francis McGovern is another example of discovery provisions tailored to a specific case.[37] Such a survey was used in an action brought by 10,000 Alabama plaintiffs alleging injuries stemming from the release of DDT into a tributary of the Tennessee River. Rather than depose these 10,000 plaintiffs, or even require them to answer interrogatories, the parties agreed upon a survey questionnaire that would be administered by neutral third-parties. The cost of this survey was less than the estimated cost of interrogatories, the survey could be answered much faster than could interrogatories, and the survey results could be transferred easily to computers for further use.[38]

Whether agreements are reduced to a formal, written stipulation or not, a great deal of cooperation among counsel is necessary for the discovery rules to work efficiently and economically. The need for counsel to work cooperatively prior to trial was noted by Judge Hall at a pretrial conference in the Buffalo Creek disaster litigation:

> [T]he Court intends to conduct this case wide open, so to speak, and discovery [is] to be broad but I don't intend to get to the point where the defendant is put to an unconscionable amount of trouble. A lot of these things can be done, it would seem to me, if counsel would talk about them a little bit more.
>
> You have got a job to do. You have got a lawsuit to try here and it is going to be hard enough if counsel get together.[39]

While the Federal Rules of Civil Procedure provide the framework within which counsel must work, Rule 29 and local custom and practice give counsel the opportunity to structure the day-to-day handling of their cases in the manner best suited to each particular action.

III. THE GENERAL SCOPE AND LIMITS OF RULE 26 DISCOVERY

Rule 26(b) sets forth the general scope of discovery obtainable through the specific discovery devices recognized by the Federal Rules of Civil Procedure. Rule 26(b)(1) provides that, unless "otherwise limited by court order," parties "may obtain discovery regarding any nonprivileged matter that is relevant to any party's claim or defense." This scope of discovery, concerning matter "relevant to any party's claim or defense," applies in all cases unless specifically limited by the court. However, Rule 26(b)(1) also provides: "For good cause, the court may order discovery of any matter relevant to the subject matter involved in the action."

Prior to the 2000 amendments to that Rule, Rule 26(b)(1) entitled parties to discovery "regarding any matter, not privileged, which is

---

37. McGovern & Lind, "The Discovery Survey," 51 *L. & Contemp. Probs.* 41 (1988).

38. *Id.* at 47.

39. *Prince v. Pittston Co.*, Civil Action No. 3052–HN (S.D.W.Va.), Proceedings of May 16, 1973, at 25.

relevant to the subject matter involved in the pending action, whether it relates to the claim or defense of the party seeking discovery or to the claim or defense of any other party." The 2000 amendment to Rule 26(b)(1) created a bifurcated scope of discovery; parties generally are restricted to non-privileged matter relevant to the claims or defenses asserted in the action, but the court can expand the scope of discovery to encompass "any matter relevant to the subject matter involved in the action." As the Advisory Committee noted, "The amendment is designed to involve the court more actively in regulating the breadth of sweeping or contentious discovery."[40] However, the Advisory Committee also "hoped that reasonable lawyers can cooperate to manage discovery without the need for judicial intervention."[41]

Rule 26(b)(1) further provides: "Relevant information need not be admissible at the trial if the discovery appears reasonably calculated to lead to the discovery of admissible evidence." This provision, too, was modified in the 2000 amendments to the Federal Rules of Civil Procedure. Prior to 2000, there was no requirement that inadmissible evidence that was reasonably calculated to lead to the discovery of relevant evidence must itself be relevant. The Advisory Committee explained the rationale for the insertion of the word "relevant" in this sentence as follows: "The Committee was concerned that the 'reasonably calculated to lead to the discovery of admissible evidence' standard set forth in this sentence might swallow any other limitation on the scope of discovery. Accordingly, this sentence has been amended to clarify that information must be relevant to be discoverable, even though inadmissible, and that discovery of such material is permitted if reasonably calculated to lead to the discovery of admissible evidence."[42]

While Rule 26(b) defines the scope of civil discovery quite broadly, it does not address the specific discovery that is appropriate in any particular case. In fact, Rule 26(b)(2)(A) explicitly gives district courts the authority to alter the otherwise applicable limits on the numbers of interrogatories and the number and length of depositions contained in the Federal Rules and to limit the number of requests for admissions. Thus while Rule 26(b) contemplates a broad scope for civil discovery, the actual discovery permitted in specific cases may be rather limited due to numerical restrictions on the use of discovery devices contained in the Federal Rules of Civil Procedure or in orders entered by individual judges.

A. RELEVANCE

Prior to the 2000 amendments to the Federal Rules of Civil Procedure, parties were entitled to discover non-privileged matters "relevant to the subject matter involved in the pending action." The Supreme Court had interpreted this standard very broadly:

---

40. Advisory Committee Note to 2000 Amendment to Rule 26, 192 F.R.D. 340, 389 (2000).

41. *Id.*

42. *Id.* at 390.

"[R]elevant to the subject matter involved in the pending action" * * * has been construed broadly to encompass any matter that bears on, or that reasonably could lead to other matter that could bear on, any issue that is or may be in the case. See *Hickman v. Taylor.* Consistently with the notice-pleading system established by the Rules, discovery is not limited to issues raised by the pleadings, for discovery itself is designed to help define and clarify the issues. Nor is discovery limited to the merits of a case, for a variety of fact-oriented issues may arise during litigation that are not related to the merits.[43]

The broad nature of discoverable information under Rule 26 was frequently blamed for many of the perceived abuses of civil discovery. For this reason, proposals were offered to limit the scope of discovery under Rule 26(b). While a 1978 Preliminary Draft of Proposed Amendments to the Federal Rules of Civil Procedure would have required that discovery be relevant to a claim or defense in an action,[44] the 1980, 1983, and 1993 amendments to Rule 26 did not contain such a restriction on the scope of discovery. Rather than limit the *scope* of discovery under Rule 26(b), the 1993 amendments to the Rules instead limited the *amount* of discovery presumptively available under those Rules. Thus, while counsel were restricted in the number of depositions they were entitled to take or interrogatories they could serve, until 2000 Rule 26(b)(1) permitted deposition questions and interrogatories seeking information "regarding any matter, not privileged, which is relevant to the subject matter involved in the pending action."

As amended in 2000, Rule 26(b)(1) restricts a party's right to discovery to nonprivileged matters "relevant to any party's claim or defense." However, upon a showing of "good cause," Rule 26(b)(1) explicitly provides for discovery "relevant to the subject matter involved in the action." Thus parties may be able to obtain discovery within the same broader scope that applied prior to the 2000 amendment to Rule 26(b)(1), but only if they can establish "good cause" for such discovery. If good cause cannot be shown, they only will be permitted to discover matters "relevant to any party's claim or defense."

NOTES AND QUESTIONS CONCERNING RELEVANCE

1. What is the practical difference between "discovery regarding any nonprivileged matter that is relevant to any party's claim or defense" and "discovery of any matter relevant to the subject matter involved in the action?" The Advisory Committee provided this guidance: "The dividing line between information relevant to the claims and defenses and that relevant

---

43. *Oppenheimer Fund, Inc. v. Sanders,* 437 U.S. 340, 351 (1978). Despite this broad definition of relevance, the Supreme Court held that the names and addresses of class members sought in discovery in the case before it were not relevant for the purposes of Rule 26. 437 U.S. at 352.

44. Committee on Rules of Practice and Procedure, Judicial Conference of the United States, *Preliminary Draft of Proposed Amendments to the Federal Rules of Civil Procedure,* 77 F.R.D. 613, 623 (1978).

only to the subject matter of the action cannot be defined with precision. * * * In each instance, the determination whether such information is discoverable because it is relevant to the claims or defenses depends on the circumstances of the pending action." Advisory Committee Note to 2000 Amendment to Rule 26, 192 F.R.D. 340, 389 (2000). Is this helpful? Magistrate Judge Paul Grimm has suggested that "the difference between discovery relevant to the 'claims and defenses' as opposed to the 'subject matter' of the pending action [may be] the juridical equivalent to debating the number of angels that can dance on the head of a pin." *Thompson v. Dept. of Housing & Urban Development*, 199 F.R.D. 168, 172 (D.Md. 2001). Magistrate Grimm therefore has suggested that "the practical solution to implementing the new [2000] rule changes may be to focus more on whether the requested discovery makes sense in light of the Rule 26(b)(2) factors, than to attempt to divine some bright line differences between the old and new rule." *Id.*

2. Assuming that there is, in fact, a true difference between discovery "relevant to any party's claim or defense" and "discovery of any matter relevant to the subject matter involved in the action," what constitutes the "good cause" required to obtain "subject matter" discovery under Rule 26(b)(1)? Professor Thomas Rowe, who served on the Advisory Committee on Civil Rules during the drafting of amended Rule 26(b)(1), has suggested that "[o]ne idea was for the injection of a good-cause contention seeking broader subject-matter discovery to trigger court involvement in complex or contentious cases." Rowe, "A Square Peg in a Round Hole? The 2000 Limitation on the Scope of Federal Civil Discovery," 69 *Tenn. L. Rev.* 13, 32 (2001). Rowe suggests, however, that this may not actually be happening in practice because the courts have been involved with discovery before the good cause issues actually have arisen. *Id.* For a discussion of "good cause" under Rule 26(b)(1), see Stempel & Herr, "Applying Amended Rule 26(b)(1) in Litigation: The New Scope of Discovery," 199 F.R.D. 396, 418–23 (2001).

3. Can a party use a lawsuit as a vehicle to obtain information for non-litigation purposes? *See* Model Rules of Prof'l Conduct Rule 3.1 ("A lawyer shall not bring or defend a proceeding, or assert or controvert an issue therein, unless there is a basis in law and fact for doing so that is not frivolous * * * ."). What if the information sought is relevant within the terms of Rule 26(b)(1)?

4. Why does Rule 26(b)(1) provide that the relevant information sought "need not be admissible at the trial if the discovery appears reasonably calculated to lead to the discovery of admissible evidence?" In what situations might inadmissible information be "reasonably calculated to lead to the discovery of admissible evidence?" What other purposes might such discovery serve?

5. Rule 401 of the Federal Rules of Evidence defines "relevant evidence" to be "evidence having any tendency to make the existence of any fact that is of consequence to the determination of the action more probable or less probable than it would be without the evidence." This does not mean that a single bit of evidence only will be considered to be relevant if it establishes a particular matter by itself. "A brick is not a wall." *McCormick on Evidence* § 185, at 308 (K. Broun ed. 6th ed. 2006).

6. There is a different standard for initial disclosures under Rule 26(a)(1) than for discovery under Rule 26(b)(1). While the latter Rule permits discovery concerning any nonprivileged matter "relevant to any party's claim or defense," Rule 26(a)(1) initial disclosures are required concerning only matters that support the claims or defenses of the party making the disclosures. Why the different standards? What difference do they make in practice?

B. PRIVILEGE

Rule 26(b)(1) specifically excludes privileged material from the scope of civil discovery, but does not define the material that falls within this discovery exclusion. Nor do the Federal Rules of Evidence provide much guidance concerning the privileges that are to be recognized within the federal judicial system. Federal Rule of Evidence 501 states that, except when otherwise provided by federal law or by state law in cases in which state law supplies the rule of decision, privileges "shall be governed by the principles of the common law as they may be interpreted by the courts of the United States in the light of reason and experience." The following case illustrates the manner in which the Supreme Court has relied upon "reason and experience" to determine the scope of the attorney-client privilege within the federal courts.

UPJOHN CO. v. UNITED STATES

Supreme Court of the United States, 1981.
449 U.S. 383.

JUSTICE REHNQUIST delivered the opinion of the Court.

We granted certiorari in this case to address important questions concerning the scope of the attorney-client privilege in the corporate context and the applicability of the work-product doctrine in proceedings to enforce tax summonses. With respect to the privilege question the parties and various *amici* have described our task as one of choosing between two "tests" which have gained adherents in the courts of appeals. We are acutely aware, however, that we sit to decide concrete cases and not abstract propositions of law. We decline to lay down a broad rule or series of rules to govern all conceivable future questions in this area, even were we able to do so. We can and do, however, conclude that the attorney-client privilege protects the communications involved in this case from compelled disclosure and that the work-product doctrine does apply in tax summons enforcement proceedings.

I

Petitioner Upjohn Co. manufactures and sells pharmaceuticals here and abroad. In January 1976 independent accountants conducting an audit of one of Upjohn's foreign subsidiaries discovered that the subsidiary made payments to or for the benefit of foreign government officials in order to secure government business. The accountants so informed petitioner Mr. Gerard Thomas, Upjohn's Vice President, Secretary, and General Counsel. Thomas is a member of the Michigan and New York Bars, and has been Upjohn's General Counsel for 20 years. He consulted with outside counsel and R. T. Parfet, Jr., Upjohn's Chairman of the Board. It was decided that the company would conduct an internal investigation of what were termed "questionable payments." As part of this investigation the attorneys prepared a letter containing a questionnaire which was sent to "All Foreign General and Area Managers" over the Chairman's signature. The letter began by noting recent disclosures that several American companies made "possibly illegal" payments to foreign government officials and emphasized that the management needed full information concerning any such payments made by Upjohn. The letter indicated that the Chairman had asked Thomas, identified as "the company's General Counsel," "to conduct an investigation for the purpose of determining the nature and magnitude of any payments made by the Upjohn Company or any of its subsidiaries to any employee or official of a foreign government." The questionnaire sought detailed information concerning such payments. Managers were instructed to treat the investigation as "highly confidential" and not to discuss it with anyone other than Upjohn employees who might be helpful in providing the requested information. Responses were to be sent directly to Thomas. Thomas and outside counsel also interviewed the recipients of the questionnaire and some 33 other Upjohn officers or employees as part of the investigation.

On March 26, 1976, the company voluntarily submitted a preliminary report to the Securities and Exchange Commission on Form 8–K disclosing certain questionable payments. A copy of the report was simultaneously submitted to the Internal Revenue Service, which immediately began an investigation to determine the tax consequences of the payments. Special agents conducting the investigation were given lists by Upjohn of all those interviewed and all who had responded to the questionnaire. On November 23, 1976, the Service issued a summons pursuant to 26 U.S.C. § 7602 demanding production of:

> "All files relative to the investigation conducted under the supervision of Gerard Thomas to identify payments to employees of foreign governments and any political contributions made by the Upjohn Company or any of its affiliates since January 1, 1971 and to determine whether any funds of the Upjohn Company had been improperly accounted for on the corporate books during the same period.

> "The records should include but not be limited to written questionnaires sent to managers of the Upjohn Company's foreign affiliates, and memorandums or notes of the interviews conducted in the United States and abroad with officers and employees of the Upjohn Company and its subsidiaries."

The company declined to produce the documents specified in the second paragraph on the grounds that they were protected from disclosure by the attorney-client privilege and constituted the work product of attorneys prepared in anticipation of litigation. On August 31, 1977, the United

States filed a petition seeking enforcement of the summons under 26 U.S.C. §§ 7402(b) and 7604(a) in the United States District Court for the Western District of Michigan. That court adopted the recommendation of a Magistrate who concluded that the summons should be enforced. Petitioners appealed to the Court of Appeals for the Sixth Circuit, which rejected the Magistrate's finding of a waiver of the attorney-client privilege, 600 F.2d 1223, 1227, n. 12, but agreed that the privilege did not apply "[t]o the extent that the communications were made by officers and agents not responsible for directing Upjohn's actions in response to legal advice ... for the simple reason that the communications were not the 'client's.'" *Id.*, at 1225. The court reasoned that accepting petitioners' claim for a broader application of the privilege would encourage upper-echelon management to ignore unpleasant facts and create too broad a "zone of silence." Noting that Upjohn's counsel had interviewed officials such as the Chairman and President, the Court of Appeals remanded to the District Court so that a determination of who was within the "control group" could be made. In a concluding footnote the court stated that the work-product doctrine "is not applicable to administrative summonses issued under 26 U.S.C. § 7602." *Id.*, at 1228, n. 13.

II

Federal Rule of Evidence 501 provides that "the privilege of a witness ... shall be governed by the principles of the common law as they may be interpreted by the courts of the United States in light of reason and experience." The attorney-client privilege is the oldest of the privileges for confidential communications known to the common law. 8 J. Wigmore, Evidence § 2290 (McNaughton rev. 1961). Its purpose is to encourage full and frank communication between attorneys and their clients and thereby promote broader public interests in the observance of law and administration of justice. The privilege recognizes that sound legal advice or advocacy serves public ends and that such advice or advocacy depends upon the lawyer's being fully informed by the client. As we stated last Term in *Trammel v. United States,* 445 U.S. 40, 51 (1980): "The lawyer-client privilege rests on the need for the advocate and counselor to know all that relates to the client's reasons for seeking representation if the professional mission is to be carried out." And in *Fisher v. United States,* 425 U.S. 391, 403 (1976), we recognized the purpose of the privilege to be "to encourage clients to make full disclosure to their attorneys." This rationale for the privilege has long been recognized by the Court, see *Hunt v. Blackburn,* 128 U.S. 464, 470 (1888) (privilege "is founded upon the necessity, in the interest and administration of justice, of the aid of persons having knowledge of the law and skilled in its practice, which assistance can only be safely and readily availed of when free from the consequences or the apprehension of disclosure"). Admittedly complications in the application of the privilege arise when the client is a corporation, which in theory is an artificial creature of the law, and not an individual; but this Court has assumed that the privilege applies when the client is a corporation, *United*

States v. Louisville & Nashville R. Co., 236 U.S. 318, 336 (1915), and the Government does not contest the general proposition.

The Court of Appeals, however, considered the application of the privilege in the corporate context to present a "different problem," since the client was an inanimate entity and "only the senior management, guiding and integrating the several operations ... can be said to possess an identity analogous to the corporation as a whole." 600 F.2d, at 1226. The first case to articulate the so-called "control group test" adopted by the court below, *Philadelphia v. Westinghouse Electric Corp.,* 210 F.Supp. 483, 485 (E.D.Pa.), petition for mandamus and prohibition denied *sub nom. General Electric Co. v. Kirkpatrick,* 312 F.2d 742 (C.A.3 1962), cert. denied, 372 U.S. 943 (1963), reflected a similar conceptual approach:

> "Keeping in mind that the question is, Is it the corporation which is seeking the lawyer's advice when the asserted privileged communication is made?, the most satisfactory solution, I think, is that if the employee making the communication, of whatever rank he may be, is in a position to control or even to take a substantial part in a decision about any action which the corporation may take upon the advice of the attorney ... then, in effect, *he is (or personifies) the corporation* when he makes his disclosure to the lawyer and the privilege would apply." (Emphasis supplied.)

Such a view, we think, overlooks the fact that the privilege exists to protect not only the giving of professional advice to those who can act on it but also the giving of information to the lawyer to enable him to give sound and informed advice. See *Trammel, supra,* at 51; *Fisher, supra,* at 403. The first step in the resolution of any legal problem is ascertaining the factual background and sifting through the facts with an eye to the legally relevant. See ABA Code of Professional Responsibility, Ethical Consideration 4-1:

> "A lawyer should be fully informed of all the facts of the matter he is handling in order for his client to obtain the full advantage of our legal system. It is for the lawyer in the exercise of his independent professional judgment to separate the relevant and important from the irrelevant and unimportant. The observance of the ethical obligation of a lawyer to hold inviolate the confidences and secrets of his client not only facilitates the full development of facts essential to proper representation of the client but also encourages laymen to seek early legal assistance."

See also *Hickman v. Taylor,* 329 U.S. 495, 511 (1947).

In the case of the individual client, the provider of information and the person who acts on the lawyer's advice are one and the same. In the corporate context, however, it will frequently be employees beyond the control group as defined by the court below—"officers and agents ... responsible for directing [the company's] actions in response to legal advice"—who will possess the information needed by the corporation's lawyers. Middle-level—and indeed lower-level—employees can, by actions within the scope of their employment, embroil the corporation in serious legal difficulties, and it is only natural that these employees would have the relevant information needed by corporate counsel if he is adequately to advise the client with respect to such actual or potential difficulties. This fact was noted in *Diversified Industries, Inc. v. Meredith*, 572 F.2d 596 (C.A.8 1977) (en banc):

> "In a corporation, it may be necessary to glean information relevant to a legal problem from middle management or non-managerial personnel as well as from top executives. The attorney dealing with a complex legal problem 'is thus faced with a "Hobson's choice". If he interviews employees not having "the very highest authority", their communications to him will not be privileged. If, on the other hand, he interviews *only* those employees with "the very highest authority", he may find it extremely difficult, if not impossible, to determine what happened.' " *Id.*, at 608–609 (quoting Weinschel, Corporate Employee Interviews and the Attorney–Client Privilege, 12 B.C. Ind. & Com. L. Rev. 873, 876 (1971)).

The control group test adopted by the court below thus frustrates the very purpose of the privilege by discouraging the communication of relevant information by employees of the client to attorneys seeking to render legal advice to the client corporation. The attorney's advice will also frequently be more significant to noncontrol group members than to those who officially sanction the advice, and the control group test makes it more difficult to convey full and frank legal advice to the employees who will put into effect the client corporation's policy. See, *e. g., Duplan Corp. v. Deering Milliken, Inc.*, 397 F.Supp. 1146, 1164 (SC 1974) ("After the lawyer forms his or her opinion, it is of no immediate benefit to the Chairman of the Board or the President. It must be given to the corporate personnel who will apply it").

The narrow scope given the attorney-client privilege by the court below not only makes it difficult for corporate attorneys to formulate sound advice when their client is faced with a specific legal problem but also threatens to limit the valuable efforts of corporate counsel to ensure their client's compliance with the law. In light of the vast and complicated array of regulatory legislation confronting the modern corporation, corporations unlike most individuals "constantly go to lawyers to find out how to obey the law," Burnham, The Attorney–Client Privilege in the Corporate Arena, 24 Bus. Law. 901, 913 (1969), particularly since compliance with the law in this area is hardly an instinctive matter, see, *e. g., United States v. United States Gypsum Co.*, 438 U.S. 422, 440–441 (1978) ("the behavior proscribed by the [Sherman] Act is often difficult to distinguish from the gray zone of socially acceptable and economically justifiable business conduct"). The test adopted by the court below is difficult to apply in practice, though no abstractly formulated and unvarying "test" will necessarily enable courts to decide questions such as this with mathematical precision. But if the purpose of the attorney-client privilege is to be served, the attorney and client must be able to predict with some degree of certainty whether particular discussions will be protected. An uncertain privilege, or one which purports to be certain but results in widely varying applications by the courts, is little better than no privilege at all. The very terms of the test adopted by the court below suggest the unpredictability of its application. The test restricts the availability of the privilege to those officers who play a "substantial role" in deciding and directing a corporation's legal response. Disparate decisions in cases applying this test illustrate its unpredictability. Compare, *e.g., Hogan v. Zletz,* 43 F.R.D. 308, 315–316 (N.D.Okla.1967), aff'd in part *sub nom. Natta v. Hogan,* 392 F.2d 686 (C.A.10 1968) (control group includes managers and assistant managers of patent division and research and development department), with *Congoleum Industries, Inc. v. GAF Corp.,* 49 F.R.D. 82, 83–85 (E.D.Pa., 1969), aff'd, 478 F.2d 1398 (C.A.3 1973) (control group includes only division and corporate vice presidents, and not two directors of research and vice president for production and research).

The communications at issue were made by Upjohn employees to counsel for Upjohn acting as such, at the direction of corporate superiors in order to secure legal advice from counsel. As the Magistrate found, "Mr. Thomas consulted with the Chairman of the Board and outside counsel and thereafter conducted a factual investigation to determine the nature and extent of the questionable payments *and to be in a position to give legal advice to the company with respect to the payments.*" (Emphasis supplied.) 78–1 USTC ¶ 9277, pp. 83,598, 83,599. Information, not available from upper-echelon management, was needed to supply a basis for legal advice concerning compliance with securities and tax laws, foreign laws, currency regulations, duties to shareholders, and potential litigation in each of these areas. The communications concerned matters within the scope of the employees' corporate duties, and the employees themselves were sufficiently aware that they were being questioned in order that the corporation could obtain legal advice. The questionnaire identified Thomas as "the company's General Counsel" and referred in its opening sentence to the possible illegality of payments such as the ones on which information was sought. A statement of policy accompanying the questionnaire clearly indicated the legal implications of the investigation. The policy statement was issued "in order that there be no uncertainty in the future as to the policy with respect to the practices which are the subject of this investigation." It began "Upjohn will comply with all laws and regulations," and stated that commissions or payments "will not be used as a subterfuge for bribes or illegal payments" and that all payments must be "proper and legal." Any future agreements with foreign distributors or agents were to be approved "by a company attorney" and any questions concerning the policy were to be referred "to the company's General Counsel." This statement was issued to Upjohn employees worldwide, so that even those interviewees not receiving a questionnaire were aware of the legal implications of the interviews. Pursuant to explicit instructions from the Chairman of the Board, the communications were considered "highly confidential" when made and have been kept confidential by the company. Consistent with the underlying purposes of the attorney-client privilege, these communications must be protected against compelled disclosure.

The Court of Appeals declined to extend the attorney-client privilege beyond the limits of the control group test for fear that doing so would entail severe burdens on discovery and create a broad "zone of silence" over corporate affairs. Application of the attorney-client privilege to communications such as those involved here, however, puts the adversary in no worse position than if the communications had never taken place. The privilege only protects disclosure of communications; it does not protect disclosure of the underlying facts by those who communicated with the attorney:

> "[T]he protection of the privilege extends only to *communications* and not to facts. A fact is one thing and a communication concerning that fact is an entirely different thing. The client cannot be compelled to answer the question, 'What did you say or write to the attorney?' but may not refuse to disclose any relevant fact within his knowledge merely because he incorporated a statement of such fact into his communication to his attorney." *Philadelphia v. Westinghouse Electric Corp.*, 205 F.Supp. 830, 831 (E.D.Pa.1962).

See also *Diversified Industries*, 572 F.2d, at 611; *State ex rel. Dudek v. Circuit Court*, 34 Wis.2d 559, 580, 150 N.W.2d 387, 399 (1967) ("the courts have noted that a party cannot conceal a fact merely by revealing it to his lawyer"). Here the Government was free to question the employees who communicated with Thomas and outside counsel. Upjohn has provided the IRS with a list of such employees, and the IRS has already interviewed some 25 of them. While it would probably be more convenient for the Government to secure the results of petitioner's internal investigation by simply subpoenaing the questionnaires and notes taken by petitioner's attorneys, such considerations of convenience do not overcome the policies served by the attorney-client privilege. As Justice Jackson noted in his concurring opinion in *Hickman v. Taylor*, 329 U.S., at 516: "Discovery was hardly intended to enable a learned profession to perform its function ... on wits borrowed from the adversary."

Needless to say, we decide only the case before us, and do not undertake to draft a set of rules which should govern challenges to investigatory subpoenas. Any such approach would violate the spirit of Federal Rule of Evidence 501. See S. Rep. No. 93–1277, p. 13 (1974) ("the recognition of a privilege based on a confidential relationship ... should be determined on a case-by-case basis"); *Trammel*, 445 U.S., at 47; *United States v. Gillock*, 445 U.S. 360, 367 (1980). While such a "case-by-case" basis may to some slight extent undermine desirable certainty in the boundaries of the attorney-client privilege, it obeys the spirit of the Rules. At the same time we conclude that the narrow "control group test" sanctioned by the Court of Appeals in this case cannot, consistent with "the principles of the common law as ... interpreted ... in the light of reason and experience," Fed. Rule Evid. 501, govern the development of the law in this area.

[The Court then held that the court of appeals had been incorrect in concluding that the attorney work-product doctrine was inapplicable to non-attorney-client communications in a tax summons enforcement proceeding such as this.]

Accordingly, the judgment of the Court of Appeals is reversed, and the case remanded for further proceedings.

It is so ordered.

CHIEF JUSTICE BURGER, concurring in part and concurring in the judgment.

I join in Parts I and III of the opinion of the Court and in the judgment. As to Part II, I agree fully with the Court's rejection of the so-called "control group" test, its reasons for doing so, and its ultimate holding that the communications at issue are privileged. As the Court states, however, "if the purpose of the attorney-client privilege is to be served, the attorney and client must be able to predict with some degree of certainty whether particular discussions will be protected." For this very reason, I believe that we should articulate a standard that will govern similar cases and afford guidance to corporations, counsel advising them, and federal courts.

The Court properly relies on a variety of factors in concluding that the communications now before us are privileged. Because of the great importance of the issue, in my view the Court should make clear now that, as a general rule, a communication is privileged at least when, as here, an employee or former employee speaks at the direction of the management with an attorney regarding conduct or proposed conduct within the scope of employment. The attorney must be one authorized by the management to inquire into the subject and must be seeking information to assist counsel in performing any of the following functions: (a) evaluating whether the employee's conduct has bound or would bind the corporation; (b) assessing the legal consequences, if any, of that conduct; or (c) formulating appropriate legal responses to actions that have been or may be taken by others with regard to that conduct. Other communications between employees and corporate counsel may indeed be privileged—as the petitioners and several *amici* have suggested in their proposed formulations—but the need for certainty does not compel us now to prescribe all the details of the privilege in this case.

Nevertheless, to say we should not reach all facets of the privilege does not mean that we should neglect our duty to provide guidance in a case that squarely presents the question in a traditional adversary context. Indeed, because Federal Rule of Evidence 501 provides that the law of privileges "shall be governed by the principles of the common law as they may be interpreted by the courts of the United States in the light of reason and experience," this Court has a special duty to clarify aspects of the law of privileges properly before us. Simply asserting that this failure "may to some slight extent undermine desirable certainty," neither minimizes the consequences of continuing uncertainty and confusion nor harmonizes the inherent dissonance of acknowledging that uncertainty while declining to clarify it within the frame of issues presented.

NOTES AND QUESTIONS CONCERNING *UPJOHN CO. V. UNITED STATES* AND THE *ATTORNEY-CLIENT PRIVILEGE*

1. Judge Charles Wyzanski's frequently cited recitation of the requirements of the attorney-client privilege provides:

> The privilege applies only if (1) the asserted holder of the privilege is or sought to become a client; (2) the person to whom the communication was made (a) is a member of the bar of a court, or his subordinate and (b) in connection with this communication is acting as a lawyer; (3) the communication relates to a fact of which the attorney was informed (a) by his client (b) without the presence of strangers (c) for the purpose of securing primarily either (i) an opinion on law or (ii) legal services or (iii) assistance in some legal proceeding, and not (d) for the purpose of committing a crime or tort; and (4) the privilege has been (a) claimed and (b) not waived by the client.

United States v. United Shoe Mach. Corp., 89 F.Supp. 357, 358–59 (D.Mass. 1950). The satisfaction of which of these requirements was at issue in *Upjohn?*

2. The Federal Rules of Evidence as submitted to Congress recognized not only the attorney-client privilege at issue in *Upjohn,* but also the following other non-constitutional privileges: required reports, psychotherapist-patient, husband-wife, communications to clergy, political vote, trade secrets, secrets of state and other official information, and identity of informer. Rule 501 as adopted represents congressional concerns that common law privileges not be modified or restricted and that federal law not supersede a state's substantive law of privilege in diversity cases. *See* H.R. Conf. Rep. No. 93–1597, 93d Cong., 2d Sess. 7–8 (1974). For discussions of the privileges recognized in the federal courts see Symposium, "Federal Privileges in the 21st Century," 38 *Loy. L.A. L. Rev.* 515 (2004); Capra, "The Federal Law of Privileges," *Litigation,* Fall 1989, at 32. *See also* 3 J. Weinstein & M. Berger, *Weinstein's Federal Evidence* Art. V (J. McLaughlin ed. 2d ed. 2008); 2 C. Mueller & L. Kirkpatrick, *Federal Evidence* Chap. 5 (3d ed. 2007). Not only have the federal courts recognized common law privileges pursuant to Rule 501, *e.g., Jaffee v. Redmond,* 518 U.S. 1 (1996) (recognizing psychotherapist-patient privilege), but Congress has created statutory privileges as well. *See* 26 U.S.C. § 7525 (recognizing privilege for "any federally authorized tax practitioner" with respect to tax advice in certain noncriminal tax matters before the Internal Revenue Service or in federal court).

3. Among those urging in amicus briefs that the Supreme Court uphold the attorney-client privilege in *Upjohn* were the American Bar Association, the Federal Bar Association, the American College of Trial Lawyers, and the

Chamber of Commerce of the United States. Why were these associations concerned about this case?

4. Seven of the individuals interviewed in this case had terminated their employment with Upjohn at the time they were interviewed. 449 U.S. at 394 n.3. Because the lower courts had not addressed the issue, the Supreme Court did not consider whether the attorney-client privilege applied to communications by these former employees concerning activities during their period of employment. *Id.* Should the attorney-client privilege be recognized in connection with attorney interviews of former corporate employees? *See generally* Section of Litigation, American Bar Association, *Ex Parte Contacts with Former Employees* (2002); Becker, "Discovery of Information and Documents from a Litigant's Former Employees: Synergy and Synthesis of Civil Rules, Ethical Standards, Privilege Doctrines, and Common Law Principles," 81 *Neb. L. Rev.* 868 (2003).

5. Once the Supreme Court decides that Upjohn's questionnaires are privileged, what should the United States do?

6. Consider some of the things that Upjohn did in order to ensure that its questionnaires would be considered protected:

(a) Upjohn's general counsel was in charge of the investigation;

(b) The Upjohn officials to whom the general counsel's questionnaire was sent were general and area managers, rather than lower level employees;

(c) Upjohn officials were instructed to treat the investigation as "highly confidential" and not to discuss it with anyone other than employees who might be helpful in providing the requested information;

(d) Responses were to be sent directly to Upjohn's general counsel;

(e) The information sought was needed to permit the general counsel to give legal advice to Upjohn;

(f) The communications concerned matters within the scope of the employees' corporate duties, and the employees were aware that they were being questioned so that the corporation could obtain legal advice; and

(g) The questionnaire responses were kept confidential by Upjohn.

7. Will the attorney-client privilege recognized in *Upjohn* lead corporate employees to freely confide in corporate attorneys? Are corporate employees primarily concerned about possible actions that may be taken against their employer by third-parties or about sanctions that may be imposed against them by members of the corporate control group? *See* D. Luban, *Lawyers and Justice* 224–25 (1988). For a study of the operation of the attorney-client privilege in the corporate setting see Alexander, "The Corporate Attorney–Client Privilege: A Study of the Participants," 63 *St. John's L. Rev.* 191 (1988).

8. Consider the views of one commentator concerning the corporate attorney-client privilege:

> In the great majority of cases, the privilege is needed neither to encourage the client to talk nor to encourage the lawyer to listen. The corporate privilege protects no moral interest in privacy or autonomy. Additionally it imposes tremendous costs not only on the litigants but also on the entire judicial system.

Thornburg, "Sanctifying Secrecy: The Mythology of the Corporate Attorney–Client Privilege," 69 *Notre Dame L. Rev.* 157, 218 (1993). Do you agree?

9. When an attorney conducts an investigation on behalf of a corporation, what should she tell corporate employees about whom she represents? Need employees be warned at the outset of the interview that the attorney's primary allegiance is to the corporation? *See* Model Rules of Prof'l Conduct Rule 1.13(d).

10. As with any privilege, the attorney-client privilege can be waived. Such waiver has become especially problematic in recent years in civil actions involving large numbers of documents or electronically stored information. To address this situation, Congress in 2008 enacted Federal Rule of Evidence 502. This new rule had two major purposes: (1) to resolve disputes "about the effect of certain disclosures of communications or information protected by the attorney-client privilege or as work product," especially concerning inadvertent disclosure and possible waiver of related, but non-disclosed material and (2) to respond to the "widespread complaint that litigation costs necessary to protect against waiver of attorney-client privilege or work product have become prohibitive due to the concern that any disclosure (however innocent or minimal) will operate as a subject matter waiver of all protected communications or information." Advisory Committee Note to Federal Rule of Evidence 502, 28 U.S.C.A. Fed. R. Evid. 502, at 31 (Supp. 2010).

In addressing these concerns, Rule 502(a) initially provides that when a disclosure is made in a federal proceeding or to a federal office or agency, the resulting disclosure only extends to related but nondisclosed matter if "(1) the waiver is intentional; (2) the disclosed and undisclosed communications or information concern the same subject matter; and (3) they ought in fairness to be considered together." Counsel should realize that the waiver of the attorney-client privilege or work-product protection can waive the privilege or protection with respect to more than the material actually disclosed, and therefore should protect all such matter accordingly.

Rule 502(b) helps counsel protect such material by providing that disclosure of privileged or protected material in a federal proceeding or to a federal office or agency does not constitute waiver if "(1) the disclosure is inadvertent; (2) the holder of the privilege or protection took reasonable steps to prevent disclosure; and (3) the holder promptly took reasonable steps to rectify the error, including (if applicable) following Federal Rule of Civil Procedure 26(b)(5)(B)." Rule 502(b) thus recognizes that attorney-client privileged or work-product protected material is sometimes inadvertently disclosed. Such disclosure, however, may not be considered to be a waiver of the privilege or protection if, before the inadvertent disclosure in a federal proceeding or to a federal office or agency, the disclosing person took reasonable steps to protect such material and, after the disclosure, the person took reasonable steps to address the disclosure.

11. In order to prevent waiver of a privilege or protection concerning inadvertently disclosed material, Federal Rule of Evidence 502(b)(3) requires that the disclosing person must take reasonable steps to rectify the erroneous disclosure, "including (if applicable) following Federal Rule of Civil Procedure 26(b)(5)(B)." Rule 26(b)(5)(B) was one of the 2006 electronic discovery amendments to the Federal Rules of Civil Procedure meant to address situations in which information (electronic or otherwise) that is arguably protected by privilege or work-product protection is mistakenly produced in discovery. Rule 26(b)(5)(B) provides:

> If information produced in discovery is subject to a claim of privilege or of protection as trial-preparation material, the party making the claim may notify any party that received the information of the claim and the basis for it. After being notified, a party must promptly return, sequester, or destroy the specified information and any copies it has; must not use or disclose the information until the claim is resolved; must take reasonable steps to retrieve the information if the party disclosed it before being notified; and may promptly present the information to the court under seal for a determination of the claim. The producing party must preserve the information until the claim is resolved.

12. While Federal Rule of Evidence 502(a) and (b) limit the situations in which intentional or unintentional disclosure will be considered to waive attorney-client privilege or work-product protection, counsel can gain even greater protection through an agreement with other parties concerning the effect of inadvertent production of privileged or protected material in discovery. *See* American Bar Association, *Civil Discovery Standards*, Standard 28 (2004) ("The parties should consider stipulating in advance that the inadvertent disclosure of privileged information ordinarily should not be deemed a waiver of that information or of any information that may be derived from it.").

The 2006 amendments to the Federal Rules of Civil Procedure explicitly recognize party agreements to deal with the mistaken production of documents arguably protected by privilege or work-product protections. Rule 16(b)(3)(B)(iv) lists among the matters that a pretrial scheduling order may include "any agreements the parties reach for asserting claims of privilege or of protection as trial-preparation material after information is produced," while Rule 26(f)(3)(D) states that the parties' discovery plan must consider "any issues about claims of privilege or of protection as trial-preparation materials, including—if the parties agree on a procedure to assert these claims after production—whether to ask the court to include their agreement in an order."

In recommending amendments to Rule 26(f), the Advisory Committee on the Federal Rules of Civil Procedure described some of the ways in which counsel address problems of inadvertent waiver:

> They may agree that the responding party will provide certain requested materials for initial examination without waiving any privilege or protection—sometimes known as a "quick peek." The requesting party then designates the documents it wishes to have actually produced. This designation is the Rule 34 request. The responding party then responds

in the usual course, screening only those documents actually requested for formal production and asserting privilege claims as provided in Rule 26(b)(5)(A). On other occasions, parties enter agreements—sometimes called "clawback agreements"—that production without intent to waive privilege or protection should not be a waiver so long as the responding party identifies the documents mistakenly produced, and that the documents should be returned under those circumstances.

234 F.R.D. 219, 324 (2006).

13. While party agreements can protect claims of privilege or work-product protection with respect to the parties to such agreements, they typically do not bind others. Federal Rule of Evidence 502(e) provides: "An agreement on the effect of disclosure in a Federal proceeding is binding only on the parties to the agreement, unless it is incorporated into a court order." Counsel, therefore, should be sure to seek a court order incorporating the parties' agreement, because Federal Rule of Evidence 502(d) provides: "A Federal court may order that the privilege or protection is not waived by disclosure connected with the litigation pending before the court—in which event the disclosure is also not a waiver in any other Federal or State proceeding."

14. Hopefully, counsel will realize that material is privileged before producing it to other parties. Once counsel decides that information sought in discovery is privileged or protected, she must assert such a claim. Rule 26(b)(5)(A) prescribes the manner in which a claim of privilege or trial preparation protection must be asserted:

> When a party withholds information otherwise discoverable by claiming that the information is privileged or subject to protection as trial-preparation material, the party must:
>
> (i) expressly make the claim; and
>
> (ii) describe the nature of the documents, communications, or tangible things not produced or disclosed—and do so in a manner that, without revealing information itself privileged or protected, will enable other parties to assess the claim.

While the detail with which an objection must be asserted under Rule 26(b)(5)(A) will vary from case to case, claims of privilege and work-product protection must be expressly asserted. "To withhold materials without such notice is contrary to the rule, subjects the party to sanctions under Rule 37(b)(2), and may be viewed as a waiver of the privilege or protection." Advisory Committee Note to 1993 Amendment to Rule 26, 146 F.R.D. 401, 639 (1993).

15. Do these potential waiver situations present ethical, as well as legal, issues for counsel? Model Rule of Professional Conduct 4.4(b) provides: "A lawyer who receives a document relating to the representation of the lawyer's client and knows or reasonably should know that the document was inadvertently sent shall promptly notify the sender." The comment to Rule 4.4, though, further provides: "Whether the lawyer is required to take additional steps, such as returning the original document, is a matter of law beyond the

scope of these Rules, as is the question of whether the privileged status of a document has been waived."

Even though an electronic document may have been produced intentionally, is it still possible that there was an inadvertent disclosure of metadata concerning this document indicating, for instance, when the document was created and by whom or showing prior versions of the document? A comment to Rule 4.4 of the Maine Rules of Professional Conduct addresses this situation directly:

> The fact a writing contains metadata does not necessarily mean the sending lawyer intended the metadata be disclosed, notwithstanding the fact the ostensible writing may have been disclosed intentionally. The embedded metadata, if it contains confidential information, or is subject to a claim of privilege or of protection as trial preparation material, may be deemed to be inadvertently disclosed, and thus subject to paragraph (b) [establishing specific duties for a lawyer who receives inadvertently disclosed confidential, privileged, or protected material].

The ethical duties of attorneys sending and receiving electronically stored information vary from state to state. King, "The Ethics of Mining for Metadata Outside of Formal Discovery," 113 *Penn. St. L. Rev.* 801 (2009). This has prompted Professor Paula Schaefer to call for the adoption of new rules of professional conduct to deal with such situations. Schaefer, "The Future of Inadvertent Disclosure: The Lingering Need to Revise Professional Conduct Rules," 69 *Md. L. Rev.* 195 (2010). *See also* J. Barkett, *The Ethics of E–Discovery* (2009).

16. In *Calvin Klein Trademark Trust v. Wachner*, 198 F.R.D. 53 (S.D.N.Y. 2000), the court refused to extend the attorney-client privilege to cover documents "many of which appear on their face to be routine suggestions from a public relations firm as to how to put the 'spin' most favorable to [Calvin Klein, Inc.] on successive developments in the ongoing litigation." 198 F.R.D. at 54. Although the public relations firm had been retained by Calvin Klein's attorneys, that firm had previously been working directly for Calvin Klein. In rejecting a claim of attorney-client privilege, Judge Rakoff concluded: "It may be that the modern client comes to court as prepared to massage the media as to persuade the judge; but nothing in the client's communications for the former purpose constitutes the obtaining of legal advice or justifies a privileged status." 198 F.R.D. at 55.

In other factual settings, however, courts have held documents shared by an attorney with a public relations firm to be protected by the attorney-client privilege. *E.g., Federal Trade Comm'n v. GlaxoSmithKline*, 294 F.3d 141 (D.C.Cir. 2002). In *In re Grand Jury Subpoenas*, Judge Kaplan held that "(1) confidential communications (2) between lawyers and public relations consultants (3) hired by the lawyers to assist them in dealing with the media in cases such as this (4) that are made for the purpose of giving or receiving advice (5) directed at handling the client's legal problems are protected by the attorney-client privilege." 265 F.Supp.2d 321, 330 (S.D.N.Y. 2003).

17. Some commentators have urged, and a few courts have adopted, a qualified self-evaluative privilege to protect internal corporate investigations. The rationale for such a qualified privilege, protecting subjective corporate

analyses but not underlying factual data, is to protect confidential internal evaluations relevant to an inquiry that is in the public interest. *See generally Internal Corporate Investigations* (B. McNeil & B. Brian 3d ed. 2007); Vandegrift, "The Privilege of Self–Critical Analysis: A Survey of the Law," 60 *Alb. L. Rev.* 171 (1996); Allen & Hazelwood, "Preserving the Confidentiality of Internal Corporate Investigations," 31 *Corp. Prac. Commentator* 76 (1989); Murphy, "The Self–Evaluative Privilege," 7 *J. Corp. L.* 489 (1982); Note, "The Privilege of Self–Critical Analysis," 96 *Harv. L. Rev.* 1083 (1983). *But see* Flanagan, "Rejecting a General Privilege for Self–Critical Analyses," 51 *Geo. Wash. L. Rev.* 551 (1983). *See also* Richmond, "Law Firm Internal Investigations: Principles and Perils," 54 *Syracuse L. Rev.* 69 (2004) (suggesting ways in which a law firm's investigation of its own conduct can be protected from later discovery).

Exercises Concerning the Attorney–Client Privilege

1.   You are the Deputy General Counsel of the Pittston Company and report to the General Counsel and Vice–President of Pittston. The General Counsel has informed you that, during his weekly golf game with Pittston's Chief of Engineering, this individual informed the General Counsel that he, the Chief of Engineering, had raised questions with a now-deceased Pittston officer concerning the safety of the dam on the Buffalo Creek that eventually failed. While plaintiffs have not yet deposed the Chief of Engineering, the General Counsel's deposition has been noticed for next month and he would like to know whether his conversation with the Chief of Engineering is protected by the attorney-client privilege. Write a memorandum to the General Counsel addressing this question.

2.   The General Counsel and Vice–President of the Pittston Company would like to survey Pittston's engineering staff concerning dam safety. He would like you to structure a mechanism by which information can be obtained from the engineering staff within the protections of the attorney-client privilege. He has asked you to write a memorandum addressing these questions:

(a) Who should conduct any interviews (the General Counsel, you, another attorney within the General Counsel's office, a paralegal, or an individual in Pittston's Engineering Department)?

(b) Should the information obtained be reported orally or in writing?

(c) If written reports are used, to whom should they be addressed, how should they be labeled, where should they be stored, and how should they be protected from inadvertent disclosure?

(d) Should the Chief Engineer sit in on interviews to help explain technical matters that may arise?

(e) Should counsel for, or the chief executive of, a potential codefendant be permitted to sit in on the interviews?

(f) If written statements or reports are prepared, should copies be given to the individuals interviewed?

(g) Should any resulting documents prepared be shown to Pittston's insurance carrier, the President of Pittston, the Chief of Engineering, the Pittston paralegal responsible for assembling documents concerning the dam failure, or individual Pittston employees mentioned in the documents?

3. You are class counsel for the plaintiffs in a major products liability action. On the eve of trial you receive a misdirected fax containing materials that one defense attorney intended to send to other defense counsel. A quick glance at the documents indicates that they are covered by the attorney-client privilege.

(a) What should you do with these documents?

(b) Who should be told that you have received the documents?

(c) What if the documents are received in the mail from an anonymous "supporter of the class action?"

(d) What if the documents are provided to you by one of your clients, who tells you that she received them from a friend who works for one of the defendants?

(e) What if the documents are not received due to a misdirected fax but are mistakenly included within documents produced by a defendant in discovery?

C. DISCOVERY LIMITS

A 1988 Harris Poll of several hundred state and federal judges revealed that these judges considered lawyers' abuse of the discovery process to be the leading cause of judicial delay.[45] Magistrate Judge Wayne Brazil has argued that "adversary pressures and competitive economic impulses inevitably work to impair significantly, if not to frustrate completely, the attainment of the discovery system's primary objectives [of insuring complete disclosure of relevant information, facilitation of settlement, and a shortening and streamlining of the trial process]."[46]

According to Magistrate Judge Brazil, the "one controlling fact" that results in discovery abuse and overuse is that "attorneys who use discovery procedures are attorneys [who are] engaged in litigation."[47] Brazil asserts:

---

45. Louis Harris & Associates, Inc., "Judges' Opinions on Procedural Issues," Study No. 874017 (1988), *reprinted in* 69 *B.U. L. Rev.* 731 (1989). Forty-seven percent of the federal judges and thirty-four percent of the state judges cited abuse of the discovery process as a major cause of judicial delay. *Id.* at 735 (Table 1.1), 736 (Table 1.2). Eighty-three percent of the federal judges and eighty percent of the state judges replied that there were either a "lot" or "some" discovery problems in their jurisdictions. *Id.* at 736 (Table 2.1).

46. Brazil, "The Adversary Character of Civil Discovery: A Critique and Proposals for Change," 31 *Vand. L. Rev.* 1295, 1303 (1978). For a more recent analysis of the "fatal flaws" and structural disincentives to discovery reform in complex, high stakes, and otherwise contentious cases see Beckerman, "Confronting Civil Discovery's Fatal Flaws," 84 *Minn. L. Rev.* 505 (2000).

47. Brazil, *supra* note 46, at 1311.

Discovery is a tool whose purposes are fixed by the purposes of the larger process of which it is a part. That larger process is litigation. Attorneys in litigation have five primary objectives: (1) to win; (2) to make money; (3) to avoid being sued for malpractice; (4) to earn the admiration of the professional community; and (5) to develop self-esteem for the quality of their performances. * * * It is not difficult to perceive that these goals make the purposes of discovery for individual litigators quite different from the purposes which the architects of the discovery system contemplated.[48]

Brazil's own empirical research, however, suggests that "discovery in smaller cases * * * is a very different animal from that in larger cases and that in the smaller matters it is afflicted by substantially less debilitating abuses and problems."[49] A Federal Judicial Center study of more than 3000 cases filed in six federal judicial districts similarly has suggested that discovery abuse may be neither as easily identified nor as widespread as is sometimes presumed.

It is possible for a single discovery request to be abusive, as it is possible for sixty-two requests to be appropriate, relevant, and facilitative in the just disposition of a particular case. The data do suggest, however, that discovery abuse, to the extent it exists, does not permeate the vast majority of federal filings. In half the filings, there is no discovery—abusive or otherwise. In the remaining half of the filings, abuse—to the extent it exists—must be found in the *quality* of the discovery requests, not in the *quantity,* since fewer than 5 percent of the filings involved more than ten requests.[50]

More recently, a study by the RAND Institute for Civil Justice concluded:

The median time lawyers spend on discovery per litigant for cases with issue joined and closed within 270 days after filing is only three hours, whereas the median is twenty hours for those cases that close more than 270 days after filing.

Overall, lawyer work hours per litigant on discovery are zero for 38% of general civil cases and low for the majority of cases.

---

48. *Id.*

49. Brazil, "Civil Discovery: How Bad Are the Problems?," 67 *A.B.A.J.* 450, 454 (1981). *See* Brazil, "Civil Discovery: Lawyers' Views of Its Effectiveness, Its Principal Problems and Abuses," 1980 *Am. B. Found. Res. J.* 787; Brazil, "Views from the Front Lines: Observations by Chicago Lawyers About the System of Civil Discovery," 1980 *Am. B. Found. Res. J.* 219.

50. P. Connolly et al., *Judicial Controls and the Civil Litigative Process: Discovery* 35 (1978). *See also* Trubek et al., "The Costs of Ordinary Litigation," 31 *UCLA L. Rev.* 72, 89–90 (1983) (finding no evidence of discovery in over one-half of 1600 federal and state cases studied); Rosenberg, "Changes Ahead in Federal Pretrial Discovery," 45 F.R.D. 481, 490 (1968) (summarizing findings of Columbia University field survey of several hundred cases from the early 1960s "that on the whole there is no sign of major disenchantment or disastrous malfunctioning in the pretrial discovery system as it now operates"). *See also* E. Lee & T. Willging, *Federal Judicial Center National, Case–Based Civil Rules Survey: Preliminary Report to the Judicial Conference Advisory Committee on Civil Rules* 8–10 (2009); Cooper, "Simplified Rules of Federal Procedure," 100 *Mich. L. Rev.* 1794, 1798 (2002) ("Empirical studies of discovery have repeatedly disclosed that for most cases in federal court no discovery occurs, or only a few hours are devoted to it."); T. Willging et al., *Discovery and Disclosure Practice, Problems, and Proposals for Change* (1997).

Discovery is not a pervasive litigation cost problem for the majority of cases. The empirical data show that any problems that may exist with discovery are concentrated in a minority of cases, and the evidence indicates that discovery costs can be very high in some cases. * * * It is the minority of the cases with high discovery costs that generate the anecdotal "parade of horribles" that dominates much of the debate over discovery rules and discovery case management.[51]

While discovery may not occur in all cases, another study by the Federal Judicial Center found that 48 percent of attorneys who had discovery in their cases reported discovery problems, and discovery expenses represented 50 percent of litigation expenses (although only 3 percent of the amount at stake in the litigation) in those federal cases studied.[52] According to a Federal Judicial Center survey of attorneys handling federal civil actions that closed in the final quarter of 2008, "in half of cases with some reported discovery, plaintiff attorneys reported that their clients' discovery costs represented no more than 1.6 percent of the clients' stakes in the case, and defendant attorneys reported that their clients' discovery costs represented no more than 3.3 percent of their clients' stakes."[53] A majority of both plaintiff attorneys and defense attorneys in this survey reported that the disclosure and discovery in their cases had generated "just the right amount" of information and that the costs of discovery to their client's stakes in the case were "just the right amount" as well.[54]

While such empirical studies do not suggest pervasive discovery abuse, perceptions of such discovery abuse have remained widespread. As a result of the modest nature of the 1980 amendments to the Federal Rules of Civil Procedure, three members of the Supreme Court dissented from the approval of those amendments. Relying in part upon a 1979 opinion of Justice Powell which asserted that the discovery rules have "not infrequently [been] exploited to the disadvantage of justice,"[55] these

---

51. Kakalik et al., "Discovery Management: Further Analysis of the Civil Justice Reform Act Evaluation Data," 39 *B.C. L. Rev.* 613, 636 (1998). These findings in federal litigation are consistent with a 1990s study in five state trial courts. Calais et al., "Is Civil Discovery in State Trial Courts Out of Control?," *St. Ct. J.*, Spring 1993, 8, 9 (finding that 42% of civil cases studied had no recorded discovery, while 37% of cases with discovery had 3 or fewer recorded discovery events). A 1999 analysis of discovery data from the Columbia University study from the early 1960s concluded: "The cases without discovery are those with small stakes, few factual issues, and where each litigant believes that the other has little factual evidence. In addition, plaintiffs will tend to conduct less, or even no, discovery either if conditions suggest that the defendant is conducting excessive discovery or if the plaintiff's lawyer is paid on contingency." Shepherd, "An Empirical Study of the Economics of Pretrial Discovery," 19 *Int'l Rev. L. & Econ.*, 245, 263 (1999).

52. T. Willging et al., *Discovery and Disclosure Practice, Problems, and Proposals for Change* 2 (1997).

53. E. Lee & T. Willging, *Federal Judicial Center National, Case–Based Civil Rules Survey: Preliminary Report to the Judicial Conference Advisory Committee on Civil Rules* 43 (2009). *See also* E. Lee & T. Willging, *Litigation Costs in Civil Cases: Multivariate Analysis: Report to the Judicial Conference Advisory Committee on Civil Rules* (2010).

54. E. Lee & T. Willging, *Federal Judicial Center National, Case–Based Civil Rules Survey: Preliminary Report to the Judicial Conference Advisory Committee on Civil Rules* 27–28 (2009).

55. *Herbert v. Lando,* 441 U.S. 153, 179 (1979) (Powell, J., concurring).

justices urged that the recommended amendments be rejected in favor of "a thorough re-examination of the discovery Rules that have become so central to the conduct of modern litigation."[56]

This was not the end of the matter, for in 1983 Rule 26 was amended to require district courts to limit discovery in certain specified situations. The 1983 amendments to Rule 26 changed the heading of Rule 26(b) from "Scope of Discovery" to "Discovery Scope and Limits." Prior to 1983, the final sentence of Rule 26(a) provided: "Unless the court orders otherwise under subdivision (c) of this rule, the frequency of use of [discovery] methods is not limited." However, Rule 26(b)(2)(C) as amended in 1983, 1993, 2006, and 2007 requires a court to limit discovery if it determines that:

> (i) the discovery sought is unreasonably cumulative or duplicative, or can be obtained from some other source that is more convenient, less burdensome, or less expensive; (ii) the party seeking discovery has had ample opportunity to obtain the information by discovery in the action; or (iii) the burden or expense of the proposed discovery outweighs its likely benefit, considering the needs of the case, the amount in controversy, the parties' resources, the importance of the issues at stake in the action, and the importance of the discovery in resolving the issues.

Rule 26(b)(2)(C) requires trial courts to consider not only the relevance of discovery sought but also the other factors set forth in that Rule. As Figure 6–4 illustrates, the greater the burden and expense of producing discovery, the more important the information sought must be for it to be discoverable. In many cases, Rule 26(b)(2)(C)(iii) may require such a balancing of likely benefit and burden.

---

56.   446 U.S. 997, 1001 (1980) (dissenting statement of Powell, J.).

FIGURE 6-4

RULE 26(b)(2)(C)(iii) DISCOVERY BALANCING

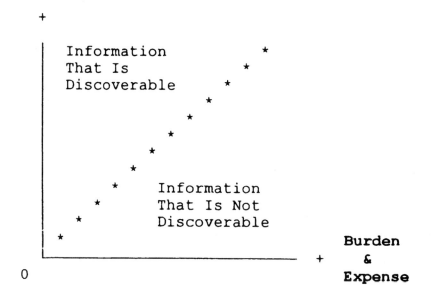

Despite the explicit focus of the 1983 amendment to Rule 26(b) on limiting discovery, perceived problems with discovery abuse and overuse persisted. A 1989 New York State Bar Association report concluded that "Rule 26(b)(1) provides such a broad definition of relevance that it encourages waves of discovery requests and objections, and results in excessive and costly motion practice without enhancing the truth-finding process."[57] This same report continued: "The reality of the current situation is that very few courts will restrict discovery practice, even when faced with numerous motions made across a span of years, resulting in lengthy and costly litigation."[58]

The 1993 amendments to the Federal Rules of Civil Procedure and efforts at expense and delay reduction undertaken pursuant to the Civil Justice Reform Act of 1990 resulted from such concerns. The Advisory Committee Note to the 1993 amendment to Rule 26(b) summarizes the 1993 amendments and their rationale.

The information explosion of recent decades has greatly increased both the potential cost of wide-ranging discovery and the potential for

57. Committee on Discovery, Section on Commercial and Federal Litigation, New York State Bar Association, *Report on Discovery Under Rule 26(b)(1)*, 127 F.R.D. 625, 625 (1989).

58. *Id.* at 631.

discovery to be used as an instrument for delay and oppression. Amendments to Rules 30, 31, and 33 place presumptive limits on the number of depositions and interrogatories, subject to leave of court to pursue additional discovery. The revisions in Rule 26(b)(2) are intended to provide the court with broader discretion to impose additional restrictions on the scope and extent of discovery * * * .[59]

Unfortunately, perceptions of discovery abuse continued even after the Federal Rules were amended in 1993 to limit discovery. As noted by the Advisory Committee on Civil Rules in proposing the 2000 amendments to Rule 26(b)(1), "Concerns about costs and delay of discovery have persisted * * *, and * * * bar groups have repeatedly renewed * * * proposals [to limit the scope of civil discovery]."[60] As a result, Rule 26(b)(1) was amended in 2000, and that provision now narrows discovery to non-privileged matter "that is relevant to any party's claim or defense," providing, however, that for "good cause, the court may order discovery of any matter relevant to the subject matter involved in the action." The Chair of the Civil Rules Advisory Committee that recommended this restriction in Rule 26 has described Rule 26 as amended in 2000 as "a three-level process—a Neapolitan Plan—in which mandatory disclosure of some type is the first layer, core discovery under attorney management is the second, and customized more extensive discovery, approved by the court pursuant to a plan submitted by the parties, is the third."[61]

Whether or not judges exercise their discretion to limit or expand discovery in particular cases, there can be real practical disadvantages to seeking every relevant bit of information through formal discovery. Discovery in major cases often resembles an arms race, with extensive discovery requests engendering extensive discovery requests from opposing counsel in return. Before deciding upon discovery requests, counsel should ask themselves whether their clients can bear the delay and expense that may result. In many cases, formal discovery may not lead to significant information beyond what could be obtained through client and witness interviews. Formal discovery requests also may reveal significant information about the requesting party's own case to other parties.

Counsel should look before they leap into the abyss that discovery has become in all too many cases. Just because information is arguably relevant under Rule 26(b)(1) does not mean that it must be requested through formal discovery.

---

59. Advisory Committee Note to 1993 Amendment to Rule 26(b), 146 F.R.D. 401, 638 (1993).

60. 192 F.R.D. 340, 388 (2000).

61. Niemeyer, "Here We Go Again: Are the Federal Discovery Rules Really in Need of Amendment?," 39 *B.C. L. Rev.* 517, 524 (1998). In addition to narrowing the scope of discovery permitted as a matter of course, the 2000 amendments built upon the 1993 amendment to Rule 26(b)(2). In offering the amendments to Rule 26 that became effective in 2000, the Advisory Committee noted: "The Committee has been told repeatedly that courts have not implemented these [Rule 26(b)(2)] limitations with the vigor that was contemplated." 192 F.R.D. 340, 390 (2000). As a result, Rule 26(b)(1) was amended by the addition of a final sentence that now reminds courts and counsel: "All discovery is subject to the limitations imposed by Rule 26(b)(2)(C)."

NOTES AND QUESTIONS CONCERNING DISCOVERY LIMITS

1. Rule 26(b)(2)(C)(iii) provides that a court can consider "the parties' resources" in determining whether "the burden or expense of the proposed discovery outweighs its likely benefit." What does this mean? Does it mean that a plaintiff can impose more of a discovery burden upon General Motors than upon a local car dealer? What if General Motors is the party requesting discovery? What implications does this provision have for litigation against governmental bodies?

2. How can Federal Rule of Civil Procedure 26(c) be used to respond to discovery requests that are unduly burdensome or expensive? Are there ways in which the burden and expense of responding to extensive discovery requests can be shifted to the requesting party? *See* Federal Rule of Civil Procedure 33(d). Are there nevertheless reasons why a responding party may choose to have its own employees produce requested information?

3. Not only did the 1993 amendments to the Federal Rules of Civil Procedure add to Rule 26(b)(2) explicit authorization for discovery limitations and presumptive numerical limitations upon discovery devices, but those amendments created a duty of disclosure in Rule 26(a). Is there any inconsistency between the amendments to these two provisions?

4. How many of the problems with excessive discovery cost, burden, and delay could be alleviated by focusing attorneys on specific "best practices" for handling discovery matters? Magistrate Judge Wayne Brazil asserts that attorney conduct is influenced by avoidance of malpractice, the desire to earn the admiration of the professional community, and the development of self-esteem, as well as the desires to win and make money. Brazil, "The Adversary Character of Civil Discovery: A Critique and Proposals for Change," 31 *Vand. L. Rev.* 1295, 1311 (1978). If this is so, might clear guidance from the profession help overcome discovery problems and abuse? The American Bar Association has adopted Civil Discovery Standards "(i) to eliminate unnecessary effort and expense, (ii) to restrict the opportunities for misusing the discovery process, both offensively and defensively, and (iii) where possible, to encourage a cooperative rather than adversarial approach to discovery." American Bar Association, *Civil Discovery Standards* 1 (2004).

5. Assuming that your discovery requests are successful and net you great amounts of discovery, what's to be done with this material at the conclusion of the civil action? Some discovery may be produced under an agreement providing that the material be returned to the party that produced it or be destroyed after a certain amount of time. At least one attorney donated discovery material to a history research center, although his attempt to take a tax deduction for this contribution ultimately was unsuccessful. *Jones v. Commissioner*, 560 F.3d 1196 (10th Cir.), *cert. denied*, ___ U.S. ___ (2009) (charitable contribution denied for donation of discovery produced by United States in Oklahoma City bombing prosecution because attorney had no taxable basis in the material).

Exercise Concerning Discovery Limits

Certain aliens who have been deported from the United States are excluded from reentry unless the Attorney General consents. 8 U.S.C. § 1182(a)(9)(A). You represent Evita Simon, whose application for reentry was denied by both the District Director and Regional Commissioner of U. S. Immigration and Customs Enforcement (ICE).

You have filed a declaratory judgment action on behalf of Ms. Simon, alleging that the denial of permission to reenter was arbitrary and capricious and therefore unlawful. In order to establish this, you have filed a discovery request asking ICE to produce each of the estimated 1395 written reentry decisions issued during the last ten years within the five-state ICE region (including the 319 decisions from the local district). ICE counsel has informed you that the specific decisions that you seek are not computerized, and it would take over 2500 hours to manually search files to locate the decisions that you have requested. Accordingly, Immigration and Customs Enforcement will not produce the requested discovery.

Write a memorandum to the associate who is helping you with this case describing the course of action that she should follow in dealing with this discovery impasse.

D. LITIGATION IN CYBERSPACE

Although they have been amended many times in recent years, the Federal Rules of Civil Procedure originally were adopted in 1938—in an era as close to the Civil War as it is to us today in the 21st Century. The Federal Rules have proven to be extremely flexible and have been used creatively by federal judges to cover many situations not foreseen by the drafters of the original Rules. In recent years, though, new technologies have stretched those Rules, which were amended in 2006 to take into account the new challenges posed by electronic discovery.[62] Similarly, modern technological advances have raised questions under other rules that govern lawyers and the practice of law and were drafted before today's technological revolution.[63]

At this time the answers that ultimately will be given to many of the significant questions posed by new technologies cannot be comfortably predicted. However, some of the more significant issues are becoming clear. These issues are sketched in the following notes and questions.

---

62. *See* Chapter 9, Section II(B) (Electronic Discovery), *infra* p. 395.

63. Technology is used many ways in modern law practices, including for communication, litigation support, client billing, case filing and management, factual investigation, and legal research. *See generally* M. Arkfeld, *The Digital Practice of Law* (5th ed. 2001); *Flying Solo: A Survival Guide for the Solo and Small Firm Lawyer* 329–438 (K. Gibson ed., 4th ed. 2005); B. Roper, *Using Computers in the Law Office* (5th ed. 2008). *See also* Marcus, "The Electronic Lawyer," 58 *DePaul L. Rev.* 263 (2009).

An extremely useful resource concerning legal technology is the Legal Technology Resource Center of the American Bar Association. http://www.lawtechnology.org. In addition, the ABA's Legal Technology Resource Center surveys law firms and issues annual trend reports concerning law office technology, litigation and courtroom technology, web and communication technology, online research, and lawyer mobility. http://www.abanet.org/tech/ltrc/survstat.html.

1. What special duties do new forms of electronic communications place upon attorneys to ensure the protection of client confidences and the preservation of the attorney-client privilege? The ABA Standing Committee on Ethics and Professional Responsibility has concluded that lawyers have a reasonable expectation of privacy in all forms of email and that unencrypted email sent to a client over the Internet does not breach an attorney's duty to protect confidential client communications. ABA Comm. on Professional Ethics and Grievances, Formal Op. 99–413 (1999). However, the Committee cautioned that in certain circumstances information may be so sensitive that extraordinary measures will be necessary to protect the confidentiality of the communication and that counsel should consult the client in such circumstances and follow the client's instructions about the appropriate mode of communication. One way in which confidentiality protections might be heightened would be to encrypt the communication before sending it. A recent ad in the *ABA Journal* for electronic encryption software showed a sinking ship and proclaimed: "Emailing Terms, Sinks Firms." *See generally* Hricik, "Lawyers Worry Too Much about Transmitting Client Confidences by Internet E-mail," 11 *Geo. J. Legal Ethics* 459 (1998).

2. One of the rationales for the ABA Committee's conclusion that email normally affords a reasonable expectation of privacy was that, because email generally is not broadcast over public airwaves, such messages are not subject to the same risks of interception as are cordless and cellular telephone technology. ABA Comm. on Professional Ethics and Grievances, Formal Op. 99–413 (1999). However, what about wireless Internet services that do actually "broadcast" the electronic communications? *See* Miller, Note, "For Your Eyes Only? The Real Consequences of Unencrypted E–Mail in Attorney–Client Communication," 80 *B.U. L. Rev.* 613, 631 (2000). While the ABA Committee also relied upon the general difficulty of intercepting email and laws making the interception and disclosure of email communications illegal, this is another example of how the law is struggling to keep up with rapidly changing technology. *See generally* Hill, "Emerging Technology and Client Confidentiality: How Changing Technology Brings Ethical Dilemmas," 16 *B.U. J. Sci. & Tech. L.* 1 (2010); Pikowsky, "Privilege and Confidentiality of Attorney–Client Communication Via E-mail," 51 *Baylor L. Rev.* 483 (1999).

3. The State Bar of Arizona's Committee on the Rules of Professional Conduct has concluded that no duty of confidentiality extends to an unsolicited email sent to an attorney who had no website and did not advertise on the Internet. Arizona State Bar Comm. on the Rules of Professional Conduct, Op. 02–04 (September 2002). Even before the attorney-client relationship is created, though, electronic communications between the attorney and prospective client may be found to be privileged. *E.g., Barton v. United States District Court*, 410 F.3d 1104 (9th Cir. 2005) (on-line questionnaires completed by prospective class members before they became attorneys' clients are nevertheless protected by attorney-client privilege).

4.   Lawyers are well-advised to maintain disclaimers on their websites to prevent unsolicited email from having to be treated confidentially. Assuming that there are appropriate disclaimers, the District of Columbia Bar's Legal Ethics Committee has concluded that attorneys may answer questions in an Internet chat room. In order to ensure that an attorney-client relationship is not formed, attorneys should only provide legal information, as opposed to legal advice tailored to the unique facts of a particular person's circumstances. The D.C. Committee noted that, because Internet communications extend beyond the District of Columbia, the ethical rules of jurisdictions other than the District of Columbia also may apply. District of Columbia Bar Legal Ethics Comm., Op. 316 (July 2002). *See also* Cal. St. Bar Standing Comm. Prof. Resp., Formal Op. 2001–155 (2001) (concluding that attorney websites must meet California lawyer advertising restrictions and suggesting that such sites state where the attorney is licensed, maintains an office, is willing to appear in court, and that she does not seek to represent anyone based only on a visit to the website). The ABA Standing Committee on Ethics and Professional Responsibility has concluded that, by the use of warnings or cautionary statements on her website, a lawyer may prevent misunderstandings and limit or disclaim her obligations with respect to the creation of the attorney-client relationship, the confidentiality of the reader's information, the rendering of legal advice, and the ability of the lawyer to represent a party adverse to the website's reader. Formal Op. 10–457 (2010). *See also* Hill, "Lawyer Communications on the Internet: Beginning the Millennium with Disparate Standards," 75 *Wash. L. Rev.* 785 (2000) (arguing for national rules governing lawyer advertising and solicitation on the Internet).

5.   Attorneys must be continuously sensitive to new technology and the implications that such technology has for the practice of law. In order to protect attorneys and their clients, it has been recommended that attorneys should (1) be aware of the technology that they use and the changing ethical and legal guidelines concerning that technology in their jurisdictions; (2) select technology that minimizes the risk of unintended disclosure of privileged and confidential communications; and (3) educate clients about how they can help to minimize disclosure (by, for instance, not calling their attorneys on cell or cordless phones or communicating highly sensitive information by voice mail messages or unencrypted email). Mills & Rothberg, "Protecting Client Confidences in the Age of High Technology," *Litigation*, Winter 2000, at 15, 20–21.

6.   Some states have enacted legislation providing that communication through certain electronic means does not destroy the attorney-client privilege. *E.g.*, Cal. Evid. Code § 917(b) (West 2011) (communication "does not lose its privileged character for the sole reason that it is communicated by electronic means"); N.Y.C.P.L.R. § 4548 (McKinney 2010) (email). However, the fact that the privilege has not been waived does not resolve the many other quite practical problems that may result if privileged or confidential information becomes known to an opposing

party or others. Attorneys should take reasonable precautions to prevent the disclosure of privileged and confidential material, and the likelihood that a communication will be found to be protected by the attorney-client privilege can be enhanced if the communication is treated as such by the attorney and office in question (for instance, by describing the electronic communication as a "privileged attorney-client communication" in the electronic communication itself and limiting access to the communication within the office).

7.   Email, in particular, may be a fertile source of impeaching statements, as evidenced by the role that the email communications of Monica Lewinsky and others played in the impeachment case against President Clinton. Communication from Kenneth W. Starr, Independent Counsel, H.R. Doc. No. 105–310, 105 Cong., 2d Sess. 52, 84, 85, 86 (1998). Because of its ease, speed, and apparent confidentiality, people say things in email that they would never otherwise say and often are more candid in such communications. "Email trails" therefore should not be overlooked in formulating pretrial discovery requests.

8.   Regardless of the rules that will be used to determine disputes in, and involving, cyberspace, it is necessary that the attorneys and judges handling these disputes have a basic familiarity with the underlying technical questions. How can this be assured? What should be done when competing experts disagree about underlying technical matters? In an effort to avoid potentially exorbitant costs of providing electronic discovery, some employment contracts now provide that any dispute involving electronic data will be handled by a qualified third-party. As a result, some mediators now specialize in the mediation of electronic discovery disputes. Nadel, "High–Tech Mediation," *U.S.L.W.*, Oct. 20, 1998, at 2212. On the other hand, when faced with a discovery dispute in a case before him, Magistrate Judge Joe Brown offered to create a Facebook account so that individuals could "friend" him and thereby permit him to conduct an in camera review of photographs and material on their Facebook pages. *Barnes v. CUS Nashville, LLC*, 2010 WL 2265668 (M.D.Tenn. 2010). In addition, at least one state court system has a presence on Facebook and YouTube and shares judicial opinions and other information through Twitter. www.judiciary.state.nj.us.

9.   Problems may result from the fact that it sometimes is difficult to determine whether electronically stored information actually exists. Although data may be "deleted" on a computer, this simply means that a portion of the computer's memory is available to be overwritten. This may or may not actually happen, and the fact that new data is entered is not itself an assurance that the original data is beyond retrieval, because the new data may be assigned to another location in memory or may not obliterate the old data if it is smaller than the original data. In addition, word processing technology may permit the retrieval of drafts of documents that were not saved in hard copy (by, for instance, "undoing" changes to a document produced in electronic format). Robins, "Computers and the Discovery of Evidence–A New Dimension to Civil Procedure,"

17 *J. Marshall J. Computer & Info. L.* 411, 414–21 (1999); Johnson, "A Practitioner's Overview of Digital Discovery," 33 *Gonz. L. Rev.* 347, 359–63 (1997/98). The production of tables and spreadsheets in electronic format also may permit such data to be reorganized electronically at a great savings in time and expense to the requesting party. *See generally* Solovy & Byman, "Digital Discovery," *Nat'l L. J.*, Dec. 27, 1999, at A16. Document histories in some word processing programs also may enable one to locate documents on an organization's network and determine when and by whom the documents were modified or downloaded. Rial & Regard, "Finding the Smoking Gun Electronically," *Nat'l L. J.*, Aug. 13, 2001, at B15, B16.

10.   Only a mirror image (sector-by-sector) copy will preserve all data, including residual data, on a disk drive, and it may be necessary in some cases to retain an expert to conduct an on-site visit to ensure that all relevant information has been obtained. Johnson, "A Practitioner's Overview of Digital Discovery," 33 *Gonz. L. Rev.* 347, 370–73 (1997/98). *See also Gates Rubber Co. v. Bando Chemical Industries, Ltd.*, 167 F.R.D. 90 (D.Colo. 1996) (in which a special master was appointed to supervise a site inspection order establishing a discovery escrow to preserve computer records as well as the parties' right to object to the production of materials from the escrow). In order to obtain all relevant email and other electronic media, counsel should send a notice to opposing counsel at the very outset of the litigation, informing the opposing party that specific steps should be taken to preserve all potentially discoverable electronic data. *See* Johnson, *supra*, at 363–66. To the extent that technologies permit the immediate destruction of electronic data, the very use of such technologies could lead to charges of destruction of evidence (spoliation)—in which case you may wish you still had the electronic data to produce to the other party. In order to avoid possible destruction of electronic evidence, one's client immediately should be told to save all relevant electronic data. If such an instruction is followed, opposing counsel should not be able to argue that your client has engaged in inappropriate or illegal document destruction due to routine electronic destruction policies. *See* Brown & Weiner, "Digital Dangers: A Primer on Electronic Evidence in the Wake of Enron," *Litigation*, Fall 2003, at 24.

11.   Presuming that client confidences and the attorney-client privilege can be maintained for email attorney-client communications, how does such instantaneous electronic communication change client expectations and the nature of legal practice? Keeping in touch with clients electronically can be much easier and quicker than telephone or mail communication, and clients may appreciate the more frequent contact that email facilitates. However, do clients (or certain clients) as a result expect frequent electronic contacts and immediate responses to their emails to counsel?

12.   State bar ethics committees have found that the manner in which LegalMatch.com facilitates the matching of attorneys and clients is consistent with attorney ethical requirements. Rhode Island Supreme

Court Ethics Advisory Panel, Op. 2005–01 (Feb. 24, 2005); North Carolina State Bar, 2004 Formal Ethics Opinion 1 (April 23, 2004). Under this service, attorneys pay an annual fee to access the legal issues electronically presented by potential clients, with any attorney-client relationships being formed apart from the LegalMatch website. In contrast to such an "anti-matching" service, a matching service that would have charged attorneys a fee for each engagement resulting from a proposed Internet site has been found to be inconsistent with the prohibitions on attorney referral fees and sharing of attorneys' fees with non-lawyers. Maryland State Bar Ass'n Comm. on Ethics, Op. 2001–03 (May 16, 2001).

13. ABA Model Rule of Professional Conduct 7.3(a) provides: "A lawyer shall not by in-person, live telephone or real-time electronic contact solicit professional employment from a prospective client when a significant motive for the lawyer's doing so is the lawyer's pecuniary gain, unless the person contacted: (1) is a lawyer; or (2) has a family, close personal, or prior professional relationship with the lawyer." Attorneys therefore should be cautious about entering online chat rooms, especially if their participation could be construed as the provision of specific legal advice or an attempt to establish an attorney-client relationship with a particular person. *See* Goehler et al., "Technology Traps: Ethical Considerations for Litigators in a 24/7 Online World," *Litigation*, Winter 2010, at 34, 35–36.

14. Does the Internet present opportunities for lawyers to serve the unmet legal needs of those who may not have the financial resources to avail themselves of traditional legal services? Professor Catherine Lanctot has traced the organized bar's reaction to uses of new technology to render legal advice (including bar efforts to successfully suppress the popular 1930s radio show *Good Will Court*) and has concluded that the giving of specific legal advice in cyberspace often results in the creation of an attorney-client relationship. Professor Lanctot suggests consideration of a more limited form of attorney-client representation in which legal services would be "unbundled" and attorneys would provide brief, specific advice electronically without any expectation of continuing and comprehensive legal assistance. Lanctot, "Attorney–Client Relationships in Cyberspace: The Peril and the Promise," 49 *Duke L. J.* 147 (1999). *See also* Schnell, Note, "Don't Just Hit Send: Unsolicited E–Mail and the Attorney–Client Relationship," 17 *Harv. J. L. & Tech.* 533 (2004); Schwartz, "Practicing Law Over the Internet: Sometimes Practice Doesn't Make Perfect," 14 *Harv. J. L. & Tech.* 657 (2001).

15. While recent advances in technology have impacted litigation in numerous ways—from electronic filing to client communication to factual investigation and legal research—one of the most significant changes in civil pretrial practice has been with respect to disclosure and discovery. A series of amendments to the Federal Rules of Civil Procedure to specifically address the discovery of electronically stored information became effective in 2006. These recent provisions of the Federal Rules are considered in Section II(B) of Chapter 9, *infra* p. 395.

16.   After reading the next section of this text concerning the work-product doctrine, consider whether computer databases should be subject to discovery under Rule 26. Is it significant whether the database organization involves only objective coding, such as the author, date, or recipient of a document, or involves subjective coding that includes document summaries, characterization of documents, or document reviews for privilege or litigation significance? What, if any, conditions should be placed upon such discovery? Are the financial resources of the requesting party relevant to the answer to this question? How significant is the availability of the documents themselves or the cost and effort that would be required to replicate the requested database? *See* Miller & Griffin, "Computer Databases: Forced Production versus Shared Enterprise," *Litigation*, Summer 1997, at 40, 43 ("[I]f significant costs would be expended in a simple duplication of effort, the argument regarding undue hardship [under Rule 26(b)(3)] almost inevitably tips in favor of disclosure of an extant database.").

IV.   THE ATTORNEY WORK-PRODUCT DOCTRINE

Not all of the limitations on civil discovery were originally spelled out in the Federal Rules of Civil Procedure. The attorney work-product doctrine was recognized by the Supreme Court twenty-three years before the Federal Rules of Civil Procedure were amended to specifically acknowledge that doctrine. The work-product doctrine is extremely important to the civil litigator and should not be confused with the "attorney work load doctrine" invented by one of the author's creative students on a civil procedure examination.

A.   THE SUPREME COURT'S RECOGNITION OF THE DOCTRINE

Did the original version of Rule 26 literally mean what it said in providing that a party could obtain discovery concerning "any matter, not privileged, which is relevant to the subject matter involved in the pending action?" Consider the following case.

HICKMAN v. TAYLOR

Supreme Court of the United States, 1947.
329 U.S. 495.

MR. JUSTICE MURPHY delivered the opinion of the Court.

This case presents an important problem under the Federal Rules of Civil Procedure as to the extent to which a party may inquire into oral and written statements of witnesses, or other information, secured by an adverse party's counsel in the course of preparation for possible litigation after a claim has arisen. Examination into a person's files and records, including those resulting from the professional activities of an attorney, must be judged with care. It is not without reason that various safeguards have been established to preclude unwarranted excursions into the privacy of a man's work. At the same time, public policy supports reasonable and necessary inquiries. Properly to balance these competing interests is a delicate and difficult task.

On February 7, 1943, the tug "J. M. Taylor" sank while engaged in helping to tow a car float of the Baltimore & Ohio Railroad across the Delaware River at Philadelphia. The accident was apparently unusual in nature, the cause of it still being unknown. Five of the nine crew members were drowned. Three days later the tug owners and the underwriters employed a law firm, of which respondent Fortenbaugh is a member, to defend them against potential suits by representatives of the deceased crew members and to sue the railroad for damages to the tug.

A public hearing was held on March 4, 1943, before the United States Steamboat Inspectors, at which the four survivors were examined. This testimony was recorded and made available to all interested parties. Shortly thereafter, Fortenbaugh privately interviewed the survivors and took statements from them with an eye toward the anticipated litigation; the survivors signed these statements on March 29. Fortenbaugh also interviewed other persons believed to have some information relating to the accident and in some cases he made memoranda of what they told him. At the time when Fortenbaugh secured the statements of the survivors, representatives of two of the deceased crew members had been in communication with him. Ultimately claims were presented by representatives of all five of the deceased; four of the claims, however, were settled without litigation. The fifth claimant, petitioner herein, brought suit in a federal court under the Jones Act on November 26, 1943, naming as defendants the two tug owners, individually and as partners, and the railroad.

One year later, petitioner filed 39 interrogatories directed to the tug owners. The 38th interrogatory read: "State whether any statements of the members of the crews of the Tugs 'J. M. Taylor' and 'Philadelphia' or of any other vessel were taken in connection with the towing of the car float and the sinking of the Tug 'John M. Taylor.' Attach hereto exact copies of all such statements if in writing, and if oral, set forth in detail the exact provisions of any such oral statements or reports."

Supplemental interrogatories asked whether any oral or written statements, records, reports or other memoranda had been made concerning any matter relative to the towing operation, the sinking of the tug, the salvaging and repair of the tug, and the death of the deceased. If the answer was in the affirmative, the tug owners were then requested to set forth the nature of all such records, reports, statements or other memoranda.

The tug owners, through Fortenbaugh, answered all of the interrogatories except No. 38 and the supplemental ones just described. While admitting that statements of the survivors had been taken, they declined to summarize or set forth the contents. They did so on the ground that such requests called "for privileged matter obtained in preparation for litigation" and constituted "an attempt to obtain indirectly counsel's private files." It was claimed that answering these requests "would involve practically turning over not only the complete files, but also the telephone records and, almost, the thoughts of counsel."

* * * The District Court for the Eastern District of Pennsylvania, sitting *en banc,* held that the requested matters were not privileged. 4 F.R.D. 479. The court then decreed that the tug owners and Fortenbaugh, as counsel and agent for the tug owners, forthwith "answer plaintiff's 38th interrogatory and supplementary interrogatories; produce all written statements of witnesses obtained by Mr. Fortenbaugh, as counsel and agent for Defendants; state in substance any fact concerning this case which Defendants learned through oral statements made by witnesses to Mr. Fortenbaugh whether or not included in his private memoranda and produce Mr. Fortenbaugh's memoranda containing statements of fact by witnesses or to submit these memoranda to the Court for determination of those portions which should be revealed to Plaintiff." Upon their refusal, the court adjudged them in contempt and ordered them imprisoned until they complied.

The Third Circuit Court of Appeals, also sitting *en banc,* reversed the judgment of the District Court. 153 F.2d 212. It held that the information here sought was part of the "work product of the lawyer" and hence privileged from discovery under the Federal Rules of Civil Procedure. The importance of the problem, which has engendered a great divergence of views among district courts, led us to grant certiorari.

The pre-trial deposition-discovery mechanism established by Rules 26 to 37 is one of the most significant innovations of the Federal Rules of Civil Procedure. Under the prior federal practice, the pre-trial functions of notice-giving, issue-formulation and fact-revelation were performed primarily and inadequately by the pleadings. Inquiry into the issues and the facts before trial was narrowly confined and was often cumbersome in method. The new rules, however, restrict the pleadings to the task of general notice-giving and invest the deposition-discovery process with a vital role in the preparation for trial. The various instruments of discovery now serve (1) as a device, along with the pre-trial hearing under Rule 16, to narrow and clarify the basic issues between the parties, and (2) as a device for ascertaining the facts, or information as to the existence or whereabouts of facts, relative to those issues. Thus civil trials in the federal courts no longer need be carried on in the dark. The way is now clear, consistent with recognized privileges, for the parties to obtain the fullest possible knowledge of the issues and facts before trial.

[The Court then noted that neither Rule 33 nor Rule 34 of the Federal Rules of Civil Procedure could be used to obtain information from attorney Fortenbaugh, because Rule 33 interrogatories and Rule 34 requests for production only can be directed to a party. The Court suggested that Hickman should have attempted to take Fortenbaugh's deposition and seek the documents in question by means of a Rule 45 subpoena *duces tecum.*]

But, under the circumstances, we deem it unnecessary and unwise to rest our decision upon this procedural irregularity, an irregularity which is not strongly urged upon us and which was disregarded in the two courts below. It matters little at this late stage whether Fortenbaugh fails to answer interrogatories filed under Rule 26 or under Rule 33 or whether he refuses to produce the memoranda and statements pursuant to a subpoena under Rule 45 or a court order under Rule 34. The deposition-discovery rules create integrated procedural devices. And the basic question at stake is whether any of those devices may be used to inquire into materials collected by an adverse party's counsel in the course of preparation for possible litigation. The fact that the petitioner may have used the wrong method does not destroy the main thrust of his attempt. Nor does it relieve us of the responsibility of dealing with the problem raised by that attempt. * * *

In urging that he has a right to inquire into the materials secured and prepared by Fortenbaugh, petitioner emphasizes that the deposition-discovery portions of the Federal Rules of Civil Procedure are designed to enable the parties to discover the true facts and to compel their disclosure wherever they may be found. It is said that inquiry may be made under these rules, epitomized by Rule 26, as to any relevant matter which is not privileged; and since the discovery provisions are to be applied as broadly and liberally as possible, the privilege limitation must be restricted to its narrowest bounds. On the premise that the attorney-client privilege is the one involved in this case, petitioner argues that it must be strictly confined to confidential communications made by a client to his attorney. And since the materials here in issue were secured by Fortenbaugh from third persons rather than from his clients, the tug owners, the conclusion is reached that these materials are proper subjects for discovery under Rule 26.

As additional support for this result, petitioner claims that to prohibit discovery under these circumstances would give a corporate defendant a tremendous advantage in a suit by an individual plaintiff. Thus in a suit by an injured employee against a railroad or in a suit by an insured person against an insurance company the corporate defendant could pull a dark veil of secrecy over all the pertinent facts it can collect after the claim arises merely on the assertion that such facts were gathered by its large staff of attorneys and claim agents. At the same time, the individual plaintiff, who often has direct knowledge of the matter in issue and has no counsel until some time after his claim arises could be compelled to disclose all the intimate details of his case. By endowing with immunity from disclosure all that a lawyer discovers in the course of his duties, it is said, the rights of individual litigants in such cases are drained of vitality and the lawsuit becomes more of a battle of deception than a search for truth.

But framing the problem in terms of assisting individual plaintiffs in their suits against corporate defendants is unsatisfactory. Discovery concededly may work to the disadvantage as well as to the advantage of individual plaintiffs. Discovery, in other words, is not a one-way proposition. It is available in all types of cases at the behest of any party, individual or corporate, plaintiff or defendant. The problem thus far transcends the situation confronting this petitioner. And we must view that problem in light of the limitless situations where the particular kind of discovery sought by petitioner might be used.

We agree, of course, that the deposition-discovery rules are to be accorded a broad and liberal treatment. No longer can the time-honored cry of "fishing expedition" serve to preclude a party from inquiring into the facts underlying his opponent's case. Mutual knowledge of all the relevant facts gathered by both parties is essential to proper litigation. To that end, either party may compel the other to disgorge whatever facts he has in his possession. The deposition-discovery procedure simply advances the stage at which the disclosure can be compelled from the time of trial to the period preceding it, thus reducing the possibility of surprise. But discovery, like all matters of procedure, has ultimate and necessary boundaries. * * * [A]s Rule 26(b) provides, * * * limitations come into existence when the inquiry touches upon the irrelevant or encroaches upon the recognized domains of privilege.

We also agree that the memoranda, statements and mental impressions in issue in this case fall outside the scope of the attorney-client privilege and hence are not protected from discovery on that basis. It is unnecessary here to delineate the content and scope of that privilege as recognized in the federal courts. For present purposes, it suffices to note that the protective cloak of this privilege does not extend to information which an attorney secures from a witness while acting for his client in anticipation of litigation. Nor does this privilege concern the memoranda, briefs, communications and other writings prepared by counsel for his own use in prosecuting his client's case; and it is equally unrelated to writings which reflect an attorney's mental impressions, conclusions, opinions or legal theories.

But the impropriety of invoking that privilege does not provide an answer to the problem before us. Petitioner has made more than an ordinary request for relevant, nonprivileged facts in the possession of his adversaries or their counsel. He has sought discovery as of right of oral and written statements of witnesses whose identity is well known and whose availability to petitioner appears unimpaired. He has sought production of these matters after making the most searching inquiries of his opponents as to the circumstances surrounding the fatal accident, which inquiries were sworn to have been answered to the best of their information and belief. Interrogatories were directed toward all the events prior to, during and subsequent to the sinking of the tug. Full and honest answers to such broad inquiries would necessarily have included all pertinent information gleaned by Fortenbaugh through his interviews with the witnesses. Petitioner makes no suggestion, and we cannot assume, that the tug owners or Fortenbaugh were incomplete or dishonest in the framing of their answers. In addition, petitioner was free to examine the public testimony of the witnesses taken before the United States Steamboat Inspectors. We are thus dealing with an attempt to secure the production of written statements and mental impressions contained in the files and mind of the attorney Fortenbaugh without any showing of necessity or any indication or claim that denial of such production would unduly prejudice the preparation of petitioner's case or cause him any hardship or injustice. For aught that appears, the essence of what petitioner seeks either has been revealed to him already through the interrogatories or is readily available to him direct from the witnesses for the asking.

* * *

In our opinion, neither Rule 26 nor any other rule dealing with discovery contemplates production under such circumstances. That is not because the subject matter is privileged or irrelevant, as those concepts are used in these rules. Here is simply an attempt, without purported necessity or justification, to secure written statements, private memoranda and personal recollections prepared or formed by an adverse party's counsel in the course of his legal duties. As such, it falls outside the arena of discovery and contravenes the public policy underlying the orderly prosecution and defense of legal claims. Not even the most liberal of discovery theories can justify unwarranted inquiries into the files and the mental impressions of an attorney.

Historically, a lawyer is an officer of the court and is bound to work for the advancement of justice while faithfully protecting the rightful interests of his clients. In performing his various duties, however, it is essential that a lawyer work with a certain degree of privacy, free from unnecessary intrusion by opposing parties and their counsel. Proper preparation of a client's case demands that he assemble information, sift what he considers to be the relevant from the irrelevant facts, prepare his legal theories and plan his strategy without undue and needless interference. That is the historical and the necessary way in which lawyers act within the framework of our system of jurisprudence to promote justice and to protect their clients' interests. This work is reflected, of course, in interviews, statements, memoranda, correspondence, briefs, mental impressions, personal beliefs, and countless other tangible and intangible ways—aptly though roughly termed by the Circuit Court of Appeals in this case as the "work product of the lawyer." Were such materials open to opposing counsel on mere demand, much of what is now put down in writing would remain unwritten. An attorney's thoughts, heretofore inviolate, would not be his own. Inefficiency, unfairness and sharp practices would inevitably develop in the giving of legal advice and in the preparation of cases for trial. The effect on the legal profession would be demoralizing. And the interests of the clients and the cause of justice would be poorly served.

We do not mean to say that all written materials obtained or prepared by an adversary's counsel with an eye toward litigation are necessarily free from discovery in all cases. Where relevant and non-privileged facts remain hidden in an attorney's file and where production of those facts is essential to the preparation of one's case, discovery may properly be had. Such written statements and documents might, under certain circumstances, be admissible in evidence or give clues as to the existence or location of relevant facts. Or they might be useful for purposes of impeachment or corroboration. And production might be justified where the witnesses are no longer available or can be reached only with difficulty. Were production of written statements and documents to be precluded under such circumstances, the liberal ideals of the deposition-discovery portions of the Federal Rules of Civil Procedure would be stripped of much of their meaning. But the general policy against invading the privacy of an attorney's course of preparation is so well recognized and so essential to an orderly working of our system of legal procedure that a burden rests on the one who would invade that privacy to establish adequate reasons to justify production through a subpoena or court order. That burden, we believe, is necessarily implicit in the rules as now constituted.

Rule 30(b), as presently written [now, Rule 26(c)], gives the trial judge the requisite discretion to make a judgment as to whether discovery should be allowed as to written statements secured from witnesses. But in the instant case there was no room for that discretion to operate in favor of the petitioner. No attempt was made to establish any reason why Fortenbaugh should be forced to produce the written statements. There was only a naked, general demand for these materials as of right and a finding by the District Court that no recognizable privilege was involved. That was insufficient to justify discovery under these circumstances and the court should have sustained the refusal of the tug owners and Fortenbaugh to produce.

But as to oral statements made by witnesses to Fortenbaugh, whether presently in the form of his mental impressions or memoranda, we do not believe that any showing of necessity can be made under the circumstances of this case so as to justify production. Under ordinary conditions, forcing an attorney to repeat or write out all that witnesses have told him and to deliver the account to his adversary gives rise to grave dangers of inaccuracy and untrustworthiness. No legitimate purpose is served by such production. The practice forces the attorney to testify as to what he remembers or what he saw fit to write down regarding witnesses' remarks. Such testimony could not qualify as evidence; and to use it for impeachment or corroborative purposes would make the attorney much less an officer of the court and much more an ordinary witness. The standards of the profession would thereby suffer.

Denial of production of this nature does not mean that any material, non-privileged facts can be hidden from the petitioner in this case. He need not be unduly hindered in the preparation of his case, in the discovery of facts or in his anticipation of his opponent's position. Searching interrogatories directed to Fortenbaugh and the tug owners, production of written documents and statements upon a proper showing and direct interviews with the witnesses themselves all serve to reveal the facts in Fortenbaugh's possession to the fullest possible extent consistent with public policy. Petitioner's counsel frankly admits that he wants the oral statements only to help prepare himself to examine witnesses and to make sure that he has overlooked nothing. That is insufficient under the circumstances to permit him an exception to the policy underlying the privacy of Fortenbaugh's professional activities. If there should be a rare situation justifying production of these matters, petitioner's case is not of that type.

* * * When Rule 26 and the other discovery rules were adopted, this Court and the members of the bar in general certainly did not believe or contemplate that all the files and mental processes of lawyers were thereby opened to the free scrutiny of their adversaries. And we refuse to interpret the rules at this time so as to reach so harsh and unwarranted a result.

We therefore affirm the judgment of the Circuit Court of Appeals.

Affirmed.

MR. JUSTICE JACKSON, concurring.

The narrow question in this case concerns only one of thirty-nine interrogatories which defendants and their counsel refused to answer. As there was persistence in refusal after the court ordered them to answer it, counsel and clients were committed to jail by the district court until they should purge themselves of contempt.

* * *

The primary effect of the practice advocated here would be on the legal profession itself. But it too often is overlooked that the lawyer and the law office are indispensable parts of our administration of justice. Law-abiding people can go nowhere else to learn the ever changing and constantly multiplying rules by which they must behave and to obtain redress for their wrongs. The welfare and tone of the legal profession is therefore of prime consequence to society, which would feel the consequences of such a practice as petitioner urges secondarily but certainly.

"Discovery" is one of the working tools of the legal profession. It traces back to the equity bill of discovery in English Chancery practice and seems to have had a forerunner in Continental practice. See Ragland, Discovery Before Trial (1932) 13–16. Since 1848 when the draftsmen of New York's Code of Procedure recognized the importance of a better system of discovery, the impetus to extend and expand discovery, as well as the opposition to it, has come from within the Bar itself. It happens in this case that it is the plaintiff's attorney who demands such unprecedented latitude of discovery and, strangely enough, *amicus* briefs in his support have been filed by several labor unions representing plaintiffs as a class. It is the history of the movement for broader discovery, however, that in actual experience the chief opposition to its extension has come from lawyers who specialize in representing plaintiffs, because defendants have made liberal use of it to force plaintiffs to disclose their cases in advance. See Report of the Commission on the Administration of Justice in New York State (1934) 330–31; Ragland, Discovery Before Trial (1932) 35–36. Discovery is a two-edged sword and we cannot decide this problem on any doctrine of extending help to one class of litigants.

* * *

To consider first the most extreme aspect of the requirement in litigation here, we find it calls upon counsel, if he has had any conversations with any of the crews of the vessels in question or of any other, to "set forth in detail the exact provision of any such oral statements or reports." Thus the demand is not for the production of a transcript in existence but calls for the creation of a written statement not in being. But the statement by counsel of what a witness told him is not evidence when written. Plaintiff could not introduce it to prove his case. What, then, is the purpose sought to be served by demanding this of adverse counsel?

Counsel for the petitioner candidly said on argument that he wanted this information to help prepare himself to examine witnesses, to make sure he overlooked nothing. He bases his claim to it in his brief on the view that the Rules were to do away with the old situation where a lawsuit developed into "a battle of wits between counsel." But a common law trial is and always should be an adversary proceeding. Discovery was hardly intended to enable a learned profession to perform its functions either without wits or on wits borrowed from the adversary.

The real purpose and the probable effect of the practice ordered by the district court would be to put trials on a level even lower than a "battle of wits." I can conceive of no practice more demoralizing to the Bar than to require a lawyer to write out and deliver to his adversary an account of what witnesses have told him. Even if his recollection were perfect, the statement would be his language, permeated with his inferences. Every one who has tried it knows that it is almost impossible so fairly to record the expressions and emphasis of a witness that when he testifies in the environment of the court and under the influence of the leading question there will not be departures in some respects. Whenever the testimony of the witness would differ from the "exact" statement the lawyer had delivered, the lawyer's statement would be whipped out to impeach the witness. Counsel producing his adversary's "inexact" statement could lose nothing by saying, "Here is a contradiction, gentlemen of the jury. I do not know whether it is my adversary or his witness who is not telling the truth, but one is not." Of course, if this practice were adopted, that scene would be repeated over and over again. The lawyer who delivers such statements often would find himself branded a deceiver afraid to take the stand to support his own version of the witness's conversation with him, or else he will have to go on the stand to defend his own credibility—perhaps against that of his chief witness, or possibly even his client.

Every lawyer dislikes to take the witness stand and will do so only for grave reasons. This is partly because it is not his role; he is almost invariably a poor witness. But he steps out of professional character to do it. He regrets it; the profession discourages it. But the practice advocated here is one which would force him to be a witness, not as to what he has seen or done but as to other witnesses' stories, and not because he wants to do so but in self-defense.

And what is the lawyer to do who has interviewed one whom he believes to be a biased, lying or hostile witness to get his unfavorable statements and know what to meet? He must record and deliver such statements even though he would not vouch for the credibility of the witness by calling him. Perhaps the other side would not want to call him either, but the attorney is open to the charge of suppressing evidence at the trial if he fails to call such a hostile witness even though he never regarded him as reliable or truthful.

Having been supplied the names of the witnesses, petitioner's lawyer gives no reason why he cannot interview them himself. If an employee-witness refuses to tell his story, he, too, may be examined under the Rules. He may be compelled on discovery, as fully as on the trial, to disclose his version of the facts. But that is his own disclosure—it can be used to impeach him if he contradicts it and such a deposition is not useful to promote an unseemly disagreement between the witness and the counsel in the case.

        * * *

The question remains as to signed statements or those written by witnesses. Such statements are not evidence for the defendant. *Palmer v. Hoffman,* 318 U.S. 109. Nor should I think they ordinarily could be evidence for the plaintiff. But such a statement might be useful for impeachment of the witness who signed it, if he is called and if he departs from the statement. There might be circumstances, too, where impossibility or difficulty of access to the witness or his refusal to respond to requests for information or other facts would show that the interests of justice require that such statements be made available. Production of such statements are governed by Rule 34 and on "showing good cause therefor" the court may order their inspection, copying or photographing. No such application has here been made; the demand is made on the basis of right, not on showing of cause.

I agree to the affirmance of the judgment of the Circuit Court of Appeals which reversed the district court.

MR. JUSTICE FRANKFURTER joins in this opinion.

NOTES AND QUESTIONS CONCERNING *HICKMAN V. TAYLOR*

1.   After the Supreme Court's ruling in *Hickman v. Taylor*, the case was tried and resulted in a $5000 verdict for Hickman's estate. At the trial Fortenbaugh offered the witness statements that he had refused to provide in discovery, but the court sustained plaintiff's objection to this evidence. Coady, "Dredging the Depths of *Hickman v. Taylor*," *Harv. L. Rec.*, May 6, 1977, at 2.

2.   What is really at stake in this action? Why would the defendant tug owners and attorney Fortenbaugh litigate the discovery issue in this case all the way to the United States Supreme Court? Both the Eastern District of Pennsylvania and the United States Court of Appeals for the Third Circuit decided this case *en banc* and the American Bar Association participated as *amicus curiae* in the Supreme Court and the lower federal courts.

3.   Why were Fortenbaugh's interviews not protected by the attorney-client privilege? What if the survivors he interviewed had been ordered to talk to Fortenbaugh by the tug owners? What if the survivors were themselves part-owners of the tug?

4.   What if the surviving crew members had given no public testimony? What if they not only had given no public testimony but, after their interviews with Fortenbaugh, they refused to talk with plaintiff's counsel?

5.   Could the plaintiff obtain the information he sought directly from the witnesses from whom Fortenbaugh had taken statements? Why did plaintiff nevertheless want the statements taken by Fortenbaugh?

6.   The Supreme Court in *Hickman v. Taylor* establishes a hierarchy of attorney work-product protections. Consider the degree of protection given the following under *Hickman:* written statements taken from a witness at the time of an interview; memoranda prepared by an attorney contemporaneously with witness interviews; the current mental impressions and recollections of an attorney concerning a witness.

7.   Why did Justice Jackson write a concurring opinion in *Hickman v. Taylor*? Justice Jackson served as the chief prosecutor for the Allies at the Nuremberg War Crime Trials, where he had observed firsthand the abuses of a legal system in which an attorney's primary loyalty was not to her client. Even prior to his service at Nuremberg, Jackson had written eloquently about the role of the lawyer, and, in particular, of the "country lawyer," in protecting individual rights within our legal system:

> [T]his vanishing country lawyer left his mark on his times, and he was worth knowing. * * * Once enlisted for a client, he took his obligation seriously. He insisted on complete control of the litigation—he was no mere hired hand. But he gave every power and resource to the cause. He identified himself with the client's cause fully, sometimes too fully. He would fight the adverse party and fight his counsel, fight every hostile witness, and fight the court, fight public sentiment, fight any obstacle to his client's success. He never quit. * * * He moved for new trials, he

appealed; and if he lost out in the end, he joined the client at the tavern in damning the judge—which is the last rite in closing an unsuccessful case, and I have officiated at many. * * * The law to him was like a religion, and its practice was more than a means of support; it was a mission. He was not always popular in his community, but he was respected. Unpopular minorities and individuals often found in him their only mediator and advocate. He was too independent to court the populace—he thought of himself as a leader and lawgiver, not as a mouthpiece.

Jackson, "Tribute to Country Lawyers: A Review," 30 *A.B.A.J.* 136, 139 (1944). Reprinted with permission from the March 1944 issue of the *ABA Journal,* the Lawyer's Magazine, published by the American Bar Association.

8. In its opinion the Supreme Court states: "Mutual knowledge of all the relevant facts gathered by both parties is essential to proper litigation." 329 U.S. at 507. Is this a self-evident proposition? Why is discovery in criminal cases, in which life and liberty are at stake, much more limited than in civil actions? Why have other countries not followed the United States in providing expansive civil discovery? Is the presumption underlying the Supreme Court's statement in *Hickman v. Taylor* one of the reasons for current problems with discovery abuse?

9. Professor Geoffrey Hazard has stated that "broad discovery is * * * not a mere procedural rule. Rather it has become, at least for our era, a procedural institution perhaps of virtually constitutional foundation." Hazard, "From Whom No Secrets Are Kept," 76 *Tex. L. Rev.* 1665, 1694 (1998). Should we attempt to turn back the clock to an earlier era in which discovery played a less dominant role? Would it be possible?

B. THE WORK–PRODUCT DOCTRINE UNDER RULE 26(b)(3)

In 1970, well after the Supreme Court's decision in *Hickman v. Taylor,* Rule 26(b)(3) was added to the Federal Rules of Civil Procedure to protect trial preparation materials from discovery. Rule 26(b)(3)(A) provides:

> Ordinarily, a party may not discover documents and tangible things that are prepared in anticipation of litigation or for trial by or for another party or its representative (including the other party's attorney, consultant, surety, indemnitor, insurer, or agent). But, subject to Rule 26(b)(4) [concerning expert discovery], those materials may be discovered if:
>
> (i) they are otherwise discoverable under Rule 26(b)(1); and
>
> (ii) the party shows that it has substantial need of the materials to prepare its case and cannot, without undue hardship, obtain their substantial equivalent by other means.

Regardless of whether trial preparation materials may fall within Rule 26(b)(3)(A), though, Rule 26(b)(3)(B) explicitly protects "core work product." Rule 26(b)(3)(B) thus states: "If the court orders discovery of

* * * materials [under Rule 26(b)(3)(A)], it must protect against disclosure of the mental impressions, conclusions, opinions, or legal theories of a party's attorney or other representative concerning the litigation."

Rule 26(b)(3) applies only to "documents and tangible things." The Advisory Committee's Note to the 1970 amendments to Rule 26 provides:

> Rules 33 and 36 have been revised in order to permit discovery calling for opinions, contentions, and admissions relating not only to fact but also to the application of law to fact. Under those rules, a party and his attorney or other representative may be required to disclose, to some extent, mental impressions, opinions, or conclusions. But documents or parts of documents containing these matters are protected against discovery by this subdivision. Even though a party may ultimately have to disclose in response to interrogatories or requests to admit, he is entitled to keep confidential documents containing such matters prepared for internal use.[64]

While *Hickman v. Taylor* involved work-product created by an attorney, Rule 26(b)(3) extends its protections beyond attorneys to other party representatives, including consultants, sureties, indemnitors, insurers, and agents. The hierarchy of work-product protections established in *Hickman v. Taylor* is preserved in Rule 26(b)(3). Thus, while there may be circumstances in which witness statements will be discoverable, "a much stronger showing is needed to obtain evaluative materials in an investigator's reports."[65] In addition, Rule 26(b)(3)(B) explicitly protects from disclosure "the mental impressions, conclusions, opinions, or legal theories of a party's attorney or other representative concerning the litigation."[66]

NOTES AND QUESTIONS CONCERNING RULE 26(b)(3)

1. Must a specific legal claim have arisen by the time that a document was created in order for that document to have been "prepared in anticipation of litigation" for the purposes of Rule 26(b)(3)? In *In Re Sealed Case*, 146 F.3d 881, 884 (D.C.Cir. 1998), the court stated: "For a document to meet this [Rule 26(b)(3)] standard, the lawyer must at least have had a subjective belief that litigation was a real possibility, and that belief must have been objectively reasonable." The court concluded that, in the case before it, this standard was met even though no specific claim was pending at the time the document in question was created.

---

64.   48 F.R.D. 487, 502 (1970). Despite the limitation of Rule 26(b)(3) to "documents and tangible things," "the *Hickman* decision continues to govern the standards for unrecorded work product protection." Special Project, "The Work Product Doctrine," 68 *Cornell L. Rev.* 760, 841 (1983). *See also United States v. One Tract of Real Property*, 95 F.3d 422, 428 n.10 (6th Cir. 1996); *Maynard v. Whirlpool Corp.*, 160 F.R.D. 85 (S.D.W.Va. 1995). *But see* Shapiro, "Some Problems of Discovery in an Adversary System," 63 *Minn. L. Rev.* 1055, 1066–69 (1979).

65.   Advisory Committee Note to 1970 Amendment to Rule 26(b)(3), 48 F.R.D. 487, 501 (1970).

66.   The courts have divided on the question of whether Rule 26(b)(3) still contemplates the possibility, as did *Hickman v. Taylor*, of "rare situations" in which opinion work-product may be discoverable. *See* cases collected in 8 C. Wright et al., *Federal Practice and Procedure* § 2026 (3d ed. 2010).

2. An accountant and lawyer is asked to evaluate the tax consequences of a contemplated merger, which is expected to generate an enormous loss and tax refund, to be challenged by the Internal Revenue Service, and to lead to litigation. The resulting memorandum analyzes likely legal challenges, discusses the governing law, recommends ways in which the transaction could be structured, and makes predictions about the likely outcome of litigation. The court of appeals held that Rule 26(b)(3) is applicable to such a litigation analysis prepared to inform a business decision that turns on the party's assessment of the likely outcome of litigation expected to result from the transaction. *United States v. Adlman*, 134 F.3d 1194 (2d Cir. 1998). The court adopted a definition of "in anticipation of litigation" focusing on whether the document in question was prepared because of the prospect of litigation. 134 F.3d at 1202. *But see United States v. Davis*, 636 F.2d 1028, 1040 (5th Cir.), cert. denied, 454 U.S. 862 (1981) (concluding that work-product protection only applies if the "primary motivating purpose behind the creation of the document was to aid in possible future litigation").

3. In the processing of insurance claims, business activity at some point may shift from general claims investigation and evaluation to efforts undertaken in anticipation of litigation. In *Lett v. State Farm Fire and Casualty Co.*, 115 F.R.D. 501 (N.D.Ga. 1987), the court held that Rule 26(b)(3) applied to documents created after a claim was assigned to an investigative unit because of suspicion of plaintiffs' involvement in the fire. It also appeared that the claim would be denied if the information in the file was confirmed to be true. The court further concluded that plaintiffs could not show the substantial need and undue hardship necessary to overcome the work-product protection; the insurer's bad faith that plaintiffs needed to establish was to be determined as of the date of trial, and plaintiffs had not identified any facts known exclusively by defendants or shown that they could not obtain the facts necessary to support their claims by deposing the individuals who wrote the reports they sought to discover.

4. Rule 26(b)(3)(C) permits any person to obtain "the person's own previous statement about the action or its subject matter." Doesn't this provision circumvent some of the protections established by *Hickman v. Taylor*? Under this Rule, could the plaintiff in *Hickman* merely have asked those who had given statements to attorney Fortenbaugh to request copies of their statements from the defendant? In this regard, consider the definition of "statement" contained in Rule 26(b)(3)(C) and the protections that Rule 26(b)(3)(B) requires to be given to "the mental impressions, conclusions, opinions, or legal theories of a party's attorney or other representative concerning the litigation."

5. Are there circumstances in which a party can depose opposing counsel concerning the investigation undertaken prior to the filing of suit? The plaintiff in *Brown v. Hart, Schaffner & Marx*, 96 F.R.D. 64 (N.D.Ill. 1982), brought a shareholders' derivative action. Although Rule 23.1 of the Federal Rules of Civil Procedure requires that the complaints in such actions be verified, plaintiff's deposition revealed that she had not "even the vaguest notion of whether or not a factual basis existed for any of the grave charges she had made against the [defendant] directors." 96 F.R.D. at 66. Instead, plaintiff had left any investigation to her attorneys (who also represented her

in five other derivative actions). The defendants then sought to depose her attorneys to ascertain the nature and extent of any investigation that was conducted prior to the filing and verification of the complaint.

The court rejected plaintiff's assertion of attorney-client privilege, because her lack of information concerning the defendants indicated that she could not have communicated any relevant information to her attorneys. Nor did the court believe that the work-product doctrine precluded the discovery sought; plaintiff had made no showing that the documents defendants requested had been prepared in anticipation of litigation and the defendants had satisfied the court of their substantial need for the information sought and their inability to obtain that information by other means. The court stressed that it was the purpose of Rule 23.1 to discourage "strike suits," which it described as "a particularly repugnant species of blackmail. Such lawsuits are the base work of rapacious jackals whose declared concern for the corporate well-being camouflages their unwholesome appetite for corporate dollars." 96 F.R.D. at 67.

6.   Does the work-product doctrine preclude the deposition of attorney-employees concerning non-privileged, pre-litigation factual matters? In *United States v. Philip Morris*, 209 F.R.D. 13 (D.D.C. 2002), the court refused to quash the depositions of defendant's senior vice president and general counsel and three in-house counsel because the depositions that had been noticed were not of trial or litigation counsel and would not expose the defendant's litigation strategy in the pending case. 209 F.R.D. at 17. Judge Gladys Kessler noted that to preclude these depositions "would allow Defendants to immunize themselves from discovery on key issues, by knowingly and strategically placing persons who happen to be attorneys in positions where they perform critical business, marketing, public relations, research, scientific and development duties." 209 F.R.D. at 19. In reaching her decision, Judge Kessler distinguished the decision in *Shelton v. American Motors Corp.*, 805 F.2d 1323, 1327 (8th Cir. 1986), which had precluded the deposition of trial counsel unless "(1) no other means exist to obtain the information than to depose opposing counsel * * * ; (2) the information sought is relevant and nonprivileged; and (3) the information is crucial to the preparation of the case."

Exercises Concerning the Attorney Work–Product Doctrine

1.   As an attorney for the plaintiffs in the Buffalo Creek disaster litigation, you desire to obtain information from residents of Logan County, West Virginia, concerning the failure of the Buffalo Creek dam. You realize that the Pittston Company's attorneys would like to obtain information from these same individuals. Your task therefore is to obtain information while at the same time ensuring that the information is protected from discovery under Rule 26(b)(3) and the work-product doctrine.

Write a short memorandum summarizing the manner in which you would obtain the information while preserving any work-product protection. Your memorandum should address specifically the following questions:

(a) Who should conduct these interviews: an attorney, a paralegal, an investigator specifically hired to conduct the interviews, or one of the plaintiffs who has volunteered her time for this project?

(b) If someone other than trial counsel conducts the interviews, to whom should any resulting memoranda be addressed, how should they be labeled, and where and how should they be kept?

(c) Should these interviews be preserved by having the individuals sign statements at the time of the interview, by tape recording the interviews, by the interviewer later dictating a memorandum of her impressions of the interview, or in some other manner?

(d) What form should the interviews take: a strictly factual narrative statement from the person interviewed, a narrative of the witness's responses to questions concerning counsel's opinions and theories about the litigation, or an interview summary including facts and the conclusions, impressions, and opinions of the interviewer?

(e) Should the persons interviewed be shown any notes of the interview or asked to sign or approve either those notes or a final interview summary?

(f) What if one of the witnesses was severely injured in the flood and is not expected to live much longer?

(g) What if a witness already has given a statement to the Pittston Company?

(h) What if one of the witnesses is a mine safety engineer whom plaintiffs might call as an expert witness at trial concerning the reasons for the collapse of the dam?

2. You represent a major corporation that is one of thirty defendants in a complex series of antitrust cases. The discovery in these cases has been consolidated and conducted in stages. During the initial document productions over 1,000,000 documents have been produced. The next stage of the discovery will be depositions, over 200 of which have been scheduled. One of plaintiffs' lead counsel has proposed a discovery management order requiring that, 30 days prior to each deposition, any attorney who plans to examine the deponent must identify all documents about which she will ask the witness at the deposition.

Write a memorandum to your senior partner concerning:

(a) possible legal questions posed by the discovery proposal; and

(b) the litigation advantages and disadvantages to your client of such an order.

3. You represent a railroad that has been sued by an employee for injuries allegedly sustained at work. While the plaintiff has complained that "he is in such intense pain he can hardly move," an investigator has provided you with a videotape of the plaintiff dancing the polka at a relative's wedding reception. Plaintiff has filed a document request seeking "any videotape recordings that the defendant may offer to show the

alleged physical condition of the plaintiff." While the plaintiff's deposition has been scheduled for next week, plaintiff's counsel has told you that this deposition will not go forward until after you have responded to plaintiff's outstanding production request. What should you do?

V. DISCOVERY CONCERNING EXPERTS

Not only does Rule 26 specifically address the discovery of insurance agreements and trial preparation materials, but that Rule also governs the pretrial discovery of experts. The 1993 amendments to the Federal Rules of Civil Procedure added Rule 26(a)(2), which provides for the pretrial disclosure of expert testimony. Furthermore, Rule 26(b)(4)(A) specifically provides that an expert who will testify at trial may be deposed after that expert's required written report has been provided. In addition to these procedural rules governing expert discovery, the federal courts have grappled increasingly with the questions as to who is, and who is not, an expert witness and the evidence that may be presented by such experts.

A. WHO IS AN EXPERT?

Under Rule 702 of the Federal Rules of Evidence, an individual may be considered qualified as an expert "by knowledge, skill, experience, training, or education." As the Advisory Committee on the Proposed Federal Rules of Evidence observed, "[W]ithin the scope of the rule are not only experts in the strictest sense of the word, e.g. physicians, physicists, and architects, but also the large group sometimes called 'skilled' witnesses, such as bankers or landowners testifying to land values."[67] While a physician might be called as an expert witness to testify about the extent of plaintiff's medical injuries, the plaintiff also might call as experts an automobile mechanic to testify concerning the condition of his car's brakes and a veteran bus driver to testify concerning bus policies and practices within the local community. However, Rule 702 was amended in 2000 to provide that expert testimony is only admissible if "(1) the testimony is based upon sufficient facts or data, (2) the testimony is the product of reliable principles and methods, and (3) the witness has applied the principles and methods reliably to the facts of the case."

An idea of the broad scope of expert witness testimony and the importance that such testimony plays in civil litigation can be gained from a glance at the classified section of any bar association journal. Among the areas of expertise identified in bar journal advertisements are "crane accident investigation," "wood scientist," "air traffic expert," "aquatic safety expert," "accounting malpractice," "addictionologist," "warning labels," "root canals/endodontist," and "otolaryngologist."[68]

---

67. 56 F.R.D. 183, 282 (1973).

68. If you have to ask what an "otolaryngologist" is, chances are that you do not need such an expert for your case.

In *Daubert v. Merrell Dow Pharmaceuticals, Inc.*,[69] the Supreme Court addressed the manner in which federal trial judges are to consider scientific expert opinion. The Court held that such expert opinion can be admissible under Federal Rule of Evidence 702 even if the scientific technique in question is not generally accepted as reliable in the relevant scientific community and the evidence therefore might not have been admissible at common law.[70] The Court, however, stressed that federal trial judges must perform a screening function concerning scientific evidence offered pursuant to Federal Rule of Evidence 702. While " 'general acceptance' is not a necessary precondition to the admissibility of scientific evidence under the Federal Rules of Evidence, * * * the Rules of Evidence—especially Rule 702—do assign to the trial judge the task of ensuring that an expert's testimony both rests on a reliable foundation and is relevant to the task at hand."[71] The 2000 amendment to Federal Rule of Evidence 702 explicitly incorporated *Daubert* into that Rule with respect to all forms of expert testimony.

Because of the broad acceptance of expert testimony under the Federal Rules of Evidence, and the resulting importance of experts in civil litigation, expert discovery has become an increasingly important aspect of pretrial practice.

B. DISCLOSURE OF EXPERT TESTIMONY UNDER RULE 26(a)(2)

Because of the importance of expert testimony in modern civil litigation, such testimony is specifically covered by the Rule 26(a) mandatory disclosure provisions. Rule 26(a)(2)(A) requires that parties disclose to other parties "the identity of any witness it may use at trial to present

---

69. 509 U.S. 579 (1993).

70. 509 U.S. at 585–89.

71. 509 U.S. at 597. In *Kumho Tire Co. v. Carmichael*, 526 U.S. 137 (1999), the Supreme Court concluded that *"Daubert*'s general holding—setting forth the trial judge's general 'gatekeeping' obligation—applies not only to testimony based on 'scientific' knowledge, but also to testimony based on 'technical' and 'other specialized' knowledge." 526 U.S. at 141.

While *Daubert* authorized the admission of expert testimony that would not have satisfied the "general acceptance" test for admissibility at common law, federal courts have taken their "gatekeeping" obligations under *Daubert* quite seriously. Parties seeking the exclusion of expert testimony typically file pretrial *"Daubert* motions," which may involve multi-day evidentiary hearings. *See* Shaughnessy, *"Daubert* After a Decade," *Litigation*, Fall 2003, at 19. According to a 2001 study by the RAND Institute for Civil Justice:

[Federal judges] are increasingly acting as gatekeepers for reliability and relevance, they are examining the methods and reasoning underlying the evidence, and they appear to be employing general acceptance as only one of many factors that enter into their reliability assessments. The rise that took place in both the proportion of evidence found unreliable and the proportion of challenged evidence excluded suggests that the standards for admitting evidence have tightened. The subsequent fall in these two proportions suggests that parties proposing evidence—and perhaps parties challenging evidence as well—have responded to the change in standards.

L. Dixon & B. Gill, *Changes in the Standards for Admitting Expert Evidence in Federal Civil Cases Since the Daubert Decision* xiii (RAND Institute for Civil Justice 2001).

evidence under Federal Rule of Evidence 702, 703, or 705."[72] Rule 26(a)(2)(D) provides that experts are to be disclosed "at the times and in the sequence that the court orders." In the absence of any such direction by the court, the disclosures are to be made "at least 90 days before the date set for trial or for the case to be ready for trial."[73]

Rule 26(a)(2) not only requires disclosure of the identity of experts, but Rule 26(a)(2)(B) requires that, except as otherwise stipulated or ordered by the court, disclosures from witnesses "retained or specially employed to provide expert testimony" are to be accompanied by a written report prepared and signed by the witness. Rule 26(a)(2)(B) is quite specific concerning the matters that are to be included in expert witness reports. This Rule requires that these reports include:

(i) a complete statement of all opinions the witness will express and the basis and reasons for them;

(ii) the facts or data considered by the witness in forming them;

(iii) any exhibits that will be used to summarize or support them;

(iv) the witness's qualifications, including a list of all publications authored in the previous 10 years;

(v) a list of all other cases in which, during the previous 4 years, the witness testified as an expert at trial or by deposition; and

(vi) a statement of the compensation to be paid for the study and testimony in the case.

To enforce these and the other Rule 26(a) disclosure requirements, Rule 37(c)(1) provides that parties who without substantial justification fail to disclose this information shall not, unless the failure is harmless, be permitted to use that information during the pretrial process or at trial. Thus, if an expert plans to offer a particular opinion at trial, she or he had better include that opinion in a Rule 26(a)(2)(B) expert witness report. In addition, the Rule 26(e) duty to supplement disclosures applies to expert witnesses. Rule 26(e)(2) specifically provides that the duty to supplement expert reports "extends both to information included in the report and to information given during the expert's deposition" and that any "additions or changes to this information must be disclosed by the time the party's pretrial disclosures under Rule 26(a)(3) are due."[74]

Not only does Rule 26(a)(2)(B) require the mandatory disclosure of expert witness reports, but that Rule quite specifically defines the experts whose reports must be disclosed. The report disclosure provision extends

---

72. This disclosure does not extend to opinion testimony offered by lay witnesses pursuant to Federal Rule of Evidence 701. In 2000 Rule 701 was amended specifically to provide that lay opinion evidence under that Rule does not include testimony "based on scientific, technical, or other specialized knowledge within the scope of Rule 702." "By channeling testimony that is actually expert testimony to Rule 702, [amended Rule 701] * * * ensures that a party will not evade the expert witness disclosure requirements set forth in Fed. R. Civ. P. 26 * * * by simply calling an expert witness in the guise of a layperson." Advisory Committee Note to 2000 Amendment to Rule 701, 192 F.R.D. 340, 416 (2000).

73. Fed. R. Civ. P. 26(a)(2)(D)(i). If, however, the expert testimony is offered for rebuttal purposes, the disclosure is to be made within 30 days after the disclosure that is being rebutted. Fed. R. Civ. P. 26(a)(2)(D)(ii).

74. Unless otherwise ordered by the court, pretrial disclosures under Rule 26(a)(3) are to be made at least 30 days before trial. Fed. R. Civ. P. 26(a)(3)(B).

to any person who may present expert testimony at trial, whether "retained or specially employed to provide expert testimony in the case or one whose duties as the party's employee regularly involve giving expert testimony." Thus the mandatory expert disclosure provisions cannot be circumvented by offering expert testimony through a party's employee rather than by retaining an independent expert.[75]

C. FURTHER EXPERT DISCOVERY UNDER RULE 26(b)(4)

In light of the requirement for the disclosure of "detailed and complete" written expert reports under Rule 26(a)(2)(B),[76] it may not be necessary to obtain additional discovery concerning some experts. Rule 26(b)(4), though, provides for the discovery of additional expert information. Rule 26(b)(4)(A) provides that a party "may depose any person who has been identified as an expert whose opinions may be presented at trial." However, that Rule further provides: "If Rule 26(a)(2)(B) requires a report from the expert, the deposition may be conducted only after the report is provided."

If a party has retained or specially employed an expert who is not expected to testify at trial, Rule 26(b)(4)(D) only permits discovery of that expert, through interrogatories or deposition, pursuant to Rule 35(b) (concerning physical and mental examinations of parties) or "on showing exceptional circumstances under which it is impracticable for the party to obtain facts or opinions on the same subject by other means." It therefore is only with respect to experts whom a party anticipates calling at trial that other parties are entitled to discovery as a matter of right. While discovery as of right concerning even trial experts traditionally was limited to interrogatories, under the 1993 amendment to Rule 26(b)(4)(A) parties may, without seeking leave of court, depose trial experts. If, however, the expert in question will not testify at trial, a showing of exceptional circumstances under Rule 26(b)(4)(D)(ii) must be made to obtain discovery concerning that expert.

Rule 26(b)(4)(E) contains specific provisions governing the costs of expert discovery. It provides:

Unless manifest injustice would result, the court must require that the party seeking discovery:

(i)   pay the expert a reasonable fee for time spent in responding to discovery under Rule 26(b)(4)(A) or (D); and

---

75. However, because Rule 26(a)(2)(B)'s expert witness report requirement extends only to experts "retained or specially employed to provide expert testimony in the case or one whose duties as the party's employee regularly involve giving expert testimony," reports are not routinely required from experts such as, for instance, treating physicians. Advisory Committee Note to 1993 Amendment to Rule 26(a)(2), 146 F.R.D. 401, 635 (1993).

76. Advisory Committee Note to 1993 Amendment to Rule 26, 146 F.R.D. 401, 634 (1993).

(ii) for discovery under (D) [of a non-testifying expert], also pay the other party a fair portion of the fees and expenses it reasonably incurred in obtaining the expert's facts and opinions.

Thus, in order to depose a non-testifying expert, a party typically will be required to pay both the expert and the party who has retained that expert.

Even when discovery concerning an expert is possible, though, there are specific limits on what can be obtained through such discovery. In 2010, the Federal Rules of Civil Procedure were amended to explicitly protect prior drafts of expert reports and disclosures, as well as communications between an expert and the attorney who retained that expert. Rule 26(b)(4)(B) provides that "Rules 26(b)(3)(A) and (B) [concerning trial preparation materials] protect drafts of any report or disclosure required under Rule 26(a)(2), regardless of the form in which the draft is recorded."

In addition, Rule 26(b)(4)(C) provides:

Rules 26(b)(3)(A) and (B) protect communications between the party's attorney and any witness required to provide a report under Rule 26(a)(2)(B), regardless of the form of the communications, except to the extent that the communications:

(i) relate to compensation for the expert's study or testimony;

(ii) identify facts or data that the party's attorney provided and that the expert considered in forming the opinions to be expressed; or

(iii) identify assumptions that the party's attorney provided and that the expert relied on in forming the opinions to be expressed.

Thus, unless the attorney-expert communications involve (1) expert compensation or (2) the provision by the attorney of facts or data considered by the expert in forming her opinions or assumptions relied upon by the expert in forming her opinions, those communications are not discoverable.

The rationale for so protecting expert report drafts and attorney-expert communications is set forth in the Committee Note to the 2010 amendments to Rule 26(a)(2) and (b)(4):

The Committee has been told repeatedly that routine discovery into attorney-expert communications and draft reports has had undesirable effects. Costs have risen. Attorneys may employ two sets of experts—one for purposes of consultation and another to testify at trial—because disclosure of their collaborative interactions with expert consultants would reveal their most sensitive and confidential case analyses. At the same time, attorneys often feel compelled to adopt a guarded attitude toward their interaction with testifying experts that impedes effective communication, and experts adopt strategies that protect against discovery but also interfere with their work.[77]

Under amended Rule 26, both attorney-expert communications and the work process of experts should be more natural, more efficient, and, consequently, less costly.

NOTES AND QUESTIONS CONCERNING EXPERT DISCOVERY

1. In what circumstances might a party be granted leave to obtain discovery concerning a non-testifying expert? In *Heitmann v. Concrete Pipe Machinery*, 98 F.R.D. 740 (E.D.Mo. 1983), the plaintiff deposed defendant's trial expert, who testified that he had read and considered the report of another expert whom defendant had retained but did not intend to call as a witness at trial. Defendant argued that this report of the non-testifying expert was protected by the work-product doctrine and that plaintiff had not shown the "exceptional circumstances under which it is impracticable for the party seeking discovery to obtain facts or opinions on the same subject by other means" pursuant to Rule 26(b)(4)(B) (now, Rule 26(b)(4)(D)(ii)). The court held that, even though the expert who had prepared the report would not testify at trial, plaintiff was entitled to that report because it had been relied upon by defendant's testifying expert and plaintiff's counsel would need this report in order to effectively cross-examine the testifying expert at trial. The court required that, pursuant to Federal Rule of Civil Procedure 26(b)(4)(C)(ii) (now, Federal Rule of Civil Procedure 26(b)(4)(E)(ii)), plaintiff pay one-third of defendant's expenses in obtaining this report from the non-testifying expert—representing a "fair portion of the fees and expenses reasonably incurred by the [defendant] in obtaining facts and opinions from the expert." 98 F.R.D. at 743.

2. *Heitmann v. Concrete Pipe Machinery* was decided prior to the 1993 amendments to the Federal Rules of Civil Procedure that created the mandatory duty to disclose expert testimony. Under the current version of Rule 26, would the plaintiff have had another argument for the disclosure of the non-testifying expert's report in *Heitmann*? *See* Federal Rule of Civil Procedure 26(a)(2)(B)(ii). What could defense counsel have done in this case to prevent the discovery of the non-testifying expert's report?

3. What if the *Heitmann* plaintiff had sought not only a copy of the non-testifying expert's report, but also wanted to depose that non-testifying expert? Would plaintiff be entitled to either the report or a deposition of the non-testifying expert if defendant's two experts merely had talked about the report and the testifying expert had not read that report?

4. The final sentence of Federal Rule of Evidence 705 provides: "The expert may in any event be required to disclose the underlying facts or data [upon which the expert relies] on cross-examination." In light of this provision, why not require plaintiff to wait until trial to receive a copy of the report upon which the testifying expert relies?

---

77. Advisory Committee Note to 2010 Amendment to Rule 26, 266 F.R.D. 502, 562–63 (2010).

5. In addition to Rule 705, Federal Rule of Evidence 612 in part provides:

[I]f a witness uses a writing to refresh memory for the purpose of testifying, either—

(1) while testifying, or

(2) before testifying, if the court in its discretion determines it is necessary in the interests of justice,

an adverse party is entitled to have the writing produced at the hearing, to inspect it, to cross-examine the witness thereon, and to introduce in evidence those portions which relate to the testimony of the witness.

Attorneys need to consider the effect of Rule 612 before giving any witness, whether an expert or not, documents to review prior to trial. Moreover, under the 1993 amendment to Rule 26(a)(2) requiring the disclosure of expert witness reports, "litigants should no longer be able to argue that materials furnished to their experts to be used in forming their opinions—whether or not ultimately relied upon by the expert—are privileged or otherwise protected from disclosure when such persons are testifying or being deposed." Advisory Committee Note to 1993 Amendment to Rule 26, 146 F.R.D. 401, 634 (1993). *See* Mickus, "Discovery of Work Product Disclosed to a Testifying Expert Under the 1993 Amendments to the Federal Rules of Civil Procedure," 27 *Creighton L. Rev.* 773 (1994).

6. Is the limited ability to obtain discovery concerning non-testifying experts relevant to the manner in which an attorney consults and uses experts during the pretrial phase of a case? Consider the following use of experts. Plaintiff's attorney retains an expert prior to trial to conduct various statistical tests in an effort to show that defendant has discriminated against women in connection with hiring and promotion decisions. While several of the tests run by this expert support plaintiff's theory of the case, two tests do not. Plaintiff's attorney then retains a second expert, who is asked by counsel to run only those tests that support plaintiff's theory of the case. It is only this second expert whom the plaintiff intends to call as a witness at trial, thus making it unlikely that the defendant will be able to obtain any discovery concerning the analyses of plaintiff's first (non-testifying) expert. Are there ethical problems with such use of "clean" experts? Are there practical problems? *Cf. Coates v. AC & S, Inc.*, 133 F.R.D. 109, 110 (E.D.La. 1990) (in which the court required the parties to identify all experts to whom tissue samples were sent "in an effort to curtail the 'shopping' of [those] samples").

7. Can an attorney ethically retain more experts than she knows she will be permitted to call as witnesses at trial? What about retaining an expert merely so an opposing party cannot retain that expert? What if an opposing counsel has retained all of the available experts in a given geographic area or specific field of expertise?

8. Plaintiffs bring an action against the operators of an oil well, and these defendants implead third-party defendants whom they allege were responsible for the "blowout" that led to the litigation. One group of plaintiffs retain expert witnesses who are expected to offer testimony critical of the defendants but, on the day that these experts are to be deposed, the defen-

dants settle with this group of plaintiffs. One term of this settlement is an agreement by these plaintiffs that their experts will no longer be listed as testifying experts. Should the plaintiffs who have not settled their claims be able to depose these "non-testifying" experts? *See Tom L. Scott, Inc. v. McIlhany*, 798 S.W.2d 556 (Tex.1990).

9. Even if a discovering party must pay "a fair portion" of the fees and expenses incurred in obtaining facts and opinions from an expert, there still will be significant costs to the party who has retained the expert. As Judge Jerome Frank observed more than fifty years ago:

> In order to prove his claim, or to defend against one, a man * * * may need the services of an engineer, or a chemist, or an expert accountant, to make an extensive—and therefore expensive—investigation. Without the evidence which such an investigation would reveal, a man is often bound to be defeated. His winning or losing may therefore depend on his pocketbook. * * * For want of money, expendable for such purposes, many a suit has been lost, many a meritorious claim or defense has never even been asserted.

J. Frank, *Courts On Trial* 94 (1949). See also Medine, "The Constitutional Right To Expert Assistance for Indigents in Civil Cases," 41 *Hastings L. J.* 281 (1990); Note, "Contingent Fees For Expert Witnesses In Civil Litigation," 86 *Yale L. J.* 1680 (1977). In The Civil Rights Act of 1991, P.L. No. 102–166, 105 Stat. 1071 (1991), Congress provided for the recovery of expert witness fees by prevailing parties in civil rights actions. 42 U.S.C. §§ 1988(c) and 2000e–5(k).

VI. DISCOVERY CONFERENCES, ORDERS AND PLANNING

Rule 26 of the Federal Rules of Civil Procedure was amended in 1980 to add a new Rule 26(f) that confirmed the power of district courts to require discovery conferences and provided that a court was to order such a conference in response to a properly supported motion filed by any party. "The [1980] amendment envisioned a two-step process: first, the parties would attempt to frame a mutually agreeable plan; second, the court would hold a 'discovery conference' and then enter an order establishing a schedule and limitations for the conduct of discovery."[78] This procedure, relying upon a party's request for a discovery conference, was rarely used in most courts.[79]

With the 1993 amendments to the Federal Rules, Rule 26(f) was changed substantially. No longer does Rule 26(f) provide for a discovery conference with the court. Instead, provisions affirming judicial control of the discovery process were added in 1993 to Rule 16,[80] which generally governs pretrial conferences, scheduling, and case management. Rule

---

78. Advisory Committee Note to 1993 Amendment to Rule 26, 146 F.R.D. 401, 641 (1993).

79. *Id.* at 641–42.

80. Fed. R. Civ. P. 16(b)(3), 16(c)(2)(F).

16(c)(2)(F) now provides that one of the subjects for consideration and action at a Rule 16(c) pretrial conference is "controlling and scheduling discovery, including orders affecting disclosures and discovery under Rule 26 and Rules 29 through 37."

Instead of providing for judicially-hosted discovery conferences, the current version of Rule 26(f) requires the parties themselves to confer to plan their discovery. Unless the case is among those types of proceedings exempted from initial disclosure under Rule 26(a)(1)(B) or the court otherwise orders, Rule 26(f)(2) requires the parties to confer to "consider the nature and basis of their claims and defenses and the possibilities for promptly settling or resolving the case; make or arrange for the disclosures required by Rule 26(a)(1); discuss any issues about preserving discoverable information; and develop a proposed discovery plan." While Rule 26(f) does not require that this discovery conference be a face-to-face meeting, Rule 26(f)(1) does provide that the parties must confer "as soon as practicable—and in any event at least 21 days before a scheduling conference is to be held or a scheduling order is due under Rule 16(b)."

Rule 26(f)(2) in part provides: "The attorneys of record and all unrepresented parties that have appeared in the case are jointly responsible for arranging the conference, for attempting in good faith to agree on the proposed discovery plan, and for submitting to the court within 14 days after the conference a written report outlining the plan."[81] The written discovery plan is to provide the basis for the court's subsequent Rule 16(b) scheduling order and any discussion of discovery at a Rule 16(c) pretrial conference.

The 2006 amendments to the Federal Rules of Civil Procedure expanded Rules 16 and 26(f) to explicitly require that parties and the court focus on issues involving electronically stored information at the early stages of a civil action. As noted by the Advisory Committee on the Federal Rules of Civil Procedure concerning these amendments, "The overall directive is broad, but specific provisions focus on three areas recognized as frequent sources of difficulty in electronic discovery: the form of producing electronically stored information in discovery; preserving information for the litigation; and the assertion of privilege and work-product protection claims."[82]

Rule 26(f)(3) specifically addresses the subjects to be considered in the parties' discovery plan. These subjects include:

> (A) what changes should be made in the timing, form, or requirement for disclosures under Rule 26(a), including a statement of when initial disclosures were made or will be made;

---

81. As amended in 2000, Rule 26(f)(2) also provides that a court "may order the parties or attorneys to attend the conference in person."

82. Report of the Advisory Committee on the Federal Rules of Civil Procedure, 234 F.R.D. 219, 312 (2006).

(B) the subjects on which discovery may be needed, when discovery should be completed, and whether discovery should be conducted in phases or be limited to or focused on particular issues;

(C) any issues about disclosure or discovery of electronically stored information, including the form or forms in which it should be produced;

(D) any issues about claims of privilege or of protection as trial-preparation materials, including—if the parties agree on a procedure to assert these claims after production—whether to ask the court to include their agreement in an order;

(E) what changes should be made in the limitations on discovery imposed under these rules or by local rule, and what other limitations should be imposed; and

(F) any other orders that the court should issue under Rule 26(c) or under Rule 16(b) and (c).

This listing of specific topics "does not exclude consideration of other subjects, such as the time when any dispositive motions should be filed and when the case should be ready for trial."[83]

Form 52 in the Appendix of Forms to the Federal Rules of Civil Procedure is illustrative of the type of discovery plan contemplated by Rule 26(f). As amended in 2000, Rule 26(f) requires only a party conference, rather than a face-to-face meeting (although an actual meeting still can be required by court order). Whether the parties actually meet or merely confer over the telephone, Form 52, which follows, can serve as a check list for their Rule 26(f) conference.

REPORT OF THE PARTIES' PLANNING MEETING

(Caption–See Form 1.)

1. The following persons participated in a Rule 26(f) conference on *date* by *state the method of conferring*:

(e.g., name representing the plaintiff.)

2. Initial Disclosures. The parties [have completed] [will complete by (date)] the initial disclosures required by Rule 26(a)(1).

3. Discovery Plan. The parties propose this discovery plan:

(*Use separate paragraphs or subparagraphs if the parties disagree.*)

(a) Discovery will be needed on these subjects: (*describe*)

(b) Disclosure or discovery of electronically stored information should be handled as follows: (*briefly describe the parties' proposals, including the form or forms for production.*)

---

83. Advisory Committee Note to 1993 Amendment to Rule 26, 146 F.R.D. 401, 643 (1993).

(c) The parties have agreed to an order regarding claims of privilege or of protection as trial-preparation material asserted after production, as follows: (*briefly describe the provisions of the proposed order.*)

(d) (Dates for commencing and completing discovery, including discovery to be commenced or completed before other discovery.)

(e) (Maximum number of interrogatories by each party to another party, along with dates the answers are due.)

(f) (Maximum number of requests for admission, along with the dates responses are due.)

(g) (Maximum number of depositions for each party.)

(h) (Limits on the length of depositions, in hours.)

(i) (Dates for exchanging reports of expert witnesses.)

(j) (Dates for supplementations under Rule 26(e).)

4. Other Items:

(a) (A date if the parties ask to meet with the court before a scheduling order.)

(b) (Requested dates for pretrial conferences.)

(c) (Final dates for the plaintiff to amend pleadings or to join parties.)

(d) (Final dates for the defendant to amend pleadings or to join parties.)

(e) (Final dates to file dispositive motions.)

(f) (State the prospects for settlement.)

(g) (Identify any alternative dispute resolution procedure that may enhance settlement prospects.)

(h) (Final dates for submitting Rule 26(a)(3) witness lists, designations of witnesses whose testimony will be presented by deposition, and exhibit lists.)

(i) (Final dates to file objections under Rule 26(a)(3).)

(j) (Suggested trial date and estimate of trial length.)

(k) (Other matters.)

(Date and sign—see Form 2.)

Because the court should have the parties' discovery plan at the time that it enters its Rule 16(b) scheduling order and, in many cases, also will have met with the parties at a Rule 16(c) conference, the discovery in a particular case can be tailored by the court to the needs of the parties and the case. This is another example of the manner in which the 1993 amendments to the Federal Rules of Civil Procedure created the potential for more active judicial involvement in the pretrial process and moved beyond the notion of "one size fits all" with respect to the procedures applicable to federal civil litigation.

Rule 16(b)(1) of the Federal Rules of Civil Procedure provides that, except in "categories of actions exempted by local rule," a district judge or magistrate judge must "issue a scheduling order: (A) after receiving the parties' report under Rule 26(f); or (B) after consulting with the parties' attorneys and any unrepresented parties at a scheduling conference or by telephone, mail, or other means." The April 11, 1973, order establishing the initial pretrial deadlines in the Buffalo Creek litigation is illustrative of Rule 16(b) scheduling orders:

IN THE UNITED STATES DISTRICT COURT FOR THE SOUTHERN DISTRICT OF WEST VIRGINIA

DENNIS PRINCE et al.,	)	
Plaintiffs,	)	
	)	
v.	)	Civil Action No. 3052–HN
	)	
THE PITTSTON COMPANY,	)	
Defendant.	)	

ORDER

Upon consideration of the various motions, affidavits, memoranda of law, and other pleadings and documents on file in this action, and the motions having been argued at a hearing and pre-trial conference on March 2, 1973, and good cause appearing therefor, * * *

IT IS ORDERED, that the parties in this action are directed to proceed with discovery and pre-trial proceedings pursuant to the following schedule:

(a) The defendant shall complete its document turnover by April 15, 1973;

(b) Plaintiffs shall file a more definite statement as to their states of citizenship and damage claims by April 15, 1973;

(c) Plaintiffs will review the documents and defendant will review the statement of damages during the period from April 15 to April 30, 1973;

(d) All depositions by the parties shall be completed during the period from May 1, 1973, to September 1, 1973;

(e) The parties (1) will file with the Court, by October 15, 1973, a joint stipulation setting forth all undisputed facts and listing or annexing copies of all exhibits to be offered at trial, and (2) will serve and file any motion on or before October 15, 1973; and

(f) The parties will serve and file their respective trial memoranda with the Court by November 1, 1973.

DATED this 11th day of April, 1973.

s/ ————

United States District Judge

APPROVED FOR ENTRY:

s/ ————

Of Counsel for Plaintiffs

s/ ————

Of Counsel for Defendant

————

Even prior to the 1993 amendments to the Federal Rules of Civil Procedure, Judge Robert Peckham of the United States District Court for the Northern District of California required attorneys to engage in "two-stage discovery planning." Under this system, the minimal discovery necessary for the parties to present any dispositive motions or resolve the case by settlement, mediation or arbitration initially is obtained. If the case is not terminated by these means, the parties engage in more complete discovery to ready the case for trial.[84] Rule 26(f)(3)(B) requires the parties to confer concerning "whether discovery should be conducted in phases or be limited to or focused on particular issues," while Rule 16(c)(2)(F) lists as a potential subject for consideration at pretrial conferences "controlling and scheduling discovery." "Phased discovery" as employed by Judge Peckham thus is fully contemplated by the Federal Rules. Indeed, Rule 26 itself provides for a form of "phased discovery," with initial information exchange restricted to Rule 26(a)(1) required disclosures and further discovery generally unavailable until those disclosures have been provided.[85]

Whether or not detailed discovery plans are negotiated with other counsel or ordered by the court, counsel should plan carefully the discovery that they will undertake in each case. Discovery planning should be a major part of the litigation plan that is developed at the very outset of each case.[86] Clients should be consulted concerning the plan, particularly concerning the costs of the anticipated discovery and the delay that this discovery may engender. Prior to estimating either discovery costs or scheduling, counsel must make an educated guess about the discovery that opposing counsel will seek. In making these estimates, the manner in which an initial set of discovery requests can lead other parties to request discovery must be kept in mind.

One of the major decisions in planning discovery is the order in which the different discovery devices will be used. Rule 26(d)(1) provides: "A

---

84. Peckham, "A Judicial Response to the Cost of Litigation: Case Management, Two–Stage Discovery Planning and Alternative Dispute Resolution," 37 *Rutgers L. Rev.* 253 (1985).

85. Fed. R. Civ. P. 26(a)(1)(C), 26(d)(1).

86. *See* Chapter 3, Section II, *supra* p. 58.

party may not seek discovery from any source before the parties have conferred as required by Rule 26(f), except in a proceeding exempted from initial disclosure under Rule 26(a)(1)(B), or when authorized by [the Federal Rules], by stipulation, or by court order." It also is quite likely that a Rule 16(b) scheduling order will restrict the sequence and timing of discovery. However, in some cases a scheduling order or discovery order may not control the sequence of discovery. Even when a court order will control the discovery sequence, counsel must make a strategic decision as to the best discovery sequence for her client. Rule 26(d)(2) provides that "[u]nless * * * the court orders otherwise * * * (A) methods of discovery may be used in any sequence; and (B) discovery by one party does not require any other party to delay its discovery."

Many attorneys begin formal discovery by serving interrogatories and document requests, then depose the key witnesses, and finally serve admission requests after all other discovery has been completed. The advantage of such a progression is that the information obtained in each stage of discovery can be used as a basis for the next stage. For example, interrogatory answers and documents produced in discovery can be very helpful in planning depositions. The disadvantage of this form of discovery plan is that opposing counsel and third-parties may learn very early in a case where the discovery is headed. In some cases it may make sense to immediately depose a key witness, before he has figured out the likely questions that he will be asked at his deposition.

Finally, no discovery plan is complete without a consideration of informal discovery. Informal discovery usually is much less expensive than the formal discovery contemplated by the Federal Rules of Civil Procedure. Informal discovery also may be faster than formal discovery and, sometimes, can be conducted without alerting opposing counsel to your discovery efforts.

Exercises Concerning Discovery Planning

1. You represent Mr. Thomas Eakins, who was introduced in exercise 1 of the Exercises Concerning Client Interviewing in Chapter 2, *supra* p. 38. Based upon the facts contained in that interview exercise and any additional information that you have obtained about Eakins or the Buffalo Creek disaster since reading that exercise, prepare a memorandum setting forth a discovery plan that you will pursue on behalf of Mr. Eakins.

For the purposes of your memorandum, presume that the Eakins complaint has been drafted and is ready to be filed in federal court. Consider the following matters in your memorandum:

(a) The sequence in which the specific discovery devices provided in Rules 27 through 36 of the Federal Rules of Civil Procedure should be utilized;

(b) The likely responses from defense counsel to your discovery initiatives;

(c) A time schedule for completion of the discovery that you anticipate will occur in the case;

(d) The cost of undertaking discovery in the manner that you propose;

(e) The litigation advantages that should be gained by the discovery plan that you propose; and

(f) The information necessary to your case that can best be gained by informal, rather than formal, discovery.

2. You represent the plaintiffs in the major lawsuit brought by attorney Gerald Stern on behalf of victims of the Buffalo Creek disaster against the Pittston Company in the United States District Court for the Southern District of West Virginia. Prepare a memorandum setting forth the manner in which you would obtain the following information:

(a) The recollections of a disgruntled former dam safety employee of Pittston, whose whereabouts you have reason to believe are unknown to Pittston;

(b) Routine business records of the Buffalo Mining Company;

(c) Routine business records of the Pittston Company;

(d) Information from Pittston executives concerning the failure of the Buffalo Creek dam;

(e) Information from executives of the Buffalo Mining Company concerning the failure of the Buffalo Creek dam;

(f) Various documents filed by both the Pittston Company and Buffalo Mining Company with state and federal mining authorities;

(g) Information concerning the insurance coverage of both the Pittston Company and Buffalo Mining Company;

(h) Documents showing the internal corporate organization of the Pittston Company and Buffalo Mining Company;

(i) Information concerning whether Pittston and Buffalo Mining officials responsible for dam safety have received any training in that area; and

(j) Older personnel records of the Buffalo Mining Company that you have reason to believe will soon be routinely destroyed by that company.

3. You represent the Pittston Company in the federal lawsuit that has been filed against it by several hundred victims of the Buffalo Creek disaster. Presume that this lawsuit has just been filed.

(a) Write a memorandum setting forth the strategy that you will pursue in connection with the Rule 26(f) discovery conference; and

(b) Draft a proposed Rule 26(f) discovery plan that you would like the parties to submit to the court after their discovery conference.

4. You represent the estate of Norman Hickman, who lost his life when the tugboat "J. M. Taylor" sank on February 7, 1943. Based on the facts set forth in *Hickman v. Taylor,* 329 U.S. 495 (1947), *supra* p. 273:

(a) Draft a Rule 26(f) discovery plan on behalf of plaintiff;

(b) Draft a Rule 26(f) discovery plan on behalf of the defendant tugboat owners.

VII. THE DUTY TO SUPPLEMENT DISCOVERY DISCLOSURES AND RESPONSES

Rule 26(e) of the Federal Rules of Civil Procedure requires the supplementation of Rule 26(a) disclosures; responses to interrogatories, requests for production, and requests for admissions; and required expert witness reports. A party is required to supplement or correct these disclosure and discovery responses to include information acquired after the disclosure or discovery response was made if the court so orders or "if the party learns that in some material respect the disclosure or response is incomplete or incorrect, and if the additional or corrective information has not otherwise been made known to the other parties during the discovery process or in writing."[87] While Rule 26(e) imposes a duty of supplementation upon a "party," this duty is triggered regardless of whether it is the party or counsel who learns that a disclosure or discovery response is materially incomplete or incorrect.[88]

As with the duty to supplement initial disclosures, there is no duty to supplement a discovery response unless it is *materially* incomplete or incorrect, and no duty of supplementation exists if the information otherwise has been provided during discovery or in a writing apart from the formal discovery process. While typically supplementation is provided in writing, such supplementation may occur in the discovery process itself, if, for instance, during a deposition a witness not formerly disclosed is identified or an expert corrects information in an earlier report.[89] However, supplementation apart from the formal discovery process must be made in writing.[90] Thus a duty to supplement under Rule 26(e) cannot be satisfied by a phone call to opposing counsel. Putting supplementations in writing also will make a record that will prevent any confusion as to whether a disclosure or response has been supplemented and, if so, the contents of that supplementation. This can be quite important, because

---

87. Fed. R. Civ. P. 26(e)(1). Rule 26(e)(2) further defines the duty to supplement Rule 26(a)(2)(B) expert witness disclosures, providing that this specific duty "extends both to information contained in the [expert's] report and to information given during the expert's deposition."

However, unless a deponent is an expert whose testimony must be supplemented pursuant to Rule 26(e)(2), deposition testimony ordinarily need not be supplemented pursuant to Rule 26(e). Advisory Committee Note to 1993 Amendment to Rule 26(e), 146 F.R.D. 401, 641 (1993).

88. Advisory Committee Note to 1993 Amendment to Rule 26(e), 146 F.R.D. 401, 641 (1993).

89. *Id.*

90. Fed. R. Civ. P. 26(e)(1)(A).

Rule 37(c)(1) provides that, unless the failure to supplement is harmless or was substantially justified, the offending party can be prohibited from using in the pretrial or trial process any witness or information not disclosed.

Whether or not there is a duty to supplement disclosures or discovery responses depends upon the facts of each particular case. A duty to supplement was found to exist under the pre–1993 version of Rule 26(e) in *Scott and Fetzer Co. v. Dile.*[91] The United States Court of Appeals for the Ninth Circuit held that the district court had abused its discretion by permitting plaintiff to offer at a preliminary injunction hearing the testimony of 20 witnesses, including an expert witness, who had not been identified in response to interrogatories. Plaintiff had not listed 26 of its 51 exhibits in its interrogatory answers and used its undisclosed witnesses and exhibits to introduce a new theory of the case. Because of these violations of Rule 26(e), the court of appeals reversed the district court's grant of plaintiff's motion for a preliminary injunction.

In contrast to *Scott and Fetzer*, the United States Court of Appeals for the Sixth Circuit refused to grant a new trial due to an alleged violation of Rule 26(e) in *Lewis Refrigeration Co. v. Sawyer Fruit, Vegetable and Cold Storage Co.*[92] The court of appeals concluded that (1) not only was the challenged trial testimony not materially different from the deposition testimony that had not been supplemented, but (2) plaintiff was not significantly prejudiced by the trial testimony and could have cured any prejudice actually suffered by seeking a continuance in the trial court.

Attorneys engaged in civil discovery must be familiar with Rule 26(g), as well as Rule 26(e), of the Federal Rules of Civil Procedure. Rule 26(g)(1)(A) provides that an attorney's signature on a Rule 26(a)(1) or (a)(3) disclosure constitutes a certification that the disclosure is "complete and correct at the time it is made," while Rule 26(g)(1)(B)(i) provides that an attorney's signature on a discovery request, response, or objection certifies that the discovery document is "consistent with these rules and warranted by existing law or by a nonfrivolous argument for extending, modifying, or reversing existing law, or for establishing new law." The requirements imposed by Rule 26(g) upon discovery papers parallel the requirements imposed upon pleadings, motions, and other papers by Rule 11.

Apart from Rule 26(e) and (g), Model Rule 3.3(a) of the Model Rules of Professional Conduct addresses the situation in which an attorney learns that her client has materially misled a party or the court by offering false evidence. Model Rule 3.3(a) provides:

A lawyer shall not knowingly:

* * *

---

91.   643 F.2d 670 (9th Cir. 1981).

92.   709 F.2d 427 (6th Cir. 1983).

(3) offer evidence that the lawyer knows to be false. If a lawyer, the lawyer's client, or a witness called by the lawyer has offered material evidence and the lawyer comes to know of its falsity, the lawyer shall take reasonable remedial measures, including, if necessary, disclosure to the tribunal. * * *

Attorneys must be familiar with the requirements of both the Federal Rules of Civil Procedure and governing ethical standards to competently and professionally engage in civil litigation.

Exercise Concerning Supplementation of Discovery

In the course of discovery in the Buffalo Creek litigation, plaintiffs have served upon the defendant Pittston Company an interrogatory seeking information concerning all accidents at earthen dams similar to the one that failed on February 26, 1972. Four specific incidents were described in the answer to plaintiffs' interrogatory.

You are an attorney for the Pittston Company and now have learned that there actually was a fifth dam that collapsed in the 1950s that was not mentioned in Pittston's interrogatory answer. Moreover, after the filing of Pittston's interrogatory answer, there was a minor accident at another Pittston dam. Due to the circumstances concerning these two dam incidents, it is likely that plaintiffs will never learn of either of the situations.

(a) Write a letter to Pittston's general counsel concerning whether Pittston must supplement its interrogatory answer or otherwise reveal these two incidents to plaintiffs.

(b) As bar disciplinary counsel, write a letter concerning the duties of counsel in this situation with respect to (1) the client Pittston; (2) the opposing parties and counsel; and (3) the court.

VIII. CONCLUSION

Rule 26 of the Federal Rules of Civil Procedure establishes the general scope and limitations of civil discovery. Regardless of the specific discovery device employed by a party, whether interrogatories, depositions, or admission or production requests, Rule 26 governs the underlying information that can be sought. Now that the general scope of discovery has been examined, the following chapters consider the specific discovery devices that can be employed to obtain information falling within Rule 26.

IX. CHAPTER BIBLIOGRAPHY

American Bar Association, *Civil Discovery Standards* (2004).

The Attorney–Client Privilege in Civil Litigation (V. Walkowiak ed. 2008).

Beckerman, "Confronting Civil Discovery's Fatal Flaws," 84 *Minn. L. Rev.* 505 (2000).

Bell et al., "Automatic Disclosure in Discovery—The Rush to Reform," 27 *Ga. L. Rev.* 1 (1992).

T. Blumoff et al., *Pretrial Discovery: The Development of Professional Judgment* (1993).

Brazil, "The Adversary Character of Civil Discovery: A Critique and Proposals for Change," 31 *Vand. L. Rev.* 1295 (1978).

Brazil, "Civil Discovery: Lawyers' Views of Its Effectiveness, Its Principal Problems and Abuses," 1980 *Am. B. Found. Res. J.* 787.

Brazil, "Views from the Front Lines: Observations by Chicago Lawyers About the System of Civil Discovery," 1980 *Am. B. Found. Res. J.* 219.

Brazil, "Civil Discovery: How Bad Are the Problems?," 67 *A.B.A.J.* 450 (1981).

Cohn, "The Work–Product Doctrine: Protection, Not Privilege," 71 *Geo. L. J.* 917 (1983).

P. Connolly et al., *Judicial Controls and the Civil Litigative Process: Discovery* (1978).

"Developments in the Law—Privileged Communications," 98 *Harv. L. Rev.* 1450 (1985).

M. Dombroff, *Discovery* (1986).

S. Easton, *Attacking Adverse Experts* (2008).

E. Epstein, *The Attorney–Client Privilege and the Work–Product Doctrine* (5th ed. 2007).

Fox, "Planning and Conducting a Discovery Program," *Litigation,* Summer 1981, at 13.

J. Gergacz, *Attorney–Corporate Client Privilege* (3d ed. 2009).

P. Grimm et al., *Discovery Problems and their Solutions* (2005).

R. Haydock & D. Herr, *Discovery Practice* (5th ed. 2009).

Hench, "Mandatory Disclosure and Equal Access to Justice: The 1993 Federal Discovery Rules Amendments and the Just, Speedy and Inexpensive Determination of Every Action," 67 *Temple L. Rev.* 179 (1994).

E. Imwinkelried & T. Blumoff, *Pretrial Discovery: Strategy & Tactics* (rev. ed. 2010).

Ingebretsen, "Crafting a Discovery Plan," *Litigation,* Summer 2007, at 26.

Issacharoff & Loewenstein, "Unintended Consequences of Mandatory Disclosure," 73 *Tex. L. Rev.*753 (1995).

Johnson, "A Practitioner's Overview of Digital Discovery," 33 *Gonz. L. Rev.* 347 (1997/98).

Kakalik et al., *Discovery Management: Further Analysis of the Civil Justice Reform Act Evaluation Data* (1998).

Keilitz et al., "Is Civil Discovery in State Trial Courts out of Control?," *St. Ct. J.*, Spring 1993, at 8.

C. Kuhne, *A Litigator's Guide to Expert Witnesses* (2006).

Lanctot, "Attorney–Client Relationships in Cyberspace: The Peril and the Promise," 49 *Duke L. J.* 147 (1999).

E. Lee & T. Willging, *Federal Judicial Center National, Case–Based Civil Rules Survey: Preliminary Report to the Judicial Conference Advisory Committee on Civil Rules* (2009).

E. Lee & T. Willging, *Litigation Costs in Civil Cases: Multivariate Analysis: Report to the Judicial Conference Advisory Committee on Civil Rules* (2010).

D. Malone & P. Zwier, *Effective Expert Testimony* (2d ed. 2006).

Manual for Complex Litigation, Fourth (2004).

McElhaney, "The Discovery Plan," *A.B.A.J.*, Dec. 1989, at 76.

Moot, "Consider Doing No Discovery," *Litigation,* Fall 1988, at 36.

Mullenix, "Adversarial Justice, Professional Responsibility, and the New Federal Discovery Rules," 14 *Rev. Litig.* 13 (1994).

Napolitano, "Showing Your Cards: Litigating in a Mandatory Disclosure Jurisdiction," *Litigation*, Winter 1994, at 26.

P. Rice, *Attorney–Client Privilege in the United States* (2d ed. 1999).

Schwarzer, "The Federal Rules, the Adversary Process, and Discovery Reform," 50 *U. Pitt. L. Rev.* 703 (1989).

Schwarzer, "In Defense of 'Automatic Disclosure in Discovery,' " 27 *Ga. L. Rev.* 655 (1993).

W. Schwarzer et al., *Civil Discovery and Mandatory Disclosure* (2d ed. 1994).

Shapiro, "Some Problems of Discovery in an Adversary System," 63 *Minn. L. Rev.* 1055 (1979).

Shaughnessy, "Dirty Little Secrets of Expert Testimony," *Litigation*, Winter 2007, at 47.

Shepard's/McGraw Hill, *Discovery Proceedings in Federal Court* (3d ed. 1995).

R. Simpson, *Civil Discovery and Depositions* (2d ed. 1994).

Slomanson, "Supplementation of Discovery Responses in Federal Civil Procedure," 17 *San Diego L. Rev.* 233 (1980).

Sorenson, "Disclosure Under Federal Rule of Civil Procedure 26(a)— 'Much Ado About Nothing?'," 46 *Hastings L. J.* 679 (1995).

Special Project, "The Work Product Doctrine," 68 *Cornell L. Rev.* 760 (1983).

Symposium, "2010 Civil Litigation Review Conference," 60 *Duke L. J.* 537 (2010).

Symposium, "Conference on Discovery Rules," 39 *B.C. L. Rev.* 517 (1998).

Symposium, "Recent Changes in the Rules of Pretrial Fact Development: What Do They Disclose About Litigation and the Legal Profession?," 46 *Fla. L. Rev.* 1 (1994).

Symposium, "Reinventing Civil Litigation: Evaluating Proposals for Change," 59 *Brook. L. Rev.* 655 (1993).

Symposium, "The Civil Justice Reform Act," 67 *St. John's L. Rev.* 705 (1993).

Thornburg, "Rethinking Work Product," 77 *Va. L. Rev.* 1515 (1991).

Thornburg, "Sanctifying Secrecy: The Mythology of the Corporate Attorney–Client Privilege," 69 *Notre Dame L. Rev.* 157 (1993).

Waits, "Opinion Work Product: A Critical Analysis of Current Law and a New Analytical Framework," 73 *Or. L. Rev.* 385 (1994).

T. Willging et al., *Discovery and Disclosure Practice, Problems and Proposals for Change* (1997).

Winter, "In Defense of Discovery Reform," 58 *Brook. L. Rev.* 263 (1992).

Wolfson, "Opinion Work Product—Solving the Dilemma of Compelled Disclosure," 64 *Neb. L. Rev.* 248 (1985).

CHAPTER 7

INTERROGATORIES:
"ASK ME A QUESTION, ANY QUESTION."

■ ■ ■

The set of interrogatories is two inches high, 381 pages long, and contains a total of 2,736 questions and subparts.

* * * A conservative estimate of the total costs of answering is $24,000.

In re U.S. Financial Securities Litigation, 74 F.R.D. 497, 497–98 (S.D.Cal. 1975) (*sua sponte* striking defendants' interrogatories).

Responding to interrogatories is like growing mushrooms: you keep them in the dark and feed them garbage.

Anon.

Analysis

I. INTRODUCTION

Having considered the duty of disclosure and general scope of discovery under Rule 26, the specific discovery devices provided by the Federal Rules of Civil Procedure now will be examined. Although any of these discovery devices could have been examined first, there are several reasons why it makes sense to consider interrogatories before the other devices. First of all, interrogatories are among the most frequently used of all

310

discovery devices.[1] In addition, interrogatories are probably the easiest, and least expensive, discovery device to utilize. A set of interrogatories can be produced by an attorney in her office very quickly. Because they can be so easily drafted, interrogatories have been abused in practice. Finally, although there is no one "right" order in which to conduct discovery, many lawyers seek interrogatory answers before utilizing other discovery devices.

II. THE RULE 33 INTERROGATORY

To effectively utilize interrogatories, attorneys must understand both when they can be used and when they should be used. These are the two subjects of this section.

A. THE GOVERNING LAW

An interrogatory is a question, and legal interrogatories resemble the questions by which we conduct "discovery" in our daily lives. The requirements for interrogatories are set forth in Rule 33 of the Federal Rules of Civil Procedure.

Rule 33 interrogatories are written questions that only can be promulgated *by* a party to a civil action *to* another party to that same action. If information is needed from a non-party, informal discovery or discovery devices such as Rule 45 subpoenas must be employed. Absent leave of court or written stipulation, interrogatories may not be served before the parties have met and conferred at their Rule 26(f) discovery conference.[2] Interrogatories therefore are treated like depositions and production and admission requests, which typically cannot be employed until after Rule 26(a)(1) initial disclosures and a discovery plan have been discussed by the parties.

---

1. One study sponsored by the Federal Judicial Center found that approximately 35% of the discovery requests filed in a sample of over 3000 federal cases from the mid–1970s consisted of interrogatories. P. Connolly et al., *Judicial Controls and the Civil Litigative Process: Discovery* 30 (Figure 1) (1978). *See also* Glaser, *Pretrial Discovery and the Adversary System* 53 (1968) (interrogatories used in 30% of 3000 cases studied). A Federal Judicial Center study of closed federal cases in the 1990s found that, in the cases in which discovery occurred, interrogatories were employed in 81% of the cases, Willging, et al., "An Empirical Study of Discovery and Disclosure Practice Under the 1993 Federal Rules Amendments," 39 *B.C. L. Rev.* 525, 530 (1998), while a study of civil cases closed in 2008 found that interrogatory filings were reported by 73.5% of plaintiff's lawyers and 76.2% of defense attorneys. E. Lee & T. Willging, *Federal Judicial Center National, Case–Based Civil Rules Survey: Preliminary Report to the Judicial Conference Advisory Committee on Civil Rules* 9 (2009).

To say that interrogatories are an extremely popular discovery device is not to say that civil discovery cannot be accomplished without them. In fact, interrogatories are not generally available in the state courts of Oregon. Or. R. Civ. P. 36(A). Nor can attorneys bring actions predicated solely upon negligence in the New York state courts and, without leave of court, both depose and serve interrogatories upon the same party. N.Y.Civ.Prac. L. & R. § 3130(1) (McKinney 1991). *See also* Luria & Clabby, "An Expense Out of Control: Rule 33 Interrogatories After the Advent of Initial Disclosures and Two Proposals for Change," 9 *Chap. L. Rev.* 29, 43–48 (2005) (suggesting that interrogatories be eliminated, with information instead being provided by required disclosures and requests for admissions); Weller et al., "What Happened When Interrogatories Were Eliminated?," *Judges' J.*, Summer 1982, at 8.

2. Fed. R. Civ. P. 26(d)(1).

Once the Rule 26(f) conference has been held, a party may, without leave of court or written stipulation, serve upon any other party "no more than 25 written interrogatories, including all discrete subparts."[3] While there is a presumptive 25 interrogatory limit in Rule 33(a)(1), that Rule also provides: "Leave to serve additional interrogatories may be granted to the extent consistent with Rule 26(b)(2)."[4]

The party upon whom interrogatories are served can (1) answer the interrogatories, (2) object to the interrogatories, or (3) answer some interrogatories and object to others. Rule 33(b)(3) provides that each interrogatory "must, to the extent it is not objected to, be answered separately and fully in writing under oath," while Rule 33(b)(4) requires that the "grounds for objecting to an interrogatory must be stated with specificity." As with Rule 34 production requests and Rule 36 admission requests, a party generally has thirty days in which to file its answers or objections to interrogatories.[5]

What if a party objects to interrogatories or refuses to answer them? The party who has served the interrogatories may file a motion pursuant to Federal Rule of Civil Procedure 37 seeking either an order compelling interrogatory answers or, if his opponent has refused to respond to an entire set of interrogatories, appropriate sanctions against that party.[6]

Interrogatories can seek any information within the scope of discovery set forth in Federal Rule of Civil Procedure 26(b).[7] Depending upon their status under the Federal Rules of Evidence, interrogatory answers may be

---

3.   Fed. R. Civ. P. 33(a)(1).

Fine distinctions may be necessary in determining what is a "discrete subpart," and thus what counts toward the 25–interrogatory limit of Rule 33(a)(1). At least two tests have been proposed to guide this determination. *Kendall v. GES Exposition Services, Inc.*, 174 F.R.D. 684, 685 (D.Nev. 1997) ("Probably the best test of whether subsequent questions, within a single interrogatory, are subsumed and related [and therefore not "discrete subparts"], is to examine whether the first question is primary and subsequent questions are secondary to the primary question. Or, can the subsequent question stand alone?"); *Cardenas v. Dorel Juvenile Group, Inc.*, 231 F.R.D. 616, 620 (D.Kan. 2005) (If interrogatory subparts do not "discuss various, unrelated topics," but instead "elicit[ ] details concerning a *common theme*," those subparts count as a single interrogatory.).

Under Federal Rule of Civil Procedure 26(b)(2)(A), a district court "may alter the limits in [the Federal Rules] * * * on the number of * * * interrogatories." Thus some courts and commentators have suggested that in at least some multi-party cases a limit of 25 interrogatories per side, rather than per party, should be applied. Yoo, Comment, "Rule 33(a)'s Interrogatory Limitation: By Party or by Side?," 75 *U. Chi. L. Rev.* 911 (2008). *See Felman Production, Inc. v. Industrial Risk Insurers*, 2009 WL 3668038 (S.D.W.Va. 2009) (per-side interrogatory limit appropriate when all three defendants share corporate relationship, are parties to relevant contract, share counsel, and interests align in case).

4.   Rule 5(d)(1) of the Federal Rules of Civil Procedure provides:

Any paper after the complaint that is required to be served—together with a certificate of service—must be filed within a reasonable time after service. But disclosures under Rule 26(a)(1) or (2) and the following discovery requests and responses must not be filed until they are used in the proceeding or the court orders filing: depositions, interrogatories, requests for documents or tangible things or to permit entry upon land, and requests for admissions.

5.   Fed. R. Civ. P. 33(b)(2). However, Rule 33(b)(2) also provides: "A shorter or longer time may be stipulated to under Rule 29 or be ordered by the court."

6.   Fed. R. Civ. P. 37(a)(3)(B)(iii), (d)(1)(A)(ii). *See* Chapter 10, *infra*.

7.   Fed. R. Civ. P. 33(a)(2).

introduced as evidence at trial.[8] For instance, a specific answer might be admissible as a prior statement of a witness or an admission by a party-opponent pursuant to Federal Rule of Evidence 801(d)(1) and (2). However, Rule 26(b)(1) provides: "Relevant information need not be admissible at the trial if the discovery appears reasonably calculated to lead to the discovery of admissible evidence."

Federal Rule of Civil Procedure 33(a)(2) explicitly provides that interrogatories can do more than seek strictly factual data from another party: "An interrogatory is not objectionable merely because it asks for an opinion or contention that relates to fact or the application of law to fact * * * ." "Contention interrogatories" therefore can be used to focus the pretrial proceedings upon the matters actually in dispute between the parties.[9]

To merely obtain information in a tort action, the plaintiff might ask the following interrogatory: "At what point did the defendant see plaintiff's car approaching?" However, the following contention interrogatory might be more useful in narrowing the parties' legal dispute: "Does the defendant contend that the plaintiff was contributorily negligent because he did not blow his horn before entering the intersection?" Contention interrogatories also can be used to determine the factual bases for a party's legal claims: "Upon what specific facts does defendant rely in contending that the plaintiff was contributorily negligent?" Some attorneys use interrogatories that track each of the paragraphs of an opposing party's pleading: "What is the factual basis for plaintiff's allegation in paragraph ___ of the complaint that [a certain fact occurred]?" With a 25 interrogatory limit, though, interrogatories generally should be targeted on the most important portions of opposing claims or defenses.

Because a party's legal and factual theories, and thus opinions and contentions, often change during the pretrial period, Federal Rule of Civil Procedure 33(a)(2) provides that "the court may order that [contention interrogatories] need not be answered until designated discovery is complete, or until a pretrial conference or some other time." In addition, the 1970 Advisory Committee Notes to Rule 33(b) make it clear that contention interrogatories "may not extend to issues of 'pure law.' "[10]

B. STRATEGIC CONSIDERATIONS

To say that Rule 33 permits interrogatories to be served upon other parties does not mean that interrogatories routinely should be employed in all cases. Even more significantly, Rule 33 gives no indication of the types of discovery that can be obtained most effectively by interrogatories or how interrogatories should be used as part of a comprehensive discovery plan.

---

8. Fed. R. Civ. P. 33(c).

9. *See generally* Johnston & Johnston, "Contention Interrogatories in Federal Court," 148 F.R.D. 441 (1993).

10. 48 F.R.D. 487, 524 (1970).

Interrogatories can be an effective and inexpensive way to obtain background information from an opposing party and lay the groundwork for other discovery devices. Early sets of interrogatories can be used to discover the organizational structure of a party-opponent, dates of meetings and conversations, and, to the extent not known from Rule 26(a)(1)(A) disclosures, people with knowledge of relevant matters. Because interrogatory answers from a corporation, partnership, association, or governmental agency are to provide the collective knowledge of the party,[11] certain information may be gained more efficiently by interrogatories than by depositions directed to individual corporate officials.

After obtaining interrogatory answers, a party should be better able to conduct further formal and informal discovery. Interrogatories seeking the identification of third-parties should request that the telephone numbers and other contact information for these individuals be supplied. The persons listed then can be contacted for interviews or, if appropriate, may be deposed.

Once the organizational structure of a business or agency has been described in interrogatory answers, an attorney may have a much better sense of which individuals within the organization might profitably be deposed. Another way to learn of those within the organization with relevant knowledge is to end a set of interrogatories with an interrogatory seeking basic background information concerning (1) the person who was assigned to answer interrogatories on behalf of the organization, (2) all those who were consulted in preparing the organization's answers, and (3) all documents relied upon in formulating interrogatory answers.

If this information has not been supplied in a Rule 26(a)(1)(B) initial disclosure, interrogatories can be an effective way of discovering the existence of documents that then can be requested pursuant to Rule 34 of the Federal Rules of Civil Procedure. Some attorneys serve interrogatories and document requests simultaneously, asking in the Rule 34 request for the production of "any documents described in answer to Interrogatories ___, ___, and ___."

While the main virtue of interrogatories is that they are extremely inexpensive, there are major disadvantages to interrogatories. Interrogatories only can be directed to parties, and a party's attorney presumably will review interrogatory answers before they are served. Interrogatory answers therefore can differ dramatically from the answers given spontaneously by a party during an oral deposition. In addition, Rule 33(b)(2) gives parties thirty days to respond to interrogatories, while deposition testimony often can be obtained much sooner.

Another major disadvantage of interrogatories is that, because an entire set of interrogatories is prepared at one time, there is no opportunity for immediate follow-up questioning as there is at a deposition. Counsel

---

11. Fed. R. Civ. P. 33(b)(1)(B); *Shepherd v. American Broadcasting Cos.*, 62 F.3d 1469, 1482 (D.C.Cir. 1995); *General Dynamics Corp. v. Selb Mfg. Co.*, 481 F.2d 1204, 1210–11 (8th Cir. 1973); *Weddington v. Consolidated Rail Corp.*, 101 F.R.D. 71, 74 (N.D.Ind. 1984).

must draft interrogatories based upon the anticipated responses of the answering party. In order to cover different potential answers, interrogatories often must be drafted in a manner similar to this: "If your answer to Interrogatory ___ is 'yes,' please state the following: * * * ." In order to stay within the interrogatory limitations of Rule 33(a)(1), such a sequence of interrogatories might be combined into a single interrogatory asking: "If [a certain matter is true], please state the following: * * * ."

While important information can be gleaned from an opposing party through the use of carefully crafted interrogatories, an opposing party may learn things about your case through the interrogatories that you have asked. Indeed, an opposing counsel who has not thoroughly investigated her own case could be directed to entirely new areas of research and inquiry by well-prepared interrogatories. Attorneys also should be aware that interrogatories may alert opposing counsel to the topics that will be pursued in later depositions, and thereby permit the "scripting" of responses in advance of deposition questioning.

By themselves, interrogatories cannot provide the total discovery necessary in most cases. However, in virtually every case they can provide at least some helpful information at a modest cost. Attorneys should plan to use interrogatories carefully as one part of an overall discovery plan.

NOTES AND QUESTIONS CONCERNING INTERROGATORIES

1. Parker brings a civil action against both Dempsey and Dooper. Can Dempsey serve interrogatories upon Parker? When? Can Dempsey serve interrogatories upon Dooper? When?

2. Is there any aspect of Rule 33 interrogatories that might influence plaintiff's counsel concerning those persons named as defendants in an action? Can an attorney name a person as a defendant merely so that interrogatories (and Rule 34 production requests and Rule 36 admission requests) can be directed to that person? Should the possible availability of interrogatories and other discovery be a consideration in a "close case" as to whether to name a person as a defendant? Consider the requirements of Rule 11 of the Federal Rules of Civil Procedure. *See also* Model Rules of Prof'l Conduct Rule 3.1.

3. Why can't contention interrogatories be addressed to matters of "pure law?" In that connection, consider an interrogatory seeking a listing of (1) "all cases in this jurisdiction that support your contention that the plaintiff was contributorily negligent" and (2) "all cases in this jurisdiction that are contrary to your contention that plaintiff was contributorily negligent."

III. THE USE, AND ABUSE,
OF INTERROGATORIES
IN PRACTICE

The following case concerns the use of contention interrogatories and illustrates the manner in which interrogatories may be abused in practice.

Might the case have been handled differently today, after the 1993 and 2000 amendments to Rules 26 and 33 presumptively limited parties to 25 interrogatories and narrowed the Rule 26(b)(1) scope of discovery? Would a Rule 26(f) pretrial party conference have prevented some of these disputes?

IN RE CONVERGENT TECHNOLOGIES SECURITIES LITIGATION

United States District Court, Northern District of California, 1985.
108 F.R.D. 328.

Order

WAYNE D. BRAZIL, UNITED STATES MAGISTRATE.

The principal issue in this discovery dispute can be simply framed: *when* (at which juncture in the pretrial period) should plaintiffs answer "contention" interrogatories served by defendants. The parties do *not* disagree about *whether* the questions should be answered. The sole question is when.

Counsel already have spent upwards of *$40,000* of their clients' money on this *one discovery dispute.* That fact strikes this court as strong evidence that there has been in this case a major breakdown in what is supposed to be the self-executing system of pretrial discovery. The spirit of Rule 26, as amended in 1983, has been violated. So has the spirit of Rule 1, which declares that the purpose of the Federal Rules of Civil Procedure is "to secure the just, speedy, and inexpensive determination of every action[.]" The discovery system depends absolutely on good faith and common sense from counsel. The courts, sorely pressed by demands to try cases promptly and to rule thoughtfully on potentially case dispositive motions, simply do not have the resources to police closely the operation of the discovery process. The whole system of Civil adjudication would be ground to a virtual halt if the courts were forced to intervene in even a modest percentage of discovery transactions. That fact should impose on counsel an acute sense of responsibility about how they handle discovery matters. They should strive to be cooperative, practical and sensible, and should turn to the courts (or take positions that force others to turn to the courts) only in extraordinary situations that implicate truly significant interests.

These are not simply the sentiments of an idealistic and frustrated magistrate. They are the law. They were clearly made so by the 1983 amendments to Rule 26. Those amendments formally interred any argument that discovery should be a free form exercise conducted in a free for all spirit. Discovery is not now and never was free. Discovery is expensive. The drafters of the 1983 amendments to sections (b) and (g) of Rule 26 formally recognized that fact by superimposing the concept of proportionality on all behavior in the discovery arena. It is no longer sufficient, as a precondition for conducting discovery, to show that the information sought "appears reasonably calculated to lead to the discovery of admissible evidence." After satisfying this threshold requirement counsel *also must* make a common sense determination, taking into account all the circumstances, that the information sought is of sufficient potential significance to justify the burden the discovery probe would impose, that the discovery tool selected is the most efficacious of the means that might be used to acquire the desired information (taking into account cost effectiveness and the nature of the information being sought), and that the timing of the probe is sensible, i.e., that there is no other juncture in the pretrial period when there would be a clearly happier balance between the benefit derived from and the burdens imposed by the particular discovery effort.

This articulation of the responsibilities counsel must assume in conducting or responding to discovery may make it appear that the 1983 amendments require counsel to conduct complex analyses each time they take action in the discovery arena. Not so. What the 1983 amendments require is, at heart, very simple: good faith and common sense. Counsel can satisfy these requirements by *not* using or responding to discovery for some ulterior purpose and by exercising straight forward judgment. The questions are simply stated: 1) what information am I really likely to need and 2) what is the most cost effective way to get it. Tailoring probes and responses to the real issues in the case at hand, rather than relying on stock questions or knee jerk objections and evasive responses, is all that is required.

The problem, one senses, is *not* that the requirements the law imposes are too subtle. Rather, the problem is more likely to be that counsel are less interested in satisfying the law's requirements than in seeking tactical advantages. At least in cases involving big economic stakes, good faith and common sense hardly seem to be the dominant forces. Instead, it appears that the root evil in complex civil litigation continues to be the pervasiveness of gaming. Civil litigation is too often civil only on the surface. Underneath, it is obsession with pursuit of procedural or psychological edge. In adopting the 1983 amendments, the rulemakers have unequivocally condemned that obsession.

The fact that counsel have spent so much money on this one discovery dispute raises troubling questions in this court's mind that reach beyond the confines of this particular litigation. In little more than a year this court has been forced to intervene in discovery disputes in many cases involving big economic stakes. I have emerged from my contacts with these matters with an uneasy sense that the discovery system in large commercial cases more than occasionally may be perverted into an arena for economic power plays, that parties use discovery tools (or cast their responses to discovery requests) not so much to learn what the facts are, but more to muscle one another into attitudes conducive to favorable settlements. While I do not have sufficient evidence to make a fair judgment about whether the discovery process has been so perverted in this case, my fear that discovery has been distorted by economic combat in this type of litigation compels me to make it absolutely clear that it is irresponsible, unethical, and unlawful to use discovery for the purpose of flexing economic muscle.

I. General Principles

Before considering specific interrogatories it is advisable to articulate some of the generalizations the court has considered *en route* to deciding matters presented by defendants' motions.

At the outset I point out that the phrase "contention interrogatory" is used imprecisely to refer to many different kinds of questions. Some people would classify as a contention interrogatory any question that asks another party to indicate *what* it contends. Some people would define contention interrogatories as embracing only questions that ask another party *whether* it makes some specified contention. Interrogatories of this kind typically would begin with the phrase "Do you contend that...." Another kind of question that some people put in the category "contention interrogatory" asks an opposing party to state all the *facts* on which it *bases* some specified contention. Yet another form of this category of interrogatory asks an opponent to state all the *evidence* on which it *bases* some specified contention. Some contention interrogatories ask the responding party to take a position, and then to explain or defend that position, with respect to *how the law applies to facts*. A variation on this theme involves interrogatories that ask parties to spell out the *legal basis* for, or theory behind, some specified contention.

     * * *

Despite assertions to the contrary by defendants, no party has an absolute right to have answers to contention interrogatories, or to any kind of interrogatory. Rule 33(b) [now, Rule 33(a)(2)], which declares that an interrogatory is "not necessarily objectionable merely because an answer ... involves an opinion or contention that relates to fact or the application of law to fact" confers no such absolute right. The sentence of [the Rule] that includes the quoted passage makes it clear that it applies only to interrogatories that are "otherwise proper." After 1983, a court can determine whether any given interrogatory is "otherwise proper" only after considering, among other things, whether it is interposed for any improper purpose, and whether it is "unreasonable or unduly burdensome or expensive, given the needs of the case, the discovery already had in the case, the amount in controversy, and the importance of the issues at stake in the litigation." * * *

[Rule 33(a)(2)] and the Advisory Committee Notes accompanying the 1970 amendments thereto clearly confer on the courts considerable discretion in deciding when (if ever) a party must answer contention interrogatories. After declaring that an otherwise proper interrogatory is not *necessarily* objectionable merely because it calls for an opinion or contention, the Rule immediately adds: "but the court may order that such an interrogatory need not be answered until after designated discovery has been completed or until a pretrial conference or other later time." Commenting on this passage, the Advisory Committee notes that "Since interrogatories involving mixed questions of law and fact may create disputes between the parties which are best resolved after much or all of the other discovery has been completed, the court is expressly authorized to defer an answer." * * *

* * *

Plaintiffs in this case argue vigorously that they should not be compelled to answer any of defendants' contention interrogatories until after defendants have substantially completed the document production the plaintiffs requested earlier in the pretrial period. * * * Plaintiffs also argue that defendants have full access to information about their own behavior, and, since it is that behavior that gives rise to the plaintiffs' claims, defendants cannot be prejudiced by having to wait until completion of some discovery before having plaintiffs systematically describe the conduct of the defendants that plaintiffs contend offends legal norms. In short, plaintiffs argue that because defendants know what their own behavior was and what the law requires, they have no real need for early answers to their contention interrogatories. Proceeding from that premise, plaintiffs go on to argue that the real purpose of the defendants interrogatories, which numbered more than 1,000 questions (counting subparts separately) as originally submitted, was to harass and pressure plaintiffs' counsel.

* * *

Plaintiffs also cite discussion of problems associated with interrogatories in the *Revised Report of the Special Committee On Effective Discovery in Civil Cases for the Eastern District of New York to the Honorable Jack B. Weinstein, Chief Judge.* According to the lawyers and law professors who drafted the *Revised Report,* "substantive interrogatories ... often lead to objections or self-serving responses which do not advance the discovery process and which can derail the lawsuit by generating time-consuming discovery litigation. Additionally, the same or similar questions are frequently repeated at later depositions. Contention interrogatories are too often used at the outset of a litigation to harass the opposition knowing that the responses at that stage will produce little useful information." The *Revised Report* goes on to suggest that "substantive or contention interrogatories [as distinguished from "identification interrogatories"] are better used, if at all, near the completion of discovery and after utilization of other discovery devices." Finally, plaintiffs point to the recently revised passages of the *Manual for Complex Litigation, II,* which clearly indicate that courts should be cautious in permitting the use of contention interrogatories in complex civil cases and which suggest that this discovery tool often may not be the most effective device for clarifying and narrowing issues (the *Manual* suggests that early pretrial conferences, stipulation procedures, and motions, e.g., for partial summary judgment, often accomplish the end of narrowing issues more effectively than contention interrogatories, especially in light of the limitations on the evidentiary use of interrogatory answers in multi-party cases).

   * * *

Defendants in this case argue that there are several different ways in which compelling parties to answer contention interrogatories early in the case development period might contribute to the efficiency of dispute resolution. First, defendants argue that by helping clarify what the issues in the case are, early answers to contention interrogatories can help parties improve the focus of their discovery and can equip courts to more reliably contain discovery excesses. * * *

Defendants further argue that in the process of crafting answers to contention interrogatories parties can be forced to systematically assess their positions earlier than they might if left to their own devices—and that such early systematic assessments might persuade parties to abandon tenuous causes of action, or to dismiss opponents as to whom proof problems seem very substantial. A systematic assessment also might persuade a litigant that the *cost* of developing the evidence to support a particular claim outweighs whatever benefits might be achieved by prevailing on it. Early answers to interrogatories seeking the factual or evidentiary bases for contentions also might serve as predicates for successful motions for summary judgment on part or all of a suit. * * *

Because the benefits that can flow from clarifying and narrowing the issues in litigation *early* in the pretrial period are potentially significant, and because it is possible that in some circumstances answers to some kinds of contention interrogatories might contribute meaningfully toward these objectives, it would be unwise to create a rigid rule, even if applicable to only certain categories of cases, that would always protect parties from having to answer contention interrogatories until some predetermined juncture in the pretrial period.

On the other hand, there is substantial reason to believe that the *early* knee jerk filing of sets of contention interrogatories that systematically track all the allegations in an opposing party's pleadings is a serious form of discovery abuse. Such comprehensive sets of contention interrogatories can be almost mindlessly generated, can be used to impose great burdens on opponents, and can generate a great deal of counterproductive friction between parties and counsel. Moreover, at least in cases where defendants presumably have access to most of the evidence about their own behavior, it is not at all clear that forcing plaintiffs to answer these kinds of questions, early in the pretrial period, is sufficiently likely to be productive to justify the burden that responding can entail.

This follows in part from the court's skepticism about the *quality* of the information that *early* responses to contention interrogatories are likely to contain. Counsel drafting responses to these kinds of interrogatories early in the pretrial period may fear being boxed into a position that later embarrasses them, or that might be used to try to limit the subject areas of their subsequent discovery. Lawyers generally attempt to maximize and preserve their options while providing as little tactical help to their opponents as possible; so motivated, they are likely to search for ways to give opponents as little information as they can get away with when they respond to contention interrogatories early in the pretrial period. The "substance" of their responses to such questions might reduce to phrases like "research and investigation continuing."

In assessing the *likelihood* that *early* answers to contention interrogatories will contribute materially to the efficiency of case development one also must consider the spirit in which courts respond *early* in the pretrial period to the kinds of motions that defendants here argue might be used to reduce the scope of the suit. Early in the case development process courts generally are reluctant to rule definitively in response to motions under Rules 12(b)(6), 12(c), or 56. Parties resisting such motions frequently can argue that it would be unfair to terminate their action without first giving them an opportunity to conduct at least some core discovery. They also can argue that pressing *early* in the pretrial period for answers to the kind of contention interrogatories that call for application of law to fact is inconsistent with the basic structure of the system for case development established by the Federal Rules of Civil Procedure. With the limited exception of matters covered in Rule 9, that system contemplates pleadings that are sufficient simply to put defendants on notice about the real world events that give rise to plaintiffs' claims. * * *

Given all of the above considerations, this court believes that the wisest course is not to preclude entirely the *early* use of contention interrogatories, but to place a burden of justification on a party who seeks answers to these kinds of questions before substantial documentary or testimonial discovery has been completed. * * *

    * * *

The court concludes that the following procedure is appropriate with respect to contention interrogatories filed before most other discovery has been completed. The propounding party must craft specific, limited (in number) questions. The responding party must examine such questions in good faith and, where it appears that answering them would materially contribute to any of the goals discussed in this opinion, must answer the interrogatories. If answering some, but not all, of the questions would materially contribute to any of the goals described above, the responding party must answer those questions. Where the responding party feels, in good faith, that providing early answers would not contribute enough to justify the effort involved, that party should telephone or write opposing counsel to explain the basis for his position. If opposing counsel continues to press for early answers, the responding party should enter objections in compliance with Local Rule 230–1 or seek permission from the Court to file an objection to the interrogatories as a group. Thereafter, the burden would fall on the propounding party to seek an order compelling answers. In seeking such an order, the propounding party would bear the burden of justification described above. To the extent, if any, that this procedure modifies the way burdens might be allocated with respect to other kinds of discovery disputes, this court believes that the problems associated with the early filing of contention interrogatories, discussed above, justify the different treatment.

[The magistrate then ordered that plaintiffs (1) answer interrogatories seeking the identity of witnesses with, and documents containing, information supporting or contradicting the allegations of the amended complaint (which now would be provided as Rule 26(a)(1) initial disclosures), (2) need not respond to interrogatories seeking to ascertain the scope of plaintiffs' factual investigation "until after the party seeking the Rule 11 discovery has shown, through traditional discovery, that there is more than a speculative basis for believing that its opponent may have violated the norms set forth in Rule 11," and (3) need not answer other interrogatories until sixty days after substantial completion of the document production by the defendant.]

NOTES AND QUESTIONS CONCERNING CONVERGENT TECHNOLOGIES

1. In 1993 Rule 33(a) was amended to limit parties to 25 interrogatories without leave of court or written stipulation. Magistrate Judge Wayne Brazil was a member of the Advisory Committee on Civil Rules that recommended this amendment. Might his frustration in cases such as *Convergent Technologies* have led to his support for such amendments? Continuing frustration with discovery costs and abuses led to the amendments to the Federal Rules of Civil Procedure in 2000, including the Rule 26(b)(1) restriction of the scope of discovery to nonprivileged matters relevant to any party's "claim or defense" and the additional sentence in Rule 26(b)(1) that now subjects all discovery "to the limitations imposed by Rule 26(b)(2)(c)."

2. It's cases such as this that cause corporate executives to complain about attorneys who are given unlimited litigation budgets and exceed them. In a footnote omitted from the preceding case report, Magistrate Judge Brazil observed:

> The 40,000 [dollars spent on this single discovery dispute] * * * does *not* include money counsel spent drafting, serving and initially objecting to the interrogatories themselves. The amount of money counsel have spent on this dispute is especially distressing in light of the fact that the briefs submitted do not substantially advance the analytical ball on the principal issue: i.e., *when* the interrogatories should be answered. None of the parties have spelled out, in anything like the detail that the court would find helpful, why it would promote interests served by the Federal Rules of Civil Procedure to have certain questions answered at one stage of the pretrial rather than at some other stage. The court was forced to press for answers to this pivotal question during oral argument. And in writing this opinion, the court has had to go well beyond the materials submitted by the parties to arrive at answers that are at least arguably more than simple-minded.

108 F.R.D. at 330 n.3.

3. Magistrate Judge Brazil notes his disappointment that "the briefs submitted do not substantially advance the analytical ball on the principal issue." In light of this fact, do the attorneys' clients have a cause of action for the work produced? Does Magistrate Judge Brazil? What about the parties to other cases that were delayed while Magistrate Judge Brazil considered this dispute?

4. In connection with Magistrate Judge Brazil's admonition that attorneys "should strive to be cooperative, practical and sensible," consider Model Rule of Professional Conduct 3.4(d), which provides that "[a] lawyer shall not * * * make a frivolous discovery request or fail to make reasonably diligent effort to comply with a legally proper discovery request by an opposing party." *See also* Model Rules of Prof'l Conduct Rule 4.4 ("In representing a client, a lawyer shall not use means that have no substantial purpose other than to embarrass, delay, or burden a third person * * * .").

5. Even in those cases in which interrogatories are answered, the answers may not be provided in a timely manner. In a study of over 3000 cases terminated in the federal courts in the 1970s, timely interrogatory responses were not generally forthcoming:

> Over 80 percent of responses to interrogatories were filed more than thirty days after requested. * * * Substantial tardiness appears to be the norm rather than the exception. The median time for response to interrogatories fell in the 61– to 90–day interval, and more than 3 percent of the responses required a year.

P. Connolly et al., *Judicial Controls and the Civil Litigative Process: Discovery* 18–19 (1978).

6. What type of showing must a party make to be entitled to early answers to contention interrogatories under *Convergent Technologies?* Does the same standard apply to both plaintiffs and defendants? Is it more likely that a plaintiff or a defendant would be found entitled to early answers to contention interrogatories?

7. In *Convergent Technologies* Magistrate Judge Brazil rejects a "rigid rule * * * that would always protect parties from having to answer contention interrogatories until some predetermined juncture in the pretrial period." What can be said in favor of such a "rigid rule?" Is it possible that Judge Brazil's flexible approach and his willingness to devote a 22–page opinion to this dispute actually might cause future discovery disputes and encourage parties to submit their disputes to the court rather than resolve those disputes themselves? Compare Judge Brazil's approach with that of Rule 33.3(c) of the United States District Court for the Southern District of New York, which precludes contention interrogatories until other discovery has been completed. *See also* the discovery order in Chapter 6, *supra* p. 238, of Judge Robert Keeton, who would "not serve * * * as a mediator for settlement of disputes over discovery in which each party takes unreasonable positions with the purpose of conceding what is plainly due under the rules only when before the court or magistrate."

8. Magistrate Judge Brazil is skeptical about "the *quality* of the information that *early* responses to contention interrogatories are likely to con-

tain." However, would it be a sufficient answer to a contention interrogatory that "research and investigation [are] continuing?" Isn't one of the purposes of contention interrogatories to "box[ ] [parties] into a position * * * [and] limit the subject areas of their subsequent discovery?"

9. Consider the following explanation as to why interrogatories are abused in practice:

> Lawyers generally do not abuse Rule 33 simply to harass the opposing party. More often, lawyers misuse interrogatories because they spend too little time on them. Interrogatories are often prepared by people who are unfamiliar with the legal and factual issues in the case, who work from forms rather than from a thoroughly researched analysis of the case, and who are given little guidance by the lawyers who are familiar with the issues.

Klenk, "Using and Abusing Interrogatories," *Litigation,* Winter 1985, at 25, 25.

10. Although such conferences were not mandatory at the time of *Convergent Technologies*, wouldn't a Rule 26(f) discovery conference have addressed many of the issues brought by the parties to Judge Brazil in that case?

IV. DRAFTING INTERROGATORIES

Before drafting interrogatories, counsel must consider both the substance and the form of those interrogatories. These two topics are considered in this section of this chapter.

A. THE SUBSTANCE OF THE INTERROGATORIES

Prior to drafting interrogatories, or seeking any other discovery, counsel must have a firm grasp of her case. She must have selected a legal theory, know the facts that must be proven in order to prevail on that legal theory, and have anticipated the contentions that opposing counsel is most likely to raise. The creation of an element check list[12] and a discovery plan[13] are essential to the effective utilization of interrogatories and all other discovery devices.

By preparing an element check list and discovery plan, counsel will have determined (1) what information must be obtained by formal discovery and (2) what portions of that information can be obtained most effectively through interrogatories. It then should be a relatively simple task to determine the substance of specific interrogatories. Consider the information that defense counsel in the Buffalo Creek disaster litigation sought with the following interrogatories. Note, however, that the basic damage calculation sought by these interrogatories would today be voluntarily disclosed pursuant to Rule 26(a)(1)(A)(iii).

---

12. *See* Chapter 3, Section II(C), *supra* p. 61.

13. *See* Chapter 6, Section VI, *supra* p. 296.

IN THE UNITED STATES DISTRICT COURT
FOR THE SOUTHERN DISTRICT OF
WEST VIRGINIA At Charleston

DENNIS PRINCE ET AL.,

              Plaintiffs,

     -against-   Civil Action No. 3052–HN

THE PITTSTON COMPANY,

              Defendant.

DEFENDANT'S INTERROGATORIES
FIRST SERIES

TO: DENNIS PRINCE and all other persons named as plaintiffs in the above-styled action, and WILLIS O. SHAY, ESQUIRE of the law firm of STEPTOE & JOHNSON, Tenth Floor, Union Bank Building, Clarksburg, West Virginia 26301 and GERALD M. STERN, ESQUIRE of the law firm of ARNOLD & PORTER, 1229 Nineteenth Street, N.W., Washington, D. C. 20036, attorneys for plaintiffs:

Defendant requests that each plaintiff in the above-styled action answer under oath, in accordance with Rule 33 of the Federal Rules of Civil Procedure, the following interrogatories; any plaintiff who sues both individually on his or her own behalf and representatively on behalf of one or more other persons is requested to answer each interrogatory for himself or herself and separately for each other person on behalf of whom such plaintiff sues:

1. State your full given name and any other names or nicknames, your date of birth, and your residence address as of February 25, 1972, and (if not the same) as of the date of the answers to these interrogatories.

2. If you were employed at any time during the period January 1, 1971, through February 26, 1972, state the nature of such employment and the name and address of your employer or employers.

3. If you have been employed at any time since February 26, 1972, state the nature of such employment and the name and address of your employer or employers.

4. If you claim damages in this action for the loss, destruction or diminution in value of real property set forth the following information with respect to such real property, as of February 25, 1972, and (if not the same) as of the date of the answers to these interrogatories:

     (a) Location and description of such real property and any improvements thereon;

     (b) Nature of your interest in such real property;

     (c) Name or names of titled owner of such real property;

(d) Date or dates upon which such person or persons became titled owner of such real property;

(e) Amount of purchase price paid by such person or persons and identity of seller;

(f) Nature and cost of improvements to such real property, if any, made subsequent to such purchase and prior to February 26, 1972;

(g) Nature and extent of damage to such real property and any improvements thereon caused by the flood on February 26, 1972;

(h) Was such real property subject to mortgage or other lien as of February 26, 1972, and, if so, the name and address of each mortgagor or other lienholder, the amount of each such mortgage or other lien, and the present status thereof;

(i) The dollar amount of damages claimed for the loss, destruction or diminution in value of such real property and the manner in which such amount is calculated.

5. If you claim damages in this action for the loss, destruction or diminution in value of personal property, set forth the following information with respect to each item of personal property as to which such claim is made (any group of items of personal property purchased for a total of $500 or less may be treated as one item):

(a) Description of such personal property;

(b) Nature of plaintiff's interest therein as of February 25, 1972;

(c) Location of such personal property immediately prior to flood on February 26, 1972;

(d) Date such personal property was purchased, amount of the purchase price and name and address of immediate seller;

(e) Nature and extent of damage to such personal property caused by flood on February 26, 1972;

(f) Was such personal property subject to a lien as of February 26, 1972, and, if so, the name and address of each lienholder, the amount of each such lien, and the present status thereof;

(g) The dollar amount of damages claimed for the loss, destruction or diminution in value of such personal property and the manner in which such amount is calculated.

6. If you claim damages in this action for personal injury or injuries, set forth the following with respect to each such personal injury:

(a) Description of the injury and the manner in which it was sustained;

(b) The date or dates upon which treatment for such injury was received, the nature of such treatment, and by whom such treatment was rendered;

(c) Are you presently being treated for such injury, and, if not, when did treatment cease?

(d) Is such injury claimed to be permanent?

(e) An itemized statement of the amount of money which you were obliged to expend for treatment of such injury, including but not limited to, expenses for hospitals, physicians, nurses and medicines, the date or dates of such payments and a description of the services or goods for which such moneys were paid;

(f) The dollar amount of damages which you claim for such injury and the manner in which such amount is calculated.

* * *

8. If you claim any damages in this action not referred to in your answers to the preceding interrogatories, itemize and describe the nature of such additional damages and state the dollar amount sought and the manner in which such amount is calculated.

9. If you claim punitive or exemplary damages in this action, state the amount claimed.

> JACKSON KELLY HOLT & O'FARRELL
> Kanawha Valley Building
> Charleston, West Virginia 25301
> By s/ _____
>   A Member of the Firm
>
> DONOVAN LEISURE NEWTON & IRVINE
> Two Wall Street
> New York, New York 10005
> By s/ _____
>   A Member of the Firm
>
> s/ _____
>   ZANE GREY STAKER
>   Box 388
>   Kermit, West Virginia 25674

B. THE FORM OF THE INTERROGATORIES

Once counsel determines the substance of the information that will be sought through interrogatories, she actually must draft those interrogatories. The major problem with drafting most interrogatories is avoiding ambiguity.

There is a quite natural tendency, and arguably a professional duty, for lawyers to provide no more information in response to interrogatories than what is explicitly sought by those interrogatories. Where interrogatories in good faith can be interpreted in more than one manner, lawyers generally interpret the ambiguities in the manner most favorable to their clients. Extra care in drafting interrogatories therefore may prevent later disappointment with less than helpful interrogatory answers.

In addition to precisely drafting individual interrogatories, counsel can guard against ambiguities by including a definitional section as a preface to the interrogatories. The United States District Courts for the Southern and Eastern Districts of New York have sought to ensure that all parties use the same definitions in their interrogatories and other discovery requests. Rule 26.3(a) of those courts provides: "The full text of the definitions and rules of construction set forth [in Rule 26.3] is deemed incorporated by reference into all discovery requests. * * * This rule shall not preclude: (1) the definition of other terms specific to the particular litigation, (2) the use of abbreviations, or (3) a more narrow definition of a term defined in [Rule 26.3]."

Included among the definitions deemed incorporated into discovery requests by Rule 26.3 are the following:

(1) **Communication.** The term "communication" means the transmittal of information (in the form of facts, ideas, inquiries or otherwise).

(2) **Document.** The term "document" is defined to be synonymous in meaning and equal in scope to the usage of this term in Federal Rule of Civil Procedure 34(a), including, without limitation, electronic or computerized data compilations.[14] A draft or non-identical copy is a separate document within the meaning of this term.

(3) **Identify (with respect to persons).** When referring to a person, "to identify" means to give, to the extent known, the person's full name, present or last known address, and when referring to a natural person, additionally, the present or last known place of employment. Once a person has been identified in accordance with this subparagraph, only the name of that person need be listed in response to subsequent discovery requesting the identification of that person.

(4) **Identify (with respect to documents).** When referring to documents, "to identify" means to give, to the extent known, the (i) type of document; (ii) general subject matter; (iii) date of the document; and (iv) author(s), addressee(s) and recipient(s).

(5) **Parties.** The terms "plaintiff" and "defendant" as well as a party's full or abbreviated name or a pronoun referring to a party mean the party and, where applicable, its officers, directors, employees, partners, corporate parent, subsidiaries or affiliates. This definition is not intended to impose a discovery obligation on any person who is not a party to the litigation.[15]

---

14. Rule 34(a)(1)(A) of the Federal Rules of Civil Procedure provides for the production of "documents or electronically stored information-including writings, drawings, graphs, charts, photographs, sound recordings, images and other data or data compilations—stored in any medium from which information can be obtained either directly or, if necessary, after translation by the responding party into a reasonably usable form."

15. Rule 26.3(c)(1)–(5) of the United States District Courts for the Southern and Eastern Districts of New York.

Rule 26.3(d) of the United States District Courts for the Southern and Eastern Districts of New York further provides:

The following rules of construction apply to all discovery requests:

(1) **All/Each.** The terms "all" and "each" shall be construed as all and each.

(2) **And/Or.** The connectives "and" and "or" shall be construed either disjunctively or conjunctively as necessary to bring within the scope of the discovery request all responses that might otherwise be construed to be outside of its scope.

(3) **Number.** The use of the singular form of any word includes the plural and vice versa.

Interrogatory instructions and definitions also can be taken from the standing orders of individual judges. William Schwarzer, during his service on the United States District Court for the Northern District of California, adopted the following guideline concerning the assertion of privilege in response to a discovery request:

A claim of privilege must be supported by a statement of particulars sufficient to enable the Court to assess its validity. In the case of a document, such a statement should specify the privilege relied on and include the date, title, description, subject and purpose of the document; the name and position of the author and the addresses of other recipients. In the case of a communication, the statement should include the date, place, subject and purpose of the communication and the names and positions of all persons present.[16]

If instructions or definitions such as these do not apply in a particular jurisdiction, counsel can include them in an introduction to a set of interrogatories or agree with other counsel that all parties will abide by them in a given case.

To ensure that interrogatories are as precise as possible, they can be limited to specific time periods or geographic areas. An interrogatory in the Buffalo Creek litigation seeking a list of "all of the defendant's documents concerning dam safety" probably would have been objected to as overbroad and unduly burdensome. To avoid this problem, the request might be rephrased to seek "all of the defendant's documents concerning dam safety from January 1, 1965, to the present time" or "all of the defendant's documents concerning the safety of coal waste dams east of the Mississippi River." So that there are no ambiguities, important terms that are used at several points in a set of interrogatories can be defined at the beginning of those interrogatories. In the Buffalo Creek litigation, an initial definition of the word "dam" as used in a set of interrogatories might avoid later problems.

---

16. Schwarzer, "Guidelines for Discovery, Motion Practice and Trial," 117 F.R.D. 273, 277 (1987). *Compare* Fed. R. Civ. P. 26(b)(5)(A)(ii) (requiring description of material not disclosed or produced "in a manner that, without revealing information itself privileged or protected, will enable other parties to assess the claim").

Whether or not instructions or definitions are used, every effort should be made to ensure that interrogatories are drafted as precisely as possible.

NOTES AND QUESTIONS CONCERNING INTERROGATORY DRAFTING

1. Should other courts adopt rules of construction and definitions similar to those adopted by the United States District Courts for the Southern and Eastern Districts of New York? Why not merely approve form interrogatories that can be used in all cases?

2. In contrast to the specific rules of construction and definitions adopted by the Southern and Eastern Districts of New York, consider the following approach in Rule 26.7 of the United States District Court for the Eastern District of New York:

> Discovery requests shall be read reasonably in the recognition that the attorney serving them generally does not have the information being sought and the attorney receiving them generally does have such information or can obtain it from the client.

Would definitional sections to interrogatories be necessary if all counsel read interrogatories reasonably?

3. In addition to carefully choosing the language used in interrogatories, ambiguities may be avoided by subdividing questions into several shorter interrogatories or interrogatory subparts. Even if one subpart of an interrogatory is found to be ambiguous or objectionable, useful answers still can be obtained in response to the other interrogatory subparts.

Exercises Concerning Interrogatory Drafting

1. You represent Thomas Eakins, the victim of the Buffalo Creek disaster who was introduced in exercise 1 of the Exercises Concerning Client Interviewing in Chapter 2, *supra* p. 38. You have filed a federal diversity action on behalf of Eakins, and you would like to obtain some initial information from the defendant Pittston Company concerning the design, construction, inspection, and compliance with applicable safety regulations of the dam on the Buffalo Creek that failed on February 26, 1972. Your assignment is to draft no more than twenty interrogatories to obtain this information. For the purposes of this exercise, presume that no discovery has been conducted yet in this action and that the Rule 26(a)(1) initial disclosures that you have received have not been particularly helpful on these subjects.

In addition to drafting these interrogatories, prepare a short memorandum setting forth:

    (a) any information related to the dam that you would *not* seek through interrogatories (and why interrogatories would not be used to obtain such information);

    (b) how the interrogatories you have drafted will relate to any other discovery devices that you intend to use to obtain information concerning the dam;

(c) other potential areas of discovery concerning the failed dam that effectively could be obtained by interrogatories; and

(d) the effect upon your use of interrogatories of the Rule 33(a)(1) provision that unless "otherwise stipulated or ordered by the court, a party may serve on any other party no more than 25 written interrogatories, including all discrete subparts."

2. You represent the estate of Norman Hickman, who died on February 7, 1943, when the tugboat "J. M. Taylor" sank in the Delaware River. You were retained soon after this accident, filed a federal civil action, and, as permitted by an order entered in this case, have decided to serve interrogatories before any Rule 26(f) discovery conference upon the defendant owners of the tugboat "J. M. Taylor." Based upon the facts set forth in *Hickman v. Taylor,* 329 U.S. 495 (1947), *supra* p. 273, draft no more than twenty interrogatories on behalf of the estate of Norman Hickman.

3. For the last five years, Shoes, Unlimited (Shoes) has operated a shoe store at the Happy Valley Mall under a lease with Developers, Inc. (Developers). There are two sporting goods stores in the Happy Valley Mall, and Shoes's lease prohibits it from "featuring athletic footwear." Shoes recently began selling a fashionable brand of walking shoes. Soon thereafter, Developers notified Shoes that it considered Shoes to have violated the terms of its lease, that the lease was terminated, and that Shoes should vacate its store within thirty days. Shoes then filed a federal diversity action against Developers and the two sporting goods stores alleging both contract and tort claims.

(a) As counsel for Shoes draft no more than twenty interrogatories to be served upon Developers.

(b) As counsel for Shoes draft no more than twenty interrogatories to be served upon the two sporting goods stores.

4. You are associated with attorney Gerald Stern in connection with the lawsuit that he filed on behalf of several hundred victims of the Buffalo Creek disaster. A new attorney in your firm has drafted a series of interrogatories to be served upon the Pittston Company. Draft a short memorandum (1) discussing any potential problems with the following interrogatories and (2) redrafting the interrogatories as necessary:

(a) These interrogatories shall be deemed to be continuing in nature and as calling for supplemental answers as necessary to correct or update answers previously given, as required by Rule 26(e)(1).

(b) State whether it would have been prudent to prevent the damming of water behind the dam that failed prior to February 26, 1972.

(c) Identify, by name and present address, all engineers, employees, and agents who planned or designed the dam that failed on

February 26, 1972. Attach to your answers copies of all such plans or designs.

(d) Identify all individuals, whether Pittston or Buffalo Mining employees, supervisors, managers, officers, or directors, who were physically within sight of the dam that failed within the thirty day period prior to its collapse.

(e) Please provide the dates of any conversations or meetings held regarding the:

    1.   design of the dam that failed on February 26, 1972;

    2.   construction of the dam that failed on February 26, 1972; and

    3.   inspection of the dam that failed on February 26, 1972.

V.   RESPONDING TO INTERROGATORIES

Parties either can answer interrogatories or they can object to them. Both of these possible interrogatory responses are considered in this section of this chapter.

A.   ANSWERS TO INTERROGATORIES

Interrogatories only can be directed to parties, and Federal Rule of Civil Procedure 33(b)(5) provides that the party to whom interrogatories are directed must sign, under oath, the answers given. If the party is a corporation, partnership, association, or governmental agency, those answers must be based on the collective knowledge of the party and its agents (including its attorneys).[17]

In the case of a corporation, partnership, association, or governmental agency, Rule 33(b)(1)(B) requires that an officer or agent must respond on that party's behalf. Because the officer or agent who answers interrogatories often will be deposed by opposing counsel, this individual should be chosen with care.

1.   Drafting the Answers

Definitions and instructions can be used as a preface to interrogatory answers, just as they can be included at the beginning of a set of interrogatories. In responding to the Buffalo Creek interrogatories set forth in the prior section of this chapter, plaintiffs filed eleven pages of "General Comments" describing the manner in which they had construed the defendant's interrogatories. These General Comments included statements such as the following:

> *Interrogatories 1, 2, and 3.* The answers to Interrogatories 1, 2, and 3 are self-explanatory. We note that Interrogatories 2 and 3 seek

---

17.   E. Imwinkelried & T. Blumoff, *Pretrial Discovery: Strategy & Tactics* § 8.9, at 8–21 (rev. ed. 2010). *See Naismith v. Professional Golfers Ass'n,* 85 F.R.D. 552, 565 (N.D.Ga. 1979); Fed. R. Civ. P. 33(b)(1)(B).

information with respect to employment *at any time* during the periods, respectively, from January 1, 1971 to February 26, 1972 and from February 26, 1972 to the present. Answers listing employment during either or both of those periods therefore do not necessarily imply continuous or steady employment throughout the periods indicated.

In addition to these General Comments served on behalf of all of the plaintiffs, each individual plaintiff filed his or her own separate answers. Because these individual answers were filed together as a group, there was not a separate case caption on each set of answers. The answers of plaintiff Steve Looney are illustrative:

ANSWERS OF STEVE LOONEY TO DEFENDANT'S INTERROGATORIES—FIRST SERIES

1. A. PLAINTIFF'S FULL NAME:
        Steve Allen Looney
    B. PLAINTIFF'S OTHER NAMES OR NICKNAMES, IF ANY:
        None
    C. PLAINTIFF'S DATE OF BIRTH:
        January 31, 1950
    D. PLAINTIFF'S RESIDENCE ADDRESS AS OF FEBRUARY
        25, 1972:
        Lundale, West Virginia 25631
    E. PLAINTIFF'S RESIDENCE ADDRESS ON THE DATE OF
        THESE ANSWERS:
        Accoville, West Virginia 25606
2. PLAINTIFF'S EMPLOYMENT, IF ANY, AT ANY TIME BE-
    TWEEN JANUARY 1, 1971 AND FEBRUARY 26, 1972:
        Timberman; Amherst Coal; Lundale, West Virginia
3. PLAINTIFF'S EMPLOYMENT, IF ANY, AT ANY TIME SINCE
    FEBRUARY 26, 1972:
        Shuttle Car; Amherst Coal; Lundale, West Virginia
4. PLAINTIFF'S REAL PROPERTY CLAIMS, IF ANY:
        None
5. PLAINTIFF'S PERSONAL PROPERTY CLAIMS, IF ANY:
        None
6. PLAINTIFF'S PERSONAL INJURY CLAIMS:
    A. DESCRIPTION OF INJURY OR INJURIES AND MANNER
        IN WHICH SUSTAINED:
        Injury A: Psychic impairment (see introductory paragraphs).
        Injury B: Hurt foot while in water.
    B. DATES OF TREATMENT, NATURE OF TREATMENT,
        AND BY WHOM TREATMENT WAS RENDERED:
        Injury A: None to date.
        Injury B: None to date.
    C. AND D.   WHETHER TREATMENT HAS CEASED AND IF
                 SO WHEN:
                 WHETHER INJURY IS PERMANENT:
        Injury A: Treatment has not ceased; expected to be permanent.
        Injury B: None to date.
    E. ITEMIZED STATEMENT OF EXPENSES:
        See attached Medical Expense Appendix for Steve Looney family.

    F. DAMAGE CLAIM:
       See introductory paragraphs.
  7. WRONGFUL DEATH CLAIMS:
       None
  8. OTHER DAMAGE CLAIMS:
       See introductory paragraphs. Plaintiff also claims for loss of 15
         days of wages—$640.00
  9. EXEMPLARY DAMAGES CLAIM:
       See introductory paragraphs.

These answers illustrate one of the ways in which interrogatories can be most useful: in seeking relatively straightforward background information concerning a party and his claims. In contrast to such straightforward information, descriptions or explanations of a party's claims and contentions usually can be most effectively probed at a deposition. The background information obtained through interrogatories, however, can be very useful in planning and taking a deposition.

2. Why Not Require the Opposing Party to Answer Its Own Interrogatories?

In 1970, Rule 33(c) was added to the Federal Rules of Civil Procedure. That subdivision became Rule 33(d) as a result of the 1993 amendments to the Federal Rules of Civil Procedure and was amended in 2006 to explicitly provide that "business records" includes "electronically stored information." Rule 33(d) provides:

> (d) *Option to Produce Business Records.* If the answer to an interrogatory may be determined by examining, auditing, compiling, abstracting, or summarizing a party's business records (including electronically stored information), and if the burden of deriving or ascertaining the answer will be substantially the same for either party, the responding party may answer by:
>
> > (1) specifying the records that must be reviewed, in sufficient detail to enable the interrogating party to locate and identify them as readily as the responding party could; and
>
> > (2) giving the interrogating party a reasonable opportunity to examine and audit the records and to make copies, compilations, abstracts, or summaries.

The requirement that the specification of records under Rule 33(d) be made in sufficient detail so that the interrogating party can locate specific documents as readily as the responding party was added to Rule 33 in 1980. The Advisory Committee explained the reason for the addition of this requirement as follows:

> The Committee is advised that parties upon whom interrogatories are served have occasionally responded by directing the interrogating party to a mass of business records or by offering to make all of their

records available, justifying the response by the option provided by this subdivision. Such practices are an abuse of the option. A party who is permitted by the terms of this subdivision to offer records for inspection in lieu of answering an interrogatory should offer them in a manner that permits the same direct and economical access that is available to the party. * * *[18]

NOTES AND QUESTIONS CONCERNING INTERROGATORY ANSWERS

1. In light of the efficiencies possible under Rule 33(d), why might a responding party decide not to produce its business records pursuant to that Rule but instead go to the extra work of answering the interrogatories in question?

2. In addition to the specification of records required by Rule 33(d)(1), some courts have required the party utilizing that subdivision to provide the interrogating party with a knowledgeable employee to assist in the location of specific documents from among the documents produced. *Robinson v. Lehman,* 33 F.E.P. Cases 710 (E.D.Pa. 1983); *Saddler v. Musicland–Pickwick Int'l, Inc.,* 31 Fed.R.Serv. 2d 760 (E.D.Tex. 1980).

3. The potential problems with respect to the production of electronic information were noted in the Advisory Committee Note to the 2006 amendment to Rule 33(d), which expanded Rule 33(d) to explicitly include "electronically stored information." The Advisory Committee noted:

> [S]atisfying [Rule 33(d)] with respect to electronically stored information may require the responding party to provide some combination of technical support, information on application software, or other assistance. The key question is whether such support enables the interrogating party to derive or ascertain the answer from the electronically stored information as readily as the responding party. A party that wishes to invoke Rule 33(d) by specifying electronically stored information may be required to provide direct access to its electronic information system, but only if that is necessary to afford the requesting party an adequate opportunity to derive or ascertain the answer to the interrogatory. In that situation, the responding party's need to protect sensitive interests of confidentiality or privacy may mean that it must derive or ascertain and provide the answer itself rather than invoke Rule 33(d).

234 F.R.D. 219, 356 (2006).

4. In the course of their own case preparation, defendant insurance companies analyzed their records related to plaintiffs' insurance claims. Subsequently, plaintiffs served an interrogatory seeking information about defendants' handling and payment of plaintiffs' claims. Can defendants utilize the Rule 33(d) option and produce business records from which plaintiffs can extract the information sought or must defendants answer the interrogatories based upon their own independent records analysis? See *Petroleum Ins. Agency, Inc. v. Hartford Accident and Indem. Co.,* 111 F.R.D. 318 (D.Mass. 1983).

---

18.   85 F.R.D. 521, 531 (1980).

5.　Consider the following problems posed by Professor David Shapiro in "Some Problems of Discovery in an Adversary System," 63 *Minn. L. Rev.* 1055, 1058 (1979):

1.　You represent A, executor of B, in a Superior Court action for negligence arising out of an automobile accident at a highway intersection in the state. The intersection contained a stop sign at all access roads. B died in the accident and C, a passenger in the car B was driving, stated to you in an interview that B did not come to a full stop before entering the intersection. C too has since died, from causes unrelated to the accident, and none of the other witnesses you have spoken to claims to have seen B enter the intersection. You have no reason to doubt the correctness of C's statement. D, the defendant in the action, has alleged contributory negligence as a defense and has submitted the following interrogatory to A under Rule 33 of the state rules of civil procedure:

> "Did B come to a full stop before entering the intersection where the accident in suit occurred?"

What should be the response to this interrogatory?

2.　The facts are as stated in question 1, but the interrogatory submitted by D reads as follows:

> "If you have any information about whether or not B came to a full stop before entering the intersection where the accident in suit occurred, please state: (a) the nature of that information; and (b) your opinion with respect to whether or not B came to a full stop at that time."

What should be the response to this interrogatory?

6.　In an employment discrimination suit, defendant serves the following interrogatory upon plaintiff:

"Were you employed during the period 1891 to 1895?"

Although plaintiff was not employed during the period in question (not having been alive from 1891 to 1895), counsel presumes that there is a typographical error in the interrogatory and that the interrogatory should have read "during the period 1991 to 1995." During the period 1991 to 1995 plaintiff's only "employment" consisted of intermittent work on his father-in-law's farm, for which he received room and board.

How should plaintiff respond to defendant's interrogatory?

B.　OBJECTIONS TO INTERROGATORIES

Not only does Federal Rule of Civil Procedure 33(b) set forth the procedure for answering interrogatories, but Rule 33(b)(4) provides for interrogatory objections so long as the grounds for any objection are "stated with specificity." Rule 33(b)(5) requires that interrogatory answers be signed by the person making them, but that any interrogatory objections be signed by counsel. Rule 33(b)(4) provides: "Any ground not stated in a timely objection is waived unless the court, for good cause, excuses the failure."[19] However, counsel should be aware of Rule 33(b)(2)'s provision that, while 30 days is the usual time for serving interrogatory answers or objections, "A shorter or longer time may be stipulated to under Rule 29 or be ordered by the court."[20]

If answers are given to some, and objections are raised to other, individual interrogatories within the same set of interrogatories, dual signature lines will be necessary. These lines might look like this:

As to the answers herein:

> Pursuant to 28 U.S.C. § 1746, I, [party's name], declare this _____ day of _____, 20__, under penalty of perjury that the above answers are true and correct.

[party's signature]

As to the objections herein:

[regular attorney signature lines]

In this example, an unsworn declaration has been used instead of the oath otherwise required of the party making the interrogatory answers by Federal Rule of Civil Procedure 33(b)(3).

Because of the requirement that interrogatory objections must be signed by counsel, Rule 26(g) of the Federal Rules of Civil Procedure is applicable to any objections raised. Rule 26(g)(1)(B) in part provides that, by signing an objection, the attorney certifies that to the best of her "knowledge, information, and belief formed after a reasonable inquiry" the objection is:

(i) consistent with these rules and warranted by existing law or by a nonfrivolous argument for extending, modifying, or reversing existing law, or for establishing new law;

(ii) not interposed for any improper purpose, such as to harass, cause unnecessary delay, or needlessly increase the cost of litigation; and

(iii) neither unreasonable nor unduly burdensome or expensive, considering the needs of the case, prior discovery in the case, the amount in controversy, and the importance of the issues at stake in the action.

Rule 26(g)(3) provides that courts must impose sanctions for certifications made in violation of Rule 26(g).

---

19. Even prior to the 1993 addition of the specific provision in Rule 33(b)(4) stating that, absent good cause, failure to assert a timely objection results in waiver of the objection, courts had found waiver in such situations. *Renshaw v. Ravert,* 82 F.R.D. 361, 362 (E.D.Pa. 1979). *But see Williams v. Krieger,* 61 F.R.D. 142, 145 (S.D.N.Y. 1973) (objections to "totally improper" interrogatories will not be deemed waived); *Bohlin v. Brass Rail, Inc.,* 20 F.R.D. 224, 225–26 (S.D.N.Y. 1957) (objections deemed waived except as to information protected by doctor-patient privilege and attorney work-product protection).

20. As the Advisory Committee Note to the 1993 Amendment to Rule 33 makes clear, though, "the fact that additional time may be needed to respond to some questions (or to some aspects of questions) should not justify a delay in responding to those questions (or other aspects of questions) that can be answered within the prescribed time." 146 F.R.D. 535, 676 (1993).

Because Rule 33(a)(2) provides that interrogatories "may relate to any matter that may be inquired into under Rule 26(b)," Rule 26(b) provides a check list of the most common interrogatory objections. Because they seek information outside the scope of discovery established by Rule 26(b)(1), objections can be raised to interrogatories that ask for privileged information or information that is not relevant to the claim or defense of any party (unless the court has, pursuant to Rule 26(b)(1), expanded discovery to "matter relevant to the subject matter involved in the action"). Similarly, objections can be raised to interrogatories seeking trial preparation materials other than those that are discoverable under Rule 26(b)(3) or expert discovery other than that provided by Rule 26(b)(4).

Aside from these particular objections, interrogatories are objectionable if (1) they are "unreasonably cumulative or duplicative, or can be obtained from some other source that is more convenient, less burdensome, or less expensive;"[21] (2) "the party seeking discovery has had ample opportunity to obtain the information by discovery in the action;"[22] or (3) "the burden or expense of the proposed discovery outweighs its likely benefit."[23] Because of the ease of drafting interrogatories and the potential burden of preparing interrogatory responses, objections based upon undue burden frequently are raised.

Objections can be made to ambiguous or confusing interrogatories. Rather than filing such an objection, however, counsel should consider contacting opposing counsel for clarification or simply answering the interrogatories as most reasonably interpreted. There usually is nothing gained by objecting to interrogatories that seek discovery to which an opponent is clearly entitled.

There can be other reasons for not raising a valid interrogatory objection. A string of objections may sour a good working relationship with opposing counsel. It takes time for the court to resolve discovery disputes. Counsel herself may want to obtain the very type of information sought by opposing counsel's arguably objectionable interrogatory. If the information sought by the interrogatory is not harmful, these may be good reasons not to raise an objection. In these situations, some counsel raise the appropriate objection (to preserve the position that the interrogatory is improper), but nevertheless answer the specific interrogatory.[24]

Once it is decided that an objection should be made to an interrogatory, that objection is quite simply raised. The following are illustrative interrogatory objections.

---

21. Fed. R. Civ. P. 26(b)(2)(C)(i).

22. Fed. R. Civ. P. 26(b)(2)(C)(ii).

23. Fed. R. Civ. P. 26(b)(2)(C)(iii).

24. Other counsel respond to objectionable interrogatories by "fighting fire with fire." Rather than object to the interrogatories, they quickly serve their own interrogatories upon the opposing party. These interrogatories are identical to the first set of interrogatories, except for such changes as interchanging the words "plaintiff" and "defendant." Opposing counsel is then faced with the prospect of answering the very interrogatories that she originally drafted.

Interrogatory No. ___. [Many local rules require that the interrogatory being answered or objected to be set forth prior to the interrogatory answer or objection.]

Objection. This interrogatory seeks information concerning conversations between the plaintiff and his counsel, which information is protected under the attorney-client privilege and is not subject to discovery under Rule 26(b)(1) of the Federal Rules of Civil Procedure.

Interrogatory No. ___. * * *

Objection. This interrogatory is unduly burdensome, because any response would require manual searches of the entire contents of approximately 535 file cabinets located in the eight regional offices of the defendant corporation. Even if such searches could be conducted, any information gathered would be of only marginal relevance to the remaining issues in this action.

As shown by these examples, an objection should include some of the specific facts upon which it is based. This specificity may dissuade opposing counsel from challenging the objection by a Rule 37 motion to compel. Specificity also may prove helpful if a motion to compel is filed and the district judge or magistrate judge has occasion to read the objection in connection with that motion.

What, though, if an entire set of interrogatories is objectionable? In this event a party, after consultation with the party serving the objectionable interrogatories, can file a motion for a protective order under Federal Rule of Civil Procedure 26(c) rather than file individual interrogatory objections.[25]

Exercise Concerning Interrogatory Responses

In the major action brought on behalf of several hundred victims of the Buffalo Creek disaster, plaintiffs have served upon the defendant Pittston Company a set of 50 interrogatories seeking detailed information concerning the design and construction of the dam on the Middle Fork that failed. Despite the 25 interrogatory limitation of Rule 33(a)(1), as Pittston's counsel you have prepared a set of 65 interrogatories that you would like to serve on plaintiffs.

Plaintiffs' 50 interrogatories are not individually objectionable, but Pittston's engineering department estimates that it would take over 200 hours for engineers in various offices in New York and West Virginia to assemble the information necessary to answer the interrogatories. Some of the individuals with direct knowledge concerning the design of the dam no longer work for either Pittston or the Buffalo Mining Company. However, the engineering expert whom you have just retained has asked for some of the same data that plaintiffs request in their interrogatories.

Write a short memorandum describing the manner in which Pittston should respond to plaintiffs' interrogatories. Attach to that memorandum

---

25. *See* Chapter 10, Section II, *infra* p. 445.

any document that you recommend should be sent to or served upon plaintiffs' counsel.

VI. FORM INTERROGATORIES

The *Convergent Technologies* case[26] illustrates one type of problem with modern discovery. Another discovery problem is the misuse of "form interrogatories" which are not tailored to the issues or subject matter of a particular case. Consider the following litigation:

> Defendants' lawyers have served a set of 94 interrogatories concerning the motion for class certification. Plaintiff's counsel, in response, vouchsafes 74 pages of purported answers. Although we have before us two highly competent law firms, there is, in this vast expanse of paper, no indication that any lawyer (or even moderately competent paralegal) ever looked at the interrogatories or at the answers. It is, on the contrary, obvious that they have all been produced by some word-processing machine's memory of prior litigation.[27]

The district court in this case, on its own motion, struck both the interrogatories and answers and ordered the parties "never to refer to them again in this litigation."[28]

Despite the potential for abuse, form interrogatories can provide helpful check lists of important areas of inquiry. Especially for newer attorneys and those inexperienced with a particular type of case, form interrogatories can be useful starting points for the drafting of interrogatories tailored to a given case. Most attorneys develop their own "form interrogatories" over time as they draw upon interrogatories they or their colleagues have filed in previous actions.

Consider the manner in which the following form interrogatories could be helpful to a new attorney:

PLAINTIFF'S INTERROGATORIES TO DEFENDANT
Mailman Bitten by Dog[29]

Identification
1. State your full name, any other names that you have been known by, your date of birth, your place of birth, and your present resident address.

---

26. *Supra* p. 316.

27. *Blank v. Ronson Corp.,* 97 F.R.D. 744, 745 (S.D.N.Y. 1983).

28. *Id.* Consider, too, the interrogatories directed to a five-year-old plaintiff seeking information about the child's marital status and driving experience. Lundquist, "In Search of Discovery Reform," 66 *A.B.A.J.* 1071, 1072 (1980).

29. 1 *Bender's Forms of Discovery,* "Animals," No. 4, pp. 15–19 (2009). Copyright © 2009 by Matthew Bender & Co., Inc., and reprinted in abridged form with permission from *Bender's Forms of Discovery.*

Description of Dog

2. With respect to the defendants' dog known as _____ which is referred to in the complaint, set forth the following:
   a. the breed;
   b. the age;
   c. the sex;
   d. the height; and
   e. the weight.

Length of Ownership

3. State the length of time that the defendants have owned this dog.

Veterinarians

4. State the names, addresses, and telephone numbers of each veterinarian who has ever examined or treated the dog.

* * *

Prior Attacks

9. State whether the subject dog ever chased, attacked and/or bit anyone on or about these premises prior to the date of the alleged incident, and, if so, state the following:
   a. whether the dog chased, attacked and/or bit the individual;
   b. the name, address and phone number of the individual;
   c. the approximate date of the incident; and
   d. a general statement describing each incident referred to in response to this Interrogatory.

10. State whether either of the defendants ever told the plaintiff, prior to the date of the alleged incident, that the dog chased mailmen or meter readers, and if so, state:
    a. which defendant made the statement; and
    b. the approximate date of the statement.

Precautions to Restrain Dog

11. State whether the dog knocked open the screen door of the subject premises on the date of the incident while the plaintiff was on the premises, and if so, state the following:
    a. the name of the individual in the house who put the dog back in the house; and
    b. the name and address of the individual.

12. State whether either defendant, prior to the date of the incident, told the plaintiff that the dog would be kept confined during the time that the mail was usually delivered.

13. State whether the defendants deny having been told by the plaintiff, prior to the date of the incident, that the dog barked at the plaintiff and knocked open the door, enabling the dog to roam freely on the premises while the plaintiff was delivering mail.

Description of Attack

14. State fully and in complete detail the defendants' version of how the dog attack occurred, beginning the description with the point in

time ten (10) minutes before the attack and completing it with a full description of the attack itself, describing in detail:
    a.   the events leading up to the attack;
    b.   how the attack occurred;
    c.   what the plaintiff and the dog did; and
    d.   what happened in the order in which the events took place.

* * *

Provocation by Plaintiff

17. State whether the defendants contend that the plaintiff, on the date of the incident, was engaged in the commission of a trespass or other tort or was teasing, tormenting or abusing the dog while on the premises, and, if so, state the following:
    a.   what the defendants specifically contend the plaintiff was committing on the date of the incident; and
    b.   a statement describing each incident.

18. State whether the defendants contend that the plaintiff teased, tormented or abused the dog prior to the date of the incident, and, if so, state the following:
    a.   the date of each incident; and
    b.   a statement as to how the plaintiff teased, tormented or abused the dog.

Violation of Statute

19. State the factual basis on which the defendants deny that the attack by the dog as alleged in plaintiff's complaint and resultant injuries to the plaintiff is in violation of _____ (statute).

Defendant's Insurance Coverage

20. State whether the defendants were covered by a homeowners' insurance policy on the date of the incident, and, if so, state the following:
    a.   the name and address of the insurance carrier;
    b.   the extent of insurance coverage; and
    c.   the amount of the policy limits.

* * *

———

Unfortunately, not all form interrogatories are as straightforward as these nor do all attorneys merely use such forms as guides or suggestions. Because of the unfocused zeal with which some attorneys use form interrogatories, at least one federal district court has attempted to discourage the use of form interrogatories (and other discovery requests) that do not pertain to the case at hand:

    Attorneys using form discovery requests shall review them to ascertain that they are relevant to the subject matter involved in the particular case. Discovery requests which are not relevant to the subject matter involved in the particular case shall not be used.[30]

Nevertheless, some courts actually have approved uniform interrogatories for use in those jurisdictions.[31] Whatever the source of form interrogatories, however, they should be appropriately tailored to the case at hand.

VII. INTERROGATORIES UNDER LOCAL RULES OF COURT

Because of the potential for abuse, interrogatory practice has been a frequent subject for regulation by the local rules of federal district courts. Prior to the 1993 amendment to Rule 33(a) creating a presumptive limit of 25 interrogatories, most districts had adopted local rules limiting the number of interrogatories that could be asked without leave of court.[32] The 1993 amendment to Rule 33, "based on experience with local rules,"[33] now limits parties to "no more than 25 written interrogatories, including all discrete subparts" absent leave of court or written stipulation.[34]

While Rule 26(b)(2) no longer permits courts to adopt local rules that alter the numerical limit on interrogatories established by Rule 33(a)(1), local rules still may govern other aspects of interrogatory practice. Rule 33.3 of the Local Rules of the United States District Court for the Southern District of New York provides:

> (a) Unless otherwise ordered by the court, at the commencement of discovery, interrogatories will be restricted to those seeking names of witnesses with knowledge of information relevant to the subject matter of the action, the computation of each category of damage alleged, and the existence, custodian, location and general description of relevant documents, including pertinent insurance agreements, and other physical evidence, or information of a similar nature.

> (b) During discovery, interrogatories other than those seeking information described in paragraph (a) above may only be served (1) if they are a more practical method of obtaining the information sought than a request for production or a deposition, or (2) if ordered by the court.

---

30. Rule 26.6 of the United States District Court for the Eastern District of New York.

31. Rule CV–33(b) of the United States District Court for the Western District of Texas. *See also* the form interrogatories approved by the California Judicial Council for use in California state courts. California Judicial Council, *California Judicial Council Forms* (Form Interrogatories–General, DISC–001, Jan. 1, 2008), http://www.courtinfo.ca.gov/forms/allforms.htm.

32. As of 1989, over 80% of the federal district courts had local rules limiting the number of interrogatories that could be served without leave of court. Coquillette et al., "The Role of Local Rules," *A.B.A.J.,* Jan. 1989, at 62, 65.

33. Advisory Committee Note to the 1993 Amendment to Rule 33, 146 F.R.D. 535, 675 (1993).

34. Fed. R. Civ. P. 33(a)(1). Rule 26(b)(2) was amended in 2000 to remove the authority that previously existed under that Rule for the enactment of local rules establishing different presumptive limits on the number of interrogatories.

(c) At the conclusion of other discovery, and at least 30 days prior to the discovery cut-off date, interrogatories seeking the claims and contentions of the opposing party may be served unless the court has ordered otherwise.

Because of the number of federal courts that have regulated the use of interrogatories, local rules always should be consulted before drafting or responding to interrogatories.

NOTES AND QUESTIONS CONCERNING LOCAL RULES GOVERNING INTERROGATORIES

1. Is there any limit on the restrictions that local district courts can place upon interrogatories or other discovery? Is there a point at which local restrictions upon discovery come into conflict with either the spirit or the letter of the discovery provisions of the Federal Rules of Civil Procedure? *See* Roberts, "The Myth of Uniformity in Federal Civil Procedure: Federal Civil Rule 83 and District Court Local Rule–Making Powers," 8 *U. Puget Sound L. Rev.* 537 (1985); Flanders, "Local Rules in Federal District Courts: Usurpation, Legislation, or Information?," 14 *Loy. L.A. L. Rev.* 213 (1981). *Cf. Eash v. Riggins Trucking Inc.,* 757 F.2d 557, 568–70 (3d Cir. 1985) (en banc).

2. What possible effect might a limitation on the number of interrogatories have upon the other discovery undertaken in a case? Has an interrogatory limitation served its purpose if it causes an increase in depositions, which generally are more expensive than interrogatories?

3. Are there alternatives other than depositions that can be used when counsel cannot convince opposing counsel or the court of the need for more than the 25 interrogatories permitted by Rule 33(a)(1)?

VIII. CONCLUSION

As with much else in life, interrogatories can be extremely beneficial if used in moderation. However, if used to excess, interrogatories can impede, rather than facilitate, effective discovery. The lawyer's job is to target interrogatories to those aspects of a case where they can be most effective and use other formal and informal discovery devices to gather information not well suited to discovery by interrogatories.

IX. CHAPTER BIBLIOGRAPHY

Berman, "Q: Is This Any Way To Write An Interrogatory? A: You Bet It Is," *Litigation,* Summer 1993, at 42.

Charfoos & Christensen, "Interrogatories: How to Use Them Effectively in Personal Injury Cases," *Trial,* June 1986, at 56.

Ehrenbard, "Cutting Discovery Costs Through Interrogatories and Document Requests," *Litigation,* Spring 1975, at 17.

Gelb, "Standard Paragraphs in Interrogatories," *Prac. Law.,* June 1, 1982, at 51.

Haydock & Herr, "Interrogatories: Questions and Answers," 1 *Rev. Litig.* 263 (1981).

Johnston & Johnston, "Contention Interrogatories in Federal Court," 148 F.R.D. 441 (1993).

Klenk, "Using and Abusing Interrogatories," *Litigation,* Winter 1985, at 25.

Luria & Clabby, "An Expense Out of Control: Rule 33 Interrogatories After the Advent of Initial Disclosures and Two Proposals for Change," 9 *Chap. L. Rev.* 29 (2005).

Mullins, "Using Interrogatories Properly," *Prac. Law.,* Dec. 1, 1983, at 59.

Schoone & Miner, "The Effective Use of Written Interrogatories," 60 *Marq. L. Rev.* 29 (1976).

Seitz, "Get More Information and Less Indigestion Out of Your Interrogatories," *A.B.A.J.,* Mar. 1985, at 74.

Shapiro, "Some Problems of Discovery in an Adversary System," 63 *Minn. L. Rev.* 1055 (1979).

Thompson, "How to Use Written Interrogatories Effectively," *Prac. Law.,* Feb. 1970, at 81.

Yoo, Comment, "Rule 33(a)'s Interrogatory Limitation: By Party or by Side?," 75 *U. Chi. L. Rev.* 911 (2008).

CHAPTER 8

DEPOSITIONS UPON ORAL EXAMINATION: "CAN WE TALK?"

■ ■ ■

[C]ases [can] be adequately prepared and tried without discovery depositions, and in fact were frequently so tried within the memory of some present members of the bench and bar. The implication of [defendant's] argument to the court was that a poor man or even a man of some means has no business bringing litigation in court unless he can afford the services of a large double-breasted law firm with platoons of young credit card-carrying associates who can fan out all over the country on a search-and-depose mission.

Uhl v. Columbia Broadcasting Systems, 476 F.Supp. 1134, 1141 (W.D.Pa. 1979).

My father was a trial lawyer, and it seems unfortunate that the heirs to his craft will come to be characterized as deposition lawyers. The reason for this is that unlike a trial, the inartful or dilatory deposition is without substantive effect. This trivialization, combined with the fact that money can be made in the bargain, has created a climate of enormous inefficiency.

Katzenbach, "Modern Discovery: Remarks from the Defense Bar," 57 *St. John's L. Rev.* 732, 734 (1983).

Analysis

Sec.

I. INTRODUCTION

Depositions are among the most frequently employed discovery device in modern civil litigation.[1] As will be seen in this chapter, there are many reasons why the deposition is frequently, and successfully, used in civil litigation. As also will be seen, oral depositions sometimes are abused.

The next section of this chapter sketches the law governing depositions. While the law (primarily Rule 30 of the Federal Rules of Civil Procedure) is relatively straightforward, the strategies and tactics used in taking and defending depositions are more complex. Sections III through VI address these strategies and tactics. Only by knowing the governing law, and developing deposition practice skills, can the oral deposition be most effectively used in practice.

II. DEPOSITIONS UNDER THE FEDERAL RULES

Before engaging in deposition practice, counsel should be familiar with the deposition ground rules contained in the Federal Rules of Civil Procedure. This section considers these rules. Specifically, the section examines the rules governing depositions, the taking of deposition testimony, and the use of that testimony in civil litigation.

A. THE GOVERNING LAW

Rule 30 of the Federal Rules of Civil Procedure governs the taking of depositions upon oral examination.[2] Rule 30(a) provides that a party may take the oral deposition of any person (party or non-party). However, Rule 30(a)(2)(B) provides that leave of court is required if the person to be

---

1. According to a major study sponsored by the Federal Judicial Center during the 1970s, depositions were the most frequently employed discovery device in those federal cases studied in which discovery was conducted. P. Connolly et al., *Judicial Controls and the Civil Litigative Process: Discovery* 30 (Figure 1) (1978). Only 48% percent of the over 3000 terminated cases in the sample study involved the use of discovery. *Id.* at 28. However, approximately 43% percent of the discovery requests made in the cases in which there was discovery were oral deposition notices. *Id.* at 30 (Figure 1). The breakdown of the deponents in these cases was: parties, 54.2%; doctors, 3.3%; other experts, 4.8%; records custodians, 5.4%; other witnesses, 25.6%; and unknown deponents, 6.8%. *Id.* at 32 n.85. A Federal Judicial Center study of closed federal cases in the 1990s found that, in the cases in which discovery occurred, depositions occurred in 67% of the cases (with document production and interrogatories occurring in 84% and 81% of the cases, respectively). Willging, et al., "An Empirical Study of Discovery and Disclosure Practice Under the 1993 Federal Rules Amendments," 39 *B.C. L. Rev.* 525, 530 (1998). In a more recent survey of attorneys in federal civil actions that closed in the last quarter of 2008, 54.8% of plaintiff's attorneys and 54.3% of defense attorneys reported that non-expert depositions had been taken in their cases. Lee & Willging, *Federal Judicial Center National, Case–Based Civil Rules Survey: Preliminary Report to the Judicial Conference Advisory Committee on Civil Rules* 10 (2009).

2. In addition to Rule 30 depositions upon oral examination, Rule 31 of the Federal Rules of Civil Procedure provides for depositions upon written questions. Rule 31 depositions are infrequently used, for they involve the same stenography costs as oral depositions but do not have the same major advantages.

Under Rule 31 a party may serve written questions upon either another party or, if a Rule 45 subpoena is used, a non-party. After other parties are given the opportunity to serve cross questions, a reporter takes down the deponent's answers to the written questions. These

deposed is confined in prison. While leave of court had been required to depose a prisoner even prior to the 1993 amendments to Rule 30, Rule 30(a)(2)(A) as amended in 1993 and 2007 requires leave of court to conduct depositions if the parties have not stipulated to the deposition and:

(i) the deposition would result in more than 10 depositions being taken under [Rule 30] or Rule 31 by the plaintiffs, or by the defendants, or by the third-party defendants;

(ii) the deponent has already been deposed in the case; or

(iii) the party seeks to take the deposition before the time specified in Rule 26(d), unless the party certifies in the notice, with supporting facts, that the deponent is expected to leave the United States and be unavailable for examination in this country after that time.[3]

Most significantly, Rule 30(a)(2)(A) limits any side in a lawsuit to ten depositions and delays all depositions until after the parties' Rule 26(f) discovery meeting has been held. However, these restrictions do not apply if the parties have agreed to alter these requirements by written stipulation or the court enters an order to the contrary.[4] Rule 30(d)(1) limits each deposition to "1 day of 7 hours" unless the court orders or the parties stipulate to the contrary. However, Rule 30(d)(1) also provides that courts "must allow additional time consistent with Rule 26(b)(2) if needed to fairly examine the deponent or if the deponent, another person, or any other circumstance impedes or delays the examination." Thus courts are given the explicit authority to extend the seven hour deposition time limit in response to attempts to delay a deposition and thereby "run out the clock" on that deposition.

In planning depositions, counsel must consider limitations placed upon the number and length of depositions by Rule 30(a)(2) and (d)(1), court order, or party stipulation. She then must consider whether the timing of her depositions is limited by Rule 26(d), court order, or party stipulation. The Rule 26(f) discovery conference can be used to reach agreement with opposing counsel upon a deposition schedule that is fair and workable for all parties and deponents.

---

questions thus are seen before the deponent's testimony is transcribed, and the spontaneity of normal deposition answers is lost. Because the questions are written in advance, there also is no possibility for immediate follow-up questioning as there is at an oral deposition. Because of these disadvantages of Rule 31 depositions, counsel should consider using interrogatories or admission requests instead of the more expensive depositions upon written questions or should, if the person with the relevant information is a non-party, depose that person pursuant to Rule 30.

3. Fed. R. Civ. P. 30(a)(2)(A)(i), (ii), (iii). Not only does Rule 30(a)(2)(A)(iii) provide for the possibility of expedited depositions when an individual is about to leave the country, but Rule 27 contemplates the taking of depositions both before the actual filing of an action and pending appeal. However, such depositions only can be taken pursuant to an order of court, based upon a finding that perpetuation of the testimony may prevent a "failure or delay of justice." Fed. R. Civ. P. 27(a)(3), 27(b)(3). *See* Kronfeld, Note, "The Preservation and Discovery of Evidence Under Federal Rule of Civil Procedure 27," 78 *Geo. L. J.* 593 (1990).

4. Fed. R. Civ. P. 30(a)(2), 26(b)(2)(A), 26(d)(1).

Presuming that a deposition is to be taken, counsel must comply with the Rule 30(b) requirements for noticing and taking the deposition. Rule 30(b)(1) provides: "A party who wants to depose a person by oral questions must give reasonable written notice to every other party." Rule 30 does not define "reasonable notice," which may vary somewhat from jurisdiction to jurisdiction and from situation to situation within any particular jurisdiction. In some federal districts, this matter is addressed in local rules of court.[5]

In most jurisdictions, counsel desiring to take a deposition will contact other counsel to arrive at a mutually-convenient time for the deposition; the deposition then will be noticed for that agreed-upon time. If this practice is not followed, multiple deposition notices may be necessary or a motion for a protective order may be filed because the deposition has been scheduled for a time when counsel or the deponent cannot be present.

Not only does Rule 30(b)(1) require written notice of a deposition, but Rule 30(b)(3)(A) requires that the deposition notice state "the method for recording the testimony." That Rule further provides that, unless the court orders otherwise, testimony "may be recorded by audio, audiovisual, or stenographic means" and that the party taking the deposition "bears the recording costs."

Leave of court is thus not required for a party to take an audio or audiovisual deposition. However, Rule 26(a)(3)(A)(ii) requires pretrial disclosure of a written deposition transcript of any testimony not taken stenographically that may be offered at trial other than solely for impeachment. In addition, if nonstenographically recorded deposition testimony is offered, Rule 32(c) requires that the court be provided with a transcript of that testimony. Because parties may want a written deposition transcript well before trial, Rule 30(b)(3)(A) permits any party to "arrange to transcribe a deposition"—whether that deposition had been taken by audio, audiovisual, or stenographic means. Moreover, Rule 30(b)(3)(B) provides: "With prior notice to the deponent and other parties, any party may designate another method for recording the testimony in addition to that in the original notice." In such cases, Rule 30(b)(3)(B) further provides that this party "bears the expense of the additional record or transcript unless the court orders otherwise."

Counsel can use a deposition to do more than ask questions. Rule 30(b)(2) provides that oral deposition notices can be accompanied by Rule 34 requests for the production of documents or other tangible things at the deposition. However, even if reasonable notice for a deposition has been given, parties retain the full thirty days provided by Rule 34 to respond to any document request accompanying the deposition notice.[6]

---

5. *E.g.*, Rule 26.1(j) of the United States District Court for the Southern District of Florida (at least 7 days notice for depositions within the state and 14 days notice for depositions outside the state); Rule 30.1 of the United States District Court for the District of Delaware (not less than 10 days notice).

6. 8A C. Wright et al., *Federal Practice and Procedure* § 2108, at 513 (3d ed. 2010). Prior to the 2007 amendments to the Federal Rules of Civil Procedure, Rule 30(b)(5) explicitly provided

The basic form for an oral deposition notice is quite simple, as shown by the following notice served by the defendant Pittston Company in the Buffalo Creek litigation. However, to comply with the current version of Rule 30(b)(3)(A), this notice should explicitly state that the deposition testimony will be stenographically recorded.

IN THE UNITED STATES DISTRICT COURT
FOR THE SOUTHERN DISTRICT
OF WEST VIRGINIA At Charleston

DENNIS PRINCE ET AL.,
              Plaintiffs,

AGAINST   Civil Action No. 3052–HN

THE PITTSTON COMPANY,
              Defendant.

NOTICE OF TAKING OF DEPOSITIONS

TO: DENNIS PRINCE and all other persons named as plaintiffs in the above-styled action, and WILLIS O. SHAY, ESQUIRE of the law firm of STEPTOE & JOHNSON, Tenth Floor, Union Bank Building, Clarksburg, West Virginia, 26301 and GERALD M. STERN, ESQUIRE of the law firm of ARNOLD & PORTER, 1229 Nineteenth Street, N.W., Washington, D.C., 20036, attorneys for plaintiffs:

Notice is hereby given that defendant will take the testimony, upon oral examination, before an officer authorized by law to administer oaths, commencing at the hour of 9:30 o'clock a.m., e.d.s.t., on May 7, 1973, and continuing from day to day thereafter, except on Saturdays, Sundays and holidays, until completed, at the offices of Jackson, Kelly, Holt and O'Farrell, Kanawha Valley Building, Capitol Street, Charleston, West Virginia, of the following parties plaintiff, in the following order:

Evan Allison
Lucille Allison
Betty Jean Boykins
John Tom Boykins
Charles Cowan

---

that the "procedure of Rule 34 shall apply" to a request to produce documents at a deposition. However, the 1970 Advisory Committee Note to Rule 30(b)(5) stated that this provision was for situations in which "documents are few and simple, and closely related to the oral examination," while "[i]f the discovering party insists on examining many and complex documents at the taking of the deposition, thereby causing undue burdens on others, the latter may, under Rules 26(c) or 30(d), apply for a court order that the examining party proceed via Rule 34 alone." 48 F.R.D. 487, 514 (1970). "In essence, a document request under Rule 30(b)[2] is a complement to a Rule 30 deposition, not a substitute for a Rule 34 document request." *BKCAP, LLC v. Captec Franchise Trust 2000–1*, 2010 WL 1710391 (N.D. Ind. 2010) (quoting *Carter v. United States*, 164 F.R.D. 131, 133 (D.Mass. 1995)). There is no suggestion in the commentary to the 2007 amendments to Rule 30 that documents requested pursuant to a deposition notice should be treated any differently under the current version of Rule 30(b)(2).

Emma Cowan
Dorothy Daily
Charles A. Daily
Willie F. Dailey
James L. Hagood
Ora Hagood
Estelle Hampton
Alfred K. Hampton
Rex Howard
Viola Howard
Phyllis Walls
Wayne Walls
Star Thomas
Cora Thomas
Keith Thomas
Delsie Scalf
Wallace Scalf

Dated this 27th day of April, 1973.

JACKSON, KELLY, HOLT & O'FARRELL
Kanawha Valley Building
Charleston, West Virginia 25301
By s/ _____
     A Member of the Firm

DONOVAN, LEISURE, NEWTON & IRVINE
Two Wall Street
New York, New York 10005
By s/ _____
     A Member of the Firm

s/ _____
     ZANE GREY STAKER
     Box 388
     Kermit, West Virginia 25674

     COUNSEL FOR DEFENDANT

———

Rather than serving separate deposition notices for each plaintiff deponent, the defendant has used a single deposition notice to schedule the depositions of an entire series of plaintiffs. Do the times set for the depositions or the timing of the deposition notice raise any questions?

In addition to deposition notices addressed to the actual deposition witness, Federal Rule of Civil Procedure 30(b)(6) provides that a deposition notice may merely "name as the deponent a public or private corporation, a partnership, an association, a governmental agency, or other entity and must describe with reasonable particularity the matters for examination."[7] It then is the task of the entity noticed to designate one or more persons to provide the requested testimony. Rule 30(b)(6) deposition notices can be extremely useful when seeking information from large agencies or corporations; without such notices a party might have to depose three or four officers until the person with the specific information sought is finally identified. Another advantage of these depositions is that, even if more than one person testifies in response to a Rule 30(b)(6) deposition notice, the deposition should be treated as a single deposition for the purposes of Rule 30(a)(2)(A)(i)'s limitation on the number of depositions.[8] Finally, Rule 30(b)(6) states that the persons responding to such deposition notices are to testify to "information known or reasonably available to the organization," which requires testimony "in accordance with the information the deposed party possesses, after due inquiry."[9]

Despite the existence of Rule 30(b)(6), specific employees of large organizations still can be singled out for depositions. Rule 30(b)(6) itself provides that that subdivision does not preclude the taking of a deposition by other means. There may be cases in which a party wants the deposition testimony of a particular corporate officer, while in other cases counsel may not want to specify in advance the matters that will be covered during a deposition or rely upon another person to designate deponents.

Not only can party depositions be taken pursuant to Rule 30, but depositions can be taken of non-parties as well. However, when the deponent is not a party, his deposition attendance must be compelled by a Rule 45 subpoena. A Rule 30 deposition notice is still prepared, and the Rule 45 subpoena should issue from the court for the district in which the deposition will be taken.[10] Unless the subpoena is issued on behalf of the United States or an officer or agency thereof, a check for one day's witness

---

7. An example of a Rule 30(b)(6) deposition notice from the Buffalo Creek litigation is contained in the Exercise Concerning the Discovery of Insurance Agreements in Chapter 6, *supra* p. 233. *See generally* Peltz & Weill, "Corporate Representative Depositions: In Search of a Cohesive & Well–Defined Body of Law," 33 *Nova L. Rev.* 393 (2009); Sinclair & Fendrich, "Discovering Corporate Knowledge and Contentions: Rethinking Rule 30(b)(6) and Alternative Mechanisms," 50 *Ala. L. Rev.* 651 (1999); Cymrot, "The Forgotten Rule," *Litigation*, Spring 1992, at 6.

8. Advisory Committee Note to 1993 Amendment to Rule 30(a)(2)(A), 146 F.R.D. 401, 662 (1993).

9. *Mitsui & Co. v. Puerto Rico Water Res. Auth.*, 93 F.R.D. 62, 66 (D.P.R. 1981), quoting 8 C. Wright & A. Miller, *Federal Practice and Procedure* § 2177, at 559 (1970).

"Rule 30(b)(6) explicitly requires [the defendant] to have persons testify on its behalf as to all matters known or reasonably available to it and, therefore, implicitly requires such persons to review all matters known or reasonably available to it in preparation for the Rule 30(b)(6) deposition." *United States v. Taylor*, 166 F.R.D. 356, 362 (M.D.N.C.), *aff'd*, 166 F.R.D. 367 (M.D.N.C.1996). *See also Federal Deposit Ins. Corp. v. Butcher*, 116 F.R.D. 196 (E.D.Tenn. 1986). Sanctions therefore can be imposed upon a corporation producing an unprepared individual pursuant to a Rule 30(b)(6) deposition notice. *Black Horse Lane Assoc., L.P. v. Dow Chemical Corp.*, 228 F.3d 275, 299–305 (3d Cir. 2000); *Resolution Trust Corp. v. Southern Union Co.*, 985 F.2d 196 (5th Cir. 1993). Another reason that Rule 30(b)(6) deponents should be well prepared is that their testimony may be considered binding on the corporation. *Rainey v. American Forest & Paper Ass'n, Inc.*, 26 F.Supp.2d 82, 93–96 (D.D.C. 1998). *Contra A.I. Credit Corp. v. Legion Ins. Co.*, 265 F.3d 630, 637 (7th Cir. 2001); *Industrial Hard Chrome, Ltd. v. Hetran, Inc.*, 92 F.Supp.2d 786, 791 (N.D.Ill. 2000) ("The testimony given at a Rule 30(b)(6) deposition is evidence which, like any other deposition testimony, can be contradicted and used for impeachment purposes.").

10. Fed. R. Civ. P. 45(a)(2)(B).

fee and mileage must be given to the witness at the time the deposition subpoena is served.[11] In addition to compelling the attendance of non-party deponents, Rule 45 deposition subpoenas can be used to require that deponents produce specified documents or other tangible things at a deposition.[12]

Once a deposition has been noticed, it is important that the party noticing the deposition (1) attend that deposition and (2) ensure that the deponent (if a non-party) is served with a deposition subpoena. Rule 30(g) of the Federal Rules of Civil Procedure provides that if a deposition does not go forward for either of these two reasons, parties appearing for the deposition are entitled to their reasonable expenses from the party that noticed the deposition.

B. THE TAKING OF DEPOSITION TESTIMONY

The deposition having been properly noticed, the deponent is to appear at the time and place specified in the deposition notice. Prior to the beginning of the deposition questioning, the court reporter makes some preliminary statements and puts the deponent under oath. The deposing attorney then asks the deponent questions, and the court reporter takes down the questions, the deponent's answers, and any objections or other statements made by the attorneys. Testimony is elicited in a manner similar to that used at trial, with the major difference being the absence of a judge at the deposition.

Because there is no judge present, objections cannot be ruled on during the deposition. Accordingly, the only objections that must be made at or before the deposition are those concerning errors that could be corrected if a timely objection were raised. For example, objections to the deposition notice or the qualifications of the reporter before whom the deposition will be taken must be made promptly or they will be considered to have been waived.[13] For similar reasons, Rule 32(d)(3)(B) provides:

> An objection to an error or irregularity at an oral examination is waived if:
>
> (i) it relates to the manner of taking the deposition, the form of a question or answer, the oath or affirmation, a party's conduct, or other matters that might have been corrected at that time; and
>
> (ii) it is not timely made during the deposition.

Rule 32(d)(3)(A), however, provides a different rule with respect to errors that cannot be cured if made before or during the deposition:

> An objection to a deponent's competence—or to the competence, relevance, or materiality of testimony—is not waived by a failure to

---

11. Fed. R. Civ. P. 45(b)(1), 28 U.S.C. § 1821.

12. Fed. R. Civ. P. 45(a)(1)(C).

13. Fed. R. Civ. P. 32(d)(1), (2).

make the objection before or during the deposition, unless the ground for it might have been corrected at that time.

Attorneys therefore need not raise objections to deposition questions that might elicit hearsay testimony or testimony that is irrelevant. If a party later seeks to introduce the deposition transcript at trial, the court at that time can exclude the portion of the deposition testimony that is hearsay or irrelevant. However, an objection that the examining attorney is asking leading questions (an objection to the form of the questions) must be made at the deposition in order to give the examining attorney a chance to reframe her questions.

Even if an attorney is not required by the Federal Rules of Civil Procedure to make certain deposition objections, these objections are made on occasion. While many attorneys will not object to a single irrelevant question, an objection becomes increasingly likely as an entire series of irrelevant questions is asked. Such objections sometimes are made in order to suggest (often not so subtly) that examining counsel not waste additional time by pursuing matters that are neither admissible nor reasonably calculated to lead to the discovery of admissible evidence. Even when such objections are made, Rule 30(c)(2) provides that "the examination still proceeds; the testimony is taken subject to any objection." Because there is no judge present to rule on the objections, the reporter merely takes down those objections and the witness answers the questions. Counsel also must remember the directive of Rule 30(c)(2) that any deposition objections must be "stated concisely in a nonargumentative and nonsuggestive manner."

In certain, limited situations, an attorney will not only make an objection but also will instruct her client not to answer a particular question. Rule 30(c)(2) permits such instructions "only when necessary to preserve a privilege, to enforce a limitation ordered by the court, or to present a motion under Rule 30(d)(3)." Rule 30(d)(3)(A) in turn provides that if a deposition is being conducted "in bad faith or in a manner that unreasonably annoys, embarrasses, or oppresses the deponent or party," either the deponent or a party can suspend the deposition and seek a court order terminating or limiting the deposition.[14]

The Rule 30(c)(2) instruction not to answer a deposition question seeking privileged information might occur in the following fashion:

Attorney Smith:	What did your doctor tell you about your medical condition?
Attorney Jones:	I object because that question seeks information privileged under the doctor-patient privilege.
Attorney Smith:	I believe that any such privilege has been waived. Mr. Witness, will you please answer my question?
Attorney Jones:	I instruct my client not to answer that question because it seeks privileged information.

---

14.   Rule 30(d)(3)(C) also provides: "Rule 37(a)(5) applies to the award of expenses" incurred in relation to such a motion. *See* Chapter 10, *infra.*

Witness: Upon the advice of my counsel, I refuse to answer that question.

Attorney Smith: I'd like to ask the court reporter to mark his notes so that my question and the witness's refusal can be transcribed in connection with a motion for an order compelling an answer to my question.

In this situation, many examining attorneys would complete the deposition and then file a Rule 37 motion seeking an order compelling the testimony in question. If, however, major areas of deposition questioning hinge on the specific testimony sought, the attorney can suspend the deposition in midcourse and seek an immediate court ruling pursuant to Rule 37(a)(3)(B)(i).

While an attorney may need to instruct a client not to answer in certain situations, there is no similar basis for instructing a third-party witness. It may be important to establish through deposition questioning whether deponents such as employees or former employees of a corporation are the clients of corporate counsel. Even if they are not, an attorney might suggest that they consult with their own counsel before divulging obviously privileged information.

C. THE USES OF ORAL DEPOSITIONS

Rule 30(e) provides that, if requested by the deponent or a party before completion of the deposition, the deponent has 30 days after notification that a deposition transcript or recording is available in which to review the transcript or recording and, if he wishes to make changes in form or substance, "sign a statement listing the changes and the reasons for making them."[15] Because the deposition transcript may be used to attempt to impeach the deponent at trial, it usually will make sense for the examining party to request this 30 day review period. If one represents the deponent, or will call the deponent as a witness, it also generally is a good idea to have him inspect and sign the deposition so that any changes in the transcript can be made well before trial. A mere request that a review period be afforded the deponent does not ensure that the deposition recording or transcript actually will be reviewed, but the deposition official is required by Rule 30(e)(2) to indicate "whether a review was requested and, if so, * * * attach any changes the deponent makes during the 30-day period."

Although deposition transcripts traditionally were filed with the court, Rule 5(d)(1) now provides that depositions are not to be filed "until they are used in the proceeding or the court orders filing." Assuming that filing is not permitted or required under Rule 5(d)(1), the court reporter is directed by Rule 30(f)(1) to send the transcript "to the attorney who arranged for the transcript or recording," and that attorney "must store it

---

15. *See* Gill, Note, "Depose and Expose: The Scope of Authorized Deposition Changes under Rule 30(e)," 41 *U. C. Davis L. Rev.* 357 (2007).

under conditions that will protect it against loss, destruction, tampering, or deterioration."

Whether or not it is filed with the court, there are numerous uses that can be made of a deposition transcript. In order to use the deposition most effectively, counsel must know its contents. For this reason, depositions often are indexed or summarized. This permits easy access to the deposition's contents and avoids the need to reread the entire deposition every time a different bit of testimony is sought. Such an index can be particularly useful if the deposition was recorded on audio or video tape. In such cases the testimony can be digitized so that it can be searched by bar coding such as is used in the supermarket checkout line.

Because of the scope of discovery under Rule 26(b)(1), discovery depositions can be used to obtain relevant information that may not itself be admissible at trial, so long as it "appears reasonably calculated to lead to the discovery of admissible evidence." For example, inadmissible hearsay may identify witnesses who can give direct, and admissible, testimony concerning certain matters.

The use of depositions at trial is governed not only by the Federal Rules of Civil Procedure, but also by the Federal Rules of Evidence.[16] Generally, depositions can be used to impeach the trial testimony of a witness.[17] If the deposition is offered against a party-deponent by an opposing party or if the deponent is unavailable at trial, the deposition may be admitted as substantive evidence.[18] Although the exact manner in which it will be used may not be clear at the time a deposition is taken, the different possible uses of depositions should be kept in mind in planning deposition discovery.

NOTES AND QUESTIONS CONCERNING ORAL DEPOSITIONS

1. While Federal Rule of Civil Procedure 30(b)(3) provides that parties may take audio or video depositions without leave of court, Rule 30 contains numerous requirements to ensure that any recording provides an accurate depiction of the deposition. Unless the parties agree to the contrary, all depositions must be conducted before an officer authorized to administer oaths and the deposition must begin with certain introductory statements by the officer and the administration of an oath or affirmation to the deponent. Fed. R. Civ. P. 28(a), 30(b)(5). Rule 30(b)(5)(B) also provides that identifying statements shall be repeated by the officer "at the beginning of each unit of recording medium" and that the "deponent's and attorney's appearance or demeanor must not be distorted through recording techniques." Finally, Rule 30(b)(5)(C) provides that at the end of the deposition "the officer must state on the record that the deposition is complete and must set out any stipulations made by the attorneys about custody of the transcript or recording and of the exhibits, or about any other pertinent matters."

---

16. Fed. R. Civ. P. 32(a).

17. Fed. R. Civ. P. 32(a)(2); Fed. R. Evid. 613.

18. Fed. R. Civ. P. 32(a)(3), 32(a)(4); Fed. R. Evid. 801(d)(2), 804(b)(1).

2. What are the relative advantages and disadvantages of video depositions? In what situations might they effectively be used? *See* Mathias et al., "Lights, Camera, Action: Taking, Defending, and Using Videotape Depositions," *Trial Practice* 8 (2007); Neubauer, "Videotaping Depositions," *Litigation*, Summer 1993, at 60; Figari & Loewinsohn, "Videotaped Depositions Come to Court," *Litigation*, Spring 1988, at 35; Underwood, "The Videotape Deposition: Using Modern Technology for Effective Discovery" (pts. 1 & 2), *Prac. Law.*, April 15, 1985, at 61, *Prac. Law.*, June 1, 1985, at 65.

Both attorneys taking and defending video depositions must remember that the deposition will be filmed for possible viewing by the judge or jury. An attorney thus should pace her examination so that the video technician doesn't need to change the recording medium or halt the deposition for another reason just as counsel reaches the most crucial part of her examination.

A good video technician is essential in ensuring that the video deposition will have the maximum impact at trial. This won't be the case if lawyer or deponent can't be heard on the recording, if the deponent doesn't look into the camera, or if the viewer's eyes are drawn to the diploma on the wall behind the deponent or to the deponent's garish clothing rather than to the deponent himself. Attorneys should confirm that the camera angle and framing of the witness are appropriate and that the camera will not be zoomed in or out during the deposition (zooming in on the witness, for instance, to emphasize particular testimony or to show nervous perspiration). Unless the camera is positioned over the shoulder of the examining attorney, the videotape will show the witness speaking to one side, and if the examining attorney asks particular questions while walking behind the camera the witness's eyes will be seen as "shifty" on the videotape. *See* McArdle, "Video Depositions: The New Weapon of Persuasion at Trial," *Lawyers Weekly USA*, Mar. 6, 2000, at S22.

In the event that another party takes the video deposition of one of your witnesses, you may want to conduct a redirect examination of that witness to create some helpful testimony to show the judge or jury in the event that another portion of the video deposition is offered at trial. Mathias et al., "Lights, Camera, Action: Taking, Defending, and Using Videotape Depositions," *Trial Practice* 8, 10 (2007).

3. Courts have approved the use of video depositions to conduct experiments and recreate accidents for courtroom viewing. In *Roberts v. Homelite Division of Textron, Inc.,* 109 F.R.D. 664, 667 (N.D.Ind. 1986), the court granted defendant's request to take a video deposition of plaintiff at the place of his accident so that he could demonstrate how he was injured by defendant's lawn mower. In *Carson v. Burlington Northern Inc.,* 52 F.R.D. 492 (D.Neb. 1971), the court permitted the defendant to take plaintiff's deposition in defendant's machine shop to show the manner in which he operated machinery prior to and at the time of his accident. *See also Emerson Electric Co. v. Superior Court,* 16 Cal.4th 1101, 946 P.2d 841, 68 Cal.Rptr.2d 883 (1997) (under California civil discovery statute, deposition "answer" at a videotaped deposition includes nonverbal as well as verbal responses, so that tort plaintiff may be compelled to reenact or diagram accident).

4. Federal Rule of Civil Procedure 30(b)(4) in part provides: "The parties may stipulate—or the court may on motion order—that a deposition be taken by telephone or other remote means." What practical problems do telephone depositions present? Why might parties nevertheless agree to such depositions? What if the witness at a telephone deposition refuses to answer a question?

5. While Federal Rule of Civil Procedure 30(c)(1) requires that deposition testimony be recorded in some fashion, it does not require that it be transcribed. Why might counsel not want to have deposition testimony transcribed?

6. Under 28 U.S.C. § 1920(2), the federal courts can tax as costs "[f]ees for printed or electronically recorded transcripts necessarily obtained for use in the case." Pursuant to this statutory provision, prevailing parties sometimes can recover deposition expenses as costs. *Templeman v. Chris Craft Corp.*, 770 F.2d 245, 248–49 (1st Cir.), *cert. denied*, 474 U.S. 1021 (1985); *Koppinger v. Cullen–Schiltz & Assocs.*, 513 F.2d 901, 911 (8th Cir. 1975). Potentially recoverable fees include the costs of video depositions. *Craftsmen Limousine, Inc. v. Ford Motor Co.*, 579 F.3d 894, 897–98 (8th Cir. 2009); *Morrison v. Reichhold Chemicals, Inc.*, 97 F.3d 460, 463–466 (11th Cir. 1996) (per curiam).

7. Recent technological advances have expanded the possibilities for taking Rule 30(b)(4) depositions by remote means. Satellite communications technology permits lawyers in one location to take the deposition of a witness located in another city. Internet deposition services now permit live deposition video, two-way audio, real-time court reporter's transcripts, and private instant messaging to communicate with other attorneys during the deposition. Chambers, "Service Allows Attorneys to Take Depositions on Internet," *Chicago Daily Law Bulletin*, Mar. 29, 2000, at 1. In determining whether to utilize such modern technology, counsel must carefully weigh the advantages of being physically present at a deposition against the savings in time and expense that electronic depositions may afford counsel and their clients. *See generally* Hecht, *Effective Depositions* 492–96 (2d ed. 2010); Parker et al., "The Paperless Deposition," *Utah Bar J.* 36 (Jan./Feb. 2007).

8. Although the objection of privilege is generally raised to specific deposition questions, there are situations in which any deposition questioning arguably may violate a recognized privilege. Consider the following opposition to a motion to compel deposition testimony:

> Richard Wade, Jr. should not be ordered to submit to oral examination, because he is the plaintiff per se in the case and is acting as his own attorney at present. To order the attorney for plaintiff to undergo oral examination is not in the best interest of justice or the plaintiff.

Plaintiff's Opposition to Defendants Motions to Extend Time to Respond to Rule 34 and to Compel Deposition of Plaintiff and for Award of Expenses, *Wade v. United States Steel Corp.*, C.A. No. 76–670 (N.D.Ohio 1977).

9. Does Rule 32(a)(3) really mean what it says in providing that an adverse party may use "for any purpose" the deposition of another party? Consider the following trial transcript:

The Court:	Next witness.
Ms. Olschner:	Your Honor, at this time, I would like to swat Mr. Buck in the head with his client's deposition.
The Court:	You mean read it?
Ms. Olschner:	No sir, I mean swat him in the head with it. Pursuant to Rule 32, I may use this deposition for any purpose, and that is the purpose for which I want to use it.
The Court:	Well, it does say that. (pause) There being no objection, you may proceed.
Ms. Olschner:	Thank you, Judge Hanes. (Whereupon, Ms. Olschner swatted Mr. Buck in the head with the deposition.)
Mr. Buck:	But, Judge.
The Court:	Next witness.

Buchmeyer, "How to Use a Deposition at Trial," *Tex. Bar J.* April 1995, at 411, 412.

Exercises Concerning Depositions Under the Federal Rules

1. Your law firm represents Global Industries, Inc., the defendant in a federal diversity action filed in the United States District Court for the Southern District of California. Plaintiff Sammy Slick lists Dr. Dean Alan as an expert witness who will testify in support of Slick's products liability claims. A partner in your firm takes Dr. Alan's deposition in Chicago, where Alan lives and works. At the deposition, the partner's questions establish both Alan's expert qualifications and several expert opinions that are quite favorable to plaintiff Slick.

This case is now in trial, and, rather than calling Alan as a witness, Slick's counsel has offered the transcript of Alan's deposition. Although you have not previously worked on this case, you have been called by trial counsel and asked to write a memorandum concerning the admissibility of Alan's deposition. Because you are not sure of the exact facts concerning the deposition, your memorandum should consider the significance of (1) the reason that Alan (who is still living and working in Chicago) is not being called to testify at trial; (2) the extent to which plaintiff's counsel questioned Alan at the deposition; and (3) the stated purposes for the deposition set forth in the deposition notice. While your memorandum is to be faxed to the partner later today, she also would like your opinion as to what she could have done to prevent the possible use of Alan's deposition transcript at trial.

2. Mark David, one of your associates in your small law firm, has just called you about the following situation. David had noticed for today the depositions of Myrtle and Michael Rocca, the plaintiffs in a consumer

protection action brought against a local car dealer that your law firm represents. David believes that this action is groundless, although he has been unable to convince the court to grant summary judgment. Today is the discovery deadline imposed by the court, and trial is set for the end of next week.

Michael Rocca's deposition was scheduled to begin at 10:00, but the Roccas' counsel insisted that Myrtle Rocca sit in on this deposition. Mark David does not want her to do so, because he believes that her testimony concerning alleged conversations with the defendant car dealer otherwise may differ from the testimony of her husband. The Roccas' counsel has refused to go forward with either Michael's or Myrtle's deposition unless the other spouse can be present. The judge to whom this case is assigned is out of town until next week.

What is your advice to your colleague?

III. PREPARING WITNESSES TO BE DEPOSED

Most lawyers wouldn't dream of putting on the witness stand at trial a person who had not been adequately prepared to testify. Nevertheless, some lawyers are less attentive to the need to prepare witnesses for depositions. Despite this fact, it can be even more important to carefully prepare witnesses for depositions than for trial. Most cases settle short of trial, and settlements often are based, at least in part, upon the performance of parties and important witnesses at their depositions. In addition, depositions are the first direct experience with civil litigation for many people, and being deposed can be an uncomfortable experience. Finally, a witness's eventual trial testimony usually is limited, as a practical matter, by the deposition testimony given by that witness.

Thorough preparation of witnesses for their depositions can directly effect the deposition testimony given. Litigation attorneys interviewed in a 1979 study stated that their deposition preparation techniques resulted in witnesses not revealing arguably significant information in approximately sixty percent of their cases.[19] This statistic may not reflect any ethical improprieties, but merely deposition witnesses who refused to volunteer information and responded only to the specific questions put to them. However, statistics such as this do indicate why current discovery practice has so often become costly and inefficient.

The two basic areas about which witnesses should be prepared are: (1) the facts and claims in the particular case (deposition substance) and (2) the nature of oral depositions (deposition procedure). It is helpful for witnesses to understand generally what the present case is about, as well as how their particular testimony fits within that case. Simply by explain-

---

19. Brazil, "Civil Discovery: How Bad Are the Problems?," *A.B.A.J.*, April 1981, at 450, 451. *See also* Brazil, "Civil Discovery: Lawyers' Views of its Effectiveness, Its Principal Problems and Abuses," 1980 *A. B. Found. Res. J.* 787, 819–21.

ing to a witness why his deposition has been noticed may help him better understand and deal with deposition questioning.

The witness should be shown important documents about which he may be questioned, including any statements he may have given that have been produced to opposing counsel. While the witness should be cautioned to completely read documents shown to him during the deposition, having reviewed the documents prior to the deposition should make him more comfortable in answering deposition questions. The witness also should be questioned concerning documents that he believes he may be asked about at the deposition.

In preparing a witness, counsel must be aware that the examining attorney may ask about documents that a witness reviewed in preparation for the deposition. Under Federal Rule of Evidence 612 that attorney may be entitled to those documents.[20] Even if opposing counsel already is aware of the documents, she may be interested in knowing the specific documents that other counsel considered important enough to review prior to the deposition. However, if the documents are important and opposing counsel is likely to ask about them, they generally should be discussed with witnesses prior to their depositions. More generally, counsel should remember that the attorney-client privilege only extends to clients and should conduct witness preparation accordingly.

The final aspect of "substantive" deposition preparation is raising with the witness the important questions that are likely to be asked during the deposition. This can be done conversationally, although many attorneys play the role of opposing counsel and conduct short examinations patterned upon the anticipated deposition questioning.

During deposition preparation, counsel should be careful not to tell the witness what his deposition answers should be. As one court has noted, "[The attorney's] duty is to extract the facts from the witness, not to pour them into him; to learn what the witness does know, not to teach

---

20. *In re Comair Air Disaster Litigation,* 100 F.R.D. 350 (E.D.Ky. 1983); *James Julian, Inc. v. Raytheon Co.,* 93 F.R.D. 138, 144–46 (D.Del. 1982). *See also In re Seroquel Products Liability Litig.,* 2008 WL 591929 (M.D.Fla. 2008) (even without reliance on Federal Rule of Evidence 612, documents reviewed by witness before deposition testimony must be produced because defendant could not establish work product protection). *But see Sporck v. Peil,* 759 F.2d 312 (3d Cir.), *cert. denied,* 474 U.S. 903 (1985); *North Carolina Electric Membership Corp. v. Carolina Power & Light Co.,* 108 F.R.D. 283, 285–86 (M.D.N.C. 1985). *See generally* Applegate, "Preparing for Rule 612," *Litigation,* Spring 1993, at 17; Robinson, "Duet or Duel: Federal Rule of Evidence 612 and the Work Product Doctrine Codified in Civil Procedure Rule 26(b)(3)," 69 *U.Cin. L. Rev.* 197 (2000).

One judge has considered the following factors in determining whether documents that otherwise would be protected from disclosure by the work-product doctrine should be disclosed under Rule 612: (1) the status of the witness (expert or non-expert); (2) the nature of the issue in dispute (general or specific and case-dispositive); (3) when the events in question took place; (4) when the documents were reviewed; (5) the number of documents reviewed; (6) whether the witness prepared the documents reviewed; (7) whether the documents contain "pure" attorney work product; (8) whether the documents previously had been disclosed; and (9) whether there are credible concerns regarding manipulation, concealment, or destruction of evidence. *Nutramax Laboratories, Inc. v. Twin Laboratories Inc.,* 183 F.R.D. 458, 469–70 (D.Md. 1998). *See also In re Managed Care Litigation,* 415 F.Supp.2d 1378, 1381 (S.D.Fla. 2006) ("[A]utomatic waiver is inconsistent with both the plain language of Rule 612 and with the advisory committee notes.").

him what he ought to know."[21] Nevertheless, deposition preparation can include work on difficult areas of anticipated questioning and possible deposition inconsistencies.

Video recording is increasingly used in deposition preparation. Commercially prepared recordings, containing portions of simulated depositions, can be used to explain deposition procedures. Some attorneys prepare their clients for depositions by video recording their responses to likely deposition questions. If a deposition itself is to be video recorded, it may be particularly helpful for an important witness to view herself on video during deposition preparation. This will permit the witness to see the importance of looking directly into the camera, not appearing evasive, and dressing appropriately for the deposition. The degree of realism injected into sample deposition questioning is dependent upon the style and preferences of the attorney preparing the witness and the characteristics and importance of the particular witness.

In addition to preparing the witness for the substance of the anticipated deposition questioning, counsel should explain deposition procedures to the witness. The witness should understand what a deposition is and the manner in which his testimony will be elicited. He must appreciate that, while no judge will be present at the deposition, the deposition will produce sworn testimony that will be very important in the case. Witnesses can be shown deposition transcripts from other cases so that they understand that everything they say during the deposition will be transcribed.

The attorney's explanation of deposition procedures should help to lessen the quite natural anxiety that witnesses have about depositions. Witnesses should be told that depositions are an ordinary part of the pretrial process and that opposing parties and their main witnesses will be deposed. Counsel also should give witnesses plenty of opportunity to ask questions and raise concerns about their upcoming depositions.

Finally, clients and important witnesses must understand that the discovery deposition is usually not the place to offer all affirmative evidence supporting a given claim. The deponent should be cautioned to respond truthfully to the questions asked during the deposition, but not to volunteer information about which the examining attorney has not asked. The deponent should understand that he will have the chance to give his complete testimony in response to the questions that you will ask him at trial.[22]

---

21. *In re Eldridge*, 82 N.Y. 161, 171 (1880). In *Ibarra v. Baker*, 338 Fed.Appx. 457 (5th Cir. 2009), the Court of Appeals upheld findings that attorneys had improperly coached witnesses prior to their depositions by having an expert witness meet with the deponents and suggest a novel defense theory and specific facts to them. See *also* Goldman & Winegardner, "The Anti–False Testimony Principle and the Fundamentals of Ethical Preparation of Deposition Witnesses," 59 *Cath. U. L. Rev.* 1 (2009); "Symposium on Witness Preparation," 30 *Tex. Tech. L. Rev.* 1333 (1999); Wydick, "The Ethics of Witness Coaching," 17 *Cardozo L. Rev.* 1 (1995).

22. Professor Steven Lubet has suggested that, because most cases settle, the traditional advice that deponents "only answer the question that is asked" may not make sense in all cases. Instead, he suggests that in some cases counsel can gain an advantage in later settlement

In explaining deposition procedures to a witness, a deposition preparation sheet such as the following can be helpful. Such a sheet can be sent to the witness prior to the deposition preparation session in order to save time at that session.

DEPOSITIONS[23]

[*CASE NAME*]

WHEN:	[TIME OF DEPOSITION]
WHERE:	[PLACE OF DEPOSITION]
ATTORNEYS:	[NAMES AND PHONE NUMBERS OF ATTORNEYS DEFENDING DEPOSITION]

GENERAL INFORMATION:

You are about to have your deposition taken. A deposition is a discovery procedure in which an individual is asked to respond under oath to questions asked by an attorney for one of the parties in a lawsuit. There are several purposes of a deposition: (1) to provide the attorney with information that can be used to establish various aspects of the case; (2) to fix the testimony of a party or a potential witness so that it is available if that person is later unable to attend the trial; (3) to impeach or discredit the testimony of a party or witness who changes his or her story at the time of trial. Therefore, it is very important that you not guess at answers or think that mistakes can easily be corrected later.

The procedure for a deposition is that you will be in a room with your attorneys [list attorney names], plaintiff's [or defendant's] attorneys [list attorney names], and a court reporter. The court reporter will put you under oath and will record the proceedings. Plaintiff's [or defendant's] attorneys will question you first; when they are done, your attorneys will have the opportunity to ask you questions if there is a need for that. You will have the opportunity to read and sign the typed transcript of the deposition before it is filed with the court.

Your attorneys will discuss the deposition with you before you are deposed. At that time, they will answer any questions that you might have. Please review this paper and the discovery responses with which you have been supplied before that meeting so that you will be prepared to discuss this matter with your attorneys.

HELPFUL HINTS:

1.   Set your own pace. You're under no obligation to respond immediately or quickly. Take sufficient time to understand the question and to

---

negotiations by encouraging her witnesses to reveal more, rather than less, information in their depositions. Lubet, "Showing Your Hand: A Counter–Intuitive Strategy for Deposition Defense," *Litigation*, Winter 2003, at 38.

23.   This sheet is based upon material that originally was obtained from attorneys within the Federal Programs Branch of the Civil Division of the United States Department of Justice. It has been modified by the author over time.

For a lengthier set of rules for the deponent see Israel, "130 Rules for Every Deponent," *Litigation*, Summer 2001, at 46.

formulate a responsive answer. You are entitled to plenty of time to think before you answer.

2. Don't begin a response before the question is completed. As a rule, allow at least 2–3 seconds (longer, if you wish) between question and answer. This allows time for your attorney to decide whether to pose an objection to the question.

3. If an objection is made, do not answer the question until your attorney tells you to do so.

4. Answer only the question that is asked. It is very important that you listen carefully and understand the question. Do not answer the question you want asked; answer the question that is asked.

5. If a question can be answered with a "yes" or "no," you should answer it that way. Do not volunteer information. For example, if the question is "Did you speak with Mr. X?" and the answer is "Yes," then say "Yes," not "Yes, I spoke with him several times" or "Yes, I spoke with him at the meeting with Y."

6. If you don't understand a question, say so. Do not try to answer a question if you don't understand what's being asked.

7. Do not be evasive. However, if you honestly can't remember, don't be afraid to say so.

8. You are to testify from your own knowledge, not from what someone else says may have happened or from what you think could have happened. Do not guess. If the answer to a question is not known to you, say so.

9. While you should not bring any documents to the deposition, you may be asked about documents by the examining attorney. Before responding to a question about a document, ask to see the document. Read it carefully before answering.

10. You may be asked if you spoke with your attorneys about your testimony or about matters that might be raised during the deposition. Because you will have discussed the deposition with your attorneys, your answer will be "Yes." Do not be embarrassed or nervous about this question. While it is unethical for an attorney to tell you what to say, it is proper and part of a lawyer's duty to explain the nature of the matters involved and to prepare you for what to expect.

11. Be courteous to the questioner. Do not argue with the questioning attorney. Resist the temptation to get "cute," angry, or defensive. Do your best to remain calm and polite.

12. Do not look at your attorneys when asked a question. It is improper for your attorneys to "coach" a witness, so they will be maintaining an impassive expression during your testimony. You should not interpret this as a sign of disinterest or a sign that you are not doing well.

13. Try to keep your voice loud, clear, and distinct so that your testimony can be taken down by the court reporter. Do not respond by head shakes or nods.

14. The most important thing to remember in answering questions is: *Tell the truth.*

15. If you have *any* questions, please call your attorneys before the deposition begins. If you have a question for your attorneys during the deposition, request permission to go off the record to ask your attorneys a question.

———

As you practice law, you no doubt will adapt deposition preparation sheets such as this one to suit your own purposes. Remember, though, that Federal Rule of Evidence 612 may give the examining party the right to a copy of any sheet with which a deponent has been prepared.

Whether you use witness preparation sheets or not, witnesses should be thoroughly prepared before their depositions. The extra time invested in deposition preparation should pay handsome dividends during later settlement negotiations or trial.

Exercises Concerning Deposition Preparation

1. As one of the counsel for the Pittston Company in the Buffalo Creek disaster litigation, you have been assigned the task of preparing for their depositions Pittston's Chief of Engineering; the engineer within Pittston's Engineering Department who is in charge of overseeing and approving dam construction; and a Pittston engineer who inspected the site of the failed dam several days after that dam collapsed. Deposition notices, accompanied by Rule 34 document production requests, have been served setting these depositions for Monday, Tuesday, and Wednesday of the week after next. Due to the document requests and the depositions of Buffalo Creek engineers that plaintiffs took last month, you have a fairly good idea of the types of questions that these individuals will be asked.

Your assignment is to write a short memorandum describing the manner in which you will prepare these individuals for their depositions. In your memorandum be sure to address (1) the specific manner in which you will prepare each of these employees; (2) whether you will give them anything to read either before or after you have met with them; (3) whether you will prepare these employees individually, in a group, or both separately and together; (4) the instructions that you will give these individuals for their depositions; (5) the extent of detail that you will go into about plaintiffs' lawsuit and where the testimony of these three employees fits within that lawsuit; (6) when you will prepare these employees and how long the preparation sessions should take; and (7) any instructions that you will give the employees about talking among themselves or with others before their depositions.

After completing the above memorandum, come to class ready to prepare the three Pittston engineers for their depositions.

2. Charles Anderson is a truck driver who is being sued for allegedly hitting seven-year-old Matthew Lawrence Mason with his truck and then speeding away from the scene of the accident. The eyewitness testimony concerning the accident is conflicting.

(a) As counsel for Mr. Anderson, prepare for their depositions:

(1) Charles Anderson;

(2) Lindsay Elisabeth Rollins, the wife of Charles Anderson (whose testimony is that Anderson was at home at the time of the accident); and

(3) Greg Murray, an eyewitness who states that it was not Anderson's truck that hit Matthew Mason.

(b) As counsel for Matthew Mason, prepare for their depositions:

(1) Matthew Mason;

(2) Matthew's parents (one of whom witnessed the accident); and

(3) Emily Katherine Pocatello, an eyewitness who states that Charles Anderson's truck hit Matthew Mason.

IV. DEPOSITION STRATEGIES FOR EXAMINING ATTORNEYS

To be successful, depositions must be well planned. This section addresses factors to be considered in planning which depositions to take and the questions that should be asked at specific depositions.

A. PRELIMINARY CONSIDERATIONS

The first strategic decision that must be made by an attorney contemplating deposition discovery is whether to depose particular individuals at all. Too many attorneys routinely "depose the usual suspects" without giving any real thought to the matter. Rather than functioning in such an automatic fashion, counsel should determine the purpose that particular depositions might serve and the potential disadvantages of taking those depositions.

One of the major potential disadvantages of deposition discovery is the cost of depositions—in attorney time, client time, and reporters' fees. Not only will your own depositions be costly, but your deposition notices may trigger a wave of deposition notices from opposing counsel. Depositions also may educate opposing counsel, both about your case (through the questions that you ask) and about their case (through their preparation for the depositions and listening to actual deposition testimony).

Another possible deposition disadvantage is that the deposition transcript may perpetuate damaging information. This should be a particular concern if the potential deponent is in ill health or for other reasons may not be available to testify at trial; in such a case the deposition transcript, which you have created, may be offered as evidence at trial pursuant to Federal Rule of Civil Procedure 32(a)(4). Nevertheless, in most cases it is better to learn the worst early on so that you can prepare to meet the evidence at trial.

Once possible deposition disadvantages have been considered, counsel must determine the purposes that would be served by a deposition and the manner in which a deposition would fit within the comprehensive discovery plan. Depositions can be used to discover information from another party or witness, to preserve testimony for trial, to support a summary judgment or other pretrial motion, to pin witnesses down to a particular version of the facts prior to trial, to evaluate the demeanor and credibility of important trial witnesses, to authenticate relevant documents or things, to learn a bit more about opposing counsel (if she is unknown to you), and, if a case is likely to settle, to use your questioning to display information and your competence and preparation to opposing counsel and parties. The extent to which these purposes can be achieved should determine whether particular depositions should be taken, the order in which they should be taken, and the types of deposition questioning that should be employed.

Regardless of the purposes that a deposition is to serve, attorneys need to prepare thoroughly for the deposition questioning. If the deponent is not represented by counsel, an informal witness interview can help counsel determine (1) whether to depose that person and (2) the questions that should be asked if a deposition is held. It's also important to talk with third-party witnesses to ensure that their depositions are scheduled at convenient times and places. In fact, the sequence and scheduling of all depositions should be carefully planned. If several witnesses are questioned about the same subject, opposing counsel may anticipate the questions that will be asked of the latter witnesses and prepare those witnesses accordingly.

In planning depositions, the examining attorney should review allegations made in the pleadings, prior statements of the deponent, and all relevant discovery responses and other documents. If an expert witness is to be deposed, the writings of that individual should be read and analyzed. For tactical reasons, an attorney may decide not to pursue at the deposition all of the areas that such investigation reveals. Nevertheless, it's helpful to have as much information about a witness as possible before taking his deposition.

Some thought should be given to where a deposition will be held. Many attorneys find it most convenient to take depositions in their own offices. Some attorneys believe that a witness gains a psychological advantage from being deposed in a familiar setting such as the witness's office or other place of business.

However, there can be advantages to "accommodating" a busy witness by taking a deposition at his office or place of work. Examining attorneys can gain information about deponents merely by observing them in their work environment. If an expert witness has hundreds of message slips on her desk, she may not have the necessary time to devote to this case. If she has copies of particular treatises on her office bookshelves, she may recognize those treatises as authoritative. It also is difficult for a witness to reject an informal request for a document discussed in a deposition if that document is in a file cabinet in the next room.

Wherever the deposition will be held, the examining attorney should be sure to reserve the location in advance. She also must arrange for a court reporter and inform him of the time, place, and expected length of the deposition. If the deposition transcript is needed on an expedited basis, this should be confirmed with the reporter in advance. Federal Rule of Civil Procedure 30(b)(1) requires that the deposition notice be sent to all parties, not merely party-deponents. If a non-party will be deposed, a Rule 45 subpoena must be issued.

On the day of the deposition, the attorney should arrive a few minutes before the time set in the deposition notice. If the deponent is not represented by counsel, this may permit the attorney to speak briefly with him and continue to build witness rapport. Court reporters also appreciate attorneys who arrive early for depositions. The reporter's job can be made easier by giving him a copy of the deposition notice (from which he can copy the case caption), the names of the deponent and attorneys, and the spellings of any unusual names or other words that are likely to come up in the deposition. If there is no tactical reason to withhold such documents, the examining attorney can use the time right before the deposition to give the reporter copies of any documents that will be marked as deposition exhibits. Counsel also should bring to the deposition copies of all anticipated deposition exhibits for other counsel so that the exhibits can be introduced during the deposition without breaking the flow of deposition questioning.

Careful thought should be given to these details of deposition preparation. As important as are the questions that counsel will ask, factors such as the deposition setting may contribute to ultimate deposition success.

B. DEPOSITION QUESTIONING

The decision has been made to depose a particular witness. It's now time to consider strategies for obtaining the most helpful deposition testimony from that witness.

1. General Strategies

At the outset of some depositions, attorneys may ask whether the "usual stipulations" are in force. In most jurisdictions, these stipulations include agreements to forego review of the deposition transcript by the deponent, to reserve all objections except as to the form of question until trial, and to dispense with the filing of the deposition transcript with the court. While there may be reasons to enter into stipulations in certain situations, there are many situations in which stipulations make no sense. A deposition may be a more powerful impeachment tool if reviewed by the deponent, Rules 30 and 32 contain specific provisions concerning the reservation of deposition objections, and Rule 5(d)(1) provides that depositions are not to be filed until they are used in the proceeding or the court orders filing. Whatever the relative advantages or disadvantages of particular stipulations in a given case, the deposition transcript should quite clearly specify the substance of any stipulations. An agreement to "the usual" (undefined) stipulations only creates the potential for future conflict among the parties.

Rule 30(b)(5)(A) specifies certain preliminary matters that are to be set forth upon the record by the court reporter or other officer before whom the deposition is being conducted. This individual is to start the deposition with a statement that includes "(i) the officer's name and business address; (ii) the date, time, and place of the deposition; (iii) the deponent's name; (iv) the officer's administration of the oath or affirmation to the deponent; and (v) the identity of all persons present." After these preliminaries, the examining attorney might begin her questioning as follows:

Examining Attorney:	Mr. Smith, my name is Clara Darrow, and, as you know, I represent the defendant in this case, Acme Exterminators. I'll be taking this deposition today pursuant to the Federal Rules of Civil Procedure and the Federal Rules of Evidence. With me today is co-counsel James Cohen, and you are represented today by attorney Janice Bell.
	Mr. Smith, have you ever had your deposition taken before?
Deponent:	No, I haven't.
Examining Attorney:	Well, then, let me explain what this is all about. The purpose of this deposition is to learn about your claims against Acme Exterminators. I will be asking you questions about those claims, and the court reporter, Mr. Clark, will take down both my questions and your answers.
	I will try to make my questions as straightforward as possible. If I ask you any question that is confusing or that you don't understand, I'll be glad to explain it for you. Will

	you agree to ask me to explain any questions that you don't understand?
Deponent:	Sure.
Examining Attorney:	I also want to be sure that the reporter gets your complete answers to all of the questions that I ask. Will you tell me if I begin to ask a new question before you've completed your answer to an earlier question?
Deponent:	Yes.
Examining Attorney:	All right, then, let me now ask you about

* * *

By setting the stage in this fashion, several things are accomplished. The examining attorney has demonstrated her general competence and knowledge of depositions. In addition, the witness has agreed on the record to note any questions that are confusing or that cut into a prior answer. These agreements can be used at trial if the witness tries to explain away deposition answers on such grounds. Finally, if opening statements such as these are followed by routine questions about the deponent's background, the witness may relax and drop his guard prior to the tougher questions that will be asked later in the deposition.

While the types of deposition questions asked will depend upon the purpose of the deposition, several general comments can be made about deposition questioning. It is extremely difficult to conduct a coherent deposition without having an outline upon which to base deposition questions. Outlines may organize deposition questioning chronologically or logically by topics. While structure is important, it may be possible to obtain more spontaneous answers from a witness if not all the deposition questions proceed in a predictable fashion. The examining attorney must be careful not to merely read questions to the witness and to carefully *listen* to all answers. This should permit counsel to pursue any answers that were not anticipated in planning the questioning.

While flexibility in questioning is essential, a deposition outline can both serve as a guide for initial questioning and as a check list that can be used to make sure that all major areas have been covered. An outline concerning an important conversation might look like this:

Date of conversation?

How do you remember the date?

Any written memorialization?

Time of conversation?

How do you remember the time?

Any written memorialization?

What were you doing before and after the conversation?

Place of conversation?

Location of conversation?

Other people present during conversation?

Where were they positioned during conversation?

Substance of conversation?

How do you know?

Any notes or other memorialization?

Length of conversation?

End of conversation?

Counsel should remember that, in most cases, only a written transcript of the deposition will be produced. Head shakes and other relevant gestures therefore should be noted for the record, and the witness should be asked to give answers that can be transcribed by the court reporter. Questions should be kept short, simple, and understandable. For example, a "no" answer to the following question will be ambiguous, at best: "Isn't it true that you never warned the citizens about the flood?" Repeated use of prefatory phrases such as "isn't it true?" or "you don't dispute the fact, do you?" may result in a confusing transcript and add to transcription expenses.

There is no one correct style for lawyers to adopt in the deposition setting. As with trial work, the best advice is to adopt a style and manner of questioning with which you are most comfortable.[24] There is little to be gained, and much to be lost, from displaying discourtesy toward opposing counsel, opposing parties, or third-party witnesses. The cooperation of these people can be quite helpful during the course of a case, especially if settlement negotiations eventually are undertaken.

The specific deposition questions asked by the examining attorney depend upon the type of deposition that is being taken. Depositions can be roughly categorized as: (1) discovery depositions, which are taken primarily to discover information, or (2) trial depositions, which are taken with the intention that they will be offered at trial in lieu of the live testimony of the deponent.

Most depositions are discovery depositions. Because their purpose is to discover information, questions asked at discovery depositions generally are very open ended (calling for a narrative answer rather than a "yes" or "no" response). If the deposition is being taken for discovery purposes, one of counsel's main jobs is to get the deponent to talk. Many of the same techniques used in client interviews can be used to encourage witnesses to talk more freely at depositions.[25]

An initial question to a witness at a discovery deposition might be: "Tell me what happened to you when the dam burst on February 26,

---

24. While the suggestion to "be yourself" is generally sound advice, Mark Twain warned that this can be the worst advice that you can give some people. Presumably those reading this are not in the small minority to whom Twain was alluding.

25. *See* Chapter 2, Section II, *supra* p. 12.

1972." The question has been asked for discovery purposes, and the witness should be given as much time as necessary to completely answer the question. Most people become uncomfortable with long silences in a room full of people. If the examining attorney occasionally pauses, witnesses may volunteer information they would not under rapid-fire questioning.

After initially obtaining a narrative statement from the witness, counsel can take the witness back through the narrative and follow up with more specific questions. In order to effectively ask follow-up questions, it helps to have notes of the witness's testimony. However, the very act of taking notes may stifle deposition testimony. One solution to this problem is to have co-counsel take notes, and then consult with her before the deposition questioning is terminated.

Because the purpose of a discovery deposition is to ascertain everything that a particular witness knows about a particular matter, the attorney should "close up" each segment of deposition questioning by summarizing the witness's testimony and asking if there is anything else that the witness can recall concerning the event in question. For example: "So you had ten minutes warning before the flood entered your house?" Even in a discovery deposition, the deponent should be pinned down to a specific version of the facts. However, the leading questions necessary to accomplish this only should be asked once the witness's narrative has been elicited.

If a witness appears to suffer from a momentary memory loss, ask him what would help him remember further details. By pinning the witness down in this manner, it is less likely that his memory will be remarkably "refreshed" after the deposition and that he will give trial testimony that was not provided at the deposition. For similar reasons, many attorneys end their examinations with questions such as: "Is there any other information about [a particular event] that you haven't yet testified about in this deposition?" or "Are there any other matters that you believe you might testify about at trial that you haven't testified about during this deposition?"

Deposition witnesses frequently hesitate to give specific estimates about matters on which they are uncertain. Follow-up questioning often can produce at least a general estimate from the witness in these situations:

Examining Attorney:	Although you've testified that you can't give an estimate of the speed of plaintiff's car, I wonder if you could tell us whether that car was traveling more than 35 miles per hour?
Deponent:	Why, sure, the car was traveling at least 35 miles per hour.
Examining Attorney:	Was it traveling more than 45 miles per hour?
Deponent:	Yes, I believe so.

Examining Attorney:	Was the car traveling more than the posted speed limit, 65 miles per hour?
Deponent:	No, based upon the speed of the other traffic, I don't believe that plaintiff's car was traveling more than 65 miles per hour.
Examining Attorney:	So plaintiff's car was traveling between 45 and 65 miles per hour, is that correct?
Deponent:	Yes, that's correct.

Consider pinning down a witness in this fashion whenever his testimony contains a characterization that is reasonably susceptible of multiple interpretations. It's usually better to try to obtain more specific answers at a deposition than to quibble with a witness at trial about what he meant by his deposition statement that a car was moving "fast."

Depositions are not just effective discovery devices. "Trial depositions" can be taken to preserve the testimony of a witness who may not be available to testify at trial. There may be a concern that a witness won't be alive at the time of trial or, less dramatically, will be outside the subpoena power of the trial court or otherwise unavailable. Federal Rule of Civil Procedure 32(a)(4) provides that depositions can be offered at trial in lieu of live testimony in these circumstances. Rule 27 also authorizes district courts to permit a deposition to be taken before the filing of an action or pending appeal if necessary to perpetuate testimony that may not later be available.

In order to know whether testimony should be preserved for trial, counsel must have a good sense of what the testimony will be. It therefore makes sense to talk to witnesses before deciding to take their depositions.[26] If a witness is sympathetic to your client, he can and should be prepared prior to the deposition. Because the deposition presumably will be introduced at trial, the questioning should be similar to that conducted in the courtroom and should not roam far and wide in random attempts to discover new facts for the first time.

Rarely will there be a single purpose or strategy applicable to a particular deposition. Even in a discovery deposition, the examining attorney usually will (1) first ask open-ended questions to uncover everything that a witness knows about a particular event and (2) then ask leading questions to pin the witness down to particular parts of his testimony.

The dynamics of a deposition can be as important as the specific questions asked or answers given. Depositions can be used to display investigative work and preparation that an attorney has put into her case. Depositions also give counsel a chance to evaluate the demeanor of the parties, important witnesses, and opposing counsel. The demeanor, as well

---

26. However, the very reason that some depositions are taken is because the witness will not talk voluntarily with an attorney. Indeed, Model Rule of Professional Conduct 4.2 generally prohibits attorneys from communicating with a person about the subject of the representation without the consent of that person's attorney.

as the testimony, of important witnesses can be significant in case settlements prior to trial.

By careful planning prior to depositions, and by keeping in mind the purposes that particular depositions are to serve, the most effective oral depositions can be ensured.

2. Depositions of Organizations and Examination of Documents[27]

Parties and witnesses in modern civil litigation often are organizations or are affiliated with an organization. When seeking information from organizations, Federal Rule of Civil Procedure 30(b)(6) can be extremely useful in requiring someone within the organization to designate a person to provide the specific deposition testimony sought. Nevertheless, there will be times when an attorney should exercise her right under Rule 30(b)(6) to specifically designate those representatives of an organization to be deposed.

Sometimes an initial deposition is held and then is followed by the depositions of specific individuals identified by the first deponent. Rule 30.5 of the United States District Court for the Eastern District of New York attempts to streamline this process in the following manner:

> (a) Where an officer, director or managing agent of a corporation or a government official is served with a notice of deposition or subpoena regarding a matter about which he or she has no knowledge, he or she may submit reasonably before the date noticed for the deposition an affidavit to the noticing party so stating and identifying a person within the corporation or government entity having knowledge of the subject matter involved in the pending action.

> (b) The noticing party may, notwithstanding such affidavit of the noticed witness, proceed with the deposition, subject to the witness' right to seek a protective order.[28]

Whether deposition testimony is sought from an organization or a specific individual, Rule 30(b)(2) provides that the deposition notice can be accompanied by a Rule 34 production request.[29] Similarly, Rule 45(a)(1)(C)

---

27. For general advice concerning the use of documents at a deposition see Wood, "Better Discovery Through Document Management," *Litigation*, Summer 2005, at 43.

28. Some states have adopted an "apex" rule, under which officers at the very top of a corporate hierarchy cannot be deposed unless the employee has special or unique knowledge or the information has first been pursued by other means. *Crown Cent. Petroleum Corp. v. Garcia*, 904 S.W.2d 125 (Tex. 1995); *Liberty Mut. Ins. Co. v. Superior Court of San Mateo County*, 10 Cal.App.4th 1282, 13 Cal.Rptr.2d 363 (1992). *Contra Ford Motor Co. v. Messina*, 71 S.W.3d 602, 607 (Mo. 2002). *See also In re Tennessee Valley Authority Ash Spill Cases*, 3:09–CV–06 (E.D. Tenn. May 13, 2010) (President and Chief Operating Officer of Tennessee Valley Authority found to have "unique personal knowledge" of ash spill supporting his deposition testimony in light of his congressional testimony that he was "on the scene of the disaster ... just hours after the breach occurred."). Sometimes, however, it is the very lack of knowledge about a particular issue by a high-ranking corporate officer that is relevant to a particular claim.

29. Even if documents have not been requested in advance of the deposition, counsel may want to ask the deponent whether he has brought any documents with him to the deposition. Whether or not they have been brought to the deposition, examining counsel has a strong

provides that documents or tangible things can be subpoenaed in connection with a non-party deposition. However, if there are a large number of documents responsive to a production request, it may be difficult for the examining attorney to review them at the time of the deposition.

Attorneys therefore should file their document requests sufficiently early so that the requested documents must be produced well before any depositions. Because this is sometimes not possible, many attorneys accommodate opposing counsel by providing documents shortly before the deposition at which they must be produced.[30] By reaching such agreements, depositions will proceed more smoothly and deponents and their counsel will not have to wait while examining attorneys review documents for the first time at the deposition.

If a relatively small number of documents have been produced in connection with a deposition, those documents can be made deposition exhibits. In other cases, the deponent can be asked to describe, during the deposition, the documents or categories of documents that have been produced. In either case, it's important to make a record of the documents that have been produced.

If a witness is questioned about an important document during a deposition, that document should be marked as a deposition exhibit and referred to by deposition exhibit number during the deposition. Because only a written transcript usually is made of the deposition, discussions of "this letter" may be ambiguous. Attorneys should attempt to create a deposition transcript that is both unambiguous and self-contained.

If a deposition witness describes documents that have not been produced, the examining attorney should ask for these documents on the record of the deposition. In some cases the documents can be located during a break or even while the deposition is continuing. While a person is not compelled to produce documents without a formal request, most attorneys will agree to informal requests made during a deposition (after they have had a chance to review the documents in question). The pressure on an attorney to agree to informal document production is increased if the witness states, on the record, that he has no objection to producing the documents. An attorney also may agree to informal document production during a deposition in order to preclude any attempt to redepose the witness if the documents are not produced until a later time.

---

argument that Federal Rule of Evidence 612 entitles her to any documents that the deponent has reviewed in preparing for his deposition testimony.

30. The production of requested documents in advance of depositions is more than a local custom in some jurisdictions. Rule 30.7 of the United States District Court for the Eastern District of New York provides:

Consistent with the requirements of Federal Rules of Civil Procedure 30 and 34, a party seeking production of documents of another party in connection with a deposition should schedule the deposition to allow for the production of the documents in advance of the deposition. If documents which have been so requested are not produced prior to the deposition, the party noticing the deposition may either adjourn the deposition until after such documents are produced or, without waiving the right to have access to the documents, may proceed with the deposition.

Both formal and informal document requests, as well as Rule 30(b)(6), should be used by examining attorneys in order to maximize the effectiveness of their depositions.

3.   Depositions of Experts

Federal Rule of Civil Procedure 26(b)(4)(A) permits parties to "depose any person who has been identified as an expert whose opinions may be presented at trial." Expert witnesses are routinely deposed because of the important role that experts play in modern civil litigation and the difficulty of cross-examining experts who have not been deposed prior to trial. Most of the same basic rules and strategies that apply to other depositions apply to the deposition of expert witnesses. However, if expert information has been provided pursuant to Rule 26(a)(2), a local disclosure rule or court order entered in the particular case, or party agreement, expert depositions should be modified accordingly. In most cases an expert witness report will have been provided pursuant to Rule 26(a)(2)(B), and the deposition can build upon and answer questions left unresolved by that report.

One of the major purposes of an expert deposition is to probe the qualifications of the expert. The examining attorney should request a copy of the expert's vita prior to the deposition if one has not been furnished pursuant to Rule 26(a)(2)(B). Deposition questioning can focus on those things that appear, and those things that do not appear, in the expert's vita. Questions should be asked concerning both formal education and any practical, hands-on experience that the expert possesses.

Particularly important is any testimony that the expert may have given in other cases. Counsel should obtain not only the expert's own description of this testimony, but the names of the prior cases and of the attorneys involved. This will permit verification of the expert's role in these earlier cases and review of the expert's actual testimony in these cases.[31]

Counsel also should inquire about the expert's role in the present case. Experts typically are asked how they came to be involved in the case, the work that they have been asked to perform, and the fee that they will receive for their work. The purpose of a discovery deposition can be defeated if the expert undertakes extensive work after the deposition. The examining attorney therefore should inquire about the status of the expert's work and be ready to state on the record that she reserves the right to redepose the expert when his work is complete. In addition, counsel might inform the expert about the duty to supplement both expert reports and deposition testimony pursuant to Rule 26(e)(1) and (2).

---

31. Prior testimony of experts can be located through electronic legal research services. In addition to databases that are generally available, specific databases may exist for plaintiffs or defense counsel with respect to particular types of litigation. For instance, the Industrial Defense Library is a computer database available to subscribing corporations and defense attorneys that contains thousands of full-text transcripts of expert witness testimony provided primarily by members and their counsel. Diemer, "Corporate Defendants Utilize Shared Database to Impeach Opponent Experts," *Litigation News*, Sept. 1996, at 2.

The bulk of an expert deposition is spent questioning the expert about his opinions. The general areas of such questioning are set forth in Federal Rule of Evidence 702, which governs the admissibility of expert testimony at trial. Rule 702 requires that "(1) the testimony is based upon sufficient facts or data, (2) the testimony is the product of reliable principles and methods, and (3) the witness has applied the principles and methods reliably to the facts of the case."

During the deposition, the grounds for the opinions should be established, as well as the facts or data underlying each opinion. Counsel should ask about all material relied upon by the expert in reaching his opinions, as well as any other material that he has reviewed. The expert should be asked to explain tests or other work that he has done in connection with the case. This is the type of information that should be included in a Rule 26(a)(2)(B) expert witness report. However, even if such a report has been provided, there generally will be good reason to pursue these matters in greater depth in the deposition. Good experts are good teachers, and one way in which an expert witness may be encouraged to talk at a deposition is by asking her to "help out" the examining attorney with difficult aspects of the expert's opinions or field of expertise.

Counsel should be sure to ask about matters not considered or relied upon by the expert and therefore not included in his report. The expert should be questioned as to why certain tests were not conducted, certain facts were not considered, and certain authorities were not consulted. The expert also might be asked if his opinion would change if the facts underlying that opinion were different than the expert had been told or had presumed.

As with other deponents, an expert can be asked to draw diagrams or perform simple calculations during the deposition. These should be attached to the deposition as deposition exhibits. A Rule 45 subpoena can be used to ensure that the expert brings to the deposition documents such as his vita, his report, and the written material upon which his opinions are based. These documents also can be attached to the deposition transcript as exhibits.

The examining attorney should ask the expert about those whom he considers to be authorities in his field. He also might be asked his opinion about other individuals who have been retained as expert witnesses in connection with the case. The expert's recognition of particular treatises as authoritative can provide a basis for reliance upon those books as learned treatises at trial pursuant to Federal Rule of Evidence 803(18).

A great deal of advance preparation is necessary to ensure a successful expert deposition. The examining attorney must familiarize herself with the expert's field of expertise, as well as with any specific writings by that expert. The examining attorney's own expert can help educate her on these matters. In many cases, counsel will agree that an attorney's own expert can be present in the deposition room while an opposing expert is being deposed. As one court has observed in connection with trial testimony, "A lawyer who undertakes to cross-examine a medical expert without having his own expert at his elbow has only himself to blame if the witness utters some arcanum that the lawyer cannot understand."[32]

As with other depositions, a successful expert deposition does not just happen. Planning, preparation, and attention to detail are necessary to make the most of the opportunities that an expert deposition affords.

Exercises Concerning the Taking of Oral Depositions

1. As counsel for Thomas Eakins in his lawsuit against the Pittston Company, you have served and received answers to the interrogatories discussed in exercise 1 of the Exercises Concerning Interrogatory Drafting in Chapter 7, *supra* p. 330. You now would like to depose the appropriate employees of the Pittston Company and the Buffalo Mining Company concerning the design, construction, inspection, and compliance with applicable safety regulations of the dam that failed on February 26, 1972. Unfortunately, you do not have the identity of the specific individuals who have the information that you seek.

Your assignment is to:

(a) draft the deposition notice(s) to obtain the deposition testimony that you seek (including requests for any documents that you would like to inspect in connection with your deposition(s));

(b) prepare an outline of the deposition examination(s) that you plan to conduct; and

(c) come to class prepared to conduct the deposition(s).

2. As counsel for the defendant Pittston Company, you are to conduct the deposition of plaintiff Steve Looney concerning his claims in the Buffalo Creek litigation. Mr. Looney's interrogatory answers are set forth in Section V(A)(1) of Chapter 7, *supra* p. 333. You should:

(a) draft a deposition notice to obtain Mr. Looney's deposition testimony (including requests for any documents that you would like to inspect in connection with the deposition);

(b) prepare an outline of the deposition examination that you plan to conduct; and

(c) come to class prepared to conduct the deposition.

3. Plan to depose plaintiff Thomas Eakins, who was introduced in exercise 1 of the Exercises Concerning Client Interviewing in Chapter 2, *supra* p. 38. Presume for the purposes of your deposition that Mr. Eakins has filed a diversity action that now is pending in the United States District Court for the Southern District of West Virginia.

4. Plan to depose the witnesses who were prepared for their depositions in exercise 2 of the Exercises Concerning Deposition Preparation, *supra* p. 366.

---

32. *Abernathy v. Superior Hardwoods, Inc.*, 704 F.2d 963, 969 (7th Cir. 1983).

5. Seven-year-old Matthew Lawrence Mason was struck by a speeding truck, which accident resulted in the lawsuit described in exercise 2 of the Exercises Concerning Deposition Preparation, *supra* p. 366. Matthew is hospitalized in critical condition. As Matthew's counsel:

(a) Write a memorandum setting forth a plan to take his videotaped trial deposition in the hospital;

(b) Prepare the documents necessary to take Matthew's videotaped deposition; and

(c) Plan and conduct Matthew's videotaped deposition.

V. DEPOSITION STRATEGIES FOR DEFENDING ATTORNEYS

The most important aspect of defending a deposition does not occur in the deposition room, but is the preparation of the deponent. When preparing deponents it is important to stress to them that once the deposition starts the active involvement of defending counsel usually will be minimal.

To say that the defending attorney will not normally be actively involved in a deposition is not to say that the attorney should not carefully listen and observe everything that occurs at the deposition. Defending depositions can be very boring, and one of the most difficult tasks in some depositions is to remain awake while the examining attorney's questioning drones on. It's embarrassing to be jolted out of an extended daydream by a question from your client such as, "Do I really have to tell her everything that we've talked about concerning this case?"

In addition to listening to the questions asked and answers given during the deposition, the defending attorney needs to be alert to the condition of her client. Depositions can be even more tiring and stressful for witnesses than for attorneys, and the defending attorney should see to it that there are sufficient breaks so that her client does not become overly tired.

Counsel should not forget that, once the deposition begins, anything said in the deposition room can become part of the deposition transcript. The defending attorney thus should be aware of, and talk with her client about, the opportunity to go "off the record" during the deposition. While in some jurisdictions counsel are given a bit more latitude in conferring with their clients, in other jurisdictions attorney and client only can go "off the record" to discuss whether to assert a privilege.[33] Counsel and

---

33. *E.g. Hall v. Clifton Precision*, 150 F.R.D. 525 (E.D.Pa. 1993). *See* Taylor, "Rambo as Potted Plant: Local Rulemaking's Preemptive Strike Against Witness–Coaching During Depositions," 40 *Vill. L. Rev.* 1057 (1995) (discussing local deposition "no-consultation" rules).

In *United States v. Phillip Morris Inc.*, 212 F.R.D. 418 (D.D.C. 2002), the court prohibited counsel from consulting with witnesses "during breaks in the deposition regarding the subject matter of the deposition" except to ascertain whether a privilege should be asserted or when the deposition extends over non-consecutive days. *See also Minebea Co. v. Papst*, 2005 WL 4821182

witness both should be sure that they understand the ground rules in their particular jurisdiction.

The attorneys who are taking and defending a deposition may decide to go off the record for discussions that need not be recorded by the court reporter. Counsel may not need several pages of (costly) transcript concerning a discussion of when the deposition will resume the next morning. Even when discussions are held off the record, a short statement can be made later on the record memorializing the parties' agreement. There also may be a reason to make a record of certain discussions between counsel. If the examining attorney refuses to adjourn a deposition at a reasonable hour or take a break for lunch, the defending attorney may want to preserve the colloquy concerning these matters.

Most court reporters record everything that is said during a deposition unless counsel agree that a particular discussion is to be off the record. An attorney therefore should never merely state "Let's go off the record" and then launch into matters that she does not want in the deposition transcript. It usually is wise for the examining attorney (who has retained the court reporter) to confirm with the reporter prior to the deposition that no statements will be considered off the record unless the examining attorney so requests.

Rule 30(c)(2) requires that deposition objections "be stated concisely in a nonargumentative and nonsuggestive manner."[34] If the examining attorney chooses not to withdraw or reformulate her question, the witness should answer the question subject to the objection. However, Rule 30(c)(2) provides that counsel may instruct a deponent not to answer a deposition question "when necessary to preserve a privilege, to enforce a limitation ordered by the court [typically pursuant to a Rule 26(c) protective order], or to present a motion [filed pursuant to Rule 30(d)(3) to prevent deposition examination conducted in bad faith or in such manner as unreasonably to annoy, embarrass, or oppress the deponent or party]."

Objections also can be made during the deposition to protect a client from lesser forms of harassment. For example, it is important to ensure that the witness has the opportunity to fully answer all deposition questions. If the defending attorney believes that examining counsel is cutting off the witness's answers, an objection should be made and the

---

(D.D.C. 2005) ("Counsel and their witnesses shall not engage in private, off-the-record conferences during depositions or during breaks or recesses, except for the purpose of deciding whether to assert a privilege. Any conferences that occur pursuant to, or in violation of, this guideline are a proper subject for inquiry by deposing counsel to ascertain whether there has been any witness-coaching and, if so, what.").

In *Strauch v. American College of Surgeons*, 2004 WL 2584794 (N.D.Ill. 2004), a defense witness changed his deposition testimony after he had consulted with counsel during a deposition break. The judge informed the parties that if such testimony were offered at trial and the defendant prevailed on the claims in question, he would consider the circumstances under which the "clarification" had occurred, "and from the present perspective that would mean the issue would have to be retried." *Id.* at 2. Shortly after this ruling, the lawsuit settled. Beckman, "Change in Deposition Testimony Leads to Preclusion," *Litigation News*, May 2005, at 5.

34. *See generally* A. Bocchino & D. Sonenshein, *Deposition Evidence, Objections, Instructions Not to Answer, and Responses—Law and Tactics* (2005).

witness asked whether he has finished his answer. If nothing else, such good faith objections should reassure the witness that you are still there to protect him during the deposition.

Although objections can be raised to deposition questions, it generally is considered improper for counsel to confer with a witness once a question has been asked. As one court has colorfully put it, "It is too late once the ball has been snapped for the coach to send in a different play."[35] Nevertheless, there will be times when a witness gives a deposition answer that his attorney believes to be incorrect. If requested by the deponent or a party pursuant to Rule 30(e), the witness should have a chance to offer changes to the deposition after it has been transcribed.

However, it usually makes more sense to deal with apparently mistaken deposition testimony during the deposition rather than wait until the deposition transcript has been prepared. Once the examining attorney has completed her questioning, the attorney defending the deposition can herself question the witness to resolve any remaining misstatements or ambiguous answers. If one portion of a deposition ultimately is offered by opposing counsel at trial, other, explanatory portions of the deposition can be introduced as well.[36] Limited questioning of one's own deposition witness can be used to correct deposition misstatements as soon as possible and blunt the possible use that opposing counsel can make of the deposition transcript at trial.

There are major risks, though, in questioning one's own witness at a deposition. Such questions provide a further chance for opposing counsel to examine the witness. By engaging in any extended examination of your own witnesses at their depositions, opposing counsel may be given a preview of your trial examinations. Other factors to be considered in deciding whether to question your own witness include:

- The possibility that the witness will be unavailable at trial

- The extent to which the witness has been damaged by opposing counsel's questioning

- The danger that needed clarifications may sound disingenuous if initially made at trial

- [The attorney's] sense of the witness's ability to defend the clarifications made in answering his questions if then subjected to further questioning by other counsel[37]

An attorney's major aim in defending a deposition should be to ensure that opposing counsel obtain only the information to which they properly are entitled. The defending attorney must fight the urge to show her cards at the deposition, realizing that there will be other occasions both before

---

35. *Eggleston v. Chicago Journeymen Plumbers' Local Union No. 130,* 657 F.2d 890, 902 (7th Cir. 1981) (en banc), *cert. denied,* 455 U.S. 1017 (1982).

36. Fed. R. Civ. P. 32(a)(6); Fed. R. Evid. 106.

37. D. Suplee & D. Donaldson, *The Deposition Handbook* 167 (3d ed. 1999).

and during trial when her own affirmative case more effectively can be displayed.

Finally, counsel should be certain that there is no ambiguity concerning the termination of the deposition. Rule 30(b)(5)(C) provides that, at the conclusion of the deposition, the court reporter is to state on the record that the deposition is complete. Counsel defending the deposition should be certain that this statement is made. Rule 30(a)(2)(A)(ii) requires leave of court to depose a single person more than one time in a case, and counsel defending the deposition therefore should object to statements that a deposition is being "recessed" or that otherwise suggest that a deposition merely is being continued rather than terminated.

Exercises Concerning the Defense of Oral Depositions

1. As counsel for the Pittston Company, you have designated a Pittston engineer to provide the testimony sought by plaintiff Thomas Eakins in the deposition notice contemplated by exercise 1 of the Exercises Concerning the Taking of Oral Depositions, *supra* p. 378. As Pittston's counsel:

> (a) prepare a short outline setting forth the strategy that you would adopt in defending this deposition; include in this outline both (i) the extent of any questioning that you would conduct at the deposition and (ii) whether any objection should be raised if the plaintiff attempts to bring an engineer he has retained to the deposition; and

> (b) come to class prepared to defend the deposition of the Pittston engineer.

2. The defendant Pittston Company has noticed the deposition of plaintiff Steve Looney in the Buffalo Creek litigation. *See* exercise 2 of the Exercises Concerning the Taking of Oral Depositions, *supra* p. 378. As plaintiffs' counsel:

> (a) prepare a short outline of the strategy that you would adopt in defending this deposition; include in this outline the extent of any questioning that you would conduct of Mr. Looney at this deposition; and

> (b) come to class prepared to defend Mr. Looney's deposition.

3. Defend the deposition of plaintiff Thomas Eakins that is contemplated in exercise 3 of the Exercises Concerning the Taking of Oral Depositions, *supra* p. 378.

4. Defend the depositions that are contemplated in exercise 4 of the Exercises Concerning the Taking of Oral Depositions, *supra* p. 378.

5. Prepare to defend the videotaped deposition of plaintiff Matthew Lawrence Mason that is contemplated in exercise 5 of the Exercises Concerning the Taking of Oral Depositions, *supra* p. 379. In this connection, write a memorandum explaining the defendant's position on whether

a videotaped deposition should be taken and describing any safeguards that should be insisted upon if a videotaped deposition is held. Come to class prepared to defend a videotaped deposition.

VI. DEPOSITION ETHICS

The oral deposition is the one discovery device in which counsel for all parties simultaneously participate. While the ability to follow up with deposition questions makes the deposition an effective discovery device, it can result in discovery abuse if this questioning is conducted by overzealous counsel. As Magistrate Judge Wayne Brazil has noted:

> An aggressive litigator bent on straining the resources and testing the will of an adversary can notice numerous depositions and can prolong each examination for extended periods. Because depositions can be used to require the presence of the deponent for lengthy periods of time, they also have great adversarial potential for harassing and embarrassing adverse parties or witnesses and for disrupting their lives and businesses.[38]

As a result of such abuse, in 1993 a limit of 10 depositions per side was imposed by Rule 30(a)(2)(A), while in 2000 Rule 30(d)(2) (now, Rule 30(d)(1)) was amended to provide that unless otherwise stipulated or ordered by the court "a deposition is limited to 1 day of 7 hours." While Rule 26(b)(2) previously had permitted these time and number limitations to be altered by local rule, the 2000 amendment to Rule 26(b)(2) removed this possibility.[39]

In addition to problems caused by the number or length of depositions, even the time of day that a deposition is to be taken can raise difficulties. Consider the following:

> One well-respected legal services attorney reported scheduling a client's deposition to be taken at the attorney's storefront offices. The offices were located in an area with a very high crime rate, and the attorney scheduled the deposition shortly before sundown in hopes of persuading his wealthier, suburban opponent to cancel the deposition, or at least to make it a short session so they would be finished before dark.[40]

Numerous examples of abusive deposition questioning are provided in *Eggleston v. Chicago Journeymen Plumbers' Local Union No. 130.*[41]

---

38. Brazil, "The Adversary Character of Civil Discovery: A Critique and Proposals for Change," 31 *Vand. L. Rev.* 1295, 1329 (1981).

39. *See* Advisory Committee Note to 2000 Amendment to Rule 26(b)(2), 192 F.R.D. 340, 391 (2000) ("There is no reason to believe that unique circumstances justify varying these nationally-applicable presumptive limits in certain districts. The limits can be modified by court order or agreement in an individual action, but 'standing' orders imposing different presumptive limits are not authorized.").

40. Weissbrod, Comment, "Sanctions Under Amended Rule 26—Scalpel or Meat-ax? The 1983 Amendments to the Federal Rules of Civil Procedure," 46 *Ohio St. L. J.* 183, 186 n.27 (1985).

41. 657 F.2d 890 (7th Cir. 1981) (en banc), *cert. denied,* 455 U.S. 1017 (1982).

Counsel in this case generated over 2600 pages of deposition transcripts, even though discovery was limited to the issue of class certification. Defense counsel asked the representatives of the class of plumbers "questions some members of the bar might have difficulty answering correctly," other questions suggesting that a deposition was "an examination to determine if [a plaintiff] should be issued a plumber's license by the State of Illinois," and other questions characterized by the court of appeals as "valueless," "argumentative and senseless," and "repetitious, or worse."[42]

Although they may not raise strictly ethical concerns, certain deposition questioning techniques can cause very real practical problems and greatly increase discovery expenses. Consider the examination techniques employed by the following types of lawyers:

> The first type of lawyers I call *sponges*. They absorb every word of testimony but only to write down as much of each answer as possible. Why they do this I do not know. It is as though what appears on the legal pad has more importance than what appears in the transcript. * * *

> Another easily recognizable type I call *scaredycats*. These are usually young lawyers who leave no fact unearthed, no matter how remote or how irrelevant, simply because they are afraid that some senior will later ask them "Why didn't you ask this or that?" * * *

> The third type I call *explorers*. They use a trial deposition for ordinary discovery. * * * The explorer fills in the few gaps left by sponges and scaredycats.[43]

Unfortunately, such conduct by one lawyer often will trigger similar tactics by other counsel in the case. It is such tactics that have caused courts to limit both the numbers and lengths of depositions under the 1993 and 2000 amendments to Rules 16, 26 and 30.

Abusive deposition tactics are not the sole province of examining counsel. In the *Eggleston* case, there were 965 refusals to answer deposition questions and 127 off-the-record conferences between plaintiffs' counsel and witnesses.[44]

Another example of deposition abuse by defending counsel occurred in *Unique Concepts, Inc. v. Brown,* in which the court considered a deposition transcript in which "it is hard to find a page on which [the defending

---

42. 657 F.2d at 899–900.

43. Mason, "The Most Forgettable Deposition I Ever Took," *Litigation,* Spring 1982, at 49, 50.

44. 657 F.2d at 901–902. Witnesses, too, can be sanctioned for abusive deposition conduct. In *Carroll v. Jaques*, 926 F.Supp. 1282 (E.D.Tex. 1996), the attorney deposition witness was fined $7000 by the court. This fine was based upon the number of times the attorney referred to opposing counsel with profanity and other uncomplimentary language (starting with $500 for each reference to opposing counsel as an "idiot" or "ass"). The substance of a deponent's testimony also can raise ethical duties for counsel. N.Y. Cty. Lawyers' Ass'n Comm. on Prof'l Ethics, Op. 741 (Mar. 1, 2010) (attorney who comes to know that her client offered material deposition evidence that is false must take reasonable remedial measures to correct false testimony). *See also* Model Rules of Prof'l Conduct Rule 3.3(a)(3).

attorney] [did] not intrude on the examination with a speech, a question to the examiner, or an attempt to engage in colloquy distracting to the examiner."[45] During the deposition, defense counsel referred to the deposing attorney as "an obnoxious little twit" and stated:

> If you want to go down to Judge Pollack and ask for sanctions because of that [deposition conduct], go ahead. I would almost agree to make a contribution of cash to you if you would promise to use it to take a course in how to ask questions in a deposition.[46]

The district judge was not amused, and fined the attorney for this behavior.

"Coaching" of witnesses is another improper tactic employed by some counsel in defending depositions. The following types of comments by defense counsel were found to be improper in *Langston Corp. v. Standard Register Co.*:

> [A question was asked by the examining attorney, Ms. Bell.]
>
> MR. ROVNER: You are asking for his personal knowledge; right?
> MS. BELL: Uh-huh.
> MR. ROVNER: I'm not sure he can answer that question, but if you [the witness] think you can—[47]

Both speeches by counsel and deposition objections suggesting an answer are now explicitly addressed by Rule 30(c)(2), which provides that any deposition objection "must be stated concisely in a nonargumentative and nonsuggestive manner."

Still another form of abuse by attorneys defending depositions is to improperly instruct witnesses not to answer deposition questions that do not seek privileged information. In *Shapiro v. Freeman*, in which third-party witnesses repeatedly refused to answer deposition questions not seeking privileged information, the court noted:

> It is not the prerogative of counsel, but of the court, to rule on objections. Indeed, if counsel were to rule on the propriety of questions, oral examinations would be quickly reduced to an exasperating cycle of answerless inquiries and court orders.[48]

For these reasons, Rule 30 was amended in 1993 and Rule 30(c)(2) now explicitly provides that a person "may instruct a deponent not to answer only when necessary to preserve a privilege, to enforce a limitation

---

45. 115 F.R.D. 292, 292 (S.D.N.Y. 1987).

46. 115 F.R.D. at 293.

47. 95 F.R.D. 386, 388 (N.D.Ga. 1982). *See also Wright v. Firestone Tire and Rubber Co.*, 93 F.R.D. 491 (W.D.Ky. 1982), in which the court found that plaintiff's counsel had "repeatedly interjected inquiries into the meaning of defendant's questions despite any indication from the witness that the questions were unclear." 93 F.R.D. at 493.

48. 38 F.R.D. 308, 311 (S.D.N.Y. 1965). *See also Ralston Purina Co. v. McFarland*, 550 F.2d 967, 971–74 (4th Cir. 1977); *United States v. Int'l Bus. Mach. Corp.*, 79 F.R.D. 378, 380–81 (S.D.N.Y. 1978).

ordered by the court, or to present a motion [to limit or terminate a deposition] under Rule 30(d)(3)."

Whether it is the attorney defending the deposition or the examining attorney who resorts to improper tactics, opposing counsel should make a record of the questioned conduct. If you anticipate that opposing counsel may resort to abusive deposition tactics, the deposition can be taken by audiovisual recording. The recording should provide a record of deposition abuse that is clearer than a written deposition transcript and, even better, may discourage abuse from ever occurring. Once a clear record is made, counsel can suspend the deposition pursuant to Federal Rule of Civil Procedure 30(d)(3)(A) and seek a protective order, other judicial assistance, or sanctions.

In virtually all of the cases discussed in this section, the court ultimately imposed sanctions. For instance, in *Shapiro v. Freeman*,[49] the court appointed a special master to preside over all depositions in the case and ordered plaintiff's counsel (without any reimbursement from his clients) to pay the costs of the master. In a more recent case, a district court required plaintiff's counsel to bear the cost of a discovery master because of deposition conduct that necessitated "the provision of day care for counsel who, like small children, cannot get along and require adult supervision."[50]

One federal district judge has offered good advice both as to how to conduct oneself in a deposition and how to deal with improper deposition behavior by other counsel:

> Counsel should never forget that even though the deposition may be taking place far from a real courtroom, with no black-robed overseer peering down upon them, * * * counsel are operating as officers of this court. They should comport themselves accordingly; should they be tempted to stray, they should remember that this judge is but a phone call away.[51]

Deposition abuse is not only unethical, but is conduct for which lawyers can be, should be, and are sanctioned.

Exercise Concerning Deposition Ethics

You represent the plaintiff corporation in a major commercial lawsuit brought against seven corporate defendants. Defense counsel have traveled from several different cities to take the deposition of plaintiff's chief executive officer in Cleveland, where the plaintiff corporation is headquartered and the action has been filed. The parties have stipulated that this deposition may take "up to two seven-hour days." Counsel for one of the major defendants examines the CEO for one and one-half days, after

---

49. 38 F.R.D. 308 (S.D.N.Y. 1965).

50. *Van Pilsum v. Iowa State Univ.*, 152 F.R.D. 179, 181 (S.D. Iowa 1993).

51. *Hall v. Clifton Precision*, 150 F.R.D. 525, 531 (E.D.Pa. 1993).

which several other defense counsel each ask 30–45 minutes of questions. At the end of the second day of this deposition, counsel for the seventh defendant informs you that she does not want to begin her questioning until tomorrow. She also tells you that, although this deposition was only scheduled to last two days, she has "perhaps as much as four to five hours of questions." You are scheduled to meet with several clients in other cases tomorrow, but counsel for the seventh defendant refuses to relent.

(a) Write a memorandum describing what you would do in this situation.

(b) Presume that you decide to contact the local judge to whom this case is assigned. His law clerk has told you that the judge will take a five minute call from you and defense counsel. Prepare an outline of the argument that you would make to the judge.

(c) Write a memorandum concerning how such a problem could be avoided in the future.

VII. CONCLUSION

Depositions can be the most effective civil discovery device for many purposes in many cases. No other device permits the inquiring attorney to directly question a witness or party. However, because of the ease with which depositions can be noticed, and the seeming ease with which they can be conducted, too many attorneys engage in "search-and-depose" missions of the type criticized in the quote at the beginning of this chapter. Counsel should avoid such deposition abuse, and instead target depositions to perform specific tasks within a comprehensive discovery plan.

VIII. CHAPTER BIBLIOGRAPHY

Applegate, "Witness Preparation," 68 *Tex. L. Rev.* 277 (1989).

Altman, "Witness Preparation Conflicts," *Litigation*, Fall 1995, at 38.

Aufses, "Documents and Depositions: The Basics," *Litigation*, Winter 1994, at 49.

Berman, "The Four–Hour Deposition," *Litigation*, Spring 1993, at 51.

A. Bocchino, *Winning at Deposition* (1998) (CD–ROM).

A. Bocchino & D. Sonenshein, *Deposition Evidence, Objections, Instructions Not to Answer, and Responses–Law and Tactics* (2005).

Charfoos & Christensen, "Depositions: A Practical Guide," *Trial*, August 1986, at 25.

B. Clary et al., *Successful First Depositions* (3d ed. 2011).

Day, "Playing Hardball in Expert Witness Depositions," *Litigation*, Summer 2000, at 19.

Dickerson, "The Law and Ethics of Civil Depositions," 57 *Md. L. Rev.* 273 (1998).

Facher, "Taking Depositions," *Litigation,* Fall 1977, at 27.

Figari & Loewinsohn, "Videotaped Depositions Come to Court," *Litigation,* Spring 1988, at 35.

Gavin, "Playing by the Rules: Strategies for Defending Depositions," 1999 *Det. Col. L./Mich. St. U. L. Rev.* 645.

Gildin, "A Practical Guide to Taking and Defending Depositions," 88 *Dick. L. Rev.* 247 (1984).

Greene, "The Folklore of Depositions," *Litigation,* Summer 1985, at 13.

Hamilton, "Taking and Defending Depositions," *Litigation,* Winter 1985, at 20.

H. Hecht, *Effective Depositions* (2d ed. 2010).

S. Israel, *Taking and Defending Depositions* (2004).

Johnson, "The 10 Deadly Deposition Sins," *A.B.A.J.,* Sept. 1984, at 62.

Kerper, "Preparing a Witness for a Deposition," *Litigation*, Summer, 1998, at 11.

Kornblum, "The Oral Civil Deposition: Preparation and Examination of Witnesses," *Prac. Law.,* May 1971, at 11.

Kuney, "Deposition Preparation: A Methodological Approach," 8 *Am. J. Trial Advoc.* 241 (1984).

P. Lisnek & M. Kaufman, *Depositions* (1990).

Liss, "Formal Discovery from Nonparties," *Litigation,* Summer 1987, at 11.

The Litigation Manual: Depositions (P. Schwab & L. Vilardo eds. 2006).

Lutz, "Multi-Level Depositions," *Litigation,* Spring 1990, at 9.

D. Malone et al., *The Effective Deposition: Techniques and Strategies that Work* (3d ed. 2006).

D. Malone, *Deposition Rules: The Essential Handbook to Who, What, When, Where, Why, and How* (4th ed. 2006).

Mathias et al., "Lights, Camera, Action: Taking, Defending, and Using Videotape Depositions," *Trial Practice* 8 (2007).

McElhaney, "Basic Deposition Techniques," *Litigation,* Fall 1994, at 43.

McElhaney, "Objecting at Depositions," *Litigation,* Summer 1988, at 51.

McNamara & Sorensen, "Deposition Traps and Tactics," *Litigation,* Fall 1985, at 48.

Miller, Note, "Taking of Depositions Conditioned Upon Payment of Opposing Attorney's Expenses," 48 *Mo. L. Rev.* 813 (1983).

A. Moore et al., *Depositions in a Nutshell* (2010).

Neubauer, "Videotaping Depositions," *Litigation*, Summer 1993, at 60.

Peltz & Weill, "Corporate Representative Depositions: In Search of a Cohesive & Well–Defined Body of Law," 33 *Nova L. Rev.* 393 (2009).

Pope & Trull, "When Your Opponent Is Difficult," *The Brief*, Summer 1991, at 30.

Salpeter et al., "Discovery from Those at the Top," *Litigation,* Summer 1987, at 15.

Schenkier, "Deposing Corporations and Other Fictive Persons: Some Thoughts on Rule 30(b)(6)," *Litigation*, Winter 2003, at 20.

Sinclair & Fendrich, "Discovering Corporate Knowledge and Contentions: Rethinking Rule 30(b)(6) and Alternative Mechanisms," 50 *Ala. L. Rev.* 651 (1999).

D. Small, *Preparing Witnesses: A Practical Guide for Lawyers and Their Clients* (2d ed. 2004).

Somers, "Deposing an Adverse Expert: Hammer and Nails," *For the Defense,* July 1989, at 24.

V. Starr, *Witness Preparation* (1998).

D. Suplee & D. Donaldson, *The Deposition Handbook* (4th ed. 2002).

Sussman & Sussman, "Electronic Depositions," *Litigation,* Summer 1989, at 26.

"Symposium on Witness Preparation," 30 *Tex. Tech. L. Rev.* 1333 (1999).

Underwood, "The Videotape Deposition: Using Modern Technology for Effective Discovery" (pts. 1 & 2), *Prac. Law.*, April 15, 1985, at 61, *Prac. Law.*, June 1, 1985, at 65.

Winik, "Strategies in Expert Depositions," *Litigation*, Spring 1998, at 14.

Zacharias & Martin, "Coaching Witnesses," 87 *Ky. L. J.* 1001 (1999).

CHAPTER 9

REQUESTS TO PRODUCE, FOR ADMISSIONS, AND FOR PHYSICAL AND MENTAL EXAMINATIONS: "YOUR REQUEST IS MY COMMAND."

■ ■ ■

The purpose of Rule 34 is to make relevant and nonprivileged documents, electronically stored information, and objects in the possession of one party available to the other, thus eliminating strategic surprise and permitting the issues to be simplified and the trial to be expedited.

8B C. Wright et al., *Federal Practice and Procedure* § 2202, at 117 (3d ed. 2010).

[In the] quintessential Rule 34 case, *United States v. IBM,* * * * [l]awyers produced over 64 million pages of documents during the first five years of discovery. One of many discovery disputes led to an appeal to the Court of Appeals for the Second Circuit, a simultaneous petition for a writ of mandamus, an attempted appeal to and a petition for a writ of certiorari from the Supreme Court, and a petition for an extraordinary writ. Almost a year and a half after the order was entered, IBM was found in contempt and assessed a fine of $150,000 per day until it produced the documents required by the pretrial order.

Pope, "Rule 34: Controlling the Paper Avalanche," *Litigation,* Spring 1981, at 28, 28.

Analysis

I. INTRODUCTION

While interrogatories and depositions may be what immediately come to mind when one thinks of discovery, the Federal Rules of Civil Procedure provide several other discovery devices that can be used effectively in preparing a case for trial. These additional discovery devices are the subject of this chapter.

The first discovery device considered is the Rule 34 request to produce documents, electronically stored information, or things and for entry upon the land of another party. While a party can be required to *tell* another party about something through Rule 33 interrogatories or a Rule 30 deposition, Rule 34 requires a party to *show* another party documents, electronically stored information, or things.

Federal Rule of Civil Procedure 35 provides for another form of party inspection, specifically, a physical or mental examination of another party to the litigation. Because of the potential sensitivity of these examinations, Rule 35 is the only discovery device that requires either party agreement or an order of court for the discovery to occur.

Rule 36 admission requests are similar to most other discovery devices because their successful use typically does not involve any judicial intervention. In fact, Rule 36 requests are deemed to be admitted automatically unless there is a timely response.

While Rules 34, 35, and 36 operate somewhat differently in practice, all three Rules should be considered in developing any comprehensive discovery plan.

II. RULE 34 REQUESTS TO PRODUCE

So that the potential uses and abuses of Rule 34 production requests can be understood, this section examines both Rule 34 and modern production practice.

A. THE PROVISIONS OF RULE 34

Rule 34 of the Federal Rules of Civil Procedure permits a party to seek from another party the production of documents or electronically stored information for inspection, copying, testing or sampling; the inspection, copying, testing, or sampling of tangible things; and the entry upon property for inspection, measuring, surveying, photographing, testing, or sampling.

The format for Rule 34 requests is quite simple, as is evidenced by Form 50 of the Appendix of Forms to the Federal Rules of Civil Procedure:

REQUEST TO PRODUCE DOCUMENTS AND TANGIBLE THINGS, OR TO ENTER ONTO LAND UNDER RULE 34[1]

(Caption–See Form 1.)

The plaintiff *name* requests that the defendant *name* respond within ___ days to the following requests:

1. To produce and permit the plaintiff to inspect and copy and to test or sample the following documents, including electronically stored information:

   (Describe each document and the electronically stored information, either individually or by category.)

   (State the time, place, and manner of the inspection and any related acts.)

2. To produce and permit the plaintiff to inspect and to copy—and to test or sample—the following tangible things:

   (Describe each thing, either individually or by category.)

   (State the time, place, and manner of the inspection and any related acts.)

3. To permit the plaintiff to enter onto the following land to inspect, photograph, test, or sample the property or an object or operation on the property.

   (Describe the property and each object or operation.)

   (State the time and manner of the inspection and any related acts.)

   (Date and sign—See Form 2.)

———

As with interrogatories, depositions, and admission requests, Rule 34 production or inspection requests generally cannot be served before the parties have held their Rule 26(f) discovery meeting unless the court provides or the parties stipulate to the contrary.[2] Rule 34(b)(1)(A) requires that the request "must describe with reasonable particularity each item or category of items to be inspected," while Rule 34(b)(1)(B) provides that the request "must specify a reasonable time, place, and manner for the inspection and for performing the related acts."

---

1. Rule 34(b)(1)(C) provides that the requesting party "may specify the form or forms in which electronically stored information is to be produced." If electronically stored information is sought, the Rule 34 request therefore should specify the form of information that would be most useful to the requesting party. Rule 34(b)(2)(E)(ii) further provides: "Unless otherwise stipulated or ordered by the court, ... If a request does not specify a form for producing electronically stored information, a party must produce it in a form or forms in which it is ordinarily maintained or in a reasonably usable form or forms."

2. Fed. R. Civ. P. 26(d)(1).

As with responses to interrogatories and admission requests, parties served with Rule 34 requests must respond within thirty days after service of the request unless a different time has been ordered by the court or been agreed to in writing by the parties pursuant to Rule 29.[3] Rule 34(b)(2)(A) requires an actual written response, while Rule 34(b)(2)(B) requires that this response either must state an objection to the request or state that the production or inspection sought will be permitted as requested. Objections to particular document production requests generally are quite similar in appearance to interrogatory objections.[4] If a party objects to any portion of a Rule 34 request, the requesting party may file a Rule 37 motion seeking a court order compelling production.

If a small number of documents are called for by a Rule 34 request, copies of the documents usually are given to the requesting party. There is no obligation to make copies, though, and when a larger number of documents are requested they may merely be produced for inspection by the requesting party. That party then determines which documents it wants copied. These copies can be made by the producing party (with the requesting party paying copying charges) or arrangements can be made for the requesting party to make its own copies under the supervision of the producing party.

To avoid later disputes about precisely what documents, electronically stored information, or things are produced, an index should be prepared listing the items produced. Many attorneys number the documents that they produce for the same reason. If the producing party does not make such a record, the attorney who requested the documents can send a letter to counsel for the producing party listing the items that have been received.

Rule 34(b)(2)(E)(i) provides: "A party must produce documents as they are kept in the usual course of business or must organize and label them to correspond to the categories in the request." The need for this provision was explained in the 1980 Advisory Committee Note to Rule 34 as follows: "The Committee is advised that, 'It is apparently not rare for parties deliberately to mix critical documents with others in the hope of obscuring significance.' "[5] It's thus not proper to hide relevant needles of information in huge haystacks of irrelevant or otherwise extraneous material. To provide further information to the requesting party, Rule 34 requests can include an instruction asking for a copy of the file folder or the label from the file drawer, notebook or other container from which requested documents have been removed.

A systematic approach to document production is necessary. Attorney Robert Ehrenbard makes the following suggestions:

---

3. Fed. R. Civ. P. 34(b)(2)(A).

4. *See* the sample interrogatory objections in Chapter 7, *supra*, p. 339.

5. 85 F.R.D. 521, 532 (1980), *quoting* Section of Litigation, American Bar Association, *Report of the Special Committee for the Study of Discovery Abuse* 22 (1977).

As litigation counsel, you cannot leave it to other people to know the contents of the documents you produce. You must know how the production request is framed, how the search was conducted, and what is in the material you are producing.

To comply with a broad request or subpoena that requires an exhaustive search of corporate files, you can organize a group within the corporation, generally supervised by the house counsel or someone on his staff. Give them a lecture on what is required and have them conduct the initial screening. Instruct them that, where there are questions of interpretation in terms of whether a document should or should not be produced, a lawyer should make the final decision. The lawyer who is consulted should prepare memoranda stating his interpretation of the request or subpoena and the reasons why certain documents or classes of documents were not produced. Many times there are perfectly sound reasons for not including certain documents. But, if no record is made, those reasons may get lost and the propriety of the decision may later be questioned.[6]

Unfortunately, Rule 34 document productions are not always handled in the professional manner suggested by Mr. Ehrenbard.

NOTES AND QUESTIONS CONCERNING RULE 34

1. Why does Rule 34(a)(1) provide that a party must produce discoverable material "in the responding party's possession, custody or control?" Can a corporation be required to produce documents to which it has no legal right, but that are in the possession of the corporation's retirees? What if the retirees are receiving periodic retirement checks from the corporation? *See In re Folding Carton Antitrust Litigation,* 76 F.R.D. 420 (N.D.Ill. 1977).

2. Rule 34 production requests only can be served on other parties to the action. What if a non-party has relevant documents or electronically stored information? If the non-party will not voluntarily produce this material, a Rule 45 subpoena can be used to require the production.

3. What does Rule 34(a)(1)(A) mean by providing that certain "data or data compilations—stored in any medium from which information can be obtained" may need to be translated by the respondent "into a reasonably usable form?" *Compare Bell v. Automobile Club,* 80 F.R.D. 228, 233 (E.D.Mich. 1978), *appeal dism'd mem.,* 601 F.2d 587 (6th Cir.), *cert. denied,* 442 U.S. 918 (1979) (defendant required to work with plaintiffs to create a computer data bank permitting retrieval of employee data) and *Stapleton v. Kawasaki Heavy Industries, Ltd.,* 69 F.R.D. 489 (N.D.Ga. 1975) (defendant required to pay costs incurred by plaintiff in translating from Japanese to English documents defendant produced in discovery) *with In re Puerto Rico Elec. Power Authority,* 687 F.2d 501, 504–10 (1st Cir. 1982) (defendant not

---

6. Ehrenbard, "Cutting Discovery Costs Through Interrogatories and Document Requests," *Litigation,* Spring 1975, at 17, 21. While written well before the advent of electronic discovery, this advice concerning attorney responsibility for the document search, organization of that search, and making a record of the search process are particularly important with respect to responses to requests for electronically stored information. *See* Section II(B), *infra.*

required to translate or pay costs of translating documents responsive to plaintiff's Rule 34 request from Spanish into English).

4. In the event that a party is required to "translate" information in response to a Rule 34 request, must the responding party bear the entire cost of the translation? As the Advisory Committee noted in its commentary on the 1970 amendment to Rule 34:

> In many instances, [the inclusion of electronic data compilations within the coverage of Rule 34] means that respondent will have to supply a print-out of computer data. The burden thus placed on respondent will vary from case to case, and the courts have ample power under Rule 26(c) to protect respondent against undue burden or expense, either by restricting discovery or requiring that the discovering party pay costs.

48 F.R.D. 487, 527 (1970).

5. Among the sanctions available if a party refuses to obey an order requiring the production of documents is an order "prohibiting [the party from whom the documents had been requested] . . . from introducing [those documents] in evidence." Fed. R. Civ. P. 37(b)(2)(A)(ii). *See Von Brimer v. Whirlpool Corp.,* 536 F.2d 838 (9th Cir. 1976).

6. In complex cases involving many parties and tens of thousands of documents, the parties may establish a joint document depository. These depositories provide a central location for storage of relevant documents and spare parties the expense of duplicative copying of every conceivably relevant document. Computerized document retrieval systems often are developed to speed access to documents in these depositories. *See* Sugarman, "Coordinating Complex Discovery," *Litigation,* Fall 1988, at 41, 42–43. Discovery in the breast implant products liability litigation was put on CD–ROM computer disks, with a single disk containing 15,000 pages of discovery selling for $25.00. DeBenedictis, "Implant Documents on CD–ROMs," *A.B.A.J.*, July 1993, at 24. *See generally Manual for Complex Litigation, Fourth* § 11.444 (2004).

By approaching electronic discovery in this fashion, the parties should be able to share (and save) costs, expedite discovery, and avoid last minute requests from other parties to "share" a database that has been created by and for a single party. In fact, parties who decline to participate in a joint database at the outset of a case will have a difficult time later arguing that they are entitled to share in such an electronic database. Miller & Griffin, "Computer Databases: Forced Production versus Shared Enterprise," *Litigation*, Summer 1997, at 40, 59.

B. ELECTRONIC DISCOVERY

The Federal Rules of Civil Procedure were amended in 2006 to take account of the increasing importance, and complexity, of electronic discovery.[7] The Report of the Judicial Conference Committee on Rules of

---

7. Another testament to the increasing importance and complexity of electronic discovery is the growing number of books, newsletters, symposia, and websites concerning electronic discovery. *E.g.*, M. Arkfeld, *Arkfeld on Electronic Evidence and Discovery* (3d ed. 2010); J. Barkett, *The Ethics of E–Discovery* (2009); A. Cohen & D. Lender, *Electronic Discovery: Law and Practice*

Practice and Procedure set forth the following rationale for these electronic discovery amendments:

> The discovery of electronically stored information raises markedly different issues from conventional discovery of paper records. Electronically stored information is characterized by exponentially greater volume than hard-copy documents. Commonly cited current examples of such volume include the capacity of large organizations' computer networks to store information in terabytes, each of which represents the equivalent of 500 million typewritten pages of plain text, and to receive 250 to 300 million e-mail messages monthly. Computer information, unlike paper, is also dynamic; merely turning a computer on or off can change the information it stores. Computers operate by overwriting and deleting information, often without the operator's specific direction or knowledge. A third important difference is that electronically stored information, unlike words on paper, may be incomprehensible when separated from the system that created it. These and other differences are causing problems in discovery that rule amendments can helpfully address.

> * * * Without national rules adequate to address the issues raised by electronic discovery, a patchwork of rules and requirements is likely to develop. While such inconsistencies are particularly confusing and debilitating to large public and private organizations, the uncertainty, expense, delays, and burdens of such discovery also affect small organizations and even individual litigants.[8]

One series of resulting amendments to Rules 16, 26(a), 26(f) and Form 35 (now, Form 52) required parties and the court to give early attention to electronic discovery issues. Rule 16(b) now explicitly states that scheduling orders may "provide for disclosure or discovery of electronically stored information" and "include any agreements the parties reach for asserting claims of privilege or of protection as trial-preparation material after information is produced."[9] Corresponding amendments to

---

(2010); J. Grenig et al., *eDiscovery & Digital Evidence* (2010); J. Kidwell et al., *Electronic Discovery* (2010); R. Losey, *Introduction to e-Discovery: New Cases, Ideas, and Techniques* (2009); S. Nelson et al., *The Electronic Evidence and Discovery Handbook: Forms, Checklists, and Guidelines* (2006); P. Rice, *Electronic Evidence: Law and Practice* (2d ed. 2008); S. Scheindlin et al., *Electronic Discovery and Digital Evidence: Cases and Materials* (2008); The Sedona Conference Working Group for Electronic Document Retention and Protection, *The Sedona Principles: Best Practices, Recommendations & Principles for Addressing Electronic Document Production* (2d ed. 2007); 2010 Conference on Civil Litigation, http://civilconference.uscourts.gov/Lotus Quickr/dcc/Main.nsf/h _ Library/9E884B4174EE27B6852576E900738E7B/?OpenDocument; Symposium, "Ethics and Professionalism in the Digital Age," 60 *Mercer L. Rev.* 845 (2009); Discovery Resources.org, http://www.discoveryresources.org ("information, resources and news ... about electronic discovery"); e-Discovery Team, http://e-discoveryteam.com ("combining the talents of Law and IT"); Electronic Discovery Law, http://www.ediscoverylaw.com ("blog on legal issues, law, and best practices relating to the discovery of electronically stored information"); Kroll Ontrack, http://www.krollontrack.com ("technology and consulting services for large scale paper and electronic discovery, computer forensics, and litigation readiness and response projects"). *See generally* Richert, "Electronic Discovery Bibliography," 42 *Akron L. Rev.* 419 (2009).

8. 234 F.R.D. 219, 272–73 (2006).

9. Fed. R. Civ. P. 16(b)(3)(B)(iii), (iv).

Rule 26(f) and Form 52 require the parties to discuss electronic discovery, the preservation of electronic and other discoverable information, and any issues related to claims of privilege or work product protection at their Rule 26(f) discovery planning conference. Rule 26(a)(1)(A)(ii) now explicitly lists "electronically stored information" along with "documents" and "tangible things" as subject to the Rule 26(a)(1) initial disclosure requirement.[10]

As amended in 2006, Rule 26(b)(2)(B) addresses the situation in which it may be possible to recover electronically stored information, but it would be unduly burdensome or costly to retrieve this data. The first sentence of Rule 26(b)(2)(B) states: "A party need not provide discovery of electronically stored information from sources that the party identifies as not reasonably accessible because of undue burden or cost." Examples of the type of "not reasonably accessible" data contemplated by Rule 26(b)(2)(B) are set forth in the Report of the Civil Rules Advisory Committee and include:

> back-up tapes intended for disaster recovery purposes that are often not indexed, organized, or susceptible to electronic searching; legacy data that remains from obsolete systems and is unintelligible on the successor systems; data that was "deleted" but remains in fragmented form, requiring a modern version of forensics to restore and retrieve; and databases that were designed to create certain information in certain ways and that cannot readily create very different kinds or forms of information.[11]

On a motion to compel the production of such data, Rule 26(b)(2)(B) requires that the party from whom the discovery is sought "show that the information is not reasonably accessible because of undue burden or cost." Even once that showing is made, Rule 26(b)(2)(B) permits the court to order discovery from these sources if "good cause" for such discovery is shown, although the court may specify conditions for such discovery (including the payment of appropriate costs by the requesting party). In determining whether good cause has been shown, Rule 26(b)(2)(B) explicitly provides that the court is to take into account the factors specified in Rule 26(b)(2)(C), such as the ability to obtain the information less expensively from another source or whether "the burden or expense of the proposed discovery outweighs its likely benefit."[12]

---

10. Nevertheless, a recent study of federal civil cases terminated in 2008 found that only 34.8% of plaintiff's counsel and 33.0% of defense counsel reported that their discovery planning conference included discussion of electronically stored information, while only about 20% of counsel reported that the discovery plan ultimately adopted by the court addressed electronically stored information. E. Lee & T. Willging, *Federal Judicial Center National, Case–Based Civil Rules Survey: Preliminary Report to the Judicial Conference Advisory Committee on Civil Rules* 15, 16 (2009).

For a comprehensive Pretrial Conference Agenda for Computer–Based Discovery see Withers, "Computer–Based Discovery in Federal Civil Litigation," 2000 *Fed. Cts. L. Rev.* 2 (appendix).

11. 234 F.R.D. 219, 331 (2006).

12. Professor Henry Noyes has argued that the "good cause" requirement has been ineffective in limiting electronic discovery and that judicial discretion should be limited with respect to

Because of the sheer volume and complexity of electronic data, the chances of inadvertently producing information that is arguably privileged or protected by the work-product doctrine is greatly heightened.[13] Rule 26(b)(5)(B) therefore was added to the Rules in 2006 to provide a procedure for asserting claims of privilege or work-product protection after information has been mistakenly produced in discovery. Once a party has been notified of a claim of privilege or work-product protection, Rule 26(b)(5)(B) requires that party to "promptly return, sequester, or destroy the specified information and any copies it has; [and] must not use or disclose the information until the claim is resolved." Rule 26(b)(5)(B) also provides that the receiving party must take reasonable steps to retrieve the information if it already has disclosed the information, while the producing party must preserve the information until the claim is resolved. Rule 26(b)(5)(B) merely creates a procedure for resolving questions of waiver and "does not address whether the privilege or protection that is asserted after production was waived by the production."[14]

Although electronic documents had been produced under the prior versions of these Rules, "electronically stored information" is now explicitly listed as falling within the definition of business records for the purposes of Rule 33(d) and information that can be requested under Rule 34(a)(1)(A).[15] In addition, the procedure for requesting electronically stored information under Rule 34(b)(1)(C) now provides that Rule 34 requests "may specify the form or forms in which electronically stored information is to be produced." Pursuant to Rule 34(b)(2)(D), the responding party may state "an objection to the requested form for producing electronically stored information." Rule 34(b)(2)(D) also provides: "If the responding party objects to a requested form—or if no form was specified in the request—the party must state the form or forms it intends to use." Rather than simply accept the form preferred by the party possessing electronically stored information, the requesting party should specify a specific form in the Rule 34 request. There may be disagreement as to the appropriate form in which electronically stored information should be produced, and Rule 26(f)(3)(C) provides that the parties' views and proposals on "the form or forms in which [electronically stored information]

---

the production of electronic discovery under the Federal Rules of Civil Procedure. Noyes, "Good Cause is Bad Medicine for the New E–Discovery Rules," 21 *Harv. J. Law & Tech.* 49 (2007).

13. *See* Report of Civil Rules Advisory Committee on 2006 Amendments to Federal Rules of Civil Procedure, 234 F.R.D. 219, 342 (2006) ("[Rule 26(b)(5)(B)] is a nod to the pressures of litigating with the amount and nature of electronically stored information available in the present age, a procedural device for addressing the increasingly costly and time-consuming efforts to reduce the number of inevitable blunders.").

14. Advisory Committee Note to 2006 Amendment to Rule 26(b)(5)(B), 234 F.R.D. 219, 346 (2006).

15. "The rule covers—either as documents or as electronically stored information—information 'stored in any medium,' to encompass future developments in computer technology. Rule 34(a)(1) is intended to be broad enough to cover all current types of computer-based information, and flexible enough to encompass future changes and developments." Advisory Committee Note to 2006 Amendment to Rule 34(a), 234 F.R.D. 219, 361 (2006). *See also* Withers, "Electronically Stored Information: The December 2006 Amendments to the Federal Rules of Civil Procedure," 7 *Sedona Conf. J.* 1, 25 (2006).

should be produced" must be included in the parties' discovery plan that is to be developed at their Rule 26(f) conference.

Rule 34(b) was amended in another significant respect in 2006. Rule 34(b) had provided since 1980: "A party who produces documents for inspection shall produce them as they are kept in the usual course of business or shall organize and label them to correspond with the categories in the request." This requirement is now found in Rule 34(b)(2)(E)(i), and Rule 34(b)(2)(E)(ii) and (iii) have been added to specifically address the form for production of electronically stored information. They provide:

> (ii) If a request does not specify a form for producing electronically stored information, a party must produce it in a form or forms in which it is ordinarily maintained or in a reasonably usable form or forms; and

> (iii) A party need not produce the same electronically stored information in more than one form.

Counsel therefore should consider the form or forms in which electronically stored information would be most useful for the purposes of the litigation.[16] This decision may be informed by discussion at the parties' Rule 26(f) discovery planning conference about the manner in which electronic information is maintained and more general discussion of electronic discovery issues.[17] In the event that no specific form for the

---

16. As noted in the Advisory Committee Note to the 2006 Amendment to Rule 34(b):

The rule recognizes that different forms of production may be appropriate for different types of electronically stored information. * * * [A] party might be called upon to produce word processing documents, e-mail messages, electronic spreadsheets, different image or sound files, and material from databases. * * * The rule therefore provides that the requesting party may ask for different forms of production for different types of electronically stored information.

234 F.R.D. 219, 363 (2006). *See also Manual for Complex Litigation, Fourth* § 11.446 (2004).

17. Even when documents are available in hard copy, there may be reasons to request that information in electronic form. The production of data in electronic form may allow the party receiving the information to electronically organize the information produced (seeking, for instance, all communications between specific people, memoranda written during a particular time period, or documents concerning a specific topic).

The electronic version of a document also may contain user-created "embedded" data that is not apparent when that document is printed in hard copy (such as, for instance, prior drafts of the document or an indication that a blind copy of an email was created). Electronic "metadata" may indicate when the document was created, modified, or deleted and by whom. Brown & Weiner, "Digital Dangers: A Primer on Electronic Evidence in the Wake of Enron," *Litigation*, Fall 2003, at 24, 25. This may permit the party receiving the information to conduct its own electronic searches of that information, although such "metadata mining" may not be permissible under the ethics rules as interpreted in some states. King, "The Ethics of Mining for Metadata Outside of Formal Discovery," 113 *Penn. St. L. Rev.* 801 (2009). On the other hand, the production of hard copy may show handwriting on a printed document or reveal a file containing other relevant documents that had not been independently produced in discovery.

While Rule 34(b)(2)(E)(iii) provides that a party "need not produce the same electronically stored information in more than one form," in some cases counsel may want to agree upon the production of both hard copy and electronic versions of certain documents. The requesting party also should not forget that it is "the master of its production requests; it must be satisfied with what it asked for." *Autotech Technologies Ltd. Partnership v. Automationdirect.com, Inc.*, 248 F.R.D. 556, 560 (N.D.Ill. 2008). *See also Aguilar v. Immigration and Customs Enforcement*, 255 F.R.D. 350, 357 (S.D.N.Y. 2008) ("[I]f metadata is not sought in the initial document request, and particularly if the producing party already has produced the documents in another form, courts tend to deny later requests, often concluding that the metadata is not relevant.").

production of such information is requested, however, the default form established by Rule 34(b)(2)(E)(ii) is "a form or forms in which [that information] is ordinarily maintained or in a reasonably usable form or forms."

The most controversial of the 2006 electronic discovery amendments to the Federal Rules did not involve the actual discovery or disclosure of electronically stored information, but a new "safe harbor" for parties who have lost electronically stored information. Rule 37(e) provides:

> Absent exceptional circumstances, a court may not impose sanctions under these rules on a party for failing to provide electronically stored information lost as a result of the routine, good-faith operation of an electronic information system.

The Report of the Civil Rules Advisory Committee described the rationale for this provision (which was Rule 37(f) at that time, but was designated as Rule 37(e) in 2007):

> Proposed Rule 37(f) [now, Rule 37(e)] responds to a distinctive feature of electronic information systems, the routine modification, overwriting, and deletion of information that attends normal use. The proposed rule provides limited protection against sanctions for a party's inability to provide electronically stored information in discovery when that information has been lost as a result of the routine operation of an electronic information system, as long as that operation is in good faith.[18]

While Rule 37(e) protects parties in certain circumstances from the imposition of sanctions under the Federal Rules of Civil Procedure, "It does not affect other sources of authority to impose sanctions or rules of professional responsibility."[19] The Advisory Committee Note to Rule 37(f) (now, Rule 37(e)) states:

> Good faith in the routine operation of an information system may involve a party's intervention to modify or suspend certain features of that routine operation to prevent the loss of information, if that information is subject to a preservation obligation. A preservation obligation may arise from many sources, including common law, statutes, regulations, or a court order in the case. The good faith requirement of Rule 37(f) means that a party is not permitted to exploit the routine operation of an information system to thwart

---

18. 234 F.R.D. 219, 370 (2006). This Report also noted: "It can be difficult to interrupt the routine operation of computer systems to isolate and preserve discrete parts of the information they overwrite, delete, or update on an ongoing basis, without creating problems for the larger system." *Id.* "Describing a worst-case scenario, [Civil Rules Advisory Committee member Judge Shira] Scheindlin said: 'Large companies have the possibility of being sued every day, which means they cannot even implement their data destruction policies.' " "Judicial Conference Panel Backs Changes to Accommodate Discovery of Electronic Data," 72 *U.S.L.W.* 2637, 2638 (Apr. 27, 2004).

19. Advisory Committee Note to 2006 Amendment to Rule 37(f). 234 F.R.D. 219, 374 (2006).

discovery obligations by allowing that operation to continue in order to destroy specific stored information that it is required to preserve.[20]

In addition to the above amendments to Rules 16, 26, 33, 34, and 37, Rule 45 was amended in 2006 to explicitly extend that Rule to "electronically stored information" and conform Rule 45, and the process for obtaining information by subpoena, with the amendments to the other discovery rules.

NOTES AND QUESTIONS CONCERNING ELECTRONIC DISCOVERY

1.   Were the 2006 amendments to the Federal Rules really necessary? Didn't judges already have sufficient discretion within the existing Rules to respond to the special challenges raised by electronic discovery? *See* Hedges, "A View from the Bench and the Trenches: A Critical Appraisal of Some Proposed Amendments to the Federal Rules of Civil Procedure," 227 F.R.D. 123 (2005) (suggesting that new amendments added unnecessary complexity to the Rules, that attorneys can resolve electronic discovery issues by conferring with other counsel, and that judges had sufficient discretion to regulate discovery prior to electronic discovery amendments); Noyes, "Is E–Discovery So Different that It Requires New Discovery Rules? An Analysis of Proposed Amendments to the Federal Rules of Civil Procedure," 71 *Tenn. L. Rev.* 585 (2004) (concluding that some of the 2006 electronic discovery amendments were unnecessary or inappropriate). *But see* Marcus, "Complex Litigation at the Millennium: Confronting the Future: Coping with Discovery of Electronic Material," 64 *L. & Contemp. Probs.* 253 (2001) (in which Special Reporter to Discovery Subcommittee of Advisory Committee on Civil Rules analyzes arguments for amending the Rules and other alternatives for dealing with electronic discovery). *See also* "Conference on Electronic Discovery," 73 *Fordham L. Rev.* 1 (2004) (sponsored by Judicial Conference Advisory Committee on Civil Rules as it considered electronic discovery amendments to Federal Rules of Civil Procedure).

2.   Prior to the 2006 electronic discovery amendments to the Federal Rules of Civil Procedure, local rules were adopted in some federal districts, and in some state courts, to address electronic discovery. *See, e.g.,* the rules collected in *Zubulake v. UBS Warburg LLC,* 229 F.R.D. 422, 439 n.123 (S.D.N.Y. 2004), and at http://www.krollontrack.com/rules-statutes/. The proliferation of such local rules was one of the reasons cited by the Judicial Conference Committee on Rules of Practice and Procedure for amending the Federal Rules of Civil Procedure and thereby providing uniform national rules in this area. 234 F.R.D. 219, 272–73 (2006).

3.   Nevertheless, since the adoption of the electronic discovery amendments in 2006, some federal courts have provided additional guidance, and created additional requirements, concerning electronic discovery. Most notably, the United States Court of Appeals for the Seventh Circuit launched an Electronic Discovery Pilot Program, formulating electronic discovery principles and a standing order to be used in selected cases by participating judges within the Seventh Circuit. Phase One of this pilot program concluded on May

---

20. *Id.*

1, 2010, and, based upon the experiences of judges and lawyers in this phase of the program, an expanded Phase Two of the program began on July 1, 2010. *See* Seventh Circuit Electronic Discovery Pilot Program—Report on Phase One, http://www.7thcircuitbar.org/associations/1507/files/05–2010%20Phase%20One%20Report%20and%20Appendix%20with%20Bookmarks.pdf. The standing order developed by the Court's Electronic Discovery Committee, *id.*, at 76, 77, initially stresses the need for counsel to approach electronic discovery cooperatively and reminds counsel that the "proportionality standard set forth in Fed. R. Civ. P. 26(b)(2)(C) should be applied in each case when formulating a discovery plan."

4. In a survey of attorneys handling federal civil actions that closed in the final quarter of 2008, plaintiff's attorneys reported that their reported median costs rose from $8126 in cases with no electronic discovery to $30,000 in cases that included electronic discovery requests; Defendant's attorneys reported an increase of median costs in such cases from $15,000 in cases with no electronic discovery to $40,000 in cases with any electronic discovery. E. Lee & T. Willging, *Federal Judicial Center National, Case–Based Civil Rules Survey: Preliminary Report to the Judicial Conference Advisory Committee on Civil Rules* 35–37 (2009). *See also* E. Lee & T. Willging, *Litigation Costs in Civil Cases: Multivariate Analysis: Report to the Judicial Conference Advisory Committee on Civil Rules* (2010).

5. Prior to its amendment in 2006, Rule 34 referred to "documents (including * * * data compilations from which information can be obtained * * *)." Rule 34 now provides for the production of "documents **or** electronically stored information." (Emphasis added.) Does this mean that Rule 34 requests should now seek both "documents and electronically stored information" in order to ensure that both electronically and non-electronically stored information are produced? *See* Advisory Committee Note to 2006 Amendment to Rule 34(a), 234 F.R.D. 219, 361 (2006) ("[A] Rule 34 request for production of 'documents' should be understood to encompass, and the response should include, electronically stored information unless discovery in the action has clearly distinguished between electronically stored information and 'documents.' ").

6. The version of Rule 34 that was published for public comment prior to the 2006 amendments had as the default form for the production of electronically stored information "a form in which it is ordinarily maintained or in an electronically searchable form." Critics of an "electronically searchable" alternative suggested that such a standard might be read to require "native format" production and that different computer systems had different search capabilities. The Advisory Committee on the Federal Rules of Civil Procedure therefore substituted for "an electronically searchable form" in Rule 34(b) "a form or forms that are reasonably usable," thus paralleling the long-standing provision in Rule 34(a) that documents may have to be "translated, if necessary, * * * into reasonably useable form." Report of the Judicial Conference Committee on Rules of Practice and Procedure, 234 F.R.D. 219, 353–54 (2006). The current version of Rule 34(b)(2)(E)(ii) provides: "If a request does not specify a form for producing electronically stored information, a party must produce it in a form or forms in which it is ordinarily maintained or in a reasonably usable form or forms."

7. Because of the complexity, volume and cost of electronic discovery, it is crucial that counsel work together in discovery planning. As the Judicial Conference Committee on Rules of Practice and Procedure noted in its report on the 2006 amendments to the Federal Rules, "The proposed rules provide support for early party management and, where necessary, effective judicial supervision. Keeping discovery manageable, affordable, and fair is a problem that litigants and judges in all courts share." 234 F.R.D. 219, 396 (2006).

Counsel are now required to discuss electronic discovery issues at their Rule 26(f) discovery planning conference. In virtually all cases, it is in the interest of all parties to agree to some ground rules concerning electronic discovery and inadvertent waiver of privilege or work-product protections. While Rule 26(b)(5)(B) does not define the parameters of either privilege or waiver, "Agreements reached under Rule 26(f)(4) [now, Rule 26(f)(3)(D)] and orders including such agreements entered under Rule 16(b)(6) [now, Rule 16(b)(3)(B)(iv)] may be considered when a court determines whether a waiver has occurred." Advisory Committee Note to 2006 Amendment to Rule 26(b)(5)(B), 234 F.R.D. 219, 346 (2006).

8. Rule 26(b)(2)(B) provides that parties "need not provide discovery of electronically stored information from sources that the party identifies as not reasonably accessible because of undue burden or cost." This amended Rule contemplates a "two-tier practice in which [lawyers] first sort through the information that can be provided from easily accessed sources and then determine whether it is necessary to search the difficult-to-access sources." Report of Civil Rules Advisory Committee, 234 F.R.D. 219, 331 (2006). Thus here, too, cooperation among counsel is contemplated, as they work through issues concerning electronic data that may not be reasonably accessible because of undue burden or cost. Advisory Committee Note to 2006 Amendment to Rule 26(b)(2), 234 F.R.D. 219, 337 (2006) ("If the requesting party continues to seek discovery of information from sources identified as not reasonably accessible, the parties should discuss the burdens and costs of accessing and retrieving the information, the needs that may establish good cause for requiring all or part of the requested discovery even if the information sought is not reasonably accessible, and conditions on obtaining and producing the information that may be appropriate.").

9. While this information should be explored in the parties' Rule 26(f) conference, in appropriate cases formal discovery should be addressed to the technological structure employed by other parties to the litigation. The early deposition of a management information systems (MIS) official can be used to establish the structure of a party's technological operations and provide the basis for future discovery seeking specific electronically stored information. Nevertheless, questions such as the following might still be asked of all witnesses in order to confirm that electronically stored information is not being withheld by another party:

Do you use e-mail at work?

Do you use your personal e-mail accounts for work?

Do you work at home on a computer?

Do you use a laptop, Palm Pilot, Blackberry, alphanumeric pager, etc., for work?

Is that laptop, etc., provided by the company?

Do you use your home computer for work?

Have you ever deleted an e-mail or other document concerning ...?

What is your best recollection of what it said?

Why did you delete it?

Have you ever asked IS staff to retrieve a deleted document?

Were they successful?

Who attempted to retrieve it for you?

Do you regularly make hard copy printouts of your e-mail?

Did you print out any e-mail regarding ...?

Flynn & Finkelstein, "A Primer on 'E–*vide*–n.c.e.,' " *Litigation*, Winter 2002, at 34, 40.

10. Because of the tremendous potential cost of electronic discovery, a significant amount of attention has focused on possible cost-shifting in the production of electronically stored information. "Under [the federal discovery rules], the presumption is that the responding party must bear the expense of complying with discovery requests, but he may invoke the district court's discretion under Rule 26(c) to grant orders protecting him from 'undue burden or expense' in doing so, including orders conditioning discovery on the requesting party's payment of the costs of discovery." *Oppenheimer Fund, Inc. v. Sanders*, 437 U.S. 340, 358 (1978). *See also Manual for Complex Litigation, Fourth* § 11.433 (2004) ("[W]here production is to be made of data maintained on computers, and the producing party is able to search for and produce the data more efficiently and economically than the discovering party, they may agree to use the former's capabilities subject to appropriate reimbursement for costs.").

As amended in 2006, Rule 26(b)(2)(B) gives the courts the authority to shift costs for the production of electronically stored information that is "not reasonably accessible because of undue burden or cost." Prior to the 2006 amendment to Rule 26(b)(2)(B), Judge Shira Scheindlin ordered the production of backup tapes that would impose a Rule 26(c) "undue burden or expense" on the producing party pursuant to the following test:

First, it is necessary to thoroughly understand the responding party's computer system, both with respect to active and stored data. For data that is kept in an accessible format, the usual rules of discovery apply: the responding party should pay the costs of producing responsive data. A court should consider cost-shifting *only* when electronic data is relatively inaccessible, such as in backup tapes.

Second, because the cost-shifting analysis is so fact-intensive, it is necessary to determine what data may be found on the inaccessible media. Requiring the responding party to restore and produce responsive documents from a small sample of the requested backup tapes is a sensible approach in most cases.

Third, and finally, in conducting the cost-shifting analysis, the following factors should be considered, weighted more-or-less in the following order:

1. The extent to which the request is specifically tailored to discover relevant information;

2. The availability of such information from other sources;

3. The total cost of production, compared to the amount in controversy;

4. The total cost of production, compared to the resources available to each party;

5. The relative ability of each party to control costs and its incentive to do so;

6. The importance of the issues at stake in the litigation; and

7. The relative benefits to the parties of obtaining the information.

Zubulake v. UBS Warburg LLC, 217 F.R.D. 309, 324 (S.D.N.Y. 2003). See *also* Advisory Committee Note to 2006 Amendment to Rule 26(b)(2), 234 F.R.D. 219, 338 (2006) (listing seven factors to be considered in determining whether to require a party to search for and produce electronically stored information that is not readily accessible because of undue burden or cost); Vainberg, Comment, "When Should Discovery Come with a Bill? Assessing Cost Shifting for Electronic Discovery," 158 *U. Pa. L. Rev.* 1523 (2010); Redish, "Electronic Discovery and the Litigation Matrix," 51 *Duke L. J.* 561 (2001) (proposing a conditional cost-shifting model for discovery involving electronically stored information that is not reasonably accessible in the ordinary course of business).

11. What, though, if it is unclear just what the burden and cost would be to produce electronically stored information that is alleged to be "not reasonably accessible?" In that situation, the drafters of Rule 26(b)(2)(B) envisioned the possibility of limited discovery to determine just what the burden and cost would be of full-scale discovery. "In such cases, the parties may need some focused discovery, which may include sampling of the sources, to learn more about what burdens and costs are involved in accessing the information, what the information consists of, and how valuable it is for the litigation in light of information that can be obtained by exhausting other opportunities for discovery." Advisory Committee Note to 2006 Amendment to Rule 26(b)(2), 234 F.R.D. 219, 338 (2006). See *also* American Bar Association, *Civil Discovery Standards*, Standard 31(b) (2004) ("At any discovery conference that concerns particular requests for electronic discovery, * * * the parties should consider, where appropriate, stipulating to the entry of a court order providing for: (i) The initial production of tranches or subsets of potentially responsive data to allow the parties to evaluate the likely benefit of production of additional data, without prejudice to the requesting party's right to insist later on more complete production.").

12. Judge Scheindlin's opinions in the *Zubulake* case have been influential with respect to other aspects of electronic discovery. In *Zubulake III* and *IV*, Judge Scheindlin dealt with spoliation and a party's duty to preserve

information (both electronic and non-electronic) in anticipation of litigation. In *Zubulake IV*, Judge Scheindlin concluded:

> Once a party reasonably anticipates litigation, it must suspend its routine document retention/destruction policy and put in place a "litigation hold" to ensure the preservation of relevant documents. As a general rule, that litigation hold does not apply to inaccessible backup tapes (*e.g.*, those typically maintained solely for the purpose of disaster recovery), which may continue to be recycled on the schedule set forth in the company's policy. On the other hand, if backup tapes are accessible (*i.e.*, actively used for information retrieval), then such tapes *would* likely be subject to the litigation hold.

220 F.R.D. 212, 218 (S.D.N.Y. 2003).

Unless she does not want a potential defendant to know that a lawsuit is coming, plaintiff's counsel might send to that future defendant a "preservation letter." In this letter counsel can state that a lawsuit is being prepared and request that specific electronic discovery be preserved. The letter may include citations to legal authority requiring a litigation hold (such as *Zubulake*), and counsel can later file a motion for a preservation order along with the complaint in the ultimate civil action. T. Mauet, *Pretrial* § 6.8(2)(a) (7th ed. 2008).

13. Judge Scheindlin's *Zubulake V* opinion was written to address the destruction and significantly-delayed production of emails in that case. She further detailed counsel's duty to communicate with her client that client's obligations concerning the identification, retention, and production of discovery:

> [O]nce the duty to preserve attaches, counsel must identify sources of discoverable information. This will usually entail speaking directly with the key players in the litigation, as well as the client's information technology personnel. In addition, when the duty to preserve attaches, counsel must put in place a litigation hold and make that known to all relevant employees by communicating with them directly. The litigation hold instructions must be reiterated regularly and compliance must be monitored. Counsel must also call for employees to produce copies of relevant electronic evidence, and must arrange for the segregation and safeguarding of any archival media (*e.g.*, backup tapes) that the party has a duty to preserve.

229 F.R.D. 422, 439 (S.D.N.Y. 2004). Relying upon the decisions of the United States Court of Appeals for the Second Circuit in *Kronisch v. United States*, 150 F.3d 112 (2d Cir. 1998), *Byrnie v. Town of Cromwell*, 243 F.3d 93 (2d Cir. 2001), and *Residential Funding Corp. v. DeGeorge Fin. Corp.*, 306 F.3d 99 (2d Cir. 2002), Judge Scheindlin found that the defendant had engaged in spoliation and agreed to instruct the jury that it could infer that the evidence that had been destroyed would have been unfavorable to the defendant. 229 F.R.D. at 429–30, 436, 439. While denying a request for an adverse inference stemming from the destruction of emails in violation of a document preservation order, the court in *United States v. Philip Morris USA*, 327 F.Supp.2d 21 (D.D.C. 2004), precluded testimony from the 11 employees who had deleted

emails and ordered Philip Morris to pay a sanction of $2,750,000 ($250,000 for each individual who had violated the court's order).

14.   More recently, Judge Scheindlin has revisited issues of spoliation due to the destruction of electronically stored information. In an opinion entitled "Zubulake Revisited: Six Years Later," Judge Scheindlin concluded:

> After a discovery duty is well established, the failure to adhere to contemporary standards can be considered gross negligence. Thus, after the final relevant *Zubulake* opinion in July, 2004, the following failures support a finding of gross negligence, when the duty to preserve has attached: to issue a written litigation hold; to identify all of the key players and to ensure that their electronic and paper records are well preserved; to cease the deletion of email or to preserve the records of former employees that are in a party's possession, custody, or control; and to preserve backup tapes when they are the sole source of relevant information or when they relate to key players, if the relevant information maintained by those players is not obtainable from readily accessible sources.

Pension Comm. of the Univ. of Montreal Pension Plan v. Banc of America Securities LLC, 685 F.Supp. 2d 456, 471 (S.D.N.Y. 2010). Although spoliation requires the showing of prejudice as a result of the destruction of relevant documents, Judge Scheindlin noted: "Relevance and prejudice may be presumed when the spoliating party acted in bad faith or in a grossly negligent manner." *Id.* at 467.

15.   In a subsequent case involving allegations of the intentional destruction of electronically stored information, Judge Lee Rosenthal, Chair of the Advisory Committee on the Federal Rules of Civil Procedure, agreed to issue an adverse inference instruction allowing the jury to infer that deleted information would have been unfavorable to the defendants. *Rimkus Consulting Group v. Cammarata*, 688 F.Supp. 2d 598 (S.D. Tex. 2010). However, she stressed: "Whether preservation or discovery conduct is acceptable in a case depends on what is *reasonable*, and that in turn depends on whether what was done—or not done—was *proportional* to that case and consistent with clearly applicable standards." *Id.* at 613. She also noted that, in at least some circuits, an adverse inference instruction could not be premised upon gross negligence, as Judge Scheindlin had concluded in her *Pension Committee* opinion. *Id.* at 615.

More recently, Magistrate Judge Paul Grimm concluded that in evaluating a motion for sanctions due to the failure to preserve electronically stored information, a court must consider "(1) whether there is a duty to preserve; (2) whether the duty has been breached; (3) the level of culpability involved in the failure to preserve; (4) the relevance of the evidence that was not preserved; and (5) the prejudice to the party seeking discovery of the ESI that was not preserved." *Victor Stanley, Inc. v. Creative Pipe, Inc.*, 269 F.R.D. 497, 502 n.7 (D. Md. 2010). Magistrate Judge Grimm also expressed concern in his opinion about the "lack of a national standard, or even a consensus among courts in different jurisdictions about what standards should govern preservation/spoilation issues." *Id.* at 516. In a subsequent opinion, Magistrate Judge

Grimm imposed on the defendants sanctions of more than $1 million. *Victor Stanley, Inc. v. Creative Pipe, Inc.,* No. MJG–06–2662 (D.Md. Jan. 24, 2011).

16. Despite the 2006 amendments to the Federal Rules and an increasing body of case law, issues involving electronic discovery will continue to proliferate. The American Bar Association amended its Civil Discovery Standards in 2004 to address the practical aspects of electronic discovery. American Bar Association, *Civil Discovery Standards* (2004). *See also* The Sedona Conference Working Group for Electronic Document Retention and Protection, *The Sedona Principles: Best Practices, Recommendations & Principles for Addressing Electronic Document Production* (2d ed. 2007).

17. Why does Rule 26(b)(5) merely establish a procedure for asserting privilege or work product protection? One of the major rationales for amending the Rules in 2006 was to establish national uniformity and to create clearer rules to guide party conduct. Why, therefore, does Rule 26(b)(5)(B) not address the circumstances under which inadvertent production actually constitutes a waiver of a privilege or work-product protection?

18. To address the substance of waiver due to inadvertent disclosure of information otherwise protected by the attorney-client privilege or work-product doctrine, Rule 502 was added to the Federal Rules of Evidence in 2008. Section (b) of Federal Rule of Evidence 502 provides:

> When made in a Federal proceeding or to a Federal office or agency, the disclosure does not operate as a waiver in a Federal or State proceeding if:
>
> (1) the disclosure is inadvertent;
>
> (2) the holder of the privilege or protection took reasonable steps to prevent disclosure; and
>
> (3) the holder promptly took reasonable steps to rectify the error, including (if applicable) following Federal Rule of Civil Procedure 26(b)(5)(B).

Section (e) of Rule 502 further provides: "An agreement on the effect of disclosure in a Federal proceeding is binding only on the parties to the agreement, unless it is incorporated into a court order." With respect to Federal Rule of Evidence 502, see also Notes 10–13 of the Notes and Questions Concerning Upjohn Co. v. United States and the Attorney–Client Privilege in Chapter 6, *supra* pp. 255–257.

19. Thus in order to ensure protection for electronically stored information produced in discovery, counsel should reach an agreement protecting the information produced by all parties and have that agreement incorporated into an order of the court. The Advisory Committee on the Federal Rules of Civil Procedure has described two standard aspects of such orders: a "quick peek" provision and a "clawback" agreement:

> [Counsel] may agree that the responding party will provide certain requested materials for initial examination without waiving any privilege or protection—sometimes known as a "quick peek." The requesting party then designates the documents it wishes to have actually produced. This designation is the Rule 34 request. The responding party then responds

in the usual course, screening only those documents actually requested for formal production and asserting privilege claims as provided in Rule 26(b)(5)(A). On other occasions, parties enter agreements—sometimes called "clawback agreements"—that production without intent to waive privilege or protection should not be a waiver so long as the responding party identifies the documents mistakenly produced, and that the documents should be returned under those circumstances.

Advisory Committee Note to 2006 Amendment to Rule 26(f), 234 F.R.D. 219, 324 (2006).

20. As electronic discovery becomes more common and more complex, lawyers are increasingly turning to electronic discovery firms or creating this expertise within their own law firms. Krause, "Don't Try This at Home," *A.B.A.J.*, March 2005, at 59; Jones, "The Surging Evolution of E–Discovery: The Cost and Scale of E–Discovery Spawns New Firms," *Nat'l L. J.*, Aug. 2, 2004, at 1. The courts also may call upon technical experts to deal with electronic discovery issues, by, for instance, the appointment of a special master to work with parties to negotiate an electronic discovery protocol or to adjudicate legal or technical disputes concerning electronic discovery. Scheindlin & Redgrave, "Special Masters and E–Discovery: The Intersection of Two Recent Revisions to the Federal Rules of Civil Procedure," 30 *Cardozo L. Rev.* 347 (2008); Krause, "The Paperless Chase," *A.B.A.J.*, April 2005, at 48, 53. *See also* American Bar Association, *Civil Discovery Standards*, Standard 31(b)(iii) (2004) ("[T]he parties should consider, where appropriate, stipulating to the entry of a court order providing for * * * The appointment of a mutually-agreed, independent information technology consultant * * * to (A) Extract defined categories of potentially responsive data from specified sources, or (B) Search or otherwise exploit potentially responsive data in accordance with specific, mutually-agreed parameters.").

21. Once electronically stored information is obtained in discovery, there may be questions as to its admissibility into evidence. The electronically stored information must be authenticated and fall within an exception to the hearsay rule (typically as a party admission, business record, or official record). Diemer, "Caught in the Web: Introduction of Electronic and Internet Evidence," *Litigation News*, March 2002, at 12. *See also Lorraine v. Markel Am. Ins. Co.*, 241 F.R.D. 534 (D. Md. 2007) (analyzing admissibility of various types of electronically stored information).

Exercises Concerning Electronic Discovery

You represent Parker Parker, who recently invested his life savings in a "Shoe Lace Boutique" franchise. This new store got off to a great start—in large part because of its location at the local shopping mall. However, after the store had been open for 15 months, another "Shoe Lace Boutique" opened across the highway from the mall. This new store has significantly cut into Parker's profits.

You have filed a breach of contract action against Franchisers International, claiming that Franchisers had agreed not to license any new "Shoe Lace Boutiques" within a five-mile radius of Parker's store. The action is filed as a diversity action in federal district court.

1.   Assume that this action has just been filed and that counsel will meet next week for the parties' Rule 26(f) discovery conference. Your senior partner, who is not familiar with the 2006 electronic discovery amendments to the Federal Rules of Civil Procedure, has asked you to draft a memorandum discussing how to address the electronic discovery issues that the parties are required to consider pursuant to Rule 26(f)(2) and (3). In your memorandum be sure to set forth any assumptions that you are making concerning the computer systems of either party and additional facts that you would need to know before taking any firm positions at the Rule 26(f) conference. In drafting your memorandum, you might consult the Pretrial Conference Agenda for Computer–Based Discovery that is an appendix to Withers, "Computer–Based Discovery in Federal Civil Litigation," 2000 *Fed. Cts. L. Rev.* 2.

2.   Although you have received some basic information about the storage of electronic information by Franchisers International, you are very interested in learning more about this company's computer systems before deposing other fact witnesses in this case. Draft a memorandum setting forth how you would develop this information. In your memorandum be sure to consider the possible application of Rule 30(b)(6), what specific questions you would ask Franchisers to answer, whether you would use any expert(s) or consultant(s) in developing this information, how your opposing counsel may react to your strategy, and what, if any, impact this should have upon the strategy that you pursue.

3.   Assume that you want to ensure that Franchisers International does not routinely (or otherwise) destroy relevant documents before this case comes to trial. You also assume that counsel for Franchisers would like to ensure that Parker's company preserves relevant documents and electronically stored information. Prepare the communication(s) that you propose should be sent to the parties by both sets of counsel asking that all relevant documents and electronically stored information be preserved.

4.   Although you have filed a Rule 34 request seeking "all documents and electronically stored information that mentions Parker Parker," you suspect that the response of Franchisers International to this request has not been complete. Wendy Witness (a former employee of Franchisers International) stated in her deposition that she received an email from Sammy Salesman asking her whether she "could believe just how stupid" Parker was to think that Franchisers wouldn't license another "Shoe Lace Boutique" within five miles of his store. However, no such email has been produced by Franchisers International.

Draft a memorandum setting forth how you would address this situation (formally or informally) with opposing counsel, in upcoming depositions of Franchisers International's employees, and with the court.

C.   DOCUMENT PRODUCTIONS IN PRACTICE

The production of documents in response to a Rule 34 request might seem at first blush to be a simple discovery task; if a document falls within a proper Rule 34 request, that document must be produced. However, in modern corporate litigation there may be thousands, or tens of thousands, of documents that arguably fall within a set of Rule 34 requests. Nevertheless, most counsel are understandably reluctant to produce documents that have not been unambiguously requested.

The following excerpt is from the book *The Partners,* by James Stewart. The document production problems described in this excerpt arose in a major antitrust suit brought by Berkey Photo, Inc. against the Eastman Kodak Company. Alvin Stein, of the New York law firm of Parker, Chapin, Flattau & Klimpl, represented Berkey Photo in this case. John Doar, Mahlon Perkins and Helmut Furth of New York's Donovan Leisure Newton & Irvine were primary counsel for the defendant Kodak in this litigation and in a related suit brought against Kodak by the GAF Corporation.

While reading this excerpt consider why the problems described arose and how they could have been prevented. The case vividly illustrates how, in the words of Judge Frankel, "a kind of single-minded interest in winning, winning, winning" can pervert the entire discovery process.

J. STEWART, THE PARTNERS

pp. 327–28; 335–51; 354–65 (1983).

Samuel Murphy, Jr., the star litigating partner at Donovan Leisure Newton & Irvine, was grim as he welcomed five of his partners, all members of the firm's executive committee, to his large corner office in Rockefeller Center early Tuesday morning, January 9, 1978. Murphy had interrupted a business trip to Atlanta and flown back to New York the night before, and the importance of the occasion was underlined by the presence of both George Leisure, Jr., and Ralstone Irvine, two of the firm's most senior partners. "I know you are finding this hard to believe," Murphy told the worried group, and proceeded to unfold a tale of scandal and intrigue which, unknown to the committee members, had been brewing within the firm for months. As he continued, "a state of shock began to take hold," Murphy recalls.

Conspicuously absent from the high-level secret meeting was John Doar, probably the firm's best-known partner as a result of his national prominence as counsel to the Senate Judiciary Committee throughout the Watergate crisis. That morning, Doar was sequestered in a Donovan, Leisure litigation office in lower Manhattan working on the closing statement to the jury in *Berkey v. Kodak,* an antitrust case he had just tried for one of Donovan, Leisure's most important corporate clients, Eastman Kodak. The closing argument, Doar realized, might be his last chance to salvage what was rapidly turning into a disaster of nightmare proportions.

That disaster had already struck was manifestly clear to the stunned executive committee members gathered in Murphy's office. And as the details of what was happening sank in, their concern quickly expanded beyond worry about losing the Kodak case. They had to face the fact that the Kodak debacle now threatened the continued existence of Donovan, Leisure itself.

* * *

During 1975, the Kodak cases settled into a routine characteristic of any litigation of such a large size and scope. Stein [counsel for plaintiff Berkey Photo] had made several discovery motions before Judge Marvin Frankel, the federal district judge to whom both the Berkey and GAF cases had been assigned; and the judge had been relatively generous in granting them. As a result, Donovan, Leisure associates began to comb through the files at Kodak, making copies of the hundreds of thousands of documents requested by the plaintiffs' lawyers. To coordinate the production of documents, the Donovan, Leisure team was assigned space in offices maintained by Kodak in New York City at 77 Broadway, known as the Wanamaker building. There, lawyers and paralegals scrutinized the documents, coded them, entered them into an elaborate computer system installed for the litigation, and then gave copies to lawyers for GAF and Berkey.

As Cravath's had been in the IBM case, the strategy was to drown the opposition in documents, most of which were harmless or irrelevant, hoping that they would lack either the manpower or the willpower to pore through each and every one of them. Similarly, litigants schedule depositions—pretrial question-and-answer sessions—with as many of the opposing party's executives as possible, as much to harass as to gain information that may later be used as evidence at trial. All such "discovery" activities are designed to minimize surprises at the trial itself.

By the end of 1975, the Donovan, Leisure lawyers under Doar's direction had produced more than 500,000 documents from Kodak's internal files. Their opponents at Parker, Chapin and at Simpson, Thacher [counsel for GAF Corporation in its antitrust suit against Kodak] had not moved nearly as quickly. They had not computerized their operation—Stein's firm couldn't afford the system—and had produced only about 100,000 documents. Furth, in particular, sensed that Donovan's heavy document production had stunned the opposition, and he moved quickly to exploit what he perceived as an advantage. He made a motion to Judge Frankel for immediate commencement of depositions of all of GAF's top executives, which Frankel—a judge who was known for his efforts to speed up lengthy litigation—granted. Simpson, Thacher's Vance tried to stop the program from going forward (he, like Murphy, was preoccupied with other cases), but when he failed, he assigned defense of the depositions to a highly regarded partner, John Guzzetta, and an associate, Eric Vitalliano.

Furth's strategy was first to depose Jesse Werner, the chairman of GAF, and James Sherwin, the executive vice president, to, as he puts it, "draw first blood." That deposition began in Kodak's office space in the Wanamaker building shortly after Frankel's order. Such procedures usually take a few days, at most a week. Werner's deposition took a solid month, and as the days wore on, Werner's temper became shorter.

To Furth's surprise, he didn't think the lawyers from Simpson, Thacher took the depositions very seriously. To the untrained eye, the lawyer who represents the person being questioned at a deposition doesn't have much to do. Occasionally, the lawyer may instruct the witness not to answer a question, but such an instruction can be appealed to the judge or a magistrate and is not often given. Ordinary courtroom objections have no effect. In many depositions, the defense counsel seems to do little more than listen, and for these reasons, corporate law firms often send their less experienced litigation associates to cover them. In Simpson, Thacher's case, the firm rotated lawyers at Werner's and Sherwin's depositions, beginning with Guzzetta, who then occasionally assigned others to take his place.

One deposition objection frequently made is that a question has already been asked and answered, but it requires a defense counsel familiar with what has already happened at the deposition. According to Furth, when he saw Simpson, Thacher sending in new lawyers, he deliberately began to ask the same questions over, prolonging the deposition and rattling Werner and Sherwin. While the witnesses became increasingly agitated, the Simpson, Thacher lawyers listened to the repetitive questions for the first time, not noticing Furth's ploy.

* * *

The next day, Furth asked Werner about the effect of government administration during and after World War II, and the chairman emphatically denied that it had had any effect on GAF's profits. But Furth was still suspicious. He later asked Guzzetta for any letter Werner had written to the wage and price council requesting an exemption. Guzzetta answered that if such a letter hadn't already been produced, it had been lost or destroyed. The next day, Furth called Vitalliano at Simpson, Thacher. Feigning innocence, he indicated that the price control issue was coming up in his questioning and said, "We're ready for that letter Werner wrote to the wage and price council." Vitalliano took the bait. Werner had indeed written such a letter, and Vitalliano answered that he'd have to review the document, but otherwise he'd be happy to send it. By Monday, Furth had a document in his hands that he hadn't even been sure existed.

As soon as he had the letter, Furth made the unsuspecting Werner repeat his sworn testimony that government administration had had no effect on GAF's profitability. Then he pulled out a copy of the document in which Werner had argued the opposite position to the wage and price council. Werner was surprised and embarrassed. Whatever he might have planned to say at trial on the subject would now be undermined. When Vance later left the firm to become Secretary of State, GAF dropped Simpson, Thacher from the case.

Furth considered his deposition campaign in GAF to be a litigation coup, but it was not so regarded by his new superior at Donovan, Leisure,

John Doar. Doar confided to one associate that Furth's technique had amounted to little more than a cheap trick, one unbecoming to the profession. Doar told Guzzetta that he was having "problems" with Furth. When Furth later offered his opinion that the Kodak cases should be tried before a judge and not a jury, his advice was disregarded. And when GAF successfully obtained an indefinite postponement of its case in order to change counsel (GAF first asked Stein to handle its case as well as Berkey's; when he declined, it turned to Skadden, Arps, Slate, Meagher & Flom in New York), Furth was left in charge of GAF. His legal staff dwindled to two associates, and he was in the law firm's equivalent of exile.

* * *

While Donovan, Leisure lawyers were busy scheduling and conducting depositions of Berkey and GAF executives, Stein was finally getting his own discovery program under way on behalf of Berkey. After conducting depositions of Fallon and most of Kodak's top executives during the course of 1976, Stein scheduled the deposition of Yale economist Merton J. Peck, whom Donovan, Leisure lawyers had chosen to be Kodak's principal economic expert witness in the case.

* * *

The care and feeding of an expert witness by lawyers takes time and money. The experts must review all of the facts in the case, thousands of documents, and must develop an economic theory which coincides with the legal theory being presented by the lawyers. For their efforts, such economic experts command fees of up to $4,000 a day; Peck received more than $100,000 for his work with Donovan, Leisure. In theory, the testimony of such an expert is supposed to represent the independent judgment of the expert, untainted by any favoritism toward either party. In practice, the economists, who otherwise subsist on academic salaries, know to whom they owe their six-figure yearly incomes. Highly respected experts have been known to ask lawyers, "Tell me what I'm supposed to say."

Early in the Kodak case, Perkins had been given the assignment of selecting and preparing Kodak's expert witnesses. It was an assignment that appealed to the scholarly side of Perkins' nature, and to assist him, he asked that associate Joseph Fortenberry be assigned to work with him. Fortenberry, too, had a professorial air, though at times it bordered on that of a mad professor. Other associates and partners at the firm describe him uniformly as an odd-ball, a loner who most enjoyed library research assignments, whose oddities concealed a shy and sensitive nature. After Perkins had selected Peck and Morris Adelman from the Massachusetts Institute of Technology as Kodak's economic experts, he and Fortenberry set about developing the economic theories, submitting various reports and analyses to the experts for their review, and developing positions through exchanges of memoranda.

On March 29, 1977, Stein finally scheduled his deposition with Peck, and Doar assigned Perkins and Fortenberry to the task of defending his deposition. While it was a logical extension of his work in developing Peck's testimony, Perkins was not looking forward to the deposition. As hard as he had tried, Perkins had never delighted in the kind of tough litigating tactics that had characterized Furth's work, for example, and that might be called for in the deposition by the opponent's lead counsel of Kodak's single most important witness. But the need to prove himself was weighing heavily on Perkins since Doar's arrival, and he went into the deposition determined to take a hard line.

Peck's deposition began on April 20 in a conference room at Donovan, Leisure's Rockefeller Center offices. Peck was nervous; Stein recalls that it was quickly apparent to him that "Peck wasn't strong in the personal sense; he seemed vulnerable, very suggestible." Stein began, however, by focusing his questions at Perkins. At the time he scheduled Peck's deposition, Stein had also made a request for all the documents that Peck had received and everything he had written about the Kodak litigation.

While the request was a broad one, it wasn't unreasonable. Over the years, courts have ruled that almost anything that a lawyer shows an economic expert witness must be disclosed to opposing counsel, the theory being that everything a witness sees relating to the case becomes a part of his thinking and should be subject to cross-examination at trial. An expert's opinion, the theory goes, is only as good as the information on which it is based. The lawyers at Donovan, Leisure had already taken a hard line about producing some of the documents that Stein had demanded, to the point that an exasperated Stein called for a special hearing before the magistrate to determine what Donovan, Leisure had to produce. Doar attended the hearing—not Perkins—and the magistrate ruled that even "interim" reports had to be produced if they had been discussed by the expert with counsel. Doar had argued that only "final" reports had to be turned over, but Doar sent a memo summarizing the ruling to Perkins in anticipation of his deposition with Peck.

When Stein began his questioning of Peck, the lawyer naturally focused on the existence and whereabouts of such documents that Donovan, Leisure might have failed to turn over to him; and in the course of his questioning, Peck told him that he had returned all of his written material, including his handwritten notes, to the lawyers at Donovan, Leisure. Stein hadn't gotten any handwritten notes. The lawyer stopped his questioning to demand that those papers be produced, and almost casually Perkins replied that the material "had not been retained."

Peck then babbled on about what had happened: "The practice I followed when I accumulated a substantial bulk of material is to send it by REA Express to Donovan, Leisure, because a lot of the material was covered by a confidentiality order, and I had no storage facilities as well as I had no room.... I just kept it in a cardboard box and when the box filled up I sent it off. I told them I didn't want it anymore and I had no further use for them." Stein's suspicions were aroused. Was Peck being defensive, a little too effusive in his explanation? Again Stein turned to

Perkins: "I ask that I be provided with the dates when materials prepared by this witness and returned to Donovan, Leisure was [sic] destroyed by Donovan, Leisure, and I ask that there be identified to me the persons who participated in that destruction."

"I have no way of knowing," Perkins answered irritably. "All I can state is that no materials were destroyed subsequent to the receipt of your notice of production." Fortenberry, Perkins' associate who was sitting beside him, interrupted to whisper in Perkins' ear, but Perkins brushed him aside as Stein asked again who at Donovan, Leisure had destroyed the Peck documents. "Well, I am the person responsible for destroying or seeing that they were destroyed," Perkins finally admitted.

Stein moved on to another area of questioning, but he had on the record what he wanted for the time being: three admissions from Perkins that a substantial number of potentially important documents had been destroyed, and an admission that Perkins himself had destroyed then. Stein thought that the situation smelled suspicious. There is nothing wrong with destroying documents in the ordinary course of business—such behavior is routine at many corporations as a result of cases like Kodak—but if they were destroyed *after* they are subpoenaed it is a crime: destruction of evidence. Even if not subject to a particular subpoena, destruction of documents related to an ongoing case by counsel seemed extraordinary. "My feeling was that all along what they'd done was so contrary to reasonable practice—this was a perfect example which would reflect seriously on the credibility of Peck's testimony," Stein recalls. He made a note to himself to again explore the subject of the missing documents at trial, before the judge and the jury.

It had been a bad day for Perkins, whose fears about the ugliness of litigation had been confirmed. When he returned to the Wanamaker building, Perkins asked to talk with Doar, and Fortenberry began examining documents for the next day's examination. Perkins told Doar what had happened at the deposition, mentioning that he told Stein that he had disposed of documents that had been returned to him by Peck. Just as Stein had been suspicious, Doar was troubled by the explanation. In a case involving hundreds of thousands of documents that had been successfully computerized and accounted for, it was inherently odd that three entire briefcases of documents had disappeared, apparently destroyed by one of the top partners in the case. Why? What could account for such extraordinary behavior?

It was a critical juncture in the case and one where Doar, with some vigorous questioning of Perkins, might have prevented all that was to happen. But inexplicably, Doar simply accepted Perkins' explanation. He didn't ask him any questions. He didn't call in Fortenberry to find out if he knew anything about the matter. He told Perkins only that he was "troubled" by the destruction of the documents, that it suggested that there was something untrustworthy about Donovan, Leisure, and by implication, Doar himself. His chief concern seemed to be his own reputation, not Perkins' shaky explanation; and he told Perkins to find other copies of the documents in question and produce them to Stein.

Doar may have been preoccupied by the fact that he had already made a more significant blunder with respect to materials relied upon by Peck. About a month earlier, Doar had prepared some looseleaf notebooks which contained all the information he would need to conduct his examination of Peck at trial, including a draft of the actual questions that he intended to ask and the answers he expected to receive from Peck—a virtual script for Peck's testimony at trial. Though trial testimony is always intended to sound spontaneous, such script preparation is common. Showing it to the witness is not. Because of strict discovery requirements, it must never be shown to an expert witness economist, from whom it could actually fall into the hands of opposing counsel. Doar had given his notebooks to Peck to read, but he had not turned them over to Stein pursuant to his discovery request. The next day, Doar planned to attend Peck's deposition and admit to Stein that he had shown the books to Peck while arguing that they were protected by a lawyer's work product privilege and didn't have to be produced. At the same time, Doar wanted Perkins to produce copies of all the documents that he could recall had been destroyed. Perhaps such a display of candor and cooperativeness would restore some of Doar's reputation for trustworthiness.

Doar made his appearance, but his explanations did not satisfy Stein, and in fact only heightened his suspicions. He took the matter to the magistrate in the case, who ordered Doar to produce the four notebooks he had shown Peck. Doar was desperately afraid of turning over those materials, and had in turn to appeal the magistrate's order to Judge Frankel, bringing the whole unpleasant business to the attention of the judge. The hearing on that appeal was set for May 5. Knowing that the issue of the destroyed documents was also likely to come up then, Doar brought Perkins along to the hearing.

The subject arose almost immediately, and Perkins delivered the explanation he had worked out with Doar. Yes, Perkins told the judge, the documents had been destroyed, but he had searched through his files and come up with duplicates; those had been turned over to Stein. The story seemed a bit implausible to Frankel. "And you are able to know just what it was that was destroyed, is that what you are saying?" the judge asked skeptically. Perkins didn't answer, and Frankel ordered Perkins to produce an affidavit, sworn under oath, explaining what had happened to the documents and how they had been reproduced. Then Stein tried to exploit what he saw as a crucial weakness in Perkins' explanation:

"The witness has testified, Peck, that over the period of years he received a whole host of documents from a whole host of sources. He has made notes and memoranda of what he saw over the years," Stein pointed out.

"He then testifies that all of this material, every shred of it, was returned to Kodak's counsel. And Kodak's counsel now says that every bit of that, or virtually all of it, was destroyed." Stein had managed to make the story sound even more implausible.

"Including memos that the expert made?" the judge asked.

"Including *handwritten* memos and drafts of what he prepared, yes," Stein emphasized. How could a handwritten memo be reproduced from Kodak's files?

"Is that right, Mr. Perkins?" the judge asked incredulously.

Perkins evaded the question, answering, "Your Honor, I haven't reviewed all of the record."

The judge, noting the still unanswered questions, ordered Perkins to have his explanatory affidavit in court by the following Monday morning.

* * *

Sunday afternoon, Doar, Perkins and Magee met in Perkins' office. But nothing further was said about Perkins' statement in court, nor were any questions asked about the document destruction. The affidavit was discussed briefly, and Doar gave Perkins a copy of the memo he had prepared, telling Perkins to make sure that his affidavit conformed to it. Then Doar changed the subject to other aspects of the case. "It never occurred to me that Mr. Perkins had in fact not destroyed the documents which he said he had destroyed," Doar later said. Nor did he realize that the documents, now stored in a large suitcase, were at that moment hidden in a closet in Perkins' office, inches from where Doar sat.

By the summer of 1977, the discovery phase of the trial was over. Despite all of its resistance, Donovan, Leisure eventually turned over nearly all the documents it had with respect to Peck, though the judge spared Doar from having to produce his notebooks. The trial began on July 18 in Federal District Court in downtown Manhattan. Stein did all of the questioning in presenting Berkey's case, which—keeping the presence of the jury always in mind—was short and to the point. Doar began his direct questioning immediately after. He did virtually all of the examination of Kodak's witnesses. Neither Perkins nor Furth was ever seen in the courtroom, though Doar was always accompanied by several associates.

* * *

Peck took the witness stand on January 5, 1978. One topic which was excluded from his examination was the 1915 case he had discussed with Furth, since the Donovan, Leisure lawyers had argued that the old ruling against Kodak might prejudice the jury if they knew about it. Then Doar, on the very first day of Peck's examination, asked him the broad question that Furth had drafted, and Stein immediately objected. If Peck was going to discuss the source of Kodak's monopoly power, he argued, he should be permitted to question him about the 1915 consent decree, which Berkey contended had contributed to Kodak's dominant position in the market. The judge let Doar proceed with his questioning, but indicated that he would rule on Stein's request to ask about the 1915 case the following day.

When Peck and the lawyers got back to the Wanamaker building, Peck went over to the drinking fountain and started talking with Furth, with whom he seemed to have established a rapport, and who had not been in court. As soon as Peck mentioned the dispute over the subject of the 1915 case, Furth's eyes lit up. Furth has an amazing memory for detail—Donovan, Leisure lawyers conceded that no one rivals Furth's command of the Kodak facts—and he immediately recalled a letter he had received from Peck that discussed the 1915 decree. "That's no problem," Furth told Peck, and proceeded to refresh the economist's memory of the now four-year-old letter.

But Peck was troubled. Already anxious that the lawyers hadn't given him enough attention during his preparation for trial, he went to Mac-Sheain and asked why he hadn't been shown the letter he had written to Furth in 1974, and asked if he could see it now. This was the first that MacSheain had heard about a 1974 letter, and she went to Doar to ask him about it. "Peck shouldn't worry about it," Doar told her. "Tell him if Stein asks him about it to identify it," Doar said, even though he had never seen the document himself.

Later that evening, around 9:00 P.M., Doar, MacSheain, Fortenberry, a lawyer from Kodak and Peck met in Doar's office to review for the next day's examination. Furth was excluded, as usual, even though he was the only one who actually recalled the substance of the 1915 memo. When the subject of the 1915 case came up, Doar finally asked to see a copy of the letter. He looked at it briefly and said that if Frankel ruled the next day that the 1915 case was relevant, he would have to give copies of the document to the judge and to Stein. Peck was upset, saying that he didn't want to be asked questions about a document he hadn't seen in more than three years, so Doar gave him a copy to review. No one bothered to ask why a copy of the document hadn't been provided Stein before during all the discovery. According to Doar, he was preoccupied with proposed instructions to the jury that would follow Peck's testimony and was busy making sure that all the documents had been properly admitted into evidence.

The next morning, Frankel began the court session with a ruling that information about the 1915 case appeared to be more prejudicial than relevant, and hence questions about the 1915 case would be barred. A sigh of relief went through the Donovan, Leisure ranks, for now it would not be necessary to unveil Peck's letter. But Stein was still suspicious that Peck had produced some work that had not been turned over to him during discovery, so he again asked the economist if he had produced any such memoranda. With the 1915 letter now fresh in his mind, Peck said, "Yes, there are." With that, Doar was forced to hand out the copies of Peck's memo on the 1915 antitrust case.

Stein's retaliation was quick and harsh: "A vital, relevant document has been deliberately withheld, and in this case I am compelled to say by counsel as well as the witness ... it is particularly shocking since it relates directly to the matters we have been wrestling with these past few days trying to find out whether there is a reason ... for bringing in the 1915 decree," Stein exclaimed. The document itself was innocuous enough, as Furth had earlier noted, but in the present context it was a disaster. Since its whole premise was whether the 1915 case had contributed to continued unlawful dominance of the market by Kodak, it indicated that the Donovan, Leisure lawyers thought that was a relevant question in the case—precisely opposite to the position they had been arguing to Judge Frankel, who had ruled in their favor that morning. The judge immediately asked why the memo hadn't been produced, and Doar— eventually facing that question for the first time—volunteered that a magistrate's ruling had exempted it from production. Incredibly, Doar couldn't remember which ruling, remembering vaguely only that one had been made. Doar was speculating, desperately, for there had been no such ruling. Judge Frankel, skeptical, noted that the case was becoming "explosive" and ordered Doar to produce an affidavit explaining why the memo had not been produced before.

The day had been a humiliating nightmare for Doar. When the glum litigation team returned to the Wanamaker building, Doar shut himself in his office and refused to see his colleagues.

The next two days in court were spent discussing the proposed jury instructions, but the incident over the 1915 memo had put all of Stein's complaints about Donovan, Leisure's discovery tactics in a new, harsh light. The destroyed documents had continued to nag at Frankel, and at the close of the day on January 8, he ordered Doar to include with his affidavit about the 1915 letter yet another affidavit explaining how and why the Peck documents had been sent to Donovan, Leisure and destroyed. Doar assigned responsibility for the preparation of the affidavits to Magee, who went to the Rockefeller Center offices to tell Perkins that he had to provide a fuller explanation.

At the Wanamaker litigation center, further concern about Perkins and his missing documents, if any, was lost in the gloom over the Peck debacle. As Furth recalls it, "There was no question that Peck had been lost at this point. He was completely at sea. He looked like a fool, he sounded terrible, he wasn't answering properly, he wasn't making any sense." A more secure witness might have staved off disaster. After all, nothing of any great substantive importance had been uncovered. But Peck lacked the strength of character to fight back from the accusations of lying and hiding evidence, and Doar offered no support. Peck crumbled before the jury's eyes, looking less believable as his testimony neared its agonizing conclusion.

But the worst revelation occurred outside the courtroom. Late on January 8, Perkins arrived at Doar's office in the Wanamaker building visibly upset. Magee had been to see him about another affidavit, he explained to Doar, and then his speech faltered. Looking tired, haggard, and with tears in his eyes, Perkins finally confessed to Doar: No documents had ever been destroyed. With his earlier affidavit, Perkins had committed perjury. He couldn't do it again.

*

As the case continued to collapse around him, Doar remained coldly professional. He immediately called John Tobin, the corporate partner who headed the firm's executive committee, at Tobin's home in Westchester, and broke the news. He told Tobin that he and Perkins were leaving then for the Rockefeller Center offices, where the documents were stored, and advised Tobin that he planned to take the entire matter before the court once he had had a chance to look at the documents. Tobin was astounded and confused—the facts were hard for him to grasp—he couldn't believe that "Perk", his friend, colleague and former classmate at Harvard Law School, was involved.

Tobin called George Leisure, Jr., the son of the firm's patriarch, who was also a litigator and was more familiar with the Kodak case. Leisure left immediately for the Wanamaker building to intercept Doar and Perkins. But by the time he had arrived, Doar's mind was already made up about the course that had to be taken. He was taking Perkins to his office to review the documents, and as soon as he had determined what had been withheld, he intended to notify the judge and opposing counsel. Doar was unwilling to wait for the advice of Donovan, Leisure's executive committee, and at about 10:00 P.M. Doar and Perkins left for the Rockefeller Center offices, where they spent the remainder of the night poring over the documents in the suitcase, trying to identify which had been produced, and numbering and indexing those which had not.

Stein was asleep in his home on Long Island at about 6:00 A.M. the next day when he was awakened by a phone call from Doar. Doar "was obviously very distressed," Stein recalls. "He told me that he'd discovered that these documents we'd been told had been destroyed were in the possession of Donovan, Leisure lawyers all along, and that he'd have them in court that morning." Stein told Doar only that he'd be interested in seeing them, concealing his surprise. "I realized instantly that it meant that obviously false affidavits had been filed. There is a limit—I mean, even with their already questionable ethics in this case, I never believed they would go that far."

The new disclosure was ammunition that Stein was prepared to use that very day in court—the last sorry day of the beleaguered Peck's testimony. Peck had spent the previous evening at the Wanamaker building getting ready for his last day, oblivious to the Perkins disclosure taking place only a few doors away from where Fortenberry and Mac-Shean were rehearsing him for his final questions. Nor did the Donovan, Leisure associates and most other partners know what had happened the night before, or why Doar was looking quite so haggard and worn. Only Magee had joined Leisure, Doar and Perkins the previous night, and all agreed to keep the matter secret until it was formally disclosed to the court. Only in the limousine heading to the courtroom in downtown

Manhattan did Doar explain to Peck that yet another miserable day lay ahead, and that the fact that Perkins had not destroyed the documents would be revealed.

The day proved to be all that Peck and Doar feared. Doar began his presentation by stating on the record that certain documents previously described as having been destroyed were actually intact, and he produced them for Stein. Frankel was expecting the admission—Doar's phone call had gotten him out of the shower that morning—but not Doar's attempt to minimize the impact of the disclosure by asking that the document destruction issue not be brought to the attention of the jury. "All the documents that I know of have been produced to Mr. Stein for his cross-examination with respect to Dr. Peck's opinion," Doar argued. "The matter of the destruction of the documents seems to me to be so prejudicial to Kodak ... that the prejudice would outweigh any issue of credibility."

But the judge's patience with respect to Donovan, Leisure's disclosure of evidence had reached its limit, especially since Stein, after looking at the documents Doar produced, noticed from their dates that some of them had been found in Peck's files *after* the time Peck testified he had sent them all back to Donovan, Leisure. Frankel snapped at Doar, "I don't understand how you can say that when a few minutes ago Mr. Stein told me that at your instance Peck looked in his files over the weekend and found some that were not sent back and not destroyed ... and if that doesn't go to his credibility, I don't know what does. For his [Peck's] $60,000 or $70,000 he ought to look in his files."

Frankel then allowed Stein, in front of the jury, to question Peck at length about the supposedly destroyed documents and Perkins' false statements under oath; and it gave Stein the material he wanted for a blistering final characterization of Peck and his testimony: "That sordid spectacle of dissembling, evasiveness, deception and concealment disgraces the dignity of this court, this proceeding, and you jurors.... And there is no doubt, I believe, based upon the evidence presented to you, and the conclusions to be drawn from that evidence, that the witness deliberately and purposefully concealed material evidence, and—I think it has got to be said—lied to you under oath. Not once, repeatedly." Stein finally concluded that Peck "has proven himself utterly unworthy of belief."

* * *

Meanwhile, within Donovan, Leisure, debate continued about how to handle the Perkins matter. As previously expressed by Murphy, the sentiment of the executive committee was still to do what it could to protect Perkins' status as a partner in the firm and as a member of the bar. But Doar soon removed that option, as he had done earlier by bringing the matter to the attention of the court and to opposing counsel. As soon as Doar finished his closing argument and the jury retired on January 13, he determined unilaterally "to make a more complete report to the Court as to what Mr. Perkins had said to me Sunday night."

Perkins, on the advice of Murphy and Tobin, had retained his own counsel, Harold Tyler, the former federal judge who had been approached to join Donovan, Leisure at the time Doar was hired. Perkins had since refused to talk to Doar about what had happened, so Doar called Perkins' lawyers and advised them that he intended to go into court the next morning and tell the judge everything Perkins had told him during their Sunday meeting. Since Perkins' earlier statement to Doar admitted that he knew he was lying when he prepared the affidavit about the destroyed documents, Doar's account was likely to result in a perjury indictment. Faced with that threat, Perkins called Tobin and said he would be willing to discuss the incident with a member of the firm and with Doar before Doar went into court the next day. That Friday night, Perkins came into the Rockefeller Center offices and met with Doar for about three hours. By the time they emerged, Perkins agreed that he would personally appear in court the next morning and make his own statement before the judge.

The next afternoon, a Saturday, Perkins, his lawyer Tyler, Doar and Stein met in private session in Judge Frankel's chambers. No one from Kodak was present, nor were other Donovan, Leisure partners. Though a transcript of the proceedings was made, it was promptly placed under seal, and Frankel stressed the need for secrecy, warning that he had already refused to take calls from several reporters. Then Perkins began his account:

"I think I should probably start by saying that the things or most of the things I am going to tell you, I haven't told anybody before now except to my lawyers," he began in a quiet, halting voice. After referring to his work with Peck and the shipment of documents, he turned to the Peck deposition. "Mr. Stein was asking Professor Peck about documents that he said he had sent to Donovan, Leisure. He asked me where the documents were and I said they had been discarded. He asked me who destroyed them, and I said, 'I did.' That was not the truth, Your Honor. As I recall it now, that answer came into my head for some reason at the deposition. I had not planned to make that answer. I don't believe that I had really considered it." Perkins explained that the evening after the deposition, his associate Fortenberry, acting on his own, had taken the briefcases containing the documents Perkins testified had been destroyed up to the Rockefeller Center offices, where the documents were stored in a locked closet. Perkins said he never looked at the documents until the night he opened the suitcase with Doar. Rather, "I know this is difficult to explain," Perkins said, "but I simply treated those documents as if they had in fact been destroyed. I did not discuss them with Mr. Fortenberry."

Perkins seemed at particular pains to explain exactly Fortenberry's involvement in the matter. After discussing his conversation with Doar about the affidavit he prepared, and the redraft he did with the help of Magee, he added, "It's my best recollection that Mr. Fortenberry had no knowledge at the time of the contents of that affidavit. Following this whole episode, I just didn't discuss the matter with Mr. Fortenberry. He didn't bring it up with me. I knew that he was aware of it, because he brought the suitcase up." And then Perkins remembered that Fortenberry had interrupted him during the Peck deposition: "During the morning of the second day of the deposition [when Stein was pursuing the matter of the destroyed documents] ... Mr. Fortenberry ... whispered in my ear, something to the effect ... 'You have forgotten about the suitcase.' "

* * *

Not long after that discussion with Doar, Perkins recalled that the judge had ordered him to draft yet another affidavit explaining the destroyed documents. "I started to revise it," Perkins recalled, referring to his affidavit, "and then it began to grow on me that I shouldn't be handing in any more affidavits to Your Honor." It had been that evening that Perkins had gone to Doar and confessed. Only when Perkins opened the suitcase with Doar that night did he learn that virtually all the documents it contained had already been produced to Stein. The few papers that hadn't been produced proved to be entirely inconsequential, and were never submitted as evidence by Berkey. The attempt to conceal them, in the end, did nothing to benefit Kodak.

"I am not going to go into my feelings on the subject of the documents which were not destroyed in the suitcase and my affidavit to you, but I understand absolutely that what I did was wrong," Perkins sadly concluded. "I injured many people as a consequence."

The following Monday, Perkins came into his office as usual, where he found a note asking him to speak with Tobin. The previous day, the Donovan, Leisure executive committee had again met to consider Perkins' status. After reading a copy of the sealed transcript of Perkins' statement to the court—and the judge's assertion that at some future point all the information would be turned over to the U.S. Attorney for possible prosecution—the committee members painfully concluded that Perkins could no longer maintain a practice within the firm. Tobin, Perkins' closest friend on the committee, was delegated to convey the decision.

Even now, Tobin finds it difficult to talk of his meeting with Perkins. "It was a very difficult thing for me to do, but I personally relieved him of all assignments within the firm. I spoke to him, I just told him that we had to ... It was painful, but he understood and agreed. We talked about replacements for his other clients (principally the Advertising Association of America). He tried to talk about what had happened, but he couldn't explain it. He was in shock." Though Perkins stopped coming into the office, he remained a partner in the firm pending a further investigation of the incident.

*

Attention was shortly diverted from the plight of Perkins by yet more bad news for Donovan, Leisure. After nine days of deliberations, the jury returned to the courtroom on January 22 and announced its verdict. It found Kodak guilty of monopolization. Judge Frankel ordered commencement of a separate trial for damages—Berkey claimed damages of approximately $300 million, which, when trebled, would result in an award of nearly $1 billion—and Walter Fallon, Kodak's chairman, quickly issued a press release denouncing the verdict and pledging an immediate appeal. Decisions about how to handle the damages trial and the appeal of the verdict had to be made quickly, so Tobin and Murphy flew to Rochester to meet with the senior Kodak executives.

It was at this meeting, the day after the verdict, that the Donovan, Leisure partners were first made aware of Kodak's displeasure with the conduct of the trial. It had nothing to do with the Perkins matter, the Kodak executives claimed; but according to Cole, sentiment had been growing for some time within Kodak that Doar was not handling the case properly. Would Donovan, Leisure consider replacing Doar as lead counsel for the damages trial? Murphy asked for some time to consider the decision, but his instinct was that Doar should not be replaced. "It didn't make any sense," he says. "The trial was in its last stages. Doar had put together the defense; no one was in a better position to go forward with it. It really was in no one's interest to replace him, and it would have been a devastating blow for Doar."

* * *

The position the firm adopted and tried to convey to Kodak was not enhanced by the reaction of Judge Frankel, who, after further reflection, made the following statement after the jury rendered its verdict: "I listened sadly and sympathetically as Mr. Perkins went out of the way to take all the blame to himself and to absolve substantially everyone else, except possibly an associate. But I was left with a nagging sense of uneasiness about that—a feeling that didn't diminish as other circumstances developed and came into focus."

Frankel proceeded to cast aspersions on the conduct of the other lawyers at Donovan, Leisure: "The strange and suspicious story of destroyed documents obviously called for inquiry. The upshot is that this matter, without questioning anybody's honesty, seems to have been characterized in its handling by defense counsel by . . . a course of self-help, mistake, and/or extreme carelessness. All of this," the judge continued, "reflects a kind of single-minded interest in winning, winning, winning, without the limited qualification of that attitude that the court, I think, is entitled to expect and which I feel must have infected Perkins." The judge's suggestions that the improper attitudes of top partners on the case—Doar obviously included—had "infected" Perkins provided ammunition for the growing group within Kodak that wanted Doar off the case. Shortly after the judge's remarks, Cole called Murphy to tell him that Kodak not only wanted Doar off the damages case, they wanted him off all Kodak matters.

* * *

Not until March 28, two weeks later, did Kodak issue a terse statement announcing that Donovan, Leisure was being replaced as counsel by

Sullivan & Cromwell. Cole justified the decision with a statement to the press saying that "an unfortunate incident" (the Perkins matter) had given rise to a potential conflict of interest with Donovan, Leisure, making necessary the change of counsel. But both Cole and the lawyers at Donovan, Leisure knew that the potential conflict had had nothing to do with the decision to drop the firm altogether. A lawyer at Sullivan & Cromwell recalls that the pretext of the conflict of interest was nothing but a face-saving fib, and that at the time Sullivan & Cromwell was assigned the case Kodak said nothing about any concern over a conflict.

* * *

Following the transition period during the spring, most of the Donovan, Leisure lawyers on the case were sent on vacation—the firm had nothing else for them to do. Doar himself went on a six-week trip to Ireland with his wife, and when he returned he submitted his resignation to the firm.

Doar was never told that Kodak had demanded that he be replaced, nor did the firm ever seek his resignation. But he realized that his position in the firm had become untenable. "It was entirely his own decision to leave," Murphy says, "and I tried to talk him out of it. I think he was held responsible by my partners for things that really weren't his fault, and because of the case, he really didn't know any of them besides me and Tobin. He undoubtedly felt pressure."

* * *

At the time he left, Doar told his partners that he missed the small practice he had had as a lawyer in Wisconsin, and had reluctantly concluded that a large firm wasn't the setting for him. Today he maintains a solitary practice in a small office in midtown Manhattan, still handling occasional matters for the Ladies Garment Workers and waiting for litigation referrals. Divorced by his wife, he is described by one lawyer who has dealt with him recently as "hiding what seems to be bitterness behind a cold and taciturn facade." Still revered by much of the public for his Watergate role, his legal career is viewed by many other lawyers as in shambles.

Furth became "of counsel" to Sullivan & Cromwell but is an outcast in his new firm. Sullivan & Cromwell partners have banished him to his office in the Wanamaker building, where he pores over files and presides over a suite of now largely deserted offices. He has no illusions about his future with Sullivan & Cromwell, and hopes that when the case is over, Kodak will reward his loyalty with a position on its in-house staff in Rochester.

Joseph Fortenberry, too, is no longer at Donovan, Leisure. Though all other senior associates who toiled on the Berkey case have been rewarded with partnerships—a visible symbol of the firm's promise that no one's future at Donovan, Leisure would be handicapped by the Perkins affair or the loss of Kodak—Fortenberry was passed over and is now a lawyer with the Justice Department in Washington. It is doubtful that, despite being implicated by Perkins, Fortenberry really knew the true story about the destroyed documents. (If he did, he would have been obligated to reveal Perkins' misconduct to the bar association, or at least to senior members of the firm.) Fortenberry claims that a paralegal, not he, carried the suitcase of documents from the Wanamaker building to Rockefeller Center, and says he "does not recall" whispering anything about the suitcase to Perkins at the deposition.

At any rate, Fortenberry's role in the scandal had nothing to do with his failure to be made a partner. The firm had actually passed him over two months before the Perkins matter ever came to light. It later lied about its decision so as to enhance Fortenberry's chances of getting another job, keeping him working so that prospective employers would not see his immediate dismissal from the firm and conclude that Fortenberry was indeed implicated in Perkins' wrongdoing. Even so, Fortenberry was not hired by every private law firm at which he applied for a job.

Ironically, Perkins may have emerged relatively well. In the fall of 1978, he appeared in Federal District Court and pled guilty to a reduced misdemeanor charge of contempt of court. His lawyer, Harold Tyler, commented that "there, possibly but for the grace of God, go I, because of the pressures which come upon men and women who practice law in big cases." Though Perkins spent 30 days in jail for the offense, he retains his firm pension and has never been disbarred. Since his release, Perkins has traveled extensively in the Far East, where he taught English to Japanese students for some time, and is now devoting himself to his duties as president of the Greenwich, Connecticut, Philharmonic Society. He has little contact with his former partners at Donovan, Leisure, but one lawyer who spoke with him recently describes him as "happier, I believe, than he had been as a practicing lawyer."

* * *

Kodak, too, has emerged unscathed. On June 25, 1979, based on the briefs submitted by Sullivan & Cromwell, the Court of Appeals for the Second Circuit, in a precedent-setting opinion that was later cited by IBM, reversed the jury's verdict for Berkey. The reversal was, in practical terms, an unqualified victory for Kodak. It eventually settled the case with Berkey for a comparatively paltry $4.75 million in cash and $2 million of credit.

Thus did the Kodak case come to an end. As in the IBM case, it is hard to say what impact the lawyers actually had on the ultimate result. The Donovan, Leisure lawyers themselves maintain that the Court of Appeals reversal of the jury verdict vindicates their own efforts at trial. In any event, the law firm of Donovan, Leisure, as an institution, has emerged relatively unscathed.

The same cannot be said for Doar, Perkins, Fortenberry and Furth. The intense pressures which exist for partners in all of the elite corporate firms forced them outside the self-contained world of Donovan, Leisure, and into the arena of public scrutiny and prosecution. At all such firms, institutional self-preservation comes first. For the lawyers within them, the resulting personal sacrifices can be great indeed.

NOTES AND QUESTIONS CONCERNING THE ETHICS OF DOCUMENT PRODUCTIONS

1. While there is a tendency among many attorneys to resist the production of documents requested by an opposing party, a somewhat differ- ent litigation strategy was employed in *Berkey v. Kodak:* "[T]he strategy was to drown the opposition in documents, most of which were harmless or irrelevant, hoping that they would lack either the manpower or the willpower to pore through each and every one of them." J. Stewart, *The Partners* 335 (1983). Is this ethical? Is it a good litigation strategy? How can opposing counsel be deterred from such conduct?

2. Consider the ethical propriety and strategic wisdom of the following deposition tactic: "[L]itigants schedule depositions * * * with as many of the opposing party's executives as possible, as much to harass as to gain informa- tion that may later be used as evidence at trial." *Id.* What about Helmut Furth taking a month to depose a Kodak executive and asking the same deposition questions when new opposing counsel appeared at the deposition? *Id.* at 336.

3. What, specifically, is wrong with "[h]ighly respected experts * * * ask[ing] lawyers, 'Tell me what I'm supposed to say.'?" *Id.* at 339. In this respect, note that Federal Rule of Evidence 706 permits the court to call its own (neutral) experts.

4. Presuming that he knew the statement to be false, what duty rested upon associate Joseph Fortenberry when he heard his senior partner state at Peck's deposition that the documents sought by Berkey had been destroyed? Was it enough to whisper in Perkins's ear at the deposition? *See* Model Rules of Prof'l Conduct Rule 8.3 ("A lawyer who knows that another lawyer has committed a violation of the Rules of Professional Conduct that raises a substantial question as to that lawyer's honesty, trustworthiness or fitness as a lawyer in other respects, shall inform the appropriate professional authori- ty.").

5. Consider the reaction of "one lawyer close to the case" to John Doar's decision to inform the court about the perjured affidavit while Merton Peck was still on the witness stand:

> There was hardly universal admiration for Doar's unilateral action. It had been hasty, seemingly without much thought for the consequences or how they might be alleviated. Was it possible, for example, to delay raising this matter until the case had already been submitted to the jury? Perhaps not, but Doar didn't even give his partners the chance to raise the question. He seemed more concerned about establishing his own innocence than about the welfare of the client, or of the firm.

J. Stewart, *The Partners* 351–52 (1983).

6. Was John Doar correct in deciding to inform the court what Mahlon Perkins had told him about the perjured affidavit? What was the effect of Doar's decision? What if Perkins's explanation to the court had differed from what he had told Doar privately?

7. Was John Doar expected to leave Donovan, Leisure because he had acted unethically, because he had lost a major case, or because he had embarrassed his law firm? Consider Rule 5.1(b) and (c) of the Model Rules of Professional Conduct:

> (b) A lawyer having direct supervisory authority over another lawyer shall make reasonable efforts to ensure that the other lawyer conforms to the Rules of Professional Conduct.

> (c) A lawyer shall be responsible for another lawyer's violation of the Rules of Professional Conduct if:

* * *

> (2) the lawyer is a partner or has comparable managerial authority in the law firm in which the other lawyer practices, or has direct supervisory authority over the other lawyer, and knows of the conduct at a time when its consequences can be avoided or mitigated but fails to take reasonable remedial action.

Did Doar have a responsibility to investigate when Perkins first told him (during Peck's deposition) that documents had been destroyed?

8. How can counsel be sure that other parties have produced all documents encompassed within a document production request? Deponents can provide useful information about the existence of documents, as did Merton Peck in the Berkey litigation. Copies of documents typically pass through many hands in a large corporation, and there may be many individuals who can be asked about the existence of documents. The "cc" lines on documents also should be checked. If a party listed as having received a copy of a document does not produce that document, questions may arise about the completeness of other aspects of the document production.

9. Judge Richard Posner has observed that "discovery of sensitive documents is sometimes sought not to gather evidence that will help the party seeking discovery to prevail on the merits of his case but to coerce his opponent to settle regardless of the merits rather than have to produce the documents." *Marrese v. American Academy of Orthopaedic Surgeons,* 726 F.2d 1150, 1161 (7th Cir.1984) (en banc), *rev'd,* 470 U.S. 373 (1985). Is this tactic ethically proper? How should opposing counsel deal with such a document request?

10. Judge Frankel ultimately denied Berkey's request to see the four notebooks that contained John Doar's synthesis of the litigation and that Doar had shown to Kodak's economic experts. *Berkey Photo, Inc. v. Eastman Kodak Co.,* 74 F.R.D. 613 (S.D.N.Y. 1977). However, Judge Frankel included a "fair warning" in his decision that, in light of newly effective Federal Rule of Evidence 612, "there will be hereafter powerful reason to hold that materials considered work product should be withheld from prospective witnesses if they are to be withheld from opposing parties." 74 F.R.D. at 617.

Waiver of privileges or work-product protections is not something that attorneys want to learn about firsthand. *See generally* Applegate, "Preparing for Rule 612," *Litigation*, Spring 1993, at 17; Ward, "The Litigator's Dilemma: Waiver of Core Work Product Used in Trial Preparation," 62 *St. John's L. Rev.* 515 (1988); Marcus, "The Perils of Privilege: Waiver and the Litigator," 84 *Mich. L. Rev.* 1605 (1986). In his article Professor Marcus suggests that broad waiver rules recognized in cases such as *Berkey* will cause attorneys to prepare witnesses in person rather than with written materials, thereby increasing litigation costs and favoring wealthier litigants. 84 *Mich. L. Rev.* at 1608–14; 1642–48. *See also* Robinson, "Duet or Duel: Federal Rule of Evidence 612 and the Work Product Doctrine Codified in Civil Procedure Rule 26(b)(3)," 69 *U.Cin. L. Rev.* 197 (2000). Are there different considerations that should apply to a determination of waiver when the witness who has reviewed otherwise protected material is an expert rather than a fact witness? *See* Staton, Note, "Discovery of Attorney Work Product Reviewed by an Expert Witness," 85 *Colum. L. Rev.* 812 (1985).

11. Although John Doar risked waiving work product protection for his trial notebooks by showing those notebooks to expert witnesses, Rule 26(b)(4)(B), as amended in 2010, would now protect the draft expert witness reports that were ordered produced in discovery. This rule provides: "Rules 26(b)(3)(A) and (B) protect drafts of any report or disclosure required under Rule 26(a)(2), regardless of the form in which the draft is recorded."

Exercises Concerning Rule 34 Production Requests

1. As counsel for the plaintiffs in the Buffalo Creek litigation, you would like to obtain information concerning safety inspections of the Pittston Company's various mining dams. You believe that Pittston has been required to file periodic reports with state and federal authorities based upon its own inspections of its dams. In addition to these official reports, you have learned that individual Pittston inspectors examine the dams twice a year and file written reports with Pittston. Unfortunately, Pittston's reports are kept for only five years, and the internal reports from the period 1965 to 1970 are scheduled to be routinely destroyed next month. Prior to the destruction of these reports, a summary of some of the information they contain is stored in Pittston's computerized records system.

In addition to examining these records, you would like to have an engineer whom plaintiffs have retained inspect the site of the Buffalo Creek dam that failed. You are concerned that this inspection be undertaken as soon as possible because of Pittston's ongoing efforts to clean up the dam site.

Write a short memorandum describing the manner in which you would (or would not) attempt to obtain:

(a) the official reports filed with the state and federal governments;

(b) the internal Pittston dam inspection reports;

(c) any computerized information Pittston may have concerning the dam inspections; and

(d) an opportunity for your engineer to inspect the site of the failed dam.

In your memorandum, be sure to address Pittston's likely responses to the discovery course that you recommend. If you choose to file any Rule 34 production or inspection requests with the court, draft those requests.

2. You recently have been hired as the general counsel of O'Brien Industries, Inc. During your first week on the job, you learn that this corporation is in the process of destroying several years of documents pursuant to longstanding records retention and destruction policies. Some of these documents may be relevant to:

(a) a business dispute that has not yet resulted in litigation;

(b) a civil action that has just been filed by consumer groups against Magus Manufacturing, a corporation that is not related to O'Brien but that manufactures some of the same products;

(c) a civil action that has just been filed against O'Brien; and

(d) a discovery request made by the plaintiff in another action pending against O'Brien.

Write a memorandum to the president of O'Brien, who is herself an attorney, setting forth your recommendations concerning these documents. In connection with your research you may wish to consult M. Koesel & T. Turnbull, *Spoliation of Evidence: Sanctions and Remedies for Destruction of Evidence in Civil Litigation* (D. Gourash ed. 2d ed. 2006); J. Gorelick et al., *Destruction of Evidence* (2010); Finkelstein et al., "Spoliation, *or* Please Don't Leave the Cake Out in the Rain," *Litigation*, Summer 2006, at 28; Huang & Muriel, "Spoliation of Evidence: Defining the Ethical Boundaries of Destroying Evidence," 22 *Am. J. Trial Advoc.* 191 (1998); Cedillo & Lopez, "Document Destruction in Business Litigation From a Practitioner's Point-of-View: The Ethical Rules vs. Practical Realities," 20 *St. Mary's L. J.* 637 (1989). *See also* Brown & Weiner, "Digital Dangers: A Primer on Electronic Evidence in the Wake of Enron," *Litigation*, Fall 2003, at 24.

III.   RULE 35 PHYSICAL AND MENTAL EXAMINATIONS

While parties can be required to answer interrogatories pursuant to Rule 33 or answer deposition questions pursuant to Rule 30, if the physical or mental condition of a party is at issue Rules 30 and 33 may not provide the discovery most needed. Fortunately, a separate provision is made in Federal Rule of Civil Procedure 35 for physical and mental examinations.

Rule 35(a)(1) provides:

The court where the action is pending may order a party whose mental or physical condition—including blood group—is in controversy to submit to a physical or mental examination by a suitably licensed or certified examiner. The court has the same authority to order a party to produce for examination a person who is in its custody or under its legal control.

The order that is necessary to obtain a Rule 35 physical or mental examination is described in Rule 35(a)(2):

The order:

(A) may be made only on motion for good cause and on notice to all parties and the person to be examined; and

(B) must specify the time, place, manner, conditions, and scope of the examination, as well as the person or persons who will perform it.

In order to obtain such examinations of the Buffalo Creek plaintiffs, attorneys for the defendant Pittston Company filed the following motion:

IN THE UNITED STATES DISTRICT COURT FOR THE SOUTHERN DISTRICT OF WEST VIRGINIA AT CHARLESTON

DENNIS PRINCE, et al.,
           Plaintiffs,
           v.   CIVIL ACTION NO. 3052–HN

THE PITTSTON COMPANY,
           Defendant.

MOTION FOR ORDER REQUIRING EACH INDIVIDUAL PLAINTIFF TO SUBMIT TO PHYSICAL AND MENTAL EXAMINATIONS

Comes defendant, and moves the Court, as authorized by Rule 35 of the Rules of Civil Procedure, for an order requiring each individual plaintiff in the above-entitled action to appear at Highlands Clinic and Williamson Appalachian Regional Hospital, at South Williamson, Kentucky, at a time and in accordance with such schedule for appearance as the Court shall deem proper, with due regard for the convenience of individual plaintiffs, there to submit to physical and mental examinations by Russell Meyers, M.D.; and that the defendant have such other and further relief for accomplishment of the aforesaid examinations of plaintiffs as may be proper. In support of this motion, the affidavit of Zane Grey Staker, one of counsel for defendant, is attached hereto and made a part hereof.

Dated this 10th day of May, 1973.

> JACKSON, KELLY, HOLT & O'FARRELL
> By s/ _____
>   Firm Member
>   Kanawha Valley Building
>   Charleston, West Virginia 25322
>
> DONOVAN, LEISURE, NEWTON & IRVINE
> By s/ _____
>   Firm Member
>   Two Wall Street
>   New York, New York 10005
>
> ZANE GREY STAKER, ESQUIRE
> By s/ _____
>   Kermit, West Virginia 25674
>
> Attorneys for Defendant

Attached to this motion was the following affidavit:

IN THE UNITED STATES DISTRICT COURT FOR THE SOUTHERN DISTRICT OF WEST VIRGINIA AT CHARLESTON

DENNIS PRINCE, et al.,
        Plaintiffs,

v.   CIVIL ACTION NO. 3052–HN

THE PITTSTON COMPANY,
        Defendant.

AFFIDAVIT

STATE OF WEST VIRGINIA,

COUNTY OF KANAWHA, to-wit:

This day appeared Zane Grey Staker before the undersigned Notary Public in and for the County and State aforesaid, and being first put upon his solemn oath did depose and state as follows:

That he is one of counsel for defendant in the above-entitled action, and that of his certain knowledge said action is, *inter alia,* an action by plaintiffs for damages for personal injuries, both physical and mental, allegedly suffered and sustained in or by reason of a Buffalo Creek flood disaster as in the complaint claimed, and as stated in plaintiffs' More Definite Statement, it being specifically alleged by plaintiffs that the physical and mental health of each and every individual plaintiff has been injured or impaired; that defendant is without means or method whatsoever of discovery of the true nature and extent of plaintiffs' alleged injuries except by examination by a physician trained and experienced in the specialized fields of medicine and psychiatry required for such examination; that Dr. Russell Meyers is widely known, and accepted, as a highly trained, thoroughly experienced and eminently qualified medical practitioner in the fields of neurology, neurosurgery and psychiatry; that the Highlands Clinic and Williamson Appalachian Regional Hospital at South Williamson, Kentucky, have available for use by Dr. Russell Meyers in connection with the examination of plaintiffs all requisite laboratory facilities and equipment for diagnostic use and utilization as may be required; that no medical facility so equipped exists in Logan County, West Virginia, nor is any physician possessed of Dr. Meyers' qualifications in the medical field aforesaid available in Logan County, West Virginia, to perform the examinations of plaintiffs; that said Highlands Clinic and Williamson Appalachian Regional Hospital is in point of fact the nearest medical facility to Logan County, West Virginia, and more specifically the area of Buffalo Creek, with the requisite facilities and equipment required for proper conduct of the examinations of plaintiffs, and less inconvenience to plaintiffs will, therefore, attend their examination at the Highlands Clinic and Williamson Appalachian Regional Hospital than at any other comparable medical facility available as a location for appearance of plaintiffs for purposes of submitting to such examinations.

And further affiant says naught.

s/ _____
Zane Grey Staker

Taken, subscribed and sworn to before me by Zane Grey Staker, this 10th day of May, 1973.

My commission expires October 5, 1975.

s/ _____
Notary Public,
Kanawha County,
West Virginia

_____

Once an examination has been conducted under Rule 35(a), the party examined may request a report of the physician or other examiner. So there is no later confusion about the request, it should be made in writing (usually in a letter to opposing counsel). Rule 35(b)(1) provides that the party who caused the examination to be made then must "deliver to the requester a copy of the examiner's report, together with like reports of all earlier examinations of the same condition."

After a copy of the examiner's report has been provided to the party who was examined, Rule 35(b)(3) provides that the party who moved for the examination is entitled to "like reports of all earlier or later examinations of the same condition." Rule 35(b)(3) continues, though, that "those reports need not be delivered by the party with custody or control of the person examined if the party shows that it could not obtain them."

Rule 35(b)(4) provides that, by requesting a copy of a report or deposing the physician or other examiner, the examined party waives any privilege in connection with any examinations of the same physical or mental condition. Because the examination reports must be obtained from doctors or other licensed or certified examiners, the examined party may be asked to execute an authorization requesting the release of his medical records to counsel.

NOTES AND QUESTIONS CONCERNING RULE 35 EXAMINATIONS

1. Rule 35 conditions a party's right to obtain discovery upon that party's provision of discovery to other parties. After a Rule 35 examination, the party who requested the examination must provide the party who was examined with a report of the examination. The examined party's right to obtain this report is conditioned upon that party's provision of any other reports of the same condition to the examining party.

2. Rule 35(a) examinations are not limited to parties, but examinations may be sought of "a person who is in [a party's] custody or under its legal control." What types of situations is this portion of Rule 35(a)(1) meant to cover?

3. A mother brings suit on behalf of her minor child against her landlord, claiming that exposure to lead paint in their apartment has caused the child's learning disabilities. The landlord seeks not only physical and mental examinations of the child but IQ and other testing of the mother and her other children. Must these non-parties submit to such examinations? *Compare Anderson v. Seigel*, 255 A.D.2d 409, 680 N.Y.S.2d 587 (1998) (yes) *with Monica W. v. Milevoi*, 252 A.D.2d 260, 685 N.Y.S.2d 231 (1999) (no).

4. The Supreme Court has held that Rule 35 is constitutional and within the scope of the Rules Enabling Act, both when applied to the examination of a plaintiff, *Sibbach v. Wilson & Co.*, 312 U.S. 1 (1941), and of a defendant, *Schlagenhauf v. Holder,* 379 U.S. 104 (1964).

5. Once a party has obtained a written report of the doctor or other person who has examined him, can he still depose the examiner? Rule 35(b)(6) provides that Rule 35(b) "does not preclude obtaining an examiner's report or deposing an examiner under other rules." Under what other rule might the deposition of an examiner be taken? *But see Cox v. Fennelly,* 40 F.R.D. 1, 2 (S.D.N.Y. 1966) ("Rule 35, by allowing an examined party to institute an exchange of written reports, should normally obviate the need for * * * depositions, and appears in fact to have done so in the run of cases.").

6. Rule 35(b)(6) also applies the Rule 35(b) discovery procedures to examinations undertaken by party agreement, unless the agreement states otherwise. A party who is voluntarily examined should realize that he is entitled to a report of the examination, but by asking for the report he waives the doctor-patient, therapist-patient, or other applicable privilege in connection with other examinations of the same condition.

7. Why should more than one examiner examine a party? Why don't counsel jointly select an expert and agree to accept her conclusions, rather than retaining separate examiners? *See* Fed. R. Evid. 706.

Exercises Concerning Rule 35 Examinations

1.　You are plaintiffs' counsel in the Buffalo Creek litigation. One of the plaintiffs, Sally Lund, has asserted a claim on behalf of her six year old daughter, Emily. Emily has complained of severe headaches and has had repeated nightmares since the flood, but the family practitioner who has seen Emily has been unable to find anything wrong with her. Emily has a very difficult time talking about the flood, in which a grandmother to whom she was very close died. The defendant Pittston Company now has sought to have Emily examined by a pediatrician, a neurologist, a psychiatrist and a child psychologist, all of whose offices are in Charleston.

Please write a short memorandum to your co-counsel addressing the following matters:

(a) Is there any basis upon which you can resist the Rule 35 examinations sought by the defendant?

(b) In the event that the court grants defendant the right to examine the child, are there any conditions that should be placed upon the examinations to make the experience less traumatic for the child?

(c) What are the relative advantages and disadvantages of asking for a copy of the examining doctors' reports?

2.　You represent the plaintiffs in the Buffalo Creek litigation. Judge Hall has told counsel that he will grant the Pittston Company's Motion for Order Requiring Each Individual Plaintiff to Submit to Physical and Mental Examinations that is set forth earlier in this chapter, *supra* p. 432. The judge has asked counsel to submit an agreed order under which the examinations can go forward.

(a) As counsel for the Pittston Company, draft an examination order for submission to plaintiffs' counsel;

(b) As counsel for plaintiffs, draft an examination order for submission to defense counsel.

(c) Presume that the examinations have been held.

(1) As counsel for the plaintiffs, draft a letter to defense counsel requesting copies of reports of the examinations;

(2) As counsel for the Pittston Company, draft the release for each plaintiff to sign authorizing defense counsel to obtain medical records of the plaintiffs to which Pittston is entitled under Rule 35.

IV.　RULE 36 REQUESTS FOR ADMISSIONS

Rule 36 admission requests often are either the first or the last discovery device employed in a comprehensive discovery plan. They are relatively inexpensive to prepare and are largely self-executing. If properly used, they can help to narrow the parties' disputes and eliminate the need for other discovery.

A. THE GOVERNING LAW

Rule 36(a)(1) of the Federal Rules of Civil Procedure provides that a party "may serve on any other party a written request to admit, for purposes of the pending action only, the truth of any matters within the scope of Rule 26(b)(1) relating to: (A) facts, the application of law to fact, or opinions about either; and (B) the genuineness of any described documents."

Form 51 of the Appendix of Forms to the Federal Rules of Civil Procedure illustrates the general format for Rule 36 requests:[21]

REQUEST FOR ADMISSIONS UNDER RULE 36

(Caption–See Form 1.)

The plaintiff *name* asks the defendant *name* to respond within 30 days to these requests by admitting, for purposes of this action only and subject to objections to admissibility at trial:

1.   The genuineness of the following documents, copies of which [are attached] [are or have been furnished or made available for inspection and copying].

(List each document.)

2.   The truth of each of the following statements:

(List each statement.)

(Date and sign-See Form 2.)

———

Rule 26(d)(1) provides that, as with Rule 33 interrogatories and Rule 34 production requests, the service of Rule 36 admission requests generally must await the parties' Rule 26(f) discovery meeting unless the court or a written stipulation provides to the contrary. Rule 36(a)(3) also provides that admission requests must be responded to within the same time period as interrogatories and production requests: thirty days, unless a different time is set by the court or agreed to in a written Rule 29 stipulation.

Admission requests are markedly different from other discovery devices in at least one respect. Rule 36(a)(3) provides that unless such requests are answered or objected to within thirty days (or a different time set by the court or in a written stipulation), they automatically are deemed to be admitted. Counsel ignore admission requests at their own peril; they are the sole discovery device that all attorneys hope their opposing counsel will mislay or otherwise neglect to answer. This may be

---

21. As with other discovery requests, it's usually wise to include a set of instructions or definitions at the beginning of admission requests to remove any possible ambiguity in those requests. *See* Chapter 7, Section IV(B), *supra* p. 328.

one of the few areas of discovery practice in which "No news is good news."

What if you are the attorney who has failed to respond to admission requests in a timely fashion? In that event, consider a motion to file admission responses out of time. This motion should attempt to convince the court that, as required by Rule 36(b) in such situations, "the presentation of the merits of the action" would be promoted by permitting admission responses to now be filed, the party seeking the admissions would not be prejudiced by untimely admission responses, and the filing of admissions responses would be consistent with Rule 16(e)'s restrictions concerning the amendment of final pretrial orders.

Admission answers and objections are to be signed by the party to whom the admission requests are addressed or that party's attorney. Admission answers must admit those portions of an admission request that are true, even if the entire request is not true. A party must set forth in detail the reasons why any portion of an admission request cannot be answered or denied, and Rule 36(a)(4) provides that an answering party "may assert lack of information or knowledge as a reason for failing to admit or deny only if the party states that it has made reasonable inquiry and that the information it knows or can readily obtain is insufficient to enable it to admit or deny." Rule 36(a)(5) also requires that the grounds for any objections must be stated, and such objections usually will be quite similar to objections that might be drafted in response to Rule 33 interrogatories.[22]

Admission requests that are not answered are deemed admitted, and Rule 36(a)(6) permits a party to ask the court to determine the sufficiency of admission answers or objections. Rule 36(a)(6) also provides that the party prevailing on such a motion may be awarded the expenses of the motion, while Rule 37(c)(2) provides that if a party refuses to admit a matter that later is proved to be true at trial, the party requesting the admission may seek the reasonable expenses incurred in making the proof at trial. Rule 37(c)(2) requires that these expenses must be awarded unless "(A) the request was held objectionable under Rule 36(a); (B) the admission sought was of no substantial importance; (C) the party failing to admit had a reasonable ground to believe that it might prevail on the matter; or (D) there was other good reason for the failure to admit."

In contrast to deposition statements or interrogatory answers, which can be disputed at trial, any matter admitted under Rule 36 is, according to Rule 36(b), "conclusively established unless the court, on motion, permits the admission to be withdrawn or amended." Thus, not only can Rule 36 admissions narrow the disputed issues that must be tried, but they also can provide a basis for the grant of summary judgment.[23]

---

22. *See* Chapter 7, Section V(B), *supra* p. 336.

23. *McCann v. Mangialardi*, 337 F.3d 782, 788 (7th Cir. 2003); *Donovan v. Carls Drug Co.*, 703 F.2d 650, 651–52 (2d Cir. 1983); *Virga v. Big Apple Construction & Restoration Inc.*, 590 F.Supp.2d 467, 471 (S.D.N.Y. 2008); *O'Bryant v. Allstate Ins. Co.*, 107 F.R.D. 45 (D.Conn. 1985).

B. STRATEGIC CONSIDERATIONS

As with other discovery devices, admission requests are good for some, but not all, purposes. Admission requests differ significantly from interrogatories and depositions, which generally are used to obtain information from another party. Admission requests, in contrast, are used to pin another party down concerning facts that the requesting party believes to be true.

Counsel's success in using admission requests often will depend upon the precision with which the requests are drafted. To the extent that the precise language of an opposing party is used in an admission request, it becomes difficult for that party to deny the admission. For example, if officials of the Pittston Company had testified before Congress that "Pittston never conducted an engineering feasibility study of the dam to be built on Buffalo Creek," an admission request might be served upon Pittston asking it to admit that "Pittston never conducted an engineering feasibility study of the dam on Buffalo Creek that failed on February 26, 1972."[24]

Another way to ensure that admission requests are treated seriously is to file along with the requests an interrogatory asking for all of the facts upon which any admission denials are based. It may be easier for opposing counsel to admit certain matters than to fully answer the interrogatory.[25]

Different lawyers use admission requests at different points in a case. Admission requests can be used effectively at the very outset of some cases, although Rule 26(d)(1) precludes service of admissions before the Rule 26(f) discovery conference unless the court orders or the parties agree to permit earlier discovery. If matters are admitted early in a case, entire areas of inquiry may be eliminated as subjects for further discovery and trial. Successive admission requests can be used to narrow the facts and issues in a case as discovery progresses. Service of admission requests prior to Rule 16 pretrial conferences may help to narrow the issues to be discussed at these conferences and may be reflected in the court orders issued after the conferences.[26]

Use of admission requests presupposes that sufficient information exists to permit the formulation of requests that another party will have to admit. For this reason, many attorneys serve admission requests at the

---

24. The drafting of such an admission request presupposes that the other party is aware of its prior statement or that there is no strategic reason why that party should not be made aware of the statement prior to trial. If this is not the case, counsel may decide to wait until trial (or at least until a deposition) to impeach the other party with the prior statement.

25. Admission requests also can be used to establish that there is no evidence supporting particular allegations in the litigation. In *McCann v. Mangialardi*, 337 F.3d 782 (7th Cir. 2003), the defendant requested that the plaintiff admit that he had no evidence supporting one of his claims. The court of appeals held that plaintiff's failure to respond to this request provided the basis for summary judgment against him on that claim. *Id.* at 788.

26. Commercial and Federal Litigation Section, New York State Bar Association, "Report on Practice under Rule 36: Requests for Admissions," 53 *Alb. L. Rev.* 33, 43–45, 46–47 (1988).

close of discovery, once the details of an opposing party's case are clearer. Before serving admission requests, counsel should review existing discovery responses to see if there are loose ends that should be nailed down prior to trial. For example, Rule 36 requests can be used to obtain unequivocal admissions about matters on which a party may have been evasive at a deposition.

If there is enough time before discovery closes, admission requests can be used to encourage an opposing counsel's good faith participation in any pretrial stipulation process. Other attorneys may be more cooperative if they realize that the failure to reach stipulations may result in the service upon them of stipulation proposals cast in the form of Rule 36 admission requests.

Exercises Concerning Rule 36 Admission Requests

1. Assume that the following admission requests have been served upon the defendant Pittston Company in the Buffalo Creek litigation:

1. No employees of either the Pittston Company or the Buffalo Mining Company made any efforts to warn the residents of the Buffalo Creek Valley of the impending failure of the dam on the Middle Fork of the Buffalo Creek on February 26, 1972.

2. Exhibit No. 1 to Plaintiffs' First Request for Admissions is a true and accurate copy of the minutes of a meeting of the Buffalo Mining Company held on March 13, 1971.

3. The defendant Pittston Company does not contend in this action that the plaintiffs were contributorily negligent with respect to the injuries that they suffered as a result of the failure of defendant's dam.

4. The defendant Pittston Company is insured in connection with dam failures such as the one that occurred on February 26, 1972.

5. More people died as a result of the failure of the defendant's dam on the Middle Fork of the Buffalo Creek on February 26, 1972, than as a result of any other dam failure in this nation's history.

6. The defendant Pittston Company is liable for the injuries suffered by plaintiffs due to the failure of defendant's dam on the Middle Fork of the Buffalo Creek on February 26, 1972.

7. Defendant Pittston's own inquiry into the reasons for the failure of its dam on the Middle Fork of the Buffalo Creek found that this dam had been improperly constructed.

8. Mr. Thomas Reid, of Logan County, West Virginia, complained to Pittston officials about the safety of the dam on the Middle Fork of the Buffalo Creek in December 1971.

As counsel for Pittston, draft that company's responses to these admission requests. Base these responses upon the following information.

(1) Although Pittston officials are not aware of any Pittston employee who made efforts to warn residents about the failure of its dam, a night shift mining supervisor employed by the Buffalo Mining Company told the seven men on his shift the night before the dam burst that it would burst and that "they had better move their families to high ground."

(2) The attached document appears to be what plaintiffs have described it to be, although it is not a document of Pittston.

(3) Pittston has not pled contributory negligence in this action, nor does it foresee that it might plead that defense at a latter stage of the proceedings.

(4) Although Pittston now is insured for legal claims arising from dam failures such as the one that occurred on Buffalo Creek, its former insurance carriers are contesting insurance coverage as of the time the dam failed in February 1972.

(5) Pittston officials are not aware of the numbers of deaths resulting from the failures of dams other than its own.

(6) Pittston's preliminary inquiries indicate that it may well be liable for plaintiffs' injuries.

(7) Pittston's internal investigation indicates that its dam was improperly constructed, not being in compliance with several mine safety regulations.

(8) Prior to his recent death, former Pittston official Charles Connor told you (as counsel for Pittston) that Mr. Reid had complained to him about the dam in December 1971. Mr. Reid is dead now, and no living officials of either Pittston or Buffalo Mining Company have any knowledge of any meeting between Reid and Connor.

2. You represent the estate of Norman Hickman in the case of *Hickman v. Taylor,* 329 U.S. 495 (1947), *supra* p. 273. This case has just been filed. Write a memorandum concerning the way in which you plan to use Rule 36 admission requests in this case. Consider in your memorandum:

(a) When you would serve any Rule 36 requests;

(b) How those requests would relate to other discovery that you contemplate taking;

(c) Any expenses or time that might be saved by using Rule 36 admission requests; and

(d) The areas to which your requests would be addressed.

To the extent now possible, attach to your memorandum at least ten specific admission requests that you would serve on the defendant tugboat owners.

V. CONCLUSION

The three discovery devices discussed in this chapter—Rule 34 production requests, Rule 35 examinations, and Rule 36 admission requests—are each designed to perform specific discovery tasks. While all of these devices may not be useful in all cases, their potential use should be considered in any pretrial discovery plan. Counsel's task is to determine whether these devices should be used in particular cases and then to target them for their most effective use within appropriate cases.

VI. CHAPTER BIBLIOGRAPHY

M. Arkfeld, *Arkfeld on Electronic Evidence and Discovery* (3d ed. 2010).

Bales & Ray, "The Availability of Rule 35 Mental Examinations in Employment Discrimination Cases," 16 *Rev. Litig.* 1 (1997).

J. Barkett, *The Ethics of E–Discovery* (2009).

Becker, Note, "Court-ordered Mental and Physical Examinations: A Survey of Federal Rule 35 and Illinois Rule 215," 11 *Loy. U. Chi. L. J.* 725 (1980).

Cagan, "Rule 34(b): Who's Organizing This Production?," *Litigation,* Winter 1994, at 41.

Carlisle, "Nonparty Document Discovery from Corporations and Governmental Entities Under the Federal Rules of Civil Procedure," 32 *N. Y. L. Sch. L. Rev.* 9 (1987).

A. Cohen & D. Lender, *Electronic Discovery: Law and Practice* (2010).

Comment, "The Dilemma of Federal Rule 36," 56 *Nw. U. L. Rev.* 679 (1961).

Commercial and Federal Litigation Section, New York State Bar Association, "Report on Practice under Rule 36: Requests for Admissions," 53 *Alb. L. Rev.* 33 (1988).

Dombroff, "Requests for Admissions: Weighing the Pros and Cons," *Trial,* June 1983, at 82.

Ehrenbard, "Cutting Discovery Costs Through Interrogatories and Document Requests," *Litigation,* Spring 1975, at 17.

Epstein, "Rule 36: In Praise of Requests to Admit," *Litigation,* Spring 1981, at 30.

Evans, "Admissions Practice," 62 *St. John's L. Rev.* 475 (1988).

Feagan, Comment, "Rule 35—Is There a Right to Choice of Physician?," 14 *N. Ky. L. Rev.* 447 (1988).

Figg et al., "Uses and Limitations of Some Discovery Devices," *Prac. Law.,* April 1974, at 65.

Finman, "The Request for Admissions in Federal Civil Procedure," 71 *Yale L. J.* 371 (1962).

J. Grenig et. al., *eDiscovery & Digital Evidence* (2010).

Haydock & Herr, "Production of Results Under Rule 34," 5 *Am. J. Trial Advoc.* 253 (1981).

Kenney, "Making Requests for Admission Work," 38 *Trial Law. Guide* 1 (1994).

J. Kidwell et al., *Electronic Discovery* (2010).

M. Koesel & T. Turnbull, *Spoliation of Evidence: Sanctions and Remedies for Destruction of Evidence in Civil Litigation* (D. Gourash, ed., 2d ed. 2006).

R Losey, *Introduction to e-Discovery: New Cases, Ideas, and Techniques* (2009).

McElhaney, "Requests for Admissions," *Litigation,* Summer 1989, at 53.

Nelson et al., *The Electronic Evidence and Discovery Handbook: Forms, Checklists, and Guidelines* (2006).

G. Paul & B. Nearon, *The Discovery Revolution: E–Discovery Amendments to the Federal Rules of Civil Procedure* (2006).

Placey, "Developing Evidence from Nonparties," *Litigation,* Spring 1999, at 32.

Pope, "Rule 34: Controlling the Paper Avalanche," *Litigation,* Spring 1981, at 28.

P. Rice, *Electronic Evidence: Law and Practice* (2d ed. 2008).

Richert, "Electronic Discovery Bibliography," 42 *Akron L. Rev.* 419 (2009).

S. Scheindlin et al., *Electronic Discovery and Digital Evidence: Cases and Materials* (2008).

Scheindlin & Rabkin, "Electronic Discovery in Federal Civil Litigation: Is Rule 34 Up to the Task?," 41 *B.C. L. Rev.* 327 (2000).

The Sedona Conference Working Group for Electronic Document Retention and Protection, *The Sedona Principles: Best Practices, Recommendations & Principles for Addressing Electronic Document Production* (2d ed. 2007).

Shapiro, "Some Problems of Discovery in an Adversary System," 63 *Minn. L. Rev.* 1055 (1979).

Symposium, "Ethics and Professionalism in the Digital Age," 60 *Mercer L. Rev.* 845 (2009).

Underwood, "Discovery According to Federal Rule 34," *Prac. Law.,* March 1, 1980, at 55.

CHAPTER 10

THE INTERVENTION OF THE COURT INTO THE DISCOVERY PROCESS: "IF WE CAN'T AGREE, I'M GOING TO THE JUDGE."

■ ■ ■

The idea that procedure must of necessity be wholly contentious disfigures our judicial administration at every point. It leads the most conscientious judge to feel that he is merely to decide the contest, as counsel present it, according to the rules of the game, not to search independently for truth and justice. It leads counsel to forget that they are officers of the court and to deal with the rules of law and procedure exactly as the professional football coach with the rules of the sport.

Pound, *The Causes of Popular Dissatisfaction with the Administration of Justice* (1906), *reprinted in* 35 F.R.D. 273, 281 (1964).

The Plaintiffs' allegations of antitrust have spilled over to the discovery process where nobody trusts anybody.

Associated Radio Service Co. v. Page Airways, Inc., 73 F.R.D. 633, 634 (N.D.Tex. 1977), in which Judge Robert Porter ordered both sets of attorneys to pay the discovery expenses incurred by the opposing parties.

Analysis

444

I. INTRODUCTION

The previous chapters of this text have considered the devices by which information within the scope of Federal Rule of Civil Procedure 26 can be discovered or is disclosed. By and large, the discussion in those chapters has presumed that counsel are cooperating with one another and that there are no disagreements between counsel as to discovery and disclosure matters. Many disputes are prevented by the Rule 26(f) conference (at which disclosures are to be made or arranged and a discovery plan is to be developed) and the Rule 16 pretrial orders which follow such conferences.

Nevertheless, discovery does not go smoothly in all cases. Even in cases in which an attorney is proceeding quite appropriately, opposing counsel may believe that a particular discovery stance is unjustified. In those cases the Federal Rules of Civil Procedure provide mechanisms for judicial resolution of the parties' differences.

There are several ways in which a court can intervene in a discovery or disclosure dispute. The court *sua sponte* can ascertain a discovery dispute or abuse and issue an appropriate order. More frequently, the parties themselves bring discovery or disclosure disputes to the court's attention. This can occur when the person from whom discovery or disclosure is sought seeks a Rule 26(c) protective order that the discovery or disclosure in question not be had. Alternatively, the party seeking the discovery or disclosure may invoke the court's assistance by filing a motion pursuant to Rule 37 seeking an order compelling discovery or disclosure, sanctions, or both. It is not unusual for both the party requesting discovery and the party from whom discovery is sought to file motions and for the court to decide Rule 26(c) and Rule 37 motions simultaneously.

Rules 26(c) and 37 are available in those extreme situations in which the parties cannot resolve their own discovery or disclosure disputes. However, those Rules are no substitute for reasoned negotiation, and parties are required by Rules 26(c) and 37(a) to attempt to resolve their differences before filing a motion for a protective order or a motion to compel. Motions for protective orders, for orders compelling discovery or disclosure, and for sanctions should be thought of as the last, rather than the first, resort for counsel involved in discovery disputes.

II. RULE 26 MOTIONS FOR PROTECTIVE ORDERS

As with other pretrial procedural devices, both governing law and practice must be understood in order to most effectively utilize Rule 26(c) protective orders.

A. THE GOVERNING LAW

Presume that a plaintiff seeks discovery from the defendant that the defendant considers to be objectionable. In this situation, the defendant need merely file appropriate objections to the discovery request.[1] The plaintiff then must decide whether to file a Rule 37(a) motion to compel the discovery or to take no further action and do without that discovery.

However, the party from whom discovery is sought can do more than merely object and wait for opposing counsel to act. Rule 26(c)(1) of the Federal Rules of Civil Procedure provides the federal district courts with the authority to enter protective orders "for good cause" in order to "protect a party or person from annoyance, embarrassment, oppression, or undue burden or expense." Protective orders can be entered based upon a motion filed by either a party to the action or a non-party from whom discovery is sought. Figure 10–1 illustrates possible responses to a discovery request, as well as the manner in which disputes concerning the propriety of the discovery can be resolved. Not only can protective orders be sought in response to discovery requests as illustrated in Figure 10–1, but Rule 26(c)(1) provides that such orders can be sought concerning discovery disclosures that otherwise would be required pursuant to Rule 26(a).

FIGURE 10–1

DISCOVERY RESPONSES AND INTERVENTION BY THE COURT

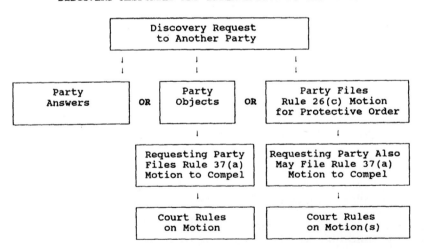

Rule 26(c)(1) provides specific examples of the types of protective orders that can be entered. These include Rule 26(c)(1)(A) orders "forbidding the disclosure or discovery," Rule 26(c)(1)(B) orders "specifying terms, including time and place, for the disclosure or discovery," Rule 26(c)(1)(D) orders "forbidding inquiry into certain matters, or limiting the

---

1. *See* Fed. R. Civ. P. 30(c)(2), 33(b)(4), 34(b)(2), 36(a)(5).

scope of disclosure or discovery to certain matters," and Rule 26(c)(1)(F) orders "requiring that a deposition be sealed and opened only on court order."

Most discovery disputes are capable of resolution by the parties, and the Federal Rules of Civil Procedure require good faith efforts to privately resolve such disputes before resort to a court. Rule 26(c)(1) provides that a motion for a protective order must "include a certification that the movant has in good faith conferred or attempted to confer with other affected parties in an effort to resolve the dispute without court action." More than a pro forma contact with opposing counsel is required. One federal court has suggested that, under a local meet and confer rule comparable to that contained in Rule 26(c)(1), a party waives arguments that are not raised in a prefiling conference with opposing parties; the court concluded that a movant "should not be raising significant arguments in a later motion to compel or motion for protective order which were not first raised with the other side, and available to it at that time."[2] Not only do judges have better things to do than resolve routine discovery disputes, but informal resolution of those disputes will be faster and less expensive than intervention by the court.

NOTES AND QUESTIONS CONCERNING RULE 26(C) PROTECTIVE ORDERS

1. Federal courts have upheld the rights of third-persons to gain access to sealed discovery for use in other litigation. *E.g.*, *Foltz v. State Farm Mutual Automobile Ins. Co.*, 331 F.3d 1122, 1132 (9th Cir. 2003) ("Where reasonable restrictions on collateral disclosure will continue to protect an affected party's legitimate interests in privacy, a collateral litigant's request * * * to modify an otherwise proper protective order * * * should generally be granted."); *Grove Fresh Distrib., Inc. v. Everfresh Juice Co.*, 24 F.3d 893 (7th Cir. 1994) (persons who are litigants in collateral lawsuits have presumptive right of access to discovery material that may overcome a protective order). *See also* Va. Code Ann. § 8.01–420.01 (2007) (limiting use in personal injury or wrongful death cases of protective orders that prohibit sharing of information with attorneys in similar cases). However, after an amendment of Rule 5 in 2000, Rule 5(d)(1) of the Federal Rules of Civil Procedure now provides that most disclosures and discovery "must not be filed [with the court] until they are used in the proceeding or the court orders filing." As the Seventh Circuit Court of Appeals subsequently concluded, "[W]hile the public has a presumptive right to access discovery materials that are filed with the court, used in a judicial proceeding, or otherwise constitute 'judicial records,' the same is not true of materials produced during discovery but not filed with the court." *Bond v. Utreras*, 585 F.3d 1061, 1073 (7th Cir. 2009).

---

2. *Ellison v. Runyan*, 147 F.R.D. 186, 188 n. 1 (S.D.Ind. 1993).

Judges prefer that parties not only raise discovery disputes with each other but actually resolve them. When faced with a motion asking him to determine the locale of a Rule 30(b)(6) deposition, Judge Gregory Presnell ordered the parties to appear on the front steps of the courthouse and "engage in one (1) game of 'rock, paper, scissors.' The winner of this engagement shall be entitled to select the location for the 30(b)(6) deposition to be held somewhere in Hillsborough County during the period July 11–12, 2006." *Avista Management, Inc. v. Wausau Underwriters Ins. Co.*, 2006 WL 1562246 (M.D.Fla. 2006).

2. Can a court prohibit attorneys from selling information obtained in discovery to attorneys handling similar litigation? *See Williams v. Johnson & Johnson,* 50 F.R.D. 31, 32–33 (S.D.N.Y. 1970). In *In re Upjohn Co. Antibiotic Cleocin Prod. Liab. Litig.,* 81 F.R.D. 482, 484–85 (E.D.Mich. 1979), *aff'd,* 664 F.2d 114 (6th Cir.1981), the court required that plaintiffs inform the court prior to the release of discovery to other litigants and disclose the terms of payment or reimbursement for such discovery. In *Kehm v. Procter & Gamble Mfg. Co.,* 724 F.2d 630 (8th Cir. 1984), the court of appeals upheld a contempt citation and $10,000 sanction imposed upon an attorney for selling documents obtained under a protective order.

Plaintiffs' attorneys have formed litigation groups or clearinghouses in situations where a defendant is being sued by many plaintiffs in connection with the same allegedly defective product. Membership in the group typically entitles the attorney to copies of pleadings, discovery, and other court documents, as well as newsletters tracking trials, settlements, and judicial decisions. *See* Rheingold, "The MER/29 Story—An Instance of Successful Mass Disaster Litigation," 56 *Cal. L. Rev.* 116 (1968). *See also* Erichson, "Informal Aggregation: Procedural and Ethical Implications of Coordination Among Counsel in Related Lawsuits," 50 *Duke L. J.* 381, 386–408 (2000) (describing coordination among plaintiffs' attorneys and among defense attorneys in major complex litigation).

3. Can a court issue a Rule 26(c) protective order prohibiting counsel in one case from using discovery in another case in which they also are counsel? *See Cipollone v. Liggett Group, Inc.,* 822 F.2d 335, 338–39 (3d Cir.), *cert. denied,* 484 U.S. 976 (1987). Can counsel be prohibited from disclosing discovery to their own clients? *See Natta v. Zletz,* 405 F.2d 99, 101–102 (7th Cir. 1968), *cert. denied,* 395 U.S. 909 (1969); *Safe Flight Instrument Corp. v. Sundstrand Data Control Inc.,* 682 F.Supp. 20 (D.Del. 1988); *Spartanics, Ltd. v. Dynetics Engineering Corp.,* 54 F.R.D. 524 (N.D.Ill. 1972).

4. Can a party post on the Internet another party's video deposition? Does it matter whether the case in which the deposition was taken is still pending? Is it significant whether or not the deposition has been filed with the court? *See* "Court Hits Pause in Case Involving Internet Video of Deposition," *Litigation News,* Spring 2009, at 21 (concerning court order to plaintiff to remove posting from YouTube of video deposition of defendant's chief financial officer).

5. Is the party who has obtained discovery free to turn over that discovery to the government in an effort to convince the government to bring a civil or criminal action against its opposing party? In *GAF Corp. v. Eastman Kodak Co.,* 415 F.Supp. 129 (S.D.N.Y. 1976), the court answered this question in the negative, expressing concern that government resources should not be enhanced by the efforts of private litigants and noting that the parties' assumption had been that the discovery was only for the present case. *But see Sharjah Investment Co. (UK) Ltd. v. P. C. Telemart, Inc.,* 107 F.R.D. 81 (S.D.N.Y. 1985) (parties' discovery stipulation did not preclude plaintiffs from disclosing deposition transcripts to SEC); Gillers, "Speak No Evil: Settlement Agreements Conditioned on Noncooperation Are Illegal and Unethical," 31 *Hofstra L. Rev.* 1 (2002) (arguing that settlement agreements restricting a

party's ability to cooperate with future litigants may constitute obstruction of justice under federal law).

6. If a court is convinced that specific discovery will cause harm to the public or to a particular person, it can order that the discovering party not disseminate the information or, if the discovery has been filed with the court, that the record of the discovery be sealed. *See* Rule 26(c)(1)(F)–(G). Even apart from Rule 26, courts have held that they have inherent equitable powers to seal a court record. *E.g., Int'l Products Corp. v. Koons,* 325 F.2d 403, 407–08 (2d Cir. 1963). However, once a court has sealed discovery, its protective order is subject to modification. *Am. Tel. & Tel. Co. v. Grady,* 594 F.2d 594 (7th Cir. 1978) (per curiam), *cert. denied,* 440 U.S. 971 (1979). *See also Martindell v. Int'l Tel. & Tel. Corp.,* 594 F.2d 291, 296 n.7 (2d Cir. 1979); *Felling v. Knight,* 211 F.R.D. 552 (S.D.Ind. 2003) (good cause no longer existed for protective order barring release of videotapes after lawsuit involving termination of basketball coach had been settled and deponents had secured other positions).

7. Despite Rule 26(c) and a court's inherent power to enter protective orders, are there constitutional limitations upon the sealing of court records? In *Seattle Times Co. v. Rhinehart,* 467 U.S. 20 (1984), the Supreme Court upheld a state court's protective order that prohibited the defendant newspaper from publishing or disseminating information obtained in discovery concerning the membership and finances of a religious foundation. The Court noted that "pretrial depositions and interrogatories are not public components of a civil trial," *id.* at 33, and that "judicial limitations on a party's ability to disseminate information discovered in advance of trial implicates the First Amendment rights of the restricted party to a far lesser extent than would restraints on dissemination of information in a different context." *Id.* at 34.

The Court concluded: "Liberal discovery is provided for the sole purpose of assisting in the preparation and trial, or the settlement, of litigated disputes. Because of the liberality of pretrial discovery permitted by Rule 26(b)(1), it is necessary for the trial court to have the authority to issue protective orders conferred by Rule 26(c)." *Id.* Accordingly, the Supreme Court upheld the validity of the protective order in the case before it.

8. Rule 26(c) protective orders can be sought not only by parties to the litigation, but also by other persons from whom discovery is requested. In what types of situations might a non-party seek a protective order? *See Silkwood v. Kerr–McGee Corp.,* 563 F.2d 433 (10th Cir. 1977) (case reversed and remanded for trial court to consider motion for protective order filed by third-party film producer to preclude defendant from seeking documents and information obtained in confidence during producer's investigation of death of Karen Silkwood). *See also Caisson Corp. v. County West Building Corp.,* 62 F.R.D. 331 (E.D.Pa. 1974); *Herbst v. Able,* 63 F.R.D. 135 (S.D.N.Y. 1972).

9. While courts often enter protective orders based upon contested motions, the parties frequently agree to stipulated protective orders. *See generally* Marcus, "Myth and Reality in Protective Order Litigation," 69 *Cornell L. Rev.* 1 (1983). For an example of a comprehensive protective order

to which the parties stipulated and which the court approved see *In re San Juan Dupont Plaza Hotel Fire Litigation*, 121 F.R.D. 147 (D.P.R. 1988).

Judge Edward Becker has stated that "[w]e are unaware of any case in the past half-dozen years of even a modicum of complexity where an umbrella protective order * * * has not been agreed to by the parties and approved by the court." *Zenith Radio Corp. v. Matsushita Elec. Indus. Co.*, 529 F.Supp. 866, 889 (E.D.Pa. 1981). Why might corporate defendants be interested in blanket protective orders? Why might plaintiffs? What incentive is there for a trial judge to enter these orders? What potential problems do such orders present? *See* Doré, "Secrecy by Consent: The Use and Limits of Confidentiality in the Pursuit of Settlement," 74 *Notre Dame L. Rev.* 283 (1999); Marcus, "The Discovery Confidentiality Controversy," 1991 *U.Ill. L. Rev.* 457; Miller, "Confidentiality, Protective Orders, and Public Access to the Courts," 105 *Harv. L. Rev.* 427 (1991); Morrison, "Protective Orders, Plaintiffs, Defendants and the Public Interest in Disclosure: Where Does the Balance Lie?," 24 *U. Rich. L. Rev.* 109 (1989).

10.   In response to concerns about blanket protective orders, some courts have required that district courts make particularized determinations before sealing discovery documents. In *Ashcraft v. Conoco*, 218 F.3d 288, 303 (4th Cir. 2000), the United States Court of Appeals for the Fourth Circuit required that the district court "must (1) provide public notice of the request to seal and allow interested parties a reasonable opportunity to object, (2) consider less drastic alternatives to sealing the documents, and (3) provide specific reasons and factual findings supporting its decision to seal the documents and for rejecting the alternatives." *See also Citizens First Nat'l Bank v. Cincinnati Ins. Co.*, 178 F.3d 943, 946 (7th Cir. 1999) (overturning a protective order as "standardless, stipulated, permanent, frozen, [and] overbroad"); *Pansy v. Borough of Stroudsburg*, 23 F.3d 772, 785 (3d Cir. 1994) ("Disturbingly, some courts routinely sign orders which contain confidentiality clauses without considering the propriety of such orders, or the countervailing public interests which are sacrificed by the orders.").

11.   In recent years legislation has been introduced in Congress that would require federal judges to make findings that no information they place under seal is (1) relevant to the protection of public health or safety or (2) the public interest in the disclosure of potential health or safety hazards is outweighed by the interest in maintaining the confidentiality of the information and the protective order is no broader than is necessary to protect the privacy interest asserted. H.R. 5419, 111th Cong., 2d Sess. (2010); S. 537, 111th Cong., 1st Sess. (2009). Texas Rule of Civil Procedure 76a establishes a presumption of public access to court records and permits courts to seal such records only upon a specific showing after publicly posting a notice of the request that the records be sealed, while Florida's "Sunshine in Litigation Act," Fla. Stat. § 69.081 (West 2004), prohibits courts from entering orders or judgments that have the purpose or effect of concealing a public hazard.

12.   In 1993 the Advisory Committee on Civil Rules recommended to the Committee on Rules of Practice and Procedure of the Judicial Conference significant amendments to Rule 26(c). 150 F.R.D. 380, 383 (1993). Included among the proposed changes was a new section 26(c)(3) providing as follows:

On motion, the court may dissolve or modify a protective order. In ruling, the court must consider, among other matters, the following:

(A) the extent of reliance on the order;

(B) the public and private interests affected by the order; and

(C) the burden that the order imposes on persons seeking information relevant to other litigation.

150 F.R.D. at 386–87.

13.   Some United States District Courts have adopted local rules restricting and governing the entry of protective orders by federal district courts. *E.g.*, Local Rule 26.2(b) of the United States District Court for the Northern District of Illinois ("restricting order" may be entered "for good cause shown"); Local Rule 105.11 of the United States District Court for the District of Maryland (order seeking protective order must set forth "specific factual representations to justify the sealing" and "an explanation why alternatives to sealing would not provide sufficient protection").

B.   PROTECTIVE ORDERS IN PRACTICE

Parties resisting discovery frequently seek protective orders because of the "undue burden or expense" of complying with a discovery request.[3] Typical of such motions is the following motion from the Buffalo Creek litigation, filed in response to the deposition notice in Chapter 8, *supra* p. 350.

IN THE UNITED STATES DISTRICT COURT FOR THE SOUTHERN DISTRICT OF WEST VIRGINIA AT HUNTINGTON

DENNIS PRINCE, et al.,	)	
Plaintiffs,	)	
	)	
v.	)	CIVIL ACTION NO. 3052–HN
	)	
THE PITTSTON COMPANY,	)	
Defendant.	)	

NOTICE OF MOTION AND MOTION FOR
PROTECTIVE ORDER WITH RESPECT TO
DEPOSITIONS OF PLAINTIFFS

TO: The Pittston Company, by service upon Daniel R. Murdock, Esquire, of the law firm of Donovan Leisure Newton & Irvine, Two Wall Street, New York, New York 10005; Zane Grey Staker, Esquire, Box 388, Kermit, West Virginia 25674; and Messrs. Jackson, Kelly, Holt & O'Farrell, Kanawha Valley Building, Charleston, West Virginia 25301; attorneys for the defendant, The Pittston Company

---

3. Fed. R. Civ. P. 26(c)(1). *See, e.g., Isaac v. Shell Oil Co.,* 83 F.R.D. 428 (E.D.Mich. 1979) (protective order entered where discovery response would cost $50,000 and plaintiff had not shown reasonable grounds to support his allegation of liability); *Frost v. Williams,* 46 F.R.D. 484 (D.Md. 1969) (motion for protective order granted concerning 200 interrogatories served by plaintiff in ordinary automobile collision case).

PLEASE TAKE NOTICE that the Plaintiffs will bring on for hearing before the Honorable K. K. Hall, Judge of this Court, at 10:00 o'clock A.M. on May 16, 1973, at Charleston, West Virginia, this motion for a protective order with respect to Defendant's depositions of Plaintiffs.

Plaintiffs respectfully move this Court, pursuant to Rule 26(c), F. R. Civ. P., for a protective order requiring that the Defendant's depositions of any Plaintiff be held (a) only upon reasonable advance notice to Plaintiffs' attorneys of the date, time, and place thereof, and (b) only at or nearby the Plaintiff's place of residence or such other suitable place as the parties may agree upon in advance.

This motion is made necessary by reason of Defendant's action in attempting to have 22 Plaintiffs travel from their homes in the Buffalo Creek area to Charleston for the purpose of having their depositions taken. In the context of this case, this action by the Defendant is clearly an harassing tactic.

The Plaintiffs in this case are, by and large, impecunious individuals who cannot readily and without great difficulty make their way to Charleston for depositions. Some of those whose depositions have been noticed are older or disabled;* others are young children.** Some are employed in jobs they should not be asked to leave unnecessarily.*** There is no good reason why any Plaintiff should be deposed in Charleston rather than in the Buffalo Creek valley.

Furthermore, Defendant has noticed 22 consecutive depositions with no indication (except as to the first) as to when any one deposition is to end and the next to begin. There is no indication whether the depositions can be expected to take several hours each or several days each. Presumably the Defendant would prefer not to be bound to a rigid schedule but rather would prefer to proceed from one deponent to the next taking as much or as little time with each deponent as that particular deponent warrants. Plaintiffs have no objection to this procedure except that, if the depositions are to be taken in Charleston, this will mean unnecessary and difficult trips back and forth from the Buffalo Creek valley for the various deponents until their depositions are completed or else the substantial inconvenience and expense of having to stay overnight in Charleston so long as the depositions are going forward.

Plaintiffs' counsel understand that beginning June 11, 1973, the facilities of the Accoville, West Virginia elementary school in the middle of the Buffalo Creek valley can be made available at all reasonable hours (including weekends, if desired) to the parties for depositions of the Plaintiffs for as long as necessary.**** Plaintiffs are agreeable to begin-

---

* For example, Rex Howard is a 63–year–old retired, disabled coal miner.

** For example, Alfred Hampton is barely 7 years old.

*** For example, both Wallace and Delsie Scalf are teachers employed by the Logan County Board of Education.

**** We understand that the school is now available on evenings and weekends.

ning the depositions of the 22 persons named by the Defendant in the order named at 9:30 A.M. on the morning of Monday, June 11, 1973 at the schoolhouse and continuing thereafter from day to day until those depositions are completed.

* * *

On Monday, April 30, 1973, Defendant mailed to the Plaintiffs' attorneys a Notice of Taking of Depositions of 22 of the Plaintiffs in this action beginning at 9:30 on the morning of Monday, May 7, 1973 in Charleston, West Virginia.

Although Plaintiffs' counsel had been in regular contact with Defendant's counsel with respect to discovery and other matters—including by telephone on April 30, 1973 (the day the Notice of Deposition was mailed)—Plaintiffs had no notice of the proposed timing of or arrangements for the depositions until the Notice arrived in the mail. Defendant's counsel made no prior effort to arrange with the Plaintiffs the timing of or the other arrangements with respect to said depositions.

Immediately upon receipt (on May 2—five days from the deposition date) of the mailed Notice, Plaintiffs' counsel in Washington, D.C. telephoned Defendant's counsel in an effort to reach more satisfactory arrangements for the depositions.***** Specifically, Plaintiffs' proposed alternatively that the depositions either (a) be taken at each Plaintiff's residence in the Buffalo Creek valley rather than in Charleston, or (b) that the depositions begin at the Accoville elementary school in the Buffalo Creek valley when the present school term ends at the beginning of June.

Defendant's counsel rejected both proposals. Plaintiffs' counsel then proposed to Defendant's counsel that this deposition matter be noticed for the hearing already set for May 16, 197[3], and Defendant's counsel assented.

Plaintiffs are fully aware of Defendant's right to take the deposition of each Plaintiff, and Plaintiffs have no desire either to delay said depositions or otherwise to obstruct them in any way. However, Defendant's unwillingness to make fair and reasonable arrangements with respect to those depositions makes the present motion necessary.******

There is no reason for holding the depositions in Charleston. The Plaintiffs are not residents of either Charleston or Kanawha County. The Defendant is not located in Charleston. This case was not filed in Charleston. No events pertinent to the case took place in Charleston, and no evidence pertinent to the depositions is located in Charleston. Access to

---

***** Plaintiffs' counsel informed Defendant's counsel that it was totally unreasonable to require that these Plaintiffs travel all the way to Charleston for depositions. Plaintiffs' counsel then was told that Defendant also intends to try and force these Plaintiffs to travel all the way to the other side of the State—to Williamson, West Virginia—for physical and psychiatric medical tests. It is difficult not to be outraged at these obvious harassment tactics.

****** Plaintiffs have been more than reasonable in cooperating with the Defendant with respect to the depositions of Defendant's officers, as the following facts show: [Facts showing accommodations made by plaintiffs' counsel in connection with the depositions of defendant's officers were then set forth.]

Charleston from the Buffalo Creek valley, where most of the Plaintiffs reside, is difficult and expensive.

The Court should not normally have to be involved in such matters as where and when depositions of parties are to take place. However, the Defendant's unwillingness to consider more suitable arrangements within the financial and physical capabilities of the Plaintiffs has made this motion necessary.

For the reasons stated, we respectfully urge the Court to enter the requested protective Order.

Respectfully submitted,

s/ _____
Gerald M. Stern

s/ _____
Harry Huge
ARNOLD & PORTER
1229 Nineteenth Street, N.W.
Washington, D.C. 20036

s/ _____
Willis O. Shay
STEPTOE & JOHNSON
Tenth Floor
Union Bank Building
Clarksburg, West Virginia
26301

Attorneys for Plaintiffs

May 4, 1973

Exercises Concerning Rule 26(c) Protective Orders

1. As counsel for the defendant Pittston Company, draft for filing with the court a memorandum in opposition to the preceding motion for a protective order. For the purposes of your memorandum presume that:

(a) Judge Hall sits in Charleston, West Virginia;

(b) while the local rules of the federal district court do not define "reasonable written notice" for the purposes of Rule 30(b)(1), local custom is to provide at least five days notice for depositions;

(c) it was not until plaintiffs filed their more definite statement with the court on April 16 that defense counsel could decide which plaintiffs should be deposed in the first round of depositions;

(d) there are depositions of Pittston officials set for May 25 in Charleston;

(e) it is your hope that some of the less serious plaintiffs will be "weeded out" of the lawsuit by refusing to travel to Charleston to have their depositions taken.

In your memorandum, you may suggest any "terms * * * for the discovery" within the meaning of Rule 26(c)(1)(B) for the plaintiffs' depositions that would be acceptable to you. You may rely upon any plausible facts concerning deposition logistics that you would have checked out in the actual case.

2. Among the products manufactured by Power Tools, Inc. is a chain saw that allegedly has led to several serious injuries in different parts of the United States. A products liability action has been filed against Power Tools in the United States District Court for the District of South Dakota by Johnny Johns, who lost two fingers in an accident involving a saw. Plaintiff's counsel has sought in discovery all documents concerning the development, design, and manufacture of the chain saw, as well as any advertisements for the saw. Defense counsel is prepared to provide this discovery, but only under a protective order that would prohibit any dissemination of the information outside the present lawsuit.

(a) As counsel for Power Tools, draft the protective order that you would like the court to enter;

(b) As counsel for the plaintiff, write a letter to defense counsel setting forth your position on the proposed protective order and your reasons for that position;

(c) As the judge to whom the case is assigned, write a short memorandum opinion granting or denying the parties' joint request for entry of a protective order.

3. You represent the defendant tugboat owners in the case of *Hickman v. Taylor*, 329 U.S. 495 (1947), *supra* p. 273. While the case is still pending in the federal district court, plaintiff's counsel files a document request seeking any witness statements taken by defense counsel. Defense counsel is not willing to surrender these statements. Without citing the Supreme Court's decision in this case (which has yet to be written):

(a) Attempt to negotiate a resolution of the parties' discovery dispute pursuant to Rule 26(c);

(b) Presuming that no resolution of the discovery dispute is reached, write a letter to plaintiff's counsel memorializing the outcome of your negotiation and informing him that a motion for a protective order will be filed if he insists upon obtaining the witness statements; and

(c) Presuming that plaintiff's counsel informs you that he still wants the witness statements, draft a motion for a protective order on behalf of the defendants.

III. RULE 37 MOTIONS TO COMPEL

The preceding section of this chapter has discussed the way in which a Rule 26(c) protective order can be sought to prevent or limit discovery or disclosure. Federal Rule of Civil Procedure 37(a) provides a corresponding mechanism by which the party *seeking* discovery or disclosure can invoke the court's assistance in the parties' dispute.

Rule 37(a)(3)(B) provides:

A party seeking discovery may move for an order compelling an answer, designation, production, or inspection. This motion may be made if:

(i) a deponent fails to answer a question asked under Rule 30 or 31;

(ii) a corporation or other entity fails to make a designation under Rule 30(b)(6) or 31(a)(4);

(iii) a party fails to answer an interrogatory submitted under Rule 33; or

(iv) a party fails to respond that inspection will be permitted—or fails to permit inspection—as requested under Rule 34.

Rule 37(a)(3)(A) similarly provides for a motion to compel disclosures required by Rule 26(a), and Rule 37(a)(1) provides that all motions to compel must "include a certification that the movant has in good faith conferred or attempted to confer with the person or party failing to make disclosure or discovery in an effort to obtain it without court action."[4] It's usually wise to send a letter to opposing counsel to memorialize attempts to resolve the discovery dispute. Such a letter can serve as evidence that a good faith attempt to resolve the dispute was made and that counsel is serious about receiving the discovery and is not sitting on her discovery rights. Some attorneys may not seriously consider a discovery request until they receive a letter stating that a Rule 37 motion will be filed with the court by a given date unless the discovery is forthcoming.

Rule 37(a)(5)(A) provides that, unless it finds that (1) the movant filed the motion before attempting in good faith to obtain the disclosure or discovery without court action, or (2) the opposing party's action was substantially justified, or (3) other circumstances make an award of expenses unjust, the district court *must* order the payment of the expenses incurred in connection with a successful Rule 37(a) motion to compel. Rule 37(a)(5)(A) also provides that these expenses can be assessed against the party or deponent whose conduct necessitated the successful motion to

---

4. In some districts, local rules contain other specific requirements for discovery motions. For instance, Local Rule 37.3 of the United States District Court for the Eastern District of New York provides that discovery motions are to be raised by telephone or by a letter not exceeding 3 pages in length. Any responsive letter can be no more than 3 pages long, although court rulings based solely upon a telephone discovery conference are subject to de novo reconsideration based upon letters of no more than 5 pages.

compel, the party or attorney who advised such conduct, or both of them. Rule 37(a)(5)(B) provides that if a motion to compel is denied, the court may enter a Rule 26(c) protective order and must require the moving party or that party's counsel or both to pay the expenses (including attorney's fees) incurred in opposing the motion, unless it finds that the motion was substantially justified or other circumstances make an award of expenses unjust. As Professors Wright and Miller have noted, "The great operative principle of Rule 37(a)(5) is that the loser pays."[5]

Despite the apparent attractiveness of Rule 37 in cases of discovery abuse, a 1978 study found that motions to compel are not as frequently sought in practice as one might suppose:

> The median time between filing an interrogatory and seeking court assistance under rule 37(a) fell in the 91– to 120–day interval; nearly 5 percent of the compelling motions were filed a year after the requests. * * *

> Delay in the use of rule 37(a)—or even its nonuse—would be understandable if compelling motions, when used, did not produce the desired results. That was not the situation, however, in the sampled cases * * * .

> More than half the compelling motions were ruled upon, and the rulings were overwhelmingly favorable to the moving parties. Although a substantial number of motions were not ruled upon, the absence of ruling often means that the motion was mooted by the filing of the desired response before the court had a chance to rule.[6]

If efforts to resolve disclosure or discovery disputes informally have proven unsuccessful, a Rule 37(a) motion for an order to compel disclosures or discovery responses should be considered. Not only may this be the only way in which needed information can be obtained, but a Rule 37(a) order may be a prerequisite to further sanctions in the event that the information is still not forthcoming.

NOTES AND QUESTIONS CONCERNING RULE 37 MOTIONS TO COMPEL

1. Why does Rule 37(a) not provide for a motion to compel answers to requests for admissions? Rule 37(c)(2) deals with the situation in which a party fails to admit a request for an admission and thereby requires the requesting party to prove the matter at trial. In these situations, Rule 37(c)(2) gives the court authority to impose the costs of proving the matter upon the party who refused to admit the admission request prior to trial. Consider the conditions under which an award of expenses can be awarded under Rule 37(c)(2). Does it appear that these awards will be assessed frequently?

2. Although Rule 37(a)(5) provides for the award of expenses in connection with the grant or denial of a motion to compel, such an award is only to

---

5. 8B C. Wright et al., *Federal Practice and Procedure* § 2288, at 515 (3d ed. 2010).

6. P. Connolly et al., *Judicial Controls and the Civil Litigative Process: Discovery* 19–20 (1978).

be assessed "after giving an opportunity to be heard." What type of opportunity to be heard does this provision require?

3. If the discovery sought to be compelled pursuant to Rule 37(a) is not sought from a party, where should the motion to compel be filed? *See* Rule 37(a)(2). Why is there a different rule for parties and non-parties?

Exercises Concerning Rule 37 Motions to Compel

1. Assume that plaintiffs did not file the motion for a protective order set forth in Section II(B) of this chapter, *supra* p. 451. Instead, plaintiffs' counsel calls you (local counsel for Pittston) one day before the depositions are to commence and tells you that plaintiffs will not attend their depositions because they have been noticed in Charleston.

Write a short memorandum describing the course of action that you will pursue, starting today (May 6, 1973). If your plan involves the drafting of any documents (either for filing with the court or otherwise), draft those documents.

2. You represent the plaintiff Ann Chung in a federal diversity action brought against Mary Oaks in the United States District Court for the Northern District of Indiana. The action stems from an automobile collision between the cars driven by Chung and Oaks. In this accident Chung was seriously injured and her young son was killed.

This is an excerpt from the 125 page deposition of Mary Oaks taken in her home town of Boston, Massachusetts:

Plaintiff's Counsel:	Were you drinking on the night of the collision, Ms. Oaks?
Oaks:	I may have had a beer or two.
Plaintiff's Counsel:	Do you have a drinking problem?
Oaks:	That's none of your business.
Plaintiff's Counsel:	You'll have to answer my question.
Oaks:	I will not.

Although discussion between counsel ensued, Mary Oaks refused to answer the question about a possible drinking problem.

(a) Write a memorandum to the attorney who took Oaks's deposition describing the steps that she should take to compel an answer to her question; and

(b) Draft the court papers that must be filed to obtain a Rule 37(a) order compelling an answer to the question.

IV. RULE 37 MOTIONS FOR SANCTIONS

An earlier chapter of this book considered Rule 11 and Rule 11 sanctions.[7] Federal Rule of Civil Procedure 37 provides for the imposition

---

7. Chapter 4, Section VI, *supra* p. 161.

of sanctions in connection with discovery disputes. It is with these Rule 37 sanctions that this section deals.

A. THE SANCTIONS AVAILABLE

In addition to its provisions for orders compelling discovery, Rule 37 contains mechanisms for dealing with persons who do not comply with such court orders. Rule 37(b)(2)(A) provides that if a party fails to obey a discovery order "the court where the action is pending may issue further just orders." Rule 37(b)(2)(A) also lists a series of specific sanctions that the courts can impose, either separately or in combination, upon disobedient parties.

These may be orders:

(i) directing that the matters embraced in the order or other designated facts be taken as established for the purposes of the action, as the prevailing party claims;

(ii) prohibiting the disobedient party from supporting or opposing designated claims or defenses, or from introducing designated matters in evidence;

(iii) striking pleadings in whole or in part;

(iv) staying further proceedings until the order is obeyed;

(v) dismissing the action or proceeding in whole or in part;

(vi) rendering a default judgment against the disobedient party; or

(vii) treating as contempt of court the failure to obey any order except an order to submit to a physical or mental examination.

Rule 37(b)(2)(B) further provides: "If a party fails to comply with an order under Rule 35(a) requiring it to produce another person for examination, the court may issue any of the orders listed in Rule 37(b)(2)(A)(i)–(vi), unless the disobedient party shows that it cannot produce the other person."[8]

In addition, Rule 37(b)(2)(C) provides that district courts are to award the expenses, including attorneys' fees, incurred as a result of a person's failure to obey a discovery order. All of the Rule 37(b)(2) sanctions can be imposed against a person who has not complied with an order compelling discovery. Rule 37 also contemplates the imposition of sanctions in cases in which no order has been entered, but there has been a virtual nonresponse to a discovery request. Rule 37(d)(3) provides that all of the sanctions listed in Rule 37(b)(2)(A) except contempt can be entered by the court if a party fails (1) to appear for a deposition, (2) to serve answers or

---

8. All of the Rule 37(b)(2)(A) sanctions can be imposed by the court in the district in which an action is pending. Rule 37(b)(1) covers the situation in which a deposition is taken in another district, providing: "If the court where the discovery is taken orders a deponent to be sworn or to answer a question and the deponent fails to obey, the failure may be treated as contempt of court."

objections to interrogatories, or (3) to serve a written response to a Rule 34 request. The dual routes to Rule 37(b) sanctions are illustrated by Figure 10–2.[9]

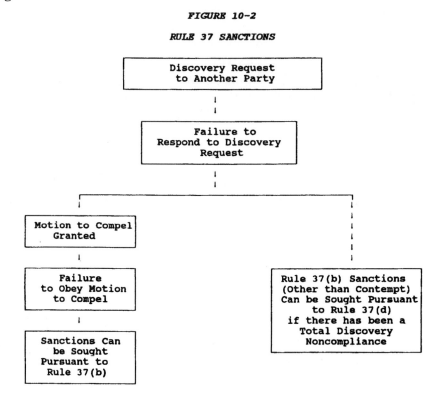

FIGURE 10–2

RULE 37 SANCTIONS

After reading Rule 37, one might presume that Rule 37(b) sanctions routinely are sought whenever a party totally fails to respond to a discovery request. However, this often is not the case, for at least two reasons. Many courts are reluctant to impose full Rule 37(b) sanctions if the recalcitrant party has not first been ordered to provide the discovery in question.[10] In addition, the party seeking the discovery sanctions may appear more reasonable if her first request is for an order compelling the

---

9. In addition to the sanctions that can be imposed for failure to respond to discovery requests or orders, Rule 37(c)(1) provides for sanctions against parties who fail to disclose information as required by Rule 26(a) or (e), "unless the failure was substantially justified or is harmless." Rule 37(c)(1) provides that substantially unjustified failures to disclose can be sanctioned by precluding use of the information or witness not disclosed on a motion, at a hearing, or at trial, by requiring payment of the reasonable expenses caused by the failure, by informing the jury of the failure to make the disclosure, and by any of the orders authorized under Rule 37(b)(2)(A)(i)–(vi).

10. *See Haskins v. Lister,* 626 F.2d 42 (8th Cir. 1980); *J. M. Cleminshaw Co. v. City of Norwich,* 93 F.R.D. 338 (D.Conn. 1981). *But see Al Barnett & Son, Inc. v. Outboard Marine Corp.,* 611 F.2d 32, 35 (3d Cir. 1979) ("a direct order by the Court, as Rule 37(a) and (b) requires, is not a necessary predicate to imposing penalties under Rule 37(d)"); *USX Corp. v. Tieco, Inc.,* 189 F.R.D. 674, 679 (N.D. Ala. 1999), *aff'd in part and rev'd and vacated in part on other grounds,* 261 F.3d 1275 (11th Cir. 2001) ("Under these circumstances, USX's misconduct has waived the usual requirement of a court order compelling production as the predicate for sanctions.").

discovery and costs, rather than for the more extreme Rule 37(b) sanctions.

The district courts have been criticized for their measured response to Rule 37 motions to compel and for sanctions.

> [S]anctions against wrongful resistance to discovery, contained in rule 37, may not provide immediate relief. The judge will usually order the recusant party to comply with the discovery request; this order leaves open the possibility of continued resistance, necessitating further resort to the court for a more severe sanction. Rule 37, then, generally offers a built-in second chance for parties resisting discovery, and the judge may in effect provide a third chance by conditioning the ultimate sanction upon further noncompliance.[11]

In an effort to encourage judges to be less hesitant in imposing Rule 37 sanctions, that Rule was amended in 1970. Rule 37 now (1) requires the district courts to award expenses incurred in unsuccessfully seeking or defending Rule 37(a) motions to compel (unless the party successfully obtaining discovery or disclosure did not first seek to obtain the information without court action, the losing party was substantially justified, or an award of expenses would be unjust) and (2) makes it clear that negligent, as well as willful, refusals to provide discovery can be sanctioned. In construing amended Rule 37, the Supreme Court has stressed that these new powers given the district courts can and should be used. In *National Hockey League v. Metropolitan Hockey Club, Inc.*,[12] the Supreme Court upheld the dismissal of an action due to the plaintiff's failure to comply with discovery orders. The Court stated that "the most severe in the spectrum of sanctions provided by statute or rule must be available to the district court in appropriate cases, not merely to penalize those whose conduct may be deemed to warrant such a sanction, but to deter those who might be tempted to such conduct in the absence of such a deterrent."[13]

Whether Rule 37 sanctions are being imposed more frequently in practice remains a disputed issue, with many lawyers complaining that judges still are too reticent to impose sanctions. One Chicago attorney interviewed in a 1979 study complained that courts "want nothing to do with discovery and never use sanctions. Rule 37 is really Rule Zero."[14] Indeed, "[p]erhaps the single most dramatic product of [this study of Chicago lawyers was] the anger and disappointment attorneys expressed

---

11. Note, "The Emerging Deterrence Orientation in the Imposition of Discovery Sanctions," 91 *Harv. L. Rev.* 1033, 1036–37 (1978).

12. 427 U.S. 639 (1976) (per curiam).

13. *Id.* at 643.

14. Brazil, "Civil Discovery: Lawyers' Views of its Effectiveness, Its Principal Problems and Abuses," 1980 *A. B. Found. Res. J.* 787, 824.

In a study of federal civil cases closed in 2008, majorities of both plaintiffs' counsel and defense counsel agreed or strongly agreed that the Federal Rules of Civil Procedure "should be revised to enforce discovery obligations more effectively." E. Lee & T. Willging, *Federal Judicial Center National, Case–Based Civil Rules Survey: Preliminary Report to the Judicial Conference Advisory Committee on Civil Rules* 63–64 (2009).

about the role played by the judiciary in the discovery stage of litigation. * * * When asked specifically whether they would favor or oppose more frequent use of sanctions for discovery abuse, fully *80 percent* of the lawyers interviewed declared that they would *favor increased* use of the *sanctioning* power."[15]

However, another study of six United States district courts sponsored by the Federal Judicial Center in the mid–1970s suggests that there may be less reluctance among judges to impose Rule 37 sanctions than many suppose:

> [D]espite the common view that federal judges will not impose sanctions under rule 37, the data show that sanctions, although rarely sought, are indeed frequently granted. Fewer than 1 percent of the requests led to motions for sanctions, but the motions were granted in about three-fourths of those that led to rulings. If analysis of data from other courts, yielding larger numbers of motions, shows the same trend, there may be cause to wonder whether the pessimism about the effectiveness of rule 37 is a self-fulfilling prophecy.[16]

Nor is it necessarily an easy task to determine where the zealous client representation demanded of all attorneys ends and sanctionable conduct begins. While it may be easy to agree on the extreme cases in which sanctions definitely should, or should not, be assessed, there remain many situations in which tough judgments under Rule 37 must be made.

NOTES AND QUESTIONS CONCERNING DISCOVERY SANCTIONS

1. In addition to sanctions under Rule 37, sanctions can be assessed against counsel or parties pursuant to Rule 26(g)(3) for discovery certifications made in violation of Rule 26(g). Pursuant to Rule 26(g)(1)(B), the signature on any discovery request, response, or objection constitutes a certification that the discovery document is (i) "consistent with [the Federal Rules of Civil Procedure] and warranted by existing law or a nonfrivolous

---

15. Brazil, "Views from the Front Lines: Observations by Chicago Lawyers About the System of Civil Discovery," 1980 *A. B. Found. Res. J.* 217, 245, 248.

16. P. Connolly et al., *Judicial Controls and the Civil Litigative Process: Discovery* xi (1978). *See also* Werner, "Survey of Discovery Sanctions," 1979 *Ariz. St. L. J.* 299, 316; Slawotsky, "Rule 37 Discovery Sanctions—The Need for Supreme Court Ordered National Uniformity," 104 *Dick. L. Rev.* 471 (2000).

If, in fact, judges are less enthusiastic about the imposition of sanctions than are many attorneys, it may be because judges are less convinced of the effectiveness of sanctions.

Many judges are not convinced that imposing monetary sanctions will significantly deter abusive conduct. While the reasons for this disbelief are seldom articulated, they include the knowledge that discovery abuse is predominantly found in a small group of cases and does not permeate the system; that ad hoc, unpublished sanctions cannot be expected to affect attorney behavior profoundly; that an adversary system must tolerate some excesses; that parties who allow their lawyers to run up huge bills in discovery are generally aware of the proceedings and approve because it is in their interest to do so; and that it seems incongruous to compensate a party for its expenses on a discovery motion at the cost of additional judicial resources that cannot be recovered from the offending party.

Sofaer, "Sanctioning Attorneys for Discovery Abuse Under the New Federal Rules: On the Limited Utility of Punishment," 57 *St. John's L. Rev.* 680, 718 (1983).

argument for extending, modifying, or reversing existing law, or for establishing new law;" (ii) "not interposed for any improper purpose;" and (iii) "neither unreasonable nor unduly burdensome or expensive, considering the needs of the case, prior discovery in the case, the amount in controversy, and the importance of the issues at stake in the litigation." Pursuant to Rule 26(g)(1)(A), the signature on a disclosure constitutes a certification that the disclosure "is complete and correct as of the time it is made."

2. The Federal Rules of Civil Procedure do not provide the only basis for discovery sanctions. Section 1927 of Title 28 of the United States Code provides:

> Any attorney or other person admitted to conduct cases in any court of the United States or any Territory thereof who so multiplies the proceedings in any case unreasonably and vexatiously may be required by the court to satisfy personally the excess costs, expenses, and attorneys' fees reasonably incurred because of such conduct.

Not only conduct at trial, but also discovery abuse, has been sanctioned under this statute. *Fritz v. Honda Motor Co.,* 818 F.2d 924, 925 (D.C.Cir. 1987); *Unique Concepts, Inc. v. Brown,* 115 F.R.D. 292, 293 (S.D.N.Y. 1987). *But see Revson v. Cinque & Cinque, P.C.,* 221 F.3d 71, 77, 79 (2d Cir. 2000) (threatening to subject opposing law firm to "legal equivalent of a proctology exam," while "offensive and distinctly lacking in grace and civility," did not provide basis for sanctions under 28 U.S.C. § 1927). *See generally* Prossnitz, "Fines Against the Trial Lawyer," *Litigation,* Fall 1983, at 36.

3. In addition to provisions in federal statutes and rules providing for the imposition of sanctions, the Supreme Court has held that the district courts possess an inherent equitable power to assess sanctions against attorneys for bad faith obstruction of the discovery process. *Roadway Express, Inc. v. Piper,* 447 U.S. 752, 764–67 (1980). *See also Chambers v. NASCO, Inc.,* 501 U.S. 32 (1991). For general treatments of the various bases upon which the courts have awarded one important sanction, attorneys' fees, see Dobbs, "Awarding Attorney Fees Against Adversaries: Introducing the Problem," 1986 *Duke L. J.* 435, and Leubsdorf, "Recovering Attorney Fees as Damages," 38 *Rutgers L. Rev.* 439 (1986).

4. In *United States v. Lundwall,* 1 F.Supp.2d 249 (S.D.N.Y. 1998), the court upheld a prosecution under the federal obstruction of justice statute, 18 U.S.C. § 1503, of two former Texaco Inc. officials for allegedly willfully destroying documents relevant to a racial discrimination suit against Texaco. Is the criminal prosecution of individuals for alleged actions within a civil lawsuit a good use of prosecutorial resources? Is it significant that those prosecuted were individuals who apparently acted independently of their employer, which was the party in the civil action?

5. In *Petroleum Ins. Agency, Inc. v. Hartford Accident & Indem. Co.,* 106 F.R.D. 59 (D.Mass. 1985), the court considered the appropriate sanction to address plaintiffs' failure to identify and produce certain documents in discovery. The magistrate judge concluded that, rather than preclude plaintiffs from introducing these documents at trial, he would (1) grant a trial continuance so that defendants could prepare to meet the documents and (2) require plain-

tiffs to pay the reasonable expenses incurred by defendants in having to prepare their case again.

Despite his conclusion that this was the appropriate sanction, the magistrate judge concluded that there was no authority to impose the sanction under Rule 37 because plaintiffs had responded, albeit incompletely, to defendants' production requests and interrogatories. 106 F.R.D. at 65–67. Nor did the magistrate judge believe he had authority to impose sanctions under 28 U.S.C. § 1927, because plaintiffs' actions were neither undertaken in bad faith nor were deliberately harassing. 106 F.R.D. at 68–69. Instead, the continuance/expense sanction was imposed pursuant to the inherent power of the court. 106 F.R.D. at 69–70.

6. Some courts have apportioned discovery sanctions between counsel and clients based upon their relative degrees of culpability. *E.g., Petroleum Ins. Agency, Inc. v. Hartford Accident & Indem. Co.,* 106 F.R.D. 59, 70 (D.Mass. 1985) (plaintiffs' counsel to pay one-half of sanction assessed, plaintiffs to pay the other one-half). *See also Stillman v. Edmund Scientific Co.,* 522 F.2d 798 (4th Cir. 1975). Some district courts have ordered that clients cannot reimburse their attorneys for sanctions levied against the attorneys. In *Associated Radio Service Co. v. Page Airways, Inc.,* 73 F.R.D. 633 (N.D.Tex. 1977), plaintiffs' attorneys were required to pay discovery expenses of defendants, defendants' attorneys were required to pay discovery expenses of plaintiffs, and the clients were prohibited from reimbursing their attorneys.

7. Despite the sanctioning authority granted by the Federal Rules of Civil Procedure and federal statutes, there are constitutional limitations upon the imposition of certain sanctions. In *Societe Internationale Pour Participations Industrielles Et Commerciales, S.A. v. Rogers,* 357 U.S. 197, 212 (1958), the Supreme Court held that plaintiff's claim could not be dismissed due to its failure to produce discovery documents because the failure was "due to inability, and not to willfulness, bad faith, or any fault of petitioner."

8. In determining whether to assess monetary sanctions under Rule 37, is it a relevant consideration that the party seeking the sanctions is not financing its own litigation costs? *See Bell v. Automobile Club of Michigan,* 80 F.R.D. 228, 229 (E.D.Mich. 1978), *appeal dism'd mem.,* 601 F.2d 587 (6th Cir.), *cert. denied,* 442 U.S. 918 (1979).

9. Parties sometimes may prefer to have Rule 37 sanctions assessed against them rather than disclose sensitive material in discovery. This may be the case if a governmental agency considers it essential to protect law enforcement information from disclosure. *See In re Attorney General of the United States,* 596 F.2d 58 (2d Cir.), *cert. denied,* 444 U.S. 903 (1979) (Attorney General held in civil contempt for refusing to comply with order to disclose FBI files concerning confidential government informants); *Alliance to End Repression v. Rochford,* 75 F.R.D. 438 (N.D.Ill. 1976) (after Chicago Police Department refused to answer interrogatories seeking information about confidential informants, court held that certain allegations of plaintiffs' complaint would be taken as established).

Are there trade secrets that private parties might refuse to disclose even in the face of a court order requiring disclosure? *See Coca–Cola Bottling Co. v.*

Coca–Cola Co., 110 F.R.D. 363 (D.Del. 1986). The trade secret at issue in this case was Coca–Cola's formula for "Merchandise 7X," which is known to only two persons and is locked in a bank vault that only can be opened by a resolution of the Coca–Cola Company's board of directors. *Coca–Cola Bottling Co. v. Coca–Cola Co.,* 107 F.R.D. 288, 289 (D. Del. 1985). What are the duties and responsibilities of counsel if a client refuses to obey a discovery order in such a situation?

10.   When can an attorney who has had discovery sanctions assessed against her challenge those sanctions? In *Cunningham v. Hamilton County,* 527 U.S. 198 (1999), the Supreme Court held that a Rule 37 sanction order was not a final decision immediately appealable by the attorney against whom it was entered, even though that attorney no longer represented a party in the case. The Court concluded that, although the order was conclusive, appellate review could not remain completely separate from the merits of the case and that immediate review of such orders pursuant to 28 U.S.C. § 1291 could lead to the very delaying and harassing tactics that Rule 37 was intended to reduce.

11.   What about the potential injury to attorneys' reputations from having discovery sanctions assessed against them? *See J. M. Cleminshaw Co. v. City of Norwich,* 93 F.R.D. 338 (D.Conn. 1981) (which contains no listing of the attorneys involved in the case and refers to the attorneys sanctioned as "Attorney S" and "Attorney Z").

12.   After the settlement of Paula Jones's sexual harassment suit against President Clinton and the conclusion of congressional impeachment proceedings, the trial judge in the *Jones* case *sua sponte* found the President in civil contempt. *Jones v. Clinton,* 36 F.Supp.2d 1118 (E.D.Ark. 1999). The judge sanctioned the President under Rule 37(b) because of his willful failures to obey the court's orders to provide discovery concerning any state or federal employees with whom he had had sexual relations. *Id.* The sanctions calculation was based upon the fees and expenses incurred by plaintiff's attorneys due to the President's denial of sexual relations with Monica Lewinsky in an interrogatory answer and in his deposition. *Jones v. Clinton,* 57 F.Supp.2d 719 (E.D.Ark. 1999).

13.   Significant sanctions have been assessed in recent years because of the destruction of emails and other electronic information. In *United States v. Philip Morris USA, Inc.,* 327 F.Supp.2d 21 (D.D.C. 2004), sanctions of $2,750,000 were assessed against Philip Morris due to its failure to preserve emails pursuant to the court's document preservation order and its own document retention policies. In addition, all of the 11 executives who had failed to retain their emails were precluded from testifying at trial.

The court in *Zubulake v. UBS Warburg LLC,* 229 F.R.D. 422 (S.D.N.Y. 2004), decided to, *inter alia,* instruct the jury that it could infer that the emails not produced by UBS Warburg LLC would have been unfavorable to that company. Not only the failure to produce electronic material, but negligent delay in such production, has been sanctioned. *Residential Funding Corp. v. DeGeorge Financial Corp.,* 306 F.3d 99 (2d Cir. 2002).

Rather than argue after the fact about whether particular conduct (or lack of conduct) is sanctionable, counsel should insure that both she and her client take their obligations seriously with respect to the preservation and production of electronic evidence. In *Zubalake* Judge Scheindlin concluded that counsel were required to "take all necessary steps to guarantee that relevant data was both preserved and produced." 229 F.R.D. at 431. Counsel must put in place a "litigation hold" to ensure the preservation of relevant documents, "communicate directly with the 'key players' in the litigation" about the preservation duty, and "instruct all employees to produce electronic copies of their relevant active files." *Id.* at 432–33.

14. In 2006 a new section was added to Rule 37 of the Federal Rules of Civil Procedure to address sanctions for failure to provide electronic discovery. Rule 37(e) now provides: "Absent exceptional circumstances, a court may not impose sanctions under these rules on a party for failing to provide electronically stored information lost as a result of the routine, good-faith operation of an electronic information system."

The "safe harbor" of Rule 37(e) does not abrogate the duty to put a "litigation hold" on relevant electronic information and presumes good faith on the part of the party with the electronic material. "The good faith requirement of Rule 37(f) [now, Rule 37(e)] means that a party is not permitted to exploit the routine operation of an information system to thwart discovery obligations by allowing that operation to continue in order to destroy specific stored information that it is required to preserve." Advisory Committee Note to 2006 Amendment to Rule 37(f), 234 F.R.D. 219, 374 (2006). Electronic sanction decisions prior to the adoption of Rule 37(f), and the need for a safe harbor provision in the Federal Rules, are discussed by a judicial leader in the response to electronic discovery in Scheindlin & Wangkeo, "Electronic Discovery Sanctions in the Twenty–First Century," 11 *Mich. Tel. & Tech. L. Rev.* 71 (2004).

15. The amount of discretion judges possess in fashioning appropriate sanctions was illustrated in the case of *In re Vivian*, 150 B.R. 832 (Bkrtcy. S.D.Fla. 1992). In this case a bank's "rouge computer" was held in contempt and fined 50 megabytes of hard drive memory and 10 megabytes of random access memory for violating a court order by sending a collection letter concerning a debt that had been discharged in bankruptcy. The computer was permitted to purge the contempt by ceasing the production and mailing of documents to the Vivians, who had received a discharge in bankruptcy.

B. ONE JUDGE'S CHANGE OF HEART CONCERNING RULE 37 SANCTIONS

Federal Judge Jerry Buchmeyer once suggested that discovery abuse was merely "the second most serious problem facing the legal profession," while "[t]he most serious problem is the Veritable Flood of speeches, paper[s], articles, and other writings about Widespread Discovery Abuse."[17] Based upon the sentiments expressed in the following opinion,

---

17. Buchmeyer, "Discovery Abuse and the Time Out Rule," *Tex. Bar J.*, Feb. 1983, at 276, 276, 277 n.1.

do you believe that Judge Robert Porter would agree with that assessment?

SCM SOCIETA COMMERCIALE S.P.A. v. INDUSTRIAL AND COMMERCIAL RESEARCH CORP.

United States District Court, Northern District of Texas, 1976.
72 F.R.D. 110.

Order

ROBERT W. PORTER, DISTRICT JUDGE.

Once again this Court has been called in to arbitrate the no show and no tell discovery games engaged in by the parties to this lawsuit. I should emphasize at the outset that this is not the only game in town. The fact pattern hereinafter recited has repeatedly surfaced in other litigation during my tenure on the bench. In fact, I have often thought that if the Federal Rules of Civil Procedure were in effect in 1492 the Indians undoubtedly would have made a motion to suppress Columbus' discovery.

This case commenced on January 27, 1975. Highlights of the discovery process are detailed below. * * *

1. March 6, 1975 the Plaintiff filed its first set of interrogatories to the Defendant;

2. May 5, 1975 this Court entered an order granting the Defendant an extension of time to answer or object to Plaintiff's first set of interrogatories;

3. May 12, 1975 Defendant answered the Plaintiff's first set of interrogatories;

4. May 19, 1975 Plaintiff moved the Court to compel the Defendants to file responsive and complete answers to the first set of interrogatories, and to award the expenses of the motion;

5. June 26, 1975 a hearing was held on discovery and other matters;

6. On July 10, 1975 the Defendant responded in opposition to the Plaintiff's motion to compel answers to interrogatories;

7. July 10, 1975 this Court entered an order granting the Plaintiff's motion to compel answer to its interrogatories;

8. August 1, 1975 the Defendant moved for an extension of time to answer interrogatories;

9. August 6, 1975 this Court entered an order granting the extension of time;

10. October 22, 1975 the Plaintiff communicated by letter that this Court's July 10, 1975 order had not been complied with;

11. February 2, 1976 the Plaintiff communicated by letter that Defendant had still not complied with the July 10, 1975 order;

12.   This Court communicated to the Defendant that the interrogatories were to be answered within ten days;

13.   May 17, 1976 the Plaintiff moved the Court to compel production of documents by Defendant, to compel answers to questions upon oral examination and to award Plaintiff's expenses;

14.   June 25, 1976 the Defendant filed an answer in opposition to Plaintiff's motion to compel production of documents and to compel answers to questions upon oral examination and to award Plaintiff's expenses;

15.   June 25, 1976 a lengthy, multi-hour hearing was conducted in chambers relating to discovery and other pre-trial matters;

16.   July 1, 1976 I entered an order compelling discovery not later than July 31, 1976. In addition I partially granted the Plaintiff's motion for a protective order and required the Defendant to comply with my July 10, 1975 order no later than July 31, 1976. Also I permitted the Defendant to depose one Mr. Aurelli;

17.   July 30, 1976 Defendants provided answers to Plaintiff's first set of interrogatories;

18.   August 6, 1976 Plaintiff moved to impose sanctions upon Defendant and its attorney for failure to comply with discovery order;

19.   August 6, 1976 I ordered Defendant to answer the motion by August 13, 1976;

20.   August 13, 1976 I celebrated my 50th birthday in relative peace there being no discovery motion filed in connection with this case as Defendant had moved for and was granted a three day extension of time to answer;

21.   August 16, 1976 Defendant filed various discovery related papers including a motion to quash Plaintiff's notice to take oral depositions, supplemental answers to Plaintiff's first set of interrogatories, a motion to reconsider my order of July 1, 1976 and finally an answer in opposition to Plaintiff's Motion to impose sanctions;

22.   August 18, 1976 the Plaintiff filed a letter brief responding to the Defendant's opposition to the Plaintiff's motion to impose sanctions;

23.   August 26, 1976 another hearing—this one lasting an hour and a half was held in chambers.

The sad part of the foregoing chronology is that the only things accomplished in this time span are the production of incomplete answers to Plaintiff's first set of interrogatories, the impregnation of my file cabinets, the generation of legal fees and the fact that I have aged a year. Or is it ten?

The effect of these vexatious discovery tactics has been to substantially hamper the speedy, just and efficient determination of legal disputes in the federal courts. These kinds of practices cost litigants large amounts of money with the collateral effect of tilting the scales of justice in the direction of the party that can best afford to pay.

This case makes abundantly clear that the supposedly self-executing federal discovery rules are being abused. Apparently my prior policy, which included a reluctance to use Rule 37 sanctions, has not worked. Henceforth, I will embark on a different course liberally using the full range of Rule 37 sanctions in appropriate circumstances. My aim is to achieve maximum discovery with minimum involvement of this Court.

There have been proposals advanced in furtherance of this aim, but I believe that the best solution to this problem is to create a climate where the lawyers are induced to exercise self-restraint and act reasonably with respect to discovery matters and each other. I know full well as do most attorneys that discovery is often used vexatiously in an effort to obtain a settlement. The case is settled in such instances for "nuisance value" and not on the relative strength of the legal rights and liabilities. I also take notice that many defendants instruct their attorneys to delay the litigation as much as possible thus making the plaintiff lose money and interest in his suit. This practice has the effect of deterring future litigation and is therefore desirable from a defense viewpoint. It is indefensible under the Federal Rules of Civil Procedure.

Henceforth, if I conclude that these practices are at the root of discovery problems or if an attorney is acting unreasonably in any other way, I will liberally impose Rule 37 sanctions.

Turning to the instant case I have several motions pending before me. The Defendant's motion to quash is denied except that the noticed deposition of Mr. Kenneth Nicholas shall take place at INCOR's place of business and he shall be required to make available all those documents he was asked to produce in the August 10, 1976 notice to take oral deposition. If he is not in possession of any or all of those documents and cannot obtain them he shall so state under oath.

The Defendant's motion to reconsider is also denied, except that my July 1, 1976 order is modified to the extent that Defendant shall be allowed to delete certain material relating to customers other than Plaintiff and to delete names of dealers that appear on the documents I have ordered to be produced. The documents shall be produced not later than September 2, 1976. The Plaintiff's motion for sanctions will now be considered.

Plaintiff contends that the Defendant has failed to obey this Court's July 1, 1976 order in several respects. First, I ordered that certain materials be provided for inspection and copying no later than July 31, 1976. Second I directed that interrogatories were to be answered not later than July 31, 1976. These were the same interrogatories the Defendant was previously ordered by the Court to answer way back on July 10, 1975. On July 30, 1976 the Defendant filed some answers to Plaintiff's interrogatories. Plaintiff in its August 6, 1976 motion alleged that these answers were incomplete and evasive. The Plaintiff specifically complained of evasive and incomplete answers to Interrogatory Nos. 41 and 45. The Defendant supplemented its answer to Interrogatory No. 41 after the motion for sanctions was filed. The Plaintiff contends that even this supplemental response is incomplete and evasive.

* * *

The Plaintiff is certainly entitled to some sanctions. He asks the Court to strike the Defendant's counterclaim for damages. He further requests that INCOR and its attorneys be required to pay SCM's reasonable expenses, including attorney fees, caused by Defendant's failure to comply with the Court's order.

While I will not grant the Plaintiff's Motion in its entirety, I have decided to grant the motion insofar as it relates to costs. I will deny the motion to strike Defendant's counterclaims. As a result, the Plaintiff shall be paid the sum of $500.00 to be taxed as costs against the Defendant.

I am always reluctant to dismiss a party's substantive claims as sanction for dilatory tactics. I am mindful of the fact that often these tactics are undertaken at the behest of the party. The defense lawyer is thus put in a difficult position between an intractable client and a diligent Plaintiff's lawyer intent on protecting *his* client's interests. That may well be the case here, but I nevertheless will not dismiss these counterclaims at this time. Costs, however, will be allowed as above set forth.

I further order that all discovery in this case shall be completed within the time frame set forth in my July 1, 1976 order. I will remain receptive to motions for sanctions as a remedy for dilatory tactics between now and then. I am hopeful that this course of action will result in the completion of discovery without further dispute. If a further dispute *does* develop and finds its way to this Court the parties will quickly discover that their games might well be over.

It is so ORDERED.

Notes and Questions Concerning *SCM Societa Commerciale S.P.A.*

1. Why does Judge Porter spend such a large portion of his opinion laying out the discovery history of this case? Are there situations in which a detailed discovery chronology might be useful to counsel in supporting or opposing a Rule 37 motion?

2. Judge Porter announces in the opinion that his "aim is to achieve maximum discovery with minimum involvement of this Court." Why has Judge Porter adopted this position? Is his aim consistent with the purposes of the Federal Rules of Civil Procedure? Is the approach taken in his opinion the best way to achieve his goal?

3. Judge Porter notes that "many defendants instruct their attorneys to delay the litigation as much as possible thus making the plaintiff lose money and interest in his suit." Are attorneys compelled to follow such instructions from their clients? *See* Model Rules of Prof'l Conduct 3.1 and 3.2. *See also* the

memorandum from the Xerox Corporation to its attorneys referred to in Note 6 of the Notes and Questions Concerning Creeds of Professionalism in Chapter 4, *supra* p. 180.

4.   Are there economic incentives that may influence some attorneys to file discovery motions rather than attempt to work out disputes between counsel?

> [A] lot of lawyers who bill by the hour . . . would rather file a motion than pick up the telephone. . . . You can only bill once for a telephone call, but if you file a motion, you can bill for drafting it, researching it, finalizing it, and filing it, and then for scheduling the hearing, preparing for the hearing, traveling to the hearing, waiting for the hearing to begin, conducting oral argument, traveling back to the firm, calling the client, and sending a confirmatory letter. Twelve things you could bill for that you would never have had to do if you just picked up the phone and said, "When can you get those discovery responses?"

Lerman, "Scenes from a Law Firm," 50 *Rutgers L. Rev.* 2153, 2165 (1998).

Should these realities be taken into account by judges in considering discovery sanctions?

5.   In this case the defendant supplemented one of its interrogatory responses after the Rule 37 motion was filed. Does this moot the possibility of sanctions concerning this interrogatory?

6.   Rule 3.4(d) of the Model Rules of Professional Conduct provides: "A lawyer shall not * * * make a frivolous discovery request or fail to make reasonably diligent effort to comply with a legally proper discovery request by an opposing party." In a survey of attorneys in civil actions closed in the last quarter of 2008, 93.1% of the attorneys representing primarily plaintiffs and 95.1% of those representing primarily defendants agreed or strongly agreed with the statement: "Attorneys can cooperate in discovery while still being zealous advocates for their clients." E. Lee & T. Willging, *Federal Judicial Center National, Case–Based Civil Rules Survey: Preliminary Report to the Judicial Conference Advisory Committee on Civil Rules* 62–63 (2009).

Exercises Concerning Rule 37 Sanctions

1.   Assume the facts described in the Buffalo Creek plaintiffs' motion for a protective order set forth in Section II(B) of this chapter, *supra* p. 451. Assume further that the court granted the Pittston Company's motion to compel the plaintiffs' deposition attendance, but denied Pittston's request for the award of expenses incurred in connection with that motion. Following entry of this order, 19 of the 22 plaintiffs whose depositions were noticed traveled to Charleston for their depositions. Three plaintiffs, however, failed to appear for their depositions. The Pittston Company has filed a Rule 37 motion requesting that these three plaintiffs be dismissed from this action and that costs be assessed against these plaintiffs and their counsel.

The following facts are established in the parties' motion papers.[18] (1) Plaintiff Martha Tombly had car trouble on the way to Charleston, and, as a result, turned back to her home in Logan County. She did not inform either her own attorneys or defense counsel that she would not be able to attend her deposition, although she now is willing to travel to Charleston for a deposition. (2) Plaintiff Mark David Grubb, age 78, does not want to leave his widowed mother to travel to Charleston. He is willing to give deposition testimony in Logan County, so long as any segment of the deposition does not take more than one hour. Although plaintiffs' counsel had been told by Grubb that he would not appear in Charleston for his deposition, they "forgot" to inform defense counsel of this fact. (3) Plaintiff Dennis Lander told plaintiffs' counsel well before his deposition was noticed that he "didn't have time for such things." Plaintiffs' counsel informed Mr. Lander, in a letter written prior to the beginning of plaintiffs' depositions, that if he did not travel to Charleston for his deposition his claims could be dismissed. Plaintiffs' counsel also informed Pittston's attorneys during the course of the first 19 depositions that there might be a problem with Lander's deposition appearance.

The depositions of these three plaintiffs were to be taken on the last scheduled day for the plaintiffs' depositions. Short deposition transcripts were made to memorialize the fact that counsel, but not these plaintiffs, appeared for the depositions. Had defense counsel known that these plaintiffs would not appear for their depositions, they could have left Charleston and returned to New York one day sooner than they actually did.

(a) Come to class prepared to argue Pittston's sanctions motion on behalf of plaintiffs;

(b) Come to class prepared to argue Pittston's sanctions motion on behalf of the Pittston Company; or

(c) As the federal magistrate judge to whom this discovery dispute has been assigned, write a short opinion ruling on Pittston's motion.

2.   Assume the facts set forth in exercise 2 of the Exercises Concerning Rule 37 Motions to Compel in Section III of this chapter, *supra* p. 458. After a telephone conference, the United States District Court for the Northern District of Indiana granted plaintiff's motion to require defendant Mary Oaks to answer the deposition question about a possible drinking problem. Counsel attempted to resume the deposition that very evening, but Mary Oaks could not be located. Plaintiff's counsel therefore remained in Boston until the next morning, at which time the deposition resumed. Mary Oaks still refused to answer the question, and plaintiff's counsel had to return to Indiana due to other commitments.

---

18. The three individuals described in this exercise were not plaintiffs in the Buffalo Creek litigation and the facts assumed in the exercise are fictional. In conducting the exercise, counsel should assume that the names of these individuals appear on defendant's April 27, 1973, deposition notice.

(a) Write a memorandum for plaintiff's counsel recommending the course of action that she should pursue;

(b) Draft any court papers that you recommend should be filed on plaintiff's behalf; and

(c) Come to class prepared to argue any motion that you have recommended should be filed by plaintiff.

V.   CONCLUSION

The discovery rules discussed in this chapter were never intended to be relied upon routinely by counsel in conducting civil discovery. The discovery provisions of the Federal Rules of Civil Procedure presuppose reasonable persons working in good faith to resolve their discovery disputes among themselves. For the discovery process to work effectively, the court's intervention into discovery disputes pursuant to Rules 26(c) and 37 must remain the exception, rather than the rule.

VI.   CHAPTER BIBLIOGRAPHY

Batista, "Defending Yourself Against Sanctions," *Litigation,* Spring 1984, at 34.

Batista, "Foreword: Symposium: Sanctioning Attorneys for Discovery Abuse," 57 *St. John's L. Rev.* 671 (1983).

Brazil, "Improving Judicial Control over the Pretrial Development of Civil Actions: Model Rules for Case Management and Sanctions," 1981 *A. B. Found. Res. J.* 875.

Cohen, Note, "Access to Pretrial Documents under the First Amendment," 84 *Colum. L. Rev.* 1813 (1984).

P. Connolly et al., *Judicial Controls and the Civil Litigative Process: Discovery* (1978).

Dobbs, "Awarding Attorney Fees Against Adversaries: Introducing the Problem," 1986 *Duke L. J.* 435.

Doré, "Secrecy by Consent: The Use and Limits of Confidentiality in the Pursuit of Settlement," 74 *Notre Dame L. Rev.* 283 (1999).

G. Joseph, *Sanctions: The Federal Law of Litigation Abuse* (3d ed. 2000).

Krupp, "Rule 37: Sanctions for Discovery Resistance," *Litigation,* Spring 1981, at 32.

Leubsdorf, "Recovering Attorney Fees as Damages," 38 *Rutgers L. Rev.* 439 (1986).

Marcus, "Myth and Reality in Protective Order Litigation," 69 *Cornell L. Rev.* 1 (1983).

Marcus, "The Discovery Confidentiality Controversy," 1991 *U.Ill. L. Rev.* 457.

Miller, "Confidentiality, Protective Orders, and Public Access to the Courts," 105 *Harv. L. Rev.* 427 (1991).

Note, "The Emerging Deterrence Orientation in the Imposition of Discovery Sanctions," 91 *Harv. L. Rev.* 1033 (1978).

Note, "Federal Rules of Civil Procedure: Defining a Feasible Culpability Threshold for the Imposition of Severe Discovery Sanctions," 65 *Minn. L. Rev.* 137 (1980).

Note, "Nonparty Access to Discovery Materials in the Federal Courts," 94 *Harv. L. Rev.* 1085 (1981).

Pepe, "Persuading Courts to Impose Sanctions on Your Adversary," *Litigation*, Winter 2010, at 21.

Pollak, Comment, "Sanctions Imposed by Courts on Attorneys Who Abuse the Judicial Process," 44 *U. Chi. L. Rev.* 619 (1977).

Prossnitz, "Fines Against the Trial Lawyer," *Litigation*, Fall 1983, at 36.

Rendall, Comment, "Protective Orders Prohibiting Dissemination of Discovery Information: The First Amendment and Good Cause," 1980 *Duke L. J.* 766.

Renfrew, "Discovery Sanctions: A Judicial Perspective," 67 *Cal. L. Rev.* 264 (1979).

R. Rodes et al., *Sanctions Imposable for Violations of the Federal Rules of Civil Procedure* (1981).

Sofaer, "Sanctioning Attorneys for Discovery Abuse Under the New Federal Rules: On the Limited Utility of Punishment," 57 *St. John's L. Rev.* 680 (1983).

Slawotsky, "Rule 37 Discovery Sanctions—The Need for Supreme Court Ordered National Uniformity," 104 *Dick. L. Rev.* 471 (2000).

Symposium, "Secrecy in Litigation," 81 Chi.–Kent L. Rev. 301 (2006).

Weissbrod, Comment, "Sanctions Under Amended Rule 26—Scalpel or Meat-ax? The 1983 Amendments to the Federal Rules of Civil Procedure," 46 *Ohio St. L. J.* 183 (1985).

Werner, "Survey of Discovery Sanctions," 1979 *Ariz. St. L. J.* 299.

CHAPTER 11

THE PRESENTATION AND ARGUMENT OF MOTIONS: "WHO GETS TO MOVE FIRST?"

■ ■ ■

[After consolidation of his sixteen separate cases] Mr. Urban
* * * filed 16 separate motions for expedition and for a change of
venue to allow the appeals to be heard in a nationally televised jury
trial before the Supreme Court.

Urban v. United Nations, 768 F.2d 1497, 1499 (D.C.Cir. 1985) (per
curiam).

Very few souls are saved after the first ten minutes.

Billy Sunday.

Analysis

I. INTRODUCTION

Previous chapters of this text have considered specific pretrial motions such as Rule 12 motions to dismiss and Rule 26(c) and Rule 37
discovery motions. These prior discussions focused primarily upon when
these particular motions can be filed and the legal standards governing
the motions. In the present chapter, pretrial motion practice is discussed
more generally.

This chapter's initial discussion of motion strategy considers whether
a motion that can be filed actually should be filed in a given case. The

second major section of the chapter discusses the manner in which a written motion should be presented to the court, while the third major section addresses the oral argument of pretrial motions.

Motion practice is a very important part of civil litigation. However, neither motion practice nor individual pretrial motions should be considered in isolation. Rather than being an end in itself, motion practice is only one of the tools by which litigation can be resolved or shaped prior to trial. The relationship of pretrial motions to one another and to other aspects of the trial and pretrial processes should be paramount in counsel's thinking and planning. In this manner, pretrial motion practice can best be used to advance the litigation interests of one's client.

II. MOTION STRATEGY

Before engaging in motion practice, counsel must determine the goals that the contemplated motion or motions will serve. The major goals of motion practice are to (1) attempt to obtain an immediate, favorable disposition of the case (perhaps through the grant of a motion for summary judgment or a motion to dismiss), (2) narrow and shape the case in the pretrial stages (perhaps through the grant of a motion for partial summary judgment), (3) obtain control of the pretrial proceedings, (4) establish with opposing counsel and the court your abilities as an attorney and the strength of your client's case, and (5) lay the groundwork for an ultimately favorable resolution of the case either at trial or by settlement. Counsel's task is to develop a motion practice strategy that will advance these goals.

A. SHOULD THE MOTION BE BROUGHT?

The initial strategy question presented in connection with any potential motion is whether the motion should be filed. If the motion is dispositive, the potential benefits of a favorable ruling are obvious. Even non-dispositive motions may be quite useful in obtaining control of the litigation or narrowing the case that ultimately will be tried. However, while most lawyers are well aware of the potential advantages of successful pretrial motions, they may not pause to consider the possible disadvantages if a pretrial motion is unsuccessful.

Just as attorneys should work to establish good rapport with their clients, rapport with judges should be high on any attorney's list of litigation objectives. Essential to good rapport is the belief that both persons will deal honestly and fairly with one another. Any time an attorney brings an unsuccessful motion, the judge may wonder if that attorney is dealing with the court in a totally honest and fair manner. For similar reasons, judges often develop a trust in attorneys who don't seek court orders unless their clients appear to be entitled to them.

While all attorneys lose motions, self-inflicted wounds should be avoided. Attorneys start every case with a certain "credibility account" with the judge. Counsel should attempt to make deposits to that account by adopting sound positions during the pretrial proceedings. Because an unsuccessful motion may constitute a "withdrawal" from an attorney's credibility account, such a motion should be avoided if possible.

The filing of pretrial motions may cause other counsel to respond with motions of their own. The filing of a motion for summary judgment may trigger the filing of a cross-motion for summary judgment by the opposing party. Counsel therefore should not only consider the court's probable response to a potential motion, but the likely reaction of other counsel (including counsel for co-parties). Rule 16 pretrial orders may set motion filing deadlines or otherwise govern motions, and counsel should be certain to adhere to any such pretrial orders.

Pretrial motions can be costly for clients and can divert attorney attention from other aspects of the pretrial process. Because of the time and expense that motions may entail, counsel always should be open to alternatives to motions by which the desired relief can be obtained. In the discovery area, counsel usually will be required to meet and confer in an attempt to settle their differences before filing a motion with the court.[1] Such consultation may reduce the need for other motions as well, or at least narrow the scope of motions that must be brought before the court.

Motions should not be considered in isolation, but a coordinated motion strategy should be adopted. Such a strategy should consider not only what motions will be filed if the current motion is successful, but should plan for the eventuality that the current motion is unsuccessful. The victory obtained from even a "successful" motion may be short-lived. For example, a judge may grant a defendant's motion to dismiss but give the plaintiff leave to file an amended complaint.

Finally, pretrial motions should not be inconsistent with a party's overall case theory. The plaintiff who has sought an expedited resolution of its claims should be selective in filing motions for extensions of time during the pretrial process. Counsel should not become so fixed upon achieving an immediate end that they lose sight of broader litigation goals.

---

1. Rule 26(c)(1) requires that motions for protective orders "must include a certification that the movant has in good faith conferred or attempted to confer with other affected parties in an effort to resolve the dispute without court action," while Rule 37(a) and 37(d) contain similar requirements for motions to compel and for discovery sanctions. Some courts have extended such meet and confer requirements beyond discovery disputes, requiring consultation with opposing counsel before filing non-discovery motions as well. *E.g.,* Rule 7.02 of the United States District Court for the District of South Carolina; Rule 7.1(a) of the United States District Court for the Eastern District of Michigan. If agreement is reached as a result of attorney consultation, this fact can be confirmed by a short thank-you letter to opposing counsel.

Although counsel may be able to handle many matters by stipulation, they may not be able to unilaterally extend the time periods for certain pretrial tasks and responses. *See, e.g.,* Rule 144(a) of the United States District Court for the Eastern District of California. *See also* Fed. R. Civ. P. 6(b) (providing for court order for an enlargement of time); Fed. R. Civ. P. 29(b) ("a stipulation extending the time for any form of discovery must have court approval if it would interfere with the time set for completing discovery, for hearing a motion, or for trial").

B. POSSIBLE PRETRIAL MOTIONS

Many of the most common pretrial motions involve the management of the discovery process. As seen in Chapter 10, parties may file motions to compel discovery under Federal Rule of Civil Procedure 37(a) or motions for a protective order under Federal Rule of Civil Procedure 26(c). The parties also may file motions to exceed discovery limitations pursuant to Rule 26(b)(2), to obtain discovery prior to their discovery meeting pursuant to Rule 26(d)(1), or to take a deposition by telephone pursuant to Rule 30(b)(4).

Chapter 5 of this book dealt with the most common preanswer motions such as motions to dismiss and for judgment on the pleadings, while Chapter 12 deals specifically with motions for summary judgment. There are, however, many other non-discovery motions that are commonly filed during the pretrial process. This section examines some of these non-discovery pretrial motions. This section's discussion of motions is not exhaustive,[2] and counsel considering the filing of any motion should do careful research before actually filing the motion.

1. Rule 41 Dismissals and Rule 55 Default Judgments

Motions to dismiss and for summary judgment are not the only pretrial motions that can result in the entry of final judgment. Dispositive motions also can be filed pursuant to Rules 41 and 55 of the Federal Rules of Civil Procedure. Rule 41 provides for the dismissal of civil actions, and Rule 55 provides for the entry of default judgments. Rule 41 is invoked against the claimant (usually the plaintiff), while Rule 55 is invoked against the party against whom judgment is sought (usually the defendant). Both of these motions typically are triggered by a party's failure to properly litigate an action.

Turning first to Rule 41 dismissals, it is important to realize that there are two quite distinct types of dismissals provided by Rule 41 of the Federal Rules of Civil Procedure. Rule 41(a) provides for the voluntary dismissal of a civil action. With certain limited exceptions,[3] Rule 41(a)(1)(A)(i) provides that a plaintiff may voluntarily dismiss its action by filing "a notice of dismissal before the opposing party serves either an answer or a motion for summary judgment." Thus, if the plaintiff acts quickly enough, he usually can change his mind and decide not to pursue the action that he has filed.[4] In addition, Rule 41(a)(1)(A)(ii) provides that

---

2.   There are many types of motions that arise in only certain types of litigation. For instance, if a class action has been filed, there may be motions to certify the proposed class or to approve a settlement that would not arise in other types of actions.

3.   Rule 41(a)(1)(A) provides that the specific requirements for court approval of dismissals set forth in Rule 23(e) (class actions), Rule 23.1(c) (derivative actions), Rule 23.2 (actions related to unincorporated associations), and Rule 66 (actions in which a receiver has been appointed), and in any federal statutes supersede Rule 41(a)(1)(A)'s provision for dismissal by the plaintiff or by stipulation of the parties.

4.   Unless the notice or stipulation of dismissal states otherwise, the first time that the plaintiff invokes Rule 41(a)(1)(A) the dismissal is considered to be without prejudice to the filing of any later action. Fed. R. Civ. P. 41(a)(1)(B). However, voluntary dismissals generally are not considered to be without prejudice if the plaintiff has previously dismissed an action based on or

a plaintiff normally can voluntarily dismiss an action without court approval if all parties to the action stipulate to such a dismissal.

Under what circumstances would a plaintiff decide to voluntarily dismiss his own action? The plaintiff may decide that he does not want to prosecute a lawsuit because of unexpected expenses, a change in the plaintiff's priorities, or other changed circumstances. The plaintiff also may decide not to pursue an action because he is unlikely to prevail in a particular forum or because there are problems with establishing personal jurisdiction or venue in that forum. One federal judge has quoted the words of Oliver Goldsmith to characterize why a plaintiff might seek a voluntary dismissal under Rule 41(a):

For he who fights and runs away

May live to fight another day;

But he who is in battle slain

Can never rise to fight again.[5]

What if the defendant has answered the complaint and the other parties will not stipulate to a voluntary dismissal? Although a unilateral voluntary dismissal is not possible, the plaintiff still can seek court approval for a voluntary dismissal. If approval is granted the court can impose "terms that the court considers proper," but unless the court specifies to the contrary the dismissal will be without prejudice.[6]

Pursuant to Rule 41(b), the court also can enter an involuntary dismissal. Such dismissals can be ordered if the plaintiff "fails to prosecute or to comply with these rules or a court order."[7] Rule 41(b) provides that involuntary dismissals pursuant to that Rule constitute an adjudication on the merits unless the dismissal order specifies otherwise or the dismissal is for lack of jurisdiction, improper venue, or for failure to join a party under Rule 19.

---

including the same claim. *Id.* Even if the first dismissal is considered to be without prejudice, the court may require the plaintiff to pay the costs of the first action as a prerequisite to the prosecution of the second action. Fed. R. Civ. P. 41(d)(1).

5. *Merit Ins. Co. v. Leatherby Ins. Co.*, 581 F.2d 137, 144 (7th Cir. 1978) (Swygert, J., dissenting). The court of appeals in *Merit Ins. Co. v. Leatherby Ins. Co.* upheld the plaintiff's right to voluntarily dismiss its action pursuant to Rule 41(a)(1) even after the district court had granted the defendant's motion to stay the civil action and compel arbitration and the arbitration had commenced.

In *Vaqueria Tres Monjitas, Inc. v. Rivera Cubano*, 341 F.Supp.2d 69 (D.P.R. 2004), *motion for reconsideration denied*, 230 F.R.D. 278 (D.P.R. 2005), plaintiffs voluntarily dismissed their action pursuant to Rule 41(a)(1) after the court denied their motion for a preliminary injunction. However, when they refiled their action approximately one hour later, the case was transferred to the judge who had denied the preliminary injunction motion in the first action and plaintiffs' attorneys were fined $1000 each for "judge-shopping."

6. Fed. R. Civ. P. 41(a)(2). However, if the defendant has pled a counterclaim prior to service of plaintiff's motion to dismiss, the action cannot be dismissed over defendant's objection unless the counterclaim can remain pending for independent adjudication by the court. *Id.*

7. Fed. R. Civ. P. 41(b). A party's failure to comply with discovery rules and orders is sanctionable under Federal Rule of Civil Procedure 37, rather than under Rule 41(b). *Societe Internationale Pour Participations Industrielles Et Commerciales, S.A. v. Rogers*, 357 U.S. 197, 206–208 (1958). Included among the sanctions that can be assessed for noncompliance with discovery rules and orders is an order dismissing an action. Fed. R. Civ. P. 37(b)(2)(A)(v).

Not only can the court dismiss an action due to the plaintiff's failure to prosecute, it can enter a default judgment under Rule 55 against a defendant who does not defend. Obtaining a Rule 55 default judgment is a two step process. First of all, Rule 55(a) requires that the party seeking judgment must show "by affidavit or otherwise" that the other party "has failed to plead or otherwise defend." Once this showing is made, the clerk enters a Rule 55(a) "default," thereby establishing the defending party's failure to defend.

The default itself cannot be translated into relief for the non-defaulting party. This party must use the default to obtain a default judgment. If the claim in question is for a sum certain or for a sum which can be made certain by mathematical calculation, the clerk can enter the default judgment.[8] Otherwise, an application for entry of the default judgment must be made to the court, which is required by Rule 55(b)(2) to hold a hearing on the application in certain circumstances. Rule 55(c) also provides that, even after a default judgment is entered, the defaulting party can move to set aside the judgment pursuant to Federal Rule of Civil Procedure 60(b).

2. Motions for a Change of Forum

One of the important determinants of litigation success is the forum in which an action is heard. Counsel, especially defense counsel, always should consider the possibility of moving an action to a forum other than the one originally chosen by the plaintiff. Motions seeking a change of forum can play an important role in the litigation and resolution of any civil case.

Counsel can seek to transfer cases within the federal district courts pursuant to 28 U.S.C. Sections 1404 and 1406. Section 1404(a) provides: "For the convenience of parties and witnesses, in the interest of justice, a district court may transfer any civil action to any other district or division where it might have been brought." Under the general federal venue statute,[9] there often are multiple districts in which venue is proper. Section 1404 is a statutory exception to the general rule that plaintiffs get to choose the court that will hear their case. Indeed, not only can defendants seek to transfer cases under Section 1404, but plaintiffs, themselves, can file transfer motions under that statutory provision.[10]

---

8. Fed. R. Civ. P. 55(b)(1). However, the clerk cannot enter a default judgment against a minor or an incompetent person. If a default judgment is sought against such a person, an application must be made to the court (which is to ensure that the person is represented in the default judgment proceedings). Fed. R. Civ. P. 55(b)(2).

9. 28 U.S.C. § 1391.

10. *Philip Carey Mfg. Co. v. Taylor*, 286 F.2d 782 (6th Cir.), *cert. denied*, 366 U.S. 948 (1961). *See also Dayton Power and Light Co. v. East Kentucky Power Coop., Inc.*, 497 F.Supp. 553, 554 (E.D.Ky. 1980).

Why would a plaintiff ever file an action in one federal district court and then seek to transfer the case to another federal judicial district? The litigation situation may have changed since the filing of the complaint or a major defendant may have been dismissed or cannot be served if the case remains in the original forum. The plaintiff also may (1) attempt to gain a favorable substantive rule of law by filing in the initial forum and then (2) seek a transfer to a second court

Because the plaintiff's initial choice of forum generally is respected, in order to be successful on a Section 1404 transfer motion a strong showing must be made that another judicial district would be more convenient for the parties, the witnesses, and the courts.[11] Although it was a *forum non conveniens* case decided before the enactment of Section 1404, the Supreme Court's decision in *Gulf Oil Corp. v. Gilbert*[12] provides a useful enumeration of the types of factors the district courts may consider in ruling on Section 1404 transfer motions.[13]

In *Gulf Oil* the Court first listed factors going to the "private interest of the litigant," such as relative ease of access to sources of proof, availability of compulsory process, the possibility of a site view by the trier of fact, and "all other practical problems that make trial of a case easy, expeditious and inexpensive."[14] The Court then considered "public interest" factors such as court congestion, the imposition of jury duty on persons from a community with no relation to the litigation, and the "local interest in having localized controversies decided at home."[15]

On balance, the necessary showing usually comes down to a matter of common sense: "Your honor, the plaintiff lives in California, the defendant is a California corporation, seven of the ten witnesses live in California, and there is related litigation pending in California. Why should this case be tried in New York?"

While 28 U.S.C. § 1404 covers situations in which venue in the initial forum is technically proper, Section 1406 of Title 28 is addressed to cases

---

to gain a favorably disposed judge or jury or a more convenient forum. Despite the transfer of a case under 28 U.S.C. § 1404, the choice of law rule of the court in which the case was originally filed continues to apply. *Van Dusen v. Barrack,* 376 U.S. 612 (1964). This is true even if it is the plaintiff who moves for the change of venue. *Ferens v. John Deere Co.,* 494 U.S. 516 (1990). However, if the action originally was filed in a district merely to take advantage of that forum's statute of limitations, transfer to another district upon the motion of the plaintiff may not be considered "in the interest of justice" for the purposes of 28 U.S.C. § 1404(a). *Frazier v. Commercial Credit Equip. Corp.,* 755 F.Supp. 163 (S.D.Miss. 1991). *See also In re Volkswagen of America, Inc.,* 545 F.3d 304, 318 (5th Cir. 2008) (en banc) (case transferred because "only connection between * * * case and the [initial venue was] plaintiffs' choice to file there").

11. A defendant thus was unsuccessful in seeking to transfer a case from Galveston to Houston because Galveston has no commercial airport. *Smith v. Colonial Penn Insurance Co.,* 943 F.Supp. 782 (S.D.Tex. 1996). The judge noted that Galveston is less than 40 miles from Houston's Hobby Airport, "that the highway is lighted all the way to Galveston, and thanks to the efforts of this Court's predecessor, Judge Roy Bean, the trip should be free of rustlers, hooligans, or vicious varmints of unsavory kind." *Id.* at 784.

12. 330 U.S. 501 (1947).

13. *Aguinda v. Texaco, Inc.,* 303 F.3d 470, 479–480 (2d Cir. 2002); *Wm. A. Smith Contracting Co. v. Travelers Indem. Co.,* 467 F.2d 662, 664 (10th Cir. 1972). Because Section 1404 provides for the transfer, rather than dismissal, of civil actions, the courts can grant Section 1404 transfers upon a lesser showing of inconvenience than that necessary for a *forum non conveniens* dismissal. *Norwood v. Kirkpatrick,* 349 U.S. 29 (1955).

14. 330 U.S. at 508.

15. *Id.* at 508–509. For critiques of district court practice and the affect upon outcome of transfers under 28 U.S.C. § 1404 see Clermont & Eisenberg, "Exorcising the Evil of Forum–Shopping," 80 *Cornell L. Rev.* 1507 (1995); Steinberg, "Simplifying the Choice of Forum: A Response to Professor Clermont and Professor Eisenberg," 75 *Wash. U. L. Q.* 1479 (1997); Clermont & Eisenberg, "Simplifying the Choice of Forum: A Reply," 75 *Wash. U. L. Q.* 1551 (1997); Steinberg, "The Motion to Transfer and the Interest of Justice," 66 *Notre Dame L. Rev.* 443 (1990).

in which venue in the first court is improper.[16] Section 1406 gives federal judges the discretion not only to dismiss these cases, but, "if it be in the interest of justice," to transfer them to a district where the action properly could have been brought in the first instance.[17] Although an action dismissed for improper venue can be refiled in another district, in some cases the statute of limitations may have run between the time the case was first filed and the time by which it can be refiled in the proper district. In these cases, transfer under 28 U.S.C. § 1406 can preserve a claim that otherwise would be barred.

If similar cases are pending in other federal judicial districts, counsel might consider a motion under 28 U.S.C. § 1407 to transfer the present action to another district court for coordinated or consolidated pretrial proceedings. The major prerequisites for transfer of multidistrict litigation are that the civil actions in question involve "one or more common questions of fact" and that transfer will result in "convenience of parties and witnesses and will promote the just and efficient conduct of such actions."[18]

In addition to these possibilities for transferring an action within the federal courts, defendants can argue that a case properly belongs in another judicial system. Under the common law doctrine of *forum non conveniens,* a court can dismiss an action over which it has jurisdiction because it would be a very inconvenient forum. A court presented with a motion for a *forum non conveniens* dismissal should consider factors similar to those relevant to transfer under 28 U.S.C. § 1404, and such a dismissal will not be granted unless there is another court that can entertain the action.[19]

If a civil action is filed in state court, defense counsel should consider the possibility of removing the case to a federal district court. Defendants generally can remove state court actions over which the federal courts

---

16. At least some courts, however, have relied upon Section 1406 to transfer cases in which venue, but not personal jurisdiction, was proper in the original court. *Dubin v. United States,* 380 F.2d 813, 816 (5th Cir. 1967). *See also Manley v. Engram,* 755 F.2d 1463, 1467 n.8 (11th Cir. 1985); *Sinclair v. Kleindienst,* 711 F.2d 291, 294 (D.C.Cir. 1983). The Supreme Court has upheld transfer under Section 1406 when both venue and personal jurisdiction do not exist in the original forum. *Goldlawr, Inc. v. Heiman,* 369 U.S. 463 (1962).

17. In appropriate cases, a party might file a motion to dismiss or, in the alternative, to transfer pursuant to 28 U.S.C. Section 1406.

18. 28 U.S.C. § 1407(a). *See generally* D. Herr, *Multidistrict Litigation Manual* (2006); Hensler, "The Role of Multi–Districting in Mass Tort Litigation: An Empirical Investigation," 31 *Seton Hall L. Rev.* 883 (2001); Herrmann, "To MDL or Not to MDL? A Defense Perspective," *Litigation,* Summer 1998, at 43; Kyle, "The Mechanics of Motion Practice Before the Judicial Panel on Multidistrict Litigation," 175 F.R.D. 589 (1998); Symposium, "The Problem of Multidistrict Litigation," 83 *Tul. L. Rev.* 2199 (2008); Tompkins, "Multidistrict Litigation Proceedings," 37 *Trial Law. Guide* 24 (1993).

19. *Piper Aircraft Co. v. Reyno,* 454 U.S. 235 (1981); *Gulf Oil Corp. v. Gilbert,* 330 U.S. 501 (1947). *See generally* M. Karayanni, *Forum Non Conveniens in the Modern Age* (2004); Samuels, "When Is an Alternative Forum Available? Rethinking the Forum Non Conveniens Analysis," 85 *Ind. L. Rev.* 1059 (2010). In *Sinochem Int'l Co. v. Malaysia Int'l Shipping Corp.,* 549 U.S. 422, 436 (2007), the Supreme Court held that "where subject-matter or personal jurisdiction is difficult to determine, and *forum non conveniens* considerations weigh heavily in favor of dismissal," *forum non conveniens* dismissal is appropriate without first determining personal or subject matter jurisdiction.

have original jurisdiction.[20] The major exception to this rule precludes removal based upon federal diversity jurisdiction if one or more of the defendants is a citizen of the state in which the action has been brought.[21]

In order to remove a case from state court, the defendant must file a notice of removal in federal court within thirty days after defendant's receipt of the state court summons, pleading or other document that indicates that the action is or has become removable.[22] Other parties can challenge the removal, arguing that the case was improperly removed and should be remanded to state court.[23]

3. Motions Affecting the Trial of the Action

Counsel should consider using pretrial motions to structure not only pretrial proceedings, but also the trial of an action. Rule 42 of the Federal Rules of Civil Procedure presents several possibilities in this regard.

Pursuant to Rule 42(a) a party can seek joint hearings, trials, or the consolidation of separate actions, while Rule 42(b) permits the court to order separate trials of any claims or issues within a single case. The court can use Rule 42 to save both itself and the parties unnecessary cost and delay, as well as to prevent possible prejudice to a party that might result if claims or issues were tried together. If lengthy trial testimony will be offered concerning damages, it may make sense to try the issue of liability first. If plaintiff loses this initial trial, there should be no need for trial of the damage issues.[24]

---

20. 28 U.S.C. § 1441(a).

21. 28 U.S.C. § 1441(b).

22. 28 U.S.C. §§ 1446(a), (b). However, 28 U.S.C. § 1446(b) also provides that actions cannot be removed on the basis of diversity of citizenship more than one year after the commencement of the action.

This statutory provision has led to attempts to manipulate party joinder to preclude removal of civil actions to federal court from plaintiff-friendly state courts. As a judge in the multidistrict litigation involving the "fen-phen" diet drugs noted: "[T]here is a pattern of pharmacies being named in complaints, but never pursued to judgment, typically being voluntarily dismissed at some point after the defendant's ability to remove the case has expired." *Anderson v. American Home Products Corp.*, 220 F.Supp.2d 414, 424 (E.D.Pa. 2002). The judge also noted that "the only pharmacy in Jefferson County, Mississippi * * * is named in hundreds of lawsuits involving the sale of allegedly defective drugs, including fen-phen." *Id.*

23. 28 U.S.C. § 1447(c).

24. While the bifurcation of liability and damages may be appealing to the defendant and the court, in some cases bifurcation may not be to the plaintiff's advantage. If the plaintiff has compelling evidence on damages, he may want that evidence before the jury at the time that it determines liability. *See generally* Granholm & Richards, "Bifurcated Justice: How Trial–Splitting Devices Defeat the Jury's Role," 26 *U. Tol. L. Rev.* 505 (1995); Schwartz, "Severance—A Means of Minimizing the Burden and Expense in Determining the Outcome of Litigation," 20 *Vand. L. Rev.* 1197 (1967).

However, scholars have argued that, while plaintiffs may be less likely to establish liability in bifurcated cases, they may actually receive larger damage awards in bifurcated trials in which liability is established. De Villiers, "A Legal and Policy Analysis of Bifurcated Litigation," 2000 *Colum. Bus. L. Rev.* 153; Gensler, "Bifurcation Unbound," 75 *Wash. L. Rev.* 705 (2000). *See also* Landsman et al., "Be Careful What You Wish For: The Paradoxical Effects of Bifurcating Claims for Punitive Damages," 1998 *Wisc. L. Rev.* 297, 335 (both incidence of punitive damage awards, and size of such awards, increased in simulated bifurcated cases); Rubin, "The Managed Calendar: Some Pragmatic Suggestions about Achieving the Just, Speedy, and Inexpensive Determination of Civil Cases in Federal Courts," 4 *Just. Sys. J.* 135, 146 n.16 (1978) (offering

While most evidentiary objections are made at trial, preliminary rulings concerning important evidentiary and procedural issues can be requested at the pretrial stage by a motion *in limine*.[25] Perhaps the most common motions *in limine* are those that seek a pretrial ruling that certain evidence may or may not be offered at trial. If counsel is concerned that highly prejudicial evidence may be offered by another party at trial, a pretrial motion *in limine* should be considered. A pretrial ruling on such a motion should prevent the prejudice that otherwise would occur if evidence slips out at trial before counsel can object or raise the matter with the court.

In some jurisdictions it may not be necessary to file individual Rule 42 motions and motions *in limine*. Instead, evidentiary objections and requests concerning the trial of specific claims are to be raised by the parties in the proposed pretrial order.[26]

4. Other Miscellaneous Motions

Motion practice is not limited to the motions formally recognized in the Federal Rules of Civil Procedure or in local rules of court. Rule 7(b)(1) provides: "A request for a court order must be made by motion." A myriad of situations arise during the pretrial process that may warrant entry of a court order. A party may seek a stay of a case or of a particular aspect of a case, the right to file a brief in excess of the page limitations contained in a local rule of court, or the service of discovery responses more expeditiously than required by the Federal Rules of Civil Procedure. In addition, many judges entertain motions for the reconsideration of pretrial rulings,[27] although counsel should get their best arguments before the judge in the first instance so that a motion for reconsideration is not necessary.[28]

---

evidence that bifurcated trials do not lead to a disproportionate number of defense verdicts). *But see* American Bar Association, *Principles for Juries and Jury Trials*, Principle 13(H) (2005) ("In civil cases the court should seek a single, unitary trial of all issues in dispute before the same jury, unless bifurcation or severance of issues or parties is required by law or is necessary to prevent unfairness or prejudice.").

25. *See generally* Mead, "Motions in Limine: The Little Motion that Could," *Litigation*, Winter 1998, at 52. *See also* Blumenkopf, "The Motion *In Limine:* An Effective Procedural Device with No Material Downside Risk," 16 *New Eng. L. Rev.* 171 (1981); Epstein, "Motions in Limine—A Primer," *Litigation*, Spring 1982, at 34; Saltzburg, "Tactics of the Motion in Limine," *Litigation,* Summer 1983, at 17.

26. Rule 281(b)(5) of the United States District Court for the Eastern District of California; Rule 16.1(d)(2)(b)(6) of the United States District Court for the Eastern District of Pennsylvania. *See* Chapter 13, *infra. See also* Fed. R. Civ. P. 26(a)(3)(B), which requires parties to list objections to trial exhibits prior to trial.

27. Motions for reconsideration or reargument are explicitly recognized in the local rules of some federal courts. Civil Rule 6.3 of the United States District Courts for the Southern and Eastern Districts of New York; Rule 7.10 of the United States District Court for the Middle District of Pennsylvania.

28. Attorneys have been sanctioned under Rule 11 for moving for reconsideration without offering new legal or factual arguments. *Magnus Electronics, Inc. v. Masco Corp. of Indiana,* 871 F.2d 626, 630–31 (7th Cir.), *cert. denied,* 493 U.S. 891 (1989); *Unioil, Inc. v. E.F. Hutton & Co.,* 809 F.2d 548, 559 (9th Cir. 1986), *cert. denied,* 484 U.S. 823 (1987). Rule 11 sanctions even have been imposed for the filing of a groundless motion to reconsider the imposition of Rule 11 sanctions. *Brown v. National Bd. of Med. Examiners,* 800 F.2d 168 (7th Cir. 1986).

Federal Rule of Civil Procedure 6(b) recognizes what may be one of the most significant motions that an attorney will file in many cases: the motion for enlargement of time.[29] While counsel should attempt to adhere to the time limitations established by rules and court orders, there inevitably will be situations when additional time is necessary. Motions for enlargement of time therefore can be extremely important in the pretrial litigation of any case. As with many other pretrial motions, the trial court has a great amount of discretion in deciding whether to grant a motion for an enlargement of time.[30]

There are numerous motions that counsel can use to resolve or narrow a case prior to trial and to establish control and credibility within the pretrial process. Careful planning and coordination of pretrial motions can maximize the effectiveness of counsel's motion practice.

C. RESPONDING TO MOTIONS

Planning is not only required in determining whether to file motions, but is necessary in deciding upon the appropriate response to the motions filed by other parties. In responding to motions, counsel's goals should be to (1) maximize the chances of a successful outcome on each particular motion and (2) not let another party's motions unduly interfere with her own motions and pretrial litigation strategy.

If a careful pretrial litigation plan has been prepared, an opponent's major motions should not be great surprises. In analyzing a case, it

---

29. Rule 6(b)(1)(A) provides that "for good cause" the court may enlarge the period of time for doing an act if a request for such enlargement is made "before the original time or its extension expires." If the enlargement is not sought until after the original time period has expired, the enlargement must be sought by a motion "if the party failed to act because of excusable neglect." Fed. R. Civ. P. 6(b)(1)(B). *See Lujan v. National Wildlife Fed.*, 497 U.S. 871, 897 n.5 (1990) (footnote in a reply memorandum did not satisfy Rule 6(b)'s requirement for a motion for enlargement of time).

The etymology of the word "deadline," as well as its significance, was made clear by one judge as follows:

The word "deadline" was coined by Union soldiers held at the Andersonville prison camp during the War of Northern Aggression. Confederate guards summarily executed any prisoner crossing a preordained line on the camp grounds; thus, the term "deadline." * * * While the Court does not contemplate as harsh a rejoinder to Appellants' counsel's crossing of this Court's preordained line, it will still be, well, "fatal" to his claim.

Brown v. McCabe & Pietzsch, P.A., 180 B.R. 325 (S.D.Ga. 1995).

30. *Yonofsky v. Wernick*, 362 F.Supp. 1005, 1014 (S.D.N.Y. 1973). *See also* the Advisory Committee Note to the 1963 Amendment to Federal Rule of Civil Procedure 6(b), 31 F.R.D. 587, 633 (1963).

Because of the judge's discretion in ruling on motions for an enlargement of time, attorneys only should seek enlargements of time when they are really needed. While judges may give counsel the benefit of the doubt the first few times an enlargement of time is sought, at some point the judge will become less receptive to these motions. We all have a finite number of second cousins, and it's unlikely that counsel will have to attend more than two or three funerals of such relatives during a single case.

The United States Court of Appeals for the Seventh Circuit has criticized "self-help" extensions of time filed on the day that a brief is due, noting: "If a party needs more time, a request for an extension must be filed in advance of the due date. If extra time has not been granted in advance, then the litigant must file its brief as scheduled." *Ramos v. Ashcroft*, 371 F.3d 948, 949–50 (7th Cir. 2004).

usually will be obvious to all counsel that, for example, a particular party probably will file a motion to dismiss or for summary judgment. Knowledge of an opposing attorney also should alert counsel to the possibility that certain pretrial motions will be filed. If defense counsel routinely files motions to dismiss, chances are good that she will file such a motion in the present case. The judge also may ask about possible motions at a Rule 16 pretrial conference, and the court's scheduling order may set motion deadlines pursuant to Rule 16(b)(3).

By considering at an early stage of the case the likely motions that opposing attorneys will file, counsel can prepare to meet these motions. This preparation can take several forms. It may mean that counsel will begin the legal research, factual investigation, or discovery that will be necessary to use in opposition to the contemplated motion. For instance, counsel may ask a few additional questions at a deposition if she believes that the deponent later may offer an affidavit in support of a motion for summary judgment.

If counsel anticipates that an opposing party will file a motion, she may decide to present her own pretrial motions in a more expeditious manner. If the opposing party is likely to file a motion for summary judgment, counsel may want to file her own summary judgment motion first so that it will be considered either before or with her opponent's motion. If opposing counsel are forced to respond to motions, they may have less time to prepare their own motions.

Once a motion has been filed, counsel need not respond in a purely defensive manner. In response to a motion to dismiss, the plaintiff may file a motion to amend the complaint (which, if granted, would fix the problem the defendant has identified in the complaint). Possible responses to a motion for summary judgment include a cross-motion for summary judgment or a motion to reopen discovery so that additional relevant evidence can be presented to the court.

Responsive motions can be made in the alternative. A plaintiff may oppose a motion to dismiss with both (1) an argument that the motion is not well-taken and, in the alternative, (2) a motion to amend (in the event that the court agrees with the argument made in defendant's motion). Counsel must think through alternative responses, however, because asking the court for leave to amend is at least an implicit concession that there may be problems with the complaint.

Nor should all motions routinely be opposed. There may be advantages to be gained from not opposing some motions. If you raise no objection to opposing counsel's motion for an enlargement of time, it will be difficult for her to object if you later seek a comparable enlargement of time. If you do not oppose the entry of a protective order covering other parties' discovery, it may be easier to obtain similar treatment for discovery produced by your client. By applying a "Golden Rule of Reciprocity," most judges attempt to treat all counsel in a roughly equivalent fashion.

Planning and consideration of the likely consequences of the responses available to your client are essential in responding to pretrial motions.

NOTES AND QUESTIONS CONCERNING PRETRIAL MOTION STRATEGY

1.   What can be done if the court refuses to rule on a pretrial motion? Should counsel for the moving party contact the court? If so, how should the contact be made? Are there other alternatives?

2.   Should clients be involved in the decision to file pretrial motions? Should they be given copies of the pretrial motions that are filed? Should clients be notified or consulted when pretrial motions are filed by opposing parties?

3.   In contemplating responses to another party's motion or request, consider not only tactical, but also ethical and professionalism, issues that the motion or request may present. When another attorney requests additional time in which to respond to a motion or meet a court deadline, never forget that you, too, may well need additional time or other consideration later in the case. Can an attorney be sanctioned for refusing to agree to a reasonable request for an enlargement of time? What if her client objects? *See Regional Transp. Authority v. Grumman Flxible Corp.*, 532 F.Supp. 665 (N.D.Ill. 1982).

4.   Can a plaintiff use Rule 41(a) as a means of evading Rule 11 sanctions? In *Cooter & Gell v. Hartmarx Corp.*, 496 U.S. 384 (1990), the Supreme Court held that district courts retain the power to impose Rule 11 sanctions due to a baseless complaint even after that complaint has been voluntarily dismissed under Rule 41(a). The Court reasoned: "Because a Rule 11 sanction does not signify a District Court's assessment of the legal merits of the complaint, the imposition of such a sanction after a voluntary dismissal does not deprive the plaintiff of his right under Rule 41(a)(1) to dismiss an action without prejudice." 496 U.S. at 396. As a practical matter, will plaintiffs have much success refiling complaints that have been found to be sanctionable under Rule 11? Will district judges be more or less likely to impose sanctions once an action has been voluntarily dismissed? Rule 11 was amended in 1993 to limit the sanctions that can be imposed after a voluntary dismissal or settlement. Rule 11(c)(5) now provides: "The court must not impose a monetary sanction . . . on its own, unless it issued the show-cause order under Rule 11(c)(3) before voluntary dismissal or settlement of the claims made by or against the party that is, or whose attorneys are, to be sanctioned."

5.   During 1983–84 the Pennzoil Company was on the verge of acquiring the Getty Oil Company, only to have Texaco Incorporated acquire Getty while the Pennzoil–Getty acquisition papers were being drafted. Pennzoil filed a lawsuit in Delaware Chancery Court, unsuccessfully seeking to enjoin Texaco's acquisition of Getty. Attorneys for Pennzoil then realized that their client would be better served by litigating Pennzoil's damage claims before a Texas jury. The following excerpt describes the manner in which Pennzoil attorney Irv Terrell was able to obtain the Texas jury that rendered a ten billion dollar Pennzoil verdict (ultimately resulting in a three billion dollar settlement for Pennzoil). While reading this excerpt consider not only the strategy adopted

by Pennzoil's attorneys in this particular case but the potential impact of such a strategy upon civility within the legal profession.

T. PETZINGER, OIL AND HONOR

261–62 (1987).

[W]hile studying the unfamiliar (to him) terrain of the Delaware courts, Terrell had come upon a seldom-used rule: If someone fails to file a formal answer to a lawsuit, the lawsuit may be dismissed at any stage of the case—without even asking the judge for permission. Getty Oil had filed a response. So had the trust and the museum. *Texaco hadn't.* As near as Terrell could tell, Pennzoil was now free to drop Texaco from the Delaware lawsuit without even having to ask the judge for permission, then refile the case anywhere in the country where both companies had operations. That, of course, meant [chairman of Pennzoil] Hugh Liedtke's Houston.

While awaiting the decision on the injunction motion, Terrell discussed the move to nonsuit Texaco with the Pennzoil local law firm in Delaware, which agreed that the move just might succeed. However, special security measures were required. The Chancery Court of Delaware is a genteel court, where local custom requires the lawyers on one side of a case to notify their adversaries in advance of any filings. Doing so in this case would obviously permit Texaco to hustle up a piece of paper formally answering Pennzoil's suit.

"Maintain silence," Terrell told his cohorts in Delaware. "We're not gonna follow this gentlemanly rule."

At midnight the day that Judge Brown finally dashed Pennzoil's hope of restoring its deal, Terrell conferred with his partner Jeffers and with Liedtke, who were in Washington appearing before the Federal Trade Commission in yet another effort to thwart the Texaco deal. (It too would fail.) Liedtke gave the go-ahead. Early the following morning, Pennzoil gave the Delaware court clerk a $25,000 check to cover its costs in the case and filed a one-sentence document: "Please take notice that plaintiff, Pennzoil Company, hereby dismisses this action without prejudice as to defendant Texaco Inc. pursuant to Chancery Court Rule 41(a)(1)(i)."

Fifteen minutes later, Terrell filed the case of *Pennzoil Company v. Texaco Incorporated,* Cause #84–05905, in the District Court of Harris County, Texas. In the last paragraph of the twenty-page document, Pennzoil made the greatest damages demand ever seen in Harris County, and probably anywhere in the world: "Pennzoil respectfully prays that upon trial by jury, this Court enter judgment against Texaco in such amount as is proper, but in no event less than $7,000,000,000 actual damages and $7,000,000,000 punitive damages."

The amounts would later be increased to $7.53 billion each, after Pennzoil had more fully refined its case.

Exercises Concerning Motion Strategy

1.   In exercise 1 of the Exercises Concerning Litigation Planning in Chapter 3, *supra* p. 65, a litigation plan was developed on behalf of Thomas Eakins, a survivor of the Buffalo Creek disaster. Reconsider the litigation plan that was developed at that time, focusing particularly on (1) the pretrial motions that should be filed on Mr. Eakins's behalf, (2) the motions that probably will be filed by the defendant Pittston Company, and (3) how to deal with Pittston's likely motions. As Eakins's attorney, draft a memorandum to the file describing the motion strategy that you intend to pursue on his behalf.

2.   You are a partner in the law firm representing the Pittston Company in the actions filed against it by victims of the Buffalo Creek disaster. Counsel for plaintiff Thomas Eakins has filed a motion for partial summary judgment on the issue of liability twenty days after the commencement of his action. This motion is based upon the public statements of Pittston and Buffalo Mining officials, the governmental investigations of the disaster, and public documents showing that the Pittston Company is the sole shareholder of Buffalo Mining. Draft a memorandum outlining the manner in which Pittston should respond to this motion. Be certain that the strategy that you adopt is consistent with the overall pretrial and trial strategy that you intend to pursue on Pittston's behalf.

3.   As counsel for the estate of a young woman killed in an automobile accident, you have brought suit against the General Motors Corporation in the United States District Court for the Eastern District of Pennsylvania. Although General Motors waived service of summons pursuant to Rule 4(d), that company has filed no answer or other response to the complaint with the court. Seventy days after sending the request for waiver of service, you called the general counsel's office of General Motors and were told by a secretary that the attorney handling the case would "get back to you." When you still heard nothing from General Motors, you wrote its general counsel attempting to bring the suit to the corporation's attention. It now has been three months since process was served upon General Motors.

Write a memorandum to the partner who heads your law firm's litigation department describing the strategy you plan to employ at this point. Consider in your memorandum:

   (a) whether any motion should be filed;

   (b) what, if anything, should be done before any motion is filed; and

   (c) what, if any, record should be created of your firm's actions.

III. THE WRITTEN MOTION PAPERS

The Federal Rules of Civil Procedure include few requirements concerning the format of pretrial motions. The major requirement contained in the Rules is that the motion must:

(A) be in writing unless made during a hearing or trial;

(B) state with particularity the grounds for seeking the order; and

(C) state the relief sought.[31]

Rule 7(b)(1)(B)'s requirement that the motion must "state with particularity the grounds for seeking the order" should not be overlooked. It is difficult for a judge to rule for an attorney if he cannot understand her argument. As one court has observed, "Judges are not like pigs, hunting for truffles buried in briefs."[32] Rule 7(b)(1)(C) additionally requires that the motion must "state the relief sought." It's a good idea to set forth the relief sought at the beginning, as well as at the end, of the brief or memorandum filed in support of a motion so that the judge can consider counsel's argument in light of the requested relief. The motion, itself, is a rather short document that usually is not difficult to prepare.[33] Local rules may require the preparation of a notice of motion or a proposed order to accompany the motion.[34]

---

31. Fed. R. Civ. P. 7(b)(1). Apart from the requirement of Rule 7(b)(1), it's a good practice to put every pretrial motion in writing so that there will be no questions (in either the trial or appellate courts) about the motion that was made. Appellate courts may refuse to consider an issue if the record does not indicate that the matter was raised in the trial court. *Terrell v. Poland,* 744 F.2d 637, 639 n.2 (8th Cir. 1984); *Alger v. Hayes,* 452 F.2d 841, 843–44 (8th Cir. 1972). Absent local practice to the contrary, requests for court orders should not be made in letters to the court. *Tate v. International Business Machines Corp.,* 94 F.R.D. 324 (N.D.Ga. 1982).

In addition to the requirements of Rule 7(b)(1), Federal Rule of Civil Procedure 7(b)(2) specifies: "The rules governing captions and other matters of form in pleadings apply to motions and other papers." The motion should include a short, descriptive title. *Venezolana Internacional De Aviacion, S.A. v. Int'l Ass'n of Machinists & Aerospace Workers,* 118 F.R.D. 151 (S.D.Fla. 1987) (lengthy and argumentative motion title stricken *sua sponte* by district court).

Finally, Rule 11(a) requires that written motions must be signed "by at least one attorney of record in the attorney's name—or by a party personally if the party is unrepresented."

32. *United States v. Dunkel,* 927 F.2d 955, 956 (7th Cir. 1991) (per curiam).

Attorneys should avoid the barebones style of argument employed in a post-trial motion in *Lynn v. Smith,* 193 F.Supp. 887 (W.D.Pa. 1961). The post-trial motion in this case provided in its entirety:

The verdict was inadequate.

The learned trial judge erred on the law.

The learned trial judge erred in rulings on the evidence.

The learned trial judge erred in his charge to the jury.

The charge of the learned trial judge to the jury was prejudicial to the plaintiffs.

193 F.Supp. at 888.

Not surprisingly, the learned trial judge found that this motion did not comply with Federal Rule of Civil Procedure 7(b)(1) and denied the motion.

33. *See* Form 40 of the Appendix of Forms to the Federal Rules of Civil Procedure, set forth in Chapter 5, *supra* p. 192.

34. Rule 6.1 of the United States District Courts for the Southern and Eastern Districts of New York (notice of motion); Rule 7.1(c) of the United States District Court for the Northern

The most time-consuming aspect of pretrial motion practice is the preparation of the brief or memorandum in support of the motion. There are no tricks or shortcuts to well-written motion briefs. The same techniques that ensure good legal writing generally should lead to well written motion papers.[35] Counsel's briefs should be as clear and concise as possible. Particularly in longer briefs, organizational techniques such as argument subheadings should be used.

Sufficient time should be set aside for careful preparation of the brief. This requires, whenever possible, that motions and supporting papers be started far enough in advance so that they can be thought through over time. The preparation and revision of multiple drafts of important briefs is essential.

The brief's opening paragraph should set the stage by describing the case and explaining how the current motion fits within the case. For example, the Pittston Company's opposition to the Buffalo Creek plaintiffs' May 4, 1973, motion for a protective order[36] might have begun as follows:

> On April 30, 1973, the defendant Pittston Company mailed deposition notices to 22 of the plaintiffs in this case. These depositions were noticed pursuant to Rule 30 of the Federal Rules of Civil Procedure, and a full five days "reasonable notice" was given plaintiffs concerning the May 7, 1973, deposition date. The depositions were noticed for Charleston, where plaintiffs have deposed officials of defendant and where this court sits. Nevertheless, on May 4, 1973, plaintiffs sought a protective order concerning these depositions.

District of Texas (proposed order). *See* Section III(A)(2) of Chapter 5, *supra* p. 192. Even when not required by local rule, the drafting of a proposed order may help to focus the written motion and oral argument upon the key issues posed by the motion.

35. The following books concerning legal writing may prove helpful: L. Bahrych & M. Rombauer, *Legal Writing in a Nutshell* (4th ed. 2009); L. Edwards, *Legal Writing: Process, Analysis, and Organization* (5th ed. 2010); E. Fajans et al., *Writing for Law Practice* (2004); B. Garner, *Legal Writing in Plain English* (2001); B. Garner, *The Elements of Legal Style* (2d ed. 2002); M. Johns, *Professional Writing for Lawyers: Skills and Responsibilities* (1998); T. LeClercq, *Expert Legal Writing* (1995); M. Ray & B. Cox, *Beyond the Basics: A Text for Advanced Legal Writing* (2003); M. Ray & J. Ramsfield, *Legal Writing: Getting It Right and Getting It Written* (4th ed. 2005); M. Smith, *Advanced Legal Writing: Theories and Strategies in Persuasive Writing* (2002); R. Wydick, *Plain English for Lawyers* (5th ed. 2005).

These books pertain specifically to written motions: I. Alterman, *Plain and Accurate Style in Court Papers* (1987); M. Fontham et al., *Persuasive Written and Oral Advocacy in Trial and Appellate Courts* (2d ed. 2007); G. Gale & J. Moxley, *How to Write the Winning Brief* (1992); B. Garner, *The Winning Brief* (2d ed. 2004); L. Jorgensen, *Motion Practice and Persuasion* (2006); M. Murray & C. DeSanctis, *Adversarial Legal Writing and Oral Argument* (2006); G. Peck, *Writing Persuasive Briefs* (1984); L. Oates & A. Enquist, *Just Briefs* (2003); E. Re & J. Re, *Brief Writing and Oral Argument* (9th ed. 2005); A. Scalia & B. Garner, *Making Your Case: The Art of Persuading Judges* (2008). *See also* Christensen, "How to Write for the Judge," *Litigation,* Spring 1983, at 25.

As courts increasingly permit the filing of "electronic briefs," counsel should take advantage of the unique advantages, and avoid the particular pitfalls, of new electronic formats. *See* Crist, "The E–Brief: Legal Writing for an Online World," 33 *N.M. L. Rev.* 49 (2003).

Whether submitting motions in hard copy or electronically, all writers should be familiar with W. Strunk & E. B. White, *The Elements of Style* (4th ed. 2000).

36. *Supra* p. 451.

Because plaintiffs cannot establish "undue burden" as required by Rule 26(c), their motion for a protective order should be denied.

This illustrative opening paragraph sets forth the governing law (which permits the party noticing depositions to choose the time and place for the depositions), the fact that the party represented acted within the governing law (in noticing the depositions at the time and place in question), and rebuts the anticipated response of the opposing party (that the noticed depositions would cause an undue burden).

After this type of an introductory paragraph, there should be a statement of the facts.[37] This statement should be preceded by a descriptive heading and should recite the facts in greater detail than is possible in the opening paragraph of a brief. The factual statement should contain facts, rather than argument or contentions, and should not omit the major facts that will be relied upon by opposing counsel. The facts, however, should be written from the client's perspective and be arranged so that they inexorably lead to the conclusion sought by counsel. The judge should be persuaded by the fact statement before he ever reaches the argument portion of the brief.

The statement of the facts should include citations to supporting evidentiary material. A sample sentence and supporting citations from a statement of the case might read as follows: "The defendant is incorporated in New York and has its principal place of business in Connecticut. April 1, 2011, Answer ¶ 4; June 1, 2011, Declaration of James Jones, ¶ 3."

The major portion of the brief, containing counsel's argument, usually follows the statement of the facts. The argument should contain both relevant facts and governing law, interwoven in as persuasive a manner as possible. As with other aspects of advocacy, it's better to understate, rather than overstate, one's case in the brief. An overstatement concerning even a minor aspect of a case can undermine counsel's credibility with the court and opposing counsel.[38]

Argument headings should be used to frame the issues presented by the motion in the fashion most favorable to the moving party. This framing of the issues may be the most important aspect of the argument. Consider this possible argument heading for the Buffalo Creek plaintiffs' motion for a protective order: "The plaintiffs should not be subjected to the undue burden and expense of traveling to Charleston when their depositions could just as easily be taken in the Buffalo Creek Valley."

---

37. In more extensive briefs, there may be a separate "statement of the case" preceding the factual statement and reciting the procedural history of the action. If a separate statement of the case is not justified, the procedural facts relevant to the present motion should be included in the brief's introductory paragraph or statement of the facts.

38. The appearance of the brief should be understated and professional as well. Thus one judge felt compelled to note in a dissenting opinion, "To the extent that BAM has successfully persuaded me of the fundamental soundness of its position, that success should not be attributed, in any degree, to its counsel's unrestrained and unnecessary use of the bold, underline, and 'all caps' functions of word processing or his repeated use of exclamation marks to emphasize points in his briefs." *B.A.M. Development, L.L.C. v. Salt Lake County*, 87 P.3d 710, 734 n.30 (Utah App. 2004) (Orme, J., dissenting).

Although legal authorities should be cited in support of the arguments made in the brief, string citations should be avoided. The judge and law clerk reading the motion papers only have a limited amount of time to devote to those papers. Rather than force the reader to go through citation after citation establishing a single, perhaps self-evident, proposition, get right to the point. Page limitations contained in local rules of court may require counsel to file brief briefs.[39] However, if the brief refers to judicial opinions or other authorities that may not be readily available to other counsel or the court, copies of this material should be submitted with the motion.[40]

The focus in the written motion papers should be on the major points upon which the motion turns. If there is a subsidiary point that must be addressed, it may be possible to handle this in a footnote. The major arguments of the opposing party should be confronted in the brief, although this is best done after affirmatively establishing the strongest arguments in support of the motion. Ignoring the difficult issues raised by opposing counsel will not make them go away. If you have no answer to your opponent's arguments, you probably should not have filed the motion in the first place. In addition, attorneys are required to reveal to the court directly adverse legal authority within the controlling jurisdiction.[41]

Finally, the brief should have a concluding section. This conclusion should not be argumentative but should merely recite in a single sentence the relief requested. A possible conclusion to a summary judgment brief in the Buffalo Creek disaster litigation might read as follows:

CONCLUSION

For the above reasons, the defendant Pittston Corporation requests that its motion for summary judgment be granted and the plaintiffs' complaint be dismissed.

In addition to the motion brief or memorandum, counsel may need to draft supporting papers such as affidavits or declarations.[42] Affidavits should be sufficiently detailed so that their assertions are credible. This is especially important with respect to the background of the affiant. The affidavit should begin with a paragraph or two describing the witness's background, and then offer the witness's substantive testimony in sepa-

---

39. Civil Rule 7(e) of the United States District Court for the District of Columbia (memoranda of points and authorities not to exceed 45 pages and reply memoranda not to exceed 25 pages); Rule 7.1(c)(2) of the United States District Court for the Southern District of Florida (no brief or legal memorandum to exceed 20 pages, except for reply memoranda, which are not to exceed 10 pages). Totally apart from such local rules, there generally is a direct relationship between the effectiveness and the brevity of trial briefs.

40. *See* Rule 7.01(e)(5) of the United States District Court for the Middle District of Tennessee ("Citations to any federal or state court decisions or administrative opinions not reported in one of the publications of the West Publishing Company shall include Westlaw or Lexis citations and shall be accompanied by a copy of the entire text of the decision.").

41. Model Rules of Prof'l Responsibility Rule 3.3(a)(3).

42. Notarized affidavits are not required in the federal courts. Instead, witnesses can execute unsworn declarations under the penalty of perjury that conform to the requirements of 28 U.S.C. § 1746.

rately numbered paragraphs. Despite the need for specificity on important points, counsel should be aware of the discovery provided to opposing parties by motion affidavits. These documents should not be cluttered with information that is not pertinent to the present motion.

If a witness drafts his affidavit in the first instance, different drafts of the affidavit may be created as the attorney and witness decide upon the affidavit's final wording. These draft affidavits later may be sought in discovery. One way to avoid this problem is for the attorney to interview the witness and then read a draft affidavit to the witness over the telephone (making changes based on the witness's comments).

Federal Rule of Civil Procedure 10(c) provides, in part, that a statement in a pleading may be "adopted by reference" in a motion. If counsel intends to rely upon other documents (such as discovery responses pertinent to a motion for summary judgment), the material in question should be packaged so as to be the most accessible and persuasive to the court. Counsel should consider gathering all relevant affidavits, discovery responses, and other evidentiary material into an evidentiary appendix. If the supporting material is voluminous, this evidentiary appendix can include a table of contents and be tabbed so that the judge can easily find particular affidavits or portions of the pretrial record. Not only does the submission of an evidentiary appendix make the job of the judge and his law clerk easier, but it may ensure that they actually will consider the (presumably favorable) evidence supporting the motion.

The documents filed in support of a motion should be as concise as possible. Violators of this rule run the risk that the judge will not read their papers. There may be times, though, when it may be as important for a judge to see, as to actually read, the motion papers. If you are opposing a motion to compel discovery, why not create an evidentiary appendix binding together all of the voluminous discovery that already has been provided? The mere volume of papers filed in connection with a motion for summary judgment may suggest that "there's a genuine issue of material fact in there somewhere." The St. Louis Cardinals supposedly paid Dizzy Dean in silver dollars at one point in his career because he believed that he was getting more money that way.

Once the motion and all supporting papers have been prepared, they must be served upon other counsel and filed with the court.[43] In some courts, oral argument must be specifically requested at the time that the motion is filed.[44] If local rules or custom require the moving party to notice the motion for a particular day, it usually makes sense to contact opposing counsel to ensure that the motion day chosen is acceptable to

---

43. Federal Rule of Civil Procedure 5(a)(1)(D) provides that "a written motion, except one that may be heard ex parte" must be served on every party, while Rule 5(d)(1) provides that, except for certain specified disclosures and discovery requests and responses, "[a]ny paper after the complaint that is required to be served—together with a certificate of service—must be filed within a reasonable time after service." A certificate of service should be appended to the motion papers evidencing compliance with the above service requirements. *See* Chapter 5, *supra* p. 195.

44. Rule 7–1(d)(2) of the United States District Court for the District of Oregon; Rule 7.5(a) of the United States District Court for the Southern District of Indiana.

everyone. Other counsel may not even oppose the motion, which should be stated in the motion papers. Such a statement can be made in the caption of the motion: "Plaintiff Acme's Unopposed Motion to Amend the Complaint." Informed of the lack of opposition in this manner, the judge may grant the motion based on the written motion papers and not require counsel to appear for a hearing.

Care should be taken to ensure that the papers are served and filed in a timely manner. Not only are motion time periods set forth in local rules,[45] but Federal Rule of Civil Procedure 6(c) provides that written motions and any notice of motion and supporting affidavits "must be served at least 14 days before the time specified for the hearing," unless the motion may be heard ex parte or the court or another provision of the Federal Rules of Civil Procedure set a different time. Rule 6(d) gives counsel an extra three days to respond to papers that have been served by mail or electronically.[46] Pretrial scheduling orders also may limit the time period for filing pretrial motions.[47]

The written opposition to a motion should follow the same general form as that suggested for briefs filed in support of a motion. However, the argument section of the opposition may be different in structure from that of the brief filed in support of the motion. While the movant may have to establish multiple points in order to be entitled to the relief sought, the most forceful opposition will be one focused on the weakest elements of the movant's motion. Counsel also should consider submitting affidavits or other evidentiary material in opposition to the motions of other parties.

Finally, in many jurisdictions the moving party is entitled, or can seek the right, to file a reply brief.[48] Reply briefs should address matters raised for the first time in the papers filed in opposition to the motion rather than merely repeat the argument made in the initial motion papers. If a reply brief is filed on the eve of oral argument, counsel may want to

---

45. *E.g.*, Rule 7.1(a) of the United States District Court for the Eastern District of North Carolina ("All motions in civil cases except those relating to the admissibility of evidence at trial must be filed on or before thirty (30) days following the conclusion of the period of discovery."); Rule 7(F)(1) of the United States District Court for the Eastern District of Virginia (responsive briefs to be filed within 11 days after service of brief supporting motion).

46. Some attorneys have been known to use Rule 6 to cut down on the time opposing counsel have to respond to motions. If mail delivery usually takes less than 3 days, these attorneys serve papers by hand so that the additional three day response period of Rule 6(d) is not triggered; if, however, mail delivery takes more than 3 days, these attorneys are sure to serve opponents by mail. Because life is too short to play such games, the attorney should contact other counsel and suggest that all papers be served by a mutually agreeable method. If the parties agree to electronic service pursuant to Federal Rule of Civil Procedure 5(b)(2)(E), they all will have an additional three days to respond to court filings. Fed. R. Civ. P. 6(d).

Many attorneys still file papers with the clerk by hand (to ensure that the papers are properly filed) and serve opposing counsel by mail. If opposing counsel follows this pattern, it may be possible to obtain copies of important motions from the clerk's office before they arrive in the office mail. It's also not a bad idea to periodically check the clerk's docket sheet to make sure that no motions or orders have been filed that you have not received.

47. *See* Fed. R. Civ. P. 16(b)(3)(A).

48. Rule 7.1.2(b) of the United States District Court for the District of Delaware; Rule 7.1(c) of the United States District Court for the Eastern District of Tennessee.

assure that the judge actually receives the brief by having a copy delivered to chambers in addition to filing the brief with the clerk's office. It's disheartening, to say the least, to have a judge state during argument that he hasn't seen your most recent brief because it still is in the clerk's office.

Exercises Concerning Written Motions

1. As in exercise 2 of the Exercises Concerning Motion Strategy, *supra* p. 489, presume that plaintiff Thomas Eakins filed a motion for partial summary judgment on the issue of liability twenty days after the commencement of his action. The motion is based upon public statements by officials of the Pittston and Buffalo Mining Companies, governmental investigations of the disaster, and public documents showing that the Pittston Company is the sole shareholder of Buffalo Mining.

    (a) Draft a short responsive memorandum on behalf of the Pittston Company, making reasonable assumptions as to the factual background of the case and the specific bases of plaintiff's motion;

    (b) Draft a proposed order to accompany Pittston's memorandum; and

    (c) If you believe that it would be to your client's advantage, draft a motion requesting oral argument on plaintiff's motion.

2. Presume that the Pittston Company has been sued in the United States District Court for the Southern District of West Virginia by (1) approximately 600 victims of the Buffalo Creek disaster in a suit brought by attorney Gerald Stern and (2) in an individual action brought by Thomas Eakins. Presume also that it is the spring of 1974, discovery in these cases has been consolidated, and this discovery is nearing completion.

Judge Hall is about to schedule the cases for trial, and has asked for counsel's suggestions. Counsel for Thomas Eakins wants Eakins's suit to be tried before those of the plaintiffs in Gerald Stern's action. Gerald Stern believes that Eakins's claims are not as strong as those of the plaintiffs whom he represents, and he does not want Eakins's suit to be among the first claims tried. Counsel for the Pittston Company agrees with Gerald Stern about the strength of the various claims and would like for Eakins's case to go to trial first.

    (a) As counsel for Thomas Eakins, draft a motion asking the court to schedule Eakins's case for trial before the claims of the plaintiffs in Gerald Stern's action;

    (b) As co-counsel to Gerald Stern, respond to the motion of Thomas Eakins;

    (c) As counsel for the Pittston Company, respond to the motion of Thomas Eakins.

3. You represent Buddy's Markets in a federal diversity action filed against it in the United States District Court for the District of Vermont by Charles Cullen, a citizen of New Jersey. While Cullen's complaint correctly alleges that Buddy's Markets has its principal place of business in Vermont, Buddy's is incorporated in New Jersey.

(a) Write a short memorandum describing the actions that you would take on behalf of Buddy's Markets;

(b) Draft the motion or motions that you would file on behalf of Buddy's Markets; and

(c) Draft a proposed order to accompany each motion that you have prepared, as well as any other appropriate motion papers.

IV. MOTION ARGUMENT

The oral argument of any motion will depend to a great extent upon the motion practice within the particular jurisdiction.[49] In some jurisdictions, pretrial motions are not argued unless the court so orders. In other jurisdictions, virtually every motion must be presented to a judge at a weekly "motion day."[50] Local rules of court and the policies of individual judges must be checked in developing a motion argument strategy.[51]

Despite the variations in motion practice from jurisdiction to jurisdiction, some general considerations concerning the argument of motions are addressed in this section. After this initial general advice, the more specific oral argument suggestions of John W. Davis are set forth.

A. GENERAL CONSIDERATIONS CONCERNING ORAL ARGUMENT

Successful oral argument hinges not only upon what attorneys do and say within the courtroom but also upon their advance preparation for the motion hearing.

1. Preparation for the Oral Argument

Before even going to the courthouse, it's a good idea to telephone the motion judge's docket or scheduling clerk to ensure that the motion is set

---

49. For examples of the different ways in which motions are handled by federal district judges see P. Connolly & P. Lombard, *Judicial Controls and the Civil Litigative Process: Motions* (1980); Devitt, "Effective Judicial Management of Motion Practice," 91 F.R.D. 153 (1981); Steckler, "Motions Prior to Trial," 29 F.R.D. 299 (1961).

50. Federal Rule of Civil Procedure 78(a) provides: "A court may establish regular times and places for oral hearings on motions." However, Rule 78(b) further provides: "By rule or order, the court may provide for submitting and determining motions on briefs, without oral hearings."

51. For instance, some judges handle motion hearings over the telephone. *E.g.*, Rule 7–1(d)(3) of the United States District Court for the District of Oregon; Schwarzer, "Guidelines for Discovery, Motion Practice and Trial," 117 F.R.D. 273, 279 (1987). Telephone hearings can save the court and counsel both time and the expense of travel to the courthouse. If the motion is important, counsel should request that the judge's court reporter be present in chambers to transcribe the hearing and the court's ruling.

for argument. In some courts oral argument must be specifically requested, while some judges grant motions prior to scheduled argument, particularly if the motion is uncontested. If the motion is set on a "motion day"
on which many motions will be heard by the court, a clerk may be able to
estimate when the motion actually will be called and thus spare attorneys
time otherwise spent waiting at the courthouse.[52]

Presuming that the motion will be heard, what should the attorney
take to the oral argument?[53] The attorney's case file, containing the
pleadings and other documents that have been filed with the court, should
be brought to any court appearance. If there are numerous documents
pertaining to the motion, it may make sense to tab or otherwise organize
the material so that counsel can quickly locate particular documents
during the argument.

A few extra copies of the motion itself should be brought to court. In
addition, counsel may want to have with her copies of any significant
cases, statutes, or other authorities upon which her motion rests. While
some judges may send their law clerks to fetch relevant volumes of the
Federal Reporter System, other judges may not read the authorities upon
which you rely unless you offer copies to them. Having copies of relevant
authorities handy may be particularly important if they are very recent or
are from a loose leaf service or another source to which the judge may not
have ready access. In fact, if such authorities are cited in the written brief
or memorandum submitted in connection with the motion, copies of them
should be appended to that document.

Some notes or an outline of the motion argument should be brought
to court. During the argument it's important that counsel engage in a
conversation with the judge, rather than attempt to impress the court
with her reading ability. Nevertheless, a short outline of the argument,
perhaps including the key supporting authorities, can be used as a check
list to ensure that all the important points are made. An outline also may
lead to a better oral argument by increasing the confidence of the
attorney, and the very process of preparing the outline should result in a
well-organized argument.

Counsel should try to avoid giving her oral argument for the very first
time at the motion hearing. She may practice the argument herself,

---

52. In some jurisdictions motions may not be called in a strictly random order on motion days,
and clerks may be willing to schedule particular motions to accommodate attorneys' scheduling
conflicts. At one time some clerks used other systems for determining the order in which cases
were called. There is a story about a young attorney who gave the clerk $20.00 so that his case
would be called at the beginning of the motion day. However, the attorney's motion was not
called despite the passage of much of the morning. The attorney therefore spoke to the clerk at a
break, asking why his motion had not been called. The clerk replied, "Why, we're still on the
$50.00 motions."

53. One thing that counsel may *not* want to have with her at the oral argument is her client.
Clients should be informed about motion hearings and should be permitted to attend these
hearings if they insist. However, the presence of the client may distract counsel from the hearing.
Some attorneys also tend to dramatize their arguments or otherwise play to their clients in a way
that they would not if their clients were not present. It's also possible that the judge may direct
questions to a client who is present in the courtroom or that opposing counsel may overhear a
chance remark by the client that will be useful in opposing that client's cause.

possibly using an audio or video recorder. An even better way to prepare for significant motion arguments is to have a moot court before other attorneys. Practicing important motion arguments before lay persons (such as a spouse or non-attorney friend) also may be helpful, especially if the "judge" of such a moot court asks pertinent questions. Moot courts can help counsel avoid becoming tied to a memorized script and instead develop the ability to address the actual concerns expressed by the judge.

2. Structure of the Oral Argument

The oral argument should not merely parrot the written brief point by point. Instead, oral argument should be focused on the most important issues raised by the motion. One of the most significant constraints upon any oral argument is the limited amount of time for argument. Counsel cannot plan to "save the best" of her argument for last. Attorneys should get to the bottom line of their arguments quickly.[54]

There should be a logical structure to the oral argument. Counsel generally begin an argument with an introductory statement such as "May it please the court, my name is Clarence Darrow and I'm appearing here today on behalf of the plaintiff, John Jones." Such an introductory statement should be modified to fit the circumstances of the particular case and motion. This formal an opening would not be given by an attorney who appears regularly before a judge or in a case in which the judge has heard numerous other recent motions.

After an introductory statement, counsel should raise and answer the main issue presented by the pending motion. For example:

> The issue posed by Mr. Jones's motion for a protective order is whether he should be required to respond to defendant's sixth set of interrogatories. We submit that he should not be required to answer these interrogatories. Mr. Jones already has answered over 100 defense interrogatories, and requiring him to answer still more interrogatories at this time would delay the trial date set by your honor.

The relevant facts then should be briefly stated. Such a factual statement should encompass both the nature of the case and of the motion that is before the court. The length of the factual statement will depend upon the judge's familiarity with the case, and counsel should carefully listen to, and watch, the judge for signals that the factual statement should be shortened.

After laying out the facts, counsel should develop in appropriate detail the reasons why the motion should or should not be granted. While this is the actual motion "argument," the statements of the issue and of the facts should have been developed so that the judge is predisposed in counsel's favor before the argument even begins.

---

54. It's also important to have an idea prior to the hearing as to how much time will be allotted for oral argument. If the time for argument is clearly insufficient, counsel may wish to request additional time before the day of the hearing.

Because counsel are communicating orally, the argument must be laid out more simply than it was in the written briefs. The judge can be referred to the briefs concerning secondary issues or for more detailed treatment of an issue than seems merited in the oral argument: "On page nine of our brief we have cited the many cases supporting this portion of our argument, and we'll rely upon the brief concerning this issue unless the court has questions." The oral argument should focus on the most important issues raised by the motion.

What are the "most important issues raised by the motion?" While this question must be answered on a case-by-case basis, the most important issues usually are those upon which a party must prevail in order to be successful on the motion. In certain cases, however, counsel also may be wise to focus upon those particular issues about which the judge seems most skeptical or those issues that are not self-explanatory or that were not adequately covered in the written briefs.

Arguments in the trial court generally should stress the facts and interweave the facts with the major legal arguments. Both factual and legal analogies may make counsel's position more easily understood by the judge. It's also important for the judge to understand just how the present motion fits within the case and the case proceedings to date. Depending upon the nature of the motion, counsel may wish to consider the use of visual aids during the argument (or the inclusion of these items in the supporting motion papers). The facts underlying a motion may be more easily understood if there are maps of the scene of the accident, photographs of the accident site, or a chart summarizing data relevant to the motion.[55]

At the end of the argument, counsel should close with a sentence or two summarizing her position for the court. For example:

> Your honor, Mr. Jones should not be required to answer still more defense interrogatories at this late stage of the case. He already has answered over 100 of defendant's interrogatories. The trial in this action should not be delayed so that the defendant can obtain still more interrogatory answers. We therefore ask you to grant Mr. Jones the protective order that he seeks.

3. Dealing With Opposing Counsel and the Court

The oral argument may be the first opportunity to deal directly with certain positions of opposing counsel and the concerns of the judge who will decide the motion. While the major arguments of opposing counsel should be addressed head-on, be sure that the argument is focused upon

---

55. Such information can be presented to the court in several ways. The material can be attached to and authenticated by affidavits submitted in connection with the motion or by the testimony of witnesses taken at the motion hearing pursuant to Rule 43(c). Opposing counsel may be willing to stipulate to the authenticity of a map, document, or physical object for the purposes of the motion hearing. Finally, material may be used at the motion hearing as demonstrative or illustrative evidence without being moved into evidence.

the opponent's factual and legal positions rather than on the opponent herself.

Counsel always should be willing to concede points that they cannot in good faith dispute. Debaters' points are not awarded during oral argument. Concessions concerning non-essential points will leave more time to deal with the points on which a motion hinges. In addition, counsel's credibility with the court will be enhanced by an honest admission that a particular argument does not support her client. Counsel can focus the oral argument by making explicit at the outset the matters that are not in dispute: "Your honor, we do not take issue with plaintiff's assertions that X, Y, and Z are true. Where we part company with plaintiff is when he contends that he can establish A, B, and C."

Not only may oral argument give counsel the chance to directly deal with the positions of opposing counsel, but argument should provide counsel with the unique opportunity to deal directly with the concerns of the judge. Counsel should be certain to focus upon and directly address all of the concerns that the judge raises. Oral argument would serve little purpose if the attorneys and judge did not engage one another during the argument. Counsel should not only respond forthrightly to all of the judge's questions, but should encourage questions. This often can be done by maintaining eye contact with the judge and pausing at important parts of the argument.

Some judges will be thoroughly prepared for oral argument, while other judges may have done little in the way of advance preparation. Counsel should attempt to draw out a judge early in the argument to determine how familiar she is with the case, the present motion, and the authorities upon which the parties rely. Premising an oral argument upon an incorrect assumption about the extent of the judge's preparation can be a mistake that the attorney very quickly will regret.

Judges' practices in ruling upon pretrial motions vary greatly. Particularly with dispositive motions or motions that are somewhat complex, the judge may "take the matter under advisement" after the oral argument and issue a written order and decision at a later time. Other judges may rule from the bench at the conclusion of the oral argument. Still other judges may announce a "provisional ruling" at the very outset of the argument, which ruling becomes the basis for the ensuing oral argument.

Sometimes judges' oral rulings are not as clear as they might be. In this situation, it may be necessary for counsel to seek clarification of the ruling. The judge may have said that he was denying a motion to compel discovery based upon an understanding that certain discovery would be provided voluntarily. If there are questions about the discovery that is to be provided or when it is to be provided, it may make sense to raise those questions while counsel are still before the judge. Later disputes between counsel about what the judge said may be resolved by a transcript of the hearing, which court reporters will be happy to produce for a fee. If the transcript does not resolve the ambiguity in the court's ruling, a motion for clarification may have to be filed with the court.

In some jurisdictions counsel (usually prevailing counsel) will be asked to draft a written order reflecting the court's ruling. While this may seem like a burdensome chore, counsel should be happy with such an assignment (and, in fact, should volunteer to draft the order if that seems appropriate). While the attorney drafting the order must remain faithful to the judge's ruling, it is best to attempt to (fairly) resolve any ambiguities yourself in the first instance.

The Scout motto "Be Prepared" is excellent advice for the attorney attending a motion hearing. Some judges will use a motion hearing to monitor the progress of a case. The judge might ask about the status of discovery, set dates for the close of discovery or for trial, or question counsel about attempts at settlement. The judge also might invite argument on pending motions other than the one actually set for argument.

Before attending any motion hearing, counsel should be thoroughly familiar with all aspects of the case and carefully consider any matters that the judge might raise at the hearing. The attorney's personal calendar always should be brought to court appearances. Counsel should be prepared for a great amount of informal give-and-take with the judge and other counsel at the hearing.

Despite the most thorough preparation, attorneys sometimes are asked questions at oral argument that they had not anticipated. If counsel is not satisfied with her immediate response to an unexpected question, some judges may permit the filing of a supplemental brief after the argument. The best course, however, is to prepare thoroughly before the hearing to reduce the likelihood that the judge will ask a question that has not been anticipated.

B. ADVICE ON ORAL ARGUMENT FROM A MASTER ADVOCATE

John W. Davis is considered by many to be one of the finest advocates that this nation has produced. Davis served in the United States House of Representatives, as Solicitor General, and ran as the Democratic nominee for President in 1924. He argued more cases in the United States Supreme Court than any lawyer since Daniel Webster. The following address by Davis to the Association of the Bar of the City of New York is one of the classic statements concerning oral argument. Although the speech is entitled "The Argument of an Appeal," virtually all of the excerpted portions of the address contain good advice for oral argument in trial, as well as in appellate, courts.

DAVIS, "THE ARGUMENT OF AN APPEAL"[56]

In the old days, when not only courts but lawyers and litigants are reputed to have had more time at their disposal, similar feats [involving extended oral argument] were performed at the American Bar. It has been stated, for instance, that the arguments of Webster, Luther Martin and their colleagues in *McCulloch v. Maryland* consumed six days, while in the *Girard* will case Webster, Horace Binney and others, for ten whole days assailed the listening ears of the Court.

Those days have gone forever; and partly because of the increased tempo of our times, partly because of the increase of work in our appellate tribunals, the argument of an appeal, whether by voice or pen, is hedged about today by strict limitations of time and an increasing effort to provoke an economy of space. The rules of nearly every court give notice that there is a limit to what the judicial ear or the judicial eye is prepared to absorb. Sometimes the judges plead, sometimes they deplore, sometimes they command. The bar is continuously besought to speak with an eye on the clock and to write with a cramped pen.

Observing this duty of condensation and selection I propose tonight to direct my remarks primarily to the oral argument. I begin after the briefs have all been filed; timely filed of course, for in this matter lawyers are never, hardly ever, belated. I shall assume that these briefs are models of brevity, are properly indexed, and march with orderly logic from point to point; not too little nor yet too much on any topic, even though in a painful last moment of proof-reading many an appealing paragraph has been offered as a reluctant sacrifice on the altar of condensation.

I assume also that the briefs are not overlarded with long quotations from the reported opinions, no matter how pat they seem; nor over-crowded with citations designed it would seem to certify to the industry of the brief-maker rather than to fortify the argument. * * *

I assume further that they are not defaced by *supras* or *infras* or by a multiplicity of footnotes which, save in the rare case where they are needed to elucidate the text, do nothing but distract the attention of the reader and interrupt the flow of reasoning. And I remark in passing that these are no more laudable in a judge's opinion than they are in a lawyer's brief.

I assume that there is not a pestilent "and/or" to be found in the brief from cover to cover; or if there is, that the court, jealous of our mother-tongue, will stamp upon the base intruder.

And finally I assume as of course that there has been no cheap effort to use variety in type to supply the emphasis that well constructed sentences should furnish for themselves. It may be taken as axiomatic that even judges, when they are so disposed, can read understandingly; and I should think that where the pages of a brief begin conversationally

---

56. 26 *A.B.A.J.* 895 (1940). Reprinted with permission from the December 1940 issue of the *ABA Journal*, the Lawyer's Magazine, published by the American Bar Association.

in small pica, nudge the reader's elbow with repeated italics, rise to a higher pitch with whole paragraphs of the text—not mere headings—in black letter, and finally shout in full capitals (and such have been observed), the judge might well consider that what was a well intentioned effort to attract his attention was in reality a reflection of his intelligence.

So it is with our briefs brought to this state of approximate perfection that we approach our oral argument. * * *

   * * *

Professing no special fitness for the task, I have ventured * * * to frame a decalogue by which such arguments should be governed. There is no mystical significance to the number ten, although it has respectable precedent; and those who think the number short and who wish to add to the roll when I have finished, have my full permission to do so.

At the head of the list I place, where it belongs, the cardinal rule of all, namely:

(1) Change places (in your imagination of course) with the Court.

   * * *

[T]hose who sit in solemn array before you, whatever their merit, know nothing whatever of the controversy that brings you to them, and are not stimulated to interest in it by any feeling of friendship or dislike to anyone concerned. They are not moved as perhaps an advocate may be by any hope of reward or fear of punishment. They are simply being called upon for action in their appointed sphere. They are anxiously waiting to be supplied with what Mr. Justice Holmes called the "implements of decision." These by your presence you profess yourself ready to furnish. If the places were reversed and you sat where they do, think what it is you would want first to know about the case. How and in what order would you want the story told? How would you want the skein unravelled? What would make easier your approach to the true solution? These are questions the advocate must unsparingly put to himself. This is what I mean by changing places with the Court.

If you happen to know the mental habits of any particular judge, so much the better. To adapt yourself to his methods of reasoning is not artful, it is simply elementary psychology; as is also the maxim not to tire or irritate the mind you are seeking to persuade. And I may say in passing that there is no surer way to irritate the mind of any listener than to speak in so low a voice or with such indistinct articulation or in so monotonous a tone as to make the mere effort at hearing an unnecessary burden.

I proceed to Rule No. 2—

(2) State first the nature of the case and briefly its prior history.

Every Appellate Court has passing before it a long procession of cases that come from manifold and diverse fields of the law and human experience. Why not tell the Court at the outset to which of these fields its attention is about to be called? If the case involves the construction of a will, the settlement of a partnership, a constitutional question or whatever it may be, the judge is able as soon as the general topic is mentioned to call to his aid, consciously or unconsciously, his general knowledge and experience with that particular subject. It brings what is to follow into immediate focus. * * *

Next in order—

(3) State the facts.

If I were disposed to violate the rule I have previously announced against emphasis by typography, I would certainly employ at this point the largest capital type. For it cannot be too often emphasized that in an appellate court the statement of the facts is not merely a part of the argument, it is more often than not the argument itself. A case well stated is a case far more than half argued. Yet how many advocates fail to realize that the ignorance of the court concerning the facts in the case is complete, even where its knowledge of the law may adequately satisfy the proverbial presumption. The court wants above all things to learn what are the facts which give rise to the call upon its energies; for in many, probably in most, cases when the facts are clear there is no great trouble about the law. *Ex facto oritur jus,* and no court ever forgets it.

    * * *

Of course there are statements and statements. No two men probably would adopt an identical method of approach. Uniformity is impossible, probably undesirable. Safe guides, however, are to be found in the three C's—chronology, candor and clarity: Chronology, because that is the natural way of telling any story, stringing the events on the chain of time just as all human life itself proceeds; candor, the telling of the worst as well as the best, since the court has the right to expect it, and since any lack of candor, real or apparent, will wholly destroy the most careful argument; and clarity, because that is the supreme virtue in any effort to communicate thought from man to man. It admits of no substitute. There is a sentence of Daniel Webster's which should be written on the walls of every law school, court room and law office: "The power of clear statement" said he, "is the great power at the bar." Purple passages can never supply its absence. And of course I must add that no statement of the facts can be considered as complete unless it has been so framed and delivered as to show forth the essential merit, in justice and in right of your client's cause.

(4) State next the applicable rules of law on which you rely.

If the statement of facts has been properly done the mind of the court will already have sensed the legal questions at issue, indeed they may have been hinted at as you proceed. These may be so elementary and well established that a mere allusion to them is sufficient. On the other hand, they may lie in the field of divided opinion where it is necessary to expound them at greater length and to dwell on the underlying reasons that support one or the other view. It may be that in these days of what is apparently waning health on the part of our old friend *Stare Decisis,* one can rely less than heretofore upon the assertion that the case at bar is governed by such-and-such a case, volume and page. Even the shadow of a long succession of governing cases may not be adequate shelter. In any event the advocate must be prepared to meet any challenge to the doctrine of the cases on which he relies and to support it by original reasoning. Barren citation is a broken reed. What virtue it retains can be left for the brief.

(5) Always "go for the jugular vein."

I do not know from what source I quote that phrase but it is of course familiar. Rufus Choate's expression was "the hub of the case." More often than not there is in every case a cardinal point around which lesser points revolve like planets around the sun, or even as dead moons around a planet; a central fortress which if strongly held will make the loss of all the outworks immaterial. The temptation is always present to "let no guilty point escape" in the hope that if one hook breaks another may hold. Yielding to this temptation is pardonable perhaps in a brief, of which the court may read as much or as little as it chooses. There minor points can be inserted to form "a moat defensive to a wall." But there is no time and rarely any occasion in oral argument for such diversions.

I think in this connection of one of the greatest lawyers, and probably the greatest case winner of our day, the late John G. Johnson of Philadelphia. He was a man of commanding physical presence and of an intellect equally robust. Before appellate courts, he addressed himself customarily to but a single point, often speaking for not more than twenty minutes but with compelling force. When he had concluded it was difficult for his adversary to persuade the court that there was anything else worthy to be considered. This is the quintessence of the advocate's art.

(6) Rejoice when the Court asks questions.

And again I say unto you, rejoice! If the question does nothing more it gives you assurance that the court is not comatose and that you have awakened at least a vestigial interest. Moreover a question affords you your only chance to penetrate the mind of the court, unless you are an expert in face reading, and to dispel a doubt as soon as it arises. This you should be able to do if you know your case and have a sound position. If the question warrants a negative answer, do not fence with it but respond with a bold *thwertutnay*—which for the benefit of the illiterate I may explain as a term used in ancient pleading to signify a downright No. While if the answer is in the affirmative or calls for a concession the Court will be equally gratified to have the matter promptly disposed of. If you value your argumentative life do not evade or shuffle or postpone, no matter how embarrassing the question may be or how much it interrupts the thread of your argument. Nothing I should think would be more irritating to an inquiring court than to have refuge taken in the familiar evasion "I am coming to that" and then to have the argument end with the promise unfulfilled. If you are really coming to it indicate what your answer will be when it is reached and never, never sit down until it is made.

* * *

[C]hief Justice Denison of the Supreme Court of Colorado puts the matter thus:

> "A perfect argument would need no interruption and a perfect Judge would never interrupt it; but we are not perfect. If the argument ... discusses the truth of the first chapter of Genesis when the controlling issue is the constitutionality of a Tennessee statute it ought to be interrupted ... It is the function of the Court to decide the case and to decide it properly ... The Judge knows where his doubts lie, at which point he wishes to be enlightened; it is he whose mind at last must be made up, no one can do it for him, and he must take his own course of thought to accomplish it. Then he must sometimes interrupt."

* * *

(7) Read sparingly and only from necessity.

The eye is the window of the mind, and the speaker does not live who can long hold the attention of any audience without looking it in the face. There is something about a sheet of paper interposed between speaker and listener that walls off the mind of the latter as if it were boiler-plate. It obstructs the passage of thought as the lead plate bars the X-rays. I realize that I am taking just this risk at present, but this is not a speech or an argument, only, God save the mark, a lecture.

Of course where the case turns upon the language of a statute or the terms of a written instrument it is necessary that it should be read, always, if possible, with a copy in the hands of the court so that the eye of the court may supplement its ear. But the reading of lengthy extracts from the briefs or from reported cases or long excerpts from the testimony can only be described as a sheer waste of time. With this every appellate court of my acquaintance agrees. A sentence here or a sentence there, perhaps, if sufficiently pertinent and pithy, but not I beg of you print by the paragraph or page.

There is a cognate fault of which most of us from time to time are guilty. This arises when we are seeking to cite or distinguish other cases bearing on our claims and are tempted into a tedious recital of the facts in the cited case, not uncommonly prefaced by the somewhat awkward phrase "That was a case where," etc. Now the human mind is a pawky thing and must be held to its work and it is little wonder after three or four or half a dozen such recitals that not only are the recited facts forgotten but those in the case at bar become blurred and confused. What the advocate needs most of all is that his facts and his alone should stand out stark, simple, unique, clear.

(8) Avoid personalities.

This is a hard saying, especially when one's feelings are ruffled by a lower court or by opposing counsel, but none the less it is worthy of all acceptation, both in oral argument and in brief. I am not speaking merely of the laws of courtesy that must always govern an honorable profession, but rather of the sheer inutility of personalities as a method of argument in a judicial forum. Nor am I excluding proper comment on things that deserve reprobation. I am thinking psychologically again. It is all a question of keeping the mind of the court on the issues in hand without distraction from without.

One who criticizes unfairly or harshly the action of a lower court runs the risk of offending the quite understandable *esprit du corps* of the judicial body. Rhetorical denunciation of opposing litigants or witnesses may arouse a measure of sympathy for the persons so denounced. While controversies between counsel impose on the court the wholly unnecessary burden and annoyance of preserving order and maintaining the decorum of its proceedings. Such things can irritate, they can never persuade.

(9) Know your record from cover to cover.

This commandment might properly have headed the list for it is the *sine qua non* of all effective argument. You have now reached a point in the litigation where you can no longer hope to supply the want of preparation by lucky accidents or mental agility. You will encounter no more unexpected surprises. You have your last chance to win for your client. It is clear therefore that the field tactics of the trial table will no longer serve and the time has come for major strategy based upon an accurate knowledge of all that has occurred. At any moment you may be called on to correct some misstatement of your adversary and at any moment you may confront a question from the Court which, if you are able to answer by an apt reference to the record or with a firm reliance on a well-furnished memory, will increase the confidence with which the Court will listen to what else you may have to say. Many an argument otherwise admirable has been destroyed because of counsel's inability to make just such a response.

(10) Sit down.

This is the tenth and last commandment. In preparing for argument you will no doubt have made an outline carefully measured by the time at your command. The notes of it which you should have jotted down lie before you on the reading desk. When you have run through this outline and are satisfied that the court has fully grasped your contentions, what else is there left for you to do? You must be vain indeed to hope that by further speaking you can dragoon the Court into a prompt decision in your favor. The mere fact that you have an allotted time of one hour more or less does not constitute a contract with the Court to listen for that length of time. On the contrary, when you round out your argument and sit down before your time has expired, a benevolent smile overspreads the faces on the bench and a sigh of relief and gratification arises from your brethren at the bar who have been impatiently waiting for the moment when the angel might again trouble the waters of the healing pool and permit them to step in. Earn these exhibitions of gratitude therefore whenever you decently can, and leave the rest to Zeus and his colleagues, that is to say, to the judges on high Olympus.

Exercises Concerning Motion Argument

1. The following is one portion of a transcript of oral argument held in the Buffalo Creek litigation on May 16, 1973.

Prince v. Pittston, Civil Action No. 3052–HN (S.D.W.Va.) Proceedings Of May 16, 1973, Pp. 2–7.

THE COURT: Prince and others versus the Pittston Company. There are several matters for consideration by the Court at this time. The Court would request counsel in addressing themselves to the questions as presented to limit any argument to not more than ten minutes on any one point and less if practicable, so the first matter that I see for consideration is the motion of the plaintiffs to file an amended complaint and to add parties. Is there any objection to that seriously?

MR. STAKER: Your Honor, the defendant has no objection to the motion to amend the complaint or to add additional plaintiffs so long as it be with the understanding that the grant of such motion shall not be in any manner prejudicial to the rights and the defenses, as they may be, of the defendant, in light of the fact that the additions are made at this juncture.

THE COURT: The motion is granted.

The second matter that the Court has noted for discussion and consideration concerns the defendant's objections to the plaintiffs' more definite statement. There are several matters that are to be considered in connection with that. The plaintiffs' more definite statement is quite voluminous but as to one point raised, a sampling taken by the Court indicates that the state of residence of plaintiffs is set forth in the particular statement and can be ascertained readily by the defendant.

If that isn't true, I'll listen to any specifics about it but it seems to me if you read those statements, each one of them tells at the end of the first paragraph where the plaintiff resides. Is that not true?

MR. STAKER: It is in the main, your Honor, but there are instances which were the basis for the objection that are reflected or exemplified, for example, in a statement that some plaintiffs have moved to Kentucky.

THE COURT: That's right.

MR. STAKER: And it is not apparent from the standpoint of what we regarded as the concise statement required in such a pleading with reference to diversity to know from the face of the pleading whether they were saying they were Kentucky residents or West Virginia residents or what.

THE COURT: What is the defendant's place of business?

MR. STAKER: The defendant's place of business is—it is a corporation with its principal offices in New York City.

THE COURT: Is there any question that any plaintiff might be a resident of New York?

MR. STAKER: That we don't know.

THE COURT: In the sampling I looked at it seemed clear that there might be some question like you say, but there still would be no question on diversity of citizenship that I could note. If there is any question about that in any case, if the defense will point it out I am sure the plaintiffs will give a specific place of residence. So that will take care of that part of it.

Another point that came up had to do with the special damages. In the amended complaint except for funeral expenses it appears that the plaintiffs have dropped the item of special damages. Is that not true, Mr. Shay?

MR. SHAY: Your Honor, we have had difficulty with this question of defining precisely what may be special damages. We do not intend by whatever was done in the more definite statement to drop whatever may be called special damages, anticipating that the interrogatories which have recently been received and are in the process of being answered, that specific dollar amounts applicable to what may be called special damages, such as medical expenses and the like, will be covered in those interrogatories. We do not intend to drop any claims for special damages, your Honor.

* * *

THE COURT: * * * What is the defendant's position on this point?

MR. MURDOCK: Your Honor, the defendant's position is simply that that's what the federal rules require and that's what we moved for initially. Practically every group of plaintiffs in the initial complaint stated a specific dollar amount of special damages and the rules require that they be itemized by category and amount and we moved, and our motion was not opposed, and the same total figure is used in the amended complaint and special damages have vanished, so all we wanted was an itemization of what had been said to be special damages.

THE COURT: Under Rule 12(e)?

MR. MURDOCK: Yes, your Honor.

THE COURT: Do you have anything further to say about that, Mr. Shay?

MR. SHAY: I don't think it would help the Court or counsel to discuss whether there has to be a categorization and identification of amount. Certainly there has to be an itemization of the types of special damages.

THE COURT: Yes, sir.

MR. SHAY: And to the extent that counsel for the defendant may not be advised of what items of special damages as against amounts of special damages may have been incurred by these plaintiffs, we can either amend again or in the answers to interrogatories they seek this information, quite properly, very specifically, and that's where we think the office of this discovery technique aptly applies.

Notice pleading is a term of art that we understand applies to complaint practice in the federal courts and I think that their interrogatories, which I say are quite proper and which is the way this information should be sought, dollar by dollar, would serve that function if the Court were so minded to permit us to proceed in that fashion. It would be awfully easy—

THE COURT: Have interrogatories already been served?

MR. SHAY: Yes, your Honor, they have.

THE COURT: And asking that specific information?

MR. SHAY: Yes, your Honor.

THE COURT: That ought to be good enough.

———

(a) Presume that you are one of plaintiffs' counsel in the Buffalo Creek litigation. In response to the request of Judge Hall, draft an order reflecting the rulings made at the May 16, 1973, hearing.

(b) Presume that you are one of the defense counsel in the Buffalo Creek litigation and that Judge Hall has asked you to draft an order reflecting his rulings at the May 16, 1973, hearing. Do so.

(c) Presume that you are one of the defense counsel in the Buffalo Creek litigation. Your senior partner has asked you to consider whether the Pittston Company should seek reconsideration of any of Judge Hall's May 16, 1973, rulings. Draft a memorandum containing your advice.

(d) Presume that you are one of plaintiffs' counsel in the Buffalo Creek litigation. You have been assigned to argue a series of non-dispositive motions before Judge K. K. Hall and, in preparation for your argument, you have reviewed the transcript of the May 16, 1973, hearing.

Write a critique of the May 16, 1973, argument, evaluating the performances of the judge, opposing counsel Zane Gray Staker and Daniel R. Murdock, and plaintiffs' attorney Willis O. Shay. Be sure to consider the manner in which, and the formality with which, Judge Hall presided at the argument. In light of what happened at this earlier argument, describe your plans concerning (1) preparation for your own oral argument and (2) the manner in which you actually will argue your own motions.

2. As in exercise 2 of the Exercises Concerning Motion Strategy, *supra* p. 489, presume that the plaintiff Thomas Eakins has filed a motion for partial summary judgment on the issue of liability twenty days after the commencement of his action against the Pittston Company. This motion is based upon the public statements of Pittston and Buffalo Mining officials, the governmental investigations of the disaster, and public documents showing that the Pittston Company is the sole shareholder of Buffalo Mining.

(a) As counsel for Thomas Eakins, draft the outline of the oral argument that you will give at the hearing on this motion and come to class prepared to argue the motion.

(b) As counsel for the Pittston Company, draft the outline of the oral argument that you will give at the hearing on this motion and come to class prepared to argue the motion.

3. The Pacific Lighting Corporation has been sued in a federal diversity action by Bigler Brothers, Inc. The complaint was filed by Bigler Brothers in the United States District Court for the District of Alaska and alleges state common law fraud claims against Pacific Lighting. During the course of discovery, the deposition of Michael Parker, a former employee of Pacific Lighting, was held. This is a portion of the deposition transcript:

Plaintiff's Counsel:	Can you describe your employment with Pacific Lighting?
Parker:	I worked for them as a first line supervisor until last September.
Plaintiff's Counsel:	Were you a part of their upper level management?
Parker:	No, not at all.
Plaintiff's Counsel:	Mr. Parker, have you ever talked with the attorneys for Pacific Lighting about this case?
Parker:	Yes, I was asked by Pacific's executive vice-president to talk to the company's general counsel about this case.
Plaintiff's Counsel:	Can you tell us what you told the general counsel?
Defense Counsel:	I invoke Pacific Lighting's attorney-client privilege and instruct the witness not to answer that question.

Based upon the instruction of Pacific Lighting's counsel, Michael Parker refused to answer the question about his conversation with Pacific's general counsel. Counsel for Bigler Brothers has filed a motion to compel an answer to her deposition question.

Assuming that there is no law in Alaska concerning the scope of the corporate attorney-client privilege, conduct the oral argument on the motion to compel on behalf of either plaintiff Bigler Brothers or defendant Pacific Lighting.

V. CONCLUSION

Pretrial motion practice requires the same attorney care, skill and resourcefulness that is required by pretrial litigation generally. Both advance planning and skillful execution are necessary to ensure pretrial motion success. However, motion practice differs from other aspects of the pretrial litigation process in at least two ways. As opposed to many other pretrial litigation tasks, counsel usually know, rather quickly, whether motion practice is successful or not; the judge rules on motions and successful counsel receive instant gratification in the form of court orders. Even more importantly, successfully briefing and arguing pretrial motions is almost always great fun. By following the suggestions in this chapter, motion practice should become even more successful and more fun.

VI. CHAPTER BIBLIOGRAPHY

Adler, "Pretrial Motion Practice," 32 *Trial Law. Guide* 405 (1988).

Bright, "The Ten Commandments of Oral Argument," 67 *A.B.A.J.* 1136 (1981).

Bright & Arnold, "Oral Argument? It May be Crucial!," *A.B.A.J.*, Sept. 1984, at 68.

Cagan, "Twelve Common Motion Practice Blunders in U.S. District Courts," *Trial Law. Q.*, Winter 1990, at 52.

P. Connolly & P. Lombard, *Judicial Controls and the Civil Litigative Process: Motions* (1980).

Devitt, "Effective Judicial Management of Motion Practice," 91 F.R.D. 153 (1981).

Edelstein, "The Ethics of Dilatory Motions Practice: Time for Change," 44 *Fordham L. Rev.* 1069 (1976).

Faruki, "The Practical Use of Motions to Structure a Complex Civil Case," 41 *Ohio St. L. J.* 107 (1980).

M. Fontham et al., *Persuasive Written and Oral Advocacy in Trial and Appellate Courts* (2d ed. 2007).

G. Gale & J. Moxley, *How to Write the Winning Brief* (1992).

Galbraith, "The Joy of Motion Practice," *Litigation*, Winter 1998, at 15.

B. Garner, *The Winning Brief* (2d ed. 2004).

B. Garner, *The Winning Oral Argument* (2009).

Hanson et al., "Telephone Hearings in Civil Trial Courts: What Do Attorneys Think?," 66 *Judicature* 408 (1983).

Hartje, "Pre–Trial Motions," 5 *Am. J. Trial Ad.* 15 (1981).

D. Herr et al., *Motion Practice* (4th ed. 2004).

Joanos, "A Few Suggestions to Beginning Lawyers Regarding Motions Hearings," 53 *Fla. B. J.* 438 (1979).

L. Jorgensen, *Motion Practice and Persuasion* (2006).

Larkins, "Oral Argument on Motions," *Litigation*, Winter 1997, at 16.

McElhaney, "Making the Most of Motions," *A.B.A.J.*, Feb. 1996, at 74.

McMahon, "How to Draft an Order," 13 *Clearinghouse Rev.* 858 (1980).

Motions in Federal Court (Lawyers Cooperative Publishing eds., 3d ed. 1996).

M. Murray & C. DeSanctis, *Adversarial Legal Writing and Oral Argument* (2006).

G. Peck, *Writing Persuasive Briefs* (1984).

E. Re & J. Re, *Brief Writing and Oral Argument* (9th ed. 2005).

Reilly, "Courtroom Advocacy," 8 *Cap.U. L. Rev.* 185 (1978).

Romano, "Motion Practice," *Trial,* Nov. 1987, at 93.

A. Scalia & B. Garner, *Making Your Case: The Art of Persuading Judges* (2008).

Stein, "Going Through the Motions," *Litigation,* Winter 1985, at 18.

CHAPTER 12

MOTIONS FOR SUMMARY JUDGMENT: "SOME OF THE BEST WITNESSES NEVER TESTIFY IN THE COURTROOM."

■ ■ ■

Summary judgment procedure is properly regarded not as a disfavored procedural shortcut, but rather as an integral part of the Federal Rules as a whole, which are designed "to secure the just, speedy and inexpensive determination of every action."

Celotex Corp. v. Catrett, 477 U.S. 317, 327 (1986), *quoting* Rule 1 of the Federal Rules of Civil Procedure.

The Fifth Circuit has traditionally been seen as so quick to reverse grants [of summary judgment] that one district judge * * * posted the sign, "No Spitting, No Summary Judgments."

Childress, "A New Era for Summary Judgments: Recent Shifts at the Supreme Court," 116 F.R.D. 183, 183 (1987).

Analysis

I. INTRODUCTION

The preceding chapter examined pretrial motion practice, including motion strategy, the written motion papers, and oral argument. While some of the common pretrial motions were discussed in Chapter 11, one very important motion was not: the Rule 56 motion for summary judgment. Although the summary judgment motion always has been a significant weapon in the pretrial litigator's arsenal, a trilogy of 1986 Supreme Court decisions focused renewed attention on summary judgment and its use to resolve cases prior to trial. Because of the increasing importance of summary judgment, it is the subject of the present chapter.

This chapter considers the most effective ways to utilize, and to defend against, the motion for summary judgment. After an initial decision is made to employ a Rule 56 motion, counsel must determine the scope and timing of the motion as well as the most persuasive evidentiary material with which to support the motion. Attorneys defending against summary judgment motions can focus on the moving party's failure to carry its summary judgment burden or otherwise comply with summary judgment requirements. These attorneys also can attempt to affirmatively structure the pretrial record to preclude summary judgment.

As with other pretrial motions, summary judgment motion strategy should be consistent with, and supportive of, a party's litigation theory and theme. Evidence should be sought in discovery that will be useful in seeking or defending against summary judgment. Counsel should look beyond any pending summary judgment motion and anticipate the next step in the litigation if summary judgment is denied. The motion for summary judgment can be an effective weapon in the pretrial process, both in shaping cases for trial and in disposing of cases at the pretrial stage.

II. THE GOVERNING LAW

In order to properly utilize, and defend against, summary judgment motions, counsel must be knowledgeable about the law governing these motions. Not only must attorneys be familiar with the basic requirements of Rule 56 of the Federal Rules of Civil Procedure, but they must be aware of judicial interpretations of, and proclivities toward, Rule 56 in order to effectively engage in summary judgment practice.

A. THE BASIC REQUIREMENTS OF RULE 56

Rule 56(b) of the Federal Rules of Civil Procedure provides: "Unless a different time is set by local rule or the court orders otherwise, a party may file a motion for summary judgment at any time until 30 days after the close of all discovery." Any party may move for summary judgment, and such judgment can be sought with respect to multiple claims or defenses, a single claim or defense, or a part of a claim or defense.[1]

Despite the fact that Rule 56(b) itself permits summary judgments to be filed "until 30 days after the close of discovery," in many cases local rules or a specific judge will establish a time table for the filing of

---

1. Fed. R. Civ. P. 56(a). While either plaintiffs or defendants can move for summary judgment, a study of 3 federal district courts found that over two-thirds of the summary judgment motions in the cases studied were filed by defendants. J. Cecil & C. Douglas, *Summary Judgment Practice in Three District Courts* 6 (1987) (Table 2).

summary judgment motions. Rule 16(c)(2)(E) lists as one of the subjects that may be discussed at a pretrial conference "the appropriateness and timing of summary adjudication under Rule 56." The Advisory Committee has recognized that "the potential use of Rule 56 is a matter that [often] arises from discussions during a [pretrial] conference. The court may then call for motions to be filed."[2] Counsel therefore should be ready to discuss summary judgment at pretrial conferences and should realize that the court may determine the timing of summary judgment motions at such conferences.

The two basic requirements for summary judgment are contained in Rule 56(a) of the Federal Rules of Civil Procedure. Rule 56(a) provides that the court "shall grant summary judgment if the movant shows that there is no genuine dispute as to any material fact and the movant is entitled to judgment as a matter of law." There is thus both a factual and a legal component to any summary judgment motion. If there are genuine disputes as to material facts, those disputes should be resolved at trial rather than on the paper record usually presented in connection with a summary judgment motion. Nor should summary judgment be granted if the governing law does not establish the moving party's right to judgment.

While summary judgment may be denied because of either factual or legal disputes, generally the real question posed by a summary judgment motion is whether there are any genuine disputes as to any material fact that require the action to be tried. This should not be surprising, because if there is no legal basis for an action the defendant usually will have sought dismissal in an earlier Rule 12(b)(6) motion. In addition, any party can seek judgment on the pleadings pursuant to Rule 12(c) to test the legal sufficiency of an opposing party's claims or defenses. In fact, if matters outside the pleadings are presented and considered in connection with a Rule 12(b)(6) or a Rule 12(c) motion, those motions are to be treated as Rule 56 motions for summary judgment.[3]

What, exactly, is a genuine dispute of material fact? First of all, only a dispute concerning a *material* fact is sufficient to preclude summary judgment. If there is no factual dispute concerning whether defendant's car struck plaintiff, summary judgment (at least as to liability) may be appropriate even though there is a factual dispute as to the exact speed at which the car was traveling. In this example, the dispute concerning the speed of defendant's car concerns a nonmaterial fact.

---

2. Advisory Committee Note to the 1993 Amendments to Rule 16, 146 F.R.D. 401, 604 (1993). The Advisory Committee also recognized that the addition of Rule 16(c)(11) to the Federal Rules (now, Rule 16(c)(2)(K)), explicitly permitting consideration of "disposing of pending motions" at pretrial conferences, "enables the court to rule on pending motions for summary adjudication that are ripe for decision at the time of the conference." 146 F.R.D. at 604. Indeed, the court can enter summary judgment in the absence of a motion. Rule 56(f) provides: "After giving notice and a reasonable time to respond, the court may: (1) grant summary judgment for a nonmovant; (2) grant the motion on grounds not raised by a party; or (3) consider summary judgment on its own after identifying for the parties material facts that may not be genuinely in dispute."

3. Fed. R. Civ. P. 12(d).

In order for a factual dispute to preclude summary judgment, not only must it be material, but the factual dispute must be *genuine*. The Supreme Court has noted that "summary judgment will not lie if the dispute about a material fact is 'genuine,' that is, if the evidence is such that a reasonable jury could return a verdict for the nonmoving party."[4] However, the "mere existence of a scintilla of evidence in support of the [party opposing summary judgment] will be insufficient" to preclude the entry of summary judgment.[5]

In determining whether a genuine dispute of material fact exists, the trial court must consider not only the parties' pleadings and discovery responses but also any summary judgment affidavits or declarations that may have been filed.[6] Federal Rule of Civil Procedure 56(c)(4) sets forth quite specific requirements for summary judgment affidavits and declarations. This Rule provides that these documents must be made on personal knowledge, set forth admissible facts, and show that the affiant or declarant is competent to testify on the matters stated in the affidavit or declaration.

Although the requirements of Rule 11 apply to summary judgment papers,[7] Rule 56(h) also specifically provides that sanctions may be imposed if summary judgment affidavits or declarations are "submitted in bad faith or solely for delay." While bad faith remains a prerequisite for the imposition of sanctions under Rule 56(h), Rule 11 requires that attorneys conduct an objectively reasonable factual and legal investigation prior to filing court papers.[8]

Rule 56(c) provides specific procedures for establishing the existence or non-existence of factual disputes. Rule 56(c)(1) provides that a party "asserting that a fact cannot be or is genuinely disputed must support the assertion by":

(A) citing to particular parts of materials in the record, including depositions, documents, electronically stored information, affidavits or declarations, stipulations (including those made for purposes of the motion only), admissions, interrogatory answers, or other materials; or

---

4. *Anderson v. Liberty Lobby, Inc.*, 477 U.S. 242, 248 (1986). In *Anderson v. Liberty Lobby* the Court held that plaintiffs must make a greater showing to defeat summary judgment if their trial burden is higher than the mere preponderance standard. "[I]n ruling on a motion for summary judgment, the judge must view the evidence presented through the prism of the substantive evidentiary burden." 477 U.S. at 254.

5. *Anderson v. Liberty Lobby, Inc.*, 477 U.S. 242, 252 (1986).

6. Fed. R. Civ. P. 56(c)(1). Even before the 2010 amendment of Rule 56 to explicitly refer to declarations, 28 U.S.C. § 1746 permitted unsworn declarations to be offered instead of sworn affidavits in federal court if the declaration was dated and signed pursuant to the form set forth in that statutory provision.

7. *Mossman v. Roadway Express, Inc.*, 789 F.2d 804 (9th Cir. 1986); *Frazier v. Cast*, 771 F.2d 259 (7th Cir. 1985); *REDD v. Fisher Controls*, 147 F.R.D. 128, 130–31 (W.D.Tex. 1993).

8. *Cabell v. Petty*, 810 F.2d 463 (4th Cir. 1987); *Burkhart v. Kinsley Bank*, 804 F.2d 588 (10th Cir. 1986); *Thornton v. Wahl*, 787 F.2d 1151, 1154 (7th Cir.), *cert. denied*, 479 U.S. 851 (1986).

(B) showing that the materials cited do not establish the absence or presence of a genuine dispute, or that an adverse party cannot produce admissible evidence to support the fact.

Thus parties must cite to specific material in the summary judgment record, or the absence of such material, to support or oppose summary judgment. In the vernacular, it's time to "put up or shut up"[9] or, as colorfully stated by the United States Court of Appeals for the Fifth Circuit, "Rule 56 * * * say[s] in effect, 'Meet these affidavit facts or judicially die.' "[10] Assuming summary judgment otherwise is appropriate, the party opposing summary judgment must offer discovery responses, affidavits, or declarations showing that there is a "genuine dispute as to [a] material fact."[11]

What if counsel cannot set forth specific facts showing that there is a genuine dispute for trial because those specific facts are inaccessible? Rule 56(d) provides that counsel, herself, may file an affidavit explaining why the necessary facts cannot be obtained. If this is done, Rule 56(d) provides that "the court may: (1) defer considering the motion or deny it; (2) allow time to obtain affidavits or declarations or to take discovery; or (3) issue any other appropriate order." Rule 56(d) oppositions typically result not in the outright denial of summary judgment motions, but in the deferral of the court's consideration of summary judgment. A continuance may be granted if, for example, the party opposing summary judgment has not had an opportunity to obtain discovery that might uncover evidence of a genuine dispute as to a material fact precluding summary judgment.[12]

Finally, Rule 56(a) provides that summary judgment may be sought, or granted, in connection with specific aspects of a party's claim. For example, a plaintiff can seek summary judgment only on the issue of liability, leaving for trial the determination of damages. Rule 56(g) further provides that when an action is not fully resolved on a summary judgment motion, the court may "enter an order stating any material fact—including an item of damages or other relief—that is not genuinely in dispute and treating the fact as established in the case." Motions for summary judgment therefore provide not only a basis for the complete resolution of civil actions prior to trial, but can be used to narrow cases by the selective

---

9. *Street v. J. C. Bradford & Co.*, 886 F.2d 1472, 1478 (6th Cir. 1989).

10. *Southern Rambler Sales, Inc. v. American Motors Corp.*, 375 F.2d 932, 937 (5th Cir.), *cert. denied*, 389 U.S. 832 (1967).

11. Fed. R. Civ. P. 56(a).

However, a party is not entitled to summary judgment merely because there is no response to that motion. *United States v. 5800 SW 74th Avenue*, 363 F.3d 1099, 1101 (11th Cir. 2004) ("[T]he district court cannot base the entry of summary judgment on the mere fact that the motion was unopposed, but, rather, must consider the merits of the motion."); *Jaroma v. Massey*, 873 F.2d 17, 20 (1st Cir. 1989) (per curiam) ("[T]he district court cannot grant a motion for summary judgment merely for lack of any response by the opposing party, since the district court must review the motion and the supporting papers to determine whether they establish the absence of a genuine issue of material fact.").

12. *E.g., Phillips v. General Motors Corp.*, 911 F.2d 724 (4th Cir. 1990) (per curiam); *Garrett v. City & County of San Francisco*, 818 F.2d 1515, 1518–19 (9th Cir. 1987).

pretrial resolution of claims or defenses about which there is no "genuine dispute as to any material fact."

B. SUMMARY JUDGMENT MOTIONS IN PRACTICE

Despite the great potential Rule 56 appears to have for the resolution of civil actions prior to trial, until fairly recently summary judgment motions were not easily obtained in many federal courts. As Professor Arthur Miller stated before a group of federal judges in 1984, "The Supreme Court has told you people time and time again: 'Oh, summary judgment is a wonderful device, but maybe you shouldn't grant it in any serious case.' "[13]

During its October 1985 term, however, the Supreme Court decided a trilogy of summary judgment cases that were heralded as the advent of a "New Era for Summary Judgments."[14] In each of these cases the federal district court had granted summary judgment, but was reversed by the court of appeals, which then, in turn, was reversed by the United States Supreme Court.[15]

While the law established in these cases was not a radical departure from either prior judicial holdings or the provisions of Rule 56, the language and tone of the majority's holdings were quite supportive of summary judgment. After these decisions, the United States Court of Appeals for the Second Circuit exclaimed:

> It appears that in this circuit some litigants are reluctant to make full use of the summary judgment process because of their perception that this court is unsympathetic to such motions and frequently reverses grants of summary judgment. Whatever may have been the accuracy of this view in years gone by, it is decidedly inaccurate at the present time * * * .[16]

The court of appeals then cited a study showing that it affirmed seventy-nine percent of district court grants of summary judgment and stated that "[w]e hope that the * * * study dispels the misperception so that litigants will not be deterred from making justifiable motions for summary judgment."[17]

---

13. A. Miller, *The August 1983 Amendments to the Federal Rules of Civil Procedure: Promoting Effective Case Management and Lawyer Responsibility* 8 (1984).

14. Childress, "A New Era for Summary Judgments: Recent Shifts at the Supreme Court," 116 F.R.D. 183 (1987). *See also* Bratton, "Summary Judgment Practice in the 1990s: A New Day Has Begun—Hopefully," 14 *Am. J. Trial Advoc.* 441 (1991).

15. *Matsushita Elec. Indus. Co. v. Zenith Radio Corp.,* 475 U.S. 574 (1986); *Anderson v. Liberty Lobby, Inc.,* 477 U.S. 242 (1986); *Celotex Corp. v. Catrett,* 477 U.S. 317 (1986).

16. *Knight v. United States Fire Insurance Co.,* 804 F.2d 9, 12 (2d Cir. 1986), *cert. denied,* 480 U.S. 932 (1987).

17. *Id. See also* Schwarzer, "Summary Judgment under the Federal Rules: Defining Genuine Issues of Material Fact," 99 F.R.D. 465, 467 n.9 (1984) (finding that, from January 1979 through June 1983, the United States Court of Appeals for the Ninth Circuit affirmed the trial court in 63% of the appeals taken from summary judgments).

Some judges and commentators have decried the perceived extension of summary judgment as a result of the Supreme Court's summary judgment trilogy.[18] However, a Federal Judicial Center study of cases in six federal district courts from 1975 through 2000 reached somewhat surprising results: "We found that when we controlled for changes over time in the types of cases being filed, the likelihood that a case contained one or more motions for summary judgment increased *before* the Supreme Court trilogy, from approximately 12 percent in 1975 to 17 percent in 1986, and has remained fairly steady at approximately 10 percent since that time."[19] This 2007 study additionally concluded:

> Although summary judgment motions have increased over this 25–year period, this increase reflects, at least in part, increased filings of civil rights cases, which have always experienced a high rate of summary judgment motions. Surprisingly, no statistically significant changes over time were found in the outcome of defendants' or plaintiffs' summary judgment motions, again after controlling for differences across courts and types of cases. These findings call into question the interpretation that the trilogy led to expansive increases in summary judgment. Our analysis suggests, instead, that changes in civil rules and federal case-management practices prior to the trilogy may have been more important in bringing about changes in summary judgment practice.[20]

A "New Era" for summary judgments may or may not have dawned with the *Celotex* trilogy. However, it seems likely that federal and state courts that are subject to caseload pressures will be increasingly receptive to the use of summary judgment to resolve cases short of trial. At the very least, attorneys defending against summary judgment may be required to present more of their proof at the summary judgment stage rather than

---

18. Bronsteen, "Against Summary Judgment," 75 *Geo. Wash. L. Rev.* 522, 551 (2007) (arguing that summary judgment is "inefficient, unfair, and unconstitutional"); Schneider, "The Dangers of Summary Judgment: Gender and Federal Civil Litigation," 59 *Rutgers L. Rev.* 705 (2007) (recent development of summary judgment law especially problematic in gender cases); Miller, "The Pretrial Rush to Judgment: Are the 'Litigation Explosion,' 'Liability Crisis,' and Efficiency Cliches Eroding our Day in Court and Jury Trial Commitments?," 78 *N. Y. U. L. Rev.* 982, 1134 (2003) (suggesting that summary judgment may have eroded the jury's duty to "make commonsense determinations about human behavior, reasonableness, and state of mind based on objective standards"); Wald, "Summary Judgment at Sixty," 76 *Tex. L. Rev.* 1897, 1941 (1998) ("Its flame lit by *Matsushita, Anderson,* and *Celotex* in 1986, and fueled by the overloaded dockets of the last two decades, summary judgment has spread swiftly through the underbrush of undesirable cases, taking down some healthy trees as it goes."); Mollica, "Federal Summary Judgment at High Tide," 84 *Marq. L. Rev.* 141, 144 (2000) (finding summary judgment "applied to every kind of legal and factual question—including such indeterminate legal standards such as intent and reasonableness—and even credibility issues").

19. Cecil et al., "A Quarter–Century of Summary Judgment Practice in Six Federal District Courts," 4 *J. Emp. Legal Studies* 861, 861 (2007).

20. *Id.* at 862. *See also* Coleman, "The *Celotex* Initial Burden Standard and an Opportunity to 'Revivify' Rule 56," 32 *S. Ill. U. L. J.* 295, 320–21 (2008) ("'[O]ne-off changes like a shift in the initial burden standard under *Celotex,* as it happens, did not create great institutional change."); Burbank, "Vanishing Trials and Summary Judgment in Federal Civil Cases: Drifting Toward Bethlehem or Gomorrah?," 1 *J. Emp. Legal Studies* 591, 620 (2004) ("Such reliable empirical evidence as we have ... does not support the claims of those who see a turning point in the Supreme Court's 1986 trilogy.").

withhold such evidence until trial. The civil litigator must know how to use summary judgment offensively, as well as how to defend against motions for summary judgment brought by opposing counsel.

NOTES AND QUESTIONS CONCERNING SUMMARY JUDGMENT

1. Plaintiff Bradley Comisky brings a tort action against the Pleasant Valley Railroad. Immediately after the filing of suit, the railroad moves for summary judgment, asserting that Comisky cannot establish one of the necessary elements of causation.

(a) Is summary judgment appropriate?

(b) What if the defendant railroad's summary judgment motion is not filed until after the parties have completed discovery? Can the defendant obtain summary judgment without offering supporting affidavits or citing to the discovery responses of either party? *See* Fed. R. Civ. Pro. 56(c)(1)(B); *Celotex Corp. v. Catrett*, 477 U.S. 317, 328 (1986) (White, J., concurring).

(c) What if Comisky, in response to the railroad's motion for summary judgment, states that he will call a witness to establish all of the elements of causation? What if this witness is deposed by defendant and states that, although he (the witness) cannot establish certain elements of causation, he believes that another person, whom he names, can? *See Canada v. Blain's Helicopters, Inc.*, 831 F.2d 920, 925 (9th Cir. 1987). *See also* Steinman, "The Irrepressible Myth of *Celotex*: Reconsidering Summary Judgment Burdens Twenty Years After the Trilogy," 63 *Wash. & Lee L. Rev.* 81 (2006); Kennedy, "Federal Summary Judgment: Reconciling *Celotex v. Catrett* with *Adickes v. Kress* and the Evidentiary Problems Under Rule 56," 6 *Rev. Litig.* 227 (1987). *But see* Shannon, "Responding to Summary Judgment," 91 *Marq. L. Rev.* 815 (2008).

2. In *Nissan Fire & Marine Ins. Co. v. Fritz Companies, Inc.*, 210 F.3d 1099, 1106 (9th Cir. 2000), the Court of Appeals reconciled the potential conflict between *Celotex* and *Adickes v. S. H. Kress & Co.*, 398 U.S. 144 (1970), as follows:

> Under *Adickes* and *Celotex*, a moving party without the ultimate burden of persuasion at trial thus may carry its initial burden of production [on a motion for summary judgment] by either of two methods. The moving party may produce evidence negating an essential element of the nonmoving party's case, or, after suitable discovery, the moving party may show that the nonmoving party does not have enough evidence of an essential element of its claim or defense to carry its ultimate burden of persuasion at trial.

The first of these methods was employed in *Kress*, while the second method was the basis of the summary judgment upheld by the Supreme Court in *Celotex*. As amended in 2010, Rule 56(c)(1) provides: "A party asserting that a fact cannot be or is genuinely disputed must support the assertion by: (A) citing to particular parts of materials in the record, including depositions, documents, electronically stored information, affidavits or declarations, stipulations (including those made for purposes of the motion only), admissions, interrogatory answers, or other materials; or (B) showing that the materials cited do not establish the absence or presence of a genuine dispute, or that an adverse party cannot produce admissible evidence to support the fact.''

3.   Plaintiffs Pat and Mike bring a tort action against defendant Homeowner because their young child entered Homeowner's yard and drowned in her swimming pool.

  (a) Presuming that there are no factual disputes concerning the drowning and Homeowner's ownership and control of the pool, can plaintiffs obtain summary judgment? Why is summary judgment generally not appropriate in negligence cases?

  (b) What if, in violation of a local ordinance, there was no fence around the pool? Can plaintiffs then successfully move for summary judgment? Can Homeowner successfully move for summary judgment if she had installed a fence and otherwise was in full compliance with all pool safety ordinances?

4.   Rachel Smith applies for a position as an associate with a law firm, but, despite her excellent academic credentials, does not receive an offer of employment. She then files a civil rights action against the law firm, claiming that she was denied employment because of her gender. After the completion of discovery, the defendant law firm moves for summary judgment. The firm supports its motion with the affidavits of several attorneys who state that, although Smith was the firm's second choice, an employment offer was extended to a more qualified male applicant. Smith files opposing affidavits showing that the law school record of the male who was hired was no better than her own and that of the twenty-five attorneys in the firm the only females are two associates. Is the defendant law firm entitled to summary judgment? What sort of evidence would make Smith's summary judgment opposition stronger? How is she to obtain such evidence?

III.   EFFECTIVE USE OF RULE 56 MOTIONS

Once the law governing Rule 56 is mastered, counsel must focus on strategic concerns in order to ensure that an effective summary judgment strategy is developed and implemented. The first strategic issue that must be confronted is whether or not to file a motion for summary judgment. If the decision is made to file a Rule 56 motion, counsel still must decide when the motion should be filed, the scope of the motion, and how the motion for summary judgment should be supported.

A.   SHOULD A MOTION FOR SUMMARY JUDGMENT BE FILED?

Although a successful summary judgment motion may result in judgment for the moving party, there may be reasons why summary judgment should not be sought in a particular case. Counsel always should weigh both the advantages and disadvantages of a summary judgment motion before filing any motion.

The major benefit of a successful summary judgment motion is obvious; it can result in the entry of judgment for the moving party. This is the ultimate goal of civil litigation, and the entry of judgment pursuant to Rule 56 will spare the client the trauma and expense of a trial.

Counsel may gain some measure of control over the pretrial proceedings by filing a summary judgment motion. If opposing counsel must concentrate upon her response to a summary judgment motion, she may not be able to initiate her own motions and discovery requests. Rule 56 motions may be coupled with other procedural motions. For instance, a defendant may be able to convince the court to stay discovery until a summary judgment motion going to a threshold defense (such as lack of jurisdiction) can be briefed and resolved by the court.

Nevertheless, there can be real disadvantages to motions for summary judgment. First of all, there are practical (and, in certain cases, ethical) problems with filing a motion that your client is unlikely to win. Counsel should be particularly careful about filing a motion where the argument relied upon in the motion will be presented at trial if the motion is denied. Once a judge has denied a motion for summary judgment, he may be predisposed to resolve the issue presented by the motion in the same manner at a later bench trial. In denying summary judgment, the court also may write an opinion that goes beyond the immediate summary judgment issues and is critical of the moving party in other respects.

Counsel must ask herself: (1) On what record (the paper record presented to the court in connection with a summary judgment motion or the record created by live witnesses at trial) will my client's case look the strongest? (2) On what record will the witnesses of the opposing party look the weakest? Some people are very convincing in person, while others are not. Counsel may have had a chance to evaluate the major witnesses in the case at their discovery depositions. If your client and his main witnesses will not be particularly convincing at trial, or if opposing witnesses can give compelling live testimony, a summary judgment motion may be in order. In other cases, you may want the judge to actually hear your witnesses if they will be more convincing in person than on the paper record that would be presented in connection with a summary judgment motion.[21]

A convincing summary judgment motion may require a great amount of time and effort to prepare. The law must be researched and summary judgment papers such as supporting affidavits must be drafted. The adoption of a summary judgment strategy may require counsel to take depositions or pursue additional discovery that otherwise would not be sought. Moreover, the filing of a motion for summary judgment may delay the pretrial proceedings, especially if the motion encourages opposing counsel to file a cross-motion for summary judgment.

---

21. A possible alternative to presenting the court with a "cold" paper record is to videotape the depositions of key witnesses. However, videotape depositions can be expensive and present logistical problems. There also can be no assurance that a judge will view the depositions rather than merely read the printed deposition transcript.

A well-supported summary judgment motion generally will require the moving party to reveal its case to opposing parties. Those witnesses who offer summary judgment affidavits become prime deposition targets. However, not only will information be provided to opposing parties by a motion for summary judgment, but the responses to the motion may reveal the contours of opponents' cases.

Sometimes, even winning a motion for summary judgment may ultimately harm the moving party. This can happen if a party is awarded summary judgment by the trial judge, but an appellate court later reverses the grant of summary judgment. If, in the time between the grant of summary judgment and the appellate reversal, witnesses or other evidence become unavailable, the party who initially prevailed on the summary judgment motion may be disadvantaged at the eventual trial.

In deciding whether to file a motion for summary judgment, counsel should consider not only the chances that the motion will be granted by the trial judge, but the likelihood that any grant of summary judgment will be upheld on appeal. In order for summary judgment to be properly granted, there must be no genuine disputes concerning material facts and no difference in the material inferences that reasonably can be drawn from the relevant facts.[22] In addition, courts are unlikely to grant or uphold summary judgment in certain types of cases.[23]

There may be alternatives to a Rule 56 motion for obtaining a favorable judgment. Accordingly, both the pros and cons of a motion for summary judgment should be considered carefully before such a motion is filed.

B.   WHEN SHOULD THE SUMMARY JUDGMENT MOTION BE FILED?

If counsel decides to file a motion for summary judgment, she still must determine when that motion should be filed. In making this determination, both governing law and strategic considerations should be explored.

Initially, counsel must be aware of explicit restrictions on when a motion for summary judgment can be filed. Rule 56(b) provides: "Unless a different time is set by local rule or the court orders otherwise, a party may file a motion for summary judgment at any time until 30 days after the close of all discovery." Local rules of court frequently do govern the

---

22. *United States v. Diebold, Inc.,* 369 U.S. 654, 655 (1962) (per curiam); *Warrior Tombigbee Transp. Co. v. M/V Nan Fung,* 695 F.2d 1294, 1296–98 (11th Cir. 1983).

23. One study of summary judgment practice in three federal district courts found that 7% of civil rights and prisoner actions and 6% of contract actions were disposed of by summary judgment, while only 1% of personal injury cases were resolved by such motions. J. Cecil & C. Douglas, *Summary Judgment Practice in Three District Courts* 7 (1987) (Table 4). *See also* Guiher, "Summary Judgments: Tactical Problem of the Trial Lawyer," 48 *Va. L. Rev.* 1263, 1272 (1962) (Table 2). *But see* McLauchlan, "An Empirical Study of the Federal Summary Judgment Rule," 6 *J. Legal Stud.* 427, 458 (1977).

timing of summary judgment motions, and may, for instance, require that summary judgment motions be filed within a reasonable period of time prior to the trial date.[24] Local rules of court also may set a time table for the responses and reply briefs filed in connection with summary judgment motions.[25] Even absent such local rules, the court may set deadlines for the filing of summary judgment papers in a Rule 16(b) scheduling order or at a Rule 16 pretrial conference.

Strategic considerations can play a large part in when a motion for summary judgment should be filed. The early filing of a motion for summary judgment may educate the judge concerning a party's theory of the case. A summary judgment motion also may help to smoke out the opposing party's case theory and evidence. If opposing counsel is concerned that you may succeed on the motion, she may file summary judgment affidavits or other documents that are quite valuable in the continued litigation of the action.[26]

Attorneys should consider the possible settlement leverage that can be generated by the filing of a motion for summary judgment. Such a motion can demonstrate to opposing counsel both the strengths of an attorney's factual and legal positions and her skills as an advocate. It also may require a substantial investment of time and money for the opposing party to respond to a well prepared summary judgment motion. Accordingly, it may make good economic sense for opposing counsel to attempt to negotiate a settlement rather than respond to a summary judgment motion and run the risk that the court will grant the motion. A good time to raise the possibility of settlement therefore may be immediately after you file a motion for summary judgment.[27]

As this discussion indicates, the timing of the motion for summary judgment is an important part of summary judgment strategy.

C. WHAT SHOULD THE SCOPE BE OF THE MOTION FOR SUMMARY JUDGMENT?

In determining the most appropriate scope for a summary judgment motion, counsel should refer back to the element check list that was developed at the outset of the case.[28] A review of the essential case elements should provide a helpful reminder of precisely what elements the plaintiff must establish in order to prevail. If plaintiff's counsel plans to

---

24. Rule 56(A) of the United States District Court for the Eastern District of Virginia.

25. Rule 6.1(d)(2) of the United States District Court for the District of Kansas (responses to be filed and served within 21 days after summary judgment motions and reply memoranda to be filed and served within 14 days after service of response).

26. There must be at least a colorable basis for any summary judgment motion. Not only are summary judgment motions subject to the strictures of Rule 11, but losing a summary judgment motion will not help your position at trial (particularly if the court had to devote a significant amount of time to the resolution of the motion).

27. Conversely, it's usually counterproductive to broach settlement with opposing counsel immediately after the court has denied your client's motion for summary judgment.

28. *See* Figure 3–1 in Chapter 3, *supra* p. 63.

seek summary judgment on behalf of her client, she must offer evidentiary support establishing each of the essential case elements.[29]

Defense counsel can be much more selective in drafting a summary judgment motion. The defendant is entitled to judgment if plaintiff cannot establish all of the elements of his claim. Defense counsel therefore can target a summary judgment motion at the weakest aspect of plaintiff's case. For example, even if the plaintiff has a strong case on damages, the defendant may be able to obtain summary judgment by focusing its summary judgment motion upon the element of causation. The defendant's summary judgment motion generally should be used as a scalpel, probing for the weakest aspects of the opposing party's case.[30]

Both plaintiffs and defendants should consider seeking partial summary judgment. On a motion for partial summary judgment the court can render judgment concerning individual claims or parties, thus simplifying the issues remaining for trial. Rule 56(g) provides that even if a motion for summary judgment, rather than for partial summary judgment, is filed, "If the court does not grant all the relief requested by the motion, it may enter an order stating any material fact—including an item of damages or other relief—that is not genuinely in dispute and treating the fact as established in the case."

Partial summary judgment can have a far-reaching impact on a civil action. If a plaintiff only can establish very nominal compensatory damages, the grant of partial summary judgment concerning plaintiff's demand for punitive damages may effectively end the litigation. Partial summary judgment also may mean that a party may not be able to offer specific favorable evidence at trial. As a result, that party's chances of obtaining a judgment at trial on its remaining claims may be greatly reduced.[31]

---

29. In addition, plaintiff's counsel can seek partial summary judgment concerning defenses asserted by the defendant. *E.g., Visa U.S.A. Inc. v. First Data Corp.,* 2006 WL 516662 (N.D.Cal. 2006); *Laker Airways Ltd. v. Pan American World Airways,* 568 F.Supp. 811 (D.D.C. 1983); *Diedrich v. Wright,* 550 F.Supp. 805 (N.D.Ill. 1982). *See also* 10B C. Wright et al., *Federal Practice and Procedure* § 2737, at 321–22 (3d ed. 1998). *Contra Uniroyal, Inc. v. Heller,* 65 F.R.D. 83, 86 (S.D.N.Y. 1974); *Bernstein v. Universal Pictures, Inc.,* 379 F.Supp. 933, 936 (S.D.N.Y. 1974), *rev'd on other grounds,* 517 F.2d 976 (2d Cir. 1975). *See also Dixie Yarns, Inc. v. Forman,* 1993 WL 227661, at *3 (S.D.N.Y. 1993) (accepting argument that "an effort to strike affirmative defenses should be brought under Rule 12(f), not Rule 56").

30. There may be specific cases in which it doesn't make sense to seek the pretrial dismissal of an opponent's weakest claims. If the plaintiff has several weak claims and one strong claim, it may be to defendant's advantage if all of plaintiff's claims are presented at trial. Not only may the weak claims blunt the force that the strong claim would if presented by itself, but there may be witnesses or evidence offered in support of the weak claims that actually may help the defendant. While such situations should rarely arise if counsel carefully evaluate their cases, this does not always happen in practice.

31. The settlement pressures created by the grant of partial summary judgment may be enhanced because "a partial summary 'judgment' is not a final judgment, and, therefore, * * * is not appealable, unless in the particular case some statute allows an appeal from the interlocutory order involved." Advisory Committee Note to 1948 Amendment to Rule 56, 5 F.R.D. 433, 475 (1946). In addition, Federal Rule of Civil Procedure 54(b) provides that, in the absence of the court's express direction to the contrary, "any order or other decision, however designated, that adjudicates fewer than all the claims or the rights and liabilities of fewer than all the parties does

In many cases, it may be best to successfully seek judgment on portions of an opposing party's claims or defenses instead of unsuccessfully seeking judgment across-the-board.

D. HOW SHOULD THE MOTION FOR SUMMARY JUDGMENT BE SUPPORTED?

As with most other pretrial motions, the actual motion for summary judgment generally is neither lengthy nor complex. The following motion filed by the defendant Pittston Company in the Buffalo Creek litigation is illustrative:

IN THE UNITED STATES DISTRICT COURT
FOR THE SOUTHERN DISTRICT OF WEST VIRGINIA
At Charleston

DENNIS PRINCE, et al.,
            Plaintiffs,

v.   Civil Action No. 3052–HN

THE PITTSTON COMPANY,
            Defendant.

MOTION FOR SUMMARY JUDGMENT

TO: RUBY DALE BAILEY; [additional plaintiffs on whose claims summary judgment was sought]; and WILLIS O. SHAY, ESQUIRE, of the law firm of Steptoe and Johnson, Tenth Floor, Union Bank Building, Clarksburg, West Virginia 26301, and GERALD M. STERN, ESQUIRE, of the law firm of Arnold & Porter, 1229 Nineteenth Street, N.W., Washington, D.C. 20036, attorneys for the above-named plaintiffs.

The defendant by its attorneys, and pursuant to Rule 56(b) and (c) [now, Rule 56(a)] of the Federal Rules of Civil Procedure, moves the Court to enter summary judgment for the defendant upon the personal injury claims of the above-named plaintiffs on the ground that there is no genuine issue as to any fact material to a determination that such injuries were not proximately caused by the defendant and that the defendant is entitled to a judgment as a matter of law.

In support of this motion, defendant refers to the complaint, to the answers of said plaintiffs or members of plaintiffs' families to the interrogatories of the defendant, and the discovery depositions of said plaintiffs or of members of plaintiffs' families all sworn to, which are on file in this action in this Court.

---

not end the action as to any of the claims or parties and may be revised at any time before the entry of a judgment adjudicating all the claims and all the parties' rights and liabilities.''

ZANE GREY STAKER, ESQUIRE

s/ _____

   Kermit, West Virginia 25674

JACKSON, KELLY, HOLT & O'FARRELL

By: s/ _____

       Firm Member
       P.O. Box 553
       1601 Kanawaha Valley Building
       Charleston, West Virginia 25322

DONOVAN, LEISURE, NEWTON & IRVINE

By: s/ _____

       Firm Member
       30 Rockefeller Plaza
       New York, New York 10025

   Attorneys for Defendant

In addition to the motion itself, counsel may be required to submit a supporting brief, a notice of motion, a proposed order, and a statement of material facts as to which there is no genuine issue.[32] Counsel also generally will want to submit evidentiary material in support of the motion for summary judgment. In determining what evidentiary material to submit to the court, counsel must decide (1) what evidence should be offered in support of the motion and (2) in what form that evidence should be offered.[33]

In deciding what evidence to offer, counsel first must determine the evidence that will be minimally sufficient to obtain summary judgment. Then counsel must decide whether to offer more than this bare minimum. While a conservative approach may be to put all favorable evidence before the court, this strategy may not be wise for two separate reasons: (1) If too much evidence is put before the judge, he may not focus on the specific

---

32. *E.g.,* Rule 7.5 of the United States District Court for the Middle District of Pennsylvania (requiring brief in support of motion); Rule 7–4 of the United States District Court for the Central District of California (requiring notice of motion); Rule 7(c) of the United States District Court for the District of Columbia (requiring submission of proposed order with motion); Rule 56.1 of the United States District Courts for the Eastern, Middle, and Western Districts of Louisiana (requiring submission of statement of material facts as to which there is no genuine issue).

Some local rules require not only that parties submit a statement of material facts in connection with a motion for summary judgment, but also copies of all affidavits and discovery to which those statements refer. *E.g.,* Rule 56.1 of the United States District Court for the District of Massachusetts; Rule CV–56(a), (d) of the United States District Court for the Eastern District of Texas. Whether or not this is required, it usually is a good practice to assemble the relevant evidence in a motion appendix for the court.

33. For an overview of evidentiary materials that may be offered, and the required form for such materials, see Brunet, "Summary Judgment Materials," 147 F.R.D. 647 (1993).

issue or issues entitling the movant to summary judgment; (2) If the motion for summary judgment is denied, the evidentiary material submitted may provide valuable discovery for the opposing party. In considering whether to offer particular evidence in connection with a summary judgment motion, counsel must balance the immediate benefits from offering the evidence against the long run detriment if the motion for summary judgment is denied and the case goes to trial.

The form in which summary judgment material is offered usually is not crucial. Despite the possibility of reliance upon declarations in the federal courts pursuant to Rule 56(c)(1)(A) and 28 U.S.C. § 1746, many counsel feel more comfortable supporting summary judgment motions with affidavits. Whether declarations or affidavits are used may depend upon the availability of a notary public and the local custom in the particular jurisdiction.

Federal Rule of Civil Procedure 56(c)(4) contains the specific requirements for summary judgment affidavits, providing: "An affidavit or declaration used to support or oppose a motion must be made on personal knowledge, set out facts that would be admissible in evidence, and show that the affiant or declarant is competent to testify on the matters stated." While Rule 26(b)(1) does not limit pretrial discovery to admissible evidence, Rule 56(c)(4) is not so liberal concerning the material that may be offered in connection with summary judgment motions.

The evidentiary material that can be submitted in connection with a motion for summary judgment is not limited to affidavits and declarations. Rule 56 gives counsel the option of submitting stipulations and discovery responses in connection with a motion for summary judgment. The most convincing summary judgment evidence often is taken from an opposing party's discovery responses ("right from the horse's mouth"). For instance, a plaintiff in a Title VII discrimination suit might be asked in his deposition to describe all specific incidents of alleged discrimination. The plaintiff's inability to describe specific incidents, or the defendant's ability to establish that the incidents described do not constitute illegal discrimination, may provide a basis for the entry of summary judgment for the defendant.[34]

Discovery requests therefore should be framed to elicit responses that will be useful in a possible summary judgment motion. After obtaining general information in a deposition, the examining attorney can use a leading question to summarize the answers given: "So the only times that you talked with Mr. Smith were on March 22, 2011, March 27, 2011, and April 1, 2010?" An affirmative answer to this question can be used in support of a summary judgment motion and will obviate the need to refer to a series of deposition questions and answers spanning several pages of transcript. Factual disputes also may be narrowed by the inclusion of

---

34. *E.g., Meiri v. Dacon,* 759 F.2d 989, 998 (2d Cir.), *cert. denied,* 474 U.S. 829 (1985) (summary judgment for defendant employer affirmed due to plaintiff's conclusory allegations of discrimination and request that she not be "ask[ed] * * * to pinpoint people, times, or places").

precise fact statements in the complaint or in a request for admissions served upon opposing parties during pretrial discovery.

Once the decision is made to move for summary judgment, great care should be taken to ensure that the most persuasive supporting evidence will be presented to the court in the most persuasive manner.

Exercises Concerning Effective Use of Summary Judgment Motions

1. In the Buffalo Creek litigation filed by plaintiffs' attorney Gerald Stern, the only defendant that was named was the Pittston Company. Pittston asserted throughout this litigation that it was not a proper defendant and that any responsibility for plaintiffs' damages was that of Pittston's subsidiary, the Buffalo Mining Company. Because the plaintiffs and the Buffalo Mining Company were all West Virginia citizens, the adoption of Pittston's argument by the federal district court would have meant that it could not exercise diversity jurisdiction over the action.

Presume that you are an associate in the law firm representing the Pittston Company in this lawsuit. Write a memorandum to your senior partner addressing the following issues:

(a) Should Pittston move for summary judgment?

(b) If a motion for summary judgment should be filed, what should be its scope?

(c) If a summary judgment motion should be filed, when should it be filed?

(d) What relation should there be between a motion for summary judgment and the parties' ongoing discovery?

(e) How should the papers supporting any motion for summary judgment be structured? For instance, what, if any, affidavits or other documents should be submitted to the court in connection with the motion?

2. You are an attorney associated with Gerald Stern in connection with the Buffalo Creek litigation that he has brought against the Pittston Company. You have been asked to write a memorandum discussing any possible motions for summary judgment that the plaintiffs might file in that action. In your memorandum, discuss plaintiffs' chances of prevailing on any motions under the governing Rule 56 standards and the manner in which summary judgment motions might or might not fit within the plaintiffs' overall case strategy.

3. In the motion for summary judgment set forth in Section III(D) of this chapter, *supra* p. 528, the Pittston Company sought summary judgment on the claims of thirty-three plaintiffs who were not physically injured in the flood, were not threatened with immediate physical injury from the flood, and did not witness any other person sustain physical injury in the flood. You are an associate in the law firm representing the

Pittston Company and have been asked for your advice concerning the wisdom of filing such a motion addressed to thirty-three of the approximately 600 plaintiffs in the action. Write a memorandum containing your advice.

4. Bart Bakki has taught as a history and driver education teacher for the Hillsborough County Schools for three years. Last fall he sent a letter to the editor of the local paper criticizing the school system's "exaltation of athletics at the expense of academic excellence." The day that the letter appeared, Bart's principal called him into her office and told him that he'd "made a big mistake with that letter" and that he'd "live to regret having gone public with those complaints." The next day the principal spoke with him again, apologized, and told him that she'd "forgotten the whole episode."

Six months later, Bart's probationary teaching contract was not renewed for the next school year. The stated reason for the non-renewal was that, because the school system had contracted for driver education classes to be taught by a private company, there was no longer any need for Bart's services. The contracts of each of the seven other probationary teachers within the school system were renewed, but Bart had been the only person teaching driver education.

After attempting to resolve the matter informally, Bart filed a federal civil rights action against his principal (who recommended that his contract not be renewed) and the superintendent of schools and members of the Hillsborough County Board of Education (who approved the principal's recommendation). Although his suit alleges that his contract was not renewed due to the exercise of his first amendment rights, at his deposition Bart stated that he has no evidence other than what is set forth in this exercise to support his claim. Discovery in the case has been completed.

As counsel for the defendant school officials, draft a motion for summary judgment and the other documents that you would file in support of that motion.

IV. DEFENDING AGAINST RULE 56 MOTIONS

The key to defending against summary judgment motions is to convince the court that the outcome of the case could be different at trial if summary judgment is denied.[35] As much as judges may welcome the judicial time-savings that summary judgments can produce, most judges are hesitant to grant summary judgment against a party whom they believe might prevail at trial. Not only does the grant of summary judgment in such cases seem unfair, but judges are rarely reversed by appellate courts for denying summary judgments (in orders that are not

---

35. This is not to say, however, that a plaintiff can defeat summary judgment "by merely asserting that the jury might, and legally could, disbelieve the defendant[ ]." *Anderson v. Liberty Lobby, Inc.,* 477 U.S. 242, 256 (1986).

final and from which interlocutory appeal is generally not available). Even after the *Celotex* trilogy, the Supreme Court has noted that "summary judgment serves as the ultimate screen to weed out *truly insubstantial* lawsuits prior to trial."[36]

Three major strategies can be employed in defending against summary judgment motions. First of all, the party opposing summary judgment can focus on the movant's failure to comply with the requirements of Rule 56 or local rules of court. Secondly, the party opposing summary judgment can itself produce evidence creating a genuine issue of material fact. Finally, in certain cases, a party can argue that affidavits or other relevant evidence are not available and that the summary judgment motion should be denied or continued pursuant to Federal Rule of Civil Procedure 56(d). Each of these possibilities will be considered in turn.[37]

A. THE MOVING PARTY'S FAILURE TO COMPLY WITH SUMMARY JUDGMENT REQUIREMENTS

Although these defenses may be of a somewhat technical nature, it may be possible to defeat, or at least delay, summary judgment by focusing upon the moving party's failure to comply with the summary judgment requirements of Federal Rule of Civil Procedure 56 or local rules of court. For instance, the moving party may not have complied with local rules concerning the timing of summary judgment or the requirements for summary judgment affidavits and declarations.

The moving party's affidavits or declarations may not be in compliance with Rule 56(c)(4). This Rule requires that affidavits or declarations be made on personal knowledge, and that they set forth admissible facts and show that the affiant or declarant is competent to testify. Summary judgment affidavits or declarations also should lay the foundation for any attached documents.

More significant evidentiary challenges can be made. Mere conclusory allegations unsupported by factual affidavits or declarations are insufficient to support summary judgment.[38] The party opposing summary

---

36. *Crawford–El v. Britton*, 523 U.S. 574, 600 (1998) (emphasis added).

37. Those counsel who believe that "If you can't beat 'em, join 'em," also might consider the filing of a cross-motion for summary judgment. Even if a cross-motion for summary judgment is not made, the court can grant summary judgment *for* the party opposing summary judgment if there is no genuine issue of material fact and that party is entitled to judgment as a matter of law. *Pueblo of Santa Ana v. Mountain States Tel. & Tel. Co.*, 734 F.2d 1402, 1408 (10th Cir. 1984), *rev'd on other grounds*, 472 U.S. 237 (1985); *SMI Communications, Inc. v. City of Flint*, No. 96–CI–72982–DT, 1998 U.S.Dist. LEXIS 2430 (E.D.Mich. Jan. 27, 1998). However, the mere fact that all parties have moved for summary judgment does not mean that judgment short of trial is necessarily warranted. *ITCO Corp. v. Michelin Tire Corp.*, 722 F.2d 42, 45 n.3 (4th Cir. 1983), *cert. denied*, 469 U.S. 1215 (1985); *McKenzie v. Sawyer*, 684 F.2d 62, 68 n.3 (D.C.Cir. 1982); *A. Brod, Inc. v. S K & I Co.*, 998 F.Supp. 314, 320 (S.D.N.Y. 1998). *See also Wermager v. Cormorant Township Bd.*, 716 F.2d 1211, 1214 (8th Cir. 1983).

38. *Fano v. O'Neill*, 806 F.2d 1262, 1266 (5th Cir. 1987); *Windon Third Oil and Gas Drilling P'ship v. Federal Deposit Ins. Corp.*, 805 F.2d 342, 345 n.7 (10th Cir. 1986), *cert. denied*, 480 U.S.

judgment can stress its lack of opportunity for cross-examination and the self-serving nature of his opponent's affidavits. Deposition testimony and other discovery are given greater weight in connection with summary judgment motions than are affidavits specifically prepared in connection with a summary judgment motion. Indeed, a genuine dispute of material fact normally cannot be created by an affidavit that conflicts with the affiant's prior unambiguous deposition testimony.[39] Counsel therefore must thoroughly prepare all witnesses for their depositions, rather than assume that any deposition "slips" or other admissions can be corrected by later summary judgment affidavits.

Summary judgment is generally inappropriate when credibility determinations must be made. Courts are reluctant to grant summary judgment when intent and motive are at issue. As the drafters of the modern version of Rule 56 recognized, "Where an issue as to a material fact cannot be resolved without observation of the demeanor of witnesses in order to evaluate their credibility, summary judgment is not appropriate."[40] If an opposing party is expected to move for summary judgment, counsel can attempt to highlight credibility issues in discovery depositions. For instance, an attorney might state to a witness during a deposition: "I see that you're nervous." While the statement is self-serving, it nevertheless could be relied upon to bolster an argument that the witness's credibility is an issue that should be determined at trial.

---

947 (1987). *See also Celotex Corp. v. Catrett,* 477 U.S. 317, 328 (1986) (White, J., concurring) ("It is not enough to move for summary judgment without supporting the motion in any way or with a conclusory assertion that the plaintiff has no evidence to prove his case."); Fed. R. Civ. P. 56(c)(1).

Rule 166a of the Texas Rules of Civil Procedure specifically provides for a "no-evidence motion" for summary judgment:

> After adequate time for discovery, a party without presenting summary judgment evidence may move for summary judgment on the ground that there is no evidence of one or more essential elements of a claim or defense on which an adverse party would have the burden of proof at trial. The motion must state the elements as to which there is no evidence. The court must grant the motion unless the respondent produces summary judgment evidence raising a genuine issue of material fact.

Cf. Fed. R. Civ. P. 56(c)(1)(B), providing for a summary judgment based upon a "showing that the materials cited do not establish the absence or presence of a genuine dispute, or that an adverse party cannot produce admissible evidence to support the fact."

39. As noted by one federal court of appeals, "A party may not create a factual issue by filing an affidavit, after a motion for summary judgment has been made, which contradicts her earlier deposition testimony." *Reid v. Sears, Roebuck and* Co., 790 F.2d 453, 460 (6th Cir. 1986). *See also Peck v. Bridgeport Machines, Inc.,* 237 F.3d 614, 619 (6th Cir. 2001); *Camfield Tires, Inc. v. Michelin Tire Corp.,* 719 F.2d 1361 (8th Cir. 1983); *Clay v. Equifax, Inc.,* 762 F.2d 952, 955 n.3 (11th Cir. 1985). *But see Kennett–Murray Corp. v. Bone,* 622 F.2d 887, 893–95 (5th Cir. 1980). *See generally* 10A C. Wright, A. Miller et al., *Federal Practice and Procedure* § 2726 (3d ed. 1998); Cox, Note, "Reconsidering the Sham Affidavit Doctrine," 50 *Duke L. J.* 261 (2000); Holley, "Making Credibility Determinations at Summary Judgment: How Judges Broaden Their Discretion While 'Playing by the Rules,' " 20 *Whittier L. Rev.* 865 (1999).

40. Advisory Committee's Note to 1963 Amendment to Rule 56, 31 F.R.D. 621, 648 (1963). *See also Anderson v. Liberty Lobby, Inc.,* 477 U.S. 242, 255 (1986) ("Credibility determinations, the weighing of the evidence, and the drawing of legitimate inferences from the facts are jury functions, not those of the judge * * * ."); *Hutchinson v. Proxmire,* 443 U.S. 111, 120 n.9 (1979); *Sartor v. Arkansas Natural Gas Corp.,* 321 U.S. 620, 628–29 (1944). *Cf. Harlow v. Fitzgerald,* 457 U.S. 800, 813–820 (1982) (in which the Court redefined the test for qualified good faith immunity in terms of objective reasonableness to "permit the resolution of many insubstantial claims on summary judgment").

"Further, '[s]ince tort actions generally encompass a multitude of factual issues and abstract concepts that become elusive when applied to varying concrete factual situations, such actions are usually not appropriate for disposition by summary judgment.' "[41] More generally, "on summary judgment the inferences to be drawn from the underlying facts * * * must be viewed in the light most favorable to the party opposing the motion."[42]

The courts have recognized that, because of the complex opinions often presented, summary judgment may be inappropriate in cases involving expert testimony.[43] In addition, although juries had been requested in at least some of the cases decided in the Supreme Court's 1986 summary judgment trilogy, trial judges may be hesitant to grant summary judgment in a case in which jury trial has been sought.[44]

Although summary judgment defenses must be tailored to the facts of each specific case, a consideration of whether the moving party has satisfied all summary judgment requirements is a good place to start when faced with an opponent's motion for summary judgment.

B. AFFIRMATIVE ATTEMPTS TO DEFEAT SUMMARY JUDGMENT

In addition to focusing upon the moving party's failure to satisfy summary judgment requirements, the opposing party can act affirmatively to defeat summary judgment. In some cases, summary judgment can be defeated by nothing more than amendment of the pleading that is being challenged. Under Rule 15(a)(1)(B) of the Federal Rules of Civil Procedure, amendment as of right is possible if the amendment is filed within 21 days after the party seeking summary judgment filed its answer or a motion to dismiss under Rule 12(b), (e), or (f). Even if amendment as of

41. *Umpleby v. United States,* 806 F.2d 812, 814–15 (8th Cir. 1986), *quoting Hughes v. American Jawa, Ltd.,* 529 F.2d 21, 23 (8th Cir. 1976). *See also Delgado v. Lockheed–Georgia Co.,* 815 F.2d 641, 644 (11th Cir. 1987).

42. *Matsushita Elec. Indus. Co. v. Zenith Radio Corp.,* 475 U.S. 574, 587 (1986), *quoting United States v. Diebold, Inc.,* 369 U.S. 654, 655 (1962) (per curiam). *See also Board of Educ. v. Pico,* 457 U.S. 853, 863 (1982); *Poller v. Columbia Broadcasting System,* 368 U.S. 464, 473 (1962).

43. *Sightsound.com Inc. v. N2K, Inc.,* 391 F.Supp.2d 321, 330–31 (W.D.Pa. 2003); *Sonobond Corp. v. Uthe Technology, Inc.,* 314 F.Supp. 878, 881 (N.D.Cal. 1970). *See also Amhil Enterprises Ltd. v. Wawa, Inc.,* 81 F.3d 1554, 1557–58 (Fed. Cir. 1996); *Ferebee v. Chevron Chem. Co.,* 736 F.2d 1529, 1534–35 (D.C.Cir.), *cert. denied,* 469 U.S. 1062 (1984); *Webster v. Offshore Food Service, Inc.,* 434 F.2d 1191, 1193 (5th Cir. 1970), *cert. denied,* 404 U.S. 823 (1971). *But see Merit Motors, Inc. v. Chrysler Corp.,* 569 F.2d 666, 672–74 (D.C.Cir. 1977).

44. *See Weinberger v. Hynson, Westcott & Dunning, Inc.,* 412 U.S. 609, 622 (1973) ("If this were a case involving trial by jury as provided in the Seventh Amendment, there would be sharper limitations on the use of summary judgment, as our decisions reveal."). In fact, Professor Suja Thomas has argued that, because there was no procedure akin to summary judgment at common law in 1791, summary judgment violates the seventh amendment. Thomas, "Why Summary Judgment is Unconstitutional," 93 *Va. L. Rev.* 139 (2007). *See also* Bronsteen, "Against Summary Judgment," 75 *Geo. Wash. L. Rev.* 522, 547–50 (2007). *Contra* Brunet, "Summary Judgment is Constitutional," 93 *Iowa L. Rev.* 1625 (2008); Nelson, "Summary Judgment and the Progressive Constitution," 93 *Iowa L. Rev.* 1653 (2008). *But see* Thomas, "Why Summary Judgment is Still Unconstitutional: A Reply to Professors Brunet and Nelson," 93 *Iowa L. Rev.* 1667 (2008).

right is no longer an option, "in the preliminary stages of the lawsuit, the trial court should permit discovery and freely grant leave to amend the complaint under Rule 15."[45]

Even if there is no factual dispute between the parties, summary judgment may be inappropriate if the party seeking judgment is not "entitled to judgment as a matter of law" under Rule 56(a). The argument against summary judgment in such a situation is basically the same as that made in opposition to a Rule 12(b)(6) motion to dismiss for failure to state a claim: although there may be no factual dispute, the party seeking summary judgment is incorrect that the governing law entitles it to judgment.

In extreme cases, the party successfully opposing summary judgment can seek sanctions under Rule 11 of the Federal Rules of Civil Procedure against the unsuccessful movant.[46] Since the amendment of Rule 11 in 1983, counsel should not use summary judgment motions merely to "educate the court" or obtain discovery from an opposing party. Rule 56(h) provides for sanctions against parties employing affidavits "submitted in bad faith or solely for delay."[47]

There are numerous ways in which to bolster summary judgment affidavits and thus defeat summary judgment. Affidavits and declarations should be carefully drafted, and both the affiant's background and the factual basis for any conclusions or opinions offered in the affidavit should be clearly stated. It's not a good idea for an affiant to just state: "My name is Dr. Donald Duck, and I believe that the plaintiff's death was caused by defendant's malpractice."

In drafting affidavits in opposition to a summary judgment motion, it may be appropriate to touch on the merits of the case. This strategy only makes sense if your client has a sympathetic case on the merits, because judges do not like to enter judgment against people whom they believe have raised meritorious claims. This is not to suggest that aspects of the merits having no possible relation to the pending summary judgment motion be dragged before the court. However, if the merits are arguably relevant to the motion (if only to put the motion in proper context), it does not hurt to remind the court of the helpful aspects of the merits.[48]

---

45. *Gary Plastic Packaging Corp. v. Merrill Lynch, Pierce, Fenner & Smith, Inc.,* 756 F.2d 230, 236 (2d Cir. 1985). *See also Foman v. Davis,* 371 U.S. 178 (1962); *Bradley v. Kemper Ins. Co.,* 121 F.App'x 468, 471 (3d Cir. 2005); Fed. R. Civ. P. 15(a)(2) ("The court should freely give leave [to amend] when justice so requires.").

46. *E.g., Mossman v. Roadway Express, Inc.,* 789 F.2d 804 (9th Cir. 1986); *Frazier v. Cast,* 771 F.2d 259 (7th Cir. 1985); *REDD v. Fisher Controls,* 147 F.R.D. 128, 130–31 (W.D.Tex. 1993). *See also* 28 U.S.C. § 1927.

47. *See Acrotube, Inc. v. J. K. Financial Group, Inc.,* 653 F.Supp. 470, 477–478 (N.D.Ga. 1987); *Dardanell Co. Trust v. United States,* 634 F.Supp. 186, 190 (D.Minn. 1986), *aff'd mem.,* 822 F.2d 1094 (8th Cir. 1987).

48. This is not to say that counsel should overreact to an opponent's summary judgment motion by putting before the court every conceivable bit of evidence that will be offered at trial. Attorneys should be careful not to defeat the summary judgment motion at the expense of ultimately losing the case on the merits at trial.

Nor need a summary judgment opposition be restricted to the filing of affidavits or other documents. Under Rule 43(c) of the Federal Rules of Civil Procedure, the district courts have discretion to take oral testimony at summary judgment hearings.[49] While it's not a frequent occurrence, witnesses can be subpoenaed for summary judgment hearings.

More generally, courts are reluctant to grant summary judgment if it appears that no time will be saved by the summary judgment procedure. Some judges may be reluctant to grant summary judgment if there is a great mass of evidentiary material that must be considered in connection with a summary judgment motion. At least a few judges still follow the apocryphal "One Inch Rule," under which a genuine issue of material fact is presumed to exist if the summary judgment papers are over one inch thick.

Judges also may be disinclined to grant summary judgment if it has not been sought in a timely manner or if a trial date is fast approaching. Rule 56(b) provides that summary judgment motions may be filed "until 30 days after the close of all discovery," unless a different time is set "by local rule or the court orders otherwise." Even if a motion is filed within such a time period, it may be possible to argue (while attempting not to whine): "Your honor, we're set to try this case in three weeks; Let's have our trial, rather than waste several months briefing and obtaining a ruling on a last-minute summary judgment motion."[50]

Whether the party opposing judgment focuses upon the movant's failure to satisfy its summary judgment burdens or attempts to bolster its own opposition affirmatively, an ounce of common sense may be worth a pound of precedent in defending against summary judgment.

---

49. *Argus Inc. v. Eastman Kodak Co.,* 801 F.2d 38, 42 n.2 (2d Cir. 1986), *cert. denied,* 479 U.S. 1088 (1987); *Walters v. Ocean Springs,* 626 F.2d 1317, 1322 (5th Cir. 1980). *But see Stewart v. RCA Corp.,* 790 F.2d 624, 629 (7th Cir. 1986) ("Because the judge may not resolve evidentiary disputes, * * * Rule 43(e) [now, Rule 43(c)] hearings on motions for summary judgment * * * should be rare.").

50. A majority of the federal courts of appeal have recognized that trial judges have discretion to deny summary judgment even when the requirements of Rule 56 are technically satisfied. Friedenthal & Gardner, "Judicial Discretion to Deny Summary Judgment in the Era of Managerial Judging," 31 *Hofstra L. Rev.* 91, 104–110 (2002) (in which the authors argue that Rule 56 should be amended to explicitly give judges the discretion to deny summary judgment and require written reasons for the exercise of such discretion).

In the 2010 amendments to Rule 56, the word "shall" was reinstated for the word "should" in Rule 56(a), the relevant sentence of which now provides: "The court shall grant summary judgment if the movant shows that there is no genuine dispute as to any material fact and the movant is entitled to judgment as a matter of law." In its note to the 2010 amendment to Rule 56, the Advisory Committee recognized the apparently conflicting statements in Supreme Court opinions as to "whether a district court has discretion to deny summary judgment when there appears to be no genuine issue as to any material fact." 266 F.R.D. 502, 580 (2010). The Committee "restored ['shall'] to the place it held from 1938 to 2007," rather than use either the words "should" or "must," which could have been perceived as changing the traditional Rule 56 standard for summary judgment. *Id.* at 579.

C. THE RULE 56(d) OPPOSITION TO SUMMARY JUDGMENT

In certain situations, the party opposing summary judgment may not be able to marshal the specific evidence necessary to defeat a Rule 56 motion at the time that the motion is filed. Rule 56(d) provides: "If a nonmovant shows by affidavit or declaration that, for specified reasons, it cannot present facts essential to justify its opposition, the court may: (1) defer considering the motion or deny it; (2) allow time to obtain affidavits or declarations or to take discovery; or (3) issue any other appropriate order."[51]

The most common situation in which Rule 56(d) is invoked is when summary judgment is sought before the completion of discovery.[52] While courts may be reluctant to grant summary judgment if it is sought too late in the pretrial proceedings, if summary judgment is sought before discovery has been completed the opposing party often can argue successfully that the motion is premature.

The courts have recognized that "sufficient time for discovery is especially important when relevant facts are exclusively in the control of the opposing party."[53] The chances for a successful Rule 56(d) summary judgment opposition therefore are heightened if the information necessary to the opposition has been sought from an opposing party through formal discovery devices. For instance, in *Garrett v. City & County of San Francisco* the United States Court of Appeals for the Ninth Circuit relied upon Rule 56(f) (now, Rule 56(d)) and reversed the grant of summary judgment in a Title VII case because the district court had not first considered plaintiff's pending motion to compel discovery.[54]

Counsel should realize that some Rule 56(d) summary judgment oppositions are merely delaying actions; once the non-movant has been given time to obtain the information specified in his Rule 56(d) affidavit, the court will consider the motion for summary judgment. Even if consideration of the summary judgment motion is only delayed, "summary judgment delayed is (at least temporarily) summary judgment denied." After a Rule 56(d) continuance has been granted, the court may decide to proceed to trial without further consideration of the summary judgment motion or the parties may be able to settle the action. Rule 56(d) can be a powerful weapon in defending against motions for summary judgment.

NOTES AND QUESTIONS CONCERNING SUMMARY JUDGMENT OPPOSITIONS

1. Why will courts generally not grant summary judgment if credibility is at issue? What if the action is to be tried to the court rather than to a jury? What if, although credibility is at issue, the relevant depositions were video-taped?

---

51. *See generally* Brunet, "The Timing of Summary Judgment," 198 F.R.D. 679 (2001).

52. *E.g., Brown v. Mississippi Valley State Univ.*, 311 F.3d 328, 332–34 (5th Cir. 2002); *Glen Eden Hosp., Inc. v. Blue Cross & Blue Shield of Michigan, Inc.*, 740 F.2d 423, 427–28 (6th Cir. 1984); *Delphi–Delco Electronics System v. M/V Nedlloyd Europa*, 324 F.Supp.2d 403, 416–421 (S.D.N.Y. 2004). *See also Fano v. O'Neill*, 806 F.2d 1262, 1266 (5th Cir. 1987).

53. *Weir v. Anaconda Co.*, 773 F.2d 1073, 1081 (10th Cir. 1985).

54. 818 F.2d 1515 (9th Cir. 1987).

2. What role, if any, should the client play in determining how much evidence should be placed into the record to defeat a motion for summary judgment? Are there reasons, apart from a reluctance to provide discovery to an opposing party in the present lawsuit, why a client may wish to withhold information from summary judgment affidavits? Should the client's wishes in such situations control?

3. How should the persons who will offer summary judgment affidavits be chosen? If a case is not resolved by summary judgment, what actions might opposing parties take with respect to those persons who have offered summary judgment affidavits?

4. Can a party oppose the entry of summary judgment for an opposing party and yet file a cross-motion seeking the entry of summary judgment for itself? Are there practical problems with such a position?

Exercises Concerning Summary Judgment Oppositions

1. In the Buffalo Creek litigation filed by plaintiffs' attorney Gerald Stern, the defendant Pittston has made a motion for summary judgment asserting that it is not a proper defendant. The grounds for this motion are described in more detail in exercise 1 of the Exercises Concerning Effective Use of Summary Judgment Motions, *supra* p. 531. You are associated with Gerald Stern in representing the plaintiffs in this action, and he has asked you to write a memorandum discussing the manner in which plaintiffs should oppose this motion. In your memorandum be sure to consider both the legal and factual arguments that should be made, as well as the specific evidentiary materials that should be offered in opposition to Pittston's motion.

2. You are an associate in the law firm that represents the Pittston Company in connection with the Buffalo Creek litigation brought against it by attorney Gerald Stern. Presume that (1) Pittston has filed the motion for summary judgment that forms the basis for the immediately preceding problem; (2) the judge has not yet ruled on Pittston's motion for summary judgment; and (3) the plaintiffs have filed a motion for partial summary judgment addressed only to Pittston's liability for the collapse of the mining dam in Logan County, West Virginia.

Write a memorandum to your senior partner with your recommendations as to how Pittston should respond to plaintiffs' motion for partial summary judgment.

3. You are associated with attorney Gerald Stern in connection with his representation of the approximately 600 plaintiffs who have brought suit against the Pittston Company seeking redress for damages suffered as a result of the Buffalo Creek disaster. Presume that the Pittston Company has filed the summary judgment motion set forth in Section III(D) of this chapter, *supra* p. 528, seeking judgment concerning the claims of thirty-three plaintiffs who were not physically injured in the flood, were not threatened with immediate physical injury from the flood, and did not witness any other person sustain physical injury in the flood. Write a

memorandum to Gerald Stern containing your recommendations as to the plaintiffs' response to Pittston's summary judgment motion.

4. You represent the plaintiff Bart Bakki in the lawsuit described in exercise 4 of the Exercises Concerning Effective Use of Summary Judgment Motions, *supra* p. 532. Draft the papers that you would file in opposition to the summary judgment motion filed on behalf of the defendant school officials in that case.

5. You represent the plaintiff Bart Bakki in the lawsuit described in exercise 4 of the Exercises Concerning Effective Use of Summary Judgment Motions, *supra* p. 532. In contrast to the situation in the immediately preceding exercise, assume that no discovery has been undertaken by any of the parties. Assume also that although he has not been deposed, Bart Bakki has no facts supporting his claim other then those specified in the prior exercises.

Draft the papers that you would file in opposing summary judgment.

V. CONCLUSION

Whether or not we have entered a "New Era for Summary Judgments," all counsel should know how to utilize and oppose motions for summary judgment. As concern with extended and expensive pretrial proceedings mounts, summary judgment may be one of the major ways in which attorneys can tailor and, in at least some cases, resolve civil litigation short of trial. In order to achieve the resultant savings for their clients, attorneys only need take advantage of the procedural tool that has been provided by Rule 56 of the Federal Rules of Civil Procedure.

VI. CHAPTER BIBLIOGRAPHY

Brunet, "Summary Judgment Materials," 147 F.R.D. 647 (1993).

Brunet, "The Timing of Summary Judgment," 198 F.R.D. 679 (2001).

Brunet, "The Use and Misuse of Expert Testimony in Summary Judgment," 22 *U. C. Davis L. Rev.* 93 (1988).

E. Brunet & M. Redish, *Summary Judgment: Federal Law and Practice* (3d ed. 2006).

Burbank, "Vanishing Trials and Summary Judgment in Federal Civil Cases: Drifting Toward Bethlehem or Gomorrah?," 1 *J. Emp. Legal Studies* 591 (2004).

J. Cecil & C. Douglas, *Summary Judgment Practice in Three District Courts* (1987).

Cecil et al., "A Quarter–Century of Summary Judgment Practice in Six Federal District Courts," 4 *J. Emp. Legal Studies* 861 (2007).

Childress, "A New Era for Summary Judgments: Recent Shifts at the Supreme Court," 116 F.R.D. 183 (1987).

Collins, Note, "Summary Judgment and Circumstantial Evidence," 40 *Stan. L. Rev.* 491 (1988).

Cox, Note, "Reconsidering the Sham Affidavit Doctrine," 50 *Duke L. J.* 261 (2000).

Currie, "Thoughts on Directed Verdicts and Summary Judgments," 45 *U. Chi. L. Rev.* 72 (1977).

Duane, "The Four Greatest Myths about Summary Judgment," 52 *Wash. & Lee L. Rev.* 1523 (1996).

Friedenthal, "Cases on Summary Judgment: Has There Been a Material Change in Standards?," 63 *Notre Dame L. Rev.* 770 (1988).

Friedenthal & Gardner, "Judicial Discretion to Deny Summary Judgment in the Era of Managerial Judging," 31 *Hofstra L. Rev.* 91 (2002).

Garner, "Summary Judgment: 'Put Up or Shut Up,'" *Litigation*, Spring 1999, at 23.

Glannon, "Civil Procedure—Summary Judgment—Suggested District Court Procedure," 69 *Mass. L. Rev.* 135 (1984).

Gordillo, Note, "Summary Judgment and Problems in Applying the *Celotex* Trilogy Standard," 42 *Clev. St. L. Rev.* 263 (1994).

Issacharoff & Lowenstein, "Second Thoughts About Summary Judgment," 100 *Yale L. J.* 73 (1990).

Kennedy, "Federal Summary Judgment: Reconciling *Celotex v. Catrett* with *Adickes v. Kress* and the Evidentiary Problems Under Rule 56," 6 *Rev. Litig.* 227 (1987).

Louis, "Federal Summary Judgment Doctrine: A Critical Analysis," 83 *Yale L. J.* 745 (1974).

Maryott, "The Trial on Paper: Key Considerations for Determining Whether to File a Summary Judgment Motion," *Litigation*, Spring 2009, at 36.

McGinley, "Credulous Courts and the Tortured Trilogy: The Improper Use of Summary Judgment in Title VII and ADEA Cases," 34 *B.C. L. Rev.* 203 (1993).

McLauchlan, "An Empirical Study of the Federal Summary Judgment Rule," 6 *J. Legal Stud.* 427 (1977).

Miller, "The Pretrial Rush to Judgment: Are the 'Litigation Explosion,' 'Liability Crisis,' and Efficiency Cliches Eroding our Day in Court and Jury Trial Commitments?," 78 *N. Y. U. L. Rev.* 982 (2003).

Mollica, "Federal Summary Judgment at High Tide," 84 *Marq. L. Rev.* 141 (2000).

Mullenix, "Summary Judgment: Taming the Beast of Burdens," 10 *Am. J. Trial Advoc.* 433 (1987).

Nelken, "One Step Forward, Two Steps Back: Summary Judgment After *Celotex*," 40 *Hastings L. J.* 53 (1988).

Pierce, "Foreword: Summary Judgment: A Favored Means of Summarily Resolving Disputes," 53 *Brooklyn L. Rev.* 279 (1987).

Pollak, "Liberalizing Summary Adjudication: A Proposal," 36 *Hastings L. J.* 419 (1985).

Redish, "Summary Judgment and the Vanishing Trial: Implications of the Litigation Matrix," 57 *Stan. L. Rev.* 1329 (2005).

Risinger, "Another Step in the Counter–Revolution: A Summary Judgment on the Supreme Court's New Approach to Summary Judgment," 54 *Brooklyn L. Rev.* 35 (1988).

Sandler & Corderman, "Winning a Summary Judgment," *Litigation,* Spring 1984, at 15.

Schwarzer, "Summary Judgment under the Federal Rules: Defining Genuine Issues of Material Fact," 99 F.R.D. 465 (1984).

Schwarzer et al., "The Analysis and Decision of Summary Judgment Motions," 139 F.R.D. 441 (1991).

Shannon, "Responding to Summary Judgment," 91 *Marq. L. Rev.* 815 (2008).

Sinclair & Hanes, "Summary Judgment: A Proposal for Procedural Reform in the Core Motion Context," 36 *Wm. & Mary L. Rev.* 1633 (1995).

Sonenshein, "State of Mind and Credibility in the Summary Judgment Context: A Better Approach," 78 *Nw.U. L. Rev.* 774 (1983).

Steinman, "The Irrepressible Myth of *Celotex*: Reconsidering Summary Judgment Burdens Twenty Years After the Trilogy," 63 *Wash. & Lee L. Rev.* 81 (2006).

Stempel, "A Distorted Mirror: The Supreme Court's Shimmering View of Summary Judgment, Directed Verdict, and the Adjudication Process," 49 *Ohio St. L. J.* 95 (1988).

Symposium: "Procedural Justice: Perspectives on Summary Judgment, Peremptory Challenges, and the Exclusionary Rule," 93 *Iowa L. Rev.* 1613 (2008).

Symposium: "The Future of Summary Judgment," 43 *Akron L. Rev.* 1107 (2010).

Wald, "Summary Judgment at Sixty," 76 *Tex. L. Rev.* 1897 (1998).

Wallance, "Summary Judgment Ascending," *Litigation,* Winter 1988, at 6.

Chapter 13

The Final Pretrial Conference, Pretrial Orders, and Judicial Management of the Pretrial Process: "Who's in Charge Here?"

■ ■ ■

[Pre-trial procedure] operates upon each separate case to eliminate all those matters which ought not to be permitted to take up time and cause expense at the trial. It substitutes an open, business-like and efficient presentation of real issues for the traditional strategy of concealment and disguise.

Sunderland, "The Theory and Practice of Pre–Trial Procedure," 36 *Mich. L. Rev.* 215, 226 (1937).

[P]re-trial is an accessory to the trial process, not itself a trial; and it should be kept in its proper subordinate position.

Clark, "To an Understanding Use of Pre–Trial," 29 F.R.D. 454, 461 (1961).

Analysis

I. INTRODUCTION

All good things must come to an end, and so it is with pretrial litigation. The pretrial process culminates in the final pretrial conference and the final pretrial order prepared in connection with that conference. Final pretrial conferences and final pretrial orders, as well as judicial management of the pretrial process, are the subjects discussed in this chapter.

One way to look at pretrial conferences and orders is in terms of control. Pretrial conferences and the orders resulting from these conferences bind the parties and restrict counsel's control over future litigation options. Judges quite rightly believe that they need control over the cases on their dockets. Rule 16 of the Federal Rules of Civil Procedure provides a framework by which the court can be assured of control over civil litigation, while permitting counsel to be the moving forces in defining the claims and issues to be tried.

The present chapter first considers the Rule 16 final pretrial conference, at which counsel and the judge reach agreement about the manner in which the case will be tried. Usually as a result of such a final pretrial conference, the judge enters a final pretrial order. These final pretrial orders govern subsequent proceedings in the action and are discussed in this chapter's second major section. The final major section of the chapter returns explicitly to the question of control and considers the questions raised by the intervention of "managerial judges" into the pretrial process.

Pretrial conferences and orders are important to the litigation attorney for two separate reasons. In order to successfully handle cases prior to trial, the attorney must understand the requirements of Rule 16 and how the final pretrial conference and final pretrial order relate to other pretrial and trial proceedings. In addition to understanding what Rule 16 requires in individual cases, counsel should reflect upon the policy issues posed by Rule 16 and the need to strike a balance between attorney and judicial control of modern pretrial litigation.

II. RULE 16 PRETRIAL CONFERENCES

Rule 16 pretrial conferences are becoming increasingly important in both federal and state litigation. Rule 16 envisions the possibility of multiple conferences during the pretrial stages of a case.[1] Initially, Rule 16 requires that, except for categories of actions exempted by local rule,[2] the district court must enter a scheduling order setting time limitations within which the parties must join other parties, amend the pleadings,

---

1. For an extreme example see *Life Music, Inc. v. Edelstein,* 309 F.2d 242, 242 (2d Cir. 1962) (23 pretrial conferences, recorded in over 1000 pages of transcript).

2. "Logical candidates for [exclusion from mandatory scheduling orders] include social security disability matters, habeas corpus petitions, forfeitures, and reviews of certain administrative actions." Advisory Committee Note to 1983 Amendment to Rule 16, 97 F.R.D. 165, 207 (1983).

complete discovery, and file motions.[3] Rule 16(b)(3)(B)(i) and (ii) provide that this scheduling order also may include modifications of the time for discovery disclosures under Rule 26(a) and (e)(1) and of the extent of discovery to be permitted. Rules 16(b)(3)(B)(iii) and (iv) provide that the scheduling order additionally may "provide for disclosure or discovery of electronically stored information" and "include any agreements the parties reach for asserting claims of privilege or of protection as trial-preparation material after information is produced."

Typically Rule 16(b) scheduling orders result from an initial scheduling conference involving the judge and counsel, which in some districts may be conducted over the telephone.[4] In most cases the parties are required to hold a Rule 26(f) discovery conference, and the report of that meeting is to be submitted to the court before the scheduling order is entered so that the court can consider that report in formulating its order.[5]

Some judges hold not only initial scheduling conferences and final pretrial conferences, but also other, intermediate conferences as deemed necessary by the court. Such conferences became more common as a result of the Civil Justice Reform Act of 1990, which, *inter alia*, required all district courts to consider as a principle of litigation management "early and ongoing control of the pretrial process through involvement of a judicial officer" in various aspects of the pretrial process.[6] Intermediate pretrial conferences often are less formal than the final pretrial conference, and Rule 16(d) provides that the orders resulting from these conferences are subject to modification by later orders of court. Even if not mandated by the court, counsel can request that the court hold a pretrial conference in order to facilitate case preparation or pretrial settlement.

In contrast to intermediate pretrial conferences, the final pretrial conference may require quite extensive preparation by counsel. This

---

3. Fed. R. Civ. P. 16(b)(3)(A). The requirement of a pretrial scheduling order was added to Rule 16 by the substantial amendments to that Rule in 1983. The requirement for scheduling orders was premised upon "[e]mpirical studies [that] reveal that when a trial judge intervenes personally at an early stage to assume judicial control over a case and to schedule dates for completion by the parties of the principal pretrial steps, the case is disposed of by settlement or trial more efficiently and with less cost and delay than when the parties are left to their own devices." Advisory Committee Note to 1983 Amendment to Rule 16, 97 F.R.D. 165, 207 (1983). *See* S. Flanders, *Case Management and Court Management in United States District Courts* (1977).

While other pretrial conferences and orders are provided for by Rule 16, they are not mandatory as are Rule 16(b) scheduling orders in most cases.

4. Fed. R. Civ. P. 16(b)(1)(B). *See also, e.g.,* Rule 16.1(b) of the United States District Court for the Eastern District of Pennsylvania. An example of a pretrial scheduling order resulting from a pretrial conference is set forth in Chapter 6, *supra* p. 300.

The Judicial Conference of the United States has recommended the use of electronic technologies such as teleconferencing and video telecommunications for appropriate pretrial conferences. Judicial Conference of the United States, *Final Report—The Civil Justice Reform Act of 1990*, 175 F.R.D. 62, 85–87 (1997). Pretrial conferences also have been held online successfully. "Pretrial Conference in Ohio Held Online," *Atlanta Journal–Constitution*, June 3, 2000, at A4.

5. Fed. R. Civ. P. 16(b)(1)(A); Advisory Committee Note to 1993 Amendment to Rule 16(b), 146 F.R.D. 401, 603 (1993).

6. 28 U.S.C. § 473(a)(2) (expired Dec. 1, 1997).

conference may be counsel's final chance to discuss the conduct of the trial with the court and opposing counsel, and, pursuant to Rule 16(e), the order resulting from the final pretrial conference may be modified "only to prevent manifest injustice."

While counsel must be ready to participate in scheduling and other preliminary pretrial conferences, this chapter's focus is on final pretrial conferences and the final pretrial orders resulting from these conferences. In the present section, the final pretrial conference is first described; then suggestions are made concerning attorney preparation for and handling of the final pretrial conference. The section ends with a portion of the transcript from an actual final pretrial conference.

A. THE FINAL PRETRIAL CONFERENCE

Over fifty years ago, Judge J. Skelly Wright remarked that "pretrial is the salvation of the administration of justice in the Twentieth Century."[7] Some attorneys, however, may not wish to be saved. As Chief Justice Warren Burger noted in 1976, "Increasingly in the past 20 years, responsible lawyers have pointed to abuses of the pretrial process in civil cases. The complaint is that misuse of pretrial procedures means that 'the case must be tried twice.' "[8]

Rule 16 does not require that any case "must be tried twice." The objectives of the pretrial conference are set forth in Rule 16, itself, and include:

(1) expediting disposition of the action;

(2) establishing early and continuing control so that the case will not be protracted because of lack of management;

(3) discouraging wasteful pretrial activities;

(4) improving the quality of the trial through more thorough preparation, and;

(5) facilitating settlement.[9]

Pretrial conferences are intended not only to enhance the efficiency with which cases are handled at the pretrial and trial stages, but to improve the quality of the end result of the case during pretrial, at trial, or by way of settlement. An early study of mandatory pretrial conferences in personal injury cases in the New Jersey state courts concluded, however, that all of these objectives may not be achieved in all cases.[10]

---

7. Wright, "The Pretrial Conference," 28 F.R.D. 141, 157 (1960).

8. Burger, "Agenda for 2000 A.D.—A Need for Systematic Anticipation," 70 F.R.D. 83, 95–96 (1976). *See also* Pollack, "Pretrial Conferences," 50 F.R.D. 449, 451–52 (1970).

9. Fed. R. Civ. P. 16(a). *See generally* Clark, "Objectives of Pre–Trial Procedure," 17 *Ohio St. L. J.* 163 (1956).

10. M. Rosenberg, *The Pretrial Conference and Effective Justice* (1964). *See also* T. Willging, *Trends in Asbestos Litigation* 73 (1987) ("Efforts to produce earlier settlement [by judicial intervention] appear justifiable only on grounds of improving the quality of settlements; efficiency grounds will support little more than a system of imposing fines for delayed settlements or a brief

This study of 1960 through 1962 cases concluded that the trial presentation was improved in some of the pretried cases, but that appreciable amounts of court time were required to conduct the pretrials.[11] The study also revealed that mandatory pretrial did not increase the frequency of pretrial settlements nor lead to a reduction in the amount of time required to try the cases.[12] The recommendation of the study was for selective, rather than mandatory, pretrial of cases, as provided by Rule 16 of the Federal Rules of Civil Procedure.[13]

Specific pretrial requirements vary greatly from court to court and judge to judge.[14] District judges have the inherent authority to require the attendance of counsel at pretrial conferences,[15] and Rule 16(c)(1) specifically provides that, if appropriate, "the court may require that a party or its representative be present or reasonably available by other means to consider possible settlement."[16]

---

judge-hosted conference."). *Cf.* J. Kakalik et al., *Just, Speedy, and Inexpensive? An Evaluation of Judicial Case Management Under the Civil Justice Reform Act* 1–2 (RAND Institute for Civil Justice 1996) ("Early judicial case management, setting the trial schedule early, shortened time to discovery cutoff, and having litigants at or available for settlement conferences are associated with a significantly reduced time to disposition. Early judicial case management also is associated with significantly increased costs to litigants, as measured by attorney work hours.").

11. M. Rosenberg, *supra* note 10, at 28–29.

12. *Id.* at 46–47, 50–53.

13. *Id.* at 124. *See also* Walker & Thibaut, "An Experimental Examination of Pretrial Conference Techniques," 55 *Minn. L. Rev.* 1113, 1133–34 (1971). Based on the simulations of pretrial conferences described in this article, the authors also recommend that pretrial judges encourage package settlement offers rather than settlement of individual issues and that pretrial conferences should begin with discussions of settlement rather than with a discussion of the issues. *Id.* This final recommendation runs counter to the recommendations and practice of some judges. "Handbook for Effective Pretrial Procedure," 37 F.R.D. 255, 270–71 (1964); Thomas, "The Story of Pre–Trial in the Common Pleas Court of Cuyahoga County," 7 *W. Res. L. Rev.* 368, 390–91 (1956). See also Judicial Conference of the United States, *Civil Litigation Management Manual* 60–63 (2001).

14. For a summary of the different approaches to pretrial conferences adopted by federal judicial districts prior to the 1983 amendments to Rule 16 see Kulasza, Note, "Pretrial Conference: A Critical Examination of Local Rules Adopted by Federal District Courts," 64 *Va. L. Rev.* 467 (1978). For descriptions of judicial activity under the amended Rule 16 see N. Weeks, *District Court Implementation of Amended Civil Rule 16: A Report on New Local Rules* (1984).

15. In *Link v. Wabash R. R. Co.*, 370 U.S. 626 (1962), the Supreme Court upheld the dismissal of an action due to the failure of plaintiff's counsel to attend a pretrial conference after earlier delays had been caused by that counsel. Rule 16(f), added to the Federal Rules of Civil Procedure in 1983, now explicitly gives federal judges this authority. One federal appellate court has described Rule 16(f) as "the judicial stick which insures that lawyers and litigants partake of the carrot of increased efficiency." *Figueroa–Rodriguez v. Lopez–Rivera*, 878 F.2d 1488, 1490 (1st Cir. 1988), *vac'd and modified on other grounds*, 878 F.2d 1478 (1st Cir. 1989) (en banc).

16. Even prior to the 1993 amendment that added this provision to Rule 16(c), the United States Court of Appeals for the Seventh Circuit had held that district judges could require the attendance of represented parties at pretrial conferences. *G. Heileman Brewing Co. v. Joseph Oat Corp.*, 871 F.2d 648 (7th Cir. 1989) (en banc). *See also In re Novak*, 932 F.2d 1397 (11th Cir. 1991) (while district court could not directly order employee of non-party insurer to appear for settlement conference, it had inherent authority to order defendant to produce individual with full settlement authority).

What, though, if the party produces a representative for the final pretrial conference but that party has an across-the-board policy against settling suits with its customers (such as the plaintiff in the lawsuit)? In *Shedden v. Wal–Mart Stores, Inc.*, 196 F.R.D. 484 (E.D.Mich. 2000), the judge ordered Wal–Mart's general counsel or other corporate officer with litigation policy authority to attend trial because of Wal–Mart's across-the-board policy that it would not settle suits brought by customers. The court noted, 196 F.R.D. at 486, "'[A]n across-the-board policy of refusing to

Local rules and standing orders requiring parties to attend pretrial conferences are premised, at least in part, upon a judicial desire to use these conferences to achieve settlements.[17] A leading judicial proponent of the pretrial conference made the following observation many years ago about requiring parties to attend pretrial conferences:

> Perhaps the presence of the parties [at the pretrial conference] has contributed most in furthering settlements. * * * It is the plaintiff who is the chief exhibit in a personal injury action. In evaluating a lawsuit there is no substitute for an opportunity for the man with the checkbook to see the plaintiff, to hear him talk, to view any residual effects of the injury. The sight of the plaintiff at the pre-trial has caused many claims men to realistically re-evaluate their figures upward, thus making settlements possible.[18]

While some attorneys may resent perceived judicial pressure to settle cases at pretrial conferences, Judge Charles Richey has suggested that clients should be present at final pretrial conferences because of the possibly conflicting interests of attorney and client. "It is an unfortunate fact that courts cannot always rely on attorneys to fairly represent to their clients the merits of a particular settlement. To overcome this tension, it is in my view critical that courts have the authority to compel the attendance at settlement conferences of clients themselves, where the clients can evaluate *for themselves* whether settlement best serves their interests."[19]

As with party attendance requirements, the timing of pretrial conferences varies from court to court and judge to judge. In some jurisdictions, the final pretrial conference often was held significantly before the scheduled trial date.[20] However, Rule 16(e) now provides that any final pretrial conference "must be held as close to the start of trial as is reasonable." Some judges hold pretrial conferences only a few days before the scheduled trial date.[21]

---

negotiate frustrates both the letter and spirit of both the Federal Rules of Civil Procedure and this Court's Local Rules, which encourage good faith settlement efforts in order to preserve scarce judicial resources."

17. Federal Rule of Civil Procedure 16(c)(2)(I) lists as one of the subjects that may be considered at pretrial conferences "settling the case and using special procedures to assist in resolving the dispute when authorized by statute or local rule." *See also* 1983 Advisory Committee Note to Rule 16, 97 F.R.D. 165, 210 (1983) ("Although it is not the purpose of Rule [16(c)(2)(I)] to impose settlement negotiations on unwilling litigants, it is believed that providing a neutral forum for discussing the subject might foster it.").

18. Thomas, "The Story of Pre-trial in the Common Pleas Court of Cuyahoga County," 7 *W. Res. L. Rev.* 368, 381–82 (1956).

19. Richey, "Rule 16: A Survey and Some Considerations for the Bench and Bar," 126 F.R.D. 599, 604 (1989).

20. Pollack, "Pretrial Conferences," 50 F.R.D. 451, 460 (1970) (pretrial orders sometimes entered one year prior to trial).

21. *E.g.*, Krupansky, "The Federal Rules are Alive and Well," *Litigation,* Fall 1977, at 10, 12 (final pretrial conference held 3 days before trial). *See also* Rubin, "The Managed Calendar: Some Pragmatic Suggestions about Achieving the Just, Speedy and Inexpensive Determination of Civil Cases in Federal Courts," 4 *Just. Sys. J.* 135, 141 (1978) (recommending holding final pretrial conference 10 to 14 days before trial). Judge Charles Richey, however, notes that "[t]o conduct

Local practice varies as to whether the judge who will try the case conducts the pretrial conference or the case is assigned to another district judge or magistrate judge for pretrial. There are obvious advantages in having the judge who will preside at trial help shape the case at the final pretrial conference. However, if one of the major purposes of the final pretrial conference is to attempt to settle the case, there may be advantages in someone other than the trier of fact conducting the pretrial conference.

B. SUGGESTIONS FOR HANDLING THE FINAL PRETRIAL CONFERENCE

The manner in which counsel should approach the final pretrial conference will depend in large measure upon the local rules and standing orders governing the conference and the expectations of the judge who will preside at the conference. This section offers advice concerning pretrial conferences generally.

First of all, attorneys should prepare for the final pretrial conference just as they would for any other court appearance. Rule 16(c)(2) contains a lengthy list of matters that may be considered at the pretrial conference. Included on this list are "formulating and simplifying the issues," "amending the pleadings if necessary or desirable," "obtaining admissions and stipulations about facts and documents," "identifying witnesses and documents," "settling the case," and "facilitating in other ways the just, speedy, and inexpensive disposition of the action."[22]

Because of the great number of matters that can be discussed at a final pretrial conference, and the binding effect of the final pretrial order, more thorough preparation for the conference may be necessary than for other, earlier and more focused, court appearances. Quite simply, counsel should come to the conference prepared for anything.[23] Counsel also should be aware that sanctions may be imposed upon attorneys, parties, or both if a party or party's attorney "is substantially unprepared to participate—or does not participate in good faith—in the conference."[24]

Attorneys should be knowledgeable about all prior proceedings in the case and should come to the conference with a file documenting all pretrial case activity. Counsel should be prepared to talk not only about prior pretrial activity, but also about all aspects of the upcoming trial. For

---

the conference too close to trial actually begets error and perhaps injustice. * * * [I]t may also increase the costs of litigation through the actual commencement of trial followed by a settlement shortly thereafter." Richey, "Rule 16: A Survey and Some Considerations for the Bench and Bar," 126 F.R.D. 599, 610 (1989).

22. Fed. R. Civ. P. 16(c)(A), (B), (C), (G), (I), (P).

23. *See, e.g., Portsmouth Square, Inc. v. Shareholders Protective Comm.,* 770 F.2d 866, 868–70 (9th Cir. 1985) (affirming district judge's *sua sponte* grant of summary judgment at pretrial conference). *But see Williams v. Georgia Dept. of Human Resources,* 789 F.2d 881 (11th Cir. 1986) (district judge reversed for granting "directed verdict" at pretrial conference based on evidence parties planned to present at trial).

24. Fed. R. Civ. P. 16(f)(1)(B).

this reason, the attorney or attorneys who actually will try the case should attend the final pretrial conference. In fact, Rule 16 requires that the final pretrial conference "must be attended by at least one attorney who will conduct the trial for each party and by any unrepresented party."[25]

Pursuant to Rule 16(c)(2)(G), final pretrial and trial dates may be set at the final pretrial conference. If there is discovery that has not yet been completed, the judge may set a date for its completion. The judge also may set a date for submission of the proposed final pretrial order (if it has not been completed prior to the final pretrial conference), as well as for the trial of the action. Because these dates may be set by the court, attorneys should bring their calendars to the final pretrial conference.

Not only will the trial of the action be discussed at the final pretrial conference, but many judges use this conference to discuss settlement. Professor Albert Alschuler has referred to the pretrial conference as an "antitrial conference" because of the settlement focus of so many of these conferences.[26] Counsel therefore should discuss settlement with her client before the conference and be prepared to respond to settlement offers or inquiries that may be made at the conference. Many judges require that clients attend the final pretrial conference.[27] Even if the client is not required to attend, he usually should be available by telephone to respond to settlement offers that may be made during the pretrial conference.

After the conclusion of the pretrial conference, counsel should be certain to follow up with respect to any remaining business. The client should be informed about the outcome of the conference and the status of final trial preparations. All witnesses should be contacted and informed of the trial date, and, if the trial date is imminent, subpoenas should be issued to ensure the attendance of all witnesses at trial. Finally, counsel may be asked to draft a proposed final pretrial order to reflect the actions taken at the final pretrial conference.

C. A TRANSCRIPT OF A FINAL PRETRIAL CONFERENCE

What happens at any pretrial conference will depend in large measure upon the district judge or magistrate judge who presides at that conference. An idea of the types of matters typically discussed at final pretrial conferences, and of the informal give-and-take characteristic of these

---

25. Fed. R. Civ. P. 16(e). In addition, Rule 16(c)(1) requires that "[a] represented party must authorize at least one of its attorneys to make stipulations and admissions about all matters that can reasonably be anticipated for discussion at a pretrial conference."

26. Alschuler, "Mediation with a Mugger: The Shortage of Adjudicative Services and the Need for a Two–Tier System in Civil Cases," 99 *Harv. L. Rev.* 1808, 1828 (1986).

27. In *Lockhart v. Patel,* 115 F.R.D. 44 (E.D.Ky. 1987), the court struck defendant's pleadings and held him in default due to the refusal of defendant's insurance carrier to send a representative with settlement authority to a pretrial conference. *See also G. Heileman Brewing Co. v. Joseph Oat Corp.,* 871 F.2d 648 (7th Cir. 1989) (en banc); *In re LaMarre,* 494 F.2d 753, 756 (6th Cir. 1974). *But see In re Novak,* 932 F.2d 1397 (11th Cir. 1991) (while district court could not directly order employee of non-party insurer to appear for settlement conference, it had inherent authority to order defendant to produce individual with full settlement authority).

conferences, can be gained from the following transcript. While pretrial conferences often are not recorded, the following transcript was made with the consent of counsel for inclusion in a law review symposium concerning pretrial.[28]

The transcript is of a 1956 pretrial conference presided over by Judge William K. Thomas in the Ohio Court of Common Pleas. The lawsuit stemmed from an accident between a car and a tractor trailer. The car's driver and passenger (Dennis and Bertha Morris) sued the owners and operators of the tractor trailer (the Baxters) and a freight company with which the Baxters had contracted (Lake Shore Motor Freight). The Baxters were insured by the Farm Bureau Mutual Automobile Insurance Company, and Lake Shore Motor Freight was insured by Great American Indemnity Company. The Morris's claims were settled for $9,250, with the two insurance companies reserving the question of their relative responsibilities for satisfying the settlement. The Farm Bureau then brought suit against Great American, seeking a declaratory judgment construing the insurance policies covering the Baxters and Lake Shore Motor Freight. The following pretrial conference was held in this declaratory judgment action.

THOMAS, "THE STORY OF PRE-TRIAL IN THE COMMON PLEAS COURT OF CUYAHOGA COUNTY"

7 W. Res. L. Rev. 368, 393–98, 400–401, 403–405, 408 (1956).

THE COURT: Gentlemen, I have gone over the pleadings in this matter and as I read them it occurred to me that there are a number of points that are admitted on both sides and I would like to record all of the points that can be admitted and then when we reach a point that is disputed we can, of course, hear from each side so stating.

* * *

THE COURT: All right. I understand gentlemen, the pleadings—it is admitted that on May 10, 1951 a collision occurred at or near the intersection of Detroit Road and Dover Road in the County of Cuyahoga, State of Ohio, and that collision involved a westbound tractor and a passenger automobile, I believe, operated in a northerly direction, if I recall correctly; is that correct?

MR. DAVIS: That is correct.

MR. WARDER: Yes.

THE COURT: The westerly-bound tractor was operated by George A. Martin, Jr.—

MR. WARDER: That is right.

---

28. "Pre–Trial—A Symposium," 7 *W. Res. L. Rev.* 367 (1956). For a simulation of the initial pretrial conference in complex civil litigation *see* Pointer, "Complex Litigation: Demonstration of Pretrial Conference," 6 *Rev. Litig.* 285 (1987). *See also* Kincaid, "A Judge's Handbook of Pre–Trial Procedure," 17 F.R.D. 437, 458 (1955) ("Exemplar of Pre–Trial Conference Procedure").

THE COURT:—and the northerly-bound automobile was being driven by Dennis Morris, and in it was his wife Bertha Morris. Are those facts agreed on?

MR. WARDER: I am agreed.

MR. DAVIS: That is correct.

THE COURT: Now, then, secondly, without going into details, it is agreed that some injuries were sustained by Bertha Morris—

MR. WARDER: Yes.

THE COURT:—and Dennis Morris; is that correct?

Mr. Warder: Yes.

THE COURT: That is correct?

MR. DAVIS: Yes, that is correct.

THE COURT: Do you care at this time to indicate the extent of those injuries?

MR. DAVIS: Do you want the extent of the money that we paid?

THE COURT: Well, we are going to get to that in a moment so perhaps we can save any discussion of injuries for that point.

MR. WARDER: I would think so.

THE COURT: All right.

MR. DAVIS: I didn't bring that file with me so I don't recall what the injuries were; the woman was laid up for several months but I don't know—

THE COURT: Now, then, the next point which appears to be admitted on both sides is that the tractor was owned by Florence Baxter and Ford Baxter, or was owned by Florence Baxter and Ford had the right to use it? Which?

MR. DAVIS: Well, that is a question.

MR. WARDER: That is a good question. We don't honestly know the answer to that.

THE COURT: What do you say, Mr. Warder, on behalf of the plaintiff?

MR. WARDER: It is my understanding it was Florence Baxter, but as there is no documentary evidence on that I am relying on what Ford Baxter told me.

THE COURT: What do you say, Mr. Davis?

MR. DAVIS: My understanding is that Florence Baxter's husband had died shortly before this time, before the time this contract was entered into in 1950—

* * *

MR. WARDER: Well, I don't think we have any disagreement here; my understanding is that Florence Baxter owned the business; that her son ran it more or less as a manager with full authority to sign any contract; and there is no question but what he had the authority to execute it; but she owned the business.

THE COURT: Just to get that relationship clear, Ford Baxter is the son of Florence Baxter, is that right?

MR. WARDER: He is her son.

THE COURT: Can it be stipulated, gentlemen, that the actual certificate of title of the tractor was in the name of Florence Baxter?

MR. WARDER: Yes.

MR. DAVIS: I assume so; yes.

THE COURT: Can that be agreed?

MR. DAVIS: I think so; yes.

THE COURT: All right. Now, then, that brings us to the contract to which you have made reference, Mr. Davis. As I understand it, there was a contract between Lake Shore Motor Freight and Ford Baxter; is that correct?

MR. DAVIS: That is right.

THE COURT: Do you have a copy of it there?

MR. DAVIS: A photostatic copy; think we furnished it—

MR. WARDER: You have.

THE COURT: Gentlemen, I am going to mark this, if I may, as Pre-trial Exhibit 1.

MR. DAVIS: We have the original some place.

THE COURT: Now, with reference to Pre-trial Exhibit 1, which appears to be in the original form a single sheet with printing on front side and back side and with the signatures on the first page, do you say, Mr. Davis, that this is the agreement which was signed by Ford Baxter and Lake Shore Motor Freight on or about the 26th day of August, 1950?

MR. DAVIS: Yes.

THE COURT: All right. Mr. Warder, are you prepared to stipulate that this is a correct photostatic copy of the original agreement?

MR. WARDER: That is what I wanted to ask the question about. This accident occurred May 10, 1951; this agreement is executed August 26, 1950. Now, was this, the same agreement in effect? That is what I want to be certain of.

MR. DAVIS: Yes, that is the same agreement that was in effect.

MR. WARDER: And there is no subsequent—

MR. DAVIS: No.

MR. WARDER: I will stipulate.

MR. DAVIS: You will note, I think, that that agreement continues in effect until cancelled by one of the parties; that there is no other agreement, that I know of, prior to May 10, 1951.

THE COURT: All right. The record may show that the parties have stipulated that Pre-trial Exhibit 1 was and continued to be the contract in full force and effect between Lake Shore Motor Freight * * * and Ford Baxter * * * .

     * * *

THE COURT: Now, that brings us, I think, to the insurance policies. First of all, with reference to the policy of Farm Bureau, Mr. Warder, what are the facts in that respect?

MR. WARDER: I have here what purports to be a copy of it—I am sure Mr. Davis has a copy of it; don't you? Do you have a copy of our policy?

MR. DAVIS: Not of yours, no.

MR. WARDER: Well, now, this is just a copy, it is not admissible—in the event we can't stipulate I will have to bring up the records from Canton, * * * but here, you can look it over (indicating); I am sure that it is the policy.

MR. DAVIS: I will admit that is a copy of the policy.

THE COURT: All right; the policy, copy which has been submitted by Mr. Warder as a true and correct copy of the original policy, will be marked as Pre-trial Exhibit 2. May it be stipulated, gentlemen, that this is the policy of casualty insurance that covered Ford Baxter in the operation of the tractor involved in the collision, and which policy was in full force and effect on May 10, 1951?

MR. WARDER: I will so stipulate; yes.

MR. DAVIS: Yes.

THE COURT: Both sides stipulate?

MR. WARDER: Yes. * * *

THE COURT: All right: Now, then with reference to the Great American Casualty policy which insured Lake Shore Motor Freight, do you have a copy of that, Mr. Davis?

MR. DAVIS: I have a copy of various forms, part of it, here (indicating).

THE COURT: Can you put it together in one composite policy, do you think?

     * * *

MR. DAVIS: Yes. To get the policy correctly before the Court it probably would have to have copied—the first sheet copied on here; then we could present a copy of the policy as issued, plus the various endorsements.

THE COURT: I am wondering if perhaps this might not be a good way to proceed: Suppose Mr. Davis were asked to agree to make up a complete policy, and together with that have an affidavit signed by a responsible officer of the corporation that that was the complete policy of insurance on Lake Shore Motor Freight as of that date of May 10, 1951? * * *

* * *

THE COURT: What do you say about that approach to it, Mr. Warder?

MR. WARDER: I am a little bit reluctant to rely on an affidavit on something like that; that really is the $64 question. Now, what is the extent of their coverage and what is the extent of our coverage, as I see it, are the only two important questions in this lawsuit.

THE COURT: In other words, putting it another way, the basic question in this lawsuit is whether the tractor that collided with the Morris car was insured, (a) by Farm Bureau, or (b) by Great American, or (c) by both?

MR. WARDER: Yes.

THE COURT: If C is correct, then you would have a further question: To the extent of proportionate responsibility of each company? Is that the basic fact or crucial issue of the case?

MR. WARDER: This is the case. Very clear.

THE COURT: Do you agree with that Mr. Davis?

MR. DAVIS: Well, I'll see. A by Farm Bureau?

THE COURT: A by Farm Bureau alone.

MR. DAVIS: That is right.

THE COURT: B by Great American alone.

MR. DAVIS: Yes.

THE COURT: C by both; and if it is C, then it becomes a question of the proportion of liability to each.

MR. DAVIS: Not of the proportion, but of their respective liabilities; whether primary or secondary.

THE COURT: Well, I think the primary or secondary question would come under A or B—no, not necessarily, because you say "alone," don't you?

MR. DAVIS: There is no question that as far as we are concerned, that we covered this tractor to the extent of $10,000; that, as I say, we, the Great American—

THE COURT: At the time of the accident?

MR. DAVIS: At the time of the accident; there is no question about that.

* * *

MR. DAVIS: * * *

Now, if the Farm Bureau, having also covered this tractor, then the question is, first, whether the Farm Bureau coverage is primary or whether the Great American coverage is primary; second, if the Great American coverage is on there at all—I will change that. If the Great American and Farm Bureau both cover, without any question as to which is primary and which is secondary, then the question would be, which is the question in the lawsuit, as to whether the $10,000 applies only on the Great American policy or whether the $200,000, which is their—or $400,000, which is their total coverage?

Our position is that, first, that the Farm Bureau is primary coverage; second, that if they should find that the Farm Bureau is not the primary coverage, then we are in there equally with the Farm Bureau on $10,000 apiece and we each owe half of the settlement.

THE COURT: What is the position of Farm Bureau, Mr. Warder?

MR. WARDER: Well, we maintain, first, that they are the primary coverer—

* * *

THE COURT: * * * Well, let's see what other additional facts, first, from the standpoint of the plaintiff, are subject to stipulation.

MR. WARDER: Well, I have been served with Notice To Take Depositions in Youngstown on Tuesday. It is my understanding you are going to take the deposition of the driver of this truck?

MR. DAVIS: Yes.

MR. WARDER: I can't imagine anything that he would say that I wouldn't stipulate to.

MR. DAVIS: Well—

MR. WARDER: What are you trying to prove?

MR. DAVIS: The only thing I am trying to prove on that, and I would say that it is probably not a very strong point, is that the reason for this collision was the complete failure of his brakes. That is his statement.

* * *

THE COURT: Let me ask this, Smith, on that point: Since you said that it is possible that maybe the deposition could be avoided, do you by any chance have and would you want to show a signed statement of Martin, which conceivably you might have on that? Now, if that is not a fair question, why, tell me so.

MR. DAVIS: No—I will tell you: I think we have, and I will tell you the reason we don't have it here: Because this file is about that big (indicating), and I separated it, the parts that I thought would be pertinent to bring down here; and the parts that deal with the Morris cases are all in the office. Now, I may have such a statement, Smith may have it, or the Farm Bureau, because they made the original investigation.

MR. WARDER: He told that to the police; there is no question about that.

MR. DAVIS: Pardon me?

MR. WARDER: George Martin told that to the police; And I wanted to check the statement we have from George Martin and here it is (indicating). * * * [The statement then was read.]

MR. DAVIS: That doesn't coincide with ours but on the basis of that statement I am perfectly willing to drop the deposition.

    * * *

THE COURT: Would the parties stipulate that without the necessity of calling Walter F. O'Malley as a witness at the trial of this action, that if he were called to testify that he would testify as he did in his deposition on January 25, 1956?

MR. WARDER: Yes, I will so stipulate, but I don't want to foreclose myself from subpoenaing Mr. O'Malley if something that I don't presently foresee comes up.

MR. DAVIS: Shall we put it here as we have got it there, to the effect that the driver of the truck received orders in Cleveland to proceed to Lorain to pick up some steel to take to Economy, Pennsylvania?

MR. WARDER: I will do better than that; I will stipulate with you that the deposition of Walter F. O'Malley taken January 25, 1956 may be read in evidence on trial without further authentication and without filing.

THE COURT: Doesn't that take care of it?

MR. WARDER: How is that?

MR. DAVIS: That is right; that takes care of it. Thank you. Now, is the contract between Baxter and Lake Shore admitted?

THE COURT: Yes.

MR. WARDER: Yes.

MR. DAVIS: Is it admitted that George Martin, Jr. was an employee of Ford Baxter?

MR. WARDER: Yes.

MR. DAVIS: Well, as far as I can see—and we have admitted the insurance policy of the Farm Bureau?

THE COURT: Yes.

MR. DAVIS: I can't think of anything else.

THE COURT: All right, gentlemen. Then that brings us to a discussion of the issues; we have already touched on those but I think that perhaps at this point it may be helpful to attempt to clarify our thinking on it a little further.

Mr. Warder, will you state, if you will please, the position of Farm Bureau? I realize you have set it forth at some length in your petition but I think it may be helpful if you give us the essence of your position.

MR. WARDER: Yes. I would like to start with where Mr. Davis left off. I make no quarrel, that is, between Lake Shore and Baxter—well, no—as between Lake Shore and Martin, that the liability of Martin is primary and that the Lake Shore is secondary. Now, I have some doubts about whether, as between Baxter and Lake Shore, that is the situation, in spite of this case (indicating).

* * *

MR. WARDER: Here is my theory of this lawsuit: That the Farm Bureau policy—let's start with that—the plaintiff's policy insures anyone legally responsible for the operation of this truck; anybody; that would include Lake Shore, that would include Baxter, that would include Martin had he been sued, and we would have had a duty to defend.

Now, by a parity of reasoning, your policy has the same provisions. I think that Lake Shore's policy affords coverage to Lake Shore, to Baxter and to Martin.

Now, the fact that those various people may as between themselves have had primary and secondary responsibility seems to me to be a wholly different thing from saying which is the primary or secondary insurer. Do you follow me on that?

MR. DAVIS: Yes.

MR. WARDER: The only authority I know of anywhere in Ohio in what is a primary and secondary insurer is Trinity Universal vs. General Accident; I think that is 138; if it is not, try 137; it is one of them. I find I always miss these things one volume; do you, Judge?

THE COURT: Gee, I am lucky if I come that close.

MR. WARDER: But that case announces the principle that where one company insures the risk in general terms, and another company insures a specific risk, that the specific insurer has the primary coverage. Now, that case involved a premises liability policy and an automobile policy, and the automobile carrier contended that there was co-extensive insurance, and the Supreme Court said that is not right here because this general insurer covers the whole field and he just covers this automobile just by happenstance because it happened to be on the premises when the accident happened, but you have got the specific risk and you were primarily liable.

Now, we don't have that situation; we have got two policies, both of which cover this trip over the road, or any trip over the road with this truck for that matter.

Now, I think as between the insurance companies it is co-extensive coverage, and your problem here is not who is primary between Baxter and Lake Shore—your problem here is if there be dual coverage as to anybody?

[Counsel and the court discussed this legal issue.]

* * *

THE COURT: * * * We have now reached that point in the pre-trial where I think that it might very well be profitable to have a separate discussion with each side looking to the possibility of an amicable adjustment of your controversy, unless you feel that this is the kind of case where you want to make some earth-shaking law establishing a principle that might conceivably have some bearing on later cases.

Would you at this time like to indulge in that discussion or would you prefer to wait until you have had an opportunity to exchange the further exhibits?

MR. DAVIS: I think, possibly, Judge, we may both be in the same position: We would have to communicate with our home offices before we could [even] talk; is that right, Smith?

MR. WARDER: I have some limited authority depending on what develops on your exhibit though. There is no use of my kidding you; we may loosen up a little bit, depending on what develops in your exhibit.

MR. DAVIS: Don't strain yourself.

THE COURT: We will leave it this way, gentlemen: Let's get that complete exhibit, and then we will resume settlement discussions, which normally would occur at this point in the pre-trial.

Notes and Questions Concerning the Pretrial Conference Transcript

1. How well were counsel prepared for this pretrial conference? Were there things that counsel should have done to prepare for the pretrial that they did not do? How might the conference have been different had the parties been required to prepare a proposed joint pretrial order prior to the conference?

2. Were counsel prepared to make significant stipulations or concessions at the pretrial? Were they too ready to do so? What role did the judge play in the stipulation process? Are there any problems with the role that he played?

3. Based on this transcript, how would you characterize the relationship between counsel in this case? How would you characterize the relationship between counsel and the court?

4. Only one of the parties had a representative other than trial counsel at this pretrial. Might the pretrial have been conducted any differently if both parties had representatives present?

5. Why did the judge probe the attorneys concerning the facts underlying this case? Isn't it the job of counsel to present the facts that they consider relevant at trial? Is it the facts or the law that appear most important at this pretrial?

6. In what manner did the judge broach the possibility of settlement? How did counsel respond to the judge's questions about settlement? How might either the judge or counsel have handled this matter differently?

7. Other than agreement to several stipulations, what was accomplished at this pretrial?

Exercises Concerning Pretrial Conferences

1. Thomas Eakins, who was introduced in exercise 1 of the Exercises Concerning Client Interviewing in Chapter 2, *supra* p. 38, filed and prosecuted a lawsuit against the Pittston Company due to the injuries that he sustained in the Buffalo Creek disaster. This lawsuit is set for trial in two months in the United States District Court for the Southern District of West Virginia. The separate action filed by attorney Gerald Stern has just settled.

Judge K. K. Hall, who will try Eakins's case, has asked the parties for their preferences concerning the final pretrial conference. The judge has asked for a short memorandum from counsel addressing the following specific questions:

(1) Should the parties be present at the final pretrial conference?

(2) Are there persons other than the parties and their attorneys who should be present at the pretrial conference?

(3) Should the case be pretried by Judge Hall or by a United States Magistrate Judge assigned specifically to that task?

(4) How soon before trial should the final pretrial conference be held?

(5) How long do the parties estimate that the final pretrial conference will last?

(6) Do the parties wish for the court to attempt to facilitate a settlement at the pretrial conference?

Based upon the facts as you presume them to be at this stage of the case, draft the memorandum requested by the court:

(a) on behalf of the plaintiff Thomas Eakins; or

(b) on behalf of the defendant Pittston Company.

2. You are a law clerk to Judge Jan Nelson, recently appointed to the United States District Court for the Southern District of New York. Judge Nelson would like to issue a standing order concerning civil pretrial conferences. The judge has asked your advice.

(a) Draft a standing order concerning pretrial conferences that can be sent to counsel in all cases assigned to Judge Nelson; and

(b) Write a short memorandum explaining the standing order that you have drafted. Be sure that this memorandum addresses such issues as the purpose of the pretrial conferences that you envision, the number of conferences in a typical civil case, the role of parties, counsel and the court at the conferences, and the timing of the conferences.

3. Draft the same standing order and memorandum described in exercise 2, but presume that Judge Nelson has just been appointed to the United States District Court for the District of Montana.

III. RULE 16 PRETRIAL ORDERS

Rule 16 not only provides for pretrial conferences between counsel and the court, but Rule 16(d) requires: "After any conference under this rule, the court should issue an order reciting the action taken." Rule 16 pretrial orders are the subject of this section of this chapter.

A. PRETRIAL ORDERS IN PRACTICE

As with pretrial conferences, the pretrial orders resulting from such conferences vary from court to court and from judge to judge. Pretrial orders can be: dictated by the judge during or at the conclusion of the pretrial conference, presented to the judge by counsel at the pretrial conference, or prepared by counsel or the judge after the pretrial conference.[29] If counsel are given the primary responsibility for preparing the proposed order, their proposal is subject to approval and entry as an order by the judge.

Many judges require that counsel prepare a proposed draft of the final pretrial order and have issued standing orders containing quite extensive and detailed requirements as to what the proposed pretrial order must contain. Counsel may be required to confer among themselves prior to the final pretrial conference with the judge and attempt to reach agreement concerning contested and uncontested factual and legal issues, the specific basis for objections that will be raised to any party's trial exhibits, the portions of any depositions that will be offered at trial, and the substance of expected testimony that will be offered by specific witnesses at trial.[30]

One federal judge who requires an extensive final pretrial order describes the benefits of those orders as follows: "The script having been completed and the roles cast, * * * the trial * * * is an anticlimax, and proceeds, absent a settlement, without surprise, confusion, or delay."[31] However, some attorneys suspect that the real reason some judges require

---

29. "Handbook for Effective Pretrial Procedure," 37 F.R.D. 255, 271–72 (1964); Christenson, "The Pre–Trial Order," 29 F.R.D. 362, 365–70 (1961). Rulings and other aspects of the pretrial conference also can be memorialized by transcription of the proceedings or the entry of individual docket orders. *Manual for Complex Litigation, Fourth* § 11.22 (2004).

30. *E.g.,* Krupansky, "The Federal Rules are Alive and Well," *Litigation,* Fall 1977, at 10, 12.

31. *Id.* at 13.

extensive final pretrial orders is to induce them to settle their cases. As a judge's secretary once said to the author upon handing him extensive pretrial order preparation requirements, "Read 'em and settle."

This issue has been addressed by Judge Robert Peckham of the United States District Court for the Northern District of California:

> If some judges use pretrial procedures simply to overwhelm attorneys with busywork in order to browbeat them into settlement, then the bar's distaste for elaborate procedures is understandable. In my experience, however, requiring the attorneys to prepare a comprehensive pretrial statement and order promotes settlement primarily because these pretrial tasks illuminate the strengths and weaknesses of each side's case. Comprehensive procedures also force the attorneys— perhaps for the first time—into a graphic confrontation with the probable cost of trial, obviously an important factor in the settlement process.[32]

Nevertheless, some judges simply do not feel that extensive pretrial orders are worth the work required by counsel or the court. In contrast to the growing size and complexity of the pretrial orders required in many courts, Judge John Grady dispensed with pretrial orders entirely and merely required stipulations concerning matters not genuinely in dispute:

> No matter how mightily the attorneys may have labored [on the pretrial order], the product is usually unimpressive. The things they have agreed upon are trivial, and most of the order is a series of recitations about why they have been unable to agree upon the items really in dispute. If the device were really to be useful, it would be necessary for the judge to monitor the preparation of the order and attempt to induce meaningful agreement. However, since the case is probably going to be settled anyway, I think this would be a misuse of the judge's time.[33]

Charles Clark, who as dean of the Yale Law School was one of the leaders of the movement that culminated in the Federal Rules of Civil Procedure, once commented: "[Rule 16], in its inception and in its wording, makes it clear that pre-trial is not intended as a substitute for trial; its whole tenor is that of proper preparation for trial."[34]

While the specific requirements for both final and interim pretrial orders vary from jurisdiction to jurisdiction, Rule 16(d) is explicit about the significance of pretrial orders, providing that such an order "controls

---

32. Peckham, "The Federal Judge as a Case Manager," 69 *Cal. L. Rev.* 770, 788 (1981). The Federal Rules of Civil Procedure also place limitations upon the pretrial procedure required by individual federal courts and judges. Prior to the 1983 amendments to Rule 16, certain pretrial order requirements were struck down by courts of appeals as contrary to that Rule. *McCargo v. Hedrick,* 545 F.2d 393 (4th Cir. 1976); *Padovani v. Bruchhausen,* 293 F.2d 546 (2d Cir. 1961). Rule 83(b) provides that the standing orders and other requirements of individual judges must be consistent with federal law, the Federal Rules of Civil Procedure, and local rules of court.

33. Grady, "Trial Lawyers, Litigators and Clients' Costs," *Litigation,* Spring 1978, at 5, 6. *See also* Costantino, "Judges as Case Managers," *Trial,* March 1981, at 56, 58.

34. Clark, "To an Understanding Use of Pre–Trial," 29 F.R.D. 454, 455 (1961).

the course of the action unless the court modifies it." This provision gives trial judges the discretion to amend pretrial orders or issue new pretrial orders as the pretrial process develops. For example, a discovery deadline set in an initial pretrial order may become unrealistic in light of pretrial developments. Under Rule 16(d) the court has the power to issue a later pretrial order extending the date for the completion of discovery.

Matters that are resolved in a final pretrial order are not so easily modified. Rule 16(e) specifically addresses final pretrial orders, providing: "The court may modify the order issued after a final pretrial conference only to prevent manifest injustice." What this often means in practice is that the parties will be precluded from offering arguments, witnesses, or exhibits that have not been identified in the final pretrial order.[35] Thus a defendant was held to have waived a statute of limitations defense that was omitted from the final pretrial order, even though that defense had been included in the answer and raised in a motion for directed verdict.[36]

Counsel not infrequently may seek to amend a pretrial order to postpone the date for trial. The following comment from Judge Robert Porter is typical of the reluctance of many judges to grant these requests:

> This trial setting will be postponed only in the event of an extreme emergency. Such emergency would arise if, while on a plea-sure cruise in the South Pacific, Plaintiffs' attorneys and Defendants' attorneys were stranded on a deserted island, became enamored of one another and decided to pursue the trials of Robinson Crusoe rather than the trial of this case.[37]

Rule 16(e) does contemplate, however, that even a final pretrial order can be modified "to prevent manifest injustice." Among the factors considered in determining whether a final pretrial order should be modified are the prejudice or surprise to the party opposing modification of the order, the ability to cure the prejudice, the extent to which modification of the order would disrupt trial, and any bad faith or willfulness on the part of the party seeking modification.[38]

Regardless of the specific pretrial order requirements imposed in a particular case, counsel should devote the time and attention necessary to ensure a carefully prepared pretrial order. In negotiating the order with other attorneys or the court, counsel should try to be cooperative without conceding important positions of the client. Volunteering to prepare the

---

35. *Ramirez Pomales v. Becton Dickinson & Co.,* 839 F.2d 1 (1st Cir. 1988); *Admiral Theatre Corp. v. Douglas Theatre Co.,* 585 F.2d 877, 897–98 (8th Cir. 1978). *See also Manual for Complex Litigation, Third* § 41.63(9) (1995) (sample final pretrial order providing: "Evidence not identified in this order may not be offered and no issues other than those identified in this order may be tried.").

36. *Youren v. Tintic School District,* 343 F.3d 1296, 1304–1305 (10th Cir. 2003).

37. *Associated Radio Service Co. v. Page Airways, Inc.,* 73 F.R.D. 633, 638 (N.D.Tex. 1977).

38. *Perry v. Winspur,* 782 F.2d 893 (10th Cir. 1986); *Smith v. Rowe,* 761 F.2d 360, 365–66 (7th Cir. 1985). Other courts have considered the importance of the evidence in question and the explanation for the party's failure to list the evidence in the final pretrial order. *Adalman v. Baker, Watts & Co.,* 807 F.2d 359, 369–70 (4th Cir. 1986). *See generally* Peckham, "The Federal Judge as a Case Manager," 69 *Cal. L. Rev.* 770, 795–800 (1981).

initial draft of the proposed order may result in an order that contains language favorable to one's client. Finally, it generally makes sense to preserve drafts of proposed orders discussed by the parties and to make a written record of disputes between counsel that later may be brought before the judge.

NOTES AND QUESTIONS CONCERNING RULE 16 PRETRIAL ORDERS

1.   What are the relative advantages and disadvantages for the judge who requires counsel to jointly draft an extensive proposed pretrial order? What are the relative advantages and disadvantages of such a requirement for counsel and their clients? Will any particular types of clients be helped or harmed by such a requirement?

2.   What if counsel refuse to cooperate in the preparation of the proposed order? How can the judge know whether counsel are acting in bad faith or merely are refusing to concede colorable positions of their clients?

3.   In addition to setting forth required pretrial order formats, some local rules of court explicitly permit judges to tailor pretrial requirements to the facts and complexity of particular cases. *E.g.,* Rule 16.1(a) of the United States District Court for the Eastern District of Pennsylvania; Rule 16(m)(2) of the United States District Court for the Western District of Washington. What is the purpose of these provisions?

4.   One of the most innovative pretrial case management orders is the "Time Out" Rule that Judge Edward Becker threatened to invoke in *Zenith Radio Corp. v. Matsushita Elec. Indus. Co.,* 478 F.Supp. 889, 959 (E.D.Pa. 1979), *vac'd on other grounds,* 631 F.2d 1069 (3d Cir. 1980). Under this rule each party would be entitled to three "time outs" during the pretrial period. These time outs were to be called by a party's "Designated Whistler," and during time out periods "all deadlines are postponed and counsel can generally goof off." *Id.* The Rule also provided that "counsel attempting to exceed the three time outs will have his, her or its desk moved five yards (in the event of a non-flagrant violation) or fifteen yards (in the event of a flagrant infraction) further from the jury box at trial." 478 F.Supp. at 960.

B.   A FORM FINAL PRETRIAL ORDER

The matters to be addressed in final pretrial orders typically are listed in local rules of court or in the standing orders issued by individual judges.[39] Many local rules and standing orders also provide the specific format to be used in the preparation of the final pretrial order. An example of such a final pretrial order form is set forth in Civil Rule 16.1 of the United States District Court for the Western District of Washington.

---

39.   *See* "Handbook for Effective Pretrial Procedure," 37 F.R.D. 255, 275–315 (1964) (containing local rules, notices, standing orders and pretrial order forms from various federal judicial districts). The local rules of federal district courts can be found through the federal judiciary's website, http://www.uscourts.gov/rulesandpolicies/FederalRulemaking/LocalCourtRules.aspx, or in *Federal Local Court Rules* (West 3d ed. 2010). Standing orders of individual judges can be located on the websites of federal district courts or in the *Directory of Federal Court Guidelines* (2010) or they can be obtained from the clerk's office or the chambers of specific judges.

Just as the Rule 26(f) Report of Parties' Planning Meeting, *supra* p. 298, is intended to provide a road map for discovery and other pretrial proceedings, orders such as the following are to govern trial.

Hon. [name of judge]

UNITED STATES DISTRICT COURT
WESTERN DISTRICT OF WASHINGTON AT _____

_____,
          Plaintiff,   No. _____
          vs.
_____   PRETRIAL ORDER
          Defendant.

JURISDICTION

Jurisdiction is vested in this court by virtue of: (State the facts and cite the statutes whereby jurisdiction of the case is vested in this court).

CLAIMS AND DEFENSES

The plaintiff will pursue at trial the following claims: (E.g., breach of contract, violation of 28 U.S.C. § 1983). The defendant will pursue the following affirmative defenses and/or claims: (E.g., accord and satisfaction, estoppel, waiver).

ADMITTED FACTS

The following facts are admitted by the parties: (Enumerate every agreed fact, irrespective of admissibility, but with notation of objections as to admissibility. List 1, 2, 3, etc.)

The plaintiff contends as follows: (List 1, 2, 3, etc.)

The defendant contends as follows: (List 1, 2, 3, etc.)

(State contentions in summary fashion, omitting evidentiary detail. Unless otherwise ordered by the court, the factual contentions of a party shall not exceed two pages in length. * * *)

ISSUES OF LAW

The following are the issues of law to be determined by the court: (List 1, 2, 3, etc., and state each issue of law involved. A simple statement of the ultimate issue to be decided by the court, such as "Is the plaintiff entitled to recover?" will not be accepted.) If the parties cannot agree on the issues of law, separate statements may be given in the pretrial order.

EXPERT WITNESSES

(a) Each party shall be limited to _____ expert witness(es) on the issues of _____.

(b) The name(s) and address(es) of the expert witness(es) to be used by each party at the trial and the issue upon which each will testify is:

(1) On behalf of plaintiff;

(2) On behalf of defendant.

OTHER WITNESSES

The names and addresses of witnesses, other than experts, to be used by each party at the time of trial and the general nature of the testimony of each are:

(a) On behalf of plaintiff: (E.g., Jane Doe, 10 Elm Street, Seattle, WA; will testify concerning formation of the parties' contract, performance, breach and damage to plaintiff.)

(b) On behalf of defendant: (follow same format).

(As to each witness, expert or others, indicate "will testify," or "possible witness only." Also indicate which witnesses, if any, will testify by deposition. Rebuttal witnesses, the necessity of whose testimony cannot reasonably be anticipated before trial, need not be named.)

EXHIBITS

(a) Admissibility stipulated:

Plaintiff's Exhibits

1. Photo of port side of ship. (Examples)

2. Photo of crane motor.

3. Photo of crane.

Defendant's Exhibits

A–1. Weather report. (Examples)

A–2. Log book.

A–3. X–ray of plaintiff's foot.

A–4. X–ray of wrist.

(b) Authenticity stipulated, admissibility disputed:

Plaintiff's Exhibits

4. Inventory Report. (Examples)

Defendant's Exhibits

A–5. Photograph. (Examples)

(c) Authenticity and admissibility disputed:

Plaintiff's Exhibits

5. Accountant's report. (Examples)

Defendant's Exhibits

A–6. Ship's log.

(No party is required to list any exhibit which is listed by another party, or any exhibit to be used for impeachment only. * * *)

ACTION BY THE COURT

(a) This case is scheduled for trial (before a jury) (without a jury) on _____, 20__, at _____.

(b) Trial briefs shall be submitted to the court on or before _____.

(c) (Omit this sub-paragraph in non-jury case.) Jury instructions requested by either party shall be submitted to the court on or before _____. Suggested questions of either party to be asked of the jury by the court on voir dire shall be submitted to the court on or before _____.

(d) (Insert any other ruling made by the court at or before pretrial conference.)

This order has been approved by the parties as evidenced by the signatures of their counsel. This order shall control the subsequent course of the action unless modified by a subsequent order. This order shall not be amended except by order of the court pursuant to agreement of the parties or to prevent manifest injustice.

DATED this _____ day of _____ [insert month], 20__ [insert year].

United States District
Judge/Magistrate Judge

FORM APPROVED

_____
Attorney for Plaintiff

_____
Attorney for Defendant

NOTES AND QUESTIONS CONCERNING THE FORM PRETRIAL ORDER

1.   What is the advantage in specifying the precise format of the final pretrial order as the federal judges in the Western District of Washington have done? Are there disadvantages to such a standard format?

2.   Is the completion of pretrial orders such as the above likely to conserve judicial resources? Legal resources? Costs to clients? What must be balanced against any potential savings?

3.   The above order requires the parties not only to stipulate to facts and exhibits to be admitted at trial, but to stipulate to "every agreed fact, irrespective of admissibility" and to exhibits as to which there is a dispute as to admissibility but not authenticity. Why does the order require such stipulations concerning matters that may not be admissible at trial?

4.   In some pretrial orders, counsel are required to estimate the number of days they need to try the case. Based upon such estimates, and, sometimes,

subsequent negotiations with the judge, counsel may be restricted to a limited number of trial days in which to present their case. *See Gen. Signal Corp. v. MCI Telecomms. Corp.*, 66 F.3d 1500, 1507–11 (9th Cir. 1995), *cert. denied*, 516 U.S. 1146 (1996); *MCI Commc'ns Corp. v. Am. Tel. & Tel. Co.*, 708 F.2d 1081, 1170–72 (7th Cir.), *cert. denied*, 464 U.S. 891 (1983).

5.   The last section of the above order contemplates the incorporation of judicial rulings into the final pretrial order. Why might judges prefer to make such rulings prior to trial? Why might counsel have a similar preference? Are there any problems presented by such pretrial rulings?

6.   Judges may require counsel to prepare additional pretrial documents beyond the final pretrial order. The final section of the above order suggests that the parties may be required to prepare trial briefs, proposed jury instructions, and proposed voir dire questions. In cases to be tried to the court, some judges require counsel to submit proposed findings of fact and conclusions of law either before or after the trial of an action. *See* Fed. R. Civ. P. 52(a).

7.   Final pretrial orders typically are prepared by counsel. After counsel have jointly prepared such an order, the proposed order is considered at a pretrial conference and approved for entry by the judge.

Exercises Concerning Pretrial Orders

1.   You represent the plaintiffs in the lawsuit filed in the United States District Court for the Southern District of West Virginia by attorney Gerald Stern on behalf of victims of the Buffalo Creek disaster. Presume that the local practice is for plaintiffs' counsel to prepare the initial draft of the proposed pretrial order, to submit this initial draft to defense counsel, and for the parties to negotiate a final proposed draft order for submission to the court.

(a) Based upon the complaint set forth in Chapter 4, *supra* p. 152, draft a proposed pretrial order for submission to defense counsel. This proposed order should comply with the form of pretrial order required by the United States District Court for the Western District of Washington.

(b) Prepare a memorandum to Gerald Stern describing your strategy in drafting the proposed pretrial order in the manner that you did. This memorandum also should set forth your plans for negotiating the final version of the proposed order with defense counsel. In this regard, be sure to note aspects of the proposed order to which either defense counsel or the court may object, as well as your plan for dealing with anticipated objections.

2.   The Supreme Court has just ruled in *Hickman v. Taylor,* 329 U.S. 495 (1947), *supra* p. 273, that the witness statements sought by the plaintiff are protected by the work-product doctrine. This case now has been remanded for trial to the United States District Court for the Eastern District of Pennsylvania. Based upon the facts set forth in the Supreme Court's opinion, draft a proposed pretrial order complying with

the form order required in the United States District Court for the Western District of Washington on behalf of:

(a) the estate of Norman Hickman (the plaintiff); or

(b) the defendant tugboat owners.

IV. JUDICIAL MANAGEMENT OF THE PRETRIAL PROCESS

Judge Marvin Frankel described the "adversary judge" as "the neutral, impartial, calm, noncontentious umpire standing between the adversary parties, seeing that they observe the rules of the adversary game."[40] Whatever general accuracy this description once may have had, many federal district judges no longer remain on the litigation sidelines as neutral umpires. Increasingly, judges have become active litigation managers.[41] As the Supreme Court has observed, "One of the most significant insights that skilled trial judges have gained in recent years is the wisdom and necessity for early judicial intervention in the management of litigation."[42]

Both the Federal Rules of Civil Procedure and federal procedural statutes contemplate at least some degree of judicial case management. Procedures for litigation management include provisions for the consolidated pretrial of multidistrict litigation,[43] for the consolidation or separate consideration of multiple claims in a single action pursuant to Rule 42, and for the assignment of related civil actions to a single judge.[44] The Judicial Conference of the United States offers federal judges an extensive *Civil Litigation Management Manual*.[45] In addition, the *Manual for Complex Litigation, Fourth* encourages federal judges to adopt efficient management techniques to resolve complex civil cases. The "General Principles" section of the *Manual* begins: "Fair and efficient resolution of complex litigation requires at least that (1) the court exercise early and effective supervision (and, where necessary, control); (2) counsel act cooperatively and professionally; and (3) the judge and counsel collaborate

---

40. Frankel, "The Adversary Judge," 54 *Tex. L. Rev.* 465, 468 (1976). *Cf. Confirmation Hearing on the Nomination of John G. Roberts, Jr. to be Chief Justice of the United States Before the Senate Committee on the Judiciary*, 109th Cong., 1st Sess. 55 (2005) ("Judges are like umpires. Umpires don't make the rules, they apply them.").

41. Nor are efforts to effectively manage litigation new. Over 60 years ago, a federal judicial committee referred to pretrial procedures as transforming the trial judge into "an active director of litigation * * * [free to] strip the controversy of nonessentials, and to mold it into such form as will make it possible to dispose of the contest properly with the least possible waste of time and expense." Committee to the Judicial Conference for the District of Columbia, "Pretrial Procedure," 1 F.R.D. 759, 761–62 (1941).

42. *Hoffmann–La Roche Inc. v. Sperling,* 493 U.S. 165, 171 (1989).

43. 28 U.S.C. § 1407.

44. *E.g.,* Rule 40.5 of the United States District Court for the District of Columbia; Rule 83.11(b)(7) of the United States District Court for the Eastern District of Michigan.

45. Judicial Conference of the United States, *Civil Litigation Management Manual* (2d ed. 2010).

to develop and carry out a comprehensive plan for the conduct of pretrial and trial proceedings."[46]

Judicial management received a boost from the 1983 and 1993 amendments to, and expansion of, Federal Rule of Civil Procedure 16. This Rule was in 1983 "extensively rewritten and expanded to meet the challenges of modern litigation" and now emphasizes "judicial management that embraces the entire pretrial phase, especially motions and discovery."[47] The Rule was further expanded in 1993, at the same time that amendments to Rule 26 resulted in a significantly broader potential role for federal judges in the pretrial process. Perhaps most telling was the 1993 amendment of Rule 1, which now provides that the Federal Rules of Civil Procedure "shall be construed *and administered* to secure the just, speedy, and inexpensive determination of every action and proceeding."

Many modern judges, acting pursuant to Rule 16 and the other Federal Rules of Civil Procedure, no longer function as Judge Frankel's "adversary judge" merely "standing between the adversary parties, seeing that they observe the rules of the adversary game." As Judge Charles Richey has observed, Rule 16 "effectively lays to rest the historical model of the passive judge * * * and replaces it with a model that is more active, and which is involved with every aspect of a lawsuit from start to finish."[48]

While judicial efforts to effectively manage civil litigation are not new, recent litigation management initiatives constitute a change in the kind, rather than merely in the degree, of judicial control of civil litigation. Continuing judicial case management may be working a basic change in the traditional common law adversary process, under which counsel determine the issues and the evidence that will be presented for adjudication.[49] As illustrated by the 1983 and 1993 amendments to the Federal Rules of Civil Procedure, some members of the bench and bar have concluded that judicial time is too precious a resource to permit attorneys free reign in its use. Congress reached a similar conclusion in the Civil Justice Reform Act of 1990, which required each United States district court to implement a civil justice expense and delay reduction plan under which judges were to take a more active role in case management.[50]

Professor Judith Resnik attributes this rise in "managerial judging" to the increasing need for judicial resolution of pretrial discovery disputes, the articulation of new rights and remedies, and judicial caseload pres-

---

46. *Manual for Complex Litigation, Fourth* § 10 (2004).

47. Advisory Committee Note to 1983 Amendment to Rule 16, 97 F.R.D. 165, 206–207 (1983).

48. Richey, "Rule 16: A Survey and Some Considerations for the Bench and Bar," 126 F.R.D. 599, 600 (1989).

49. Judicial management efforts may represent merely one aspect of a more general trend away from traditional civil litigation, in which courts determine the private rights of private parties, to the "public law litigation" of the last several decades. Chayes, "The Role of the Judge in Public Law Litigation," 89 *Harv. L. Rev.* 1281 (1976).

50. The Civil Justice Reform Act of 1990 is Title I of the Judicial Improvements Act of 1990. Pub. L. No. 101–650, 104 Stat. 5089 (1990) (originally codified at 28 U.S.C. §§ 471–482; all but 28 U.S.C. § 476 expired Dec. 1, 1997).

sures.[51] In her article addressing both the reasons for, and the questions posed by, managerial judging, Professor Resnik raises the following concerns:

> Management is a new form of "judicial activism," a behavior that usually attracts substantial criticism. Moreover, judicial management may be teaching judges to value their statistics, such as the number of case dispositions, more than they value the quality of their dispositions. Finally, because managerial judging is less visible and usually unreviewable, it gives trial courts more authority and at the same time provides litigants with fewer procedural safeguards to protect them from abuse of that authority. In short, managerial judging may be redefining *sub silentio* our standards of what constitutes rational, fair, and impartial adjudication.[52]

While managerial judges may become actively involved in all phases of a lawsuit, Professor Resnik is particularly concerned with judicial management of the pretrial phases of civil litigation: "[B]ecause pretrial management is judge initiated, invisible, and unreviewable, it breaks sharply from American norms of adjudication."[53]

Professor Resnik is not alone in her criticisms. Professor Donald Elliott has observed: "Managerial judging is evolving rapidly from a set of techniques for narrowing issues to a set of techniques for settling cases."[54] Professor Elliott notes: "Managerial judges believe that the system does not work; only that *something* must be done to make it work; and that the only plausible solution to the problem is *ad hoc* procedural activism by judges."[55]

Other commentators have defended active judicial management of the federal civil caseload as a modern necessity. One judicial administrator who has extensively studied federal judicial management has challenged Professor Resnik's critique for ignoring the quite effective management techniques that federal district judges have tailored to the individual cases before them.[56] This administrator faults Professor Resnik for advocating

---

51. Judith Resnik, "Managerial Judges," 96 *Harv. L. Rev.* 374, 391–402 (1982).

52. *Id.* at 380.

53. *Id.* at 414. *But see* Thornburg, "The Managerial Judge Goes to Trial," 44 *U. Rich. L. Rev.* 1261 (2010) (discussing extension of judicial management from pretrial to civil trials).

54. Elliott, "Managerial Judging and the Evolution of Procedure," 53 *U. Chi. L. Rev.* 306, 323 (1986).

55. *Id.* at 309.

56. Flanders, "Blind Umpires—A Response to Professor Resnik," 35 *Hastings L. Rev.* 505, 514–520 (1984).

An extensive study by the RAND Institute for Civil Justice reached the following conclusions concerning time to disposition, cost, attorney satisfaction, and perceptions of fairness due to a combination of pretrial case management techniques:

> If early case management and early setting of a trial schedule are combined with shortened time to discovery cutoff, the increase in lawyer work hours predicted by early management can be offset by the decrease in lawyer work hours predicted by judicial control of discovery. We estimate that under these circumstances, litigants on general civil cases that do not close within the first nine months would pay no significant cost penalty for reduced time to disposition on

"blind justice," arguing that it is neither possible nor desirable for judges to be totally uninvolved with the cases before them during the pretrial process.[57] As Judge Learned Hand observed in 1945, "A judge is more than a moderator; he is charged to see that the law is properly administered, and it is a duty which he cannot discharge by remaining inert."[58]

There is some truth to the positions of both the supporters and the critics of managerial judges. Managerial judging and the entire pretrial process raise the basic tension between fairness and efficiency that is endemic to our system of civil procedure. While our judicial system must attempt to ensure that every litigant is treated fairly, backlogs in many federal district courts raise questions about fairness to those individuals who must wait several years for the adjudication of their claims.[59] In addition, judicial intervention in the pretrial process may result in an improved presentation in those cases that ultimately reach trial.[60]

In its final report to Congress pursuant to the Civil Justice Reform Act of 1990,[61] the Judicial Conference of the United States concluded:

> Through the history of our civil justice system, independent judicial officers have been called upon to strike the balance between efficiency and justice. The consequences of tilting that balance in favor of standardized procedures cannot be measured solely in numbers and percentages. The "quality of justice" delivered in our courts must remain foremost in the minds of judicial policy makers.[62]

In the final analysis, we must rely upon the wisdom and integrity of our judges to manage their caseloads pursuant to Rule 1 of the Federal Rules of Civil Procedure "to secure the just, speedy, and inexpensive determination of every action and proceeding."

NOTES AND QUESTIONS CONCERNING MANAGERIAL JUDGING

1. Is it surprising that many judges have resorted to "managerial judging?" Professor Donald Elliott suggests not and makes the following suggestion for reform: "[W]e should think about civil procedure less from the

---

the order of four to five months. None of these policies has any significant effect on lawyers' satisfaction or perceptions of fairness.

J. Kakalik et al., *Just, Speedy, and Inexpensive? An Evaluation of Judicial Case Management Under the Civil Justice Reform Act* 28 (RAND Institute for Civil Justice 1996).

57. Flanders, *supra* note 56, at 520.

58. *United States v. Marzano,* 149 F.2d 923, 925 (2d Cir. 1945).

59. *See generally Civil Case Backlogs in Federal District Courts: Hearings Before the Subcomm. on Courts of the Senate Comm. on the Judiciary,* 98th Cong., 1st and 2d Sess. (1983, 1984); Action Committee to Reduce Court Costs and Delay, American Bar Association, *Attacking Litigation Costs and Delay* (1984). *See also* Civil Justice Reform Act of 1990, Pub. L. No. 101–650 § 102 (containing congressional findings concerning cost and delay in federal civil litigation).

60. *See* Rosenberg, *The Pretrial Conference and Effective Justice* 29–44 (1964).

61. Judicial Improvements Act of 1990, Pub. L. No. 101–650, tit. I, 104 Stat. 5089, originally codified at 28 U.S.C. §§ 471–482; all but 28 U.S.C. § 476 expired Dec. 1, 1997.

62. Judicial Conference of the United States, *Final Report—The Civil Justice Reform Act of 1990,* 175 F.R.D. 62, 109 (1997).

perspective of powers granted to judges, and more from the perspective of incentives created for lawyers and clients. Our current system of civil litigation creates perverse incentives for lawyers, and then relies on judges to police litigant behavior through techniques like managerial judging. If we are not satisfied with the results, we should redesign the system to provide direct incentives for appropriate behavior." Elliott, "Managerial Judging and the Evolution of Procedure," 53 *U. Chi. L. Rev.* 306, 308 (1986).

2.   How, specifically, could our judicial system be reformed to provide "direct incentives for appropriate [litigant] behavior?" How, specifically, could these reforms be instituted? What groups might be mobilized to push for these reforms? Are there groups that might oppose reform?

3.   What implications does managerial judging have for present methods of judicial selection? For the manner in which judges are, or are not, trained? Is the life tenure of federal district judges relevant to the debate concerning managerial judges?

4.   Do the 1983 and 1993 amendments to Rule 16 give federal district judges additional managerial powers that they did not have before? Is the more significant factor in controlling and managing litigation the governing rules or the judges who administer those rules? Consider the sentiments of District Judge Elizabeth Kovachevich of the United States District Court for the Middle District of Florida:

> Implementation of solutions must ultimately come from the individual trial captains of the courtrooms. . . . We cannot manufacture time; we can only manage the time that we have. A litigant is entitled to *his* [day] in court, but not to somebody else's day.

American Law Institute, *Proceedings* 36, 41 (1984) (address of Chief Justice Warren Burger).

5.   In her 1982 article, Professor Resnik suggested that the federal judiciary might be moving from the traditional common law adversarial system toward a civil law inquisitorial system. Judith Resnik, "Managerial Judges," 96 *Harv. L. Rev.* 374, 445 (1982). After considering judicial developments since 1982, Professor Thomas Rowe concluded that "there has been some such movement [of federal courts in America toward convergence with civil-law systems], but less than may have been assumed by some, and with more variation among civil-law systems themselves than is sometimes recognized on this side of the Atlantic." Rowe, "Authorized Managerialism Under the Federal Rules—and the Extent of Convergence with Civil–Law Judging," 36 *Sw. U. L. Rev.* 191, 193 (2007).

Exercises Concerning Judicial Management of the Pretrial Process

1.   You are the law clerk to Judge K. K. Hall, who has been assigned the action that has just been filed by Gerald Stern on behalf of victims of the Buffalo Creek disaster. Write a memorandum to Judge Hall with your suggestions concerning management policies that he should adopt in the pretrial stages of this lawsuit.

2.   Gerald Stern has just filed a lawsuit on behalf of the victims of the Buffalo Creek disaster, and Judge Hall has scheduled a conference to discuss pretrial case management. The judge has asked counsel for both plaintiffs and the Pittston Company to file a short memorandum prior to this conference suggesting management policies that should be adopted by the court. Draft such a memorandum:

(a) on behalf of the plaintiffs; or

(b) on behalf of the Pittston Company.

3.   The United States Department of Justice has filed a major anti-trust action against the Busy Bakers Company, alleging that this baking company has attempted to monopolize the bread market in Southern California in violation of Section 2 of the Sherman Act, 15 U.S.C. § 2. Within three weeks after the filing of this action, four other baking companies filed their own private antitrust actions against Busy Bakers. At an initial pretrial conference, counsel estimated that pretrial proceedings in these cases would take "three to four years, if we're lucky."

You are a newly appointed United States Magistrate Judge, and the district judge to whom these cases have been assigned has asked your advice as to how the cases should be handled. In particular, the judge has asked that you examine the *Manual for Complex Litigation, Fourth* (2004) to see what case management suggestions might be adopted from that manual. The judge is interested in delegating as many case management tasks to you as possible and would like your suggestions concerning what pretrial tasks you, rather than the judge, most effectively can undertake.

Write a memorandum to the judge containing your recommendations for the pretrial management of these antitrust cases.

V.   CONCLUSION

Counsel frequently complain about the burdens posed by final pretrial conferences and orders. While these conferences and orders may require major investments of attorney time, they can present litigation opportunities for conscientious counsel. The attorney who has prepared her case carefully during the pretrial process should be able to comply with Rule 16's requirements without major difficulty. If the pretrial litigation of the action has gone according to plan, the final pretrial order should do no more than memorialize the attorney's own litigation planning. These concluding aspects of the pretrial process should be used to ensure a successful resolution of the litigation, either at trial or by settlement short of trial.

VI.   CHAPTER BIBLIOGRAPHY

Brazil, "Improving Judicial Controls over the Pretrial Development of Civil Actions: Model Rules for Case Management and Sanctions," 1981 *A. B. Found. Res. J.* 873.

Buxton & Glover, "Managing a Big Case Down to Size," *Litigation,* Summer 1989, at 22.

Clark, "Objectives of Pre–Trial Procedure," 17 *Ohio St. L. J.* 163 (1956).

Elliott, "Managerial Judging and the Evolution of Procedure," 53 *U. Chi. L. Rev.* 306 (1986).

Flanders, "Blind Umpires—A Response to Professor Resnik," 35 *Hastings L. Rev.* 505 (1984).

S. Flanders, *Case Management and Court Management in United States District Courts* (1977).

Flanders, "Case Management in Federal Courts: Some Controversies and Some Results," 4 *Just. Sys. J.* 147 (1978).

Gensler, "Judicial Management: Caught in the Crossfire," 60 *Duke L. J.* 669 (2010).

"Handbook for Effective Pretrial Procedure," 37 F.R.D. 255 (1964).

Judicial Conference of the United States, *Civil Litigation Management Manual* (2d ed. 2010).

Judicial Conference of the United States, *Final Report—The Civil Justice Reform Act of 1990*, 175 F.R.D. 62, 85–87 (1997).

Kahn, "Local Pretrial Rules in Federal Courts," *Litigation,* Spring 1980, at 34.

J. Kakalik et al., *Just, Speedy, and Inexpensive? An Evaluation of Judicial Case Management Under the Civil Justice Reform Act* (RAND Institute for Civil Justice 1996).

Krupansky, "The Federal Rules are Alive and Well," *Litigation,* Fall 1977, at 10.

Manual for Complex Litigation, Fourth (2004).

Markey, "Judicial Administration—The Human Factors," 1981 *B. Y. U. L. Rev.* 535.

McDermott, "The Pretrial Order and *McCargo v. Hedrick:* Effective Management or Unproductive Formalism?," 4 *Just. Sys. J.* 245 (1978).

Miller, *The August 1983 Amendments to the Federal Rules of Civil Procedure: Promoting Effective Case Management and Lawyer Responsibility* (1984).

Peckham, "The Federal Judge as a Case Manager: The New Role in Guiding a Case from Filing to Disposition," 69 *Cal. L. Rev.* 770 (1981).

Pointer, "Complex Litigation: Demonstration of Pretrial Conference," 6 *Rev. Litig.* 285 (1987).

Pollack, "Pretrial Conferences," 50 F.R.D. 449 (1970).

Pollack, "Pretrial Procedures More Effectively Handled," 65 F.R.D. 475 (1974).

Resnik, "Managerial Judges," 96 *Harv. L. Rev.* 374 (1982).

Richey, "Rule 16: A Survey and Some Considerations for the Bench and Bar," 126 F.R.D. 599 (1989).

Richey, "Rule 16 Revised, and Related Rules: Analysis of Recent Developments for the Benefit of Bench and Bar," 157 F.R.D. 69 (1994).

Richey, "Rule 16 Revisited: Reflections for the Benefit of the Bench and Bar," 139 F.R.D. 525 (1991).

Rosen & Hennessy, "Rule 16, the Litigator's Forgotten Ally," *Litigation*, Summer 2008, at 42.

M. Rosenberg, *The Pretrial Conference and Effective Justice* (1964).

Rowe, "Authorized Managerialism Under the Federal Rules—and the Extent of Convergence with Civil–Law Judging," 36 *Sw. U. L. Rev.* 191 (2007).

Rubin, "The Managed Calendar: Some Pragmatic Suggestions about Achieving the Just, Speedy and Inexpensive Determination of Civil Cases in Federal Courts," 4 *Just. Sys. J.* 135 (1978).

Schwarzer, "Managing Civil Litigation: The Trial Judge's Role," 61 *Judicature* 400 (1978).

W. Schwarzer & A. Hirsch, *The Elements of Case Management* (1991).

Shapiro, "Federal Rule 16: A Look at the Theory and Practice of Rulemaking," 137 *U. Pa. L. Rev.* 1969 (1989).

Tigar, "Pretrial Case Management under the Amended Rules: Too Many Words for a Good Idea," 14 *Rev. Litig.* 137 (1994).

Walker & Thibaut, "An Experimental Examination of Pretrial Conference Techniques," 55 *Minn. L. Rev.* 1113 (1971).

Wright, "The Pretrial Conference," 28 F.R.D. 141 (1960).

CHAPTER 14

NEGOTIATION AND SETTLEMENT: "I'LL TAKE THE BIGGER HALF."

■ ■ ■

Discourage litigation. Persuade your neighbors to compromise whenever you can. Point out to them how the nominal winner is often the real loser—in fees, expenses, and waste of time. As a peacemaker the lawyer has a superior opportunity of being a good man.

Abraham Lincoln, "Notes for Law Lecture," *in* 2 *Complete Works of Abraham Lincoln* 140, 142 (J. Nicolay & J. Hay ed. 1905).

All negotiation is an attempt to replace uncertainty with certainty.

Rubin & Will, "Some Suggestions Concerning the Judge's Role in Stimulating Settlement Negotiations," 75 F.R.D. 227, 228 (1976).

Analysis

———

I. INTRODUCTION

Until now this text has focused on material about which most lay persons have little knowledge or experience. It is the unusual non-lawyer who has the background to talk intelligently about modern pleading requirements, civil discovery, or Rule 12 motions.

The present chapter deals with negotiation, with which lawyers and lay persons alike have extensive experience. This experience may have come from buying a house or a car, deciding what movie or restaurant a group of people should attend on a given evening, or negotiating with a

577

teacher about the scope of a proposed term paper. Students should bring to this chapter, and to the negotiations that they will conduct in their legal practices, the experiences and common sense they have acquired in non-legal negotiation settings.

Building on such common negotiation experiences, this chapter considers negotiation in the legal context. Initially considered are negotiation strengths and weaknesses and the negotiation techniques by which civil litigation so often is resolved. A specific examination of the ethics of legal negotiation then is undertaken. Even after a settlement of a lawsuit has been negotiated, the attorneys must draft the documents necessary to effectuate that settlement. Accordingly, the next section of the chapter deals with settlement documents. Finally, judicial intervention into the negotiation process is covered in the last major section of the chapter.

Legal negotiation should build not only on non-legal negotiation experiences, but should be based upon the strategic positions taken by counsel during the earliest stages of a lawsuit. The manner in which the complaint was drafted, discovery was sought or provided, and pretrial motions were argued all can enhance a party's position both in negotiations and at trial. Because many more cases are settled than are tried, counsel always should consider the impact that particular pretrial decisions will have upon a negotiated settlement of the action.

II. PRETRIAL SETTLEMENT NEGOTIATIONS

While there is a great amount that can be said about negotiation strategy and techniques, much of it already has been said. Those in search of comprehensive treatment of legal negotiation should consult the many fine books on this subject.[1] Rather than constituting a primer on legal negotiation, this chapter merely introduces the subject of negotiated settlement and raises some of the issues legal negotiations most commonly present.

A. THE SIGNIFICANCE OF PRETRIAL NEGOTIATION

Pretrial negotiation is one of the most important tasks in which modern litigators engage. One study has found that attorneys devote

---

1. *E.g.*, W. Brazil, *Effective Approaches to Settlement: A Handbook for Lawyers and Judges* (1988); C. Craver, *Effective Legal Negotiation and Settlement* (6th ed. 2009); H. Edwards & J. White, *The Lawyer as a Negotiator* (1977); J. Folberg & D Golann, *Lawyer Negotiation: Theory, Practice, and Law* (2006); D. Gifford, *Legal Negotiation: Theory and Applications* (2d ed. 2007); R. Korobkin, *Negotiation: Theory and Strategy* (2d ed. 2009); E. Lynch et al., *Negotiation and Settlement* (2005); C. Menkel–Meadow et al., *Negotiation: Processes for Problem Solving* (2006); M. Nelken, *Negotiation: Theory and Practice* (2d ed. 2007); G. Williams & C. Craver, *Legal Negotiating* (2007). *See also* H. Cohen, *You Can Negotiate Anything* (1980); R. Fisher & W. Ury, *Getting to Yes* (2d ed. 1991); C. Karrass, *The Negotiating Game: How to Get What You Want* (rev. ed.1994); M. Mnookin et al., *Beyond Winning: Negotiating to Create Value in Deals and Disputes* (2000); H. Raiffa et al., *Negotiation Analysis: The Science and Art of Collaborative Decision Making* (2002); H. Raiffa, *The Art and Science of Negotiation* (1982); G. Shell, *Bargaining for Advantage* (1999).

15.1% of their time to settlement discussions, which is about as much time as is devoted to any other single litigation task.[2] This study found that the only tasks on which attorneys spent more time than settlement discussions were conferring with clients (on which attorneys spent 16.0% of their time) and discovery (to which 16.7% of attorney time was devoted).[3]

Not only are great amounts of attorney time devoted to settlement negotiation, but modern civil litigation increasingly is resolved by informal settlement rather than by formal adjudication. "[B]argaining and settlement are the prevalent and, for plaintiffs, perhaps the most cost-effective activity that occurs when cases are filed."[4] Because of the expense of modern litigation, many clients should find negotiated settlement a welcome alternative to formal adjudication.[5] In addition, many judges encourage counsel to discuss settlement, and local rules often require counsel to negotiate disputed issues within a lawsuit before bringing those disputes to the court.[6]

Attention to legal negotiation makes sense because of the large number of cases resolved by settlement and the great amount of attorney time devoted to settlement negotiations. In addition, there are both ethical and strategic negotiation pitfalls into which inexperienced counsel may fall. Settlements typically are negotiated outside the presence of the judge, and there are few rules governing legal negotiation. Counsel often is on her own in the negotiation process.

Legal negotiation also is worthy of study because all attorneys can become better negotiators. Those who negotiate repeatedly with the same opposing counsel should attempt to learn the negotiation strategies and

---

2. Trubek et al., "The Costs of Ordinary Litigation," 31 *UCLA L. Rev.* 72, 91 (Table 3) (1983).

3. *Id.*

4. *Id.* at 122. This study found that less than 8% of the federal and state cases sampled went to trial. *Id.* at 89. *See also* Chapter 1, *supra*, notes 1–3. This does not mean, however, that over 90% of civil cases are voluntarily settled. Flanders, "Blind Umpires—A Response to Professor Resnik," 35 *Hastings L. J.* 505, 517 n.56 (1984) (estimating that no more than about 60% of federal civil cases are settled). *See also* W. Brazil, *Effective Approaches to Settlement: A Handbook for Lawyers and Judges* 394–97 (1988); Eisenberg & Lanvers, "What is the Settlement Rate and Why Should We Care?," 6 *J. Em. Legal Studies* 111 (2009) (finding different settlement rates by case type and location, a general settlement rate of about two-thirds of civil cases, and no material increase in settlement rates over time); Eisenberg et al., "Litigation Outcomes in State and Federal Courts: A Statistical Portrait," 19 *Seattle U. L. Rev.* 433, 444 (1996) (1991–92 settlement rates in contract and non-asbestos tort cases of 62.2% in urban state courts and 64.6% in federal courts). In fact, the percentage of federal civil cases resolved by settlement actually may have decreased since 1970, while nontrial judicial adjudications have increased significantly. Hadfield, "Where Have All the Trials Gone? Settlements, Nontrial Adjudications, and Statistical Artifacts in the Changing Disposition of Federal Civil Cases," 1 *J. Em. Legal Studies* 705 (2004).

5. Thus the Chicago law firm of Jenner & Block pioneered the establishment of a separate negotiation/dispute resolution department in 1982. C. Craver, *Effective Legal Negotiation and Settlement* § 12.18 (6th ed. 2009). For a description of the alternative dispute resolution services provided by other law firms see Dick, "CPR Survey: Law Firm ADR," 13 *Alternatives to High Cost Litig.* 57 (1995); Burch, Comment, "ADR in the Law Firm: A Practical Viewpoint," 1987 *Mo. J. Disp. Resol.* 149.

6. *E.g.,* Rule 7.1(a) of the United States District Court for the Eastern District of Michigan; Rule 26.1(f) of the United States District Court for the Eastern District of Pennsylvania; Rule 7.02 of the United States District Court for the District of South Carolina. *See also* Fed. R. Civ. P. 26(c)(1), 37(a)(1) (requiring that discovery motions be accompanied by a certification that movant has conferred with other parties in an effort to resolve the dispute).

ploys of those individuals. All attorneys should critique their own negotiation performance in order to better their negotiation skills.

Finally, despite, or perhaps because of, the importance of settlement in modern civil litigation, concerns have been raised about the propriety of resolving certain types of legal disputes by informal settlement. Professor Owen Fiss, the most prominent critic of the movement to resolve cases by settlement, has argued:

> Settlement is for me the civil analogue of plea bargaining: Consent is often coerced; the bargain may be struck by someone without authority; the absence of a trial and judgment renders subsequent judicial involvement troublesome; and although dockets are trimmed, justice may not be done. Like plea bargaining, settlement is a capitulation to the conditions of mass society and should be neither encouraged nor praised.[7]

Professors Andrew McThenia and Thomas Shaffer have responded that "Fiss comes close to equating justice with law. * * * We do not believe that law and justice are synonymous. * * * Justice is not usually something people get from the government. And courts * * * are not the only or the most important places that dispense justice."[8] Professor David Luban has suggested that "the question cannot be 'for or against settlement?' but 'how much settlement?' " and that some of the public values promoted by adjudication also can be vindicated by settlements that are open to the public.[9]

Whatever one's beliefs concerning negotiated settlements, such settlements are, and will continue to be, a major means of legal dispute resolution. Virtually all litigators spend a significant amount of time in legal negotiations. Some of these attorneys are skilled negotiators, while others are not. By adopting a conscious and critical attitude toward one's own negotiations, counsel should be able to improve the skills required by this most important lawyer task.

B. NEGOTIATION STRENGTHS AND WEAKNESSES

As in much of the rest of life, the best (*i.e.*, the strongest) team generally comes out on top in legal negotiations. In formulating a negotiation strategy, attorneys therefore must evaluate both their own and their opposing counsels' negotiation strengths and weaknesses. Negotiation

---

7. Fiss, "Against Settlement," 93 *Yale L. J.* 1073, 1075 (1984). *See also* Mnookin, "When Not to Negotiate: A Negotiation Imperialist Reflects on Appropriate Limits," 74 *U. Colo. L. Rev.* 1077 (2003) (suggesting that it is appropriate to refuse to negotiate some conflicts, such as between the Taliban and the United States immediately after September 11, 2001).

8. McThenia & Shaffer, "For Reconciliation," 94 *Yale L. J.* 1660, 1664–65 (1985). Professor Fiss's reply is set forth in Fiss, "Out of Eden," 94 *Yale L. J.* 1669 (1985). Various arguments favoring settlement are analyzed in Galanter & Cahill, " 'Most Cases Settle': Judicial Promotion and Regulation of Settlements," 46 *Stan. L. Rev.* 1339 (1994).

9. Luban, "Settlements and the Erosion of the Public Realm," 83 *Geo. L. J.* 2619, 2620 (1995).

strengths and weaknesses depend upon (1) the strengths and weaknesses of the parties' *legal positions,* (2) the strengths and weaknesses of the *parties* themselves, and (3) the strengths and weaknesses of the parties' *attorneys.* Not only will one's negotiation power depend upon a balance of these three factors, but the strength of one's position is only significant as compared with the strength of one's opponent. Thus *relative* negotiation strengths and weaknesses ultimately must be assessed by counsel.

This subsection considers the assessment of relative strengths and weaknesses of the negotiator's position, as well as means by which one's position can be enhanced relative to the position of opposing counsel.

1. Evaluation of Negotiation Strengths and Weaknesses

Most attorneys intuitively realize that their bargaining power in a negotiation depends to a large extent upon the strength of their client's legal position.[10] For instance, if the judge has indicated that he will grant the defendant's dispositive motion, the plaintiff's negotiating power usually is quite minimal.[11]

In many cases it will not be so easy to determine the relative strengths of the parties' legal positions. If the law clearly supported one of the parties, the parties' dispute may not even have resulted in contested litigation. In the types of cases that typically end up in court, in which uncertainty plays a major role, counsel need to continue the legal analysis and planning that was done in the very early stages of the case. The same sort of element check lists that are useful in planning litigation also are quite useful in settling litigation.[12]

Not only must counsel determine the legal elements that each party must establish to succeed in the litigation, but she must estimate the probabilities that each party will be able to establish these legal elements. Because of the many uncertainties present in most cases, this assessment is not a simple matter. For this reason, some attorneys employ decision trees and other business techniques in an attempt to quantify the likelihood of various litigation outcomes.[13]

---

10. The strength of the parties' legal positions has a tremendous impact upon private settlements because if settlement of a case is not reached, the case will be resolved at trial according to the governing legal rules. Thus private negotiation has been described as "bargaining in the shadow of the law." Mnookin & Kornhauser, "Bargaining in the Shadow of the Law: The Case of Divorce," 88 *Yale L. J.* 950 (1979).

11. However, a sophisticated analysis of the case may indicate that plaintiff's legal position is not as weak as it initially seems. Even after the judge has said he will grant the defendant's motion, plaintiff's counsel should consider the possibility of persuading the judge to change his mind (by a supplemental brief or a motion for reconsideration) as well as the chance of obtaining an appellate reversal of the judge's ruling.

12. *See* Figures 3–1 and 3–2, *supra,* pp. 63, 64.

13. *See* Senger, "Decision Analysis in Negotiation," 87 *Marq. L. Rev.* 723 (2004); Victor, "The Proper Use of Decision Analysis to Assist Litigation Strategy," 40 *Bus. Law.* 617 (1985); Nagel, "Applying Decision Science to the Practice of Law," *Prac. Law.,* Apr. 15, 1984, at 13; Greenberg, "The Lawyer's Use of Quantitative Analysis in Settlement Negotiations," 38 *Bus. Law.* 1557 (1983).

Jury verdict reporters may be helpful in providing counsel with recent verdicts for the same type of case within the jurisdiction in question. In major cases, some attorneys present an abbreviated version of their case to a mock jury that is representative of an actual jury within the jurisdiction. These mock juries can help an attorney value a case for settlement and provide useful feedback on particular arguments and evidence that may be offered at trial. Whatever means are used to determine the likely trial outcome, any assessments must be continuously updated to reflect ongoing litigation developments.

In addition to considering the relative strengths and weaknesses of the parties' legal positions, counsel should consider the relative strengths and weaknesses of the parties, themselves. The fact that the plaintiff has an overwhelming chance of succeeding at trial may be of little significance if he cannot afford to wait three years until the case can be tried.

In assessing a settlement offer, plaintiffs should consider the time value of money and the costs of litigation. Not only is $1000 today worth more than $1000 three years from now, but the value of any future judgment must be discounted by additional legal and emotional costs that must be incurred to obtain the judgment. These litigation costs can be quite significant. The trial of an action may not only require payment of trial counsel, but also payments to expert witnesses and costs and inconveniences incurred by the parties and their witnesses.

The negotiation position of a major corporation or governmental entity generally is enhanced because of its ability to withstand lengthy and expensive pretrial proceedings. Such "non-legal" factors can affect a party's negotiating strength far more than the likelihood of ultimately prevailing at trial.

There are numerous non-legal factors that can affect a party's negotiating strength. A party may be afraid of testifying at a deposition or at trial, may wish to avoid trial publicity or the revelation of confidential business information in the litigation, or may want to settle the present case because of its relation to other ongoing or potential litigation. An apparent client weakness may be turned to the client's advantage in certain situations. If a defendant corporation is in financial difficulty, plaintiff's counsel may be convinced to accept a smaller settlement than might be obtained at trial; judgments are of little value if entered against persons unable to satisfy them.

Not only must these factors be assessed in determining the bargaining position of one's own client, but counsel always should consider whether the opposing party's position may be influenced by such non-legal factors. Counsel must remember that it is up to the client to ultimately accept or reject a settlement offer,[14] and the client's settlement decisions may be influenced by both legal and non-legal factors.

Decision analysis is just one of many traditionally "non-legal" fields of study that is increasingly used, and useful, in analyzing legal negotiation. *See* Symposium: "The Emerging Interdisciplinary Canon of Negotiation," 87 *Marq. L. Rev.* 637 (2004).

14.   Model Rules of Prof'l Conduct Rule 1.2(a).

Negotiation strengths and weaknesses also can be greatly affected by the attorneys involved in the litigation. An experienced trial attorney may obtain better settlements when negotiating against an inexperienced attorney because of the latter attorney's desire not to try a case against such an experienced trial lawyer.

Many attorney factors other than trial experience will influence negotiation strength. In fact, the inexperienced attorney may be able to turn that very inexperience to her advantage. Consider the following negotiation posture: "As you know, I've never tried a case before. Not only is this case very important to me personally, but I really want try my first case. Your settlement offers are going to have to improve significantly if this case is going to settle."

This example suggests some of the other attorney factors that can enhance a negotiation position. The attorney's commitment to a case, a client, or a cause may enhance her bargaining power, as will the amount of case preparation that she has undertaken. Expertise in the governing substantive law, as well as experience in similar types of cases, in the same court or before the same judge, may be as significant as general trial experience. Some counsel may have conflicting personal or professional obligations that make them predisposed to settle certain cases. Finally, the amount of time and attention that counsel devote to the settlement negotiations may have a direct bearing upon the quality of the settlement ultimately obtained.

Counsel's aim in analyzing a case for settlement should be to place a dollar value on the case by establishing a range of acceptable settlement offers. One method of calculating acceptable settlement ranges has been described as follows:

> To compute his bargaining limit, defendant will (1) multiply the expected damage award by the probability that it will be rendered against him, (2) add to the result in (1) the amount of his anticipated litigation costs, (3) subtract his settlement costs, and (4) subtract his opportunity costs of settling now as opposed to paying later.

> To compute his bargaining limit, plaintiff will (1) multiply the expected damage award by the probability that the court will award it to him, (2) subtract from the product in (1) the amount of his anticipated litigation costs, (3) add his settlement costs, and (4) subtract his opportunity gains from receiving payment now as opposed to a judgment later.[15]

If the defendant's bargaining limit is equal to or greater than plaintiff's bargaining limit, rational parties should, and usually do, settle

---

15. Friedman, Note, "An Analysis of Settlement," 22 *Stan. L. Rev.* 67, 79–80 (1969) (c) 1969 by the Board of Trustees of the Leland Stanford Junior University.

Professor Thomas Mauet suggests that the settlement value of a case should be determined by considering the likely verdict that plaintiff will receive if the case goes to trial, the likelihood that plaintiff will be successful at trial, the additional costs that must be borne if the case is tried, the time value of money, and the extent of the defendant's insurance coverage. T. Mauet, *Pretrial* 394–95 (7th ed. 2008).

(knowing that they can achieve a more favorable outcome by settling within their bargaining limits than by taking the case to trial). However, certain types of cases are more likely to go to trial than are others,[16] and attorneys should never presume that a particular lawsuit will settle.[17] If the action doesn't settle, the attorney may not be fully prepared for trial. Even if the action settles, a party's negotiating position may be severely compromised if opposing counsel realizes that the party or his attorney is counting on a settlement.

2. Attempts to Change Negotiation Strengths and Weaknesses

Negotiation strengths and weaknesses are not unchanging or unchangeable. Counsel not only should evaluate relative negotiation strengths and weaknesses, but should consider ways in which (1) their own strengths can be enhanced and weaknesses reduced and (2) their opponent's weaknesses can be enhanced and strengths reduced.

Counsel should realize that negotiation success often is determined by the perceived, rather than the actual, strength of the parties.[18] A plaintiff's negotiating position will be greatly compromised if the defendant knows that the plaintiff is desperately in need of funds and must reach an immediate settlement. Despite this reality, the plaintiff may do well in the negotiation if the defendant isn't aware of plaintiff's actual situation but perceives the plaintiff as ready and able to endure a lengthy and costly trial.

All counsels' perceptions of their relative bargaining strengths are influenced by their information concerning the case at hand. Thorough pretrial investigation and discovery enhances the chances of negotiation success by providing counsel with a better picture of the parties' relative negotiation strengths and weaknesses. Conversely, the attorney who is able to successfully resist discovery may thereby weaken the bargaining position that opposing counsel otherwise would have obtained. Under the discovery disclosure provisions of Rule 26(a)(1), however, there may be a

---

16. Admin. Office of the U.S. Courts, *Statistical Tables for the Federal Judiciary: March 31, 2010* (2010) (Table C4). *See also* Gross & Syverud, "Getting to No: A Study of Settlement Negotiations and the Selection of Cases for Trial," 90 *Mich. L. Rev.* 319 (1991); Kiser et al., "Let's Not Make a Deal: An Empirical Study of Decision Making in Unsuccessful Settlement Negotiations," 5 *J. Em. Legal Studies* 551 (2008).

17. One of the factors that influences whether a party will accept a particular settlement is the degree to which that party is risk averse. While most people are more likely to accept a monetary gain that is certain instead of a chance to obtain an even greater amount of money, they are more ready to risk a substantial monetary loss than to accept a certain, smaller loss. Kahneman & Tversky, "The Psychology of Preferences," *Scientific American,* Jan. 1982, at 160. *See also* Guthrie, "Better Settle Than Sorry: The Regret Aversion Theory of Litigation Behavior," 1999 *U. Ill. L. Rev.* 43 (1999). In negotiating settlements of civil lawsuits, counsel should recognize that psychological factors may affect themselves as well as their clients, Birke & Fox, "Psychological Principles in Negotiating Civil Settlements," 4 *Harv. Negot. L. Rev.* 1 (1999), although attorneys may be less influenced by non-economic factors than are their clients. Korobkin & Guthrie, "Psychology, Economics, and Settlement: A New Look at the Role of the Lawyer," 76 *Tex. L. Rev.* 77 (1997).

18. H. Cohen, *You Can Negotiate Anything* 53–55 (1980). Cohen argues that the major determinants of negotiation outcome are perceived power, time, and information. *Id.* at 19.

duty to automatically disclose certain basic information at the very outset of a lawsuit.

Not only can pretrial discovery and investigation result in an enhanced negotiation position, but virtually every action taken during the pretrial proceedings should have the aim of increasing the client's position for the ultimate resolution of the case by way of settlement or trial. A sloppy initial client interview may deprive counsel of relevant facts that would increase negotiation strength, and expenditures on peripheral discovery early in a case may preclude later discovery on topics more directly related to the parties' real strengths and weaknesses.

Rule 68 of the Federal Rules of Civil Procedure can be used by defense counsel to focus plaintiffs' counsel on the true merits of their cases and cause them to "think very hard" about settlement.[19] Rule 68 permits defense counsel, at any time more than ten days before trial, to serve upon plaintiff an offer to allow a specific judgment to be taken against the defendant. If this offer is accepted, judgment is entered thereon. If the plaintiff does not accept the offer of judgment, and does not ultimately obtain a judgment more favorable than that offer, he must "pay the costs incurred after the making of the offer."[20]

Rule 68's major impact is on civil rights and other cases in which statutes define "costs" to include attorneys' fees in certain circumstances. In these cases, Rule 68 operates to deprive prevailing plaintiffs of attorneys' fees for work done after they turn down an offer of judgment that is greater than or equal to the amount they ultimately recover at trial.[21] Defense counsel therefore can use Rule 68 offers of judgment to significantly alter the relative bargaining positions of the parties in some cases.[22]

---

19. *Marek v. Chesny,* 473 U.S. 1, 11 (1985). *See generally* "Symposium: Revitalizing FRCP 68: Can Offers of Judgment Provide Adequate Incentives for Fair, Early Settlement of Fee–Recovery Cases?," 57 *Mercer L. Rev.* 717 (2006); Bone, " 'To Encourage Settlement': Rule 68, Offers of Judgment, and the History of the Federal Rules of Civil Procedure," 102 *Nw. U. L. Rev.* 1561 (2008).

20. Fed. R. Civ. P. 68. If judgment is ultimately entered for the defendant, cost shifting under Rule 68 is not triggered. *Delta Air Lines, Inc. v. August,* 450 U.S. 346 (1981).

21. *Marek v. Chesny,* 473 U.S. 1 (1985). By its terms, Rule 68 does not deprive prevailing claimants of pre-offer costs they otherwise are entitled to recover. In addition, presuming a fee shifting statute that only awards attorneys' fees to prevailing parties, the post-offer costs that prevailing plaintiffs may be required to pay pursuant to Rule 68 should not include any of the defendants' attorneys' fees. *Champion Produce, Inc. v. Ruby Robinson Co.,* 342 F.3d 1016 (9th Cir. 2003); *Harbor Motor Co. v. Arnell Chevrolet–Geo, Inc.,* 265 F.3d 638, 645–47 (7th Cir. 2001); *Crossman v. Marcoccio,* 806 F.2d 329, 333–34 (1st Cir. 1986), *cert. denied,* 481 U.S. 1029 (1987). *But see Jordan v. Time, Inc.,* 111 F.3d 102 (11th Cir. 1997) (because "prevailing party" may receive reasonable attorneys fees as costs under Copyright Act, plaintiff who did not recover at trial more than Rule 68 settlement offers must pay defendant's post-offer costs and attorneys fees). Finally, a Rule 68 offer of judgment offering the maximum statutory relief to named class representatives does not moot a putative class action if made before plaintiffs have had a reasonable chance to file a class certification motion. *Weiss v. Regal Collections,* 385 F.3d 337 (3d Cir. 2004); *Nasca v. GC Services Limited Partnership,* 53 Fed.R.Serv.3d 1089 (S.D.N.Y. 2002).

22. Defendants in the United Kingdom and Ireland can make "offers into court" that are similar to Rule 68 offers; empirical studies suggest that such rules do not increase the propensity to settle but do lower the size of the settlements reached. Main & Park, "The Impact of Defendant Offers into Court on Negotiations in the Shadow of the Law: Experimental Evidence," 22 *Int'l Rev. Law & Econ.,* 177 (2002).

Because the parties' relative bargaining positions change over time, counsel should carefully consider when serious settlement negotiations should be undertaken.[23] A party's settlement leverage may be at its greatest immediately after the filing of a strong pretrial motion or immediately before or after an opposing party has been deposed. Indeed, a party's maximum settlement leverage may exist prior to the filing of suit. That is, the threat of litigation may itself be a powerful factor in inducing settlement. Once a lawsuit is filed this leverage will be lost, and the parties' positions may harden and make settlement difficult. The timing of events outside the scope of the lawsuit also should be considered. Plaintiffs may be most ready to settle immediately before major bills, such as income tax payments, are due.

Achieving favorable settlements often takes time. Opposing counsel may be working under time constraints that can be used to a client's advantage in negotiations.[24] Opposing counsel may wish to settle an action because of a personal need for the attorneys' fees that settlement will bring. If an attorney has traveled from out of town to discuss settlement, she may wish to settle the case before returning home.[25] Some attorneys attempt to create time pressures on opposing counsel by scheduling negotiations immediately before a holiday weekend or on a Friday afternoon.

If a settlement deadline is approaching, some attorneys may try to increase their bargaining leverage by claiming that their client is out of town until after the deadline has passed. They then insist that if there is going to be any settlement, it must be on the last terms approved by the client before leaving town. When faced with such a position, counsel should explore the possibility of (1) extending the settlement deadline or (2) encouraging opposing counsel to reach the "inaccessible" party. If, however, her own client is truly inaccessible, counsel should recognize that this may increase her bargaining position.

---

23. Local rules of court may affect the timing of settlement negotiations. Some courts require counsel to meet to discuss case settlement within a certain period of time after the issue is joined or after discovery is complete. *E.g.,* Rule 16.3 of the United States District Court for the Northern District of Georgia. Other local rules assess court and juror costs against the parties if the court is not notified of settlement more than a certain amount of time before the date set for trial. Flanders, "Local Rules in Federal District Courts: Usurpation, Legislation, or Information?," 14 *Loy. L.A. L. Rev.* 213, 265 n.252 (1981) (collecting such local rules). *See also Martinez v. Thrifty Drug & Discount Co.,* 593 F.2d 992 (10th Cir. 1979); *Manual for Complex Litigation, Fourth* § 13.12 (2004).

24. When there are several opposing counsel, the possibility of conflicting individual desires and interests, as well as the potential sources from which to gather information, are multiplied. For this reason, Branch Director David Anderson of the United States Department of Justice was known to wish: "Let me always negotiate against a committee." On the other hand, some attorneys may feel insecure, and therefore not negotiate most effectively, if they are outnumbered at the negotiating table.

Counsel should be conscious of any personal desires that might affect their own negotiation positions and be sure to subordinate those desires to the wishes and best interests of their clients.

25. In this situation, why not offer to arrange for a cab to the airport for opposing counsel? Not only will such a friendly gesture be appreciated by that attorney, but it will give you an indication of exactly what the time constraints are on opposing counsel.

Counsel should not feel compelled to respond immediately to negotiation discussions attempted over the telephone. If a call from opposing counsel catches you off guard, it may be best to promise to get back to her as soon as possible and then become thoroughly familiar with the file before returning the call.[26] Before you discuss settlement in a telephone call, be sure that you have carefully reviewed the case and have planned the negotiation as thoroughly as you would a face-to-face negotiation session.

Counsel should not only prepare the case during pretrial so as to maximize settlement leverage, but should carefully prepare for all settlement negotiations. There should be a well thought-out plan for any negotiations, and counsel should have researched both the relevant facts and law prior to the negotiations. This familiarity with the case will strengthen counsel's position in more ways than one. Not only may the information gained prove valuable in the negotiations, but the process of information gathering should increase counsel's self-confidence in the negotiations and convince her of the reasonableness of her own negotiation positions.

Some attorneys engage in mock negotiations prior to particularly difficult or important negotiation sessions. Mock negotiations should help counsel to emphasize the strong points of her case, as well as to deal comfortably with the case's weaknesses.[27] Counsel also should reflect upon actual negotiation sessions after the fact. Techniques used in one negotiation are likely to be used, or be useful, in future negotiations.

Consideration should be given to the relative advantages of possible locales for the negotiation session. Many attorneys seek the "home court advantage" supposedly gained by negotiating in their own offices. Meeting in her office may give an attorney both added control and confidence during a lengthy negotiation. If an agreement is reached, counsel can call in her secretary to immediately prepare the settlement documents for signature.

On the other hand, valuable information can be gained by negotiating on opposing counsel's home turf. By meeting at another attorney's office, chance remarks by that attorney's employees or associates may be overheard and a sense of that law firm's commitment to the case may be gleaned. In addition, if a stormy negotiation session is anticipated, counsel should recognize that it's difficult to walk out of negotiations conducted in your own office.

---

26. Professor Charles Craver suggests that counsel can disconnect the telephone while she, herself, is talking in order to gain time in a telephone negotiation. C. Craver, *Effective Legal Negotiation and Settlement* § 12.07[3][b] (6th ed. 2009).

27. However, because negotiations are more of a free-form exercise than are trials, counsel must be prepared to be extremely flexible during negotiating sessions. For this reason, mock negotiations should not be used to perfect a fixed negotiation "script," but instead to practice the assertion and maintenance of one's basic negotiating positions when faced with differing approaches from opposing counsel.

If more than one attorney is representing a party, counsel should consider which attorney should discuss settlement with opposing counsel at any given time. Factors that should be considered in this regard include the relative negotiating skills and experience of counsel, the relative seniority of counsel, and whether the opposing party will treat settlement offers coming from particular counsel more or less seriously than offers from co-counsel.

Not only may offers from particular attorneys carry more weight, but opposing counsel may not believe in the sincerity of settlement overtures coming from particular attorneys. If the relations between lead counsel are strained, it may make more sense for a settlement offer to come from associate counsel. Junior attorneys also can be used to keep communication channels open between the parties throughout contentious phases of pretrial and trial.

Counsel's job during the pretrial process is to build a strong trial and negotiation position for her client relative to the position of the opposing party. It does not take much skill or creativity for an attorney to achieve a favorable settlement for a client who enters litigation with an extremely strong position. The skillful attorney is the one who can obtain favorable settlements for clients who are not initially in strong positions, but whose relative position is enhanced by skillful use of the pretrial process.

Exercises Concerning Negotiation
Strengths and Weaknesses

1. You represent the Pittston Company in the litigation that attorney Gerald Stern has filed against that company.

(a) Presume that it is April 1, 1972, and the Buffalo Creek disaster has just occurred. Based upon the facts previously set forth in this text and reasonable assumptions about other relevant facts, write a memorandum analyzing the relative strengths and weaknesses of the parties. In addition to analyzing the negotiating strengths and weaknesses of the Pittston Company and the plaintiffs, the memorandum should recommend a negotiation strategy for Pittston.

(b) Write the memorandum described in exercise 1(a), but presume that it is September 15, 1972, and plaintiffs' lawsuit has just been filed.

(c) Write the memorandum described in exercise 1(a), but presume that discovery has been completed and the trial date is one month away.

2. It is April 1, 1972, and you represent several hundred victims of the Buffalo Creek disaster. These individuals have asked you to pursue a strategy that will result in a speedy negotiated settlement of their claims against the Pittston Company. Write a memorandum setting forth the negotiation strategy that you would adopt.

3. It is January 15, 1977, and the Internal Revenue Service has issued an administrative summons seeking all files of the Upjohn Company concerning an investigation by Upjohn's general counsel into corporate political contributions and payments to foreign governments. The summons and the facts underlying this case are set forth in *Upjohn Co. v. United States,* 449 U.S. 383 (1981), *supra,* p. 245. Upjohn has notified the IRS that it will not voluntarily comply with the summons. However, both Upjohn and the Internal Revenue Service would like to avoid litigation, and a meeting of counsel has been scheduled to discuss a possible settlement of the parties' dispute.

(a) As counsel for the Internal Revenue Service, write a memorandum analyzing the relative negotiation strengths and weaknesses of the IRS and Upjohn and recommending a negotiation strategy that the Internal Revenue Service should pursue.

(b) As counsel for the Upjohn Company, write a memorandum analyzing the relative negotiation strengths and weaknesses of Upjohn and the IRS and recommending a negotiation strategy that the Upjohn Company should pursue.

4. You represent Walmart, which has just been sued by Sam Samuels, one of its employees in suburban St. Louis, in an action alleging racial discrimination. Samuels, a 30 year old Caucasian male, has had numerous run-ins with his African–American supervisor at Walmart, and he has filed at least two other unsuccessful claims against prior employers.

Although you have concluded that Samuels' chances of ultimately succeeding in this law suit are virtually nil, you estimate that it will cost you approximately $20,000 to complete discovery and file a successful motion for summary judgment. Samuels' attorney has suggested that, because Samuels has decided to move to California, he'd "like to put this lawsuit behind him." Counsel suggests that she "might be able to get Samuels to accept $5000" in settlement.

Write a memorandum to your client recommending whether Walmart should accept the $5000 settlement offer. With respect to the issues posed by "nuisance-value settlements," see Kozel & Rosenberg, "Solving the Nuisance–Value Settlement Problem: Mandatory Summary Judgment," 90 *Va. L. Rev.* 1849 (2004) (suggesting that the filing of "nuisance-value" claims would be discouraged by a requirement that judicial settlement agreements cannot be approved before the filing of a motion for summary judgment).

C. NEGOTIATION STYLE, SUBSTANCE, AND TECHNIQUE

Many of the books concerning negotiation focus on negotiation styles that can be used to enhance negotiation success. Many attorneys become preoccupied with negotiation styles and techniques, to the exclusion of the actual substance of negotiations. The successful negotiator, however, must be concerned with both substance and style. Indeed, the hallmark of the successful negotiator frequently is the substantive positions, rather than the personal style, adopted by that individual.[28]

This should be a comfort to the new attorney. If she has built a strong case during pretrial, a favorable settlement should be obtainable regardless of her lack of negotiation experience. The discovery of a previously unknown witness during pretrial investigation or skillful deposition questioning of an opposing party will advance one's negotiation position more than bargaining table theatrics.

Counsel also should not be unduly concerned about negotiation style because of the fact that it is often difficult to assume a style that is different from one's own. If one's personality is pleasant and non-confrontational, it may be very hard, and self-defeating, to feign aggression during negotiations. Rather than attempt to radically alter a personal style, counsel should become cognizant of that style and attempt to use it to one's best advantage in pretrial negotiations.

While effective negotiators differ in personal styles, studies indicate that certain negotiation positions tend to result in more successful negotiations. Specifically, those negotiators who start with a high, yet reasoned, initial demand and make smaller concessions during the negotiation typically obtain better negotiation results.[29]

Some have described the negotiator's job as finding, and attempting to change, the other negotiator's settling point without revealing her own settling point.[30] Techniques that help counsel find and change her opponent's bottom line settlement position while not revealing her own should be considered by all negotiators. Counsel should not presume that an opponent's bottom line is only monetary, but should consider the non-monetary needs and desires of the opposing party as well.

Some of the same techniques used in client and witness interviews are quite helpful for the legal negotiator. If the goal of the negotiator is to obtain information without revealing information in return, counsel will

---

28. Not only should counsel differentiate negotiation substance from style, but they should recognize that effective negotiation substance and style may vary depending upon the stage of a particular negotiation. D. Gifford, *Legal Negotiation: Theory and Applications* 35–38 (2d ed. 2007). Professor Carrie Menkel–Meadow suggests that the effectiveness of one's approach to negotiation will depend upon such things as the subject matter of the dispute, the content of the issues involved, the relationship of the parties, the visibility of the negotiation, how routine the problem being negotiated is, and the alternatives to negotiation. Menkel–Meadow, "Toward Another View of Legal Negotiation: The Structure of Problem Solving," 31 *UCLA L. Rev.* 754 (1984).

29. C. Karrass, *The Negotiating Game: How to Get What You Want* 19–20, 26 (rev. ed. 1994); M. Schoenfield & R. Schoenfield, *Legal Negotiation: Getting Maximum Results* § 3.06 (1988); C. Craver, *Effective Legal Negotiation and Settlement* § 4.01[3][g] (6th ed. 2009); Korobkin, "Aspirations and Settlement," 88 *Cornell L. Rev.* 1 (2002). *See also* Orr & Guthrie, "Anchoring, Information, Expertise, and Negotiation: New Insights from Meta–Analysis," 21 *Ohio St. J. Disp. Resol.* 597 (2006).

30. H. Edwards & J. White, *The Lawyer as a Negotiator* 112–13 (1977). One's own settling point should be based upon a careful case analysis. *See* Section II(B)(1), *supra*, p. 581. Such a principled case analysis should help counsel from falling into the "split the difference" pattern that many negotiations take.

want to spend most of her time in negotiations listening rather than talking. The use of questions, pauses, and active listening devices can be effective in obtaining information about an opponent's settling point. Many negotiators also attempt to elicit the first serious negotiation offer from the opposing negotiator.

Counsel should be conscious of nonverbal communication. If the opposing negotiator is raptly intent on your opening offer, this may indicate that she considers your initial position to be reasonable. If opposing counsel is constantly looking at her watch or has a huge pile of message slips on her desk, it may indicate that she has other cases to attend to and would just as soon settle the present lawsuit.

It may be best to begin negotiations with a consideration of the issues upon which agreement is most likely. The creation of a cooperative climate at the outset of the negotiations may make agreement on other, more difficult, issues more likely as the negotiations progress.

Negotiation threats, on the other hand, may stifle the cooperative communication process upon which successful negotiations usually are built. In addition, if attorneys become angry during negotiations, they may lose their perspective and not only miss opportunities to settle the lawsuit but inadvertently say things that will strengthen the position of the other side.

Counsel must be prepared to carry through with any negotiation threat or risk losing credibility with opposing counsel. To the extent that threats are useful in negotiations, it usually is the implied, rather than the explicit, threat that generates maximum settlement leverage. Little is gained by constantly threatening "If you don't agree to our offer, we're going to take this case to trial!" Consider, instead, telling opposing counsel: "Here are copies of several motions *in limine* that we'll bring before the judge at the pretrial conference next week. We also wondered if you had completed your list of trial witnesses and exhibits?"

Because counsel must not only estimate her opponent's settling point, but attempt to change that point, she, too, must provide information to the opposing attorney. However, any information provided may help an opponent to determine your own settling point. In addition, if the case doesn't settle but goes to trial, the information provided may prove helpful to an opposing party. Counsel therefore should carefully plan exactly what information to share during settlement negotiations.[31] This decision should take into account the likelihood that the case will settle, the effect on the settlement negotiations of the information in question, and the

---

31. Federal Rule of Evidence 408 provides that settlement offers, as well as conduct or statements made during settlement negotiations, are not admissible to prove liability for or the invalidity of the underlying claim or its amount. However, Rule 408 does not preclude evidence of settlement conduct or statements when offered for a purpose other than proving or contesting the validity or the amount of the claim or impeaching through a prior inconsistent statement or contradiction.

advantage that would be gained if the information were not revealed and the case goes to trial.[32]

The selective exchange of information concerning settlement and litigation costs and, especially, the likely trial outcome is a typical focus of legal negotiation. In dealing with certain defense counsel, the job of plaintiff's attorney will be to convince that counsel that plaintiff's case is not a "routine" civil action for which a predetermined amount of settlement dollars should be paid. Only by having an intimate grasp of the facts can an attorney successfully argue that a case doesn't fall within the pigeonhole in which opposing counsel has mentally placed the case.

One way in which settlement leverage may be increased is by documenting a settlement offer in a letter that marshals the factual and legal grounds supporting that offer. Such a letter might contain, for instance, the life or work expectancy calculations upon which plaintiff's expert witness will rely at trial to establish plaintiff's losses.

Some attorneys present opposing counsel with a settlement brochure or videotape summarizing their most persuasive trial evidence.[33] A plaintiffs' personal injury lawyer might produce a videotape containing interviews with key witnesses and permit opposing counsel to examine photographs, models or other trial exhibits prior to the time that the court has set for the exchange of exhibits. Before presenting opposing counsel with such information, counsel must weigh the potential gain in settlement leverage against the potential loss if the settlement is not achieved and the case must be tried.

Despite the risk in providing detailed information to the other party, counsel should be aware that settlement documents often have much greater impact upon settlement than mere oral offers. The attorney who presents the other side with an expert witness's detailed breakdown of economic damages may be rewarded by the opposing counsel's acceptance of these figures as a starting point for further negotiations. Counsel should draft settlement letters and other documents with the realization that they may be read by the opposing party as well as by opposing counsel. Settlement letters should be persuasive without needlessly offending the opposing party and creating a barrier to settlement. Counsel also should realize that every document she drafts may be seen by her

---

32. In determining the information that should be imparted to an opposing party, counsel may wish to consider the economic models which have been developed to predict when parties will settle, rather than litigate, a particular dispute. Posner, "An Economic Approach to Legal Procedure and Judicial Administration, 2 *J. Legal Stud.* 399 (1973); Priest & Klein," "The Selection of Disputes for Litigation," 13 *J. Legal Stud.* 1 (1984); Priest, "Reexamining the Selection Hypothesis: Learning from Wittman's Mistakes," 14 *J. Legal Stud.* 215 (1985).

The basic factors considered in these models include the parties' settlement and litigation costs, their stakes in the case, and their estimates of the likelihood of success at trial. Posner, *supra,* at 417–20. Professor Peter Schuck has suggested that the models also include a consideration of the effect of judicial intervention in the settlement process. Schuck, "The Role of Judges in Settling Complex Cases: The Agent Orange Example," 53 *U. Chi. L. Rev.* 337 (1986).

33. Branson & Branson, "Documenting the Demand," *Litigation,* Winter 1988, at 14; 3 M. Belli, *Modern Trials* §§ 50.2–50.18 (2d ed. 1982).

own client and should draft even preliminary settlement documents with that fact in mind.

Concessions, as well as offers, should be made on a principled basis. For instance, an attorney might justify a specific concession based on the likelihood that the judge will rule a particular way on a pretrial motion or that the case will be transferred to another judge. Concession patterns should be planned in advance, at least tentatively, to move the negotiations to the final settlement figure that counsel is attempting to achieve. If concessions are not made and justified on a principled basis, the negotiation may degenerate into an exercise in splitting the difference with opposing counsel. By planning concessions in advance, counsel is less likely to make impulsive offers or be swayed by the emotions of the negotiating room and make a concession that she later regrets.

Recently attention has focused on ways in which to facilitate cooperative or problem-solving negotiations and settlements.[34] A cooperative negotiator considers negotiations to be more than a zero sum game in which one party's gain requires a corresponding loss for the other party. Instead of making negotiation demands, the needs of the parties are seen as negotiating problems that all counsel will work to solve. Viewed from such a cooperative perspective, negotiations are seen as both affecting and being affected by the parties' ongoing relationships.[35]

Counsel always should search for cooperative negotiation solutions from which all parties can benefit. Assume, for instance, that a plaintiff has brought a civil action against a local merchant. An alternative to a strictly monetary settlement of this dispute might be for the merchant to offer the plaintiff the chance to purchase certain merchandise at dealer cost. Such a settlement could provide the plaintiff with more than he would have obtained in a strictly monetary settlement and yet would cost the defendant less than a monetary settlement.

Structured settlements, in which the defendant in a tort suit purchases an annuity that will provide the plaintiff with tax free periodic payments for an extended period of time, are another example of settlements in which the plaintiff's gain is greater than the defendant's loss. Nor should counsel rule out the possibility of partial settlements, resolving some, but not all, of the issues between the parties. The parties also may desire to lessen the uncertainty of the trial outcome by agreeing before

---

34. *See, e.g.* R. Fisher & W. Ury, *Getting to Yes* (2d ed. 1991); R. Fisher & S. Brown, *Getting Together* (1988); M. Mnookin et al., *Beyond Winning: Negotiating to Create Value in Deals and Disputes* (2000). *See also* Menkel–Meadow, "Toward Another View of Legal Negotiation: The Structure of Problem Solving," 31 *UCLA L. Rev.* 754 (1984). *But see* Wetlaufer, "The Limits of Integrative Bargaining," 85 *Geo. L. J.* 369 (1996).

35. R. Fisher & S. Brown, *Getting Together* 132–148 (1988). *See also* Eisenberg, "Private Ordering Through Negotiation: Dispute–Settlement and Rulemaking," 89 *Harv. L. Rev.* 637 (1976). Any ongoing relationship between the parties can be either an inducement to settlement ("Let's work this thing out; we'd like to do more business with the defendant in the future.") or a settlement barrier ("If we raise our offer to the plaintiff that guy will think that he can dictate the terms of his employment."). The parties also may be concerned that their settlement will serve as a precedent in similar disputes that either may encourage or discourage similarly situated individuals to bring suit.

trial to a "high-low" settlement, under which the plaintiff's minimum and maximum recoveries are fixed. Regardless of the jury's verdict, these agreements guarantee the plaintiff a specified, minimum recovery and protect the defendant from a damage award greater than a specified maximum amount.

As with other lawyering tasks, the most successful legal negotiations require careful planning, hard work, and a good deal of imagination, flexibility, and creativity.

Exercises Concerning Negotiation Style, Substance, and Technique

1. You are a relatively new attorney, practicing in a small law firm in Nashville, Tennessee. One of your first substantial cases is the civil action that you have brought on behalf of Thomas Eakins, the victim of the Buffalo Creek disaster who was introduced in exercise 1 of the Exercises Concerning Client Interviewing in Chapter 2, *supra,* p. 38. The defendant in this action, the Pittston Company, is represented by a major New York law firm.

(a) Prepare a memorandum setting forth the negotiation style and strategy that you would adopt in trying to settle this case, which has just been filed. Consider in this memorandum such matters as when settlement should be discussed with opposing counsel and the manner in which settlement should be raised.

(b) Presume that, immediately after the judge entered a discovery scheduling order in the Eakins lawsuit, you approached opposing counsel in the courthouse and asked whether Pittston might be interested in settlement. The senior partner representing Pittston snapped back, "You've got to be joking. You brought this suit; now let's see you try it!" Although you were greatly offended by this outburst, your client, Thomas Eakins, does not want to go to trial or even have his discovery deposition taken. Write a short memorandum describing the course of action that you would pursue in this situation.

2. Presume the facts set forth in the transcript of the pretrial conference in Section II(C) of Chapter 13, *supra,* p. 550. The claims of Bertha and Dennis Morris, for personal injuries and damages to their car, have been settled for $9250. The two insurance companies have reserved the question of their respective liabilities for that settlement.

The Farm Bureau Mutual Automobile Insurance Company insured the Baxters, who owned and operated the trailer that struck the Morrises. Presume that the limits on this policy were $20,000 for bodily injury and $20,000 for property damages. The Great American Indemnity Company insured Lake Shore Motor Freight, with whom the Baxters had contracted to carry freight. Presume that the limits of the Great American policy were $400,000 for bodily injury and $100,000 for property damages.

A final pretrial conference is set tomorrow in the declaratory judgment action that has been filed by Farm Bureau, whom your law firm represents. The partner in charge of this case just entered your office and asked you to "call Great American's counsel and see if we can't settle this case this afternoon."

(a) Draft a memorandum setting forth the strategy that you plan to pursue in your call to the attorney for Great American; and

(b) Come to class prepared to conduct a telephone negotiation with this attorney.

III. NEGOTIATION ETHICS

Settlement negotiations typically occur quite informally, outside the presence of the judge. The procedural rules and statutes that apply to other aspects of the civil litigation process generally do not apply to the negotiated settlement of litigation. Negotiation ethics have received a significant amount of attention in recent years,[36] and the Litigation Section of the American Bar Association has adopted guidelines specifically focused on the ethics of settlement negotiation.[37]

Professor Thomas Shaffer has posed the problem of negotiation ethics starkly:

> The judiciary, operating with an adversary system, is the source of justice. However, a dispute that will never see the inside of a courtroom is never exposed to the system that determines what is just. No one can know what result justice would have required. Thus, the only significant component of negotiation is the power, overt or subtle, to obtain results for clients.[38]

Is power the only significant component of negotiation or are there ethical limitations that govern counsel's negotiation behavior? This is the question that is examined in the following subsections of this chapter. Negotiation ethics are explored by focusing upon the conflicting duties that typically arise in settlement negotiations. While the attorney's primary duty is to her client, ethical proscriptions impose duties upon counsel in her dealings with other counsel and parties, as well as in situations in which counsel is representing multiple clients.

---

36. *E.g., What's Fair: Ethics for Negotiators* (C. Menkel–Meadow & M. Wheeler, eds. 2004); Craver, "Negotiation Ethics for Real World Interactions," 25 *Ohio St. J. On Disp. Resol.* 299 (2010); Richmond, "Lawyers' Professional Responsibilities and Liabilities in Negotiations," 22 *Geo. J. Legal Ethics* 249 (2009); Young, "Sharks, Saints, and Samurai: The Power of Ethics in Negotiations," 24 *Negotiation Journal* 145 (2008). *See also* Reilly, "Was Machiavelli Right? Lying in Negotiation and the Art of Defensive Self–Help," 24 *Ohio St. J. on Disp. Resol.* 481 (2009) (suggesting strategies to avoid being exploited by negotiation lies).

37. Section of Litigation, American Bar Association, *Ethical Guidelines for Settlement Negotiations* (2002). *See also* "A Symposium: Ethical Issues in Settlement Negotiations," 52 *Mercer L. Rev.* 807 (2001).

38. Shaffer, "Negotiation Ethics: A Report to Cartaphila," *Litigation,* Winter 1981, at 37, 39.

A. COUNSEL'S DUTY TO HER CLIENT

The very first rule of the American Bar Association Model Rules of Professional Conduct provides: "A lawyer shall provide competent representation to a client. Competent representation requires the legal knowledge, skill, thoroughness and preparation reasonably necessary for the representation."[39] Whether attorneys are involved in legal negotiations or other aspects of the pretrial process, professional competence, including preparation for the particular task at hand, is expected.

Counsel must never forget that they are negotiating on behalf of their clients. Client interests must be placed ahead of (1) the personal desires of the attorney ("If this case doesn't settle, I'll have to reschedule my vacation."); (2) the desires of other attorneys in the law firm ("We've already put too much time and money into your case."); and (3) the desires of the judge ("I don't care how you do it, but settle this case!").

Counsel always should remember precisely who her client is in any legal negotiation. Attorneys generally are not permitted to accept payment for their services from someone other than their client.[40] However, despite the fact that insurance defense counsel are paid by an insurance company, the insurance company is not their client. Such legal representation is permitted so long as the client has consented to the arrangement (typically in the insurance contract), attorney-client confidences are preserved, and "there is no interference with the lawyer's independence of professional judgment or with the client-lawyer relationship."[41] In negotiating a settlement on behalf of an insured, insurance defense counsel, as well as all other attorneys, must keep the interests of their clients paramount.

Because the attorney is negotiating on behalf of her client, all settlement offers must be transmitted to the client for approval or rejection.[42] Unless the offer is not serious, it is best to relay offers to the client in writing. By putting the offer in a letter to the client, later confusion can be avoided concerning precisely what the client was told about the offer. The attorney's letter should not only describe the total offer made, but should list the expenses and fees that would be subtracted from the gross offer and the net amount that the client actually would receive under the terms of the offer. The client can be asked to sign and date a copy of the attorney's letter if the settlement is acceptable.[43]

---

39. Model Rules of Prof'l Conduct Rule 1.1.

40. Model Rules of Prof'l Conduct Rule 1.8(f).

41. Model Rules of Prof'l Conduct Rule 1.8(f)(2).

42. Model Rules of Prof'l Conduct Rule 1.2(a). Nevertheless, if an attorney without actual, but with apparent, authority agrees to the settlement of an action, principles of agency law may bind the client to that settlement. *Capital Dredge & Dock Corp. v. City of Detroit,* 800 F.2d 525 (6th Cir. 1986); *Int'l Telemeter Corp. v. Teleprompter Corp.,* 592 F.2d 49, 55–56 (2d Cir. 1979).

43. Because a lawyer is to explain matters to her client so that the client can make informed decisions concerning those matters, Model Rules of Prof'l Conduct Rule 1.4(b), the client letter can summarize the advice given the client concerning the merits of the settlement offer. Attorneys should be sure to counsel clients about the non-monetary incidents of trial, including

B. COUNSEL'S DUTY TO MULTIPLE CLIENTS

While attorneys must put the interests of their clients above the interests of others, what if more than one client is represented by the same counsel? Rule 1.7 of the Model Rules of Professional Conduct permits attorneys to represent multiple clients if they can adequately represent the interests of each and the clients consent to the multiple representation.

In addition to this general guideline concerning multiple representation, Model Rule 1.8(g) specifically addresses the attorney's role in the settlement of similar claims of multiple clients:

> A lawyer who represents two or more clients shall not participate in making an aggregate settlement of the claims of or against the clients * * * unless each client consents after consultation, including disclosure of the existence and nature of all the claims * * * involved and of the participation of each person in the settlement.[44]

Thus, in a lawsuit such as that brought by attorney Gerald Stern on behalf of survivors of the Buffalo Creek disaster, the plaintiffs should consent to multiple representation as well as to the individual monetary award that each plaintiff will receive under any proposed settlement.

Other, more subtle, conflicts between multiple clients may arise in the context of settlement negotiations. For instance, an attorney involved in a trial on behalf of one client may not have the time to try, or even properly negotiate settlements of, cases in which she represents other clients. A similar problem may occur if an attorney's caseload is so large that, as a practical matter, she must settle almost all of her cases regardless of the interests and desires of particular clients. An attorney's caseload should be managed to prevent these possible conflicts from arising.

C. COUNSEL'S DUTY TO OPPOSING PARTIES AND COUNSEL

Are there ethical constraints on counsel's attempts to negotiate the most favorable settlements for their clients? In particular, are counsel

---

the possible disruption of business or personal affairs and the tensions inherent in the trial process, and to keep the client informed about negotiation developments as they occur.

44. Model Rules of Prof'l Conduct Rule 1.8(g). ABA Formal Ethics Opinion 06–438 concluded:

> In seeking to obtain the informed consent of multiple clients to make or accept an offer of an aggregate settlement * * * as required under Model Rule 1.8(g), a lawyer must advise each client of the total amount or result of the settlement or agreement, the amount and nature of every client's participation in the settlement or agreement, the fees and costs to be paid to the lawyer from the proceeds or by an opposing party or parties, and the method by which the costs are to be apportioned to each client.

ABA Formal Ethics Opinion 06–438 (Feb. 10, 2006). *See also* Silver & Baker, "I Cut, You Choose: The Role of Plaintiffs' Counsel in Allocating Settlement Proceeds," 84 *Va. L. Rev.* 1465 (1998). *But see Principles of the Law of Aggregate Litigation* § 3.17(b) (2009) (permitting individual claimants, before receipt of settlement offer, to agree in writing to be bound by a vote of a substantial majority of claimants concerning an aggregate settlement proposal in certain circumstances).

under any duties to the opposing parties and counsel with whom they negotiate?[45] Indeed, they are.

Rule 4.1(a) of the Model Rules of Professional Conduct provides: "In the course of representing a client a lawyer shall not knowingly * * * make a false statement of material fact or law to a third person." Does this mean that during settlement negotiations an attorney cannot engage in "puffing" when describing the strengths of her client's position? Not only is puffing considered ethically proper, but it is a common negotiation practice. In fact, a comment to Rule 4.1 of the Model Rules of Professional Conduct provides: "Under generally accepted conventions in negotiation, certain types of statements ordinarily are not taken as statements of material fact. Estimates of price or value placed on the subject of a transaction and a party's intentions as to an acceptable settlement of a claim are in this category * * * ."

The ethical line that attorneys must draw is between "estimates" and "intentions," on the one hand, and "facts," on the other. Unfortunately, no bright-line tests exist to help counsel differentiate between these types of negotiation statements. It may be helpful, though, to separate statements concerning the negotiation itself ("He won't take a penny less!") from statements concerning objective facts outside the context of the negotiation ("He paid $29,546.78 for the car back in 2007."). Statements concerning the negotiation are more likely to be estimates or intentions that are not governed by the ethical proscriptions on attorney misrepresentation. Attorneys should attempt to put themselves in the shoes of opposing counsel in assessing whether a negotiation statement is an unethical misrepresentation. If you would feel misled or abused if opposing counsel made similar statements to you, the statement probably is one that you should not make.

The Model Rules of Professional Conduct are not the only limits on counsel's negotiation conduct. The United States Court of Appeals for the Second Circuit has upheld a fraud action against attorneys for misrepresenting insurance policy limitations during settlement negotiations.[46] Nor are material misstatements the only negotiation conduct that can lead to later judicial relief. In some cases, misrepresentation has been found not based upon affirmative attorney misstatements, but because counsel has not conveyed certain information to opposing counsel.[47] Thus the Minnesota Supreme Court upheld the vacation of a settlement due to defense

---

45. When counsel is dealing with an unrepresented opposing party, special ethical constraints are applicable. Model Rule of Professional Conduct 4.3 provides, in part, that "[i]n dealing on behalf of a client with a person who is not represented by counsel, a lawyer shall not state or imply that the lawyer is disinterested." Can an attorney submit a proposed waiver of rights to an unrepresented party if she does not attempt to persuade that party to sign it? *See Dolan v. Hickey*, 385 Mass. 234, 431 N.E.2d 229 (1982) (drafting documents for unrepresented parties to sign does not constitute "advice" and is not improper so long as attorney does not engage in misrepresentation or overreaching).

46. *Slotkin v. Citizens Casualty Co.*, 614 F.2d 301 (2d Cir. 1979), *cert. denied*, 449 U.S. 981 (1980).

47. *See* Temkin, "Misrepresentation by Omission in Settlement Negotiations: Should There Be a Silent Safe Harbor?," 18 *Geo. J. Legal Ethics* 179 (2004).

counsel's failure to disclose that plaintiff was suffering from an aneurysm that had not been discovered by his own physicians.[48]

Finally, apart from what is stated or implied during negotiations, governing contract law may proscribe settlements that are unconscionable.[49] Unfortunately, there are no simple definitions of which settlements are so one-sided as to be considered unconscionable. Perhaps the best advice in this regard is the old adage that if something seems too good to be true, it probably is.

NOTES AND QUESTIONS CONCERNING NEGOTIATION ETHICS

1. When driving home from work one day, Paul is involved in a collision with another car driven by Driver. Paul sues both Driver and Mechanic, Inc., the business that serviced Driver's car immediately before the accident. Prior to trial Driver agrees to pay Paul $50,000 minus any recovery that Paul ultimately obtains at trial against the non-settling defendant Mechanic. This settlement is kept secret, and Driver agrees to remain as a defendant in the lawsuit. At the trial Driver's testimony is quite supportive of Paul's claim against Mechanic, which claim is the focus of Paul's proof. The jury returns a verdict for defendant Driver and a verdict against defendant Mechanic for $100,000.

What are the incentives for Paul and Driver to enter into such a "Mary Carter" settlement agreement? What are the problems that such an agreement creates for defendant Mechanic? What ethical issues do such agreements pose? How, if at all, should the courts regulate these agreements? Although many courts have required that such agreements be disclosed to the jury, can such a rule be defeated by including in the agreement information damaging to the non-settling defendant? *See generally* Entman, "Mary Carter Agreements: An Assessment of Attempted Solutions," 38 *U. Fla. L. Rev.* 521 (1986); Quinn & Weaver, "Mary Carter Agreements," *Litigation*, Spring 1994, at 41.

2. Perjured files a personal injury action against Dutiful. In this suit Perjured, a self-employed carpenter, asserts in both his complaint and at his deposition that he earned $40,000 per year during the three years prior to the accident upon which he bases his suit. However, when Perjured produces his

---

48. *Spaulding v. Zimmerman,* 263 Minn. 346, 116 N.W.2d 704 (1962). At the time the trial court approved the parties' $6500 settlement it had not been informed about plaintiff's aneurysm. 263 Minn. at 350, 116 N.W.2d at 708. *See* Cramton & Knowles, "Professional Secrecy and its Exceptions: *Spaulding v. Zimmerman* Revisited," 83 *Minn. L. Rev.* 63 (1998). *See also Kath v. Western Media, Inc.,* 684 P.2d 98 (Wyo. 1984) (order confirming settlement vacated because plaintiffs' attorney did not reveal in settlement negotiations letter in which major witness contradicted important deposition testimony he had given); *Virzi v. Grand Trunk Warehouse & Cold Storage Co.,* 571 F.Supp. 507 (E.D. Mich.1983) (settlement set aside because plaintiff's counsel failed to disclose to defense counsel or the court at time settlement was reached that plaintiff was dead). *But see Brown v. County of Genesee,* 872 F.2d 169 (6th Cir. 1989) (per curiam) (unilateral mistake by plaintiff's counsel as to highest wage level at which plaintiff could have been paid by defendant did not constitute fraud sufficient to vacate settlement). *Compare* Comment to Model Rule 4.1 of the Model Rules of Professional Conduct ("A lawyer * * * generally has no affirmative duty to inform an opposing party of relevant facts.") *with* Comment to Model Rule 3.3 of the Model Rules of Professional Conduct ("There are circumstances where failure to make a disclosure is the equivalent of an affirmative misrepresentation.").

49. *Restatement (Second) of Contracts* § 208 (1981). *See also* Fed. R. Civ. P. 60(b).

income tax returns for this same time period, they only show reported income of $30,000 per year.

Can Dutiful's attorney make use of these facts in settlement negotiations? What, if any, duty rests upon Dutiful's attorney to report this discrepancy or take other action? What, if any, duty rests upon Perjured's attorney? What if, rather than being a self-employed carpenter, Perjured is a self-employed attorney? What if Perjured's attorney makes an offer of settlement that is very favorable to Dutiful, on the condition that Dutiful and his counsel not report the apparent discrepancy in Perjured's income?

3. While representing a woman seeking a divorce, counsel learns of the criminal adultery of the woman's husband. What use can the woman's attorney make of this information during the divorce negotiations? *See State v. Harrington,* 128 Vt. 242, 260 A.2d 692 (1969).

4. Presume that you represent some of the victims of the Buffalo Creek disaster and are attempting to negotiate a settlement of their claims against the Pittston Company. Your particular clients are interested only in maximizing the monetary recovery that they receive from Pittston. Nevertheless, you insist in negotiations that a term of any settlement must be that Pittston will never build another coal waste dam in the Buffalo Creek Valley, a term that you know is unacceptable to Pittston. Is such negotiation conduct ethically proper? Why might counsel adopt such a position? What strategic problems might be raised by such tactics?

5. Rule 3.3(a)(2) of the Model Rules of Professional Conduct requires counsel to disclose to the court "legal authority in the controlling jurisdiction known to the lawyer to be directly adverse to the position of the client and not disclosed by opposing counsel." What if during negotiations opposing counsel appears unaware of governing legal authority? Are there situations in which counsel is required to correct misperceptions of opposing counsel concerning the governing law? What if the negotiations are with an opposing party who is not represented by counsel?

6. Presume that attorney Jane Justice has filed a civil rights class action, seeking exclusively injunctive relief, and that the governing statute provides for the recovery of attorneys' fees by prevailing plaintiffs. Prior to trial, defense counsel offers a settlement under which the defendant will provide all of the injunctive relief plaintiffs seek, if they will waive their right to any attorneys' fees. Is it ethical for defense counsel to make such an offer? How should plaintiffs' counsel respond to such an offer? How could plaintiffs' counsel have avoided being placed in such an apparent conflict between herself and her clients? See *Evans v. Jeff D.,* 475 U.S. 717 (1986). *See also* Note, "Fee as the Wind Blows: Waivers of Attorney's Fees in Individual Civil Rights Actions Since *Evans v. Jeff D.,*" 102 *Harv. L. Rev.* 1278 (1989); Stedman, Note, "*Evans v. Jeff D.:* Putting Private Attorneys General on Waiver," 41 *Vand. L. Rev.* 1273 (1988). *But see Pinto v. Spectrum Chemicals and Laboratory Products,* 200 N.J. 580, 985 A.2d 1239 (2010) (While defendants in state consumer protection and employment cases may insist on simultaneous negotiation of settlement of the merits and attorneys' fees, they may not insist on fee waivers in such fee-shifting cases involving public-interest counsel).

7. Are attorneys forbidden from revealing client confidences during negotiations? Model Rule 1.6(a) of the Model Rules of Professional Conduct provides, generally, that a lawyer shall not reveal information relating to the client representation unless the client has consented to the revelation. However, the comment to that Rule provides that, "except to the extent that the client's instructions or special circumstances limit that authority," attorneys are impliedly authorized to make negotiation disclosure about a client that "facilitates a satisfactory conclusion to a matter."

8. Immediately after the Buffalo Creek disaster, the Buffalo Mining Company offered monetary settlements to victims of the flood. Similar settlements typically are offered immediately after airline accidents and other mass disasters. Are any ethical problems raised by the involvement of legal counsel in such settlement offers? Does the ethical propriety of the offers depend upon the mental and emotional condition of the victims? Are there advantages to potential plaintiffs from such offers? Are there disadvantages?

9. Presume that in a labor negotiation the attorney representing the employees tells management's attorney that her clients will go on strike unless a settlement is reached, even though this is not really the employees' bottom line position. Is such a statement ethically permissible?

Consider the following scenario. Labor and union attorneys are involved in face-to-face bargaining at the offices of management counsel. Labor counsel arranges for the leader of the union to send her a telegram saying "If settlement is not reached by 5:00, union will strike." Although she knows that this is not true, upon receiving the telegram the labor attorney hands it to management counsel.

Is such conduct ethically improper? What if the employees' attorney had not arranged in advance for the telegram to be sent? What if the employees' attorney does not hand the telegram to management counsel, but places it alongside her brief case and then says she needs to make a telephone call in another room?

10. Adam Admirable does insurance defense work for the Acme Insurance Company. In that role, he is assigned to defend Donna Douglas in an automobile negligence suit brought against her by plaintiff Parker Paulson. Although she is the only defendant named in this action, Douglas was running an errand for her employer, Deep Pocket, Inc., at the time of the accident. Acme has issued both a small policy covering Douglas and a much larger employer's policy covering Deep Pocket.

Admirable is aware of all of these facts, but Paulson's counsel only knows about the Acme policy covering Douglas. Paulson's attorney has scheduled a conference to discuss the possibility of settlement with Admirable. What advice would you give Admirable prior to that conference?

11. In addition to possible conflicts of interest posed by counsel's duties to existing clients, must attorneys be wary of conflicts between present clients and potential future clients? In the negotiations leading to the settlement of the lawsuit brought by Gerald Stern on behalf of victims of the Buffalo Creek disaster, the Pittston Company insisted that Stern not represent any other potential plaintiffs. G. Stern, *The Buffalo Creek Disaster* 269 (1976). Are there

ethical problems with such a settlement term? *See* Model Rules of Prof'l Conduct Rule 5.6(b). Why shouldn't Gerald Stern be able to use Pittston's concerns about potential future litigation to gain a better settlement for his present clients? Is Model Rule 5.6(b) intended to protect clients or attorneys? Virginia's counterpart to Model Rule 5.6(b) forbids agreements "in which a restriction on the lawyer's right to practice is part of the settlement of a controversy, except where such a restriction is approved by a tribunal or a government entity." Va. Sup. Ct. R. 5.6(b) (2006). *See generally* Gillers & Painter, "Free the Lawyers: A Proposal to Permit No–Sue Promises in Settlement Agreements," 18 *Geo. J. Legal Ethics* 291 (2005).

12. The jury awards plaintiff a verdict of $1,000,000. Under her contingent fee contract, plaintiff's counsel is entitled to thirty-five percent of this verdict. The defendant appeals, raising some strong points in its appellate brief. After filing this brief, the defendant offers to settle the case for $750,000. Plaintiff's counsel strongly recommends that plaintiff accept this settlement, but plaintiff declines to do so unless counsel will lower the percentage of her contingent fee. Counsel refuses to do so, the plaintiff refuses to settle, and the trial court's judgment is reversed on appeal. What should plaintiff's counsel do? *See Hagans, Brown & Gibbs v. First Nat'l Bank*, 783 P.2d 1164 (Alaska 1989).

IV. MEMORIALIZING THE SETTLEMENT

Once a settlement has been negotiated, the terms of that settlement still should be reduced to writing and the appropriate legal documents drafted to effectuate the settlement. It is these settlement documents that are considered in this section.

Often the formal documents that finalize a settlement will have been preceded by other settlement documents. Counsel should obtain written settlement authority from their clients before engaging in settlement negotiations. Letters may be exchanged between counsel summarizing settlement offers or tentative agreements. If oral settlement offers are made, a record of them should be kept.[50]

In contrast to such internal documents that should be kept in counsel's case file, this section concerns the formal settlement documents that reflect the parties' final settlement agreement.

A. THE SETTLEMENT DOCUMENTS[51]

Typically there are at least two separate documents that must be drafted to effectuate the settlement of a lawsuit. The first of these

---

50. Due to his failure to keep such a record, a defense counsel once offered the author (who was representing a plaintiff) more money in settlement than the plaintiff had previously demanded. Some time had passed since the plaintiff's last demand, and defense counsel apparently had forgotten that plaintiff had made an intervening, and lower, demand.

51. As with other contracts, there may be no requirement that a particular settlement be put in writing. However, a written memorialization of the settlement terms can prevent later

documents contains the parties' actual settlement agreement, while the second document is the notice or court order dismissing the pending litigation. Two documents generally are used so that the public documents filed with the court need not recite the specific settlement terms.[52]

The parties' settlement agreement may be encompassed in a release executed by the plaintiff. The release is just what its title implies; it is the legal document in which the plaintiff relinquishes all underlying claims against the defendant. The execution of a release is the bottom line condition for the settlement of most civil actions.[53]

If a plaintiff has potential tort claims against more than one person and a settlement has been reached with fewer than all of these potential defendants, a covenant not to sue, rather than a release, may be executed with the settling defendants. The covenant not to sue provides that, in return for a valuable consideration, the plaintiff will not sue or continue suit against a particular defendant. These covenants historically were used to avoid the possibility of inadvertently releasing all tortfeasors from liability through the execution of a release with only a single defendant. While the tort law in most states now prevents such an inadvertent release of non-settling defendants,[54] out of an abundance of caution many attorneys still use covenants not to sue rather than releases in cases involving multiple tortfeasors.

In some jurisdictions, settling defendants may be concerned that other potential defendants who have not settled will seek contribution from them with respect to a later judgment. In such jurisdictions, the settlement documents may include an agreement by the plaintiff to indemnify the settling defendant if contribution is sought by other potential defendants who are not a party to the present settlement.[55] Because the law of contribution varies from state to state, the law governing a

---

misunderstandings and thus protect both counsel and their clients. It also may be difficult to enforce a settlement agreement that hasn't been reduced to writing.

52. Parties desiring confidentiality also may file the settlement agreement with the court but request that it be sealed from public scrutiny. The increasing use of sealed settlements has been criticized, however, and courts have upheld the right of private parties to have settlements unsealed in certain circumstances. *E.g., Bank of America Nat'l Trust & Sav. Ass'n v. Hotel Rittenhouse Associates,* 800 F.2d 339 (3d Cir. 1986). *See also Janus Films, Inc. v. Miller,* 801 F.2d 578 (2d Cir. 1986). If, rather than sealing the settlement agreement, the parties include the terms of the settlement in the (public) court order dismissing the case, and make compliance with those terms a condition of settlement and dismissal, they can ensure that the court dismissing the action will have jurisdiction over any later action for breach of the settlement agreement. W. Brazil, *Effective Approaches to Settlement: A Handbook for Lawyers and Judges* 303 (1988). *See also Kokkonen v. Guardian Life Ins. Co.,* 511 U.S. 375, 381–82 (1994); Parness & Walker, "Enforcing Settlements in Federal Civil Actions," 36 *Ind. L. Rev.* 33 (2003); DiSarro, "Six Degrees of Separation: Settlement Agreements and Consent Orders in Federal Civil Litigation," 60 *Am. U.L. Rev.* 275 (2010).

53. The release signed by the plaintiffs in the Buffalo Creek litigation is set forth *infra* at p. 609.

54. D. Dobbs, *The Law of Torts* § 388 (2000). *See also* Unif. Cont. Among Tortfeasors Act § 4(a), 12 *U.L.A.* 284 (2008).

55. *See Pierringer v. Hoger,* 21 Wis.2d 182, 124 N.W.2d 106 (1963). The plaintiff's agreement to indemnify a settling tortfeasor should be unnecessary in states that have adopted the Uniform Contribution Among Tortfeasors Act or similar statutes restricting the right to contribution. Unif. Cont. Among Tortfeasors Act § 1(b), 12 *U.L.A.* 201 (2008).

particular case should be researched carefully before drafting the settlement documents. In addition, a choice of law clause should be used in the covenant or release to ensure that there is no question as to which state's law governs the settlement.

While a release or covenant not to sue may be sufficient to memorialize routine settlements, if the settlement involves significant mutual promises by the parties it is best to draft an actual settlement agreement. Such a settlement agreement should be signed by the parties and should set forth all of the promises underlying the settlement.[56]

Because releases and settlement agreements generally are not filed with the court, a notice, stipulation, or court order dismissing the lawsuit must be prepared and filed with the clerk's office. Rule 41(a)(1)(A)(ii) of the Federal Rules of Civil Procedure provides that, in most cases, "the plaintiff may dismiss an action without a court order by filing * * * a stipulation of dismissal signed by all parties who have appeared."

Rule 41(a)(1)(B) also provides: "Unless the notice or stipulation states otherwise, the dismissal is without prejudice."[57] In most cases a precondition to settlement will be the plaintiff's agreement not to refile the same claim against the defendant at a later date. To ensure that there is no later question on this point, the notice of dismissal should state explicitly that dismissal either is with, or without, prejudice to the refiling of the action.[58]

More complex documentation may be required if the parties have agreed to a structured settlement of the action.[59] Under such a settlement, the defendant agrees to provide the plaintiff with periodic settlement payments rather than merely give the plaintiff a lump sum payment at the time of settlement. Often structured settlements are designed to ensure long term care for tort victims, as well as prevent the plaintiff from squandering a large lump sum settlement, by providing for the payment of monthly benefits to the plaintiff for the rest of his life.[60]

---

56. The settlement agreement executed in the Buffalo Creek litigation is set forth *infra* at p. 606.

57. However, Rule 41(a)(1)(B) further states that a notice of dismissal operates as an adjudication upon the merits if the plaintiff had previously filed and dismissed an action based on or including the claim now being dismissed.

58. If the settlement is without prejudice and the parties contemplate the possible refiling of the action at some future time, the settlement agreement should specify the parties' understanding concerning the statute of limitations applicable to any future action. A dismissal without prejudice will be of little use to a plaintiff if the statute of limitations has run during the pendency of the first action.

59. Concerning structured settlements *see* 3 M. Belli, *Modern Trials* §§ 50.25–50.34 (2d ed. 1982); Danninger, Johnson & Lesti, "The Economics of Structuring Settlements," *Trial,* June 1983, at 42; J. Eck & J. Ungerer, *Structuring Settlements* (1987); P. Lesti et al., *Structured Settlements* (1986); Winslow, "Drafting for Reliability and Favorable Tax Treatment," *Trial,* Dec. 1988, at 21.

60. It thus is ironic that a major market has developed in which companies purchase the right to future structured settlement payments in return for a discounted lump sum payment to the plaintiff. *See* Scales, "Against Settlement Factoring? The Market in Tort Claims has Arrived," 2002 *Wis. L. Rev.* 859. Many states permit such arrangements despite anti-assignment provisions in structured settlement contracts. Neil, "Fading Resistance: Rulings Rejecting Purchases of

Any structured settlement agreement should be carefully drafted and tailored to the particular case. Because payments under a structured settlement may continue well into the future, the defendant generally agrees to buy from a reputable insurance company an annuity that will provide the plaintiff with payments at periodic intervals. In order to account for inflation, the annuity payments may increase in amount over time. Many structured settlements also are drafted to include an initial lump sum payment to the plaintiff, out of which sum attorneys' fees, the costs of the litigation, and other existing expenses such as medical bills are paid.

Structured settlements can be advantageous to both plaintiffs (who receive periodic payments) and defendants (who can purchase an annuity that will provide a greater sum of money to the plaintiff over time than could be provided in a single lump sum).[61] Another major advantage of a structured settlement is that, under 26 U.S.C. § 104(a)(2), the interest earned on the annuity is not taxable income to the recipient so long as the annuity represents compensation (and not punitive damages) for personal physical injuries or physical sickness. However, if the plaintiff is compensated with a lump sum payment, interest earned from the investment of that payment is generally taxable income.

While structured settlements can have great advantages for both plaintiffs and defendants, the assessment of such settlements requires not only careful legal analysis, but a consideration of tax and economic issues beyond those typically posed by a lump sum settlement.

B.   THE BUFFALO CREEK SETTLEMENT DOCUMENTS

The following documents were prepared to effectuate the settlement of the Buffalo Creek litigation. While settlement documents always should be tailored to the particular case that is being settled, these documents provide examples of a settlement agreement, release, and court order dismissing a civil action.

Structured Settlements Are an Endangered Species," *A.B.A.J.*, Sept. 2002, at 26. Court approval is usually required for such transfers, *id.*, and there is a significant federal tax on sales of structured settlements that occur without court approval. 26 U.S.C. § 5891.

61.   For this reason, statutes in some states provide for the award of periodic payments in certain types of judgments. *See* Elligett, "The Periodic Payment of Judgments," 46 *Ins. Couns. J.* 130, 133–34 (1979); Unif. Periodic Payment of Judgments Act, 14 *U.L.A.* 223 (2005). Without benefit of a periodic payment statute or suggestion by counsel or the court, at least one jury has returned a verdict requiring periodic payments by the defendant. *M & P Stores, Inc. v. Taylor,* 326 P.2d 804 (Okla. 1958).

IN THE UNITED STATES DISTRICT COURT FOR THE SOUTHERN DISTRICT OF WEST VIRGINIA AT CHARLESTON

DENNIS PRINCE, et al.,   :
           Plaintiffs, :
           :
           v.   :   CIVIL ACTION NO. 3052–HN
           :
THE PITTSTON COMPANY,   :
           Defendant. :

SETTLEMENT AGREEMENT

WHEREAS, the above-captioned action is presently pending in the United States District Court for the Southern District of West Virginia; and

WHEREAS, the defendant in the aforesaid action has denied and does continue to deny liability under each of the causes of action asserted therein; and

WHEREAS, the parties to the aforesaid action recognize the element of uncertainty which exists in all litigation and consider it desirable and in the best interest of all concerned finally to dispose of that action; and

WHEREAS, the parties to the aforesaid action desire finally to dispose of all of their differences, disputes, claims or controversies which are asserted or which might have been asserted in this action in order to avoid the further and inevitable diversion of efforts, inconvenience, expense and distraction common to protracted litigation;

NOW, THEREFORE, IT IS HEREBY STIPULATED AND AGREED by and between Arnold & Porter, as counsel for the plaintiffs in the aforesaid action, including Sylvia Jean Davis, Anna Gay Canterbury, and the duly appointed representatives of the estates of Frank Brown, Dixie Alice Holt, and Grant White who are hereby deemed to be plaintiffs herein, and Zane Grey Staker and Donovan Leisure Newton & Irvine, as counsel for the defendant in the aforesaid action, and counsel being fully authorized by their respective clients to enter into this agreement, that all claims now asserted or which could have been asserted by any plaintiff in the aforesaid action be and the same hereby are compromised, settled and released on the following terms and conditions:

1. The defendant agrees to pay to the law firm of Arnold & Porter, as attorneys in fact for each and every plaintiff, the total amount of $13.5 million, in complete settlement of this action, as more fully provided hereafter.

2. All claims by plaintiffs for exemplary or punitive damages are herewith withdrawn and abandoned and the parties hereto acknowledge that no portion of the amount to be paid in settlement is or properly can be attributable to any such claims.

3. The allocation and distribution to and among plaintiffs of said monies to be paid by the defendant shall be the obligation and sole responsibility of the law firm of Arnold & Porter, and said firm agrees to indemnify and hold the defendant harmless with respect of any claim whatsoever against the defendant respecting said allocation and distribution.

4. Plaintiffs' counsel will file a petition with the Court herein setting forth the aforesaid allocation and requesting a determination by the Court that the allocation as to each infant plaintiff is fair and reasonable and in the best interest of each such infant plaintiff, and requesting a hearing on said petition. It is understood and agreed that plaintiffs' counsel may petition the Court requesting a determination that the allocation is fair and reasonable as to each other plaintiff in this action. It is also understood and agreed that defendant shall have no responsibility whatsoever concerning said petitions or any allocation set forth therein.

5. Upon entry of an order by the Court declaring that the allocation is fair and reasonable and in the best interest of each infant plaintiff in this action, counsel agree that the following procedures shall be followed:

a) the respective attorneys of record for the parties herein will approve an order of prejudicial dismissal in the form annexed hereto as Exhibit A, which shall be submitted to the Court for entry; and

b) counsel for the defendant shall deliver one or more bank cashier checks, made payable to a single payee to be designated by the law firm of Arnold & Porter, which checks shall total the amount of $13.5 million.

6. Arnold & Porter, as counsel for the plaintiffs herein, agree that they will not distribute to any plaintiff herein any portion of the settlement amount allocated to such plaintiff unless and until such plaintiff shall have properly executed a release in the form annexed hereto as Exhibits B–1 or B–2, it being understood that this Settlement Agreement is in addition to, and in no way limits, the generality of the releases executed by plaintiffs in the forms annexed hereto. Arnold & Porter agrees to deliver to Zane Grey Staker, as counsel for defendant, all such releases promptly upon receipt thereof. It is understood and agreed that in the case of any plaintiff under the age of eighteen as of July 15, 1974 said release shall be sufficient if executed by such person or class of persons as shall be specifically empowered by the Court's Order approving the allocation.

7. Within thirty days after the entry of the order of dismissal, unless some other date is mutually agreed upon, counsel for the parties shall exchange letters confirming that they have complied with paragraphs 4, 5, and 6 of the "Stipulation with Respect to Document Production and Documentary Discovery by Authorization of a Party" herein dated December 15, 1973.

IN WITNESS WHEREOF, the undersigned have caused this Agreement to be duly executed this 3rd day of July, 1974.

ARNOLD & PORTER
1229 Nineteenth Street, N.W.
Washington, D.C. 20036
By s/ _____
    A Member of the Firm

ZANE GREY STAKER, ESQUIRE
Kermit, West Virginia 25674

s/ _____

STEPTOE & JOHNSON
Tenth Floor
Union Bank Building
Clarksburg, West Virginia 26301

DONOVAN LEISURE NEWTON
  & IRVINE
30 Rockefeller Plaza
New York, New York 10020

JACKSON, KELLY, HOLT &
  O'FARRELL
1601 Kanawha Valley Building
Charleston, West Virginia 25322

Attorneys for Plaintiffs

Attorneys for Defendant

———

EXHIBIT A

IN THE UNITED STATES DISTRICT COURT FOR THE SOUTHERN DISTRICT OF WEST VIRGINIA AT CHARLESTON

DENNIS PRINCE, et al., :
                    Plaintiffs, :
                                 :
         v.   :   CIVIL ACTION NO. 3052–HN
                                 :
THE PITTSTON COMPANY,   :
                  Defendant. :

ORDER OF DISMISSAL

Counsel for the parties having made known to the Court that all matters in difference herein have been made the subject of an agreed settlement, and plaintiffs having thereupon moved for dismissal of this action, and the Court being in all respects advised, it is

ORDERED that this action be and the same hereby is dismissed with prejudice and the defendant shall go hence without day; that the parties shall each bear the costs of action by them respectively expended herein; and that the Clerk is directed to omit this cause from the docket as forever ended.

DATED: this ___ day of ___, 1974.

                    _____
                    UNITED STATES DISTRICT COURT

APPROVED FOR ENTRY:

_____
Of Counsel for Plaintiffs

_____
Of Counsel for Defendant

———

EXHIBIT B–1

GENERAL RELEASE

KNOW ALL MEN BY THESE PRESENTS that the undersigned, _____, for and in consideration of the sum of $1.00 and for other good and valuable consideration to him/her in hand paid, the receipt and sufficiency of which is hereby acknowledged, has remised, released and forever discharged and by these presents does for himself/herself and for his/her heirs, executors, administrators, and assigns, hereby remise, release and forever discharge The Pittston Company, Buffalo Mining Company, Pardee Land Company (hereinafter collectively known as "Releasees"), as well as the officers, directors, stockholders, agents, servants and employees of said corporations, their predecessors and successors, present and former subsidiaries, affiliates, parents and assignees, and as well all other persons, firms, corporations and other legal entities whatsoever, of and from all manner of actions, causes of action, suits, debts, dues, sums of money, accounts, reckonings, bonds, bills, specialties, covenants, contracts, controversies, agreements, promises, variances, trespasses, damages, judgments, extents, executions, claims and demands whatsoever, in law, in admiralty or in equity, whether or not well founded in fact or in law and whether or not presently known to the undersigned, which against the Releasees or any of them he/she ever had, now has, or can, shall or may have for, upon or by reason of any matter, cause or thing whatsoever connected with, arising out of, or in any way relating to the flood which occurred on February 26, 1972 on Buffalo Creek, a tributary of the Guyandotte River, in Triadelphia District, Logan County, West Virginia.

The undersigned does further declare that he/she is over the age of eighteen (18) years, and that this Release is executed by him/her upon the express understanding that the same shall operate to extinguish, and the undersigned declares extinguished, now and forever, any and all claims which the undersigned now has or may in the future have in the premises.

IN WITNESS WHEREOF, I have hereunto set my hand and seal this ___ day of ___, 1974.

_____

(L.S.)

STATE OF
COUNTY OF

On the _____ day of _____, 1974, before me personally came _____, to me known, and known to me to be the individual described in, and who executed the foregoing instrument, and duly acknowledged to me that he/she executed the same.

_____

Notary Public

_____

EXHIBIT B–2

[Exhibit B–2 is a general release virtually identical to Exhibit B–1 although it is for a corporate, rather than a natural, plaintiff.]

NOTES AND QUESTIONS CONCERNING THE BUFFALO CREEK SETTLEMENT DOCUMENTS

1. Because of the large number of plaintiffs in the Buffalo Creek litigation, a general settlement agreement was signed by counsel for plaintiffs and the Pittston Company and the individual plaintiffs executed separate releases. When this can more easily be done, it generally makes sense for the parties and their counsel to all sign the settlement agreement.

2. Why all of the archaic language in the release? Couldn't the release merely say that the plaintiff releases every claim which he now has or which may later accrue that arises from the flood in the Buffalo Creek Valley of February 26, 1972?

3. The releases signed by the Buffalo Creek plaintiffs recite that they are being entered into "for and in consideration of the sum of $1.00 and for other good and valuable consideration." Why didn't the releases recite the actual consideration that each plaintiff received?

4. The releases cover not only the claims the plaintiffs may have raised in the underlying lawsuit, but also claims that they *could have raised.* Why are such terms standard in settlement releases? What implications does such a term have for counsel in fashioning a lawsuit? In counseling a plaintiff concerning a proposed settlement?

5. The releases covered any claims that the plaintiffs had arising from the Buffalo Creek disaster "whether or not presently known" to the plaintiffs. Is this release term enforceable? Why might it have been inserted in the release? While such releases generally have been found sufficient to bar the later assertion of even unknown claims, in *E.I. DuPont de Nemours & Co. v. Florida Evergreen Foliage,* 744 A.2d 457 (Del.1999), the Delaware Supreme Court held that a general release extending to "any and all causes of action, claims, demands, actions, obligations, damages, or liability, whether known or unknown" did not bar a claim for fraudulent inducement of this release. The court held that the plaintiffs could retain the $2.3 million for which the action originally had been settled and maintain a new action for fraudulent inducement based upon plaintiffs' allegations that defendant had fraudulently withheld material information from discovery and testified falsely in related litigation. *But see Metrocall of Delaware, Inc. v. Continental Cellular Corp.,* 246 Va. 365, 375, 437 S.E.2d 189, 194–95 (1993) ("Even fraud cases can be settled. When one party, under these circumstances, freely and for consideration, releases and promises not to sue for failure to disclose material facts

and for misrepresentation, that party will not be heard to claim that the promise was fraudulently induced because material information was, in fact, not disclosed.'').

6. Why was an order of dismissal, requiring the judge's approval, prepared in the Buffalo Creek litigation? Doesn't Rule 41(a)(1)(A)(ii) of the Federal Rules of Civil Procedure permit the parties to dismiss the action by filing a stipulation of dismissal? While Rule 41(a)(1)(A) voluntary dismissals generally do not require court approval, that Rule is subject to "Rules 23(e), 23.1(c), 23.2, and 66 and any applicable federal statute." However, this litigation was not subject to these Rules or any federal statute requiring court approval of a settlement.

In addition to the explicit limitations on voluntary dismissal contained in Rule 41, the settlement of actions involving minor parties typically requires court approval. In the Buffalo Creek litigation a guardian ad litem was appointed for the minor plaintiffs to investigate the adequacy and fairness of the proposed settlement. Based upon the guardian's testimony and written petition, the court approved the settlement and, on August 1, 1974, entered the order that is set forth above as Exhibit A to the parties' settlement agreement. *Prince v. The Pittston Co.*, Civil Action No. 3052–HN (S.D.W.Va. 1974). Were there special reasons why counsel and the parties may have wanted a court-approved settlement in the Buffalo Creek case?

7. While the Buffalo Creek documents are typical of those drafted by the parties to civil litigation, what if the injured person was insured for the injuries he suffered? When an insurer settles an insurance policy claim, it typically is subrogated to any claims that the insured may have against a third-party tortfeasor. However, if an outright settlement is made with the insured, the resulting suit against the tortfeasor may have to be brought in the name of the injured party's insurance company.

Because American juries are thought to be less than sympathetic to insurance companies, these companies may merely "loan" their insureds the amount to which they are entitled under their insurance policies. The "loan," however, need only be repaid out of the proceeds of any lawsuit brought against the defendant tortfeasor, and this lawsuit then can be prosecuted in the name of the injured party rather than that of the insurance company. *See* R. Keeton & A. Widiss, *Insurance Law* § 3.10(c)(1) (1988).

8. What is the purpose of paragraph 7 of the settlement agreement? Should counsel and the courts accede to such attempts to seal discovery or settlement terms? *See* the Notes and Questions Concerning Rule 26(c) Protective Orders in Chapter 10, *supra* p. 447; Knutsen, "Keeping Settlements Secret," 37 *Fla. St. U. L. Rev.* 945 (2010); Symposium, "Secrecy in Litigation," 81 Chi.–Kent L. Rev. 301 (2006); Zitrin, "The Case Against Secret Settlements (Or, What You Don't Know *Can* Hurt You)," 2 *J. Inst. Stud. Legal Ethics* 115 (1999); Rooks, "Settlements and Secrets: Is the Sunshine Chilly?," 55 *S. C. L. Rev.* 859 (2004).

Richard Zitrin unsuccessfully proposed to the ABA's Ethics 2000 Commission a new provision in the Model Rules of Professional Conduct that would have made it unethical for an attorney to participate in offering or making an agreement restricting the public availability of information the attorney reasonably believed directly concerned a substantial danger to the public health or safety. Waldbeser & DeGrave, "Current Development 2002–2003: A Plaintiff's Lawyer's Dilemma: The Ethics of Entering into a Confidential Settlement," 16 *Geo. J. Legal Ethics* 815, 823–24 (2003). The United States District Court for the District of South Carolina has prohibited the sealing of settlement agreements filed with the court, Rule 5.03(E) of the United States District Court for the District of South Carolina, but Rule 5.03 provides that its prohibition does not extend to documents that are not filed with the court.

9. In addition to providing information relevant to public health and safety, settlements may be crucial in determining the prevalence of, for instance, discrimination and the effectiveness of private enforcement actions in addressing such discrimination. Because many of the settlements in such actions are sealed or not filed with the court in the first instance, useful aggregate data may not be available to policy-makers and the public. Kotkin, "Invisible Settlements, Invisible Discrimination," 84 *N.C. L. Rev.* 927 (2006).

10. In an effort to deal with the desire of many defendants for settlement confidentiality clauses, a law firm provides in its retainer agreements that clients will not accept settlements with the health care industry that contain "gag clauses." In the event that the client nevertheless agrees to accept such a confidentiality provision, the client will pay the firm's full fee rather than the reduced fees charged those who do not accept settlement confidentiality clauses. Are there ethical difficulties with such fee agreements? Are there practical difficulties? *See* "Engagement Contract May Offer Reduced Fee If Client Rejects Gag Clause in Settlement," 69 *U.S.L.W.* 2215 (Oct. 17, 2000).

11. Despite the controversy that they sometimes engender, sealed settlement agreements in federal district courts are rare (occurring in less than one-half of one percent of civil cases) and "generally the only thing kept secret is the amount of settlement." R. Reagan et al., *Sealed Settlement Agreements in Federal District Court* 8 (Federal Judicial Center 2004).

C. DRAFTING THE SETTLEMENT DOCUMENTS

Releases, covenants not to sue, and settlement agreements represent contractual understandings between the parties. Accordingly, these documents should be drafted with the same care and attention to detail that is afforded any legal contract. The time devoted to carefully drafting these documents is time well spent, and it should prevent later misunderstandings concerning the settlement terms and make it easier to establish a breach of the settlement in any later enforcement action. For similar reasons, a clause can be included in the settlement agreement specifying that the agreement is governed by the substantive law of a particular jurisdiction.

Because they are contracts, settlement agreements, releases, and covenants not to sue should contain an integration or merger clause, explicitly providing that the document represents the entire agreement between the parties. It also makes sense to explicitly recite the consideration provided by all parties to the settlement, the parties' claims and denials in the lawsuit, and the transaction or occurrence from which the settled claims arose.

Any assumption underlying the settlement should be stated explicitly in the written settlement documents. For instance, if the plaintiff is concerned that a covenant not to sue might be construed as a release of its claims against other potential defendants, the settlement agreement should explicitly state that plaintiff is merely executing a covenant not to sue and does not intend to discharge claims against any person other than the settling defendant. If fewer than all defendants settle, the parties should consider the possible impact of the release upon contribution rights among the parties and other potential tortfeasors.

The stipulation or court order dismissing the action should be quite specific concerning whether the dismissal is with or without prejudice. In the absence of an explicit provision to the contrary, Rule 41(a)(1)(B) and (a)(2) provide that dismissal stipulations or orders are considered to be without prejudice.[62] The order or stipulation dismissing the action also should specifically set forth the parties' agreement as to who will bear the court costs of the dismissed action.[63]

Because of the possible ambiguities in any agreement, there are benefits to be gained from offering to draft the initial settlement documents. Often there will be minor settlement terms that are not explicitly covered in the parties' oral negotiations. By drafting the settlement documents, counsel can include the terms that are the most advantageous to her client. To the extent that the other party has no objection to these terms, they have been obtained for one's client without having to offer anything in exchange. There also is a certain inertia inherent in the legal drafting process. Even though opposing counsel may not be happy with a minor term of a settlement document, she may be hesitant to ask that the entire document be reworked merely to correct one, minor point.

The characterization of settlement terms may be quite significant for third-parties. Because the Internal Revenue Code does not consider compensatory damages received on account of personal physical injury or physical sickness to be taxable income,[64] it is usually important that the settlement documents unambiguously denominate any portion of the settlement attributable to personal physical injury damages.[65]

---

62. Rule 41(a)(1)(B), however, provides: "But if the plaintiff previously dismissed any federal- or state-court action based on or including the same claim, a notice of dismissal operates as an adjudication on the merits."

63. Under Rule 54(d)(1) of the Federal Rules of Civil Procedure, "Unless a federal statute, these rules, or a court order provides otherwise, costs—other than attorney's fees—should be allowed to the prevailing party." Dismissal stipulations and orders typically provide that each party will bear its own court costs. *See* the Order of Dismissal in the Buffalo Creek litigation, *supra* p. 608.

64. 26 U.S.C. § 104(a)(2). A defendant often will be able to deduct damage payments as ordinary and necessary trade or business expenses or trade or business losses. 26 U.S.C. §§ 162(a), 165(a).

65. *See generally* Kahn, "Ensure Tax Advantages in Case Settlements," *Trial,* June 1990, at 62; Isleib & Kahn, "Tax Strategies Can Increase the Value of Settlements," *Trial,* June 1994, at

A major settlement concern of the defendant may be that no portion of the settlement be designated as punitive damages.[66] Because the defendant's insurance coverage presumably extends to only compensatory damages, it may be quite important that the settlement documents explicitly designate any monetary settlement as such.[67] The parties also must consider the possibility that attorneys' fees might be considered income to the plaintiff, which, although deductible as a miscellaneous itemized deduction, could trigger significant federal tax liability through the operation of the Alternative Minimum Tax.[68]

In the settlement of the Buffalo Creek litigation, it was impracticable for each of the plaintiffs to sign the settlement agreement. In cases involving a more limited number of parties, all parties should sign the actual settlement agreement. If an association, corporation, partnership, or governmental agency is a party to the settlement, the person signing the settlement documents should be someone with authority to sign on behalf of that party.

Reading and signing the agreement should impress upon the parties just what they are agreeing to, and counsel should take the time to answer any questions that their clients have about the details of the agreement. Some counsel insert language in settlement documents that the parties have read and understand the legal document that they are signing. This is done so that clients will not later raise objections to the settlement or claim that their attorneys' signatures do not bind them to its terms.

At least one copy of settlement documents should be complete and self-contained. Usually this is done by attaching all other settlement documents to the settlement agreement as appendices. The agreement

---

36. *See also* Burch & Fowles, "Traversing the Swamp: Understanding the Tax Implications of Settlements and Awards in Employment–Related Litigation," 17 *S.C. Lawyer* 28 (2006). Non-tax considerations, particularly state law concerning contribution among joint tortfeasors, sometimes may lead to a different apportionment of settlement damages than the one suggested by the tax code. *See* Dewey, "Traps in Multifeasor Settlements," *Litigation,* Summer 1987, at 41, 42. *See also* Kornhauser & Revesz, "Settlements under Joint and Several Liability," 68 *N.Y.U. L. Rev.* 427 (1993).

66. For tax purposes it also may be advantageous to the plaintiff if any money received pursuant to the settlement is designated as compensatory, rather than punitive, damages. 26 U.S.C. § 104(a)(2) (limiting that section's exclusion from income to "damages (other than punitive damages) received * * * on account of personal physical injuries or physical sickness").

67. *See* the Buffalo Creek Settlement Agreement, ¶ 2, *supra* p. 606.

68. In *Commissioner v. Banks*, 543 U.S. 426 (2005), the Supreme Court held that the portion of a judgment or settlement paid to plaintiff's attorney under a contingent fee agreement is income to the plaintiff. Section 62(a)(20) of Title 26, added to the Internal Revenue Code after the cases before the Court arose, now permits a taxpayer to deduct from gross income "attorneys fees and court costs paid by, or on behalf of, the taxpayer in connection with any action involving a claim of unlawful discrimination * * * or a claim made under section 1862(b)(3)(A) of the Social Security Act." Other claimants therefore still may be subject to taxation on attorneys' fees without receiving an equivalent tax benefit from the deduction of those fees from income. *See* Schrack, "Winning Plaintiffs May Become Losers in the End: Award Recipients Taxed on Contingent Fees Paid to Attorneys," 30 *Vt. L. Rev.* 221 (2006); Jackson, "Won the Legal Battle, But at What Cost to your Client: The Tax Consequences of Contingency Fee Arrangements Leading up to and after *Commissioner v. Banks*," 57 *Baylor L. Rev.* 47 (2005).

should refer to, and have attached to it, a copy of the notice of settlement that the parties have agreed to file with the court.[69]

Finally, counsel should provide their clients with copies of all settlement documents, and plaintiff's counsel should give the plaintiff an itemization of the distribution of all settlement proceeds. While the client should have received the breakdown of costs, fees and plaintiff's net recovery at the time that the settlement offer was relayed to him, reaffirmation of these terms once the settlement documents have been executed should obviate any questions about the size of the settlement check plaintiff ultimately will receive.

Exercises Concerning Negotiation

1.   Thomas Eakins is the victim of the Buffalo Creek disaster who was introduced in exercise 1 of the Exercises Concerning Client Interviewing in Chapter 2, *supra* p. 38. In the present exercise you are to attempt to negotiate a settlement of Eakins's claims against the Pittston Company. Counsel can, and should, rely on all information concerning Thomas Eakins and the Pittston Company developed in the earlier chapters of this book or during class simulation exercises. Presume that Eakins's case was filed in the United States District Court for the Middle District of Tennessee, but has been transferred to Judge Hall's docket in the Southern District of West Virginia.

Presume the following facts for the purposes of your negotiations. Eakins's case has been set for trial on July 15, 1974, and it is now June 1, 1974. Frustrated at getting the parties to agree on representative plaintiffs in the action brought by attorney Gerald Stern, Judge Hall has decided to try Eakins's action first and treat it, in effect, as a representative case. While all parties have sought an extension of the trial date, Judge Hall has remained adamant that the trial will start on July 15 and expects that the case should take no more than one week to try. Thomas Eakins's attorneys are representing him on a contingent fee basis that entitles them to one-third of any net recovery (total recovery minus litigation expenses).

Although they disagreed as to the extent of care that will be needed, both parties' medical experts stated at their depositions that Mr. Eakins may need some form of psychological counseling for at least the next ten years due to the trauma he experienced as a result of the death of his nephew, Matthew.

Counsel for Thomas Eakins and the Pittston Company should:

(a) Attempt to negotiate a settlement of Eakins's action;

(b) Prepare all documents necessary to execute the settlement to which the parties have agreed, including documents that would, and would not, be filed with the court; and

---

69.   *See* the Buffalo Creek settlement documents, *supra* p. 605.

(c) Write individual memoranda setting forth negotiation strategies, evaluating the success of those strategies, and explaining the rationale for the manner in which the settlement documents were drafted.

2. Presume that the plaintiffs in the Buffalo Creek litigation have prepared the Motion for a Temporary Restraining Order set forth in the Exercise Concerning the Relief Requested in Chapter 4, *supra* p. 136. As counsel for either the plaintiffs or the defendant, attempt to negotiate a settlement of plaintiffs' motion and draft the necessary documents to effectuate the settlement. Conduct your negotiations under one of the following sets of presumed circumstances:

(a) plaintiffs' counsel has not yet filed the motion, but has sent a copy of the proposed motion to defense counsel one day before the motion is to be filed;

(b) the motion has been filed, and the court will hold a hearing on the motion tomorrow; or

(c) at the hearing on the motion, the judge talked informally with both sides for about five minutes and then walked off the bench saying "I'm sure you lawyers can work something out on this."

3. You represent the victims of the Buffalo Creek disaster in the lawsuit that Gerald Stern filed against the Pittston Company. Presume that you have negotiated the settlement documents that were actually drafted in that litigation and that are set forth starting on page 605, *supra*. Write a letter to the plaintiffs explaining the settlement terms and the settlement documents to your clients. In drafting this letter, keep in mind the lawyer's duty to "explain a matter to the extent reasonably necessary to permit the client to make informed decisions." Model Rules of Prof'l Conduct Rule 1.4(b).

4. Sandra Summers was a recreational mountain climber who is now paralyzed from the waist down as the result of a climbing fall that occurred when a rope she was using broke. The rope was made from a new synthetic fiber that in rare cases breaks down due to extended exposure to sunlight. Summers cannot positively identify the manufacturer of the rope that failed, and the rope was not retrieved at the time of Summers's accident. At her deposition she stated that, because the rope was dirty from a prior outing, she had kept it in her backyard for several weeks before she went on her last climb. She also stated that she knew that climbing ropes should not be stored outdoors, but that the rope appeared to be fine when she packed it for her trip.

Based upon Summers's description of the rope, it could have been manufactured by three companies: Climbers, Inc., The Charles Smith Company, or Recreational Industries, Inc. Climbers, Inc. is a small, self-insured company in Seattle that manufactures and sells fifty percent of the climbing rope in this country. The Charles Smith Company is located in Scranton, Pennsylvania and is a division of American Sporting Goods, a national sporting goods manufacturer. Smith sells fifteen percent of the climbing rope in this country, and carries $15,000,000 in products liability insurance from the Global Insurance Company. Recreational Industries, Inc. is a seventy-five year old sporting goods company headquartered in Bloomington, Minnesota that sells thirty-five percent of the climbing rope in this country. It is insured for $1,000,000 for products liability claims.

Because of the uncertainty concerning the manufacturer of the rope, Summers has named Climbers, Inc., The Charles Smith Company, and Recreational Industries, Inc. as defendants in her federal diversity suit in the United States District Court for the Northern District of California. The twenty-seven year old plaintiff has asked for $25,000,000 in damages, and the court has denied the defendants' motions to dismiss. Discovery is almost complete, and the case is set for a jury trial in sixty days. The judge has asked counsel to make a final attempt to settle the case before trial.

(a) Write a memorandum describing the negotiation strategy that you would pursue on behalf of the plaintiff or one of the three defendants;

(b) Conduct settlement negotiations on behalf of the plaintiff or one of the three defendants; and

(c) Draft the documents necessary to execute any settlement to which some or all of the parties agree.

V.   COURT INTERVENTION IN SETTLEMENT NEGOTIATIONS

While counsel generally negotiate case settlements among themselves, there is another individual who is extremely interested in the resolution of cases short of trial: the judge. Indeed, the judge may be even more interested in pretrial case settlement than are counsel. Over ninety-five percent of federal civil cases are resolved short of trial.[70] If this figure were only ninety percent, federal judges would be faced with more than twice as many trials as they now handle (presuming that the volume of

---

70. For the 12 month period that ended on March 31, 2010, only 1.2% of the civil actions, other than land condemnation cases, that were terminated in the federal courts reached trial. Admin. Office of the U.S. Courts, *Statistical Tables for the Federal Judiciary: March 31, 2010* (2010) (Table C4).

This does not mean, however, that all cases that do not reach trial are settled by the parties. Flanders, "Blind Umpires—A Response to Professor Resnik," 35 *Hastings L. J.* 505, 517 n.56 (1984) (finding that, while more than 95% of federal civil cases studied did not reach trial, only about 60% of these federal civil cases were settled). *See also* Eisenberg & Lanvers, "What is the Settlement Rate and Why Should We Care?," 6 *J. Em. Legal Studies* 111 (2009) (finding different settlement rates by case type and location, a general settlement rate of about two-thirds of civil cases, and no material increase in settlement rates over time); Eisenberg et al., "Litigation Outcomes in State and Federal Courts: A Statistical Portrait," 19 *Seattle U. L. Rev.* 433, 444 (1996) (1991–92 settlement rates in contract and non-asbestos tort cases of 62.2% in urban state courts and 64.6% in federal courts). Indeed, it may be that the percentage of federal civil cases resolved by settlement may actually have decreased since 1970, while nontrial judicial adjudications have increased significantly. Hadfield, "Where Have All the Trials Gone? Settlements, Nontrial Adjudications, and Statistical Artifacts in the Changing Disposition of Federal Civil Cases," 1 *J. Em. Legal Studies* 705 (2004).

federal civil case filings remained unchanged). Judges, too, have a very practical interest in facilitating the settlement of cases prior to trial.[71]

It thus is not surprising that many judges take an active interest in facilitating the settlement of cases on their dockets.[72] This judicial involvement may take many forms. At one extreme, the judge may set a settlement conference or otherwise require counsel to report concerning the status of any settlement discussions. A common portion of many pretrial orders is a section summarizing the parties' efforts to achieve voluntary settlement. Some judges also assign certain cases to other judicial personnel to discuss settlement with counsel and to attempt to achieve a pretrial settlement. In the United States district courts, federal magistrate judges often are asked to conduct settlement conferences.[73]

Many federal and state judges personally discuss and encourage settlement. Because the full authority and weight of the judge is thus brought to bear on counsel, these judicial efforts often are rewarded with settlements. Moreover, it is usually helpful for counsel to get a sense of how the judge who will try the case evaluates its strengths and weaknesses. This, too, can result in the settlement of cases that otherwise would be tried.

Direct judicial involvement in settlement has its downsides, however. Counsel may be reluctant to anger the judge who will ultimately try their case and may settle cases that they believe would be better resolved by trial. If a case is not settled despite judicial intervention, it may be difficult for the judge to preside evenhandedly at trial. Even if the judge is able to disregard information learned during settlement discussions, counsel still may believe that he has been unable to do so.

Professor Leo Levin, a former Director of the Federal Judicial Center, has noted:

> Judicial intervention to promote settlement casts the trial judge in a delicate role. Many lawyers desire more assistance from judges in removing psychological and informational barriers that stand in the way of settlement, but they do not want to lose control over their

---

71. Many judges also favor settlement because of their belief that it results in greater party satisfaction and higher quality dispute resolution than do judgments imposed upon the parties by the courts. As Judge Hubert Will stated at a 1976 seminar for newly appointed federal judges, "One of the fundamental principles of judicial administration is that, in most cases, the absolute result of a trial is not as high a quality of justice as is the freely negotiated, give a little, take a little settlement." Will et al., "The Role of the Judge in the Settlement Process," 75 F.R.D. 203, 203 (1976).

Although many judges and attorneys share this belief, whether this or other purported settlement benefits actually exist is an open question. Gallanter, "The Quality of Settlements," 1988 *J. Disp. Resol.* 55.

72. Witness the discussions of settlement at the seminars for newly appointed federal district judges sponsored by the Federal Judicial Center. F. Lacey, *The Judge's Role in the Settlement of Civil Suits* (1977); Will et al., "The Role of the Judge in the Settlement Process," 75 *F.R.D.* 203 (1976); Fox, "Settlement: Helping the Lawyers to Fulfill Their Responsibility," 53 *F.R.D.* 129 (1971). *See also* D. Provine, *Settlement Strategies for Federal District Judges* (1986).

73. *E.g.*, Rule 72.1(I)(e)(2) of the United States District Court for the Eastern District of Pennsylvania; Rule 72.1(b) of the United States District Court for the District of Nebraska. *See* 28 U.S.C. § 636(b).

lawsuits or forgo their rights to proceed to trial. To serve the interests of the parties effectively, the judge must alter the relationship between the disputants so as to encourage—but not coerce—an early settlement. To serve the interests of the court, and indirectly the interests of the public, the judge must not spend more of the court's time than is warranted by the savings in trial time and litigation costs.[74]

The following excerpt from Professor Peter Schuck's book *Agent Orange on Trial* illustrates both the potential advantages and disadvantages of direct judicial involvement in the pretrial settlement process. Schuck's book describes the litigation brought on behalf of American servicemen, their families, and others who alleged various cancers and other injuries due to exposure to the herbicide Agent Orange, which had been used by the United States Army to defoliate jungle cover during the Vietnam War.

Although originally filed by a single plaintiff in New York state court, in 1979 an amended class action complaint was filed in the United States District Court for the Southern District of New York.[75] This action, brought against the chemical companies that manufactured Agent Orange and the United States, ultimately was transferred to the United States District Court for the Eastern District of New York and assigned to United States District Judge Jack Weinstein.

The following excerpt describes Judge Weinstein's efforts to settle the Agent Orange litigation in the spring of 1984. Although these claims were unique in many respects, the issues raised by judicial involvement in settlement negotiations extend well beyond cases of the magnitude and complexity of the Agent Orange litigation. While reading this excerpt, consider how these negotiation and settlement issues might arise in other, more typical, civil cases. Consider, too, how negotiation changes when counsel must not only negotiate with one another but with the judge assigned to preside over the case.

P. SCHUCK, AGENT ORANGE ON TRIAL

143–147, 149–166 (1987).

Fashioning a Settlement

From the moment Weinstein entered the Agent Orange case, the goal of settlement was uppermost in his mind. He had said as much to the lawyers on October 21, [1983] and those who best knew his thinking—the special masters and his law clerks—believe that purpose guided his every action in the months that followed. For Weinstein, the attractiveness of

---

74. Levin, "Foreword" to D. Provine, *Settlement Strategies for Federal District Judges* v (1986). To address such concerns with judicial involvement in settlement, Professor Jeffrey Parness has suggested the adoption of written guidelines governing judicial settlement conferences. Parness, "Improving Judicial Settlement Conferences," 39 *U. C. Davis L. Rev.* 1891 (2006).

75. *Reutershan v. Dow Chemical Company,* No. 78–CV–4253 (S.D.N.Y. 1979).

settlement had much to do with his belief that a mass toxic tort with the special problematic features of a case like Agent Orange should not be litigated, at least under traditional rules. To try such a case, he felt, would consume an almost unthinkable amount of time (he predicted a very long trial), money, talent, and social energy, and with the inevitable appeals and possible retrials, the outcome might well be uncertain for many years to come. In the end, the only people who would surely benefit from such an endless litigation would be the defendants' lawyers, who were paid by the hour. And for all his courage and independence of mind, the liberal Weinstein must have dreaded the prospect that his genuine doubts about the veterans' causation evidence might oblige him to withhold their case from the jury or, if he submitted it to the jury and the jury found for plaintiffs, he might enter judgment for the chemical companies, notwithstanding that verdict. Finally, a negotiated settlement offered the prospect of everybody obtaining something rather than one side losing everything.

* * *

Weinstein knew he could not settle a case as large, complex, and symbolically explosive as Agent Orange without employing agents to act as eyes, ears, tongues, and buffers. He also knew that with the highly competitive, aggressive lawyers gearing up for trial, he could only brake the emotional momentum toward conflict by diverting their attention to shared goals. Convinced that unusual political skills and contacts would be essential, Weinstein turned to several Washington insiders for help. * * *

* * * In February, he told the Agent Orange lawyers that he wanted their permission to retain, at the defendants' expense, an unnamed consultant to develop a settlement strategy and plan. They agreed. Weinstein recruited Kenneth Feinberg, a lawyer in his late thirties who had been Senator Edward Kennedy's chief of staff, to develop a plan to settle the case and distribute the proceeds. * * *

* * * Feinberg energetically set to work and by mid-March had drafted an eighty-page settlement plan, which the judge, after making some changes, distributed to the lawyers. Perhaps not coincidentally, the PMC [Plaintiffs' Management Committee] itself broached the possibility of settlement discussions at about this time.

Feinberg's plan, which did not state any dollar amount, consisted of three parts. The first focused on the elements for determining the aggregate amount of a settlement, especially the various sources of uncertainty and the nature and number of the claims. The second discussed alternative criteria—litigation costs, market shares, dioxin content of their Agent Orange, and voluntary agreement—for allocating any settlement amount among the defendants. The third part analyzed alternative criteria for distributing the settlement fund among the plaintiff class members; these included the likelihood that particular diseases were caused by dioxin, economic need, objective disability, and priority for children with birth defects. * * *

On Good Friday, April 20, 1984, Weinstein met in his chambers with the lawyers for both sides and introduced them to his two special masters for settlement—Feinberg and David I. Shapiro. Shapiro's assignment from Weinstein (whom he had never met before) was to actually negotiate the settlement (in Shapiro's unvarnished words, to "get a deal done"). * * *

During the 1960s and early 1970s, Shapiro had been celebrated by many in the plaintiffs' bar as "the father of the consumer class action"; this reflected his ingenuity in engineering massive antitrust actions on behalf of state and local governments against the drug and other industries, winning enormous recoveries for his clients and lavish fee awards for himself. He knew little about toxic tort cases and had soured on plaintiffs' class action litigation in recent years (out of disgust, he claims, with the ways in which judges set fees and plaintiffs' lawyers often receive fee awards out of all proportion to their contribution). No one, however, was more knowledgeable than Shapiro about the design, trial, administration, and settlement of complex class actions. In addition, he was an exceedingly skillful, experienced negotiator and mediator. * * *

* * *

At the Good Friday meeting, Weinstein told the assembled lawyers to regard Feinberg and Shapiro * * * as his agents; he was making the masters available to help the parties reach a settlement if they wished to do so. Shapiro then took over, with a cocky, irreverent, no-nonsense style that would have seemed inappropriate in a judge. He asked the PMC members to leave Judge Weinstein's chambers so that the masters could talk to the chemical companies' lawyers. He then turned to Weinstein, asking him to leave as well. Now alone with defendants' lawyers, Shapiro asked them whether they wanted to settle. They replied that they did but that the plaintiffs' lawyers were "crazy and unrealistic." Shapiro shot back, "They probably say the same about you." Suddenly, one of the Monsanto lawyers interjected: "We won't pay a penny more than $100 million, and only if the government kicks in the same amount." At that moment Shapiro became convinced that a deal would eventually be made.

But although Feinberg and Shapiro met with both sides frequently for the next two weeks, enormous obstacles to settlement remained. First, the parties' initial positions were separated by astronomical distances. Prior to this conversation, the defendants had mentioned a maximum figure of $25 million, while the PMC, which had appointed Chesley and Locks to be its spokesmen in any settlement negotiations, was talking internally in terms of a minimum of $700 million. At the end of April, the parties were still more than $250 million apart; Chesley and Locks were still demanding $360 million, while the defendants had come up to $100 million. A second problem was the internal conflict within each camp. The chemical companies were at loggerheads over whether to settle, on what terms, and how to divide responsibility for any settlement amount among themselves. The PMC, a hastily organized "rump group" (as Feinberg later described it), was divided by egos and reputational concerns and was cautious lest talk of settlement prompt a rush by plaintiffs to opt out of the class.

* * *

Although the settlement masters continued to meet with the other parties during this period, the momentum generated by the need to gear up for trial now seemed irresistible. The veterans' lawyers were thirsting to go before the jury, and the chemical companies, while always concerned about their potential liability exposure, nevertheless felt confident that the plaintiffs' already fragile case would disintegrate under the pressures of trial. Barring some new development, settlement before trial now seemed out of the question.

On Thursday morning, May 3—four days before jury selection was to begin—John Sabetta, Monsanto's lawyer, called Len Rivkin, Dow's lawyer. Sabetta said that Judge Weinstein's chambers had instructed all counsel to appear at the courthouse early Saturday morning and to bring whoever was necessary to authorize settlement on behalf of their clients. The judge, they were told, would provide each side with separate rooms and would be available to them at all times. They should "bring their tooth-brushes" and be prepared to stay all night Saturday and Sunday, if necessary. (During a fruitless midweek meeting with defendants' counsel, Shapiro had privately suggested to Feinberg that they try to break the logjam by requiring the lawyers and their principals to attend an around-the-clock negotiating marathon that weekend. Shapiro called Weinstein to ask his approval, but the judge was in court and unavailable. Shapiro then brazenly told the lawyers what was being required of them, assuring them that Weinstein had ordered it. He quickly telephoned the judge again, this time with some trepidation. "Don't get sore, Judge," Shapiro began, "but this is what I've done and you've got to cover for me." Weinstein burst out laughing. "You tell them that that's my order." Shapiro laughed even harder. "I already did," he said.)

* * *

When the lawyers arrived Saturday morning, they found that an entire floor of the deserted courthouse had been set aside for their use. Part of each contingent went off to continue their *voir dire* (jury challenges) with Magistrate Scheindlin that had begun on Friday. Judge Weinstein, ever the innovator, had approved Scheindlin's recommendation for an extremely detailed questionnaire for prospective jurors, one that probed for bias in unusual ways. (More than four hundred prospective jurors had been called in during that week to complete the questionnaire; at a cost of over \$20,000, the clerk's office, now assisted by about a dozen temporary employees, had devised a random number system to protect the jurors from intrusive press inquiries.) When Dean and his colleagues reviewed the questionnaire with jury psychologists and polling experts, they were impressed by Weinstein's acuity but distressed that the prejudices of most prospective jurors, who they assumed would favor the veterans' cause, would now be revealed. The defendants' lawyers, who thought they discerned a pro-veteran bias in the responses of most of the prospective jurors, moved to strike the jury panel, which Weinstein firmly refused to do.

The masters initiated the negotiation process by meeting with all of the lawyers together. In the two weeks since April 20, Shapiro and Feinberg—the "strong-arm man" and the "fine tuner" (as some defendants' lawyers viewed them)—had already done some important spade work with both sides. Initial discussions centered on two issues: opt-outs and a "structured settlement." Weinstein previously had allowed class members to file opt-out forms by April 30; less than a week later, however, it remained unclear how many had actually done so. The defendants' lawyers feared that a settlement would be worthless if a large number of veterans decided to opt out and sue the chemical companies on their own. Shapiro suggested a simple solution: the parties could stipulate that if an unacceptable number of veterans opted out, the chemical companies could "walk away" from the settlement and the trial would resume.

Although the defendants' lawyers were attracted by the idea, the PMC initially rejected it, fearing that this would weaken their hand and also give Yannacone [an attorney who helped fashion the litigation originally but who was not on the plaintiffs' management committee], who was watching from the wings and could persuade many veterans to opt out, the power to torpedo the settlement and thus perhaps dictate its terms. Shapiro expressed astonishment at the lack of sophistication on both sides:

> Settlement negotiations usually pit pros against pros. Here, neither the defendants' lawyers nor the PMC seemed to have any feel for the dynamics of class actions. They failed to realize that with a class action settlement, a defendant greatly reduces and puts a finite limit on its potential liability; even if a thousand veterans ultimately opted out, they would represent a very small percentage of the class, and defendants would have substantially limited their exposure. No defendant will walk away from that because for them, exposure limitation is what the game is all about.

Shapiro eventually persuaded the PMC to go along. In his long experience with class actions and opt-outs, he told them, he had never known a defendant to walk away from a settlement; the advantages of settlement were simply too great. Furthermore, he hinted, Judge Weinstein had ways to encourage the opt-outs to return to the class and join in the settlement.

The structured settlement issue was more complicated. When the masters had met with the defendants' lawyers in late April, Feinberg had indicated that a structured settlement was possible. The lawyers had understood him to be using that term in its conventional tort litigation sense: an arrangement under which a fixed settlement amount would be paid out over many years, beginning with the date the settlement order became final after appeals were exhausted. * * *

Although this was the kind of structured settlement the defendants thought they were negotiating, the special masters had something very different in mind; they envisioned giving the defendants a choice between paying the full amount immediately and paying on the date the settlement order became final the full amount plus interest at the prime rate, running from the date of the settlement *agreement.* Shapiro emphasized this point to the PMC at his first meeting with them in the courthouse on Saturday. Shapiro listened to the PMC's demands, writing them on a blackboard. He urged the PMC lawyers to compromise on some items even as they insisted on others. He attempted to persuade them to lower their new settlement target, which he figured to be $250 million, to $200 million plus interest running from the date of the agreement. This, he argued, would really amount to $225 million or more by the time the settlement order became final.

The special masters' structured settlement approach initially encountered fierce resistance from both sides. It would of course be very expensive for the chemical companies. First, an immediate payout would mean that they could not enjoy the use of most of the settlement amount for years to come; the present value of these funds during the interim, however, was substantial. On the other hand, if they deferred payment, the additional cost could perhaps be even higher, depending on changes in interest rates. Second, even as they negotiated, Congress was rewriting the tax law to prohibit defendants in tort cases from deducting the entire amount of a settlement during the first year unless that amount was actually paid out. * * *

The PMC's resistance to Shapiro's approach was perhaps more surprising. "They were very worried about the veterans' reactions to a settlement figure," he recalled. "They seemed willing to accept a later date for triggering interest payments by the defendants in exchange for a higher initial settlement amount, even though the combination of an earlier trigger date and a lower amount up front could ultimately net the veterans a higher recovery. They figured that the up-front amount was what the media and the veterans would pick up on."

When Weinstein came to the courthouse Saturday morning, he first brought all the lawyers together for a pep talk about settlement, eloquently appealing to their patriotism. He then spoke to each side separately. Meeting with the defendants' lawyers late Saturday morning, he gave each an opportunity to speak, but Rivkin, representing Dow, did most of the talking. Rivkin enumerated ten elements of settlement that had to be addressed. First, the defendants wanted the judge to recertify the class as (b)(1)(B) mandatory (no opt-outs permitted), thereby ensuring that any settlement would be binding on all members. If the judge insisted on a (b)(3) class (opt-outs permitted), however, defendants wanted a walk-away provision. Second, Rivkin noted that defendants wanted protection against the "tail" of the case—claims by children yet unborn and by civilians. Third, they wanted a provision that if a settlement were reached but subsequently reversed, the ensuing trial would be nonjury; if not, they argued, the publicity surrounding a settlement would deprive them of a fair trial. Fourth, they wanted the class definition broadened to include all U.S. and Vietnamese civilians in Vietnam and all spouses and children of all U.S., Australian, and New Zealand soldiers. This would bind more potential claimants to the settlement. Fifth, they wanted the settlement agreement to stipulate that Agent Orange had not caused injuries. Sixth, they wanted the judge to make a "low, fair" fee award to plaintiffs' counsel in order to discourage such suits in the future. Seventh, they wanted the settlement agreement to take account of insurance coverage triggers by requiring that claimants against the settlement fund provide detailed information on exposure, manifestation of injuries, and so on. Eighth, they wanted no payment from the settlement fund to be made until the settlement had cleared final appellate court review. Ninth, the problem of numerous opt-outs must be resolved. Finally, plaintiffs' counsel must return all documents and agree not to use them publicly.

The judge, as always, had done his homework. He immediately responded to each of these demands. He indicated that he would insist on a (b)(3) class but that a walk-away provision was possible; that the tail problem would be addressed; that the nonjury trial contingency was a "good idea"; that he would not redefine the class by sending out a new class notice but in the notice of settlement would define it to include all veterans, whether claiming injury or not; that the settlement agreement would state that causation had not been proved; that the fee award would be "reasonable"; that insurance considerations would be respected; that no payments would be made until the settlement had cleared appellate review; and that he would approve whatever arrangements the parties could negotiate about documents.

Four additional points were then raised. First, the defendants argued that they should be indemnified from the settlement fund for any payments they might be obliged to make on Agent Orange claims as a result of judgments in other actions brought by veterans in *state* courts. Weinstein indicated that he had no objection. Second, they expressed concern about punitive damage claims, to which Weinstein replied that he was not allowing such claims. Third, Weinstein read to them Maskin's letter of April 24, indicating the government's unwillingness to participate in the settlement discussions, and Feinberg's May 4 letter to Maskin, informing him that unless the government negotiated the matter with the other parties, the court's settlement order would not release any claims against it. Fourth, Weinstein indicated that if no settlement was reached, he intended to adopt the theory, long advanced by plaintiffs, that any manufacturer that knew its product would be mixed with others that might contain dangerous levels of dioxin should be treated as if its product were identifiable by plaintiffs. This was an important point; it was tantamount to ruling that as a matter of law, all defendants were potentially liable if causation could be proved.

In the early afternoon, the judge met with the plaintiffs' lawyers. He talked to them like a Dutch uncle, sympathetic but pulling no punches. He began by saying that he understood the veterans' plight and that "my heart bleeds for deformed children." Nevertheless, he emphasized, their case on causation was very weak. Even if he was wrong about that, his rulings on their behalf, such as his decisions on choice of law and class action, might well be reversed on appeal, especially by the Burger Court. He predicted that they could go broke litigating the case for several more years and urged them to take what they could get now. The lawyers then caucused again and decided to hold firm at $250 million. But Musslewhite, sensing that important money decisions would soon have to be made, telephoned Schwartz and O'Quinn, two of the financiers on the PMC, to urge that they immediately fly up from Houston to join in the deliberations.

Meanwhile, Shapiro and Feinberg were meeting with the defendants' lawyers concerning how to allocate any settlement amount among each of the companies. This question had not previously been discussed by the group as a whole. As in most multiple-defendant cases, it proved to be exceedingly delicate, perhaps the most divisive issue of all. * * *

Three contending allocational criteria were discussed: dioxin content, favored by Dow and Hercules; product volume or market share, favored by Monsanto and Diamond Shamrock; and ability to pay, favored by the smaller companies. These criteria implied very different allocations. For a company that was part of a conglomerate, for example, a small market share might be linked to a large ability to pay. Although there was substantial agreement as to the facts—the product volumes were established by government records and there was no longer any real dispute over the general dioxin content of each product—no consensus on the allocation formula could be forged. To break the impasse, one of them said, "We'll never get agreement on this. Let's let the judge do it; he's fair." Each of the companies then argued its case separately to the special masters, who agreed to ask Weinstein to make a recommendation.

At 4:30 p.m., Weinstein called in the defendants' lawyers. He told them he was recommending that the allocation [be] based on a combination of product volume and dioxin content * * *.

Weinstein's statement brought squeals of pain and shrieks of delight from the lawyers. The economic stakes that these dry percentages implied were enormous, even for corporate giants like Dow, Monsanto, and Diamond Shamrock; each percentage point ultimately represented almost $1.8 million of liability. * * *

* * *

On Sunday morning, the weary lawyers for both sides returned to the courthouse and caucused again. Monsanto, facing the possibility that it would have to litigate against the plaintiffs alone, fell into line. The defendants agreed to accept the Weinstein allocation up to $150 million, subject to their approval of the terms of the settlement structure, and they so informed the masters. They had surmounted their most difficult obstacle, the allocation formula.

Now it was the plaintiffs' group that began to fracture. When Shapiro met with them and the lawyers repeated their $250 million figure, Shapiro shook his head. "This case won't settle for $250 million. If you insist on that, you'll lose everything." To drive the point home, he told them about a case in which plaintiffs had rejected a $100 million class action settlement offer, then had gone on to lose the case. He also pressed once again for acceptance of the lower initial amount coupled with an early trigger date for interest. Moved by Shapiro's arguments, the PMC then decided to discuss a $200 million figure. Dean argued passionately for staying at $250 million and going to trial if necessary. "Let's hurt them in front of the jury for a few weeks," he urged. "Let's let *them* bleed, let *their* stocks go down. Let's go to work for a while and talk later." The lawyers then voted one by one and approved a $200 million counteroffer; Dean was the only dissenter. Shapiro said he would try to sell their proposal and left the room. Dean, keyed up for trial and overcome by feelings of frustration and betrayal, fled to an empty courtroom, where he sobbed. * * *

At four o'clock on Sunday afternoon, after discussing the structural elements of the plaintiffs' position, Shapiro and Feinberg returned to the defendants' lawyers and reported on each of the elements of the PMC's counteroffer. The PMC would not agree to waive a jury trial under any circumstances; defendants' insistence on a waiver would be a "deal breaker." The PMC was firm at $200 million. It would agree to the "reverse indemnification" of defendants from the settlement fund in the event of adverse state court judgments, subject to a limit of 50 percent of the verdicts up to a total of $10 million. The PMC would allow the defendants to walk away if a substantial number of class members opted out. It wanted the defendants to assign to plaintiffs half of their claims against the government. It agreed to return all documents after retaining them long enough to sue the government. It agreed to broadening the class to include civilians. It agreed that the fund could not make payments until appeals were fully exhausted but wanted reimbursement for its expenses at an early date. Finally, the PMC demanded that interest be paid on the settlement amount from the date of the agreement.

After an hour of discussion, the defendants' lawyers authorized the masters to return to the PMC with a counterproposal. If the settlement were reversed, trial would be before a jury whose findings would be advisory, not binding, on the judge. Reverse indemnification must be for 100 percent of state court verdicts up to $25 million. Defendants would not assign their claims against the government. They wanted their documents returned in one year if the plaintiffs failed to sue the government. They wanted Judge Weinstein to certify an appeal immediately on any challenge to the settlement. They agreed to allow reimbursement of the lawyers' expenses even before appeals were final. They insisted that *all* parties release each other from future claims, including codefendants and corporate subsidiaries. They insisted on detailed, insurance-relevant information on all claim forms. And they demanded a ten-year reversionary interest in any moneys left unclaimed in the fund. Defendants agreed to negotiate in the $150–$180 million range; they would not go higher so long as they remained exposed to liability to American civilians, Vietnamese, foreign nationals, opt-outs, and after-born children. But they remained divided over the question of the trigger date for interest on the settlement amount, with Dow agreeable to the earlier date and Diamond Shamrock adamantly opposed.

Before returning to the PMC, Shapiro and Feinberg conferred with Judge Weinstein. The three men sensed that the time had come to make or break the settlement. At this point, the structural issues seemed readily resolvable; only the settlement amount really divided the parties. As Shapiro viewed the situation, it would be very difficult to move the PMC away from their $200 million figure. Several factors—their belief that they could damage the defendants at trial, Dean's opposition to even that amount, and the lawyers' fear that Yannacone would denounce such a settlement in the media as a sell-out and damage their reputations—together created political tensions within the group that made further compromise unlikely. Shapiro believed that the defendants, facing the specter of trial the very next day, could easily be convinced that $200 million would be a cheap settlement; indeed, he had heard that Dow had revealed to the other manufacturers a secret study it had commissioned indicating that a jury would award far more than that to the veterans. Moreover, he strongly suspected that defendants' insurance coverage would cover most or all of that amount.

* * *

Judge Weinstein [ultimately] called in the PMC and the special masters. In a sworn statement later filed as part of a challenge to the propriety of the settlement, Benton Musslewhite described the judge's remarks at that meeting:

> He would say: "Now, I am not going to hold it against you if you don't settle. I am not going to penalize you. I am going to conduct this trial on a fair basis to everybody," and then came the "but" ... "But," he would say, "I have carried you plaintiffs all this time. I have decided a lot of questions in your favor that I could have decided the other way. And I want you to know that at nine o'clock Monday morning I am through carrying you. You are on your own. I will do my duty as a judge."
>
> Then a little conversation would take place and then he would come back and say: "You know, remember, I just don't think you have got a case on medical causation. I don't think you have a case on punitive damages."

According to Musslewhite, he and the other lawyers understood these and other remarks to mean that if they did not settle for $180 million, the judge intended to direct a verdict against plaintiffs on the causation issue at least as to the "big-ticket" claims for birth defects and miscarriages, leaving at most only the cancer, chloracne, and liver disease claims. Musslewhite, echoing others on both sides of the case, also emphasized that Weinstein exploited their fatigue and other psychological factors.

> Not only were you tired and not your usual self in terms of resistance, of having control, you know, of what was going on, but it made you feel a kind of helplessness. I mean, you are there and you have got to stay in the negotiations ... I could see how psychologically it was affecting all the members of the committee, particularly the ones who were going to have to try the case, to get to be ready to go on Monday. So many things that we had to do, and here we were down at the courthouse negotiating this settlement on an around-the-clock basis ... the judge wore us all down with that tactic ... the judge made us negotiate around the clock knowing that we had a difficult time being ready for trial, we were thin on manpower, and we were working night and day to get ready, and to lose the last 48 to 72 hours just before the trial was going to adversely affect us, and we knew it. You had to be dumb not to know that. Plus the fact that it tired us and made us less resistant to pressure, and he knew that, I think.
>
> * * *

After Weinstein had explained his position to the PMC, he asked each of the lawyers to give their views. Several, including Locks, Chesley, and Schwartz, indicated that they favored settlement; the others resisted. When O'Quinn, one of the Houston financiers, expressed his opposition, Weinstein told him that although he respected O'Quinn's views, he would hold him and the others "personally responsible" if they rejected the settlement and the case went to trial: "I don't care what the committee's internal fee agreement says, I will expect you to stay with this case until the bitter end, no matter what the cost." As the PMC left Weinstein's chambers, O'Quinn was visibly upset. "I am changing my vote," he told Musslewhite. "The judge is saying that I will be personally responsible for $180 million if we try this case and lose it. He won't sit still until we settle." Although some of the lawyers understood Weinstein merely to be reminding them of the obligations of being on the PMC, O'Quinn was taking no chances. When interviewed almost a year and a half later, O'Quinn remained convinced (despite a skeptical questioner) that Weinstein was threatening the lawyers with possible financial ruin through malpractice actions by the veterans if, after rejecting settlement, they then lost at trial.

* * *

The PMC caucused. The resisters now switched sides, and after several hours of passionate debate the group approved the $180 million figure. Only Dean dissented. Emotionally and physically exhausted and literally in tears, Dean had gone to Weinstein's chambers, where the judge, Shapiro, and a law clerk were gathered. Dean told them he opposed what his colleagues were about to do and wanted to go home and get some rest. (A momentary break in the tension occurred when a messenger arrived with Chinese food that the defendants' lawyers had ordered. Laughing, the punctilious Weinstein refused it, saying, "Do you think I'm going to accept food from lawyers?") Meanwhile, at Henderson's suggestion, the PMC had assigned Locks to make one last effort to split the defendants, offering to settle with all but Monsanto and Diamond Shamrock at the already agreed-upon amounts and allocations. Lock's overture, however, was rebuffed; the defendants would deal with the PMC only through the settlement masters and would remain united. The PMC then reported to the masters its agreement on the $180 million.

Late Sunday evening, Judge Weinstein called in the defendants' lawyers. "Here is the deal," he began, "$180 million plus interest beginning this morning." When one of the lawyers protested that this would cost considerably more than $200 million, Shapiro responded that if they did not accept this, they would end up having to pay $200 million plus interest. The judge again emphasized the costs to defendants even if their case was strong—the vagaries of a trial, the risks to the defendants of trying the case before a Brooklyn jury, the uncertainties of appellate review, the damage to their reputations that intensive press coverage of the trial would inevitably cause. Impressed by these now-familiar arguments, the defendants agreed to the amount. (According to a Monsanto lawyer, the defendants also understood Weinstein to be hinting that he would not award substantial fees to the plaintiffs' lawyers, an understanding to which the defendants attached great importance, hoping that such a stand would discourage future mass tort claims.)

* * *

At one in the morning, only hours before jury selection was to begin, Weinstein called the defendants' lawyers back in. He confirmed that agreement had been reached on the amount and discussed the outstanding structural issues. After a further discussion with the PMC, he called both sides in to announce that a deal had been struck. He read a document that he had swiftly drafted, which enumerated the terms of the settlement, as follows: (1) Defendants would pay $180 million plus interest running from May 7; all codefendants would release each other, their subsidiaries, and parent companies from liability to one another. (2) The settlement fund would advance moneys to pay class notice and settlement administration expenses. (3) No other distribution of settlement funds would be made until appeals from a final settlement order had been exhausted. (4) Defendants could obtain reverse indemnification for veteran opt-out claims upheld by state courts up to $10 million until January 1, 1999. (5) The class definition would be interpreted to include service people whose injuries had not yet been manifested. (6) Plaintiffs could retain defendants' documents for one year. (7) All parties reserved all rights to sue the United States. (8) Defendants denied all liability. (9) Defendants reserved the right to reject the settlement if a "substantial" number of class members opted out. (10) Any class member who had previously opted out would have an opportunity to opt back in. (11) Unclaimed funds would revert to the defendants after twenty-five years. (12) The settlement agreement was subject to a Rule 23(e) "fairness" hearing. (13) Although after-born claimants were not included in the class and could therefore sue, the distribution plan would make special arrangements to address their needs. (14) The court would retain jurisdiction until the settlement fund was exhausted.

What Weinstein read, of course, was only a statement of settlement principles. Once the deal had been cut and the media had turned to other stories, it took two weeks of intensive, often around-the-clock negotiations to hammer out and agree upon the details. * * *

But on May 7, only hours before jury selection was to begin, these problems seemed too distant and difficult for the exhausted lawyers to get excited about. What mattered was the settlement, and when the lawyers murmured their weary assents sometime after three o'clock in the morning, a grinning Judge Weinstein broke out several bottles of champagne to celebrate the agreement that he had sired. After a half hour of awkward conviviality, the bleary-eyed, punch-drunk lawyers straggled out of the room. The defendants' group met briefly to sign an internal agreement specifying the previously negotiated allocation among them and to discuss the Thompson Chemicals problem further. They then informed their clients.

NOTES AND QUESTIONS CONCERNING THE AGENT ORANGE SETTLEMENT

1. Because the Agent Orange litigation was certified as a class action, Judge Weinstein held a series of nationwide fairness hearings to determine whether to approve the settlement pursuant to Rule 23(e) of the Federal Rules of Civil Procedure. The settlement ultimately was approved by Judge Weinstein, *In re Agent Orange Product Liability Litigation,* 597 F.Supp. 740 (E.D.N.Y. 1984), and upheld on appeal. *In re "Agent Orange" Product Liability Litigation,* 818 F.2d 145 (2d Cir. 1987), *cert. denied,* 484 U.S. 1004 (1988). The first checks were sent to class members on March 1, 1989, more than ten years after the filing of the lawsuit. "Payments for Families of Defoliant's Victims," *N.Y. Times,* Mar. 3, 1989, at A23.

2. Agent Orange litigation continued for decades after the settlement was approved in this case. *See In re "Agent Orange" Product Liability Litigation,* 373 F.Supp.2d 7, 23–27 (E.D.N.Y. 2005). The settlement approved by Judge Weinstein specifically included individuals who had not yet manifested injury. However, two Vietnam veterans whose injuries manifested after the depletion of the settlement funds in 1994 successfully argued that they were not bound by that settlement. The United States Court of Appeals for the Second Circuit concluded that these veterans were not adequately represented in the initial litigation due to the inherent conflict between class members who could seek compensation from the settlement fund and those whose injuries only manifested after the fund was exhausted. *Stephenson v. Dow Chemical Co.,* 273 F.3d 249 (2d Cir. 2001), *aff'd by an equally divided Court,* 539 U.S. 111 (2003) (per curiam). Judge Weinstein, however, ultimately granted summary judgment for the defendants based upon the government contractor defense, thus dismissing these claims. *In re "Agent Orange"*

Product Liability Litigation, 304 F.Supp.2d 404; 344 F.Supp.2d 873 (E.D.N.Y. 2004).

3.　In addition to the Agent Orange litigation, Congress in 1991 enacted the Agent Orange Act, Pub. L. No. 102–4, 105 Stat. 11 (1991) (codified as amended at 38 U.S.C. § 1116), lessening the showing required of Vietnam Veterans to obtain disability compensation with respect to certain illnesses that may have resulted from exposure to Agent Orange. *See generally* Brown, "The Role of Science in Department of Veterans Affairs Disability Compensation Policies for Environmental and Occupational Illnesses and Injuries," 13 *J. L. & Pol'y* 593 (2005).

4.　Although the settlement of $180,000,000 was the largest tort settlement in history up to that time, it was bitterly denounced by many veterans and their families. To many of the veteran class members, the central purpose of the lawsuit had not been the recovery of monetary relief but the public assignment of legal and moral responsibility for their injuries. As one of the veteran leaders explained, "The settlement doesn't establish the truth. * * * How am I supposed to explain to [my daughter] what happened to her? Where was her day in court?" Michael Ryan, *quoted in* P. Schuck, *Agent Orange on Trial* 171 (1986).

5.　Another criticism of the Agent Orange settlement focused on Judge Weinstein's award of $10,767,000 in attorneys' fees to plaintiffs' counsel. *In re "Agent Orange" Product Liability Litigation*, 611 F.Supp. 1296 (E.D.N.Y. 1985), *modified*, 818 F.2d 226 (2d Cir. 1987). In his attorneys' fee opinion, Judge Weinstein made clear that he wished to encourage "the legal profession * * * to think at least twice before initiating sprawling, complicated cases of highly questionable merit that will consume time, expense, and effort on the part of all concerned, including the courts, in a degree vastly disproportionate to the results eventually obtainable." 611 F.Supp. at 1312. Will his fee award have such an effect? Are there other problems with such judicial statements?

6.　In addition to this award of fees to plaintiffs' counsel, defense counsel were compensated by their corporate clients. One of plaintiffs' counsel estimated that the defense lawyers were spending $2,000,000 per week in the weeks prior to the settlement. P. Schuck, *Agent Orange on Trial* 201 (1986). *See also* J. Kakalik et al., *Costs of Asbestos Litigation* vi–vii (1983) (As of August 26, 1982, on which date the Manville Corporation filed for Chapter 11 bankruptcy protection, of the $661,000,000 in total expenses and compensation paid by defendants and their insurers to resolve 3800 claims, only $400,000,000 was compensation paid to the plaintiffs; of this $400,000,000, plaintiffs received only $236,000,000 after deduction of legal fees and other expenses.).

7.　The Agent Orange litigation was unique in many ways, and perhaps Judge Weinstein's intervention in the case can be justified because of the singular nature of the case. The real problems with the case may stem from the institutional limitations of our judicial system rather than from the judge's handling of the case. In addition to the case's size and complexity, the likelihood of active judicial involvement in the case was heightened because it had been certified as a class action. As a result, any pretrial settlement had to be approved by the court pursuant to Rule 23(e) of the Federal Rules of Civil

Procedure. Why is there a specific requirement for judicial approval of class actions? Is a judge who has been as active in settlement negotiations as Judge Weinstein likely to find that the resulting settlement agreement is unfair? In what circumstances does a judge have the authority to reject the parties' settlement in a non-class action? *See* Navarro, "U.S. District Court Approves Ground Zero Health Settlement," *N.Y. Times*, June 23, 2010, at A28 (federal judge approves settlement for 9/11 first responders after initially rejecting settlement negotiated by the parties).

8. In affirming Judge Weinstein's approval of the Agent Orange settlement, the United States Court of Appeals for the Second Circuit noted that once this case had been certified as a class action "a settlement * * * , dramatically arrived at just before dawn on the day of trial after sleepless hours of bargaining, seems almost as inevitable as the sunrise." 818 F.2d 145, 166 (2d Cir. 1987), *cert. denied*, 484 U.S. 1004 (1988). Why is this? If the observation of the Second Circuit is true, what implications does it have for the judicial supervision of class actions?

9. Due to the many plaintiffs and defendants involved in the Agent Orange litigation, there were not only negotiations between the opposing parties but also bargaining among parties on the same side of the case. How did Judge Weinstein use the differences among the co-parties to achieve a settlement?

10. Under what authority did Judge Weinstein require counsel to meet with the settlement masters he had appointed? What purposes were those masters to serve? What problems did the use of settlement masters create?

11. Was Judge Weinstein justified in determining that a $180,000,000 settlement was fair and that the defendants should pay no more? Consider the contrasting view of settlement master David Shapiro: "As a negotiator, I did not regard any particular figure as objectively 'fair' or 'right.' Instead I was guided by the principle that the parties themselves are the best judges of what is fair, and I asked myself, 'What is the most I can get defendants to agree to without squeezing them for every last cent?' " P. Schuck, *Agent Orange on Trial* 159 (1986).

12. Did Judge Weinstein really "coerce" any of the counsel in the Agent Orange litigation to settle? What input did the plaintiffs have concerning the settlement? What practical problems may have limited their involvement in the formulation of the settlement?

13. Regardless of the attorneys' evaluation of Judge Weinstein's settlement efforts in the *Agent Orange* litigation, judicial intervention in the settlement process often is welcomed by counsel. In one study of almost 1900 attorneys in four different federal judicial districts, 85% responded that "involvement by federal district judges in settlement discussions [is] likely to improve significantly the prospects for achieving settlement," while 70% believed that "federal judges [should] try to facilitate settlement in cases where they have been asked to do so." W. Brazil, *Settling Civil Suits* 39 (1985). As discussed in the next chapter, many attorneys voluntarily seek the intervention of third-party neutrals in mediation or other alternative dispute resolution proceedings that may facilitate settlement. Counsel also can avail themselves of on-line settlement services that compare settlement offers and

demands electronically and "settle" cases when the parties' offers and demands are within an agreed-upon range. Marquess, "Point, Click—Settle Quick," *A.B.A.J.*, April 2000, at 82.

14. Had counsel not agreed to a scttlement, would Judge Weinstein have had difficulty in trying the case? Counsel for those plaintiffs who had opted out of the Agent Orange class action later unsuccessfully sought Judge Weinstein's recusal from hearing the opt-out cases because, in part, of Judge Weinstein's involvement with the class settlement. P. Schuck, *Agent Orange on Trial* 232 (1986). Rule 2.6(B) of the ABA Model Code of Judicial Conduct provides: "A judge may encourage parties to a proceeding and their lawyers to settle matters in dispute but shall not act in a manner that coerces any party into settlement." *See also* Cratsley, "Judicial Ethics and Judicial Settlement Practices: Time for Two Strangers to Meet," 21 *Ohio St. J. Disp. Resol.* 569 (2006).

15. Even absent direct involvement in settlement discussions, there are many ways in which judges can encourage settlement. The judicial action that perhaps most frequently results in settlement is the setting of a firm date for trial. In the Agent Orange litigation, Judge Weinstein was adamant that the case would be tried on the date he had set, at one point refusing a continuance when defendant Monsanto's lead trial counsel suffered a nervous collapse. P. Schuck, *Agent Orange on Trial* 118 (1986). He also placed a large calendar in the courtroom with the trial date circled and had carpenters expand the jury box in order to accommodate extra alternate jurors for the trial. *Id.* at 119. Consider the other management tools given judges by the 1983 and 1993 amendments to Rule 16 and the affect that these tools can have upon settlement. *See* Chapter 13, *supra.*

16. Apart from the possible misuse of individual inducements to settlement, should our system of civil justice encourage settlements of actions such as the Agent Orange litigation? *See* Fiss, "Against Settlement," 93 *Yale L. J.* 1073 (1984). Does the judge have any stake in settlements? Are the parties or counsel likely to react differently to a settlement that the judge has encouraged or helped to craft? Reconsider these questions after reading Chapter 15 of this book dealing with alternative dispute resolution.

17. In his book Professor Schuck offers differing assessments of Judge Weinstein's handling of the Agent Orange litigation. First, consider Schuck's analysis of the program Judge Weinstein adopted to govern the distribution of the settlement fund to individual claimants:

> Unlike legislated benefit programs, Weinstein's was drawn to his personal specifications and was not vulnerable to modification or repeal, budgetary review, administrative oversight, public control through the representative organs of government, or any other mechanism of political accountability. In effect, Weinstein had fused in himself legislative, administrative, and judicial powers, subject to no checks and balances and no higher authority than his own conscience and the unlikely intervention of the appellate court.

P. Schuck, *Agent Orange On Trial* 223 (1986).

A later analysis of the settlement is quite different:

On another view, however, Weinstein's extraordinary moves were no more than was demanded by an extraordinary case like Agent Orange. His legal innovations—his propensity to "make things up as he goes along"—can be seen as the quintessential work of the common-law judge, "working the law pure" as it is applied to unforeseen cases in unprecedented circumstances, devising judicial solutions in an area of policy in which legislatures have been content to permit the courts to take the lead.

Id. at 259–60.

With which analysis do you agree?

18. Judge Weinstein's own thoughts on the issues suggested in the preceding paragraphs can be found in J. Weinstein, *Individual Justice in Mass Tort Society: The Effect of Class Actions, Consolidations, and other Multiparty Devices* (1995).

19. What pressures does litigation of the scope and intensity of the Agent Orange cases place upon the attorneys handling the lawsuits? Attorney Stephen Schlegel was one of the lead counsel in the Agent Orange litigation, and, during one thirteen month period, he spent only four evenings at home in Chicago with his wife and daughters. Eight days after Judge Weinstein awarded him $1,200,000 in attorneys' fees, Schlegel's wife filed for divorce. Schlegel believes that the Agent Orange litigation was largely responsible for the subsequent divorce. Wagner, "The New Elite Plaintiffs' Bar," *A.B.A.J.,* Feb. 1986, at 44, 48–49.

Whether stemming from megacases such as Agent Orange or from other cases or legal tasks, the stresses of legal practice have become a major issue for both individual attorneys and the law firms and others that employ them. For possible individual and law firm responses to these issues see N. Levit & D. Linder, *The Happy Lawyer: Making a Good Life in the Law* (2010); Young Lawyers Division, American Bar Association, *Life in the Balance: Achieving Equilibrium in Professional and Personal Life* (2003); Commission on Women in the Profession, American Bar Association, *Balanced Lives: Changing the Culture of Legal Practice* (2002); Symposium, "Perspectives on Lawyer Happiness," 58 *Syracuse L. Rev.* 217 (2008).

VI. CONCLUSION

Some attorneys are naturally gifted negotiators. Others subconsciously have developed negotiation skills in non-legal settings from a very early age. The rest of us, however, have to develop our negotiation skills the old fashioned way—we have to work at it.

This is not a major problem, because of the constant opportunities for practicing and perfecting negotiation skills that a litigation practice provides. In order to become a skillful negotiator, attorneys must pay the same attention to this aspect of their practices that they do to the other aspects of modern civil litigation. Through self-conscious critique of one's own negotiation performances, the novice attorney can hone her negotiation skills and the experienced attorney can become an even more accomplished negotiator.

VII.   CHAPTER BIBLIOGRAPHY

R. Bastress & J. Harbaugh, *Interviewing, Counseling, and Negotiation* (1990).

Bone, " 'To Encourage Settlement': Rule 68, Offers of Judgment, and the History of the Federal Rules of Civil Procedure," 102 *Nw. U. L. Rev.* 1561 (2008).

W. Brazil, *Effective Approaches to Settlement: A Handbook for Lawyers and Judges* (1988).

W. Brazil, *Settling Civil Suits* (1985).

H. Cohen, *You Can Negotiate Anything* (1980).

C. Craver, *Effective Legal Negotiation and Settlement* (6th ed. 2009).

Dahl, "Ethics on the Table: Stretching the Truth in Negotiations," 8 *Rev. Litig.* 173 (1989).

Dewey, "Traps in Multifeasor Settlements," *Litigation,* Summer 1987, at 41.

DiSarro, "Six Degrees of Separation: Settlement Agreements and Consent Orders in Federal Civil Litigation," 60 *Am.U. L. Rev.* 275 (2010).

H. Edwards & J. White, *The Lawyer as a Negotiator* (1977).

Eisenberg, "Private Ordering Through Negotiation: Dispute–Settlement and Rulemaking," 89 *Harv. L. Rev.* 637 (1976).

Eisenberg & Lanvers, "What is the Settlement Rate and Why Should We Care?," 6 *J. Em. Legal Studies* 111 (2009).

R. Fisher & S. Brown, *Getting Together* (1988).

R. Fisher & W. Ury, *Getting to Yes* (2d ed. 1991).

Fiss, "Against Settlement," 93 *Yale L. J.* 1073 (1984).

X. Frascogna & H. Hetherington, *Negotiation Strategy for Lawyers* (1984).

Friedman, Note, "An Analysis of Settlement," 22 *Stan. L. Rev.* 67 (1969).

D. Gifford, *Legal Negotiation: Theory and Applications* (2d ed. 2007).

Gross & Syverud, "Getting to No: A Study of Settlement Negotiations and the Selection of Cases for Trial," 90 *Mich. L. Rev.* 319 (1991).

R. Haydock, *Negotiation Practice* (1984).

Kahn, "Ensure Tax Advantages in Case Settlements," *Trial,* June 1990, at 62.

C. Karrass, *The Negotiating Game: How to Get What You Want* (rev. ed. 1994).

Kiser et al., "Let's Not Make a Deal: An Empirical Study of Decision Making in Unsuccessful Settlement Negotiations," 5 *J. Em. Legal Studies* 551 (2008).

R. Korobkin, *Negotiation: Theory and Strategy* (2d ed. 2009).

Lynch & Levine, "The Settlement of Federal District Court Cases: A Judicial Perspective," 67 *Or. L. Rev.* 239 (1988).

Madden, "Drafting Settlement Agreements in Commercial Litigation," *Litigation,* Fall 1978, at 40.

Menkel–Meadow, "Toward Another View of Legal Negotiation: The Structure of Problem Solving," 31 *UCLA L. Rev.* 754 (1984).

H. Miller, *Art of Advocacy—Settlement* (1987).

M. Mnookin et al., *Beyond Winning: Negotiating to Create Value in Deals and Disputes* (2000).

M. Nelken, *Negotiation: Theory and Practice* (2d ed. 2007).

Nolan, "Settlement Negotiations," *Litigation,* Summer 1985, at 17.

J. Parness, *Advanced Civil Procedure: Civil Claim Settlement Laws* (2000).

Parness, "Improving Judicial Settlement Conferences," 39 *U.C. Davis L. Rev.* 1891 (2006).

Peters, "The Use of Lies in Negotiation," 48 *Ohio St. L. J.* 1 (1987).

D. Provine, *Settlement Strategies for Federal District Judges* (1986).

H. Raiffa, *The Art and Science of Negotiation* (1982).

H. Raiffa et al., *Negotiation Analysis: The Science and Art of Collaborative Decision Making* (2002).

A. Rau et al., *Negotiation* (3d ed. 2006).

Richmond, "Lawyers' Professional Responsibilities and Liabilities in Negotiations," 22 *Geo. J. Legal Ethics* 249 (2009).

Rubin, "A Causerie on Lawyers' Ethics in Negotiation," 35 *La. L. Rev.* 577 (1975).

Section of Litigation, American Bar Association, *Ethical Guidelines for Settlement Negotiations* (2002).

G. Shell, *Bargaining for Advantage* (1999).

Shaffer, "Negotiation Ethics: A Report to Cartaphila," *Litigation,* Winter 1981, at 37.

M. Schoenfield & R. Schoenfield, *Legal Negotiations: Getting Maximum Results* (1988).

Steele, "Deceptive Negotiating and High–Toned Morality," 39 *Vand. L. Rev.* 1387 (1986).

Symposium, "Revitalizing FRCP 68: Can Offers of Judgment Provide Adequate Incentives for Fair, Early Settlement of Fee–Recovery Cases?," 57 *Mercer L. Rev.*717 (2006).

Symposium, "The Emerging Interdisciplinary Canon of Negotiation," 87 *Marq. L. Rev.* 637 (2004).

Tornquist, "The Active Judge in Pretrial Settlement: Inherent Authority Gone Awry," 25 *Willamette L. Rev.* 743 (1989).

W. Ury, *Getting Past No* (1993).

Wetlaufer, "The Ethics of Lying in Negotiations," 75 *Iowa L. Rev.* 1219 (1990).

What's Fair: Ethics for Negotiators (C. Menkel–Meadow & M. Wheeler ed. 2004).

Will et al., "The Role of the Judge in the Settlement Process," 75 F.R.D. 203 (1976).

White, "Machiavelli and the Bar: Ethical Limitations on Lying in Negotiation," 1980 *Am. B. Found. Res. J.* 926 (1980).

G. Williams & C. Craver, *Legal Negotiating* (2007).

CHAPTER 15

ALTERNATIVE DISPUTE RESOLUTION: "ARE YOU SURE YOU WANT TO FILE A LAWSUIT?"

■ ■ ■

I must say that as a litigant I should dread a lawsuit beyond almost anything else short of sickness and death.

Judge Learned Hand, "The Deficiencies of Trials to Reach the Heart of the Matter," *in* 3 Association of the Bar of the City of New York, *Lectures on Legal Topics* 87, 105 (1926).

Blessed are the peacemakers * * * .

Matthew 5:9.

Analysis

I. INTRODUCTION

This book has focused on both modern pretrial litigation and the system of civil adjudication within which pretrial litigation is practiced. The basic rules for adjudicating civil disputes in the federal and in many state courts are contained in the Federal Rules of Civil Procedure. These rules, and the court systems in which they apply, have served us well for many years. Today, however, federal and many state systems of civil adjudication are under great strain. Costs and delays, in particular, have led to calls for reform and increasing criticism of civil adjudication.

In addition to calls for reform, there have been efforts to develop alternatives to our current systems of civil adjudication. The resulting proposals and experiments have become so widespread that they have become loosely lumped together as the "alternative dispute resolution," or "ADR," movement. These alternatives to traditional civil adjudication are the subject of this chapter.

The chapter is divided into four main sections. Initially, alternatives to the filing of a civil lawsuit are considered. The ADR movement has not, though, merely advanced dispute resolution devices totally separate and apart from current systems of civil litigation. ADR techniques have been developed to aid in the resolution of existing lawsuits within the civil justice system. The second major section of the chapter considers these ADR techniques for resolving civil cases. Now that the initial enthusiasm for alternative dispute resolution has subsided somewhat, questions have been raised about ADR. The third major section of the chapter deals with these second thoughts about alternative dispute resolution. The fourth and final major section of the chapter is a postscript on the Buffalo Creek disaster litigation, which illustrates some of the inherent limitations of modern civil adjudication.

A single chapter cannot do more than present a broad survey of the alternative dispute resolution techniques currently being utilized across the country. A great many books[1] and newsletters and journals[2] are devoted to alternative dispute resolution. The American Bar Association has a Dispute Resolution Section, the Association of American Law Schools has a Section on Alternative Dispute Resolution, and organizations such as the International Institute for Conflict Prevention and Resolution encourage the use of ADR to resolve disputes in many settings. Alternative dispute resolution programs frequently are featured at bar association and continuing legal education sessions. Law firms also have shown an interest in ADR, at least in part because of client resistance to the costs and delays that civil litigation increasingly entails.

This chapter is intended as an introduction to the subject of alternative dispute resolution and to some of the ADR techniques currently utilized by judges, lawyers and disputants.

---

1. *Alternative Dispute Resolution: Practice and Perspectives* (M. Matthews ed. 1990); *Alternative Dispute Resolution: The Litigator's Handbook* (N. Atlas et al. eds. 2000); E. Brunet et al., *Alternative Dispute Resolution: The Advocate's Perspective* (3d ed. 2006); J. Folberg et al., *Resolving Disputes: Theory, Practice, and Law* (2d ed. 2010); S. Goldberg et al., *Dispute Resolution: Negotiation, Mediation, and Other Processes* (5th ed. 2007); J. Grenig, *Alternative Dispute Resolution* (3d ed. 2005); M. Moffitt & A. Schneider, *Dispute Resolution: Examples & Explanations* (2008); A. Ordover & A. Doneff, *Alternatives to Litigation: Mediation, Arbitration, and the Art of Dispute Resolution* (2d ed. 2002); A. Rau et al., *Processes of Dispute Resolution: The Role of Lawyers* (4th ed. 2006); L. Riskin et al., *Dispute Resolution and Lawyers* (4th ed. 2009); B. Roth et al., *The Alternative Dispute Resolution Practice Guide* (1993); K. Stone, *Private Justice: The Law of Alternative Dispute Resolution* (2000); S. Ware, *Principles of Alternative Dispute Resolution* (2d ed. 2007).

2. *Alternatives to the High Costs of Litigation*; *World Arbitration and Mediation Report*; *Dispute Resolution Magazine*; *Journal of Dispute Resolution*; *Ohio State Journal on Dispute Resolution*.

II. ALTERNATIVES TO LITIGATION

Alternatives to civil litigation are not a new phenomenon.[3] In fact, our current systems of civil adjudication were at one time "alternative dispute resolution" systems themselves. Whatever our frustrations with modern civil litigation, no one seriously suggests that we revert to some of the dispute resolution devices that existing systems replaced, such as trial by combat, trial by ordeal, or the technicalities of common law pleading.

Today there is an interest in mechanisms to resolve disputes more quickly and efficiently than may be possible with civil lawsuits. The major alternatives include private judges, arbitration, mediation, and negotiation.[4] These ADR processes differ greatly in their formality and expense. There generally is a direct relation between the formality of a particular alternative dispute resolution process and the expense to the parties of that process.

Having a dispute resolved by a private judge can be just as expensive as traditional adjudication, and the procedures employed by private judges may be identical to those used in the civil courts. At the other extreme, negotiation is usually an inexpensive way to resolve a dispute, and there are few formal rules regulating negotiation conduct.[5] While alternative dispute resolution procedures are discussed individually, they should be

---

3. The historical development of alternatives to formal adjudication in this country is traced in J. Auerbach, *Justice Without Law?* (1983).

4. In addition, specific administrative structures have been developed to handle particular types of disputes. Most states have established administrative bodies to handle at least the initial processing of claims involving workers' compensation. 7 L. Larson, *Larson's Workers' Compensation Law* § 124.01 (2010). State and federal administrative agencies have been established to resolve discrimination, Social Security, and tort claims. 42 U.S.C. § 2000e–5(b)–(d); 42 U.S.C. § 1383; 28 U.S.C. § 2672. Some states and public and private institutions have established the office of ombuds, an individual specifically charged with resolving disputes with governmental bodies and institutions. *See generally* Wiegand, "A Just and Lasting Peace: Supplanting Mediation with the Ombuds Model," 12 *Ohio St. J. Disp. Resol.* 95 (1996); Verkuil, "The Ombudsman and the Limits of the Adversary System," 75 *Colum. L. Rev.* 845 (1975).

Not only have such structures been established to handle specific types of disputes, but administrative mechanisms can be utilized to settle claims within a particular lawsuit or series of lawsuits. Administrative procedures for processing and determining the claims of class members are a prime example of such mechanisms. *See Manual for Complex Litigation, Fourth* § 21.66 (2004). Over fifty asbestos manufacturers and insurers created an Asbestos Claims Facility to speed settlements and reduce legal costs in the nationwide asbestos litigation. This claims facility resolved over 21,000 claims before manufacturers began to withdraw from the facility. Holzberg, "Novel Settlement Experiment Fails," *Litigation News*, Dec. 1988, at 2. *See also* Wellington, "Asbestos: The Private Management of a Public Problem," 33 *Clev. St. L. Rev.* 375 (1984–85).

More recently, Congress established the September 11th Victim Compensation Fund, through which more than $7,000,000,000 was paid to those who were physically injured in the attacks of September 11, 2001, and to the families of those who died in those attacks. *See* Ackerman, "The September 11th Victim Compensation Fund: An Effective Administrative Response to National Tragedy," 10 *Harv. Negot. L. Rev.* 135 (2005). The Special Master appointed to administer the September 11th Victim Compensation Fund was Kenneth Feinberg, who had been appointed by Judge Weinstein to attempt to achieve a settlement in the Agent Orange litigation considered in Chapter 14, Section V. *See* K. Feinberg, *What Is Life Worth?: The Unprecedented Effort to Compensate the Victims of 9/11* (2005).

5. In most cases, the formality of procedures is inversely related to the amount of party control over the dispute resolution mechanism. Once a lawsuit is filed, formal rules govern the method by which the lawsuit will be resolved and the parties must play by those rules. At the

thought of as points on a broad continuum based upon their formality and expense. This continuum is illustrated by Figure 15–1.

FIGURE 15–1

FORMALITY, EXPENSE, AND PARTY CONTROL OF DISPUTE PROCESSING

	More Formal, More Expensive & Less Party Control	Less Formal, Less Expensive & More Party Control	
← ← ←			→ → →

| Private Judges | Arbitration | Mediation | Negotiation |

It is somewhat misleading to speak of alternative dispute resolution structures such as mediation or arbitration as if there is only a single variant of these devices. Many alternative dispute resolution techniques are hybrids of the processes described in this chapter. Counsel contemplating use of an ADR technique should consider the ways in which a standard technique can be tailored to best resolve the case at hand.[6]

Alternative dispute resolution must be considered against the backdrop of traditional civil litigation. The possibility of civil litigation is what usually shapes disputes. The hackneyed threat remains "I'll see you in court," not "I'll see you in mediation." Because parties may not be aware of non-litigation alternatives, counsel should be sure to explore with clients ADR possibilities. While it is up to the client to choose the means by which his dispute will be resolved, a client cannot even consider ADR techniques if he is not aware of their existence.

Four of the major alternatives to traditional civil litigation now will be considered.

A. PRIVATE JUDGES

One major concern with current systems of civil adjudication is that the delays and inconveniences in those systems have made them an impractical method of dispute resolution for many litigants. For this reason, among others, litigants in some states have hired private judges to resolve their civil claims. Private judges can be retained to hear a case at the convenience of the parties, even in the evenings or on weekends. This

---

other extreme, the contours of a negotiation are up to the parties to the negotiation. In addition, more informal ADR techniques may be less likely than litigation to rupture existing party relationships. *See* Galanter, "Reading the Landscape of Disputes: What We Know and Don't Know (And Think We Know) About Our Allegedly Contentious and Litigious Society," 31 *UCLA L. Rev.* 4, 24–26 (1983). Finally, the representation of parties by attorneys may increase both the formality and expense of proceedings.

6. Indeed, to the extent that parties do not attempt to tailor dispute resolution techniques to their particular dispute and their conflict resolution needs, they have forfeited one of the major advantages of alternative dispute resolution. *See* Stipanowich, "Arbitration: The 'New Litigation,'" 2010 *U. Ill. L. Rev.* 1 (2010) (more nuanced approach to arbitration is necessary to achieve full benefits of this dispute resolution technique).

dispute resolution technique has received significant attention in the state courts of California and New York.[7]

In jurisdictions in which private judging has taken hold, retired judges or experienced attorneys serve as the private judges (or "rent a judges" as private judges have been called by some). The parties can choose as a private judge an individual in whom they have confidence and perhaps someone who has familiarity with the general subject matter of their dispute. Private judges can sit by themselves or in panels, and the tribunals over which these judges preside typically apply the rules of evidence and procedure applicable in the state courts. The judgments rendered by private judges can be entered on the dockets of the state trial courts and appealed to state courts of appeal in the same manner as judgments of that state's own trial courts.[8]

Despite the attractiveness of private judging to some private litigants, there are potential problems posed by this means of dispute resolution. One of the reasons that private judging is attractive to some litigants is that the proceedings generally are closed to the public. However, if a "private" dispute has implications for other parties or for the general public, there may be a public interest in resolving that dispute in a public forum.[9]

Permitting wealthy litigants to opt out of our civil justice system could lead to a dual system of justice, in which well-to-do litigants hire private judges while other parties are relegated to the public courts and the delays that have become increasingly common in some of those courts. Parties who can afford to have their disputes litigated outside the public courts may have less interest in the quality of justice rendered in those courts.

Despite these concerns about the use of private judges, this alternative to litigation appears to be gaining acceptance in some states. Indeed, the use of private judges is a good illustration of the manner in which parties can devise their own procedures to resolve their disputes.

---

7. Cal. Civ. Proc. Code §§ 638–645.2 (West 1976 & Supp. 2006); N. Y. Civ. Prac. Law §§ 4301–4321 (McKinney 1992 & Supp. 2007). *See* Shapiro, "Private Judging in the State of New York: A Critical Introduction," 23 *Colum. J. L. & Soc. Probs.* 275 (1990); Kim, Note, "Rent–A–Judges and the Cost of Selling Justice," 44 *Duke L. J.* 166 (1994); Note, "The California Rent–A–Judge Experiment: Constitutional and Policy Considerations of Pay–As–You–Go Courts," 94 *Harv. L. Rev.* 1592 (1981). Both the California and New York statutes permitting private judging were adopted as part of the Field Codes in those states over 100 years ago. They were rediscovered as civil dockets became increasingly crowded in recent years.

8. Cal. Civ. Proc. Code §§ 644, 645 (West Supp. 2006); N. Y. Civ. Prac. Law § 4319 (McKinney 1992).

9. Gnaizda, "Secret Justice for the Privileged Few," 66 *Judicature* 6 (1982). *Contra* Coulson, "Private Settlement for the Public Good," 66 *Judicature* 7 (1982). Not only may the public have an interest in the resolution of specific cases, but there may be a general public interest in having disputes publicly litigated so as to create precedents to guide future conduct of parties, lawyers, and the courts. *See generally* Symposium, "Secrecy and Transparency in Dispute Resolution," 54 *U. Kan. L. Rev.* 1211 (2006).

B. ARBITRATION

In addition to the development of new dispute resolution devices such as private judges, the ADR movement has focused attention on some well-established alternatives to civil litigation. Arbitration thus has received increased attention as a means of alternative dispute resolution; it is perceived as a more flexible dispute resolution mechanism than traditional civil litigation and less subject to litigation delays and costs.[10]

Arbitration has been used for many years to resolve disputes in the construction industry and between labor and management. In these situations, and many others, the parties' contract contains a term providing that any disputes arising under the contract will be resolved by arbitration rather than by resort to the courts. This arbitration clause also specifies the procedures that will govern any resulting arbitrations. Often, rather than drafting their own rules, the parties simply agree that the arbitration rules of the American Arbitration Association will apply.

In a typical arbitration, the parties present witnesses and evidence as they would in a civil lawsuit. However, the rules of evidence that apply in arbitrations usually are not as strict as those applied in court. For example, the hearsay rule usually is not applicable in arbitration proceedings. Arbitration is favored by some disputants because there often is not the same extensive discovery, with its attendant costs and delay, as in civil adjudication. To the extent that contractual arbitration clauses guarantee extensive procedural protections, though, arbitration can become as costly and time-consuming as the civil litigation that it is intended to supplant.

Another distinctive feature of arbitration is that the parties choose the arbitrator, who is usually someone with expertise in the subject matter of the parties' dispute or the industry in which the parties do business. The arbitrator also may be someone who has handled other arbitrations involving these same parties and therefore is familiar with their course of dealing under the contract from which the dispute arises. In addition, the parties may prefer to air their dispute privately in an arbitration hearing rather than in a public courtroom.

While the parties are expected to amicably arbitrate and comply with the arbitrator's decision, if they do not, both an agreement to arbitrate[11] and the arbitration award[12] usually are judicially-enforceable. The Federal

---

10. *See generally* T. Carbonneau, *The Law and Practice of Arbitration* (2d ed. 2007); J. Cooley & S. Lubet, *Arbitration Advocacy* (2d ed. 2003); O. Fairweather, *Practice and Procedure in Labor Arbitration* (4th ed. 1999); A. Rau et al., *Arbitration* (3d ed. 2006); A Reuben et al., *How Arbitration Works: Elkouri & Elkouri* (6th ed. 2003); K. Stone & R. Bales, *Arbitration Law* (2d ed. 2010).

In adjudicatory arbitration such as is described in the text, the arbitrator renders a decision in the same basic manner as does a judge in a civil lawsuit. Final offer arbitration differs from traditional arbitration because the parties each submit a proposed resolution of the dispute and the arbitrator chooses the most reasonable offer. Final offer arbitration has been successfully used to resolve professional baseball salary disputes and disputes involving public employees. *E.g.,* Mich. Comp. Laws Ann. § 423.238 (West 2001); Iowa Code Ann. § 20.22 (West 2001); N. J. Stat. Ann. § 34:13A–16 (West 2000). *See also* P. Feuille, *Final Offer Arbitration* (1975); Perlman, Note, "Final Offer Arbitration: A Pre–Trial Settlement Device," 16 *Harv. J. Legis.* 513 (1979).

11. 9 U.S.C. § 2.

12. 9 U.S.C. § 9.

Arbitration Act[13] has been held to establish "a liberal federal policy favoring arbitration agreements,"[14] which requires that the courts "rigorously enforce agreements to arbitrate."[15]

The Supreme Court has been quite receptive to the resolution of private disputes by arbitration, enforcing predispute contractual clauses requiring the arbitration of alleged violations of federal antitrust and securities laws,[16] as well as claims brought under the Age Discrimination in Employment Act.[17] However, the employee's agreement to arbitrate such claims does not preclude the EEOC from seeking victim-specific relief on that employee's behalf in the federal courts.[18] The Supreme Court also has suggested that certain statutory schemes may present "an inherent conflict between arbitration and the statute's underlying purposes."[19]

While it would be neither possible nor wise to require arbitration in all cases, arbitration has proven to be a quite effective means of resolving many disputes. Arbitration therefore should be considered both at the time that a contract is drafted on behalf of a client and once any later dispute has arisen.

C. MEDITATION

An alternative dispute resolution device that is usually less formal, and thus less expensive, than arbitration is mediation.[20] Mediation is a

---

13. 9 U.S.C. §§ 1–15.

14. *Moses H. Cone Mem'l Hosp. v. Mercury Constr. Corp.*, 460 U.S. 1, 24 (1983).

15. *Dean Witter Reynolds, Inc. v. Byrd*, 470 U.S. 213, 221 (1985).

16. *Rodriguez de Quijas v. Shearson/American Express, Inc.*, 490 U.S. 477 (1989); *Shearson/American Express, Inc. v. McMahon*, 482 U.S. 220 (1987); *Mitsubishi Motors Corp. v. Soler Chrysler–Plymouth, Inc.*, 473 U.S. 614 (1985).

17. *Gilmer v. Interstate/Johnson Lane Corp.*, 500 U.S. 20 (1991). The Supreme Court has held that state courts may be required to enforce predispute contractual agreements to arbitrate state law claims as well. *Circuit City Stores, Inc. v. Adams*, 532 U.S. 105 (2001); *Allied–Bruce Terminix Cos., Inc. v. Dobson*, 513 U.S. 265 (1995); *Southland Corp. v. Keating*, 465 U.S. 1 (1984).

However, the Court has cautioned that "courts should remain attuned to well-supported claims that the agreement to arbitrate resulted from the sort of fraud or overwhelming economic power that would provide grounds 'for the revocation of any contract.'" *Mitsubishi Motors Corp. v. Soler Chrysler–Plymouth, Inc.*, 473 U.S. 614, 627 (1985) (quoting Federal Arbitration Act, 9 U.S.C. § 2). Thus upon remand from the Supreme Court, the Ninth Circuit Court of Appeals held that the arbitration clause at issue in *Circuit City Stores, Inc. v. Adams* was unconscionable under state contract law because it only required the employee to arbitrate claims, limited the relief available to the employee under state law, required the employee to split the arbitrator's fees, and precluded the employee from invoking a continuing violation doctrine available under state law. 279 F.3d 889 (9th Cir. 2002).

18. *Equal Employment Opportunity Commission v. Waffle House, Inc.*, 534 U.S. 279 (2002).

19. *Shearson/American Express, Inc. v. McMahon*, 482 U.S. 220, 227 (1987). In addition, the Supreme Court has held that arbitration pursuant to a collective bargaining agreement does not preclude employees from filing federal claims under the Fair Labor Standards Act, *Barrentine v. Arkansas–Best Freight System, Inc.*, 450 U.S. 728 (1981); Section 1983 of Title 42 of the United States Code, *McDonald v. City of West Branch*, 466 U.S. 284 (1984); and Title VII of the Civil Rights Act of 1964, *Alexander v. Gardner–Denver Co.*, 415 U.S. 36 (1974).

20. *See generally* H. Abramson, *Mediation Representation: Advocating in a Problem–Solving Process* (2004); J. Alfini et al., *Mediation Theory and Practice* (2001); M. Bennett & S. Hughes, *The Art of Mediation* (2d ed. 2005); J. Cooley, *Mediation Advocacy* (2d ed. 2002); D. Golann, *Mediating Legal Disputes: Effective Strategies for Lawyers and Mediators* (1996); K. Kovach,

process in which a neutral third-party is called upon by the parties to a dispute to help them resolve that dispute. The mediator acts as a facilitator, helping the parties reach their own agreement.

Because of his neutrality and detachment, the mediator may see and suggest possible resolutions of a dispute that the parties have not considered. Although he may recommend solutions to the parties' dispute, the mediator does not issue a ruling as does an arbitrator.[21] Mediation is basically negotiation that involves a neutral third-party facilitator. Mediation represents a break from the adversary model of dispute resolution, because it is not as rule-bound as adjudication and it seeks common ground between the parties rather than culminating in an award under which one party gains at the other party's expense.[22]

Mediation has been used to facilitate settlements of private disputes (such as family disputes) and public disputes (such as labor disputes involving public employees). Some state and federal statutes encourage or require public employees[23] and railroad and airline workers[24] to submit their disputes to mediation to prevent strikes that might result if no settlement of the parties' dispute is reached.

In addition to mediators, some states provide for the appointment of third-party fact finders.[25] These individuals investigate a dispute and issue findings of fact (with or without accompanying recommendations). The parties then use these facts to negotiate a settlement of their dispute, either by themselves or with the assistance of a third-party such as a mediator.

Mediation and arbitration sometimes are melded in a "med-arb" combination. Under these combined dispute resolution devices, a mediator initially attempts to facilitate a settlement of the parties' dispute. If the parties do not reach agreement during the mediation process, the dispute is submitted to, and resolved by, arbitration. An issue presented by such a combination of mediation and arbitration is whether the person who

---

Mediation: Principles and Practice (3d ed. 2004); C. Menkel–Meadow et al., *Mediation* (2005); C. Moore, *The Mediation Process: Practical Strategies for Resolving Conflict* (3d ed. 2003); J. Murray et al., *Mediation and Other Non–Binding ADR Processes* (3d ed. 2006); N. Rogers & C. McEwen, *Mediation: Law, Policy, Practice* (2d ed. 1994).

21. However, mediators may ask the parties to present their positions, through evidence or otherwise, and then explore possible solutions with them. For a comparison of arbitration and mediation see Cooley, "Arbitration vs. Mediation—Explaining the Differences," 69 *Judicature* 263 (1986).

22. The terms "mediation" and "conciliation" sometimes are used interchangeably or in combination. *E.g.* 29 U.S.C. § 172 (establishing Federal Mediation and Conciliation Service). In other situations, "conciliation" is used to refer to a dispute resolution mechanism in which a neutral third-party attempts to facilitate an agreement but does not recommend any solution (as do many mediators). Conciliation may be used in situations such as labor or marital disputes where the disputants are unwilling to talk to one another due to party tensions and distrust. *See generally* L. Kanowitz, *Alternative Dispute Resolution* 77–82 (1986).

23. Cal. Govt. Code § 3505.2 (West 1995); Mich. Comp. Laws Ann. § 423.207 (West 2001); Wis. Stat. Ann. § 111.87 (West 2002).

24. 45 U.S.C. §§ 151–188 (Railway Labor Act).

25. *E.g.,* Mass. Gen. Laws Ann. ch. 150E, § 9 (West 2004); Wis. Stat. Ann. § 111.88 (West 2002).

initially serves as the mediator should serve as the arbitrator. The advantages and disadvantages of using the same person for both purposes are similar to the issues raised by a judge's active involvement in settlement discussions.[26]

By itself or combined with particular elements of arbitration, mediation can be a useful dispute resolution device. Mediation's particular strength is in fostering a dialogue between disputants and encouraging them to view the dispute through the eyes of a neutral mediator or of the other disputants. Such a perspective usually is a necessary prerequisite to the settlement of any dispute.

D. NEGOTIATION

Most disputes are resolved, informally and privately, by negotiation. Because of their importance to modern civil litigation, the entire preceding chapter is devoted to negotiation and settlement. Only a few points will be made concerning negotiation in this chapter.

First of all, negotiation is a dispute resolution mechanism that can, and does, occur at any stage of a dispute. Negotiation can occur prior to the filing of a lawsuit, prior to trial, or while a case is on appeal. Negotiation can be used to prevent a formal dispute from ever arising. Negotiation can occur at a single point in a particular dispute or the parties may continuously negotiate as their dispute is processed by the judiciary or through alternative dispute resolution mechanisms.

In addition, negotiation is a dispute resolution technique that can be uniquely tailored to the needs of the disputants. Parties to a dispute can negotiate by and among themselves, through lawyers, or with the aid of a judge or mediator. The timing, structure, and costs of negotiations are generally up to the parties.

Finally, many of the other dispute resolution alternatives to litigation and alternatives within litigation have as their ultimate goal the negotiated settlement of disputes. For example, one way to measure the efficacy of mediation is by the negotiated settlements that result from that process.

While not a new dispute resolution device, negotiation promises to continue to be the major alternative to formal litigation for the resolution of disputes.

NOTES AND QUESTIONS CONCERNING ALTERNATIVES TO LITIGATION

1. With such a wealth of choices, how is a disputant to know which dispute resolution process to choose? Professor Frank Sander has advocated the creation of dispute resolution centers which house various dispute resolution processes, from traditional courts to arbitrators, mediators and ombuds. Sander, "Varieties of Dispute Processing," 70 F.R.D. 111, 130–32 (1976). The American Bar Association has sponsored experimental Multi–Door Court-

---

26. *See* Chapter 14, Section V, *supra* p. 617.

house Centers based on this premise. At these dispute resolution centers counselors help disputants select the most appropriate dispute resolution process, taking into consideration a dispute's characteristics, the dispute resolution options available, and the party's desires. Ray, "Emerging Options in Dispute Resolution," *A.B.A.J.*, June 1989, at 66, 68. *See also* Fla. Stat. Ann. §§ 44.1011–44.406 (West 2003 & Supp. 2007) (permitting Florida courts to refer civil actions to mandatory mediation, non-binding arbitration, or voluntary binding arbitration); Tex. Civ. Prac. & Rem. Code Ann. §§ 154.021–154.027 (Vernon 2005) (permitting Texas courts to refer cases to mediation, mini-trials, moderated settlement conferences, summary jury trials, and arbitration). The development of the multi-door courthouse concept and the ways in which this concept has been successfully implemented and could be improved are discussed in Stempel, "Reflections on Judicial ADR and the Multi–Door Courthouse at Twenty: Fait Accompli, Failed Overture, or Fledgling Adulthood?," 11 *Ohio St. J. Disp. Resol.* 297 (1996).

2. Courts may have a major influence even on disputes that are not filed as civil lawsuits. Professor Marc Galanter has observed:

> Disputes may be prevented by what courts do, for instance by enabling planning to avoid disputes or by normatively disarming a potential disputant. Also, courts may foment and mobilize disputes, as when their declaration of a right arouses and legitimates expectations about the propriety of pursuing a claim, or when changes in rules of standing suggest the possibility of pursuing a claim successfully. Further, courts may displace disputes into various forums and endow these forums with regulatory power. Finally, courts may transform disputes so that the issues addressed are broader or narrower or different than those initially raised by the disputants.

Galanter, "Reading the Landscape of Disputes: What We Know and Don't Know (and Think We Know) About Our Allegedly Contentious and Litigious Society," 31 *UCLA L. Rev.* 5, 34 (1983).

3. Not only courts, but legislatures, can encourage or discourage litigation. If laws are ambiguous or poorly drafted, litigation concerning the meaning of those laws may be inevitable. If standards for private conduct are not clear, litigation may be engendered. Inducements to suit (such as the provision of attorneys' fees to prevailing plaintiffs) or access barriers (such as bond and filing requirements) represent legislative attempts to encourage or discourage litigation. Finally, laws establishing no-fault insurance and divorce systems can take entire categories of claims out of the judicial system.

4. Lawyers, too, may want to resolve potential disputes with their own clients by non-judicial techniques. The American Bar Association's Standing Committee on Ethics and Professional Responsibility has determined that the inclusion of a mandatory arbitration provision in a client retainer agreement is acceptable under the Model Rules of Professional Conduct so long as the attorney has explained to the client both the advantages and disadvantages of mandatory arbitration and the client has given voluntary consent to such an arbitration clause. ABA Comm. on Prof'l Ethics and Grievances, Formal Op. 02–425 (2002).

5. Attorneys must be careful to separate their role as an ADR intermediary from their duties to individual clients. Model Rule of Professional Conduct 1.12(a) provides that a lawyer generally "shall not represent anyone in connection with a matter in which the lawyer participated personally and substantially as a judge or other adjudicative officer, arbitrator or law clerk to such a person, unless all parties to the proceeding consent after disclosure." Why might one or both of the parties to a dispute want an attorney to continue representation after a failed attempt at mediation? What problems can arise due to continuing representation? Should waiver be permitted in these situations? *See Barbour v. Barbour*, 146 Vt. 506, 511–12, 505 A.2d 1217, 1220–21 (1986); Tex. Eth. Op. 583, 2008 WL 4897790 (Tex. Prof. Eth. Comm. 2008) (lawyer cannot enter into agreement to mediate divorce settlement between unrepresented parties and prepare settlement documents to effectuate mediated settlement). *See also* Sato, Comment, "The Mediator–Lawyer: Implications for the Practice of Law and One Argument for Professional Responsibility Guidance—A Proposal for Ethical Considerations," 34 *UCLA L. Rev.* 507 (1986); Purnell, Comment, "The Attorney as Mediator—Inherent Conflict of Interest," 32 *UCLA L. Rev.* 986 (1985).

6. Alternative dispute resolution may present many other ethical issues for attorneys. *See* Symposium, *Ethics in the Expanding World of ADR: Considerations, Conundrums, and Conflicts*, 49 *S. Tex. L. Rev.* 787 (2008); Symposium, *ADR and the Professional Responsibility of Lawyers*, 28 *Fordham Urban L. J.* 887 (2001); Symposium, *The Lawyer's Duties and Responsibilities in Dispute Resolution*, 38 *S. Tex. L. Rev.* 375 (1997). Indeed, attorneys increasingly may be faced with new issues as states recommend or require that attorneys advise their clients about ADR possibilities in matters likely to result in litigation. *E.g.*, Colorado Rules of Professional Conduct Rule 2.1; Georgia Aspirational Statements on Professionalism (Specific Aspirational Ideals as to Clients). *See also* Breger, "Should an Attorney be Required to Advise a Client of ADR Options?," 13 *Geo. J. Legal Ethics* 427 (2000); Cochran, "ADR, the ABA, and Client Control: A Proposal that the Model Rules Require Lawyers to Present ADR Options to Clients," 41 *S. Tex. L. Rev.* 183 (1999).

7. In recent years attorneys have developed collaborative law and cooperative law practice models. In a collaborative law agreement the parties and their attorneys establish a negotiation process and agree to use that process in a good faith attempt to settle the parties' dispute. This agreement, however, contains a provision that, in the event that settlement is not achieved, the lawyers will be disqualified from party representation in the ensuing litigation. Cooperative law agreements also are used in an effort to achieve the settlement of disputes before the filing of litigation. In contrast to collaborative law agreements, though, cooperative law agreements do not disqualify the lawyers from representing their clients if settlement is not reached and the dispute enters the litigation process. *See* Lande, "Practical Insights From an Empirical Study of Cooperative Lawyers in Wisconsin," 2008 *J. Disp. Resol.* 203, 204–205.

The Colorado Bar Association Ethics Committee has concluded that the disqualification clause of collaborative law agreements, by establishing a duty of withdrawal owed to the opposing party, creates a conflict of interest under

Rule 1.7(b) of the Colorado Rules of Professional Conduct to which a client cannot consent. Colo. Bar Ass'n, Formal Eth. Op. 115 (2007). However, a later ABA Formal Ethics Opinion concluded that the disqualification clause of a collaborative law agreement did not create a conflict of interest that a party could not waive but, with informed client consent, was a limited scope agreement valid under Rule 1.2(c) of the Model Rules of Professional Conduct. ABA Comm. on Ethics and Prof'l Responsibility, Formal Op. 07–447 (2007).

8. In addition to considering methods of alternative dispute resolution, counsel should attempt to prevent disputes from ever arising. Future disputes often can be prevented by careful and unambiguous drafting of documents and by planning for future client contingencies. Attorneys can include clauses in contracts, settlement agreements, and other documents providing that any disputes will be resolved by a specific ADR technique. The old adage "An ounce of prevention is worth a pound of cure" is as applicable to the law as to other areas of life. *See generally* L. Brown & E. Dauer, *Planning by Lawyers* (1978).

9. Consider the implications of the following story for the manner in which attorney conduct may encourage or discourage litigation.

> I gave my contracts students a hypothetical. *Seller* is continually late in making his deliveries. *Buyer*, after pleas and much patience, finally cancels the contract. After stating the problem, I asked:
>
> "If you were *Seller*, what would you say?"
>
> I was looking for a discussion of the various legal theories that throw *Buyer* into breach for cancelling the contract, legal arguments that would allow *Seller* to crush *Buyer*.
>
> I looked around the room. As is so often the case with first-year students, they were all inspecting their shoes. There was, however, one eager face: that of the eight-year-old son of one of my students. He had been biding his time, drawing pictures. Suddenly he raised his hand. Such behavior, even from an eight-year old, must be rewarded.
>
> "Okay," I said, "What would you say if you were *Seller*?"
>
> "I'd say 'I'm sorry'."

K. Hegland, *Introduction To The Study And Practice Of Law In A Nutshell* 358–59 (5th Ed. 2008).

> What if the Pittston Company had said "I'm sorry" immediately after the Buffalo Creek disaster? *See* Cohen, "Advising Clients to Apologize," 72 *S. Cal. L. Rev.* 1009 (1999). *But see* Taft, "Apology Subverted: The Commodification of Apology," 109 *Yale L. J.* 1135 (2000).

A Veterans Administration hospital that adopted a policy of revealing malpractice, apologizing in a face-to-face meeting with the patient and family, and offering compensation for actual loss found that its liability payments under this policy were quite moderate. Kramman & Hamm, "Risk Management: Extreme Honesty May Be the Best Policy," 131 *Annals of Internal Medicine* 963 (1999). *See also* Robbennolt, "Attorneys, Apologies, and Settlement Negotiation," 13 *Harv. Neg. Rev.* 349 (2008); Robbennolt, "Apologies and Legal Settlement: An Empirical Examination," 102 *Mich. L. Rev.* 460

(2003); Zemil, "ABA Resolves to Protect Apologies of Health Care Providers," 32 *Litigation News* No. 6, at 3 (Sept. 2007) (ABA House of Delegates adopts resolution encouraging states to amend evidentiary rules to exclude apologies of health care providers). *See generally* "Symposium: The Role of Forgiveness in the Law," 27 *Fordham Urban L. J.* 1347 (2000).

10. After the 1985 crash of a Delta Air Lines plane on which 137 people died, Delta's insurers immediately sought ways in which to comfort the families of those who had died in the crash. Delta employees visited with families, helped with medical, funeral and other expenses, and, in at least one case, sent the sister of a crash victim flowers on her birthday and attended a family funeral. As a result of these efforts, significantly fewer claims were filed than in comparable airline crashes.

Those individuals who did sue Delta encountered "hardball" defense litigation tactics. In the resulting trials, Delta's attorneys attempted to bring out the fact that one of the crash victims was gay, another had been having an extramarital affair, and the wife of a third victim had had an abortion and had used cocaine. At least some of this information had been gained by Delta's insurers in the initial efforts to comfort the families of the deceased. Bean, "Damage Control," *Wall St. J.,* Nov. 7, 1986, at A1.

11. Rather than submit their business dispute to the courts, two aviation executives decided to resolve the matter (concerning the use of an advertising slogan) in an arm wrestling match. The parties not only saved the costs that formal litigation would have entailed, but gained favorable nationwide publicity from the media accounts of the arm wrestling. Ramstad, "Bosses Arm Wrestle to Settle Fuss," *Knoxville News–Sentinel*, Mar. 21, 1992, at C6.

12. A burgeoning area of ADR in recent years is ODR—online dispute resolution. This can take the form of assisted negotiation (with software that visually shows the specific proposals requested by each party, the reasons for these proposals, and the status of the proposals), automated negotiation (in which a computer attempts to settle disputes by determining whether the parties' offers and demands overlap or are reasonably close), online mediation (with the mediation being conducted on-line), or online arbitration (in which arbitration is conducted electronically rather than in person). *See generally* G. Kaufmann–Kohler & T. Schultz, *Online Dispute Resolution: Challenges for Contemporary Justice* (2004); E. Katsh & J. Rifkin, *Online Dispute Resolution: Resolving Conflicts in Cyberspace* (2001); Krause, "Settling It On the Web," *A.B.A.J.*, Oct. 2007, at 42.

13. In 2001 the Michigan Legislature enacted legislation to create the nation's first "cybercourt." When funded, the court would have had concurrent jurisdiction over business and commercial actions with more than $25,000 in controversy. Because hearings and trials would have been held electronically, attorneys would not have had to travel to court nor would both local and national counsel have needed to be present for court proceedings. Ponte, "The Michigan Cyber Court: A Bold Experiment in the Development of the First Public Virtual Courthouse," 4 *N.C. J. L. & Tech.* 51 (2002); Drummond, "Michigan Legislation Creates First Virtual Courtroom," *Litigation News*, March 2002, at 6. However, this court did not begin operations

because it was not funded by the Michigan Legislature. Pappas, "ONLINE COURT: Online Dispute Resolution and the Future of Small Claims," 12 *UCLA J. L. & Technology* (www.lawtechjournal.com) 10–11 (2008).

Exercises Concerning Alternatives to Litigation

1.   Reconsider the litigation plan that was developed in either of the first two Exercises Concerning Litigation Planning in Chapter 3, *supra,* p. 65. Did that plan consider the possibility of *non*-litigative dispute resolution techniques? Write a memorandum discussing why you did, or did not, consider alternatives to formal adjudication in your earlier litigation plan.

2.   It is March 1972 and your law firm has just been retained by victims of the Buffalo Creek flood to institute a civil action against the Pittston Company. Write a memorandum to your senior partner concerning the appropriateness of submitting your new clients' claims to alternative dispute resolution. In your memorandum consider the advantages and disadvantages of applying particular ADR techniques to resolve the claims of the Buffalo Creek claimants.

3.   It is March 1972 and your law firm represents the Pittston Company and the Buffalo Mining Company. Write a memorandum to your senior partner concerning the possibility of applying alternative dispute resolution techniques to the expected claims that will result from the Buffalo Creek dam failure.

4.   Either as counsel for the victims of the Buffalo Creek dam collapse or as counsel for the Buffalo Mining Company and the Pittston Company, write a letter to your clients suggesting that they consider submission of the disputes stemming from the Buffalo Creek disaster to alternative dispute resolution.

5.   Either as counsel for the victims of the Buffalo Creek dam collapse or as counsel for the Buffalo Mining Company and the Pittston Company, write a letter to opposing counsel attempting to interest that attorney in using alternative dispute resolution techniques to resolve the claims resulting from the Buffalo Creek disaster.

6.   You have been asked by the partners in your law firm to consider whether your firm should begin offering ADR services. Write a memorandum containing your response. You may make any reasonable factual assumptions in your memorandum, but be sure to consider whom you would talk with in formulating your advice, what information you would need, and what specific ADR mechanisms you would consider providing. Your memorandum should address the manner in which ADR services should be marketed, any problems with such marketing, possible conflicts of interest or other problems that might be created by offering ADR services, and whether non-attorneys should be used in connection with these services.

7.   Your law firm provides alternative dispute resolution services and you have been consulted concerning possible ADR techniques that might

be adopted to resolve the following disputes. Write a letter to the parties to each of the disputes recommending whether ADR should be considered in connection with the disputes. If you recommend an ADR mechanism, specify how that mechanism should be designed, considering such matters as whether the procedure should be public or private, whether attorneys should participate in the proceedings, what discovery should be permitted, who will pay for the proceedings, and how any third-party neutral should be selected.

(a) A dispute has arisen among the insurers of a corporation that has been named as a defendant in a series of major products liability actions; the dispute concerns the relative responsibilities of the insurers to defend the corporation and to cover any recovery eventually obtained by the plaintiffs;

(b) A dispute has arisen between local, state, and federal authorities concerning responsibility for the clean-up of a community that has been struck by a major natural disaster and the amount of governmental funds that will be provided to rebuild public and private structures in that community;

(c) A dispute has arisen between a chemical company and the residents of a community in which it has a major manufacturing facility concerning the siting and design of chemical storage facilities;

(d) A dispute has arisen between a local textile mill and its non-union employees concerning wages, salaries, and other terms and conditions of employment;

(e) A dispute has arisen between the unionized employees of a local automobile parts supplier and that company concerning the handling of employee grievances related to plant working conditions;

(f) A dispute has arisen among the plaintiffs in a major class action lawsuit concerning the proper apportionment of any recovery that plaintiffs may receive at trial or in settlement of their action.

III. ALTERNATIVE MEANS OF RESOLVING LITIGATION

Attention in recent years not only has focused on alternatives to the filing of civil litigation, but on judicial management techniques to resolve such litigation once a civil complaint has been filed.[27] States have enacted alternative dispute resolution statutes, giving state courts the explicit authority to employ non-adjudicatory techniques to resolve civil litigation.[28] A widespread movement to ADR within the federal courts was

---

27. *See, e.g.,* Comm. on Court Admin. & Case Mgt., Judicial Conference of the United States, *Civil Litigation Management* (2001); CPR Legal Program, *ADR and the Courts: A Manual for Judges and Lawyers* (E. Fine & E. Plapinger eds. 1987); R. Niemic et al., *Guide to Judicial Management of Cases in ADR* (Federal Judicial Center 2001); D. Steelman, *Improving Caseflow Management: A Brief Guide* (Nat'l Ctr. for State Cts. 2008).

28. *E.g.,* Tex. Civ. Prac. & Rem. Code Ann. §§ 151.001–173.004 (Vernon 2005 & Supp. 2006); Fla. Stat. Ann. §§ 44.1011–44.406 (West 2003 and Supp. 2007).

sparked by the Civil Justice Reform Act of 1990, which required every federal district court to consider authorizing the reference of appropriate cases to alternative dispute resolution programs.[29]

More recently, Congress provided in the Alternative Dispute Resolution Act of 1998: "Each United States district court shall devise and implement its own alternative dispute resolution program, by local rule adopted under [the Act], to encourage and promote the use of alternative dispute resolution in its district."[30] Alternative dispute resolution is defined in this Act as "any process or procedure, other than an adjudication by a presiding judge, in which a neutral third party participates to assist in the resolution of issues in controversy, through processes such as early neutral evaluation, mediation, minitrial, and arbitration * * * ."[31] Each district court is to "provide litigants in all civil cases with at least one alternative dispute resolution process," although districts that elect to require the use of alternative dispute resolution in certain cases "may do so only with respect to mediation, early neutral evaluation, and, if the parties consent, arbitration."[32]

Many of the ADR techniques recently adopted by state and federal courts are quite similar to those employed outside the judicial process, while others are unique to the federal and state court systems. All of these court-annexed ADR techniques, however, attempt to build upon the strengths of the judicial process while simultaneously providing a more efficient dispute resolution mechanism than that provided by traditional adversarial litigation.[33]

Within the confines of traditional civil litigation, there are many opportunities for judges to attempt to resolve disputes. Pretrial conferences held pursuant to Rule 16 of the Federal Rules of Civil Procedure are used by many judges to discuss and promote settlement. Rule 16(c)(2)(I) provides that one of the subjects that may be considered at pretrial conferences is "settling the case and using special procedures to assist in resolving the dispute when authorized by statute or local rule." As seen in Chapter 14, judges also can appoint magistrate judges or masters to facilitate settlement.[34] This section of the present chapter deals with other, alternative means of resolving civil litigation.

---

29.   28 U.S.C. § 473(a)(6) (expired Dec. 1, 1997).

30.   28 U.S.C. § 651(b). Pursuant to the Civil Justice Reform Act of 1990, P. L. No. 101–650, 104 Stat. 5089 (1990), the great majority of federal district courts had established alternative dispute resolution programs prior to the Alternative Dispute Resolution Act of 1998. E. Plapinger & D. Stienstra, *ADR and Settlement in the Federal District Courts* (1996) (describing ADR programs in individual federal district courts).

31.   28 U.S.C. § 651(a).

32.   28 U.S.C. § 652(a).

33.   For an analysis of court-connected ADR programs by a national leader in the development of such programs see Brazil, "Comparing Structures for the Delivery of ADR Services by Courts: Critical Values and Concerns," 14 *Ohio St. J. Disp. Resol.* 715 (1999). *See also* Brazil, "Court ADR 25 Years After Pound: Have We Found a Better Way?," 18 *Ohio St. J. Disp. Resol.* 93 (2002).

34.   Chapter 14, Section V, *supra*, p. 617. *See also* Fed. R. Civ. P. 16(c)(2)(H); "The Role of Special Masters in the Judicial System," 31 *Wm. Mitchell L. Rev.* 1193 (2005). Federal Rule of

A. COURT–ANNEXED ARBITRATION

One major dispute resolution technique that many courts recently have employed is arbitration. This "court-annexed arbitration" is distinguishable from traditional arbitration due to the manner in which the arbitration is initiated. Traditionally, arbitration is invoked by the parties to a dispute, often under the terms of a collective bargaining or other agreement. Court-annexed arbitration, in contrast, has been established as an alternative to, or prerequisite for, judicial consideration of certain types of cases in some courts. The rationales for court-annexed arbitration are that cases resolved by arbitration will not have to be adjudicated by the courts and that the parties will be spared at least some of the expense otherwise incurred in discovery, pretrial and trial.

Federal district courts have experimented with court-annexed arbitration for many years. Most recently, in the Alternative Dispute Resolution Act of 1998,[35] Congress provided all federal district courts with the authority to permit the referral of certain cases to arbitration with the parties' consent.[36] Several states also have established court-annexed arbitration programs.[37]

Once a case has been referred to court-annexed arbitration, the procedure is basically the same as for any other arbitration. Because arbitration procedures are less formal than those applicable to judicial actions, disputes often can be resolved more quickly and less expensively by arbitration.[38] If, however, one or more of the parties do not agree with the arbitration award, they can request a judicial trial. At least some court-annexed arbitration systems provide that if the party who refuses to accept the arbitration award does not obtain a significantly more favorable

---

Civil Procedure 16(c)(2)(L) provides that a possible subject for consideration at pretrial conferences is "adopting special procedures for managing potentially difficult or protracted actions that may involve complex issues, multiple parties, difficult legal questions, or unusual proof problems."

35. Pub. L. 105–315, 112 Stat. 2993 (1998).

36. 28 U.S.C. § 654. This Act precludes the referral to arbitration, even with the parties' consent, of civil rights actions, cases asserting constitutional violations, and actions seeking more than $150,000 in damages. 28 U.S.C. § 654(a). However, the 1988 Judicial Improvements and Access to Justice Act permitted a limited number of federal judicial districts to require arbitration of certain damage claims pursuant to local rules of court, Pub. L. 100–702, Sec. 901, 102 Stat. 4642, 4659 (1988), and these existing mandatory arbitration programs were permitted to continue under the 1998 Act. 28 U.S.C. § 654(d).

37. *E.g.,* Cal. Civ. Pro. Code §§ 1141.10–1141.32 (West 1982 & Supp. 2006); Del. Super. Ct. R. 16.1. *See generally* P. Ebener & D. Betancourt, *Court–Annexed Arbitration: The National Picture* (1985). Some states also have established medical malpractice screening panels, to which medical malpractice actions must be presented before resort to state courts. *E.g.,* Md. Cts. & Jud. Proc. Code Ann. §§ 3–2A–01—3–2A–10 (Michie 2006); Alaska Stat. § 09.55.536 (2006).

38. There is evidence suggesting that court-annexed arbitrations may facilitate settlement because of the faster hearing dates that these arbitrations impose upon the parties. E. Lind & J. Shapard, *Evaluation of Court–Annexed Arbitration in Three Federal District Courts* 78–83 (rev. ed. 1983); B. Meierhoefer, *Court–Annexed Arbitration in Ten District Courts* 103 (1990). *See also* T. Willging, *Trends in Asbestos Litigation* 71 (1987) (finding that not only ADR procedures but also the scheduling of firm trial dates produces settlements).

outcome at trial, he is liable for specified costs of the arbitration, the trial, or both.[39]

While court-annexed arbitration may not be appropriate for all claims or all parties, initial studies suggest that litigants and counsel have been favorably impressed with this process.[40] Depending upon the success of the many recent court-annexed arbitration programs, such arbitration may become an increasingly common means of resolving civil litigation.

B. SUMMARY JURY TRIALS AND MINI-TRIALS

Two other promising means for resolving civil litigation are the summary jury trial and the judicial mini-trial. Although both of these devices are referred to as "trials," they are not trials in the traditional sense. Instead, summary jury trials and mini-trials are judicial proceedings whose purpose is to facilitate the private settlement of civil actions.

The summary jury trial was pioneered by Judge Thomas Lambros of the United States District Court for the Northern District of Ohio.[41] Under the procedure developed by Judge Lambros, selected cases are set for summary trials before individuals chosen from the court's existing jury pool. Rather than calling witnesses to testify, the attorneys are given limited amounts of time (usually one-half to one day) in which to themselves summarize anticipated trial testimony.

In order to focus the attorneys' presentations, trial briefs and proposed jury instructions typically are required. Some judges permit the jurors to question the attorneys about the case during or after the attorney presentations. At the conclusion of this summary testimony and argument, the jury renders an advisory verdict, after which there may be the opportunity for informal discussions between jurors and attorneys.

The rationale for summary jury trials is that the evaluation of a case by a representative group of jurors will narrow the uncertainty concerning how an actual jury would decide the case. Having received the advisory jury's verdict, attorneys and their clients realistically can evaluate the case and, having done so, settle the lawsuit. The advisory jury's "verdict" therefore becomes the starting point for settlement negotiations. The attorneys and their clients (who are required to attend the summary jury trial) may decide to settle an action after they have witnessed the

---

39. *E.g.,* Cal. Civ. Proc. Code § 1141.21 (West Supp. 2006).

40. B. Meierhoefer, *Court–Annexed Arbitration in Ten District Courts* 63–83 (1990); A. Lind et al., *The Perception of Justice: Tort Litigants' Views of Trial, Court–Annexed Arbitration, and Judicial Settlement Conferences* (1989); A. Lind & J. Shapard, *Evaluation of Court–Annexed Arbitration in Three Federal District Courts* 56–69 (rev. ed. 1983); Simoni et al., "Litigant and Attorney Attitudes Toward Court–Annexed Arbitration: An Empirical Study," 28 *Santa Clara L. Rev.* 543 (1988). *But see* J. Thibaut & L. Walker, *Procedural Justice, A Psychological Analysis* 72–80; 87–96 (1975) (finding a preference among litigants for adversarial dispute resolution).

41. *See* Lambros, "The Summary Jury Trial—An Alternative Method of Resolving Disputes," 69 *Judicature* 286 (1986); Lambros, "The Summary Jury Trial and Other Alternative Methods of Dispute Resolution," 103 F.R.D. 461 (1984); Lambros & Shunk, "The Summary Jury Trial," 29 *Clev. St. L. Rev.* 43 (1980). *See also* M. Jacoubovitch & C. Moore, *Summary Jury Trials in the Northern District of Ohio* (1982).

strengths of their opponent's case and any difficulties in their own case presentation.[42]

A federal district judge has noted another advantage of summary jury trials:

> [T]he summary jury trial gives the parties a taste of the courtroom and satisfies their psychological need for a confrontation with each other. * * * When emotions run high, whether between parties or attorneys, cases may not settle even when a cost-benefit analysis says they should. A summary jury trial can provide a therapeutic release of this emotion at the expenditure of three days of the court's time instead of three weeks.[43]

Several federal district courts have relied upon their inherent powers to manage their dockets and Rule 16 of the Federal Rules of Civil Procedure in ordering summary jury trials.[44] Policy questions, however, have been raised about using the federal judicial system to conscript "private juries" to render advisory verdicts and whether, and when, jurors should be told that they have not been called to hear a "real" trial.[45]

The summary jury trial presents the same tactical issue to counsel that is typically posed by other settlement devices: How much information about one's case should be revealed to opposing parties? A party's ultimate

---

42. Judge Lambros calculated that over 90% of the cases set for summary jury trial in the Northern District of Ohio settled, at a savings in juror costs of approximately $1500 per case. Lambros, "The Summary Jury Trial and Other Alternative Methods of Dispute Resolution," 103 F.R.D. 461, 472–74 (1984). Based on a study of summary jury trials in the North Carolina state courts, Professor Thomas Metzloff has recommended that parties be permitted to consent to binding, rather than merely advisory, summary jury trials. Metzloff, "Reconfiguring the Summary Jury Trial," 41 *Duke L. J.* 806 (1992).

43. *McKay v. Ashland Oil, Inc.,* 120 F.R.D. 43, 50 (E.D.Ky. 1988) (Bertelsman, J.).

44. *Federal Reserve Bank v. Carey–Canada, Inc.,* 123 F.R.D. 603 (D.Minn. 1988); *McKay v. Ashland Oil, Inc.,* 120 F.R.D. 43 (E.D.Ky. 1988); *Arabian Am. Oil Co. v. Scarfone,* 119 F.R.D. 448 (M.D.Fla. 1988). *See also Home Owners Funding Corp. of Am. v. Century Bank,* 695 F.Supp. 1343, 1347 n.3 (D.Mass. 1988).

However, two federal courts of appeal have held that district courts do not have the power to mandate participation in summary jury trials. *In re NLO, Inc.,* 5 F.3d 154, 156–58 (6th Cir. 1993); *Strandell v. Jackson County,* 838 F.2d 884 (7th Cir. 1987). These cases, though, were decided prior to the 1993 amendment to Rule 16(c)(9) (now Rule 16(c)(2)(I)) authorizing pretrial consideration of "special procedures to assist in resolving the dispute when authorized by statute or local rule." *Ohio v. Louis Trauth Dairy, Inc.,* 164 F.R.D. 469, 470 (S.D.Ohio 1996). *See* Woodley, "Saving the Summary Jury Trial: A Proposal to Halt the Flow of Litigation and End the Uncertainties," 1995 *J. Disp. Resol.* 213, 234–64 (1995); Ponte, "Putting Mandatory Summary Jury Trial Back on the Docket: Recommendations on the Exercise of Judicial Authority," 63 *Fordham L. Rev.* 1069, 1092–94 (1995). *See also In re Atlantic Pipe Corp.,* 304 F.3d 135 (1st Cir. 2002) (district court had inherent power to order mandatory mediation, so long as court sets reasonable limits on duration of mediation and mediator's fees). *But see* 28 U.S.C. § 652(a) ("Any district court that elects to require the use of alternative dispute resolution in certain cases may do so only with respect to mediation, early neutral evaluation, and, if the parties consent, arbitration.").

45. Posner, "The Summary Jury Trial and Other Methods of Alternative Dispute Resolution: Some Cautionary Observations," 53 *U. Chi. L. Rev.* 366 (1986). One federal district judge has held that there is no statutory authority for requiring jurors to hear summary jury trials. *Hume v. M & C Management,* 129 F.R.D. 506 (N.D.Ohio 1990). *See also* Posner, *supra,* at 385–86; Woodley, *supra* note 44; Maatman, "The Future of Summary Jury Trials in Federal Courts: *Strandell v. Jackson County,*" 21 *J. Marshall L. Rev.* 455 (1988); Wiegand, "A New Light Bulb or the Work of the Devil? A Current Assessment of Summary Jury Trials," 69 *Or. L. Rev.* 87 (1990).

position at trial may be weakened if it presents all of its most powerful evidence during a summary jury trial and a settlement is not forthcoming. On the other hand, the chances of a favorable settlement can be greatly enhanced by a favorable summary jury verdict. Furthermore, summary jury trials are held after discovery is complete and the case is otherwise ready for trial. If the case has been thoroughly pretried, there should be few significant matters about which all attorneys are not aware.

Related to the summary jury trial is the judicial mini-trial.[46] As at summary jury trials, a truncated version of the facts is presented during the mini-trial. Typically these facts are presented by way of attorney statements and arguments and summary testimony by experts and other key witnesses. Experts also may be permitted to question one another directly, and the rules of evidence usually are relaxed.

In contrast to summary jury trials, which are presented to a judge and jury, mini-trials usually are presented to a private, neutral person outside the judicial process. In many cases, this neutral person is not to issue a judgment in the first instance, but merely presides over the presentation of evidence and argument. The parties are all required to attend the mini-trial and thereby are exposed to the expected proof at trial. Having heard a detailed preview of the other parties' evidence, clients are presumably more ready to talk seriously, and concretely, about settlement.

If settlement cannot be reached based upon the presentation of the parties' summary evidence, they may ask the presiding neutral to render a non-binding decision that will serve as a basis for further party negotiation. Whether or not an opinion is offered, the hope is to achieve a settlement that will preserve existing relationships between the parties. Such a settlement may be suggested by the business executives who attend the mini-trial as party representatives, and it need not be limited to the remedies from which a court must choose.

Some federal judges themselves have presided over mini-trials. In a judicial mini-trial held before Judge Robert Keeton of the United States District Court for the District of Massachusetts, the parties stipulated that if the mini-trial did not result in a settlement each side would offer a proposal as to the terms upon which the case should be resolved. Judge Keeton then would choose the proposal that he believed represented the best resolution of the case.[47]

Both summary jury trials and mini-trials are best suited to lengthy cases, rather than cases that can be fully tried in a few days. Cases must be quite carefully selected for summary jury trial or mini-trial treatment,

---

46. See E. Green, *The CPR Legal Program Mini–Trial Handbook* (1982), *in* Center for Public Resources, *Corporate Dispute Management 1982* (1982); E. Fine, *CPR Legal Program Mini–Trial Workbook* (1985); Henderson, "Avoiding Litigation with the Mini–Trial: The Corporate Bottom Line as a Dispute Resolution Technique," 46 *S.C. L. Rev.* 237 (1995); Fox, "Mini–Trials," *Litigation*, Summer 1993, at 36; Green et al., "Settling Large Case Litigation: An Alternate Approach," 11 *Loy. L.A. L. Rev.* 493 (1978).

47. D. Provine, *Settlement Strategies for Federal District Judges* 78 (1986). *See also* Rule 16.7 of the United States District Court for the Western District of Michigan (providing for summary jury trials and summary bench trials).

for additional resources will be expended, rather than conserved, if substantial numbers of the cases selected for summary jury trials and mini-trials ultimately are fully tried.

These techniques are not well-suited to cases that require major credibility determinations (unless key witnesses can be presented live or on videotape) or to cases with pending issues or motions. In both situations, the outcome of the summary jury trial or mini-trial might be a poor predictor of the likely judgment after a full trial. The confidentiality of summary jury trials and mini-trials also can be crucial to their success. Party participants may need the assurance that the statements made and evidence offered in these proceedings cannot be directly used by other parties at a later trial or for other purposes.[48]

The exact contours of summary jury trial and mini-trial procedures vary from district to district and from judge to judge. For example, Judge William K. Thomas of the United States District Court for the Northern District of Ohio successfully settled cases by requiring the presentation of opening statements, in the courtroom and in front of the parties, at Rule 16 pretrial conferences. In the right cases, many other judges successfully have used summary jury trials and mini-trials, or variants of those devices, to resolve major cases.[49] There is an increasing interest in these devices from judges, attorneys, and clients alike. Continued experimentation with the summary jury trial and the judicial mini-trial can be expected.

C. JUDICIAL MEDIATION AND SETTLEMENT FACILITATION

The summary jury trial and judicial mini-trial are two of the more promising devices that recently have been employed to settle civil cases. Many other settlement devices have been utilized, however, some of which now will be considered.

The local rules of many federal district courts provide for court-annexed mediation of certain civil cases.[50] Such mediation is often quite

---

48. The United States Court of Appeals for the Sixth Circuit has held that summary jury trials are not proceedings to which a first amendment right of access attaches and that such trials can be closed to the public. *Cincinnati Gas & Elec. Co. v. General Elec. Co.,* 854 F.2d 900 (6th Cir. 1988), *cert. denied,* 489 U.S. 1033 (1989).

49. While most commonly used with major cases, variants of summary jury trials and mini-trials have been utilized with other cases as well. With party consent, "short trials" are heard in a Nevada trial court, with parties given no more than three hours to present their cases. A local lawyer presides over these cases, which are heard by a four-person jury that resolves the case by a majority vote. Sternlight, "Separate and Not Equal: Integrating Civil Procedure and ADR in Legal Academia," 80 *Notre Dame L. Rev.* 681, 720–21 (2005).

50. *E.g.,* Rule 16.2(c)(2)(b) of the United States District Court for the Eastern District of Washington; Rules 9.01–9.07 of the United States District Court for the Middle District of Florida; Rule 16.3 of the United States District Court for the Eastern District of Michigan. *See also Rhea v. Massey–Ferguson, Inc.,* 767 F.2d 266 (6th Cir.1985) (per curiam) (upholding mandatory court-annexed mediation in the Eastern District of Michigan).

similar to the mediation in which disputants may engage outside the litigation process. It may be conducted by the same individuals who handle non-litigation related mediation or by attorney-mediators certified by the court. The local rules of one federal district court suggest the type of individual best-suited to act as a mediator: "The mediator is an attorney, certified by the chief judge in accordance with these rules, who possesses the unique skills required to facilitate the mediation process including the ability to suggest alternatives, analyze issues, question perceptions, use logic, conduct private caucuses, stimulate negotiations between opposing sides and keep order."[51]

Judicial settlement activity may paint the judge, himself, in the role of mediator. Many of the potential advantages and disadvantages of judicial mediation are illustrated by the description in the previous chapter of Judge Jack Weinstein's efforts to settle the Agent Orange litigation.[52] Some of the potential problems with judicial involvement in settlement may be avoided if the judge presiding over the settlement discussions is not the judge who will try the case if no settlement is reached.

Judges have been very creative in utilizing other devices to resolve civil litigation short of trial. For instance, Rule 706 of the Federal Rules of Evidence permits district judges to appoint expert witnesses. The appointment of a neutral expert may not only help a judge master complex statistical or technical issues but may force the parties to reevaluate their litigation positions, perhaps question their own experts, and reach a voluntary settlement.[53]

Since 1985 the United States District Court for the Northern District of California has had an "Early Neutral Evaluation" program. Under this program, the court can order the parties in certain civil cases to attend a confidential review session at which a private attorney with relevant

---

Some states also provide for mandatory mediation, either across-the-board or in specific types of cases such as those involving child custody determinations. *E.g.*, Cal. Fam. Code § 3170 (West 2004).

51. Rule 9.01(a) of the United States District Court for the Middle District of Florida.

52. Chapter 14, *supra* p. 619. *See also* Galanter, "The Emergence of the Judge as a Mediator in Civil Cases," 69 *Judicature* 257 (1986).

As did Judge Weinstein in the *Agent Orange* litigation, judges can use special masters to mediate disputes and help facilitate settlement under Federal Rule of Civil Procedure 53 or comparable state rules. *See generally* Tractenberg, "Court–Appointed Mediators or Special Masters: A Commentary," 12 *Seton Hall Legis. J.* 81 (1988). Under certain circumstances, cases can be heard by a master or magistrate judge, whose findings are subject to district court review. Fed. R. Civ. P. 53; 28 U.S.C. § 636(b). In addition, the parties may consent to the trial of an action by a federal magistrate judge, with a right of appeal to the court of appeals. 28 U.S.C. § 636(c).

53. *See, e.g., San Francisco NAACP v. San Francisco Unified School Dist.*, 576 F.Supp. 34, 39–40 (N.D.Cal. 1983) ("settlement team" of educational experts designated by parties and appointed by the court to attempt to fashion settlement in school desegregation case); *Ohio Pub. Interest Campaign v. Fisher Foods, Inc.*, 546 F.Supp. 1, 4 (N.D.Ohio 1982) (expert appointed by court to facilitate settlement of antitrust class actions); *In re Swine Flu Immunization Prod. Liab. Litig.*, 495 F.Supp. 1185 (W.D.Okla. 1980) (panel of medical experts appointed to examine each plaintiff and report to court and counsel). *See generally* T. Willging, *Court–Appointed Experts* (1986); Thorpe et al., "Court–Appointed Experts and Technical Advisors," *Litigation*, Summer 2000, at 31.

subject matter expertise provides a neutral evaluation of that particular case. The evaluation comes at the very early stages of a case, in an effort to force the parties to confront the merits of their cases, help them plan further pretrial proceedings, and facilitate settlement before substantial resources have been devoted to discovery or motion practice.[54]

Both bar associations and courts have successfully sponsored "settlement weeks," during which various alternative dispute resolution techniques are used to attempt to reduce judicial dockets. During these periods, settlement efforts often are targeted at older cases on the docket and settlements are facilitated by experienced attorneys who meet with opposing parties and counsel.

Counsel should consider requesting a conference with the court to discuss the possible resolution of an action by ADR techniques.[55] In some federal district courts, the judge, on his own initiative, may order that counsel, and perhaps their clients, participate in a mandatory settlement conference.[56] In addition, several courts and judges have experimented with "fast track" procedures to expedite the judicial resolution of civil cases.[57]

Many judges believe that one of their duties is to attempt to resolve cases by party settlement. The ingenuity of these judges, utilizing their inherent judicial powers and the powers given them by governing rules and statutes, undoubtedly will result in still more devices to facilitate the settlement of civil litigation in the years to come.

Exercises Concerning Alternative Means of Resolving Litigation

1. You are the law clerk to Judge K. K. Hall, who has been assigned the litigation brought on behalf of approximately 600 victims of the Buffalo Creek disaster. It is the fall of 1972, and the judge has scheduled an initial status conference with counsel in this case in two weeks. In anticipation of this conference, Judge Hall has asked you to write a memorandum discussing possible alternative means of resolving the Buf-

---

54. *See* Levine, "Early Neutral Evaluation: The Second Phase," 1989 *J. Disp. Resol.* 1; Levine, "Early Neutral Evaluation: A Follow–Up Report," 70 *Judicature* 236 (1987); Brazil et al., "Early Neutral Evaluation: An Experimental Effort to Expedite Dispute Resolution," 69 *Judicature* 279 (1986). Early Neutral Evaluation also has been utilized by the United States District Court for the District of Columbia, "ADR in D.C. Circuit Shows Promise," *The Third Branch*, March 1990, at 1, and all district courts are authorized to adopt this procedure under the Alternative Dispute Resolution Act of 1998, 28 U.S.C. § 651(a).

55. *See* Fed. R. Civ. P. 16(c)(2)(I), (L), (P).

56. *E.g.,* Rule 16.3 of the United States District Court for the Southern District of California; Rule 16(c) of the United States District Court for the District of Connecticut.

57. *E.g.,* Kaufman, "Fast–Track Courts with Part–Time Judges," *Litigation*, Fall 1982, at 31; Horner, "Trials in the Fast Lane—Is the Length of Trial Affected by 'Fast Track' in San Diego?," 2 *J. Contemp. Legal Issues* 89 (1989); McKelson, "Fast Track: Are We on the Right Track?," 2 *J. Contemp. Legal Issues* 229 (1989). *See also* McMillan & Siegel, "Creating a Fast–Track Alternative Under the Federal Rules of Civil Procedure," 60 *Notre Dame L. Rev.* 431 (1985).

State small claims courts have been used for some time to resolve relatively small disputes in a less expensive and more expeditious fashion than otherwise would be possible.

falo Creek litigation. Judge Hall ideally would like to convince the parties to engage voluntarily in ADR, so your memorandum should discuss not only the fairness and effectiveness of possible ADR techniques, but also arguments the judge can use to "sell" ADR to counsel for plaintiffs and the defendant. Be sure to consider in your memorandum any resources that the court might offer the parties to help them attempt to resolve this litigation by alternative means.

2.   You are an attorney representing the Pittston Company in the Buffalo Creek litigation. Although this litigation has just been filed, Pittston officials believe that they will lose a jury trial in federal district court and that media coverage of the trial will greatly injure Pittston. Accordingly, you have been asked to draft a motion seeking resolution of this litigation by non-traditional means in a closed proceeding.

   a.   Write a memorandum to your client discussing alternatives such as a mini-trial (to the judge or to independent experts), summary jury trial, arbitration, and mediation. Consider the possibility of fee and cost shifting provisions in connection with the ADR proceedings;

   b.   Draft the motion asking the judge to employ the ADR technique that you believe will be most advantageous to your client. Anticipate in this motion the likely objections that plaintiffs may raise to your proposal; and

   c.   Draft the order detailing the specific procedures that you believe should be employed to implement the ADR technique that you have chosen.

3.   You are an attorney in private practice in Charleston, West Virginia. You have been called by the Charleston *Gazette,* which has learned that Judge Hall has ordered a summary jury trial that will be closed to the public in the Buffalo Creek litigation. Write a letter to the newspaper's editor outlining the course of action that you recommend the paper follow to attempt to open the summary jury trial to the public.

4.   Judge Hall has informed counsel in the Buffalo Creek litigation that he wants them to attempt to agree upon an alternative means of resolving that litigation. As counsel for either the plaintiffs or the defendant, write a memorandum setting forth the strategy that you will pursue in the upcoming negotiations with opposing counsel.

5.   The parties in the Buffalo Creek litigation have agreed upon a settlement of $13,500,000. Defense counsel does not want to become involved in apportioning this settlement among the individual plaintiffs. As plaintiffs' counsel, write a memorandum to your clients setting forth the manner in which you believe this lump sum settlement should be apportioned. Be sure that you include in your memorandum the procedures for plaintiffs' approval of the apportionment method that you propose.

6.   The judges of your local United States District Court have been considering adoption of a local rule concerning alternative dispute resolu-

tion. The reasons the judges are interested in ADR vary, but among their concerns are the length of time necessary to resolve the small number of extremely complex civil cases filed in your district, the amount of time devoted to the many smaller federal cases, and the time the judges must devote to *pro se* cases (particularly those filed by inmates of the local prison).

The chief judge of the district has asked you to draft a local rule providing for alternative dispute resolution. She has left up to you whether to draft a general rule applicable to all cases, to single out specific categories of cases for ADR treatment, or to establish monetary floors or ceilings for cases subject to ADR. She also has left up to you whether the ADR you recommend should be compulsory and whether particular proceedings may or must be open to the public.

    a. Draft the local rule requested;

    b. Draft a memorandum discussing why you drafted the proposed rule in the fashion that you did; and

    c. Draft a second memorandum discussing the manner in which you believe the proposed local rule should be presented to the public and the local bar for notice and comment before becoming final.

IV. SECOND THOUGHTS ABOUT ADR

Interest in, and the actual use of, alternative dispute resolution have grown tremendously in recent years, growing even faster than the judicial caseloads cited as one of the primary reasons for adopting ADR. However, amid the enthusiasm for alternative dispute resolution, concerns and questions have been raised. Is alternative dispute resolution the revolutionary breakthrough that its proponents claim or instead "an unenlightened step backwards"[58] as some of its critics contend? This section considers some of the second thoughts that have been raised about ADR. The section initially considers some of the fundamental criticisms that have been lodged against the ADR movement and then examines some of the practical problems that must be addressed in order to implement a system of alternative dispute resolution. As with many debates, a fair analysis of ADR lies somewhere between the most extreme claims made by ADR proponents and the criticisms leveled by its detractors.

A. ALTERNATIVE DISPUTE RESOLUTION CONCERNS

Before adopting alternatives to any system of civil adjudication, the rationale for such alternatives should be enunciated. Only if there are problems with current adjudicatory systems should alternatives be considered and adopted. In the vernacular, "If it ain't broke, don't fix it."

---

58. *Hume v. M & C Management,* 129 F.R.D. 506, 508 n. 3 (N.D. Ohio 1990).

A major rationale for adoption of ADR techniques is that these techniques are necessary to deal with large increases in civil caseloads and the delays and costs that result from such caseload increases. However, the relevant studies do not establish a monolithic pattern of caseload increases. Civil filings in federal district courts increased dramatically from the 1950s until the mid–1980s, fell from the mid–1980s until the early 1990s, and then rose again from the early 1990s until 1995 (declining about nine percent from 1984 to 1995).[59] Annual federal civil filings also declined from 1996 to 2004, only to increase in 2005 to a level that was only five percent more than in 1996.[60] While federal civil filings increased 10.9% from 2001 to 2010, federal question filings actually declined by 0.09% over this period while diversity actions increased by 113.1%.[61]

Civil filings in state courts of general jurisdiction rose twenty-nine percent from 1984 to 1995 (although filings actually decreased in some years during this period),[62] while total civil filings rose by 15 percent from 1995 to 2004.[63] Not only do different court systems show different patterns, but the filing patterns for different types of cases within a single court system have not changed uniformly.[64] The argument that this country is suffering from a nationwide "litigation explosion" thus cannot support the adoption of ADR techniques to resolve all types of cases in all jurisdictions.

This is not to say, though, that caseload pressures in particular court systems should not be considered in determining whether to experiment with alternative dispute resolution. One federal judge has explained the potential benefits to him of alternative dispute resolution procedures as follows: "I used the time saved [from settlements stemming from summary jury trials] to work six days a week instead of seven for awhile, perhaps saving me from a heart attack."[65] It is not just judges who are

---

59. B. Ostrom & N. Kauder, *Examining the Work of State Courts, 1995: A National Perspective from the Court Statistics Project* 95–96 (1996).

60. Admin. Office of the U. S. Courts, *Federal Judicial Caseload Statistics 2005* (2005) (Judicial Caseload Indicators: 12–Month Periods Ending March 1996, 2001, 2004, and 2005).

61. Admin. Office of the U. S. Courts, *Federal Judicial Caseload Statistics: March 31, 2010* (2010) (Judicial Business, at 10 (Civil Case Filings Percentage Change Over Time)).

62. Ostrom & Kauder, *supra* note 59, at 95–96. *Compare also* R. Posner, *The Federal Courts: Crisis and Reform* 59–77 (1985) and Federal Courts Study Commission, *Report of the Federal Courts Study Commission* 4–10 (1990) *with* National Center for State Courts, *State Court Caseload Statistics: 1987 Annual Report* 26–33 (1989). *See also* Catenacci, "Hyperlexis or Hyperbole: Subdividing the Landscape of Disputes and Defusing the Litigation Explosion," 8 *Rev. Litig.* 297 (1989).

63. R. Schauffler et al., *Examining the Work of State Courts, 2005: A National Perspective From the Court Statistics Project*, 22 (2006).

64. Galanter, "The Day After the Litigation Explosion," 46 *Md. L. Rev.* 3, 14–28 (1986). *See also* Ostrom & Kauder, *supra* note 59, at 26–29; Clark, "Adjudication to Administration: A Statistical Analysis of Federal District Courts in the Twentieth Century," 55 *S. Cal. L. Rev.* 65 (1981).

65. *McKay v. Ashland Oil, Inc.,* 120 F.R.D. 43, 49 n.19 (E.D.Ky. 1988). But what if these summary jury trials had not resulted in settlements? Judge Bertelsman commented in this same case that he was "gambling a five-day summary jury trial against a six-week real trial. Six to one is pretty good odds." 120 F.R.D. at 49.

paying the price for overcrowded dockets in certain jurisdictions. As Judge Elizabeth Kovachevich of the United States District Court for the Middle District of Florida has noted, "Litigants are entitled to their day in court, but not, to somebody else's day."[66] Even if rising caseloads have not created judicial gridlock in a given jurisdiction, both litigants and the judicial system can benefit from dispute resolution mechanisms that fairly resolve cases more quickly and less expensively than full scale judicial adjudication.

Unfortunately, there is real uncertainty as to whether ADR has uniformly resulted in more and faster case settlements. Professor Kim Dayton, after comparing ten years of judicial workload data from federal districts which had, and had not, adopted ADR techniques, concluded:

> [C]laims concerning ADR's potential to reduce costs and delays are greatly exaggerated. The data analyses indicate that ADR districts do not differ from non-ADR districts with respect to the variables that are indicators of cost and delay. The data analyses also show that ADR has not significantly reduced overall delay, decreased the incidence of civil trials, increased the number of civil trials that individual judges are able to conduct, nor influenced the pending caseload in the districts using ADR over the ten-year period involved in the analyses.[67]

More recently, the evaluation by the RAND Institute for Civil Justice pursuant to the Civil Justice Reform Act "provided no strong statistical evidence that the mediation or neutral evaluation programs as implemented in [the six districts studied] significantly affected time to disposition, litigation costs, or attorney views of fairness or satisfaction with case management."[68]

Even if it were established that ADR leads to more and faster settlements, questions about a wholesale movement to ADR remain. Professor Owen Fiss has argued that formal adjudication serves purposes that go well beyond the resolution of particular disputes between private parties. According to Fiss, a judge's job "is not to maximize the ends of private parties, nor simply to secure the peace, but to explicate and give force to the values embodied in authoritative texts such as the Constitution and statutes: to interpret those values and to bring reality into accord with them."[69] Professor Fiss equates the settlement of civil cases with the

---

66. *Arabian Am. Oil Co. v. Scarfone*, 119 F.R.D. 448, 449 (M.D.Fla. 1988).

67. Dayton, "The Myth of Alternative Dispute Resolution in the Federal Courts," 76 *Iowa L. Rev.* 889, 916 (1991) (reprinted with permission). *See also* Dayton, "Case Management in the Eastern District of Virginia," 26 *U.S.F. L. Rev.* 445, 489 (1992) (concluding that, rather than ADR, "[f]irm judicial control of the docket * * * is the key to reduced expense and delay in federal civil litigation").

68. J. Kakalik et al., *Just, Speedy, and Inexpensive? An Evaluation of Judicial Case Management Under the Civil Justice Reform Act* 18 (RAND Institute for Civil Justice 1996). *See also* Kakalik et al., *An Evaluation of Mediation and Early Neutral Evaluation Under the Civil Justice Reform Act* (RAND Institute for Civil Justice 1996).

69. Fiss, "Against Settlement," 93 *Yale L. J.* 1073, 1085 (1984). *See also* Lederman, "Precedent Lost: Why Encourage Settlement, and Why Permit Non–Party Involvement in Settlements,"

plea bargaining of criminal cases and suggests that "although dockets are trimmed, justice may not be done."[70]

Unfortunately, lengthy delays, and the costs that they often engender, mean that formal judicial adjudication is not a realistic method for resolving all disputes.[71] These delays and costs may prevent the courts from rendering the public judicial pronouncements that Professor Fiss seeks.

The rationality of decisions reached in overcrowded courts also can be questioned. Consider Professor Arthur Miller's description of modern federal civil litigation:

> In many ways, contemporary federal litigation is analogous to the dance marathon contests of yesteryear. The object of the exercise is to select a partner from across the "v," get out on the dance floor, hang on to one's client, and then drift aimlessly and endlessly to the litigation music for as long as possible, hoping that everyone else will collapse from exhaustion.[72]

A move away from formal adjudication has been supported by the argument that less formal dispute resolution processes yield "better" outcomes than those produced through formal adjudication.[73] While adjudication pits parties against one another, alternative dispute resolution devices may bring the parties together and preserve or create relationships that will prevent future disputes from arising. There also may be advantages from having disputes resolved by neutral third-parties who have expertise in the substantive area underlying the present dispute and who are not bound by overly rigid legal rules and doctrines.

However, some have questioned the assumption that the compromise outcomes possible through ADR are necessarily superior to the more rigid decisions produced by formal litigation.[74] Questions can be raised concerning the "accuracy" of alternative dispute resolution outcomes based upon cases in which disparate outcomes were reached in these proceedings and

---

75 *Notre Dame L. Rev.* 221 (1999); Fiss, "The Supreme Court, 1978 Term—Foreword: The Forms of Justice," 93 *Harv. L. Rev.* 1 (1979).

70.   Fiss, "Against Settlement," 93 *Yale L. J.* 1073, 1075 (1984).

71.   Civil litigation can be a very expensive means of compensating injured parties. J. Kakalik & N. Pace, *Costs and Compensation Paid in Tort Litigation* 66–71 (1986) (plaintiffs in 1985 received only 56% of the total national expenditures on tort litigation); S. Carroll et al., *Asbestos Litigation* 104–105 (2005) (asbestos claimants from 1960s through 2002 received only about 42% of amount paid by defendants and insurers on such claims).

72.   Miller, "The Adversary System: Dinosaur or Phoenix," 69 *Minn. L. Rev.* 1, 9 (1984).

73.   *E.g.,* Menkel–Meadow, "Toward Another View of Legal Negotiation: The Structure of Problem Solving," 31 *UCLA L. Rev.* 754, 763–64 (1984); McThenia & Shaffer, "For Reconciliation," 94 *Yale L. J.* 1660 (1985). *See generally* "Quality of Dispute Resolution Symposium," 66 *Den. U. L. Rev.* 335 (1989).

74.   Golann, "Is Legal Mediation a Process of Repair—or Separation? An Empirical Study, and Its Implications," 7 *Harv. Negot. L. Rev.* 301 (2002) (finding "repaired relationship" between parties occurring in only 17% of 60 mediations studied); Brunet, "Questioning the Quality of Alternative Dispute Resolution," 62 *Tul. L. Rev.* 1 (1987) (arguing that ADR procedures undermine norms to be advanced by substantive law).

in later trials.[75] In addition, Professor Kevin McMunigal argues that we should consider the effect upon lawyers of the current movement away from adversarial adjudication.[76]

Less formal procedures generally mean fewer procedural protections for disputants. This can become a problem if the disputants are not equal in bargaining power. Parties who litigate frequently may have special insights into who are the most favorable neutrals. Neutrals, whose livelihood may depend upon being chosen by parties to resolve their disputes, may tend to favor those litigants who will be involved in the future selections of neutrals. It also has been suggested that racial and ethnic minorities and women may be more likely to be prejudiced in an informal ADR setting than in formal adjudication.[77]

However, the powerless may be disadvantaged under existing systems of formal litigation. If ADR procedures are more expeditious and less expensive, less powerful parties may be better able to prosecute their claims than under formal adjudicatory systems that place a premium upon a party's ability to withstand extended and expensive proceedings. In fact, to the extent that alternative dispute resolution techniques reduce the time and expense necessary to process disputes, they may lead to an increase in the number of disputes that are submitted for third-party processing.

There is no simple "yes" or "no" answer to the debate concerning alternative dispute resolution. Instead, the focus should be upon when alternative dispute resolution techniques are appropriate. Even if ADR is not appropriate for all disputes, it may be extremely useful in resolving many disputes. Judge Harry Edwards has suggested that we consider (1) whether ADR is being proposed as an alternative or merely an adjunct to

---

75. *E.g., Compressed Gas Corp. v. United States Steel Corp.,* 857 F.2d 346, 348 (6th Cir. 1988), *cert. denied,* 490 U.S. 1006 (1989) (summary jury trial verdict of $200,000 followed by additional discovery and full trial resulting in jury verdict of more than $1,750,000). *See also Muehler v. Land O'Lakes, Inc.,* 617 F.Supp. 1370, 1372 (D.Minn. 1985) (one summary jury panel rendered defense verdict, while other panel returned plaintiff's verdict in excess of $2,000,000); T. Willging, *Trends in Asbestos Litigation* 77 (1987) (in a cluster of asbestos cases presented to summary jury panels, one panel returned all defense verdicts while another panel returned plaintiff's verdicts in six of ten cases totaling over $8,000,000); Maatman, "The Future of Summary Jury Trials in Federal Courts: *Strandell v. Jackson County,*" 21 *J. Marshall L. Rev.* 455, 464–67 (1988) (one summary jury panel returned almost $3,000,000 verdict for plaintiff while other panel returned a defense verdict). One reason to split summary jurors into two panels is to obtain a range of verdicts.

76. McMunigal, "The Costs of Settlement: The Impact of Scarcity of Adjudication on Litigating Lawyers," 37 *UCLA L. Rev.* 833 (1990). Professor McMunigal's concern is with the decreasing opportunities for modern litigators to obtain trial experience. Among the possible effects of the decrease in civil trials are (1) decreasing attorney competence in trial advocacy skills; (2) a distortion of settlement outcomes because of attorneys' inability to predict trial outcomes and their personal desires to try, or avoid trial in, particular cases; (3) attorney incentives to inflate claims that presumably will be settled rather than tried; (4) abuses stemming from discovery that is not focused by the likelihood of a soon and certain trial; and (5) psychological costs to "trial lawyers" whose job is to settle, rather than try, cases. *Id.* at 848–77. *See also* J. Macfarlane, *The New Lawyer: How Settlement is Transforming the Practice of Law* (2008).

77. Delgado et al., "Fairness and Formality: Minimizing the Risk of Prejudice in Alternative Dispute Resolution," 1985 *Wis. L. Rev.* 1359; Grillo, "The Mediation Alternative: Process Dangers for Women," 100 *Yale L. J.* 1545 (1991). *Contra* Rosenberg, "In Defense of Mediation," 33 *Ariz. L. Rev.* 467 (1991).

the judicial process and (2) whether the dispute involves public or private rights. Judge Edwards believes that we should be particularly concerned about the reference of public disputes to ADR mechanisms that are independent from existing court structures.[78] Other factors that might be considered include the amount at stake in a dispute, the relative costs to process a dispute in different fashions, the relative speed for dispute processing, and the quality of the final outcomes under ADR and formal adjudication.

It should be possible to design ADR mechanisms so that the advantages of ADR are achieved while the parties and the public are protected from potential problems posed by certain ADR techniques.[79] Cases generally should be screened for ADR treatment, rather than requiring that all cases of a particular variety or description be processed by ADR techniques. Courts must be sensitive to the possible delays and costs of ADR.[80] Judges should be wary of creating a system under which substantial numbers of cases go through elaborate ADR proceedings as well as trial.

We should ask whether ADR techniques are being proffered merely in an attempt to clear judicial dockets or because an ADR technique appears to provide a better means of resolving a particular dispute. If ADR is thought to provide a better dispute resolution mechanism, the specific fashion in which an ADR device will function in a given case must be considered. If the only purpose of ADR is to predict the likely outcome of a judicial trial, perhaps a "real" trial should be held instead. On the other hand, there are situations in which ADR may permit the parties to explore cooperative solutions to their dispute, solutions that are unlikely to result from formal adjudication.

Nor should we underestimate the degree to which public acceptance of a method of dispute resolution is affected by the similarity of that procedure to a "real" trial. Consider the conclusion of one study of litigant satisfaction with various methods of dispute resolution:

> [T]he findings raise questions about how strong and how widespread is the desire for very informal, high-participation, simplified procedures of the sort advocated by some critics of court procedures. * * *

---

78. Edwards, "Alternative Dispute Resolution: Panacea or Anathema?," 99 *Harv. L. Rev.* 668 (1986). *See also* Ward, "Mandatory Court–Annexed Alternative Dispute Resolution in the United States Federal Courts: Panacea or Pandemic?," 81 *St. John's L. Rev.* 77 (2007).

79. The challenge is to ensure that ADR devices are both fair and efficient. *See* Note, "Mandatory Mediation and Summary Jury Trial: Guidelines for Ensuring Fair and Effective Processes," 103 *Harv. L. Rev.* 1086 (1990) (suggesting that ADR enabling legislation should ensure meaningful client participation, guard against coercion during confidential ADR processing, not significantly delay trial, and provide a screening mechanism to send disputes requiring full trials directly to court). *See also* Norton, "Justice and Efficiency in Dispute Systems," 5 *Ohio St. J. Disp. Resol.* 207 (1990).

80. *See, e.g., Federal Reserve Bank v. Carey–Canada, Inc.,* 123 F.R.D. 603, 604 (D.Minn. 1988) (parties estimated that three day summary jury trial would cost them $50,000 each and divert their attention from preparation for full trial). *See also* Bernstein, "Understanding the Limits of Court–Connected ADR: A Critique of Federal Court–Annexed Arbitration Programs," 141 *U. Pa. L. Rev.* 2169, 2253 (1993) (concluding that court-annexed arbitration may "decrease access to justice for poorer and more risk-averse litigants by either adding an additional layer of costly procedure or * * * by forcing them to take more risk").

Alternative procedures less formal than trial appear to be quite acceptable to litigants—witness the generally favorable reactions to court-annexed arbitration—but not *because* they are less formal, more participatory, or easy to understand. Our study suggests that whatever procedure—formal or informal—is used, it must be perceived to be enacted well and seriously if it is to be viewed as fair.[81]

Excitement about ADR should not obscure the need to monitor, and consider reforms related to, modern civil adjudication. There are at least two major possible responses to concerns with our current systems of civil litigation: (1) develop alternatives to the present systems and (2) work to improve the existing systems. Rather than focusing exclusively on one of these approaches, efforts should be made on both fronts simultaneously. ADR and traditional adjudication should not be seen as competing modes of dispute resolution. Instead, both traditional adjudication and more recent ADR techniques should be carefully developed so that they complement one another and build on each other's strengths.

Like it or not, the current systems of civil adjudication in many federal and state courts are changing, as evidenced by the turn to managerial judging in some jurisdictions. Continuing efforts and experiments in this regard should be encouraged.[82] Model Rule of Professional Conduct 6.1(b)(3) provides that lawyers should provide services through, inter alia, "participation in activities for improving the law, the legal system or the legal profession." Even if increasing numbers of cases are diverted to ADR mechanisms, court systems will be necessary to resolve the many remaining cases and to enforce non-judicial decisions. In systems in which a majority of cases are resolved by party negotiation, it may be misleading to speak of a "move" to alternative dispute resolution.

B.　PRACTICAL PROBLEMS POSED BY ALTERNATIVE DISPUTE RESOLUTION MECHANISMS

After agreement is reached that alternative dispute resolution should be used to resolve a particular dispute or class of disputes, a specific ADR mechanism must be designed and implemented. The ultimate success or failure of ADR in a given case may well depend upon the specific design of the ADR mechanism adopted. Questions may arise concerning, for instance, the parties' rights to discovery, who will pay for the ADR, and the

---

81. A. Lind et al., *The Perception of Justice: Tort Litigants' Views of Trial, Court–Annexed Arbitration, and Judicial Settlement Conferences* 76 (1989). *See also* Symposium: "Suppose It's Not True: Challenging Mediation Ideology," 2002 *J. Disp. Resol.* 81; J. Thibaut & L. Walker, *Procedural Justice: A Psychological Analysis* (1975).

82. For interesting conceptual approaches to the reform of our existing systems of civil adjudication see Langbein, "The German Advantage in Civil Procedure," 52 *U. Chi. L. Rev.* 823 (1985); Newman, "Rethinking Fairness: Perspectives on the Litigation Process," 94 *Yale L. J.* 1643 (1985). *See also* Rowe, "Authorized Managerialism Under the Federal Rules—and the Extent of Convergence with Civil–Law Judging," 36 *Sw. U. L. Rev.* 191, 212 (2007) (emphasis on judicial management in federal courts in recent decades still leaves parties with major initiative with respect to fact-gathering, with court's pretrial management focus primarily on discovery).

extent of attorney and party participation in the ADR procedure. Rather than deal with all of the many issues of ADR design and implementation, this subsection considers just two of the major issues: the extent to which alternative dispute resolution devices should be (1) voluntary and (2) confidential.

One of the major controversies surrounding ADR is whether parties to a civil lawsuit can be compelled to participate in attempts to resolve their litigation by non-traditional means.[83] Although several federal district courts have upheld mandatory participation in summary jury trials,[84] two federal courts of appeal have held that federal district judges cannot compel parties to participate in these trials.[85] Moreover, if a court mandates participation in ADR, it then may be required to determine in particular cases whether a party has meaningfully participated in the ADR proceeding.[86]

Issues of compulsion can arise even in connection with "voluntary" ADR. A concern raised by ADR critics is that alternatives to civil litigation will not be voluntarily chosen by litigants but will be imposed by judges more concerned with the state of their dockets than with achieving justice in individual cases. There inevitably are great pressures upon judges to suggest, sometimes not too subtly, that parties resolve their disputes by means other than full-scale adjudication.

Compulsion may be a matter of degree rather than of kind. At some point, judicial encouragement of ADR can become judicial coercion. Not only can the choice to participate in ADR be less than freely made, but practical pressures can push litigants to accept the outcome of "non-binding" ADR processes. Cost and fee shifting provisions are intended to

---

83. *See generally* Golann, "Making Alternative Dispute Resolution Mandatory: The Constitutional Issues," 68 *Or. L. Rev.* 487 (1989).

84. *Federal Reserve Bank v. Carey–Canada, Inc.,* 123 F.R.D. 603 (D. Minn. 1988); *McKay v. Ashland Oil, Inc.,* 120 F.R.D. 43 (E.D.Ky. 1988); *Arabian American Oil Co. v. Scarfone,* 119 F.R.D. 448 (M.D.Fla. 1988). *See also Home Owners Funding Corp. of Am. v. Century Bank,* 695 F.Supp. 1343, 1347 n.3 (D.Mass. 1988). *Cf. Firelock, Inc. v. District Court,* 776 P.2d 1090 (Colo. 1989) (upholding mandatory court-annexed arbitration).

85. *In re NLO, Inc.,* 5 F.3d 154, 156–58 (6th Cir. 1993); *Strandell v. Jackson County,* 838 F.2d 884, 887 (7th Cir. 1987). However, both of these cases were decided prior to the 1993 amendments to Rule 16 of the Federal Rules of Civil Procedure. *Ohio v. Louis Trauth Dairy, Inc.,* 164 F.R.D. 469, 470 (S.D.Ohio 1996). *See also* Posner, "The Summary Jury Trial and Other Methods of Alternate Dispute Resolution: Some Cautionary Observations," 53 *U. Chi. L. Rev.* 366, 385–87 (1986); Webber, Comment, "Mandatory Summary Jury Trial: Playing by the Rules?," 56 *U. Chi. L. Rev.* 1495 (1989). *Cf.* 28 U.S.C. § 652(a) ("Any district court that elects to require the use of alternative dispute resolution in certain cases may do so only with respect to mediation, early neutral evaluation, and, if the parties consent, arbitration."). *But see In re Atlantic Pipe* Corp., 304 F.3d 135 (1st Cir. 2002) (district court had inherent power to order mandatory mediation, so long as court sets reasonable limits on duration of mediation and mediator's fees); *Rhea v. Massey–Ferguson, Inc.,* 767 F.2d 266 (6th Cir. 1985) (per curiam) (upholding mandatory mediation rule).

86. *Gilling v. Eastern Airlines, Inc.,* 680 F.Supp. 169 (D.N.J. 1988) (defendant sanctioned for failure to participate in court-annexed arbitration in a "meaningful manner" as required by local rules of court). *See generally* Lande, "Using Dispute System Design Methods to Promote Good–Faith Participation in Court–Connected Mediation Programs," 50 *UCLA L. Rev.* 69 (2002); Sherman, "Court–Mandated Alternative Dispute Resolution: What Form of Participation Should Be Required?," 46 *SMU L. Rev.* 2079 (1993).

have exactly that effect.[87] If mandatory court-annexed ADR procedures result in substantial additional costs and delay, a litigant's right to a jury trial could be compromised.[88]

As the United States Court of Appeals for the Second Circuit has recognized, "Rule 16 of the Fed.R.Civ.P. was not designed as a means for clubbing the parties—or one of them—into an involuntary compromise."[89] Whether or not courts have the power to require summary jury trials, there is at least some empirical evidence that lawyers and parties may be more amenable to, and satisfied with, summary jury trials in which they voluntarily have chosen to participate.[90] Alternative dispute resolution systems generally should be devised to ensure that parties (1) freely choose ADR processing for their disputes and (2) voluntarily accept ADR outcomes as the final resolution of their claims.[91]

Another major question posed by at least some ADR techniques is the extent to which proceedings should be, or even can be, confidential. Many ADR proceedings are confidential, in order to permit the parties to freely air their disputes without fear that statements or evidence might be used against them later in another setting.[92] Nevertheless, persons who are not parties to the dispute or the general public may have an interest in the hearing and resolution of certain claims.

A case from the United States Court of Appeals for the Sixth Circuit, *Cincinnati Gas and Electric Company v. General Electric Company*,[93] illustrates the confidentiality problem. This case, involving the design and

---

87. *But see Tiedel v. Northwestern Michigan College*, 865 F.2d 88 (6th Cir. 1988). The court in *Tiedel* struck down a local rule taxing attorneys' fees against parties who received no better verdict from a jury than from the mediation panel established under a district's mandatory mediation plan. However, the concern of the court of appeals was with the district court's power under Rule 83 of the Federal Rules of Civil Procedure to enact such a rule, rather than with the wisdom of the rule itself. This same court of appeals had previously upheld a local rule requiring mandatory mediation of certain types of cases. *Rhea v. Massey–Ferguson, Inc.*, 767 F.2d 266 (6th Cir. 1985) (per curiam).

Even without a specific provision in an ADR rule or statute, costs can be shifted by basing a Rule 68 offer of judgment upon the outcome of an ADR proceeding.

88. *Mattos v. Thompson*, 491 Pa. 385, 421 A.2d 190 (1980).

89. *Kothe v. Smith*, 771 F.2d 667, 669 (2d Cir. 1985).

90. Alfini, "Summary Jury Trials in State and Federal Courts: A Comparative Analysis of the Perceptions of Participating Lawyers," 4 *Ohio St. J. Disp. Resol.* 213 (1989).

91. In the Alternative Dispute Resolution Act of 1998, Congress required all federal district courts to implement alternative dispute resolution programs. 28 U.S.C. § 651(b). Absent party consent, participation in only mediation and early neutral evaluation can be compelled pursuant to this Act. 28 U.S.C. § 652(a). However, the voluntary nature of ADR programs affects the numbers of cases in which these procedures are actually used. As the RAND Institute for Civil Justice concluded in its study conducted pursuant to the Civil Justice Reform Act, "Neither lawyers nor judges have used any type of ADR extensively when its use is voluntary." J. Kakalik et al., *Just, Speedy, and Inexpensive? An Evaluation of Judicial Case Management Under the Civil Justice Reform Act* 18 (RAND Institute for Civil Justice 1996).

92. *E.g.*, 42 U.S.C. § 2000g–2(b) (conciliation by federal Community Relations Service); Cal. Fam. Code § 3177 (West 2004) (child custody mediation); Am. Arb. Ass'n, *Commercial Mediation Procedures*, Rule M–12 (2005). The Alternative Dispute Resolution Act of 1998 specifically provides that ADR conducted under the authority of that Act is to be confidential. 28 U.S.C. § 652(d).

93. 854 F.2d 900 (6th Cir. 1988), *cert. denied*, 489 U.S. 1033 (1989).

construction of a nuclear power plant, was brought by electric utility companies against the General Electric Company and an architectural and engineering firm. The district judge ordered the parties to participate in a summary jury trial, and several newspapers attempted to intervene to challenge the order closing the proceedings to the public. The court of appeals upheld the trial court's confidentiality order. The court based its decision upon its characterization of the summary jury trial as a settlement proceeding and concluded that public access would undermine the effectiveness of the summary jury trial.[94]

Even if the summary jury trial in *Cincinnati Gas and Electric Company* constitutionally could be closed, a major policy question exists as to the wisdom of banning the public from such proceedings. Despite the parties' desire for confidentiality, the legitimacy of dispute resolution is ensured, at least in part, by public proceedings and public statements of the reasons for decisions. Public, written decisions provide notice to interested third-persons, permitting them to conform their conduct to the governing rules announced in specific cases. Major litigants, themselves, may desire precedents that they can rely upon to plan their future conduct. As a result, future disputes may be resolved without resort to third-party processes or may be prevented from ever arising. The general public, too, should be informed of the outcome of cases involving public issues, so that public debate and policy-making can be shaped accordingly.

Whether or not a particular ADR proceeding should be confidential will depend upon the specific dispute and the parties in question. There may be no reason to require that some parties, such as individuals disputing the terms of a divorce or child custody, publicly air their private disputes. Disputes in which the public has a legitimate concern or those involving public bodies, though, may best be resolved in a public forum. The confidentiality issues raised by these cases are similar to those posed by the increasing use of protective orders to seal material produced in discovery and case settlements.[95]

Good ADR processes are better than poor adjudication. The bench, bar, and the public should work to increase the quality of justice rendered by both systems of formal adjudication and alternative dispute resolution. The goal, in the words of Rule 1 of the Federal Rules of Civil Procedure, should be to secure the "just, speedy, and inexpensive determination" of all disputes.

NOTES AND QUESTIONS CONCERNING ADR

1. Are we expecting too much from our current systems of dispute resolution? Should we expect that health and safety standards, such as those involving dam safety that were at issue in the Buffalo Creek litigation, will be enforced by private, after-the-fact litigation? What roles should government licensing, inspection, regulation, and litigation play?

---

94. 854 F.2d at 903–904.

95. *See* the Notes and Questions Concerning Rule 26(c) Protective Orders in Chapter 10, *supra* p. 672.

2.   No matter how well planned a particular dispute resolution system is, specific individuals will have to implement and administer that system. For this reason, some ADR statutes require that those who provide such services be properly trained. *E.g.,* Fla. Stat. Ann. § 44.106 (West 2003) (requiring Florida Supreme Court to establish training standards for state mediators and arbitrators); Or. Rev. Stat. § 36.175 (2005) (requiring establishment of minimum qualifications and training for those providing dispute resolution services). The expertise or training required for dispute resolution professionals should encompass both the procedural aspects of dispute resolution and the substance of particular categories of disputes.

3.   The Federal Rules of Civil Procedure were intended to be a single body of rules for the adjudication of all civil actions. The current movement to alternative means of dispute resolution may be fueled, at least in part, by the belief that not all disputes need, or should be resolved by, identical procedures. Whether in the area of discovery, case management, or dispute resolution, individual approaches are being tailored to the specifics of individual disputes. Many lawyers and judges no longer agree with the sentiment that "If you've seen one case, you've seen 'em all." What are the costs and benefits of the breakdown of "trans-substantive" procedural rules? *See generally* Cover, "For James Wm. Moore: Some Reflections on a Reading of the Rules," 84 *Yale L. J.* 718 (1975); Carrington, "Making Rules to Dispose of Manifestly Unfounded Assertions: An Exorcism of the Bogy of Non–Trans–Substantive Rules of Civil Procedure," 137 *U. Pa. L. Rev.* 2067 (1989); Subrin, "The Limitations of Transsubstantive Procedure: An Essay on Adjusting the 'One Size Fits All' Assumption," 87 *Denv. U. L. Rev.* 377 (2010). *See also* Cooper, "Simplified Rules of Civil Procedure?," 100 *Mich. L. Rev.* 1794 (2002) (describing "Simplified Rules" project of the United States Judicial Conference Advisory Committee on the Federal Rules of Civil Procedure, exploring possibility of separate civil rules for a subset of federal civil cases).

4.   Judge Richard Posner has made a strong argument that we should attempt to measure the success or failure of ADR techniques by applying the empirical methods of the social sciences. Posner, "The Summary Jury Trial and Other Methods of Alternative Dispute Resolution: Some Cautionary Observations," 53 *U. Chi. L. Rev.* 366 (1986). He suggests that social science methodologies can help us compare the relative superiority of different ADR techniques; for instance, whether a judge is better advised to spend a full day in connection with the summary jury trial of a single case or in settlement conferences or other efforts to encourage settlement of other pending cases. *Id.* at 382. *See also* Symposium, "Empirical Studies of Mandatory Arbitration," 41 *U. Mich. J. L. Reform* 777 (2008).

5.   The United States Court of Appeals for the Sixth Circuit has stated that summary jury trials perform a "purely settlement function" and therefore are not analogues to civil jury trials. *Cincinnati Gas and Elec. Co. v. General Elec. Co.,* 854 F.2d 900, 904 (6th Cir. 1988), *cert. denied,* 489 U.S. 1033 (1989). If this is the case, under what authority can jurors be required to hear summary jury trials? *See Hume v. M & C Management,* 129 F.R.D. 506, 509 (N.D.Ohio 1990).

V. POSTSCRIPT ON THE BUFFALO CREEK LITIGATION

The strengths and weaknesses of contemporary dispute resolution are illustrated by the litigation brought on behalf of the survivors of the Buffalo Creek disaster. The Buffalo Creek flood occurred on February 26, 1972, and the settlement agreement in the action brought by attorney Gerald Stern was executed on July 3, 1974. The pretrial proceedings moved quite rapidly for a case of this size and complexity. In large measure this was due to a judge who set a firm trial date and to attorneys who worked diligently to adhere to the court's pretrial deadlines.

Nevertheless, there were survivors of the disaster who did not believe they could await the outcome of formal litigation and as a result settled with the Pittston Company soon after the flood. Other survivors didn't trust local attorneys, many of whom represented coal companies, or thought it unfair that these attorneys sought one-third contingency fees.[96]

The Buffalo Creek litigation was an expensive means of compensating those injured by the flood. The case brought by Gerald Stern settled for $13,500,000.[97] However, more than $3,000,000 of this $13,500,000 settlement went to plaintiffs' attorneys under their contingent fee arrangement and another $500,000 was used to defray the costs of the suit. The plaintiffs received approximately $9,500,000 of the $13,500,000 paid in settlement,[98] under a contract giving counsel a smaller than average contingent fee percentage. If we assume that the costs and fees charged Pittston were comparable to plaintiffs' ($4,000,000), it cost approximately $8,000,000 to transfer $9,500,000 in compensation to the plaintiffs.

In addition to the lawsuit brought by Gerald Stern, the Washington, D. C. law firm of Williams & Connolly brought a later action on behalf of 1500 minor children who were victims of the Buffalo Creek flood. This litigation settled for $4,800,000, with Williams & Connolly receiving a fee of $1,200,000.[99] The state of West Virginia also brought an action against the Pittston Company for damages to roads and other state structures resulting from the flood. This lawsuit, seeking $100,000,000 in damages, was settled for $1,000,001.[100] The United States never sued Pittston, although it sued the state of West Virginia for $4,200,000 for work done by the Army Corps of Engineers in preparing sites for the mobile homes provided to disaster victims by the federal government.[101]

---

96. Walton, "After the Flood," *Harper's Magazine,* March 1973, at 78, 83.

97. Of the $13,500,000 settlement, $5,500,000 was distributed among the plaintiffs for psychic impairment ($2,000,000 of which was placed in a trust fund for the 226 plaintiffs who were children under the age of eighteen). G. Stern, *The Buffalo Creek Disaster* 271–72 (1976).

98. *Id.;* G. Gleser et al., *Prolonged Psychosocial Effects of Disaster* 121 (1981).

99. Rudnitsky & Blyskal, "Getting Into Those Deep Pockets," *Forbes,* Aug. 1, 1980, at 59, 61.

100. "Pittston Settles Suit in West Virginia Flood, Will Pay $1,000,001," *Wall St. J.,* Jan. 17, 1977, at A12.

101. A unanimous Supreme Court ultimately upheld the claim of the United States for prejudgment interest on this sum, noting at the conclusion of its opinion that "our holding may

Even after the litigation was settled, many of the Buffalo Creek survivors could not return to the sites of their former homes because of cleanup operations and a new state highway that was built in the valley.[102] The United States Department of Housing and Urban Development established temporary trailer parks in the valley for flood survivors, but former neighbors and friends were not necessarily housed in the same parks.[103]

Disabling psychiatric symptoms were present in over ninety percent of the survivors interviewed more than two years after the flood.[104] A psychological study of adult litigants found that the anxiety and depression of approximately one-third of those sampled had not improved in the three years after the settlement of the Buffalo Creek lawsuit.[105] Other survivors interviewed thirty months after the flood suffered from anxiety and fear so strong as to be classed as "permanent inner terror" by the psychologists and psychiatrists who interviewed them.[106]

NOTES AND QUESTIONS CONCERNING THE BUFFALO CREEK SETTLEMENT

1. The complaint filed by Gerald Stern sought extensive injunctive relief and alleged that plaintiffs suffered from "loss of community." Nevertheless, the ultimate settlement, monetary damages, was a personal and individualistic remedy. Is it possible that the damage awards themselves may have contributed to a further breakdown in community, as families and friends quarreled over the recoveries?

2. Did the joinder of over 600 plaintiffs in a single lawsuit create a vehicle for building or rebuilding community? Is it significant that plaintiffs' counsel were not members of the community of plaintiffs whom they represented?

3. Were there litigation advantages from the joinder of 600 plaintiffs in a single lawsuit? Was the litigation brought by Gerald Stern more efficient because his firm represented so many plaintiffs? Were there potential conflict of interest problems presented as a result of the joinder of so many plaintiffs?

4. Could injunctive relief have redressed the underlying problems in the Buffalo Creek Valley? Could injunctive relief have extended beyond Pittston's operations in the Buffalo Creek Valley? What about the use of the criminal law to ensure public safety and corporate responsibility? Why didn't the federal government sue Pittston as a result of the dam collapse?

---

work a hardship upon the citizens of West Virginia, who have already suffered greatly as a result of the tragedies that gave rise to this litigation." *West Virginia v. United States,* 479 U.S. 305, 313 (1987).

102. Kaib, "Buffalo Creek, 10 Years Later," *Clev. Plain Dealer,* Feb. 14, 1982, at A1.

103. Gleser, *supra* note 98, at 3.

104. Titchener & Kapp, "Family and Character Change at Buffalo Creek," 133 *Am. J. Psychiatry* 295, 296 (1976).

105. Gleser, *supra* note 98, at 136.

106. Lifton & Olson, "The Human Meaning of Total Disaster: The Buffalo Creek Experience," *Psychiatry,* Feb. 1976, at 1, 2.

5. Should suit have been brought against the state and federal governments due to their lack of zeal in enforcing existing dam and mine safety regulations? Or was the problem with the laws that the state and federal authorities were charged with administering? As of May 1972 the Pittston Company had been cited over 5000 times for violations of the federal Coal Mine Health and Safety Act. *Buffalo Creek (W.Va.) Disaster, 1972: Hearings before the Subcomm. on Labor of the Senate Comm. on Labor and Public Welfare*, 92d Cong., 2d Sess. 293–95 (1972).

6. What role should insurance play in providing compensation to victims of mass disasters? Should we rely upon individuals to procure insurance from private companies? Although there were almost 1500 houses that were either demolished or extensively damaged by the Buffalo Creek flood, only two homeowners had flood insurance. Walton, "After the Flood," *Harper's Magazine,* March 1973, at 78, 82.

7. What impact would a public trial have had in this case? Would a trial have resulted in greater efforts to ensure the safety of dams in other locations? Would legislative action have been more likely as a result of a public trial? Didn't the settlement offered by Pittston include, in effect, a premium for plaintiffs' waiver of their right to a public trial? Although there was no trial, plaintiffs' attorney Gerald Stern filed (and thereby made public) a comprehensive trial brief setting forth what plaintiffs intended to prove at trial. G. Stern, *The Buffalo Creek Disaster* 262–63 (1976).

8. What were Gerald Stern's duties in this case? Could he have turned down a good settlement offer so that there would be a public trial? Could he have counseled his clients to do so? Does an attorney have any different loyalties in "public interest" litigation than in other cases?

9. What impact did the action brought by Gerald Stern have upon potential suits by other victims of the Buffalo Creek disaster? Did this action make it more likely that the law firm of Williams & Connolly would represent plaintiffs in a second federal action? Did the fee received by Stern's law firm make Williams & Connolly's representation more likely?

10. Was a contingent fee appropriate in this case? The rationale for contingent fees is that the attorney receives a substantial percentage of any recovery in return for bearing the risk that there will be no recovery at all. Was there such a risk in this case?

11. Gerald Stern has characterized the Buffalo Creek litigation that he handled as a pro bono case. G. Stern, The Buffalo Creek Disaster 20–21 (1976). Are there problems with this characterization of a case in which several million dollars in attorneys' fees were received? If not, is the entire plaintiffs' personal injury bar performing pro bono service? Would Stern's lawsuit have been a pro bono case if plaintiffs had lost the case?

12. Are there limitations on what any single lawsuit can accomplish? Consider the following comment concerning the Buffalo Creek litigation:

> In spite of the number and proximity of the plaintiffs, there was no direct encounter with the antagonists, or any form of collective action, or any sense that plaintiffs were caught up in a struggle outside the bounds of

the lawsuit. Their lawyers, notwithstanding their intense identification with the victims' cause, remained remote and professional.

Galanter, "Reading the Landscape of Disputes: What We Know and Don't Know (and Think We Know) About Our Allegedly Contentious and Litigious Society," 31 *UCLA L. Rev.* 4, 32 (1983).

Is it a criticism or a tribute to the lawyers who handled the Buffalo Creek litigation that they remained "remote and professional?"

VI.   CONCLUSION

The ADR movement presents a two-fold challenge to the practicing attorney. First of all, attorneys should be aware of alternative dispute resolution possibilities that can be utilized in their individual cases. Not only may counsel be required to utilize ADR procedures in particular cases, but they should be ready to request the use of such devices where appropriate. Second, attorneys should think about the systemic problems of modern civil adjudication and the means by which those problems can be alleviated by reforms of, and the creation of alternatives to, current procedural systems.

VII.   CHAPTER BIBLIOGRAPHY

J. Alfini et al., *Mediation Theory and Practice* (2001).

Alternative Dispute Resolution: Practice and Perspectives (M. Matthews ed. 1990).

Alternative Dispute Resolution: The Litigator's Handbook (N. Atlas et al. eds. 2000).

American Bar Association, *Alternative Dispute Resolution: A Handbook for Judges* (2d ed. 1991).

"American Law Institute Study on Paths to a 'Better Way': Litigation, Alternatives, and Accommodation," 1989 *Duke L. J.* 808.

Brazil, "A Close Look at Three Court–Sponsored ADR Programs: Why They Exist, How They Operate, What They Deliver, and Whether They Threaten Important Values," 1990 *U. Chi. Legal F.* 303.

Brazil et al., "Early Neutral Evaluation: An Experimental Effort to Expedite Dispute Resolution," 69 *Judicature* 279 (1986).

Brown, "Some Practical Thoughts on Arbitration," *Litigation,* Winter 1980, at 8.

E. Brunet et al., *Alternative Dispute Resolution: The Advocate's Perspective* (3d ed. 2006).

Brunet, "Questioning the Quality of Alternative Dispute Resolution," 62 *Tul. L. Rev.* 1 (1987).

Burger, "Isn't There a Better Way?," 68 *A.B.A.J.* 274 (1982).

T. Carbonneau, *The Law and Practice of Arbitration* (2d ed. 2007).

Coulson, "Private Settlement for the Public Good," 66 *Judicature* 7 (1982).

Dayton, "The Myth of Alternative Dispute Resolution in the Federal Courts," 76 *Iowa L. Rev.* 889 (1991).

Edwards, "Alternative Dispute Resolution: Panacea or Anathema?," 99 *Harv. L. Rev.* 668 (1986).

E. Fine, *CPR Legal Program Mini–Trial Workbook* (1985).

Fiss, "Against Settlement," 93 *Yale L. J.* 1073 (1979).

Fox, "Mini–Trials," *Litigation*, Summer 1993, at 36.

Galanter, "The Emergence of the Judge as a Mediator in Civil Cases," 69 *Judicature* 257 (1986).

Gnaizda, "Secret Justice for the Privileged Few," 66 *Judicature* 6 (1982).

Golann, "Making Alternative Dispute Resolution Mandatory: The Constitutional Issues," 68 *Or. L. Rev.* 487 (1989).

D. Golann, *Mediating Legal Disputes: Effective Strategies for Lawyers and Mediators* (1996).

S. Goldberg et al., *Dispute Resolution: Negotiation, Mediation, and Other Processes* (5th ed. 2007).

Guill & Slavin, "Rush to Unfairness: The Downside of ADR," *Judges J.*, Summer 1989, at 8.

M. Jacoubovitch & C. Moore, *Summary Jury Trials in the Northern District of Ohio* (1982).

Kickham, Note, "Court–Annexed Arbitration: The Verdict is Still Out," 8 *Rev. Litig.* 327 (1989).

K. Kovach, *Mediation: Principles and Practice* (2d ed. 2004).

Lambros, "The Summary Jury Trial and Other Alternative Methods of Dispute Resolution," 103 F.R.D. 461 (1984).

A. Levin et al., *Dispute Resolution Devices in a Democratic Society* (1985).

Levine, "Early Neutral Evaluation: The Second Phase," 1989 *J. Disp. Resol.* 1.

Lieberman & Henry, "Lessons from the Alternative Dispute Resolution Movement," 53 *U. Chi. L. Rev.* 424 (1986).

Lubet, "Some Early Observations on an Experiment with Mandatory Mediation," 4 *Ohio St. J. Disp. Resol.* 235 (1989).

B. Meierhoefer, *Court–Annexed Arbitration in Ten District Courts* (1990).

Nejelski & Zeldin, "Court–Annexed Arbitration in the Federal Courts: The Philadelphia Story," 42 *Md. L. Rev.* 787 (1983).

Note, "Mandatory Mediation and Summary Jury Trial: Guidelines for Ensuring Fair and Effective Processes," 103 *Harv. L. Rev.* 1086 (1990).

A. Ordover & A. Doneff, *Alternatives to Litigation: Mediation, Arbitration, and the Art of Dispute Resolution* (2d ed. 2002).

Posner, "The Summary Jury Trial and Other Methods of Alternative Dispute Resolution: Some Cautionary Observations," 53 *U. Chi. L. Rev.* 366 (1986).

Ponte, "Putting Mandatory Summary Jury Trial Back on the Docket: Recommendations on the Exercise of Judicial Authority," 63 *Fordham L. Rev.* 1069 (1995).

"Quality of Dispute Resolution Symposium," 66 *Den. U. L. Rev.* 335 (1989).

A. Rau et al., *Processes of Dispute Resolution: The Role of Lawyers* (4th ed. 2006).

Resnik, "Failing Faith: Adjudicatory Procedure in Decline," 53 *U. Chi. L. Rev.* 494 (1986).

A. Reuben et al. *How Arbitration Works: Elkouri & Elkouri* (6th ed. 2003).

L. Riskin et al., *Dispute Resolution and Lawyers* (4th ed. 2009).

Riskin, "Mediation and Lawyers," 43 *Ohio St. L. J.* 29 (1982).

N. Rogers & C. McEwen, *Mediation: Law, Policy, Practice* (2d ed. 1994).

B. Roth et al., *The Alternative Dispute Resolution Practice Guide* (1993).

Sander, "Varieties of Dispute Processing," 70 F.R.D. 111 (1976).

Shapiro, "Private Judging in the State of New York: A Critical Introduction," 23 *Colum. J. L. & Soc. Probs.* 275 (1990).

Special Edition, *Alternative Dispute Resolution and Procedural Justice*, 46 *SMU L. Rev.* 1889 (1993).

K. Stone, *Private Justice: The Law of Alternative Dispute Resolution* (2000).

Symposium, "Ethics in the Expanding World of ADR: Considerations, Conundrums, and Conflicts," 49 *S. Tex. L. Rev.* 787 (2008).

Symposium, "Suppose It's Not True: Challenging Mediation Ideology," 2002 *J. Disp. Resol.* 81.

Symposium, "The Future of ADR," 2000 *J. Disp. Resol.* 3.

Symposium, "The Impact of Mediation: 25 Years after the Pound Conference," 17 *Ohio St. J. Disp. Resol.* 527 (2002).

Tractenberg, "Court–Appointed Mediators or Special Masters: A Commentary," 12 *Seton Hall Legis. J.* 81 (1988).

Trubek, "Turning Away from Law?," 82 *Mich. L. Rev.* 824 (1984).

Verkuil, "The Ombudsman and the Limits of the Adversary System," 75 *Colum. L. Rev.* 845 (1975).

S. Ware, *Principles of Alternative Dispute Resolution* (2d ed. 2007).

Weinstein, "Warning: Alternative Dispute Resolution May Be Dangerous to Your Health," *Litigation,* Spring 1986, at 5.

Wiegand, "A New Light Bulb or the Work of the Devil? A Current Assessment of Summary Jury Trials," 69 *Or. L. Rev.* 87 (1990).

T. Willging, *Court–Appointed Experts* (1986).

INDEX

References are to Pages

681

†